W9-CPG-512

STRAND PRICE
$5.00

HOLLYWOOD ALBUM

HOLLYWOOD ALBUM

LIVES AND DEATHS
OF
HOLLYWOOD STARS
FROM
THE PAGES OF
The New York Times

Edited by
ARLEEN KEYLIN
and
SURI FLEISCHER

ARNO PRESS

NEW YORK · 1977

A Note to the Reader

Original copies of *The New York Times* were not available to the publisher. This volume, therefore, was created from 35mm microfilm.

Library of Congress Cataloging in Publication Data

Main entry under title:

Hollywood album.

1. Moving-picture actors and actresses--United States--Biography. 2. Obituaries.
I. Keylin, Arleen. II. Fleischer, Suri.
III. New York times.
PN1998.A2H59 791.43'028'0922 [B] 77-2492
ISBN 0-405-10311-5

Editorial Assistant: Maria Casale

Book design by Stephanie Rhodes

Manufactured in the United States of America

CONTENTS

FOREWORD

Excitement—almost everything concerning movie stars has it! Their rise to fame, their loves and flirtations, their successes and failures, the clothes they wear, the homes they live in—even their choice of night clubs, vacation spots, and friends—are all subjects of concern and importance to millions of motion picture fans the world over. Little they do can be hidden from the public eye, and if this aspect of their glowing triumph is sometimes painful to them, it is the price of success.

The fabulous personalities of the *Silver Screen* became just as familiar—and often just as cherished—as the members of immediate families. They filled mere humdrum lives with adventure, passion, heroism, and warmth. Only when they were no longer around to lend their giant personalities to new screen roles or to engage in their larger-than-life private activities—only then did we realize just how much we missed them. For with their passing they *were* missed—as much as a beloved friend.

Just as everything they did in life was subject to public curiosity and the scrutinizing eye of the reporter, so was their death also an opportunity to assess, in retrospect, their achievements. In obituaries and special articles, *The New York Times* reported the deaths of hundreds of superstars and film personalities with more detail than a simple notification that they had died. Here was a chance to recapitulate the important details of their public and private lives, how they became film stars, and the roles for which they would best be remembered.

In preparing this unusual book, the editors selected more than 200 Hollywood stars whose obituaries appeared in *The New York Times.* These include love gods and goddesses, stars of the silent screen, character actors and consistently favorite supporting players, comedians, hoofers and singers, foreign stars, and personalities associated with the film industry. During the selection, there were difficult choices to make, but the final assemblage of motion picture "greats" as they were portrayed in these detailed and sensitive obituary articles is indeed impressive.

Informative, often filled with little-known or forgotten facts, these articles will offer the reader a panoramic insight into the lives of familiar motion picture personalities. Some of them may be immediately remembered. Others may have been forgotten but are now joyfully recalled. There will also be instances of pleasurable nostalgia as marvelous films and wonderful characters are brought to mind—each and every one an integral and intimate part of our lives.

Maurice Chevalier's comment regarding his reluctance to retire—even at an advanced age—was included in his *New York Times* obituary. "I'm traveling through old age without being unhappy, without being forgotten." Thanks to HOLLYWOOD ALBUM, we can now review the lives and achievements of many beloved personalities.

Sanford L. Chernoff

The New York Times THURSDAY, APRIL 25, 1974

Bud Abbott, Straight Man To Lou Costello, Is Dead

Bud Abbott, the tall, thin, I-am-not-amused straight man who fed Lou Costello the lines and the situations that got the pair into trouble and laid their audiences into the aisles with laughter, died of cancer yesterday in his home in Woodland Hills, a Los Angeles suburb. He was 78 years old.

The team split up in 1957, and Mr. Costello died two years later. For the decade after their first big success, "Buck Privates," in 1941, they were among the top ten moneymaking stars.

During the years of World War II, the team's reworking of comedic routines, slapstick, pratfalls and pies in the face seemed to be just what Americans needed.

Mr. Abbott was tall, thin, sardonic, insulting, ever ready to slap down his partner for some idiotic prank, while Mr. Costello was the buffoon, short, fat and always the sympathetic character—the classic partnership in the classic comedy formula that dates as far back as Aristophanes and his comedy, "Lysistrata," in the fifth century B.C.

Together the pair created a new mass audience on the radio, in the movies, and, later, on television for the slapstick comedy that once had audiences howling in burlesque theaters and in vaudeville performances.

The older the gag, the better it went over, so far as the team was concerned. For example:

"Hey, Abbott, where do all the little bugs go in winter?"

"Search me."

"No, thanks. I just wanted to find out."

Resisted Analysis

The pair resisted attempts at subtle analysis. In 1941, when Frank S. Nugent of The New York Times was interviewing them and speculating on "the weird, yeast-like forces responsible for their rise in the world," Mr. Costello, combative, asked, "What's the matter? You don't like our stuff?" And Mr. Abbott, with a modest wave of his hand, said, "Why try to explain it? We're doing all right, aren't we?" Mr. Nugent noted that "he wasn't asking."

Even audiences that know them only from television replays of their most famous routine, "Who's on first?," would probably agree. (This routine—the wise-guy versus dumbbell dialogue about a baseball lineup—was placed on permanent display in the National Baseball Hall of Fame museum in Cooperstown, N.Y., in 1956 in the form of a gold recording and copy of the text.)

William A. Abbott was born into show business in Asbury Park, N.J. His father, Harry Abbott Sr., was an advance man for the Ringling Brothers circus; his mother was a bareback rider. He grew up on Coney Island and left Public School 100 for good, as he put it, when he got big enough to outrun the truant officers.

On Brooklyn's Red Hook waterfront, the youth remembered emptying a couple of schooners of beer with strangers. He woke to find himself a shanghaied stoker on a ship headed for Norway. When he made it home his father got him a job as assistant cashier at the Casino Theater in Brooklyn.

Saving the pennies, Mr. Abbott organized "tab shows" — typically four girls, a pianist, a straight man and a comic — touring burlesque houses as far away as Cleveland and Toronto. But he was back at the Casino box office four years later in 1931 when Lou Costello was on stage and needed a substitute straight man. "We clicked from the start," Mr. Abbott said.

They kept going through the Depression years until 1938, when the big breaks came in an avalanche. A booker for the Loew's circuit liked their act in Washington and signed them for a week at Loew's State. Kate Smith's scout saw them there and invited them to a guest spot on her radio show.

Appearances multiplied. In 1939 they had a chance to do their stuff in a Broadway show, "The Streets of Paris," with veteran clowns like Bobby Clark and a wiggly new Brazilian named Carmen Miranda. Brooks Atkinson, theater critic of The New York Times, welcomed the new young pair of Abbott and Costello as reassurance of "the future of low comedy."

"They go the whole hog in buffoonery," he wrote "—slaps on the face, splashing water, literally upsetting the apple cart for a climax."

They were grabbed by Universal for a spate of Hollywood pictures—four in 1941, four in 1942 and one in 1943. Critics complained that they were wearing out their welcome with repetitive material and quickie productions. The pace eased when an illness that Mr. Costello suffered idled them for a year.

Meanwhile, pictures such as "Pardon My Sarong" and "Who Done It?" gave audiences the laughter they craved.

Their antics produced a financial reward as well as approval from the audiences. In 1944 the Treasury Department published earnings figures for the 12 months ended Aug. 31, 1943. Universal Pictures paid the team $789,628. Later, they earned more.

"They thought it would never stop," their long-time manager, Eddie Sherman, said yesterday. "They spent it all each year, forgetting that they had a partner, Uncle Sam."

Struck with tax bills when their careers were waning, Mr. Abbott was forced to sell his $250,000 house and property. He cleared up all his debts by 1960.

Offstage, the two comics often argued, just as they did onstage, and their conflicts were serious. Mr. Abbott liked arguing, while Mr. Costello was just plain stubborn.

Fretted Over Confusion

One of their steady disagreements was on the subject of which was which. Mr. Costello was annoyed that the public often confused them as performers, while Mr. Abbott felt that vague identifications were good for a team because public confusion meant public wonder and talk.

Mr. Costello also felt neglected when people called him Abbott.

The team's association with Universal ended in 1955 after the production of "Abbott and Costello Meet the Mummy." The next year they did "Dance With Me, Henry" for United Artists. The partnership was amicably dissolved in 1957.

Mr. Abbott continued to make occasional television appearances and in 1961 revived some of the old acts on stage with a new partner, Candy Candido, impersonating the Costello role as closely as possible.

He suffered a series of strokes in recent years and lived in a modest home contrasting with the high living he enjoyed in his heyday.

Surviving are his widow, Betty; a son, a daughter and four grandchildren.

Bud Abbott and Lou Costello in *Buck Privates.*

The New York Times FRIDAY, OCTOBER 6, 1933.

RENEE ADOREE, 31, FILM PLAYER, DEAD

Born in Circus Tent in France, She Was Toe Dancer, Horsewoman and Acrobat at 10.

WON FAME IN 'BIG PARADE'

Came Here Soon After Flight From Germans in Belgium—On Stage Before Movies.

Special to THE NEW YORK TIMES.

HOLLYWOOD, Calif., Oct. 5.—Renée Adorée, 31-year-old screen actress, who was one of the most popular members of the film colony and who will long be remembered for the rôle of Mélisande in "The Big Parade," died today after an illness of three years with a respiratory ailment.

The actress succumbed early this morning at a Sunland health resort.

"Call of the Flesh," in which she played in support of Ramon Novarro, was her last screen play. Against the advice of her physicians she continued with the picture until it was finished. She was then rushed to a sanitarium in Prescott, Ariz., where she lay flat on her back for more than two years in an effort to regain her health.

Six months ago she was released from the sanitarium and at the time it was thought she was sufficiently recovered to attempt a comeback on the screen, but almost immediately her strength began to fail and day by day she grew weaker. Although passing her time quietly in her modest little home in the Tujunga Hills, near the film city, it finally became necessary to remove her to the Sunland health resort a few weeks ago.

The funeral will be held at 11 o'clock on Saturday morning in the Hollywood Cemetery Chapel, with the Rev. James Hamilton Lash officiating. Burial will be in a vault at the mausoleum there.

Traveled for Years in Europe.

The earliest recollection of the actress as a child were of the hurriedly erected tents in which she slept while her mother and father performed with one of the small circuses of which they were members during the first fifteen years of her life. She was born in such a tent at Lille, France.

She was christened Renée de la Fointe, and the name Adorée, given to her by a showman when she made her first appearance in a circus shortly before she was 10 years old, was used to advantage when she made her initial attempt to enter the movies.

With two sisters and a brother, she traveled in circuses throughout most of Europe. Her father taught her acrobatics and horseback riding; her mother prepared her as a toe dancer. As a toe dancer she made her first public appearance a few months before she was 10.

Renée Adorée

At 12 she was a performer in the small nomad circuses with which she and her family traveled. She later said that in one season she had appeared as toe dancer, acrobat, equestrienne and clown.

Watching other performers as a child she developed a talent for pantomime, and shortly after she had passed her fifteenth birthday she left the circus lot to join a company of pantomimists in a tour of Europe. She spoke five languages, but at her début in the movies had never attended school.

Had Appeared in England.

In 1914 when war was declared she was appearing as a dancer in a Brussels theatre. With other refugees, she fled before the German Army advance in a freight car to France. From there she went to England, where she appeared in musical comedy.

With a small sum of money saved, the actress came to the United States and appeared in three musical shows in New York. They were "Oh Uncle," "O What a Girl" and "The Dancer and Sunny."

A casting director of the Fox Film Company met her one night at a theatre and asked her to take a screen test. The test was a failure and she gave up her interest in the movies. Friends, however, urged her to take a second test, and as a result of it she received a part in 1921 in "The Strongest," a French war play.

From then until 1925 she played a number of parts with varying success. In that year "The Big Parade" was released, with her and John Gilbert in the principal rôles. Few pictures have been received with such acclaim.

Miss Adorée was married twice. Her first husband was Tom Moore, the actor. They were divorced in 1926 and a year later she married William Sherman Gill, a Los Angeles business man. They were divorced in 1929.

Among the pictures in which she appeared were: "The Bandolero," "Excuse Me," "Man and Maid," "Parisian Nights," "Exchange of Wives," "The Black Bird," "La Boheme," "Tin Gods," "The Flaming Forest," "The Show," "Mr. Wu," "Back to God's Country," "The Cossacks," "The Mating Call," "The Spieler," "The Pagan," "Redemption" and "Call of the Flesh."

Renée Adorée and John Gilbert in *The Big Parade*.

The New York Times THURSDAY, JANUARY 21, 1971

Bronco Billy Anderson Is Dead at 88

HOLLYWOOD, Jan. 20 (AP)—Gilbert M. (Bronco Billy) Anderson, who made his debut in the first movie with a story, "The Great Train Robbery" in 1903, and became the first star of Westerns, died in a sanitarium here today. He was 88 years old.

Mr. Anderson, long retired, won a special honorary Oscar in 1958 for his pioneering work in films.

He is survived by his widow, Molly, and a daughter, Maxine.

Began Western Cycle

Mr. Anderson's place in the history of the cinema is assured, if for no other reason, by the fact that "The Great Train Robbery" ran for all of 13 minutes—800 feet of film when such a time frame was unheard of. It was thus credited with being motion picture with a plot.

Mr. Anderson came from not very far west of the Mississippi—Little Rock, Ark.—and did not know how to ride a horse or shoot a pistol until after his film debut. But his mounting a saddle attached to a sawbuck in the Fort Lee, N. J., studio was the event "commencing the cycle of Western cowboy films," according to Bosley Crowther, film historian and former New York Times motion picture critic.

His real name was Max Aronson. He and his sister tried to get on the stage in New York, but the best he could do was to be a model for illustrators, including Howard Chandler Christy. In 1902 he moved up to the Edison Studio, a second story loft on Twenty-third Street that was turning out 50-foot peep-show films.

50-cent-an-hour Star

His first starring role at 50 cents an hour was in "The Messenger Boy's Mistake," about a young man who was acutely embarrassed when a messenger delivered pajamas instead of flowers to his girl friend.

His director, Edwin S. Porter, was ready next year for "The Great Train Robbery." Mr. Anderson recalled years later that he played not only the bandit but the brakeman who tried to fight him off in the caboose, and the passenger whom he shot. Some of the railroad footage was shot on location in Dover, N. J.

The one-reel film was a great success on the nickleodeon circuit and Mr. Anderson moved on to a bigger job as a $25-a-week director, actor and factotum with the Vitagraph Company. He said he made the first two-reeler in 1904. Moving on to Pittsburgh and Chicago, he formed a partnership, Essanay, (S. and A.) with George K. Spoor, a distributor of screen equipment.

Moved West in 1907

The production team, consisting of Mr. Anderson, the vaudeville veteran Ben Turpin and a cameraman, went to Los Angeles in 1907. Their first script called for Mr. Turpin as a hungry hobo to dive into the pond in Westlake Park in pursuit of a duck. As Mr. Anderson spun out the story later, a real policeman plunged in after him, the camera kept turning, and when the situation was explained to the policeman Mr. Turpin got off and the comedy was complete.

Moving on to Niles Canyon near San Francisco for its Wild West scenery, the group built a small studio and shot "The Bandit Makes Good" in 1908. Mr. Anderson played Bronco Billy, who got caught robbing a bank. He gave the money to the sheriff, who lost it gambling. Billy held up the gamblers, returned the money to the sheriff, and was named deputy. The fan response was so great that Mr. Anderson started a series around the Robin Hood type of bandit.

375 Films in 7 Years

"I directed, wrote and acted in 375 of those dang things in seven years," he recalled. In those days, a film budgeted at $800 might bring in $50,000, and Mr. Anderson's income rose to $125,000 a year.

In 1915, he recalled, Essanay hired Charlie Chaplin at a phenomenal $1,250 a week to shoot comedies such as "A Night Out," "Give and Take," "The Pugilist" and "Carmen." Mutual came along with a $10,000-a-week offer and Chaplin left.

Mr. Anderson sold out his interest in the company and made his second attempt to break into the legitimate theater—as an investor. With H. H. Frazee he bought the Longacre Theater on West 49th Street. He produced several plays but never became firmly established. When he returned to the Western scene William S. Hart and other new cowboy actors had won away Bronco Billy's old fans.

Mr. Anderson produced some comedies with Stan Laurel but drifted out of the film business after 1920, living frugally in Los Angeles. He enjoyed telling of the old days and still considered movies "the maximum amount of entertainent for the minimum amount of price."

He still liked cowboy pictures—except for singing Westerns.

Bronco Billy Anderson, the first Western Star.

Bronco Billy Anderson (center) in *Bronco Billy's Oath*, 1913.

Fatty Arbuckle and Mabel Normand in *He Did and He Didn't*.

The New York Times FRIDAY, JUNE 30, 1933.

FATTY ARBUCKLE DIES IN HIS SLEEP

Film Comedian, Central Figure in Coast Tragedy in 1921, Long Barred From Screen.

ON EVE OF HIS 'COME-BACK'

Succumbs at 46 After He and Wife Had Celebrated Their First Wedding Anniversary.

Roscoe C. (Fatty) Arbuckle, film comedian, died of a heart attack at 3 o'clock yesterday morning as he slept in his suite in the Park Central Hotel. A few hours before he and his third wife, Mrs. Addie McPhail Arbuckle, had celebrated their first wedding anniversary. He was 46 years old.

The comedian and Mrs. Arbuckle went to bed about midnight. She awoke three hours later and spoke to him. She got no answer. A few minutes later the house physician had pronounced Arbuckle dead.

"Only yesterday," said Macklin Megley, a friend of the actor, "he finished the last of a series of shorts for Warner Brothers. He came off the set in the studio in Astoria and said to Ray McCarey, the director, 'Do you mind if I knock off for a few minutes? I can't get my breath; I want a breath of fresh air.'"

He finished the picture, however, and came home to prepare with Mrs. Arbuckle, for the party. At dinner they were the guests of William La Hiff, restaurant owner, along with Johnny Dundee and Johnny Walker, prizefighters, and other Broadway folk. From the dinner they returned to their suite.

Called It His "Happiest Day."

Joseph Rivkin, Arbuckle's manager, seemed broken up over the news. "He said to me only yesterday, 'This is the happiest day of my life, Joe; it's a second honeymoon.'"

Megley and other friends spoke with some bitterness of "the bad break" that put Arbuckle out of the films at the height of his career, when he was making $1,000 a day.

The body was moved to the Campbell Funeral Church at Sixty-sixth Street and Broadway. It will lie in state in the Gold Room of the establishment in a gray cloth casket until the funeral service is held tomorrow (Saturday) afternoon at 1 o'clock. Rudolph Valentino, Jeanne Eagels and June Matthews occupied the same room in death.

Falstaffian in size, if not in subtlety, Fatty Arbuckle had figured in many minor escapades before the fatal party at which he was host in the St. Francis Hotel, San Francisco, on Sept. 5, 1921. It was one of his specialties to be arrested for speeding; he was known the world over by his nickname, but every police court appearance added more publicity and the public laughed indulgently.

His popularity was universal, especially with the children. Arbuckle went to Paris and was much fêted on the boulevards. He placed a wreath on the Tomb of the Unknown Soldier beneath the Arc de Triomphe. He returned to this country in triumph, hailed as a sort of fat, funny man of good, clean fun.

Held $3,000,000 Contract.

Arbuckle's last contract in 1921 called for twenty-two films for which he was to receive $3.000.000. Some of the pictures had been completed, but were scrapped by Paramount Pictures Corporation after the San Francisco affair.

Virginia Rappe, young actress and model, died as the result of injuries she received during that drinking party and Arbuckle was arrested and charged with murder on Sept. 10. After he had spent eighteen days in a death cell, the grand jury passed an indictment for manslaughter, and Arbuckle was tried three times. Twice juries disagreed upon the verdict; the third trial resulted in an acquittal.

Then came long years of Fatty Arbuckle's trial before public opinion. His efforts at rehabilitation were entirely unsuccessful until quite recently, when he had been working hard on four comedy "shorts" for Warner Brothers. The Arbuckle affair resulted in his pictures being banned everywhere.

Roscoe Conkling Arbuckle was born at Smith Centre, Kan., on March 24, 1887.

In 1913 he was very fat and comparatively affluent. Then he met Mack Sennett of bathing beauty fame, and he played in comedy films with the late Mabel Normand, Charles Chaplin, Chester Conklin, Ford Sterling and others. In 1917 he formed a partnership with Joseph M. Schenck for the release of his comedies through Famous Players Lasky Corporation.

Arbuckle is reputed to have made $1,000 a day in his heyday. He returned to the stage in 1927 as Jimmy Jenks in "Baby Mine," and was tolerably well received at Chanin's Theatre in this city. Later he made several vaudeville appearances.

The comedian was married three times. Aminta Durfee Arbuckle, his early vaudeville partner, after standing by him for two years after the tragedy, sued for divorce in 1923. His second wife, Doris Deane Arbuckle, obtained a divorce in 1929. He married Addie Oakley Dukes McPhail last year.

Roscoe (Fatty) Arbuckle and Buster Keaton in *Good Night Nurse*, 1918.

Roscoe (Fatty) Arbuckle

The New York Times

MONDAY, MARCH 29, 1976

Richard Arlen, Actor, Dies; Star of First Oscar Film

NORTH HOLLYWOOD, Calif., March 28 (UPI) — Richard Arlen, a silent screen actor who made the transition to "talkies" and starred in "Wings" in 1927, the first motion picture to win an Academy Award, died here today at the age of 75.

A family spokesman said Mr. Arlen died at Riverside Hospital, where he had been hospitalized four weeks ago with emphysema.

He is survived by his wife, the former Margaret Kinsella; a daughter, Rose Marie, by his first wife; a son, Richard, by his second wife; two grandchildren and two great-grandchildren.

Won Coveted Role

By ROBERT E. TOMASSON

Five years after he had joined Paramount Pictures, the 26-year-old Richard Arlen won the coveted role of a young World War I aviator, which he had himself been, in "Wings," co-starring Clara Bow, Buddy Rogers and another young star, Gary Cooper.

While he was to make about 250 movies, the 1927 film, regarded as the last of the silent spectaculars about World War I, remained a high point of his career. In an era of fierce competitiveness among the Hollywood studios, the young actor made as many as five movies a year. In an interview several years ago, he recalled:

"It used to be that 15,000 fans would greet a star at the railroad station when he returned to Hollywood. Nowadays, the star's family doesn't even bother to meet him."

The former Van Mattimore, Mr. Arlen was born on Sept. 1, 1900, in Charlottesville, Va. Most of his childhood was spent in St. Paul, where he attended St. Thomas College.

When he was 17 he went to Canada, where he joined the Royal Canadian Flying Corps and became a pilot, but saw no combat. After the war, he was briefly a sports writer in Duluth, Minn., and later worked in the oil fields of Texas before going to Hollywood.

A story told about his entry into the movies, whether the creation of the Paramount publicity department or fact is unknown, is that while he was working as a messenger for a film laboratory he was struck by a studio car and taken to the studio hospital. After being released, he went to express appreciation for his treatment and was offered roles as a bit player.

Before he was picked for the role in "Wings," he had received billing in six films.

The New York Times reviewer, citing "amazing air duels," went on to write: "This feature gives one an unforgettable idea of the existence of these daring fighters—how they were called upon at all hours of the day and night to soar into the skies and give battle to enemy planes."

4 Decades in Films

In the year after "Wings," Mr. Arlen appeared in four movies, which gave an indication of the fast-action, and fast-made, movies he was to appear in over the next four decades. His 1928 movies were "Feel My Pulse," "Ladies of the Mob," "Beggars of Life" and "Manhattan Cocktail."

His other movies included "Thunderbolt" (1929); "Only Saps Work" (1930); "Come on Marines (1934); "Mutiny in the Arctic" (1941); "Kansas Raiders (1951); "Warlock (1959) and "Fort Utah" (1967), which is believed to have been his last film.

In the 1920's and 30's, his yearly salary was estimated at $200,000 and he invested in a series of successful business ventures.

His interest in flying remained strong. Between the world wars, he was part owner of a flying service and in 1942 was a civilian liaison air safety expert with the Army Air Corps.

In May 1947 he appeared before the House Committee on Un-American Activities investigating Communist infiltration in the movie industry. He told the panel that "there are certain groups of parlor pinks or influences that we would be better off without in Hollywood and we are all aware of it."

He described these influences as "people who are dissatisfied with their progress, are frustrated and are opportunists." They were, he said, mainly screen writers.

In his later years, Mr. Arlen appeared in television roles and commercials.

Charles "Buddy" Rogers, Clara Bow and Richard Arlen in *Wings*, 1927.

The New York Times WEDNESDAY, FEBRUARY 6, 1946.

GEORGE ARLISS, 77, NOTED ACTOR, DEAD

60-Year Veteran of British and American Stage and Screen —'Disraeli' Among His Hits

MONOCLE HIS TRADEMARK

Series of Successes in Plays Led to Film Bid in 1920— 'Dr. Syn' Last Picture

By Cable to THE NEW YORK TIMES.

LONDON, Feb. 5—George Arliss, a veteran of sixty years on the British and American stage and screen, died tonight at his home here of a bronchial ailment. His age was 77. With him at his death was his wife, Florence, who played Lady Beaconsfield to his Disraeli in his most famous film.

Mr. Arliss, who first appeared on the stage in this city, started his motion-picture career in the United States in 1920. His last film, "Dr. Syn," was made in England in 1937.

Creator of Character Roles

George Arliss was first and foremost the creator of character roles, and where other stars of the stage have imposed their personalities by sheer force of dramatic power, Mr. Arliss sought and found success by subtlety and finesse. His physical appearance was not prepossessing, and, unlike an Irving, a Forbes-Robertson or a John Barrymore, he realized that he could not dominate his audiences by attractiveness of face and figure.

The thin, polished face and the ever-present monocle so familiar to the English-speaking theatregoers was never made up, except in classical roles. Instead, he relied upon his extremely mobile features, his sensitive mouth and expressive eyes. His preference was for sinister parts. The heroic he shunned, but he created parts in comedy that endeared him to thousands and helped to make his name famous both in Great Britain and the United States.

After his apprenticeship in England, years of patient study, he rose to sudden success in his native country. Then came his first visit to America and his great triumph in New York in 1902, when he conquered his audiences here in the part of Cayley Drummle in "The Second Mrs. Tanqueray," playing with Mrs. Patrick Campbell at the Republic Theatre.

George Arliss was born in London on April 10, 1868. His father was William Arliss-Andrews, printer and publisher, in whose office he worked for a short time. The sedentary life appalled him, and at 18 he began his theatrical career as a super with an obscure company, playing at the old Elephant and Castle. For this he received a salary of 6 shillings ($1.50) per week, and he was on the stage for almost a year before he was given a line to speak.

His first part was that of the jailer in "Vidocq," but of his success or failure there is no record. The fact that he joined the organization of J. A. Cave, however, would indicate that he had promise.

After making his first West End appearance on Jan. 21, 1890, as Markham in "Across Her Path," he toured the English provinees. His first substantial success came in 1900, when, playing with Mrs. Patrick Campbell, he scored a distinct hit as Keane in "Mr. and Mrs. Daventry" at the Royalty Theatre, and later as the Duke of St. Olpherts in "The Notorious Mrs. Ebbsmith."

In November, 1901, Mr. Arliss crossed the Atlantic for the first time, and after starring in "The Second Mrs. Tanqueray" was engaged by David Belasco to support Blanche Bates at the Belasco Theatre. There he scored a great success as Zakkuri in "The Darling of the Gods."

Later he appeared under the management of Harrison Grey Fiske, with Mrs. Fiske in several plays. During the season of 1907-08 he played in repertoire at the Lyric Theatre with Mrs. Fiske, taking the parts of Ulrik Brendel in Ibsen's "Rosmersholm," the title role in Molnar's "The Devil," "Septimus" and, finally, with tremendous success his famous part in Louis N. Parker's play "Disraeli."

Toured for Three Years

After appearing in the same play here, in Chicago and on tour from 1912 to 1915, Mr. Arliss appeared successively as Nicolo Paganini in "Paganini," as Professor Goodwillie in "The Professor's Love Story" and as Alexander Hamilton in his own play, "Hamilton."

In "The Green Goddess" he reconquered his English audiences at the St. James Theatre, London, after an absence of twenty-two years. The play ran for twelve months. In 1924 he returned to America, and in December of that year introduced Sylvanus Heythorp in Galsworthy's delightful comedy, "Old English," at the Ritz Theatre. From 1925 to 1927 he toured in "Old English" and in January, 1928, he played Shylock in "The Merchant of Venice" at the Broadhurst Theatre.

In 1919 Mr. Arliss received the honorary degree of M. A. from Columbia University. His autobiography "Up the Years From Bloomsbury," published in 1927, was written in charming conversational style and revealed his keen insight into human nature. He wrote a number of plays, including "The Wild Rabbit," "There and Back," "The West End" (with Sir George Dance), "Widow's Weeds," "Hamilton" (with Mrs. Hamlin) and "What Shall It Profit?" (with Brander Matthews).

This was his last formal stage appearance.

The next year he entered seriously upon the cinema career for which he was probably better known by more people than for all his former stage successes. His first appearance before the cameras had been in 1919, but it was ten years later, in the film version of "Disraeli," that he established himself as a motion picture star. He received the Photoplay Gold Medal for the outstanding performance of 1929 for his work in "Disraeli."

His subsequent film appearances were in "The Green Goddess," "The Ruling Passion," "Old English," "The Millionaire," "Alexander Hamilton" and many others. But he is probably best remembered for his succession of biographical portrayals in "Volaire," "The House of Rothschild," "The Iron Duke" and "Cardinal Richelieu."

Mr. Arliss was the first president of the Episcopal Actors Guild in New York, and held the office for fifteen years, retiring in 1938 as honorary president. He was succeeded by the late Otis Skinner.

George Arliss in *Old English.*

COMPARED STAGE, SCREEN

In Autobiography Arliss Asserted Actor's Technique Remained Same

In "My Ten Years in the Studios" (1940), a continuation of his autobiography, George Arliss talked of Hollywood and compared its world with the stage. He had not meant to quit the old theatre when he agreed to appear in "Disraeli," nor did Hollywood think he would become one of its most remunerative assets. "Harry Warner told me," he recalled, "that when he decided to do 'Disraeli' he did not expect it to pay, but he was using me as an expensive bait to hook people into the cinema who had never been there before."

Mr. Arliss disagreed with the opinion that the technique of screen-acting is different from that of the stage. The actor's technique, he says, "remains the same; it is merely a matter of how to employ it." He introduced his own system of rehearsals to overcome the obstacle of the actor's separation from the audience, and he advised screen aspirants to get stage experience, for "there is only one almighty teacher and that is an audience."

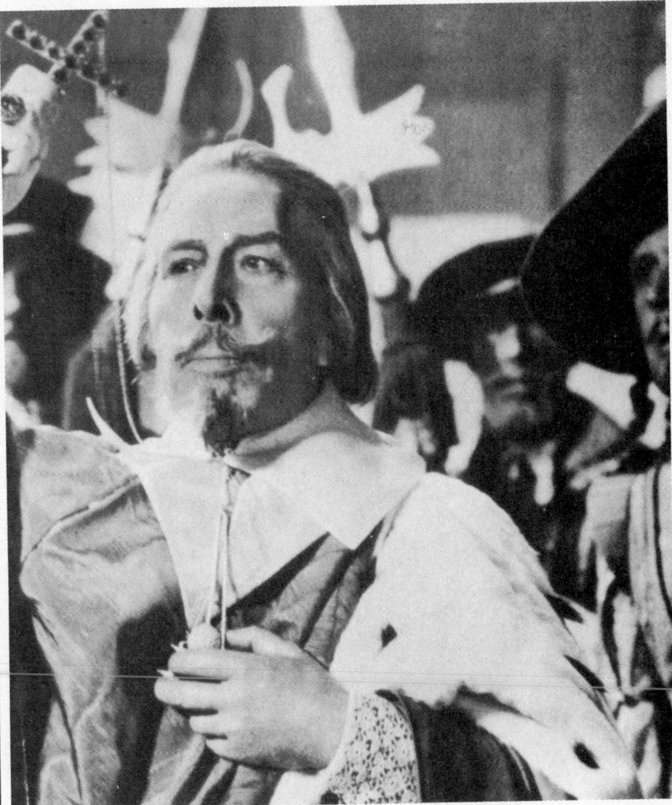

George Arliss in *Cardinal Richelieu*, 1935.

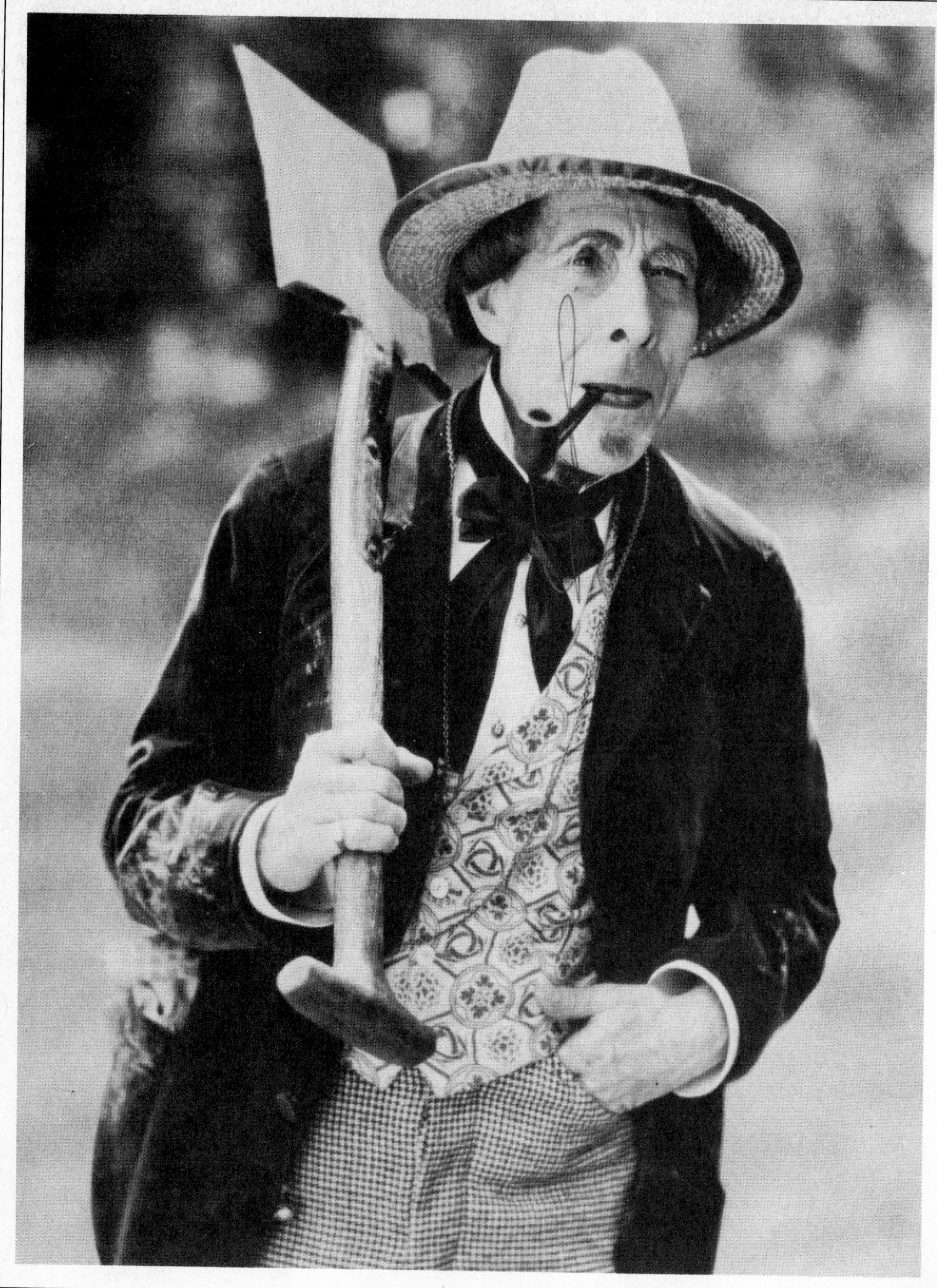

George Arliss in *Disraeli*, 1930.

The New York Times FRIDAY, APRIL 27, 1956.

EDWARD ARNOLD, ACTOR, DIES AT 66

Star Performer of Character Roles in Many Movies Began Career in '05

Special to The New York Times.

HOLLYWOOD, Calif., April 26 —Edward Arnold, actor whose career spanned fifty-one years on the stage, in films, on radio and on television, died today of a cerebral hemorrhage at his home in Encino. His age was 66.

Versatile 'Tycoon' of Films

The portly performer often remarked that the best decision he ever made was classifying himself as a character actor. After ten years as a leading man in theatrical touring companies, he became a "tycoon" of just about everything in the movies.

Mr. Arnold began his film career as a tycoon of crime. As his fame spread, he became a tycoon of lumber, land, politics and just plain money. He finally rose to the radio rank of President of the United States, many of whom he portrayed on the series "Mr. President."

Mr. Arnold linked his success to his size. "The bigger I got, the better character roles I received," he recalled. He was 5 feet 11 inches in height, weighed about 200 pounds, had blue eyes and dark brown hair.

To reach his top weight of 225 pounds to play Diamond Jim Brady in the movie "Diamond Jim" in 1935, the actor filled up on beer. Then came a rigorous diet to trim down to 200 pounds for the part of Barney Glasgow, the timber man in the screen version of Edna Ferber's "Come and Get It." Back came Mr. Arnold's avoirdupois for his return as Diamond Jim in "Lillian Russell" in 1940.

As a 12-year-old amateur he had played Lorenzo in "The Merchant of Venice." His name then was Guenther Schneider. He had become an orphan at the age of 11, a year after quitting school to go to work. Among his jobs was one as tender of the boilers in the engine room of Columbia University. But his heart was with the acting troupe at the East Side Settlement House about four miles north of his birthplace on New York's Lower East Side.

First Professional Part

John D. Barry, a playwright who later became a newspaper editor, encouraged the lad and got him his first professional part with a company in Trenton in 1905. Then, as Edward Arnold, the boy joined the Ben

Edward Arnold

Greet Players at $25 a week. Maxine Elliott thought he was worth $50 a week with her troupe, which he eventually left to join Ethel Barrymore on Broadway.

Silent film work in Chicago at $125 a week at the Essanay Studios and playing extras for $5 and $10 a day at the Old World Film Company in New Jersey inspired Mr. Arnold to return to Broadway in 1925. There he became the millionaire of the Owen Davis farce "Easy Come, Easy Go." Six years later he played a lead opposite Beatrice Lillie in "The Third Little Show."

He was a gangster the next year in "Whistling in the Dark," the same role he played later in the movie version. The film was made in 1933, a year after Mr. Arnold had made his debut in sound pictures in "Okay, America."

Mr. Arnold was so sought after that he often worked in two pictures at the same time. From gangster roles he rose to a priest in "White Sister," a sheik in "Barbarian," and then a Senator in "Jennie Gerhardt." He became King Louis XIII in "Cardinal Richelieu" with George Arliss in the title role. From then on his film interest was mainly money.

He was the gold-hungry John Sutter in "Sutter's Gold," the land-hungry John Meade in "John Meade's Woman," the millionaire who threw his wife's mink coat at Jean Arthur in "Easy Living," and again a tycoon in "You Can't Take It With You." His real-life income then was estimated at $100,000 a year.

Headed Actors Guild

In 1941 he appeared with Edward G. Robinson in "Unholy Partners." That year he also fought the devil for his soul as Daniel Webster in "All That Money Can Buy."

Mr. Arnold was a president of the Screen Actors Guild and had written an autobiography, "Lorenzo Goes to Hollywood." During World War II, he became a leader in the sale of war bonds and in the establishment of United Service Organizations camp shows for the armed forces. He was co-founder of the "I Am An American" Foundation and an officer of the movie industry's Permanent Charities Committee.

His films during and after the war included "Eyes in the Night" and "The Hidden Eye," in both of which he played Bayard Kendricks's blind detective, Duncan MacLain; "Meet John Doe," "Standing Room Only," "Janie," "Janie Gets Married" and "Three Wise Fools."

Others were "Dear Ruth," "Dear Wife," "The Hucksters," "Command Decision" and "John Loves Mary." Mr. Arnold recently finished "The Ambassador's Daughter" in Paris and had appeared in a television play two weeks ago.

Clark Gable, Ava Gardner and Edward Arnold in *The Hucksters.*

The New York Times
MONDAY, MARCH 6, 1967

Mischa Auer, Comedian in Scores of Movies, Dies

ROME, March 5 (AP) — Mischa Auer, the movie character actor and comedian, died of a heart attack at his nome here today. He was 62 years old.

Mr. Auer leaves his fourth wife, the former Elsie Souls Lee, whom he married in 1965.

A Familiar Figure

"Confidentially," intoned the Russian balletmaster, his eyes large in his gaunt face as he regarded the ballerina, "she steenks."

He was wearing a beard and an alpaca lining under his clothes that swelled his slender girth by 12 sizes. But the inflection and those shoulders that seemed to have started life with a shrug in them were unmistakable. It was Mischa Auer, familiar to millions of moviegoers from a score of comic roles where he played Borises or Stanislauses or even Mischas.

His appraisal of the dancer, delivered in the 1938 film of "You Can't Take It With You," the comedy by George S. Kaufman and Moss Hart, became one of Mr. Auer's most quoted lines.

The next year, at the crest of his movie popularity, he—or, rather, his pants—became the object of contention in the famous catfight of "Destry Rides Again." Battling it out in Bloody Gulch were Marlene Dietrich as Frenchy and Una Merkel, playing Mr. Auer's screen wife, Mrs. Boris Callahan.

Child in Siberia

Mr. Auer began as a Continental comic in the 1935 film "My Man Godfrey," whose stars were William Powell and Carole Lombard. He played a piano-tinkling gigolo, always with an eye out for something to eat. The role had some resemblance to Mr. Auer, who off the screen had a passion for marinated herring ("Be sure it's in sour cream").

But his roles had not been comic before that, nor had his life, and he had not always been well-fed.

He was born Nov. 17, 1905, the son of a naval officer who was killed in the Russo-Japanese War, in St. Petersburg—now Leningrad—and was named Mischa Ounskowski. Separated from his mother during the Bolshevik revolution, he became a member of a band of parentless children who roamed Siberia.

"We were such a problem they finally sent us back to St. Petersburg to find our families," Mr. Auer recalled in an interview many years later. "I found my mother by chance, and we went to the south of Russia, to

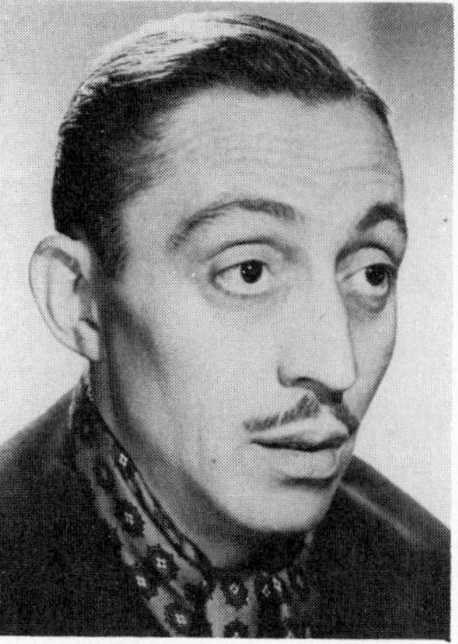

Mischa Auer

a town near the front which had been taken by the White Russians. There still wasn't enough to eat. I learned then that there are no morals, no conventions, when your stomach is empty. You'll even eat dead horses. We did."

They managed to escape with the help of the British Expeditionary Force in South Russia.

His mother helped to found a refugee hospital with the British forces. She contracted typhus and died. Mischa, at the age of 13, sold his mother's jewels and fled to Florence, Italy. There, a girlhood friend of his mother's notified Mischa's grandfather, the violinist Leopold Auer, then in New York. The grandfather, Mrs. Ounskowski's father, cabled money for him to travel to America. The boy was then 15 years old.

In New York, he was adopted by his grandfather, whose name he took. Leopold Auer, a well-known musician of his time, taught Jascha Heifetz, Mischa Elman and Efrem Zimbalist.

The grandfather sent him to the Ethical Culture School. "I couldn't do the work and I didn't care," Mr. Auer remembered. "When the teacher asked me what was the matter, I said, 'After seeing death and torture, suppose I don't do algebra?'"

But he showed an interest in the stage. In 1925, he became an extra with Helen Chandler in the Dudley Digges production of Ibsen's "The Wild Duck."

Not long after, he appeared on stage with Eva Le Gallienne, Walter Hampden and Bertha Kalich.

It was in 1928, while touring with Miss Kalich in Los Angeles, that Mr. Auer entered the movies. His first film, a silent, was "Something Always Happens." He was to play villains, old men and a succession of nondescript roles for eight years before "My Man Godfrey" and success came along.

After his arrival on the West Coast, he said later, "it took me three years to make a living. But it's a wonderful country. You can live on oranges and credit and have a car to boot."

Once established, he had no shortage of roles as impoverished princes, distraught waiters, superstitious chefs or excitable playwrights. Mr. Auer acted in "Three Smart Girls," "100 Men and a Girl," "The Rage of Paris," "Winterset," "Hellzapoppin'" and "Brewster's Millions."

His Hollywood career waned after World War II. He acted briefly on Broadway, in summer stock and on television, but most of his film work was abroad, chiefly in France and in Italy. He was given comedy and character roles because of his long professional background and his fluency in several languages.

Mr. Auer appeared with the late Martine Carol in "The Foxiest Girl in Paris" and with Brigitte Bardot in "Mam'zelle Pigalle." In 1962, he acted in "Mr. Arkadin," an Orson Welles film.

From time to time, he was in the news as he went back and forth from the West Coast to Europe.

In 1945, Mr. Auer broke a leg when he responded to screams from his next-door neighbor in Encino, Calif. He vaulted a 6-foot fence only to find that the neighbor's dog had fallen into the swimming pool.

In Monte Carlo in 1956, he was asked to lead a band at a nightclub and was warmly received. After bowing to the applause, he walked from the stage and fell down the steps, breaking his collarbone.

Mischa Auer does his monkey imitation in *My Man Godfrey,* 1936, while Alice Brady, Eugene Pallette and Carole Lombard look on.

The New York Times WEDNESDAY, APRIL 17, 1968

Fay Bainter, Actress, Dies at 74; Won Academy Award in 1939

HOLLYWOOD, April 16 (AP)—Fay Bainter, stage and Academy Award-winning screen actress who was long popular in roles as wife, understanding mother or faithful friend, died today at her home. She was 74.

Her husband of 42 years, Navy Lieut. Comdr. Reginald Venable, died in 1964. Their actor son, Reginald Jr., survives.

Miss Bainter was a Los Angeles native who entered movies at 41 after long stage experience.

Five years later, in 1939, she won the Academy Award for a supporting actress as Auntie Belle in "Jezebel," whose star, Bette Davis, also received an Oscar.

Nominated 2 Other Times

Miss Bainter was nominated for the prize for two other roles—as Claude Rains's housekeeper in "White Banners" and as a grandmother deceived by a child in the 1962 film "The Children's Hour."

She appeared in a total of 39 films. On television she co-starred with Thomas Mitchell in "A Child Is Born."

In "The Shining Hour" Miss Bainter had her first unsympathetic screen role as an unmarried older sister who despises Joan Crawford.

She was a mother in "Young Tom Edison," "Our Town" and "State Fair," Katharine Hepburn's loyal friend in "Woman of the Year" and a kindergarten teacher in "Journey for Margaret."

She made her first appearance on the New York stage at Daly's in 1912.

In 1914 she toured with Mrs. Fiske in "Mrs. Bumpstead-Leigh." She made a remarkable hit as Ruth Sherwood in "Arms and the Girl" in 1916.

A long string of successes followed—"The Willow Tree," "The Kiss Burglar, East Is West," "The Other Rose," "The Dream Girl" and others—before she went to Hollywood.

In the nineteen-fifties she toured with the national company of Eugene O'Neill's "Long Day's Journey Into Night."

Fay Bainter, Jeanne Crain and Dana Andrews in *State Fair*.

The Shining Hour, 1938, with Fay Bainter, Robert Young, Margaret Sullavan, Melvyn Douglas and Joan Crawford.

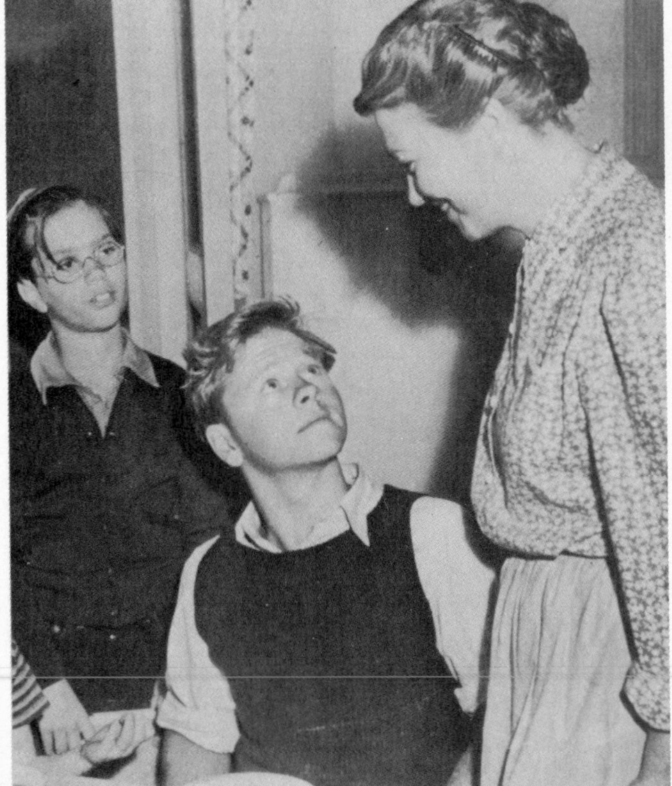

Darryl Hickman, Mickey Rooney and Fay Bainter starred in *The Human Comedy*.

Bette Davis and Fay Bainter both won Oscars for Best Actress for their roles in *Jezebel*.

Theda Bara as *Cleopatra,* 1917.

The New York Times FRIDAY, APRIL 8, 1955.

THEDA BARA DIES; SCREEN STAR, 65

'Siren' of Silent Films Was Top Box-Office Attraction During the Twenties

DENOUNCED IN CHURCHES

'Cleopatra,' 'The Vampire,' 'Salome' and 'Madame Du Barry' Among Her Hits

Special to The New York Times.

LOS ANGELES, April 7—Theda Bara, the silent screen's vamp, died tonight in California Lutheran Hospital. She was 65 years old. Critically ill with abdominal cancer, Miss Bara entered the hospital Feb. 13. She had been under treatment for many months before that.

The film empire of William Fox was built on the appeal of Miss Bara. She was his first great star. "A Fool There Was" made movie history and was one of the biggest box-office hits of the day.

The actress was the wife of Charles J. Brabin, to whom she was married in 1921. Mr. Brabin directed many of his wife's movies and later several notable sound films. After their retirement they resided in Beverly Hills.

In addition to her husband, Miss Bara leaves her mother, Mrs. Pauline Louise Bara, and a sister, Lori Bara, both of Westwood.

The 'Vampire' Type

Theda Bara was a symbol and personality—the "vampire" type created by the screen and zany publicity men to bewitch enormous movie audiences.

To millions of Americans from 1915 until the mid-Twenties she was the ageless siren, luring men to tragedy with rolling eyes, heavy make-up and scanty costumes. For her movie fans she was the perfect star in "Cleopatra" and "Salome" and her magnetism at the box office was unquestionable.

Her impassioned embraces put fire into warmed-over plots and gave meaning to even the most trite situations. Miss Bara excited her audiences to the point where she became a subject of denunciation from church pulpits; she was once mobbed by women in a department store and received hundreds of letters seeking advice about love.

Away from cameras, however, she gave a different impression. Thus, when she decided to try the Broadway stage in 1920, as the star of "The Blue Flame," the critic of The New York Times, Alexander Woollcott, wrote:

"She speaks her lines distinctly and rather like a young girl at a high school commencement exercise. * * * She displays a fine self-possession which enabled her to proceed last evening with unflinching gravity even when the audience lost control of itself and shook with laughter."

'Victim of Press Agents'

Interviewers came away with the over-all impression that they had met a rather sweet young woman with what one reporter described as a "slight, girlish figure," instead of the voluptuous siren of "The Vampire," "A Fool There Was," "Her Double Life," "Madame Du Barry," "The Tiger Woman," "Her Greatest Love," "Forbidden Path," "The Rose of Blood" and dozens of other movies.

Miss Bara never pretended that her private life was anything but simple. She called herself "the victim of overzealous press agents" who had circulated innumerable lies about her parents, birthplace, name, background.

The actress' name actually was Theodosia Goodman. She was born in 1890 in Cincinnati. Press agents told the nation she was born in the Sahara Desert and that her first name was an anagram of death and her second name was Arab spelled backward.

In changing her name officially in court, Miss Bara said her first name was an abbreviation of Theodosia and the second name came from her maternal grandfather, Francis Bara de Coppet, a Swiss.

Bara in *Salome,* 1918.

Theda Bara as Poppaea in *When A Woman Sins,* 1918.

"All the News That's Fit to Print"

The New York Times

LATE CITY EDITION

Weather: Fair, very cold today and tonight. Chance of snow tomorrow. Temp. range: today 24-14; Sunday 33-26. Full U.S. report on Page 30.

VOL. CXVIII . No. 40,501 — NEW YORK, FRIDAY, DECEMBER 13, 1968 — 10 CENTS

Tallulah Bankhead Dead at 65; Vibrant Stage and Screen Star

By MURRAY SCHUMACH

Tallulah Bankhead, the star whose offstage performances often rivaled her roles in the theater, film and television, died at St. Luke's Hospital yesterday of pneumonia, complicated by emphysema. She was 65 years old.

The actress, a member of one of the most famous political families of Alabama, was admitted to the hospital last Friday after contracting influenza. The influenza developed into pneumonia.

With her when she died were her sister, Eugenia Bankhead, and a nephew, William Brockman Bankhead 2d. Her marriage to John Emery, an actor, ended in divorce in 1941.

To admirers — and gossip mongers — for more than 40 years, Miss Bankhead was a personality as much as a star. Her vibrant energy, sultry voice, explosive speech and impetuous behavior seemed at times a phenomenon better suited for study by physicists than by journalists, who chronicled her antics with and without script.

The raw power and uninhibited style she discharged into even poor plays—and she had many—once prompted Arnold Bennett, the novelist, to write:

"I have seen Tallulah electrify the most idiotic, puerile plays into some sort of realistic coherence by her individual force."

The same force was described, from another point of view, by an awed observer who knew her socially, and said: "A day away from Tallulah is like a month in the country."

One of Miss Bankhead's many feuds with producers resulted in a famous exchange with Billy Rose during rehearsals of "Clash by Night." She called him "a loathesome little bully," and he responded, "How can you bully Niagara Falls?"

Miss Bankhead's personal life had such flair that in recent years, when she did so little stage work, there was a tendency to underestimate her talent by a generation that had never seen her as the eternal

The New York Times

Tallulah Bankhead

Continued on Page 42, Column 1

CITY HIGH SCHOOLS TO GIVE STUDENTS A VOICE IN POLICY

Donovan Sets Up a Panel to Recommend the Guidelines for Involving Youths

ADVISORY ROLE PLANNED

McCoy Ignores State Order Removing Him as Head of His Office

By JAMES ...

The Superintendent ... New York City Schools ... yesterday the formation of a committee to recommend city-wide guidelines ... high school students ... to make administrative policy decisions in their schools.

While some school ... dismissed suggestions ... committee was being formed in response to recent student outbreaks here, they said the ... did recognize growing ... school student unrest and ... the committee might find ... of avoiding serious outbreaks of violence.

In another development involving the city's schools, Rhody A. McCoy ignored a state order removing him as administrator of the Ocean Hill-Brownsville district in Brooklyn. He went to his office yesterday morning as usual, but the district's state trustee said that Mr. McCoy would be barred—by the police if necessary—if he showed up today.

A Representative Panel

The 12-member committee, called the Committee on Student Participation in School Management, will be made up of four high school principals, three students, two teachers, two representatives of parent groups and a deputy superintendent of schools, said Superintendent Bernard E. Donovan.

"This committee has no boundaries on where it can go," he said in an interview.

Seelig L. Lester, deputy superintendent of schools in charge of instruction, stressed, however, that the committee would deal with involving students as advisers in the decision-making process. The principals would continue to have final authority.

Mr. Lester, who will head the committee, said it would explore the most effective ways of giving students a voice in all matters of school policy, including curriculum, student

Continued on Page 40, Column 7

Columbia Hecklers Bested by Lindsay In Moderation Plea

By RICHARD REEVES

Mayor Lindsay outlasted a dozen radical hecklers at Columbia University yesterday and won the applause of 1,500 other students with a warning that ... names" ...

... reign ... lem," ... to include ... year prison ... gers, was ... by the N... the Nation... the Advance... People.

Vincent Bak... the branch's an... tee, said that n... was the product o... evils" that dem... "but with people ... beaten, robbed ... something should ... about crime right no...

A six-page report ... from studies initiated ... ary and approved a ... by the branch's executive committee, was made public ... news briefing in the b... headquarters at 261 ... 125th Street.

The report said that "... attitude toward crime ... criminals must change" ... Harlem.

"There are people known to cheer when some offender rushes from a store" with his loot, Mr. Baker told newsmen. "They seem to have the idea that these are some sort of 20th century Robin Hoods. With the hoods, we agree."

Among the report's demands were these:

¶Added protection, including more policemen on Harlem beats and "armed guards in every house in all public housing projects."

¶Harsher sentences, including a 10-year minimum for narcotics sellers and at least 30 years for those convicted of first-degree murder. The report

Continued on Page 39, Column 3

CARNEGIE PANEL ASKS U.S. TO SEND POOR TO COLLEGE

Plan Simi...

STATE APPROVES RYE-NASSAU SPAN

The New York Times Dec. 13, 1968

Route of proposed bridge

By JOSEPH C. INGRAHAM

J. Burch McMorran, the State Transportation Commissioner, yesterday announced approval of the controversial Long Island Sound bridge-causeway between Westchester and Nassau Counties.

He said the approach roads for the six-mile-long, $140-million span would be in Oyster Bay on the Nassau side and in the Rye-Portchester area in Westchester, but he did not specify any exact alignment.

However, the favored route would have the bridge touch Long Island at Bayville, in Oyster Bay Town.

Public hearings will start in January to help the department select the best corridors and alternative route locations, the Commissioner said. The hear-

Continued on Page 35, Column 3

New Drive Planned For Negro Self-Aid

By JOHN HERBERS
Special to The New York Times

WASHINGTON, Dec. 12 — Members of Congress, business leaders and Negro militants met here today to push a bi-partisan "community self-determination" bill that fits Richard M. Nixon's campaign promises to give Negroes "a piece of the action."

Republican Senators assured the group that the bill would receive favorable consideration in the new Administration.

Roy Innis, national director of the Congress of Racial Equality and one of the originators of the bill, and Joseph C. Wilson, board chairman of Xerox Corporation, announced separate plans to mount a national campaign for the proposed legislation.

Opposition was registered

Continued on Page 38, Column 3

Tallulah ... whose ... often ri... theater, ... died at ... terday ... cated by ... 65 years old.

The actress ... one of the m... cal families of ... admitted to th... Friday after co... enza. The influe... into pneumonia.

With her when sh... her sister, Eugenia ... and a nephew, Willi... man Bankhead 2d. ... riage to John Emery ... ended in divorce in 1...

To admirers — and ... mongers — for more ... years, Miss Bankhead ... personality as much as ... Her vibrant energy, ... voice, explosive speech ... impetuous behavior seem... times a phenomenon ... suited for study by phy... than by journalists, who ch... icled her antics with and wi... out script.

The raw power and uninhibited style she discharged into even poor plays—and she had many—once prompted Arnold Bennett, the novelist, to write:

"I have seen Tallulah electrify the most idiotic, puerile plays into some sort of realistic coherence by her individual force."

The same force was de-

... exchange ... during rehears... Clash by Night." She called him "a loathesome little bully," and he responded, "How can you bully Niagara Falls?"

Miss Bankhead's personal life had such flair that in recent years, when she did so little stage work, there was a tendency to underestimate her talent by a generation that had never seen her as the eternal

Continued on Page 42, Column 1

... ting at the White House yesterday

Associated Press

...pport Voiced ...binet Choices

...W. FINNEY ... New York Times

With a team of moderate Re... ...dent-elect Richard M. Nixon ...he political foundations for

F.C.C. SAID TO PLAN ...RB ON CABLE TV

...sional Sources See ...n Applications— ...ision Backed

... well in... foreign affairs, more receptive to Senate advice on foreign policy.

The first test of Mr. Rogers's success on Capitol Hill may well come with his reaction to a renewed assertion by the Senate of its constitutional prerog-

Continued on Page 36, Column 6

...ssador W. Harriman, chief United States negotiator in the Paris talks, had received a message from the North Vietnamese chief negotiator, Xuan Thuy, conveying Hanoi's authorization. The message said:

"On the occasion of Christmas, 1968, the Government of the Democratic Republic of Vietnam, acting in pursuit of humanitarian policies, authorizes United States pilots in

Continued on Page 6, Column 4

NEWS INDEX

...Luxury, ...rn Italy

...WALTER SULLIVAN

... Italian arche...ogists believe they have found the long-sought site of Sybaris, the seat of proverbial luxury in the ancient world.

Its inhabitants, the Sybarites, were so attentive to their own comfort that, according to classic accounts, they built roofs over roads leading out of the city to provide shade for travelers.

Likewise, it is said that according to local law, invitations to public functions had to be issued a year in advance. This was to allow the ladies time to attire themselves in suitable opulence.

Hence the word sybarite has come to mean anyone devoted to a life of luxury.

The discovery of the city, which was destroyed in civil strife in 510 B.C. after flourish-

ing for 200 years, was announced in Philadelphia last night at the University Museum of the University of Pennsylvania.

The find was described there by Dr. Froelich G. Rainey, director of the museum, and Prof. Giuseppe Foti, superintendent of antiquities of Calabria, in southern Italy.

Sybaris was situated in Calabria. Ancient writers placed it between the rivers Crathis (or Crati) and Sybaris (or Coscile), where they emptied into the sea.

In the 25 centuries that have passed since then the terrain has changed. The two rivers now meet before they reach the sea, and the ancient Greek col-

Continued on Page 2, Column 7

NIXON AGAIN PAYS CALL ON JOHNSON; TALK FAR-RANGING

Middle East, Vietnam and Missile Curb Parley With Soviet Are Discussed

CHAFEE WEIGHING OFFER

Post for Gov. Boe Indicated —President-Elect Meets With Cabinet Choices

By R. W. APPLE Jr.
Special to The New York Times

WASHINGTON, Dec. 12 — President-elect Richard M. Nixon discussed a wide range of foreign and domestic issues with President Johnson this evening in a White House meeting that lasted more than an hour and a half.

One question touched upon, according to qualified sources, was whether the Johnson Administration should begin negotiating with the Soviet Union on the limitation of nuclear missiles before it leaves office in 38 days.

Without the concurrence of Mr. Nixon, Mr. Johnson is believed to be unwilling to begin the long-delayed talks in any form. With concurrence, he would be ready to begin with a summit meeting if the Russians agreed.

Commitment Uncertain

It was not known whether the President-elect had given any commitment.

George Christian, the White House press secretary, said Mr. Nixon and Mr. Johnson had talked in the President's office about the Middle East, Vietnam "and other world problems," Mr. Johnson's forthcoming State of the Union and Budget Messages, and Mr. Nixon's Cabinet, as well as "housekeeping" matters.

Asked whether the subject of a possible summit meeting had been among the items discussed, Mr. Christian said. "I have no idea."

The meeting between the incoming and outgoing Presidents was the second since Election Day. They last talked at the White House on Nov. 11, and Mr. Nixon pledged then to allow Mr. Johnson to speak for both the old and the new Administrations on foreign policy until inauguration day.

Joined by Mrs. Nixon

Mr. Nixon took his wife, Patricia, and his elder daughter, Tricia, to the White House, and members of the new Presidential staff came along. While Mr. Nixon met privately with President Johnson, the families and staffs also talked.

The Nixon entourage arrived at 6:42 P.M., 12 minutes late. ... Johnson, who was ... stood at the south portico ... Mrs. Johnson and their ... daughter, Mrs. Pat... Nugent, to welcome ...

...e close to the Presi... reported. mean... ...t Mr. Nixon had se... ...etting Governor to ...ffice of Emergency ... specifically ex...

...ge 36, Column 1

Tallulah Bankhead Dies Here at 65

Continued From Page 1, Col. 4

prostitute, Sabrina, in Thornton Wilder's "The Skin of Our Teeth," or as the mercenary Regina in Lillian Hellman's "The Little Foxes."

The young were able to appraise her talent fairly only from revivals or television screenings of Alfred Hitchcock's "Lifeboat," in which, as the foreign correspondent, she won the best acting award in 1944 from the New York Film Critics.

In the latter phase of Miss Bankhead's hectic career, radio and television projected into millions of living rooms the personality more than the talent.

Better known to this vast new audience than any of the lines she uttered in plays was her throaty "Daaahling," with which she greeted friends and strangers. In the one word were blended her energy and sensuality, the Alabama drawl to which she was born and the London insouciance she acquired in the theater in the nineteen-twenties.

Always in Spotlight

Miss Bankhead's ability to consume liquor became a subject for public appraisal and her ownership of a lion cub, or flamboyant love of baseball became better known than the fact that she had won important critical awards.

Miss Bankhead's unabashed style emerged very often in interviews and press conferences, where she needed no help from publicity men to make startling comments. During one press gathering in 1964, she said:

"The last beau I had, let's see, someplace in California, I think. Well, this man said: 'Look here Tallulah, you don't need a man, you need a caddy.' That's the way I am honey. I have a lot of stuff I leave around, that's just the way I am. I just can't think in terms of remembering gloves and furs and things."

Tennessee Williams saw her in a different light. He came to know her when she appeared in a revival of his "A Streetcar Named Desire," and a revised revival of "The Milk Train Doesn't Stop Here Anymore."

"Tallulah," he asserted, "is the strongest of all the hurt people I've ever known in my life."

He looked upon her as the result of "fantastic cross-breeding of a moth and a tiger." He extolled her "instinctive kindness to a person in whom she senses a vulnerability that is kin to her own."

Mr. Williams scoffed at Miss Bankhead's periodic comments—out of pique or frustration—that she hated the theater and did it solely "to keep out of debtor's prison."

"She loves it with so much of her heart," the playwright said, "that in order to protect her heart she has to say that she hates it. But we know better when we see her onstage."

But those she had hurt with her biting tongue and her aggressiveness did not look upon her with such sweetness. During rehearsals for "The Skin of Our Teeth" in 1942, Elia Kazan, who had not yet attained his later stature as a director, was subjected to tantrums and abuse he did not forget for many years. Before the play opened, the actress's behavior had put the producer, Michael Myerberg, in the hospital with nervous prostration.

Long Democratic Line

Disparaging comments about Miss Bankhead sometimes stemmed from ignorance or malice. Thus, those who spoofed her campaigning for Democratic candidates for the White House forgot that her father, William, had been Speaker of the House of Representatives and that a grandfather and an uncle had been United States Senators—all Democrats from Alabama.

There were many stories about Miss Bankhead's stormy friendships with men. Generally, she ignored comments about her morals But once she summed up her attitude:

"I'd rather go on like I do than be like a lot of women I know who only look clean."

Another time she retorted:

"I'm as pure as the driven slush."

Indicative of her restrained behavior were her antics at parties. At one, she threw the shoes of the women guests into the street. At another, she did a strip tease.

On another occasion, when there had been an accumulation of tales about her behavior, or of her having given away a necklace worth thousands, or of her having gone for days without sleep as part of her dread of loneliness, she said, with a satiric flutter of eyelashes:

"I'm not the confidential type."

Contrary to widespread belief, the animal spirits of this actress were generated by a woman only 5 feet, 3 inches tall and weighing less than 130 pounds. In her prime, her beauty, with the blue eyes, voluptuous mouth, honey-colored hair that fell in waves to her shoulder, impelled Augustus John to do her portrait.

Jokes were made of her name. Bugs Baer, the humorist, once wrote that the man who christened her must have been chewing bubble gum.

Actually, she was named for a paternal grandmother, who was named after Tallulah Falls, Ga.

Born into a wealthy Southern family, Miss Bankhead was reared by an aunt after the death of her mother.

As a child her tantrums were notorious among the Bankheads. Later, her sense of mischief and resentment of discipline caused her transfer through several finishing schools.

Not until she got a bit part in a Broadway show, in 1918, did Miss Bankhead find a constructive channel for her talent. However, New York showed no great enthusiasm for her during her first few years in the theater, when she appeared in "Squab Farm," "Footloose," "39 East," "Nice People," Everyday," "Danger," "Her Temporary Husband" and "The Exciters."

Impatient with her progress, Miss Bankhead left for London in 1923, where she became a sensation in "The Dancers."

Her fame spread throughout England and her clothes, her hair, her speech, became the rage with thousands of young girls as she drew acclaim in "The Green Hat," "Fallen Angels," "They Knew What They Wanted," "The Gold Diggers," "Her Cardboard Lover" and "The Lady of the Camellias."

Movies brought her back to the United States in 1931. But her films were not successful. She returned to Broadway in 1933 in "Forsaking All Others."

For a time, it seemed that Broadway would bring her nothing but bad luck, as she performed in "Dark Victory," "Reflected Glory," "I Am Different" and "The Circle."

She received some encouragement by doing Sadie Thompson, the prostitute, in a revival of "Rain." But she was derided for her Cleopatra in a revival of "Antony and Cleopatra."

In 1939, Miss Bankhead found the play that was worthy of her artistry, "The Little Foxes." In Miss Hellman's drama, she overwhelmed the critics with her performance of Regina Giddens, a woman of extraordinary selfishness and cruelty, who goads her husband to death for money.

Words like "superb" and "magic" were used to describe her performance.

Some of those acquainted with Miss Bankhead's love of talk said this was not much of a strain on her. One writer said she was so fond of talking that she had led "a lifelong filibuster."

Miss Bankhead, however, had a different summary of her life.

"Live," she said, "in the moment."

Tallulah Bankhead in *The Devil and the Deep*, 1932.

The New York Times SATURDAY, MAY 12, 1973

LEX BARKER DIES; TARZAN OF MOVIES

Was 10th to Play the Role, Succeeding Weissmuller

Lex Barker, the 10th actor to play the role of Tarzan in Hollywood films, collapsed and died yesterday.

Mr. Barker, who was 53 years old, was found unconscious on Lexington Avenue near 61st Street about midday. He was taken to Lenox Hill Hospital, where he was pronounced dead. The body was taken to the city morgue for an autopsy.

The police said that two women with whom he apparently had had a luncheon date came to the East 67th Street station, concerned that he had not appeared.

Meanwhile, the actor's body was found and identification was established through a wristwatch inscribed "Alexander C. Barker, 205 South Beverley Drive, Beverly Hills, Cal."

The actor was a member of a Social Register family of this city and Rye, N. Y.

His full name was Alexander Crichlow Barker Jr., and he succeeded Johnny Weissmuller, the Olympic swimming star, in the Tarzan role in 1949 after Mr. Weissmuller had played it for some 17 years.

He was born in New York and educated at Phillips Exeter Academy and at Princeton University, and had had considerable training as an actor before Sol Lesser, the Hollywood producer, signed him for the Tarzan role.

He appeared in summer stock and briefly on Broadway before he tried the Hollywood film factories in 1945. He had small roles in "The Farmer's Daughter," "Mr. Blandings Builds His Dream House" and "Velvet Touch," and then made his first Tarzan film, "Tarzan's Magic Fountain."

A reviewer in The New York Times called him "a younger, more streamlined apeman with a personable grin and a torso guaranteed to make any lion cringe," but termed the picture itself "a matter of stale peanuts at the same old jungle stand." Later pictures—"Tarzan and the Slave Girl" and "Tarzan's Peril" among them—drew no better critical acclaim.

Switched to Westerns

Eventually, Mr. Barker dropped the Tarzan role, made a few westerns in which his Tarzan fame was exploited and then left the country to make a film in England. This led to a series of Westerns in Italy, France and especially in Germany, where he became a top box-office star.

Mr. Barker married five times. His wives were Constance Thurlow, a graduate of the Todhunter School and the Mount Vernon Junior College in Washington; Arlene Dahl and Lana Turner, the actresses; Irene Labhart, a Swiss drama student, and Maria del Carmen Cervera, a former Spanish beauty queen.

He served five years in the Army in World War II, and was discharged as a major.

Lex Barker

Lex Barker and Vanessa Brown starred in *Tarzan and the Slave Girl*, 1950.

Keith Andes, Lex Barker, James Arness, Joseph Cotten and Loretta Young in *The Farmer's Daughter*.

"All the News That's Fit to Print"

The New York Times.

LATE CITY EDITION
U. S. Weather Bureau Report (Page 50) forecasts: Chance of occasional rain today and tonight. Some cloudiness tomorrow.
Temp. range: 65—55; yesterday: 67.9—52.0. Temp.-Hum. Index: mid 60's; yesterday: 65.

VOL. CVIII. No. 37,036. NEW YORK, FRIDAY, JUNE 19, 1959. FIVE CENTS

10 cents beyond 50-mile zone from New York City except on Long Island. Higher in air delivery cities.

Ethel Barrymore Is Dead at 79; One of Stage's 'Royal Family'

Famed Actress Began Career at 14, Captivating Audiences With Voice and Manner

Special to The New York Times.

HOLLYWOOD, Calif., June 18—Ethel Barrymore, last of the trio known to Broadway and Hollywood as "The Royal Family" of acting, died here today of a heart ailment. She would have been 80 years old on Aug. 15.

Miss Barrymore started on the stage at 14 and made her last public appearance on television during a testimonial to her on her seventy-eighth birthday. The two others in the Barrymore triumvirate were her brothers, John, who died in 1942, and Lionel, who died in 1954.

Although Miss Barrymore talked amusingly of the past, she refused to live in it and had little patience for those who resented changes in drama brought on by movies and television. In one of her last interviews, several weeks ago, she said:

"We must recognize that change is not going to appeal to us personally if we are irrevocably determined to abide by the traditional standards of taste."

The square-jawed actress with the classical profile had done no acting for movies since 1954, when she made "Young at Heart," with Frank Sinatra and Doris Day. She took her final acting role on television in a "Playhouse 90" dramatization in 1956.

While no longer active as a performer, Miss Barrymore maintained a strong interest in the theatre, movies and television. Leading stars of Broad-

Ethel Barrymore

Continued on Page 25, Column 2

HOSPITAL ACCORD REACHED TO END 42-DAY WALKOUT

Settlement Accepted After 5 Hours of City Hall Talks—Picketing May Continue

UNION TO VOTE MONDAY

Officials Say They Will Urge Adoption of Peace Formula —Terms Not Disclosed

By RALPH KATZ

A memorandum of understanding to end the forty-two-day hospital strike was reached at City Hall at 2:30 A. M. to...

The agreement follow... hours of joint negoti... Mayor Wagner and... labor aides assisting.

The Mayor called... into the second-floo... where the talks had be... to announce that a "mem... dum of understanding" been mutually accepted by union and the struck hospita...

The terms of agreement were not announced.

Mayor Wagner said that the terms would not be made public until the union had acted on the agreement at a membership meeting Monday night.

Officials of Local 1199 of the Retail Drug Employes Union, which began the strike May 8, assured the Mayor that they would recommend acceptance of the peace formula at the meeting.

Favorable Comment Pledged

Harry A. Van Arsdale Jr., president of the city's Central Labor Council, who headed a labor negotiating team, said that his group would also comment favorably on the memorandum at the drug union's membership meeting.

Mr. Van Arsdale said, however, that picketing by the non-professional workers at the seven struck voluntary hospitals might continue until the union members had acted on the peace proposals.

He said that the picketing might be subject to change before that time.

"Both sides have agreed to the principles of the formula," Mayor Wagner said.

He thanked the negotiating teams for their long efforts to end the strike that passed its forty-second day yesterday.

He also thanked the three-man fact-finding committee for the city that he had appointed

Continued on Page 26, Column 2

SHOW WILL GO ON IF PAPP GETS BOND

Moses Writes Producer He Needs $20,000 Guarantee

By LOUIS CALTA

If Joseph Papp, producer of the New York Shakespeare Festival, can raise $20,000 he will be allowed to operate in Central Park this summer.

In a conciliatory mood, Robert Moses, Commissioner of Parks, made this announcement yesterday. But Mr. Papp, through a spokesman, said he doubted he could raise the money on such short notice.

Mr. Moses made his offer on the heels of an Appellate Division decision on Wednesday that called him "clearly arbitrary, capricious and unreasonable" in not permitting Mr. Papp to stage plays in the park unless admission were charged.

After being advised yesterday that the Corporation Counsel did not intend to appeal the decision, Mr. Moses said that he would "of course abide by the court's decision."

Later, he sent a letter by messenger to Mr. Papp disclosing his willingness to issue a permit "on the basis of the Appellate Division decision."

Mr. Moses' letter said:

"This means that funds in the minimum amount of $20,000 must be provided by you to put the area in condition for safe, controllable and reasonably satisfactory temporary use. There are other operational expenses including restoration of the area at the end of the season which must be met in some way by the Park Department."

The Commissioner stressed the need for "these funds or a

Continued on Page 11, Column 3

Queen and Prince Arrive in Canada to Open Tour

POL... OWNS...

But Goldw... Control... Moses Ba...

By WAYN...

The private sec... roe Goldwater, long... Democratic politics... revealed yesterday as... of record of most of... slum clearance site in...

Mr. Goldwater, fo... partner of the late Ed... Flynn, Democratic lea... the Bronx, met the disc... head on in a fiery press c... ence.

"I have no financial inte... in the property, never have h... and never expect to have," t... 73-year-old Mr. Goldwater d... clared.

He identified the true owners as eight business men, all but three of them clients of his law firm.

"Big Profits" Denied

On another front the Mayor's committee that directs the city's slum clearance program was embroiled in a controversy over a mortgage transaction between a bank headed by the committee's vice chairman and one of the sponsors of a project.

Robert Moses, chairman of the Slum Clearance Committee, issued a statement expressing the "complete confidence" of the committee in its vice chairman, Thomas J. Shanahan, and denying that Mr. Shanahan would get "big profits" out of committee projects.

However, James Felt, one of

Continued on Page 10, Column 1

... wa... mar... ch... to the... rides... of Estim... 100 taxi... There was... twenty-fiv... the bill.

The bill... board and... call for:

¶A gross-rec... from one-fourth... two-fifths of 1 pe...

Continued on Page 1...

McElroy Hints North Kore... Made the Attack on U. S. P...

By JACK RAYMOND

Special to The New York Times.

WASHINGTON, June 18—The two Communist planes that attacked a United States patrol aircraft Monday appeared to be North Korean, Neil H. McElroy, Secretary of Defense, said today.

He added that positive identification had not been made. However, the fact that the incident took place off North Korea over the Sea of Japan suggests that the assailants were "more than likely North Korean," he said.

It was learned from another source that United States experts had ascertained that the attacking MIG's, bearing red star markings, were based at a North Korean airfield.

Secretary McElroy said Soviet, North Korean and Chinese Communist planes, which could not always be specifically identified, often flew their own patrols over the intern... waters of the Sea of...

"Our patrolling craft... craft of the other side... great regularity in that... where both sides want to k... an eye on each other," said M... McElroy.

The latest incident, in which... the United States tail gunner was wounded and the plane badly riddled before reaching safety in Japan, has aroused the capital.

Leading officials and legislators have condemned the attackers for having molested the United States plane over international waters. According to the Pentagon, the incident occurred about thirty-eight miles from North Korea.

President Eisenhower and many Congressmen expressed

Continued on Page 4, Column 4

GOV. LONG SEIZED AFTER AUTO DASH; PUT IN AN ASYLUM

Deputies Intercept Fighting Official on Way to Capital After He Fle...

... been mentioned to Mr. Gromyko ... adjournment had ... and he had neither accepted nor rejected it.

Communist sources professed amazement at the gloom evident in the Western camp tonight. These Communist sources said the delay in responding indicated that Moscow was giving "serious study" to the Western proposals.

However, Mr. Gromyko found nothing pleasant to say about them during his luncheon with

Continued on Page 2, Column 3

SENATE REJECTS STRAUSS, 49-46, AT NIGHT SESSION; VOTE FORCED BY JOHNSON

DEFEAT ACCEPTED

...uss Sure History ... Be Just'—He ...nks Supporters

... to The New York Times. ...GTON, Friday, June ... L. Strauss, the ...inet appointee in ... history to be re... Senate, early to... his "confidence ... be just."

... the news of ... is Commerce ... Before leav... ...nt at the ... A. M., Mr. ... following ... he Presi... ...rving as ... e since ... Senate ... con...

LOSES VOTE: Lewis L. Strauss, whose nomination for Secretary of Commerce was rejected by the Senate.

The New York Times

HOUSE APPROVES 3.5 BILLION IN AID

271-142 Roll-Call Authorizes $366 Million Less Than the Bill President Asked

By RUSSELL BAKER

Special to The New York Times.

WASHINGTON, June 18—...ouse of Representatives ...ed today a $3,542,600,000 ... aid authorization for ... fiscal year. The roll-... was 271 to 142.

...y important cut was ... of $100,000,000 from ...000 that had been ... by the House ...rs Committee for ...nt Loan Fund. ...t, however, rep... ...ack for the Ad... ...hich had origi... ...only $700,000,...

...ome twenty-... ...ffered from ...gn Affairs ... beat off ...mpts to ... a net ... Presi... ...ts. ... pre... ...ear with ... progressive re... of grant-aid programs.

This is similar to a provision tacked on by the Senate Foreign Relations Committee requiring the Administration to submit plans next year for the eventual abolition of all grant aid provided under special assistance and defense support.

The foreign-aid debate now switches to the Senate, where a bill authorizing a $4,100,000,000 program for the fiscal year 1960, which begins July 1, 1959, is pending.

Following is a breakdown of the House bill's categories com...

Continued on Page 9, Column 3

A BITTER BATTLE

G. O. P. Stalls Ballot Until 2 Absentees Fly to Capital

By ALLEN DRURY

Special to The New York Times.

WASHINGTON, Friday, June 19—The Senate rejected early today the nomination of Lewis L. Strauss to be Secretary of Commerce. The vote was 49 to 46.

Two Republicans, Senators Margaret Chase Smith of Maine and William Langer of North Dakota, joined forty-seven Democrats to defeat the controversial nominee.

The dramatic repudiation of the President's choice for the Commerce post was only the eighth time in history that a Cabinet appointment had been defeated.

The last such occurrence was on March 16, 1925, when the Senate rejected President Coolidge's nomination of Charles B. Warren of Michigan to be Attorney General.

A Dramatic Conclusion

The vote was the climax of one of the longest and bitterest considerations of a Cabinet appointment in history. It came with dramatic suddeness after a day and evening of parliamentary jockeying.

Democrats opposed to the nomination sought an early vote and Republicans filibustered desperately to prevent it until three absentee Republicans could fly in from the West.

When two of the Senators had arrived early today, Democratic and Republican leaders agreed to a vote on the nomination.

The agreement involved thirty minutes more of debate, to be followed by a quorum call and then the roll-call vote. Senator Lyndon B. Johnson of Texas, the Democratic leader, announced the agreement. It was concurred in by the Republican leader, Senator Everett McKinley Dirksen of Illinois.

It was Senator Johnson who forced the issue by threats yesterday to call a surprise vote at any time.

For President Eisenhower,

Continued on Page 12, Column 4

FAUBUS CLOSINGS OF SCHOOLS UPSET

...S. Court Declares State Law Unconstitutional

By The Associated Press.

...TLE ROCK, Ark., June 18—...hree-judge Federal court ...Gov. Orval E. Faubus a ... today in his fight ...racial integration of ...ock's public high ... declared a state ...ng law unconstitu...

...ock School Board ... with plans for ... four schools in ... fall.

Mr. Faubus, who closed the schools last fall with legislative backing, conceded that it looked as if he had lost his authority to keep them closed.

The Federal court reminded the school board it was under a "continuing mandate" to integrate the schools.

The court enjoined Governor Faubus, the school board and other public officials from interfering with the "approved plan for the gradual integration" of all schools in the Little Rock district.

The Little Rock school board, through its president, Everett Tucker Jr., announced it would proceed on the premise all schools here would be opened in the fall.

An integration plan submitted by a former school board was first approved by the Federal courts in 1956.

In September, 1957, United States District Judge Ronald N. Davies of Fargo, N. D., here on a temporary assignment, ordered Mr. Faubus to cease his

Continued on Page 13, Column 5

Ethel Barrymore

Associated Press

...re triumvirate were ... brothers, John, who died in 1942, and Lionel, who died in 1954.

Although Miss Barrymore talked amusingly of the past, she refused to live in it and had little patience for those who resented changes in drama brought on by movies and television. In one of her last interviews, several weeks ago, she said:

"We must recognize that change is not going to appeal to us personally if we are irrevocably determined to abide by the traditional standards of taste."

The square-jawed actress with the classical profile had done no acting for movies since 1954, when she made "Young at Heart," with Frank Sinatra and Doris Day. She took her final acting role on television in a "Playhouse 90" dramatization in 1956.

While no longer active as a performer, Miss Barrymore maintained a strong interest in the theatre, movies and television. Leading stars of Broad-

Continued on Page 25, Column 2

NEWS INDEX

Lionel Barrymore and Ethel Barrymore teamed up for the first and only time in *Rasputin and the Empress,* 1932.

Ethel Barrymore, the Famed Actress, Is Dead at 79

Continued From Page 1, Col. 6

way and Hollywood would visit or telephone her about show business.

More Regal Than Royalty

Born to the theatrical purple, but by her own right and dramatic genius holder of the stage's brightest scepter, Ethel Barrymore once received this crowning accollade: "More regal than royalty."

The star, descended from two of the theatre's great families—the Barrymores and the Drews—achieved her dramatic fame in the golden era of the American theatre and held her grip on the hearts of theatregoers long after she had moved from glamorous roles to mature characterizations.

Critics have written of weeping from the beginning to the end of a play Miss Barrymore acted and forgetting completely to follow the plot. Clifford Odets has told the story of trying to select a pathetic little hat for her to wear in her role as the poor London charwoman in the movie "None But the Lonely Heart." After trying on countless hats, Miss Barrymore turned for approval of the latest headgear and Mr. Odets burst into laughter.

"You still look like a queen," he told her.

She was then 65 years old and Hollywood passed over the glittering array of fine talent that year to give its own Academy Award for acting to Broadway's still-reigning sovereign.

Held Audiences Enthralled

Miss Barrymore was described by Harold Clurman, author and critic, as possessing a naturally regal quality that was as easy and organic for her as breathing.

"It is a spiritual rather than a social quality," he observed. "Very few kings and queens have possessed it."

Her acting held her audiences enthralled and silent. And so did her manner. She was asked once what she did when playgoers began coughing in the theatre. "I never let them cough," she replied, then added: "They don't dare!"

Throaty and vibrant, her voice captivated audiences through half a century and more. But, as one admirer noted, it did not merely make a rich sound—it was the echo of an inexhaustible wealth of experience. It was the echo of a life Miss Barrymore once thought of describing as "Too Many Tears" in her biography, but later decided to call "Memories" because of her reticence about the expression of her private emotions.

Hailed by Truman

The actress, who had a theatre named after her—on Forty-seventh Street, west of Broadway—and who on her seventieth birthday was hailed by former President Harry S. Truman as "a great lady and a great artist," recalled once that she had never really wanted to be an actress.

"I always hoped to be a pianist," she confided. "But I had to eat, and acting seemed like the natural thing to do, since the family was already in it." Long after she had achieved fame she said she was "always scared to death" because of her shyness when she went on stage.

Miss Barrymore, who was born in Philadelphia on Aug. 15, 1879, was 14 when she decided it was time to think about earning a living. She left the Convent of the Sacred Heart in Philadelphia to join her grandmother, Mrs. John Drew Sr., one of the first of the outstanding American actresses. Miss Barrymore made her debut in New York in the role of Julia in "The Rivals," at the now defunct Empire Theatre on Jan. 25, 1894.

Elite of the Theatre

She was watched, carefully, by the critics. Her father was Maurice Barrymore, a matinee idol and a Beau Brummel of his day, and her mother was the lovely Georgiana Drew, whose family for generations had been among the élite of the theatre. Her mother's brother was John Drew and her great-grandmother, Eliza Lane, was an English actress and singer of note. These were her antecedents, and the critics were curious.

It was not a particularly brilliant debut, and managers did not rush to add this latest Barrymore to their lists of stars. But John Drew, whose leading lady then was the celebrated Maude Adams, found a small part for her in his vehicle "The Bauble Shop," and Charles Frohman, the producer, saw her and thought she might do.

She was on her way. A few years, first, of small parts, tours and little cash. But she began to attract favorable attention and, in 1901, rose to stardom when Mr. Frohman gave her the leading role of Mme. Trentoni in "Captain Jinks of the Horse Marines."

Then, for a decade or more, she appeared in some of the hits of the day, including "Cousin Kate," "Sunday," "A Doll's House," "Alice Sit-by-the-Fire" and "The Silver Box." It was for "Sunday" that Miss Barrymore came out on stage to quiet the thunderous applause and announced: "That's all there is, there isn't any more"—a line that became a part of the national language.

Among her notable roles were in the plays "The Corn Is Green," "The Constant Wife," "School for Scandal" and "The Kingdom of God." She also appeared on the screen with her brothers in "Rasputin and the Empress."

It was in the early Nineteen Hundreds that Miss Barrymore became the idol of her public. Just as schoolgirls of later periods copied the late Jean Harlow's platinum-blonde hair, Joan Crawford's eyebrows and Hedy Lamarr's coiffure, young girls of Miss Barrymore's earlier days solemnly adopted what they called the "Ethel Barrymore voice," "Ethel Barrymore walk" and a dozen other mannerisms of the star.

Rumors of Marriage

On March 14, 1909, after it had been rumored at various times that she was to be married to a dozen or more men—among them Prince Ranjitsinihi, famous British-Indian cricket player; Gerald du Maurier, Capt. Harry Graham of the Scots Guards, and others—Miss Barrymore surprised her public with her marriage to Russell G. Colt, son of Col. Samuel Pomeroy Colt, then board chairman of the United States Rubber Company.

Three children, Samuel Colt, John Drew Colt and Ethel Barrymore Colt, all of whom have since made efforts toward theatrical careers, were born to them. In 1923, after numerous separations and reconciliations, Mr. Colt and Miss Barrymore finally were divorced.

About the time the motion pictures began raiding Broadway for stars, Miss Barrymore accepted a year's contract in Hollywood. Of her career in the silent films, Miss Barrymore once said that the only picture she ever made that she could bear to look at was "The Awakening of Helena Ritchie." She was very happy to return from the silents to the stage.

'Retired' in 1936

In 1936 she announced that she was "definitely" retired from the stage and intended to devote the rest of her life to the business of being a mother to her children. But a year later she was back on Broadway in the Theatre Guild's "The Ghost of Yankee Doodle." In 1938 she starred in the role of a 101-year-old matriarch in Mazo de la Roche's "Whiteoaks." In "Constant Wife" she gave a long run of 295 performances on Broadway, but later "The Corn Is Green" ran for more than a year in the initial showing.

Miss Barrymore could be very blunt. In 1933 she told an audience of Philadelphia clubwomen that they were "moronic" and that she did not know why she bothered to speak to them at all. On her seventy-fifth birthday she was asked what she thought of television. Her reply: "It's hell."

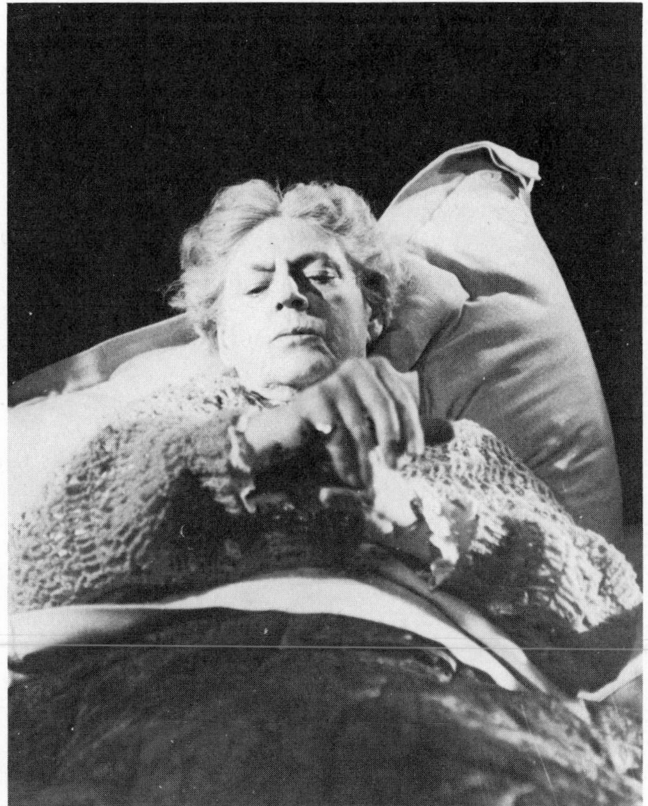

Ethel Barrymore in *Pinky,* 1949.

"All the News That's Fit to Print."

The New York Times.

LATE CITY EDITION

Continued warm today.

Temperatures Yesterday—Max., 76; Min., 56

Copyright, 1942, by The New York Times Company.

VOL. XCI..No. 30,807. Entered as Second-Class Matter, Postoffice, New York, N. Y. NEW YORK, SATURDAY, MAY 30, 1942. THREE CENTS NEW YORK CITY and Vicinity

JOHN BARRYMORE DIES IN HOLLYWOOD

Actor, 60, in Stage and Screen Career, Kept the Tradition of Famous Theatre Family

By The Associated Press.

HOLLYWOOD, May 29—John Barrymore, veteran star of the stage, screen and radio, died tonight at 10:20 o'clock Pacific war time. His age was 60.

Only his brother, Lionel, also a veteran actor, was at his bedside, in addition to his professional attendants, when the end came after several hours of unconsciousness.

His physician, Dr. Hugo M. Kersten, said the immediate cause of death was myocarditis, with chronic nephritis, cirrhosis of the liver and gastric ulcers as recent contributing factors.

Barrymore's daughter, Diana, had returned to the Hollywood Presbyterian Hospital a few minutes before his death, but was not in her father's room at the end. She had visited the hospital several times previously today, as had several of the actor's close friends, and sheafs of letters and telegrams were received from other relatives and friends over the nation.

It was not until 10:40 o'clock,

Continued on Page Six

MISS WEBB GUILTY BUT ESCAPES CHAIR; TWO OTHERS TO DIE

Recommendation of Mercy by Jury in Murder of Mrs. Reich Saves Ex-Model

NEW OUTBREAK IN COURT

'Murderer!' Shrieks Shonbrun to Prosecutor—Cullen Is Unshaken by Verdict

Madeline Webb escaped the electric chair when at 5:58 o'clock last evening a jury in General Sessions found her guilty of first-degree murder as a participant in the murder of Mrs. Susan Flora Reich, middle-aged Polish refugee, in the Hotel Sutton, but recommended to Judge Jonah J. Goldstein that she be imprisoned for the rest of her life.

"Oh, Judge Goldstein! Oh, Judge Goldstein, please, I did not do it!" cried the 28-year-old former model at the announcement of the verdict.

She was the second to be convicted, the jury two minutes before having found John D. Cullen, the first of her co-defendants, guilty of murder without a mercy recommendation, and following it two minutes later with a similar verdict for Eli Shonbrun, ex-convict.

As each was convicted after a poll of the jurors, Judge Goldstein announced he would impose the mandatory sentences on June 19, Shonbrun and Cullen to die in the electric chair.

Miss Webb accompanied her words to Judge Goldstein with repeated pounding of both fists on the defense counsel table before her, Shonbrun shouting at the same time: "She is as innocent as my mother." After court attendants had shoved him back in his chair, Shonbrun moaned, "Oh, my God! I love that girl: I love that girl!"

Then yelling to the other end of the defense table to his counsel, Jacques Buitenkant, Shonbrun continued: "Oh, Jacques, come to me! That poor girl's innocent!"

Cullen Still Enigmatic

Cullen had taken his conviction with the same enigmatic expression on his face that had characterized him during the entire trial. He flushed a little as a court attendant began to interrogate him on his past for the court record.

Cullen resumed his seat calmly after he had said he was 45, his home was at 360 Forty-fifth Street, Brooklyn, described himself as a salesman and single. He was a moderate drinker and had been sentenced to the workhouse for two months in 1939 as a petty thief.

Shonbrun's attitude when he was being questioned was just the opposite. He was violently belligerent. He said he was 33, and when asked his home address, sneered: "The City Prison."

Answering a query on his business, Shonbrun roared: "My business is a murderer, just like Grumet's," referring to Assistant District Attorney Jacob Grumet, who had presented the evidence at the trial.

Resenting the admonition of the attendant to "take it easy," Shonbrun again roared: "He just crucified that girl as they did 2,000 years ago. He could have killed me five times over, but he framed that girl." He emphasized this by pointing to Miss Webb.

When asked if he ever had been convicted before, Shonbrun blurt-

Continued on Page Eight

If in Doubt, Put It Out

Within a few days the Army expects to begin reporting violators of the new dim-out regulations to the police, it was learned yesterday.

Meanwhile, Army experts under Major Gen. T. A. Terry, commander of the Second Corps Area, are continuing their surveys of the extent to which the regulations are or are not being observed in different parts of the city and vicinity.

The Army continues to emphasize that every unnecessary light should be put out and that all other lights should be dimmed to prevent light from being projected upward and causing a glow in the sky to silhouette American ships for lurking Axis submarines. The lives of American seamen and precious cargoes are still being endangered by the carelessness of some.

"If in doubt, put it out," remains the slogan of the Second Corps Area.

Vineland Empties Its Pockets For $560,000 of War Bonds

Jersey Town of 25,000 Parades and Dances $75,000 Goal Into Oblivion as It Tests System Devised by the Treasury

Special to THE NEW YORK TIMES.

VINELAND, N. J., May 29—The good people of Vineland dug into their savings today, literally turning their pockets inside out to show the rest of the country what a small community can do when it buckles down to the serious business of buying war bonds and stamps.

The 25,000 inhabitants knew they were on the spot because the Treasury Department had told them that Vineland was to be a test case. If the sale was successful, the same methods would be applied throughout the nation.

By 10 P. M. more than $560,000 worth of bonds and stamps had been sold and it looked a[s if the] total sale would reach $60[0,000 ...] almost $25 a person. Thi[s ...] seems almost incredible con[sidering] that the experts of the T[reasury] Department believed their estimate of $75,000 optimisti[c. It] was as if New Yorkers had bou[ght] $175,000,000 worth in a single da[y.]

However, the human adding ma[chines of the Treasury Department] apparently failed to list on the credit side of the ledger that great intangible—community spirit. The way Vinelanders tackled their problem a visitor would have thought they were celebrating a victorious armistice rather than a Victory Day campaign dedicated to bringing that armistice in the shortest possible time.

Vineland's main street, Landis Avenue, was all decked out in flags and bunting. Every fifty fee[t ...] were open-air booth[s ...] speakers ca[me ...] pep talk[s ...] store[s ...]

DISTRIBUTORS FIRM ON MILK PROGRAM

Every Other Day Delivery Plan Pushed Under ODT Order Despite Strike Threat

Despite threats of a general strike of 14,000 milk drivers and maintenance workers, spokesmen for the metropolitan milk industry announced late yesterday afternoon that they would go ahead with their plan to curtail deliveries to conserve tires, gasoline and equipment, pursuant to Order 6 of the Office of Defense Transportation. Call-back and special delivery service will be discontinued on Mondays. Every-other-day deliveries will start on Wednesday.

Michael J. Cashal, vice president of the International Brotherhood of Teamsters, A. F. of L., parent of the Milk Wagon Drivers Union, asserted that while no strike call had been voted by Local 584, Units 1, 2 and 3, in protest against the plan to cut deliveries which the union declares will mean the loss of 5,000 drivers' jobs, "some men" might refuse to report for work Monday morning. Sheffield Unit 3, authorized the executive board to call a strike.

Borden's, Sheffield's the Dairy-

Continued on Page Twelve

Ac[tor, 60, in Stage and Screen] Car[eer ...] F[amous Theatre Family]

HOLL[YWOOD ...] Barrymor[e ...] stage, scr[een ...] night at 1[0:20 ...] His a[ge ...] Only his br[other ...] veteran actor, in addition to tendants, when several hours of His physician, Kersten, said the of death was m[yocarditis] chronic nephritis, liver and gastric u[lcers] contributing factors. Barrymore's daug[hter] had returned to the Presbyterian Hospital utes before his death, in her father's room a[t] She had visited the hosp[ital] eral times previously toda[y] several of the actor's close and sheafs of letters and tele[grams] were received from other rela[tives] and friends over the nation. It was not until 10:40 o'cl[ock]

Continued on Page Six

War News Summarized

SATURDAY, MAY 30, 1942

General George C. Marshall, the Army's Chief of Staff, declared yesterday that American troops "will land in France." His prediction, made in an address to the graduation class at West Point, came as the first concrete statement by an American official that the United Nations would launch a ground offensive against the Continent. General Marshall disclosed also that the Army had grown by 300,000 men in the last four weeks and that 4,500,000 would be in the ranks by the year's end, an increase of 900,000 over the previous estimate. [1:8.]

On the war's oldest active front—Libya—Axis forces cut a bewildering pattern of tank movements into the desert battlefield, but the British reported the situation satisfactory, with their fixed positions still intact. The main tank battle appeared to be raging at a desert crossroads thirty mi'es southwest of Tobruk after the British had repulsed an Axis thrust within fifty miles of the Egyptian border. The R. A. F. extended its attacks. [1:5; map, P. 2.]

Russian forces still fought fierce defensive engagements in the Izyum-Barvenkova region south of Kharkov, it was reported in a Soviet communiqué that indicated no major changes on the Kharkov front itself. Frontline dispatches said the Russians were still advancing there, while the Germans declared the battle of Kharkov had ended in a Soviet defeat. [1:7.]

British bombers raided the Gnome-Rhone airplane engine factory near Paris during the night after strong formations had struck at German targets in Northern France in daylight sweeps yesterday. During the previous night British raiders set fire to four ships in an enemy convoy off the Netherland coast. [2:2.]

Czechoslovakia groaned under new Nazi strictures as German authorities executed twelve more persons for failure to aid in the search for Reinhard Heydrich's assailant. The Deputy Gestapo Chief was reported dying: rumor had him dead. The Germans pressed their mass arrests. [1:6-7.]

The Orient's main battlefront lay in China's Chekiang Province, where Chungking reports said that Chinese groups still held the important cities of Kinhwa and Lanchi in the face of repeated Japanese assaults. Chinese diversionary attacks seemed to be developing 600 miles inland. [4:1, with map.]

Mexico's Chamber of Deputies gave unanimous approval last night to a bill authorizing President Avila Camacho to declare a state of war with the Axis powers. The Senate was expected to act today. [1:5-6.]

In Argentina, where a sharp clash loomed in Congress over the administration's neutrality policy, Acting President Castillo forbade the press to print the speeches made in Congress on foreign affairs or even to publish the news that such a prohibition had been ordered. [3:1.]

In Washington, the Navy Department announced the torpedoing of three more medium-sized American merchant ships—two in the Atlantic and one in the Caribbean area. [5:5.]

RAILROADS UNITE IN DRIVE TO MEET GREAT TRAVEL NEED

Decide at Chicago Meeting to Eliminate Some Types of Luxury Accommodations

SPECIAL TRAINS ARE OUT

Carrying Capacity in Regular Service Will Be Increased in Every Way Found Po[ssible]

[...] they [...] "luxu[ry ...] disco[ntinued ...] obser[vation ...] provid[ed ...] will be [...] coache[s ...] used on [...] dropped.

Some Sp[ecial ...]

It is expec[ted ...] accommodatio[ns ...] tained on some [...] when they do no[t ...] mands for coach [...] there be a demand [...] the luxury cars w[...] in favor of the coa[ches.]

It is planned to in[crease] cars in a train as po[ssible] of train service, th[e] speed and several [...] problems will be dis[cussed ...] committee headed by E[...] the passenger car secti[on of the] Association of American Railroads.

Mr. Pelley said that the freight load on the railroads has increased more than 80 per cent since the war started in Europe in 1939 and the passenger load has increased 40 per cent.

So far the railroads have been able to meet all demands and there has been no serious congestion in freight operations. He said that the railroads on April 1 had 3,686 more locomotives and 232,000 more serviceable freight cars than on Sept. 1, 1939, when the war began. He added that there was little hope of getting additional equipment because of restrictions on materials.

OUR SOLDIERS WILL LAND IN FRANCE, MARSHALL TELLS WEST POINT CLASS; BRITISH REPEL LIBYAN TANK ATTACKS

DESERT WAR RAGES

Axis Thrusts Beaten Off [as] Battle Goes On 28 [M]iles From Tobruk

[...] POUNDED BY R. A. F.

[...] Short of Forward [...] Positions—London [...] Optimistic View

[By ROBE]RT P. POST

[Wireless to THE] NEW YORK TIMES.

[LONDON, May] 29—The opera[tions ...] going fairly well [...] was believed in [...] it was stressed [...]ly to draw any [...]use obvious[ly ...] have some[...]heless, the [...] lieut. Gen. [...] countered [...] cessfully [...] appears [...] southern [...] the [...] fifty [...] and [...]s al[...]ruk, [...] the [...] had [...]

[...]usly [...] decla[ration ...] in a state of [war] with Germany, Italy and Japan since May 22.

It then unanimously passed a measure giving President Manuel Avila Camacho sweeping emergency power and suspending for the duration of the war many individual rights guaranteed by the Constitution, but with Congress remaining as a check on the Executive.

The declaration of war is expected to be passed promptly by the Senate tomorrow, as well as the emergency powers measure.

President Avila Camacho will then proclaim the state of war, which he asked for in his address to Congress yesterday. May 22 was the date of the Cabinet's decision for hostilities with the Axis.

The Deputies gave a loud cheer when the result of the voting was announced at 9:02 P. M. One hundred and thirty-eight Deputies were present out of a total of 168.

The vote came after two and one-half hours of speechmaking, which revealed no division and consisted of denunciations of the Axis and pleas for national and hemispheric unity.

The names of President Roosevelt and Vice President Henry Wallace were cheered when mentioned by Alejandro Carillo, editor of Popular and a Labor Deputy, who made the outstanding speech of the evening. Señor Carillo urged the organization of North

Continued on Page Three

GENERAL MARSHALL SPEAKS OF INVASION

The Chief of Staff addressing the West Point graduates yesterday

The New York Times

Heydrich Is Expected to Die; Nazis Slay 12 More Czechs

By DANIEL T. BRIGHAM

By Telephone to THE NEW YORK TIMES.

BERNE, Switzerland, Saturday, May 30—Twelve more Czechs were executed yesterday, according to official German announcements, for failing to give information to the authorities concerning the identity of the two assassins responsible for Wednesday's attack on Reinhard Heydrich, [De]puty Gestapo chief and deputy [Re]ich Protector for Bohemia-[Mo]ravia.

[G]estapo Chief Heinrich Himm[ler's] "vigilante committee" on its [...] however, appears to be as [...] discovering the perpetra[tors as] it was before the German police group left Berlin [for Cze]choslovakia. As for Herr [Heydric]h, his life was stated to be [...] of after two transfu[sions ...]erday had failed to have [...] results.

[...]eported to be suffering [...] one bullet wound in [...] bullet lodged in his [...] peritoneum, accord[ing to anoth]er report, had been [...]xplosion of the bomb [...] the car. The chauf[feur ...]st one member of [...]tapo leader's body[guard ...]day morning from [...] during the at[tack ...]ned.

[...]nt of yester[day ...]ine at Bruenn, [Moravska]-Ostrava—was [...] report from [...]ht of a con[...] tests through[...] the circle [...] from city [...] according [...]t, have [...] or[...] ical po[...] the [...] ire [...]

NEW RUSSIAN GAINS MADE AT KHARKOV

Nazi Blows Reported Repulsed South of City—Berlin Says the Battle Is Ended

By The United Press.

MOSCOW, Saturday, May 30—The Red Army advancing on the Kharkov front has captured a village and several strategic positions, and in the Izyum-Barvenkova area has repulsed two strong German attacks, one of which cost the enemy 1,400 men, front dispatches said today.

The midnight Soviet communiqué said the Red Army continued defensive battles in the Izyum-Barvenkova area and repulsed attacks by German tanks and infantry. It reported 113 German planes destroyed over the Russian front Wednesday and Thursday—sixty the first day instead of the twenty-eight previously reported, and fifty-three the next, when twenty-one Soviet planes were lost.

[The German High Command reported that the battle of Kharkov was over and that remnants of the defeated Soviet forces were being mopped up south of the Ukraine city. The Vichy radio broadcast a report that Russian artillery had shelled Kharkov for the first time in three months, according to The Associated Press.]

Under a curtain of artillery fire [a] solid line of German tanks and [mo]torized infantry charged the So[v]iet positions in one sector of Marshal Semyon Timoshenko's left flank, reports said. Russian trench-mortar and machine-gun fire at point-blank range stopped the drive and sent the Germans reeling back in confusion.

A second tank-led thrust on the twenty-five-mile Izyum-Barvenkova front seventy-five miles southeast of Kharkov likewise fell apart under Red Army counter-fire, which left the field heaped with the bodies of 1,400 enemy troops, front-line reports said.

Marshal Timoshenko, launching a new offensive north of Kharkov, was reported to have advanced about twelve miles from the region of Liptsi, eighteen miles northeast of Kharkov, to the area of the railroad running north to Belgorod in a drive threatening the main German supply line of the Northern Ukraine.

Soviet units fighting in one sec-

Continued on Page Four

CADETS CHEER HIM

Army Chief Says Staging Great Offensive Requires Courage of Youth

HAILS NEW CITIZEN-ARMY

Officers Completing Courses Are Told They Will Find Themselves 'in Fast Company'

The text of General Marshall's address is on Page 3.

By HUGH O'CONNOR

Special to THE NEW YORK TIMES.

WEST POINT, N. Y., May 29—Speaking as Chief of Staff of the Army to the graduating class of the Military Academy, General George C. Marshall declared today for the first time explicitly that "American soldiers will land in France."

He did not say when, but he set the declaration in a speech which suggested the near future rather than the indefinite.

General Marshall revealed that the Army had been increased by 300,000 men during the last four weeks and that the previous total figures of the War Department had been raised from 3,600,000 men to 4,500,000 in ranks by the end of this year.

He described the new "citizen-army of the United States" as "a virile, highly developed force" which had been organized "to fight anywhere with a minimum of delay."

"The possibilities were not overdrawn," said General Marshall, "for today we find American soldiers throughout the Pacific, in Burma, China and India. Recently they struck at Tokyo. They have wintered in Greenland and Iceland. They are landing in Northern Ireland and England—and they will land in France."

Promise of Action Cheered

The announcemen of this decision at the end of such an enumeration of our present expeditions seemed so plainly to indicate it as the next step that cheers burst from the new officers.

He then told them that their "utmost aggression" would be required and he concluded that "it is on the young and vigorous that we must depend for the energy and daring and leadership in staging a great offensive."

In accordance with the War Department security measure of concealing the movements of high officers, the Chief of Staff appeared today at West Point unannounced, as he explained, to acquaint not only the graduating class but the entire cadet corps of 1,830 with the present state of the new Army of the United States and its intentions.

General Marshall warned the 374 new second lieutenants that they would have to work "very hard" to justify themselves. He said the citizen-soldiers in the ranks were "the finest personnel in the world," and that the citizen-officers among whom they were being assigned had "won their commissions because they proved conclusively in a grueling test that they were leaders, and that they had the necessary intelligence and initiative."

"In other words," the Chief of Staff told the West Pointers, "you will be in fast company."

Motto of the Corps Stressed

In the ground forces and in the air, which will split the new West Point officers half and half, he said their contribution would be their "viewpoint, molded on four years in the corps of cadets, including a full understanding of the military intangibles which are epitomized in the motto of the corps."

The motto of the corps is "Duty, Honor, Country."

The Chief of Staff offered as an example, to both citizen and career soldiers, "the same determination that inspired Jimmie Doolittle and his gallant band."

"And I do not know anything," he continued, "which has impresse[d]

Continued on Page Three

Barrymore's Death Ends Brilliant Stage Career

Continued From Page One

twenty minutes after Barrymore's death, that Dr. Kersten notified reporters on another floor of the hospital.

Dr. Kirsten said Barrymore's last word was spoken to his brother Lionel yesterday, when he greeted him with a weak "hello." He lapsed into unconsciousness and did not regain his faculties again.

Close associates said funeral plans had not been concluded but that the ceremony undoubtedly would be held next Monday.

Barrymore, before his death, received the last sacraments of the Catholic faith, from which he had been away many years. They were administered by the Rev. John O'Donnell, pastor of a church a few blocks from the Hollywood Presbyterian Hospital. Father O'Donnell, a frequent visitor to the actor's bedside, was reluctant to discuss the matter, but said:

"Yes, it's so. It's no more than we do for a thousand others, but I suppose that because Barrymore is an international celebrity it's news."

The priest, formerly pastor of a church opposite the Metro-Goldwyn-Mayer studio, often was called as technical adviser on motion pictures. He met scores of stars, among them Barrymore. And so, he said, he only went to call on Barrymore as a friend.

"I was there the other night and he was in fine shape," Father O'Donnell said. "Lionel was visiting him, too, and John spent a long time talking about his college days. He was very gay."

Last Role On the Radio

Barrymore had confined his activities lately to the radio where he was the butt of comedy on Rudy Vallee's program. He got many of the laughs, but veteran theatregoers who had seen him in his prime, dominant as the greatest Shakespearean actor of his day, winced at his burlesque of former roles.

Occasionally, Lionel had to come to John's assistance on the air lanes, for illness kept getting in its licks, but on May 19 came the finishing siege. John showed up at the broadcasting station for rehearsal although reeling from pain. When every one was ready to go ahead he came from his dressing room, took a few steps toward the studio, then staggered backward. Vallee rushed to him. He turned his once magnificent face upward, tears streaming down his sallow, deeply lined cheeks.

"I guess," he faltered, "this is one time I miss my cue."

John Barrymore was through. Taken to a hospital, he failed to make any gain from grave complications in chest, liver and kidneys. He was conscious only part of the time. His tired heart, overtaxed by excesses of living, began to fail and stimulants had to be used to keep it going.

Of Famous Stage Lineage.

John Blythe Barrymore was born in Philadelphia on Feb. 15, 1882, of a family of troupers, but of troupers decidedly in the grand manner, his parents being the late Maurice and the late Georgianna (Drew) Barrymore. (His father had simply appropriated the name Barrymore because of its grandiloquence.) In view of his aristocratic stage lineage, it is no wonder if the young man was unable to become anything but an actor, try as he would. And he did try.

In his young manhood Mr. Barrymore had tried desperately hard to become an artist. He had dreamed of bringing the world to his feet by executing serious and even macabre masterpieces, in the style of Gustave Doré. And instead, somewhat to his own surprise, he very soon found himself to be turning out stage scenery and flamboyant posters: betraying, in his very efforts to escape it, a congenital predisposition for the stage.

One of these early Barrymores once hung in the studio-apartment of Daniel Frohman, along with other colorful odds and ends of the theatre, on the top floor of the old Lyceum Theatre building. It was a poster frankly designed to entice customers for E. H. Sothern's production of the operetta "If I Were King." The central figure was that of the poet, François Villon, depicted against a swirling, romantic and unmistakably theatrical background. Even in his art, the theatre had marked the heir of all the Barrymores and of all the Drews for its own.

In good time, of course, the theatre won. It won by the proverbial expedient of giving to a favorite and headstrong child plenty of rope, with—it is needless to add—the proverbial result. Outside the theatre misfortune and failure hounded even the most laudable efforts of the prodigal. It was a period in which he was constantly having to screw his courage up to the point of wiring to his sister, Ethel, for financial assistance.

As a cartoonist, for example, he worked for the whole of twenty minutes on The New York Telegraph. And as an illustrator for Hearst editorials he was summarily discharged one day by Arthur Brisbane, with the pious injunction that he return immediately to the stage and to the faith of his fathers. The one consolation of this period was the unexpected sale of a gruesome picture entitled "The Hangman" to Andrew Carnegie for $10—a sum which, he reflected, scarcely justified his faith in the Doré manner. It was shortly after this "encouragement" that Jack Barrymore gave up trying to go against nature and humbly bowed to his destiny.

Entrance Upon Birthright.

In its maternal astuteness, however, the theatre did not immediately kill the fatted calf. On the contrary, when the young master in October, 1903, entered upon his birthright in Chicago, in a play called "Magda" starring Nance O'Neill, he was greeted by anything but pipes and timbrils. In fact, there was only one of the Chicago reviewers—Amy Leslie by name—who seemed to be aware of the young man's presence on the stage. To this writer, possibly, the grandeur of the Barrymore name seemed a little incommensurate with the slightness of the Barrymore part. At any rate, in yellowing newspaper files, her laconic dismissal of a future Hamlet, a future Richard III, has been reverently preserved for the ages.

Later on, when the sentimentalists no longer shook their heads over him, this boisterous flippancy was transposed into the more adult key of irony. A characteristic anecdote of his later period, illustrating this tongue-in-the-cheek attitude toward extravagant praise, is the one about his being introduced to an audience as America's foremost actor. Lifting his famous left (or Drew) eyebrow, Mr. Barrymore faced his audience and said: "I like to be introduced as America's foremost actor. It precludes the necessity for further effort."

Greta Garbo and John Barrymore in *Grand Hotel.*

He made his first New York appearance at the Savoy Theatre on Dec. 28, 1903. His part was that of Corley in a play called "Glad of It," and he subsequently took the part of Polk in the same play, which could hardly be called a "vehicle." These were still impecunious days, with "art" not yet altogether lived down. But stage appearances in New York and throughout the country followed each other in rapid-fire order.

In 1906 he happened to be playing with Willie Collier in San Francisco, having arrived just in time for the earthquake, which later provided him with an inexhaustible stock of anecdotes, some of them probably imaginary. In the midst of this violent upheaval of nature Diamond Jim Brady caught sight of Barrymore elegantly strolling among the ruins, in evening dress, and gleefully brought back to New York the report that "Jack Barrymore dressed for the earthquake."

Being perpetually in need of funds at that time, and wanting to make as much capital as possible out of the earthquake, Barrymore wrote a long, imaginative letter ("one good for at least a hundred dollars") to his sister Ethel. He told in a most affecting manner how he had been thrown out of bed by the first tremor, and later, weak from exhaustion and privation, had been cruelly "put to work sorting stones by the soldiers."

Miss Barrymore (the tale goes) read this story aloud to their uncle, John Drew, who listened with mounting incredulity. "What's the matter, Uncle Jack? Don't you believe it?" inquired Miss Barrymore. "I believe every word of it," replied Mr. Drew, fervently. "It would take a convulsion of nature to get him out of bed and the United States Army to make him go to work."

Barrymore's first big "matinee idol" success was in Winchell

(continued)

Smith's "The Fortune Hunter" at the Gaiety on Sept. 4, 1909—a comedy rôle. In a chorus of mounting feminine "ahs" from pit and gallery he jumped, with characteristic lightness of heart, to dizzier and ever dizzier heights of popularity. Women swooned at the mere sight of him; his profile—which he was always extremely careful to have photographed only from the left side—became, and even in the more competitive cinema days remained, the very last word in profiles. And then, one day, the originator of the "Barrymore collar" (with the ultra long points) underwent a serious change. He began to think about his tragic heritage.

It was at the Candler Theatre, in April, 1916, that he appeared as William Falder, in Galsworthy's "Justice," "thus announcing," according to Alexander Woollcott in THE NEW YORK TIMES of March 21, 1920, "that he was about to claim his inheritance, about to enter upon the enjoyment and the responsibility of his great estate.

"Whereupon," Mr. Woollcott continued, "there was a delighted clucking from the fond nurse, from Old Nelly in the dairy, from the apple-cheeked wife of the lodge-keeper, bobbing curtseys in the lane, from all the old women of the theatre that he, the young master—bless 'is 'eart, and me that knowed 'im when 'e was a young rascal up to all manner o' tricks—that the wandering son and hope of a great house had decided to come home at last."

Of the play itself, Mr. Woollcott, the reviewer, had written (with an eye on Barrymore): "It is interesting not only as a fine and moving play, extraordinarily well staged, but as a heartening evidence of the eternal renewal of the theatre. When that old gentleman next door writes a long and lachrymose essay to prove that the last of the great Shakespearean players has made his final exit from the stage—under his very window at the time there may be dancing to the music of the hurdy-gurdies a mite of a girl destined in her day to be the greatest Juliet of them all."

At the Sam H. Harris Theatre, in November, 1922, Barrymore appeared as Hamlet, the rôle which marked the climax of his second, or tragic, phase. During 1923-24 he toured in the same play, and in 1925 stormed London itself, where he enjoyed a pronounced success. Incongruously enough, his departure from the Shakespearean into his final (and highly remunerative) cinema phase, was signalized by the recitation of the Duke of Gloucester's soliloquy in one of the earliest Vitaphone "talkies," "Show of Shows," at the Winter Garden in November, 1929. The soliloquy was sandwiched in between comedians and female dancers: a prophetic proximity.

His principal motion-picture rôles were taken in "Sherlock Holmes," "The Sea Beast," "Beau Brummel," "Don Juan," "Dr. Jekyll and Mr. Hyde," "Moby Dick," and "Rasputin."

Appeared in "Grand Hotel" Film

He also appeared in film versions of the plays "Grand Hotel," "A Bill of Divorcement," "Topaz," "Reunion in Vienna," "Dinner at Eight," "Counsellor at Law" and "Twentieth Century."

If it was true, as gossip had it, that Barrymore had dreamed of doing Shakespeare rôles for the films, his dream was never realized. In September, 1934, it was reported that he had signed a contract to appear in a motion picture version of one of Shakespeare's tragedies, under the direction of Alexander Korda, in London. But the picture was never made.

Barrymore's favorite sport was yachting and he did it on a luxurious scale. His $150,000 pleasure cruiser, the Infanta, was a familiar sight in Alaskan waters every Summer, and its launching in January, 1930, at Long Beach, Calif., was a movie colony sensation.

Amid spectacular ceremonies the vessel was named in honor of Barrymore's infant daughter, Dolores Ethel Mae Barrymore, whose birth had recently been hailed in news stories and photographs throughout the country like that of a royal princess. Barrymore was wearing a prodigious black beard then, but was as careful as ever to allow only his left profile to be photographed. (He always maintained that the right was not up to the Barrymore standard.)

He was known for his exuberant temperament and racy vocabulary, both of which were duly celebrated in "The Royal Family," a play about the three Barrymores, Ethel, John and Lionel, which enjoyed a long run at the Selwyn Theatre in 1927-28. It was written by Edna Ferber and George S. Kaufman. Barrymore was fond of paying incognito visits to New York, like a prince of the blood royal on a spree, shielding his blazing fame under obscure aliases to throw newspapers off the scent, making whirlwind tours of all the fashionable drinking places, in which he took care to exhibit only the right and comparatively little known side of his famous profile. He loved to confuse his interviewers with extravagant statements and unprintable "wisecracks," but he was liked by newspaper men, and considered good "copy," though he was one of the most carefully "edited" celebrities of the age.

In the Summer of 1934, he came down with a serious illness. Shortly after regaining his health he went on a voyage to India.

Barrymore's first wife was Miss Katherine Corri Harris, daughter of Mr. and Mrs. Sidney Harris of New York. They were married in New York on Sept. 1, 1910, though Mr. Harris objected to the match on the ground that his daughter, who was then 18, was too young. Mrs. Harris, on the other hand, favored the marriage and because she supported the plans of the young couple, was deprived of alimony by her husband and also of a large income paid her by her husband's aunt, Mrs. Herbert Harriman (formerly Mrs. Albert Stevens of Stevens Castle) prior to the marriage. Seven years later Mrs. Barrymore obtained an interlocutory decree of divorce in Santa Barbara, Calif.

In 1920, Barrymore married Mrs. Leonard Thomas, the former Blanche Oelrichs, whom Helleu, the French artist, had declared to be the most beautiful woman in the United States. Mrs. Thomas, who had divorced her husband a short time before, was considered one of the most gifted intellectuals of New York society and was the author of poetry and plays under the pen name "Michael Strange." She, too, divorced Mr. Barrymore, after a separation of three years. They had one daughter, Diana.

His third wife was Dolores Costello, the leading lady in a number of his screen successes, who retired from professional life on the birth of her daughter in 1930. Their wedding (Miss Costello's first) took place in 1928. A son, John Blythe Barrymore Jr., was born to them on June 4, 1932.

Nor was Barrymore's marriage to Miss Costello any more successful. On May 25, 1934, at Los Angeles, the latter brought suit for divorce on the grounds of cruelty, habitual intemperance and failure to provide. She asked that the entire community property be awarded to her, together with $10,000 for attorneys' fees. The divorce was granted several months later.

Enter Caliban and Ariel

Barrymore then entered upon the Caliban and Ariel phase of his career. When Miss Costello had filed suit for divorce it was noted that he had just left New York on his yacht for a cruise in the West Indies.

With him was Miss Elaine Jacobs, a 19-year-old New York actress, and her parents. Miss Jacobs had recently taken the stage name of Elaine Barrie. It was reported at the time that she and Barrymore had met as the result of a fan note addressed by the young woman to the actor, who was then in a New York hospital.

When the West Indian cruise was ended Barrymore undertook to sponsor the stage and radio career of Miss Jacobs-Barrie and frequently was seen in her company. Within a few weeks Miss Barrie announced that she planned to marry the 54-year-old actor as soon as Miss Costello obtained a divorce from him. Barrymore did not immediately confirm the announcement. When he left New York for Hollywood Miss Barrie set out upon a bewildering chase of the man with whom she had said she planned marriage. Barrymore made the trip by plane and train with Miss Barrie close behind him. She was alternately coy and effusive with the newspaper men who followed the chase. She caught up with Barrymore in California. She disclosed that she called Barrymore Caliban and that he called her Ariel.

Miss Barrie and the actor flew from Los Angeles to Yuma, Ariz., on Nov. 6, 1936, and were married by a justice of the peace.

The frequent temporary separations of the couple provided food for the gossip-loving public for several weeks. Miss Barrie announced that she planned to continue her career on the stage, adding that she would, in all probability, appear opposite her husband in several new screen and stage productions. Questioned about the aspirations of his wife, Barrymore was vague.

About two months after the marriage, Miss Barrie filed suit for divorce in Los Angeles. She charged mental cruelty. An interlocutory decree of divorce was granted. Within a few weeks Barrymore and Miss Barrie were seen in public once more and there were rumors that they planned to be re-wed. Miss Barrie confirmed these rumors although Barrymore was silent. After another more or less public reconciliation Caliban and Ariel had the decree set aside.

John Barrymore had not appeared on a legitimate stage for fourteen years when he decided to forego the more lucrative employment of Hollywood, where his salary through 1938 was in the upper brackets. There was much publicity concerning the play in which he would appear. Finally it was announced that the vehicle would be "My Dear Children," a comedy by Catherine Turney and Jerry Horwin.

The comedy opened at Princeton, N. J., on March 25, 1939, at the McCarter Theatre. It concerned the first meeting of a thrice-married actor with his daughters, now grown up. In the cast was Miss Elaine Barrie, Mr. Barrymore's fourth wife. Critics found the play inconsequential but amusing. Barrymore was accorded a five-minute ovation at the final curtain. The company then went on the road.

Barrymore by this time had become weary and seemed aged, and his health was not good. The tour was halted in Washington because of an attack of laryngitis which kept Barrymore from reading his lines. When the tour resumed the company went to St. Louis. There Barrymore and Miss Barrie had a disagreement and she quit the cast, claiming she had been "fired" and through Actor's Equity sought back pay. After arbitration she received $4,062.50 and $500 weekly until the expiration of her contract at the end of 1939.

John Barrymore and Joan Bennett in a scene from *Moby Dick.*

"All the News That's Fit to Print"

The New York Times.

LATE CITY EDITION
Increasing cloudiness today; rain tonight and tomorrow.
Temperature Range Today—Max., 55; Min., 40
Temperatures Yesterday—Max., 49; Min., 38
Full U. S. Weather Bureau Report, Page 59

Copyright, 1954, by The New York Times Company.

VOL. CIV..No. 35,360. Entered as Second-Class Matter. Post Office, New York, N. Y. NEW YORK, TUESDAY, NOVEMBER 16, 1954. Times Square, New York 36, N. Y. Telephone LAckawanna 4-1000 FIVE CENTS

U.S. ALLOTS ATOMS TO OTHER NATIONS IN PEACE PROGRAM

220 Pounds of Fissionable Material Being Allocated, Lodge Announces in U. N.

HE REPLIES TO VISHINSKY

Denies Eisenhower Plan Has Lost Scope—Confers With Russian on Proposals

By THOMAS J. HAMILTON
Special to The New York Times.

UNITED NATIONS, N. Y., Nov. 15—The United States delegation, with the authorization of President Eisenhower, announced today that the Atomic Energy Commission had allocated 220 pounds of fissionable material for use by other countries under the United States' atoms-for-peace program.

Henry Cabot Lodge Jr. told ... Political and Security Co... of the General Assem... material would ... considerable ... small experiment... are to be emphasi... stages of the p... larger amounts are ... reactors that produce ...

Neither Mr. Lodge no... members of the United ... delegation provided any ... tional information. However ... clear experts attached to ... Western delegations said ... understood that the fissionable material would not be of the ... used in nuclear weapons.

These experts said they ... lieved that the fissionable ma... rial would be either plutonium or U-235, probably the latter. They explained that while some experimental reactors use "weapon-grade" material, it is too concentrated for efficient use in most experimental or power reactors. Mr. Lodge said that "in the immediate future" no "weapon-grade" material would be supplied.

Transfers to Come in 1955

Also, since the announcement referred solely to material to be supplied with the approval of the proposed international atomic energy agency, the United States will not actually transfer any of it to a foreign country before some time next year.

The United States representative's dramatic announcement was in agreement with a suggestion last Wednesday by Brig. Gen. Carlos P. Romulo of the Philippines, who had appealed to the Soviet Union and the United States to contribute 220 pounds of fissionable material each to the United Nations. General Romulo said the organization could use it for the production of isotopes, which have wide uses in medicine, industry and agriculture, and for the training of nuclear technicians.

However, it was understood that for some time the United States delegation had been pressing the various authorities concerned in Washington to authorize the announcement, and got permission to do so only late this afternoon.

Last summer Congress authorized the Government to supply nuclear materials and information to friendly countries after arrangements had been made through bilateral negotiations. However, Congress did not authorize transfers to an international agency, so the proposed

Continued on Page 8, Column ...

Tunis Exile Warns French Invite War

By HENRY GINIGER
Special to The New York Times.

PARIS, Nov. 15—The leader of the Tunisian nationalist movement, Habib Bourguiba, accused the French today of obstructing talks and forcing the Tunisians to fight for their independence. He is negotiating indirectly with the French Government for internal autonomy for Tunisia.

Mr. Bourguiba, who is living under French guard in a hotel in Chantilly, twenty-five miles from Paris, said in an interview that French negotiators had put down conditions for granting autonomy that were "unacceptable." He said "a miracle" was needed to make the negotiations succeed.

There is a note of pessimism on the French side, too. Each side is accusing the other in advance of responsibility for the failure of the negotiations. The cordial

Continued on Page 4, Column 3

Eden Rejects Offer Of Soviet for Talks

By DREW MIDDLETON
Special to The New York Times.

LONDON, Nov. 15—Sir Anthony Eden told his countrymen tonight that changes in Soviet tactics did not mean changes in Soviet objectives.

Earlier in the day the Foreign Secretary, speaking for the Government in the House of Commons, rejected the latest Soviet bid for a European conference.

The Government hopes this rejection, and Sir Anthony's warning in a speech in Leicester, will counter the growth of the popular belief that this is the time to negotiate with the Soviet Union.

The continuous Soviet propaganda on the benefits of coexistence between the East and the West, and the sudden increase in Russian visitors to Britain, all of whom repeat the propaganda slogan about peace

Continued on Page 10, Column ...

BONN ...

... an... into... Spe... the Se... cation of ... Germany ... it into t... for one" ... Organization...

The Preside... cols were "fou... found yearning ... is shared by all t... ples." Moreover, ... "one of history's fi... tical experiments ... tional control of ar... President added.

President Eisenho... appeal for immediate ... tion on the protocols ... sovereignty to West G... and admitting it as a mem... the North Atlantic Treat... ganization. Instead he sai...

"I hope these instruments ... be studied with a view to ... abling the Senate to act promp... ly on these matters when ... meets for its new session in January."

Wiley Not to Press Issue

Senator Alexander Wiley, Republican of Wisconsin, present chairman of the Senate Foreign Relations Committee, said he would not urge consideration of the Paris protocols before January unless the Administration requested him to do so.

Mr. Wiley's view was that he would prefer to have the European nations involved ratify the protocols before the United States Senate was asked to act.

As the President sent the protocols to the Senate, the Soviet Union was urgently attempting to delay or sidetrack the whole project by proposals of its own for a European peace conference to be held this month.

President Eisenhower's message to the Senate was accompanied by a memorandum from Secretary of State Dulles. Mr. Dulles recommended that the President pledge to the Europeans, conditioned upon the full establishment of the new kind of defense community now in preparation, that the United States would maintain a "fair share" of the armed forces to stand guard in Europe.

The President sought to give reassurance that arming the West Germans would not mean a revival of German militarism. What is afoot will not endanger any nation, he said.

"On the contrary they [the arrangements] represent one of history's first great experiments in the international control of armaments," he added.

"Moreover, their fundamental significance goes far beyond the combining of strength to deter aggression. Ultimately, we hope that they will produce a new understanding among the free peoples of Europe and a new spirit of friendship which will inspire greater cooperation in many fields of human activity."

KNOWLAND WARNS OF POLICY DANGER; CALLS FOR REVIEW

Bids Congress Summon Top Leaders—Says Coexistence of Reds Is 'Trojan Horse'

Text of the Knowland statement is printed on Page 18.

By JAMES RESTON
Special to The New York Times.

WASHINGTON, Nov. 15—Senator William F. Knowland of California, the Republican leader in the Senate, today issued a vigorous dissent to his own Administration's foreign policy.

Senator Knowland did not ... to present his vi... House ... Wedne...

... Cor... there... to pe... happy ... Earlie... vetoed a ... bers of the ... —Admiral ... the chairma...

Continued on P...

Committee Unanimity Is Broken on McCarthy Censure Charges

Associated Press Wirephotos

...V. Watkins, who said Senator McCarthy's ... names of Peress case principals since June.

Lionel Barrymore Is Dead at 76; Actor's Career Spanned 61 Years

Veteran Screen and Stage Star Also Gained Fame as Scrooge on Radio

Special to The New York Times.

LOS ANGELES, Nov. 15—Lionel Barrymore died tonight at Valley Hospital in Van Nuys. He was 76 years old. His physician, John Paul Ewing, attributed his death to a heart ailment.

The actor was stricken last night at the home of Mrs. J. E. Wheeler. He had resided with Mrs. Wheeler and her two daughters, Miss Benson Wheeler and Miss Florence Wheeler, for the last eighteen years.

Mr. Barrymore was taken to the hospital and placed in an oxygen tent. Dr. Ewing said he lapsed into unconsciousness about midnight and failed to respond to treatment.

Lionel Barrymore once estimated that members of his famous family of the Drews and the Barrymores had appeared on the stage for 200 continuous years. He, himself, despite his protests that his interest in acting had arisen only from a necessity to eat, accounted for 61 of these years.

Mr. Barrymore, although he would have preferred to be an artist and composer, became an outstanding success of stage, screen and radio. His yearly radio interpretation of Scrooge in Dickens' "Christmas Carol" became traditional. In his later years, when a hip injury confined him to a wheel-

Continued on Page 29, Column 2

1947

Lionel Barrymore

Lionel Ba... Actor's C...

Veteran Screen and ... Star Also Gained Fame ... Scrooge on Radio

Special to The New York Times.

LOS ANGELES, Nov. 15—Lionel Barrymore died tonight at Valley Hospital in Van Nuys. He was 76 years old. His physician, John Paul Ewing, attributed his death to a heart ailment.

The actor was stricken last night at the home of Mrs. J. E. Wheeler. He had resided with Mrs. Wheeler and her two daughters, Miss Benson Wheeler and Miss Florence Wheeler, for the last eighteen years.

Mr. Barrymore was taken to the hospital and placed in an oxygen tent. Dr. Ewing said he lapsed into unconsciousness about midnight and failed to respond to treatment.

Lionel Barrymore once estimated that members of his famous family of the Drews and the Barrymores had appeared on the stage for 200 continuous years. He, himself, despite his protests that his interest in acting had arisen only from a necessity to eat, accounted for 61 of these years.

Mr. Barrymore, although he

Lionel Barrymore 1947

would have preferred to be an artist and composer, became an outstanding success of stage, screen and radio. His yearly radio interpretation of Scrooge in Dickens' "Christmas Carol" became traditional. In his later years, when a hip injury confined him to a wheel-

Continued on Page 29, Column 2

...lay ...ion

... active ... for the war's ... Elihu Root Jr. resigned his membership on Sept. 30, to become counsel to the firm of Cleary, Gottlieb, Friendly & Ball.

Until his appointment to the Federal Court of Appeals last year, Judge John Marshall Harlan, who was recently nominated by President Eisenhower for the United States Supreme Court, was a member of the firm.

Mr. Dewey said yesterday that he had known many members of the firm for almost thirty years. His decision to join the firm, he explained, was made as the result of conversations extending back four, five or six months. He added that he was looking forward to resuming the practice of law "with very great pleasure."

The Governor indicated that his main interest in government and politics would be in national and international affairs. But he will also concern himself, he said, with measures for improving the administration of justice and will

Continued on Page 24, Column 3

M'CARTHY ASSAILS WATKINS ON ARMY

Disputes Antagonist's Advice That Own Files Hold Data on Peress' Discharge

...xcerpts from transcript of the committee session, Page 16.

...SHINGTON, Nov. 15—Sen... ...seph R. McCarthy was ... where he could find ...oted Maj. Irving Peress, ... dentist whom he has ...eing a Communist. ...ntagonist in the cen... Senator Arthur V. ...publican of Utah, ...ation was right in ...Republican's own ...

... not satisfy Mr. ...d he was seek... ..." in the De... who allowed ...ntist to be ...ably dis...

...vened at ... wheth... ...d be ...ning ... ...ld ...

...uld not ...obably in... ...idential order ...cker had said ...m from answering some questions about the Peress case.

...should fol... ...its constitution... ...etting the cases for

Senator Watkins told Senator McCarthy that if he did not sub...

Continued on Page 26, Column 3 Continued on Page 16, Column 7

West Point and Annapolis Forbid Debates on Recognition of Peiping

By ELIE ABEL
Special to The New York Times.

WASHINGTON, Nov. 15—The Academy ban on debates of the China question the Army said: United States Military Academy at West Point and the Naval Academy at Annapolis have forbidden participation by cadets or midshipmen in college debates on whether the United States should recognize Communist China.

The Army and Navy policies were made known today in response to inquiries prompted by the withdrawal of a West Point team from a scheduled debate with the Newark Colleges of Rutgers University.

West Point expressed regrets that its team could not debate the issue of United States diplomatic relations with the Peiping regime as scheduled and suggested an alternative topic — the merits of agricultural subsidies.

Confirming the existence of an

"It is Department of the Army policy not to have U. S. M. A. cadets involved in debate on such a controversial subject, on which in any event national policy has already been established."

West Point's most prominent living graduate, President Eisenhower, enunciated a different philosophy at his news conference last Wednesday, when he was asked to comment on "the anti-intellectual trend in our country which expresses itself in hostility to new ideas or different ideas or even traditional ideas."

The President's reply was that the United States system could stand on its own feet and would be upheld by the people in the

Continued on Page 15, Column 5

CASE NOW OPPOSES M'CARTHY CENSURE ON ZWICKER COUNT

Asserts He Reversed Position on Basis of 'New Evidence' Not Fully Explored in Inquiry

ERVIN URGES EXPULSION

Calls Charge Watkins Group Imitated Methods of Reds 'Fantastic and Foul'

Excerpts from debate; Case and Stevens letters, Page 16.

By ANTHONY LEVIERO
Special to The New York Times.

WASHINGTON, Nov. 15—Senator Francis Case said today he would not vote to censure Senator Joseph R. McCarthy on charges of having abused Brig. Gen. Ralph W. Zwicker.

This apparently completes the reversal of Senator Case, a South Dakota Republican who had joined in the unanimous recommendations of a special Senate committee to censure the Wisconsin Republican. Last week Mr. Case had proposed that the two other charges on which censure was recommended — contempt of a Senate Elections subcommittee and abuse of its five members—could be wiped out by an apology from Mr. McCarthy.

Senator McCarthy has said he will not apologize and he showed no sign of relenting today. Instead he interrogated Senator Arthur V. Watkins of Utah, chairman of the Censure Committee, before his own Senate Permanent Subcommittee on Investigations and got into a hot but inconclusive argument with him over the Peress case.

Senator Case's new proposal was regarded as the latest move by a group of Republican Senators who were seeking to soften the pending censure resolution.

Asks More Drastic Action

While Mr. Case made his move, another member of the Censure Committee, Senator Samuel J. Ervin Jr., Democrat of North Carolina, said the Senate should go one step farther than censure and expel Mr. McCarthy.

Senator Ervin declared that Senator McCarthy's "fantastic and foul" charge that the censure committee imitated Communist methods indicated his "moral or mental incapacity to perform the duties of a Senator."

Senator McCarthy's fundamental defense is that he is under attack because he is a symbol of the fight against communism. Today his friend, Senator William E. Jenner, Republican of Indiana, made a major speech in his behalf, declaring that "the strategy of censure was initiated by the Communist conspiracy."

Senator Case's new insistence on a course different from the action of censure seemed only to harden the attitude of the five ... members of the Censure Committee.

...rly this evening, as the session was ending, Senator Watkins was prepared for a new attack on Mr. McCarthy for having referred to the Senate session as a "lynch session" and for having called him a "coward" over the week-end. Mr. Watkins, however, postponed the speech until tomorrow.

Explains Change of Mind

Senator Case explained his change of mind on the basis of "new evidence," in an incident not fully explored by the censure committee, he said, in the case of Maj. Irving Peress. Dr. Peress is the former Army dentist who was promoted from captain and later honorably discharged although he had written "Fifth Amendment" across part of a form instead of answering questions about his associations.

When the dentist's invocation of the Fifth Amendment was discovered, the Defense Department ordered him discharged within ninety days. He asked to be discharged at the end of sixty days but, after his appearance before the McCarthy subcommittee, asked General Zwicker, former commanding officer of Camp Kilmer, N. J., for immediate discharge. That was on last Feb. 1.

On that same day Senator McCarthy sent to Robert T. Stevens, Secretary of the Army, by messenger a letter requesting that Captain Peress be court-martialed. Mr. McCarthy has denounced Dr. Peress as a "Fifth Amendment Communist," stating that a New York undercover

Continued on Page 17, Column 1

BARRYMORE DEAD ON THE COAST AT 76

Continued From Page 1

chair, it was a tribute to his popularity and ability that parts were written around him and audiences never questioned the appearance of an actor in a wheelchair. Born in Philadelphia April 28, 1878, he was the eldest of the three children of Maurice (Blythe) and Georgie (Drew) Barrymore. He was also later to be known as the quietest of the triumvirate of Lionel, Ethel and John, born in that order.

His reluctant stage debut came at the age of 6 when the Barrymores were on tour. He was pressed into action when a child actor became ill. When he followed up his cue with a good cry instead of his lines, he was retired from the stage by his famous parents until he was 15.

At that time another of his family, his grandmother, the prominent Louisa (Mrs. John) Drew, ventured on the stage with him in "The Rivals." His debut with the famous Mrs. Malaprop of her time was apparently successful, for he next appeared with her in "The Road to Ruin."

Took to Painting

Mr. Barrymore, who was already proclaiming his desire not to act, then left the stage to study painting for three years. The attempt was not outstanding and he returned to acting, appearing in "Squire Kate," "Cumberland '61" and several plays with Nance O'Neil's company.

He toured with the late J. A. Herne in "Sag Harbor," was cast with his uncle, John Drew, in "Second in Command," and by 1904 had appeared in many more works and was counted as a star.

In 1904, having married Doris Rankin, the young sister of his uncle Sidney Drew's wife, Mr. Barrymore, still determined to become an artist, went to Paris with his bride where he continued his painting studies for several years.

Returning to New York and still plagued with the need to earn a living, he heard of D. W. Griffith's movie-making enterprise in the Biograph Studios on Fourteenth Street. He asked for a job. Disclaiming an interest in "stars" Mr. Griffith, according to Mr. Barrymore's account of the incident, reluctantly hired the six-foot, dark-haired young man at $10 a day.

One of the first pictures made by Mr. Barrymore in those early days of silent movies was "The New York Hat," with a young actress, Mary Pickford. The script, her first, was written by Anita Loos. Others of his co-workers were Mabel Norman, Lillian and Dorothy Gish, Mack Sennett and James Kirkwood. Many of the scripts of the first two-reelers were written by actors. Mr. Barrymore himself admitted to having written "dozens" at $25 apiece.

When, as he said, he was brought "kicking and protesting back to the stage," it was one of his most famous roles, that of Colonel Ibbetson in "Peter Ibbetson," in 1917. The next year he was persuaded to leave the play for the role of Milt Shanks in "The Copperhead," described by the late Heywood Broun as "the best piece of acting I ever saw."

It was to see Lionel in this part that John Barrymore, the incorrigible brother, bought out the whole house of his own play, "Peter Ibbetson," in which he was appearing in Hartford. It developed later that John's boss, Lee Shubert, had refused to let John pay for the expensive $3,000 ticket to his brother's opening night.

Lionel followed up this success in 1921 with "Macbeth," described as the hit of the season. The same year, starring in "The Claw," Mr. Barrymore met Irene Fenwick, who became his second wife July 14, 1923, after his divorce from Doris Rankin. The marriage was known as a happy one. Mrs. Barrymore retired from the stage soon after the marriage. She died Christmas Eve in 1936.

Before he "escaped permanently to California" in 1925, he had also played in "Laugh, Clown, Laugh," "The Piker" and "Man or Devil." In the movies he made what was known as "quickies" until the Thirties, when he again became a star in that medium.

"Free Soul," in which he portrayed a drunkard lawyer defending his daughter against a murder charge, won him an Academy Award for the best performance of the year in 1931. From then on, his movies, made with some of the biggest stars in Hollywood, included "Grand Hotel," "Reunion in Vienna," "Dinner at Eight," "Treasure Island" and "David Copperfield."

Three Appear in 'Rasputin'

The three Barrymores appeared together in "Rasputin and the Empress." It was Lionel and Ethel's first appearance together since Ethel staged a production of "Camille" when she was 10. That early performance, with Lionel starred as Armand, also marked his first and last appearance in a romantic role. He declined to be cast in such a part after the experience.

In 1938, "Young Dr. Kildaire," the first in the well-known series, appeared. This was the year that Lionel, after several years' in and out of his wheelchair with a hip injury had the final accident that confined him to the chair for the rest of his career.

While he was gaining his reputation on the stage, screen and in radio, he also received recognition for his artistic and musical achievements. Several of his etchings were grouped with the "Hundred Prints of the Year," and he was elected to the Society of American Etchers.

In the summer of 1944, his symphony, "Partita," was performed at Lewisohn Stadium by Fabien Sevitzky. "In Memoriam," a tone poem in memory of his brother, John, who had died in 1942, was performed by the Philadelphia Orchestra under Eugene Ormandy. "Tableau Russe," another of his compositions, was presented in the Hollywood Bowl. The theme song for the "Mayor of the Town" radio feature, in which he played the sage and samaritan mayor, was also his composition.

As recently as 1952 another of his compositions was presented on records. This was a musical setting of "Ali Baba and the Forty Thieves" with the composer as the narrator.

Narrator for Record Album

He was narrator for an album of records made during World War II by the Armed Forces Radio Service, entitled "Great Music." He was active in community affairs, often appearing in benefits for special civic causes. At one time he was chairman of the national board of sponsors of the National Arthritis Research Foundation.

Mr. Barrymore's political activity in behalf of Governor Dewey during the 1944 Presidential campaign was reported to have brought a protest from the Roosevelt family when Metro-Goldwyn-Mayer announced him for the role of Franklin Delano Roosevelt in the film "The Beginning of the End," in 1946. He was withdrawn from the picture.

In May, 1951, Mr. Barrymore added writing to his creative achievements. His book, "We Barrymores," written with Cameron Shipp, was published by Appleton-Century-Crofts, Inc.

Mr. Barrymore also wrote a novel, "Mr. Cantonwine: A Moral Tale," published by Little, Brown & Co. The story was about a snake-oil peddling preacher.

Last March, he was one of a group of motion-picture stars who received Treasury Department citations for cooperation in helping to promote investment in United States Savings Bonds.

His sister, Ethel, survives.

Lionel Barrymore in *Body and Soul* with Aileen Pringle.

The New York Times SUNDAY, AUGUST 18, 1963.

Richard Barthelmess, 68, Dies; Boyish Idol of Silent-Film Era

Actor Rose to Fame in 1919 With 'Broken Blossoms'— Academy Award in '28

Special to The New York Times

SOUTHAMPTON, L. I., Aug. 17—Richard Barthelmess, the boyish matinee idol of the silent-film era died of cancer today at his summer home. He was 68 years old and lived at 800 Park Avenue in New York City.

For more than 25 years, the appearance of Mr. Barthelmess on the screen brought great sighs from women in movie houses throughout the country. He was the clean-cut American hero; not strikingly handsome, but good-looking; masculine, but gentle, modest and unassuming.

His shy smile and sleek black hair brought him an average of 6,000 fan letters a month at the height of his career.

From 1916, when he began his career, until 1941, when he retired because "the fun had gone out of picture making," he made 76 pictures and a sizable fortune.

Mr. Barthelmess said he had only one regret after he stopped acting—selling his production company in the nineteen-twenties to accept a lucrative contract with the First National Film Corporation. He was proud of the 12 financially successful films he produced for Inspiration Pictures.

But he was best remembered as the dashing leading man. Three years after his arrival in Hollywood, and after many small parts, he starred opposite Lillian Gish in "Broken Blossoms," which was widely acclaimed after opening in New York. He played a young Chinese.

In New York for the premiere of the film, the 24-year-old bachelor found himself surrounded by women. He fell in love with Mary Hay, a Ziegfeld girl, and they were married in the city in June of 1920, after having appeared together in the film "Way Down East."

Mr. Barthelmess's next role was his most famous—Tol'able David, a Southern mountain boy who saw that the United States mail got through.

It was one of the big money makers for the young actor. He bought the rights to the film from the producer D. W. Griffith with $250,000 he had borrowed and formed Inspiration Pictures.

Shortly after divorcing his wife in 1926, he gave up the company and began making three films a year for National Films at a reported $375,000 a year.

His first film for the company, "Patent Leather Kid," in which he played a prizefighter, was one of his finest roles. In 1928, the first year the Academy Awards were presented, he won a special award for distinguished achievement in that film and in "The Noose."

That year he married Jessica Stewart Sargent of Los Angeles, adopting her son by a former marriage.

During the nineteen-thirties he traveled a great deal. He returned to Hollywood in 1939 to appear in "Only Angels Have Wings."

Meanwhile Mr. Barthelmess acquired substantial real-estate holdings. In 1955, he sold a 50-acre beachfront estate, The Dunes in Southampton, to Henry Ford 2d.

While in Hollywood, Mr. Barthelmess was active as an athlete. He played tennis, swam, rode horseback and was a keen yachtsman.

In 1938, Mr. Barthelmess received an honorary degree from Trinity College in Hartford, which he attended. The lure of acting made him quit college to accept his first contract at a salary of $50 a week.

"When I saw my friends earning $7 and $8 a week in banks, I decided I'd better go after it," he said later.

At this time Dorothy Gish, the actress and sister of Lillian, was asked by her producer to look at one of Mr. Barthelmess's pictures. She did and then said that he was too short to be a leading man. Later, however, she played opposite him in "The Beautiful City."

His mother, Caroline Harris, a stage actress, helped teach Alla Nazimova, the Russian actress, to speak English when she first came to America. Miss Nazimova helped Mr. Barthelmess obtain his first role—opposite her in "War Brides."

During World War II, he served as a lieutenant commander in the Navy. When he retired, the comfortable life of a New York socialite suited him well. His winter days were spent on Park Avenue and his summers on the shore here. Many of his fans still wrote to him. Five years ago, he developed throat cancer and underwent several operations, eventually losing his voice.

At his bedside, when he died was his wife, Jessica. He is survived also by his adopted son, Stewart of Paris, and a daughter, Mrs. Mary Hay Bradley.

Richard Barthelmess with Lillian Gish in *Way Down East.*

Barthelmess with Dorothy Gish in *I'll Get Him Yet,* 1919.

WARNER BAXTER, 59, FILM STAR, IS DEAD

Winner of 'Oscar' in 1929—Best Known for Cisco Kid and 'Crime Doctor' Portrayals

BEVERLY HILLS, Calif., May 7 (P)—Warner Baxter, veteran motion-picture actor, died at his home tonight after a long illness. His age was 59. He had suffered from arthritis for years and a lobotomy was performed three weeks ago to alleviate his pain. Bronchial pneumonia set in recently.

In recent years, he was chronically ill, suffering pain which made eating difficult and induced malnutrition. In April, he underwent cranial surgery at St. John's Hospital in Santa Monica, then returned to his Beverly Hills home.

He and his second wife, the former Winifred Bryson, stage actress, celebrated their thirty-third wedding anniversary in January.

Began as Juvenile Lead

Mr. Baxter, whose career began with the talking films, was most widely remembered for his creation of the Cisco Kid movie role. In 1929 the Academy Award for the best actor of the year went to him for his portrayal of this role in "In Old Arizona."

Well known as a juvenile lead in his early screen days, Mr. Baxter attained even greater popularity as a character actor. In 1949 he appeared in the role of Victor Burnell in "Prison Warden," a Columbia Pictures production.

Although he received some acclaim for his part in "Lady in the Dark" in 1944, it was as the Cisco Kid that he established himself in the hearts of America's more romantic film-goers. The Cisco Kid was a Robin Hood with a six-gun. In later years the role of Dr. Robert Ordway in the "Crime Doctor" series kept him before the nation's motion-picture fans.

Mr. Baxter was born in Columbus, Ohio, on March 29, 1893. A star in amateur theatricals, he was graduated from high school in Columbus and then became a salesman of farm implements. His big chance came when the partner of Dorothy Shoemaker became ill while the company was playing in Louisville and it was necessary to draft young Baxter to take his place. He remained on the stage in small parts for about four months until his disapproving mother found out what he was doing and made him return home.

Played Stock in Dallas

To please his mother he became an insurance man and before he left the business was head of the Philadelphia office of the Travellers Insurance Company. With the money he saved on the job he struck out for the West. In Tulsa, Okla., he invested his money in a garage and lost all of it.

His next move was to Dallas, Tex., where he joined the North Brothers stock company at $30 a week, a fair salary in those days. With a little stake saved from the Dallas stock company venture he went on to California, where he tried to get into motion pictures. He played on the stage for seven more years before he crashed Hollywood.

His nearest approach to a stage success was in Oliver Morosco's "Lombardi, Ltd.," in which he played the feature role in New York. After that Mr. Baxter again tried Hollywood, this time with success. He appeared with Ethel Clayton in a Paramount picture, "Her Own Money," and after one return to the stage in Morosco's "A Tailor Made Man," he began his long series of successful Hollywood roles.

Pictures in which he appeared included "The Cisco Kid," "Six Hour to Live," "Paddy, the Next Best Thing," "Forty-second Street," "Stand Up and Cheer," "King of Burlesque," "Slave Ship" and "Kidnapped."

Elizabeth Patterson, Warner Baxter, Janet Gaynor in *Daddy Long Legs*.

Dorothy Burgess and Warner Baxter in *In Old Arizona*. Baxter won an Academy Award for his performance in this film.

NOAH BEERY SR., 62, FILM VETERAN, DIES

Villain on Screen for Many Years, Star of Todd Stage Show, Succumbs on Coast

HOLLYWOOD, Calif., April 1 (AP)—Noah Beery Sr., veteran film actor, died here today in the arms of his brother, Wallace Beery. He was at Wallace's home on a leave from his engagement in a New York stage play, "Up in Central Park." His death occurred on Wallace's birthday. He was 62 years old.

The two brothers, with Wallace's daughter, Carol Ann, were scheduled to appear on a radio show tonight. Wallace and Carol Ann went on as planned.

In New York, Morton Nathanson, press representative for Michael Todd productions, said Mr. Beery had been scheduled to return next Sunday to his role of Boss Tweed in "Up in Central Park." Mr. Beery left the show on March 21 for a two-week vacation after playing the role since the première on Jan. 27, 1945.

Disliked Parts He Played

During his long career in professional villainy Noah Beery's repertoire of malevolence ranged from a child beater in "The Godless Girl" to hard-boiled army sergeant in "Beau Geste."

Mr. Beery took his cinematic misdeeds seriously and once confessed that the man who plays the role of villain continuously suffers. "If he puts his heart into his work he can't throw off his characterizations promptly and at will," he said, adding that "they linger hours, sometimes days, in his mind." He always regretted playing the fiendish guard who beat and tortured the helpless children of the reformatory in "The Godless Girl."

Mr. Beery was born on a farm in Western Missouri. He led the life of a farm boy until his fourteenth birthday, when he left home to hawk newspapers in Kansas City. Subsequently he ran errands and sold peanuts and candy at circuses and in theatres.

His turn to the stage as a professional was due chiefly to a business in lemon drops that took him nightly to the old Gillis Theatre in Kansas City. He paid $10 a week for the privilege of selling his drops there and he made the deal pay by strolling up and down the aisles between acts, shouting the merits of "Noah's Delicious Lemon Drops."

Booming Voice Gained Attention

One night his booming voice penetrated backstage to the dressing room of Ned Risley, actor, who came out to see the man who could make so much noise. Risley called young Beery to his room and told him the voice was not only loud but worthy of cultivation for singing on the stage. The boy took a few singing lessons and started his stage career. He sang for a season at Electric Park in Kansas City and had a week at Hammerstein's Roof in this city, but drifted into melodrama under William A. Brady.

He had achieved only a moderate success after an earnest apprenticeship on the stage when in 1912 his young son, Noah Jr., emerged from a serious illness with an $8,000 bill. In an effort to wipe out this debt Mr. Beery decided to try his luck with the movies. He arrived in Los Angeles broke and had to sell his extra suit to buy food. Making the rounds of the studios he landed a day's work in a suit of armor with Cecil B. De Mille's "Joan of Arc."

A second role in Mae Murray's "The Mormon" gave him another opportunity and it led to a contract with Paramount. Thereafter he was sought constantly by directors for the most important villain roles. Money was no longer a problem to the Missouri farm boy.

Noah Beery and Mae West in *She Done Him Wrong*, 1933.

Ronald Colman, Noah Beery and Ralph Forbes in *Beau Geste*.

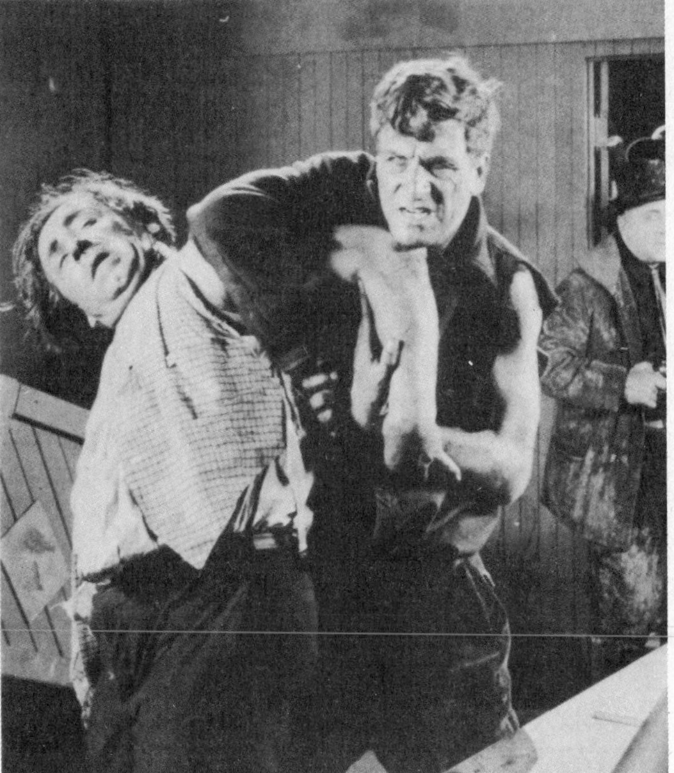

Milton Sills and Noah Beery in *The Spoilers*, 1922.

The New York Times SUNDAY, APRIL 17, 1949.

WALLACE BEERY, 64, SCREEN STAR, DIES

Leading Performer 30 Years Won 'Oscar' in 1931 for His Role in 'The Champ'

Special to THE NEW YORK TIMES.

HOLLYWOOD, Calif., April 16—Wallace Beery, veteran screen star, died last night at his home in Beverly Hills at the age of 64.

After eating dinner alone at Romanoff's Restaurant, a gathering place for film folk, Mr. Beery went home and read a newspaper. Suddenly, he slumped to the floor, and at 10 P. M. Dr. Myron Prinzmetal, who had been summoned, pronounced him dead of a myocardiac ailment.

He had been in good spirits and apparent good health, according to his permanent nurse. Members of his immediate family were notified of the heart attack at once and came to the house.

Mr. Beery planned to make his next film appearance in a picture about a reform school, "Johnny Holiday," for Willis Goldbeck, an independent producer. His last picture, "Big Jack," which he made at Metro-Goldwyn-Mayer at the end of 1948, is awaiting release.

Louis B. Mayer, head of the M-G-M studio, to which Mr. Beery had been under contract for twenty years, said today: "With the passing of Wallace Beery, the screen loses one of its most lovable figures, who brought pleasure to millions for many years."

A funeral service will be held on Tuesday.

Made 250 Pictures

Wallace Beery, who won fame on the screen as a lusty, hard-boiled, lumbering character, continued as a top-flight screen performer for more than three decades.

He had played in more than 250 pictures since 1913, and had portrayed everything from a Swedish maid to a submarine commander. Hollywood called him "the lovable old rascal."

The actor had estimated that in his years with Metro-Goldwyn-Mayer, he had made more than $50,000,000 for the company.

In 1931 Beery won an Academy Award for his performance in "The Champ." He received the Italian award for his characterization in "Viva Villa," in 1934. Four years earlier he had begun his unforgettable teaming with Marie Dressler to produce a series of pictures, the first being "Min and Bill."

In his youth Beery was a chorus boy, an elephant trainer, an engine wiper in a railroad roundhouse. He was on the dramatic stage before he became a motion-picture star.

A lover of the outdoors, he spent much of his time in later years on his two ranches—one in the Jackson Hole country of Wyoming and the other in Idaho. He had flown his own airplane for a number of years and was a lieutenant commander in the United States Naval Reserve.

Born in Kansas City, Mo., Beery was the son of a policeman, Noah Webster Beery. When a youth he was dubbed "Jumbo," because of his size. He did not enjoy classes in Chase School, Kansas City, nor the piano lessons at home, so he got a job as an elephant trainer in the Ringling Brothers circus.

After a few years with the circus, young Beery landed in New York. He had a fine baritone voice and a flair for acting, so he joined his brother Noah as a chorus man in a Broadway show. Later he had a small part, and in less than a year he replaced Raymond Hitchcock as the star in "The Yankee Tourist."

He toured the country with the Henry W. Savage company and played dramatic roles in summer stock companies in St. Louis, Kansas City and elsewhere.

It was in 1913 that Beery decided to try the movies, signing up with the Essanay studios in Chicago. In 1915 Essanay sent him to open their studios in Niles, Calif. Later he went to Hollywood and became a comedian in Keystone pictures.

While he was with Essanay he met Gloria Swanson, a shy little extra girl, and they were married in 1916. There was a divorce a year later, although they remained good friends. In 1930 Beery married Rita Gilman.

Wallace Beery in *The Champ* (1931) with Jackie Cooper.

Having no children, Beery adopted the 18-month-old daughter of a friend. The actor was devoted to his adopted daughter, who made her screen bow in "Mutiny on the Bounty."

Beery's first villain role was in "Behind the Door," made in 1917. From that time on he was cast as a villain in scores of pictures, including "The Three Musketeers," "Richard the Lion-Hearted," "Robin Hood" and "The Lost World." Eventually he returned to more likable roles of comedy portraying the kindly character behind a rough exterior.

Among his sound pictures for Metro-Goldwyn-Mayer were such hits as "Tugboat Annie," "Ah Wilderness," "The Bad Man" and "The Mighty McGurk."

Throughout the years Beery's box-office following showed an unswerving loyalty, especially in the smaller cities and towns.

Wallace Beery faces the firing squad in *The Prisoner of Zenda.*

The New York Times THURSDAY, APRIL 30, 1970

Ed Begley, Actor, Dead at 69; Noted for Character Portrayals

Won Oscar in '63 for 'Sweet Bird of Youth' — Starred in 'Inherit the Wind'

Special to The New York Times

LOS ANGELES, April 29—Ed Begley, the versatile character actor who won an Academy Award in 1963 for his portrayal of a malevolent redneck political boss in "Sweet Bird of Youth," died last night, apparently of a heart attack. The 69-year-old actor collapsed at a party in the Hollywood home of Jay Bernstein, his publicity man.

A Compulsion to Act

"I was an actor before I called myself an actor," Mr. Begley once said. "I ran away from home when I was 11 to join a traveling carnival. They dragged me back, and I ran away again. I had to act. I could no more control that than I could breathing."

Following his compulsion to act, Mr. Begley ultimately became one of the most versatile and hardworking performers of his time. He appeared on more than 12,000 radio programs and more than 250 television shows, made about 40 motion pictures, and acted on Broadway in a dozen plays.

Mr. Begley created the role of Joe Keller, the pathetic father in Arthur Miller's first stage success, "All My Sons," in 1947, and that of the crude, choleric father in Robert Anderson's "All Summer Long" in 1954.

His greatest Broadway success came in 1955, when he starred in Jerome Lawrence and Robert F. Lee's "Inherit the Wind," a fictional account of the Scopes monkey trial of 1925. During 789 performances, he played the colorful prosecutor, a character based on William Jennings Bryan, opposite Paul Muni's Clarence Darrow-like defense attorney. Then, when Mr. Muni retired from the show, Mr. Begley stepped into his role.

"The versatile Mr. Begley eased himself out of the role

Associated Press

Ed Begley

of the fundamentalist prosecutor and became the free-thinking defense counsel as though he were changing suits," Newsweek wrote.

Mr. Begley was born March 25, 1901, in Hartford, Conn. His father, Michael, was an Irish immigrant hod carrier, his mother was the former Hannah Clifford. Young Ed ran away from home several times, and at the age of 13, with only five years of grammar school behind him, gave up the idea of getting a formal education.

For many years, with time out for Navy service in World War I, he was a jack-of-all trades. He made leather knapsacks for the Army, ran a peanut roaster in a fruit store and worked as an errand boy, telegraph messenger, drayman's helper, steamfitter, pin boy and hospital attenant. finally, in 1931, he got a job as an announcer at station WTIC in Hartford.

By 1942 he had decided to try his luck in New York. Radio jobs came easy, but the would-be stage actor, already 43, had to wait a year before getting his first Broadway role, in the short-lived "Land of Fame". William Saroyan's satire, "Get Away, old Man," and other plays followed.

For five years in the mid nineteen-forties, Mr. Begley was heard on radio in the title role in "The Adventures of Charlie Chan," while at the same time he was appearing in two other radio serials and in various plays and movies.

Among his movies were "Boomerang," "Sorry, Wrong Number," "Sitting Pretty," "Deadline U.S.A." "The Great Gatsby" and "The Unsinkable Molly Brown," in which he sang, danced, and "clowns it up handsomely," according to Bosley Crowther, writing in The New York Times.

Of his dozens of television roles, Mr. Begley was most acclaimed for "Patterns," in which he played an alcoholic businessman, and "Twelve Angry Men," in which he was a bigoted juror. He re-created both roles for the screen.

Mr. Begley's bulky frame, his toothy grin, and heavy-browed eyes were familiar to millions of Americans. He stood only 5-feet-9-inches tall, but onstage often wore 3-inch elevator shoes to give an impression of bigness.

Invariably, Mr. Begley was a critic's favorite, seldom getting bad reviews, even when he was in less than good plays and roles. Of his performance in "All Summer Long," Brooks Atkinson wrote in The Times: "Ed Begley's stormy, driving, callous father is perfectly expressed." Walter Kerr, in The New York Herald Tribune, said that his performance in "Inherit the Wind" "has been widely praised but is likely never to be praised enough."

Mr Begley usually played villains, but in private life he was regarded as a jovial, warm-hearted family man who liked to tell stories about the Irish. He once described himself as "the laziest man in the world in everything except acting," and said that because of this, "I've never thought about hobbies."

Jack Warden, Edward Binns, E.G. Marshall, John Fiedler, Henry Fonda, Ed Begley, Robert Webber, Jack Klugman, George Voskovec, Martin Balsam and Joseph Sweeney in *12 Angry Men.*

WILLIAM BENDIX, ACTOR, 58, IS DEAD

Stage and Screen Veteran Capped Career With Riley

LOS ANGELES, Dec. 14 (AP) William Bendix, the actor, who played the father in "The Life of Riley" radio and television series, died today in Good Samaritan Hospital. He was 58 years old.

Mr. Bendix, who entered the hospital last Tuesday, was suffering from lobar pneumonia and malnutrition resulting from a stomach ailment.

'Good Guy' and 'Bad Guy'

On the stage, the screen and television, where a handsome face and figure can spell fortune, William Bendix parlayed into a fortune a face and figure admirably suited to the central role in Eugene O'Neill's "The Hairy Ape," a part he played in films.

The curly hair, the moon face, the jutting jaw, the low brows and the bulbous, broken nose that topped a 200-pound physique were familiar to screen and TV audiences in a succession of good-guy and bad-guy characterizations over the last 24 years.

The role of funny, shadow-boxing barkeep, with which Mr. Bendix made his Hollywood debut in "Woman of the Year" in 1941, was counterbalanced by the hired thug and killer who manhandled Alan Ladd in "The Glass Key." And television viewers knew him best for the long-run "Life of Riley" series, in which he played an amiable Brooklynite who had become a California aircraft worker and a happy, if harassed, family man.

Born at 45th and 3d

The series is said to have brought him more than $3 million, but this was not a sudden reward. Returns on Mr. Bendix's talents were slow in appearing.

He was born in a cold-water tenement at Third Avenue and 45th Street here on Jan. 14, 1906, the only son of Oscar and Hilda Carnell Bendix.

His father was a veteran of the Spanish-American War and a musician who performed in local bands. Other members of his father's family were also musicians, among them Max Bendix, a violinist who also once conducted the Metropolitan Opera Orchestra. William Bendix's only connection with music was listening to records, both popular and classic.

Several years ago he recalled that though he grew up in a tough New York neighborhood, he never got into any serious trouble. And for this he thanked his mother's firm discipline.

"My mother was strict on honesty," he said. "One time my father had $1.50 on the mantelpiece that he was saving to see a fight. I took it and bought lollipops and chocolates for the kids in the neighborhood.

"I was about 7. My mother gave me a whipping I will never forget, and to this day I have never taken anything else. Maybe she had the right idea."

Bat Boy at Polo Grounds

After graduation from Public School 5 in the Bronx and a short spell at Townsend Harris High School, Mr. Bendix went out to earn his livelihood at a variety of odd jobs. But his greatest interest was baseball, and most of the time he went to the Polo Grounds, eventually becoming a bat boy for the New York Giants and the Yankees, both of which played there.

In later years Mr. Bendix recalled fetching dozens of hot dogs for Babe Ruth, who consumed them as regularly as he hit home runs. He also attested to having watched the Bambino put more than 100 of his blasts into the stands. This and a physical resemblance added authenticity to his portrayal of the title role in "The Babe Ruth Story" in 1948.

Mr. Bendix had his first acting job when he was 5. His father, who was a handyman at the old Vitagraph Studio in Brooklyn at the time, managed to get his son a stint as the son of Lillian Walker in a silent film. Between the ages of 17 and 21, Mr. Bendix shuttled between odd jobs and semiprofessional baseball and football.

Became a Henry St. Player

He received his first taste of theatricals when he visited the Henry Street Settlement on the Lower East Side, and later he became a member of the Henry Street Players. He also did bits and songs as a singing waiter, for which he received small payments and sometimes "only a beer."

At the age of 22, on Oct. 22, 1927, Mr. Bendix married a childhood friend, Theresa Stefanotti, and, through the good offices of her father, got his first steady job—as the manager of a chain grocery store in Newark. Not quite five years later, with the Depression and mushrooming supermarkets, the chain failed and he was out of work.

Occasional cabaret jobs followed until he was able to join the New Jersey Federal Theater Project, where he earned the regular $17.50 scale.

At this point, Mr. Bendix attracted the attention of Cheryl Crawford of the Theater Guild. He had roles in six plays she produced, none of them of great moment. He appeared in "The Trial of Dr. Beck" and "One Thing After Another" and in summer stock. In between he had to go on relief.

A local agent relayed the information that the Theater Guild was seeking an actor for the role of Policeman Krupp in William Saroyan's "The Time of Your Life," which was a success for two years and became Mr. Bendix's first real break in a heretofore lean career. The late Hal Roach, veteran producer of screen comedies, saw his performance and signed him to a film contract calling for $300 a week and half of everything Mr. Roach earned

(continued)

William Bendix in *Hostages*, 1943.

Luis Van Rooten, Kirk Douglas and William Bendix in *The Detective Story,* 1951.

in excess of $600. The first film role, as the tavernkeeper in "Woman of the Year," followed.

From then on Mr. Bendix appeared in about 50 feature films, among them "Wake Island," "Guadalcanal Diary," "Lifeboat," "The Brooklyn Orchid," "Hostages," "Two Years Before the Mast," "Sentimental Journey," "Where There's Life," "The Life of Riley," "A Connecticut Yankee in King Arthur's Court," "Johnny Holiday," "Detective Story," "The Big Steal," "Blackbeard the Pirate" and "Crashout." His last movie was a Paramount production, "Invitation to a Hanging."

Four years ago the actor told an interviewer that he had played just about every role that could be imagined. But after his many years in films, he still felt that the theater was the place "where an actor gets his real satisfaction."

No 'Pressure' in Films

"Films," he said, "take tremendous pressure off—you can always reshoot a scene. But on the stage you can work with a part, build it from performance to performance."

Mr. Bendix's greatest success in three decades of radio work was his portrayal of Chester Riley in "The Life of Riley" series, which began in January of 1944 and ran for eight seasons before moving to television in January, 1953. He was assured of the sympathy of millions of radio listeners and later television viewers when he appraised the events of his fictional life, stared in bewilderment and groaned: "What a revoltin' development dis is!"

He once said that for him the most difficult role to play was that of the lovable Riley. "You've always got to strive for laughs as a bumbler," he explained. "Now, I like to play heavies, too. Once I was a psychopathic killer. You get lots of letters, but you don't have to worry about making the audience like you."

Because of contract limitations, Mr. Bendix was prevented from doing the role on TV and it went to Jackie Gleason. The show did not do well and soon Mr. Bendix took over the lead. It meant giving up a film contract worth $104,000 a year. Mr. Bendix also appeared in a Western TV series, "Overland Stage."

Took Over Gleason Role

He returned to the legitimate theater in 1960 when he succeeded Mr. Gleason in the starring role of the Broadway musical "Take Me Along."

Unlike many of his colleagues, Mr. Bendix had no yearning to be a director or a producer as his career advanced. He even disliked studying his roles in advance and for the most part he was guided by a simple professional credo: "Save a buck or two and keep on acting—that's me."

Plans for a special television series, "Bill and Martha," in which he was to have starred with Martha Raye starting in the fall, were canceled last May. Mr. Bendix filed suit against the Columbia Broadcasting System and James T. Aubrey Jr., president of C.B.S.-TV, for $2,658,000. In addition to breach of contract, the suit accused Mr. Aubrey of spreading rumors that Mr. Bendix was physically unable to do the show. It was settled for an undisclosed amount. Mr. Bendix described the settlement as "amicable."

His last television appearance was in this season's first episode of "Burke's Law."

Last June Mr. Bendix was doing a six-hour daytime radio show and appearing in the stage production "Take Her, She's Mine" at St. Charles, Ill.

'I'll Take Now'

In an interview in 1960, Mr. Bendix summed up his life:

"I've had a long, varied, pleasant, eventful career," he said. "I don't hate anybody and I don't have any bitter thoughts. I started out without any advantages, but I've been lucky and successful and I've had fun."

On another occasion, remembering his humble start and the long, lean years before success arrived, he said, "You can have the good old days. I'll take now."

Mr. Bendix, who lived in Palm Springs, Calif., is survived by his widow, a daughter, Lorraine, and an adopted daughter, Stephanie.

The New York Times MONDAY, JULY 26, 1965.

Constance Bennett Is Dead at 59; A Star Since the Silent Movies

Ghost in the 'Topper' Series Resamed Her Career Only Recently After 11 Years

Constance Bennett, whose sophisticated appearance in the films of the nineteen-thirties set standards of beauty and fashion throughout the land, died Saturday night.

The 59-year-old actress, whose career spanned four decades, died of a cerebral hemorrhage in the Walson Army Hospital at Fort Dix, N.J. She was the wife of Brig. Gen. John Theron Coulter, commander of the New York Air Defense Sector, with headquarters at Maguire Air Force Base.

She is probably best-remembered for her portrayal of the bewitching and sultry ghost in the "Topper" film series, which was adapted from Thorne Smith's novel. She played in the first "Topper" picture opposite Cary Grant in 1937.

Like the Barrymores and the Fairbankses, Miss Bennett was surrounded by the traditions of the theater from earliest childhood.

Daughter of Stage Couple

Her father was the popular Broadway stage actor Richard Bennett, and her mother was the actress Adrienne Morrison, who some time before Oct. 22, 1905, had to leave the cast of "The Squaw Man" to give birth to Constance, the eldest of her three daughters.

Although the Bennett home was constantly visited by theater people and talk of plays was daily fare, efforts were made to steer the Bennett girls clear of the stage.

Under the direction of her mother, Miss Bennett was sent to the best girls' schools in New York and Europe. Any thoughts she may have had of making the theater her life were quickly discouraged.

T'ere was an elopement in 19? with Chester Hirst Moorhead, a student at the University of Chicago. It was followed two years later by an annulment.

Then, in 1924, came the development that undid all her mother's work and brought Constance Bennett to the movies.

Won to Films by Goldwyn

In that year, she attended a ball with her father, and her blond, blue-eyed beauty caught the eye of Samuel Goldwyn, the film producer.

He persuaded her to take a screen test. She did and played a part in the movie "Cytherea." The part was small, but the critics agreed that the willowy blonde had run away with the picture.

It might be added that Miss Morrison was no more successful in keeping her other daughters from the stage. One of them became Joan Bennett, the actress; the other was Barbara Bennett, the actress and dancer who died in 1958.

After "Cytherea," there came appearances in other silent films, "Into the Net," "Code of the West," "The Goose Hangs High," "My Son," "My Wife and I," "Wandering Fires" and "Marriage."

Miss Bennett's private life soon became as familiar to movie fans as her screen roles. In 1925 she was married to the second of her five husbands, Phil Plant, a multimillionaire. They adopted a son, Peter, who in 1946 gave her away to her fifth husband, General Coulter.

Her marriage to Mr. Plant ended in divorce after four years. Next, after repeated denials of any romantic interest, she and the Marquis de la Falaise de la Coudray were married. The Marquis had previously been married to Gloria Swanson, Miss Bennett's chief rival for supremacy on the Pathe lot in Hollywood.

Rated a Shrewd Investor

At about this time Miss Bennett was reputed to be the most highly paid Hollywood star with an income of $30,000 a week. Her investment adviser said of her:

"She's the shrewdest woman in the picture industry. I used to think Mary Pickford was, but she can't hold a candle to Constance. She knows the earning power and dividend record behind every bond and every share of stock she owns."

In 1941, an article in a film magazine reported that Miss Bennett had spent a quarter of a million dollars on her wardrobe that year. This drew a sharp denial from the actress, who said that if it were so, she would have had to buy diamond-studded dresses and emerald-trimmed kimonos. Whatever the cost of her clothes, she was generally judged to be one of the mostly smartl dressed women in Hollywood.

Miss Bennett's off-screeen adventures included a court fight with Willy Pogany, a painter she had commissioned to do her portrait. She refused to pay him, complaining that he had made her thighs and waist too thick.

During the thirties she appeared in several movies every year. Among them were "Sally, Irene and Mary," "Tailspin," "This Thing Called Love," "Three Faces East," "Our Betters," "Centennial Summer," "Smart Woman" and "Madame Spy."

Her marriage to the Marquis lasted nine years. A year after they were divorced she was married to Gilbert Roland, the matinee idol whose name had been linked with hers by gossip columnists for some time. They had two daughters, Lorinda and Gyl.

Miss Bennett made her first stage appearance in 1940, in Noel Coward's "Easy Virtue." Appearances with repertory groups increased as her movie output tapered off in the late forties and early fifties.

In 1946 she was married to General Coulter, who was then a colonel. At the Officers Club at the Air Force Base in Colorado Springs she earned a reputation as an able poker player, and several times joined in card table sessions that lasted through the night and past sunrise.

Miss Bennett retained her reputation for fashionable dress, and designed many of her own clothes. In her fifties, she had not added to her 5-foot 4-inch, 97-pound figure, changed her long blond hairdo or abandoned the gold barrette and matching cigarette holder that had become her trade marks.

Credited Working Hard

When asked about her youthful appearance and enormous drive, Miss Bennett replied:

"If there's a secret to it, it's working like a beaver to be happy. What I mean is I've always been interested in everything I did, or else I wouldn't do it. When you're that interested in anything you're happy."

Constance Bennett and Cary Grant played the ghosts to Roland Young's *Topper* in the 1937 movie.

Constance Bennett, Melvyn Douglas, Greta Garbo (seated) and Robert Sterling in *Two-Faced Woman*.

"All the News That's Fit to Print"

The New York Times

LATE CITY EDITION

Weather: Partly cloudy today; cold tonight. Cloudy and cold tomorrow. Temperature range: today 35-48; Friday 33-40. Details on Page 44.

VOL. CXXIV ... No. 42,707 · © 1974 The New York Times Company · NEW YORK, SATURDAY, DECEMBER 28, 1974 · Price higher in air delivery cities. · 20 CENTS

3 Boston School Officials In Contempt Over Busing

Federal Judge Cites Foes of a Citywide Plan for Racial Desegregation

By JOHN KIFNER
Special to The New York Times

BOSTON, Dec. 27—Federal District Judge W. Arthur Garrity Jr. held three Boston School Committeemen in civil contempt of court today for refusing to approve a citywide busing plan for school desegregation.

The judge took under advisement until Monday what sanctions he might impose on the recalcitrant committee members.

Lawyers for the National Association for the Advancement of Colored People, the original plaintiffs, suggested that proper sanction might be ... a-day fines ...

... the ... a pl... — he ... —and ... 16. But ... was due ... voted 3 ... it.

In the c... day-long he... Garrity appe... ing a soluti... committee "submit" the... cial School ... without "appr...

But only m... under the judg... the three comm...

FORD AND 15 AIDES NARROW OPTIONS ON ENERGY POLICY

Nessen Says 'No Definitive Decisions Were Made,' but Calls Parley 'Intense'

By JOHN HERBERS
Special to The New York Times

VAIL, Colo., Dec. 27—President Ford met with 15 advisers today in an effort to formulate new policy proposals on energy that would increase the supply and restrict ... sumption.

Ron Ne...

... International ... Federal

PROSECUTOR BIDS WATERGATE JURY CLOSE THE LEDGER

Neal Winds Up Arguments, Declaring 'People Must Be Called to Account'

SUMMATIONS ARE ENDED

Sirica Will Give Case to the Jurors on Monday After Instructions in Law

By LESLEY OELSNER
Special to The New York Times

WASHINGTON, Dec. 27—The prosecution wound up the final arguments at the Watergate cover-up trial today by telling the jurors that it was now up to them to "balance the accounts" and close the ledgers on Watergate.

The jurors are to begin their deliberations on Monday after instructions in the law by Federal Judge John J. Sirica.

"It's no fun casting stones," the chief prosecutor, James F. Neal, told the jury this afternoon. "This Government that's represented here does not cast stones with joy or happiness.

"But to keep society going, stones must be cast. People must be called to account."

Calling to Account

If Government officials commit crimes, Mr. Neal said, if they "cover up" their mistakes, ... "strike foul blows," or "as... ult the temples of justice," ...n, "when these things occur, ...iety must call those respon... to account."

...o one at this table," he ... gesturing toward the one ... six assistant prosecutors ...tting, would suggest a ...

...s representatives of ... in a free society, ... ones who must now ... accounts and close ...lates of Watergate." ...cutor said later that ...nt "ledger," not ...

...appeal, made in ...ts of his closing ...ury, concluded ... stage of the ... instructions ...eliberations.

...nal Day

...ll and often ...ay in which ... lawyers, ... before his ...nd one of ...ming up ...t's case, ... coun... strong ...el.

...b A. ... his ...kin... ...nd ... of ... of... ...is ...y ...d ...

... summer of ... the legal problems stemming from the break-in at Democratic national headquarters in the Watergate complex on June 17, 1972.

Mr. Stein began to weep when he told the jury, toward the end of his argument, of Mr. Parkinson's good reputation, built up over more than 20 years as a lawyer.

"What is good character worth?" he asked.

Is it to be "thrown away," he asked, "and cynically tossed out in favor of the testimony of confessed perjurers? ... Doesn't a lifetime where you built it up grain by grain weigh against that?"

Mr. Stein was followed to the lectern by Richard Ben-Veniste, who presented the Government's rebuttal to the closing

Continued on Page 9, Column 1

Jack Benny, 80, Dies of Cancer on Coast

By RICHARD F. SHEPARD

Jack Benny, whose brilliant gift for self-deprecating caricature brought laughter to the nation for 40 years, died late Thursday at his home in Beverly Hills, Calif. He was 80 years old.

Irving Fein, Mr. Benny's manager and associate for many years, said that the comedian died of cancer of the pancreas. The cancer was not discovered until it appeared on X-rays last Friday. Mr. Fein said that Mr. Benny's physician had said the case was inoperable.

After word Thursday that Mr. Benny had terminal cancer, Gov. Ronald Reagan, Frank Sinatra, Bob Hope, Danny Kaye and George Burns, who was Mr. Benny's friend for 50 years, visited the Benny home.

Funeral services have been scheduled for noon tomorrow at Hillside Memorial Cemetery in Culver City, Calif. Mr. Hope and Mr. Burns will deliver eulogies. A special tribute to Mr. Benny will be televised by CBS tomorrow from 7:30 to 8:30 P.M.

The pallbearers will be Mr. Fein; Mervyn Leroy; Hilliard Marks, his wife's brother; Gregory Peck; Mr. Sinatra; Mil-

Continued on Page 26, Column 1

1959

Jack Benny

House U... As Slug...

By ...

A House committee ... conducted a nine-month ... of air hazards accuse... Federal Aviation Admi... tion yesterday of avoiding ... ership and showing sig... "sluggishness which at ti... approaches an attitude of in... ference to public safety."

The Special Subcommittee on Investigations said that the agency had "needlessly and unjustifiably put at risk" thousands of lives by failing to deal properly with dangers of the DC-10 for almost two years.

The F.A.A. began adopting stronger measures only after a McDonnell Douglas DC-10 crashed near Paris last March following sudden loss of the rear cargo door. The death toll of 346 was the largest in aviation history. The committee called on the F.A.A. to re-examine the basic design of the door's much-modified locking system.

In a 245-page report, the House group also charged the Federal agency with "foot-dragging" in allowing a long delay before ordering airliners to be equipped with a cockpit warning device designed to prevent the most common type of accident—one in which the crew inadvertently flies a properly functioning plane into a

... a... tw... ily... edi...

T... cent... jobs ... in ce... to fly... improv...

The ... recomm... F.A.A. ...

Continued ...

Jack ...

By RICHA...

Jack Benny... gift for self-de... ture brought la... tion for 40 y... Thursday at ... Beverly Hills, Ca... years old.

Irving Fein, Mr. B... ager and associate... years, said that the... died of cancer of the... The cancer was not d... until it appeared on X... Friday. Mr. Fein said ... Benny's physician had s... case was inoperable.

After word Thursday ... Mr. Benny had terminal c... Gov. Ronald Reagan, F... Sinatra, Bob Hope, Danny Kaye and George Burns, who was Mr. Benny's friend for 50 years, visited the Benny home.

Funeral services have been scheduled for noon tomorrow at Hillside Memorial Cemetery in Culver City, Calif. Mr. Hope and Mr. Burns will deliver eulogies. A special tribute to Mr. Benny will be televised by CBS tomorrow from 7:30 to 8:30 P.M.

The pallbearers will be Mr. Fein; Mervyn Leroy; Hilliard Marks, his wife's brother; Gregory Peck; Mr. Sinatra; Mil-

Continued on Page 26, Column 1

Jack Benny 1959

Amy Vanderbilt, 66, Falls to Death Here

By JUDITH CUMMINGS

Amy Vanderbilt, the syndicated columnist on etiquette, fell or jumped to her death last night from a second-story window of her residence at 438 East 87th Street, the police said.

Miss Vanderbilt, who was 66 years old, was pronounced dead on arrival at Metropolitan Hospital shortly before 8 P.M., minutes after her body was found lying near the front steps of the four-story building by a passer-by.

Miss Vanderbilt sent her interpretation of proper manners and mores into millions of American homes through her column, called "Amy Vanderbilt's Etiquette" distributed beginning in 1954 by the United Features Syndicate and later by

Continued on Page 20, Column 7

... ...tors who ...

... on Page 7, Column 1

... Industry Is in Crisis

By ... RANDELL
Special to The New York Times

BUENOS AIRES, Dec. 27 — The sweet smell of roasting beef drifted through the muggy summer air in the downtown area. Parking-lot attendants, construction workers and street repairmen have once again taken to cooking slabs of prime sirloin on crude charcoal grills on top of empty paint cans.

When the Peronist Government came to power 18 months ago, it promised to put a price freeze on beef, the staple of the Argentine diet, and to raise yearly per-capita consumption to 165 pounds within a three-year period.

The Government has succeeded beyond its wildest dreams. Today, the average Argentine eats his way through 240 pounds of beef a year, about three times as much as a Western European and twice as much as a citizen of the United States.

However, behind the prosperous veneer of crowded riverside beef restaurants and outdoor barbecues, the livestock industry has entered one of its most serious crises in recent years.

Agronomists and cattlemen agree that herds are being depleted at an alarming rate and that it is only a matter of time before there is another beef shortage — repeating the cycle that plagues the country's agriculture and explains the mysterious inability of Argentina to realize her vast agrarian potential.

"The cattle livestock industry is already in grave crisis and presents such a bleak panorama in the immediate future that urgent measures are necessary," says the Argentine Rural Society, the country's most prestigious agricultural association, in a year-end report.

The current livestock problems are partly the result of a decision earlier this year by the European Common Market countries to limit Argentine beef sharply in favor of European farmers. As a result, Argentina this year will export less than half the 556,000 tons she did in 1973.

Exports usually account for only about a third of beef production here, so it is little wonder that cattlemen have attacked the Government for the impact of its policies on the domestic market.

The freeze on meat prices was part of a general agreement negotiated by the Peronist Government between big business and labor to hold down prices and wages. But the farmers point out that the wage-

Continued on Page 2, Column 1

NEWS INDEX

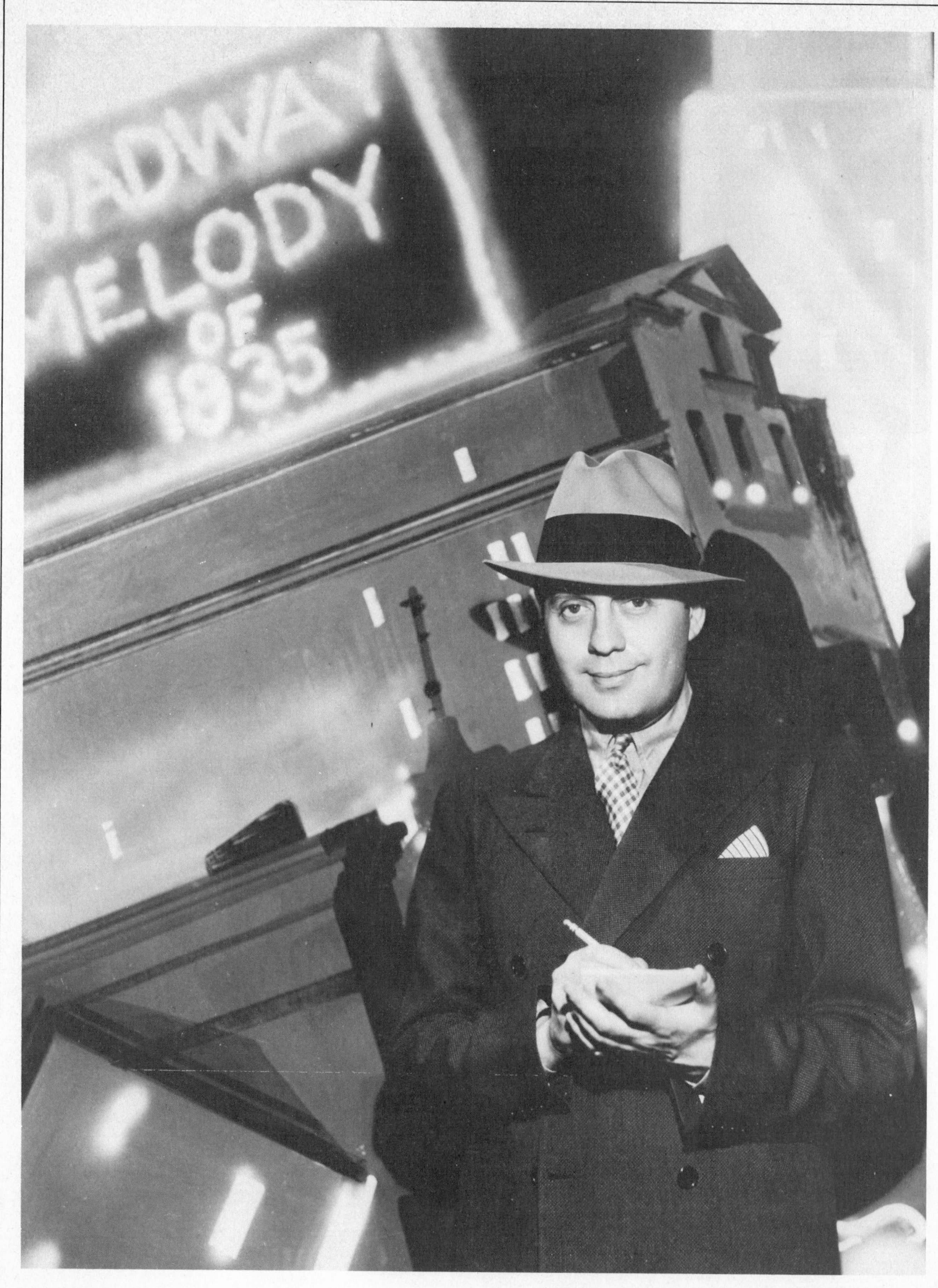

Jack Benny

Jack Benny, 80, Dies of Cancer

Continued From Page 1, Col. 2

ton Berle; Billy Wilder; Leonard Gershe; Fred Decordova and Armand Deutch.

In a telegram to the comedian's widow, President Ford said, "If laughter is the music of the soul, Jack and his violin and his good humor have made life better for all men."

Jack Benny's very special talent for the comic was, according to his own analysis, an ability to mirror the failings people recognized in themselves or their acquaintances. Decades of insistence on the air that he was only 39 years old made the joke better rather than cornier; it was one of show business's most durable bits.

A Permanent Prop

A masterly sense of timing, worthy of the violin virtuoso he realized he would never be, made him the only performer who could evoke laughter from intervals of silence. He carefully developed a performing character as a tight-fisted, somewhat pompous fellow who walked with a mincing, almost effeminate gait, and often expressed exasperation merely by resting his chin in his hand and making his blue eyes stare, martyrlike, at his viewers. His violin became his most permanent prop, and he performed nicely for fund-raising with Isaac Stern, President Truman and the New York Philharmonic.

Just as Charlie Chaplin represented the "little fellow," Mr. Benny also caught the frustrations of the average man, maybe a middle-class American, whose aspirations were always being leveled by family, friends and others.

It was not so much in his lines and in his delivery that he scored successes. His philosophy of humor shed little light on the art but it told something about the man.

It was not the words that brought the house down. It was the peerless execution of little things that became perpetually funny clichés, such as his piqued utterance of "hmmm," or his fussy, angered riposte to ribbing, "Now cut that out!"

"Never laugh at the other fellow; let him laugh at you," he said. "I try to make my character encompass about everything that is wrong with everybody. On the air, I have everybody's faults. All listeners know someone or have a relative who is a tightwad, show-off or something of that sort. Then in their minds I become a real character."

As a result, he was often the butt of his second bananas, who devastated him with their barbs. Eddie Anderson, as Rochester, his valet, lacked a shred of servility but always complained to the boss, man to man, about the Benny thrift. Mary Livingstone, his wife, Don Wilson, the announcer, and Phil Harris, the orchestra leader, also shared in the laugh lines. But Mr. Benny somehow came out ahead. Mel Blanc, the man of many voices, among them "Mr. Kitzel," and Sheldon Leonard had choice supporting parts.

Meticulous in Preparation

Mr. Benny was meticulous in preparation. Although it was widely known that he possessed a ready wit and a wonderful humor, which he often demonstrated in off-the-cuff observations on off-the-air occasions, he never—well, almost never—deviated from the script his highly paid writers had created for him.

"There is no tranquilizer like a prepared script," he once explained. For years he kept a good-humored "feud" running with Fred Allen, the humorist noted for his quick wit. Once when Mr. Allen had demolished him with a line, Mr. Benny blurted that if his scriptwriters had been there, Mr. Allen would never have gotten away with that.

He was absolutely serious about his work, in a way that many other comedians were not. At rehearsal, Mr. Benny would be sober-faced and worried about details. He was not a monster—it has always been impossible to find a colleague or even a former colleague to speak ill of him—but he was an earnest, hard-working funny man.

This was an attitude born of experience.

'Timing Was The Key'

"I soon discovered that telling jokes was not a breeze, after all," he reminisced. "Sometimes you could throw a punch line away. Other times you had to ride it hard. A pause could set up a joke—or bury it. Timing was the key."

And there was, indeed, a sort of lucky timing that determined the course of the life of this comedian out of the Midwest, a timing that found him at the right age in the right age, an age of broadcasting that made reputations overnight, as against the age of vaudeville, when it took years.

Jack Benny was named Benjamin Kubelsky when he was born in Chicago on Valentine's Day, 1894. He grew up in Waukegan, Ill., where his father Meyer, had a store, and Mr. Benny often, for laughs, used to say that this was the town where he was born.

Meyer Kubelsky, a Jewish immigrant from Russia, loved music, and when his son was 8 the father gave him a $50 violin. The boy was soon giving concerts at the town's Barrison Theater.

Got Violin at 8

The young violinist quit school in the ninth grade and, at the age of 18, went into vaudeville. He worked with a woman pianist, Cora Salisbury, and soon teamed up with Lyman Woods, also a pianist. It was during an appearance with her that Mr. Benny, who then called himself Ben K. Benny, told a joke.

"The audience laughed," he later recalled. "The sound intoxicated me. That laughter ended my days as a musician, for I never again put the violin back where it belonged except as a gag."

Life became the customary round of one-night stands in the Midwest, and the young performer was not, at least not yet, the man to startle the vaudeville bookers. When World War I came along, he joined the Navy and was assigned to "The Great Lakes Review," a sailors' road show. Here his comic genius made an impression, and his decision to renounce music became irrevocable.

After the war, he embarked on the highly competitive career of the ad libber, where his greatest asset soon proved to be his instinct for proper timing. His silence was eloquent and his double-takes were the envy of his profession. By 1926, he had a part in a Broadway musical, "The Great Temptations."

Led Popularity Polls

This led to the most coveted assignment of all: master of ceremonies at the Palace Theater, citadel of the two-a-day. Soon he went on to Hollywood, and in 1932, he found his most durable niche: radio. It started with a guest shot on Ed Sullivan's radio show and before the year was out, he had his own program on the National Broadcasting Company network.

From 1934 through 1936 he was the champion of the radio popularity polls, and for many years he was always among the top 10 programs. His wife, Sadie Marks, whom he married in 1927, became Mary Livingstone, the wife of the radio Jack Benny, as he had been calling himself for a number of years.

'The Best Format'

He still sawed away at his violin, and his never-completed rendition of "Love in Bloom" became a hallmark of the show. His writers alone received a total of $250,000 a year. In 1948, Mr. Benny took his show from NBC to CBS. As part of the move, CBS paid $2,260,000 for Mr. Benny's Amusement Enterprises organization, as part of a capital gains deal. He got $1,356,000 of this but had to pay more than $1-million in income taxes when he was unable to sustain his argument that the money did, indeed, fall into the capital gains category.

CBS kept the radio show until 1955, when, 23 years after Mr. Benny had done his first program, it went off the air. Even earlier, however, he had made the acquaintance of the new medium, television. He had been a bit wary of the tube, and his fears seemed to be substantiated by the critical reception of that first telecast, on Oct. 28, 1950.

The critics said the show had little visual attraction, that it relied too heavily on the radio tradition. But Mr. Benny made the grade with his third telecast the next April when he drastically altered his old routines and caused one critic to observe, "Mr. Benny has the best format, no format at all."

He stepped up his television schedule from irregularly scheduled shows, to semiweekly programs to weekly telecasts, which lasted from 1960 to 1965. When he "retired," he found himself almost as busy as ever, on television and in personal appearances. He appeared in many special telecasts. The last one, last Jan. 24, was billed as "Jack Benny's Second Farewell," because it came not many months after the first.

Made Many Films

Viewers of late show or midday movies occasionally glimpse Mr. Benny in many of the films he made. Among them were "Hollywood Revue of 1929" (his first), "Chasing Rainbows," "The Medicine Man," "It's in the Air," "College Holiday," "Artists and Models," "Transatlantic Merry-Go-Round," "Buck Benny Rides Again," "Charley's Aunt," "To Be or Not to Be," "George Washington Slept Here," "The Meanest Man in the World" and "The Horn Blows at Midnight."

The New York Times MONDAY, MARCH 15, 1976

Busby Berkeley, the Dance Director, Dies

By ROBERT HANLEY

Busby Berkeley, the dance director of the gaudy, grandiose Hollywood musical that awed and charmed Depression-weary filmgoers in the 1930's, died yesterday in his modest retirement home near Palm Springs, Calif. He was 80 years old.

Flamboyant, energetic, ingenious, Busby Berkeley created and perfected a musical genre of extravagant fantasy—multiple spectaculars bulging with outsized props and battalions of beautiful girls dancing in kaleidoscopic patterns or posed in elaborate geometric formations.

"My philosophy was purely—call it gigantic entertainment," he said seven years ago in an interview. "A lot of people used to say I was crazy. But I can truthfully say one thing: I gave 'em a show."

Film critics and historians never disputed that. His productions glorified girls playing 100 lighted violins in "Gold Diggers of 1933"; girls as human harp frames in "Fashions of 1934"; girls playing 100 white baby grand pianos in "Gold Diggers of 1935"; girls cascading down the sides of a pyramided fountain and swimming in unison in a large reflecting pool in "Footlight Parade" (1933); and Ruby Keeler, Mr. Berkeley's favorite leading lady, tap dancing atop a taxicab in "42d Street" (1933).

Gimmickry with the cameras was another of his hallmarks. He invented a monorail to make his cameras more mobile. He devised the so-called top-shot, the technique of filming from just above the action. And he shot through holes in the floor in his most notable works, all produced by the mid-1940's.

After that period, demand for Mr. Berkeley subsided as soaring production costs and the advent of television helped doom the big Hollywood musical.

But, in the late 1960's, the appearance of his major works on late-night television helped spark a Berkeley revival and assessments by a new generation of his contribution to film. Some admired it as a manifestation of camp.

Vincent Canby, the movie critic of The New York Times, questioned that viewpoint. Although he found some of the symmetry in Berkeley productions overbearing, he argued that Mr. Berkeley had "liberated movie musicals from a sense of oppressive realism, from the restraints of theatrical logic."

Ruby Keeler in one of Busby Berkeley's imaginative musical constructions in *42nd Street*.

Mr. Berkeley, whose original name was William Berkeley Enos, was born in Los Angeles on Nov. 29, 1895. His parents, both show people, moved to New York soon afterward, and the boy made his stage debut at the age of 5.

In 1919 he appeared in the hit musical "Irene." Two years later he began a Broadway directing career that saw him create chorus numbers in 21 musicals before he was brought to Hollywood in 1930 by Samuel Goldwyn as a dance director.

Mr. Berkeley's numbers in "Whoopee," with Eddie Cantor, were the most notable work at that studio. In 1932, he began a seven-year association with Warner Brothers that brought him to the pinnacle of hiis fame.

His eclipse began in the war years, though he continued with dance production, and some directing, through the early 1950's.

The renewed interest in Mr. Berkeley's extravaganzas was highlighted with the 1971 Broadway revival of the 1925 musical "No, No, Nanette." He supervised production for the musical. The assignment reunited him with Miss Keeler, who returned to Broadway after an absence of 41 years to play the lead role.

In recent years United Artists revived some of the Berkeley films to capitalize on the high-camp craze that swept the film industry.

At the reopening of one such replay six years ago, Mr. Berkeley reflected on the tone of his old films.

"You know, if someone came along today and made a 'Gold Diggers of 1970' he'd make himself a bloody fortune. And I'd like to do it. Wow! What I could do with wide screen and color! I didn't have those things back in the 30's."

In Busby Berkeley's *Gold Diggers of 1933*, Joan Blondell sings to a chorus of the unemployed.

The New York Times FRIDAY, NOVEMBER 10, 1967

Charles Bickford Dies on Coast; Actor Nominated for 3 Oscars

Performer's Career Spanned Almost 40 Years on Stage, in Films and on TV

HOLLYWOOD, Nov. 9 (UPI) —Charles Bickford, the actor whose crinkled hair, gruff voice and granite features made him a well-known figure on Broadway and in Hollywood for more than three decades, died tonight at the age of 78.

Mr. Bickford had been a patient at the University of California at Los Angeles Medical Center since last July, when he checked in for treatment of emphysema. His illness became complicated by pneumonia and then by a blood infection, a hospital spokesman said.

Aged With Character Parts

"Actors," Mr. Bickford once said, "seem to attach some kind of personal importance to heroism and youth, and insist on clinching in the sunset, first making sure that that touch of gray on top has been carefully shoe-polished out. If they want to stay on the screen and make money, which is a point, too, they ought to be willing to grow old and act out villainy."

In keeping with that philosophy, Mr. Bickford manifested an apparent indifference toward becoming or remaining a leading man or romantic idol. The length of his career in Hollywood—nearly 40 years —testified to his willingness to "grow old and act out villainy."

Millions came to know him in recent years for his television portrayals in "The Virginian" series, but he was also known to millions for his countless and versatile character portrayals in scores of movies.

On at least three occasions his artistry was recognized with Academy Award nominations—for "Song of Bernadette," "Johnny Belinda" and "The Farmer's Daughter"—but he never won an Oscar.

Mauled by Lion in 1935

His career nearly ended prematurely in 1935, when a 400-pound lion mauled him as they were rehearsing a jungle scene for "East of Java" at the Universal-International studios.

Handlers hauled the lion away, but not before the animal had torn Mr. Bickford's throat close to the jugular vein. Nearly a year was required to repair the injuries to Mr. Bickford's neck and shoulders.

Charles Ambrose Bickford (he used his middle initial early in his career) was born in Cambridge, Mass., on Jan. 1, 1889. He was the youngest of four sons of Lorettus E. Bickford, a coffee importer, who also had three daughters.

Intending to become an engineer, he enrolled in the Massachusetts Institute of Technology following a world cruise as a coal passer for the Navy. At one point, he found himself in San Francisco, penniless. As he later told an interviewer, a date with a burlesque queen led to an introduction to her show's impresario, who offerd him a job.

Judy Garland, James Mason and Charles Bickford starred in *A Star is Born*, 1954.

It was his introduction to the theater, and, after a hitch as a lieutenant in the Army Corps of Engineers in World War I, he returned to acting. He reached Broadway 10 years later, and in 1925 gained recognition as Oklahoma Red in Maxwell Anderson's picaresque drama of hobo life, "Outside Looking In."

After further successes on Broadway, Mr. Bickford was lured to Hollywood, for Cecil B. DeMille's first venture in sound, "Dynamite." From then on, Mr. Bickford became a familiar screen figure.

While pursuing a busy career in films, Mr. Bickford found time to develop his talent as an amateur painter and to devote himself to such business ventures as a gold mine in San Bernardino County, Calif.

But acting remained his principal interest, and he told an interviewer once that he intended to continue in that profession "as long as I can get up on my feet."

No person with acting in his blood ever wants to retire, or is happy if he does, he commented. "He is an actor to the last."

After several years in Hollywood, however, he grew dissatisfied with the parts he was playing. "Gradually I noticed that I was slipping into those cruel, gravel-voiced roles of the chief jailer and the backwoods father and the escaped convict. I made lots of pictures—mostly 'B's'—and then I began thinking of parts which would take me out of prison cell blocks and off quarterdeck of a hell ship and out of those seven-day epics into which I had gravitated."

In 1941, he began turning down "B" pictures and seeking better roles.

He campaigned for, and won, the role of the priest in "The Song of Bernadette" and his portrayal led the way to the more serious work he had been seeking.

Despite his successes, Mr. Bickford said that he rarely watched himself. "Perhaps it's because I'm too critical that I don't usually see my stuff," he said. "Very often it's a weird experience, and sometimes it's a little nauseating."

In 1919, he married Beatrice Loring, an actress. They had two children, Doris Marie and Rex Albert.

Joseph Cotten, Loretta Young, Charles Bickford and Ethel Barrymore in *The Farmer's Daughter*.

The New York Times SUNDAY, MARCH 9, 1975

Ben Blue, Sad-Faced Comedian, A Performer Five Decades, Dies

HOLLYWOOD, March 8 (UPI) —Ben Blue, the sad-faced comedian who performed for more than five decades in music halls, on the vaudeville stage, in films, nightclubs and on radio and television, died last evening at the age of 73.

He leaves his second wife, the former Axie Dunlap, a one-time George White's "Scandals" girl, and two sons, Tom and Robert.

Artist in Pantomime

From the time Ben Blue entered show business as a 15-year-old chorus boy in George M. Cohan's musical comedy "Irene," trying out in Montreal, where Mr. Blue was born, he was more of a pantomime artist than a talker.

A few years ago he explained why he became more of a mime than a speaking comedian.

"As a kid," he said, "I didn't talk very well. It was difficult to understand me because I talked too fast and ran my words into each other. So I had to use my face and body to make people understand what I meant."

He had uncanny timing and a sad face that made people laugh as, playing a simpleton in baggy pants, with straw hat and cane, he ran into one hilarious situation after another.

The pants, the hat and the cane were borrowed, in a way, from Chaplin and an early job pretending to be the Little Tramp in front of a movie house playing a Chaplin film.

Featured in Films

Over the years his was a standard vaudeville act, playing the Palace in New York and theaters throughout the country. He once explained that he changed his name from Ben Bernstein to Ben Blue because it was easier to fit on the Palace's marquee.

In the early nineteen-forties, Mr. Blue was featured in several Metro-Goldwyn-Mayer films, among them "Panama Hattie," "College Rhythm," "High, Wide and Handsome," "For Me and My Gal" and "Two Sisters From Boston." Others, later, were "My Wild Irish Rose," "It's a Mad Mad Mad Mad World," "Turn Off the Moon," "The Russians Are Coming, The Russians Are Coming" and "Where Were You When the Lights Went Out?"

In the "Russians" film Mr. Blue did a classic routine, a running gag of trying and failing repeatedly to catch a horse.

Earlier, he had appeared in a number of quickly made two-reel comedies, and between films he was a top attraction in nightclubs throughout the country.

With the advent of television Mr. Blue became a regular performer, appearing with Imogene Coca and Sid Caesar, Frank Sinatra, Perry Como and others.

In the late fifties and early sixties he operated a nightclub in Santa Monica, where he was his own top star, often drawing on waiters and busboys to help him out. The club closed in 1967 as patronage dwindled.

In 1964 Mr. Blue was indicted on six counts of evading a total of $39,334 in taxes. The case was continued for five years, when he pleaded no contest to a single count involving corporate income. He was fined $1,000, with payment suspended.

Ben Blue, Red Skelton, Ann Sothern and Rags Ragland in *Panama Hattie*.

June Allyson, Jimmy Durante and Ben Blue in *Two Girls and a Sailor*.

"All the News That's Fit to Print"

The New York Times.

LATE CITY EDITION
Condensation of U. S. Weather Bureau forecast: Mostly fair and very cold today; snow flurries likely tonight.
Temperature range today: 22—5
Temperature range yesterday: 24—7.5
Full U. S. Weather Bureau Report, Page 34

VOL. CVI..No. 36,151. Entered as Second-Class Matter, Post Office, New York, N. Y. NEW YORK, TUESDAY, JANUARY 15, 1957. Times Square, New York 36, N. Y. Telephone LAckawanna 4-1000 FIVE CENTS

PRESIDENT VISITS 4 DROUGHT STATES AND PLEDGES AID

Views Damage in Southwest and Promises 'Everyone Will Do His Best'

PEOPLE ARE OPTIMISTIC

Eisenhower Hails 'Chins-Up' Attitude—Flies to Tucson After Inspecting Farms

By W. H. LAWRENCE
Special to The New York Times.

TUCSON, Ariz., Jan. 14—President Eisenhower took a hard day-long look today at what searing sun and little or no rain have done to farms and ranches over a large section of the Southwest.

The President made inspection tours in the areas around San Angelo, Tex., Woodward, Okla., and Clovis, N. M., before flying into Tucson late this afternoon. Tomorrow he will visit Pueblo, Colo., and Garden City, Kan., before attending a fifteen-state drought conference in Wichita, Kan.

From automobiles and from a high-flying aircraft he saw burned-out crops and gaunt cattle, eloquent testimonials of the fearful economic cost of this natural disaster.

But the people he met were perpetual optimists, their spirit not unlike that of Brooklyn Dodger baseball fans in the lean years between National League pennants.

"Just wait until next year," was the refrain throughout the Southwest, just as it used to be in Brooklyn.

Praises Attitude

But, the experts say, these people require more than rain in the next crop season; they also need more generous short and long-term assistance than the Federal Government now is providing.

The President congratulated them for a "chins-up" attitude and said "everyone will do his best."

But it remained uncertain whether this signaled a reversal in current Administration policy against huge expenditures for more water conservation projects.

Everywhere President Eisenhower went he was confronted with pleas for Federal help in building new conservation projects that would trap flood waters in the spring to save them for the hot summer months.

Projects Are Urged

In Texas alone, projects totaling more than $1,000,000,000 were proposed on a self-liquidating basis over a fifty-year term. Gov. Raymond Gary of Oklahoma also turned in a sizable list of new reservoirs needed to re-establish agriculture in his state on a more normal basis to withstand the years when rains do not fall in normal quantities.

Nearly every local committee urged longer term loans at lower interest rates than the Government now is providing.

Although these droughts have persisted over many years and in some areas are the worst on record, the people the President visited remained determined to solve their problem.

An illustrated appeal on behalf of the Clovis area put the problem this way:

"When a crisis such as flood,

Continued on Page 22, Column 4

FIRST-HAND VIEW OF DROUGHT AREA: President Eisen... parched farm of Carl Peoples, left, in Woodward, Okla., ... Agriculture, who is accompanying the President on ...

Six Months on ... Required of A...

By JACK RA...
Special to The New Y...

WASHINGTON, Jan. 14—You... tional Guard or the Army Reserv... April 1 to take at least six months...

The A... and o... traini... change... tary co...

Until no... ing in the ... been require... active duty ... seven and on... Reserve. Na... had the optio... for the six mo...

The new pl... would apply on... join the Guard ... April 1.

Under the ne... youths who volunt... six months' active ... in the Guard or Rese... required to serve onl... one-half years in the R... stead of seven and one-... This provision will be... tive to Aug. 9, 1955, ... National Reserve A... passed.

The new order will a... listees between the ages ... and 25 to take the six ... training duty with a sub... Reserve duty obligatio... would enable them to es... draft altogether. This h... open to youths between ... 18½ previously.

Youths who are drafte... the Selective Service ... be required to serve ... years instead of three ... ready reserve after th...

Continued on Page 20, Column 5

LEGISLATORS' PAY EXPECTED TO RISE

Harriman Indicates He Would Not Veto an Increase—Urges Court Reform

By DOUGLAS DALES
Special to The New York Times.

ALBANY, Jan. 14—Governor Harriman has given state legislators reason to hope for a pay increase. The legislators now are talking in terms of a rise of $1,500, bringing the salaries of the 150 Assemblymen and fifty-eight Senators to $9,000 a year.

The subject came up at a Democratic caucus last week during a discussion by the Governor of the need for court reform, it was learned today.

The Governor made a strong bid for Democratic support of legislation simplifying and modernizing the court structure along lines proposed by the Temporary Commission on the Courts, headed by Harrison Tweed.

So far, no enthusiasm for court reform has been shown among legislators of either party. The only court measure for which there is optimism is a bill, still to be introduced, to increase the number of Supreme Court Justices by twenty-one.

Measures Vetoed

A similar measure was approved by the Legislature last year, along with a bill increasing the salaries of Supreme Court Justices by $2,000. They were vetoed, however, on the plea of Mayor Wagner that New York City did not have the funds to pay for its additional judges.

In expressing himself as friendly to a pay increase for legislators, there was no suggestion that the Governor's attitude was contingent upon approval of court-reform legislation.

The Governor said he understood that there was some opposition among the Democrats to changes in the court structure, but expressed the hope the reforms would have Democratic support. He also was reported to have suggested that legislators try to make more of a career out of the Legislature for longer periods.

At this point, a county leader interrupted to say that "they [the legislators] all want to become judges."

Mr. Harriman was reported to have replied that in that case perhaps an increase in pay would make the Legislature more attractive.

To this, the Assembly minority leader, Eugene F. Bannigan of Brooklyn, said that if the Governor were disposed favorably toward a pay increase, a bill would be forthcoming.

The Governor was said to have replied that if the bill came to him, he would not oppose it.

Any pay increase approved by the Legislature this year or next year could not become effective until 1959. The State Constitution bars Legislators from increasing their salaries for the

Continued on Page 26, Column 8

CHOU IS ASSURING POLES OF SUPPORT IN LIBERAL TREND

In Return, Warsaw's Leaders Are Promising Not to Hurt Solidarity of Red Bloc

By SYDNEY GRUSON
Special to The New York Times.

WARSAW, Jan. 14—Premier Chou En-lai of Communist China has given assurances of continued support for efforts to evolve a more democratic form of communism in Poland.

In return the Polish Government has accepted the Chinese view—a view to which it was slowly coming around on its own—that nothing should be done by Poland to disturb the solidarity of the Communist camp.

Reliable Communist sources ... points were the es... an understanding ... the first three days ... between the Poles ... Premier Chou was ... day and will re... tomorrow for ... the talks.

...es Amity

...Mr. Chou to... day, Premier ... assured him ... build social... that "we ... with Social... basis of ...

... Chinese ... hey fully ... d of re... pleases ... iewicz ...

Dulles Calls Mideast Peril 'Most Serious in 10 Years'

He Advises Senators That Eisenhower's Plan for Troops and Aid Funds Is Vital to Parry Red Threat

By WILLIAM S. WHITE
Special to The New York Times.

WASHINGTON, Jan. 14—John Foster Dulles declared today that in possible international Communist aggression in the Middle East lay "the most serious threat we have faced over the past ten years."

With this grave language the Secretary of State opened before

Texts of the Dulles and Green statements, Page 10.

the Senate Foreign Relations and Armed Services Committees the Administration's request for Congressional backing of a new policy involving:

¶The right of the President to use the United States armed forces as he might see fit to sustain peace in the Middle East.

¶Special Presidential authority to use in the area up to $200,000,000 of foreign aid funds, without existing restrictions, to combat economic disorder—and thus indirectly to combat Communist subversion.

Ultimately $400,000,000 more will be sought for the purpose, but that is not directly at issue now.

Secretary Dulles appeared before two of the Senate's most powerful committees.

He was hard-pressed on the economic aspect of the Administration's proposal. He agreed to some revision of the Administration's resolution that would make it plain that Congress was not committing itself to any long-range assistance. Another

Continued on Page 11, Column 3

Israel Plans to Hold Gaza, Report to U. N. Indicates

By KATHLEEN TELTSCH
Special to The New York Times.

UNITED NATIONS, N. Y., Jan. 14—The Israeli authorities have restored law and order in the Gaza Strip, a United Nations military officer said in a report today. He also gave the impression that Israel planned to occupy the area permanently.

The sandy Gaza Strip, with its crowded settlements of Pales-

Text of report on Gaza Strip appears on Page 14.

tinian Arab refugees, was taken over by Israeli troops invading Egypt last October.

[Israeli troops were blowing up Egyptian military installations at El Arish in the Sinai area Monday, according to a dispatch from headquarters of ...e United Nations Emergency ...orce. A spokesman for the ...raeli delegation to the Unit... Nations said the report was ...founded".]

...somber and more critical ...t of conditions resulting ...rael's military actions in ...as given in a second re... circulated today at the ...tions, from Henry R. ... head of the United ...ief and Works Agen... ...stine refugees.

...uisse gave a report ...ualties among the ...lting from the Is... ...ction, which, he ... fear and tension ... population.

...rthy sources ... dead in two ... Khan Yunis ...itional sixty-

...14, Column 3

AID TO CAIRO TIED TO MIDEAST PLAN

U. S. Economic Help Depends, Officials Say, on Egypt's Cooperation on Issues

By DANA ADAMS SCHMIDT
Special to The New York Times

WASHINGTON, Jan. 14—United States officials indicated today that future United States relations with Egypt in the economic field depended in large part on Egypt's cooperation in solving Middle East political problems.

Ambassador Ahmed Hussein of Egypt made another vain attempt to unfreeze the more than $40,000,000 worth of Egyptian assets in the United States.

This was the most specific point in the day's round of the general compiaint the Egyptians have been making to the State Department in recent weeks, more or less as follows:

¶The United States has been at some pains since the invasion of Egypt to help the invaders, especially Britain, to weather the economic effects of their act; but it has not lifted a finger to help Egypt.

¶The Egyptian assets, which Egyptian sources say are valued as high as $80,000,000, were frozen after Egypt nationalized the Universal Suez Canal Company last July.

Americans' Interests

United States officials say the Egyptian assets were frozen to protect the interests of American holders of Suez Canal company stock and the action cannot be reversed until the Suez Canal problem is settled.

The Egyptian Ambassador conferred for forty-five minutes with William M. Rountree, Assistant Secretary of State for Near Eastern, South Asian and African Affairs, and Raymond A. Hare, United States Ambassador just back from his Cairo post.

In reply to questions as to Egypt's attitude toward President Eisenhower's Middle East plan, Ambassador Hussein said that his Government had decided not to make any official comment until after the plan had taken final form. He said he did not know anything about newspaper comment in Cairo, which, after a period of restraint, has turned sharply critical of President Eisenhower and his program.

The Egyptian Ambassador declined to comment on his talk with Mr. Rountree and Mr. Hare.

But United States officials other than Messrs. Rountree and Hare made it pretty clear that the future of United States economic relations with Egypt, in matters of aid, surplus sales, release of frozen assets and the like, depended very much on the degree of Egyptian cooperation in solving the political problems of the Middle East.

In denying a report that the United States had rebuffed an

Continued on Page 10, Column 5

U.S. GIVES THE U.N. NEW 5-POINT PLAN ON DISARMAMENT

It Urges Missile Control and Curbs on Experiments for War From Outer Space

SOVIET CONDEMNS MOVE

Kuznetsov Asks for Special Assembly Session to Deal With Arms Problem

Excerpts from speeches will be found on Page 4.

By LINDESAY PARROTT
Special to The New York Times.

UNITED NATIONS, N. Y., Jan. 14—The United States presented to the United Nations today a new five-point proposal for world disarmament. It included international control of intercontinental missiles and of experiments for warfare in new regions of space.

The program was explained before the United Nations Political Committee by Henry Cabot Lodge Jr., head of the United States delegation.

It immediately elicited a vigorous attack from the Soviet Union on the new Eisenhower policy for the Middle East, on British and French "aggression" in Egypt, and on the alleged intention of the West to profit from such incidents as "the revolutionary conspiracy in Hungary."

[In Moscow, the newspaper Pravda renewed the suggestion for a meeting of the Big Four and India to consider the problem of world disarmament.]

Larger Body Proposed

The Soviet spokesman, Vasily V. Kuznetsov, called on the powerful committee to recommend a special session of the General Assembly to deal exclusively with disarmament. He suggested also that the United Nations Disarmament Commission and its working subcommittee be enlarged, including states not in possession of atomic weapons.

Later, Mr. Lodge called Mr. Kuznetsov's speech "bitterly discouraging" and "contemptuous of the work of the United Nations."

The United States, the Soviet Union, Britain, France and Canada are the members of the subcommittee, which has considered all disarmament plans for the last several years. The full commission includes all members of the Security Council, as well as the major countries producing nuclear energy.

Special Body Is Suggested

The United States proposal again emphasized the necessity for a working system of inspection and control to eliminate the possibility of evasion of disarmament pledges.

In a new development, however, it suggested the formation of a special body to undertake this responsibility.

"The United States proposes that such an international agency for the regulation of armaments should be installed concurrently with the beginning of the [disarmament] program," Mr. Lodge told the committee. "It can constitute a nucleus of hope at the center of the grim implications which radiate from the

Continued on Page 5, Column 3

Fare Rises Spark Barcelona Violence

By BENJAMIN WELLES
Special to The New York Times.

MADRID, Jan. 14—Three policemen were injured and at least eight persons arrested today in violent demonstrations at Barcelona University.

The demonstrations were believed to have been held in connection with a city-wide boycott of public bus, street car and subway systems, called to protest higher fares.

Gen. Felipe Acedo, Civil Governor of Barcelona, issued two statements in which he charged that students of the city's university had demonstrated and had uttered shouts of a "subversive nature."

"The demonstrators were dispersed," he announced "and some arrests were made."

Earlier in the day, the Governor charged that a group of "students and unidentified persons" had gathered at the doors of the University and had

Continued on Page 13, Column 3

Humphrey Bogart, 57, Dies of Cancer

Special to The New York Times.

HOLLYWOOD, Calif., Jan. 14—Humphrey Bogart died in his sleep early this morning in the bedroom of his Holmby Hills home. The 57-year-old movie actor, an Academy Award winner, had been suffering for more than two years from cancer of the esophagus.

In the latter part of February, 1956, he underwent surgery at Good Samaritan Hospital for removal of a malignant growth. He recovered from the operation and gained back some of the weight he had lost. But, in November, 1956, he was admitted to St. John's Hospital in Santa Monica for treatment of nerve pressure caused by the growth of scar tissue on his throat.

Mr. Bogart leaves his wife, Lauren Bacall, actress, whom he married in 1945. The couple had two children, a son, Stephen Humphrey, born in 1949, and a

Continued on Page 29, Column 2

Humphrey Bogart, 57, Dies of Cancer

Special to The New York Times.

HOLLYWOOD, Calif., Jan. 14—Humphrey Bogart died in his sleep early this morning in the bedroom of his Holmby Hills home. The 57-year-old movie actor, an Academy Award winner, had been suffering for more than two years from cancer of the esophagus.

In the latter part of February, 1956, he underwent surgery at Good Samaritan Hospital for removal of a malignant growth. He recovered from the operation and gained back some of the weight he had lost. But, in November, 1956, he was admitted to St. John's Hospital in Santa Monica for treatment of nerve pressure caused by the growth of scar tissue on his throat.

Mr. Bogart leaves his wife, Lauren Bacall, actress, whom he married in 1945. The couple had two children, a son, Stephen Humphrey, born in 1949, and a

Continued on Page 29, Column 2

The New York Times (by Edward Hausner)

NOT RUNNING: Low temperatures yesterday turned trickling water into ice on the spillway of Croton (N.Y.) Dam

Humphrey Bogart and Ingrid Bergman in *Casablanca*.

Humphrey Bogart Is Dead at 57; Movie Star Had Throat Cancer

Continued From Page 1

daughter, Leslie, born in 1952. The actor is survived also by a sister, Frances Rose Bogart of New York.

Miss Bacall was Mr. Bogart's fourth wife. His previous marriages were also to actresses. He married Helen Menken in 1926 and divorced her a year later. His marriage to Mary Philips the next year lasted until 1937. In 1938 he took Mayo Methot as his third wife. The couple was divorced shortly before Mr. Bogart wed Miss Bacall.

Deflated Publicity Balloons

Mr. Bogart was one of the most paradoxical screen personalities in the recent annals of Hollywood. He often deflated the publicity balloons that keep many a screen star aloft, but he remained one of Hollywood's top box-office attractions for more than two decades.

On the screen he was most often the snarling, laconic gangster who let his gun do his talking. In private life, however, he could speak glibly and wittily on a wide range of subjects and make better copy off the cuff than the publicists could devise for him.

He had a large, seemingly permanent following among the mass audience. Yet he said he deplored "mass activities." Furthermore, he did everything he could to confound the popular image of a movie star.

Mr. Bogart received an Academy Award in 1952 for his performance in "The African Queen." Still, he made it clear he set little store by such fanfare. Earlier he had established a mock award for the best performance in a film by an animal, making sure that the bit of satire received full notice in the press.

Proud of Profession

But despite this show of frivolity, he was fiercely proud of his profession. "I am a professional," he said. "I have a respect for my profession. I worked hard at it."

Attesting to this are a number of highly interesting characterizations in such films as "The Petrified Forest" (1936), "High Sierra" (1941), "Casablanca" (1942), "To Have and Have Not" (1944), "Key Largo" (1948), "The Treasure of Sierra Madre" (1948), "The African Queen" (1951), "Sabrina," "The Caine Mutiny" (1954) and "The Desperate Hours" (1955). The actor's last film, "The Harder They Fall," was released last year.

Mr. Bogart's high sense of responsibility toward his profession may have stemmed from the fact that both his parents were highly successful professional persons. His mother was Maud Humphrey, a noted illustrator and artist. His father was Belmont DeForest Bogart, a prosperous surgeon. Their son, born on Christmas Day in 1899, was reared in fashionable New York society.

He attended Trinity School and Phillips Academy at Andover, Mass., but an early note of discord crept into this genteel strain when he was expelled from Andover for irreverence to a faculty member.

Mr. Bogart enlisted in the Navy in 1917 and crossed the Atlantic several times as a helmsman aboard a transport ship. As a civilian he was a tugboat inspector and saw brief service in an investment house.

Next, he had a job with World Films for a short while and then appeared as a stage manager for an acting group. It was an easy step to his first roles in the early Nineteen Twenties. His rise to fame over the next fifteen years, however, was a hard road, often lined with critical brickbats.

He appeared in "Swifty" and plugged on in drawing-room comedies, appearing in "Hell's Bells, "The Cradle Snatchers," "Its a Wise Child" and many others in which he usually played a callow juvenile or a romantic second lead.

He accepted a movie contract with Fox in 1931, but roles in a few Westerns failed to improve matters and soon he was back on Broadway, convinced that his hard-bitten face disqualified him in the close-ups as a matinee idol.

In 'Petrified Forest'

But toward the end of 1934 he used this granite-like face to rebuild, with enormous success, a new dramatic career. Having heard that Robert E. Sherwood's "The Petrified Forest" had a gangster role, he approached Mr. Sherwood for the important part. The playwright referred him to the director, who told Mr. Bogart to return in three days for a reading.

When Mr. Bogart reappeared before the director he had a three-day growth of beard and was wearing shabby clothes. His reading and appearance brought him the supporting role of Duke Mantee, his most memorable Broadway part. Leslie Howard was the star of the play. Mr. Bogart later did the same part for the movie to considerable critical acclaim.

This was the first of more than fifty pictures that Mr. Bogart made, most of them for Warner Brothers. A spate of crime dramas followed, including "Angels With Dirty Faces," "The Roaring Twenties," Bullets or Ballots," "Dead End," "San Quentin" and, finally, "High Sierra" in 1941.

Mr. Bogart then insisted on roles with more scope. They were forthcoming in such films as "Casablanca," "To Have and Have Not" and "'Key Largo," wherein Mr. Bogart's notorious screen hardness was offset by a latent idealism that showed itself in the end.

Won New Followers

In "The Treasure of Sierra Madre," as a prospector driven to evil by a lust for gold, the range of his characterization won him new followers.

A further range of his talents was displayed also in "The African Queen," wherein his portrayal of a tropical tramp with a yen for gin and Katharine Hepburn won him an "Oscar." Another distinguished portrait was that of the neurotic Captain Queeg in the movie version of "The Caine Mutiny." His aptitude for romantic comedy became clear when he played the bitter business man who softens under the charms of Audrey Hepburn in "Sabrina." Mr. Bogart also appeared in "The Barefoot Contessa," made in 1954.

The movie actor made no secret of his nightclubbing. He was also a yachting enthusiast. At one point in his career he reportedly made $200,000 a film and he was for years among the top ten box-office attractions.

Mr. Bogart joined other actors in 1947 in a flight to Washington to protest the methods of the House Un-American Activities Committee, which was investigating communism in the movie colony. He was often a supporter of Democratic political causes.

Lauren Bacall with Bogart in *The Big Sleep*, 1946.

Bogart as the classical Sam Spade, with Mary Astor, in *The Maltese Falcon,* 1941.

Katharine Hepburn and Humphrey Bogart in *The African Queen.*

Bogart in the film version of *The Petrified Forest.*

"All the News That's Fit to Print"

The New York Times.

INTERNATIONAL EDITION

Algeria ...... DI. 0.70	Austria .... Sch. 5	Belgium ...... B. Fr. 7	Canary Isl. Pts 12.00
Cyprus Mils 70	Denmark ... D.Kr. 1.25	Egypt. ..... Piastres 10	Finland ..... F.M. .70
France .... F. 0.60	Germany ... D.M. 0.60	Great Britain 1s	Greece .... Dr. 6
India .... Rps. 1.25	Iran .... Rials 20	Ireland 1s	Israel ...... Agurath 80
Italy .... Lira 100	Lebanon ... Piastres 60	Libya ...... Piastres [illegible]	Luxembourg ... L. Fr. 7
Netherlands .. F. 0.60	Norway .... N.Kr. 1.25	Poland ...... Zlotys 3	Portugal ...... Esc. 5
Spain (SGEL) .. Pts. 8	Sweden .... Sw. Kr. 1	Switzerland . S.Fr. 0.60	Turkey .... Kurus 1.75
U.S. Mil-Europe .. $0.10	Yugoslavia ..... Dl. 80		

VOL. CXV .... No. 39,329 © 1965 by The New York Times Company. PARIS, TUESDAY, SEPTEMBER 28, 1965.

TODAY'S WEATHER—PARIS: Sunny. LONDON: Variable. BERLIN: Cloudy. ROME: Cloudy. NEW YORK: Sunny. CHANNEL: Choppy. Details, Page 2.

REDS' EXECUTION OF 2 AMERICANS ASSAILED BY U.S.

Authorities Deplore 'Brutal Conduct' of Vietcong—Cite Geneva Accord

DEATHS WERE REPRISAL

Bombings of Neutral Zone Linked to Weather and Similarity to Target

By NEIL SHEEHAN
Special to The New York Times.

SAIGON, Sept. 27—A United States spokesman denounced today as "acts of wanton murder" the execution yesterday by Vietcong guerrillas of two American prisoners.

The Liberation Radio, the clandestine voice of the guerrillas, said the two men, Army Capt. Humbert R. Versage of Baltimore, Md. and Army Sgt. Kenneth M. Roraback of Fayetteville, N.C., were shot by firing squad in retaliation for the execution in Danang on Wednesday of three accused Communist agitators by the Vietnamese Government.

The executions yesterday were the second time the Vietcong have taken reprisals against American prisoners for the shooting of their accused agents by the Vietnamese Government.

[South Vietnam's Premier, Air Vice Marshal Nguyen Cao Ky, said he planned to continue executing Communist terrorists despite the Vietcong reprisal, Reuters reported. He said that most of the executions would be carried out quietly, but that a few would be made public to act as a deterrent.]

Raid on Buffer Zone

An American military spokesman announced today the results of an investigation into the bombing of a bridge and village in the demilitarized zone between North and South Vietnam on Sept. 16 and 17. He said "the bridge was accidentally bombed through a navigational error caused by bad weather and an unfortunate similarity of terrain situated in North Vietnam."

It was understood that the pilots had been assigned, as an alternate target, a bridge about 20 miles north of the buffer strip. Navy planes carried out the first raid, Air Force planes the second.

Naval and Air Force officers who conducted a 10-day investigation said they had been unable to pinpoint exactly which planes had been involved. All pilots who were in the area, apparently convinced that they had hit the correct target, denied bombing in the demilitarized zone.

Three North Vietnamese were killed in the first strike, and 21 South Vietnamese in the second. The Hienluong bridge and a number of buildings destroyed.

Officials of the United States Embassy said that the government of South Vietnam would pay indemnities to the families of the persons killed in the second strike. American supplies and equipment will help to rebuild the blasted village.

The previous Vietcong reprisal execution occurred last June, when guerrillas slew Army Sgt. Harold G. Bennett of Perryville, Ark., a few days after an accused Communist terrorist died publicly before a firing squad in Saigon.

Sergeant Bennett was an adviser to a Vietnamese Ranger battalion and was captured in a battle at Binhgia, 45 miles east of Saigon, last September.

Captain Versace served as an intelligence adviser to the Vietnamese chief of Vietcong-dominated Camau Province, 150 miles south of Saigon, until he was captured during a battle there in 1963.

Sergeant Roraback was taken prisoner a few months later when the American Special Forces camp at Hiephoa, about 20 miles west of Saigon, was overrun in a Vietcong attack.

"As in the case of the Vietcong's execution of Sgt. Harold Bennett last June," the spokesman said today, "the Vietcong have carried out two more acts of wanton murder against American military prisoners."

"These acts show their utter disregard for humanitarian principles and for the provisions of the 1949 Geneva prisoner-of-war convention of whom the Vietcong's masters, the Hanoi regime [North Vietnamese Government] are an adherent."

"The Vietcong's brutal conduct can in no way be justi-

Continued on Page 2, Column 2

Ky Hints at Change In Saigon's Regime

By R. W. APPLE Jr.
Special to The New York Times.

SAIGON, Sept. 27 — Premier Nguyen Cao Ky suggested today that there might be a number of changes in his three-month-old Government in the coming weeks.

The Premier, hinting that the country's military command might also be realigned, said that he would make a "major policy speech" on a nationwide radio network soon, possibly on Friday. He gave no details. His comments were made in an informal conversation with reporters at Saigon's Tansonnhut Airport this afternoon. He was at the airport to greet the South Korean Premier, Il Kwon Chung, who arrived here for a two-day state visit.

On another subject, Premier Ky expressed concern about recreation facilities for front-

Continued on Page 2, Column 3

PROTRACTED WAR SEEN B...

Vi... tell... ther... war... the build-...

In a ... ganda l... year, po... cong h... about 1... decision." or 20 years ... icans and ... does not succ... the Vietcong ... now told.

This positio... peated Vietco... casts, has pro... tions for United ... Among United St... in Saigon there ... ceptance of the ... protracted war and ... negotiations with th... nists has diminishe... prevailing mood in S... preoccupation of th... Administration in ... pronouncements with... sibility of negotiatio... somewhat unreal ... observers.

Strategy Change

When the bombing of N... Vietnam began last Febru... it was looked upon as a me... of forcing the Communists ... the conference table. Subseque... landings of American comba... troops were to some extent an extension of this concept. Gradually, however, the intransigence of the Communists has discouraged this idea and officials have begun to regard the application of American power as simply a means of breaking the back of the Vietcong main force.

The evident change in Vietcong strategy is no less fundamental. In January the Vietcong were busy rapidly expanding their forces. Villagers were drafted on a large scale

Continued on Page 2, Column 3

U.S. CATHOLIC UNIT URGES A RESTUDY OF BIRTH CONTROL

But Group's Effort to Get Views to Papal Commission Have Been Frustrated

By JOHN COGLEY
Special to The New York Times.

ROME, Sept. 27—A group of 37 American Roman Catholic scholars has given qualified endorsement to contraception and suggested a change in the church's traditional position on birth control.

The conclusions were reached after three lengthy meetings held at the University of Notre Dame in Indiana over a period of 18 months. The meetings, sponsored by Notre Dame ... the Family Life Edu... partment of th... Chi... F...

... be ... the ... sex... ma... no ... pills ... of cont...

A m...

Contin...

Associated Press

...pare to leave Helsinki for New Delhi yes... ...the cease-fire between India and Pakistan.

Clara Bow, the 'It' Girl, Dies at 60; Film Actress Set Vogue in 1920's

Flapper-Styled Star Retired in 1930's After Marriage —Widow of Rex Bell

Special to The New York Times.

LOS ANGELES, Sept. 27—Clara Bow, the flaming red-haired "It" girl of the silent screen, died last night at the age of 60 in her Hollywood home.

She had been in ill health for several years and until recently had been under treatment in a rest home for insomnia.

Clara Bow

Typified an Era

Special to The New York Times.

NEW YORK, Sept. 27 More than any other woman entertainer of her time, Clara Bow perhaps best personified the giddier aspects of an unreal era, the "Roaring Twenties."

Hollywood's contribution to the period of bathtub gin and flappers was a series of appropriate movies and the emergence of such cinema queens as Pola Negri, Constance Bennett, Gloria Swanson, and Kay Francis. But America frankly preferred the vibrant earthiness of the lithe young redhead from Brooklyn.

Miss Bow became a national screen phenomenon in Paramount's 1927 version of Elinor Glyn's lightweight, romantic novel, "It." To many people, the title pronoun still signifies Miss Bow's toss of a boyish bob, her brazen sauciness and the energy of her Charleston high kick.

She was born Jan. 29, 1905, in Bay Ridge, Brooklyn, of English, Scottish and French lineage. Miss Bow once said that her parents, Robert and

Continued on Page 3, Column 4

...Mission in Pakistan ...rms-Aid Decision

...y PAUL GRIMES
...o The New York Times.

...About of warfare that preceded it, ...y of- United States officers who felt ...are they had a right to information in view of the aid program were repeatedly denied access to rudimentary battle data.

Reliable sources say that some of the highest ranking Americans in Pakistan, both military and civilian, were told curtly that if they wanted to know about the war they could listen to the Government radio ... read the Government-controlled newspapers.

Resentment shown Americans ...ms largely from Washing...'s decision late in 1962 to ... military aid to India. Re...s between American and ...ani military officers ... described as reasonably ... however, until fighting ... India and Pakistan ...t in the Rann of Cutch ...s year.

Restraints Before

...hen," a high-ranking ...fficer said, "we had ... no difficulty in ... we wanted and ... the use of the ... supplied."

...mission to visit ...efront was ...siderable de... sources in ...nspection on ... that both ...were using ...ipment in ... this aid ...eter any ... India ...t she ...rican

Japan Launches 150,00...

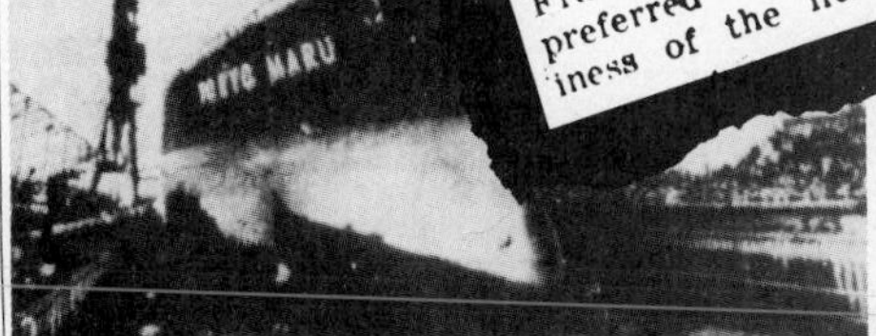

Associated Press

The Tokyo Maru is launched in ceremonies yesterday from shipyard in Yokohama harbor

By EMERSON CHAPIN
Special to The New York Times.

YOKOHAMA, Japan, Sept. 27 — The world's largest tanker, a 150,000-deadweight ton vessel that will ply between the Persian Gulf and Japan, was launched here today in a gala ceremony. The keel of the huge Tokyo Maru was laid at the new Wegishi dockyard of Ishikawajima-Harima Heavy Industries Company here on May 6, only 140 days ago. After fitting at a dock adjoining the big building berth, the ship will go into service in late December or early next year for the Tokyo Tanker Company, the ocean-transport operation for the Caltex group in Japan. The Tokyo Maru is 18,000 deadweight tons more than the present biggest tanker, the Idemitsu Oil Company's 132,000-deadweight-ton Nissho Maru. But she will be eclipsed

Continued on Page 2, Column 7

... in ... of ca... ...and in labor ... wage regulations. A session of the Supreme Soviet (Parliament) has been convened for Friday to ratify the Central Committee's changes in the structure of industrial planning and management agencies.

The delivery of major reports by Mr. Kosygin and Mr. Brezhnev reflected both the special interests and functions of the two men and the stability of their position in the Soviet hierarchy.

Their sharing of the keynote speeches seemed as if in answer to rumors in recent months that high level changes may be made in the Kremlin leadership at the current session.

The abolition of regional industrial councils announced by Mr. Kosygin puts an end to the system of decentralized management introduced by Mr. Khrushchev in 1957. About 100

Continued on Page 2, Column 8

... health ...years and until re... ...had been under treatment in a rest home for insomnia.

Typified an Era

Special to The New York Times.

NEW YORK, Sept. 27 More than any other woman entertainer of her time, Clara Bow perhaps best personified the giddier aspects of an unreal era, the "Roaring Twenties."

Hollywood's contribution to the period of bathtub gin and flappers was a series of appropriate movies and the emergence of such cinema queens as Pola Negri, Constance Bennett, Gloria Swanson, and Kay Francis. But America frankly preferred the vibrant earthiness of the lithe young redhead from Brooklyn.

Miss Bow became a national screen phenomenon in Paramount's 1927 version of Elinor Glyn's lightweight, romantic novel, "It." To many people, the title pronoun still signifies Miss Bow's toss of a boyish bob, her brazen sauciness and the energy of her Charleston high kick.

Clara Bow, shown at the height of her film career.

United Press International

Miss Bow in 1962

She was born Jan. 29, 1905, in Bay Ridge, Brooklyn, of English, Scottish and French lineage. Miss Bow once said that her parents, Robert and

Continued on Page 3, Column 4

U.N. BIDS INDIA, PAKISTAN HEED CEASE-FIRE EDICT

Thant Says New Delhi Has Yet to Reply to Demand for Troop Withdrawal

ACTION IS UNANIMOUS

Aide of Shastri Reports 76 Troops Lost in Gravest Incident in Truce

UNITED NATIONS, N. Y., Sept. 27 (Reuters)—The United Nations Security Council demanded tonight that India and Pakistan honor their commitments to the Council to observe a cease-fire.

The Council, summoned tonight for a special meeting, also called on the two principals to withdraw promptly all armed personnel as necessary steps in the further implementation of last Monday's cease-fire resolution.

The resolution was adopted unanimously without a formal vote.

U Thant, the Secretary General, told the Council that India had failed to reply to two requests by him for the withdrawal of her troops to pre-Aug. 5 positions.

Pakistan replied that no withdrawals were possible until both sides had agreed on a withdrawal plan, Mr. Thant said.

Indian Objects

India's representative, G. Parthasarathi, objected that tonight's resolution should have been directed exclusively to Pakistan. Pakistan, he said, had refused unconditionally to observe the cease-fire.

He said it was clear Pakistan had launched an offensive on Aug. 5 with the intention of enforcing a settlement of the Kashmir problem.

Until Pakistan was made to observe the cease-fire no useful purpose could be served by any discussion in the council or elsewhere as to further useful steps, he said.

Pakistan continued to attack Indian troops and positions, and the council could not expect Indian troops to stand idly by, Mr. Parthasarathi said.

In the "Indian state of Jammu and Kashmir," hundreds of armed Pakistani raiders continued their attacks and were spurred on by the Pakistani radio, he charged.

Futility Seen

In such circumstances, it would be futile for the council to waste its valuable time on the question of withdrawals and he hoped it would concentrate on the cease-fire question, he declared.

Informed sources said tonight's resolution had resulted from private consultations among the members prior to the emergency meeting of the 11-nation council.

Plans had called for a brief statement by the President, Arthur J. Goldberg of the United States, and quick adoption of the new draft, these sources said.

India Reports Raid

By J. ANTHONY LUKAS
Special to The New York Times.

NEW DELHI, Sept. 27—...ia reported today that 11 of ... soldiers had been killed and 65 were missing following a "treacherous" Pakistani attack in the Fazilka area.

A Defense Ministry spokesman said the attack, which occured yesterday morning, was "by far the most serious" violation of the cease-fire since it went into effect last Thursday.

He said United Nations observers had been informed of the violation and two observers had arrived in the area today. Fazilka is 60 miles southwest of Ferozepore and about 3 miles from the Pakistani border.

[Pakistan accused India Monday of pursuing a program of genocide against Moslems in Kashmir, The Associated Press reported.]

According to the spokesman, yesterday's incident occurred when a company of Indian troops went out to ask the intruders to leave Indian territory.

Without warning, the spokesman said, the Pakistani troops had attacked the greatly outnumbered Indian patrol.

He said one officer, one junior commissioned officer and nine soldiers had been killed in the attack. Two officers, four junior commissioned officers and 59 soldiers were

Continued on Page 3, Column 3

Clara Bow and Buddy Rogers in *Wings*.

Clara Bow, the 'It' Girl, Dies at 60; Film Actress Set Vogue in 1920's

Continued From Page 1

Sarah Bow, were extremeley poor.

"No one wanted me in the first place," she added.

She entered films as a beauty-contest winner while still in high school. A small part in "Beyond the Rainbow," starring Billie Dove, was cut from the picture. Three months later, as a young stowaway in "Down to the Sea in Ships," Miss Bow found herself almost immediat-ely fraduated to leading roles.

She appeared in such films as "Grit," "Black Oxen," "Get Your Man" and "Rough House Rosie." In 1926, under a new, long-term Paramount contract, she appeared in "Mantrap" and "Kid Boots." The next year she played the uninhibited brain-child of Miss Glyn.

Set Feminine Styles

Many female moviegoers accepted Miss Bow's hair style and her hoydenish pout as the vogue during the 1920's.

As an ideal subject for the devices of press agents, Miss Bow was given a background of constant romance and many broken engagements. At least seven men prominent in the film industry or in business were reputed to be her suitors simultaneously.

Miss Bow eventually married a cowboy actor, Rex Bell, in 1931 at Las Vegas, Nev. and retired to his cattle ranch at Spotlight, Nev. Mr. Bell also gave up the screen and was elected Lieutenant Governor of Nevada in 1954. He died in 1962 while seeking the Govern-orship.

A son, Toni, was born to the couple in 1934 and another son, George, was born in 1938.

Miss Bow came out of re-tirement in the early 1930's to make her two final films, "Call Her Savage" (1932) and "Hoopla" (1933). Neither was successful.

In 1947, Miss Bow was on the national scene once more, but unseen, when a Lock Haven, Pa., housewife won $18,000 for correctly identifying the actress's voice on the ra-dio giveaway program, "Truth or Consequences."

Clara Bow with Antonio Moreno in *It,* 1927.

Bow in William Wellman's *Wings*, 1927.

Bow in *Hoopla*.

The New York Times MONDAY, SEPTEMBER 23, 1974

Walter Brennan Dead at 80; Winner of 3 Academy Awards

Character Actor in Over 100 Films — Appeared on TV in 'The Real McCoys'

OXNARD, Calif., Sept. 21 (AP)—The veteran actor Walter Brennan, who won three Academy Awards, died Saturday night after a long battle with emphysema. He was 80 years old.

Mr. Brennan died at St. John's Hospital here, a hospital spokesman said. He had been under treatment since July 25 for respiratory problems.

His wife, Ruth, and three children were with him when he died.

A Hard Worker

By WILLIAM M. FREEMAN

Walter Brennan liked work, and looked forward to it. In his seventies, long after most men have given up a daily grind in favor of a porch and a rocking chair, he remarked:

"I'd rather do television than movies because there aren't any long layoffs between working days. You make a movie and then wait around for another good part.

"Not in television. You go to work five days a week for most of the year. That's what I like. By Sunday night I can hardly wait to get started on Monday morning. It's a shame most people don't feel the same way about their jobs."

For years Mr. Brennan's schedule went something like this: Up and on his way (by chauffeur, a concession to his advancing years) to the studio by 7 A.M. The drive took 45 minutes from his 11-acre ranch in Ventura County, and he was not often home by 7 P.M. The 12-hour day was generally standard.

He was before the cameras for more than half a century, and he had three Oscars to show for it, although to hear him tell it, he would have trouble finding which closet held the statuettes.

Each award was for "best supporting actor," in "Come and Get It," 1936; "Kentucky," 1938, and "The Westerner," 1940.

Over the years Mr. Brennan made more than 100 movies, many of them Westerns — although he was from Massachusetts — 224 segments of "The Real McCoys" for television and scores of miscellaneous television, industrial and government films.

He was born in Lynn, Mass., the son of an $18-a-week engineer who held about two dozen patents, all controlled by big companies. The elder Brennan was blind for the last four years of his life, but learned Braille at the age of 67.

After high school the future actor was a lumberjack, a ditch-digger and a bank messenger, and enlisted in the Army in World War I the day after war was declared.

After his return from Europe he returned to the bank and became a financial reporter. Then came a job as a real-estate salesman in California.

One of his colleagues liked his sales pitch and persuaded him to try the movies as a $7.50-a-day extra. His first big job was nine roles in the Paul Whiteman film, "The King of Jazz," for which he got $125 a week.

Of this film, in which Bing Crosby appeared, Mr. Brennan remarked:

"When I went to the preview I sneezed and missed myself."

He did so well later in a small role as the station agent in "The Wedding Night," a film that Samuel Goldwyn had hoped would make Anna Sten a star, that Mr. Goldwyn called for an expansion of his part after a preview.

After this came the part of an old Swede in "Come and Get It." He sought Scandinavians to help him with the accent and found six Swedes, each with a highly individual accent. Nevertheless, the picture brought him his first Oscar.

Mr. Brennan apparently did well in terms of financial reward. In addition to the "small" ranch in the San Fernando Valley he had a 12,000-acre ranch in Joseph, Ore., where he had a large cattle herd and owned a small movie house and a motel.

A bit unlike Grandpa McCoy and some of the other characters he played, he also liked a martini very cold and very dry, his automobiles fast and powerful and his beef cattle plentiful and heavy.

While he often expressed himself in salty language, he once remarked:

"Boy, let me tell you, there's no risqué stuff in my show. No sir, I won't allow it. In a TV series, you're going right into the living room, and families are watching you. It sure burns me up to see some of the stuff they let get by on other shows."

John Wayne and Walter Brennan in *Red River*, 1948.

Walter Brennan as Judge Roy Bean in *The Westerner* which starred Gary Cooper.

The New York Times WEDNESDAY, MAY 30, 1951.

FANNY BRICE DIES AT THE AGE OF 59

Comedienne, Famed in Role of Baby Snooks, First Scored With Song, 'My Man'

'DISCOVERED' BY ZIEGFELD

She Got $75 a Week to Play in 'Follies'—Also Starred on Radio and in Movies

Special to THE NEW YORK TIMES.

HOLLYWOOD, Calif., May 29—Fanny Brice, stage and screen comedienne and the Baby Snooks of radio, died at 11:15 A. M. today at the Cedars of Lebanon Hospital. Her age was 59.

Miss Brice suffered a massive cerebral hemorrhage last Thursday morning and was rushed to the hospital from her home in Beverly Hills. She never again regained consciousness, although she was placed in an oxygen tent.

With Miss Brice when she died were her son, William Brice, and her daughter, Mrs. Frances Stark, the children of her marriage to Jules W. Arnstein, and her son-in-law, Ray Stark, and daughter-in-law, Mrs. Shirley Brice.

Also surviving are a brother, Lew Brice of Hollywood; a sister, Mrs. Caroline Russak of New York, and three grandchildren, John Brice and Peter and Wendy Stark.

Torch Song Brought Fame

Although known chiefly as a comedienne, Fanny Brice first became internationally famous for singing a torch song, "My Man." Channing Pollock wrote English words to the French tune, "Mon Homme," which Miss Brice introduced in "The Ziegfeld Follies." It proved a "natural," since it appealed to every woman who had ever been in love.

Her classic burlesque and pointed satire formed a hardy perennial of the "Follies" almost every year starting in 1916, when she first did a comic version of a dying swan ballet. Her lampoon of sultry Theda Bara, her take-off of "Camille," with W. C. Fields as the maid, and her travesty on fan dancers and the modern dance, were part of the repertoire of the actress whom Brooks Atkinson of THE NEW YORK TIMES described as "a burlesque comic of the rarest vintage."

She was billed with Eddie Cantor, Will Rogers, W. C. Fields, Willie Howard and other top Broadway performers through the years, in which she appeared in such shows as the "Follies," "Music Box Review of 1924," "Sweet and Low" and Billy Rose's "Crazy Quilt." She also put across the song, "Rose of Washington Square."

She created the character Baby Snooks, originally acting the part of the annoying little girl at parties for the entertainment of friends. Later Snooks was regularly featured in sketches in the "Follies" and was introduced to radio in 1938.

After an eleven-year run, Baby Snooks went off the air when its sponsorship on the Columbia Broadcasting System network was withdrawn by General Foods. In November, 1949, however, Miss Brice resumed the role under a long-term contract with the National Broadcasting Company. The company announced yesterday that the program would be off the air for the remainder of the season, the spot being filled by an orchestra.

She was really Fannie Borach, daughter of a saloon-keeper on Forsythe Street in the crowded Lower East Side, where she was born in 1892. Her first appearance on any stage took place when she was 13 at Keeney's Theatre in Brooklyn, where she won an amateur night contest singing, "When You Know You're Not Forgotten by the Girl You Can't Forget." The prize was $5 and numerous coins hurled by the audience, and from that night on Miss Brice gave up school for the stage.

Then followed a job as jack-of-all-trades in a movie house, playing the piano, singing and helping out in the projection room. When she was 16 she applied for the chorus of the George M. Cohan-Sam Harris review, "Talk of New York." She remained in the chorus until Mr. Cohan found out she could not dance and fired her.

She then sang in various burlesque houses in New York. One night Florenz Ziegfeld "caught" her act and offered her a job at $75 a week. When she left the stage after introducing "My Man," Ziegfeld gave her a check for $2,500 and said, "You've earned it." Her weekly salary soon reached $3,000.

She first went to Hollywood to appear in the silent film, "My Man." She returned to Broadway only to find herself in Hollywood again when talkies came in, playing herself in "The Great Ziegfeld" and appearing in "Everybody Sing" and "Be Yourself."

She was married three times. Her first husband was Frank White, a barber, whom she met in 1911 in Springfield, Mass., when she was touring in "College Girl." The marriage lasted only a few days and she brought suit for divorce. In 1918 she was married to Jules W. (Nicky) Arnstein, only to divorce him in Chicago in 1927, after she had stood by him during his two years' imprisonment, starting in 1924, in Leavenworth, in connection with the mysterious disappearance of $5,000,000 worth of securities.

Two years after her divorce she was married to Billy Rose, the showman, by Mayor James Walker in New York. In 1937 she sued Mr. Rose for divorce, and shortly after it was granted he married Mrs. Eleanor Holm Jarrett, swimming champion.

Fanny Brice and Robert Armstrong in *Be Yourself.*

Fanny Brice played herself in *The Great Ziegfeld.* She is seen here with Esther Muir.

Fanny Brice in *My Man*.

The New York Times SATURDAY, NOVEMBER 16, 1974

Johnny Mack Brown, 70, Dies; Cowboy Star and Football Hero

WOODLAND HILLS, Calif., Nov. 15 (UPI)—Johnny Mack Brown, who went from All-America college-football player and Rose Bowl hero to become the star of hundreds of Saturday-matinee Western movies in the nineteen-thirties and forties, died yesterday. He was 70 years old.

Mr. Brown died of kidney failure, according to a spokesman for the Motion Picture Country Home and Hospital, where he had been under treatment for a month.

He was a halfback on the University of Alabama team tha beat the University of Washington, 20 to 19, in the Rose Bowl in 1926, in which Mr. Brown caught two touchdown passes. He was named to the College Football Hall of Fame in 1957.

Mr. Brown went on to become an actor and once said he had appeared in more than 300 pictures, mostly B-grade Westerns with his horse, Reno.

Money-Making List

His first Western was "Billy the Kid" with Wallace Berry in 1930. From 1942 to 1950 he was consistently named to The Motion Picture Herald's list of the 10 top money-making Western actors. Almost all of his films were aimed at the Saturday-afternoon children's market.

He retired in the fifties and was host and manager of a restaurant in the San Fernando Valley.

Mr. Brown was born in Dothan, Ala., and had his first brush with the movies while still a college football player. It lead eventually to his acting career. Movie crew members on location in Birmingham in the early filming "Men of Steel" with Victor McLaglen, attended a football game and were introduced to the players afterward.

George Fawcett, a character actor, remembered Mr. Brown, especially after his Rose Bowl exploits. He returned to California in 1927 as an assistant football coach from the University of Alabama and looked up Mr. Fawcett.

Met Von Stroheim

Mr. Fawcett introduced Mr. Brown to Erich Von Stroheim, the director, who, according to one story, cupped Mr. Brown's face in his hands, gazed into his face and said, "You could be an actor."

The Rose Bowl game in 1926 was the highlight of Mr. Brown's football career, he said in later years, because "we were the first Southern team ever to participate. We were supposed to be kind of lazy down South—full of hookworms and all. Nevertheless, we came out here and beat one of the finest teams in the country, making it a kind of historic event for Southern football. We didn't play just for Alabama, but for the whole South."

Mr. Brown is survived by his Widow, Cornelia, and four children.

In *Montana Moon*, 1930, Johnny Mack Brown played opposite Joan Crawford.

Johnny Mack Brown and Greta Garbo in *The Single Standard*, 1929.

"All the News That's Fit to Print"

The New York Times

LATE CITY EDITION

Weather: Partly cloudy, cool today; thundershowers tonight, tomorrow. Temp. range: today 63-53; Friday 70-52. Full U.S. report on Page 50.

VOL. CXIX . . No. 41,020 — NEW YORK, SATURDAY, MAY 16, 1970 — 10 CENTS

WAR-CURB MOVES IN SENATE SCORED BY WHITE HOUSE

Constitutional Responsibility of Nixon as Commander in Chief Is Stressed

INFRINGEMENT CHARGED

Plan of Cooper and Church on Troops in Cambodia Is Termed Unacceptable

By JAMES N. NAUGHTON
Special to The New York Times

KEY BISCAYNE, Fla., May 15—The White House strongly asserted today its view that a move in the Senate to cut off funds for future military involvement in Cambodia would be an infringement of the President's constitutional powers as Commander in Chief.

Ronald L. Ziegler, the White House press secretary, said that "it is our feeling there should be no restraint on the powers of the President as Commander in Chief" as "stated under the Constitution."

He said that the Administration could not accept the language of such legislation, proposed in the form of an amendment to a foreign military sales bill by Senator John Sherman Cooper, Republican of Kentucky, and Senator Frank Church, Democrat of Idaho. The Administration holds this view, he said, even though the amendment is in keeping with Mr. Nixon's pledge to have all United States forces out of Cambodia by June 30.

Aide Cites Article II

Article II of the Constitution gives the President the responsibility for protecting United States troops in the field, Mr. Ziegler said and the Cooper-Church amendment would be "an infringement on that constitutional responsibility."

Although the Administration expressed its opposition to the Cooper-Church Amendment on Tuesday, Mr. Ziegler's statements today represented a more definitive attempt to clarify the White House view that there was a constitutional issue involved.

There were reports yesterday that Administration spokesmen were arguing that the amendment could impair the President's credibility abroad, but Mr. Ziegler's remarks were regarded as a strong reassertion that the real issue was one of a constitutional conflict.

Mr. Ziegler said the White House opposition to the Cooper-Church amendment did not indicate any intention of keeping United States forces in Cambodia beyond June 30 or any plans for another incursion into Cambodia.

The President spent the day here in discussions with aides at his home on Key Biscayne.

G.O.P. Seeks Compromise

By JOHN W. FINNEY
Special to The New York Times

WASHINGTON, May 15—The Senate Republican leadership cast about today for a compromise on an amendment to restrict the use of troops in Cambodia that could win over uncommitted Senators in

Continued on Page 8, Column 5

Stock Rise of 17.43 Is Best in 2 Years

Stock prices moved ahead along a broad front yesterday to register their best one-day advance in more than two years. The Dow-Jones industrial average gained 17.43 points at 702.22.

In the previous session, this market barometer had closed at a seven-year low of 684.79, after dropping 100 points since mid-April.

Yesterday's rebound, which took place in the absence of any significant news developments, was the biggest since the Dow advanced 18.61 points on April 8, 1968, in response to President Johnson's move to de-escalate the war in Vietnam.

Brokers attributed the rally to technical market factors.

Details on Page 39.

First 2 Women Generals In Nation Picked by Nixon

United Press International
Cols. Elizabeth P. Hoisington, left, and Anna Mae Hays

By The Associated Press

WASHINGTON, May 15—President Nixon nominated today the first two women generals in United States history.

The Pentagon said that Col. Elizabeth P. Hoisington, director of the Women's Army Corps, and Col. Anna Mae Hays, chief of the Army Nurse Corps, had been selected by the President for promotion to the temporary rank of brigadier general.

Congress authorized general officer rank for women three years ago, but this is the first time that any woman in uniform has been picked to wear a star.

Colonel Hoisington, a native of Newton, Kan., enlisted in the Women's Army Auxiliary Corps in 1942 and was commissioned a year later. She became director of the WAC in August, 1966.

Colonel Hays, born in Buffalo, N.Y., also entered the Army in World War II, first serving in 1942 as an operating room nurse. She became chief of the Army Nurse Corps

Continued on Page 8, Column 4

U.S. Favors Joint Defense By Saigon and Pn…

By TAD SZU…
Special to The New Y…

WASHINGTON, May 15—The U… couraged South Vietnam and Camb… a joint plan for the defense of the … Nol in… munist…

But w… was bei… briefing … ment spo… other Adm… indicated tha… reserved the r… plans if they… conduct of the…

Reports from… terday said that… itary alliance … Bartch insisted, … the Administratio… been informed of th…

[In Vientiane, a sp… for the Laotian Defen… istry suggested that … Vietnamese forces inte… to help Laos, accordin… Agence France-Presse. … 9.]

Mr. Bartch said that … United States was awaiting th… outcome of discussions between South Vietnam and Cambodia to see what kind of plans emerged.

He said that he had not "seen anything" to suggest that President Nguyen Van Thieu and Premier Lon Nol had reached an agreement.

Other Administration sources said the United States favored an agreement. They recalled that Secretary of State William P. Rogers had implied this when he said Wednesday that the Nixon doctrine provided that "Asians should work with each other to take care of their common problems."

But today was the first time

Continued on Page 7, Column 1

POPE REPROACHES BELGIAN CARDINAL

'Grieved Astonishment' Is Expressed Over Prelates' Criticism of His Actions

By PAUL HOFMANN
Special to The New York Times

ROME, May 15—Pope Paul VI today sternly reproved members of the Roman Catholic hierarchy who have criticized his way of dealing with important theological issues. He mentioned no names, however.

With unusual bitterness, the Pope voiced "grieved astonishment" at comments by prelates who, he said, seemed to lack the brotherly spirit that must prevail among the episcopacy.

From the context it was clear to virtually all churchmen here that the main target of the Pontiff's rebuke was Leo Cardinal Suenens, Archbishop of Mechlin-Brussels and primate of Belgium. In an interview Monday with Le Monde of Paris, the Cardinal called for an open dialogue among the church's bishops on the problem of the celibacy of priests.

Churchmen here said they could not recall a recent precedent for public controversy between a Pope and a Cardinal.

Pope Paul's personal reaction

Continued on Page 17, Column 2

U.S. BRIEF BACKS TAX-EXEMPT ROLE OF WHITE SCHOOLS

Holds Segregated Classes Would Not Be Getting a Government Subsidy

By EILEEN SHANAHAN
Special to The New York Times

WASHINGTON, May 15—The Justice Department contended today that the segregated private schools that have grown up recently in the South should be allowed to keep their tax-exempt status. It said that the exemption did not constitute any form of Government "support" for these schools.

It was the first time the Justice Department had used this argument in the months of legal struggles over the tax-exempt status of these schools.

Previously, it had simply taken the position that the parents of black children who were suing for termination of the tax-exemptions had no legal standing to bring such suits.

Blacks File Suit

The department's views we… contained in a brief fi… the United State… for the …

pa… are… subs… ment… "T… exem… 'bene… fit th… educa… exemp… not c… tenan… recipients." The argu… a new one f… partment but…

Continued on …

Billie Burke Dead; Movie Comedienne

By The Associated Press

LOS ANGELES, May 15—Billie Burke, a great Broadway beauty when the century was young and later renowned as a movie comedienne, died last night at the age of 84.

While starring in New York musicals, she met and was married to Florenz Ziegfeld.

A Sophisticated Beauty

Addlepated, scatterbrained, twittery, jittery or skittish, Billie Burke appeared in scores of comedies on the stage and screen in a style that was a combination of naiveté and wit.

"I never was the great-ac-

Continued on Page 25, Column 1

Associated Press
…indow of women's dormitory at state college shows effect of … police say, in reply to sniper fire. Two died, nine were wounded.

F.B.I. Investigating Killing Of 2 Negroes in Jackson

By ROY REED
Special to The New York Times

JACKSON, Miss., May 15—A barrage of police gunfire …sted 30 seconds and consisted of at least 140 shots …o students dead and nine other persons wounded …t night. All the dead …nded were Negroes.

… youth, a student at …ate College, was …n front of a wom- … and the other, …n high school, …e dining hall … dormitory at …lege, a pre- …nstitution of …dents, was … from top …lash with … left un- … end of … Lynch …ed total …rolmen … shot- …0 to … looking …gs. The Justice … said it was send- …eam to investigate.

Richard G. Kleindienst, the Deputy Attorney General, told Mayor Russell C. Davis of Jackson by telephone today that the Federal investigators

Continued on Page 15, Column 4

…ntrasted …his commit- …s with that of the …zens he expected Mayor Lindsay to appoint to the pro-

Continued on Page 51, Column 4

United Press International
IN MEMORY OF UNION LEADER: Men at Ford Motor plant in St. Paul, one of many where silent tribute was paid to Walter P. Reuther. Article on funeral service on Page 25.

South African Teams Expelled From All Olympic Competition

By MICHAEL KATZ
Special to The New York Times

AMSTERDAM, the Netherlands, May 15—South Africa was expelled today from the International Olympic Committee. That means the country cannot compete in the Olympic Games.

The 69th International Olympic Committee's congress went one step further than it had in 1963, when it banned South Africa from participating in the 1964 games at Tokyo or in 1968, when it prohibited the country from taking part in the games at Mexico City.

By a vote of 35 to 28, with three abstentions, the I.O.C. "withdrew recognition" of the South African National Olympic Committee, thereby severing all ties with the country. Withdrawal of recognition also means, of course, that South Africa will not be permitted to take part in any further Olympics until its national committee, which is not a government body, is recognized anew.

This is the first time any nation has been expelled from the Olympic movement since Baron Pierre de Courbertin revived the games in 1896.

South Africa was expelled for violating Rule One of the Olympic charter, which states that "no discrimination is al-

Continued on Page 36, Column 1

WARREN DECRIES DIVIDED SOCIETY

Says Failure to Realize Ideal of Equality Has Produced Worst Crisis in Century

Excerpts from Warren speech will be found on Page 5.

By MARTIN ARNOLD

Former Chief Justice Earl Warren said yesterday that the United States was in a crisis greater than any "within the memory of living Americans."

This crisis, he said, is largely attributable "to our failure to enforce adequately" the due process and equal protection sections of the 14th Amendment of the Constitution.

"A number of factors contribute to it — war, inflation, unemployment with resulting poverty," he said, and "an atmosphere for repression."

Justice Warren, speaking at a luncheon of the N.A.A.C.P. Legal Defense and Educational Fund, Inc., said that there was "a divisiveness in our society to a degree of intensity that has not been equaled in the past 100 years."

He did not place the blame for this divisiveness on any particular segment of society, but rather indicated that society as a whole, including most particularly the judicial process, was at fault.

"There are many causes of the crisis, but none I believe as basic as our neglect in reaching the ideal we fashioned for ourselves in the Declaration of Independence that 'All men are created equal.'"

Justice Warren's speech was

Continued on Page 5, Column 3

NEWS INDEX

U.S. JURY ASSAILS POLICE IN CHICAGO ON PANTHER RAID

Asserts They Exaggerated Resistance by Blacks, 2 of Whom Were Slain

INDICTMENTS RULED OUT

3 High Officers Demoted—Panel Discerns 'Posturing' in Panthers' Attitudes

Excerpts from commission's report are on Page 14.

By FRED P. GRAHAM
Special to The New York Times

WASHINGTON, May 15—A special Federal grand jury in Chicago reported today that the police there had grossly exaggerated Black Panthers' resistance in a shooting incident last Dec. 4 in which two of the militants were killed and four others wounded.

The jury said the police had riddled the Panthers' apartment with at least 82 shots, while only one shot was apparently fired from inside.

But the jury, speculating that the policemen could have been returning one another's fire, said it could not find evidence on which to indict the policemen for violations of the gunshot victims' civil rights.

Three high-ranking Chicago police officers were demoted last night, apparently as a result of the controversy over the raid on the Panther apartment. [Details on Page 14.]

Hands Tied, Jury Says

In a 250-page report, the grand jury said that its hands had been tied because the Panthers who survived the shooting incident refused to testify, asserting that they would talk only to a "peer group."

Branding this "political posturing" by the Black Panthers to dramatize their demands for black juries, the grand jury declared that it would not permit itself "to be used as an instrument of publicity and recruiting by the Panthers."

The special grand jury was composed of 22 whites and one Negro, a woman.

Findings of Jury

Among the grand jury's findings were the following points:

¶That the initial information that the Black Panthers were thought to be stockpiling weapons in Chicago had come to the Chicago officials from the Federal Bureau of Investigation. This disclosure was the first official substantiation of charges by black leaders that Federal officials had played a part in the investigation that led to a raid on the apartment and the fatal shooting. According to the grand jury, the two F.B.I. tips were routine transmittals of information obtained from a "confidential source."

¶That Mr. Hampton's body had not contained huge amounts of the drug seconal, as reported by a pathologist who performed an autopsy on his body. Later tests on the body by F.B.I. experts showed that the drug report was a mistake, according to the jury's report.

¶That the Chicago police

Continued on Page 14, Column 6

Billie Burke Dead; Movie Comedienne

By The Associated Press

LOS ANGELES, May 15—Billie Burke, a great Broadway beauty when the century was young and later renowned as a movie comedienne, died last night at the age of 84.

While starring in New York musicals, she met and was married to Florenz Ziegfeld.

A Sophisticated Beauty

Addlepated, scatterbrained, twittery, jittery or skittish, Billie Burke appeared in scores of comedies on the stage and screen in a style that was a combination of naiveté and wit.

"I never was the great-ac-

Continued on Page 25, Column 1

Billie Burke, Film Comedienne And Once a Stage Beauty, Dies

Continued From Page 1, Col. 8

tress type," she remarked years later. "I generally did light, gay things. I often had cute plays but never a fine one."

In 1922, the year she won first place in the Motion Picture Popularity Contest, she was described by one observer this way:

"Her eyes [are] a lovely blue, her eyebrows fair and skin soft, smooth and well nourished, a cameolike delicacy of feature and a youthful figure."

But she found fault if others did not. "Ah, yes," she would sigh, her voice frosted with an adopted English accent, "I have a deep and penetrating sorrow. My freckles. I have tried everything under the sun, but they cling to me faithfully."

When she toured with a play, her press agent traveled ahead and took a house or apartment in every city along the way. The actress's dressing room would be routinely refurbished, no matter how short the engagement, most often in the style of her room at the Lyceum Theater in New York, "covered wherever possible with baby blue, the true ingénue color."

Pajamas, cigars, perfume and soaps were named for her. Billie Burke dresses with flat collars and lace and Billie Burke curls that could be attached to the back of a young woman's head became fads.

She was piquant, effusive—the darling of the day. And, one observer wrote, "she shakes hands frantically."

Ruffles and Ribbons

In the early 1900's, when women's fashions were often heavy and dark, Billie Burke was dressed in ruffles and ribbons. Her powder was made of crushed French chalk, applied to the tip of her nose and then carefully wiped off.

In her bath, she placed a small bag of yellow bran meal to soften the water. A maid brushed her hair every morning and night; some 10 years later, Florenz Ziegfeld himself poured imported champagne over her hair after every shampoo, a method he considered appropriate for a redhead.

She exercised with Indian clubs and a bar bell and walked five miles every day.

When she played on Broadway, Mark Twain was a frequent backstage visitor. From his gilded box, Enrico Caruso threw a bouquet of American Beauty roses to the stage every night during the Boston run of "Love Watches" in 1908. He was, Miss Burke later recalled, impetuous.

"He made love and ate spaghetti with equal skill and no inhibitions. He would propose marriage several times each evening."

Also in attendance were James M. Barrie and W. Somerset Maugham; it was the latter who escorted the actress to a party at the Astor Hotel on New Year's Eve, 1913. They arrived after midnight. She descended the red-carpeted staircase to the ballroom; at the foot of the stairs stood Florenz Ziegfeld Jr. Miss Burke described her reaction this way:

"He had a Mephistophelian look, his eyebrows and his eyelids lifting, curved upward, in the middle. Slim and tall and immaculate in full evening dress, he was in black and white contrast to the rest of the costumed party, and so—and for who knows what other reasons—I noticed him at once." And he noticed her.

Ziegfeld courted her in extravagant style and while she was falling in love with him, self-appointed advisers were saying that he would break her heart, that he had no money, that such a marriage could only ruin her career.

Charles Frohman, her manager, threatened to drop her. But Billie Burke had no intention of ending the affair and she and Ziegfeld met at Grant's Tomb, among other places, until they eloped to Hoboken in April, 1914. The wedding ceremony took place in the stuffy back room of a parsonage.

Mary William Ethelbert Appleton Burke was born on Aug. 6, 1886, in Washington, the only child of Blanche Beatty Hodkinson of New Orleans and William (Billy) Burke, a singing clown in the Barnum and Bailey circus.

Billy Burke was a clown of the 1880's and 1890's, an era in which clowns were artists, the masters of wit and pantomime. He was of Irish descent, with red hair, blue eyes and a fine singing voice.

When "Little Billie" was born, Billy Burke sent this telegram to his wife: "I don't care whether it's a boy or a girl, but does it have red hair?" She said she did.

Billie Burke (left), Wallace Beery and Jean Harlow in *Dinner at Eight.*

When she was 8, tthe family sailed for England, where Billy Burke organized his own troupe; soon he was playing the music halls. His daughter studied at the Misses Baillie's School where she enjoyed music and "was the dullard of the world" in mathematics.

Billie Burke was a pretty child, shy, polite and not particularly talented. But Blanche Burke decided that her daughter would be an actress or an opera singer or a dancer. And a star.

Billie studied singing in French and Italian, elocution, the piano, fencing and ballet—an undertaking that was short-lived because she could not get up on her toes.

When she was 14, she made her debut singing songs in a weak, whispery voice and doing imitations. The audience hooted, but her mother, who had undoubtedly exerted some pressure in arranging the performance, insisted on a second attempt; this time the audience applauded.

On May 9, 1903, opening night, Billie Burke stole the show with her rendition of "The Canoe Song." She was to sing the song and paddle an imaginary canoe for the next two years.

In 1907, Frohman brought her and her newly widowed mother to New York at a weekly salary of $500 to appear with John Drew in "My Wife," the play that established her as a comedienne.

Soon after Frohman's death in 1915, his office put Billie Burke under written contract as punishment for having married against his wishes. She was the only Frohman star ever under contract, and she was now delayed from embarking on the film career she desired.

But Thomas H. Ince, a Hollywood pioneer, had offered her $300,000 for her first film and she decided to forsake the stage for the screen. Florenz Ziegfeld became his wife's manager.

She made her screen debut in "Peggy," the playing the part of a girl from Scotland "who, for some plot motivation I cannot for the life of me recall, dressed as a boy."

In 1916, she made "Gloria's Romance," and then about a dozen more silent films. The next year, she returned to the New York stage.

Florenz Ziegfeld was now managing Miss Burke's theatrical career, but his choice of plays was not always good. The comedies that marked her return, including "The Rescuing Angel," "Rose Briar" and "Caesar's Wife," received bland notices.

Between 1917 and 1944, Billie Burke starred in 12 plays on Broadway, including three by W. Somerset Maugham, two by Booth Harkington and one by Noël Coward—"The Marquise" in 1927.

By 1930, in "The Truth Game," she was already established as a character actress. "Oh," she wrote, "that sad and bewildering moment when you are no longer the cherished darling but must turn the corner and try to be funny!

The Wall Street crash of 1929 destroyed Flo Ziegfeld, and Billie Burke had to try harder than ever to be funny. The Ziegfelds mortgaged Burkely Crest and the actress determined to keep working.

In 1931, she and her daughter left for California, while Ziegfeld stayed in New York trying desperately to rally.

Her favorite means of communication was the telegrams, a habit she inherited from her husband, who was known to send dozens a day.

"All the News That's Fit to Print"

The New York Times.

LATE CITY EDITION
U. S. Weather Bureau Report (Page 90) forecasts: Fair and less humid today; cool tonight. Fair tomorrow.
Temp. Range: 83—65; yesterday: 85—75. Temp.-Hum. Index: 73; yesterday: 79.

VOL. CXV..No. 39,659. © 1966 by The New York Times Company. Times Square, New York, N. Y. 10036 NEW YORK, WEDNESDAY, AUGUST 24, 1966. TEN CENTS

O'CONNOR CLAIMS VOTES FOR VICTORY ON FIRST BALLOT

He Picks Up 161 Delegates In Manhattan and Bronx and Puts Total at 706

573 ARE NEEDED TO WIN

But Roosevelt and Samuels Say They Will Remain in Governorship Contest

By TERENCE SMITH

City Council President Frank D. O'Connor said yesterday that he had gained enough pledged delegate strength to win the Democratic nomination for Governor on the first ballot.

He picked up 161 delegates from New York and Bronx counties yesterday and now claims a total of 706 publicly committed delegates. Only 573 will be needed for nomination at the convention Sept. 7 and 8 in Buffalo.

Despite Mr. O'Connor's view that only the formalities remained, the two other contenders—Howard J. Samuels and Franklin D. Roosevelt Jr.—announced that they were in the fight to stay.

The support of 75 Manhattan delegates for Mr. O'Connor was announced in the late morning by J. Raymond Jones, the county leader. Less than two hours later, a jubilant Mr. O'Connor said at a hastily summoned news conference:

"I'm now certainly the obvious nominee of the party."

Buckley Speaks for Bronx

He said his delegate strength at that moment totaled 620 and emphasized that it had reached that point without the support of the Bronx and Brooklyn delegations.

The Bronx support was announced four hours later by Charles A. Buckley, the party's county leader. He broke a long silence on the gubernatorial situation with a statement that 86 of the county's 112 delegates would vote for Mr. O'Connor.

Assemblyman Stanley Steingut has yet to disclose the sentiment of the Brooklyn delegation, although it is generally assumed that the Council President will command a healthy majority.

Mr. O'Connor's supporters have contended for some time that he would be able to accumulate the required delegate strength without the help of the organizations headed by Mr. Buckley and Mr. Steingut. And it was with obvious satisfaction that they announced the 620-vote total in the early afternoon.

Charges Denied

The most difficult moments in Mr. O'Connor's drive have resulted from charges that he agreed to step out of the 1965 Democratic Mayoral primary in exchange for the support of the Bronx and Brooklyn leaders in the governorship race.

Mr. O'Connor has repeatedly denied the charges, which were made by Mr. Roosevelt, but his aides have been eager to show that he could win the nomination without the Bronx-Brooklyn backing.

The Council President was in unusually high spirits at the press conference—held in a red-carpeted suite in the Commodore Hotel — despite lengthy questioning on the decision of the Liberal party not to endorse his candidacy.

The Liberals formally announced their opposition Monday night, explaining that they considered Mr. O'Connor "evasive on issues of substance,"

Continued on Page 24, Column 3

Stocks Dip in Busy Day

Stock prices swung erratically and declined slightly at the close yesterday in the heaviest trading in three months.

Volume on the New York Stock Exchange surged to 9.83 million shares from 8.69 million on Monday. The turnover was the highest since May 17, when 9.87 million shares were traded.

Prices rose and fell and then rose and fell again. The losses were relatively minor compared with the sharp declines in the general selloff on Monday. The Dow-Jones industrial average dipped 1.89 points, to a new 1966 low of 790.14. On Monday, the average fell 12.59 points.

Details on Page 59

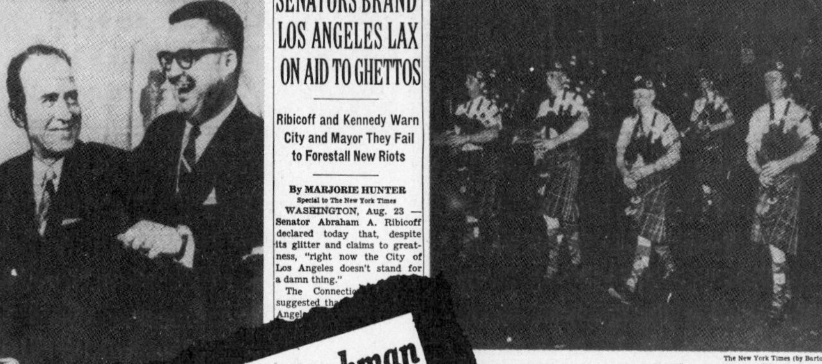

VOICES CONFIDENC[E] ... Council President, as he ... for Democratic gubern[atorial] ... James H. Glavin 3d, Dem[ocratic] ...

... 64TH STREET AT 12:08 THIS MORNING: Bagpipers taking part in the Vet[erans of] Foreign Wars parade make their music after turning east from Fifth Avenue.

The New York Times (by Barton Silverman)

CONGRESS RUSHES TO HELP BUILDERS

Quick Agreement Reached on $4.76-Billion in Funds for Home Mortgages

By The Associated Press

WASHINGTON, Aug. 23—Senate-House conferees agreed today on a compromise bill to pump $4.76-billion more of Government mortgage purchase funds into the sagging home-building industry.

In coming to a quick agreement on the legislation at their first meeting, the conferees wrote in the highest possible figure by accepting all the devices carried in both the House and Senate versions.

Sponsors said the compromise measure probably would be called up in the Senate tomorrow and could be signed into law by the end of this week.

Transit Subsidy Favored

The new funds would be channeled through the Federal National Mortgage Association. They would apply to mortgages insured by the Federal Housing Authority and guaranteed by the Veterans Administration.

The same set of conferees also agreed on a second measure — a mass-transit subsidy bill authorizing an additional $300-million to carry on this program in fiscal 1968 and 1969.

This followed the Senate version. The House had voted only for $150-million in 1968.

The extra purchasing authority for the Federal National Mortgage Association would be

Continued on Page 68, Column 6

Francis X. Bushman Of Silent Films Dies

Associated Press

Francis X. Bushman

Special to The New York Times

LOS ANGELES, Aug. 23—Francis X. Bushman, the romantic hero of the silent screen, died today after an accident in the kitchen of his home in suburban Pacific Palisades. An ambulance crew, summoned by his wife, Iva, pronounced him dead. He was 83 years old.

Mr. Bushman, who on Sunday had suffered a fall in his bath-

Continued on Page 45, Column 1

SENATORS BRAND LOS ANGELES LAX ON AID TO GHETTOS

Ribicoff and Kennedy Warn City and Mayor They Fail to Forestall New Riots

By MARJORIE HUNTER

Special to The New York Times

WASHINGTON, Aug. 23 — Senator Abraham A. Ribicoff declared today that, despite its glitter and claims to greatness, "right now the City of Los Angeles doesn't stand for a damn thing."

The Connecti[cut] ... suggested th[at] ... Angel[es] ...

B[y] ...

WA[SHINGTON] ... Presi[dent] ... W. ... Healt[h] ... today ... of rising ...

Mr. G[ardner] ... President ... mit reports ... and on Fede[ral] ...

Following ... Gardner told ... cost of such m[edical] ... hospital and ... risen 3.4 per cen[t] ... months.

"I am not say[ing] ... abuses," he decla[red] ... want to take a ve[ry] ... very quick look at ... move rapidly."

The study will be ... cooperation with the ... partment, the Preside[nt's Coun]cil of Economic Ad[visers] ... with other Federa[l] ... Mr. Gardner said.

Mr. Gardner named ... Gorham, Assistant S[ecretary] for Program Coordina[tion] ... head the study.

To Seek the Facts

Mr. Gardner sidestepped q[ues]tions on specific actions ... Government could take ... abuses were found. He stres[sed] that the first problem was ... ascertain the facts.

However, he confirmed tha[t] the investigation would cover doctors' fees, the cost of medicines, hospital charges and related medical expenses.

In one of his reports to the President, Mr. Gardner said that $4.1-million for initial planning grants had been awarded to 10 states toward the establishment of regional medical projects to combat the nation's three major killer diseases — heart disease, cancer and stroke.

Linked to Medicare

In another report he noted that Federal funds had helped build or remodel classrooms, libraries and laboratories in a third of the nation's campuses during the fiscal year ended June 30. A total of $627-million was granted to 864 colleges and universities, he said.

The President's directive for an inquiry followed reports that physicians had raised their fees for patients 65 and over by as much as 300 per cent since Medicare began on July 1.

Under the Medicare program, the Federal Government pays 80 per cent of a physician's fees after the first $50 a year under Part B of the program. The monthly cost to subscribers is $3 in premiums.

According to the Labor Department, physicians' fees have mounted steadily over the last year. Fees for family phy-

Continued on Page 23, Column 1

NEWS INDEX

[V.F.]W. Night Parade Stirs Outcries

[By ...] T. KAUFMAN

... and bagpipes ... [af]ter midnight, ... Foreign Wars ... Fifth Avenue ... complaints ... [res]idents who ... [rea]dy to march ...

... [start]ed at 96th ... An hour ... [drum]s, drum ... [Aven]ue cars ... started ... [w]alls of ... [a]ll and ... [[1]]0,000 marchers were still moving past the avenue's big apartment houses.

One man trying to get to sleep irately told the police, "If I were marching down the middle of a block blowing a bugle at this time of night, I damned well would be arrested."

Another protested that the parade was "outrageous." "I don't like it," he said. "Even the Vietnam protest was better than this—at least it was in the middle of the day." There were complaints, too, from motorists who had been bogged in traffic and from residents who told of brass bands that left the parade but went right on playing.

Still others objected to the parade-parking regulations that forced them to keep their cars off Fifth Avenue and many of the blocks between Fifth and Third.

The parade finally ended on Fifth Avenue at 12:09 A.M. and at the dispersal

Continued on Page 20, Column 1

Slaughter of Reds Gives Indonesia a Grim Legacy

Following is the third of a series of four dispatches on [I]ndonesia by The New York Times's chief correspondent in [S]outheast Asia, who recently traveled through the country.

By SEYMOUR TOPPING

Special to The New York Times

JAKARTA, Indonesia—From the terraced rice fields of [Cent]ral Java to the exquisite island of Bali, from the rub[ber pl]antations of Sumatra to the fishing villages of remote ... the Indonesian people ... [trou]bled by the heritage ... [viol]ence bequeathed by ... [stagg]ering mass slaughter ... [Commu]nists.

... [Ta]gs of uncounted ... Communists in an ... [ritu]als and blood lust ... [s]urface tensions ... [Indonesi]ans that may ... [f]or generations. ... of Indonesians ... [ac]tly to collect ... [in]calculable. ... [ne]ver know how ... members of ... Communist ... [sym]pathizers and ... [fal]sely accused ... [retal]iation for ... [Comm]unist-sup... power in ... best... [es]timate ... they ... [cou]ld be ... [mi]llion.

[Continued on Page ..., Colum]n 4

M'NAMARA PLANS TO 'SALVAGE' 40,000 REJECTED IN DRAFT

Says 100,000 a Year Will Be Taken Later by Services for Special Training

SCORES APTITUDE TESTS

Secretary, in Talk to V.F.W. Here, Links Program to the Antipoverty Drive

Excerpts from the McNamara speech appear on Page 18.

By HOMER BIGART

Defense Secretary Robert S. McNamara disclosed yesterday that 40,000 draft rejects and substandard volunteers, most of them with "poverty-encrusted" backgrounds, would be "salvaged" for military duty in the next 10 months.

The number of the "salvaged" will reach a rate of 100,000 in the next fiscal year and in succeeding years, Secretary McNamara told the annual convention of the Veterans of Foreign Wars at the New York Hilton Hotel.

The rehabilitation of young men who fail to pass the standard aptitude tests because of physical or education deficiencies, or both, will be accomplished by special training programs, Mr. McNamara explained.

His disclosure caught the Pentagon by surprise. A spokesman called the proposal an attempt to revive, in expanded form, a controversial program that was killed by Congress last year.

Fund Request Denied

Congress did not appropriate the $16,375,000 requested by President Johnson in 1964 for a three-year experiment called the Special Training Enlistment Program. The program would have involved about 11,000 men at the start.

Detractors referred to the project, known as STEP, as the "moron corps." Some critics charged that it was simply an adjunct to the President's antipoverty program and questioned whether the Army was the proper vehicle for socio-economic experiments.

Again yesterday Secretary McNamara linked the "salvage" plan to the nation's antipoverty drive. He did not contend, as did the Pentagon in 1964, that the program would reduce reliance on the draft by expanding the pool of qualified volunteers available for enlistment.

He told the veterans that the armed services' vast educational system could be the medium for preparing "tens of thousands" of substandard draftees and volunteers for "productive military careers and later for productive roles in society."

Currently, the military rejects 600,000 young men a year for failure to meet minimum

Continued on Page 18, Column 1

PEKING CHURCHES SHUT AND DEFACED

Flowers and Philatelists Are Also 'Red Guard' Targets —New Politburo Hinted

By Reuters

PEKING, Aug. 23 — Thousands of teen-agers enforcing China's tough new drive for a stricter Communist way of life closed and defaced Christian churches today.

Red flags fluttered from the dome and western tower of the South Cathedral, the main Roman Catholic center, and demonstrators curtly refused to let foreign newsmen enter the walled compound.

From across the street it could be seen that some of the cathedral's windows had been shattered. Communist slogans were pasted on its walls and Biblical pictures were mutilated.

[A report by the Chinese Communist press agency [in]dicated that a new Politburo [w]as elected by the party's [Ce]ntral Committee earlier [this] month. Page 6.]

[B]ust of Mao in Church

... the Protestant church ... [dow]n were again kept out... it was possible to see [that] the interior had been completely rearranged, with a larger - than - life white bust of China's leader, Mao Tse-tung, at the center.

The campaign to change street names and other signs continued. The capital's huge Heavenly Peace (Tien An Men) Square, where major rallies and parades are held, is now East Is Red (Dong Fang Hung) Square, according to a proclamation pasted over the old signs.

The campaign to oppose bourgeois tendencies has taken some unexpected forms.

A poster outside a depot for pedicabs—tricycles pedaled by a driver with a seat behind him for his passenger — said that they might still be hired but that the passenger should pedal himself while the driver sits in the passenger seat.

Posters outside flower shops declare that having flowers in the house is not revolutionary.

Continued on Page 6, Column 4

Asian Peace Parley Is Backed by Nixon

By JOSEPH A. LOFTUS

Special to The New York Times

WASHINGTON, Aug. 23—Republicans were moving quickly today toward a new Vietnam policy that emphasizes peace negotiations in an all-Asian conference instead of a hard line of stepped-up military activity.

Richard M. Nixon joined a growing number of Republican leaders in advancing the peace conference idea as a campaign issue this fall. The strategy seemed designed to leave the impression that President Johnson was irrevocably wedded to reconvening the nine-nation 1954 Geneva Conference, which ended the French Indochina war. The conference included European as well as Asian nations and the United States.

The Administration has spoken favorably, though cautiously, for such an all-Asian conference, explaining that it would be tactless for the United States to act as if it were an Asian leader.

That position would make the peace conference less than a clear-cut partisan issue, but Mr. Nixon and other Republicans spoke today with confi-

Continued on Page 3, Column 9

United Press International Telephoto

THUNDER OVER LOS ANGELES: Mayor Samuel W. Yorty, right, and Senator Abraham A. Ribicoff, back to camera, Democrat of Connecticut, during angry exchange over Los Angeles' slum policies. Scene is Senate subcommittee hearing on problems of cities.

Francis X. Bushman Of Silent Films Dies

Associated Press

Francis X. Bushman

Special to The New York Times

LOS ANGELES, Aug. 23—Francis X. Bushman, the romantic hero of the silent screen, died today after an accident in the kitchen of his home in suburban Pacific Palisades. An ambulance crew, summoned by his wife, Iva, pronounced him dead. He was 83 years old.

Mr. Bushman, who on Sunday had suffered a fall in his bath-

Continued on Page 45, Column 1

Francis X. Bushman, Actor, Dies at 83

Continued From Page 1, Col. 2

room, had gone into his kitchen this morning to get a cup of coffee when he slipped and fell again, striking his head on a cupboard.

A coroner's autopsy indicated that his "death was due to a rupture of the heart."

The actor had re-established himself as the courtly master of ceremonies of a late movie television show on a local station in recent years. He was scheduled to have started a role today in a feature film at Paramount. Mr. Bushman was to have portrayed a saloon owner in "Huntsville," but the fall on Sunday had postponed it.

His agent, Louis Shurr, said that the actor had just completed an assignment in television's "Voyage to the Bottom of the Sea" and was recently cast as a guest villain in the "Batman" series.

Charlton Heston, president of the Screen Actors Guild and who, like Mr. Bushman, starred in a film version of "Ben-Hur," said: "His passing marks the fall of one of the landmarks of Hollywood history. He represented all that was best in the tradition of Hollywood as well as of his own profession."

Mr. Bushman's death came on the 40th anniversary of the death of another romantic silent-screen actor, Rudolph Valentino.

'Handsomest Man in the World'

Years before the women of America sighed over such film idols as Wallace Reid and Rudolph Valentino, they adored Francis X. Bushman, star of more than 400 films and known as "the handsomest man in the world."

From 1911 until 1918, moviegoers by the millions paid their nickels and dimes to gaze upon his classic profile and his muscular physique as he made passionate love to such actresses as Beverly Bayne, Billie Dove and Corinne Griffith in two-reelers that brought him more than $6-million.

Mr. Bushman's off-screen performance matched the grandiloquence of his film roles. He spent his way into bankruptcy with $100 tips to waiters, a lavender limousine, lavender cigarettes, servants in lavender. He had 18 secretaries for his fan mail and on his 280-acre estate outside Baltimore he kept Great Danes and race horses.

But it was not his extravagance that caused Mr. Bushman's downfall. His film career was ruined by the revelation in 1918 that he was a married man with five children, a secret that had been kept from his vast public in accordance with a clause in his movie contract.

The shattering truth emerged when his wife, the former Josephine Fladuene, brought a successful suit for divorce so that he could marry Beverly Bayne, his leading lady. As a result, his romantic identity was destroyed and his mail and movie offers vanished.

Capacity for Enjoyment

Looking back on this phase of his life more than four decades later, Mr. Bushman said, with the florid speech he had acquired in his early years of working in stock companies:

"I was unknown and on a side road, picking my way through villages and hamlets. A genuine Via Dolorosa. Once a man like myself begins to slip there are kicks, bludgeons, blows."

Mr. Bushman was not seeking pity. For by then he had begun the radio and television careers that were to enable him to live in comfort.

"I have no regrets," he once said. "People look on me as a legend. It's pretty nice to be a legend and alive."

Another time, when he was asked if he wished he had saved some of his millions, he replied:

"When you have the capacity for enjoyment, that's the time to enjoy life. As you get older, you begin to think before you enjoy, and that spoils everything."

Nor was Mr. Bushman embarrassed by the fact that he continued to think highly of the flamboyant style of acting that was to become known as "ham."

"Nowadays," he said not too long ago, "people say without changing expressions: 'Hello, dear, mother's dead.' In the old days we gave it lots of feeling, breast-beating and arm-waving."

Nevertheless, Mr. Bushman was able to see himself and his style in perspective. Thus, in the middle nineteen - forties, when he was being interviewed by Pete Martin for The Saturday Evening Post, he recalled seeing a re-issue of one of his movies:

"When my face flashed on the screen, I laughed so hard I cried. I said: 'Look at that. I'm putting all of my emotions in my jaw.'"

Francis Xavier Bushman was born on Jan. 10, 1883 in Baltimore. His theatrical career began with stock companies in the East and he made his Broadway debut in 1907 in "Queen of the Moulin Rouge."

Portraits Gained Attention

Countless publicity releases and gimmicks in which Mr. Bushman participated confused the chronicles of his life. There were reports that he had run away to join a circus as a boy. But there is no reason to doubt accounts that showed that his acting career was preceded, or accompanied, by work as a wrestler, a weight - lifter, a bicycle-rider and a sculptor's model.

By Mr. Bushman's own account, his posing for sculptors, more than his many months in theatrical stage companies brought him to the attention of the filmmakers.

Pictures of these poses attracted the attention of a movie scout and gained his entrance into the movie business as an actor for the Essanay Film Company, which then had studios in Camden, N. J.

His first film, "Lost Years," in 1911, attracted considerable praise, and since the two-reelers were often ground out in a couple of days, his fame grew rapidly with his subsequent films. A few years later he was with the Metro Film Company, which was later to become part of Metro-Goldwyn-Mayer.

Among Mr. Bushman's films were "When Soul Meets Soul," "The Spy's Deceit," "Blood Will Tell" and "Social Quicksand." He starred with Miss Bayne in "Under Royal Patronage," "Graustark," "Red, White and Blue," "Romeo and Juliet" and the Mayer serial "The Great Secret."

His earnings became stupendous. And so did his appetites for the luxuries that this income could buy.

"Once in pictures," he recalled many years later, "I was on the Main Line. I raced always with abandon. There were thrills, hills, curves, ecstasy. It was glorious."

After his divorce, he made only one movie in 1919 and had no more film work until 1926, when he was the villainous Roman, Messala, in Lewis B. Mayer's silent version of "Ben-Hur," starring Ramon Novarro.

Although Mr. Bushman's performance was well received, Mr. Mayer accused the actor of trying to steal scenes from Mr. Novarro, whose career Mr. Mayer was pushing. As a result, Mr. Mayer would not give Mr. Bushman any more film roles. That and the advent of sound, which made obsolete the silent lovers that Mr. Bushman played, crushed his comeback attempt.

Mr. Bushman's fortune was wiped out by the stock market collapse of 1929 and he filed a bankruptcy petition that showed him to be more than $100,000 in debt.

2,500 Bit Parts

In the next 20 years he appeared in few movies and in none of them did he have big roles. He played Bernard M. Baruch, the financier, in "Wilson" in 1943 and King Saul in "David and Bathsheba" in 1951.

But radio, and then television, gave him new opportunities. He was said to have had more than 2,500 bit parts in radio "soap operas" alone before he began getting television work.

Once more, large audiences began seeing his face. It was still handsome though the jaw was jowly and the thick hair was white. He was recognized more often at Hollywood premieres and it seemed there was once more a market for the man of whom Arthur Brisbane had once written:

"His is the best-known name and face in the world."

Mr. Bushman's third wife was the former Norma Atkins, who died in 1956. He is survived by his widow, whom he married in 1956; 6 children by his first and second marriages; 12 grandchildren and 2 great-grandchildren.

Francis X. Bushman and Beverly Bayne, shown here in *Romeo and Juliet,* 1916, kept their marriage secret so as not to deflate the illusions of their fans.

"All the News That's Fit to Print"

The New York Times.

LATE CITY EDITION

U. S. Weather Bureau Report (Page 95) forecasts: Sunny, cool today and tomorrow. Clear and cold tonight. Temp. Range: 52—35; yesterday: 56—38.

NEWS SUMMARY AND INDEX, PAGE 95

SECTION ONE

VOL. CXIV—No. 38,977.

NEW YORK, SUNDAY, OCTOBER 11, 1964.

40c beyond 50-mile zone from New York City, except on Long Island. 50c beyond 200-mile zone from New York City, higher in air delivery cities.

THIRTY CENTS

RUSH ON LAST DAY OF REGISTRATION POINTS TO RECORD

Total in City Is Expected to Exceed the Previous High of 3.5 Million Voters

OPERATION IS SMOOTHER

But Some Are Still Waiting at 2 A.M.—Impeding of Negroes Is Charged

By EMANUEL PERLMUTTER

New Yorkers turned out by the tens of thousands yesterday on the last day of voter registration, and incomplete tabulations early today indicated that the total enrollment was headed for a record.

The present record of 3,556,377 was set in 1944.

People were reported still standing in line at 2 A.M. in at least one district. Although the polls closed at 10:30 P.M., those in line then were allowed to register.

At 3 A.M., Richmond was the only borough in which the tabulations were complete. It showed that 7,896 were enrolled yesterday, the fourth and final day to register for the Nov. 3 election. The four-day total for the borough was 16,062, making an over-all registration there of 107,908.

The rush to register across the city was particularly marked in late afternoon and early evening. There were complaints by some civil rights spokesmen that unreasonable delays were preventing Negroes from registering.

15½ Hours to Register

Thomas Mallee, a Republican member of the Board of Elections, noting that voters had 15½ hours to register yesterday, said late in the day that reports from polling place inspectors indicated the final day's total would be considerably above the total of 114,824 registered in Friday's five-hour period.

The total registration up to yesterday was 3,340,674, or 215,703 below the record. Registrants who had changed their address were required to reregister, as were new voters and those who had not voted since 1961.

Typical of the trend was the situation in the 15th Election District of Brooklyn's 10th Assembly District, which has had a large influx of Negroes and Puerto Ricans in recent years. An inspector said approximately 100 persons had registered this year, or about twice the number listed for the 1960 Presidential election.

The large registration over the city was viewed with pleas-

Continued on Page 45, Column 1

9 MILLION IN STOCK PLEDGED CORNELL

Maxwell Upson, Ex-Trustee, Plans Gift as Bequest

By JOHN SIBLEY

Stock currently worth $9 million has been pledged to Cornell University by Maxwell M. Upson, an 88-year-old alumnus and former trustee.

Mr. Upson, a self-made man who acquired his fortune as head of the Raymond Concrete Pile Company, has made numerous gifts to Cornell, including $1.5 million in 1956 for the construction of a mechanical engineering building.

His latest gift, announced yesterday by James A. Perkins, president of Cornell, is in the form of a bequest. Mr. Upson pledged $8.5 million to the university's centennial campaign, and at the same time pledged $500,000 to the Cornell University Medical College in New York City.

The industrialist stipulated that $500,000 of his contribution to the centennial drive be used to establish "a professorship in the free enterprise system."

"I'm very keen about this," he said yesterday. "A great many people don't realize how important free enterprise is."

He recalled having given $150,000 to the University of North Dakota, from which he was graduated in 1896, to bring in lecturers on free enterprise, economics and government. Mr.

Continued on Page 33, Column 1

Yankees Beat Cards, 2-1, On Mantle's Homer in 9th

Mickey Mantle hit the first pitch in the ninth inning for a home run to give the New York Yankees a 2-1 victory yesterday over the St. Louis Cardinals in the third game of the World Series at Yankee Stadium. The Yanks took a 2-1 edge in the four-of-seven series.

The New York Times

Mickey Mantle after game

Barney Schultz had just entered the game in relief of Curt Simmons, who had held the New Yorkers to one run and four hits through eight innings. Mantle smacked the ball well back into the right-field stands.

Simmons and Jim Bouton of the Yanks pitched out of frequent dificulties. Nine Cardinals were left on base.

The New Yorkers opened the scoring in the second. Elston Howard singled with one out and moved to second after Joe Pepitone had walked. Howard scored on Clete Boyer's double to left.

Simmons drove in the Cards' run in the fifth, singling home Tim McCarver from third. McCarver had singled and advanced on an error and infield out. A crowd of 67,101 saw the game.

FOOTBALL

Penn State defeated Army, Harvard beat Columbia and Princeton routed Dartmouth. Scores of leading games:

Cornell ....35 Penn .... 0 | Pittsburgh .14 West Va.... 0
Florida .....30 Mississippi .14 | Princeton ..37 Dartm[...]
Harvard .... 3 Columbia ... 0 | Purdue ...[...]
Iowa ....21 Indiana ....20 | Syra[...]
Michigan ...17 Mich. St....10
Notre Dame.34 Air Force... 7
Ohio St.....26 Illinois 0
Penn St..... 6 Army 2

HORSE R[...]

Queen Empress overcame Ma[...] the $124,375 Frizette Stakes at [...] returned $3.80 for $2 to win. Th[...] 2-year-old fillies was 1:37 2/5. [...] was disqualified and placed third [...]

Details in Secti[...]

CURTIS SUSPENDS 2 CULLIGAN CRITICS

Blair and Kantor Relieved of Duties in Policy Rift After Making Charges

By DOUGLAS ROBINSON

Two top officials of the Curtis Publishing Company were relieved of their duties yesterday in a continuing policy difference with Matthew J. Culligan, chairman and president of the publishing empire.

The two, Clay Blair Jr., editor in chief of all Curtis publications, including The Saturday Evening Post, and Marvin D. Kantor, head of the company's magazine division and the company's chief administrative officer, had recently leveled charges of mismanagement at Mr. Culligan.

An announcement by the company said the two had been placed on "inactive status with temporary leaves of absence, pending further action by the executive committee or the board of directors."

A company spokesman said the decision to relieve Mr. Blair and Mr. Kantor had been made at an emergency meeting of the executive committee of the board of directors in Philadelphia on Friday. Mr. Culligan was said to have attended the meeting.

The two executives were informed of the decision yesterday morning by Mr. Culligan in telephone conversations and by telegram. The talks were reported to have been "businesslike."

The Curtis spokesman said both men would remain on full salary pending any further action. Both, he said, have contracts with the company.

A source close to the Curtis

Continued on Page 42, Column 3

Eddie Cantor Dead; Comedy Star Was 72

By United Press International

HOLLYWOOD, Oct. 10—Eddie Cantor, banjo-eyed vaudevillian whose dancing feet and double-takes brought him stardom in movies, radio and television, died of a coronary occlusion today at the age of 72.

The comedian, famed for his charitable works, continued to be a show-business figure a decade after giving up public appearances.

Semi-retired since suffering a heart seizure in 1953, Mr. Cantor wrote books and took pride in his discovery of new talent. His energy and drive, which led to the severe heart condition, made him one of the best-loved performers of his generation.

For years Mr. Cantor joked

Continued on Page 85, Column 3

Dela[...] Olymp[...] Irrita[...]

By J[...]

A United[...] handling of [...] opening telecast [...] Games has creat[...] Japan.

The broadcast [...] from Tokyo by th[...] com III, was delay[...] hours by the Nat[...] casting Company be[...] shown on the West C[...] United States.

As a result, the cerem[...] seen on tape at 1 A.M. [...] day, Pacific time—outside [...] viewing hours—rather tha[...] 10 P.M. Friday, while it [...] happening.

Qualified sources said [...] State Department was de[...] concerned by the West Co[...] delay because live televis[...] coverage of the Olympics is [...] matter of national pride to th[...] Japanese Government.

Japan was reliably reported to have voiced surprise and disappointment to Washington officials.

The State Department had taken the initiative in encouraging the live telecast to illustrate scientific collaboration between the countries and to improve Far Eastern relations.

N. B. C., acknowledging that the historical telecast had been delayed, said the aim had been

Continued on Page 25, Column 1

ANTI-WEST VIEWS VOICED AT CLOSE OF CAIRO PARLEY

But Moderates Hold Down Pro-Peking Efforts—U.S. Scored on Guantanamo

By United Press International

CAIRO, Oct. 10—Heads of state at the conference of 47 nonaligned nations signed tonight a strongly anti-Western final declaration, which included a demand that the United States withdraw from the Guantanamo Bay base in Cuba.

The declaration is to be formally made public at noon tomorrow, but most of its points already were known. They previously had been approved by the foreign ministers of the nonaligned countries, which have been in session here since Monday.

The closing session ended just before midnight. Dele[...] members, showing [...] from the Cai[...] torium [...]

[...] ti[...] to [...] atta[...] Afri[...] A [...] to re[...] Com[...] edly w[...] olution[...]

Conti[...]

Associated Press Wirephoto

[...]ECTS HONOR GUARD: Queen Elizabeth talks with Maj. J. M. Four[...] of the guard that met her upon her arrival yesterday in Quebec.

[...]LEA [...]RCH

[...]ld [...] used [...]rations [...] hand. [...] were [...]it by [...]rk Schleifer, [...]oadcaster from

[...]umn 3

Queen, in Quebec, Appears To Back Moderate Change

By JOHN M. LEE

Special to The New York Times

QUEBEC, Oct. 10—Queen Elizabeth II, greeted here by mild protest demonstrations, indicated sympathy in a speech to the provincial Legislature today for moderate French-Canadian demands for a changed role within the Canadian confederation.

The protest demonstrations, [...]s of which had prompted [...] greatest security precau[...]s ever given a visitor to [...]ada, were staged primarily [...] about 100 youths and were [...]ly dispersed. Some cheers [...]e raised among the sporadic [...] that greeted the Queen, [...]he crowds were small.

[...]ueen appeared smiling [...]red despite the pro[...] [...]er address to the pro[...] [...]egislature, delivered [...] French, the Queen [...]nadian unity and [...]take sympathetic [...]derate French Ca[...] [...]n, which calls for [...]omy.

[...]rests Made

[...]state should not [...]s its political [...] Queen said. [...]t worked out [...]s not neces[...] needs of the [...] be surpris[...] [...] shouting [...]ested on [...]egislative [...]re were [...]ternoon

Continued on Page 3, Column 1

SAIGON HOLDS OFF EXECUTION OF RED

Fate of American, Hostage in Venezuela, Is Linked to That of Vietnam Terrorist

By PETER GROSE

Special to The New York Times

SAIGON, South Vietnam, Oct. 10—The Foreign Ministry assured the United States Embassy today that no date had yet been set for execution of a Vietcong terrorist whose death might cost the life of an American colonel kidnapped in Venezeula.

The kidnappers of Lieut. Col. Michael Smolen were reported to have threatened to kill him if South Vietnam carried out its death sentence against Nguyen Van Troi, a young Vietcong terrorist. The terrorist was convicted of having plotted to kill Robert S. McNamara when the United States Defense Secretary visited South Vietnam last May.

Colonel Smolen, the deputy chief of the United States Air Force mission in Caracas, was kidnapped near his home yesterday morning by two men, one armed with a submachine gun. Later several Caracas newspapers received anonymous telephone calls warning that the

Continued on Page 24, Column 1

VIETNAM CHARTER REPLACING KHANH IS DUE THIS WEEK

Special 17-Member Council Ends Work on Proposals for a Civilian Regime

VOTE SEEN EARLY IN '65

New Governing Committee of 6 or 7 Would Function Until Assembly Sits

By JACK LANGGUTH

Special to The New York Times

SAIGON, South Vietnam, Oct. 10 — The High National Council of South Vietnam announced today that it would make public next week the Constitution that is to put a civilian government in place of Maj. Gen. Nguyen Khanh.

Qualified sources said that the Constitution, which was completed yesterday by the council of 17 civilian members, would provide for a governing committee of six or seven. The committee chairman would serve as Acting Premier until elections are held, the sources added.

The High National Council was created after Premier Khanh's attempt Aug. 16 to assume full governmental powers was thwarted by rioting throughout the country.

Most of the members, who were selected by Maj. Gen. Duong Van Minh, South Vietnam's acting chief of state, are elderly professional men who demonstrated their opposition to the regime of President Ngo Dinh Diem before he was overthrown and slain last November.

Age of Members Stressed

Because of the age and frailty of some of them, the council has been termed a "national museum" by some younger political and military figures. One council member, Tran Dinh Nam, from central Vietnam, has been in a hospital and has not been replaced.

Members of the council are known to have been deeply concerned that the military government would not step aside for civilian appointees.

The involved procedures the council has developed are intended to remove as completely as possible any taint of dictatorship or military rule.

In an apparent effort to allay misgivings, General Khanh wrote today to the council, saying, "I urgently ask you to choose someone to replace me."

Pointing out that he had promised to terminate military rule Oct. 27, the Premier added: "I am entirely confident that the Vietnamese armed forces will support a government that

Continued on Page 22, Column 1

Today's Sections

Index to Subjects

United Press International Cablephoto

OLYMPIC SALUTE: Yoshinori Sakai raises torch after lighting caldron at Tokyo stadium. Curve in horizon results from distortion by 180-degree lens.

Eddie Cantor Dead; Comedy Star Was 72

By United Press International

HOLLYWOOD, Oct. 10—Eddie Cantor, banjo-eyed vaudevillian whose dancing feet and double-takes brought him stardom in movies, radio and television, died of a coronary occlusion today at the age of 72.

The comedian, famed for his charitable works, continued to be a show-business figure a decade after giving up public appearances.

Semi-retired since suffering a heart seizure in 1953, Mr. Cantor wrote books and took pride in his discovery of new talent. His energy and drive, which led to the severe heart condition, made him one of the best-loved performers of his generation.

For years Mr. Cantor joked

Continued on Page 85, Column 3

EDDIE CANTOR, 72, IS DEAD ON COAST

Comedy Star of Vaudeville, Screen, Radio and TV Was a Discoverer of Talent

Continued From Page 1, Col. 2

about the fact that he had five daughters and no sons. But he leaves only four of those daughters: Mrs. Natalie Metzger of Los Angeles; Mrs. Edna McHugh of Malibu, Calif.; Marilyn Cantor of New York City, and Mrs. Janet Gari of New York. His fourth daughter, Marjorie, who was also his secretary, died of cancer May 17, 1959, at the age of 44.

Ida Cantor, his wife, died Aug. 8, 1962, at the age of 70. She became known to millions of Americans because of her husband's theme song, "Ida," and the jokes he used to tell about his family. Mrs. Cantor died of a series of heart seizures.

Vaudeville in Character

Pop-eyed, peppy, exuberant Mr. Cantor was one of the most successful vaudeville comedians who ever lived. His song-and-dance specialties, his nonstop patter of puns and gags, his farce remained essentially vaudeville in character all through his years of success in musical comedy, in films, radio and television.

That success was tremendous. By the time vaudeville succumbed to sound movies in the late nineteen-twenties, Mr. Cantor set records for long runs at all major variety houses in the United States, including Keith's Palace, capital of them all. He earned millions of dollars by his art, and Florenz Ziegfeld once boasted he paid Mr. Cantor the largest salary ever given to a comedian "in the history of the world."

No one could have started to achieve fame and wealth by his own efforts with fewer advantages than the comedian. As he pointed out in his autobiography, "My Life Is in Your Hands," in 1928, he was one of many poor boys from the lower East Side of the '90's who turned out to be celebrated actors, politicians or gangsters.

Eddie Cantor was born in a crowded tenement flat over a Russian tearoom in Eldridge Street on Jan. 31, 1892. His real name was Isidor Iskowitch, and his parents were impoverished young Russian-Jewish immigrants. He never really knew them, since his mother died in childbirth when he was 1 year old, and his father, an unemployed violinist, perished of pneumonia a year later.

Eddie Cantor in *Whoopee.*

The orphan was brought up by his grandmother, Esther, a widow, who supported herself and the baby by peddling. She lived to see her grandson become a star, and he always revered her.

Mr. Cantor grew up a tough, unambitious kid in the dirty ghetto. A poor scholar, he quit school without finishing and hung around poolrooms, working at odd jobs only when hunger compelled him. His sole talent seemed to be for giving comic impersonations of personalities of the day. Ashamed to sponge on his grandmother, Eddie often left home for weeks, leaving one job after another, sleeping on roofs, singing on the street for pennies.

Won Amateur Contest

He and a friend managed to work for one week, in 1907, as a song and dance team at the old Clinton Music Hall in their home neighborhood. The next year, accepting a dare from taunting friends, Eddie Cantor, as he now called himself for "stage" purposes, entered the weekly amateur contest at Miner's Theatre on the Bowery. He was dead broke, hungry, ragged, and counted on the $1 consloation prize paid even to contestants who "got the hook" as demanded by the howling, drunken audience.

Even at the age of 16, however, his native talent asserted itself. He won first prize of $5.

On the strength of that triumph, Mr. Cantor got a job as a blackface comedian with a touring burlesque show, but it soon stranded him in Shenandoah, Pa. His grandmother came to the rescue again.

Back in New York, Mr. Cantor found his mark as a singing waiter in Carey Walsh's saloon in Coney Island, where the piano player was a clever, big-nosed tunesmith named Jimmie Durante.

Adolph Zukor and Marcus Loew had recently quit the fur business to buy four vaudeville houses in the suburbs. Mr. Cantor was booked to do a single turn on this circuit for 16 weeks at $20 a week. The managers would not permit him to repeat his act, so he blacked his face and changed a few lines to get a repeat booking.

As a comedian, he attracted the attention of Roy Arthur, fellow East Sider, who was half of the successful comedy juggling team of Bedini and Arthur. Mr. Cantor was taken on by this team, at first as valet, then silent assistant onstage, and finally as a junior member of the act. At last he was in big time, even playing Hammerstein's Victoria Theatre at Broadway and 42d Street.

Trouped With Other Stars

In 1912, after touring two years with Bedini and Arthur, Mr. Cantor was seen by Gus Edwards, who offered him a place in his "Kid Kabaret," a popular act composed of talented youngsters. Mr. Cantor picked a quarrel with Bedini so as to leave him and was immediately hired by Mr. Edwards as the star at $75 a week. Mr. Cantor never forgot his debt to Mr. Arthur, however; it was said he supported his early benefactor for 20 years after the Depression ruined the old vaudevillian.

In the "Kid Kabaret," Mr. Cantor trouped for two years with George Jessel, Eddie Buzzell, Georgie Price, Leila Lee and Gregory Kelly. Again he was in blackface, a make-up that became associated with his early success but a role that he never actually liked.

When the tour ended, he accomplished an ambition of many years by marrying his childhood sweetheart, Ida Tobias, a neighbor on the old East Side. Her parents opposed the match, sniffing at the youth as a harum-scarum, irresponsible actor, and preferring the rising young business men among Ida's suitors.

But the comedian's charm won the girl and the marriage was one of the most successful in show business. His wife bore him five daughters, Marjorie, Natalie, Edna, Marilyn and Janet; all members of the family remained devoted to one another, and there was never a hint of disharmony.

(continued)

In 1914 Eddie took Ida to Europe for a honeymoon, appearing in one of Charlot's musicals in London. But World War I stopped the show cold, and the Cantors returned home, where he toured with Al Lee in a song, dance and comedy routine billed as Cantor and Lee.

Earl Carroll admired the act in Los Angeles, recommending Mr. Cantor to Oliver Morosco, the producer, who featured Mr. Cantor in a touring company of "Canary Cottage," a musical show, in 1916. The great Ziegfeld saw him in that and engaged him for his "Midnight Frolic" on the New Amsterdam Roof in 1917.

Well-started now, he was a hit. His frenetic, nervous style on-stage, prancing about, clapping his hands, rolling his eyes, his gay enthusiasm, all made up for a poor singing voice. His energy was inexhaustible; he could play five shows a day of 40 minutes each and entertain at a house party afterward for hours. Mr. Ziegfeld engaged him for his "Follies" of 1917, 1918 and 1919. He was a featured player with Will Rogers, one of his closest friends; W. C. Fields, Ann Pennington and other stars.

Never modest, Mr. Cantor was talking Ziegfeld into starring him in a musical comedy with a "book," not just a revue.

"There isn't a part on earth that I can't play," he assured the doubtful impresario seriously.

The producer was almost convinced, when legitimate actors formed the Actors Equity Association and closed all theatres on Broadway in their historic organizational strike. Mr. Cantor never hesitated. Jeopardizing his own future, he assumed a leading part in the strike. Furious, Mr. Ziegfeld cancelled all plans to star him.

Fortunately Actors Equity won, but Mr. Ziegfeld simmered for years. The Shuberts cast Mr. Cantor in a revue the "Midnight Rounders," in 1920, and for the first time in his life he saw his name in electric lights on the marquee of a theatre. In this show he did a travesty on a Grand Street "puller-in" clothing store called "Moe's Blue Front" that many show people still consider one of the funniest turns of its kind ever produced.

The comedian continued as a star for the Schuberts in a succeeding revue, "Make It Snappy," in 1922. Then Mr. Ziegfeld had to relent. He engaged Mr. Cantor to star in "Kid Boots," a musical comedy, nonchalantly leaving most of the star's material for him to write. The show was a smash when it opened in 1923 and ran three years.

He was the star of the Ziegfeld "Follies" of 1927, the first time anyone had been starred in those annual revues. He also starred in "Whoopee," another Ziegfeld hit, from 1928 to 1930, at a reported salary of $5,000 a week. In 1928 Nathan S. Jonas, president of the Manufacturers Trust Company and Mr. Cantor's banker, said to him, "Eddie, you are a millionaire."

The stock market crash of 1929 ended the distinction. Mr. Cantor was depressed for a while, but his irrepressible vitality buoyed him up, aided by his wife's sympathetic loyalty. Giving up the stage, he went to Hollywood to make films. In 1926 he had made a silent movie version of "Kid Boots," with Clara Bow; now the movies talked and that proved better for his style.

The first year after his financial collapse the comedian earned $450,000. His wife and the girls were not going to starve after all. He made pictures until 1940 in rapid succession for the big studios. Among the hits were "Palmy Days," in 1932; "The Kid from Spain," 1933; "Roman Scandals," 1934; "Kid Millions," 1935; "Strike Me Pink," 1936, and "Ali Baba Goes to Town," 1937.

Also Introduced Hit Songs

All these were musicals and comedies, of course. Under the aegis of Sam Goldwyn, Mr. Cantor was surrounded by hordes of "Goldwyn Girls," beautiful and stereotyped creatures who filled in the background for his antics.

In 1931 Mr. Cantor entered radio work and devoted more and more time to it as the medium developed through the next two decades. He became one of the biggest stars of radio. After television attracted major sponsors, he began on a monthly show. Radio had consumed most of his time in this period, although he made a few films. The last was "If You Knew Susie" in 1948, named for a song he had made enormously popular.

He made other songs so familiar that they were associated with him as distinctively as his own name. When radio audiences heard the lyric, "Potatoes are cheaper, tomatoes are cheaper, now's the time to fall in love" or "Ida, sweet as apple cider," they knew at once Eddie Cantor was on the air.

Mr. Cantor worked as hard at philanthropy as at his theatrical career. It was said he never refused a legitimate request for aid, either personal or organizational. He played as many as six benefit shows in one night, and toured endlessly for the United Service Organizations during World War II.

He raised hundreds of thousands of dollars for Jewish refugees from Hitler, for Palestine, for Christian and non-denominational causes. He was said to have coined the phrase "March of Dimes" in his campaigns for the Warm Springs Foundation for Infantile Paralysis.

In addition to his work for Actors Equity, he was a founder and former president of the Screen Actors Guild, American Federation of Radio Artists and the Jewish Theatrical Guild.

His "loans" to impecunious actors were uncountable. His hospitality to friends was equally noted. His wife complained genially that she had to be prepared for eight of nine unexpected guests her husband might bring home for dinner any night to their large home in Beverly Hills, Calif.

When not working, Mr. Cantor was at home. He never drank, smoked or gambled and hated night clubs and parties.

The comedian suffered his first serious heart attack in 1952 and he collapsed from heart ailments several times after that. In 1956, he underwent a serious operation for the removal of kidney stones, and often joked about his ailments by quipping, "Nobody lives forever."

A book of his reminiscences, "As I Remember Them," was published last year.

Earlier this year, Mr. Cantor received a service medal from President Johnson for his service to the United States and to humanity.

Eddie Cantor and Lyda Roberti in *The Kid From Spain.*

Eddie Cantor in *Palmy Days.*

The New York Times THURSDAY, JANUARY 3, 1963.

Jack Carson Dead of Cancer; Comedian of Screen, TV, 52

Special to The New York Times.

ENCINO, Calif., Jan. 2 — Jack Carson, the chunky, moon-faced comedian, and dancer of motion pictures, night clubs and television, died of cancer at his home here tonight. He was 52 year old.

He had been ill since Oct. 26 when he collapsed during a rehearsal with what was then announced as stomach trouble.

Mr. Carson was born in Carmen, Manitoba. He attended Carleton College in Northfield, Minn. He first appeared in films in the late 1930s, specializing in the pudgy-comic sort of roles identified up to then with Jack Oakie.

His scores of pictures included "Destry Rides Again," "Mildred Pierce," "Gentleman Jim," "Arsenic and Old Lace." His recent films had included "Rally 'Round the Flag," "Cat on a Hot Tin Roof," and "A Star Is Born."

Mr. Carson got his start in the theater in vaudeville, with Dave Willock, in the team of Willock and Carson. The experience was recalled in one of his most memorable film bits as a member of the hoofing team of "Adams and Runkel" in the George M. Cohan film comedy, "Give My Regards to Broadway," made in 1942.

Mr. Carson was the third prominent Hollywood figure to succumb to cancer in less than three weeks. Both Charles Laughton and Thomas Mitchell died in mid-December.

Mr. Carson was preparing to appear in a stage production of "Critics' Choice" at Andover, N. J. when he was stricken.

With him when he died were his wife, the former Sandra Tucker, whom he married 1961, and his manager, Frank Stempel. He was divorced from Lola Albright in 1958.

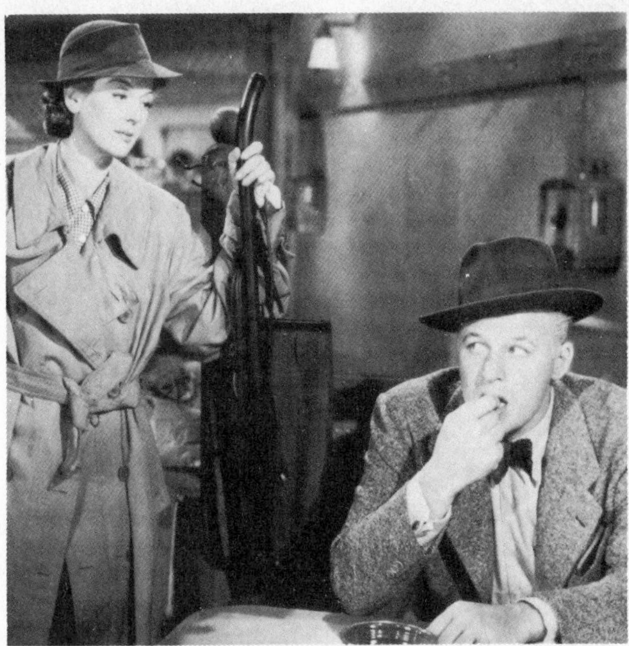

Rosalind Russell and Jack Carson in *Roughly Speaking.*

Zachary Scott, Jack Carson and Joan Crawford in *Mildred Pierce.*

The New York Times SUNDAY, JUNE 18, 1961.

JEFF CHANDLER, FILM ACTOR, DIES

He-Man Star, 42, Succumbs After Three Operations

HOLLYWOOD, June 17 (AP)—Jeff Chandler, the movie actor, died today in Culver City Hospital of blood poisoning following spinal surgery. He was 42 years old.

Mr. Chandler, who underwent three operations, was hospitalized May 13 for correction of a slipped spinal disc. Five days later, he experienced severe abdominal bleeding.

Tall, square-jawed and youthful despite his steel-gray wavy hair, Jeff Chandler was one of the group of "he-man" movie stars who rocketed to fame during the Fifties.

His real name was Ira Grossel. He was born in Brooklyn, where he attended Eramus Hall High School. He went to art school, dramatic school, and then spent two years playing summer stock before entering the Army at the outbreak of World War II.

He rose from private to lieutenant during four and one-half years and resumed his acting career in 1946, playing a variety of roles on radio programs.

He played his first movie role in "Johnny O'Clock," starring Dick Powell. Mr. Chandler had one line in the film and was seen only for a few seconds as a surly gambler.

His biggest break came in the film "Broken Arrow," when he played the Indian chief Cochise. For a while after that movie, Mr. Chandler told friends that

Jeff Chandler

he thought he would continue to get Indian parts only.

After starring roles in such films as "Sign of the Pagan," "Away All Boats," "Jeanne Eagels," and "Raw Wind in Eden," Mr. Chandler joined the growing ranks of stars who formed their own companies.

His partner in the company, Earlmar Productions, was his agent and friend, Meyer Mishkin.

Mr. Chandler also had some success as a popular singer. He wrote music, played the violin and had his own music publishing company, Chandler Music.

He was divorced in 1960 from the former Marjorie Hoshelle. They had two daughters, Jamie and Dana.

His father, Philip Grossel, and his mother, Mrs. Ann Shevelew, also survive.

Joan Crawford and Jeff Chandler in *Female on the Beach,* 1954.

Debra Paget, Jeff Chandler and James Stewart starred in *Broken Arrow.*

Kim Novak as Jeanne Eagels, and Jeff Chandler in *The Jeanne Eagels Story.*

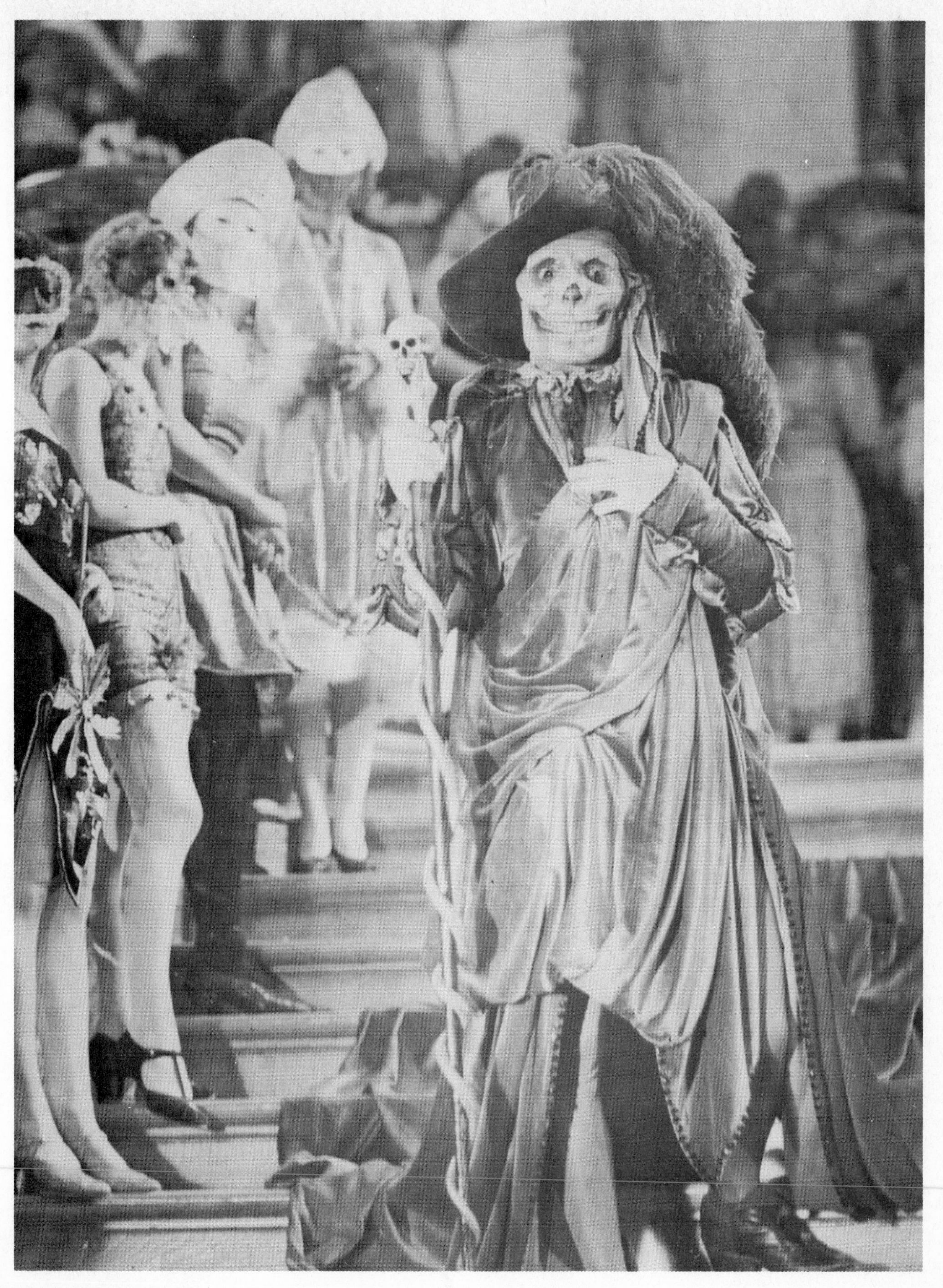

Lon Chaney in *The Phantom of the Opera.*

The New York Times WEDNESDAY, AUGUST 27, 1930.

LON CHANEY DIES AFTER BRAVE FIGHT

On Road to Recovery, Screen Actor Is Stricken by Hemorrhage of the Throat.

WAS A MASTER OF MAKE-UP

Son of Deaf and Dumb Parents, He Began Career as Property Boy—Excelled in Vivid Personations.

Special to The New York Times.

LOS ANGELES, Cal., Aug. 26.—Although he was believed to be on the road to recovery, Lon Chaney, screen actor, who had been making a valiant fight against anemia and bronchial congestion, died at 12:55 this morning in St. Vincent's Hospital before medical aid could reach him. A hemorrhage of the throat was the immediate cause of death. His wife, Hazel Hastings Chaney; Creighton Chaney, his son by an early marriage, and a nurse were at the bedside. His wife, who believed that he had passed the crisis, was prostrated by his unexpected passing.

Doctors knew that his months were numbered by bronchial cancer but he was thought temporarily to be out of danger, following a successful blood transfusion Saturday, his third in forty-eight hours.

News of the actor's serious illness became generally known in the film colony when he finished "The Unholy Three," his first talking picture.

He went to New York to consult specialists and returned here three weeks ago, retiring to his cabin in the high sierras. The first hemorrhage forced him to the hospital last Wednesday, when his condition was pronounced critical.

Funeral services for Mr. Chaney will be held Thursday, at 8 P. M. Among the honorary pallbearers will be Louis B. Mayer, Nicholas Schenck, Irving G. Thalberg, General Smedley D. Butler, Tod Browning, Harry Carey, Lionel Barrymore, Ramon Novarro, William Haines, Laurence Tibbett, Fred Niblo, Edgar Selwyn, Wallace Beery, Jack Benny and Sammy Lee.

Acted as Pike's Peak Guide.

Lon Chaney was born in Colorado Springs, Col., on April 1, 1883. He attended public school in that city, but left to earn his living as a guide, conducting tourists along the tortuous trail to Pike's Peak. He was next employed as a property boy in the opera house at Colorado Springs, his first contact with the theatre.

Chaney was the second of four children born to deaf and dumb parents. The father, who immigrated from Ireland, owned a barber shop in Colorado Springs. When the boy was nine, in the fourth grade at school, his mother became permanently helpless from inflammatory rheumatism, and for three years Lon devoted most of his time to nursing her. He had to exchange thoughts with his parents by means of his hands in the sign language. This use of hands and facial expression is said to have been the groundwork of Chaney's ability as an actor and for his unusually expressive gestures.

He made his first theatrical appearance at the age of 17, appearing in "The Little Tycoon," a play which he and his brother wrote. His brother was a theatre manager and together they followed their first offering with a cycle of Gilbert and Sullivan operas in their home city.

The little company attempted a short tour, but soon found itself without funds. Chaney then went to Chicago after having prepared himself as a dancer and comedian. He carried a stage hand's union card and during his engagements with smaller companies he would help move the scenery backstage. This interest in the machinery of the theatre led him later to become a stage director.

From Chicago he traveled West with a vaudeville troupe and in San Francisco joined the Ferris Hartmann Opera Company. He married Hazel Hastings—the present Mrs. Chaney—who was a member of the company. By a previous marriage, about which little is known, he had a son Creighton, who is now 27 years old.

With the Hartmann players he proceeded to Los Angeles where he became interested in motion pictures. He began work with a picture company and later played Western "heavy" rôles. His name appeared for the first time in the credit sheet of a film in 1914 when Universal billed him in "Hell Morgan's Girl."

Appeared in Slap-Stick Comedy.

Chaney's previous appearances in pictures, as early as 1912, before he was listed in the cast of players, included small parts in "False Faces," "Riddle Gawne," and others. He was also in an Allan Curtis slapstick comedy for Universal which was released in 1912. Later he supervised and directed J. Warren Kerrigan, then a Western star, in seven pictures.

Lon Chaney's fame rested largely on his ability to make-up his face and distort his body. The first rôle which brought him national recognition was that of the frog in "The Miracle Man."

He acquired his knoweldge of make-up as a property boy when he watched Richard Mansfield through a crack in a dressing room door as the famous actor applied the grease paint. He later made a serious study of make-up until he became an authority on the subject. He is the author of the article on make-up in the Encyclopedia Britannica and wrote the preface on a textbook of screen make-up by Cecil Holland.

In "The Road to Mandalay" he created the effect of a scar by the use of a chemical that, as it was applied to the face, dried quickly and dre wthe flesh together. By this means he also simulated wounds and burns.

Wore Straitjacket as "Hunchback."

As Quasimodo in "The Hunchback of Notre Dame" he constructed high cheek bones and remodelled his face with plastic gum. Over one eye he applied a shell, which he covered with flesh-colored material. In this grotesque portrayal he also wore a straitjacket to twist his frame. It became so painful that it had to be removed periodically to relieve him. He acquired the knack of throwing his shoulder out of joint, a feat that left him with a permanently lamed shoulder after making "The Miracle Man."

In "The Blackbird" he effected his posture by curving his spine, drawing up one leg and having the tailor accentuate this apparent bodily deformity by making one side of his suit of clothes longer than the other.

Chaney's familiar appellation was "The Man of a Thousand Faces." In almost every one of his pictures he adapted a new disguise. However, in "Tell It To the Marines," when he appeared as his natural self, without even the benefit of powder, a critic wrote that he didn't seem quite natural and that one of the lines on his face seemed misplaced.

He and Chaplin were the last of the stars to stick to silent pictures. It was rumored consistently that Chaney would not make an audible film because of his throat affliction, which would not permit him to talk. Tod Browning, director of many of the actor's successes, said that Chaney was holding out because of his shrewd business sense and not on account of a vocal disability. Chaney proved this to be true when he made a sound version of "The Unholy Three," in which he not only affected a number of disguises but talked in five different voices as well, including an imitation of a parrot.

So that the public might believe this to be true the performer had a notary attest to the fact that he used only his own voice in the making of the film.

In Hollywood he lived a quiet life in a Spanish model house in Beverly Hills. He owed three cars, but had no chauffeur. His hobbies were fishing and amateur photography. He became skillful with a small motion-picture camera. He was interested in various businesses besides films. He was himself exceedingly fond of the quip that had sprung up about him because of his various make-up feats, warning one: "Don't step on it; it may be Lon Chaney."

Mr. Chaney's personal fortune was estimated conservatively at $1,500,000. His weekly salary was $5,000.

Lon Chaney threw millions of ticket-buyers into spasms of terror in *London after Midnight.*

The New York Times SATURDAY, JULY 14, 1973

Lon Chaney Jr., Actor, Is Dead at 67

SAN CLEMENTE, Calif., July 13 (AP)—Lon Chaney Jr., the film actor, died yesterday at the age of 67.

A long series of illnesses had put Mr. Chaney in and out of hospitals for the last year. He was released from a San Clemente hospital last April after surgery for cataracts and treatment for beriberi. Friends said he had also suffered from liver problems and gout and had recently undergone acupuncture treatments to relieve pain.

Mrs. Chaney, his wife of 36 years, declined to disclose the cause of death or to tell the funeral plans.

Camera Press, 1960

Lon Chaney Jr.

Portrayed Monsters

By WILLIAM M. FREEMAN

While Lon Chaney Jr. was in the shadow of his famous father, who played the title roles in the movies "The Hunchback of Notre Dame" and "The Phantom of the Opera," he built a massive reputation of his own.

Most moviegoers thought of him as an interpreter of "monster" roles, and he did many of them, but to the critics his most noted role was Lennie in the film "Of Mice and Men," based on John Steinbeck's novel.

In that film, he was Lennie, stupid, unable to care for himself, protected by Burgess Meredith as George. Lennie liked the feel of smooth things, but he was so clumsy in his strength that he killed them, a bird, a mouse, a white-and-brown puppy and finally Mae, the foreman's wife, who was soft and had silky hair. At the film's end George told Lennie once again how the two would have their own place and then pulled a trigger behind Lennie's happily nodding head.

The critics approved Mr. Chaney's portrayal, although some said he did not quite erase the memory of Broderick Crawford's earlier interpretation on the stage, with Wallace Ford as George.

Mr. Chaney, who was 6 feet 3½ inches tall and weighed 225 pounds, played many monsters. In one film, in which he changed from a conventional appearance to a wolf man, he was pictured as he lay dying, changing in minutes from the monster to his ordinary guise.

This was achieved by shooting a few frames in the full make-up, then a slight alteration, a few more frames, further changes in the make-up and so on. The process took some 24 hours for the few minutes on the screen in which the dying wolfman became an ordinary citizen.

Played Count Dracula

He also had appeared as Count Dracula, a role usually associated with Bela Lugosi; as Frankenstein's Monster, created by Boris Karloff, and as the Mummy.

Mr. Chaney joined forces in the late nineteen-forties with Bela Lugosi, as Dracula and himself as the Wolf Man, in "Abbott and Costello Meet Frankenstein."

He also appeared in support of Bob Hope in "My Favorite Brunette," with Jerry Lewis in "Pardners" and with Gary Cooper in "High Noon." The last named, a 1952 film in which he portrayed an arthritic old marshal, won Mr. Cooper an Academy Award.

Mr. Chaney once told an interviewer: "All the best of the monsters were played for sympathy. That goes for my father. Boris Karloff, myself and all the others. They all won the audience's sympathy. The Wolf didn't want to do all those things. He was forced into them."

Born on Feb. 10, 1906, in Oklahoma City, Mr. Chaney was named Creighton Tull Chaney. He made his first stage appearance when he was only 6 months old.

He did not become Lon Chaney Jr. until after he had achieved considerable recognition on his own. As a youngster, despite his father's fame, he worked in various jobs—as a butcher boy, a boilermaker, a plumber and a fruit picker.

He did watch his father making up for his roles, and so learned the art himself. Like his father, he would spend six or seven hours in make-up preparation and became known as a perfectionist in make-up detail.

Took Small Roles

Mr. Chaney first appeared in stock companies in the Middle West and then began playing small roles in the movies as Creighton Chaney.

Some of the early films were "Man-Made Monster," "Northwest Mounted Police," "One Million B.C." "Billy the Kid," "Son of Dracula," "Calling Dr. Death," "The Mummy's Curse," "Strange Confession," "Cobra Woman" and "Here Come the Co-eds."

More often than not he was the hero's sidekick or the heavy—rarely the one who got the girl.

It was not until "Of Mice and Men," made in 1939 and released in 1940, that he achieved full stardom.

In 1937, he married Patsy Beck, a former photographic model, who survives him. He also had two sons, Ronald and Lon Jr. by a former marriage, and nine grandchildren.

Lon Chaney, Jr. as Lennie and Burgess Meredith as George in *Of Mice and Men*, 1939.

Lon Chaney, Jr. and Gary Cooper in *High Noon*.

"All the News That's Fit to Print"

The New York Times

LATE CITY EDITION

Weather: Cloudy, rain likely today; partly cloudy tonight, tomorrow. Temp. range: today 29-46; Saturday 20-35. Full U.S. report on Page 63.

SECTION ONE

VOL. CXXI . . No. 41,616 · NEW YORK, SUNDAY, JANUARY 2, 1972 · NJ · 50 CENTS

Maurice Chevalier Dead; Singer and Actor Was 83

Special to The New York Times

PARIS, Jan. 1—Maurice Chevalier, probably the most popular and best-known entertainer that France has produced this century, died here tonight. He was 83 years old.

The singer and actor, whose stage and screen career covered well over half a century, entered Necker Hospital Dec. 13 in critical condition from kidney failure. Despite several false alarms he amazed both doctors and the public with his vitality. Yesterday morning a hospital bulletin was still able to talk of "his good general condition."

The thousands of messages that he received at the hospital attested to the fact that although he belonged to another generation he was still remembered and still popular.

According to an official hospital communiqué, the cause of death was heart failure. After his death the body was taken to his home at Marnes-la-Coquette, west of Paris. His impresario, François Vals, said that though many admirers of Mr. Chevalier had already appeared at the house hoping to pay their last respects, the funeral would be "extremely discreet" in keeping with his wishes.

Camera Press

Maurice Chevalier

The Elegant Boulevardier

By ALDEN WHITMAN

No French entertainer was so jaunty, so debonair, so burnished yet so saucy, so much the elegant boulevardier of an idealized Paris as Maurice Chevalier. Attired in a one-button, dark blue suit, sporting a springtime boater and singing and talking in his magical Gallic accent, he was America's No. 1 Frenchman, the bubbling personification of a glass of champagne. He was also France's No. 1 chanteur, whose renditions of "Ma Louise," "Mimi," "Valen-

Continued on Page 54, Column 3

SUPPLIES FLOWN TO BASE IN LAOS RINGED BY ENEMY

Ammunition Is Lifted Into Long Tieng After Planes Curb Foe's Artillery

TRAIL NET IS ATTACKED

U.S. Makes 200 Air Strikes Against Supp...

. VIE... Commu... their pre... encircled ... northern ... of heavy ... American pla... munition to th... there.

A military so... that the enemy's ... been cut when U... planes destroyed th... 130-mm. cannons. ... forces were believed ... ing their remaining fo... guns to new positions.

[American planes ... more than 200 strikes ag... the Ho Chi Minh trail ... work of North Vietname... supply lines in Laos and Cambodia, the Associated Press reported from Saigon.]

Evacuation Apparently Off

The evacuation of Long Tieng's 30,000-man garrison also appeared to have been put off. The commander of the Military Region II, Gen. Vang Pao, and his more than 30 American advisers remained at the base.

Although losses in men were reported light, the base has suffered considerable damage during the last two days.

Communist shells have destroyed the ammunition dump and radio transmission center as well as the headquarters of Military Region II and a joint operations center manned by the Laotians and the Americans.

While the net remained tight around Long Tieng, which lies across the line of Communist advance towards Vientiane, 73 miles to the south, the North Vietnamese and the Pathet Lao guerrillas mounted another offensive against Pakse, the country's second largest city.

Government troops have been driven back 11 miles and the main defense line is now 21 miles from Pakse.

Earlier today, 61 American

Continued on Page 3, Column 1

Sadat Raises New Arab Union Flag

Special to The New York Times

CAIRO, Jan. 1—President Anwar el-Sadat raised a new banner of Arab unity — the red, white and black flag with a golden hawk of the Federation of Arab Republics—over Cairo today amid the contrasting sounds of ... gun military salute ... fluttering of ...

The Bowl Games

ORANGE—Nebraska, sparked by a 77-yard punt return by Johnny Rodgers and the aggressive defensive play of Rich Glover, reaffirmed its claim to the mythical national championship by overwhelming Alabama, 38-6, before a crowd of 78,151 at Miami.

COTTON—Penn State rallied from a 6-3 half-time deficit to trounce Texas, 30-6, before a crowd of 72,000 at Dallas. A 1-yard touchdown plunge by Lydell Mitchell early in the third quarter gave Penn State a 10-6 lead. The Nittany Lions increased their advantage to 17-6 moments later on a 65-yard scoring pass from John Hufnagel to Scott Skarzynski.

ROSE—Rod Garcia kicked a 31-yard field goal with 12 seconds to play to give Stanford a 13-12 upset triumph over Michigan. A crowd of 103,154 at Pasadena, Calif., saw the 155-pound kicking specialist give the Wolverines their first setback of the season.

SUGAR—Oklahoma, with Jack Mildren scoring three touchdowns, rolled to a 40-22 triumph over Auburn before 84,031 at New Orleans. The Sooners, the third-ranked college team, scored five touchdowns in the first half, a Sugar Bowl record.

Details in Section 5

NEW ORLEANS PAGEANTRY: Tennessee float roll... into Sugar Bowl Stadium in half-time show yesterda... Floats representing many Southern states joined parade...

At Half Time in Football, A Big and Costly Show

By STEVEN V. ROBERTS

Special to The New York Times

PASADENA, Calif., Jan. 1—In 1869, when Rutgers defeated Princeton in the first college football game, reports do not indicate what happened between halves of the game. Probably there was a lot of gasping for breath. But there is a record of the first college football cheer: "Siss Boom Bah, Prince-ton!"

One hundred and two years of fumbles and fractures later, football is a national institution. So is half time, 20 minutes of pep or pageantry (depending on one's viewpoint), fast-stepping marchers and high-kicking majorettes, gaggles of twirlers and gobs of tradition, the essential hole in the doughnut of football.

Half-time shows are a big and expensive business. The total cost of the extravaganzas at the four major bowl games today—Rose, Orange, Sugar and Cotton—probably approaches $500,000.

But that is only a tiny fraction of what is spent annually at thousands of shows from the high school to the professional level. Just the

Continued on Page 50, Column 1

The Elegant Boulevardier

By ALDEN WHITMAN

No French entertainer was so jaunty, so debonair, so burnished yet so saucy, so much the elegant boulevardier of an

...-button, dark ... sporting a springtime ... and singing and talking ... his magical Gallic accent, he was America's No. 1 Frenchman, the bubbling personification of a glass of champagne. He was also France's No. 1 chanteur, whose renditions of "Ma Louise," "Mimi," "Valen-

Continued on Page 54, Column 3

... New York ... major American ... have methadone ... nance programs has found that in all of them there is some trafficking in the synthetic, addictive drug.

The precise fluctuations of supply and demand in the methadone black market, which is much smaller than its better-organized heroin counterpart, are hard to gauge. But both supply and demand appear to be growing.

Supply has several origins: outpatients on methadone maintenance programs who sell part ... of ... pharmacies ... nance programs, by addicts and employes, and a small but disturbing number of private physicians who prescribe or dispense overgenerous quantities of the drug, which then finds its way into the black market.

Two years ago, agents from the Federal Bureau of Narcotics and Dangerous Drugs arrested a chemist in Tupelo, Miss., and seized 22 pounds of pure methadone that he had allegedly manufactured for distribution by underworld elements on the East Coast. But since then the bureau has had no evidence that organized crime has found

Continued on Page 52, Column 1

...ropolitan Transportation Authority. ...Sovern, another mediator. Behind ...s L. MacMahon, union executive.

The New York Times/Donal F. Holway

...e Situation

...ty's subways and buses will ...east 35 cents and possibly ...f the new transit contract. ...ill be determined by the ...e Transit Authority that ...Legislature resumes its ...y. ...tropolitan Transporta- ...e Transit Authority, ... The increase will ... Commission. ...o the purchase of ...stiles were being ...to say whether ... fare was 20 ... when the

...oday

150-MILLION PACT AVERTS WALKOUT ON TRANSIT LINES

But Fare of at Least 35c Is Certain if Legislature Approves City Package

ACCEPTANCE PREDICTED

T.W.U. and 5 Private Bus Companies Later Reach a Similar Settlement

By DAMON STETSON

A new transit labor agreement costing an estimated total of $150-million averted a bus and subway strike in the city yesterday, but an early fare increase of at least 5 cents is certain.

The new labor costs and a previous operating deficit calculated at $152,972,825 for the current fiscal year accentuated the Transit Authority's financial plight, leaving no doubt that the fare would be raised soon—to 35 cents if the State Legislature approves a proposed transit package.

The new agreements with the Transport Workers Union and the Amalgamated Transit Union were announced shortly before 3 A.M., well ahead of the 5 A.M. deadline set for a strike if no settlement had been achieved. In 1970, the agreement was not announced until three hours after the deadline.

Referendum by Mail

Matthew Guinan, president of the Transport Workers Union, representing 38,000 bus and subway workers, described the settlement as "fair and reasonable"—and forecast approval by his membership in a mail referendum. The Amalgamated Transit Union represents 2,000 bus drivers in Queens and on Staten Island.

Dr. William J. Ronan, chairman of the Metropolitan Transportation Authority, noted that the Transit Authority, which operates under the M.T.A., was assured of improved performance by its personnel under the new contract. He also said that officials of the Transit Authority were convinced that the settlement met Federal guidelines, which generally call for a limitation to about 5.5 per cent in annual increases.

Terms of Accord

Last night, the T.W.U. reached a settlement with five ...rivate bus lines in the city ...at was virtually identical to ... earlier accord with the ...nsit Authority. [Page 57.] ...th settlements provide for ... cent in pay increases ... months, in contrast to ...o-year contracts that ...evailed for years. This ...n end, at least for a ...he cliff-hanging nego-

...on Page 57, Column 4

...'s Sections

...s Sections

Because of a revised printing schedule, The Week in Review section is folded inside the Financial section.

Maurice Chevalier, Singer and Actor, Is Dead in Paris at 83

Continued From Page 1, Col. 5

tine," "Ma Pomme," "Ca Va, Ca Va," "Place Pigalle" and "Paris Oui Oui" reflected the bittersweet of life and the careless rapture of the nineteen-twenties and thirties.

Mr. Chevalier was, moreover, ageless: a headliner at the Folies-Bergère in 1909, he was still without a peer as a revue artist almost 60 years later.

"Le Grand Maurice" he was called in the fall of 1966 when he appeared, full of zest in his 79th year, in the Empire Room of the Waldorf-Astoria Hotel. Although the years had etched his once-smooth face into a faint resemblance of Will Rogers, Mr. Chevalier, once he started to perform, became in the twinkling of an eye a well-preserved man of no more than 55. His voice was full and strong, his step was spry and his light blue eyes shimmered.

His way with an audience, an observer noted, was unaffected and unforced. He enchanted them by being their Maurice, and when he departed waving his boater after an hour of songs and gentle patter about the joys of senescence it was to a spontaneous standing ovation.

Discussing his artistic longevity, Mr. Chevalier once remarked:

"I believe in the rosy side of life. I know that life has many, many dark sides for everybody. It has been for me at many moments of my life. But I believe in bringing to the people the encouragement of living, and I think I am lasting so long in the interest of the people through something that comes out of my personality and out of my work, which is just to be sort of a sunshine person, see."

$20,000-a-Week Star

At his best in songs and skits, in which his joie de vivre and personality bedazzled, Mr. Chevalier was only somewhat less renowned as a motion picture actor. In the thirties he starred at $20,000 a week in such Hollywood romantic classics as "The Love Parade" and "The Merry Widow," which were directed by Ernst Lubitsch. In these he was the gay, sophisticated and irresistible lover, the leading man to such actresses as Jeanette MacDonald, Claudette Colbert and Evelyn Brent.

There was a 10-year hiatus in his film career that ended with the French movie "Le Silence Est d'Or" in 1947, which won the grand prize at the Brussels World Film Festival. His comeback in American films — now as a dramatic and character actor — occurred in 1957 in "Love in the Afternoon." And playing with Leslie Caron in 1958, he stole the show as the aging ladies' man in "Gigi," a film that added the song "Thank Heaven for Little Girls" to his repertory. His performance won him an honorary Oscar. There followed character roles in "Can-Can," "Fanny," "Jessica" and "The Castaways" that gained him additional acclaim.

In all Mr. Chevalier appeared in 40 films, the first released in 1914, and achieved an international reputation. He was a hard and self-centered worker. "I could never say that working with him was anything more than agreeable," Miss MacDonald remarked of their association. "All he cared about was his career and his mother."

Once when Mr. Chevalier was in Hollywood he was a house guest of Mary Pickford. "He would go out on the lawn every day with his straw hat and rehearse his entire music-hall act," the actress recalled. "He leaves nothing to chance."

Although he made a lot of money in the movies and reached a world audience through them, Mr. Chevalier's métier was the revue and the one-man show. In these he mesmerized his listeners, who were transfixed by his long underlip, dancing eyes and roguish smile. American and English audiences might suspect that his fractured English was a shade too carefully preserved and that his accent was too perfect, but such skepticism melted before his warmth. Indeed, his appeal was so irresistible that he once got the august Charles de Gaulle, President of France, to join him at a charity ball in a refrain of "Ma Pomme."

As a singer Mr. Chevalier was no great shakes. He could carry an uncomplicated tune, phrase a line and be sly at the proper time, but that was about all. By unending practice, however, he converted his vocal deficiencies into assets.

"Thank God, it was my good luck not to have any voice," he said. "If I had, I would have

Maurice Chevalier and Jeannette MacDonald were stars of the 1929 hit *The Love Parade*.

tried to be a singer who sings ballads in a voice like a velvet fog, but since I am barely able to half-talk and half-sing a song, it made me look for something to make me different from a hundred other crooners who are neither good nor bad. If I had any voice, I would have been content to rest on my voice and learn nothing else. Since I had no voice, I had to find something that would hold the interest of the public."

"Any third-rate chanteur de charme [a crooner] has a better voice than I," he said on another occasion. "But they sing from the throat while I sing from the heart."

Mr. Chevalier's handling of a song, as well as the songs themselves, contributed to the spell he cast on the stage or in supper clubs. A favorite was "Ma Louise," written for him in the twenties; another was "Ca Va, Ca Va," which he wrote for himself in the forties. Still another was "Valentine." It is the story of a girl who was so little and so sweet. The years go by and Valentine is encountered again, but she is no longer petite and she has a double chin into the bargain.

"It is a very human story," he said of the song, and by accenting that quality he gave it a special character. Audiences never seemed to tire of it.

As an entertainer Mr. Chevalier considered himself in the tradition of Sir Harry Lauder, the Scottish balladeer, and Al Jolson, the American song-and-dance man. He admired both for the intimacy they established with their audiences and for their artistic intensity.

A similar intensity appeared to account for Mr. Chevalier's reluctance to retire. "Often people ask me how it feels to be 78," he said shortly after he reached that age. "And I say wonderful, considering the alternatives."

"I'm traveling through old age without being unhappy, without being forgotten," he said another time, adding:

"I get my energy from the audience."

Energy, ambition and drive for stage success characterized

(continued)

Mr. Chevalier from early childhood. Born Sept. 12, 1888, in the impoverished Paris working-class quarter of Ménilmontant, he was the youngest of nine children of Victor Charles and Josephine Bossche Chevalier. His father was a ne'er-do-well house painter who deserted the family when Maurice was 8, and his mother was a lacemaker, to whom he was devoted throughout her life. Her death, in 1932, was a severe emotional blow, but he kept her memory alive by naming his Paris villa La Louque, a nickname he had given his mother.

Maurice ended his formal schooling at the age of 10, when he was apprenticed to an engraver, and he later worked briefly in a tack factory. But he wanted to be an entertainer, first as an acrobat with his brother, Paul, and then as a singer. An accident nipped his acrobatics, and he made his vocal debut in a neighborhood cafe on amateur night. It was un grand succès d'hilarité, for he was laughed off the stage for singing in a different key from that of the pianist.

Unfazed, the Chaplinesque ragamuffin persisted, and he began to sing in the hurly-burly variety halls and cafés-concert in Paris and in the provinces. His comic efforts were based on his youth, his extravagant attire and earthy songs. When he was 15 he began to play in the boulevard revues as a singing comedian. He was billed as "Le Petit Jesus" ("The Wonder Boy") and he started to make an impression.

"Records and radio and movies did not exist at that time," Mr. Chevalier later said of those hansom-cab-and-gaslight days. "It took years of traveling and playing to a few hundred people a night to build a reputation."

Partner of Mistinguett

His big break came in 1909, when he was 21: He was hired by the Folies-Bergère to be the legendary Mistinguett's partner in a revue. Mistinguett began life as a flower girl and achieved fame on account of her pungent personality, her slender, sexy legs and a song called "Mon Homme." When Mr. Chevalier met her she was 36 and at the top of her career.

The two did something called "The Flooring Waltz," in which they rolled themselves up in a carpet, fell to the stage, rose and unrolled. One evening early in the revue's run, they were a little slower than usual in unrolling, and they emerged from the tapestry in love.

"She was very attractive and I loved her madly," Mr. Chevalier said later of their liaison. "People have said that she made me a star. That is not true. I was already a star of the younger generation. However, I learned much from her because she was a great artiste. She also brought me the dearest and biggest love a man can have."

Called up for compulsory military duty in late 1913, Mr. Chevalier was at Mélun when World War I broke out. In the German invasion, he was hit in the right lung by shrapnel and was captured. After 26 months in a prisoner-of-war camp in Germany, during which he learned English from a fellow inmate, he was released in a prisoner exchange and went home to Mistinguett and to a Croix de Guerre.

Overcoming his lung wound, he played at the Olympia in Paris, returned to the Folies-Bergère and appeared at the Théâtre Femina and the Casino de Paris. After his first trip to London, in 1919, he adopted a dress suit, top hat and white gloves to accentuate his new smoothness as a singer and comedian.

"Then one day in London I saw a young fellow in a tuxedo and a straw hat," he later recalled. "He looked so smart that I thought, 'I do not need to look farther. There is my hat. It's a man's hat. It's a gay hat. It's the hat to go with a tuxedo.' From that moment I was never without a straw boater if I could help it, even when those hats went out of fashion."

Back in Paris, he played in a musical, did a further stint at the Folies-Bergère with Mistinguett, then appeared in a song-and-dance revue with Yvonne Vallée, to whom he was subsequently married for about six years. After playing the lead in the operetta "Dédé," Mr. Chevalier was brought to the United States by Charles B. Dillingham, the New York producer, but he was too frightened or too awed to perform and was released from his contract.

His first working visit to this country was in 1928, and in the following seven years he made 12 films. This film stint ended in 1935 when Irving Thalberg, the producer, wanted to give Grace Moore top billing in a Chevalier picture.

"I told Thalberg I had never been second on any bill since I was 20," Mr. Chevalier said. "I left for Paris. It was the end of my first American movie career."

New York Debut

Between pictures, however, he had made his New York debut at the New Amsterdam Roof Garden and played the Fulton Theater. His song repertory even then captivated New Yorkers.

Returning to Paris, Mr. Chevalier was again a hit in the music halls. He entertained King George VI and Queen Elizabeth on their state visit to France in 1938 and was decorated as a Chevalier of the Legion of Honor. By 1940, when World War II embroiled France, he was a friend of Nita Raya, a young actress. Fearing Nazi persecution because Miss Raya was Jewish, the couple moved to Mr. Chevalier's villa at Cannes, in the Free French Zone.

After touring Belgium, the Netherlands, Switzerland and the Scandinavian countries, Mr. Chevalier brought his one-man show to New York in 1947. Critical acclaim was undiminished, and he toured the United States and Canada for almost a year.

Mr. Chevalier planned to return to the United States in 1951, but he was refused a visa because he had signed the Stockholm Appeal, a plea against the use of thermonuclear weapons. On the ground that Communists had been energetic in circulating the appeal, the State Department adjudged the entertainer potentially dangerous to the security of the United States. The matter was considered of such moment at the time that Secretary of State Dean Acheson sought to justify the visa ban. The barrier was not lifted until 1954 despite Mr. Chevalier's protest that he had signed the appeal out of a sense of humanity.

After that he was in the country several times, either to make films or to play theater and club dates. He also appeared on a number of television shows, none of lasting note.

Unostentatious Life

Off stage Mr. Chevalier lived a relatively quiet and unostentatious life. In his early years he liked to box and sparred from time to time with Georges Carpentier, the French pugilist and a close friend. He kept his 5-foot-11½-inch figure in trim with calisthenics and by playing golf.

With advancing years he also practiced moderation. "Until the age of 50," he remarked to a friend, "I lived from the belt down to the heels; since then I have oriented myself toward the part that lies between the belt and the head."

In 1970, he published one more book of thoughts about things, "Les Pensées de Momo" ("Momo's Thoughts" — Momo being a Parisian abbreviation for Maurice). This followed the completion of his memoirs, "Ma Route et Mes Chansons" ("My Road and My Songs").

His most recent activity was the recording of the theme song for the French version of the Walt Disney production "The Aristocats."

In the last couple of years, he also occasionally put out a record containing a few new songs. He could occasionally be seen at an opening night, theater or movie. And he would attend the major horse racing events, striking people by his impeccable dress, looking jaunty and fit as ever with his red cheeks and seeming no more than a well-preserved 60.

Maurice Chevalier, Leslie Caron and Louis Jourdan in a scene from *Gigi*.

The New York Times SUNDAY, JULY 24, 1966.

Montgomery Clift Dead at 45; Nominated 3 Times for Oscar

Completed Last Movie, 'The Defector,' in June—Actor Began Career at Age 13

Montgomery Clift, a moody, sensitive actor who often played moody, sensitive young men on the screen, died yesterday of a heart ailment in his house at 217 East 61st Street. He was 45 years old.

He was found in bed, apparently near death, at 6 A.M. by his secretary, Lorenzo James. After failing to rouse Mr. Clift, Mr. James summoned a doctor, who pronounced the actor dead.

An autopsy performed by Dr. Michael M. Baden, an associate medical examiner, indicated that Mr. Clift died of "occlusive coronary artery disease." The actor's personal physician, Dr. Howard Kline, said he had been treating Mr. Clift for the last three years for a hormone deficiency that affected the calcium balance in his body.

The movie public first got to know him in 1948, first as a lonely G.I. who befriends an even more lonely war orphan in "The Search," then as a tough, fair-minded cowpuncher in "Red River."

Mr. Clift won an Academy Award nomination for his sensitive and appealing performance in "The Search" and later was nominated as best actor for two other films—"A Place in the Sun," in which he played opposite Elizabeth Taylor, and "From Here to Eternity," in which he more than held his own playing against such veteran performers as Burt Lancaster and Deborah Kerr.

But he never won the coveted award.

Though efforts were made to make the slender, darkly handsome actor into a romantic screen idol, Mr. Clift refused to conform to this kind of role. He took roles he liked, turned down others, refused to live in California and went his own way.

"I don't have a big urge to act," he once said. "I can't play something I'm not interested in. And if I'm not interested, how can I expect the audience to be?"

Intrigued Magazines

His unorthodox attitudes toward Hollywood and success intrigued the fan magazines. Soon after his first film successes he was photographed in a $40-a-month walk-up in New York. He was shown having dinner at a Hamburger Heaven counter. He was pictured listening dreamily to classical music. He was shown reading a book.

The Hollywood reporters said he did not go to parties, did not chase starlets, was not interested in food and dressed like a man on the unemployment rolls.

To all of which Mr. Clift replied: "I'm not odd. I'm trying to be an actor. Not a movie star—just an actor.

He said that he did a lot of reading because he had a lot to catch up with, explaining that his brother had gone to Harvard, his sister had gone to Bryn Mawr, but that he had never got to high school.

Before his movie career began, he appeared in 13 Broadway plays, among them "Our Town," "The Skin of Our Teeth" and "There Shall Be No Night."

Appeared With Lunts

He played two seasons and went on the road with "There Shall Be No Night," working night after night with the stars of the production, Alfred Lunt and Lynn Fontanne. He said later it was an invaluable opportunity to study the art of acting under two such accomplished veterans.

Mr. Clift was born in Omaha, and in his early years moved with his family first to Chicago and then to New York.

In 1928, with his older brother and twin sister, he attended a private school in St. Moritz, Switzerland. At the age of 13, in Sarasota, Fla., he played a bit role in an amateur production of "As Husbands Go" and, in the words of the future box-office phenomenon, "that did it."

The following summer he obtained an insignificant role in a stock production of "Fly Away Home" at Stockbridge, Mass., and he advanced from no salary at all to $50 a week when the play moved to Broadway, with Thomas Mitchell as the star.

After two seasons in "Fly Away Home," Mr. Clift got a part in "Jubilee," a Cole Porter-Moss Hart musical success.

After two flops, "Monty" was cast as the lead in "Dame Nature," a month before his 18th birthday. He played a 15-year-old French schoolboy suddenly involved in parenthood and was hailed by critics.

His performance soon thereafter in "There Shall Be No Night" marked the beginning for Mr. Clift of a series of dramatic roles in which he voiced youth's protest against war. Among his enthusiastically received performances were those in "The Searching Wind" and "You Touched Me."

Injured in Accident

Among the 10 movies in which he starred were "Raintree Country," "The Young Lions" and "Miss Lonelyhearts."

In 1956 Mr. Clift was seriously hurt when his automobile struck a power pole in Hollywood. He recovered and returned to filmmaking.

In 1961 Stanley Kramer, the producer, offered Mr. Clift $300,000 to take the major role as the American war-crimes prosecutor in "Judgment at Nuremberg." The actor preferred a smaller part as a Jewish concentration-camp inmate and performed it for nothing, since the $100,000 offered him was $200,000 less than his usual salary and he thought the lower figure might hurt his market value.

Views on Profession

Mr. Clift bypassed the usual off-stage customs of film stars and preferred New York to Hollywood and trips on his boats to either. He was a realist about his profession and once said:

"One tries one's best to become a part of what one has to do. If you fail, you fail." Concerning the limitations of acting, he said:

"If you can play Hamlet, you can't play a peasant. If you can play a peasant, you can't play Hamlet."

His last starring role was in "Freud" four years ago. "The Defector," which he completed in June, has not yet been released.

Surviving the actor, a bachelor, are his mother, Mrs. Ethel Clift of New York; a brother, Brooks of Atlanta, and a sister, Mrs. Ethel McGinnis of Austin, Tex.

Shelley Winters and Montgomery Clift in *A Place in the Sun.*

Clift, Burt Lancaster and Frank Sinatra in *From Here to Eternity.*

The New York Times THURSDAY, FEBRUARY 12, 1976

Lee J. Cobb, the Actor, Is Dead at 64

LOS ANGELES, Feb. 11 (AP) —Lee J. Cobb, the actor best known on stage for "Death of a Salesman," on screen for "On the Waterfront" and on television for "The Virginian," died today at his home in Woodland Hills. He was 64 years old.

A Veritable Landmark

By JOHN T. McQUISTON

Lee J. Cobb created the role of Willy Loman in Arthur Miller's "Death of a Salesman" 27 years ago on Broadway. Critics called his portrayal of the aging, crushed salesman "epic" and "a towering accomplishment."

Mr. Miller said: "Lee is the greatest dramatic actor I ever saw."

Mr. Cobb repeated the portrayal of Willy in 1966 for television in what was described as a veritable landmark in studio drama. Critics said his performance was richer and deeper than it was on the stage.

It was through television that Mr. Cobb reached his largest public as Judge Garth in the series "The Virginian." He referred to the series as a "rather routine life on the TV range" but acknowledged that it made him a wealthy man.

However, it was in Hollywood movies that Mr. Cobb got his start, making more than 80 films in his long career. "The Exorcist" was among his most recent.

He was born on New York's Lower East Side on Dec. 8, 1911. His father, Benjamin Jacob, was a compositor on The Jewish Daily Forward, and as a child Lee studied to be a concert violinist. He was also a virtuoso on the harmonica, winning contests and a modicum of fame until a broken wrist ended his thoughts of a musical career.

He decided to become an actor when he was 16, although his mother argued against it. "At least study to be an accountant, she told me, so you'll have something to fall back on. But I was stubborn," he once told an interviewer.

Ran Away at 17

At 17, he ran away to Hollywood and made the rounds, unsuccessfully. So, in two months he was back in New York selling radios and studying accounting at New York University at night. "I didn't get very far because accounting and I became mortal enemies," he said.

Still obsessed by show business, he went back to California, this time to the Pasadena Playhouse, where he played small parts.

He was 23 when he again returned to New York and joined the Group Theater for a succession of plays, among them Clifford Odets's "Waiting for Lefty" and "Golden Boy." During this time he married an actress, Helen Beverly, and they had two children, a daughter and a son.

In 1943, he joined the Army Air Forces, hoping to become a pilot. Instead, he was assigned to a radio unit. Next he joined the cast of Moss Hart's "This Is the Army" and played in it for six months.

After his discharge from the service, he returned to Hollywood, where he continued to act a variety of parts in films. During a period of great frustration, he received the script of "Death of a Salesman" from Elia Kazan. Mr. Cobb said he was quick to realize that "there was no living until I played Willy Loman."

"Willy Loman is part of my existence. He isn't anyone I can have any objective opinions about," he said. His performance at the Morosco Theater became theatrical history.

Fateful Testimony

All turned sour, however, in the mid 1950's when he testified as a cooperative witness before the House Un-American Activities Committee and admitted joining the Communist Party briefly in New York as a result of contacts he had made while he was with the Group Theater.

He left the party, he said, because of a general pattern of acquiescence demanded of the members. Not long after he testified, Mr. Cobb suffered a massive heart attack that almost killed him. The experience also left him deeply in debt.

During the 1960's, he lived what he called his "new life" without much fanfare. He performed notably in such films as "The Brothers Karamazov," which he said was one of his favorites, in TV specials like "12 Angry Men" and "Don Quixote" and in his lucrative series "The Virginian."

In 1952, he and Helen Beverly were divorced, and in 1957 he married a former schoolteacher, Mary Hirsch, who had a 3-year-old son by a previous marriage. They had a son in 1960.

In November 1969, Mr. Cobb returned to the stage to play "King Lear," presented by the Repertory Theater of Lincoln Center. Again, he opened to critical acclaim, although he was playing Shakespeare for the first time in his professional life.

He was given a standing ovation at the end of the performance, and one critic described Mr. Cobb's Lear as "the finest performance in a distinguished career."

Mr. Cobb was then reluctant to compare Lear to Willy Loman, nor would he go into what constitutes true tragedy.

"If you must compare," he told an interviewer, "Loman is a half-beaker as against Lear's full, overflowing beaker of poetry and emotion."

"The great difference is that in a production of 'Lear' there is challenge to continual growth. There is no such thing as perfection," he said.

In looking back, Mr. Cobb said he did not believe that "Death of a Salesman" was "a socially significant play, as some have said. The Miller play, according to Mr. Cobb, is a love affair between a father and son, a play about the foibles, weaknesses and strengths of one man.

"Willy Loman is nobody's hero, but we are all his bereaved." said Mr. Cobb.

Mr. Cobb appeared briefly on the New York stage in the short-lived production of "The Emperor's Clothes" in 1953.

His numerous film credits included "The Moon Is Down (1943), "Song of Bernadette" (1945), "Anna and the King of Siam" (1946), "Boomerang" (1947), "Captain From Castile" and "Call Northside 777" (both 1948), "But Not for Me," "The Trap" and "Green Mansions" (1959); "Exodus" (1960), "How the West Was Won" (1962), "Come Blow Your Horn" (1963) and "The Man Who Loved Cat Dancing" (1973).

Joanne Woodward and Lee J. Cobb in *The Three Faces of Eve*.

The New York Times THURSDAY, AUGUST 31, 1961.

Charles Coburn Dies Here at 84; Stage and Movie Actor 68 Years

Repertory Company Leader Early in Century Entered Films at 60—Won Oscar

Charles Coburn

Charles Coburn, whose career in show business covered sixty-eight years, died yesterday in Lenox Hill Hospital. He was 84 years old.

Last week Mr. Coburn had been appearing in Indianapolis in the summer-stock production of "You Can't Take It With You," a show that broke an eight-year attendance record for one week at the Avondale Playhouse.

On Monday he registered at the Lenox Hill Hospital for a check-up, during the course of which he underwent minor throat surgery, a spokesman said yesterday. He died at 2 P. M. yesterday of heart failure.

Three aspects of Mr. Coburn's long and distinguished career were legendary even while he lived.

To his acting record of almost seven decades, spanning the oldtime stock company, the Broadway stage, motion pictures, radio and television, Mr. Coburn brought a deep respect and affection for his chosen craft that was as contagious to colleagues as to audiences.

Secondly, until his second marriage, in 1959, to Mrs. Winifred Jean Clements Natzka, forty-one years his junior, Mr. Coburn's thirty-one-year marriage to the late Ivah Wills remained one of the most famous love stories of the American stage. Together, the couple were responsible for training, in their own repertory company, some of America's finer acting talent.

Finally, there was the well-known youthful vitality of Mr. Coburn's private and public life during his twilight years on the West Coast, where he began a screen career in 1937, at the age of 60. The favorite pastimes of the stylishly stout actor were dancing the latest ballroom steps and attending sports events. His stable for the breeding of race horses reportedly cost him $24,000 a year to maintain.

Mistaken for Program Boy

Mr. Coburn was born on June 19, 1877, in Macon, Ga. The family moved to Savannah when he was 9. At 13, while he was standing in front of the old Savannah Theatre, young Coburn was mistaken by the manager for a program boy and was ordered inside.

Already an avid playgoer, he had saved pennies to attend shows. By the time he was 16, he had risen from program boy, without salary, to manager of the theatre.

He came to Broadway four years later, hoping to act. Instead, in discouragement, he wrapped bundles, then turned usher and bicycle racer.

Just before the turn of the century, Mr. Coburn received his first acting chore, as the giant slave in "Quo Vadis" with a small road company. He joined the troupe at Ames, Iowa, under an agreement that paid him "$12 a week and cakes (room and board)."

There followed two years of road appearances with various companies, with Mr. Coburn interpreting more than 400 different roles, including some in Shakespeare and the Greek classics.

In 1905, while touring upper New York State, he met and married his leading lady in "As You Like It," Ivah Wills. Until her death the couple refused to be separated professionally and always addressed each other as "Orlando" and "Rosalind."

Came to Broadway in 1918

Organizing the Coburn Players, devoted to "poetic drama," the couple and their charges toured the country for twelve years. In 1910 they staged a two-day performance of "Twelfth Night" and "As You Like It" on the White House lawn at the request of President and Mrs. William Howard Taft.

In 1918 the Coburns invaded Broadway, producing and starring in "The Better 'Ole," a comedy dramatization of a famous British wartime cartoon. The show was so successful that Mr. Coburn placed four companies on the road while playing the lead in New York for two years.

Other of the team's Broadway appearances were in "So This Is London," "The Yellow Jacket," "The Bronx Express," "Lysistrata," "The Rivals," and "The Canterbury Pilgrims."

In 1934 the Coburns helped to found the Mohawk Drama Festival at Union College. Each subsequent summer found them settling on the campus at Schenectady, N. Y., to perform the classics and develop young actors.

Mrs. Coburn's death in 1937 was a great blow to her husband. Later the same year Mr. Coburn accepted a Hollywood offer to appear in Metro-Goldwyn-Mayer's "Of Human Hearts." The film, a "sleeper," solidly established the aging newcomer to the medium.

Over the years, Mr. Coburn, whose ever-present monocle was worn not as an affectation but to combat an astigmatism, became one of the most popular and prolific character actors—and scene stealers—in the industry. He played roles ranging from the blackest of villains to the kindliest of paternal types.

In 1943 he won an Academy Award for a supporting role in "The More the Merrier," a light satire of housing conditions in wartime Washington.

His Films Listed

He was an award nominee for two other pictures, "The Green Years" (1946) and "The Devil and Miss Jones" (1941). Other films were "In This Our Life," "The Lady Eve," "Mr. Music," "The Road to Singapore," "Louisa," "Trouble Along the Way," "How to Be Very, Very Popular" and "Yes Sir, That's My Baby."

His other film credits included "Idiot's Delight," "The Story of Alexander Graham Bell," "Stanley and Livingstone," "Princess O'Rourke," "Paradine Case," "B. F.'s Daughter," "Wilson" and "Around the World in 80 Days."

Mr. Coburn managed to fit occasional radio and television performances into a constantly crowded film agenda. Except for a nation-wide Theatre Guild tour in 1946, when he played Falstaff in "The Merry Wives of Windsor," he never returned to the Broadway stage after having settled in Hollywood, although he did appear in summer stock.

In June, 1955, the National Theatre Arts Council presented to him a scroll in tribute to his seventy-eighth birthday and "unexcelled contributions to the theatre, films, radio and television as actor, director and producer over a span of sixty years."

Charles Coburn, Gene Tierney and Don Ameche in *Heaven Can Wait.*

The New York Times TUESDAY, MAY 20, 1958.

Ronald Colman, Actor, Is Dead; Won '48 Oscar for 'Double Life'

British-Born Star of Debonair Charm and Distinctive Voice Had 40-Year Career

Special to The New York Times.

SANTA BARBARA, Calif., May 19—Ronald Colman, noted actor, died at St. Francis Hospital early this morning of a virus lung infection. His age was 67. He was stricken last night at his home, San Ysidro Ranch, Montecito.

Surviving are his widow, Benita Hume, British actress, and his daughter, Juliet.

Long-Lasting Popularity

Few Hollywood actors remained in constant popularity as long as Ronald Colman. A leading man for more than three decades in silent and sound films and more recently on radio and television, he had a distinctive voice, debonair charm and restraint that insured the success of virtually every venture in which he appeared.

Although the actor invariably suggested a weary but whimsical sophisticate adhering to a strict gentleman's code, he produced a richly varied gallery of characterizations. His career spanned such dashing adventure roles as "Under Two Flags" and "Kismet," undiluted drama, as in "The Light That Failed" and "Condemned to Devil's Island," and frothy farce, such as "Lucky Partners" and "Champagne for Caesar."

The mention of the actor's name, however, often conveyed five specific images to the typical moviegoer. There was his elegant thief in "Raffles" and the equally suave detective role in "Bulldog Drummond," which Mr. Colman once said "saved me" when the talkies arrived. His philosophical diplomat of "Lost Horizon" underscored this towering film adaptation of a modest-scale James Hilton novel.

Of his Sidney Carton in "A Tale of Two Cities" one critic actually deemed it, "more powerful than Dickens' creation." This part and the unforgettable "Beau Geste" remained Mr. Colman's two favorites, even after he had won an Oscar, the award of the Academy of Motion Picture Arts and Sciences, for "A Double Life" in 1948.

Fought in World War

Mr. Colman was born in Richmond, Surrey, England. He attended the Hadley School at Littlehampton, Sussex, appearing in amateur theatricals and continuing his hobby at nights with the Bancroft Amateur Dramatic Society.

When World War I began, Mr. Colman rejoined his regiment, the London Scottish Guards, in which he had enlisted four years before, and saw action in the first battle of Ypres.

In 1916 he made his professional stage debut in "The Maharanee of Arakan," at the London Coliseum, and appeared in other plays as well as films. Four years later, he arrived in this country with "$37, three clean collars and two letters of introduction."

The actor lived in Brooklyn rooming houses while he toured various stage and film casting offices. He finally got a small part in support of Robert Warwick in "The Dauntless Three." In 1922, while he was supporting Ruth Chatterton in "La Tendresse," Henry King, director, offered him the male lead opposite Lillian Gish in "The White Sister."

There followed "Kiki" opposite Norma Talmadge, and a series of romantic movies opposite Vilma Banky, including "Two Lovers," "The Winning of Barbara Worth" and "The Dark Angel." But Mr. Colman really captured the hearts of American movie fans in 1929 with "Beau Geste."

Other films Mr. Colman appeared in were "The Light That Failed," "Random Harvest," "Arrowsmith," "The Prisoner of Zenda," "If I Were King," "Clive of India" and "The Talk of the Town."

His Last Two Roles

In recent years Mr. Colman appeared in two motion pictures: a small role in the late Mike Todd's production of "Around the World in 80 Days," and as the Spirit of Man in Warner Brothers' "The Story of Mankind," produced last year.

His first wife was Thelma Victoria Maud, an English actress whom he married in London in 1918. They were divorced in 1935. In 1938 he married Miss Hume.

In 1949 the Colmans began a series of radio programs, "The Halls of Ivy," which won high critical and public acclaim. The couple's performances as president and first lady of a fictional American college, and the program itself, were deemed literate and amusing.

The program was transformed into a television series in 1954 but ran for only one season.

In 1950 Mr. Colman tied in second place with Sir Laurence Olivier, one of his best friends, as "best actor of the half-century" in a poll of film workers conducted by Daily Variety, the trade publication. Another old friend, Charles Chaplin, won first place.

Two legends about Mr. Colman persisted in a town already abounding with them. One was his unflagging directness, candor and courtesy in dealing with the press. The other, as an illustrious list of co-actors and co-actresses learned, had to do with billing.

His contract always specified that Mr. Colman alone must be "starred" above a film's title. Consequently, no matter how many names of colleagues preceded the title, his always came first. Immediately after it, often in microscopic lettering, there followed the parenthesized word "starring."

Ronald Colman as Francois Villon in *If I Were King*.

Colman in *Bulldog Drummond*, in the title role, with Joan Bennet.

"All the News That's Fit to Print"

The New York Times.

LATE CITY EDITION

U. S. Weather Bureau Report (Page 95) forecasts: Mostly fair, humid today and tonight. Chance of thunderstorms tomorrow. Temp. range: 80—64; yesterday: 70—55.

SECTION ONE

NEWS SUMMARY AND INDEX, PAGE 95

VOL. CX—No. 37,731. © 1961 by The New York Times Company. Times Square, New York 36, N. Y. NEW YORK, SUNDAY, MAY 14, 1961. 35c outside New York City, its suburban area and Long Island. 50c in 17 Western states, Canada: higher in air delivery cities. THIRTY CENTS

GOVERNOR SEEKS LIBERAL SUPPORT FOR CITY FUSION

Republican and Democratic Choices for Mayor Are Considered at Parley

WAGNER MOVE AWAITED

Rose Expects 'Considerable Support' for Him if He Runs as Independent

By DOUGLAS DALES

Governor Rockefeller took the lead yesterday in trying to negotiate a "good government" ticket in New York City that the Liberal party would support.

For an hour and a half he explored the possibility of a fusion ticket with Alex Rose, vice chairman of the Liberal party, at a meeting in the Governor's city residence at 810 Fifth Avenue.

Mr. Rockefeller said a number of possible fusion candidates for Mayor had been discussed, including Republicans and Democrats. No understandings were reached, and further conferences between the two will be held, he said.

As a result of yesterday's meeting, Republican city leaders are expected to postpone a meeting they had scheduled for this week to announce their choice of Attorney General Louis J. Lefkowitz for Mayor.

One Chance Lost

Governor Rockefeller now appears to have assumed the top role in the attempt to fashion a fusion ticket. As a consequence, the five borough leaders may be expected to defer any action that could upset the negotiations he has undertaken.

The chance for a Republican-Liberal ticket suffered a setback last week when Senator Jacob K. Javits, a Republican whose political career was made possible by Liberal support, asked that his name be withdrawn from consideration as a candidate for Mayor. Republican leaders accepted his refusal as final.

There are two obstacles to an early decision on fusion. One is the uncertainty created by the refusal of Mayor Wagner, a Democrat, to say whether he will seek a third term. He had the Liberal nomination four years ago.

3 Democrats Mentioned

The second is the fact that the policy committee of the Liberal party, which will have the final say on fusion, will not meet until after May 27, when Prof. Paul R. Hays, Liberal party state chairman, returns to the United States from Turkey.

At a press conference with Mr. Rose after yesterday's meeting, Governor Rockefeller said he had introduced the names of Mr. Lefkowitz, Representative Paul A. Fino of the Bronx and Representative John V. Lindsay of Manhattan as

Continued on Page 40, Column 1

DISCUSS CITY ELECTION: Alex Rose, vice chairman of the Liberal party, with Governor Rockefeller talked to reporters at ...

Associated Press

sup...
has ...

AMU... PLA...

Amphith... for 'Hig... Mus...

By IRA H...

The New ... of 1964-65 ... amusement ... though it w... thing else an... cheap, vulgar h...

Until recently ... had not set aside ... licly—any area o... on Flushing Mea... cifically for amu...

Robert Moses, ... the fair, had ofte... pected that industri... the various states ... exhibitors would pr... in connection with th... scattered throughout ...

In outlining plans on ... five-foot model of the fai... group of thirty visiting ... bers of Congress and ... wives and children yester... J. Anthony Panuch, vice p... dent of the fair, mentio... space around the amphithea... at the north end of Mea... Lake as "our amusement ar...

Samples of Programs

When asked after his tal... explain this, Mr. Panuch sa...

"Well, we still don't call ... that—we call it the lake are... on the map—but that's wha... it's going to be. You can't close down a fair at 6 o'clock on a summer night. Of course, we shall insist, as Mr. Moses has said from the first, that everything be high-class entertainment."

Mr. Panuch gave some examples of what he meant.

In an area on the lake shore east of the amphitheatre Hawaii is planning to set up its state exhibit, featuring a typical native show of music and hula dancing. This space was formerly reserved for a nature and conservation exhibit by New York State, which has withdrawn that idea.

Musical on Aquacade Site

On the other side of the amphitheatre Florida intends to mount a water-skiing show by acrobatic bathing beauties similar to that in Cypress Gardens.

In the amphitheatre itself, which has been used for water shows every summer since Billy Rose produced his Aquacade there in the 1939-40 World's Fair, a new musical extravaganza will be produced by Meyer Davis, the orchestra leader, and Leon Leonidoff, the stage-show producer.

Larger areas, between the Long Island Expressway and the water shows on the lake shore, which on former maps were designated for automobile parking, are now for lease to show producers or commercial concerns that wish to sponsor theatrical entertainment.

Variety, the show-business

Continued on Page 54, Column 8

FOREIGN AID UNIT TO ASK 7.3 BILLION FOR 5-YEAR LOAN

Kennedy To Seek Authority to Borrow From Treasury for Long-Term Projects

By E. W. KENWORTHY

Special to The New York Times.

WASHINGTON, May 13—President Kennedy will ask Congress to permit a new, consolidated foreign aid agency to borrow $7,300,000,000 from the Treasury over five years, informed sources said today.

This request for Treasury borrowing authority, it is agreed, will be the most controversial item in the President's new for... eign aid legislation... scheduled...

United Press International Radiophoto

... Andrei A. Gromyko, left, Soviet Foreign Minis... ... Rusk. At the right is W. Averell Harriman.

Gary Cooper Dead of Cancer; Film Star, 60, Won 2 Oscars

Honored for 'Sergeant York' and 'High Noon'—Played Movie Leads 35 Years

Special to The New York Times.

HOLLYWOOD, Calif. May 13—Gary Cooper died today of cancer at his home in the Holmby Hills section of Los Angeles. He was 60 years old last Sunday.

The tall, lean actor, whose cowboy roles had made him a world symbol of the courageous, laconic pioneer of the American West, had been critically ill for several weeks.

The seriousness of his illness was revealed on April 17 when the Motion Picture Academy of Arts and Sciences was bestowing its Oscars on artists and technicians. A special statuette was ready for Mr. Cooper for his contributions during his long career in the movie business. He had previously won two Oscars for acting—in the title role of "Sergeant York" in 1941 and as the courageous sheriff in "High Noon" in 1953.

However, James Stewart, the actor, accepted the honor for his close friend and gave a short, emotional tribute. Reporters, who had accepted the explanation that Mr. Cooper was unable to attend the ceremony because of a pinched nerve in his back, later learned that he was critically ill with cancer.

A funeral service will be held Tuesday morning at the Roman Catholic Church of the Good Shepherd in Beverly Hills. There

Continued on Page 86, Column 4

Gary Cooper

...Will Give More Arms ...Money to Vietnamese

By ROBERT TRUMBULL

Special to The New York Times.

...ay 13—South Vietnam and the United ...n an eight-point program for increased ... and economic assistance. Long-range ... the Com... ...t and ...itions ...e an... ...ué is... ...sident ...n. ...e pub... ...d ar... ... Sai... ... his ...half ...

CONGO TO CONVENE PARLIAMENT SOON

Kasavubu Calls for Session Within Few Weeks—U. N. Asked to Act as Guard

By HENRY TANNER

Special to The New York Times.

LEOPOLDVILLE, the Congo, May 13—The Congolese Parliament will be called back into session within the next few weeks.

President Joseph Kasavubu, ...n an announcement at Coquil...tville last night, declared that ... had decided to reconvene ... Assembly and Senate, which ...uspended for an indefinite ... last fall during his show... with Patrice Lumumba, ...Premier.

... President said he planned ... the United Nations to ...tee the personal safety ...bers of Parliament and ...milies and to assist in ... them to the capital.

...d the time of the new ...ould be "immediately ... conclusion" of the ... of Congolese politi... ...s at Coquilhatville. ...ence had been ex... ...ose at the end of ...ut observers feel ...st longer.

...Being Drafted

...icted that the ... bring the ...liament to... ...ake several ...expected the ...ll on consti... ...from several ...out the pre... ...w Constitu... ...ting it to ...ation of the ... now being ...lhatville is ...rliament's ... call for ...liament ...Govern... ...aign to ...ereign... ...win over ...factions.

The reconvening of Parliament was interpreted as a challenge and a major concession to Antoine Gizenga, head of the regime in Stanleyville, who has repeatedly requested the reopening of Parliament.

The Central Government evidently hopes that Mr. Gizenga and his followers will accept United Nations guarantees and take their seats in Parliament.

Specialists believed Mr. Gizenga would control about forty votes in the Assembly [the lower chamber] if he heeded the call. He would need sixty-nine votes to get a majority in the 137-member Assembly.

The last time the chambers were in session they gave a majority to Patrice Lumumba in his fight for the revocation of a Presidential order issued by Mr. Kasavubu to depose him as Premier. The chambers acted

Continued on Page 9, Column 1

GROMYKO REFUSES TO YIELD ON SEATS FOR LAOS REBELS

Geneva Deadlock Continues —Rusk Says U.S. Is Ready to Accept Neutralists

COMPROMISE IS SOUGHT

Ministers at Parley Look to Talks in Asian Land for Hopes of Solution

By SEYMOUR TOPPING

Special to The New York Times.

GENEVA, May 13—Foreign Minister Andrei A. Gromyko conferred with Secretary of State Dean Rusk today but refused to budge from his insistence that the Pathet Lao rebels be seated as an equal at the conference on Laos here.

With this deadlock blocking the opening of the international parley here, the foreign ministers looked to a meeting scheduled in a Laotian jungle village for a solution.

[In Laos, representatives of the pro-Western, neutralist and pro-Communist factions agreed to begin negotiations Sunday for the political and military settlement of the Laotian civil war. The talks are to be held at Namone in territory controlled by the neutralists and the pro-Communist Pathet Lao movement.]

U. S. for Two Delegations

In his meeting with Mr. Gromyko, Secretary Rusk said he was agreeable to the seating of a delegation of the pro-Western Government of Premier Boun Oum and of another delegation representing the former neutralist Premier, Prince Souvanna Phouma.

The Secretary said, however, that he would not countenance the pro-Communist Pathet Lao representatives at the table except as observers or consultants to Prince Souvanna Phouma, who is recognized by Moscow as the rightful Premier of Laos.

Mr. Rusk was understood to feel that acceptance of the Soviet demand for a tripartite Laotian delegation would prejudice the prospect that the conference might create a truly independent and neutral Laos.

Compromise Sought

Mr. Gromyko was no less adamant in insisting that the Soviet Union had invited both the Souvanna Phouma and the Pathet Lao factions to the conference and that there could be no compromise on the seating of both.

The Soviet Union issued its invitations as co-chairman with Britain of the 1954 Geneva conference on Indochina. In the negotiations for the pending conference it was not defined specifically how the Laotian representation should be made up.

The United States was accused by the delegation of Communist China of obstructing the opening of the conference.

Wu Leng-hsi, the delegation spokesman, maintained at a

Continued on Page 3, Column 5

Sports News

BASEBALL

The Detroit Tigers increased their American League lead over the Yankees to four and one-half games by beating New York again yesterday at the Stadium, 8—3. Jim Gentile's eleventh homer paced the Baltimore Orioles to a 4-1 victory over the Cleveland Indians. Tom Sturdivant pitched a one-hitter against the Boston Red Sox as the Washington Senators won, 4—0. The Minnesota Twins defeated the Los Angeles Angels, 13—6. Willie Mays hit two homers, one with the bases loaded, to help the San Francisco Giants, the National League leaders, gain an 8-5 victory over the Milwaukee Braves. The Pittsburgh Pirates routed the Cincinnati Reds, 13—5. The Los Angeles Dodgers beat the Chicago Cubs, 7—3.

HORSE RACING

Hitting Away, paying $35.40 for $2, captured the $59,900 Withers Mile before 44,279 at Aqueduct.

TRACK AND FIELD

Manhattan College retained the Metropolitan Intercollegiate championship at Downing Stadium with 85½ points. St. John's was second with 74½. The Heptagonal title went to Yale for the fourth time in five years.

Details in Section 5.

... o... za... So... in ... pou... "... dum... "F... The... that ... from ... lack o...

Contin...

Toot... A B...

By HARO...

There is ... in Bethesd... no tooth d...

They ha... not becau... ...etic trait, nor ... ...diet, but apparently ...ause of something that happened to the maternal founder of their family tree. She was given enough penicillin to free her mouth completely of certain types of bacteria.

Those among her descendants who have been kept free from the same bacteria have had virtually no tooth decay ever since. Those exposed have had cavities.

The family constitutes part of the evidence built up by scientists at the National Institute of Dental Research to show that

Continued on Page 68, Column 4

...of the American West, had been critically ill for several weeks.

The seriousness of his illness was revealed on April 17 when the Motion Picture Academy of Arts and Sciences was bestowing its Oscars on artists and technicians. A special statuette was ready for Mr. Cooper for his contributions during his long career in the movie business. He had previously won two Oscars for acting—in the title role of "Sergeant York" in 1941 and as the courageous sheriff in "High Noon" in 1953.

However, James Stewart, the actor, accepted the honor for his close friend and gave a short, emotional tribute. Reporters, who had accepted the

Associated Press

Gary Cooper

explanation that Mr. Cooper was unable to attend the ceremony because of a pinched nerve in his back, later learned that he was critically ill with cancer.

A funeral service will be held Tuesday morning at the Roman Catholic Church of the Good Shepherd in Beverly Hills. There

Continued on Page 86, Column 4

By United Press International.

TEHERAN, Iran, May 13—Iran's new Government arrested five generals, including two former Cabinet ministers, today on charges of corruption, embezzlement and other abuses of power, authoritative sources said.

The move appeared to be a first step in Premier Ali Amini's reform campaign. High-level corruption was a factor in the fall last week of the Government of Premier Jafar Sharif-Imami.

Reports, as yet unconfirmed, said 140 other persons, including many officials, were arrested. Officials identified the arrested generals as:

Gen. Mehdigholi Alavi-Moghadam, Interior Minister under Mr. Sharif-Imami and long a chief of police. He was recently

Continued on Page 21, Column 1

Today's Sections

Index to Subjects

Gary Cooper in his Academy Award portrayal of *Sergeant York* in the 1940 film of the same name.

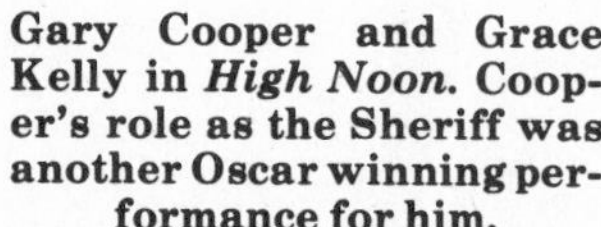

Gary Cooper and Grace Kelly in *High Noon*. Cooper's role as the Sheriff was another Oscar winning performance for him.

Ingrid Bergman with Gary Cooper in *For Whom the Bell Tolls*, 1943.

Gary Cooper Dead of Cancer; Film Star, 60, Won 2 Oscars

Continued From Page 1, Col. 5

will be a high requiem mass. Burial will be private.

The All-American Man

To millions of Americans, Gary Cooper represented the All-American Man.

He was called the "indestructible, incorruptible Galahad of moviedom." It was said that his "screen decalogue has been a combination of the Bill of Rights, the Ten Commandments and the Atlantic Charter."

He was an American frontier hero in "The Plainsman," an O. S. S. hero in "Cloak and Dagger," a Naval hero in "Task Force," a homespun, millionaire hero in "Mr. Deeds Goes to Town," a common-man, political hero in "Meet John Doe," a baseball hero in "The Pride of the Yankees," a medical hero in "The Story of Dr. Wassell" and a national hero in "Sergeant York."

He was the strong, silent man not only of the great outdoors, where he was one of its slowest-talking and fastest-drawing citizens, but also of powerful dramas and sophisticated comedies.

"Ungainly, ungrammatical, head-scratching, ineloquent men draw comfort and renewed assurance from Gary Cooper," a writer once said.

Much the Same Off Screen

Some Hollywood observers said that the off-screen Gary Cooper bore more than coincidental resemblance to the characters he usually portrayed on the screen.

Long, lean and broad of shoulder, he walked gingerly. His eyes were of chilly blue. He was handy with a gun, not a six-gun, but a shotgun or rifle.

One writer said that in only two major respects did Mr. Cooper differ markedly from his screen self: he didn't go around wearing a horse and he didn't say "They went that-a-way." Mr. Cooper reportedly would say, "Thet way."

Mr. Cooper's screen affinity for "Yup" prompted many fans, he once recalled, to stop him on the street and ask him to please say "Yup" for them.

"Yup is a convenient word," he said, "and I've learned that people don't expect too much from a man with a one-word vocabulary. And now that I think of it, it's come in handy because when people ask me personal questions they don't expect an answer."

Mr. Cooper had no illusions about his acting ability. But the men who directed his pictures said he had an instinctive sense of timing, a quick intelligence, the wit to think a role through and get to the heart of a character.

"I recognize my limitations," he once said. "For instance, I never tried Shakespeare." He paused and grinned slowly. "That's because I'd look funny in tights."

His Own Formula

Mr. Cooper was once asked to give the reasons for his success. He replied: "I don't really know but maybe it's because once in a while I find a good picture, the happy combination of director and actors, which gives me a fresh start. Mostly I think it's because I look like the guy down the street."

Mr. Cooper was born May 7, 1901 in Helena, Mont., and christened Frank James Cooper. His father, Charles Henry Cooper, was a British lawyer who had gone to Helena, married a Montana girl, managed a ranch while practicing law and became a justice of the Montana Supreme Court.

The family went to England when young Cooper was 9 and returned to Montana four years later. During the manpower shortage of World War I he worked on the family ranch.

"Getting up at 5 o'clock in the dead of winter to feed 450 head of cattle and shoveling manure at 40 below ain't romantic," he once recalled.

For two years Mr. Cooper attended Grinnell College in Iowa. He left in 1924 and went to Los Angeles. He had done some cartoon work in Helena and he thought that he might go to art school or eventually get a job in advertising.

His first job in California was door-to-door solicitation for a photography studio. He also sold advertising space on a theatre curtain. One day Mr. Cooper met two friends from Helena who told him the Fox Western Studios were looking for riders. He got a job—at $10 a day.

Emulated Tom Mix

Then he heard that Tom Mix, the cowboy star, was making $15,000 a week. Mr. Cooper decided to devote a year to make good in the movies.

A friend suggested that he change his name because there already were several Frank Coopers in pictures. Frank Cooper became Gary Cooper when the friend, who came from Indiana, suggested that Gary was a city whose name always sounded poetic to her.

Mr. Cooper got several bit parts, and just before the year ran out, got his first big role, opposite Vilma Banky in the 1926 film, "The Winning of Barbara Worth."

Among his other films were "It," with Clara Bow; "The Lives of a Bengal Lancer," "Wings," "The Virginian," "The Westerner," "For Whom the Bell Tolls," "Saratoga Trunk," "Desire," "Beau Geste," "Friendly Persusasion," "Along Came Jones" and "A Farewell to Arms." More recently he had appeared in "They Came to Cordura," "The Hanging Tree" and "The Wreck of the Mary Deare."

Mr. Cooper equaled, if not surpassed, Tom Mix' $15,000 a week, although he was generally paid by the picture—reportedly around $300,000 in recent years—not by the week.

Underwent 2 Operations

In April, 1960, he underwent prostate-gland surgery in Boston. A major intestinal operation was performed five weeks later in Hollywood.

After his recovery, the actor went to England to make his last film, "The Naked Edge," in which he portrayed a murderer opposite Deborah Kerr. When he returned to Hollywood in January, he was honored at a testimonial dinner by the Friars Club, an entertainers fraternal organization, for his thirty years in the motion-picture industry.

In 1933, Mr. Cooper married the socially prominent Veronica Balfe, who had a brief screen career as Sandra Shaw. The couple had one daughter, Maria.

In 1959, Mr. Cooper became a member of the Roman Catholic Church, of which his wife and daughter already were members.

Also surviving Mr. Cooper is his 85-year-old mother, Mrs. Alice Bracia Cooper of Los Angeles.

Marlene Dietrich and Cooper in *Morocco*.

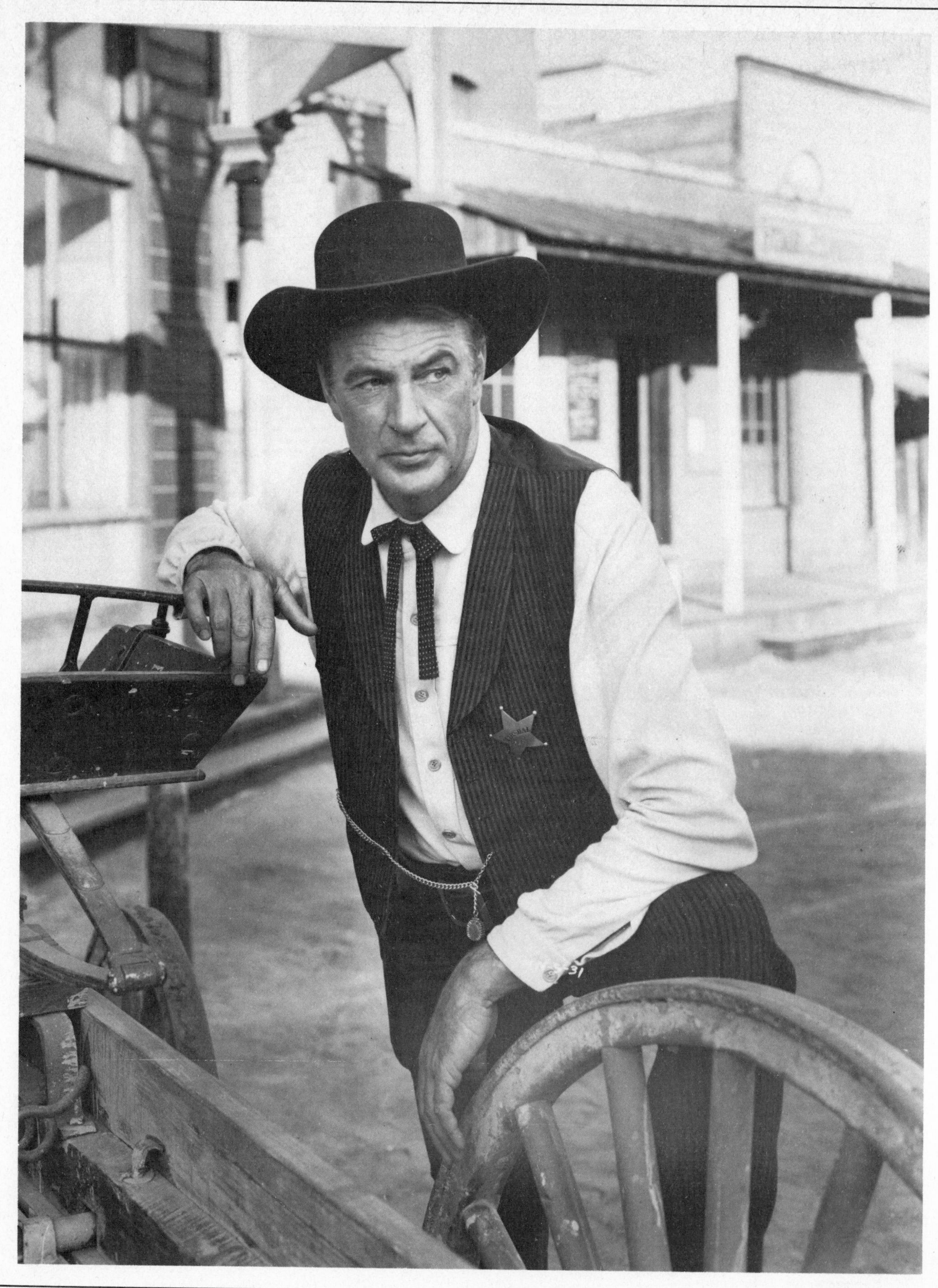

Gary Cooper in *High Noon*

The New York Times WEDNESDAY, MARCH 4, 1959.

Lou Costello, 52, Dies on Coast; Comic Had Teamed With Abbott

'Little Guy Trying to Be a Big Shot' in Films and on TV—Partners Broke Up in '57

Special to The New York Times.

BEVERLY HILLS, Calif., March 3—Lou Costello, the roly-poly funnyman of the comedy team of Abbott and Costello, died of a heart attack today in Doctors Hospital. He had suffered a previous attack five days ago, but seemed to be improving. He would have been 53 years old on Friday.

Survivors include his widow, Ann, and three daughters, Patricia Anne, Carole Lou and Christine.

'Ba-a-ad Boy' of School

Lou Costello was a big overgrown kid, who never got over having been "the ba-a-ad boy" of Public School 15, Paterson, N. J. With Bud Abbott as his straight man, he parlayed his failure to grow up into a sizable share of fame and fortune.

The great success of Abbott and Costello was attributed by the critics to their old-fashioned knock-about style, combined with a modern toughness of talk. Abbott was the lean and hawk-eyed wise guy, the sharpshooter who always got the last word; Costello the good-natured dimwit who always got it in the neck—except when the worm occasionally turned. The average viewer never analyzed them—he just laughed.

The team broke up amicably in 1957.

"Costello is a truly lovable character with patient eyes, a normally plaintive voice and the clumsily aggressive manner of a little guy trying to be a big shot," a screen critic wrote in 1941. "His moods change. At one time he is pleading pitifully with all his distressed soul in his eyes for the keeper of the brig in which he is confined to bring him a sponge cake—with a file in it.

"Then he is racing about madly in an oversize admiral's uniform, maneuvering a battleship in a desperate attempt to impress his girl. Or he's falling prey to Abbott's iniquitous shell game * * *"

Or, as others saw it, he is just stealing an apple from a pushcart and getting caught—in such a manner as to make the average viewer howl.

Famous Baseball Routine

A gold recording of Abbott and Costello's famous "Who's on First?" baseball routine was placed on permanent display at the National Baseball Hall of Fame museum at Cooperstown, N. Y., in 1956. Also placed on exhibition there was a framed copy of the dialogue. The two comedians gave the skit thousands of times in the course of twenty years.

Mr. Costello always maintained that the ludicrously tragic things that happened to him on television and in movies sometimes occurred in real life.

"Me and animals just don't get along," he once told an interviewer. "I gotta horse on my ranch who's so old he hasn't gone faster than a walk for seven years. I gotta figure he's safe for me to ride now because he's too feeble to object. My daughters can hit him and kick him and he loves it. But as soon as I get on his back he begins to rear and buck like a rodeo bronc. He throws me. But I still love horses."

"When I was a stunt man I was clawed on the top of the head by an eagle and bitten by a vulture. I wonder if anyone else in the world was ever bitten by a vulture. I was once supposed to lead a hundred Cossacks in a mob scene. I fell off my horse and all hundred rode over me."

It was always like that, on screen or off, for Mr. Costello.

Lou Costello and Bud Abbott with Martha Raye in *Keep 'Em Flying.*

Invariably, he was the fall guy for Abbott, the audience and anyone else.

'I Been to College'

Mr. Costello's name was originally Louis Francis Cristillo. He was born in Paterson, where his family owned a small silk mill. His father wanted him to be a physician, but his fate was sealed while he was still in public school by the teacher who made him write "I am a bad boy" one thousand times for mixing up the hats and coats in the cloak room.

"It was like college to me," he said—and it became one of his familiar lines—"I been to college!"

Lou worked his way West toward Hollywood after he left school by doing chores in a haberdashery, a slaughterhouse and the prize ring. He met William Abbott, called Bud, while he was a $40-a-week comic in a Brooklyn burlesque theatre, in the early Nineteen Thirties.

Their first break came in 1938, when they appeared on the Kate Smith radio show. Then they did "Streets of Paris" on Broadway, and soon afterward were signed by Universal-International for the movies. Their first screen effort was not very successful, but the second, "Buck Privates," made them stars almost overnight, and grossed nearly $10,000,000.

Abbott and Costello in a scene from their famous "Who's On First" routine.

"All the News That's Fit to Print"

The New York Times

LATE CITY EDITION

Weather: Sunny today; not so cool tonight. Sunny, warmer tomorrow. Temperature range: today 45-68; Tuesday 41-58. Details on page B9.

VOL. CXXVI . . No. 43,572 · © 1977 The New York Times Company · NEW YORK, WEDNESDAY, MAY 11, 1977 · 20 CENTS

CALIFANO SAYS SHIFT ON SOCIAL SECURITY COULD BE PERMANENT

BACKS USE OF TREASURY FUNDS

Comments by Congressmen and Criticism From Business Hint Long Fight on Carter Plan

By EDWARD COWAN

Special to The New York Times

WASHINGTON, May 10—Joseph A. Califano Jr., the Secretary of Health, Education and Welfare, told Congress today that the Carter Administration would eventually like to make a permanent part of the Social Security system the limited transfer of general revenues from the Treasury that it proposed yesterday for an experimental five-year period.

Mr. Califano stressed the belief that such shifts, for years of high unemplo[yment], were fundamentally soun[d] ... comments were made ... House Social Se[curity] ... an appare[nt] ... ministrati[on] ...

Since it was aut[horized] ... Social Security syst[em] ... nancing. It has paid ... to more than 33 millio[n] ... month—out of Social ... taxes. Employers and ... paid equal taxes on a limi[t] ... now $16,500 a year. Each ... of 5.85 percent.

Mr. Carter proposed to ... wage-base limit for employ[ers] ... they would pay taxes on all ... salaries, to make small increa[ses] ... wage base on which workers ... and to shift Treasury revenues ... Social Security system for years i[n] ... unemployment exceeds 6 percent.

Small Company Problems

Republican Representatives William Ketchum of California and Richard Schulze of Pennsylvania said that t[he] heavier employer taxes would be most burdensome for small companies, not just the corporate giants Mr. Califano had mentioned at a White House briefing.

"There's no way an employer can be made to absorb the tax out of profits," Mr. Schulze said. "His cost of business rises and he passes it on."

Mr. Califano expressed the hope that competition would "hold prices to some degree." But Representative Al Ullman, Oregon Democrat who is chairman of the Ways and Means Committee, expressed profound reservations about the Adminis-

Continued on Page A18, Col. 3

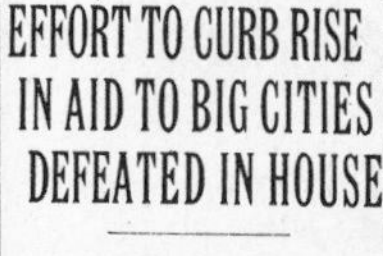

EFFORT TO CURB RISE IN AID TO BIG CITIES DEFEATED IN HOUSE

Rider to Kill New Formula Rejected, 261 to 149—Chamber May Pass Block Grant Program Today

PRESIDENT BIDS NATO RESPOND FORCEFULLY TO RUSSIANS' BUILDUP

RETURNS HOME AFTER SPEECH

Tells London Meeting of U.S. Allies Soviet Strength in Europe Is More Than Is Needed

By R. W. APPLE Jr.

Special to The New York Times

LONDON, May 10—President Carter urged America's allies in the North Atlantic Treaty Organization today to respond forcefully to a 12-year Soviet buildup in Europe that has created forces he described as "much stronger than needed for any defense purpose."

In a speech that contained his most searching analysis of East-West relations since taking office almost four months ago, the President said that the United States would prefer to reduce tensions

Text of Carter's speech, page A14.

in Europe through disarmament agreements and mutual and balanced force reductions. But until those goals could be attained, he said, "our military strength must be maintained."

Mr. Carter, who flew back to the United States tonight after his first trip overseas as President—a five-day journey that brought him considerable acclaim—promised that NATO would remain "the heart of our foreign policy." He told the NATO meeting, a regular ministerial gathering that was attended in this case by government leaders as well, that the United States would always be a "reliable and faithful ally."

White House Is Concerned

[B]ut those comments, as well as the [Pres]ident's statement that "the state of [the a]lliance is good," masked the real ... felt in his Administration about ... capacity to respond to potential aggression. Unless NATO is mod[ernized] rapidly, a senior White House ... said earlier this month, the al[liance wi]ll soon be inadequate as an in[strument o]f Western defense policy.

... [Pit]tsburgh ... the ministerial meet[ing of the] North Atlantic Treaty Organization because his language seemed to confirm this more modest approach.

Referring to a 35-nation conference that will take place in Belgrade, Yugoslavia,

Continued on Page A15, Col. 1

Joan Crawford Dies at Home

By PETER B. FLINT

Joan Crawford, who rose from waitress and chorus girl to become one of the great movie stars, died yesterday of a heart attack in her apartment at 158 East 68th Street. She gave her age as 69, but some reference works list her as two to four years older.

Miss Crawford had been a director of the Pepsi-Cola Company since the death of her fourth husband, Alfred N. Steele, the board chairman of the company, in 1959, but she had not been actively involved in the business in recent months.

A spokesman for Pepsi-Cola said Miss Crawford had no history of cardiac trouble and had appeared to be in good health except for recent complaints of back pains.

Miss Crawford was a quintessential superstar—an epitome of timeless glamour who personified for decades the dreams and disappointments of millions of American women.

With a wind-blown bob, mocking eyes and swirling short skirt, she spun to stardom in 1928, frenziedly dancing the Charleston atop a table in the silent melodrama "Our Dancing Daughters."

As a frivolous flapper she quickly made a series of spin-offs, including "Our Modern Maidens," "Laughing Sinners" and "This Modern Age." Endowed with a low voice, she easily made the transition to

Continued on Page B8, Col. 2

Joan Crawford

Joan Crawford Dies at Home

By PETER B. FLINT

Joan Crawford, who rose from waitress and chorus girl to become one of the great movie stars, died yesterday of a heart attack in her apartment at 158 East 68th Street. She gave her age as 69, but some reference works list her as two to four years older.

Miss Crawford had been a director of the Pepsi-Cola Company since the death of her fourth husband, Alfred N. Steele, the board chairman of the company, in 1959, but she had not been actively involved in the business in recent months.

A spokesman for Pepsi-Cola said Miss Crawford had no history of cardiac trouble and had appeared to be in good health except for recent complaints of back pains.

Miss Crawford was a quintessential superstar—an epitome of timeless glamour who personified for decades the dreams and disappointments of millions of American women.

With a wind-blown bob, mocking eyes and swirling short skirt, she spun to stardom in 1928, frenziedly dancing the Charleston atop a table in the silent melodrama "Our Dancing Daughters."

As a frivolous flapper she quickly made a series of spin-offs, including "Our Modern Maidens," "Laughing Sinners" and "This Modern Age." Endowed with a low voice, she easily made the transition to

Pictorial Parade

Joan Crawford

Continued on Page B8, Col. 2

... [o]n that ... to one indictment ... defendants and ... [term]s for race fixing at ... [Garden State Park] race track in February, ...

The Garden State indictments charged one count of conspiracy and 16 for race fixing and payments of between $52,000 and $58,200 to the defendants for fixing eight exacta and eight trifecta races between Dec. 21, 1974, and May 27, 1975.

State Attorney General William F. Hyland, in announcing the indictments, said that Anthony Ciulla of Stoneham, Mass., now serving a four-to-six year sentence for the Atlantic City race-fixing conviction, was the state's chief witness in the current charges.

Mr. Ciulla, an unindicted co-conspirator in the present indictment, has been moved from a state prison to a secret ... protection. His ... in protective custody. [The attor]ney general said the state made a deal with Mr. Ciulla under which it would recommend against additional prison time beyond his sentence. He noted that Mr. Ciulla faced an additional five years in prison in Rhode Island on a similar conviction there.

John Kevin Daly of Cornwells Heights, Pa., and Ralph Baker of Barrington, N.J., among the 12 indicted, received probationary terms for race fixing last year at Pocono Downs in Pennsylvania.

John Salvaggio, a suspended trainer from Mount Holly, N.J., also indicted, is currently serving a two-to three-year term for his conviction in the Atlantic City race-fixing case.

"There were daily meetings between Ciulla and some of the other defendants," said Tom Cannon, a spokesman for Mr. Hyland by telephone from

Continued on Page D19, Col. 5

... [S]oviet dis[sident] ... made that Mr. ... [did n]ot answer the letter. Dr. ... physicist who helped develop ... nuclear weapons, wrote to Mr. Carter on Jan. 21, one day after the inauguration, and Mr. Carter replied.

Some of the leaders who met with the President here had expressed alarm, mostly in private, that his outspoken criticism of political repression in the Soviet Union might endanger the atmosphere of détente and the prospect for successful negotiations to limit strategic arms.

More Cautious Attitude

However, Mr. Carter had apparently already begun to swing around to their view that more could be accomplished by quiet diplomatic pressures than by open criticism of the Kremlin. Mr. Carter has continued to say that he "reserves the right" to speak out about human rights violations but he has not done so with regard to any specific case since March 1, more than two months ago.

But even on that occasion Mr. Carter was beginning to show a more cautious attitude. He permitted Vice President Mondale to be photographed with Vladimir K. Bukovsky, an outspoken and now exiled Russian political dissident, but forbade photographs of himself with the dissident when he joined the conversations. There is no record that Mr. Carter or

INSIDE

Budget Talks Deadlocked

House and Senate budget conferees deadlocked on defense spending and were in danger of missing Sunday's deadline for spending ceilings. Page A18.

Reading Test Given

Thirty school districts gave the city reading test, but use of the results is blocked by the courts since advance copies were widely available. Page B2.

The Pillbox vs. the Law

The case of the eight Librium pills in Jerry Schwam's jacket, the neighbor's dog, the good deed and the Woodbridge, N.J. police. Page B2.

Joan Crawford, Screen Star, Dies in Manhattan Home

Continued From Page A1

sound pictures and went on to become one of the more-endurable movie queens.

Her career, a chorine-to-grande dame rise, with some setbacks, was due largely to determination, shrewd timing, flexibility, hard work and discipline.

Self-educated and intensely professional, Miss Crawford studied and trained assiduously to learn her art. She made the most of her large blue eyes, wide mouth, broad shoulders and slim figure and eventually became an Oscar-winning dramatic actress.

From Youth to Aged

In more than 80 movies, she adapted easily to changing times and tastes. When audiences began to tire of one image, she toiled to produce a new one. She made the changes with pace-setting makeup, coiffures, costumes—and craftsmanship.

From a symbol of flaming youth in the Jazz Age, she successively portrayed a shopgirl, a sophisticate, a tenacious woman fighting for success in love and/or a career in a male-dominated milieu, and later a repressed and anguished older woman.

Exhibitors voted her one of the 10 top money-making stars from 1932 through 1936, and in the late 1930's she was one of the highest-paid actresses. With a finely structured, photogenic face and high-style gowns usually designed by Adrian, she idealized what many women wished to be.

In 1945, when her career seemed to be foundering, she rebounded as a doting mother and ambitious waitress who rises to wealthy restaurateur in "Mildred Pierce," a role that won her an Academy Award as best actress.

'A Script Stealer'

Despite the Cinderella-type roles in many of her early movies, which many reviewers came to term "the Crawford formula," she fought tenaciously for varied and challenging parts, just as she later fought to remain a great star, with what one writer called "the diligence of a ditchdigger."

In her autobiography, "A Portrait of Joan," written with Jane Kesner Ardmore and published in 1962 by Doubleday & Company Inc., she acknowledged that "I was always a script stealer," which got her into "Our Dancing Daughters." She boldly cajoled producers, directors and writers to gain good roles.

When Norma Shearer refused to play a mother in the 1940 drama "Susan and God," Miss Crawford was offered the role. She responded, "I'd play Wally Beery's grandmother if it's a good part!"

Her major portrayals included a wanton stenographer in the star-studded adaptation of Vicki Baum's "Grand Hotel"; Sadie Thompson, W. Somerset Maugham's vulgar but vulnerable prostitute, in "Rain"; Crystal, a husband-stealing siren in Clare Boothe Luce's satire "The Women"; a scarred blackmailer in "A Woman's Face"; a schizophrenic in "Possessed," and the target of a homicidal husband in "Sudden Fear."

Quarrels Publicized

With dedication and skill, she also made commercial successes of what many reviewers scored as inferior vehicles with implausible plots and synthetic dialogue. In 1962 she began a new career in the horror genre, with "What Ever Happened to Baby Jane?" co-starring Bette Davis.

In later years, the indomitable Miss Crawford was involved in a number of publicized quarrels because of what some colleagues called her imperiousness, and her admitted bluntness toward actors that she regarded as incompetent, undisciplined or unprofessional.

She reveled in being a star and exhaustively cultivated her fan clubs and fans, predominantly women, with gifts and personally written notes—key efforts in maintaining their steadfast loyalty. She expressed delight in having "a hundred people clutching at my coat, clamoring for autographs."

Life imitated art in the late 1950's when, between movies, she embarked on a career as a businesswoman—a representative-in-glamour for the Pepsi-Cola Company.

In 1955 she married Alfred N. Steele, the company's board chairman and chief executive officer. Her previous marriages to three actors—Douglas Fairbanks Jr., Franchot Tone and Phillip Terry—had ended in divorce.

Mr. Steele logged more than 100,000 miles a year in revitalizing the soft-drink company's worldwide activities. She started traveling with him, flying to gala openings of new bottling plants and conventions and serving as hostess of parties on their trips, as well as in their spacious East Side Manhattan penthouse.

Joan Crawford in *Our Dancing Daughters*, 1928.

In 1959, two days after her husband died of a heart attack, she was elected the first woman director of the company's board.

She made scores of national tours, promoting Pepsi-Cola and her films. Accompanying her were large entourages and at least 15 trunks and suitcases for a wardrobe of up to 10 costume changes a day.

In New York, Miss Crawford became

Crawford in *Sudden Fear*, 1952.

a leading benefactor, fund-raiser and honorary official of dozens of philanthropies, explaining to an interviewer in 1971, "I've been on the receiving end of so much good that I feel I have to give something back."

Among her many honors were election as a fellow of Brandeis University and designation in 1965 as the first Woman of the Year by the United Service Organizations of New York for her qualities as "an actress, an executive, humanitarian."

The actress had long wanted to have children, but, she wrote, she was plagued by miscarriages. She adopted four children: Christina, who also became an actress; Christopher, and Cynthia and Cathy, who were twins.

Of French and Irish descent, Miss Crawford was born Lucille LeSueur in San Antonio. She listed her birth date as March 23, 1908, but many reference works put it at two to four years earlier. Her parents, Thomas and Anna Johnson LeSueur, separated before her birth, and her mother soon married Henry Cassin, owner of a vaudeville theater in Lawton, Okla. She was known for years as Billie Cassin.

Quit Stephens College

Her youth was harsh. Her family, including her elder brother, Hal LeSueur, moved to Kansas City, Mo., about 1916. Her mother and stepfather soon separated and, from the age of 9, she had to work, first in a laundry, helping her mother, and then in two private schools, St. Agnes Academy and the Rockingham School, where she was the only working student, cooking, washing dishes, waiting on tables and making beds for 30 other youngsters. She did not object to working, she recalled, but to being treated as a slave.

Work prevented her from attending classes. The wife of Rockingham's headmaster often punished her, with broom-handle floggings, she wrote, and falsified her records, which enabled her to enter Stephens College in Columbia, Mo., as a working student. After about three months, aware that she was not academically prepared, she withdrew.

Dancing was her main outlet, and in her early teens she won a Charleston contest in a Kansas City cafe. She worked as a salesgirl, pinching pennies for dancing lessons.

M.-G.-M. Screen Test

Vowing "to be the best dancer in the world," she went to Chicago, where she danced and sang in a cafe, and then to Detroit, where J. J. Shubert, the producer, picked her from a nightclub chorus line to dance on Broadway in his 1924 revue "Innocent Eyes."

Spotted by Harry Rapf, a talent scout for Metro-Goldwyn-Mayer, she was offered a screen test. Passing it, she signed a six-month contract for $75 a week and, on Jan. 1, 1925, set out for Hollywood.

The freckle-faced, 5-foot-4½-inch-tall dancer was a little plump, but soon slimmed down by daily jogging, decades before it was voguish.

She plunged into her movie apprenticeship as a chorus girl in "Pretty Ladies," a Zasu Pitts comedy; an ingénue in "Old Clothes" with Jackie Coogan, and a featured dancing role in "Sally, Irene and Mary." She was voted a Wampas "baby star," won a new contract and, because Lucille LeSueur was regarded as awkward to pronounce, was given the name Joan Crawford, the winning entry in a movie-magazine contest.

Joan Crawford and Ann Blyth in *Mildred Pierce*, 1945.

She gained experience and billing playing opposite such actors as Lon Chaney, William Haines and John Gilbert, and rocketed to fame in "Our Dancing Daughters." She passed the talking and singing test in 1929, in "Untamed," co-starring Robert Montgomery and made eight movies over the years with Clark Gable, most of them box-office hits. They included "Dancing Lady," gliding with Fred Astaire in his movie debut, and "Strange Cargo."

At M.-G.-M. Miss Crawford occasionally broke away from stereotyped casting and won acclaim for distinctive performances. But the best roles went to Greta Garbo and Norma Shearer, the wife of Irving G. Thalberg, the studio's executive production manager. After the two actresses retired, Greer Garson got the plums. Frustrated by formula films, which she termed "undiluted hokum," Miss Crawford asked Metro to drop her contract in 1942, and she left the studio after 17 years.

She joined Warner Brothers, but rejected scripts for more than two years until her triumphal return in "Mildred Pierce," adapted from a mordant novel by James M. Cain.

Image Is Ageless

In this and many other movies, she showed, as Richard Schickel wrote in "The Stars," published in 1962, a mastery "of what the trade knows as the 'woman's picture'," in which "she suffers incredible agonies of the spirit in her attempts to achieve love and/or success. The women suffer along with Miss Crawford, but are reassured by what they know of her own career, which clearly states that a woman can triumph in a man's world."

In her later career she projected a kind of ageless image. Her roles included the emotionally confused "Daisy Kenyon," a carnival girl and convict in "Flamingo Road," a shrew in "Harriet Craig," a hoofer in "Torch Song," a western ranch-gang leader in "Johnny Guitar," a lonely spinster who marries a psychotic youth in "Autumn Leaves" and many other vehicles of ordeal and anguish.

After ". . .Baby Jane," Miss Crawford, tenaciously holding on to stardom, made a number of thrillers, some of them grisly, and appeared occasionally in television dramas and episodes. She long talked of going on the stage, but uncharacteristically said later that she lacked "the guts" to appear before a large live audience.

In Hollywood she had determinedly improved herself, developing culture and polish. Her first marriage, to Douglas Fairbanks Jr., introduced her to the exotic social world of Pickfair, the home of Douglas Sr. and Mary Pickford. Franchot Tone helped her study classical drama and innovative acting techniques. Miss Crawford later described her marriages to them and to Phillip Terry as "dollhouse" unions. But her marriage to Mr. Steele, she said, gave her greater emotional stability than she had ever known.

Some years ago, leaving Manhattan's "21" Club, she was greeted by a group of construction workers, one shouting, "Hey, Joanie!" She cordially shook hands with several of them. One surveyed her carefully and remarked: "They don't make them like you anymore, baby."

Miss Crawford is survived by her four children: Mrs. Cathy Lalonde, Mrs. Cynthia Jordan Crawford, Christina Crawford, and Christopher, and four grandchildren.

The New York Times THURSDAY, SEPTEMBER 9, 1965.

Dorothy Dandridge Found Dead At Her Apartment in Hollywood

Singer and Actress, Star of 'Carmen Jones,' Was 41—Cause of Death Unknown

HOLLYWOOD, Sept. 8 (UPI)—Dorothy Dandridge, the actress and singer, was found dead today in her fashionable Sunset Strip apartment.

The cause of death was not immediately determined but the police said there was no evidence of "suicide, accident or foul play." An autopsy was ordered.

Earl Mills, Miss Dandridge's personal manager for 15 years, said he found the body of the 41-year-old star on the bathroom floor after forcing his way into the second-story apartment when she did not answer his ring.

Although Miss Dandridge had some career troubles in recent years, "she was never happier," Mr. Mills said. She had just returned from Mexico and was preparing for an engagement at Basin Street East in New York.

The star's mother, Ruby Dandridge, also an actress, arrived at the apartment about an hour after the body was found. She broke into tears as detectives led her to her daughters body.

Reached Top in 50's

At the pinnacle of her career in the nineteen-fifties, Dorothy Dandridge was called the most beautiful Negro singer to make her mark in nightclubs and motion pictures since Lena Horne.

On stage and on the screen, the slender, willowy actress with huge dark eyes played roles that were inevitably sultry—roles that Miss Dandridge often discussed with candor and just a shade of amusement.

"I have a nice voice and it's pleasant," she once said. "It's got a lot of soul in it. Besides, people just seem to like to look at me."

Miss Dandridge climbed to motion picture stardom in 1954 in the all-Negro musical "Carmen Jones," for which she won an Academy Award nomination. She also appeared as Bess in "Porgy and Bess" (1959), and among her other films were "Island in the Sun" and "Tamango."

A Turning Point

Her role in "Carmen Jones," was, she said later, a turning point in her career.

"I never worked harder in my life, and it was the best break I've ever had," she told an interviewer in 1954. Then, musingly, she added:

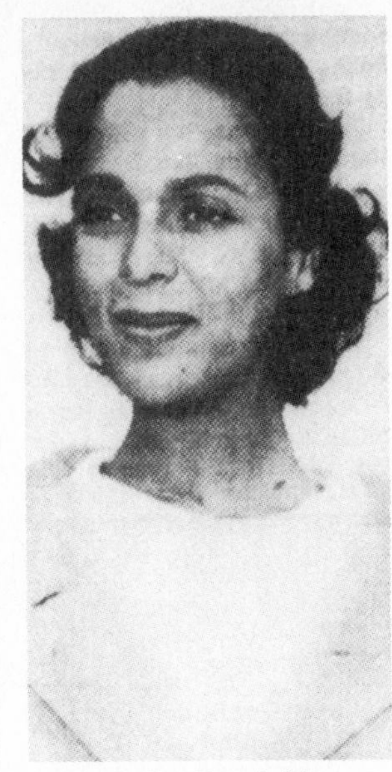

Dorothy Dandridge

"Carmen was quite a person, wasn't she? Before I was tested, Mr. Preminger [the producer-director] told me I seemed too sweet, too regal, that he didn't think I'd do. I said, 'Look, I know I can do it. I understand this type of woman. She's primitive, honest, independent, and real—that's why other women envy her.'"

Ironically, Miss Dandridge's voice in "Carmen Jones" as well as "Porgy and Bess" was dubbed.

Miss Dandridge was born in Cleveland, the daughter of a minister. She and her sister, Vivian, learned singing and dancing from her mother, Ruby, and were billed as "The Wonder Children," before school, church and social groups.

At the age of 4, Miss Dandridge was taken to Los Angeles. "I was one of those musical movie kids you hear about, with parts in pictures like the Marx Brothers' "A Day at the Races."

She dropped out of high school and with her sister and another girl formed a trio that sang with Jimmy Lunceford, a top band leader of the big band era of the nineteen-thirties.

In 1945, Miss Dandridge was married to Harold Nicholas, part of the Nicholas Brothers dance act. She retired from show business.

Before the marriage broke up six years later, Miss Dandridge had a daughter, who was born with a brain injury.

"I think it was really the heartache over my child and the failure of my marriage that forced me to make a success of my career," she said in 1954. "I had to keep busy. I threw myself into my work. It's a wonderful therapy. You don't have time to feel sorry for yourself."

She enrolled in a drama school whose students included Marilyn Monroe and Charles Chaplin Jr. She also sought work in the movies. "No producers knocked on my doors," she once recalled. "There just aren't that many parts for Negro actresses."

As a nightclub performer, however, Miss Dandridge rose quickly from a small Hollywood club to the Mocambo in 1951. Her appearance at the La Vie en Rose in New York in 1952 was a sellout.

Her gold lamé costumes, her sensuous delivery, her songs ("Love Isn't Born, It's Made," and "Talk Some Sweet Talk to Me") left fans, according to one observer, "goggle-eyed."

Quickly, Miss Dandridge became an international star, appearing in night clubs in London, New York, San Francisco, Los Angeles, Rio de Janeiro and São Paulo.

When Miss Dandridge was selected to play the title role of "Carmen Jones," her motion picture stardom was assured.

'Prejudice Is Such a Waste'

Miss Dandridge received a wave of publicity, and more often than not disarmed interviewers with her candor and no-nonsense approach.

"When you reach a certain position," she said, discussing racial bias, "people accept you more. And there are places where you are acclaimed as a performer, yet you know the doors would be shut if you walked in as plain Mrs. Sally Smith."

"It [prejudice] is such a waste," she continued. "It makes you logy and half-alive. It gives you nothing. It takes away. And it is superficial, like so many of our reactions today."

After "Porgy and Bess" was released, Miss Dandridge appeared in several films produced in France and England. She was married in 1959 to Jack Denison, a restaurant owner. They were divorced in 1962. They had no children.

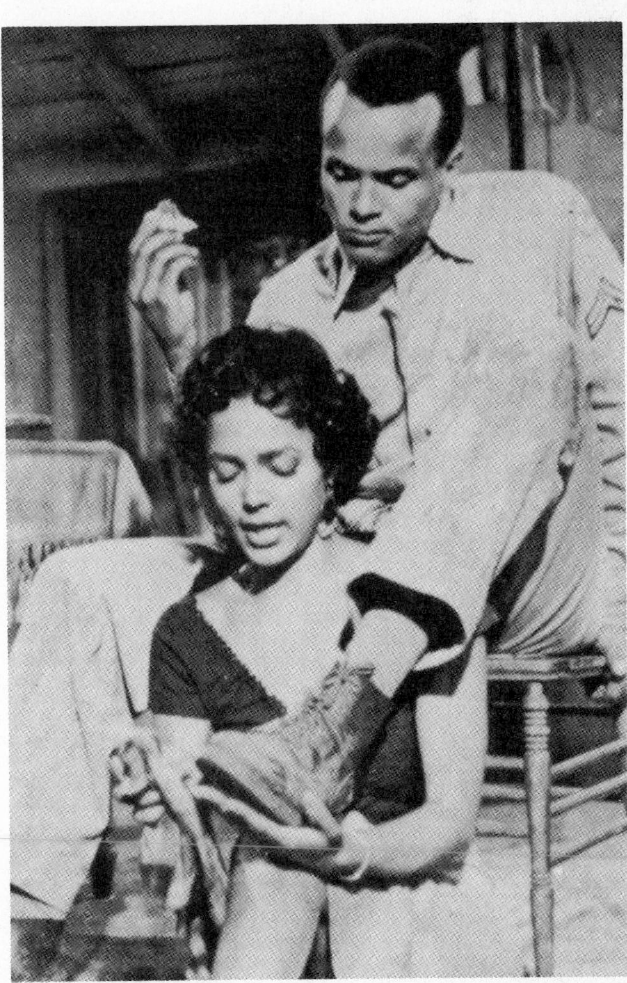

Dorothy Dandridge and Harry Belafonte starred in *Carmen Jones*.

The New York Times SUNDAY, APRIL 11, 1965.

Linda Darnell Dies of Burns at 43

CHICAGO, April 10 (AP)—Linda Darnell, who was regarded as one of the great natural beauties of the motion pictures, died in Cook County Hospital today of burns that covered 80 per cent of her body.

Death came at 2:25 P.M., Central standard time, to the 43-year-old brunette who had been seen by millions in such pictures as "Forever Amber" and "Letter to Three Wives."

She had been under intensive care in the hospital's Burn Treatment Center.

Her burns were suffered early Friday in a fire that damaged the home in suburban Glenview of Mrs. Jane Curtis, 38, her former secretary. Mrs. Curtis and her daughter, Patricia, 16, were burned less severely, and a neighbor was cut trying to reach the actress.

Firemen found Miss Darnell on the living room floor.

Mrs. Curtis said that she, her daughter and Miss Darnell had remained up late watching a television presentation of one of Miss Darnell's movies, "Star Dust."

Later, she said, Patricia was awakened by smoke, and awakened her mother and Miss Darnell.

"Intense heat was coming from the living room," Mrs. Curtis said. "Linda told us to grab wet towels, so we grabbed wet towels."

She said smoke was dense and flames drove her and her daughter back from the stairs, and they went to a second floor window, from which the girl jumped. She was assisted out by firemen.

"I thought she was behind me, but she was not," Mrs. Curtis said. "Linda went into the living room, apparently thinking we had gone downstairs."

Out of Public Eye

In recent years, Miss Darnell, a beautiful, brunette Texan who starred in "Forever Amber," edged toward show-business oblivion, occasionally appearing with minimum impact on live television and the summer stage.

However, as Miss Darnell's professional star dimmed, repeated television showings of her old movies, among them "Summer Storm," "Hangover Square" and particularly "No Way Out" and "A Letter to Three Wives," were firm reminders of her special flair for portraying sultry vixens before the Hollywood cameras.

Miss Darnell was a gifted actress—even in many bad pictures—who was prodded into the movie limelight in her early teens. She gained a career foothold but never quite made the big league of major box-office performers.

Miss Darnell was born in Dallas on Oct. 16, 1921, one of five children of a postal clerk. Her ambitious mother arranged dancing lessons for the girl who, at the age of 11, was modeling clothes and giving her age as 16. At 13 she had acquired brief experience with little-theater groups in Dallas and her alert mother saw to it that the girl was auditioned during the visits of talent scouts from the Hollywood studios.

The teen-ager aroused studio interest but was sent home from Hollywood and told to come back when she was 15. She did, and made her movie debut in a minor picture, "Hotel for Women." She was put under contract to 20th Century-Fox, where she continued to appear before the cameras, with occasional loan-outs, for the next 14 years. Her second film, equally trivial, was "Daytime Wife," opposite Fox's leading box-office property, Tyrone Power.

Films that followed included "Star Dust," "Brigham Young" and "Blood and Sand." By now Miss Darnell was known as one of Hollywood's young beauties. In frequent interviews she made it plain that she was dissatisfied with her successive roles of "sweet young things."

She also struck out for personal independence, leaving the home she shared with her family, who had moved from Dallas, and in 1944 marrying a studio cameraman, Peverell Marley. The couple adopted a daughter, Charlotte Mildred Marley, who is also called Lola. They were divorced eight years later.

In 1944 a United Artists film called "Summer Storm" made Hollywood and movie audiences aware of Miss Darnell's talent. As a scheming Russian peasant, in an adaptation of Chekhov's "The Shooting Party," she stole the picture. Three years later her big chance came in "Forever Amber," but the adaptation of Kathleen Winsor's best-selling novel was one of Hollywood's biggest flops. As the sensual lass who moved from a tavern to royal favor in Restoration England, Miss Darnell histrionically held her own. But the actress remained the focal point of an expensive, lumbering film that died at the box office. Consequently, Miss Darnell's prestige and career suffered a serious dent, although she acquitted herself professionally in such roles as the can-can dancer-victim of Jack the Ripper in the musicalized "Hangover Square."

Miss Darnell hit her stride and gave her best performances in two films directed by Joseph L. Mankiewicz, "No Way Out" and "A Letter to Three Wives." In the first, a 1950 drama about racial prejudice, the actress played a bitterly anti-Negro widow who changed her attitude. The second picture, a comedy made the previous year and the winner of several Oscars, found Miss Darnell perfectly cast as a wise-cracking girl of modest means out to snag herself a rich husband.

Linda Darnell in *Forever Amber*, 1947.

"Why don'cha show more of what you got?" advised Thelma Ritter in one scene. "Wear some beads."

"What I got don't need beads," Miss Darnell snapped.

For once the critics and the public, and Hollywood and Miss Darnell, all were in solid agreement.

In 1954 the actress was married to Phillip Liebmann, a New York brewer. She obtained a divorce in 1955.

Left Fox in '52

Miss Darnell ended her association with Fox in 1952. Toward the end of her contract her films had been less than notable and the actress fared little better as a free-lance performer in such movies as "Second Chance" and "Dakota Incident." She went to Italy and made two pictures there, including "Forbidden Women," a drama, and "The Last Five Minutes," a comedy with Vittorio De Sica.

Her last film shown here was "Zero Hour," opposite Dana Andrews, in 1957. Another Paramount drama, a Western called "Black Spurs" and co-starring Rory Calhoun, is due for release in May.

Miss Darnell made her stage debut in 1956 in Phoenix, Ariz., in "A Roomful of Roses." Her notices were also generally good in "Tea and Sympathy," in which she toured. Her one subsequent Broadway appearance was in the brief "Harbour Lights." She made appearances in four television dramas in 1956 and won favorable personal reviews.

In 1957 the actress was married to Merle Roy Robertson, an airline pilot. They were divorced five years later.

Miss Darnell made her debut as a supper club entertainer in 1960 and toured with brief success. In recent years she toured on the summer theater circuit, often attended by her daughter, now 17 years old, who attends a private school.

Linda Darnell, Ann Sothern and Jeanne Crain in *A Letter to Three Wives*, 1949.

The New York Times SATURDAY, SEPTEMBER 23, 1961.

Marion Davies, Film Actress, Dead of Cancer

One of the Last Survivors of an Ultra-Lavish Period—Protegee of Hearst

HOLLYWOOD, Calif., Sept. 22 (AP) — Marion Davies, a movie actress in a fabulous era, died today of cancer after a three-year illness.

Death came at 7 P. M. at Cedars of Lebanon Hospital, where she had been a patient since May 16. She had undergone jaw surgery June 7 for osteomyelitis—inflammation of the bone marrow.

A friend said that early in her illness Miss Davies had been told she had cancer but she had tried not to believe it. Her age has been given variously as either 61 or 64.

At her bedside were her husband, Capt. Horace Brown, a physician and two nurses. Her sister, Mrs. Rose Adlon, was also at the hospital.

Tired, Sad and Lonely

Marion Cecilia Davies, a Brooklyn girl of gamin qualities and porcelain prettiness, rose to Hollywood's heights as one of the wealthiest and most publicized of its movie nobility. Death, however, claimed a tired, sad and lonely woman.

While fame, in the sense of the public's awareness, came early to the former chorus girl for whom a fortune literally in the millions was spent in attempts to turn her into a high-magnitude dramatic star, frustration was also the reward of that costly search for serious, artistic success.

Miss Davies was one of the last survivors of the ultra-lavish era of Hollywood, that period of the great extravagances: the gold-plated Hispano-Suiza, the marble palaces transplanted from Europe to the sands of California, the sudden champagne decisions by hosts to take their week-end yachting guests on six-month excursions (all expenses paid) around the world.

It was a real-life spectacular for which Miss Davies, bubbly in spirits and enormously generous, needed no special coaching, and she played her role of a self-appointed movie queen with a skill seldom evident in her camera roles.

For a time during her career struggle the vivacious, blue-eyed, blonde beauty held court in a fourteen-room "bungalow" on the movie lot. She insisted on long luncheon breaks, at which she served champagne to one and all. Often an orchestra was hired to play mood music for her while she was on the film set.

The turning point in Miss Davies' life that changed her from just another attractive girl in a long line of kicking chorines was the evening that William Randolph Hearst, the late publisher, walked into Florenz Ziegfeld's Follies of 1917 and fell in love with her.

There is a report that he went to the show every night for eight weeks, just to gaze at her. She was 17 years old then (or 20, depending on which of two birth dates appearing in reference books is accurate) and Mr. Hearst, rich, powerful, willful, was either thirty-four or thirty-seven years her senior.

That meeting started a relationship that lasted thirty-two years, until his death in August, 1951. They lived together and traveled together (Mr. Hearst died at her home in Beverly Hills), and although in Beverly their relationship a secret initially, there was no effort to hide it as the years passed.

They wanted to marry each other, according to the new biography recently published on Mr. Hearst—"Citizen Hearst," by W. A. Swanberg—but Mrs. Hearst refused to give him a divorce. Mr. Swanberg writes that Mr. and Mrs. Hearst, parents of five sons, remained on friendly terms, but Mr. Hearst continued his relationship with Miss Davies through the years. He used his vast wealth and his great chain of newspapers and magazines to foster Miss Davies' career as an actress.

Marion Davies was one of four daughters of Bernard J. Douras, a New York lawyer who was a City Magistrate from 1918 to 1930. She followed her three older sisters, Reine, Ethel and Rose, onto the stage, taking the name Davies, which also had been selected by Reine.

The future actress attended Public School 93 in Brooklyn, where she was captain of a championship basketball team. Later she was a student at the Convent of the Sacred Heart at Hastings, N. Y.

Her first stage role was that of a chorus girl in "Chu Chin Chow." Next, she was a featured dancer in "Oh, Boy." Early in her career Miss Davies also posed for artists, modeling for magazine covers and illustrations painted by Harrison Fisher and Howard Chandler Christy. Mr. Ziegfeld saw her in "Oh, Boy" and hired her for his Follies, where Mr. Hearst first saw her.

Miss Davies, who was described as fun-loving, gay, warm and sentimental, captivated Mr. Hearst, who decided to make the mass plunge into the moviemaking world and establish his protégée as a great star.

Mr. Swanberg writes:

"Although both Hearst and the young lady herself knew that she had things to learn about acting, he had no doubt about his ability to transform her into a vibrant Galatea. She had beauty and talent. He would supply the instructors, the writers and directors to bring it out, and the publicity to exploit it.

"His creative instinct, so entangled with jimcrack tricks to beguile the public, was excited. **He was possessive about everything he owned. Miss Davies was his most prized possession whom he would train, groom, push, and publicize until she** reached the heights, eclipsing the reigning Mary Pickford."

Mr. Hearst hired the most expensive talent he could find to groom Miss Davies. He paid Miss Frances Marion, a top scenarist of the day, $2,000 a week to write for her. He purchased a former amusement center at Second Avenue and 127th Street, in New York, as a movie studio, and hired costly directors and publicity men.

Later he transferred his operations to Culver City, purchasing Cosmopolitan Pictures in order to set up a studio for Miss Davies.

But she was not a great actress and the films she made were not among the more impressive or profitable releases handled for Cosmopolitan by Metro-Goldwyn-Mayer. Bosley Crowther, the movie critic for The New York Times, tells this anecdote in his biography of Louis B. Mayer, "Hollywood Rajah":

"At a company sales convention in Los Angeles in 1927, the displeasure (over the frothy, unprofitable films starring Miss Davies) was brought to the floor when Mayer made so bold as to ask the salesmen if any of them had questions they would like to put to him.

"'Why do we handle Miss Davies' pictures?' one intrepid salesman bluntly asked.

"The question startled the gathering, and for a moment Mayer did not reply. He obviously had not expected to be so candidly taxed. But he bravely rose to the occasion. First he mentioned the modest success of one of Miss Davies' pictures. Then he reminded his audience that the actress was the close, dear friend of Mr. Hearst, the powerful publisher whose friendship and newspapers were of help to the studio.

"'Furthermore,' Mayer continued, 'I would like to remind you gentlemen that Mr. Hearst is the son of that great patriot, former United States Senator from California, the late George Hearst.' And with that he launched into an eloquent account of how George Hearst had left Missouri as a young man, made the perilous overland journey to California, opened great mining territory and contributed vastly to the building of the American West.

"'This,' said Mayer, 'is the point I wish to impress upon you gentlemen here today. We

(continued)

Marion Davies in *The Cardboard Lover*, 1928.

live in a land of opportunity. God bless America!'

"Tears sprang to his eyes and his voice quavered, as he addressed himself directly to the salesman. 'Does that answer your question?'

"'It does,' said the poor guy and sat down."

Miss Davies wanted to try heavy dramatic roles and once asked Mr. Hearst to let her play Sadie Thompson in "Rain." He was indignant and refused to consider her in a prostitute's role. Mr. Swanberg writes that Mr. Hearst had a "weakness for mawkish sentimentality" about Miss Davies' parts. He would not let her play the role of a mother, for example, because he did not want her to appear as a mature woman.

Another attempt of Miss Davies' to get a more taxing role set off a famous vendetta in Hollywood. She wanted to play in "The Barretts of Wimpole Street," but Irving Thalberg insisted on giving the part to Norma Shearer, and the two actresses became enemies. Miss Shearer's name, incidentally, was kept out of the Hearst newspapers and magazines for a long period.

Among the motion pictures in which Miss Davies starred between 1920 and 1938 were "When Knighthood Was in Flower," "Little Old New York," "Beverly of Graustark," "Bachelor Father," "The Cardboard Lover," "Floradora Girl" and "Operator 13." A number of her pictures, including "Cain and Mabel" and "Ever Since Eve," were not box-office successes.

She had a stutter, and was afraid with the advent of the talkies that she would be able to act no longer in films, but the impediment proved to be no special handicap. When Miss Davies gave up acting after eighteen years of film making it was estimated that Mr. Hearst had lost $7,000,000 in his futile attempt to make her the nation's top star.

Miss Davies had an audience for her films as long as Mr. Hearst was alive. It has been reported that during his last years, when they were alone and watched films together in her home, he sat by the hour looking at her old movies with tears in his eyes.

She was said to have been less perturbed than Mr. Hearst was when Orson Welles produced his film "Citizen Kane," a movie that bore a remarkable likeness to the events in Mr. Hearst's life. Many persons assumed that the powerful publisher Charles Kane in the film was Mr. Hearst, the huge castle Xanadu was in reality Mr. Hearst's fabulous estate San Simeon and the blonde young singer he tried to turn into a diva, although she had no voice, was in reality Miss Davies.

Although frustrated in her dramatic ambitions, and in his for her, Miss Davies became financially enriched. She had extensive real estate holdings in New York and California. She began to buy Manhattan real estate in the middle Nineteen Thirties on the advice of Arthur Brisbane, who was real estate adviser as well as editor for Mr. Hearst.

Among her properties in New York were the twenty-two-story aluminum-sheathed Davies Building, erected recently at Park Avenue and Fifty-seventh Street; the new seventeen-story Douras Building at Madison Avenue and Fifty-fifth Street, and Fifth Avenue's Squibb Building.

In 1955 Miss Davies bought the $2,000,000 Desert Inn at Palm Springs, but she sold it in 1960. She also owned residential acreage in Bel Air, Beverly Hills and Santa Monica.

In 1957 a mansion that Miss Davies had owned on the West Coast was torn down to make way for a modern hotel. That landmark was Ocean House at Santa Monica, built in 1928 for $2,000,000 and furnished with entire rooms imported from Europe at a cost of $1,250,000.

The residence had fifty-five rooms, a 110-foot swimming pool, a projecting room and a theatre. She sold the home in 1945 for only $600,000.

After Mr. Hearst's death, Miss Davies lived in a slightly smaller Spanish-style castle on a hilltop in Beverly Hills.

Mr. Hearst never forgot that when he was once in financial trouble and bankers refused to lend him money Miss Davies saved him with a loan of $1,000,000, without a note of any kind and with no request for interest.

Trust Fund Established

Before his death, Mr. Hearst had established a trust fund of 30,000 preferred shares (15 per cent) of the Hearst Corporation. Miss Davies received the income from the stock during her lifetime, and at her death the principal reverted to Mr. Hearst's five sons. In his will, Mr. Hearst referred to her as "my loyal friend, Miss Marion Douras . . .".

Two months after Mr. Hearst died, Miss Davies was married to Captain Brown, a former sea captain. Eight months later, Miss Davies filed for divorce, but withdrew the suit. She again sued for divorce in 1954, but again withdrew her suit.

Miss Davies served for several years as president of the Motion Picture Relief Fund. She also contributed both time and money to various charitable enterprises. Her benefactions, especially to sick children, brought her a citation as "woman of the year" in 1958 from the Hollywood Chamber of Commerce.

Among these benefactions, a gift of $1,500,000 to build a children's wing at the Medical Center of the University of California at Los Angeles in 1957 was notable. The wing was named for her.

Marion Davies in *Show People.*

Marion Davies and Robert Montgomery in *Blondie of the Follies,* 1932.

The New York Times SATURDAY, OCTOBER 1, 1955.

James Dean, Film Actor, Killed in Crash of Auto

PASO ROBLES, Calif., Sept. 30 (AP)—James Dean, 24-year-old motion picture actor, was killed tonight in an automobile accident near here.

A spokesman for Warner Brothers, for whom Mr. Dean had just completed "The Giant," said he had no details of the accident except that the actor was en route to a sports car meeting at Salinas. He was driving a small German speedster.

The actor had appeared in "East of Eden," released last April, and in "Rebel Without a Cause," still unreleased.

Mr. Dean was the star of Elia Kazan's film, "East of Eden," taken from John Steinbeck's novel. It was his first starring role in films. The year before he had attracted attention of critics as the young Arab servant in the Broadway production of "The Immoralist." His portrayal won for him the Donaldson and Perry awards.

James Dean and Elizabeth Taylor in *Giant*.

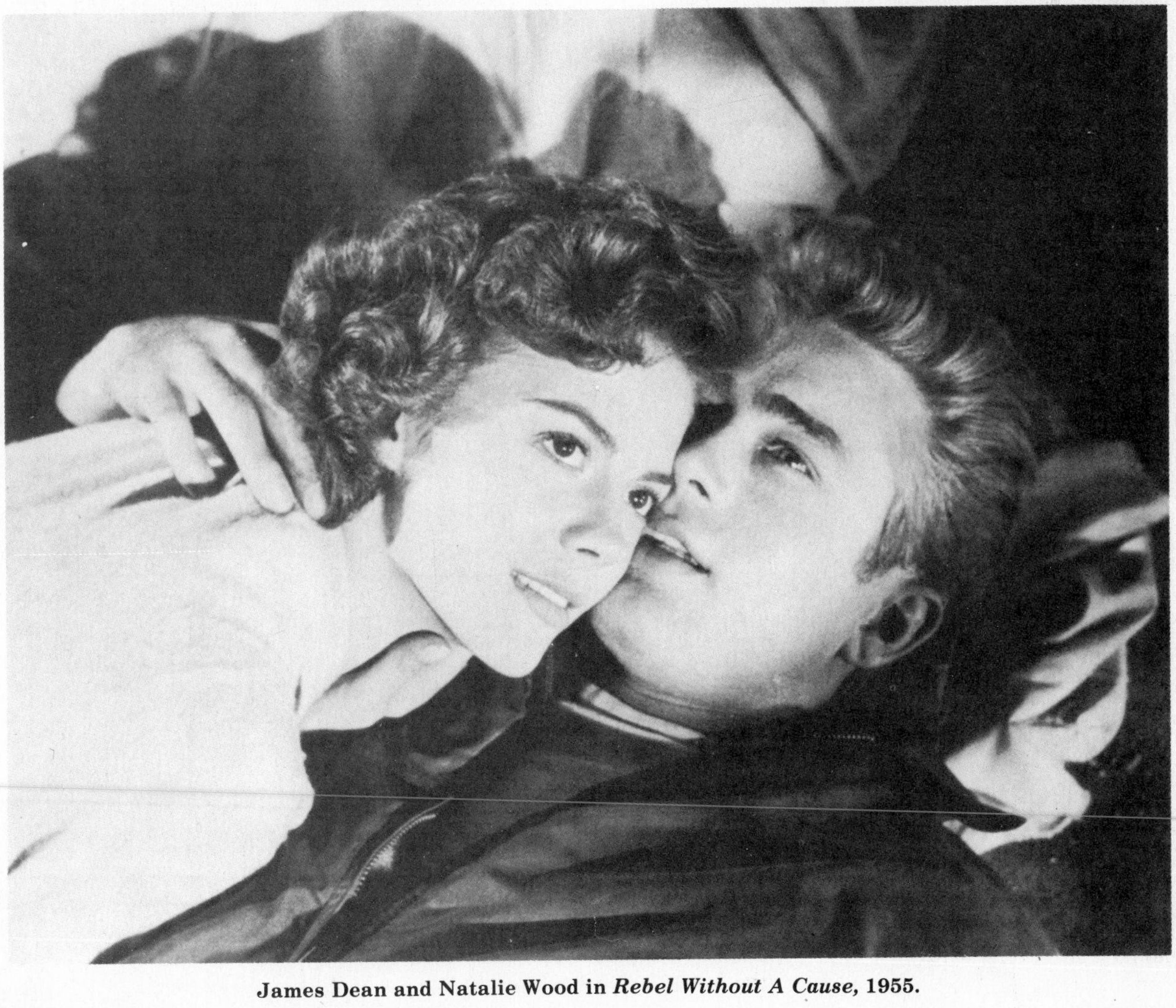

James Dean and Natalie Wood in *Rebel Without A Cause*, 1955.

James Dean in *Giant*.

"All the News That's Fit to Print"

The New York Times.

LATE CITY EDITION

U. S. Weather Bureau Report (Page 62) forecasts: Rain followed by partly cloudy and colder today. Fair, cold tomorrow. Temp. range: 58—25. Yesterday: 56.3—38.4

VOL. CVIII..No. 36,888. NEW YORK, THURSDAY, JANUARY 22, 1959. FIVE CENTS

10c beyond 100-mile zone from New York City, higher in air delivery cities.

Cecil De Mille, 77, Pioneer of Movies, Dead in Hollywood

Special to The New York Times.

HOLLYWOOD, Calif., Jan. 21—Cecil B. De Mille died of a heart ailment today in his home on De Mille Drive here. He was 77 years old.

At his bedside when he died were a daughter, Cecilia, and her husband, Joseph Harper. Mrs. De Mille, who is 85 and has been ailing for several years, was not informed until later in the morning. They had been married for fifty-six years.

Although confined to his home since last Saturday, Mr. De Mille continued to work. He was preparing to start filming "On My Honor," a history of the Boy Scout movement and its founder, the late Lord Baden-Powell.

More than 1,000 messages of condolence from persons in all walks of life had been received by late afternoon at the Hollywood office of Western Union.

In addition to their own daughter Cecilia, Mr. and Mrs. De Mille adopted three children. They are Mrs. Katherine Quinn, a former actress and wife of Anthony Quinn; Richard De Mille, who is studying for a doctorate in psychiatry at the

Continued on Page 31, Column 2

PRESIDENT SEES 'SCHIZOPHRENIA' IN BUDGET CRITICS

Says They Are 'on All Sides' of the Question—Supports Estimate of Revenue

INFLATION FIGHT URGED

Eisenhower Tells Newsmen He Still 'Despises' Controls on Wages and Prices

By EDWIN L. DALE Jr.
Special to The New York Times

WASHINGTON, Jan. 21—President Eisenhower said today that critics of his $77,030,000,000 budget were suffering from "budgetary schizophrenia."

The President described the new political malady as being "on all sides" of the budget question. Some critics, he said, want more spending, while some complain that the budget is too high.

In popular terminology, schizophrenia is known as a split personality. That was clearly the sense in which the President used it today at his news conference. [Question 13, Page 14.]

The President took up various complaints about the budget in turn.

To those who charge its revenue estimate of $77,100,000,000 is overoptimistic, the President retorted that the estimates of "the greatest experts that I know of" ranged from $75,000,000,000 to $78,000,000,000, with some running higher than $78,000,000,000.

Cites 1921 Budget Act

To those who complain that it cannot be balanced without certain Congressional actions affecting revenue, the President replied that he is "not only authorized but directed" by the Budget and Accounting Act of 1921 to include revenue legislation if revenues under existing law will not cover the expenditures he believes are necessary.

And to those who complain that the budget is "political," the President recalled that "I am not running for anything." He said his budget represented his view of what was best for America.

"Now if we get down to this business of who is using the budget as a political football," he concluded, "I assure you it is not I."

Defense Issue Avoided

The President did not address himself specifically to one common criticism of the budget—that it does not provide for enough defense or enough domestic services of the Government. His Budget Message said, however, that the budget "will effectively and responsibly carry out the Government's role in dealing with the problems and the opportunities of the period ahead."

Early maneuvering for the first skirmishes in the battle of the budget continued today. Republican Senators introduced airport construction and housing bills for the Administration—each of them requiring considerably less immediate and future spending than Democratic bills with leadership backing.

On other economic subjects today the President took long-familiar positions.

He said he did not think there was any conflict between

Continued on Page 14, Column 6

Governor Indicates A 2 Billion Budget

By LEO EGAN
Special to The New York Times

ALBANY, Jan. 21—Governor Rockefeller estimated today that state expenditures in the next fiscal year would be $235,000,000 greater than in the current year.

On the basis of his budget preview, next year's state budget would go above $2,000,000,000 for the first time. Expenditures in the current year are now estimated at $1,801,000,000. The current year ends March 31.

Among the reasons given for the prospective increase were an "urgently needed" $18,500,000 rise in state assistance to local governments, including New York City, and an "urgently needed" $20,000,000 pay increase for state employes.

All but $1,500,000 of the bal-

Continued on Page 20, Column 3

Bankers Trust Co. And Manufacturers Discuss a Merger

By ALBERT L. KRAUS

The Manufacturers Trust Company and the Bankers Trust Company, New York City's third and sixth largest banks, are weighing a merger.

The proposal, still in the exploratory stages, would create a fourth New York City institution with more than $5,000,000,000 in total resources.

It would join Manufacturers Trust's branch system, the largest in the city, with that of Bankers Trust to give the resulting institution undisputed place as the city's most extensive "retail" ... ing system.

In contrast to "w... banks that serve larg... ness customers, ... banks also seek the d... and loans of small saver... borrowers. Confirmation...

Continued on Page 52, Colu...

EISENHOWER WARY ON JOHNSON'S BILL

He Asserts Racial Disputes Are Rights Unit's Concern, but Says Mind Is Open

By ANTHONY LEWIS
Special to The New York Times.

WASHINGTON, Jan. 21—Doubts about the wisdom of Senator Lyndon B. Johnson's proposal for a Federal conciliation service on racial matters were expressed today by President Eisenhower.

The President told his news conference that conciliating racial controversies was part of the Civil Rights Commission's job and that a new organization now would not be "fruitful." But he said his mind was open on the idea and he could be convinced. [Question 12, Page 14.]

The comment reflected the lengthy effort within the Administration to work out its own civil rights legislative package.

The Justice Department has been pressing hard for proposals broader than Senator Johnson's, and dealing specifically with problems arising from school integration.

It is now probable that at least a substantial part of the Justice Department package, including some school proposals, will win the President's approval. The Administration program may be announced next week.

The President touched on several aspects of the racial issue. Five of the nineteen questions at the news conference dealt with that subject.

The President showed particular concern for the children of military personnel shut out of

Continued on Page 24, Column 5

M'ELROY DEFENDS CUTBACKS IN ARMY SLATED THIS YEAR

Argues Before Senators—Asks House Unit to Allow Smaller Reserve Force

By JACK RAYMOND
Special to The New York Times

WASHINGTON, Jan. 21—Neil H. McElroy, Secretar... Defense, argued energ... before the Sena... ices ...

la... by... Ar... ma...

Con... prop... prov... Rese... through...

It is ... propriati... to recomm... this year. ... voiced h's ... Budget Me... Mr. McElro... again in his...

The forced ... "an unpreced... from past policy... ditionally recogn... executive branch... ernment must hav... bility in providin... forces," the Secret... fense wrote.

Plea May Be Ign...

However, Congressio... ers, particularly Repres... Carl Vinson, Democrat ... gia, chairman of the ... Armed Services Committee... made it clear that they wi... heed the Administration's ... peal.

The Pentagon is worried a... more than the size of the ... serve forces. It is known to f... that a formidable principle... involved, because the Congres... sional action might be used in... other parts of the budget and further curtail Executive control over the armed forces.

The House Armed Services Committee, meanwhile, made extension of the military draft its first major business of this session.

It made plans for hearings next Monday to cover a four-year extension of the Selective Service Act, the doctors' draft

Continued on Page 10, Column 4

Associated Press Wirephoto

...s gathered yesterday outside the Presidential Palace in Havana. ...enter is statue of Maximo Gómez, a hero of Cuban independence.

Fuller Soviet News of U. S. Likely From Mikoyan Trip

By HARRISON E. SALISBURY

Anastas I. Mikoyan's trip to the United States seems ...ly to produce a shake-up in Soviet diplomatic and news ...orting because of the sharp contrast between the real ...rica and the America ...he Soviet press has been ...bing.

...Mikoyan, a Soviet First ... Premier, said nothing ... on this question. Pri... ...wever, he indicated a ...ness of it in con... ...nd comments with ...ccompanied him on ...the United States. ...an arrived in Co... ...ly today after a ...gentia, Nfld. His ...w York made a ... there Tuesday

...ications that ... Khrushchev ... some time ...dership is ... the Unit-

...ntrast

...oviet re... ...s condi... ...n after ... Khru... ...iption

...ided ...e... ...d ...e

...y would

...n Page 3, Column 4

...etary Surrenders ...nquiry on Hotel Loan Fraud

By EMANUEL PERLMUTTER

The missing secretary of George A. Brenner surrendered yesterday for questioning about the alleged loan frauds of the former Westchester surrogate. She had been sought by New York and Westchester authorities for a week.

Mrs. Norma Bucher arrived voluntarily late yesterday at the office of District Attorney Frank S. Hogan, accompanied by Maurice K. Siegel, her lawyer.

She is secretary of the Shelton Towers Hotel, 522 Lexington Avenue, for whose lease and refurbishment Mr. Brenner is accused of having committed larcenies and forgeries totaling $318,000.

Westchester officials, who also have been investigating Mr. Brenner, said unofficially yesterday that they believed a complete audit of his tangled financial operations would disclose about $1,300,000 in frauds.

Last night, on application by Assistant District Attorney Allen Harris of Mr. Hogan's staff, General Sessions Judge John A. Mullen held Mrs. Bucher in $2,500 bail as a material witness. She posted bond and was released.

In another development, the independent International Longshoremen's Association was injected into the Brenner investigation. Mr. Brenner, former county judge and surrogate in Westchester, was attorney for the union until 1955.

William B. Mischo, general counsel to the I. L. A., said yesterday he had informed Mr. Hogan's office that an audit of the union's books disclosed "a number" of promissory notes to banks, factors and discount

Continued on Page 16, Column 4

Heavy Fog Creeps Over City, Causing Delay

The New York Times (by Ernest Sisto)

View of midtown Manhattan, looking south toward Empire State Building, upper center

By GEORGE BARRETT

Fog closed down on the city yesterday, delaying planes and forcing midday motorists in some sections to use their headlights. The billowing gray curtain delighted photographers but proved a hazard for travelers. About thirty flights were held up at New York International Airport, Idlewild, Queens; some incoming planes were delayed up to two hours. Several flights bound for International Airport were diverted to La Guardia Airport or to Newark, and some were sent to Washington. The slow-up in operations began at International at 12:30 P. M. and continued for almost two hours before full

Continued on Page 43, Column 4

WEST TO PREPARE FOR A BERLIN TALK

Committee Will Re-examine Policy in Expectation of May Parley With Soviet

By E. W. KENWORTHY
Special to The New York Times.

WASHINGTON, Jan. 21—A committee of the United States, Britain, France and West Germany will set to work soon on a re-examination of policy on Germany in preparation for an expected conference with the Soviet Union this spring.

It is taken for granted here that events of the last three months—the succession of Soviet notes and the United States visit of Anastas I. Mikoyan, Soviet First Deputy Premier—have made a conference on Germany, Berlin and European security virtually certain.

The Western powers would like the conference to take place ...n May so that active discus...ons might be in progress ...ound May 27. This is the dead... that the Soviet Union set ...s note of Nov. 27 for turn... occupation functions over ...t Germany unless the ...n Allies had by that date ... to talks on the German ...

...e Factor Is Cited

"Time is pressing," one official emphasized today. "It is not simply a matter of agreeing to a conference with the Russians. The Western position must be thoroughly prepared."

The committee that will re-examine the Western position is actually an extension of the so-called Working Group on German Unification and European Security.

This group was set up in the fall of 1955 following the foreign ministers' conference in Geneva, a conference designed to carry further the agreement in principle reached by the heads of Government in July of that year to unify Germany by free elections within the context of European security. The foreign ministers' conference got nowhere.

The working group set up by the United States, Britain, France and West Germany has met periodically since then, usually in Paris or London. The European nations were usually represented by officials on the level of chiefs of the political divisions in the foreign minis-

Continued on Page 3, Column 2

EISENHOWER SAYS MIKOYAN IS AWARE U.S. BARS COERCION

Describing Chat, He Reports Russian Knows Nation Will Explore Any Peace Path

SOVIET LINE IS DECRIED

President Notes It Was 'Hard to Swallow' View Moscow Alone Is Seeking Amity

Transcript of news conference and summary, Page 14.

By FELIX BELAIR Jr.
Special to The New York Times.

WASHINGTON, Jan. 21—President Eisenhower gave Anastas I. Mikoyan to understand last week that the United States stood ready to explore all avenues toward peace any time and any place, but "simply won't be pushed around."

In making this known at his news conference today, the President said it appeared to be the chief purpose of Mr. Mikoyan, a Soviet First Deputy Premier, to persuade him that all of Moscow's proposals in the foreign-policy field were intended to promote peace and that the United States was hindering peace in opposing them. [Questions 2 and 10, Page 14.]

President Eisenhower said he found this thesis "a little bit hard to swallow."

He said he was quite certain that the Soviet leader had been convinced by his two-week tour that the United States wanted peace and that Congress and the people were united behind the Administration's foreign policy. But he insisted that Mr. Mikoyan had made no concrete proposals during their talk last Saturday. [Question 15.]

Dillon Tells of Trade Bid

The President's brief review of his conversation with Mr. Mikoyan coincided with testimony by a high State Department official that the Soviet leader had shown no interest in expanding trade "except on his own terms."

C. Douglas Dillon, Under Secretary of State for Economic Affairs, told the Senate Foreign Relations Committee that these terms included the following:

¶"Repeal of Congressional prohibitions on most-favored-nation treatment for the Soviet Union and on the importation of Russian furs."

¶"The grant of large-scale, long-term credits to cover Soviet purchases."

Soviet Purpose Noted

Mr. Dillon told the committee in closed session that he had been disappointed at Mr. Mikoyan's lack of interest when he suggested to him "some of the things the Soviet might do to promote increased trade."

Mr. Dillon said the Government would be glad to see an increase in peaceful trade with the Soviet Union.

"We must also realize that the purpose of the Soviets is to procure the advanced types of critical and industrial equipment they need to hasten their industrial development," he added.

"The Soviet exports offered in exchange for these imports are primarily industrial raw

Continued on Page 2, Column 3

Downtown Renewal Gets City's Backing

By PAUL CROWELL

Private interests supporting the proposed $1,000,000,000 redevelopment of lower Manhattan received assurance yesterday that the city would cooperate with their plans.

The assurance was given by Mayor Wagner and Manhattan Borough President Hulan E. Jack as they jointly made public a favorable report by a nine-member committee. The project was referred to the committee by the Board of Estimate in October.

The $1,000,000,000 redevelopment plan was sponsored by the Downtown - Lower Manhattan Association. The committee that studied it was headed by Mr. Jack.

The redevelopment plan affects 564 acres south of Canal Street. It calls for wholesale razing of old buildings, the

Continued on Page 18, Column 5

Cecil B. De Mille Dies on Coast; Film Industry Pioneer Was 77

Continued From Page 1, Col. 4

University of Southern California, and John De Mille, who is in the real estate business here. Also surviving are thirteen grandchildren and two great-grandchildren.

Barnum of the Movies

Cecil Blount De Mille was the Phineas T. Barnum of the movies—a showman extraordinary.

A pioneer in the industry, he used the broad medium of the screen to interpret in "colossal" and "stupendous" spectacles the story of the Bible, the splendor that was Egypt, the glory that was Rome. He dreamed in terms of millions, marble pillars, golden bathtubs and mass drama; spent enormous sums to produce the rich effects for which he became famous.

During his lifetime, Mr. De Mille produced more than seventy major films, noted for their weight and mass rather than for subtlety or finely shaded artistry.

In 1953 he won an Academy Award for "The Greatest Show on Earth," which had been released a year earlier. Previously he had won neither an Oscar nor the New York Film Critics annual award.

Won Box-office Awards

The fact that his first Oscar did not come until forty years after he had produced one of the earliest four-reel feature films, "The Squaw Man," was brushed off with a characteristic De Millean gesture:

"I win my awards at the box office."

This was true. His pageants and colossals awed the urban, suburban and backwoods audiences. By 1946 his personal fortune, despite his regal spending habits, was estimated at $8,000,000.

The producer basked in publicity's intense glare in late 1944-45 when he made a heroic issue of a demand by the union of which he was a member that he pay a $1 contribution to its political action fund. He had **been in radio about a decade by that time, staging shows for** a soap company at a reported salary of $5,000 a week.

Mr. De Mille carried the fee fight to the courts, was defeated, and then went on a one-man campaign against political assessments by unions. He later sought reinstatement in the union, but failed to get it.

Mr. De Mille was born at De Mille Corners, a backwoods crossroads in Ashfield, Mass., on Aug. 12, 1881, while his parents were touring New England with a stock company. His father, Henry Churchill De Mille, was of French-Dutch ancestry; his mother, the former Matilda Beatrice Samuel, of English stock.

At 17 he went on the stage. He played in "Lord Chumley," "The Warrens of Virginia" (which he adapted to the screen later), "The Prince Chap" and "Hearts Are Trumps."

In the cast of "Hearts Are Trumps," was Constance Adams, daughter of a New Jersey judge, engaged in a small part. They were married Aug. 16, 1902, four days after Mr. De Mille's twenty-first birthday.

In 1913 he was having lunch with Jesse Lasky when the talk turned to movies. Mr. De Mille **threw in his lot with the ambitious Lasky and with a newcomer in the theatre, Sam Goldwyn. All three reached the top rung in the movie world, though finally along separate paths.**

The first product of the new movie company—The Jesse L. Lasky Feature Play Company —was a screen version of "The Squaw Man." It was turned out in an abandoned stable in Los Angeles with crude equipment, but it bore Mr. De Mille's mark.

He was credited with many motion picture innovations. Indoor lighting was first tried out on an actor in "The Squaw Man." This picture, besides being the screen's first epic, was also the first to publicize the names of its stars.

On his first day as head of the Lasky-Goldwyn-De Mille combine, Mr. De Mille signed three unknowns—a $5 cowpoke named Hal Roach, an oil-field hand named Bill (Hopalong Cassidy) Boyd and a thin-nosed teenager who called herself Gloria Swanson. This was the nucleus around which he built his galaxy of screen stars.

To Mr. De Mille was attributed the inspiration for doing different versions of a popular picture, a possibility everyone else had overlooked. He is also supposed to have conceived of opening films with a printed cast of characters. The so-called "sneak preview"—showing a film to a test audience—was another contribution.

Switched to Americana

The first "Ten Commandments," produced in 1923 at a cost of $1,400,000, made money. From that time on Mr. De Mille wallowed in extravagant props and super-gorgeous sets. It was a good formula. It worked in "The Crusades." "The Sign of the Cross." "King of Kings," "Cleopatra" and a long list of other De Mille spectaculars.

In the latter part of his career Mr. De Mille switched from Scriptural subjects to the American scene. He turned out flamboyant chunks of Americana in "The Plainsman," taken from the lives of Wild Bill Hickok and Buffalo Bill; "The Buccaneer," a dramatic account of the life of the pirate Jean Lafitte; "Union Pacific," and "Reap the Wild Wind," a story about Key West.

"The Buccaneer," originally produced in 1937, was remade last year, with Mr. De Mille acting in a supervisory role. Unlike the new "The Ten Commandments," "The Buccaneer" was what the trade called a "remake."

"The Ten Commandments," however, was a completely new version of the Bible story and differed greatly from his first film of that title. "The Ten Commandments," issued in 1956, had grossed a reported $60,000,000 here and abroad by last fall.

Other expensive pictures Mr. De Mille produced were "Unconquered," in 1947, and "The Greatest Show on Earth," which cost an estimated total of $4,000,000 each. In 1949 he produced "Samson and Delilah" for about $3,000,000. During that same year he was named chairman of the Motion Picture Industry Council.

Mr. De Mille, who gave the University of Southern California a theatre in memory of his parents, was lavish with gifts to other institutions.

In June, 1958, he learned that plans to place translations of the hieroglyphics on the Egyptian obelisk in Central Park were being put aside for lack of funds. He offered to pay the cost of erecting four bronze plaques at the base of "Cleopatra's Needle," saying:

"As a boy, I used to look upon the hieroglyphics as so many wonderful pictures."

Two weeks ago, the Department of Parks announced that Mr. De Mille had donated $3,760 for the project.

Estelle Taylor as Miriam in Cecil B. DeMille's 1923 production of *The Ten Commandments*.

andy Dennis, Veteran Actress And Prize Winner, Is Dead at 54

By LEE A. DANIELS

andy Dennis, who as a young ac-s in the 1960's entranced Broadway Hollywood with performances that her two Tony Awards and an demy Award, died on Monday at home in Westport, Conn. She was 54 rs old.

lthough the exact cause of her h was not known, Ms. Dennis had fighting a long battle with cancer, Doris Elliott, a longtime friend. Dennis's death was confirmed by a esman for the Lewis Funeral e in Westport.

s. Dennis, born and raised in Ne-ka and blessed with an aura of ealing fragility, came to New York ge 18. Within a decade she had ioned a string of outstanding per-ances, and had earned the awards ove it.

Successive Tonys

ter making her movie debut in in a supporting role in "Splendor e Grass," she won a Tony Award in for her performance on Broad- opposite Jason Robards, as a so-worker in "A Thousand Clowns." A later she won another Tony as the tly offbeat mistress of a tycoon, played by Gene Hackman, in "Any Wednesday."

Then in 1966, she won an Academy Award as best supporting actress for her portrayal of Honey, the mousy, scared-of-her-own-shadow half of a young faculty couple alternately seduced and browbeaten by Elizabeth Taylor and Richard Burton in Edward Albee's scalding "Who's Afraid of Virginia Woolf."

She also drew critical praise for her 1967 role as the idealistic schoolteacher in the film "Up the Down Staircase."

Bosley Crowther, reviewing that film in The New York Times, praised her portrayal as "engagingly natural, sensitive, literate and thoroughly moving." He said that Ms. Dennis gave "a vivid performance of emotional range and depth," and added that she "sincerely acquaints us with a genuine loving person we can believe wants to find her pupils' wounds and, what's more, try to heal them, which she can't."

Her performance won the Moscow Film Festival prize for best actress.

Ms. Dennis's success was extraordinary for any actor or actress, but she seemed to recognize that such oversize fame might be ephemeral. In one interview she remarked that acting "isn't like painting a picture or writing a book."

"When you finish an acting stint, there's nothing except money," she said. "You have to keep going, giving the best you've got to get something intangible."

First Successes Not Duplicated

In her later roles, Ms. Dennis was never able to match the dazzling successes of her earlier years in terms of either public acclaim or favorable reviews. Where critics had once been charmed by her freshness and girl-next-door innocence, many later seemed to detect a mannered nervous quality that drove them to distraction.

This affected even Walter Kerr, the longtime Broadway critic, who had praised Ms. Dennis's performance in "Any Wednesday" with the lines: "Let me tell you about Sandy Dennis. There should be one in every home."

But in 1967, Mr. Kerr wrote tolerantly but pointedly of Ms. Dennis's "habit" of speaking onstage as though sentences "were poor crippled things that couldn't cross a street without making three false starts from the curb." Still, she continued to work steadily in films and plays and in summer stock.

The New Yorker film critic Pauline Kael once complained that Ms. Dennis "has made an acting style of postnasal drip," an assessment Ms. Dennis herself said was correct and worked to change.

Mr. Burton once described her as "one of the most genuine eccentrics I know of."

The New York Times THURSDAY, NOVEMBER 14, 1974

Vittorio De Sica, 73, Dies; Neorealist Movie Director

Special to The New York Times

PARIS, Nov. 13—Vittorio De Sica, the director of such film classics as "Shoeshine" and "The Bicycle Thief," died here today at the age of 73.

He had undergone surgery in recent months for the removal of cysts from his lungs, but family members here said they did not know the cause of death.

Leader of 'New Realism'

By MICHAEL T. KAUFMAN

As he himself once remarked, the life of Vittorio De Sica would have made a poor subject for one of his movies.

"The professional actor," said Mr. De Sica, who had been a professional actor for more than 50 years, "lives the life of a bourgeois, and he carries with him, even in his acting, something of the bourgeois attitude."

Mr. De Sica, a handsome and adored matinee idol and ladies' man, became the highest paid star in the Italian film, performing mostly in musical comedies. Impeccable in his dress, tall and handsome, with a following of adoring women, he was the model of the suave and urbane Roman sophisticate.

He was a collector of art, proud of his Modiglianis, Utrillos and Renoirs. He was a gambler addicted to roulette who frequently lost as much as $10,000 an evening at Monte Carlo.

And yet, in seeming conflict to all this, he was also the film maker who, well into middle age, moved from his highly successful acting career to focus on the harsh, small, painful dramas of the poor. With Roberto Rossellini and Luchino Visconti, he became a leader in the "new realism" movement that developed in Italy after the war.

"I love poor people," he said, adding that it was in their lives that drama could be found. "After all, if you exclude adultery, what drama is there in the bourgeoisie."

Mr. De Sica more or less stumbled into the theater against his will. As a child in Sora, a town between Naples and Rome, where he was born on July 7, 1901, he had aspired to follow in the footsteps of his father, a clerk with the Bank of Rome.

His father, a former journalist with many bohemian friends, had other ideas and prodded his shy son to perform, taking him to sing Neapolitan songs to wounded soldiers during World War I.

Still, Mr. De Sica, the oldest of two sons, hoped for the bureaucratic life and graduated from the University of Rome with a degree in accounting. After service in the army, he was casually recommended to Tatiana Pavlova, a well known Russian actress, whose troupe was performing in Rome. Impressed by the good looks of the 6-foot young man, she hired him for a walk-on role as a waiter.

'An Easy Business'

His career on the stage developed and flourished almost casually. "Acting is an easy business that I sometimes find very boring," he said in 1957. Last year, however, he said with a sigh, "If I had continued acting on the stage, I would have become a great actor."

In any case, Mr. De Sica rapidly became a highly successful and, in the opinion of many critics, highly polished actor. By the late nineteen-twenties he headed a very popular troupe with his first wife, Giuditta Rissone. In 1931 he appeared in his first movie, scoring an enormous success playing a romantic young dreamer. He played a succession of romantic young dreamers and developed a passionate army of women admirers.

Just before the war, he directed his first movie, "Twenty-Four Roses," starring in it as well. It was a conventional comedy that proved a commercial success. During the war he played in several "white telephone" movies, films that centered on the living rooms of the upper classes.

During this time Joseph Goebbels offered Mr. De Sica a post in the Nazi-dominated Italian film industry. Mr. De Sica begged off, saying he was working on a film in cooperation with the Vatican. He dawdled on that film for the duration of the war, finishing it three weeks after the American occupation.

Sophia Loren and Eleanora Brown in Vittorio De Sica's *Two Women*, 1960.

"What else could I do? I was not a Fascist," he recalled of that time, an era he documented in his latest success here, "The Garden of the Finzi-Continis." That movie was awarded an Oscar in 1972 as the best foreign film. It was Mr. De Sica's fifth Academy Award.

His first Oscar was for "The Bicycle Thief" in 1949. That had been preceded by "Shoeshine," a film shot in documentary style that told the story of the waifs of Rome scavenging and stealing to survive in the wake of war. The film was scorned by the Italian public. "Poor people do not like to look at poverty. It is not surprising," commented Mr. De Sica.

The film languished in obscurity until it was discovered by art-house audiences in New York and Paris. Despite the snowballing success of the film, Mr. De Sica had great difficulty raising funds for "The Bicycle Thief," which took him three years to make. It, like "Shoeshine," was written by Cesare Zavattini, Mr. De Sica's favorite writer and collaborator.

As in his other realist films, Mr. De Sica drew the actors he used from shops, streets and slums. Lamberto Maggiorani, who played the workman whose bicycle was stolen, was a factory worker.

In directing these people Mr. De Sica was often brutal, and at one point in the filming of "The Bicycle Thief" he traded sharp blows with Mr. Maggiorani, who burst into tears. That was the effect that Mr. De Sica had sought, and with the leading man streaming tears he ordered the cameras to roll.

Directed Sophia Loren

Awards and praise continued for subsequent De Sica films. There were "Miracle in Milan," a fantasy, and "Umberto D," and "The Roof." There was "Two Women" in which Sophia Loren's acting was acclaimed by the critics. Her emergence as a fine comedienne is generally attributed to Mr. De Sica's direction.

Miss Loren and her husband, Carlo Ponti, the producer, were with Mr. De Sica just before he died. His latest film, "The Voyage," in which she starred, opened yesterday in Paris.

In the meantime he continued to act, and in Italy, at least, was more acclaimed for that than for his direction. He also made a number of movies that were, in the view of the critics, less than memorable. Among these were "Indiscretions of an American Wife," "Yesterday, Today and Tomorrow," "Marriage, Italian Style" and "After the Fox."

The New York Times SUNDAY, FEBRUARY 20, 1977

ANDY DEVINE, FILM AND TV STAR, IS DEAD

Squeaky-Voiced Actor, 71, Suffered From Leukemia—Had Appeared In 300 Movies in 25 Years

ORANGE, Calif., Feb. 19 (AP)—Andy Devine, the squeaky-voiced deputy of television's "Wild Bill Hickok" series, died yesterday in a local hospital, a family spokesman said.

Mr. Devine, who was 71 years old, had suffered from leukemia and periodically required hospital treatment.

Football Saved His Career

By ROBERT HANLEY

Hollywood's transition from silent films to talkies in the late 1920's almost ended Andy Devine's movie career.

He had had some success in the silents, but, with the film industry's transition, his high-pitched, crackly voice—his ultimate trademark—made casting directors cringe.

But his background as a college football player saved him. One day in late 1930, he went to a Universal studio during casting for "The Spirit of Notre Dame," a football story dedicated to Knute Rockne, the coach at Notre Dame.

Mr. Devine pointed out that he had once been a college football star. That won him a part. His raspy-voiced, comic-tinged performance drew critical acclaim, and he won a long-term contract in 1931.

300 Movies in 25 Years

He was always cast in the same secondary roles—the bulky (300-pound), bumbling sidekick of fst-shooting, flashy cowboys; the misery-loving tramp; the slow-witted jolly man providing comic re-eyed soft tough for con artists.

Film makers' demand for Mr. Devine seemed unsatiated. Each year in the late 1930's and early '40's, he appeared in at least six films, and sometimes as many as nine. By 1950, he once said, he made about 300 movies in 25 years.

But with all that screen work, he believed that he gained his widest exposure and popularity playing Jingles, the merry buddy of actor Guy Madison, in the "Wild Bill Hickok" western series on television in the 1950's. Millions of children tuned in weekly to chuckle at Jingles, as their parents had at Mr. Devine's screen characters a generation earlier.

A Frequent Guest of Jack Benny

Mr. Devine was also a frequent guest on both the radio broadcasts and television shows starring the late Jack Benny.

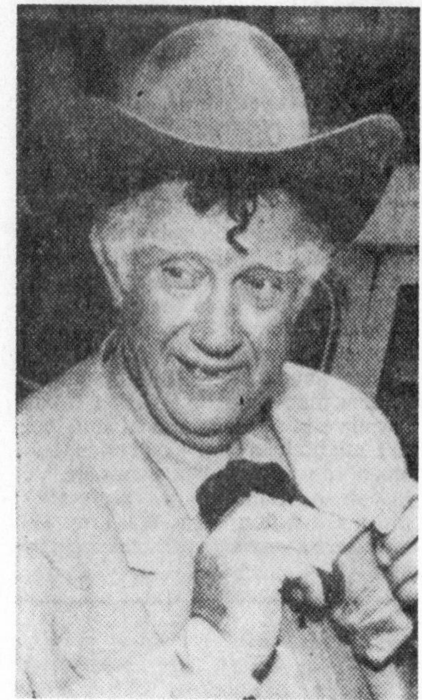

Associated Press

Andy Devine

Mr. Benny noted that on many occasions Mr. Devine would appear in place of Eddie Anderson, who played the role of Rochester, the comedian's valet.

For his own part on the shows, Mr. Devine would represent an amiable hayseed who would come in from the country to visit Mr. Benny.

In an unusual piece of type-casting, Mr. Devine was once selected by Irving Thalberg, the producer, to play the role of Peter in "Romeo and Juliet," starring Mr. Thalberg's wife, Norma Shearer, and the late Leslie Howard.

The stars and John Barrymore were present when, Mr. Devine later said, "I walked into this elegant room and the dramatic coach—a fellow they imported from England—asked me if I understood Shakespeare.

"I said, 'Understand hin? I haven't even read him.' At that, John Barrymore, who had been sprawled out n his chair, cocked an eyebrow, and we became close friends to the very end."

A Fall Affected Vocal Cords

Though his roles were limited, Mr. Devine, always good-humored and content, told interviewers that he "loved every minute" of his career.

He never had an acting lesson. His ability, he said, was traceable to a "lot of Arizona hayseed."

Andrew Devine was born in Flagstaff, Ariz., on Oct. 7, 1905. His father, Tom, ran a hotel there. His mother, Amy, was the daughter of Adm. James Harmon Ward, who was instrumental in founding the United States Naval Academy at Annapolis.

He was not born with his distinct voice. It resulted from a childhood mishap when he fell while he had a stick in his mouth. The roof of his mouth and his vocal cords were injured.

Another "accident"—or stroke of fate—was instrumental in launching his film career. One day in 1925, Mr. Devine came to Hollywood, where his father had died, and was walking along in his football sweater from Santa Clara University, where he starred in football and baseball.

A casting agent from Universal who was driving past saw him, stopped his car, and asked if he played baseball. Mr. Devine, then a strapping 20-year-old youth 6 feet 2 inches and about 210 pounds, said he did, and the agent hired him as one of the athletic "extras" for the silent serial, "The Collegians," produced in 1926 and starring George Lewis and Dorothy Gulliver.

Talkies Cost Him Job

Mr. Devine had other small roles in silent films until the onset of the talkies made him expendable. Despairing, he joined the crew of a supply ship that delivered food, fuel and mail to lighthouses in the Bering Sea. Later he returned to Venice, Calif., and worked as a lifeguard.

It was about that time that he talked his way into the cast of "The Sirit of Notre Dame." In later years, Mr. Devine fondly recalled his role as Truck McCall, who insisted on playing in the football game, broken ribs and all.

On Oct. 28, 1933, his career firmly established, Mr. Devine and Dorothy Irene House, whom he had met on a movie set, were married in Las Vegas. In November 1934, they had a son, Timothy. In January 1939, their other son, Dennis, was born.

The Devines settled in a house in Van Nuys, Calif., started accumulating real estate, and avoided the hectic, highlife of Hollywood, cncentrating on raising their sons.

Devoted to His Family

Mr. Devine seemed a devoted father. "I made a deal with my boys years ago," he said in 1957. "If they'd do nothing to embrass me, I'd do nothing to embarrass them. It's worked out fin"

He seldom ventured away from home for any extended period. Probably the longest period was in thesummer of1957 when—his wealth established from residuals of theHickok western—he came to theJones Beach, L.I., Marine Theater to play "Cap'n Andy" in Guy Lombardo's production of · the Hammerstein-Kern musical, "Show Boat."

"This is the first time I've ever acted in a play," he said then, "andI'm loving every minute of it."

Surviving are his wife, Dorothy, and sons, Timothy and Dennis.

"All the News That's Fit to Print"

The New York Times.

LATE CITY EDITION

U. S. Weather Bureau Report (Page 93) forecast: Becoming cloudy today through tonight. Fair, seasonable tomorrow. Temp. Range: 40—27; yesterday: 38—31.

VOL. CXVI..No. 39,773. © 1966 by The New York Times Company. Times Square, New York, N. Y. 10036 NEW YORK, FRIDAY, DECEMBER 16, 1966. 10 CENTS

DEMOCRATS GAIN CONVENTION RULE IN STATE CANVASS

Conservatives Obtain Third Line on the Ballot When They Outpoll Liberals

HARRINGTON IS CRITICAL

Court Fight Is Possible on Democrats' 102-84 Edge in Constitutional Parley

By RICHARD L. MADDEN

Special to The New York Times

ALBANY, Dec. 15—Five men sat around a conference table here today and signed a stack of tally sheets giving ... ocrats control of th... stitutional Conventi... Conservative party ... line on the voting ma... the next four years.

The five-member Sta... of Canvassers certified ... sults of the Nov. 8 e... which showed that Dem... delegates would outnumb... Republicans, 102 to 84, a... Constitutional Convention w... it convenes here next April 4.

The official canvass gave th... Democrats 89 district delegates to the convention, and the Republicans 82.

In addition, Democratic-Liberal candidates won 13 of the 15 places as delegates at large, elected on a statewide basis. Two Republicans running with Conservative support won the remaining at-large seats.

Challenge Still Possible

The head of the Republican at-large slate, Senator Jacob K. Javits, who also had Liberal endorsement, fell about 14,000 votes short of election.

Today's canvass was the first definitive tally of the election of delegates, but the possibility of a court suit remained because of the tangled count of write-in votes for the at-large delegates.

The canvass also verified earlier reports that the four-year-old Conservative party had displaced the 22-year-old Liberal Party as the state's third-ranking political party.

The Conservatives won the right to Line C on future ballots when their candidate for Governor, Dr. Paul L. Adams, edged the Liberal candidate, Franklin D. Roosevelt Jr., by 2,789 votes.

The canvass, which was based on final tabulations by county boards of elections, showed 510,-023 votes for Dr. Adams and 507,234 for Mr. Roosevelt. Unofficial tallies on election night had given Mr. Roosevelt a slight lead over Dr. Adams.

Police Board a Factor

Surprisingly, the Conservatives outpolled the Liberals in New York City, but trailed them in upstate New York, where Conservative sentiment tends to be strong.

The vote for Governor in New York City was put at 234,590 for the Conservatives and 218,-740 for the Liberals. Outside the city, the vote was 288,494 for Dr. Adams and 275,433 for Mr. Roosevelt.

Politicians attributed the relatively strong Conservative showing within New York City to the Conservative-supported campaign to defeat the Police Department Civilian Complaint Review Board in a local referendum on Nov. 8.

Questioning the differences in the official canvass and the unofficial tallies on election night,

Continued on Page 55, Column 1

Consumer Council Calls for Reforms

By WILLIAM M. BLAIR

Special to The New York Times

WASHINGTON, Dec. 15—Consumers, through "confusion and ignorance, some deception and even fraud," often fail to get their money's worth in the market place, a consumer panel said today.

The Consumer Advisory Council, in a long-delayed report to President Johnson, proposed reforms in a number of areas, including the automobile industry, health care, credit and home maintenance and repair.

The report was completed last June 12 and was submitted to the President a few days later. It was released today by the council with no explanation for the delay of nearly six months.

Some sources attributed the delay to the President's desire for a "consensus" report, al-

Continued on Page 82, Column 3

Museum May Name Hoving as Director

The New York Times

Thomas P. F. Hoving

By RICHARD ...

Dem... Elec... Risin...

By WA...

WHITE S... W. Va., Fr... resentment ... leadership o... broke into th... among the n... Governors.

All but two ... ernors who m... three hours las... that Democratic ... 1966 election wer... tributable to a gro... hostility toward ... Administration.

The Governors a... the National Gover... ference.

Gov. Harold E. Hu... Iowa, chairman of the... cratic Governors' cauc... that the state leaders we... vinced they would have to... a greater part in devel... party policy.

Governor Hughes said ... the Democratic Governors w... largely agreed that the Gr... Society was moving tow... realization too rapidly.

He was particularly critic...

Continued on Page 25, Column 1

A SLOWER GROWTH OF ECONOMY SEEN FOR NEXT 3 YEARS

Labor Department Lays Cut From 5.5% a Year to 4 to Low Jobless Figure

By EDWIN L. DALE Jr.

Special to The New York Times

WASHINGTON, Dec. 15—The American economy can grow no faster than about 4 per... year between now ... Labor Depart... cluded...

Coppolino Acquitted of Murdering Farber

But Still Faces Trial in Death of First Wife

By RONALD SULLIVAN

Special to The New York Times

FREEHOLD, N. J., Dec. 15—Dr. Carl A. Coppolino was acquitted today of the charge that he murdered Lieut. Col. William E. Farber.

The verdict caused ... uproar in th...

Associated Press Wirephoto

...reaction after his acquittal in Freehold, N. J.

...r is expected to ... bail when he ... Even Judge Sim-... greed that F. Lee ... ppolino's defense ... ented good rea-... the doctor now. ... de his acquit-... d in Florida. ... wever, that ... greement ... nors.

"What happens to him in Florida, I don't know," the judge said.

John Gawler, chief of county detectives here, said tonight that he would take Dr. Coppolino under guard to Florida tomorrow.

Frank Schaub, a Florida state attorney who attended the trial

Continued on Page 54, Column 5

Portion of Highwa...

Policemen inspect area of Franklin D. Rooseve... occurred. A 20-foot slab of concrete—pieces of ... eight feet from upper level of the highway during...

The New York Times (by Neal Boenzi)

The slab crushed one automobile (above) and damaged another, injuring two motorists

... illegal ... and illegal elec-... eavesdropping resulted yesterday in 11 indictments against 28 persons charged with various crimes dealing with invasion of privacy.

Mr. Hogan said he was amazed that there had been no leak to those under surveillance in the lengthy inquiry since those indicted were, in the main, private investigators, employes of detective agencies and electronics experts.

Alfred J. Scotti, chief assistant district attorney, who has been in charge of the investigation with the assistance of two aides, Peter D. Andreoli and David T. Austern, said those named as defendants were involved in

Continued on Page 36, Column 1

SOVIET INCREASES DEFENSE SPENDING

Rise for '67, Second in Two Years, Is Linked to Cost of Arms for Hanoi

By RAYMOND H. ANDERSON

Special to The New York Times

MOSCOW, Dec. 15—The Soviet Government announced today that its military spending ... year would be increased ... billion rubles, or 8.2 per ... this year's arms budg-... billion rubles ($14.8-...

... Minister Vasily F. ... declared in a report ... eme Soviet that the ... necessary because ... ve monopolist cir-... ited States have ... ed international ... reased the dan-... ld war."

... the Govern-... rp statement ... States bomb-... the capital ... Moscow ... assistance ... mese and ... at it was ... lunteers"

Walt Disney, 65, Dies on Coast; Founded an Empire on a Mouse

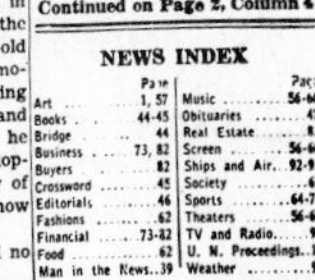

Walt Disney

Mickey Mouse

Special to The New York Times

LOS ANGELES, Dec. 15 — Walt Disney, who built his whimsical cartoon world of Mickey Mouse, Donald Duck and Snow White and the Seven Dwarfs into a $100-million-a-year entertainment empire, died in St. Joseph's Hospital here this morning. He was 65 years old.

His death, at 9:35 A.M., was attributed to acute circulatory collapse. He had undergone surgery at the hospital a month ago for the removal of a lung tumor that was discovered after he entered the hospital for treatment of an old neck injury received in a polo match. On Nov. 30 he re-entered the hospital for a "post-operative checkup."

Just before his last illness, Mr. Disney was supervising the construction of a new Disneyland in Florida, a ski resort in Sequoia National Forest and the renovation of the 10-year-old Disneyland at Anaheim. His motion-picture studio was turning out six new productions and several television shows and he was spearheading the development of the vast University of the Arts, called Cal Art, now under construction here.

Although Mr. Disney held no

Continued on Page 40, Column 1

Walt Disney

Mickey Mouse

Special to The New York Times

LOS ANGELES, Dec. 15 — Walt Disney, who built his whimsical cartoon world of Mickey Mouse, Donald Duck and Snow White and the Seven Dwarfs into a $100-million-a-year entertainment empire, died in St. Joseph's Hospital here this morning. He was 65 years old.

His death, at 9:35 A.M., was attributed to acute circulatory collapse. He had undergone surgery at the hospital a month ago for the removal of a lung tumor that was discovered after he entered the hospital for treatment of an old neck injury received in a polo match. On Nov. 30 he re-entered the hospital for a "post-operative checkup."

Just before his last illness, Mr. Disney was supervising the construction of a new Disneyland in Florida, a ski resort in Sequoia National Forest and the renovation of the 10-year-old Disneyland at Anaheim. His motion-picture studio was turning out six new productions and several television shows and he was spearheading the development of the vast University of the Arts, called Cal Art, now under construction here.

Although Mr. Disney held no

Continued on Page 40, Column 1

U.S. SAIGON AIDES ASSERT NO BOMBS FELL INSIDE HANOI

Westmoreland's Office Says Raids This Week Struck Only Military Targets

PILOT REPORTS STUDIED

Washington Produces Map to Show What Was Hit—Mistake Still Possibility

By The Associated Press

SAIGON, South Vietnam, Friday, Dec. 16—United States military headquarters in Saigon said today that no United States bombs fell in the city of Hanoi in the American raids on the Hanoi area Tuesday and Wednesday.

A special announcement from the headquarters of Gen. William C. Westmoreland, the United States commander in Vietnam, said:

"A complete review of pilot reports and photographs of the 13-14 December air strikes on the Vandien truck depot and the Yenvien railroad classification yard showed that all ordnance expended by U.S. strike aircraft was in the military target areas.

"None fell in the city of Hanoi.

"On December 14th, pilots reported seeing a SAM missile hit a North Vietnamese junk."

The reference to the Soviet-built surface-to-air missile was not further explained, but there has been speculation here that antiaircraft weapons fired by the North Vietnamese might accidentally have dropped shells inside Hanoi.

Two Targets Hit

The chief targets of the American raids Tuesday and again Wednesday were the Vandien depot five miles south of Hanoi and the Yenvien yards six miles northeast of the Communist capital.

The vehicle depot is a sprawling complex of more than 30 maintenance buildings, garages and storage structures as well as a motor pool area. Before the first raid in early December, the depot was reported to have contained 500 vehicles.

The rail yard northeast of Hanoi is a major junction of three rail lines, two of which link North Vietnam with Communist China.

Both installations were described by United States pilots as heavily damaged in this week's raids.

The North Vietnamese and Communist newsmen in Hanoi repeatedly claimed that Hanoi itself was bombed. Dispatches from Hanoi asserted that there were numerous civilian casualties and that a workers' residential quarter was bombed.

Raids Defended by U.S.

By HEDRICK SMITH

Special to The New York Times

WASHINGTON, Dec. 15—...e Administration today de-...ded American air raids on ...gets in the Hanoi region and ...uced a map to show that ... of those targets was in-...e city limits.

...als confirmed reports ...re had been damage to ...areas inside Hanoi dur-... this week, but the ...f whether American ...ght have been acci-...sponsible was not ...resolved here.

Some officials had said yesterday that targets hit by American planes could be considered, in the parlance of the man in the street, as within metropolitan Hanoi. Other officials insisted today that this was not the case.

The map made available by the Administration indicated the political limits of Hanoi and showed villages and built-up areas adjacent to several target areas raided recently. Officials said boundaries had been drawn on a 1965 United States Army map on the basis of North Viet-

Continued on Page 2, Column 4

NEWS INDEX

Walt Disney, Who Built Entertainment Empire on a Mouse, Dies

Continued From Page 1, Col. 7

formal title at Walt Disney Productions, he was in direct charge of the company and was deeply involved in all its operations. Indeed, with the recent decision of Jack L. Warner to sell his interest in the Warner Brothers studio, Mr. Disney was the last of Hollywood's veteran moviemakers who remained in personal control of a major studio.

Roy Disney, Walt Disney's 74-year-old brother, who is president and chairman of Walt Disney Productions and who directs its financial operations, said:

"We will continue to operate Walt's company in the way that he had established and guided it. All of the plans for the future that Walt had begun will continue to move ahead."

Besides his brother, Mr. Disney is survived by his widow, Lillian, two daughters, Mrs. Ron Miller and Mrs. Robert Brown.

Weaver of Fantasies

From his fertile imagination and industrious factory of drawing boards, Walt Elias Disney fashioned the most popular movie stars ever to come from Hollywood and created one of the most fantastic entertainment empires in history.

In return for the happiness he supplied, the world lavished wealth and tributes upon him. He was probably the only man in Hollywood to have been praised by both the American Legion and the Soviet Union.

Where any other Hollywood producer would have been happy to get one Academy Award—the highest honor in American movies—Mr. Disney smashed all records by accumulating 29 Oscars.

"We're selling corn," Mr. Disney once told a reporter, "and I like corn."

David Low, the late British political cartoonist, called him "the most significant figure in graphic arts since Leonardo."

Mr. Disney went from seven-minute animated cartoons to become the first man to mix animation with live action, and he pioneered in making feature-length cartoons. His nature films were almost as popular as his cartoons, and eventually he expanded into feature-length movies using only live actors.

The most successful of his non-animated productions, "Mary Poppins," released in 1964, has already grossed close to $50-million. It also won an Oscar for Julie Andrews in the title role.

From a small garage-studio, the Disney enterprise grew into one of the most modern movie studios in the world, with four

(continued)

Famous Disney characters are, clockwise from top left, Donald Duck, Snow White and two of the Seven Dwarfs, Pluto and Pinocchio. *Snow White,* the first feature-length cartoon, became one of the biggest money-makers in movie history.

sound stages on 51 acres. Mr. Disney acquired a 420-acre ranch that was used for shooting exterior shots for his movies and television productions. Among the lucrative by-products of his output were many comic scripts and enormous royalties paid to him by toy-makers who used his characters.

Mr. Disney's restless mind created one of the nation's greatest tourist attractions: Disneyland, a 300-acre tract of amusement rides, fantasy spectacles and re-created Americana that cost $50.1-million.

By last year, when Disneyland observed its 10th birthday, it had been visited by some 50 million people. Its international fame was emphasized in 1959 by the then Soviet Premier, Nikita S. Khrushchev, who protested, when visiting Hollywood, that he had been unable to see Disneyland. Security arrangements could not be made in time for Mr. Khrushchev's visit.

Even after Disneyland had proven itself, Mr. Disney declined to consider suggestions that he had better leave well enough alone:

"Disneyland will never be completed as long as there is imagination left in the world."

Ideas Met Skepticism

Repeatedly, as Mr. Disney came up with new ideas he encountered considerable skepticism. For Mickey Mouse, the foundation of his realm, Mr. Disney had to pawn and sell almost everything because most exhibitors looked upon it as just another cartoon. But when the public had a chance to speak, the noble-hearted mouse with the high-pitched voice, red pants, yellow shoes and white gloves became the most beloved of Hollywood stars.

A scene from Walt Disney's *Snow White*.

When Mr. Disney decided to make the first feature-length cartoon—"Snow White and the Seven Dwarfs"—many Hollywood experts scoffed that no audience would sit through such a long animation. It became one of the biggest money-makers in movie history.

Mr. Disney was thought a fool when he became the first important movie producer to make films for television. His detractors, once again were proven wrong.

Mr. Disney's television fame was built on such shows as "Disneyland," "The Mickey Mouse Club," "Zorro," "Davy Crockett" and the current "Walt Disney's Wonderful World of Color."

He was, however, the only major movie producer who refused to release his movies to television. He contended, with a good deal of profitable evidence, that each seven years there would be another generation that would flock to the movie theaters to see his old films.

Mickey Mouse would have been fame enough for most men In France he was known as Michel Souris; in Italy, Topolino; in Japan, Miki Kuchi; in Spain, Miguel Ratoncito; in Latin America, El Raton Miguelito; in Sweden, Muse Pigg, and in Russia, Mikki Maus. On D-Day during World War II Mickey Mouse was the pass-word of Allied Supreme Headquarters in Europe.

But Mickey Mouse was not enough for Mr. Disney. He created Donald Duck, Pluto and Goofy. He dug into books for Dumbo, Bambi, Peter Pan, The Three Little Pigs, Ferdinand the Bull, Cinderella, the Sleeping Beauty, Brer Rabbit, Pinocchio. In "Fantasia," he blended cartoon stories with classical music.

Though Mr. Disney's cartoon characters differed markedly, they were all alike in two respects: they were lovable and unsophisticated. Most popular were big-eared Mickey of the piping voice; choleric Donald Duck of the unintelligible quacking; Pluto, that most amiable of clumsy dogs, and the seven dwarfs, who stole the show from Snow White: Dopey, Grumpy, Bashful, Sneezy, Happy, Sleepy and Doc.

His cartoon creatures were often surrounded with lovely songs. Thus, Snow White had "Some Day My Prince Will Come" and the dwarfs had "Whistle While You Work." From his version of "The Three Little Pigs," his most successful cartoon short, came another international hit, "Who's Afraid of the Big Bad Wolf?" Cliff Edwards as Jiminy Cricket sang "When You Wish Upon a Star" for "Pinocchio." More recently, "Mary Poppins" introduced "Supercalifragilisticexpialidocious."

Exhibition at Museum

Mr. Disney seemed to have had an almost superstitious fear of considering his movies as art, though an exhibition of some of his leading cartoon characters was once held in the Metropolitan Museum of Art in New York. "I've never called this art," he said. "It's show business."

One day, when Mr. Disney was approaching 60 and his black hair and neatly trimmed mustache were gray, he was asked to reduce his success to a formula. His brown eyes became alternately intense and dreamy. He fingered an ashtray as he gazed around an office so cluttered with trophies that it looked like a pawn shop.

"I don't really know," he said. "I guess I'm an optimist. I'm not in business to make unhappy pictures. I love comedy too much. I've always loved comedy. Another thing. Maybe it's because I can still be amazed at the wonders of the world.

"Sometimes I've tried to figure out why Mickey appealed to the whole world. Everybody's tried to figure it out. So far as I know, nobody has. He's a pretty nice fellow who never does anybody any harm, who gets into scrapes through no fault of his own, but always manages to come up grinning. Why Mickey's even been faithful to one girl, Minnie, all his life. Mickey is so simple and uncomplicated, so easy to understand that you can't help liking him.

But when Dwight D. Eisenhower was President, he found words for Mr. Disney. He called him a "genius as a creator of folklore" and said his "sympathetic attitude toward life has helped our children develop a clean and cheerful view of humanity, with all its frailties and possibilities for good."

Honored by Universities

When France gave to Mr. Disney its highest artistic decoration as Officier d'Académie, he was cited for his "contribution to education and knowledge" with such nature-study films as "Seal Island," "Beaver Valley," "Nature's Half Acre" and "The Living Desert."

From Harvard and Yale, this stocky, industrious man who had never graduated from high school received honorary degrees. He was honored by Yale the same day as it honored Thomas Mann, the Nobel Prize-winning novelist. Prof. William Lyon Phelps of Yale said of Mr. Disney:

"He has accomplished something that has defied all the efforts and experiments of the laboratories in zoology and biology. He has given animals souls."

By the end of his career, the list of 700 awards and honors

(continued)

that Mr. Disney received from many nations filled 29 typewritten pages, and included 29 Oscars, four Emmys and the Presidential Freedom Medal.

There were tributes of a different nature. Toys in the shape of Disney characters sold by the many millions. Paris couturiers and expensive jewelers both used Disney patterns. One of the most astounding exhibitions of popular devotion came in the wake of Mr. Disney's films about Davy Crockett. In a matter of months, youngsters all over the country who would balk at wearing a hat in winter, were adorned in 'coonskin caps in midsummer.

In some ways Mr. Disney resembled the movie pioneers of a generation before him. He was not afraid of risk. One day, when all the world thought of him as a fabulous success, he told an acquaintance, "I'm in great shape, I now owe the bank only eight million."

A friend of 20 years recalled that he once said, "A buck is something to be spent creating." Early in 1960 he declared, "It's not what you have, but how much you can borrow that's important in business."

Mr. Disney had no trouble borrowing money in his later years. Bankers, in fact, sought him out. Last year Walt Disney Productions grossed $110-million. His family owns 38 per cent of this publicly held corporation, and all of Retlaw, a company that controls the use of Mr. Disney's name.

Mr. Disney's contract with Walt Disney Productions gave him a basic salary of $182,000 a year and a deferred salary of $2,500 a week, with options to buy up to a 25 per cent interest in each of his live-action features. It is understood that he began exercising these options in 1961, but only up to 10 per cent. These interests alone would have made him a multimillionaire.

Mr. Disney, like earlier movie executives, insisted on absolute authority. He was savage in rebuking a subordinate. An associate of many years said the boss "could make you feel one-inch tall, but he wouldn't let anybody else do it. That was his privilege."

Once in a bargaining dispute with a union of artists, a strike at the Disney studios went on for two months and was settled only after Government mediation.

Did Not Draw Mickey Mouse

This attitude by Mr. Disney was one of the reasons some artists disparaged him. Another was that he did none of the drawings of his most famous cartoons. Mickey Mouse, for instance, was drawn by Ubbe Iwerks, who was with Mr. Disney almost from the beginning.

However, Mr. Iwerks insisted that Disney could have done the drawings, but was too busy. Mr. Disney did, however, furnish Mickey's voice for all cartoons. He also sat in on all story conferences.

Walt Disney was born in Chicago on Dec. 5, 1901. His family moved to Marceline, Mo., when he was a child and he spent most of his boyhood on a farm.

He recalled that he enjoyed sketching animals on the farm. Later, when his family moved back to Chicago, he went to high school and studied cartoon drawing at night at the Academy of Fine Arts. He did illustrations for the school paper.

When the United States entered World War I he was turned down by the Army and Navy because he was too young. So he went to France as an ambulance driver for the Red Cross. He decorated the sides of his ambulance with cartoons and had his work published in Stars and Stripes.

After the war the young man worked as a cartoonist for advertising agencies. But he was always looking for something better.

When Mr. Disney got a job doing cartoons for advertisements that were shown in theaters between movies, he was determined that that was to be his future. He would say to friends, "This is the most marvelous thing that has ever happened."

In 1920 he organized his own company to make cartoons about fairy tales. He made about a dozen but could not sell them. He was so determined to continue in this field that at times he had no money for food and lived with Mr. Iwerks.

In 1923 Mr. Disney decided to leave Kansas City. He went to Hollywood, where he formed a small company and did a series of film cartoons called "Alice in Cartoonland."

After two years of "Alice in Cartoonland," Mr. Disney dropped it in favor of a series about "Oswald the Rabbit." In 1928 most of his artists decided to break with him and do their own Oswald. Mr. Disney went to New York to try to keep the series but failed. When he returned, he, his wife, his brother Roy and Mr. Iwerks tried to think of a character for a new series, but failed. They decided on a mouse. Mrs. Disney named it Mickey.

Added Sound to Cartoon

The first Mickey Mouse cartoon, "Plane Crazy," was taken to New York by Mr. Disney. But the distributors were apathetic. "Felix, the Cat" was ruler of the cartoon field, and they saw nothing unusual in a mouse.

When Mr. Disney returned from New York he decided that sound had a future in movies. He made a second Mickey Mouse, this one with sound, called "Steambot Bill." In October, 1928, the cartoon opened at the Colony Theater in New York. Success was immediate and the Disney empire began.

The Dream Merchant

Disney, the Fantasist of Our Times, Was Both Cinema Artist and Tycoon

By BOSLEY CROWTHER

An Appraisal

The popular image of Walt Disney as a shy and benign miracleman who performed varied feats of movie magic to entertain young and old does not do justice nor honor to this remarkable cinema artist and tycoon who rightly achieved an eminence as great as that of any star in Hollywood.

Shy and benign he was, at one phase of his extraordinary career. That was when he was ginning as a maker of animated cartoons. That was when he was conceiving and giving birth to Mickey Mouse, his miraculous cartoon character, which took the world by storm. And that was even into the bright years of the creation of Pluto and Donald Duck and all that swarm of zoological creatures that were so greatly enjoyed and loved.

As a weaver of juvenile fancies with his anthropomorphic cartoons, which turned out to be as delightful to grown-ups as they were to the young, Mr. Disney was toiling in the medium that gave him the greatest joy and stimulated his inventiveness and skill to its finest works. There isn't much question among artists that his most original and tasteful films were his animated shorts made in the nineteen-thirties, when he was still fairly diffident and benign.

It is not to Mr. Disney's discredit that, when success and fame rightly came to him, he began to expand as a person and as an ambitious businessman. It was natural that he should have flourished under the warm and tinkling rain of public praise, that he should have managed to throw off his shyness, that he should have found it quite pleasant to take bows. Mr. Disney himself often noticed that there was "a lot of the Mouse in me." He was indigenously an actor. He loved to act the father of his brood.

Furthermore, he loved success and what went with it. And, as he and his brother, Roy, took stock, they agreed that the future of their business and of Walt's creative energies lay in the direction of the then undreamed-of feature-length story cartoon. That was a terra incognita that Mr. Disney approached with the delight of a pioneer. For his first venture in this area he chose the familiar fairy-tale, "Snow White and the Seven Dwarfs."

The enterprise was successful. But it marked a major departure in Mr. Disney's work. It was not an original Disney story, worked out by him and his genii on their story-board, and it called for animation of human figures as the principal characters.

This, as we now look back upon it, was the Continental Divide in Mr. Disney's creative career. It marked his fateful migration into a new and less personal fantasy realm. He began working with the stories of other people—old familiar ones mostly—and he took to a kind of representational animation that was not esthetically felicitous. Not to him.

He was now moving in the area of the big producer, the Hollywood tycoon, and this was a role that he managed with more pretension than with comfort and ease. More work was delegated to others. His associates, whom he credited, did the things that he himself formerly executed. The Disney plant was a factory.

In this situation, which was inevitable, you might say, and pressed by economic circumstances that were discouraging to the making of cartoons, it might well have been that Mr. Disney would have quietly withdrawn into a shell, committed his business to his brother, and lived happily ever after on television residuals. And, indeed, I recall an occasion of a visit to him at his studio back in the early nineteen-fifties when I got the distinct impression that something of this sort was going on.

He seemed totally disinterested in movies and wholly, almost weirdly, concerned with the building of a miniature railroad engine and a string of cars in the workshops of the studio. All of his zest for invention, for creating fantasies, seemed to be going into this plaything. I came away feeling sad.

I needn't have been. Mr. Disney, the cinema artist and tycoon, was even then joyously gestating another Mouse. It was born as Disneyland. This great amusement park may be a symbol of mass commercialism in our day. It may be an entertainment supermarket. It may be many things that high-brow citizens frown on. But it is tasteful, wholesome and clean. It is a place of delight for millions, who escape into its massive fantasies.

It and "Mary Poppins," which he produced and in which he took a hand, were the final achievements of Mr. Disney, the most persistent and successful fantasist of our age. He managed to come out very nicely for an artist in Hollywood.

The New York Times MONDAY, JUNE 9, 1958.

Robert Donat, Actor, Dead at 53; Starred in 'Goodbye, Mr. Chips'

Briton Won Oscar for Role of Teacher—Recently Made Come-Back to Screen

LONDON, Monday, June 9 (AP)—Robert Donat, the star of the movie "Goodbye, Mr. Chips," died early today in a London hospital. He was 53 years old.

The actor had been in poor health for more than twenty years. He collapsed May 18 and was taken to the hospital critically ill. He had long suffered from asthma. Only a week before his collapse he had finished his first film role in five years.

His last role was that of the Mandarin in "The Inn of the Sixth Happiness," in which he starred with Ingrid Bergman and Curt Jurgens.

He was stricken with a serious attack of asthma on the set but carried on. Because of the strain, he was helped with a prompting board on which his lines were written in large letters. A nurse attended him at the studios, and he had a specially air-conditioned dressing room. After finishing the film he entered the hospital.

Mark Robson, the director, flew here just after Christmas, showed Mr. Donat the script and urged him to try a comeback.

"I'll read the script and let you know," replied Mr. Donat. "I can promise nothing more."

The part of the Mandarin appealed to him, and when his physicians encouraged a return to acting he began filming March 31.

"It is good to see life again," he said. "There have been long times during the last years when I have been so desperate, so afraid, that I could not face anybody."

On the first day of work he said: "I kept thinking I might break down and everyone would see me racked with coughing, racked with despair."

Mr. Donat was married twice. His first marriage to Ella Annesley Voysey was dissolved in 1946. They had two sons and a daughter. In 1953 he married Renee Asherson, actress. They were separated two years ago.

Tall and Deep-Voiced

Mr. Donat was best known here for his portrayal of the old English school teacher in "Goodbye, Mr. Chips" in 1939. This won for him the "Oscar" of the Academy of Motion Picture Arts and Sciences as the best male actor of that year.

In February, 1956, the tall, deep-voiced actor was seen here in a somewhat similar role in the British film "Lease of Life." He played a poor country vicar with but a short while to live. The rôle was said by one critic to have been enacted "with such fervor and gentle sincerity as to recall his touching performance" as Mr. Chips.

Other well-known films in which Mr. Donat had leading parts included "The Thirty-nine Steps," "The Magic Box," "The Winslow Boy," "The Young Mr. Pitt," "The Ghost Goes West," "Knight Without Armor" and "The Citadel."

Born in Withington, Manchester, England, Mr. Donat studied for the stage with James Bernard in Manchester. He made his first appearance in Birmingham in 1921. His debut was followed by several years in stock, repertory theatres and companies touring the English provinces.

Mr. Donat's first London appearance was in "Knave and Queen," produced in this country as "Children of Darkness." He also played the leading role in a London presentation of "The Sleeping Clergyman."

In the spring of 1933 Mr. Donat was selected by the late Sir Alexander Korda for the role of Culpepper in "The Private Life of Henry VIII," with Charles Laughton. Later he played Edmond Dantes in United Artists' "The Count of Monte Cristo."

At the height of his career Mr. Donat's illness increased in severity. It forced him to reduce his appearances, and temporary retirements, such as that which he ended in March to take his last movie role, became more frequent.

Robert Donat in Alfred Hitchcock's *The Thirty-Nine Steps.*

Robert Donat in *Goodbye Mr. Chips,* with Terry Kilburn.

The New York Times

THURSDAY, APRIL 6, 1972

Brian Donlevy, Film Tough Guy, Dies

HOLLYWOOD, April 5 (AP) —Brian Donlevy, who played tough guy roles in motion pictures during most of his career, died of cancer tonight in the Motion Picture Hospital here. He was 69 years old.

Broad-shouldered and muscular, Brian Donlevy played a prize fighter in his first screen role, "The Milky Way," in which he had starred on Broadway.

"The Milky Way" was a comedy about boxing, and in it, Mr. Donlevy mastered two aspects of character that were later to be part of his career—the tough guy who was nonetheless appealing and sometimes sentimental.

The mustached Mr. Donlevy was a popular he-man in a variety of movie formats—Westerns, World War II dramas, detective stories. His voice was coarse, but critics lauded his likability.

Mr. Donlevy was nominated for an Academy Award for his supporting role as a martinet in "Beau Geste," and he was also well-known for his performances in "What Price Glory," "The Great McGinty," "I Wanted Wings," "Jesse James," "Union Pacific" and "Wake Island."

His second film, "Barbary Coast, helped mark him as an exceptional actor. One critic later referred to him as the ideal "hard-boiled sentimentalist."

Mr. Donleavy married Marjorie Lane, a singer, in 1936. The marriage ended in divorce in 1947. He married Lillian Lugosi, the ex-wife of Bela Lugosi, in 1966. He had one daughter, Judy, from his first marriage.

After starring in an early television series, "Dangerous Assignment," Mr. Donlevy played in few movies and retired to Palm Springs to write short stories. He also owned a prosperous tungsten mine in California.

Barbara Stanwyck and Brian Donlevy appeared in *The Great Man's Lady*, 1941.

Brian Donlevy, Millard Mitchell, Victor Mature and Karl Malden in *Kiss of Death*.

The New York Times SATURDAY, SEPTEMBER 12, 1959.

PAUL DOUGLAS, 52, FILM STAR, DEAD

Actor Won Fame on Stage In 'Born Yesterday' Role —Ex-Sports Announcer

Special to The New York Times.

HOLLYWOOD, Calif., Sept. 11—Paul Douglas, stage, film and television actor, died of a heart attack today at his home in Hollywood Hills. He was 52 years old.

His wife, the actress Jan Sterling, said Mr. Douglas had just left his bed this morning when he collapsed on the floor. He had not been ill.

Mr. Douglas, a onetime radio announcer, first gained theatrical prominence in "Born Yesterday" on Broadway in 1946. His final work, completed last week, was the role of an umpire in "The Mighty Casey," a television drama produced by Rod Serling. He was scheduled to start work here Nov. 15 in a starring part in the Billy Wilder motion picture "The Apartment."

His last Broadway appearance was in "A Hole in the Head" in 1957. His last motion picture was "The Mating Game," made this year.

Besides his wife, Mr. Douglas leaves two children, a son, Adams, 3 years old, and a daughter, Margaret, 15, of his third marriage, to Virginia Field, an actress. His first and second marriages were to Elizabeth Farnsworth of Grand Island, Neb., and Geraldine Higgins of New York. All three previous marriages ended in divorces.

A private funeral service will be held Monday morning at the Pierce Brothers Mortuary here.

Big, Burly, Outspoken

Mr. Douglas was big, burly and outspoken and had the voice of a boss stevedore. He also had few pretensions about himself or the acting profession.

Of his personal appearance, Mr. Douglas once said that he had an Adam's apple that would kill the sale of collars, a nose that looked as if it had been left over from a bargain sale and the build of one of those post offices that were constructed during the depression days of the Nineteen Thirties.

The studio camera man, he told an interviewer, enjoyed working with him. "You know why?" he asked, and then answered his own question:

"It's because he doesn't have to worry about my bad angle—they're all bad. He doesn't have to fuss with the lights or anything, because nothing he could do could make me look better. I'm a cinch for the make-up men, too. They figure nothing can be done, so that's what they do."

Mr. Douglas considered himself more at home in New York than any other place. Although he spent much time in Hollywood, he was not overly fond of the movie capital.

"If you live in Hollywood," he once said, "you have to get fed up with hearing characters at parties saying 'I'd love to do a play' when you know they never will, and would be scared out of their wits to try Broadway."

And on another occasion he explained to a New York interviewer:

"By and large theatre actors are better than movie actors because they understand responsibility. When the curtain goes up on a play you're on your own, you're trapped. I think that the two mediums to look forward to working in are the theatre and television, but I must say that Hollywood isn't a dead city by any means. I'll surely be going back some time."

Comment on Popularity

As for his popularity with movie audiences, Mr. Douglas had this to say:

"The public's so relieved to see somebody besides a junior Adonis in the boy-meets-girl set-up they give me a cheer. Guys look at me and say, 'If that mug can win a gal, it's a cinch for me.' Gals look at me and thank God for the guy they're with."

Mr. Douglas' breakthrough as an actor came almost as an accident, but not for lack of trying. From his adolescent years he had aimed at the theatre. He was born in Philadelphia on April 11, 1907, and attended high school there.

A 6-foot, 200-pounder, Mr. Douglas played professional football briefly with the old Frankford Yellow Jackets, a Philadelphia team, and then, heeding the lure of the footlights, acted with stock companies in various parts of the country. In 1936 he was in a show called "Double Dummy," which ran here for twenty-one performances.

In the Nineteen Thirties, Mr. Douglas became one of the country's top sports announcers. Later he turned to comedy on radio, working with the Jack Benny and George Burns and Gracie Allen shows. But his heart was still in the legitimate theatre.

His break came in 1945, when Garson Kanin, the playwright, was looking for an actor to fill the role of Harry Brock, the tough junk tycoon of "Born Yesterday." According to the Broadway legend, Mr. Kanin thought the role needed someone loud, like Paul Douglas. When, it is said, Mr. Kanin suggested this to his wife, Ruth Gordon, the actress, she is reported to have replied, "Well, why don't you get Paul Douglas?"

"Born Yesterday" opened at the Lyceum Theatre in February, 1946, and was considered one of Broadway's most successful comedies. After his 1,024th performance in the play, Mr. Douglas was on his way to Hollywood, where he created a notable success in the movie "A Letter to Three Wives."

In Hollywood he played in a score of films, including "Fourteen Hours," "Clash by Night," "Executive Suite," "The Solid Gold Cadillac," "High and Dry," "Beau James" and "This May Be the Night." His latest film success, "The Mating Game," a comedy, opened here last April. In it he played a farmer who beguiles a tax man to drink in order to avoid paying back taxes.

Of Mr. Douglas' role in "A Hole in the Head," Brooks Atkinson wrote in The New York Times of March 1, 1957, that his "bluffing, shifty black sheep is obviously a good egg. There's not a mean bone in his body."

A penchant for blunt statements frequently involved Mr. Douglas in controversies. One of the most notable occurred in 1955, when he was touring in the South in the play "The Caine Mutiny Court Martial."

A North Carolina newspaper quoted him as saying: The South stinks; it's a land of sowbelly and segregation." Mr. Douglas contended that he had been misquoted. But the play's tour was canceled.

Shelley Winters confronts Paul Douglas in *Executive Suite.*

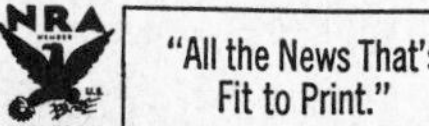

"All the News That's Fit to Print."

The New York Times.

LATE CITY EDITION

WEATHER—Fair today; tomorrow possibly showers. Temperature Yesterday—Max., 79; Min., 73

Section 1

Copyright, 1934, by The New York Times Company.

VOL. LXXXIII....No. 27,945. Entered as Second-Class Matter, Postoffice, New York, N. Y. NEW YORK, SUNDAY, JULY 29, 1934. Including Rotogravure Picture, Magazine and Book Sections. F TEN CENTS | TWELVE CENTS Beyond 200 Miles. Except in 7th and 8th Postal Zones.

AUSTRIA REBUFFS GERMANY BY INACTION ON VON PAPEN; DUCE REPORTED URGING HER

HITLER IS EMBARRASSED

Berlin Now in Position of Pleading With Austria to Be Friendly.

VIENNA NOTABLES SEIZED

Apold, Styrian Industrialist, Is Arrested After His Employes Battle With Troops.

REBEL BANDS ARE FLEEING

Government Forces Continue to Use Artillery to Rout Few Remaining Groups.

By G. E. R. GEDYE.

Wireless to THE NEW YORK TIMES.

VIENNA, July 28.—The Italian Minister to Austria was said to have called on the Acting Chancellor, Prince Ernst von Starhemberg, today to convey to him the advice of Premier Mussolini not to agree to the request of the German Government to accept Lieut. Col. Franz von Papen as Minister to Austria.

Premier Mussolini, it is understood, expressed some surprise at the readiness with which most of the Austrian press had characterized this as a German peace offer and warned the Austrians that to accept Colonel von Papen might weaken Austria's position in the pending international representations in Berlin on the subject of Germany's policy toward Austria.

Germany had hoped, it is understood, to inform the world that Austria had already forgiven and forgotten and had also hoped that Colonel von Papen would represent Germany today at the funeral of Chancellor Engelbert Dollfuss. But Berlin was disappointed. The Austrian Government has made no response to the German suggestion that Colonel von Papen be the next envoy.

Austria Delays Decision.

Herr von Erbach, German Chargé d'Affaires, called yesterday at the Chancellery and requested Austrian agreement to Berlin's proposal. The Cabinet subsequently met, but no agreement was given. The Foreign Office said tonight no reply would be made until Tuesday or Wednesday, when the new Cabinet is formed.

A new Chancellor will be designated by President Wilhelm Miklas on Monday. Dr. Kurt Schuschnigg, Education Minister, is believed to be the leading candidate.

Chancellor Hitler's precipitate recalling of Dr. Kurt Rieth, Minister to Vienna, not merely to ask an explanation of his rôle as intermediary in the negotiations for a safe conduct for Nazi rebels but to remove him from his post for an action which no one here believes he would have taken without instruction from headquarters, has placed Germany in a strange position. She is now a suppliant to little Austria, anxiously awaiting permission to show that all is right again. Austria is in no hurry.

Leading Austrians who have long been notorious because of their Nazi sympathies were arrested here today. The best known, Herr Apold, is chairman of the board of directors of Alpine Montan, which dominates the industrial life of Styria. Herr Apold was at first an ardent Heimwehr patron and terrorized his workers into joining the Heimwehr. Later he went over with most of the Styrian Heimwehr members to the Nazis, forcing his employes to follow him or be dismissed. From this concern's factories at Donawitz were drawn the strongest Nazi warriors in the three days' fighting.

General Also Arrested.

General Bardolf, former aide de camp to Archduke Francis Ferdinand, also was arrested today. General Bardolf never was a member of the Nazi party but is a pan-German of strong Nazi sympathies and an ardent supporter of Anschluss [union with Germany]. Behind the scenes he tried on various occasions to act as intermediary between Chancellor Hitler and Chancellor Dollfuss with the object of persuading the latter to fall in line with Herr Hitler's plans.

Professor Hugelmann of Vienna University, formerly a Senator and a member of Dr. Dollfuss's clerical party, who afterward became a pan-German, was another captive

Continued on Page Three.

The Austrian Situation

Chief developments yesterday in the Austrian situation and its international ramifications were:

Italy was reported to have advised Austria not to accept Franz von Papen as the new German envoy to Vienna. The Cabinet put off its decision until Tuesday or Wednesday despite German pressure for a favorable reply to Chancellor Hitler's move for reconciliation.

Berlin understood there had been a break of friendly relations between Germany and Italy. The press ... Italian troop movements and editor... that country. A renewed attac... ernment in Munich and ... Nazis be taken int... ing further o... future poli...

Intense diplo... understood, ... to Germany ... fied by her ... proval by th... dence.

In Austria the rebe... of the Starhem... Carinthia and S... fled across the ...

Great crowds assem... Dollfuss as funera... him as a man of pe... pledged loyalty to ...

HOSTILITY TO ITAL[Y] IS SHOWN IN BERLI[N]

Breach in Friendly Relations Is Reported—Press Joins in Attacks on Rome.

NAZIS THREATEN AUSTRIA

Insist Their Party Must Share in the Government—Munich Propaganda Renewed.

By OTTO D. TOLISCHUS.

Wireless to THE NEW YORK TIMES.

BERLIN, July 28.—The grave international situation precipitated by the murder of Chancellor Dollfuss took a decided turn for the worse today. The comparative easing of tension felt in diplomatic quarters here yesterday, following Chancellor Hitler's apparent disavowal of a policy of force toward Austria and his appointment of Franz von Papen as his personal peace delegate to Vienna, gave way to new alarm as the attitude of all powers involved seemed stiffening—that of Germany included.

The outstanding factor as viewed from Berlin is the apparent break of friendly relations between Germany and Italy. Up to now the Germans had hoped to reconcile Italian anger at the Nazi putsch attempt in Austria. They scolded the Italian newspapers for their violent language and pleaded with them to stop it. This attempt has been given up.

Tonight German newspapers printed under banner headlines reports from Vienna about Italian troop movements toward the Austrian border. These reports are a few days old and were suppressed heretofore. That they are now released for publication is taken as evidence of the fact that the German Goverment no longer tries to disguise the real situation and is beginning to prepare the people for whatever may develop.

German Press More Violent.

At the same time the German press is beginning to adopt a more violent tone toward Italy. Minister of Agriculture Walter Darre's Deutsche Zeitung talks about "Italian slanderers"; the Kreuz Zeitung reminds Fascists that they should be the last to reproach Germany with violence, and Der Angriff, in countering Italian charges of German agents in Vienna, reminds them of Premier Mussolini's special representative in that capital.

The Foreign Office disclaims any official knowledge of Italian troop movements. "There is no occasion for it," its spokesman said, "and the responsibility for such reports must be left to their originators."

But since Chancellor Hitler is more or less his own Foreign Minister and has in particular taken relations with Austria into his own hands, the Foreign Office has been sidetracked more than ever.

Strong Italian feeling is taken here as confirmation of the report that at Venice Chancellor Hitler promised Premier Mussolini to keep his hands off Austria and that Premier Mussolini considers this promise broken by events in Austria.

Whether or not Germany is taking any military counter measures

Continued on Page Two.

A... IT M...

Cash ... Trees, ... Roosevelt ...

Special to THE N...

LYNCHBURG, ... Warning that "the ... coming," Senator G... dress in his home c... ridiculed as "a delu... tem of Federal relief g... nounced "free silver an... fanatics."

At the same time, in ... of an impassioned plea fo... currency, he declared th... dent Roosevelt was "a sound ... man" and added:

"He has made some mistakes, ... any man would, but no man, however partisan, ever impugned the integrity and good purpose of Franklin Roosevelt.

"The Democratic party, at its worst, is better than the Republican party at its best, so there is really no occasion to discuss these matters."

Paying for Federal Aid.

Speaking before the State convention of the Young Democratic Clubs, the Senator said:

"Pay day is coming and it will be pay for all this Federal aid. See if it really is aid. Where does the government get the money? Does the Secretary of the Treasury pluck it from trees?

"That's what the free silver and greenback fanatics talk like. Dr. White's account of the French revolutionary period of inflated currency sounds like the Congressional Record now.

"We need sound money, the sort of sound money the party declared for. I wrote it into the platform myself and I'm never going to vote for any greenbacks.

"The President doesn't want it done. He accepted power to do it, but did not exercise the power; and, if he has half the sense I think he has, he won't do it. He had to take the power for fear the fanatics might make printing-press money mandatory."

For a Return to Jefferson.

Rebuking Lynchburg for taking a PWA grant when its credit was high, the Senator continued:

"These grants seem to be gifts, but we'll pay them all. We in Virginia will pay ours and we'll help pay for fourteen Western States that altogether do not pay as much Federal tax as Virginia.

"Farmers have been paid for having their sows killed to keep them from having little pigs. They got paid for plowing under their cotton and they're pleased. And you're not much bothered. But wait until we raise taxes. They are already high in other countries.

"I know there's a pay day coming and it won't be pleasant. I want to appeal again for the Jeffersonian democracy of States' rights and I resent the proposition that Virginia, whose bonds sell higher than the

Continued on Page Twenty-two.

PRESIDENT LEAVING HAWAII PLEDGES AMERICA TO PEACE

Stresses 'Defense' in Talk in Honolulu, Praising Spirit of Army and Navy.

LAUDS ISLANDS' PROGRESS

Greeting T... Governor's P... a From ...t.'

... He ... front ... were backed ... the eng... ship ... Hawaiian Oe."

The Pre... ing 'the ... shoulder... had be... them over ... wail wh... to the Island... With the ...

Continued on ...

RAIN SWEEPS CITY, FLOODING STREETS; ONE KILLED BY BOLT

Thunderstorm Brings 2-Inch Downpour—Cellars Filled as Sewers Are Choked.

SUBWAY LINES BLOCKED

Lightning Damages Homes—Humid Heat Continues—Today to Be Fair.

A violent thunderstorm, marked by almost torrential rain, struck the city shortly after noon yesterday, flooding thousands of cellars, inundating streets, hampering traffic and damaging buildings. One man was killed by lightning ... the suburbs.

Although the rainfall for the day ...easured about two inches, it ...d to clear the atmosphere of ...sive humidity. Instead, it in...ed the mugginess. The mer... hovered in the 70s all day, with the moisture in the air ...ning near the saturation ... the weather seemed oppres... hot.

...igh temperature for the day ...degrees at 10:40 A. M. and ...was 73 at 12:30 P. M. The ...erage was 76, one above ...

...er with moderate north... was forecast for today ... change in tempera...

... was so heavy that ...ked within a few ... a result, streets ... flooded. Crews ...re summoned to ... city to open ...arry away ...er débris ...ng to the ...

...ded. ...reet, the ...p. Auto... borough... umbus ...

Results ...

Tennis—Henry W... umphs at Wimbledon to ... States in the Davis Cup ... Frank Shields, 6—4, 6—... Wood Jr. in a five-set thri... wrenched his right side a... women's singles final at ... Miss Helen Jacobs, national ...

Golf—Eddie Driggs Jr. wo... defeating C. Everett Bacon 1... Bolton Landing. Three down ... match at the 36th, then took th... chip shot. In the national P. G. ... Wood and Paul Runyan reached t... 2 and 1, and Gene Kunes, 4 and 2, ...

Baseball—The Yankees broke eve... delphia, but lost the American League ... first game, 4 to 3, while the Yankees to... At Chicago the Tigers downed the White So... gained first place. Rain kept the Giants and Do...

Racing—Below Zero won the East View Stakes at Empire City, beating Morpluck by four lengths with Abner third. Toro Nancy finished a half length ahead of St. Bernard in the $57,820 Arlington Futurity before 20,000 at Arlington Park. Special Agent was third. At Rockingham Park C. V. Whitney's Roustabout won the feature race before 20,000.

(Complete details of these and other events in Sports Section.)

STRATOSPHERE FLIERS JUMP TO SAFETY IN PARACHUTES; BIG BAG RIPS 60,000 FEET UP

Log of Balloon's Voyage

Following is the log of the voyage of the balloon into the stratosphere and its descent, as told by The Associated Press, the time being Central standard time, or two hours behind Eastern daylight time:

6:45 A. M.—The world's largest balloon, with Major W. E. Kepner and Captains A. W. Stevens and O. A. Anderson, soared from a valley near Rapid City, S. D.

6:52—The voyagers radioed "Everything O. K." from an altitude of 7,400 feet.

8:00—A radio message gave the balloon's position at the 14,000-foot stage. This was a drop from the 16,000 feet reported a few moments before, when one of the crew messaged: "We had a hell of a list!"

8:10—Kepner advised Brig Gen. Westover, Assistant Chief of Army Air Corps, that the balloon was at a height of 14,000 feet and over the Cheyenne River, thirty-two miles southeast of Rapid City, and that conditions were "all right."

8:58—Kepner reported to Chicago that the bag had reached 15,000 to 15,460 feet. He said they were having a "hard pull," and added: "Everything hasn't gone perfectly." The direction then was given as "almost due south."

9:40—Kepner reported: "We are closing up," indicating that preparations were starting to seal gondola for second lap of the ascent.

10:00—Weather reports were broadcast from Chicago and Rapid City.

10:35—Balloonists reported that they were "practically stalled" at a 14,000-foot stage about twelve miles south-southeast of Manderson, S. D., and about 120 miles southeast of Rapid City.

10:50—Stevens announced that the craft had lifted to a 17,000-foot

Continued on Page Twenty.

MARIE DRESSLER, NOTED ACTRESS, DIES

Succumbs at the Age of 64 to a Long Illness at Santa Barbara, Calif.

'BEST FILM ACTRESS' IN '31

Became Motion Picture Star at Age of 61 After Waiting 14 Years for a Comeback.

Special to THE NEW YORK TIMES.

SANTA BARBARA, Calif., July 28.—Marie Dressler, beloved star of stage and screen, died at 3:35 o'clock this afternoon.

The end came in the guest cottage on the Montecito estate of C. K. G. Billings, her lifelong friend, which had been her home for the three months of her last illness. At the bedside were Dr. Franklin R. Nuzum, who has been tireless for the last six weeks; Dr. H. S. Schwalenberg, recently called into consultation; Mr. and Mrs. Allen Breed Walker, friends who left their desert home to assist in her nursing; Minnie Cox, her maid for twenty-five years, and James Cox, the maid's husband.

Miss Dressler had been in a deep coma for eighteen days. The statement of the physicians is as follows:

Miss Dressler passed away at 3:35 P. M., the immediate cause of death was uremia (failure of the kidney function). This was complicated by congestive heart

Continued on Page Twenty-two.

MARIE DRESSLER, NOTED ACTRESS, DIES

Succumbs at the Age of 64 to a Long Illness at Santa Barbara, Calif.

'BEST FILM ACTRESS' IN '31

Became Motion Picture Star at Age of 61 After Waiting 14 Years for a Comeback.

Special to THE NEW YORK TIMES.

SANTA BARBARA, Calif., July ...Marie Dressler, beloved star of ...e and screen, died at 3:35 ...this afternoon.

...nd came in the guest ...n Montecito estate of ...G. Billings, her lifelong ...hich had been her home ...hree months of her last ...t the bedside were Dr. ... Nuzum, who has been ...last six weeks; Dr. ...berg, recently called ... Mr. and Mrs. ...ker, friends who ...to assist in ... Cox, her maid ... James ... in a deep ... The state... as fol-

...away at ...e cause ...ilure of ...is was ... heart ...ancer ... the ...ead.

...ng in ...y as the ...agement. For ...nty years engage... had come along one after another. She had been earning not less than $2,500 a week and saving reasonably, so she was not disturbed. She was a favorite of the American and English audiences and 47 years old.

The Ziegfeld-Dillingham management announced on Nov. 7, 1916: "In the necessity of eliminating certain scenes from 'The Century Girl' in order to shorten an overlong performance, Miss Marie Dressler has retired from the cast."

Miss Dressler's public explanation

Continued on Page Twenty-two.

DRAMATIC DESCENT TOLD BY THE PILOT

Kepner Recounts to Chief at Capital the Battle With Rips in Falling Balloon.

JUST 'HOLDING TOGETHER'

From Dawn Start Till Leap by Parachute, Story of Flight Is Told Direct Over Radio.

By radio from the gondola of the stratosphere balloon, Major William E. Kepner told graphically at 6:47 P. M. last night of the difficulties against which he and his aides struggled before they were forced to take to their parachutes.

"The bottom of this balloon is pretty well torn out and it is just a big hole in the bottom here," Major Kepner told Brig. Gen. Oscar Westover, assistant chief of the Army Air Corps in Washington.

"I don't know how long she is going to hold together," Major Kepner said, adding: "But there's nothing to do about it but come down as long as we can, and come down as easy as we can."

"I think you are very wise to make your rate of descent very slowly," General Westover broke in.

"We are doing that as much as we can," Major Kepner replied in a conversational tone. "It is pretty hard to control it. It seems to hit areas of cold air and bounces back up."

Dropping 500 Feet a Minute.

"What is your rate of descent right now, how fast?"

"About 500 feet a minute. It goes faster and occasionally stops descent altogether and goes back up in the air a little piece. It is a very discouraging sort of a business."

"How much is your balloon still ...d up? Is the upper half of it ...tty well filled out?"

"...Well yes, about, not half of it, ...se you see, the bag is so big ... only had about 7 per cent ... we left Rapid City, and at ... time this is probably ...ite full.

...bric—there is so much ...partly torn and com...see, it acts as a para...t lets go and occa... extra chunk out ...s getting to look ... a huge sieve on ... side—probably fifty ... hole there, a yard wide."

"Well, you have, of course, no idea as to what caused this, whether it was due to expansion or whipping of the fabric?" General Westover asked.

"No, I don't," Major Kepner responded. "The balloon was going up very slowly at the time that this happened and it didn't make any particular noise. We just happened to hear a rip on top of the gondola and saw a big hole there."

"Have you anything further to report?" the General inquired.

"No, I haven't, General. We'll go ahead and do the best we can. Nothing else to do except the best to do under such circumstances."

"I know you will have to do that," General Westover said. "We

Continued on Page Twenty-one.

LEAP FROM FALLING CRAFT

Occupants Jump From the Gondola at 3,000, 2,000 and 500 Feet.

ALL LAND WITHOUT HURT

Car Is Only Slightly Damaged and the Scientific Instruments Are Saved.

STALLED AT 14,000 FEET

Craft Then Continued On, Reached Stratosphere and Was Up Ten Hours.

By Telephone to THE NEW YORK TIMES.

LOOMIS, Neb., July 28.—The huge stratosphere balloon which rose into the dawn at Rapid City, S. D., at 6:45 A. M., Central standard time, today, thudded into the black dust of a cornfield, four and one-half miles north of here, at 5 P. M. Central standard time (7 P. M. New York daylight saving time).

The metal gondola was crumpled and broken and the rubberized fabric of what had been the world's largest balloon was piled in a torn and tumbled mass amidst the furrows.

The balloon's crew of three—Major William E. Kepner, the pilot; Captain Albert W. Stevens, scientific observer, and Captain Orvil A. Anderson, co-pilot, all of the United States Army—landed safely in parachutes not far from the wreck of their strange craft.

The skymen "bailed out" just as the balloon, its fabric ripped to shreds, collapsed, and started to drop like a plummet, drawn by the weight of the metal gondola, toward the earth.

Trouble at 60,000 Feet.

Sealed in their metal 'sphere, swaying by rope girdles beneath the pear-shaped bag, the men had risen in their eleven-hour flight to an approximate altitude of 60,000 feet—well under the world's altitude record, but in an atmosphere far too rarefied to support life.

The balloon was still rising in the cold still air when a rent appeared in the lower surface of the gas bag. It grew wider.

Speaking calmly into a short-wave transmitter, which carried his words to a nation-wide audience, Major Kepner, swaying almost twelve miles high, described his experience.

Then as the bag rushed toward the earth, gaining momentum as the hydrogen escaped, he reported to his chief in Washington, Brig. Gen. Oscar Westover, Assistant Chief of Staff of the Army Air Corps:

"We are having a great deal of difficulty in coming down; for some reason or other, this thing doesn't act like it has in other balloons, and the bottom of this balloon is pretty well torn out, and it is just a big hole in the bottom here. I don't know how long she is going to hold together, but nothing to do about it but to come on down as long as we can and come down as easy as we can."

Kept Calm in Descent.

They came down—"as long as they could," and as "easy"—at the rate of a mile a minute toward the last, and all the time the calm voices—now of Major Kepner, now of Captain Stevens—reported to their chief in Washington and to a tense public the progress of their fight for life.

The tear grew wider; the gaps opened; great ribbons of rubberized fabric flapped in the breeze; through the glass portholes at the top of the gondola the crew of three could see the air sucking upward into the vast open belly of the bag; could watch the sides rip open, the balloon gradually collapse.

At 20,000 the ports were opened; they were down in the region where man could live.

"We waited until we were within 20,000 feet of the earth," Major Kepner said later. "The lungs of no human being could stand that higher altitude. But at 20,000 we prepared to abandon the ship, and all three climbed out on top of the gondola."

With parachutes strapped to their backs, hanging on to the straining, swinging rope girdles which locked the gondola to the torn and gaping fabric, the three men rode the plunging derelict down to 5,000 feet.

"At 5,000 feet that big balloon,

Continued on Page Twenty.

MARIE DRESSLER, NOTED ACTRESS, DIES

Continued From Page One.

failure and by cancer. Cancer was found July, 1931. During the latter part of the illness it spread.

FRANKLIN R. NUZUM,
H. S. SCHWALENBERG.

Earlier in the afternoon it was announced that there was no change from yesterday when her temperature varied between 100 and 101 degrees.

Hollywood knew for a long time that her health was failing. She had recovered from previous attacks, however, and long after she became gravely ill in the cottage here, there was hope that she would yet return to the screen.

Arrangements for the funeral have not been made. Mr. and Mrs. Walker are in communication with other friends.

Became Screen Star at 61.

Marie Dressler became a motion picture star in 1930, at the age of 61, after waiting fourteen years for an opportunity to show that she was not too old to make the world laugh.

When the Ziegfeld-Dillingham management dropped her from the new show they were rehearsing in 1916 she regarded it only as the judgment of one management. For more than twenty years engagements had come along one after another. She had been earning not less than $2,500 a week and saving reasonably, so she was not disturbed. She was a favorite of the American and English audiences and 47 years old.

The Ziegfeld-Dillingham management announced on Nov. 7, 1916: "In the necessity of eliminating certain scenes from 'The Century Girl' in order to shorten an overlong performance, Miss Marie Dressler has retired from the cast."

Miss Dressler's public explanation was that she had worked so long that she wanted a chance to play, and was going to Europe. She expected to be called back to a good engagement. She came back after America's entry into the war in 1917 to plunge into war work, entertaining the soldiers, making Liberty Loan speeches, welcoming home the returning troops. That kept her busy until 1919.

She bought a house and furnished it, explaining that an actress always has an accumulating desire for a home running parallel to an artistic career which forces her to live in thousands of hotels and sleep in 10,000 Pullman berths. It had not occurred to any manager to offer her an engagement. Her retirement was accepted as an established fact. She appeared as often as she thought wise in charity pageants, benefit performances, society theatricals, concealing her eagerness for the opportunity to appear.

In 1923 she gave up waiting and, as she expressed it years later, "communicated delicately and indirectly to various managers that she was ready to return." There was no response.

Marie Dressler as Carlotta Vance and Lionel Barrymore as Oliver Jordan in *Dinner at Eight*.

In 1924, with her savings dwindling, she sold her home and furniture and gave interviews announcing that her domestic instincts had been appeased at the expense of her artistic soul, and that she was about to return to the footlights. She did not give the name of the play. She moved into the Ritz, however, in accordance with a belief which she afterward recorded that "your public front and your self-confidence are your most important assets."

To "occupy the time" before her new play went into production she made a five-week vaudeville tour in 1925. "I made them laugh," she told her friends proudly, and sent them to tell the managers.

The managers said they could not ask any one to put money into a play for Marie Dressler at her age. The public, they said, was clamoring for youth—for new-love. For a while Miss Dressler despaired.

Retirement Announced.

On Oct. 13, 1925, she made a speech at a dinner of the American Woman's Association, which she had aided in raising funds for its new clubhouse. She said she was going to retire from the stage. Up to that time she had considered herself as still occupying it.

The next day she revealed in an interview that she was going to sell Florida real estate. "The other night," she said, "during a speech which I made at a dinner, I said, 'I've left the stage.' The sound of those words in my own voice gave me a strange sickening feeling. But it is done and I am glad to be through with the terrible nerve strain of theatrical work. No one except those who have experienced it knows what it is to go through with a performance, especially in a new part. For days before the opening, one wonders whether people are going to like it, whether it is going to get across. It is a never-ceasing strain, amounting at times almost to agony."

"Do you always take your work so seriously and feel so anxious about your reception?" she was asked.

"Ever since I began to realize that something was expected of me," said Miss Dressler, "and that was a long time ago. I've had my name in electric lights for twenty-eight years. You can't do that without working and keeping on working. Stars who are made overnight without much trouble on their own part may last for eight or ten years, but they're bound to go out in a short time, because they lack sound training and don't know how to work."

She said any number of business concerns wanted her to join them before she decided on the Florida real estate firm.

Unfortunately she knew nothing about mortgages, taxes or any of the things which must be explained in closing a real estate sale. Her education consisted only of what her mother had taught her, principally reading and writing, before she left home for the stage at the age of 14. She could not sell real estate even to the customers whom her many friends produced.

She came back to New York and took stock of her abilities in 1926. She had always been a good cook, who loved to concoct unusual and delicious dishes. She decided the best thing she could do with the remainder of her life was to go to Paris and open a hotel where Americans who were always complaining could get the American cooking they craved. She was dissuaded by a friend, who was an amateur astrologer and who assured her that Jupiter was preparing something else for her.

Shortly afterward, Allen Dwan called her to take a part in a film which he was producing in Florida. In the account of her life which she later supplied to "Who's Who in America," she recorded this as "returned to screen, 1926." It was a one-day engagement.

When the film was shown, however, a mention of Marie Dressler's appearance in a minor rôle recalled her to the mind of a young woman in a Hollywood casting office. She was summoned in 1927 for the comic part in "The Callahans and the Murphys." After that she returned to New York to await another summons. It came almost immediately, for a picture with Constance Talmadge.

Convinced that she had at last returned to the stage, she settled down thereafter in Hollywood ready to fill all engagements. She could not afford to travel back and forth from New York for each one. For eighteen months she waited before she got another. Then she was called for small character parts—a ponderous widow, a dowager—on which she concentrated her skill so much that reviewers noticed and said this performance was "splendid"; that one "stood out."

Her great opportunity came in 1930, when she played in "Anna Christie" with Greta Garbo. Critics said she took the picture away from Garbo. Motion-picture producers recognized her at last as a star.

In 1931 the Academy of Motion Picture Arts and Sciences voted her performance in "Min and Bill" the finest acting in motion pictures during the last year.

President and Mrs. Roosevelt were the first to sign a huge parchment scroll of greetings for Miss Dressler's sixty-fourth birthday on Nov. 9, 1933. The creator of "Tugboat Annie" was fêted in New York at a dinner given by the Actors' Dinner Club and later at

(continued)

Hollywood, where more than 700 persons cheered her and where she was presented with a cake that weighed 500 pounds.

"Best Screen Actress" of 1931-32.

Marie Dressler was adjudged the best screen actress in 1931 and in 1932. She scored new triumphs in such film plays as "Dinner at Eight," "Christopher Bean" and "Tugboat Annie."

She created a sensation when she visited NRA headquarters at Washington on Sept. 20, 1933, and offered her help to General Hugh S. Johnson. So great was the excitement that a police escort had to be provided.

Miss Dressler spoke over the radio last year to appeal for relief in the campaign staged by the Mobilization for Human Needs.

In February, 1932, Mordaunt Hall, in a critical review for THE NEW YORK TIMES, wrote of her performance in "Emma," that "her film work has earned for her the highest praise throughout the English-speaking world" and added that her Emma was "one of the finest character studies that have come to the screen."

In November of the same year, Mr. Hall, in a criticism of "Prosperity," wrote: "To accommodate the thousands who are always attracted to a Marie Dressler picture, the management opened the doors of the theatres as early as 9:30 yesterday morning and soon afterward the house echoed with the merriment of the audience. This performer who can boast of having made the world laugh a lot, and also cry, never failing to elicit admiration by her natural and able portrayals, once more scores in this present contribution."

By that time, at the age of 63, her involuntary retirement was behind Miss Dressler, and she was so assured that no one would ever again say she was too old that she told in a Saturday Evening Post article, entitled "Down and Up Again," how it felt to wait and work fourteen years for an opportunity to get back to the lights.

She said the managers who dropped her had made the mistake of thinking she made people laugh only because she was young and exuberant. She said they did not realize how she had studied people since she was a child because she wanted friends, and discovered early that people want to laugh.

"But they want to be forced to laugh," she said, "and you must find out how to do it. You must be patient and do the best you can with any situation and store up the understanding you get from it. At the bottom of it all is the fact that comedy is not far from pathos."

A Church Cupid at 5.

She recalled the laugh she got at her first public appearance at the age of 5 in a church theatrical performance, where she was Cupid on a pedestal and accidentally fell off. Thereafter she amused people by falling. Her childhood ambition was to be a woman chariot driver in a circus.

When she decided at the age of 14 to join a roving stock opera company, her parents suggested that she should change her name. She was born Leila Koerber in Coburg, Canada, Nov. 9, 1869. Her father was the last surviving officer of the Crimean War. Her mother was Anne Henderson Koerber, a musician. The name they gave their daughter for stage use was the name of a deceased aunt, Marie Dressler.

Her mother also warned her that her education needed completion and made her promise that each morning she would buy the best newspaper in any town where she happened to be and read it thoroughly so that she would have something to say when she met people.

Maurice Barrymore Praised Her.

With this equipment, she played every part on the stage from the chorus up, rising steadily from $8 a week to stardom. Maurice Barrymore, father of Lionel and John, was the first to recognize her as a great comic artist and to counsel her to develop her laugh-making technique and character studies. She was featured with Weber & Fields, Fay Templeton and Lillian Russell in the old Weber & Fields Music Hall; she played with Leo Ditrichstein and Eddie Foy.

She was a star before the motion picture was heard of, when she and Lillian Russell used to exercise every morning by bicycling around the reservoir in Central Park. She made and held a long friendship with Mrs. Stuyvesant Fish, as well as with other social leaders. In London, the Prince of Wales used to call on her. In America she was invited to the White House and knew all the Presidents since Cleveland.

In her own judgment, her greatest success was "Tillie's Nightmare," in which she introduced the song which went around the English-speaking world: "Heaven Will Protect the Working Girl." In 1916 she played the same rôle in the Mack Sennett screen comedy "Tillie's Punctured Romance," with Charlie Chaplin, Mabel Normand and others.

During the period in which she waited for theatrical managers to call her back to the stage Miss Dressler was able to earn some money by writing her life story in book and serial form under the title "The Life Story of an Ugly Duckling." She wrote: "I was too homely for a prima donna and too big for a soubrette."

During this period also, she participated actively in the struggle between the managers and the actors which attended the organization of the Actors Equity Association. When she recovered stardom in the motion pictures, however, she opposed the attempt of Equity to extend its control to the motion-picture stage. She said that times had changed and that motion pictures involved considerable investment which could not be dealt with as easily as a theatre company.

As she entered her sixtieth year, refusing vaudeville offers at $10,000 a week, she said: "I am content."

According to a report of The Associated Press, Miss Dressler was married about 1900 to George Hoppert, who soon afterward became an invalid and used to watch her perform, sitting in a wheelchair in the wings. He died a few years later. Who's Who in the Theatre states that Miss Dressler was married to James H. Dalton. The ceremony is reported to have taken place in 1914.

Rôles of Marie Dressler.

Miss Dressler first appeared on the stage in 1886 as Cigarette in "Under Two Flags." During the next few years she toured with several light opera companies playing thirty-eight different rôles. She made her début in New York on May 28, 1892, as Cunigonde in "The Robber on the Rhine" by Maurice Barrymore. She also played a number of rôles with the Bennett Moulton Opera Company at the Casino Theatre in New York.

Among her other rôles in play and operettas were the Duchess i "The Princess Nicotine," in N vember, 1893; Aurore in "Girofl Girofla," in March, 1894; Mar Douclee in "Madeleine or the Magi Kiss," 1895; Georgia West in " Stag Party," 1895; the next yea she scored a great success as Fl Honeydew in "The Lady Slavey, and played the part for some time

In 1896 she played Mrs. Malapro in "The Rivals" and appeared a Flora in "Hotel Topsy Turvy" i 1898. In 1899 she appeared as Viol Alum in "The Man in the Moon" and the following year as Heler Print in "Miss Print."

In 1905 Miss Dressler joined Joe Weber at Weber's Music Hall playing in "Higgledy-Piggledy," "The College Widower," "Twiddle Twaddle" and "The Squaw Man's Girl of the Golden West." In the next year, after appearing at the Palace Theatre in London, she played in "Philopoena" and "The Collegettes," but neither play was successful.

Returning to the United States she toured in "The Boy and the Girl" and played Tillie Blobbs in "Tillie's Nightmare" in 1910. She was with Weber and Fields in 1912 and played in "Without the Law" and "Roly Poly." In 1913 she appeared in vaudeville in San Francisco, but returned to New York the next year to play in "The Merry Gambol" and "A Mix-up."

After the World War she toured in "Tillie's Nightmare," and played in "The Passing Show of 1921" at the Winter Garden. In 1923 she appeared as Gloria Seabright in "The Dancing Girl," and during the same year played several rôles in London.

Marie Dressler with George F. Marion in *Anna Christie*.

The New York Times MONDAY, SEPTEMBER 4, 1967

James Dunn, Actor, Dies at 61; Academy Award Winner in '46

Honored as Tippling Father in 'A Tree Grows in Brooklyn' —Shirley Temple Co-Star

James Dunn, the film actor whose expression of slightly battered wistfulness became his trademark, died yesterday in Santa Monica, Calif. His age was 61.

Although Mr. Dunn made occasional film, stage and television appearances in recent years, he is perhaps best remembered for three movies in a career that flickered, dimmed and finally found him relegated to minor character portrayals.

The pictures were "Bad Girl" (1931), which brought him overnight fame opposite Sally Eilers; the 1934 musical "Stand Up and Cheer," in which he twirled a moppet named Shirley Temple before a Depression - weary world; and "A Tree Grows in Brooklyn," for which Mr. Dunn won an Academy Award as the best supporting actor of 1946.

Mr. Dunn was born near 146th Street and Broadway. After selling lunch wagons in New Rochelle, N. Y., he presented himself at the old Paramount studio in Astoria, Queens, and promptly was hired for bit extra roles.

After obtaining parts in two Broadway plays, "The Nightstick" and the Helen Morgan musical "Sweet Adeline," he was signed to a Fox studio contract and sent to Hollywood, where he played in "Bad Girl," Vina Delmar's drama of a young married couple. The film was a hit.

'Good Ship Lollipop'

Mr. Dunn subsequently appeared in "Over the Hill," "Take a Chance" and "Change of Heart." And having scored so solidly with Miss Temple in their song-and-dance duet in "Stand Up and Cheer," it was only natural that they team again in such films as "Baby Take a Bow" and "Bright Eyes," in which Mr. Dunn piloted the child aloft for her midair rendition of "On the Good Ship Lollipop."

His career dipped earthward, however, in mediocre comedies and melodramas, although his return to the stage in "Panama Hattie" in 1940 was well received.

A singer-friend, hearing of casting trouble with the screen version of Betty Smith's novel, "A Tree Grows in Brooklyn," insisted that the actor be tested for the part of Johnny Nolan, the tippling, shiftless father adored by the young heroine, played by Peggy Ann Garner. Critics agreed that it was Mr. Dunn's finest performance.

Again his career declined, although he won praise as Mickey Rooney's father in the 1948 prizefight drama, "Killer McCoy." One critic wrote that Mr. Dunn "played a disagreeable character with such expert guile that he develops a lot of sympathy." Later that year Mr. Dunn succeeded Jack Buchanan on Broadway as the hero of "Harvey." He also appeared in the television series "It's a Great Life."

Played Willy Loman

Cast in a key part in the Theatre Guild's presentation of Eugene O'Neill's "A Moon for the Misbegotten," Mr. Dunn was praised during the out-of-town tryouts for his performance as a sad man, driven to drink to forget a melancholy past. He left the play before its Broadway opening.

In October, 1951, three months after he portrayed Willy Loman in "Death of a Salesman" at the Norwich (Conn.) Summer Theater, he filed a petition in bankruptcy, describing himself as unemployed. Mr. Dunn reportedly had lost $40,000 in a stage work that failed to reach Broadway.

After an eight-year absence he returned to the screen in 1960, playing a conscience-stricken alcoholic in "The Bramble Bush." Among his last films was "The Adventures of a Young Man," derived from short stories by Ernest Hemingway.

Mr. Dunn is survived by his widow, the former Edna Rush, a singer, and a stepson, William Tick. A previous marriage, to Frances Gifford, an actress, ended in divorce in 1938.

James Dunn as Johnny in "A Tree Grows in Brooklyn."

James Dunn and Shirley Temple in *Baby Takes a Bow*, 1934.

The New York Times SATURDAY, JUNE 8, 1968

Dan Duryea, Actor, Dies at 61; Played Unsavory Characters

Toughness Stirred Fan Mail —In Real Life, He Aided Community Activities

HOLLYWOOD, June 7 (AP) —Dan Duryea, famed for his movie and television portrayals of the heel with sex appeal, died today. He was 61 years old.

Mr. Duryea, who had undergone surgery for a malignancy several months ago, was pronounced dead at his hilltop home. He had collapsed in his bathroom. According to a preliminary autopsy report, the actor died of cancer.

Mr. Duryea's wife, Helen Bryan, died of a heart ailment in 1957. They had two sons, Peter, an actor, and Richard, a talent manager now touring with the Beach Boys, a singing group.

A funeral service will be held 12:30 P.M. Monday at Forest Lawn Memorial Park.

Two Different Worlds

Six-foot one-inch tall, slim, blond and blue-eyed, Dan Duryea made a fortune by allowing Hollywood to typecast him as a movie villain. In his 28 years in Hollywood, he made more than 60 motion pictures and 75 television shows, in the vast majority of which he played unsavory characters.

Most recently, he was seen in the role of Eddie Jacks, the wandering confidence man in television's nighttime soap opera, "Peyton Place."

As movie publicity agents loved to point out, Mr. Duryea's real-life personality was quite the opposite from the one he displayed in films.

He was soft-spoken, a dedicated father and family man who went out of his way to correct his professional image in his private activities. He lived a quiet life, devoting himself to gardening, boating and community activities that included, at various times, active membership in the local parent-teachers association and command of a Boy Scout troop.

Mr. Duryea was born Jan. 23, 1907, in White Plains, where he attended high school. He majored in English at Cornell University and in his senior year succeeded Franchot Tone as president of the college drama society. He did not turn to acting professionally, however, until six years after his graduation.

Dan Duryea

When he first got out of college, Mr. Duryea worked as a space salesman for an advertising firm in New York and Philadelphia.

After being bedridden for almost a year following a heart attack, he decided to go into the theater as a comparatively easy way to make a living. Through Sidney Kingsley, a Cornell classmate, Mr. Duryea obtained a walk-on role in Mr. Kingsley's "Dead End" for $40 a week.

During that play's long Broadway long run, the actor worked up to a featured role that led, in turn, to roles in "Stepping Sisters," "Many Mansions," "Missouri Legend" and "The Little Foxes."

When Samuel Goldwyn bought the screen rights to the Lillian Hellman play in 1940, he brought Mr. Duryea to Hollywood to recreate the role of Leo, the sniveling nephew of the greedy Hubbard family. The actor never again appeared on Broadway.

He quickly gained a reputation with the public as a tough guy with a penchant for beating up women, a penchant that many female patrons apparently translated into sex appeal. He told a reporter once that "my fan mail goes up everytime I tee off on a girl." His salary went up, too, and in 1948 it was reported that he was earning more than $100,000 a year.

Among the films in which he displayed this antisocial bent were "Woman in the Window," "Scarlet Street," "The Whip," "Johnny Stool Pigeon" and "Along Came Jones."

Convincing as Blackmailer

Bosley Crowther, then film critic for The New York Times, wrote of his performance in "Woman in the Window," released in 1945, that "Dan Duryea is so good in the role of the blackmailer that you feel like actually hissing him."

The star occasionally attempted sympathetic roles, as in "Sahara" in 1943, with Humphrey Bogart, and "Battle Hymn," in 1957, with Rock Hudson, but these performances were never particularly popular with the public.

Mr. Duryea's acting style was not subtle, but it was always disciplined. His trademark was a tight-lipped vocal delivery of lines that were often punctuated with a sneer. Of his role in "Thunder Bay," a 1957 drama of offshore oil digging in which he co-starred with James Stewart, he said with some awe: "I'm legal and almost likable this time."

When his sons were young, the actor did not allow them to see his films, explaining, "I don't want them to get any wrong ideas."

In 1952, he had his own TV show, "The Adventures of China Smith," which ran for 26 episodes. Another set of 26 was made in 1955 under the title of "The New Adventures of China Smith."

His last films included "River of Dollars," "Five Golden Dragons," "The Bamboo Saucer" and "Flight of the Phoenix."

Dan Duryea and Joan Bennett in *The Woman in the Window.*

"All the News That's Fit to Print."

The New York Times.

THE WEATHER
Mostly fair today and tomorrow; continued cool.
Temperatures Yesterday—Max. 57, Min. 51.
U. S. Weather Forecast—For details see Page 56.

VOL. LXXIX....No. 26,186. ****** NEW YORK, FRIDAY, OCTOBER 4, 1929. TWO CENTS In Greater New York | THREE CENTS Within 200 Miles | FOUR CENTS Elsewhere Except 7th and 8th Postal Zones

MACDONALD TO BE GREETED BY CITY TODAY; HOOVER SENDS WELCOME BY WIRELESS; PLANS TO TAKE PREMIER TO HIS CAMP

CRUISERS ESCORTING LINER

Mayor to Meet Visitor After He Is Taken Off Berengaria in Bay.

ONLY TWO-HOUR STAY HERE

At Capital the President Will Invite Him to Rapidan for 'Campfire Talks.'

PREMIER TELLS OF HOPES

Says He Is Coming Not Only to Take Up Cruiser Question but to Aid Good-Will.

DISTING...
J. Ramsay ...

J. Ramsay MacDonald will land on American soil this morning, the first British Prime Minister to visit this country while in office. The Premier will pause here for two hours to receive the freedom of the city and an official welcome. Then he will continue on to Washington to join President Hoover for informal conversations on the Anglo-American viewpoint on international affairs.

The Berengaria, carrying its most distinguished foreign passenger since the crossing of the Prince of Wales, was steaming at reduced speed last night so as not to arrive ahead of schedule. Two United States cruisers, their ports shining through the clear night, were acting as escort. The vessel was expected off Quarantine between 8 and 9 A. M., and Mr. MacDonald and his party will step ashore at the Battery an hour later.

A message of greeting and good wishes was flashed to the Prime Minister yesterday by the President and another was sent by Secretary of State Stimson. The Premier radioed replies conveying his thanks and his assurance that the greetings would be appreciated by his fellow-countrymen.

Last Day at Sea Uneventful.

Mr. MacDonald's last day at sea was uneventful. It was shadowed somewhat by receipt of the news of the death of Dr. Gustav Stresemann, German Foreign Minister. The British Minister paid tribute to Dr. Stresemann's achievements. He had often worked side by side with the German statesman in conferences abroad.

Miss Ishbel MacDonald, daughter of the Premier and his official hostess at 10 Downing Street, submitted to an interview by the correspondents traveling with the party. In what might be termed a prelude to the press experiences which await her today she expressed her belief that she was going to like America very much.

While the leader of his Majesty's Government was approaching these shores it became known in Washington that the momentous conferences between him and the President probably would be launched at Mr. Hoover's camp. The camp is located in not readily accessible country on the Rapidan River in Virginia in surroundings which for wildness may recall to Mr. MacDonald the rugged bleakness of his own North Scotland.

Literally at a camp fire, removed from all intrusion, these leaders of government, each with his own ideals for world betterment, will exchange their views. In this simple setting the President and the Prime Minister will undertake their efforts, free of the red tape and formality and cross-currents of the conventional conference.

City's Plans Completed.

The city's plans to welcome Mr. MacDonald were completed yesterday. They were approved by Secretary Stimson, who arrived at 5 o'clock and went to the Belmont Hotel. Mr. Stimson refused to talk, saying that until this morning he was not "officially" here. He was accompanied by James C. Dunn of the Division of International Conferences and of Protocol of the State Department, and by his military aide, Captain Eugene A. Regnier, U. S. A.

A representative committee, including leaders in finance, industry, journalism and politics, will welcome the British Labor party chief in conjunction with the official greeters. The committee was chosen by Police Commissioner Grover A. Whalen, as chairman of the Mayor's Committee on Reception of Distinguished Guests.

Members of the committee, Secretary Stimson and representatives of the British Embassy and consulate will be aboard the municipal boat Macom when she leaves Pier A at the Battery at A. M. to go down the bay to meet the Berengaria. Chairman Whalen and the Federal and foreign representatives will board the Berengaria, extend a pre-

Continued on Page Two.

BISHOP ... IN CHURC...

Protestant Epis... This Country Fa... Prelates' Se...

HAD SPOKEN OF W...

Amassed Fortune in ... Before Entering Minis... Was 72 Years Old

Special to The New York T...

ATLANTIC CITY, N. J., O... The Right Rev. John Gardne... ray, presiding Bishop of the ... tant Episcopal Church in the ... States, died this afternoon ... suffering a stroke while presi... over the House of Bishops in ... James Church here.

He collapsed while reading fro... the canon laws in ruling on a poin... of order and fell to the floor. Several Bishops rushed to his aid, and not realizing that the stroke had been fatal, began praying, kneeling beside the body. Three physicians arrived quickly and found that he was dead.

Bishop Murray, whose rank in the Episcopal Church corresponds to that of the Archbishop of Canterbury in the Church of England, had complained of indigestion, but had worked with great energy during the meeting. It was he who decided that a session should be held last night, and he was up and about early this morning after having spent a sleepless night.

He was to have officiated tomorrow at the consecration of the Rev. Dr. Francis Taitt as Bishop Coadjutor of Pennsylvania and had expressed a desire to complete the business early so that he and Mrs. Murray might take an early train for Philadelphia, where the ceremony was to be held. He had complained of being weary physically, though he would not spare himself.

To Elect Successor Nov. 13.

One hundred and five Bishops have attended the sessions. They were shocked by their leader's death but it was necessary to hold a special meeting in the afternoon to fix a date for the selection of a successor to Bishop Murray. A special meeting of the House of Bishops will be held at Washington, D. C., on Nov 13 to elect a new Presiding Bishop, who will hold office until the next general convention two years hence.

The senior Bishop by consecration is the Right Rev. William Andrew Leonard of Ohio, who was consecrated in 1889 and who is 81 years old. He presided at the afternoon session. The law of the Church provides for 45-days' notice for a special election, but the proviso was modified at the suggestion of Bishop Freeman of Washington, D. C.

The Right Rev. Hugh L. Burleson missionary Bishop of South Dakota, who was chief assistant to Bishop Murray, will remain in that capacity, and it was said here today that he probably would be chosen to succeed Bishop Murray. He is a member of the National Council of the Episcopal

Continued on Page Twenty-seven.

Jeanne Eagels Collapses, Dies in Hospital On Visit to Be Treated for Nerve Ailment

Jeanne Eagels, star of "Rain" and other theatrical and motion picture successes, died suddenly last night in the Park Avenue Hospital at 591 Park Avenue. Accompanied by her maid, Miss Eagels left her home at 1,143 Park Avenue just before 8 P. M. and went to the hospital, where she has been receiving regular treatments from her personal physician, Dr. Edward Cowles.

Dr. Cowles had not yet arrived at the hospital when she got there, but his assistant, Dr. Alfred Pellegrini, conducted Miss Eagles to his examination room on the top floor. She had just sat down on a bed to prepare for the examination when she was seized with a convulsion. She collapsed and died almost instantly. Dr. Pellegrini notified the Medical Examiner's office and Dr. Thomas A. Gonzales, Assistant Medical Examiner, hurried to the hospital. He ordered an immediate autopsy. Dr. Gozales said later the aptopsy showed death was caused by alcoholic psychosis.

Miss Eagels was born in Kansas City in 1894 and made her first appearance on the stage at the age of 7 as Puck in "A Midsummer Night's Dream." She first attracted attention when she appeared in New York in 1911 as Miss Renault in "Jumping Jupiter." She played Olga Cook in "The Mind-the-Paint Girl," toured with Julian Eltinge in "The Crinoline Girl," played Kate Merryweather in "The Great Pursuit" and toured with George Arliss as Lady Clarissa in "Disraeli." She also had leading rôles in "The Professor's Love Story," "Hamilton," "Daddies," "A Young Man's Fancy" and "In the Night Watch." But her best known rôle was as Sadie Thompson in "Rain," which ran for two years in New York.

In the Spring of 1928 Miss Eagels was suspended by the Actors' Equity Association for failure to appear for star rôle of "Her Cardboard Lover" at performances in Milwaukee and St. Louis. Her suspension ended Sept. 1, and she was preparing to reappear soon under the management of Sam H. Harris in a new play.

About three weeks ago she was operated on in St. Luke's Hospital for ulcers of the eyes caused by a sinus infection. Her condition improved steadily after the operation and she was able to leave the hospital ten days later.

Miss Eagels was married in 1925 to Edward H. (Ted) Coy, former Yale football star. She obtained a divorce on June 14, 1928, in Chicago on the ground of cruelty.

Jeanne Eagels Collapses, Dies in Hospital On Visit to Be Treated for Nerve Ailment

Jeanne Eagels, star of "Rain" and other theatrical and motion picture successes, died suddenly last night in the Park Avenue Hospital at 591 Park Avenue. Accompanied by her maid, Miss Eagels left her home at 1,143 Park Avenue just before 8 P. M. and went to the hospital, where she has been receiving regular treatments from her personal physician, Dr. Edward Cowles.

Dr. Cowles had not yet arrived at the hospital when she got there, but his assistant, Dr. Alfred Pellegrini, conducted Miss Eagles to his examination room on the top floor. She had just sat down on a bed to prepare for the examination when she was seized with a convulsion. She collapsed and died almost instantly. Dr. Pellegrini notified the Medical Examiner's office and Dr. Thomas A. Gonzales, Assistant Medical Examiner, hurried to the hospital. He ordered an immediate autopsy. Dr. Gozales said later the aptopsy showed death was caused by alcoholic psychosis.

Miss Eagels was born in Kansas City in 1894 and made her first appearance on the stage at the age of 7 as Puck in "A Midsummer Night's Dream." She first attracted attention when she appeared in New York in 1911 as Miss Renault in "Jumping Jupiter." She played Olga Cook in "The Mind-the-Paint Girl," toured with Julian Eltinge in "The Crinoline Girl," played Kate Merryweather in "The Great Pursuit" and toured with George Arliss as Lady Clarissa in "Disraeli." She also had leading rôles in "The Professor's Love Story," "Hamilton," "Daddies," "A Young Man's Fancy" and "In the Night Watch." But her best known rôle was as Sadie Thompson in "Rain," which ran for two years in New York.

In the Spring of 1928 Miss Eagels was suspended by the Actors' Equity Association for failure to appear for star rôle of "Her Cardboard Lover" at performances in Milwaukee and St. Louis. Her suspension ended Sept. 1, and she was preparing to reappear soon under the management of Sam H. Harris in a new play.

About three weeks ago she was operated on in St. Luke's Hospital for ulcers of the eyes caused by a sinus infection. Her condition improved steadily after the operation and she was able to leave the hospital ten days later.

Miss Eagels was married in 1925 to Edward H. (Ted) Coy, former Yale football star. She obtained a divorce on June 14, 1928, in Chicago on the ground of cruelty.

GERMANY MOURNS STRESEMANN DEATH; WORLD PAYS TR...

MILLIONS WERE LOST IN DIS...

... There were ... factors. One was fea... the brokers' loan statement, to be issued after the market's close, would show an increase of $150,000,000 to $200,000,000. Actually it reflected a further gain of $43,000,000, putting the security loans to a new high of $6,840,000,000. Other factors were the statement by Phillip Snowden, Chancellor of the British Exchequer, that the "orgy of speculation" in the New York market over the last year had been responsible for the advance of the British rediscount rate and the financial difficulties abroad; the weakening, by continued declines, of thousands of brokerage house accounts and the necessity for many customers of these firms to sell their stocks for what they would bring.

The greatest damage was inflicted on stocks in the final hour, and so heavy was the selling in this period that it was not until forty minutes after the hour that the final quotation had been tapped out on the tickers. Sales had been only moder-

Continued on Page Twelve.

... decisive. ... obeyed and followed ... always willingly—while the extreme opponents to the Right and Left, that is to say the Nationalists and Socialists, found him more than a match in his ready political wit and persuasive logic, and none of his opponents on the floor of the Reichstag could successfully challenge his mounting international prestige.

Death Called Irreparable Loss.

"His death," says the Vorwaerts, a Socialist organ, "is an irreparable loss, for Germany cannot produce another man who enjoys an equal measure of respect abroad and who at the same time can command the same following at home for the continuation of our foreign policies along present lines. For no matter how much ground Germany has gained in the past few years, it is yet not strong enough to indulge in the experiment of carrying on with an inferior Foreign Minister."

This newspaper considers the question of finding a successor to Dr. Stresemann one of life and death to Germany. While the Nationalist press is obviously tolerantly polite in their estimates of the dead Foreign Minister, the verdict of the Liberal press constitutes an impressive flow

Continued on Page Four.

COLORADO CONVICTS KILL TEN GUARDS, HOLD PRISON AND TOSS HOSTAGES' BODIES FROM WINDOWS AFTER ESCAPE IS BALKED

'Big Brother' Head Condones Prison Riots; Conditions Drive Men to Mutiny, He Says

Special to The New York Times.

GLENS FALLS, N. Y., Oct. 3.—Branding conditions in the State and Federal penitentiaries of the United States as the most degrading and impractical of any prisons in the world, Charles Brandon Booth, son of General Ballington Booth, and head of a "Big Brother" movement, tonight addressed more than 150 members of the Glens Falls Chamber of Commerce at their annual banquet here.

"I can show you a cell block where over 600 men are incarcerated and where the warden in putting in each new man knows that he is dooming that man to consumption," Mr. Booth said.

"I am not trying to lower your opinion of the wardens of our institutions. Contrary to that, I tell you that there is not a more capable, efficient group of officials in this country.

"They strive their utmost to do their duty, themselves fettered ... system which prevents them from carrying out even ... justice.

... uprisings in your State prisons were absolutely ... would have done the same thing. In the Federal ... Leavenworth, where a riot took place, there are at ... 000 men confined in buildings constructed for ..., but the officials are obliged to feed those ... appropriation made for 1,800 men. No wonder ... they were starved.

... must eventually have, is a system by which ... to work in prison in a gainful occupation."

...HELD ...RGE

... and bought ... for cash in ...3.50. ... and $50,000, repre-

Continued on Page Twenty.

... dent of the Baldwin ...; John Snoddy and Webb Fender, foremen; Forrest Smith and Will Twigg, mill employes, and Broad Roppins, Bill Biggerstaff, Charles Tate, L. S. Steppe, Dave Jarrett, Webb Jim Owens, Taylor Green, Ed

Continued on Page Nineteen.

Tallest Building to Rise in Times Square Area; Lefcourt Will Erect 1,050-Foot Skyscraper

The tallest building in the world is being planned for the Times Square area, it was made known yesterday by A. E. Lefcourt, New York builder, when he announced that he had purchased the northwest corner of Broadway and Forty-ninth Street as a site for the structure.

The building will tower 1,050 feet above the street level, according to the plan, and with the land will represent an investment of $30,000,000. An arrangement already settled between the builder and his client, said to be one of the largest business institutions in the country, is that the building shall not be less than the height announced. This will make it some fifty feet taller than the eighty-story Empire State Building planned for the old Waldorf-Astoria Hotel site and also much higher than the new City Bank Farmers Trust Building, which is to rise 925 feet in the financial district.

Mr. Lefcourt is to take possession of the Forty-ninth Street corner next March, he said, and demolition of the present two-story building now there will proceed immediately thereafter. This building is occupied by Brill Brothers, owners of the site, and was built in 1908. Brill Brothers will occupy a store in the new building, it was announced, but most of the structure will be occupied by the enterprise for whom the skyscraper is to be built.

Mr. Lefcourt has erected some of the tallest buildings on Manhattan Island. The highest he has built so far is the forty-two story Lefcourt-National, on the site of the old Temple Emanu-El, at Fifth Avenue and Forty-third Street. A still taller one is under construction at Madison Avenue and Forty-first Street, the forty-five story Lefcourt-Colonial. He also is planning the immediate beginning of a forty-five story apartment hotel on Central Park South.

Mr. Lefcourt would not even estimate the number of stories the newest building would contain. He spoke of the height in terms of feet.

LIQUOR PURCHASER NOT GUILTY OF PLOT

Federal Appeals Court Frees A. E. Norris of New York of Conspiracy in Transporting.

CHIDES PROHIBITION UNIT

...hiladelphia Ruling Will Be ...en Up to Supreme Bench, ...owman Says at Capital.

...ial to The New York Times.

...ADELPHIA, Oct. 3.—Alfred ...is of 55 East Seventy-second New York City, a broker, was ...ed by the United States Court of Appeals here today ...city in the case of Joel D. ...so-called "society bootleg... ...versing the verdict of the ...t, which held that a pur... liquor could be penalized ...or of illegal transporta... Appeals Court ruled that ... could not be punished ...deral law even if trans... involved.

... was found guilty of ...olate the prohibition ...trict Judge William ... and fined $200. ...ded guilty, was sen... months in the Fed... at Atlanta and

... two men followed ...deral prohibition ... New York that ... liquor in ca... the Norris

...ower court's ... by Circuit ... and Judge ... is on the ... to service ... dissenting ... filed, was ... Buffington, ... Appeals Court.

...ion Bureau Rebuked.

... majority opinion, written by Judge Thomson, the court held that a purchaser of illicit liquor was not amenable to the charge of conspiracy when a bootlegger delivered the liquor to him, even with his consent and at his specific request.

Not only does it reverse Judge Kirkpatrick's ruling, which was considered important by virtue of its extension of the government's control over the purchasers of bootleg liquor, but it also chides the Prohibition Bureau for overzeal in attempting control over the purchaser, which it declares, was not intended in any of the national prohibition statutes.

On this point the opinion says:

"It appears that while the legislative department of the government has deliberately and intentionally made the purchaser of liquor guiltless of any offense under the prohibition law, the executive department of the government seeks here, by indirection, to make of the same fact, namely the purchase, a crime subjecting the purchasers to a maximum fine of $10,000, and imprisonment for a term of two years.

"Such a condition is scarcely conceivable and yet it is the position of the Government."

"The clear purpose was, as frankly stated and repeated by the government's counsel in their argument to bring before the court for decision ... or seller of liquors, where transportation and delivery is made in pursuance of the sale, can be together indicted for a conspiracy to transport," the opinion continues.

"In the case of seller and buyer, transportation by the seller is a mere incident in the sale and necessary to its completion by delivery to the purchaser. It could not be said that a conspiracy would lie to do some-

Continued on Page Fifteen.

CONVICT DEAD ARE PUT AT 10

Troops Dynamite Cellhouse and Order Up Artillery Piece.

PRIEST PLACES THE BLAST

Rioters' Ultimatum Said They Would Kill Captives and Themselves Unless Freed.

SLEW VICTIMS ONE BY ONE

Flames From Four Burning Buildings Light Last Stand of 150—Warden Wounded.

By The Associated Press.

CANON CITY, Friday, Oct. 4.—At 2:30 o'clock this morning, Mountain Time (4:30 New York Time) National Guard troops, police and sheriffs' deputies were still besieging the State prison held by 150 convicts who mutinied yesterday, killed three guards outright and hour by hour slew four, and possibly three more, whom they held as hostages. Dynamite failing to blast a way to the cellhouse held by the convicts, a .75-millimeter gun had been sent for from Golden, 190 miles away.

Warden Francis E. Crawford was shot and badly wounded in the fighting between besiegers and mutinous convicts early today. The Warden was reported shot through the head and body and it was feared the wounds might prove fatal. John Allen, chief clerk of the penitentiary and Detective Sergeant Reth of Colorado Springs were also wounded.

Three More Hostages Slain.

Three more guards held prisoners within the cellhouse were believed to have been killed shortly before 1:30 o'clock this morning. This would increase to seven the number of hostages slaughtered by ringleaders of the revolt in their effort to force prison officials to set them free. Conviction that the guards, Osborne, Roache and Hollinger, had been killed grew when, after their deaths had been threatened, shots were heard within the cellhouse. John Pease, a guard who was sent out by the convicts with their final ultimatum, declared the convicts said that if this were rejected they would immediately kill Roache, Osborne and Hollinger.

The embattled convicts soon after 12:30 o'clock this morning renewed their demand that they be furnished automobiles and a clear road to escape. The demand was refused again. This followed the appearance of a party of convicts who came to the cell house for a parley.

John Pease, one of the guards captured by the convicts, came from the cell house with a message from Danny Daniels, leader of the mutineers. The refusal was shouted back to the convicts.

Priest Dares Bitter Gun Fire.

An immediate barrage of gunfire was opened. Under cover of this fire, Father O'Neil, a priest, who already had placed a blast which failed to explode, again advanced to the cellhouse and placed another charge of dynamite. A blanket of fire covered the doorway of the cellhouse to prevent the prisoners from firing on Father O'Neil.

From every point of vantage—buildings, walls, entrance way and windows—guards and militiamen poured a relentless barrage into the cellhouse.

Father O'Neil made a hard run with the heavy charge of dynamite and returned safely to the warden's house just outside the walls. The firing then died down preparatory to the exploding of the blast.

Convict Leader Fires Last Shot.

All the windows in the warden's house crashed in and the chandeliers fell as the charge of dynamite heralding the final advance exploded. Hats were blown off men outside the walls.

Danny Daniels, leader of the convicts, was seen at the window of the cell house just before the dynamite was exploded. It is believed that Daniels fired upon the priest. So quickly was the charge exploded after he was seen that he may have been caught in the débris.

A heavy pall of smoke rushed over the cellhouse.

Meanwhile, firing continued from the gate and the cellhouse was constantly swept with bullets. The two machine guns sprayed at full speed over the heads of the guardsmen as they advanced.

Militia Men Charge.

The west gate was opened as the charge exploded and the militiamen charged through it toward the cell-

REPORTS A SEDATIVE KILLED MISS EAGELS

City Toxicologist Finds That Actress Died From Overdose of Chloral Hydrate.

Jeanne Eagels, motion picture and stage star, who died Thursday night at the Park Avenue Hospital, 891 Park Avenue, died from an overdose of chloral hydrate, a nerve sedative and soporific, according to the findings of Alexander O. Goettler, city toxicologist. Dr. Charles Norris, Medical Examiner, announced the results of the chemical analysis yesterday afternoon.

Dr. Thomas A. Gonzales, Assistant Chief Medical Examiner, had conducted an immediate autopsy after Miss Eagels's death and reported the cause had been alcoholic psychosis, but final decision was withheld until after the chemical examination conducted by Dr. Goettler.

Body to Be Sent to Kansas.

A simple funeral service will be held at the Campbell Funeral Church, Sixty-sixth Street and Broadway, at 11 o'clock this morning. Then the body will be sent to her former home at Kansas City, Mo., where she will be buried. Miss Eagels's sister, Helen, her only relative in this city, made the funeral arrangements, and will meet her mother, Mrs. Julia Sullivan Eagels; her brothers, George and Paul, and a sister, Mrs. W. K. Ackerly, who are now in California, at Kansas City.

The public was permitted to view the body yesterday afternoon at the Campbell Funeral Church. Several hundred persons filed past the coffin and as many or more visited Loew's Lincoln Square Theatre, almost directly opposite, where posters blazoned forth "Jeanne Eagles in Jealousy," her latest talking motion picture.

Theatrical people who had known Miss Eagels and a steady sprinkling of curiosity seekers filed through the funeral church late yesterday afternoon and last night to see her body. Clifton Webb, the dancer, and his mother, old friends of the actress, were among those who stayed beside the silver and bronze coffin during the afternoon.

Many Floral Tributes.

Many floral tributes were received, including offerings from Barry O'Neal, who had appeared with Miss Eagels in "Her Cardboard Lover" on tour; Grace and Marie Savage and Maybelle and Clifton Webb.

David Belasco, in commenting on Miss Eagels's death, said last night: "I probably knew her better than most people here in New York. She had gone through many varied experiences. At the time she first came to my notice we had few managers who would take any chances with new talent. This girl couldn't get any employment, so she was obliged to take a job in the chorus. I remember her coming to me in a very happy frame of mind because a manager had given her several lines to speak. Her first real opportunity came in 'Daddies.' She made a hit in this production of mine.

"As I remember the girl she was charming, sympathetic, kind and gentle. She had been told that she was consumptive, but she led a quiet and a sweet life. She had spasms of pain which caused her great concern; she wasn't a bit like the temperamental star many probably thought her to be.

"She did not take a drink except when it was ordered by her physician, and this was necessary for h health. In the latter days of her li she did not drink for the pleasu of it."

Sam H. Harris, theatrical manage who was to have produced a pl starring Miss Eagels this season, sued a statement in which he sai "I had the highest regard for Mi Eagels as an artist and a woman. think the American stage has lost greatest actress."

Jeanne Eagels with Fredric March in *Jealousy*, 1929.

Jeanne Eagels with Reginald Owen in *The Letter*, 1929. Miss Eagels made her talkie debut in this film.

The New York Times TUESDAY, MARCH 7, 1967

Nelson Eddy, Baritone of the Movies, Dead at 65

Singer Who Had Appeared With Jeanette MacDonald Is Stricken During Act

MIAMI BEACH, March 6 (AP)—Nelson Eddy, the deep-throated baritone who thrilled a generation of movie-goers 25 years ago singing the romantic songs of Sigmund Romberg and Victor Herbert with Jeanette MacDonald, died at Mount Sinai Hospital here today a few hours after being stricken during a nightclub show at the Sans Souci Hotel. He was 65 years old.

Mr. Eddy had just finished a song to an audience of 400, and had started another when his voice suddenly failed.

"Will you bear with me a minute?" Mr. Eddy asked his audience. "I can't seem to get the words out."

With a look of puzzlement, he turned to Theodore Paxson, the pianist who accompanied him for many years, and asked: "Would you play 'Dardanella?' Maybe I'll get the words back."

Mr. Paxson and Mr. Eddy's singing partner, Gale Sherwood, helped him to his dressing room. A doctor from the audience administered first aid before Mr. Eddy was rushed to the hospital, where he died this morning.

He outlived Miss MacDonald by little more than two years. She died in January 1965.

Mr. Eddy is survived by his widow, Ann, his father, William D. Eddy of Jamestown, R. I., his stepmother, and a half-sister, Mrs. J. Lloyd Brown of Pawtucket, R. I.

Funeral arrangements will be made on the West Coast, where the Eddys lived.

Favorite of the Ladies

A sturdily built, brilliantly blond baritone, Mr. Eddy often sang romantic numbers, either clutching the reins of a horse or Miss MacDonald, his red-haired singing partner of eight major money-making films.

His open, clear-eyed face was usually as dispassionate as Miss MacDonald's was expressive. But it really did not matter. From "Naughty Marietta" in 1935 to "I Married an Angel" in 1942, the pair sang their way to stardom.

For Mr. Eddy, it was a success certified by the accountants. He earned $5-million from his movies, it was reported in 1944, and was making $15,000 a week from concert appearances and $5,000 a week on radio.

With or without Miss MacDonald, Mr. Eddy was a natural romantic lead for the colorful musicals of the late nineteen-thirties and early forties. Handsome, blessed with a resounding voice that breathed masculinity, the very model of a wholesome all-American type of hero, he drew the ladies to the movie houses. It was estimated that 85 per cent of his fan mail came from women.

Nelson Eddy and Jeannette MacDonald in *The Girl of the Golden West*, 1938.

Whether the backdrop was Old Vienna ("Bitter Sweet"), old New Orleans ("Naughty Marietta"), old Paris ("Sweethearts") or the Old West ("The Girl of the Golden West") did not matter. Audiences flocked to the theaters to hear him sing "Ah, Sweet Mystery of Life," "Sweetheart, Will You Remember Me?" "Rose Marie, I Love You," "Stout Hearted Men" and "Tramp, Tramp, Tramp."

Fondness for 'Short'nin' Bread'

On radio, where he soon established a popularity that rivaled the one he had achieved in films, his trademark was "Short'nin' Bread," which was not only the song most loved by the listeners but also the one that provided a topic for joshing when he appeared with such comedians as Edgar Bergen, who used his wooden friend, Charlie McCarthy, to kid Mr. Eddy about it ceaselessly.

Between his box-office success and his vulnerability, because of his success, to critics and comics, Mr. Eddy always remained a pleasant, sociable man who referred to his work as his "business" and enjoyed what went with it.

During the nightclub engagements that occupied the last years of his life, he and his partner, Miss Sherwood, sometimes tried to spoof his big film numbers.

"I kid myself and I let Gale kid me," he told an interviewer. "I think it breaks down some resistance. People might think I take myself too seriously.

"You know, some people resent our kidding around a little bit. People come up to me and say, 'Look, this is sacred. Sing 'Indian Love Call' but sing it straight.' "

He and Miss MacDonald were approached with a plan for a screen reunion, he once recalled.

"We've been asked to do what might be called B pictures," he said. "Rather than do that, we decided we'd like to leave it on a high note."

This emphasized the fact that, while he could chuckle at himself, he had a good deal of respect for the music he sang and the movies in which he appeared.

Altogether, there were 16 major films in which Mr. Eddy starred. He played opposite Ilona Massey in "Balalaika;" opposite Miss Massey and Eleanor Powell in "Rosalie," a West Point football story, and opposite Risë Stevens in a durable serving of whipped cream called "The Chocolate Soldier."

Nelson Eddy was born June 29, 1901, in Providence, R. I., to parents who traced their ancestry back, on one side, to President Martin Van Buren.

In 1915, the family moved to Philadelphia. Young Nelson had to go to work and never finished high school. He worked as a telephone operator, a classified ad salesman and an advertising copywriter. He lost his job when his employer found him more interested in music than in ads.

Partial to Wagner

In 1924 he made his debut at the Metropolitan Opera House in the role of Tonio in "Pagliacci." He had learned 32 operatic parts and could sing in English, French, Spanish, Italian, German, Russian and Yiddish. He was always partial to Wagner.

In 1928 he performed his first concert recital, in Philadelphia. From then on, it was concert touring for a number of years—"hoping for $50 a concert and glad to get $25," he later recalled.

In 1933 Nelson Eddy and Hollywood found each other through another singer's illness in Los Angeles. Mr. Eddy was flown in from San Diego as a substitute. He had 14 encores, innumerable curtain calls and, most important, the ear of Ida Koverman, who was in the audience.

Miss Koverman was private secretary to Louis B. Mayer, head of the Metro-Goldwyn-Mayer studio. She persuaded Mr. Mayer to give Mr. Eddy a nine-year contract. His first role, in "Broadway to Hollywood," a vaudeville-family account, scarcely made history.

Another film, "Dancing Lady," with Joan Crawford, also failed to establish him.

"I engaged a dramatic coach and began to study the technique of acting on the screen," he recalled. "That same day I discovered how little I really knew."

Mr. Mayer persuaded Hunt Stromberg, producer, to cast Mr. Eddy in the lead of "Naughty Marietta," opposite Miss MacDonald. The picture had been awaiting the solution of casting problems and Mr. Stromberg, somewhat hesitantly, gave in.

He warned Mr. Eddy that he had an uphill job. If nothing else, "Ah, Sweet Mystery of Life" was the theme song of Forest Lawn Cemetery, and he would have to sing it well enough to re-establish its identity.

From that time, in 1935, Mr. Eddy had only to look forward and at Miss MacDonald.

In 1939, Mr. Eddy married Ann Denitz Franklin. The wedding caused some concern at the studio, where it was feared that the singer's female fans might not be so happy about a handsome blond married man.

The couple lived in a colonial house in Brentwood, Calif., where Mr. Eddy made a hobby of sculpturing and collected ancient pewter and porcelain Tang horses.

The New York Times FRIDAY, OCTOBER 15, 1976

Dame Edith Evans Is Dead at 88; A Legend of the English Theater

By JOSEPH COLLINS
Special to The New York Times

LONDON, Oct. 14—Dame Edith Evans, a legend of the English theater in her own lifetime, died at her home in Cranbrook, Kent, today. She was 88 years old. She died after a brief illness.

Dame Edith, the little milliner's apprentice whose subtle cadences accounted for much of the magnetism of her performances, lost little of her force with the passing years.

In 1968, at the age of 80, she walked away with all the acting awards as the lonely, unwanted Margaret Ross in Bryan Forbes's movie "The Whisperers."

She died only a few months after Dame Sybil Thorndike, her great contemporary. They were widely considered the two greatest actresses of this century.

Wide Range of Parts

Dame Edith's talent shone in a wide range of parts, but perhaps never so brightly as in comedy—Shaw, Wilde, and the Restoration comedies, which sprang into sophisticated, bawdy life after the monarchy was restored in England and Charles II ascended the throne.

A role with which her name will always be linked was the formidable Lady Bracknell in Oscar Wilde's "The Importance of Being Earnest."

When her prospective son-in-law confesses that he did not know his parents and had been found in a station baggage room in a handbag, she exploded: "a ha-and-baaag!" Rarely have three syllables run up the scale so deliciously to express disbelief, horror, shock and distaste. And rarely can a playwright have been so well served.

William Poel, the producer, saw her in an amateur production of "Much Ado About Nothing" and invited her to join his company. In 1912, she made her London debut as Cressida in "Troilus and Cressida."

Studied Drama at 16

"I never wanted to be on the stage," she once said. "But once I was there I knew that's where I belonged."

At 16, while learning to make ladies' hats in a London millinery shop, she began attending a drama class, which developed into a club known as the Streatham Shakespeare Players. It was there that Mr. Poel saw her on the stage.

But it was not until 1924, after a Shakespearean tour in Ellen-Terry's Company and acting in some Shaw plays in repertory, that she gained recognition and acclaim. This was as Millamant in Congreve's "The Way of the World," a part that she made her own.

"The Way of the World" was put on at the Lyric Theater, in suburban Hammersmith. However, West End audiences flocked out to see it and the newspaper reviewers loved it. She played Millamant again three years later.

As in all her work, it was difficult to be sure where pure technique stopped and innate artistry alone took over. She was as at home with the soliloquies of Shakespeare, giving them her own lilt, as she was with the mocking brittleness of Millament.

Played Two Cleopatras

She played Cleopatra in two different plays, Dryden's "All for Love" (1922) and Shakespeare's (1925 and 1946). Her Viola and her Rosalind are remembered with no less pleasure than her more earthly characters of good King Charles's golden day. Edith Evans was born in London on Feb. 8, 1888. Despite the name Evans, the family was not of Welsh descent. Her father was a civil servant in the Post Office.

She married George Booth, an engineer, in 1925. He died 10 years later. One of Dame Edith's few failures was her venture as an actress-manager in 1930. She put her savings into a production of "Delilah" in London, but it ran for only five performances.

During World War II, she entertained the troops at home and overseas, returning to Britain in 1945 for a production of Sheridan's "The Rivals." She played Mrs. Malaprop, for which praise was heaped upon her.

The next year, she was created a Dame Commander of the Order of the British Empire for services to the theater.

Best Remembered Roles

Among some of her best remembered roles were the Nurse in "Romeo and Juliet," which she played several times here and in New York to Katharine Cornell's "Juliet" in 1934, "Daphne Laureola" (London 1949; New York 1950), "Waters of the Moon" (1951) and "The Chalk Garden" (1956).

She performed in some Shakespeare plays in her first season at the Old Vic and returned there in 1958—a magnificent Queen Katherine in Henry VIII. She starrred in New York in 1931 in "Lady with a Lamp" and in "Evensong" two years later.

She made her first movie in 1948 and her versatility extended easily to the screen; her parts ranged from a Welsh mother in "Dolwyn," in which a young actor named Richard Burton played her son, to "The Chalk Garden" in which Hayley Mills acted her granddaughter.

Her work in "The Whisperers" won her the Silver Bear Award at the Berlin Film Festival, the Golden Globe in Hollywood, the New York Film Critics Award, the British Film Academy Award and the Variety Club of Great Britain Award.

Dame Edith Evans in *The Whisperers.*

The New York Times WEDNESDAY, DECEMBER 13, 1939.

DOUGLAS FAIRBANKS DIES IN HIS SLEEP

Stage and Screen Actor Is Victim of a Sudden Heart Attack at Santa Monica

SAW FOOTBALL SATURDAY

Special to THE NEW YORK TIMES.

HOLLYWOOD, Calif., Dec. 12—Douglas Fairbanks Sr., stage and screen actor, died in his sleep at 12:45 A. M. today at his residence at 705 Ocean Front, Santa Monica, at the age of 56. The cause of death was a sudden heart attack, following a slight one on Monday morning.

At his bedside when the end came were his widow, the former Lady Ashley; her sister, Mrs. Basil Bleck; Mr. Fairbanks's brother, Robert, and a nurse.

Douglas Fairbanks Jr. was called immediately but did not arrive until after his father's death.

C. E. Erickson, business manager for Mr. Fairbanks for the past twenty years, said the actor seemed in good spirits and health Saturday when he attended the football game at Los Angeles between the University of Southern California and the University of California at Los Angeles.

He Complained of Pains

On Sunday Mr. Fairbanks seemed nervous, Mr. Erickson said, and on Monday morning he complained of pains in his arms and chest. Shortly afterward he suffered a slight heart attack.

Canceling an intended visit to downtown Los Angeles, Mr. Fairbanks went to bed and Dr. Stanley Granger and Dr. Philip Sampson were called.

After an examination, it was not thought the illness was critical, but complete rest was ordered and a nurse placed on duty.

Last night, Mr. Erickson said, Mr. Fairbanks seemed much improved. The family retired, but were aroused shortly before 12:45 o'clock this morning by the nurse. The end came at that hour.

Mrs. Fairbanks collapsed at news of her husband's death and was immediately placed under the care of Dr. Sampson.

Friends of the family arranged tentatively to remove the body to Forest Lawn Cemetery, last resting place of such movie notables as Jean Harlow, Will Rogers and many others.

Body Lies Before Window

SANTA MONICA, Calif., Dec. 12 (UP)—The body of Douglas Fairbanks Sr. lay tonight in an ornately carved bed before a window of his Santa Monica mansion which looked out on the vast Pacific.

Douglas Fairbanks starred in *The Thief of Bagdad.*

Through the night and day came a procession of Hollywood great and the forgotten who had worked with and known Fairbanks in his swashbuckling days.

For hours Mr. Fairbanks's 150-pound mastiff Marco Polo whined beside the deathbed, refusing to move.

Although several years retired from roles which made him a world celebrity, Fairbanks continued as a bon vivant and a noted host.

He was a millionaire and movie producer, and had two objectives. One was to film the greatest adventure picture of all time; the other to complete his Shangri La, an estate at Rancho Santa Fé, 100 miles from Santa Monica and so elaborate with waterfalls and game preserves that his friends laughingly told him he never would live to finish it.

The film was to have been called "The Californian."

FAIRBANKS A STAR OF SILENT MOVIES

Most Spectacular Actor of Era Before Talking Films Noted for Acrobatics

Of all the glittering stars and sensational personalities which the silent screen gave to the world, Douglas Elton Fairbanks was, by far, the most spectacular. Other of his contemporaries at a time when film fame was as potent as regal glory may have shared equal popularity with him—Mary Pickford as "America's Sweetheart," Charles Chaplin as the world's beloved comedian. But Mr. Fairbanks, with his flashing smile and the vaulting agility of an acrobat, was the romantic personification of a male perfection, the athletic idol of small boys and the screen's most adored superman.

In the years of his greatest film accomplishments—those elaborate and fantastic costume dramas such as "Robin Hood," "The Thief of Bagdad," "Don Q" and 'The Black Pirate"—he was known throughout the world, unable to travel any place without attracting swarms of admirers for whom he generally performed some hair-raising stunt. Off screen, as well as on, he seemed to go through life leaping balustrades, scaling walls and beaming his never-to-be-forgotten smile—the 'million-dollar smile' which he once confessed to hating.

In those years, too, Mr. Fairbanks and Mary Pickford, whom he married in 1920, were the most idealized couple in America in the eyes of the motion picture fans. Millions of words were written about them, thousands of pictures were spread before the world. Their home, Pickfair, was the gathering place of the Hollywood elite, and they ruled the uncrowned monarchs of that fabulous El Dorado. But through such flamboyant publicity and the popularity of such early stars, the hold of motion pictures upon the masses was unquestionably sealed.

Last Picture Was in 1934

Later, when the "talkies" arrived and fashions in films began to change, Mr. Fairbanks, like many other "silent" stars, began to lose his great popular appeal. He wisely read the handwriting on the wall and refrained from further screen appearances after "The Private Life of Don Juan" in 1934.

His separation and later divorce from Mary Pickford in 1935 brought an end, also, to that romantic phase of his career. But his early investments in producing organizations and his partnership in United Artists had made him a wealthy man and kept him actively interested in the industry. At the time of his death, he was planning a return to film production.

But in spite of the important place which he held in the motion picture world, Mr. Fairbanks often said that he considered himself a failure. He had started out to be a Shakespearean actor, he said, and he had ended up "as an acrobatic clown." His only consolation was the fact that he brought more happiness to more people through his romantically comic roles than he ever could have afforded as a dark Othello or the "gloomy Dane" in Hamlet.

Mr. Fairbanks was born in Denver, Col., on May 23, 1883, the son of H. Charles Ulman, a New York lawyer who had gone west to look after some mining interests and remained there. Mr. Ulman was a Shakespearean scholar, and his son Douglas had begun to recite from the works of the Bard at the age of 7. At 12, he could repeat whole plays by heart and delighted to perform on those occasions when Shakespearean actors were entertained at his father's home.

At Denver he attended the Jarvis Military Academy, the East Denver High School and the Colorado School of Mines. When he was 17 years old his father moved to New York and Frederick Warde gave Douglas a part in one of his plays which was going on tour. His first stage appearance was made in Richmond, Va., on Sept. 10, 1900, playing a small role in "The Duke's Jester." Shortly thereafter he had his name legally changed to Fairbanks.

He Studied at Harvard

After a season with the Warde repertory company, during which the stage-struck boy wrestled with several classic roles, he went to Harvard, where he was briefly enrolled as a special student. But his enthusiasm for higher education was not as great as his flair for the theatre, and he soon returned to Broadway to obtain a small part in "Her Lord and Master," supporting Effie Shannon and Herbert Kelcey.

However, a touch of the wanderlust, which stayed with him throughout his life, took young Fairbanks off to Europe with a couple of friends. On his return to New York some months later he got a job in the brokerage firm of De Coppet & Doremus, gave it up to take a fling at the hardware manufacturing business, and then went back to the stage for a role in "Mrs. Jack," with Alice Fisher.

A heated encounter with the stage manager ended this engagement, however, and he took up the study of law—briefly. But soon he was back on Broadway, working for William A. Brady in "The Pit."

(continued)

Douglas Fairbanks with Mary Astor in *Don Q, Son of Zorro.*

Mary Pickford and Douglas Fairbanks in *The Taming of the Shrew*.

Upon the close of that play he went to London, appeared over there in his first and only musical comedy, "Fantana," for Lee Shubert, and then returned to New York when Mr. Brady offered him a five-year contract.

He appeared successively for Mr. Brady in "Frenzied Finance," supporting Grace George; "Clothes," "Man of the Hour," "As Ye Sow" and other light comedies, establishing himself as one of the leading juveniles of the New York stage. While playing in "A Gentleman of Leisure" in 1911, he was released from his contract with Brady and overnight signed with Cohan & Harris. For this firm, he starred in such plays as "Hawthorne, U. S. A.," "Officer 666" and "He Comes Up Smiling."

Smile Discovered by Accident

It was at about this time that Mr. Fairbanks discovered the attraction of his smile—quite by accident, he once said. At a tense moment in a play, he remembered a story he had heard at luncheon and, despite all efforts not to, he grinned. The effect was electric; the audience cheered. Thereafter he developed this asset into the amazing personal trade-mark it later became.

His penchant for athletic expansiveness came natural, however, and he was always noted for his extreme activity on stage. Medium in height and fairly stocky, young Fairbanks devoted much time to his physical development. It is reported that he entered the motion pictures on the insistence of D. W. Griffith after that prominent director had seen him vault a hedge while walking in Central Park.

However that may be, Mr. Fairbanks did quit the stage for Hollywood in 1914, appearing in his first picture, "The Lamb," under Griffith's direction. The firm was the old Triangle-Fine Arts, and the Fairbanks salary was publicized as $2,000 a week, a large sum in those early days. Pictures which followed were "Double Trouble," "Reggie Mixes In," "The Americano" and other fast comedies in which Mr. Fairbanks showed to fine effect his exuberance and acrobatic adroitness.

In 1917—the year that Yale seniors voted him their favorite actor, Forbes-Robertson second—Mr. Fairbanks broke with the old Triangle firm because he felt he wasn't receiving sufficient publicity, and with his director, John Emerson, set up his own producing company. This concern—the Douglas Fairbanks Pictures Corporation—made about a dozen successful films, among them "In Again, Out Again," "Wild and Woolly," "Down to Earth" and "Mr. Fix It."

Two years later, in 1919, Mr. Fairbanks joined with Griffith, Chaplin, Miss Pickford and Charles Ray to form the original United Artists Company, the intention being that each should produce his own pictures and release through this combined distributing unit. The organization has proved, through the years, one of the most successful and profitable in Hollywood, despite changes in partners and some discouraging phases. Miss Pickford, Mr. Fairbanks and Chaplin are still listed as partners.

It was under this new set-up that Mr. Fairbanks's urge for romantic spectacle took flower. First with "The Mark of Zorro" and later with "Robin Hood," "The Three Musketeers," "Don Q" and many others, he filled the Nineteen Twenties with a succession of brilliant costume pictures in which he, against spectacular backgrounds, was just about the whole show. He rode horses, scaled walls, leaped from windows and made sensational escapes. His films of this period were the height of romantic fantasy and were frequently marked by interesting technical innovations.

"The Taming of the Shrew" and "Reaching for the Moon," in 1929 and 1931, marked the end of Mr. Fairbanks's long reign as master of spectacle. "Mr. Robinson Crusoe" in 1932 was disappointing and

Douglas Fairbanks with Charlie Stevens in *Robin Hood.*

"The Private Life of Don Juan," made in England in association with Alexander Korda in 1934, marked the end of his acting career. Among other pictures in which he appeared was "The Gaucho."

The marriage of Mr. Fairbanks and Miss Pickford (Gladys Mary Smith), which took place in Los Angeles on March 28, 1920, was one of the most sensational events of that post-war decade. Mr. Fairbanks previously had been married to Beth Sully, daughter of Daniel N. Sully of New York, a cotton broker. This marriage had occurred in 1907 and ended in divorce in 1919. The former Mrs. Fairbanks is now married to Jack Whiting. Miss Pickford had been married and divorced from Owen Moore.

The Fairbanks-Pickford wedding, which was actually performed in comparative secrecy, was followed by a six-weeks' honeymoon in Europe, which became perhaps the most publicized wedding trip in history. A corps of publicity men preceded the newly wed couple; crowds were attracted every place they went.

Couple Cheered in London

In London, Mr. Fairbanks straddled a balcony of the Ritz Hotel while thousands cheered in the street below; in Venice, the couple went for a moonlight ride in a gondola, with an accompanying barge-load of cameramen, and Mr. Fairbanks scaled the side of an American warship in the harbor. Their union was hailed as "the greatest screen romance ever."

Rumors of a separation between Mr. Fairbanks and Miss Pickford preceded the formal petition for divorce filed by the latter in 1933. Their breakup was attributed to the fact that Mr. Fairbanks preferred to travel, Miss Pickford to remain in Hollywood. There was some talk of a reconciliation in 1934, but the divorce was granted by Judge Ben Lindsay in Los Angeles in January, 1935. The final papers were signed on Jan. 14, 1936, as the two sat together in a business conference.

Meanwhile, Mr. Fairbanks had been seen frequently in the company of Lady Ashley, wife of Lord Ashley of London, heir of the Earl of Shaftesbury. And, on Nov. 28, 1934, Lord Ashley had obtained a divorce in London, naming Mr. Fairbanks as co-respondent. The suit was not contested and Mr. Fairbanks was ordered to pay the costs. On March 7, 1936, Mr. Fairbanks and Lady Ashley were married in Paris, and had spent most of their time abroad since then. She was the former Sylvia Hawkes, musical comedy actress.

In recent years, there has been considerable talk of a shake-up in the partnership holdings in United Artists, and in May, 1937, it was reported that Samuel Goldwyn and Alexander Korda would buy up the Fairbanks - Pickford - Chaplin holdings for $10,000,000. This sale was not arranged, however, and the three original partners, who have not been active of late, remained in the company. Control, however, is reported to have fallen into the hands of Goldwyn and Korda.

About a year ago, Mr. Fairbanks announced his intention of returning to production with a new unit to be called Fairbanks International. He said he would make three pictures in 1939, the first of which was to be "The Californians." Unsettled conditions held up the schedule.

Fairbanks in one of his best films, *The Gaucho,* 1927, with Lupe Velez.

W.C. Fields and Alison Skipworth in *If I Had A Million.*

The New York Times THURSDAY, DECEMBER 26, 1946.

W. C. FIELDS, 66, DIES; FAMED AS COMEDIAN

Mimicry Star of the Films Since 1924 Got Start as a $5-a-Week Juggler

RARELY FOLLOWED SCRIPT

PASADENA, Calif., Dec. 25 (AP) —W. C. Fields, the comedian whose deadpan gestures, raspy remarks and "never give a sucker an even break" characterizations made him a showman beloved the nation over, died today at the age of 66.

He was equally well known in show business for his ad libbing and complete disregard for prepared scripts, either in the movies or radio. Once he said that the only lines he followed truly were those of Charles Dickens.

Fields got his first job in show business as a juggler at a summer park in Norristown, Pa., at $5 a week.

Left Home at Age of 11

Few men have contributed as much to the world's merriment as W. C. Fields. The comedian who ran away from home when he was 11 years old, who starved and suffered and was forced to live on his wits, kept his sense of the ridiculous—developing it, indeed, it would seem, with every hard knock he received in his youth.

His capital consisted of a highly expressive face, with a bulbous nose as the main feature, a fine voice for comedy purposes and a profound capacity for punishment. Of earthly goods he had little until he blossomed forth as one of the really great comedians about the year 1924.

His art has been described erroneously as that of the slapstick and clownerie. It is true that he could out-slapstick and out-clown most funny men of stage, circus or screen, but he possessed just a little more than his contemporaries. He was a master mimic, inimitable in his droll asides, an improviser and innovator of new tricks.

Some years ago when a whole cast of screen stars were picked to take parts in "Alice in Wonderland" he easily outshone the others in his conception of Humpty-Dumpty. The voice alone carried him to one of his greatest artistic triumphs in that egg disguise.

Career a Series of Struggles

It took many long years for Fields to reach the top. There are recorded struggles and infinite patience to master the art of juggling tennis balls and saucepans, night after night of sleeping under the stars, day after day of little or no food. A weaker man would have whined, begged, asked for governmental relief of some sort. Fields fought his fight against tremendous odds and won—and he never lost his humor. Even in life's darkest moments he saw something funny, for he had the true comedian's ability to laugh at himself.

Claude William Dukenfield—for that was his real name—was born in Philadelphia on Jan. 29, 1880. His father was severe, austere and very poor; also he had old-fashioned ideas about using the rod on his offspring.

There was nothing of the sentimental love-your-father complex in the lad's make-up, and the family ties were snapped forever one afternoon when the elder Dukenfield stepped on a toy shovel. The shovel smacked up against his shin. Thereupon the father used it as a paddle on the boy. The next day the lad waited for his father to arrive and then smacked his pater with a heavy wooden box. Then he ran away.

Developed Art of Juggling

The lad was then a homeless waif. His clothes were so many rags, his outlook most desolate. But he began to juggle anything he could find: stones, apples, tennis balls knocked over fences by beflanneled overprivileged youth and adroitly caught by the future star. Fields practiced for hours, gradually acquiring the exact sense of balance, and he finally managed to get himself engaged in his first theatrical venture.

It is recorded that he went abroad and performed juggling acts in Europe, Asia, South Africa, Australia and even at Pago Pago in the South Sea Islands. He was in Johannesburg while the guerrilla end of the Boer War was still on, juggling clubs and other sundry articles.

Dawn of success began to break when he was engaged for the Ziegfeld Follies. He filled in while the beautiful girls were changing costumes and drew plaudits from everybody except Flo Ziegfeld. The "Great Ziegfeld" knew about as much as there is to know about beautiful women, but he lacked appreciation of comedy. Field's act was cut from twenty-five to five minutes and he was more or less out in the cold again.

Soon after he went into motion pictures under the direction of D. W. Griffith. His many years in pantomime proved invaluable. He was an overnight success, and in 1926 he went on the staff of the Paramount-Famous Players-Lasky Corporation.

He is remembered for his notable presentation of Micawber in "David Copperfield." Other successes of the screen in which he played major parts include "The Great McGonigle," "Tillie and Gus," "Six of a Kind," "Mrs. Wiggs of the Cabbage Patch," "Mississippi" and "The Man on the Flying Trapeze."

During the last ten years the principal Fields films were "Poppy," "The Big Broadcast of 1938," "You Can't Cheat an Honest Man," "My Little Chickadee," written by Mae West and Mr. Fields and starring both; "The Bank Dick" and "Never Give a Sucker an Even Break."

W. C. Fields with Mae West in *My Little Chickadee.*

W.C. Fields triumphed in a daring bit of casting as Micawber in the 1934 production of *David Copperfield.* Freddie Bartholomew played the young David.

The New York Times SATURDAY, JANUARY 15, 1977

Peter Finch Is Dead on Coast at 60; British Actor on Stage and Screen

By MURRAY ILLSON

Peter Finch, the British actor and star of the widely acclaimed recently released movie "Network," died yesterday at a hospital in Los Angeles, after collapsing in the lobby of the Beverly Hills Hotel. He was 60 years old.

Mr. Finch, who appeared in more than 35 films in an acting career that started in Australia in 1938, was said to have suffered a massive heart attack while sitting in the hotel lobby, waiting to appear on a television show.

It was said that he was to have appeared on ABC's "Good Morning America" with Sidney Lumet, director of "Network."

After futile attempts to revive him, Mr. Finch was taken, unconscious, to the medical center of the University of California's Los Angeles branch, where he was placed in the intensive-care unit.

Appeared on Carson Show

The actor's most recent public appearance was on the "Tonight Show," with Johnny Carson, televised from the West Coast Thursday night. Speaking of Mr. Finch, a spokesman for the show said, "He looked old to me, older than I had expected."

Mr. Finch was also seen last weekend on NBC's television broadcast of the second version of the Israeli rescue last July 4 of hostages in Uganda, "Raid on Entebbe." In the film he played Yitzhak Rabin, Prime Minister of Israel.

A suave, literate man who exuded an air of wordly grace, Mr. Finch was the winner of numerous acting awards in this country and abroad. His rousing performance as Howard Beale, the demented news commentator in "Network," was seen as virtually certain to win him an Academy Award nomination for best actor. He had previously been nominated for his role as the homosexual doctor in the 1971 film "Sunday Bloody Sunday."

Mr. Finch was born on Sept. 28, 1916, in London, where, as he once put it, his father was a professor of science "at the university." He spent his early childhood in France and at the age of 10 was taken by his grandmother to India, where under her guidance he settled down to study with a Buddhist priest. That phase did not last long and he was sent to Australia to live with cousins.

After attending schools in Australia during the Depression, he worked at various occupations, including those of a newspaper reporter, waiter, magazine salesman and straight man for a comedian.

"If I was going to be broke," Mr. Finch told an interviewer some years ago, "I decided I might as well do it with actors as anyone else. They were cheerful idiots and seemed to take it better."

After serving with the Australian forces in World War II, Mr. Finch organized his own traveling dramatic company that put on classical plays in little theaters and in factories during lunchtime. "It failed," he once observd, "because people wanted to lie on the beach."

However, it was at that period, during a performance of Molière in a Sydney factory, that he was seen by Sir Laurence Olivier, who was touring Australia with the Old Vic company. A personal contract to Sir Laurence followed, as did Old Vic appearances.

Mr. Finch made his English debut on the stage in 1949, playing with Edith Evans in "Daphne Laureola." "I was lucky—it was a whacking success—people stood up and cheered," he recalled.

Preferred Film Roles

Later he appeared in plays with John Mills and Diana Wynyard, in "Othello" with Orson Wells and in "Romeo and Juliet" at the Old Vic.

However, Mr. Finch preferred acting in films; he said he did not have the patience for appearing in long-run plays.

"It would be ghastly if you got yourself into one of those three-year things," he said in an interview. "I think after three months your performance must deteriorate. That's why I prefer movies—three or four months and you are finished. I like to change steps if I can. You stultify as an actor if you get stuck in a groove."

Among the films Mr. Finch appeared in were "The Miniver Story" with Greer Garson and Walter Pidgeon (1950), "Gilbert and Sullivan" with Robert Morley and Maurice Evans (1953), "Elephant Walk" with Elizabeth Taylor and Dana Andrews (1954), "The Detective," with Alec Guinness (1954), "The Heart of the Matter" with Trevor Howard (1954), "The Warriors" with Errol Flynn (1955), "The Nun's Story" with Audrey Hepburn (1959), "The Sins of Rachel Cade" with Angie Dickinson (1961), "In the Cool of the Day" with Jane Fonda (1963), "The Pumpkin Eater" with Anne Bancroft (1964), "Judith" with Sophia Loren (1966), "The Legend of Lylah Clare" with Kim Novak (1968), "The Nelson Affair" with Glenda Jackson (1973) and "Lost Horizon" with Liv Ullmann (1973).

Mr. Finch was married three times, and his first two marriages ended in divorce. He leaves a daughter, Anita, by his first wife, Tamara Tchinarova; a daughter, Samantha, and a son, Charles, by his second wife, Yolande Turner, and a daughter, Diana, by his third wife, Eletha Barrett, who survives. Mr. Finch also leaves his mother, Alicia Gladys Fisher of London.

Peter Finch in *The Green Carnation.*

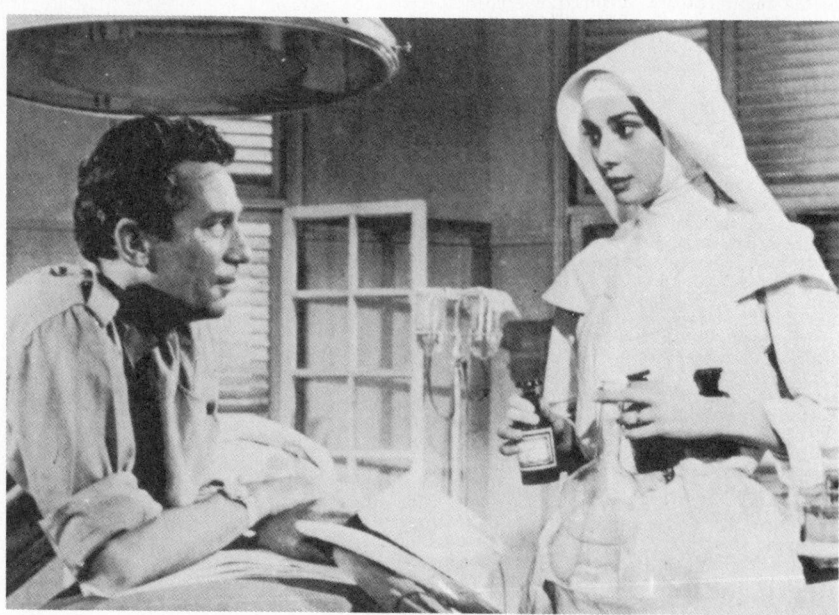

Peter Finch and Audrey Hepburn in *The Nun's Story.*

The New York Times THURSDAY, JANUARY 5, 1961.

Barry Fitzgerald Is Dead at 72; Stage and Film Star Won Oscar

Priest in 'Going My Way' Noted for Roles as Drunken and Rumpled Irishman

Special to The New York Times.

DUBLIN, Jan. 4—Barry Fitzgerald, one of Ireland's outstanding stage and screen actors, died in a hospital here tonight after an illness of several months. He was 72 years old.

His brother, Arthur Shields, the Hollywood actor, survives.

Fighting Movie Figure

To the moviegoer, Barry Fitzgerald was the cocky little bantam of an Irishman, inevitably getting into barroom discussions that grew more heated with each passing beer.

Just as inevitably the discussions reached a climax with Mr. Fitzgerald's striking a classical boxing pose and challenging one or more of his antagonists to "Come on now, put up your dukes; come on now, put up your dukes."

Yet, ironically, he won his greatest film honor—an Academy Award as best supporting actor in 1944—for his performance as a lovable, if irascible, parish priest with Bing Crosby in "Going My Way."

To the theatregoer, he was any one of a dozen or more characters, but perhaps most memorably "Captain" Jack Boyle in Sean O'Casey's "Juno and the Paycock"—a braggart rogue, a royal-mannered ne'er-do-well, a salty buffoon, dressed in wrinkled rags that clung uncertainly to his portly figure, a huge belt carelessly buckled around his waist, a squalid cap at an angle on his head.

As "Captain" Boyle, stern on the surface and all bluff underneath, Mr. Fitzgerald was more than a caricature of the Ireland so affronted by the portrait. He endowed the role, as one critic put it, "with the exasperating stubbornness, the lawlessness, the bridge-burning pride, the maudlin moods, the volatile beauty of the Irish heart."

Comic Spirit Incarnate

For many, on stage and screen, Mr. Fitzgerald was the incarnation of the comic spirit. People started laughing the moment he poked his squint face into view and began choking the English language into the back of his mouth.

As Brooks Atkinson, former drama critic of The New York Times, said of Mr. Fitzgerald's comic appearance in Louis D'Alton's "Tanyard Street":

"No one else can tangle himself up so grotesquely in shirts, suspenders and trousers, and no one can look so bedraggled when he is dressed in his best for churchgoing. Mr. Fitzgerald must sleep in his clothes for weeks to achieve the ripeness of his appearance on the stage."

As a member of Dublin's Abbey Theatre Players, Mr. Fitzgerald received a scroll in New York in 1934 acclaiming him as "the most versatile character comedian in the world today." Yet he came by his acting art relatively late in life and by chance.

Mr. Fitzgerald, whose real name was William Joseph Shields, was born in Dublin on March 10, 1888. His family claimed a vague sort of relationship to William Orr, the Irish hero who was hanged in 1798. Mr. Fitzgerald was frankly skeptical of the claim. "Everybody in Ireland wants to be related to a patriot," he once said.

Among the youngster's playmates were James Joyce's younger brothers. Joyce himself was not included and was regarded by the group rather suspiciously as "a young man with a beard and very clever."

After graduation from Civil Service College, where for three years "they stuffed our heads with enough to pass the competitive exams," Mr. Fitzgerald passed the examinations and became a junior executive attached to the Unemployment Insurance Division. He explained the choice of his profession by saying:

"It was the one into which most of the families of our grade in my young days tried to stow away their progeny, as it gave security, a fair living and a certain social status."

Mr. Fitzgerald found the work dull, if secure, and devoted much of his spare time to sports—boxing, swimming and football. He went often to the Abbey Theatre, had a chance meeting with one of the actors while out for a walk and then took a walk-on part when not enough players showed up for a crowd scene.

That was in 1915 and a few weeks later he got a speaking part with four words in it: "'Tis meet it should." They came out "'Tis sheet it mood." The audience laughed and Mr. Fitzgerald became a comedian.

By 1918, he was playing major roles, but it was not until 1929, fourteen years after his first part, that he felt secure enough in the theatre to give up his job with the Unemployment Insurance Division. In fact, he had had the Abbey Theatre pick out the name Barry Fitzgerald so that the Civil Service would not know that he was not devoting full time to his government job. He was 41 years old when he became a full-fledged actor.

The Abbey was an exciting place at the time. Backstage came such men as A. E. (George William Russell), Shaw, Synge, Yeats. There was also Sean O'Casey, of whom Mr. Fitzgerald once said, "When he wrote, he wrote in full spate and his lines carried an actor with them." Later he shared an apartment in London with Mr. O'Casey, who in 1929 wrote "The Silver Tassie" for Mr. Fitzgerald.

Came to U. S. in 1932

Mr. Fitzgerald came to the United States with the Abbey Theatre in 1932 and stayed in this country on and off for the rest of his life.

Memorable role followed memorable role, in Dublin, London, New York and later in Hollywood. He appeared in plays by Synge, Yeats, Dunsany, Pirandello, Molnar and Strindberg, among others.

Mr. Fitzgerald also appeared in many notable roles in motion pictures, including "The Plough and the Stars," "The Long Voyage Home," "Naked City," "The Quiet Man," "How Green Was My Valley" and "None But the Lonely Heart." During his years in Hollywood, Mr. Fitzgerald, a bachelor, shared an apartment with his stand-in, Angus D. Taillon, who died in 1953.

Because of his convincing appearance as a Roman Catholic priest in "Going My Way," many people were surprised to learn that Mr. Fitzgerald was a Protestant. He said that he based his convincing characterization on several of his clerical friends.

Fittingly, Mr. Fitzgerald's last two films, "Rooney" and "Broth of a Boy," both comedies, were made in Ireland. The latter opened in New York in December, 1959, two months before he underwent brain surgery in Dublin.

Barry Fitzgerald, Rise Stevens and Bing Crosby starred in *Going My Way*.

Barry Fitzgerald, John Wayne and Maureen O'Hara in *The Quiet Man*, 1952.

The New York Times THURSDAY, OCTOBER 15, 1959.

ERROL FLYNN DIES; SCREEN ACTOR, 50

Stricken in Canada While Arranging Sale of Yacht—Had Adventurous Career

VANCOUVER, B. C., Oct. 14 (AP)—Errol Flynn died here tonight, apparently of a heart attack, on the way to a hospi-tion-picture actor was 50 years old.

Mr. Flynn was in Vancouver to sell his $100,000 schooner Zaca. He had come here last week to complete the deal with a Vancouver business man.

Perennial Glamour Boy

Errol Flynn was a perennial Hollywood glamour boy, whose light-hearted escapades ran the gamut from real adventures in the wilds of New Guinea to what read like fictional encounters with a series of beautiful women.

Sailor, novelist, prize-fighter, newspaper correspondent, soldier of fortune and world traveler, he found time to become one of the ten best money-making stars in motion pictures. Every time that it seemed that he had taken a knock-out punch in some unfortunate misadventure, he bounced back apparently more hale, hearty and ready for serious work as an actor than before.

Mr. Flynn was born in Hobart, Tasmania, on June 20, 1909, a son of Theodore Thomson and Mrs. Marelle Young Flynn. He attended the Lycee Louis le Grand in Paris, St. Paul's School, London, the North Shore Grammar School, Sydney, Australia, and also schools in Ireland and South Western London College. He started his career with a characteristic serio-comic gesture of farewell to all that—by taking a post as second cook on an ocean-going schooner.

Took Newspaper Job

After that he turned up in succession as a member of the New Guinea Constabulary in Papua, as an overseer of a tropical copra plantation, and then — and here everyone thought he had finally settled down—as a newspaper correspondent in Sydney.

Mr. Flynn's father had served as a Professor of Marine Biology at Queen's College, Belfast, Northern Ireland, and perhaps some of the ocean trips of his now almost legendary early life were explainable in that light—that the elder Flynn felt that his chronic habit of running away from school could be cured by travel to strange places. But Errol soon outstripped his father in the variety and daring of his job changes and adventures.

Flynn in *The Charge of the Light Brigade*, 1936.

Errol Flynn

He was living a life of romantic adventure in the South Seas when the moving picture world suddenly caught up with him.

His small schooner was chartered one day in the early Nineteen Thirties by a group of Americans who had come to the South Pacific to make moving picture of the New Guinea head-hunters. The movie men were impressed with the appearance of the boat's skipper and took ample footage of him, which was shown in Australia.

The matter might have ended there but Errol Flynn had suddenly become alive to the prospects of moving picture work and went to England to study acting.

Mr. Flynn began his professional acting career in 1934 with the Northampton Repertory Company in England. He played major roles in such dramas as John Drinkwater's "A Man's House," and in 1935 he was spotted by a Warner Brothers talent scout and signed up. After several inconsequential roles, he was starred in "Captain Blood," a swashbuckling adventure picture for which he seemed ideally cast.

From that time on he was typed as a sometimes unscrupulous but usually golden-hearted leader of small adventurous bands and squads of daring cavaliers. His other starring vehicles included "Robin Hood," "Gentleman Jim," "Dawn Patrol," "The Sea Hawk," "Adventures of Don Juan," "Against All Flags," "Green Light," "The Prince and the Pauper," and "Objective Burma."

Mr. Flynn married Lilliane Carré (the actress Lili Damita) in 1935. They were divorced in 1942. He met his second wife, Nora Eddington, in the Los Angeles County Hall of Justice while standing trial on a statutory rape charge. Miss Eddington, who worked behind the cigar counter in the hall, was married to him in 1943 in Mexico, after his acquittal.

They were subsequently divorced and in 1950 he married an aspiring actress, Patrice Wymore at Monte Carlo. A son, Sean, was born of the first marriage, and two daughters, Deirdre and Rory, of the second. He also had one daughter, Anella Roma, by his third wife.

At various times the actor was charged with other acts of misbehavior, including numerous fist fights, but there often remained after the trials, at which he seemed to be invariably acquitted, a considerable cloud of doubt as to whether his accusers had been in earnest, or seeking publicity by embarrassing him.

Mr. Flynn took it all with a light heart. After he had been called a "charming rogue," stories, possibly press agent-inspired, came out that he was "about to turn over a new leaf," and "a new and serious Errol Flynn" was about to be born.

Don't believe a word of it," the actor exclaimed with a laugh.

The New York Times TUESDAY, AUGUST 27, 1968

Kay Francis, Actress, Dies at 63; Epitome of Glamour in the '30's

Her 50 Films Included 'Give Me Your Heart,' 'Raffles' and 'I Found Stella Parish'

Kay Francis, one of the foremost motion picture actresses of the 1930's, died vesterday of cancer in her apartment on East 64th Street. She was 63 years old.

Miss Francis had returned to her home on Saturday after having been a patient at New York Hospital. At her request, there will be no funeral service.

The actress, who quite frankly wanted to make it to the top, went from the Broadway stage to Hollywood, where she was quickly established as one of the screen's busiest, best-paid and most popular actresses.

Her tall slender figure and raven black hair, which framed a face dominated by large, moist eyes, were seen in more than 50 motion pictures from 1929 to 1945, and were frequently admired as of an almost regal beauty.

When she started, the lexicon of the screen had not jelled, and talking pictures were sometimes called "audible pictorial transcriptions" and actresses were said to "impersonate" characters. In 1931, as in one or two subsequent years, Miss Francis made seven pictures, whose titles suggest their distinction:

"Ladies' Man" (with William Powell); "Scandal Sheet," "Twenty-Four Hours," "The Vice Squad," "Transgression," "Girls About Town" and "Guilty Hands" (with Lionel Barrymore).

More Than a Living

It was, as it proved, more than a living. In 1937, Miss Francis received $227,800 in salary, in a year when F. A. Cudahy Jr., president of the Cudahy Packing Company, received $75,000 and Harvey S. Firestone, chairman of the Firestone Tire and Rubber Company, got $85,000.

The actress, who sometimes submitted to but who loathed interviews, held strongly to the right of personal privacy for public figures, but there was a point in the mid-thirties when hardly a wink of her eyelash went unreported—especially if the wink seemed to be aimed at one or another of her swains or suitors.

Miss Francis, who could at times blaze up in anger, was not always at pains to be polite

Kay Francis in 1948, when she appeared in "The Last of Mrs. Cheyney" on stage.

to reporters and film crew members. In 1934 it was reported that she "flew at a news photographer who snapped her picture" at Newark Airport.

The actress had a way of landing near the top of various lists. In addition to the salary list, she was often included on the lists of the best-dressed women in films and, in 1933, Maxwell Arnow included her, with Katharine Hepburn and Helen Hayes, as one of "the 10 brainiest women" in motion pictures.

Her stately figure was sometimes wrapped in silken fur to the ear lobes; she would appear in a broad-brimmed hat with a pheasant's feather curling smartly from its band; she was deemed the epitome of glamour and sexiness in the slinky evening gowns in which she often portrayed "the other woman" on the screen.

Miss Francis, who was afflicted with a faint lisp and could not always count on pronouncing her r's correctly, tried something a little different in playing Florence Nightingale in "The White Angel."

The New York Times critic called the film "dignified, reasonably accurate, deeply moving and dismayingly pompous" and wrote that Kay Francis as the founder of modern nursing "talks, walks and thinks like a historical character; when she speaks she is speaking for posterity."

Miss Francis played top roles in "Raffles," "First Lady," "One Way Passage," "Mandalay," "British Agent," "Wonder Bar" (with Al Jolson) and "The House on 56th Street."

"The Goose and the Gander" proved to be an especially perilous venture since, as a critic wrote, its chief impediment to an evening pleasantly unimportant in the cinema comes from its insistence on cramming the dialogue with r's, which have an embarrassing habit of becoming w's when Miss Francis goes to work on them."

Some of the most popular of her films had to do with frustrated mother love, as in "I Found Stella Parish "(1935" and "Give Me Your Heart" (1936).

In 1941 she appeared with Jack Benny in "Charley's Aunt." Miss Francis's film career, which had been so notable, ended rather sadly with her departure from the major studios to Monogram, where she made what one film collector here described yesterday, with grim sarcasm, as "The Monogram Trilogy:" "Divorce" (1945), "Allotment Wives" (1945) and "Wife Wanted" (1946), low-budget melodramas, in which she acted and was co-producer with Jeffrey Bernerd.

Before going to Hollywood, Miss Francis had appeared on Broadway in "Venus," "Crime" and "Elmer the Great," opposite Walter Huston. In 1946, she returned to the stage after an 18-year absence in "State of the Union," the Howard Lindsay-Russel Crouse Pulitzer Prize comedy.

She ended her acting career in summer stock

Oklahoma City Native

Verity is rarely stressed in motion picture biographical data, and Miss Francis was listed as having been born at three places, but Oklahoma City appears to have been the site, on Jan. 13, 1905. She was educated in private schools and convents. A teen-age marriage to Dwight Francis, scion of a socially prominent Massachusetts family, ended in divorce, as did her marriages to William A. Gaston, a lawyer, and Kenneth McKenna, a Broadway actor.

Miss Francis had lived a rather secluded life here lately and expressed some bitterness at how her Hollywood fortunes had risen so high and sunk so low.

Lilyan Tashman and Kay Francis in *Girls About Town.*

Clark Gable and Deborah Kerr in *The Hucksters*.

"All the News That's Fit to Print"

The New York Times.

LATE CITY EDITION
U. S. Weather Bureau Report (Page 72) forecasts: Mostly fair, not as warm today; fair, cold tonight. Fair, mild tomorrow. Temp. range: 55—45; yesterday: 62.2—52.1.

VOL. CX.. No. 37,553. NEW YORK, THURSDAY, NOVEMBER 17, 1960. FIVE CENTS

10 cents beyond 50-mile zone from New York City except on Long Island. Higher in air delivery cities.

Clark Gable Dies in Hollywood Of Heart Ailment at Age of 59

'King' of Film Capital Was One of Ten Top Boxoffice Attractions for Years

By The Associated Press.

HOLLYWOOD, Calif., Nov. 16—Clark Gable, for thirty years "king" of Hollywood actors, died tonight of a heart ailment that first struck him Nov. 6. He was 59 years old.

The film star died at 11 P. M. Pacific Coast Time (2 A. M. New York time) at Hollywood Presbyterian Hospital.

His wife, Kay, and his physician, Dr. Fred V. Cerini, were with him when he died.

Leader for Two Decades

As the "King of Hollywood" for more than two decades, Mr. Gable was one of the most popular actors in the world.

He held the affection of moviegoers longer than most other stars. For many years he was among the ten top boxoffice attractions. Theatre marquees would announce simply, "This week: Clark Gable."

To millions the tall, handsome man with the mustache, broad shoulders, brown hair and gray eyes was the symbol of masculinity, "naughty but nice."

He did not think he was a great actor. "I can't emote worth a damn," he said. "When I die they'll put on my tombstone, 'He was lucky—and he knew it.'"

When he was earning $7,500 a week he hung in his dressing room reminders of the days when he was a struggling actor or piling lumber in Oregon for $3.20 a day. Across the mementos he wrote: "Just to remind you, Gable."

There were many Gable legends. One was that in "It Happened One Night" (1934) he had sabotaged the undershirt industry overnight by peeling off his shirt in the picture and revealing nothing under his shirt but himself.

"I didn't know what I was do-

Continued on Page 37, Column 4

Clark Gable

U.S. WILL REDUCE SPENDING ABROAD BY A BILLION TO STEM GOLD DRAIN; DEPENDENTS AT BASES TO BE CUT

CALIFORNIA IS PUT IN NIXON'S COLUMN BY ABSENTEE VOTE

But Kennedy Is Still Assured of Presidency With Total of 300 Electoral Ballots

POPULAR MARGIN SLIM

President-Elect Is in Texas to Hold Conference With Johnson and Rayburn

By The Associated Press.

SAN FRANCISCO, Nov. 16—Vice President Nixon captured California's thirty-two electoral votes from President-elect Kennedy tonight ...

[Senator Kennedy flew to Johnson City, Tex., Wednesday for a major policy conference at the ranch home of Vice President-elect Lyndon B. Johnson near-by. They will be joined by House Speaker Sam Rayburn.]

Los Angeles County, which had most of the remaining absentee votes, was giving Mr. Nixon a consistent edge of better than 63 per cent.

Los Angeles expects its absentee ballots to total about 80,000. About 200 observers from Republican and Democratic party organizations are watching the count.

Mr. Nixon has consistently

Continued on Page 28, Column 3

POLICE HEAD RIPS P.B.A. CARD IN TWO

But Cassese Says Ouster Move Will Continue

By GUY PASSANT

In view of reporters and television cameras yesterday, Police Commissioner Stephen P. Kennedy tore up his membership card in the Patrolmen's Benevolent Association and dropped it into an ash tray.

"It seems to me that this whole business is somewhat ridiculous," he said with a smile.

"Does this mean that you are resigning from the P. B. A.?" he was asked.

"The act speaks for itself," he replied. "You can read into it any meaning you wish."

Later, with the two halves of the torn card taped back together, Commissioner Kennedy repeated his performance for television cameramen and photographers who had arrived late.

Patrolman John J. Cassese, president of the association, said that the group nevertheless would go ahead with a move to oust the Commissioner as a member.

"The Commissioner can do anything he wants with the card," Patrolman Cassese said. "That's his business.

"But, in keeping with the rules and by-laws of the association, and carrying out the mandate of the membership, he will be served with charges and specifications within a week, and at the next meeting he can plead his case.

"He will get a fair hearing at the next meeting. Of course he can lose by default."

On Tuesday night at a membership meeting in the base-

Continued on Page 32, Column 4

ALLIES AFFECTED

Vote in France on Algeria Set for 1961 by de Gaulle

President Plans Referendum on Policy of Giving Moslems Choice of Links With Paris or Independence

By ROBERT C. DOTY
Special to The New York Times.

PARIS, Nov. 16—President de Gaulle will ask France to approve by referendum, probably early in January, his plans for letting the Algerians make their choice between independence and continued association with France. ...

... prove to be decisive. If the "activists" among the Europeans of Algiers plan a new insurrectional movement such as those in May, 1958, and January of this year, it will probably come to a climax in that period, according to this view.

In any new emergency, as in the previous two, the attitude of the French Army in Algeria probably would be decisive. Government circles in Paris were hopeful, if not confident, that the army as a whole would refuse to follow the minority of career officers that has made common cause with the dissident civilians in the past.

There were authoritative reports that up to 80 per cent of the officers were shocked and alarmed by General de Gaulle's Nov. 4 speech in which he fore-

Continued on Page 18, Column 2

HELP FOR DOLLAR

Directive of President Curtails Families of Troops by 284,000

Statement, directive and news conference, Page 10.

By FELIX BELAIR Jr.
Special to The New York Times.

AUGUSTA, Ga., Nov. 16—President Eisenhower ordered all Federal agencies today to cut their foreign spending to the bone to stem the increasing deficit in the United States' balance of payments and the consequent drain on the nation's gold reserves.

The President said the moves were necessary to prevent other nations from becoming fearful that the dollar was weakening.

It was estimated that his directives would save at least $1,000,000,000 a year. The balance-of-payments deficit is currently running at an annual rate of almost $3,800,000,000 and the President said it might reach $4,000,000,000.

A principal directive, which would produce almost half the total savings, provides a mandatory reduction in the total of dependents of military personnel abroad. General Eisenhower ordered the Secretary of Defense to reduce the dependents abroad from the current level of 484,000 to 200,000 at the rate of 15,000 a month, beginning Jan. 1.

C. I. A. Also Affected

The State Department, the Central Intelligence Agency and the International Cooperation Administration as well as the Defense Department were ordered to reduce civilian staffs wherever possible.

Referring to allied nations that have gained strength as a result of United States assistance, the President remarked: "We should insist that they carry their part of the economic programs and help to meet the payments which we find so burdensome."

To emphasize the importance he attached to the continued deficit in the nation's balance of international payments, President Eisenhower put in an unexpected appearance at the Richmond Hotel in downtown Augusta to talk with White House newsmen about his directives. The President is vacationing here.

At his news conference, summoned on half an hour's notice, the President hinted strongly that a reduction in troop

Continued on Page 10, Column 7

U. S. TO REASSURE NATO ON ATOM USE

Plans to Tell Allies It Would Fight an Attack in Europe With Nuclear Weapons

By JACK RAYMOND
Special to The New York Times.

WASHINGTON, Nov. 16—The United States is planning to reassure the North Atlantic Treaty Organization that it will not hesitate to use nuclear weapons to fight aggression in ...

... States soil was not under attack. The United States is not committed to use nuclear forces in Europe under any existing treaty.

The statements that the United States plans to make before the NATO meeting are being fashioned to deal with the suspicion that Washington

Continued on Page 4, Column 5

Anthony Montagu Brown, Sir Winston's secretary, said tonight "there is no cause for anxiety" after disclosing news of the injury. Sir Winston was described as "quite cheerful" and resting comfortably.

The former Prime Minister will have to remain in bed for some days, however. Sir Winston will be 86 years old Nov. 30. Since his return to London Oct. 25 from a vacation in the south of France he has appeared livelier than he had been for some time.

Lord Moran, who has been Sir Winston's personal physician since before World War II, visited his patient at his home at Hyde Park Gate this afternoon.

Continued on Page 6, Column 4

MAYOR QUESTIONS CITY TUITION PLAN

... steps had been recommended Tuesday in a report to Governor Rockefeller by his three-man Committee on Higher Education, headed by Dr. Henry T. Heald, president of the Ford Foundation and former chancellor of New York University.

The suggestion that tuition-free higher education be ended brought sharp protests from alumni groups and students at the city's colleges, and plans were announced to carry their opposition to Albany.

The Heald report, which called for a long-range program to revamp higher education in the state, proposed tuition "rebates" to students with limited incomes. It also urged state aid for all institutions of higher learning, public and private, including church-related colleges.

Mayor Wagner commended the proposal for a strengthened state university, "not the sprawling substitute for it that the Legislature gave to us a ...

Continued on Page 32, Column 6

City ... Testify

By LAYHMOND ...

Frank Sinatra and other entertainers may testify in the city's widening investigation into charges of police ... in the issuance of cabaret permits.

This possibility arose yesterday when Investigation Commissioner Louis I. Kaplan said at a news conference that he intended to call in Mr. Sinatra and other entertainers in a search of nightclub records that showed they had performed without permits from the city police.

Noting that Mr. Sinatra, who lives in California, was outside the jurisdiction of his office, Mr. Kaplan said: "I'll telephone him. I think he will respond. I think he's just that public spirited."

The singer said through a spokesman on Tuesday that he

Continued on Page 32, Column 5

Contempt of Congress is a misdemeanor, punishable by a fine of not more than $1,000 and up to a year in jail. But there is a special statute that says that any contempt of Congress shall be reported to the "appropriate United States Attorney, whose duty it shall be to bring the matter before the grand jury for its action."

Representative Celler argued that this statute required initiation of a case by a grand jury through an indictment. He said the purpose of the law was "to remove all discretion from the United States Attorney," and he added:

"It was intended that ...

Continued on Page 72, Column 6

... week he hung in his dressing room reminders of the days when he was a struggling actor or piling lumber in Oregon for $3.20 a day. Across the mementos he wrote: "Just to remind you, Gable."

There were many Gable legends. One was that in "It Happened One Night" (1934) he had sabotaged the undershirt industry overnight by peeling off his shirt in the picture and revealing nothing under his shirt but himself.

"I didn't know what I was do-

Continued on Page 37, Column 4

NEWS INDEX

Clark Gable Dies in Hollywood Of Heart Ailment at Age of 59

Continued From Page 1, Col. 5

ing to the undershirt people," he recalled. "That was just the way I lived. I hadn't worn an undershirt since I started to school."

Some said that his ears had been pinned back when he became a star. His reply: "Never." Early in his career, however, he was turned down by one top studio. He quoted an executive as saying: "Gable won't do. Look at his big ears." The executive later hired him.

A Native of Ohio

William Clark Gable (he dropped his first name after he entered the theatre) was born in Cadiz, Ohio, on Feb. 1, 1901. His father was an oil contractor. His mother died before he was 1 year old.

At 15, after his father had remarried, the family moved to Ravenna, Ohio. His father quit oil drilling for farming. Young Gable forked hay and fed hogs wanted to be a physician.

With a friend he went to Akron. While taking premedical courses in the evening he worked for a tire company molding treads on tires. He saw his first play and decided to be an actor. He got a job as a callboy at a theatre—running errands and doing assorted jobs. He received no salary—just tips.

At 16, after his stepmother died, he and his father went to the Oklahoma oil fields. After working as a tool dresser, he got a job with a troupe that played everything from "Uncle Tom's Cabin" to "Her False Step."

When the company closed in Montana, he took a freight train to Oregon. He worked in a lumber company, sold neckties, and was a telephone company linesman.

In 1924 Mr. Gable joined a theatre company in Portland. He made his first appearance on the screen in a silent film starring Pola Negri. He appeared in two Los Angeles stage productions and then headed for Broadway.

Portrayer of Villains

In three years, he portrayed mostly villains. Then he returned to Los Angeles, where was a hit in the role of Killer Mears in "The Last Mile."

This led to a movie role again as a heavy, in "The Painted Desert," with William Boyd for Pathé in 1930. The story is that Mr. Gable was interviewed and asked if he could ride a horse. He said he could, and got the job; then he went out and learned how to ride.

His effort won him a contract with Metro-Goldwyn-Mayer. He

Associated Press

Clark Gable

first became a leading man in "Dance, Fools, Dance," with Joan Crawford. His first big hit was "A Free Soul," in which he slapped Norma Shearer.

Women by the thousands wrote in that they, too, would like to be slapped around by Mr. Gable. "For two years I pulled guns on people or hit women in the face," he later recalled.

He was a workhorse. His pictures included "Hell Divers," "Susan Lennox," Polly of the Circus," "Strange Interlude," "Red Dust," "No Man of Her Own," "The White Sister," "Hold Your Man," "Night Flight," and "Dancing Lady."

Mr. Gable's roster of leading ladies included Greta Garbo, Jean Harlow, Carole Lombard and Helen Hayes.

In 1934, overwork led to his being hospitalized. M-G-M decided he was evading a picture. When he got out, he was sent to Columbia Pictures on loan, supposedly as a punishment.

Won Oscar in Columbia Film

Columbia starred him in a comedy—"It Happened One Night." Claudette Colbert played a runaway heiress, and Mr. Gable a newspaperman, traveling by bus from Miami to New York. Both won Academy Awards for the best performances of the year.

Mr. Gable had broken out of a type-casting rut.

The next year, he played Fletcher Christian in "Mutiny on the Bounty," which won an Academy Award as the best film of the year.

In the next seven years, Mr. Gable appeared in more than twenty-five films, including "China Seas," "San Francisco," "Saratoga," "Test Pilot," "Idiot's Delight," "Gone With the Wind," "Boom Town," "They Met in Bombay" and "Somewhere I'll Find You."

From 1932 through 1943, he was listed among the first ten money-making stars in the yearly surveys by The Motion Picture Herald. After time out for military duty, he regained that ranking in 1947, 1948, 1949 and 1955.

Observers believe his films have grossed more than $100,000,000, including $50,000,000 for "Gone With The Wind". He had roles in at least sixty pictures.

After his third wife, Miss Lombard, was killed in a plane crash during a bond tour in World War II in 1942, Mr. Gable enlisted in the Army Air Forces as a private. He was then 41.

He rose to major, took part in several hazardous bomber missions over Europe, filmed a combat movie on aerial gunnery and won the Distinguished Flying Cross and the Air Medal.

After the war, he returned to Hollywood, and a Metro slogan, "Gable is back and Garson's got him" spread across the country. He starred with Greer Garson in "Adventure."

Then followed such films as "The Hucksters," "Mogambo," "The King and Four Queens," "The Tall Men," "Soldier of Fortune," "Teacher's Pet," "Run Silent, Run Deep," and "But Not for Me." He had been a freelancer since leaving Metro in 1954.

"It Started in Naples," a comedy with Mr. Gable and Sophia Loren, opened in New York in September, 1960. The film concentrated on the voluptuous attractions of Miss Loren, and a review in The New York Times said "the screen play has him shaded from the outset."

In July, 1960, Mr. Gable had begun work with Marilyn Monroe on "The Misfits." The film, reportedly budgeted at $3,500,000, was interrupted when Miss Monroe became ill five weeks later, but resumed in the fall.

Mr. Gable married five times. His first two marriages — to Josephine Dillon and Rhea Langham—ended in divorces in 1930 and 1939. Mr. Gable next married Miss Lombard. His fourth marriage, to the former Lady Sylvia Ashley, resulted in divorce in 1952.

In 1955, he married Mrs. Kay Williams Spreckels, former model and screen actress. Last Sept. 30, Mr. Gable announced that she was to have a child in the spring making Mr. Gable a father for the first time. She had had two children by her marriage to Adolph Spreckels 2d.

Clark Gable and Claudette Colbert in *It Happened One Night*, for which they both won Academy Awards.

The New York Times THURSDAY, MAY 22, 1952.

JOHN GARFIELD DIES AT HOME OF FRIEND

Actor, 39, Famed for 'Tough' Roles on Stage and Screen, Had Cardiac Ailment

John Garfield, stage and screen actor noted for his portrayal of tough characters, died of a heart ailment in the apartment of a friend, Miss Iris Whitney, at 3 Gramercy Park yesterday morning. He was 39 years old.

Miss Whitney, an actress and interior decorator, said Mr. Garfield had visited her Tuesday night and had become ill. She let him stay overnight in the bedroom, while she slept in the living room, she added. After trying vainly to waken him in the morning, she telephoned Dr. Charles H. Nammack, a private physician, who pronounced the actor dead at 9 A. M. The Medical Examiner's office ascribed Mr. Garfield's death to a cardiac condition and said there was "nothing suspicious" about it.

Mr. Garfield had been living until recently at his home at 88 Central Park West with his wife, the former Roberta Seidman, whom he married in 1932. They have two children, David 8, and Julie, 5. A third child, Katherine, died in 1945 at the age of 6. It was said that Mr. Garfield had had a minor disagreement with his wife about ten days ago and moved into the Warwick Hotel, 65 West Fifty-fourth Street.

The actor had starred recently in a successful nine-week revival of Clifford Odets' play "Golden Boy." It was in a smaller role in this same play in 1937 that Mr. Garfield gained the prominence that led to Hollywood roles.

His husky physique, shock of dark hair and his truculent manner made him a natural choice for "type casting" as gangster, criminal or "grown-up Dead-End kid."

In Hollywood he was known as an actor with no taste for night clubs, the social whirl, fancy cars and other frills.

"Screen acting," he once said, "is my business. But I get my kicks on Broadway." He made movies for money, but acted on the stage because it was his love. Once he turned down a studio offer reputed to be $250,000 a year to go into a little theatre production of "Skipper Next to God" at $80 a week.

Aided by Angelo Patri

Born Julius Garfinkle in New York, he was the son of David and Hannah Garfinkle. "My father," he said, "was a presser in a factory during the week, but a cantor on week-ends and holidays." Later the family moved to the Bronx.

After the death of his mother when he was 7 years old, the future actor played hookey so often that he was expelled from several schools. Finally he was sent to Public School 45, the Bronx, of which Angelo Patri, who was noted for his rehabilitation of problem pupils, was principal.

"That was the beginning of everything for me," Mr. Garfield said. With Mr. Patri's encouragement, he took up boxing, in which he attained sufficient prowess to rank as a semi-finalist in a Golden Gloves tournament, and studied oratory and dramatics. He attended the Heckscher Foundation dramatic school on a scholarship. To pay his expenses, he earned $6 a week as a newsboy and received $5 more from Mr. Patri.

With the Heckscher Theatre group he appeared in "A Midsummer Night's Dream" and other plays while attending Roosevelt High School. He also studied for the theatre under Mme. Maria Ouspenskaya and Richard Boleslavsky. Next he joined Eva Le Gallienne's Civic Repertory group, where he played minor roles.

Later, as Jules Garfield—the first change in his name—he became associated with the Group Theatre Acting Company, which had been formed in 1930-31. As an apprentice he worked with the regular company at Ellenville, N. Y., where the group's plays were prepared for the stage.

Won Lead in 'Wonderful Time'

His first chance was as a member of the road company of "Counselor at Law," with Otto Kruger. Later he played in the Broadway production, starring Paul Muni. Then he was offered the lead in Marc Connelly's production of Arthur Kober's "Having a Wonderful Time."

The play was a hit, but Mr. Garfield, feeling obligated to the Group Theatre, left his $300-a-week role to accept a $40 bit part in "Golden Boy." "It seemed to me," he said, "that in the Group lay the future of American drama." He appeared in such plays as "Waiting for Lefty," "Awake and Sing," "Weep for the Virgins" and "Peace on Earth."

Mr. Garfield signed a contract with Warner Brothers in 1938 but specified that he be allowed to do one stage play a year. His first assignment was in "Four Daughters." Much of the credit for the success of the picture went to John Garfield — as Warner's had renamed him.

His protests about pictures with prison atmosphere and suspensions from scheduled roles led to better parts in "Juarez," "Saturday's Children," "The Sea Wolf" and "Out of the Fog," and "Tortilla Flat."

More recent pictures include "The Postman Always Rings Twice," "Gentleman's Agreement" and "Body and Soul."

During the war he went on many overseas tours to entertain troops and was a leader in the Hollywood Canteen, West Coast center for servicemen.

In 1951 Mr. Garfield testified before the House Committee on Un-American Activities as "a co-operative" witness. "I am no Red," he insisted. "I am no pink. I am no fellow traveler." He described himself as a Democratic party member and a political liberal and said Communist front organizations that had used his name had done so without his authorization.

In 1948 he won the La Guardia Award for stage and screen, established by the Non-Sectarian Anti-Nazi League to Champion Human Rights.

John Garfield in the recent revival of the play 'Golden Boy.'

John Garfield, Lana Turner and Alan Reed in *The Postman Always Rings Twice.*

"All the News That's Fit to Print"

The New York Times

LATE CITY EDITION

Weather: Possible showers today. Showers likely tonight, tomorrow. Temp. range: today 83-65; Sunday 80-62. Temp.-Hum. Index yesterday 71. Complete U.S. report on Page 78.

VOL.CXVIII...No.40,693 © 1969 The New York Times Company. NEW YORK, MONDAY, JUNE 23, 1969 10 CENTS

POWELL DECLINES ELECTION SUPPORT FOR PROCACCINO

Hails Lindsay as Probably Only Man Able to Calm the Troubled Waters

'DEAL' ON PAY IS DENIED

Representative Says Court Studies Congress Issue—Mayor Asks Coalition

By WILLIAM E. FAR[illegible]

WarrenEraEndingToday After 16 Years of Reform

Burger's Seating to Close a Time of Controversy and Mixed Results

By FRED P. GRAHAM
Special to The New York Times

WASHINGTON, June 22—The Warren era ends at the Supreme Court tomorrow, after 16 years of bold reforms that have brought raging controversy and mixed results.

When Chief Justice [illegible]

Judy Garland, 47, Found Dead

Special to The New York Times

LONDON, June 22 — Judy Garland, whose successes on stage and screen were later overshadowed by the pathos of her personal life, was found dead in her home here today.

The cause of death of the 47-year-old singer was not immediately established, and an autopsy was scheduled. [Reuters reported that police sources said a preliminary investigation revealed nothing to suggest that Miss Garland had taken her own life.]

Miss Garland's personal life often seemed a fruitless search for the happiness promised in "Over the Rainbow," the song she made famous in the movie "The Wizard of Oz."

Her father died when she was 12 years old; the pressures of adolescent stardom sent her to a psychiatrist at the age of 18; she was married five times; she was frequently ill; her singing voice faltered, and she suffered from the effects of drugs she once said were prescribed either to invigorate or tranquilize her.

She came here at the end of last year to play a cabaret in another of the "comeback" performances that dotted her last 15 years.

Three months ago she married Mickey Deans, a discothèque manager. It was Mr. Deans, her fifth husband, who

Continued on Page 31, Column 1

Frank Donato from Impact

Judy Garland during an appearance at the Palace in 1967

SCHUMANN NAMED FOREIGN MINISTER, REPLACING DEBRE

Pompidou Picks Advocate of European Unity Despite Gaullist Objections

BIG CABINET APPOINTED

Giscard, Who Backs British Bid to Join Market, Gets French Finance Post

By HENRY TANNER
Special to The New York Times

PARIS, June 22 — President Pompidou today removed Michel Debré from the Foreign Ministry and replaced him with Maurice Schumann, a European-minded internationalist.

The shift of Foreign Ministers, made against the strong objections of orthodox Gaullists, was the most spectacular feature in the announcement of a new French Cabinet that comprises an unusually large total of 18 ministers and 20 secretaries of state. Mr. Debré was named Defense Minister.

Mr. Schumann, a prominent member of the Gaullist Resistance during World War II, became a close associate of Premier Robert Schuman, the "father of Europe," after the war.

The two men were among [t]he leaders of the Popular Re[p]ublican Movement, the Roman [Ca]tholic party that led the fight [for] European unity together [w]ith the West German and Ital[ia]n Catholic leaders of the time, Chancellor Konrad Adenauer [a]nd Premier Alcide de Gasperi.

Giscard in Finance Post

Maurice Schumann is not ex[pec]ted to be a "strong" Foreign [Min]ister but to take his orders [from] the President.

[Th]e "European" tendency in [the] Cabinet was reinforced by [the c]hoice of Valéry Giscard [d'Estain]g as Minister of Econ[omy an]d Finance. Mr. Giscard [illegible] recently joined the [Co]mmittee for the Unit[ed States] of Europe, an inter[national gr]oup headed by Jean [illegible]

Representative Ad[am Clayton] Powell, [illegible]

Told [illegible] ell's co[illegible] sued th[illegible] from Gra[illegible] spokesma[n]

"I would [illegible] support of [illegible] who feels a[illegible] gressive mo[illegible] city must c[illegible] coalition for th[illegible] people."

Mr. Powell c[illegible] conference to de[illegible] The New York P[illegible] agreed not to d[illegible] in back pay in re[illegible] statement of his [illegible] seniority in the Ho[illegible] resentatives.

Last Monday, the [illegible] Court ruled that the [illegible] violated the Constitut[ion] [illegible] it excluded Mr. Powell [illegible] 90th Congress on the [illegible] that he had misused [illegible] funds and was contemp[illegible] of New York courts and [illegible] gressional committees.

Mr. Powell said that the [illegible]

Continued on Page 28, Colum[n]

Cairo, Ill., Divide[d] By Racial Conflic[t]; City Fears Futu[re]

By DONALD JANSON
Special to The New York Times

CAIRO, Ill., June 22—"Our image has been devastated, our economy is crippled and our future, if there is one, is dark."

For a Chamber of Commerce, hardly a glowing assessment. Yet this is the conclusion of "The Cairo Story," written and published by the local chamber two months ago.

Nothing has happened since to brighten the image. This former capital of water and rail commerce at the confluence of the Mississippi and Ohio Rivers has regressed enough in recent years to recall the impression of "this dismal Cairo" by Charles Dickens after an 1842 visit: "an ugly sepulchre, a grave uncheered by any gleam of promise."

Cairo (pronounced CARE-o) has more problems than most cities its size, but compounding them is a racial polarization that has divided the town of 8,800 persons into two separate communities, with each race at the other's throat.

The latest chapter in Cairo's racial trouble began today when the Rev. Jesse L. Jackson of the Southern Christian Leadership Conference arrived from Chicago for a rally and a march on the city hall to protest local practices in law enforcement and employment. He also plans to lead protests on Tuesday and Wednesday against hunger among blacks.

Arriving separately today

Continued on Page 29, Column 1

The [illegible] a 20 pe[illegible] reduction [illegible] to doctor[illegible] effective [illegible] cost of th[illegible] program.

The cutb[illegible] eral oppos[illegible] gists say [illegible] hard hit be[illegible] payments ap[illegible] their services [illegible] they must pay [illegible] they dispense.

Dr. Lowell Be[illegible] first deputy co[illegible] the city's Healt[h] [illegible] which handles [illegible] said the druggis[ts] [illegible] against the state [illegible] valid." He said the [illegible] put a "difficult e[co]no[mic] [illegible]

Continued on Page 27, Column 3

NEWS INDEX

[illegible] when she [was 12 years old]; the pressures [of ado]lescent stardom sent her to a psychiatrist at the age of 18; she was married five times; she was frequently ill; her singing voice faltered, and she suffered from the effects of drugs she once said were prescribed either to invigorate or tranquilize her.

She came here at the end of last year to play a cabaret in another of the "comeback" performances that dotted her last 15 years.

Three months ago she married Mickey Deans, a discothèque manager. It was Mr. Deans, her fifth husband, who

Continued on Page 31, Column 1

Frank Donato from Impact

Judy Garland during an appearance at the Palace in 1967

[illegible] truck. The [illegible]ls said intelligence had spotted the radar facility a few days ago but conceded it might have been moved before the raid.

According to the Israeli spokesmen, 30 Egyptian soldiers armed with light weapons guarded the base, which consisted of five one-story buildings. How the commandos reached the target was not revealed.

Some Egyptians racing toward the sea were also attacked by the raiders, the spokesmen said. The raiders said later they did not know how many Egyptians got away but that at least half the unit was left dead. Demolition squads then set charges to the

Continued on Page 9, Column 1

United Press International

NAMED TO NEW CABINET POST: Michel Debré declining to talk with newsmen after conferring yesterday with Georges Pompidou, French President. Mr. Debré, who had been Foreign Minister, was shifted to Defense Minister.

Judy Garland, 47, Star of Stage and Screen, Is Found Dead in Her London Home

Continued From Page 1, Col. 5

found Miss Garland dead on the bathroom floor in their home in the Belgravia district.

Also surviving are three children, Liza Minnelli, the singer and actress, and Lorna and Joseph Luft.

Funeral arrangements were incomplete tonight.

Moved by Compulsion

Judy Garland's career was marked by a compulsive quality that displayed itself even during her first performance at the age of 30 months at the New Grand Theater in Grand Rapids, Minn. Here, the story is told, Frances Gumm—both her parents were vaudeville players—sang "Jingle Bells" on a Christmas program. She responded so favorably to the footlights that her father was forced to remove her after she had repeated the song seven times.

The other side of the compulsively vibrant, exhausting performances that were her stage hallmark was a seemingly unquenchable need for her audiences to respond with acclaim and affection. And often they did, screaming, "We love you, Judy—we love you."

She made more than 35 films, once set a New York vaudeville record with an engagement of 19 weeks and 184 performances, cut numerous records and in recent years made frequent television appearances.

Her other films include, "Every Sunday," "Babes In Arms," "Little Nellie Kelly," "For Me and My Gal," "The Harvey Girls," "Meet Me in St. Louis," "The Pirate," "Easter Parade," "A Star Is Born," "Judgment at Nuremberg," and "A Child Is Waiting."

Miss Garland's early success was firmly rooted in an extraordinary talent. She was an instinctive actress and comédienne with a sweet singing voice that had a kind of brassy edge to it, which made her something of an anachronism: a music hall performer in an era in which music halls were obsolete.

In an earlier era, or in another society, she might have grown up slowly, developing her talent as she disciplined it, and gone on like other, tougher performers to enjoy a long and profitable career.

Instead, Judy became a star at 15 in the relentless world of motion pictures. Movies—which are put together in bits and pieces—do not particularly require rigid discipline, and she therefore never had a chance to acquire the quality that could have sustained her talent over the years.

Perhaps the most remarkable thing about the career of Judy Garland was that she was able to continue as long as she did — long after her voice had failed and long after her physical reserves had been spent in various illnesses that might have left a less tenacious woman an invalid.

She was the kind of movie personality whose private life defined much of her public response. Whenever she stepped out on a stage in recent years, she brought with her, whether she welcomed it or not, all the well-publicized phantoms of her emotional breakdowns, her career collapses and her comebacks.

The pressures of performing began for her at an early age. When she was 18 and Louis B. Mayer's favorite at Metro-Goldyn-Mayer Studios making $150,000 a picture, she was already seeing a psychiatrist.

Recounts Experience

She wrote about the experience years later: "No wonder I was strange. Imagine whipping out of bed, dashing over to the doctor's office, lying down on a torn leather couch, telling my troubles to an old man who couldn't hear, who answered with an accent I couldn't understand, and then dashing to Metro to make movie love to Mickey Rooney."

It was during this period that she also began taking stimulants and depressants. "They'd give us pep pills," she wrote. "Then they'd take us to the studio hospital and knock us cold with sleeping pills . . . after four hours they'd wake us up and give us the pep pills again . . .

"That's the way we worked, and that's the way we got thin. That's the way we got mixed up. And that's the way we lost contact."

Less than 10 years after these experiences, at the age of 28, the singer attempted suicide.

The unhappiness that plagued her during the last few years alone included the breakup of her 13-year marriage to Sid Luft, a film director and the third of her five husbands; a subsequent bitter custody fight over their children, Lorna and Joseph, with Mr. Luft accusing her of having attempted suicide on at least 20 occasions; sudden hospitalizations for causes ranging from paralysis to unconsciousness after a fall in a hotel room, and the breaking of her voice during appearances in several cities.

Judy Garland with frequent co-star, Mickey Rooney, in *Andy Hardy Meets a Debutante,* 1940.

Miss Garland was born in Grand Rapids on June 10, 1922, the youngest of three daughters of Frank Avent and Ethel Marian Gumm. Her parents billed themselves in vaudeville as Jack and Virginia Lee.

After her debut with "Jingle Bells," she performed with her sisters, Suzanne and Virginia, until, according to theatrical legend, their act was erroneously billed at a Chicago theater as "The Glum Sisters."

Garland was her mother's maiden name. When the family arrived in Hollywood in 1936, the 14-year-old singer, who made her feature film debut in "Pigskin Parade," was billed as Judy Garland.

She made a short subject with another adolescent singer, Deanna Durbin. Louis B. Mayer was impressed, and when he learned that M-G-M had allowed Miss Durbin's contract to lapse and lost her to a rival studio, he determined to give Miss Garland a major build-up.

She sang "Dear Mr. Gable" in "Broadway Melody of 1938." Then she made a bigger hit as a gawky adolescent with a crush on Mickey Rooney in "Love Finds Andy Hardy."

In "Dear Mr. Gable" she confessed her hopeless adolescent love for an idealized movie star in special lyrics added to the ballad "You Made Me Love You."

At 17, playing the pig-tailed girl in "The Wizard of Oz," she sang the song that became her trademark, "Over the Rainbow"—a wistful pursuit of happiness that seemed, to her, unattainable.

In 1939, "The Wizard of Oz" earned her a special Oscar.

Ray Bolger, the dancer, actor and singer, who played the Scarecrow in "The Wizard," made it plain yesterday that Miss Garland's charisma was notable even when they made that film.

Three months after she had signed the contract with M-G-M, Judy's father died of spinal meningitis. In a newspaper article in 1964, Miss Garland wrote that her father's death "was the most terrible thing that ever happened to me in my life." "I can say that now," she went on, "because I'm more secure than I was then."

"But the terrible thing about it," she wrote, "was that I couldn't cry at my father's funeral. I'd never been to a funeral. I was ashamed because I couldn't cry, so I feigned it. But I just couldn't cry for eight days, and then I locked myself in a bathroom and cried for 14 hours.

"I wasn't close to my father, but I wanted to be all my life. He had a funny sense of humor, and he laughed all the time—good and loud, like I do. He was a gay Irish gentleman and very good-looking. And he wanted to be close to me, too, but we never had much time together."

(continued)

Judy Garland with Tom Drake, in what is often called the best movie of her career, *Meet Me In St. Louis*.

By 1942, Miss Garland had passed the awkward age through a popular series of musical comedies with Mr. Rooney, and was playing love scenes with Gene Kelly in "For Me and My Gal." She was already one of the top box-office stars at the most celebrated star studio in Hollywood.

Her personal troubles had already begun. She was married to the composer-pianist David Rose in 1941. They were divorced three years later. The next year she was married to her director, the gifted musical specialist, Vincente Minnelli.

Under her husband's guidance, her career flourished. She sang "The Trolley Song" in "Meet Me in St. Louis" and was praised for her first nonsinging dramatic performance, in "The Clock."

By 1948, when Miss Garland played with Gene Kelly in "The Pirate," and Fred Astaire in "Easter Parade," she was indisputably the leading musical star in films.

The next year she failed to report for work on three successive films and was reported to be suffering from a nervous breakdown. The one film she did finish in this period, "Summer Stock," attracted much comment because of her increased weight.

It was during the next year, 1950, that she slashed her wrists after M-G-M suspended her contract. She and Mr. Minnelli were divorced the next year.

In 1951 Miss Garland returned to the stage in England, doing a solo singing show with great success. She had another success with a vaudeville engagement at the New York Palace.

Frequently, however, she complained of laryngitis, and critics noted that her voice had lost some of its quality. At the same time they noted that her personality retained its full impact.

In reviewing a later performance at the Palace, Vincent Canby wrote in The New York Times of Aug. 1, 1967, that "that the voice—as of last night's performance, anyway—is now a memory seems almost beside the point." He concluded that all the performers on the bill were good, "but it is Judy who is great. And let's not worry about her voice."

Another writer called a typical Garland appearance "more than a concert . . . it is a tribal celebration." The crowds often screamed during her frenzied finales for "More! More!" and began the ritual chants of "We Love You, Judy!"

When she left the stage for intermission, Miss Garland often staggered to her dressing room, sometimes gasping, panting that she could not possibly finish the show, that she was exhausted or that her throat ached. But back she went.

Miss Garland described her feelings toward the audience for a magazine interviewer in 1961:

"A really great reception makes me feel like I have a great big warm heating pad all over me. People en masse have always been wonderful to me. I truly have a great love for an audience, and I used to want to prove it to them by giving them blood. But I have a funny new thing now, a real determination to make people enjoy the show. I want to give them two hours of just pow."

Return Impressive

The performer made an impressive return to films in 1954 with "A Star Is Born," with James Mason. But her erratic work habits had caused the production to take months longer than planned, at great expense. A commercial disappointment, the film represented a personal triumph for her.

Her best song in "A Star Is Born," a torch ballad called "The Man That Got Away," joined "Over the Rainbow" as a Garland trademark. She was expected to win an Academy Award for her performance, but Grace Kelly won it instead, for "The Country Girl."

For the next few years Miss Garland was plagued by throat troubles and marital difficulties. She was overweight for a star, consistently ill and more temperamental than ever. Hollywood would not risk employing her.

By the autumn of 1959 she was unable to work at all. She felt sick, frightened and mentally confused. In late November she was admitted to a New York hospital, where doctors found she was suffering from hepatitis.

They said she might have had the illness for as long as three years and that the hepatitis was attributed at least in part, to the combined effects of certain tranquilizers and diet pills that previous doctors, treating earlier breakdowns, had prescribed for her.

Miss Garland admitted at the time to having taken a great many drugs over the last 15 years, including sleeping pills, pep pills, diet medicines and nerve tonics.

Then, in 1960, she came back again. During a concert at London's Palladium, she was more successful than ever. She followed it with a spectacular, sobbing performance at Carnegie Hall.

Miss Garland signed for a weekly television series, with much fanfare, in 1963, but it was a failure. The carefully nurtured emotional impact that made each of her performances a special event was lost in the weekly program.

The Columbia Broadcasting System dropped the show after one season, amid loud complaints from the voluble legion of Garland fans.

Seemingly undaunted, she set out for Australia on another concert tour. Again she was plagued by "laryngitis."

When Miss Garland left Australia, she spoke wistfully about retiring and devoting herself to her three children, Liza Minnelli, 18, Lorna Luft, 11, and Joseph Luft, 9.

After her divorce from Mr. Luft, Miss Garland admitted to friends that she sometimes felt "like I'm living in a blizzard."

In 1965 she married Mark Herron, an actor. Two years later, they were divorced.

She went to London at the end of 1968 for a five-week cabaret appearance and announced she would marry Mr. Deans.

Looking slim and relaxed, Miss Garland won a standing ovation at her first London appearance. But then she began to appear late for performances, and one night walked off the stage when she was heckled by the audience, whom she had kept waiting for an hour and 20 minutes.

A few days later it was announced she was ill and would not finish the last week of the run. Unpredictable as ever, Miss Garland appeared on the stage that night, gave a smash performance and announced that she had married Mr. Deans three weeks earlier in a secret church ceremony.

The confusion from which Miss Garland often seemed to suffer in her personal life apparently extended to her performance in "The Wizard of Oz." Harold Arlen, who composed the score for the film, said she felt most deeply about the song "Over the Rainbow."

He quoted yesterday from a letter he said he had received from Miss Garland. She wrote:

"As for my feelings toward 'Over the Rainbow,' it's become part of my life. It is so symbolic of all my dreams and wishes that I'm sure that's why people sometimes get tears in their eyes when they hear it."

But recently recalling her role in "The Wizard" in another context, she said, "I was really little tortured Tillie in the whole damn thing."

Judy Garland and Ray Bolger in *The Wizard of Oz.*

The New York Times THURSDAY, DECEMBER 9, 1954.

GLADYS GEORGE, 50, ACTRESS, IS DEAD

Autopsy Will Be Performed Today—Stage and Film Star Had Been Recluse

HOLLYWOOD, Calif., Dec. 8 (AP)—Gladys George, stage and screen actress, died in a hospital today under circumstances the police described as mysterious. She was 50 years old.

She was sent to the hospital on advice of her physician, Dr. Russell Jones, but died a few hours after being admitted. Her landlady, Mrs. Emma Colfax, had found her in her apartment. Detectives from the police homicide detail were sent to the hospital to check on the death. The police said Miss George was unconscious when she was found.

An autopsy will be performed tomorrow. The police and her physician said there was a possibility that barbiturate poisoning was the cause of death.

Treated for Throat Cancer

Dr. Jones said Miss George died "before tests could be completed that would have determined if she had taken a barbiturate." He said the actress had been treated, successfully, for cancer of the throat.

Miss George, whose real name was Gladys Clare, was born in Patten, Me., and made her stage debut when 3 years old. She was in a touring stock show with her parents.

She was acclaimed one of the best performers of 1936 by the Motion Picture Academy for her role in "Valiant Is the Word for Carrie." Among her best-known roles were in "The Way of All Flesh," "Marie Antoinette," "A Child Is Born," "Madame X," "Best Years of Our Lives" and "Lullaby of Broadway."

One of her last stage appearances in Hollywood was in "Rain," in which she played the role of Sadie Thompson.

Miss George married four times. Her last husband was a Los Angeles bellboy, Kenneth C. Bradley. They were married in 1946 and divorced four years later. Her other husbands were Arthur Erway, an actor; Edward Fowler, paper manufacturer, and Leonard Penn, an actor.

A neighbor of Miss George said she had become a recluse in recent years and seldom ventured out except to walk her dog.

Starred on Broadway

Her first starring role on Broadway was in Brock Pemberton's "Personal Appearance."

Among other better known roles was Sabina, the ageless maid of all work in Thornton Wilder's "The Skin of Our Teeth." She was the third Sabina, having been preceded in the part by Tallulah Bankhead and Miriam Hopkins.

Returning to the screen in 1944, she appeared in "Christmas Holiday" and "Minstrel Man." In 1949, she was in "Flamingo Road" and in 1950 in "Bright Leaf" and "Undercover Girl."

In 1950 she also played in the Broadway play "The Velvet Glove," with Walter Hampden. The next year she had a part in the technicolor screen production "Lullaby of Broadway."

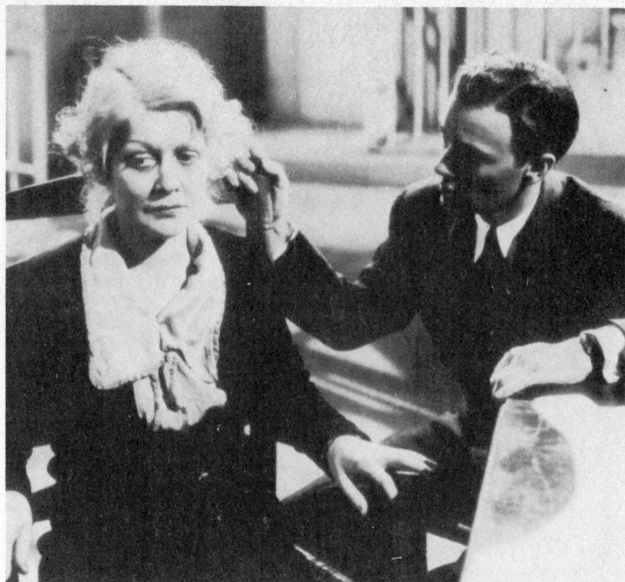

Gladys George and John Beal in *Madame X*, 1937.

Spencer Tracy with Gladys George and Franchot Tone in *They Gave Him a Gun*.

The New York Times FRIDAY, AUGUST 24, 1962.

Hoot Gibson, Film Cowboy, Dies; Made His First Movie in 1915

Broke Into Motion Pictures as a Stunt Man—Last Role Was in 'Horse Soldiers'

Special to The New York Times.

HOLLYWOOD, Calif., Aug. 23—Hoot Gibson, one of Hollywood's most famous cowboy stars, died early this morning of cancer at the Motion Picture Country House and Hospital, in Woodland Hills, Calif. He was 70 years old.

Mr. Gibson, whose real name was Edmund Richard Gibson, had been ill for a long time and had re-entered the home on Sunday. His last film appearance was in 1959 in a bit part in John Wayne's "The Horse Soldiers."

He is survived by his widow, the former Dorothy Dunstan, a singer he married in 1941; a daughter, Mrs. Lois Flanders; three sisters, Mrs. Jessie Gassaway, Mrs. Bettie Bedoian and Mrs. Jeanette Shaeffer, and a brother, Leon.

Gun-Toting Immortal

Hoot Gibson rode through the cinematic sagebrush for nearly fifty years—chasing villains, dispatching Indians and rescuing sloe-eyed ranch girls. He was one of that rapidly vanishing breed of screen cowboys who made the Western the only indigenous American motion-picture form.

Along with such gun-toting immortals as Tom Mix, Ken Maynard, William S. Hart and Col. Tim McCoy, Mr. Gibson thrilled several generations of Saturday matinee gum-chewers with his straight-shooting.

When Hoot Gibson rode across the gullies and arroyos of the Wild West, his thousands of fans were assured it was their hero behind the pommel for he was one of Hollywood's few genuine horsemen.

He was born in Tekamah, Neb., where his father had a ranch. It was here that he learned to ride, rope and wrangle, although he once jokingly said, "If you don't know how to ride a horse, you can be a cowboy actor and it doesn't make any difference."

And it was in Tekamah that he was given the nickname Hoot.

"I used to go out in caves and hunt owls," he once explained. "The kids started hollering 'hoot' at me and the name stuck."

As a young man, he toured Australia with a vaudeville act and, in 1915, he rode into the movies as a stunt man.

"In those days all they made was Indian pictures," Mr. Gibson recently recalled. "I got $20 a week, plus a bonus. We got an extra $2.50 for being Indians, getting shot and falling off a horse.

"If I played a cowboy and got shot, I got $5—it was harder to fall out of a saddle."

He was soon one of the growing industry's best stuntmen, performing all kinds of daredevil tricks, such as speeding off an open drawbridge on a motorcycle.

Once asked if he would risk a spectacular fall from a horse for an extra $5, he told the director:

"Make it ten bucks and I'll let him kick me to death."

In 1920, Mr. Gibson was signed by Universal Pictures to star in a number of five-reel silent Westerns. His director was John Ford, who also had just been promoted. Mr. Ford also directed the cowboy star in "The Horse Soldiers."

Mr. Gibson's film career blossomed in 1925 and for about five years he was one of Hollywood's leading stars. His salary during these golden days was $14,500 a week and he was surrounded by fast cars, race horses and planes.

It was during this period that the intrepid film cowboy appeared in films with such typical Western titles as "Smilin' Gun," "The Long, Long Trail," "Trigger Tricks" and "Spurs."

In 1933, Mr. Gibson was seriously injured while piloting an airplane in a special match race against Ken Maynard at the National Air Races in Los Angeles. He suffered three fractured vertebrae and broken ribs and physicians feared his film career had ended.

Like the heroes of his Western epics, however, Mr. Gibson refused to let his injuries end his performing. Although he never again attained the film heights and always walked with a slight limp, he returned to ride horses after many months in the hospital.

Ran a Dude Ranch

He retired in 1944 after starring in about 200 silent movies and seventy-five talkies. He operated a dude ranch in Nevada for a while, then tried a live television program. Neither worked out. In recent years he appeared occasionally in cowboy pictures, but spent most of his time as a greeter in a Las Vegas hotel.

He Rode the Horse Himself

Edmund Richard "Hoot" Gibson, who died this week in California, was a motion picture cowboy who rode the horse himself. He had been brought up on his father's ranch and he not only knew how to stay on horses when he wanted to; he also knew how to fall off. In the late Twenties he is said to have earned $14,500 a week. In the early days he used to fall off horses for $2.50 if he was pretending to be an Indian, and for $5 if he was a cowboy and had to ride a saddle with a high pommel. He took risks in other means of conveyance, including one airplane which cost him three fractured vertebrae and some broken ribs. Between 1915 and his partial retirement in 1944 he starred in a couple of hundred silent movies and seventy-five talkies.

Mr. Gibson belonged in that famous school of Wild Western heroes that included Tom Mix and William S. Hart, both of whom could ride, as well as "Bronco Billie" Anderson, who never even pretended to do much more than stay on a stationary horse.

Some oldsters, remembering these favorites of the silent days, will be wondering whether the films we have today are any more entertaining or take us out of our worries more effectively than those of thirty or forty years ago. The whole thing may be a matter of habit. What amused the younger generation's fathers and grandfathers might not amuse anyone today. But the imaginary West of the pictures in which Mr. Gibson took a noble part stirs nostalgia in us just as does the equally imaginary West on which its romances were based.

Hoot Gibson, 1922.

Lillian Gish and John Gilbert gave passionate performances in *La Boheme*.

The New York Times FRIDAY, JANUARY 10, 1936.

JOHN GILBERT, 38, MOVIE STAR, DIES

Romantic Silent Screen Star Lost Public When Voice Was Found Unsuited to Talkies.

HE MARRIED FOUR TIMES

Ina Claire and Virginia Bruce Among Brides—Leading Man for Greta Garbo.

Special to THE NEW YORK TIMES.

LOS ANGELES, Jan. 9.—Succumbing to a heart attack despite efforts of a Fire Department rescue squad to revive him with an inhalator, John Gilbert, 38-year-old screen star, died at his home near Beverly Hills today.

Only a few servants were present this morning when the attack occurred. Several days ago Mr. Gilbert became ill.

Virginia Bruce, his fourth wife, who divorced him in 1934, wept at news of his death and said:

"This is the most terrible shock I've ever known. I cannot realize Jack is gone."

His Career Disappointed Him.

John Gilbert, idol of the silent screen, who for years made a weekly salary of $10,000, who married and divorced four celebrated beauties, was essentially a bitter and unhappy man.

Wealth and fame, apparently, were as naught, according to a short account of his life written by himself some years ago for a motion picture magazine.

In that autobiography, the man who had been dubbed "the screen's perfect lover" revealed that he had had a miserable childhood and that he had, at times, "been hungry enough to eat out of garbage cans."

Gilbert stood, undisputed, the favorite of filmdom, the logical lover in screen dramas where Greta Garbo and Lillian Gish were heroines, when his star fell as abruptly as it had risen. The talking pictures proved his undoing.

A high-pitched voice, difficult to control, spoiled the otherwise fine performances of John Gilbert. The thousands of admirers gasped when they heard him for the first time in "Redemption" and "His Glorious Night"—Gilbert's first ventures in talking pictures.

From then on, despite his lucrative contract with Metro-Goldwyn-Mayer, he was on the downward road, and was soon replaced by other screen lovers. Gilbert remained a memory, and a fast-fading memory to a more or less fickle public.

Parents Were on Stage.

In the comparatively short history of motion pictures, however, John Gilbert remains a notable figure. He was extremely handsome and equally graceful—a son of the stage—for he came of actor stock and had, indeed, whimpered as an infant in shows where his mother appeared with long-forgotten traveling companies.

John Gilbert

His last picture—in which he took a secondary rôle—was produced in New York in November, 1934. He appeared as Steve Bramley in a production called "The Captain Hates the Sea" and his performance was greeted with indifference by the critics.

Whether it was for sentimental or other reasons, Greta Garbo insisted that he take an important part late in 1933. He played with the Swedish actress in "Queen Christina," and his performance was recorded as quite creditable.

"Quite creditable," however, was a melancholy "come-down" from the superlative gush that hailed his work of other days. It was John Gilbert "the incomparable" in "The Merry Widow," John Gilbert "the sublime" in "The Big Parade," John Gilbert the darling of the female audiences in love drama after love drama in those days.

John Gilbert caught the public interest no less in his matrimonial ventures. He married four times. The last three of his wives were famous motion-picture actresses.

First Married at 21.

Gilbert was only 21 when he married Olivia Burwell, a motion-picture "extra," from whom he was divorced some months later. He then married Leatrice Joy, the actress, by whom he had a daughter. That union broke up, and his next wife was Ina Claire, who divorced him in 1931.

Gilbert's fourth bride was Virginia Bruce, blond motion-picture star, whom he married on Aug. 10, 1932, and who divorced him on May 25, 1934. Another daughter was born of that union.

His former wives, it was said, remained his close friends.

John Gilbert was born at Logan, Utah, the son of Walter B. and Sarah Ida Apperley Gilbert. His parents were "on the road," and young John was baptized in Montreal. The lad's education was of the occasional and sporadic kind.

When he was 14, his mother having died, he was obliged to go to work, first in San Francisco, where he sold rubber goods at $7 a week, and later in Spokane, Wash., and Portland, Ore.

His first real part in motion pictures was with the old Triangle.

Gilbert attempted scenario writing, and he appeared many years later in "Downstairs," which he had sold originally for $1. He busied himself also with directing on a small scale and was engaged as a cutter of motion pictures.

Gradually he became known to the screen audience. In 1927, he appeared in an adaptation of Tolstoy's "Anna Karenina," which was shown under the title "Love," with Greta Garbo in the leading part.

Ina Claire yesterday said she was shocked at the news of her former husband's death.

"Naturally, I am terribly sorry to hear of it," she said. "We were divorced, but we were good friends. I last heard from him at Christmas, when he wired me greetings."

Gilbert and Aileen Pringle in *His Hour*, 1924.

Dorothy Gish in *Orphans of the Storm*.

The New York Times THURSDAY, JUNE 6, 1968

Dorothy Gish, Actress, Is Dead; In Theater and Films 50 Years

Starred With Sister, Lillian, in Griffith Silent Classics—Many Broadway Roles

RAPALLO, Italy, June 5 (AP)—Dorothy Gish, one of the two sisters who entertained motion picture audiences and theatergoers for more than a half-century, died here last night. She was 70 years old.

Her sister, Lillian, who has been making a movie in Rome, was at her bedside. Dorothy had been in a clinic here for nearly two years. She died of bronchial pneumonia.

The United States consulate in Genoa said that Miss Gish's body would be cremated and that the ashes would be returned to the United States.

Extra in Films in 1912

Although Dorothy and Lillian often worked together and had careers that were in many ways parallel, they were not a team. In the highly competitive world of acting, they remained a harmonious pair of sisters who admired each other.

The Gish sisters reached the peak of popularity during the silent screen days, but Dorothy was only 4 and Lillian 6 when they went on stage professionally.

They started in movies in 1912 under the wing of D. W. Griffith, the grandmaster of silent-screen films. They got their jobs through Mary Pickford, a friend whom they only knew by her real name, Gladys Smith, when they sought her out at Griffith's Biograph Company at 11 East 14th Street in New York. They had seen Gladys in movie and thought they would like to try the new medium.

Griffith started them as extras. In order to tell them apart at first, he had Lillian wear a blue ribbon and Dorothy, then 14, a red one. He was so impressed with their talents that he took them to California for his customary West Coast fall season at $50 a week, a sound wage for those silent days.

'Familiar With Tempo'

"Mr. Griffith spent months in rehearsing his players and plots before a camera turned," Dorothy recalled years later. "By the time a photoplay went into actual production an actor was thoroughly familiar with his own part as well as the tempo, approach and reactions of other members of the cast.

"Most of Mr. Griffith's films were shot without scripts and were improvised in the manner of the commedia dell'arte," she continued. "Individual scenes were staged and restaged until a maximum effect was realized and footage was closely checked with a stop watch. This saved large sums in raw film and time and kept production cost from soaring."

During her years in films, Miss Gish appeared in "An Unseen Enemy," "Hearts of the World," "The Orphans of the Storm," "Tip-Toes," "London," "Nell Gwynn," "Romola," and "Madame Pompadour." Of all her screen roles, Miss Gish preferred playing the Little Disturber in "Hearts of the World," which Griffith made in England and France during World War I.

In 1918, she worked for a while in New York with Paramount Pictures, making "Battling Jane," "I'll Get Him Yet" and "Remodeling Her Husband." The last had Richard Barthelmess as her leading man and her sister as director. After 1928 and the advent of talkies, she made only three films, "Our Hearts Were Young and Gay," (1944) "Centennial Summer" (1946) and "The Whistle at Eaton Falls" (1951).

As much as she was gratified by her film career, Miss Gish's first love, as with many performers, was the stage. Her string of credits through 1956 was long and respectable.

They included Fay Hilary in "Young Love," (1928); Maria in "The Inspector General" (1930), Emily Dickinson in "Brittle Heaven" (1934), Fanny in "Autumn Crocus" (1932), Fanny Dixwell Holmes in "The Magnificent Yankee" (1946), and Mrs. Gillis in "The Man" (1950), her last Broadway role. She succeeded Dorothy Stickney for almost a year in the starring role of Vinnie, the patient mother, in the Broadway hit "Life With Father." In 1956, she starred in "The Chalk Garden" at The Spa in Saratoga, N. Y.

Dorothy Gish was born March 11, 1898. She once told how she came to her stage career:

"Mother came up from Massillon, Ohio, where we were born, partly to look for our father, who had left us, and partly to try to earn a living for all three of us. We were practically destitute. She rented one of the old-fashioned railroad apartments, and advertised for 'genteel lady roomers.'

"One of the genteel ladies who rented a room was an actress, and after she had been with us a few weeks, she had an offer for a part in a road-company production of 'East Lynne,' provided she could find a small child . . . to play the part of Little Willie."

Mrs. Gish found someone—Dorothy. Four years later, in 1906, she made her debut at the Lincoln Square Theater with Fiske O'Hara in "Dion O' Dare."

She played juvenile parts until 1912 when she and Lillian went into the movies.

Miss Gish was once described, much later in life, by a writer who called her "a deep-voiced woman . . . with an unabated zest for life, a faintly ribald sense of humor and an uncompromising faculty for self-appraisal."

In 1951, when she was making "The Whistle at Eaton Falls," she said that she particularly enjoyed making the film because it "reminded me so much of the way we made pictures in the old days of Mr. Griffith."

She explained further: "To me, there's too much spit 'n' polish about today's film technique. When Lillian and I were in silent films, we did everything for ourselves — mother made our costumes, we did our own hair, put on our own make-up.

"Nowadays, you have a couple of people getting you into costume, another couple fussing around on your hair, others with your face. You feel, somehow, like Marie Antoinette—even with the best will in the world, rather aloof and removed."

Miss Gish loved to travel and she stipulated that her career should not interfere with her wanderings. She lived for months in England, Italy, Yugoslavia and Africa. She also had a home at Wilson Point, near Newport, Conn.

Dorothy (right) and Lillian Gish in *Orphans of the Storm.*

"All the News That's Fit to Print"

The New York Times

LATE CITY EDITION

Weather: Sunny, colder today; fair and cold tonight. Cloudy tomorrow. Temp. range: today 33-38; Thursday 44-60. Additional details on Page 58.

VOL. CXXIII ... No. 42,377 © 1974 The New York Times Company NEW YORK, FRIDAY, FEBRUARY 1, 1974 15 CENTS

KISSINGER EXPECTS SOME ARABS TO ASK OIL EMBARGO'S END

Faisal Said to Have Assured Nixon He'd Back Lifting of the Ban on U.S.

ASSESSMENT IS BRIGHT

Washington Officials Look to Key Ministers' Meeting in Tripoli Feb. 14

By BERNARD GWERTZMAN

Special to The New York Times

WASHINGTON, Jan. 31—Secretary of State Kissinger said today that several Arab leaders would recommend the lifting of the oil embargo when the Arab oil-producing nations met in Tripoli, Libya, on Feb. 14—or on an earlier date. O... of the leaders was ... to be King Faisal ... Arabia.

Mr. Kissinger's as... was his most optimisti... the prospects for ending ... embargo. It followed P... Nixon's statement, in hi... of the Union address last ... that "an urgent meeting ... be called in the immediate f... ture to discuss the lifting o... the oil embargo."

[According to a dispatch from Beirut, Arab leaders are linking an end of the embargo to progress in achieving an Israeli troop pullback on the Syrian front. Page 7.]

U.S. Role Held a Factor

Mr. Kissinger, speaking to newsmen after he had testified behind closed doors before the House Ways and Means Committee, declined to say which leaders would call for the end of the embargo.

But it was reliably reported that King Faisal, whose country is the largest Arab oil exporter, had told Mr. Nixon that, as a result of the American effort in bringing about the agreement between Egypt and Israel on separation of forces, he would support the move to end the embargo.

In his address to Congress, Mr. Nixon seemed to suggest that the Arab oil producers were going to call a special meeting to deal with the lifting of the embargo. But today officials in the Middle East and in Washington said that the only meeting of Arab oil producers scheduled so far was one set for Tripoli on Feb. 14, and that this had been made known last week.

This prompted intensive questions today from newsmen covering the White House and the State Department. In reply, official spokesmen insisted that Mr. Nixon's statement was carefully drafted after close

Continued on Page 6, Column 5

FREED: Gerald E. Kosh... tween Chin... from ...

FARM PRICES SOAR BY 9% IN MONTH; MEAT LEADS WAY

Mid-January Level Exactly Double the 1967 Average —Retail Rises Signaled

By WILLIAM ROBBINS

Special to The New York Times

WASHINGTON, Jan. 31 — Prices received by farmers rose sharply again from mid-December to mid-Janu... point ...

The New York Times/George Tames

...odino Jr., right, chairman, and Edward Hutch... ...ouse Judiciary Committee meeting yesterday.

RODINO UNIT ASKS A HOUSE MANDATE FOR NIXON INQUIRY

Subpoena Power Requested in Study on Impeachment —Approval Expected

EARLY HOUSE VOTE SEEN

Judiciary Chief Says No One Would Be Excluded From Resolution's Authority

By BILL KOVACH

Special to The New York Times

WASHINGTON, Jan. 31—The House Judiciary Committee unanimously adopted a resolution today asking that full constitutional authority for the impeachment inquiry on President Nixon, including subpoena power, be given the committee by the House of Representatives.

The adoption of the resolution, which is expected to win House approval next week, was, in effect, the Congressional response to President Nixon's promise of limited cooperation in his State of the Union address last night.

President Nixon said that his cooperation with the impeachment inquiry would be limited by precedent and his desire not to erode Presidential authority.

Several Republican members of the Judiciary Committee, while encouraged by the President's words, suggested that it remained to be seen how open the President would be to demands for evidence in the inquiry.

Exclusions Ruled Out

Peter W. Rodino Jr., New Jersey Democrat who is the committee chairman, alluded to the President's position when he told newsmen that once the authority requested in the resolution was granted, "no one is excluded from its authority."

The unanimous action on the resolution, after nearly three hours of discussion and debate, supported the general impression on Capitol Hill today that President Nixon's nationally televised address had done little to distract or delay the determination of Congress to investigate the Watergate scandal and its aftermath.

Senator Sam J. Ervin Jr., North Carolina Democrat who is chairman of the Senate Watergate Committee, said he had not changed his position that hearings should resume on matters remaining before that committee.

Ronald L. Ziegler, the President's press secretary, reinforced President Nixon's indications of limits on his cooperation with the inquiry.

"His remarks last night were

Continued on Page 10, Column 2

...s Credibility Backed ...tergate Prosecution

By ANTHONY RIPLEY

Special to The New York Times

...n. 31—The White House documents that ... Watergate prove the allegation. ... in Fed- The credibility issue was ... reason raised today by Jacob A. Stein, ... Dean lawyer for Dwight L. Chapin, ...ergate who has been charged with four counts of perjury growing ...ement from his testimony before one ... Mr. of the Watergate grand juries. ...tor Mr. Chapin, President Nixon's former appointments secretary, is charged with falsely testifying under oath about his relations with Donald H. Segretti, confessed political saboteur and spy.

Both Mr. Segretti and Mr. ...an are scheduled to be ...ong the Government wit...ses against Mr. Chapin. Mr. ... made it clear in court to ...at Mr. Dean's credibility ... be a major issue. ...ked Judge Gerhard A. ... to turn over any prose-

... on Page 10, Column 6

...ave ... por... gas... York... be a... amou... 1972, ... Turets... tor of ... fice. This ... reports ... levels ha... the same ... The Mo... — under ... mitting co... higher cos... previous mo...

Senato... And U...

WASHINGTON, J... The oil companies' f... stand together and bun... the State Department w... jor factors in the sharp... world petroleum prices, s... Frank Church declared ... Senate hearing today.

The Idaho Democrat said ... a "leap-frog" price effect ... resulted from the falling-o... among the big oil companies and ... the smaller independent produc... ...ers, and from the State Depart... ment's "undercutting" of the

...d Budget

...to "open gov... ...listing for the first ... of dollars of items ... camouflaged in ... budgets, things ... training and ... companying ... of the ... ved trans... ...st place ... the total, ... 23 and ... on third ... first.

... Column 1

Samuel Goldwyn Dies at 91

By ALBIN KREBS

Samuel Goldwyn, one of the last of the pioneer Hollywood producers, died early yesterday at his Los Angeles home at the age of 91. He had been in frail health since 1968 and two weeks ago had been released from a hospital after several weeks of treatment for an undisclosed illness.

In a distinguished career that spanned a half-century, Mr. Goldwyn became a Hollywood legend, a motion picture producer whose films, always created on a grand scale, were notable for those most elusive of traits—taste and quality.

Truly one of the last tycoons, who even looked the part, Mr. Goldwyn was a driving perfectionist, a man with a titanic temperament whose great gift was the ability to bring together, for each of his productions, the very best writers, directors, cinematographers and other craftsmen.

Having assembled these talented professionals, Mr. Goldwyn would dominate their work and their lives like a benign tyrant, praising them, goading them, encouraging them, browbeating them, as he personally supervised even the tiniest details of each of his productions.

This quest for the excellent often enraged Mr. Goldwyn's employes, but more often than not it gave his productions that sheen of quality and good taste that became known in the motion picture industry as "the Goldwyn touch."

Among the more than 70 movies to which he imparted that touch were "The Best Years of Our Lives," "Wuthering Heights," "The Pride of the Yankees," "Arrowsmith," "Dodsworth," "Stella Dallas," "Dead End." "The Westerner," "The Little Foxes," "Street

Continued on Page 34, Column 1

Samuel Goldwyn

Samuel Goldwyn Dies at 91

By ALBIN KREBS

Samuel Goldwyn, one of the last of the pioneer Hollywood producers, died early yesterday at his Los Angeles home at the age of 91. He had been in frail health since 1968 and two weeks ago had been released from a hospital after several weeks of treatment for an undisclosed illness.

In a distinguished career that spanned a half-century, Mr. Goldwyn became a Hollywood legend, a motion picture producer whose films, always created on a grand scale, were notable for those most elusive of traits—taste and quality.

Truly one of the last tycoons, who even looked the part, Mr. Goldwyn was a driving perfectionist, a man with a titanic temperament whose great gift was the ability to bring together, for each of his productions, the very best writers, directors, cinematographers and other craftsmen.

Having assembled these talented professionals, Mr. Goldwyn would dominate their work and their lives like a benign tyrant, praising them, goading them, encouraging them, browbeating them, as he personally supervised even the tiniest details of each of his productions.

This quest for the excellent often enraged Mr. Goldwyn's

employes, but more often than not it gave his productions that sheen of quality and good taste that became known in the motion picture industry as "the Goldwyn touch."

Among the more than 70 movies to which he imparted that touch were "The Best Years of Our Lives," "Wuthering Heights," "The Pride of the Yankees," "Arrowsmith," "Dodsworth," "Stella Dallas," "Dead End." "The Westerner," "The Little Foxes," "Street

Continued on Page 34, Column 1

Samuel Goldwyn

95 A... Of a...

A Pan Americ... ways 707 jetline... burned yesterday... tempting to land i... er at Pagopago,... Samoa, and a Sam... ment spokesman sa... of the 101 perso... were killed.

A Pan American s... said 10 survivors we... from the wreckage,... of them soon died in... pital.

The government spo... for Samoa, Neil Corbett,... three more persons died ... in hospital and most of ... remaining six survivors w... in very critical condition.

Corbett did not release names of the three who died later, and Pan American said it could not immediately confirm the report. According to Mr. Corbett, 94 persons were known to

...o a City Sewer

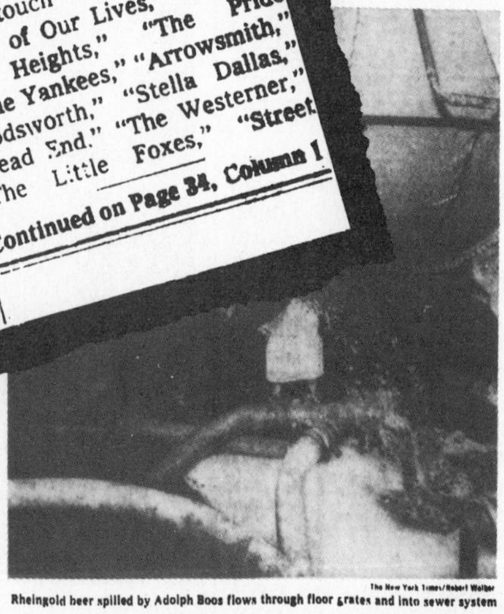

...ph Boos, a ... has worked in the ... for 38 years, as he watched the foaming beer spill onto the floor.

But at the end of the eventful day, which included a series of court actions and hearings about the 1,500 employes who are being laid off, company officials turned off the spigots and announced that an unnamed buyer was negotiating to buy the beer. A total of

Continued on Page 39, Column 4

The New York Times/Robert Walker

Rheingold beer spilled by Adolph Boos flows through floor grates and into sewer system

Samuel Goldwyn, Pioneer Film Producer, Noted for 'Goldwynisms,' Dies on Coast

Continued From Page 1, Col. 2

Scene," "Hans Christian Andersen," "The Secret Life of Walter Mitty," "Guys and Dolls" and "Porgy and Bess."

Although he was one of the flashiest and most controversial of the independent producers, to the general public he was probably best known for his "Goldwynisms," the malapropisms, mixed metaphors, grammatical blunders and word manglings that included the now classic "Include me out" and "I'll tell you in two words — im-possible!"

In recent years Mr. Goldwyn had insisted that he was not the originator of half the Goldwynisms attributed to him and, indeed, many were no doubt put into his mouth by press agents, friends and enemies. But the Goldwynisms, whether genuine or apocryphal, gave color to his personality and became part of the legend that was Sam Goldwyn.

Among the more famous Goldwynisms were:

"An oral agreement isn't worth the paper it's written on."

"A man who goes to a psychiatrist should have his head examined."

"This atom bomb is dynamite."

Another one supposedly evolved from a director's complaint that a film script in which Mr. Goldwyn was interested was "too caustic," to which the producer replied:

"Never mind the cost. If it's a good picture, we'll make it."

Until he decided that, as a pioneer and elder statesman of the motion picture industry, the Goldwynisms no longer lent his image the proper amount of dignity, Mr. Goldwyn shrewdly used them to gain publicity for himself and his pictures.

"People say that whenever I have a picture coming out I always start a controversy about something that gets into the papers," he said. "Well, in all sincerity, I want to assure you that, as a general proposition, there's not a single word of untruth in that."

Urged Better Pictures

Among the controversies that swirled about Mr. Goldwyn's bald head were his campaign against double features and his efforts to persuade his fellow producers to make fewer, better pictures. He once said that Hollywood was grinding out 600 pictures a year when "there are not brains enough in Hollywood to produce more than 200 good ones."

Mr. Goldwyn was born Aug. 27, 1882, in Warsaw. Little was known of his family background, but he was the son of poor parents who died when he was young. At the age of 11, the boy left Poland. After spending two years in England, he migrated to Gloversville, N.Y., where he took a job sweeping floors in a glove factory.

The youth already had the drive for which he was to become noted in Hollywood. By the time he was 17 he was the foreman of 100 workers in the glove plant and at 19 he went on the road as a glove salesman. Four years later he became a partner in the company, and before he was 30, Mr. Goldwyn was making more than $15,000 a year.

It was almost by accident that Mr. Goldwyn got into movie making. In 1910 he married Blanche Lasky, whose brother, Jesse, was a vaudeville producer. Mr. Lasky, at the urging of a lawyer, Arthur S. Friend, toyed with the idea of film making and tried to interest his brother-in-law in such a venture. Mr. Goldwyn, who had moved to New York, was cool to the idea until one cold day in 1913, when he stepped into a Herald Square movie house to warm up and, only incidentally, saw a Western starring Broncho Billy Anderson. He was impressed not only with the movie but also with all the dimes the management was raking in.

Enthusiastic Approach

With the enthusiasm that was typical of him, Mr. Goldwyn took up the idea of forming a film company of his very own. He and Mr. Lasky each put up $10,000 and between them Mrs. Goldwyn and Mr. Friend pledged the rest of the $26,500 capitalization for the new Jesse L. Lasky Feature Picture Play Company.

Mr. Friend had his law practice to attend to, Mr. Lasky his vaudeville management chores, and so it was up to Mr. Goldwyn to do most of the work in the new company and get little of the glory. As a friend was to observe years later, "Sam had a self-effacing streak then, but he soon pinned it to the mat for all time."

Samuel Goldwyn and two of his stars, Eddie Cantor and Miriam Hopkins.

The company set out to produce long films that told romantic stories, even if they took an hour to unfold. Most "flickers" at the time were two-reelers, lasting about 20 minutes.

The Lasky company's first movie was a milestone in more ways than one. It was a five-reeler, the first feature-length movie, and one of the first films to be made in Hollywood. Called "The Squaw Man," it starred a well-known Broadway actor, Dustin Farnum, and it was directed by a young stage manager and unsuccessful playwright named Cecil B. DeMille, who had never worked on a movie before.

"The Squaw Man" was a tremendous success, but only after its producers had gone through a major crisis. Halfway through the filming, they ran out of money. "I felt like we were on the brink of the abscess," said Mr. Goldwyn, uttering what was probably the first recorded Goldwynism. The master salesman raised additional money by selling theater owners all over the country exhibition rights of "The Squaw Man" and 11 other future pictures. He collected in advance.

The company's initial success resulted in a sudden intense interest in it from Mr. Goldwyn's partners, which, as it turned out, was exactly what he didn't want. The partners — who by then included Mr. DeMille — battled constantly and Mr. Goldwyn seemed to be in a permanent rage. Shortly after the company merged with Adolph Zukor's Famous Players Company, Mr. Goldwyn sold out his shares for nearly a million dollars.

A Name Is Born

In 1917 he joined forces with Edgar and Arch Selwyn, who as Broadway producers had built up a library of plays that might make good films.

At that time, Mr. Goldwyn's name was still Goldfish, the nearest equivalent to his Polish name that immigration officials could think of when he came to this country. Goldwyn Pictures Corporation took its name from the "Gold" in Goldfish and the "wyn" in Selwyn.

Mr. Goldwyn liked the name so much that he had his own name legally changed to it, an action that displeased the Selwyns. Two years after the partnership was formed and had gone bankrupt, one of the Selwyns is said to have told Mr. Goldwyn: "Sam, you not only broke us but took half of our good name as well."

Years later, Judge Learned Hand said of Mr. Goldwyn's adopting the neologism, "A self-made man may prefer a self-made name."

Merger With Metro

When the bankrupt Goldwyn company was merged with Metro Pictures, out of which Metro-Goldwyn-Mayer grew, Mr. Goldwyn withdrew with a substantial financial settlement, but he had to agree that he could never use the name of Goldwyn Pictures Corporation on any films he made. Thus, his productions flashed on the screen with "Samuel Goldwyn

(continued)

Presents . . ." to identify them.

In 1922, Mr. Goldwyn became an independent producer, convinced that he would never be able to get along with partners or boards of directors. "It's dog eat dog in this business, and nobody's going to eat me," he said.

In 1926 Mr. Goldwyn became a member of United Artists, a cooperative formed by independent producers to distribute their pictures. In 1939 he had a falling-out with Mary Pickford, one of the other members, and in 1941, after a bitter court fight, he sold his stock to the corporation at a reported loss of $500,000.

From the time he became an independent producer, Mr. Goldwyn was noted for the reverence in which he held creative talent. He coddled actors, writers and directors, but when he felt they were not producing what he had expected of them, he switched tactics and heaped invective upon them.

The late Ben Hecht, who worked on the script of "Wuthering Heights," compared Mr. Goldwyn's treatment of writers to "an irritated man shaking a slot machine."

Lavish Spender on Scripts

But Mr. Goldwyn always believed that the story was the thing that made good movies, and he spent lavishly on scripts written for him by writers such as Rupert Hughes, Mary Roberts Rinehart, Moss Hart, Rex Beach, Lillian Hellman and Robert E. Sherwood.

His courting of the Belgian poet Maurice Maeterlinck resulted in disaster. Mr. Goldwyn commissioned him to write a scenario based on Mr. Maeterlinck's "Life of a Bee," which the producer had not read. After seeing the finished script, the story goes, Mr. Goldwyn ran from his office screaming, "My God, the hero is a bee!"

One of several great directors with whom Mr. Goldwyn did not get along was William Wyler, yet Mr. Wyler made some of his best films, including "The Best Years of Our Lives," under the Goldwyn banner.

During the filming of "These Three," Mr. Wyler changed a night scene to a daytime shot. A furious Mr. Goldwyn rebuked him with the fiat that "Nobody can change night into day, or vice versa, without asking me first."

Let Cooper's Option End

George Cukor refused to work for Mr. Goldwyn at all, which so exasperated the producer that he is reported to have said: "That's the way with these directors — they're always biting the hand that lays the golden egg."

Among the stars Mr. Goldwyn discovered were Tallulah Bankhead, Robert Montgomery and Gary Cooper. He let Mr. Cooper's option expire, however, and later had to hire him for "The Adventures of Marco Polo" for a hundred times the amount it would have cost him had the actor remained under contract.

Perhaps Mr. Goldwyn's worst talent-finding gaffe was his import of the Polish actress Anna Sten, upon whom he spent hundreds of thousands of dollars to build up as a star. Miss Sten, he felt, had an enigmatic beauty, or, as he put it, "the face of a spink." She failed to pass muster with the public, however, and he was finally forced to admit, to everyone's amusement but his own, that "She's colossal in a small way."

But his judgment was much better in the case of Vilma Banky, whom he teamed with Ronald Colman in a series of highly successful films, among them "The Night of Love" and "The Dark Angel"; Miss Bankhead, whom he discovered in a beauty contest and starred in "Thirty a Week" long before she won Broadway fame; and several of the "Goldwyn girls" —the leggy chorines he personally chose to decorate his musicals—who later attained stardom, among them Betty Grable.

When Sam Goldwyn made a picture, he spent only his own money and never resorted, as do most producers, to big studio or Wall Street financing. That was one reason he had a hand in every aspect of his productions, from acquiring the story to editing the film to planning its promotion campaign.

"I am the producer," he said. "I do not shove the money under the door and go home." He spent money freely, often on inefficient underlings who, he didn't mind admitting, were yes men. "I'll take 50 per cent efficiency," he explained, "to get 100 per cent loyalty."

So jealously did he guard his reputation for making high-quality pictures that he would stop at no expense to make improvements. In 1947, for example, he halted production of "The Bishop's Wife," starring Cary Grant, Loretta Young and David Niven, after he had spent more than $1-million on it. He simply wasn't satisfied with the way the film was turning out, and started all over again. It was a hit.

A $1-Million Halt

When he wasn't haunting his sound stages, Mr. Goldwyn was out selling his pictures, both in this country and abroad. "I've got a great slogan for the company," he once said — giving birth to another Goldwynism — "'Goldwyn pictures griddle the earth.'"

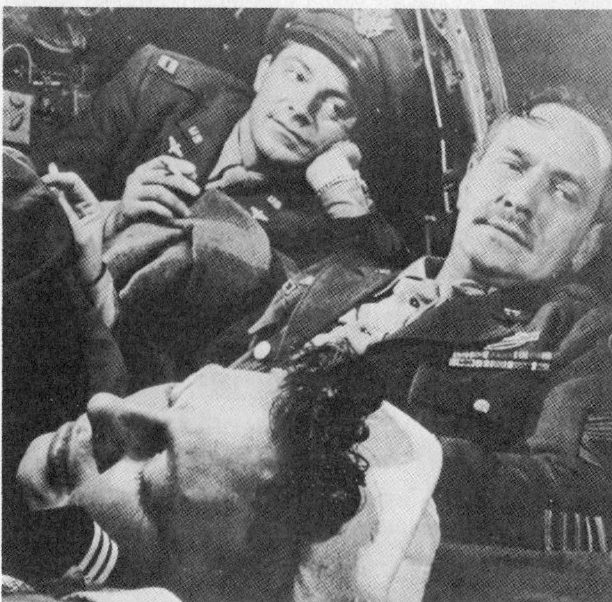

Samuel Goldwyn won the best-picture Oscar in 1947 for *The Best Years of Our Lives*. The stars included Dana Andrews, Fredric March and Harold Russell.

They not only girdled the earth, they were immensely popular. In a 20-year period before television started giving mass exposure to films, more than 200 million people paid to see Goldwyn productions. Many of the films were nominated for Academy Awards, but Mr. Goldwyn did not receive an Oscar for best picture until 1947, when "The Best Years of Our Lives" won all the major awards. Mr. Goldwyn was also presented, at that time, with the Irving Thalberg Memorial Award for his contributions to the film industry.

"Wuthering Heights" received the New York Film Critics' Award in 1939, the year "Gone With the Wind" swept the Academy Awards.

Mr. Goldwyn's films won dozens of Oscars in several categories — direction, writing, scenic design, music, color and acting. Five were winners for set design, a reflection of Mr. Goldwyn's care in that field. He was the first producer to use realistic, three-dimensional sets rather than painted flats.

Mr. Goldwyn was divorced in 1915 from Blanche Lasky, by whom he had a daughter, Ruth. In 1925 he married Frances Howard, a stage and screen actress. They had a son, Samuel Jr., who is a movie producer. They both survive.

Mrs. Goldwyn gradually became her husband's unofficial second-in-command at the studio. She also did a splendid job of keeping her husband's personal life in order, according to friends. Whenever the couple went out, she paid all restaurant checks and cab fares. She had to, because Mr. Goldwyn never carried change or a wallet. He was an extremely careful dresser and believed that his conservatively tailored suits would look lumpy if he put anything in his pockets.

Several years ago Mrs. Goldwyn installed a croquet field on the seven-acre Goldwyn estate in Beverly Hills, and it soon became a mark of distinction in Hollywood to be invited to play croquet at the Goldwyns' huge Georgian mansion.

Made Last Film at 78

Mr. Goldwyn came out of semiretirement in 1959 to make his last film, "Porgy and Bess." Although he was already 78 years old, he held his chesty, 6-foot-tall body erect, and his swinging walk seemed as always to be jet-propelled as he strode through his studio streets. His eyes, deep-set in his rather plain face, could still flash with anger, and his Polish-accented voice had lost little of its deep vibrancy.

In recent years, Mr. Goldwyn rented his studio to independent film and television productions, but he was not pleased with much of the product that emanated from there and other parts of Hollywood. He believed movies and TV had become trashy.

Summing up his career, Mr. Goldwyn said, "I was a rebel, a lone wolf. My pictures were my own. I financed them myself and answered solely to myself. My mistakes and my successes were my own. My one rule was to please myself, and if I did that, there was a good chance I would please others."

The funeral service for Mr. Goldwyn will be private.

The New York Times

WEDNESDAY, JULY 4, 1973

Betty Grable, Movie Pin-up of '40's, Dies

Special to The New York Times

SANTA MONICA, Calif., July 3 — Betty Grable, the star of a score or more of Hollywood musicals in the nineteen-forties and one of the movies' enduring sex symbols, died yesterday at St. John's Hospital here. She was 56 years old.

The cause of death was listed as lung cancer. The actress, according to friends, was "a very heavy smoker" of cigarettes.

For the last several years Miss Grable had lived in Las Vegas. She retired from the movies about 15 years ago.

'My Legs Made Me'

By ALDEN WHITMAN

Thirty years ago, Betty Grable, a shapely, straw-blond blue eyed film actress and singer of admittedly modest talents was the country's supreme pop culture idol. Not only did the star of lavish Technicolor musicals lure millions of moviegoers to the box office, but she also captured the fancy of American servicemen the world over. Indeed, three million photographs of Miss Grable, clad in a white bathing suit and displaying an inviting smile and curvaceous legs, were distributed in the armed forces, and G.I.'s acclaimed her as their favorite pin-up.

"People like to hear me sing, see me dance and watch my legs," Miss Grable once remarked with a directness that was refreshing in Hollywood. And she added, "My legs made me."

They achieved, in fact, a sort of immortality in 1948 when a print of them was committed to concrete in the forecourt of Grauman's Theater in Hollywood, not far from a cast of Clark Gable's ears and John Barrymore's profile.

Miss Grable was quite frank about her abilities. "My voice is just a voice," she said. "When it comes to dancing, I'm just average, maybe a little bit below."

Nonetheless, her more than 40 films, many of them for 20th Century-Fox, grossed about $100-million; and she herself earned at least $3-million in her career. At $300,000 a year, she was the highest-salaried American woman in 1946-47, according to the Treasury Department.

Some Films Listed

The money and the fame—10,000 admirers a week were said to have written fan letters to Miss Grable in her heyday—

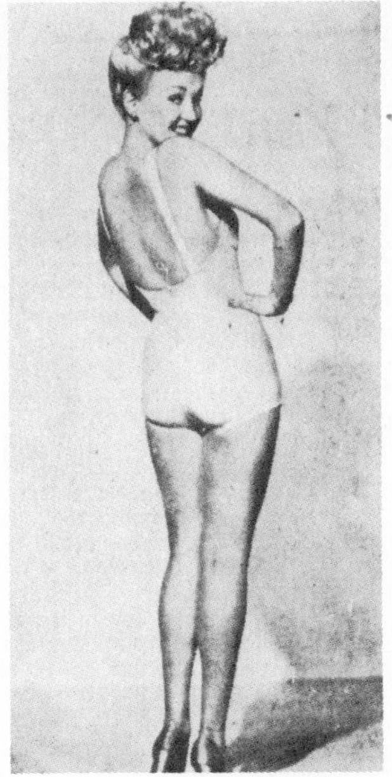

Betty Grable

came from such pictures as "Down Argentine Way," "Moon Over Miami," "A Yank in the R.A.F.," "Song of the Islands," "Springtime in the Rockies," "Million Dollar Legs," "Mother Wore Tights," and "Coney Island." Her last film, released in 1955, was 'How to Be Very Very Popular."

Miss Grable's musicals were not long on plot. In "Coney Island," for example, she was the diamond-in-the-rough boardwalk entertainer who reached Broadway with the help of two carnival men.

Her songs bore such titles as "Miss Lulu From Louisville," "I had the Craziest Dream" and "For You, for Me, for Ever More." Cavorting with Miss Grable in her films were Don Ameche, Tyrone Power, Alice Faye, Victor Mature, Cesar Romero, John Payne, Jack Oakie and Dan Dailey, among other luminaries of the day.

Reviewers thought Miss Grable's films pleasant and buoyant. In World War II and the years that immediately followed, she could be counted on to tantalize and divert audiences, to take their minds off the grimness of armed conflict. She was, as a New York Times reviewer said, "a lot of fun."

Darryl F. Zanuck, the 20th Century-Fox producer, considered Miss Grable such a sure-fire drawing card that he pressed her to play a dramatic role. She refused, saying:

"I'm strictly a song-and-dance girl. I'm no Bette Davis nor am I out to prove anything with histrionics. I just want to make pictures that people will like."

The daughter of a frustrated actress and a bookkeeper, Ruth Elizabeth Grable was born Dec. 18, 1916, in South St. Louis, Mo. At her mother's urging the child studied the saxophone and various kinds of dancing. "I don't think I missed a thing except eccentric dancing," she recalled. "I dreaded every lesson."

By 1930 Miss Grable's mother had taken her to Hollywood, where she landed some bit parts on the Sam Goldwyn lot. Then there was a comic dance number in "The Gay Divorcee" in 1934 and a string of pictures starring her in Betty coed roles.

Miss Grable's catapult to stardom was a true Hollywood fairy tale. In 1939 Mr. Zanuck saw a routine cheesecake photograph of the actress in a newspaper and signed her to a contract without ado.

And when Alice Faye, then the reigning musical comedienne, fell ill, Miss Grable took her place in "Down Argentine Way." The film was a hit, and for the next dozen years she had the Midas touch.

Part of her filmic appeal was a restrained sensuousness. In "Tin Pan Alley," for instance, she danced through a harem scene, clad in a sequined bra and panties, with her legs sinuous under transparent pantaloons. The scene was comic enough to disarm the Hollywood censors.

For another thing, Miss Grable was pert and petite. She was a little over 5 feet 3 inches tall, weighed about 110 pounds and maintained a trim figure. "Girls can see me in a picture and feel I could be one of them," she once said. To men she was concededly sexy.

Married Twice

Miss Grable was the center of three highly press-agented romances. One was with Jackie Coogan, the former child movie star, to whom she was once married in 1937. The union ended in divorce two years later.

Afterward, the actress's name was linked with George Raft, who was her frequent escort. Then in 1943 she married Harry James, the trumpeter and band leader. They were divorced in 1965.

With Mr. James she raised race horses and operated two ranches and two estates. In recent years Miss Grable attempted various comebacks, but without notable success. She was often seen in television commercials for Geritol, a reputed elixir for the middle-aged.

Betty Grable (R) and Sheree North dancing the honky-tonk number from *How To Be Very Very Popular*, 1955.

The New York Times WEDNESDAY, JANUARY 20, 1954.

S. H. GREENSTREET, 'THE FAT MAN,' DIES

Stage Actor for 35 Years Was Cited for Film Bow in 'Maltese Falcon' at 62

HOLLYWOOD, Calif., Jan. 19 (UP)—Sydney H. Greenstreet, the actor who was noted in later years for his portrayal of movie villains, died last night after a long illness. He was 74 years old.

Mr. Greenstreet had been suffering from Brights Disease and diabetes for a number of years. Recently he suffered new attacks.

The English actor did not get Hollywood roles until he was 62. Before that, he appeared on the New York stage.

Mr. Greenstreet frequently was co-starred with diminutive but equally sinister Peter Lorre. The 280-pound actor wanted to play comedy roles, but during his entire Hollywood career he remained a "heavy."

On Stage Forty Years

After treading the boards for forty years in more plays than he could remember, Sydney Hughes Greenstreet achieved almost instantaneous international recognition in 1941 for his portrayal of Kaspar Gutman, the ponderous, sinister and cultivated English crook in Warner Brothers' film version of the Dashiell Hammett mystery story, "The Maltese Falcon."

Intrigued by the role but not interested enough to continue his career before the cameras, Mr. Greenstreet rejoined the Lunts in "There Shall Be No Night," then touring on the West Coast.

But Warner Brothers, realizing that Mr. Greenstreet's appeal was not casual and that audiences were clamoring for more of "the Fat Man," prevailed upon him to accept the role of Gen. Winfield Scott in the Errol Flynn picture, "They Died With Their Boots On." This time, too, he expected that his sojourn in Hollywood would be only for as long as it took to complete the film.

In the next three years he appeared in a dozen pictures—generally in a "heavy" role—among which were "Casablanca," "Across the Pacific," "Background to Danger," "Passage to Marseille," "The Mask of Dimitrios," "Between Two Worlds," "Conflict," "The Conspirators" and "Christmas in Connecticut."

As a free-lance in recent years, he appeared in a dozen feature films including "The Hucksters," "The Velvet Touch," "Three Strangers," "Devotion" and "Flamingo Road."

Born in Sandwich, Kent, England, on Dec. 27, 1879, he was the son of John Jack Greenstreet, a tanner, and the former Ann Baker. He attended the Dane Hill Preparatory School at Margate and in 1899 went to Ceylon, where he supervised a tea plantation for two years. Returning to England, he tried selling beer for a brewery, unsuccessfully.

Encouraged by his mother, he began his theatrical career with the Ben Greet Players. He made his professional debut in 1902 in the then sensational "Sherlock Holmes," appearing as Craigen, the murderer in the gas chamber.

Came to U. S. in 1904

The next year he was seen in "The Eternal City," and in 1904 he came to this country with the Ben Greet Players. For five years thereafter he was a leading comedian in Shakespearean repertory, with assignments in eighteen different plays. Thoroughly steeped in the Bard's works, Mr. Greenstreet knew more than 12,000 lines of Shakespeare at his death.

Over this forty-year period he appeared with such notables as Sir Herbert Beerbohm Tree, Julia Marlowe, Lou Tellegen, Margaret Anglin, Viola Allen, David Thorndike and Alfred Lunt and Lynn Fontanne.

He trouped with the Lunts for more than six years, and for a three-year period was a mainstay of the Theatre Guild's companies. He was seen in such varied offerings as "Lady Windermere's Fan," Eugene O'Neill's "Marco Millions," Karel Capek's "R. U. R.," Robert Sherwood's "Idiot's Delight" and "There Shall Be No Night," Chekhov's "The Sea Gull," "The Admirable Crichton," with Walter Huston, and "Roberta."

Mr. Greenstreet's tours brought treasured associations with Presidents Wilson and Theodore Roosevelt. He met Woodrow Wilson, then a Princeton professor, on a trans-Atlantic liner. And it was during Roosevelt's term at the White House, when a benefit performance of Hawthorne's "Wonder Tales" was being presented on the lawn, that Mr. Greenstreet, playing the god Zeus, used the White House as a dressing room.

He married the former Doroth Marie Ogden on Aug. 12, 191 A son, John Ogden Greenstree survives.

Sydney H. Greenstreet

Sydney Greenstreet (R), in *The Maltese Falcon,* with Humphrey Bogart, Peter Lorre and Mary Astor.

The New York Times SATURDAY, JULY 24, 1948

DAVID W. GRIFFITH, FILM PIONEER, DIES

Producer of 'Birth of Nation,' 'Intolerance' and 'America' Made Nearly 500 Pictures

SET SCREEN STANDARDS

Co-Founder of United Artists Gave Mary Pickford and Fairbanks Their Starts

Special to THE NEW YORK TIMES.

HOLLYWOOD, Calif., July 23—David Wark Griffith, one of the first and greatest contributors to the motion picture art, died this morning in Temple Hospital after suffering a cerebral hemorrhage. His age was 73.

The producer of "The Birth of a Nation," and pioneer in such techniques as closeups, fadeouts and flashbacks, was stricken in his rooms at the Hollywood Knickerbocker Hotel, where he lived alone.

He was divorced last November from his second wife, the former Evelyn Marjorie Baldwin, whom he married in 1936 after the dissolution by divorce of his marriage to Linda Avidson, an actress.

Although an erstwhile titan of the industry, Mr. Griffith had been inactive in recent years and lived unostentatiously in relative obscurity working on his memoirs, emerging chiefly for meals in Hollywood restaurants, where he was a familiar figure, and for sessions of reminiscing with his old-time industry cronies.

A niece and nephew, Ruth and Willard Griffith of Santa Ana, spent several hours at his bedside before he succumbed.

Surviving also are a brother, Albert Griffith of New York; three other nieces, Mrs. Marie Duncan, Mrs. Earl Butler and Miss Myrtle Griffith of Kentucky, and another nephew, Lynn Griffith of Ontario, Calif.

Burial probably will take place in La Grange, Ky.

"Father of the Film Art"

The name of David Wark Griffith, the master producer and director of silent motion pictures, is synonymous with "father of the film art" and "king of directors."

He produced and directed almost 500 pictures costing $23,000,000 and grossing $80,000,000, of which his most famous film, "The Birth of a Nation," has grossed to date more than $48,000,000.

Although Mr. Griffith did not, according to research authorities, originate all of the technical devices formerly accredited to him, he did originate many of them, and he vastly improved others. Chief, perhaps, among his improvements was his development of the close-up, which had first been employed in 1895 in an early American film, "The Kiss," into a dramatic psychological contribution that shaped the entire art of the cinema down to the present day.

Among the multitude of advanced methods which he started and which have long been an established part of film technique were the long shot, the vista, the vignette, the iris or eye-opener effect, the cameo-profile, the fade-in and fade-out, soft focus, back lighting, tinting, rapid-cutting, parallel action, mist photography, high and low angle shots, night photography, and the moving camera.

Fought for Innovations

In making his innovations Mr. Griffith had to contend with the conservatism of the owners, for, despite the fact that the industry was still something of a novelty when he entered it as an actor-director, it was already stereotyped. Great courage, persistence and vision on Mr. Griffith's part were needed to convince cinematic leaders of the rightness of his ideas.

He was the first director to depart from the standard 1,000-foot film. This caused a break between him and the officers of the old Biograph Company. He then made the first four-reeler, "Judith of Bethulia," which had instantaneous success in America and Europe. When Mr. Griffith ordered a close-up shot of a human face his cameraman of long standing, Billy Bitzer, quit his job in disgust. At the first close-up there were some hisses and cries of "Where are their feet?" but soon the Griffith improvement of the close-up emerged triumphant.

It was as a creator of significant content in the films themselves, aside from their technique, that Mr. Griffith was a mighty force in the cinema. Even before "The Birth of a Nation," that epic of the Civil War and the Reconstruction Period, which, directed by a man whose family had been ruined by the fall of the Confederacy, was most biased but was filled with great sweep and movement, he had exercised his bold conception of the exalted purpose which the medium might serve.

Long before the names of Sergei Eisenstein of Russia, Fritz Lang of Germany, Alfred Hitchcock of England, and Frank Capra of Hollywood were heard of, Mr. Griffith brought to the screen important historical and philosophical themes, challenging social questions, visionary prophecies. His films were emotional, dramatic, intellectual and esthetic.

16,000 "Extras" on One Scene

In 1916 his "Intolerance" appeared on a grand scale, with four parallel stories, a stupendous re-creation of the Ancient World and an apocalyptic image-prophecy of the Second Coming of Christ. This film, in which Griffith used 16,000 "extras" in a single scene, still stands as an example of what can be done with masses of people and architecture on the screen.

The fantastic Babylon set from D.W. Griffith's film, *Intolerance*, 1916.

Mr. Griffith brought lyric poetry and high tragedy to the screen in 1919 in "Broken Blossoms," a passionate plea for a renewal of the Christian ideal in interracial relations. His "Way Down East," a folk-melodrama of New England in the Nineties, produced in 1920, used landscapes and natural backgrounds as vital psychological and dramatic elements of a story. "Dream Street," produced the next year, contained allegoric symbolism, and experimented with talking-film apparatus.

In "Orphans of the Storm," in 1922, Mr. Griffith combined magnificent spectacle with a social theme, using the French Revolution as a platform from which to attack communism and Soviet Russia, and citing the historic fruits of the revolution as a vindication of liberal democracy.

In 1924, Mr. Griffith produced the mammoth "America," another great historical pageant, this time of the American Revolution. In "America" as in "The Birth of a Nation," he set permanent standards, copied by film-makers the world over, in the technique of battle scenes.

His Methods Copied by Europe

His last important film, which came out in 1925, was "Isn't Life Wonderful!" a grim tale of Polish refugees in post-World War I Germany, which was a forerunner of

(continued)

the present-day documentary films with the difference that it transcended the latter's frequent flatness. This film, like "America," was studied and copied by the Russian film directors, especially Rudovkin. In 1931 appeared Griffith's first all-talking film, "Abraham Lincoln," and his final film, "The Struggle," a study of alcoholism.

In the days of his greatest glory Mr. Griffith never used a shooting script. "Intolerance," for example, although it was twenty-two months in production and consumed 125 miles of film, was photographed entirely from his "mental notes."

To the world at large Mr. Griffith was hailed for the many fine screen actors and actresses he molded into stars. Mary Pickford and Lillian Gish were outstanding examples of his genius in choosing and training performers for the new art. It was he, also, who induced the famous Douglas Fairbanks to leave the stage for the screen.

Dorothy Gish, Blanche Sweet, Mae Marsh, Owen Moore, Alice Joyce, Mabel Normand, Robert Harron, Arthur Johnson, Richard Barthelmess, James Kirkwood, Lionel Barrymore, Harry Carey and Mack Sennett—all these owed their film careers to David Wark Griffith.

Others were Henry B. Walthall, Louis Wolheim, Joseph Schildkraut the Talmadge sisters, Norma, Constance and Natalie; Donald Crisp, Tully Marshall, Lowell Sherman and Neil Hamilton.

Mr. Griffith's judgment of ability was remarkable, as has been said by his biographer, Seymour Stern. He changed careers and destinies overnight, turning workmen into directors and schoolgirls into actresses. He saw more potential drama in wistful maidens than in the plump type of the time, and the millions who composed his audience backed him in this belief.

They took his best-known actress, Mary Pickford, to their heart and called her "Our Mary" and "America's Sweetheart."

Born at La Grange, Ky., on Jan. 22, 1875, the son of Colonel Jacob Wark Griffith and Margaret Oglesby Griffith, he started work at the age of 16 on a local newspaper and as correspondent for The Louisville Courier-Journal.

After seeing Julia Marlowe in "Romola," he decided to become an actor, and eventually obtained the role of a dunce in a play presented by the Meffert stock company. His performance won him additional roles, but his pay was so small that he had to work as an elevator boy and later as a clerk and a book salesman in order to make ends meet.

Wrote Play for Stage

Eventually he was taken into John Griffith's Strolling Players and later joined Ada Gray's traveling troupes. After he had worked in half a dozen other stock companies, a play he had written called "A Fool and a Girl" was produced in 1907 by James K. Hackett at the Columbia Theatre in Washington.

After the failure of his play, Mr. Griffith saw his first flickering film and immediately wrote a scenario of the opera "La Tosca." The scenario, although not accepted, won him entry to moving pictures as an actor.

He worked first at the Edison studio in the film "The Eagle's Nest," under Edwin S. Porter's direction, and then shifted to Biograph, where he appeared in "When Knighthood Was in Flower" and other one-reelers.

In June, 1908, he was made an assistant director, and in July of that year made his first film, "The Adventures of Dollie," which was billed as "one of the most remarkable cases of child stealing."

In 1919, with Mary Pickford, Douglas Fairbanks and Charles Chaplin, he formed United Artists Corporation, under whose seal some of the outstanding productions of the screen were released. He sold his United Artists partnership in 1933.

D.W. Griffith (right) with his cameraman, Billy Bitzer.

The New York Times FRIDAY, AUGUST 7, 1964.

Sir Cedric Hardwicke Is Dead; Actor on Stage and in Films, 71

Created Roles in Shaw Plays and Excelled in Character Parts for Many Years

Sir Cedric Hardwicke

Sir Cedric Hardwicke, the actor, died here yesterday of a chronic lung ailment. He was 71 years old.

Sir Cedric had been admitted to University Hospital three weeks ago after a long illness. His doctors said he suffered from emphysema, a distension of the lung sacs, which makes breathing difficult.

When Cedric Hardwicke earned a knighthood in 1934 for his Shavian performances, he was the youngest theatrical performer ever to have achieved that honor. In the years that followed, he became known to American audiences for mature and dignified characterizations entirely suitable for a "Sir."

At the time he received Britain's high honor he had never appeared in America. After that, he rarely acted anywhere else. While he proudly guarded the English citizenship that gave him his title, he became one of the most familiar personalities in Hollywood films—the personification of the British gentleman, conservative, aloof and impeccably polite.

A Familiar Face

It was a rewarding characterization, and he played it well. Sir Cedric was never a movie star, and in the ranks of supporting actors he usually did exactly that—support. His notices were sometimes excellent, invariably respectful. To the general public, he was a familiar face whose name hovered on the tip of the tongue.

In the theater, Sir Cedric was very much a star. Typically, however, two of his most notable Broadway successes, in "Caesar and Cleopatra" and as the Japanese businessman in "A Majority of One," were in complementary adjunction to glittering actresses, Lilli Palmer and Gertrude Berg.

Quite possibly the finest acting he ever did was in Charles Laughton's staged reading of "Don Juan in Hell." In that George Bernard Shaw exercise in dialectic, he played the statue. Most of his performance, and certainly his most memorable effects, consisted of attitudinizing, with an eloquent "harrumph" and a devastating flip of a page, while Mr. Laughton, Charles Boyer and Agnes Moorehead articulated the meaty Shavian hyperbole.

Cedric Webster Hardwicke was born in Lye, Stourbridge, Worcester, on Feb. 19, 1893. His father, a physician, experienced the traditional British horror of his son's chosen profession in the theater, but nevertheless financed him through his studies at the Royal Academy of Dramatic Arts.

Sir Cedric credited George Bernard Shaw with helping to make the actor an acceptable member of society. "He fought as nobody else did for recognition of the actor as an intelligent member of the community," the actor recalled a few years ago.

Created Shaw Characters

Shaw became a personal friend when the young actor was appearing in his plays at the Birmingham Repertory Theater. "Shaw was a sort of godfather to me," Sir Cedric said. The playwright closely supervised the productions as the actor created the roles of Captain Shotover in "Heartbreak House" and the He-Ancient in "Back to Methuselah."

This high point in Sir Cedric's career came after he had followed the usual fledgling actor's route, touring the provinces in small parts in classics and trivia. "I played Hamlet at 14, and got *that* out of my system," he said. His London debut was in 1912, in a walk-on as a gentleman of the court in "The Monk and the Woman." Then came World War I, and seven years with the army, ending as a captain in France.

He joined the Birmingham company early in 1922, and created there, in addition to the other plays, the role of King Magnus in the first production of Shaw's "The Apple Cart." He moved on to London in this play, and began the series of diversified roles that led to his knighthood. Critics admired him as Captain Andy in "Show Boat," the sadistic father in "The Barretts of Wimpole Street," a sympathetic doctor in "The Late Christopher Bean" and the exiled Russian prince in "Tovarich."

"Dreyfus" was his first leading film assignment, in 1931. Hollywood called him for the priest in "Les Miserables," with Mr. Laughton and Fredric March in 1935, and then he appeared in one of the early Technicolor films, "Becky Sharp." He made his Broadway debut in Henri Bernstein's "Promise" in 1936. It failed, and so did "The Amazing Dr. Clitterhouse." His first Broadway long run was as Canon Skerritt in Paul Vincent Carroll's "Shadow and Substance," in 1938.

Since then he alternated between Broadway and Hollywood, sometimes directing—he had a notable success with Gertrude Lawrence in "Pygmalion" in 1946—but usually just acting. "I'm the only actor I know who never wanted to do anything else," he once said.

Among his better film roles were "The Moon Is Down;" "Wilson"; as Mr. Brink in "On Borrowed Time"; and Livingstone in 'Stanley and Livingstone," "The Keys of the Kingdom" and "A Womans Vengeance." He was particularly praised in Anthony Asquith's British-made 'The Winslow Boy," playing a determined father whose son is expelled from school for petty theft, and who fights the case over a period of years to victory in Parliament.

He acted for Alfred Hitchcock in "Rope" and for George Stevens in "I Remember Mama." In these films, he had small roles and gave well-received performances. He also appeared, to lesser applause, in "The Ten Commandments" and "Around the World in 80 Days," and as a somewhat senile king in Laurence Olivier's "Richard III."

He acted often on television, but without outstanding success. He also wrote his autobiography twice — "Let's Pretend: Recollections and Reflections of a Lucky Actor" in 1932, and, while playing in "A Majority of One," "A Victorian in Orbit." He wanted to call the last one "Fifty Years Without Being Found Out."

In private, Sir Cedric was a dry wit, a club man and a raconteur. He married and was divorced twice. Both wives were actresses — Helena Pickard, 1928 to 1950, and Mary Scott, 1950 to 1961. He had sons by both wives, Edward, now 32 and an actor, and Michael.

Although Sir Cedric made a considerable amount of money during his career, he was not well off financially in his later years, according to his friends. One friend said yesterday that Sir Cedric liked to spend money as fast as he earned it and being "flat broke" did not really disturb him.

An associate said that Sir Cedric did not let financial problems make him unhappy. He would smile and shrug his shoulders, the associate said, because it was a regular part of his life and his friends understood.

Three years ago, he summed up his private life: "The more I see of life, the more I prefer the world of the theater to the real world."

Laurence Olivier, Ralph Richardson and Cedric Hardwicke in *Richard III*, 1954.

The New York Times THURSDAY, AUGUST 8, 1957.

Oliver Hardy of Film Team Dies; Co-Star of 200 Slapstick Movies

Portly Master of the Withering Look and 'Slow Burn'—Features Popular on TV

Special to The New York Times.

HOLLYWOOD, Calif., Aug. 7—Oliver Hardy, the fat, always frustrated partner of the famous movie comedy team of Laurel and Hardy, died early today at the North Hollywood home of his mother-in-law, Mrs. Monnie L. Jones. Mr. Hardy, who was 65 years old, suffered a paralytic stroke last Sept. 12.

His widow, Lucille, who had worked as a script girl on his movies before their marriage in 1940, said Mr. Hardy never regained the power of speech after the stroke and required constant nursing care.

Stan Laurel, the frail, sad-looking member of the team, said today: "What's there to say. It's shocking, of course. Ollie was like a brother. That's the end of the history of Laurel and Hardy." Mr. Laurel suffered a stroke in June, 1955, but reported that he was steadily regaining strength.

Surviving, in addition to Mrs. Hardy, is a sister, Mrs. Elizabeth Sage of Atlanta.

Found New Audience

In recent years Mr. Hardy had found an entirely new audience through the appearance of the old Laurel and Hardy films on television. In particular, "Babes in Toyland" has become a regular offering during the Christmas season.

Until ill health intervened, he and his yawn-faced colleague were planning a movie comeback to capitalize on their renewed popularity.

Their joint career, begun in 1926 by a chance appearance in a silent two-reeler, spanned nearly 200 films. At one time their movies for Hal Roach were filmed in English, German, French, Spanish and Italian to keep pace with an expanding world audience.

Sound was only incidental to Mr. Hardy's comedy. His actions were essentially pantomime, based on the Mack Sennett silent vocabulary of the delayed and double takes. He was a master of the tailspin, the slow burn, or—when surveying the disasters wrought by his well-meaning partner—the withering look.

Although the team concentrated on feature-length films such as "The Devil's Brother," "Swiss Miss" or "Blockheads" in later years, most critics felt that the two-reelers were a more suitable mold for their hectic efforts.

Oliver Hardy as he usually appeared in motion pictures.

Scripts meant little in Laurel and Hardy comedies, as much of the plot and byplay were improvised as the shooting proceeded. The team was among the first to slow the unnaturally fast pace so characteristic of the early comedy movies.

Mr. Hardy made his first picture at the age of 21 in Jacksonville, Fla. His displacement, well on the way to its eventual 300 pounds, happened to catch the eye of a Lubin Film Company unit on location there.

At the time he had just finished four years with a stock company in Atlanta, where he was born in 1892. He had drifted into the profession by performing on showboats and in vaudeville during vacations from his law studies at the University of Georgia.

The Jacksonville role was followed two years later, in 1915, by a series of comic films with the Pathé Studios, then situated in Ithaca, N. Y. From 1918 until 1925, when it was bought by Warner Brothers, Mr. Hardy worked at Vitagraph as a director, often with Larry Semon, who later went on to earn $100,000 a year for stopping custard pies with his face.

A year later at the Hal Roach Studios Mr. Hardy was cast with a mournful-eyed Englishman named Arthur Stanley Jefferson Laurel, who had been Charlie Chaplin's understudy in London music halls. Within ten years their series had become the studio's major industry.

Laurel and Hardy as convicts in *The Second Hundred Years.*

Laurel and Hardy in *Beau Hunks,* 1931.

"All the News That's Fit to Print."

The New York Times.

LATE CITY EDITION
Generally fair today, temperature unchanged. Tomorrow scattered showers, temperature unchanged.
Temperatures Yesterday—Max., 86; min., 66.

VOL. LXXXVI....No. 28,990. Entered as Second-Class Matter, Postoffice, New York, N. Y. NEW YORK, TUESDAY, JUNE 8, 1937. P TWO CENTS In New York City. | THREE CENTS Within 200 Miles. | FOUR CENTS Elsewhere Except in 7th and 8th Postal Zones.

Jean Harlow, Film Star, Dies in Hollywood At 26 After an Illness of Only a Few Days

Special to THE NEW YORK TIMES.

HOLLYWOOD, Calif., June 7.—Jean Harlow, blond beauty of the screen, died in the Good Samaritan Hospital here today after taking a sudden turn for the worse in the illness of uremic poisoning which had confined her to bed for a week. Her age was 26.

Apparently convalescent from the uremic poisoning, the actress suffered an unexpected relapse last night, and succumbed shortly before noon today from a cerebral oedema.

Blood transfusions, intravenous injections and artificial respiration from a Fire Department inhalator were employed throughout the night in a desperate effort to save her life.

At the star's bedside when she died were William Powell, Metro-Goldwyn-Mayer star; her mother, Mrs. Jean Bello; her stepfather, Marino Bello, and Jimmie Chadney, her cousin. Working over her during the last few hours were her physicians, Dr. E. T. Fishbaugh and Dr. Leland Chapman.

Miss Harlow had been in poor health for a year. Last Fall she became so weak from an acute case of sunburn that she was forced to postpone her film work and receive special medical treatment. Shortly after returning to normal condition, Miss Harlow suffered a throat infection. This weakened her to such an extent that she became a victim of the Winter epidemic of influenza.

The uremic poisoning was first observed last week-end. Miss Harlow soon responded favorably to treatment and was thought well on the road to recovery when she lapsed into a coma last night.

By The Associated Press.

HOLLYWOOD, Calif., June 7.—Jean Harlow, who was earning approximately $4,000 a week, was reported to have left an estate of nearly $1,000,000, largely in insurance policies and annuities.

The funeral services will be private.

A Hollywood press agent lifted Jean Harlow into gaudy prominence some years ago when he called her "The Platinum Blond" to describe her hair, which was a compromise between gold and white. Platinum blond, meaning an over-bleached blond head, was the most popular exhibit at a hairdressers' convention that season. Platinum blonds made their appearance among the new dancers, show girls and blues singers. Every floor show had one or two. They appeared also in the subways, in

Continued on Page Thirty

63 PLANES BOMB SUBURB OF BILBAO; GUNS RAKE MADRID

Lezama Target of Air Raid—Insurgent Artillery Opens on Capital at Midnight

SHIP FIRES ON PALAMOS

Shore Batteries Reply North of Barcelona—Skirmishes Continue at La Granja

MADRID TRUCE IS HINTED

Report Is Loyalists Would Quit City Upon Agreement by Rebels Not to Enter

The Spanish Situation

THE FRONT—A fleet of sixty-three Insurgent planes was reported to have bombed Lezama, a suburb of Bilbao. Hard fighting continued near strategic Lemona. Rebel guns opened up on Madrid after midnight. Page 1.

HENDAYE—Insurgents said a plan for the evacuation and neutralization of Madrid was under consideration. (With the above story.) Page 1.

LONDON—Consultations were [...] by Britain, France, Germany and Italy on plans to revise the non-intervention plan and to deal with future attacks on foreign warships. Page 17.

Mass Attack of Airplanes

By The Associated Press.

HENDAYE, France, June 7.—A massed fleet of sixty-three Insurgent war planes was reported today to have bombed the suburb of Lezama, only two miles from beleaguered Bilbao Spain.

Communiqués of both sides reported their forces were locked in the struggle for the strategic highway junction at Lemona, about six miles southeast of Bilbao. The Insurgents flatly declared "the hill is entirely in our hands." The Basque Government asserted "the enemy tried to attack our positions on the hill but was easily repulsed."

Six thousand Basque troops have been killed in the last few days, the Insurgent communiqué declared.

The Insurgent attack had the double objective of occupying the commanding peaks near the valuable Lemona coal mines and the communications center at Galdacano, two miles beyond.

The Insurgents also pressed against Galdacano from Larrabezua in the Lezama sector to the northeast. No estimate of the damage inflicted by the huge air fleet was contained in the dispatches reaching here.

Madrid Truce Hinted

Wireless to THE NEW YORK TIMES.

HENDAYE, France, June 7.—A "gentlemen's agreement" between the Loyalists and Insurgents providing for evacuation of Madrid by General José Miaja's troops on the understanding that General Francisco Franco's troops shall not march in, is being talked about in Insurgent quarters.

The idea, it appears, would be that Madrid would become a neutral demilitarized city and would thus be saved from further destruction by shelling and bombing.

Whether such a plan is seriously under consideration anywhere is not known, but the San Sebastian Falangist [Fascist] newspaper Unidad asserts that it was prepared by the new Loyalist Ambassador to Paris, Angel Ossorio y Gallardo.

Madrid Heavily Shelled

MADRID, Tuesday, June 8 (AP).—Insurgent batteries opened an intensive fire upon Madrid early today after a day in which not a shot was heard on the capital front for the first time in many weeks.

Replying to a government bombardment from within the city, Insurgent artillerymen began their cannonading soon after midnight. Every ten seconds a shell could be heard screeching through the air and into the capital. The missiles exploded in scattered parts of the city.

Shouts of panic-stricken women and the sound of persons running through houses to basement refuges mingled with the din of the bombardment.

Details of casualties and damage could not be ascertained immediately.

The shelling accompanied an Insurgent attack on the Carabanchel sector southwest of Madrid. Government forces, aided by artillery, repulsed the assault.

Refugees in the United States Embassy building spent a restless night. During the bombardment, which lasted an hour and was one of the most violent since the siege of Madrid first began, two shells

Continued on Page Seventeen

Chamberlain Proposes to Compel Electric Companies to Combine

Prime Minister Would Standardize Rates and Practices of 626 Producers, Requiring Stronger to Buy Out Weaker Groups and Others to Unite Under Government Supervision

By FERDINAND KUHN Jr.

Wireless to THE NEW YORK TIMES.

LONDON, June 7.—Prime Minister Neville Chamberlain gave the nation another example of "Tory Socialism" tonight when he made public his government's recommendations for reorganization of Great Britain's electric industry.

The plans provide for the compulsory purchase or transfer of existing power companies by methods that already have raised an outcry of protest from the vested interests concerned. Clamor against the scheme is rising rapidly, and it would not be surprising if Mr. Chamberlain soon found himself facing another fight with the reactionary elements among his own supporters.

At present there are as many as 626 separate organizations supplying electricity in Britain, not including the Central Electricity Board created by the government. Of these, 371 are municipal authorities and 247 are private companies.

There is such a complexity of voltages, charges and other factors of supply that the voltage of lines varies on different sides of many London streets and [...] price ranges from a[...] a unit in some are[...] 2 pence in [...]

would be consolidated. Where one private company is clearly the most efficient in the area, it would be required to acquire all its competitors under government supervision. Where amalgamation on this basis would be too difficult, the government would authorize transfer of all existing companies in a given area to a newly constituted distribution board appointed by the government. Where two or more municipal power companies are competing in any given area they would be put under the control of a joint board.

Not only does the government propose to dictate which little companies shall be swallowed by big ones, but the Lord Chancellor would appoint an arbitral tribunal to determine the purchase price in case of dispute.

Obviously the governm[...] made up its min[...] number of elect[...] abolish overla[...] resultan[...] in [...]

Driv[...] Off[...] to [...]

STENCH [...]

Another W[...] Two Descr[...] Attack[...]

Seven thugs be[...] that he was disable[...] after his brother, w[...] employer, had refuse[...] ders from one of the [...] on trial as leaders of[...] racket, Nathaniel Brow[...] driver, testified yesterd[...] Supreme Court.

Brown, a mild-mannere[...] with horn-rimmed glasse[...] peared as a witness against [...] Plumeri, alias Jimmy Doyle, John Dioguardi, alias John [...] who are accused of assault, c[...]spiracy, extortion and malicio[...] mischief in a ten-count indictme[...] obtained by Special Prosecuto[...] Thomas E. Dewey.

Corroborating the story told las[t] week by his brother, Brown sa[id] that Plumeri, Dominick Didato, alias Dick Terry, who was murdered a few months later, and a third man went to his brother's office at 34 West Twenty-first Street in March, 1933, and threatened to ruin him, beat his drivers and cripple his trucks unless he gave up a business account.

Seven Men Invade Office

Nevertheless his brother refused, and about two weeks later seven men went into the office in the evening, just as Brown was changing from his working clothes, he testified under the questioning of Murray I. Gurfein. Mr. Gurfein, who is one of Mr. Dewey's chief assistants, is conducting the prosecution with Jacob Grumet and Paul Lockwood.

"One of them grabbed a hatchet, another grabbed a chair," the truck driver continued. "There were a lot of tools on a work bench and each man grabbed something and came at me. They hit me with everything they had. A helper named Nick was with me, and they beat him up, too."

Brown said he was left unconscious on the floor, but after about twenty minutes revived and went to his brother's home three blocks away. An ambulance surgeon treated him for fractured ribs and cuts and bruises all over his body, he said, and it was two weeks before he could stand up.

The use of stench bombs to intimidate truckmen who failed to give up accounts at the direction of the Five Boroughs Truckmen's Service Association, which the defendants are alleged to have dominated, was narrated by Herbert Gardner, a truckman of 101 Spencer Street, Brooklyn.

When he refused to give up the account of the National Silver Company at the bidding of the association, several bombs were thrown into the garage where his trucks were being loaded, forcing a cessation of activities for the night,

Continued on Page Ten

Mr[...] "T[...] the r[...] gover[...] the o[...] court. mined t[...] its New[...] tion's N[...] propose to[...] chess. We w[...] tlement of the [...] restraining order[...]

Cites "Publ[...]

Section 28 of [...] States Code, he a[...] that the case, beca[...] interest, must be g[...] over others and in e[...] dited for hearing s[...] practicable day be[...] than three of the ci[...] the circuit."

This section of the [...] added, makes mandatory [...] lishment of a special co[...] the filing by the Attorney [...] of a certificate that the c[...] general public importance[...]

The certificate to be [...] the government attorneys—A[...] Attorney General Robert H. Jackson and Special Assistant Attorney Walter L. Rice—will recite that the case has become recently of general public importance because of the restraining order issued by Judge Gibson April 29 "without notice or hearing" and the preliminary injunction granted May 14 prohibiting the government's counsel from proceeding with the suit instituted in New York.

The ex parte proceeding of April 29, the prepared certificate said, sought to make the Attorney General and other United States counsel "parties defendant" and was an expression by the court that the attorneys had so placed themselves

Continued on Page Twelve

REICH COURT RULES CHURCH IS SUBJECT TO SECRET POLICE

Declares There Is No Appeal From Any Action Taken in the 'Interest of the State'

NO REASON NEED BE GIVEN

Nazi Press Lashes Out at Vienna Cardinal for Attack on the Trials of Clergy

Wireless to THE NEW YORK TIMES.

BERLIN, June 7.—Both Protestants and Catholics here a[...] turbed over a decision [...] perior Prussian Cour[t] [...] can receive no [...] courts again[st] [...] action.

DOCTORS OF NATION MOVE TO ENDORSE PUBLIC MEDICINE

Association to Act on Plan for Government Part in a New Health System

STEP TOWARD SOCIAL IDEA

Leaders at Jersey Session Point to Changed Conditions—Resolution Up To[...]

By WILL[...]

[...]ctress suf[fered an unexpected] relapse last [night, and succu]mbed shortly be[fore noon today fr]om a cerebral [oedema.]

[Blood tr]ansfusions, intravenous injections and artificial respiration from a Fire Department inhalator were employed throughout the night in a desperate effort to save her life.

At the star's bedside when she died were William Powell, Metro-Goldwyn-Mayer star; her mother, Mrs. Jean Bello; her stepfather, Marino Bello, and Jimmie Chadney, her cousin. Working over her during the last few hours were her physicians, Dr. E. T. Fishbaugh and Dr. Leland Chapman.

Miss Harlow had been in poor health for a year. Last Fall she became so weak from an acute case of sunburn that she was forced to postpone her film work and receive special medical treatment. Shortly after returning to normal condition,

[...] Har[low soon responded fav]orably to [treatment and] was thought well on the road to recovery when she lapsed into a coma last night.

By The Associated Press.

HOLLYWOOD, Calif., June 7.—Jean Harlow, who was earning approximately $4,000 a week, was reported to have left an estate of nearly $1,000,000, largely in insurance policies and annuities.

The funeral services will be private.

A Hollywood press agent lifted Jean Harlow into gaudy prominence some years ago when he called her "The Platinum Blond" to describe her hair, which was a compromise between gold and white. Platinum blond, meaning an over-bleached blond head, was the most popular exhibit at a hairdressers' convention that season. Platinum blonds made their appearance among the new dancers, show girls and blues singers. Every floor show had one or two. They appeared also in the subways, in

Continued on Page Thirty

C.I.O. SEIZES MICHIGAN CAPITAL TO PROTEST PICKETS' ARREST; SNARLS TRAFFIC, SHUTS MILLS

STEEL AREA IS HIT

Both Sides Seek Aid of the Public in Youngstown

[NE]W DEPRESSION FEARED

[C]alls on State to Clear [O]f Non-Strikers—Asks [Sei]zure of Munitions

[V]OTE BACK TO JOB

[R]esult Will Try to [...] Works—Claims [C]anton Test

[...] DANIELL

[...]ORK TIMES.

[...], June 7.— [...] and their [...]ly today in [...] the sup[...] [ne]w depres[sion] [...]producing [...]nning to [...]ike be[...] [...]curtail[...] [...]pping [...] new [...] and [...]

[...]nd at [...]in unof[ficial] [...]ted by sup[...] [...]es, in favor of [...]rk. It was an[...] [...]d at the Cleveland offices of [Re]public Steel Corporation.

At Canton, Ohio, the vote was conducted by the Chamber of Commerce. It mailed 6,465 ballots to employes of the company, which alone among the independent steel producers fighting against recognition of the C. I. O. has attempted, with 40 per cent success, to maintain production. At the Newton plant at Monroe, a wholly owned subsidiary of Republic, the balloting was conducted by the public election officials of that city.

The Monroe balloting, according to the statement issued by the company's spokesmen, showed that 95 per cent of the 70 per cent of employes who participated favored a return to work, while 88 per cent disapproved of the strike.

The balloting was held under the supervision of Mayor Daniel Knaggs, who, the company said, "will take the certified results of the election to Lansing tomorrow to present them to Governor Frank Murphy, with the request that the Governor furnish protection, if needed, to keep the road open to the plant."

At Canton three clergymen, the

Continued on Page Five

Rail Labor Heads Oppose Roosevelt Pay-Hour Bill

Special to THE NEW YORK TIMES.

CHICAGO, June 7.—The Railroad Labor Executives Association, representing more than 1,000,000 unionized railroad employes, voted "no" here today to President Roosevelt's minimum-wage, maximum-hour bill. It adopted a recommendation that the bill be amended to exclude railroad labor from its operation.

"Our industry is highly organized," said George M. Harrison, president of the association. "Collective bargaining is almost universal and we believe wages should be fixed by collective bargaining wherever industry is organized and not by government fiat as they would under the Black-Connery (Wage and Hour) Bill.

"There are other objections to the bill. It legalizes strikebreaking in public service industries, a classification which includes the railroads."

HANDS OFF STRIKE IS ROOSEVELT AIM

Steel Union's Appeal for His Intervention Is Referred to Labor Relations Board

MAIL INQUIRY DEMANDED

Senator Bridges Attacks Postoffice—Farley Aide Defends 'Normal' Service Policy

By TURNER CATLEDGE

Special to THE NEW YORK TIMES.

[WA]SHINGTON, June 7.—The [...]l Government, from Presi[dent] Roosevelt down, was studi[ously m]aintaining a hands-off pol[icy in th]e Midwestern steel strike [in] the face of what admin[...] authorities considered an [...] by both sides to have [...]n solve their difficulties. [...] President contemplated [...] intervention now or in [...] future was indicated [...] House as announce[d] [...] that he had sent to [...]r Relations Board [...]uest from eighty [...] Calumet region [...]vene to compel [...] to sign a con[...]

[...]ns Board de[...] for the time [...]rmal action [...] would give [...] officials [...]l deliv[...] [...]th by [...]ed by [...]part[...]

[...]ed his de[...] [...]n the mails [u]pon advice [...]stal inspectors on the scene.

His statement was directed generally at the assertions, first made by steel company officials and later repeated by newspaper columnists, that mail addressed to workers in strike-bound plants was held up or "censored" by pickets. Mr. Donaldson's remarks were aimed specifically at a resolution introduced in the Senate by Senator Bridges of New Hampshire, calling for an investigation into the alleged interference with mail deliveries at the steel plants.

"We investigated this through our local representatives and today I received a wire from our postoffice inspector saying this charge was false and erroneous," Mr. Donaldson said.

"Claims that mail deliveries are being interfered with in steel strike areas are absolutely unfounded."

Holds Inquiry Is Unnecessary

Mr. Donaldson added that he did not believe a Congressional investigation was necessary.

"I assume Senator Bridges is trying to indicate that we ought to arm our trucks and drivers and force deliveries," Mr. Donaldson added. "Well, the Postoffice Department is not a strike-breaking agency."

Mr. Donaldson and other postal authorities put emphasis on their assertions that the "normal" course of the mails was maintained. This

Continued on Page Four

BLOCKADE STREETS

U. A. W. A. Strikers Halt Business for 'Labor Holiday' in Lansing

CLOSE ALL AUTO PLANTS

Invade City Hall and Leaders Direct Operations From Capitol Balcony

STUDENTS ROUT ONE GROUP

Order Is Restored After Gov. Murphy Speaks to Crowd and Starts Inquiry

Day's Strike Developments

Between 2,000 and 5,000 U. A. W. A. members and sympathizers seized the business section of Lansing, Michigan's capital, forced the closing of factories and stores and blocked all traffic in protest over the arrest of pickets. Governor Murphy's intervention stopped the demonstration. Page 1.

President Roosevelt maintained a hands-off policy in the steel strike, referring the strikers' appeal for his intervention to the Labor Relations Board. An inquiry into the Postoffice Department's refusal to accept other than "normal" mail for steel companies whose employes are on strike was demanded in the Senate. The department defended its policy. Page 1.

Both sides in the Youngstown steel strike began a drive for public support as a delegation of workers appealed to the Republic company to let them go back to their jobs. Page 1.

At South Chicago the company met a city order against housing workers in the plant buildings by moving twenty-one Pullman cars into the yards. Page 8.

A. F. of L. union was recognized as sole bargaining agency by a New York utility. Page 10.

Take Control of City

Special to THE NEW YORK TIMES.

LANSING, Mich., June 7.—Members of the United Automobile Workers of America, affiliate of the John L. Lewis C. I. O., marched on downtown Lansing early today and in the ensuing hours seized virtual control of Michigan's capital city.

Incensed by the arrest of eight pickets, the union members halted all downtown traffic and nearly all business, picketed police headquarters, the City Hall and the Capitol, threatened a jail delivery, staged a pitched battle with college students at East Lansing, and in the end yielded only to intervention by Governor Frank Murphy.

After the Governor had conferred [wi]th union representatives and [wi]th civic authorities in the afternoon, and after the last of the eight pickets had been released from jail, the marchers were withdrawn and the city assumed a normal aspect. Lester Washburn, local head of the U. A. W. A., refused tonight, however, to say that the action of the union was ended.

One of the arrested pickets was Mr. Washburn's wife. He declared that deputy sheriffs visited his home at 2 A. M. today, called Mrs. Washburn from bed and forced her to accompany them to jail, despite her pleas that her three children would be left without care.

"Labor Holiday" Is Decreed

The other prisoners were arrested under similar circumstances in the early morning hours.

The executive board of the U. A. W. A. issued a statement saying that the "labor holiday" was in "celebration" of the "superlatively brave action of Sheriff MacDonald in dragging a harmless and decent woman out of bed in the middle of the night, in terrorizing and leaving alone in the house her three young children and in throwing her into a filthy jail."

The Sheriff's action, it was asserted, "will continue to meet undying resentment of every worker and every decent citizen."

The arrests grew out of picketing at the plant of the Capital City Wrecking Company, strike-bound for the last ten days.

An anti-picketing injunction was issued in the strike Thursday by

Continued on Page Six

JEAN HARLOW, STAR OF THE FILMS, DIES

Continued From Page One

the streets and in the audiences at motion-picture theatres.

The actress's success at that time in the war film "Hell's Angels" brought her a succession of similar rôles, in which the possession of ultra-blond hair became confused in the mind of the film-going public with the possession of a talent for luring diamonds and apartments from impressionable playboys and sentimental gangsters. Miss Harlow's garish and spectacular career in the publicity spotlight swept to a tragic climax two years later when her second husband, Paul Bern, a film executive at Metro-Goldwyn-Mayer, committed suicide in September, 1932, two months after their marriage. The young actress retired thereafter to a serious pursuit of her film career.

Miss Harlow was born in Kansas City, Mo., on March 3, 1911. She was the daughter of Dr. and Mrs. Montclair Carpenter and was named Harlean. When she was 10 her parents separated and her mother took her to live in Hollywood. During her three years there the girl studied at the Hollywood School for Girls along with the daughters of film actors, and absorbed the motion-picture atmosphere. Then mother and daughter went to Highland Park, Ill., where Harlean entered the Ferry Hall Seminary.

Entrance Into Films

In 1927, when she was only 16, she eloped from school with Charles F. McGrew 2d, a young Chicago bond broker. The couple took a Spanish bungalow in Beverly Hills in 1928. Restless and bored, the young wife decided to go into the films, but her husband objected. At last she enrolled at the Central Casting Bureau, adopting her mother's maiden name of Harlow. She appeared briefly in a film starring Lois Moran, and when her wealthy grandfather added his protests to those of her husband, temporarily abandoned her career.

Seven months later she and her husband separated, and Miss Harlow became a film extra. At that time "Hell's Angels" had just been completed as a silent picture. The advent of the talking films made it necessary to produce the film over again. As Greta Nissen, its star, could speak only broken English, the producer, Howard Hughes, looked around for a new actress to play the part. Miss Harlow persuaded her friends, Ben Lyon and James Hall, who were the featured male leads, to help her get the part. The film and its previously unknown star became much-publicized successes.

In September, 1933, the actress was married to her third husband, Harold G. Rosson, a film cameraman. By May, 1934, it had become generally known that she had separated from Rosson, and in March, 1935, Miss Harlow brought a divorce action, in which she charged that her husband had kept her awake by reading in bed, thereby preventing her obtaining the rest she needed to carry on her work in pictures.

An Extra in Two Pictures

Although "Hell's Angels" and the "platinum blond' catch-phrase skyrocketed the young actress to the sort of overnight fame which occurs more frequently in books than in life, Miss Harlow had served a brief apprenticeship as an extra. She worked for $15 a day (the top-of-the-boom salary for extras) in Clara Bow's "The Saturday Night Kid" and "Paramount on Parade." She appeared in a Hal Roach pie comedy. In "Moran of the Marines" she had a part which was so infinitesimal that those who blinked never saw her at all.

After her success in "Hell's Angels" she became a sort of minor Mae West, a sentimentalized and naïve variation, in such pictures as "Iron Man," "The Secret Six," "The Public Enemy," "Goldie" and "The Beast of the City."

It was in "Red-Headed Woman," in which she appeared with Clark Gable, that Miss Harlow created the type that was to make her real cinema reputation, that of the frankly unabashed and humorously imprudent woman of the world. Subsequently she appeared in "Red Dust," also with Mr. Gable, and in "Hold Your Man," "Dinner at 8," and "Bombshell."

More recent screen work included "Girl From Missouri," "Reckless," "China Seas," "Riffraff," "Wife Versus Secretary," "Suzy," "Libeled Lady" and "Personal Property." Miss Harlow's characterizations continued to be in the light comical vein with the usual overtones of amusingly self-conscious allure. Her indignant flounce and habit of striding about wildly in her angers were familiar and, on the whole, rather endearing qualities to the critical fraternity. She added little that was new to comedy, but she intensified in her person several comical ideas of her day: the gold-digger type, the under-educated, utilitarian, quick-tongued, slightly unaware females then in vogue among cartoonists, magazine writers, jokesters.

Jean Harlow gave a witty, wise-cracking performance as Wallace Beery's wife in *Dinner at Eight*, 1933.

Miss Harlow with Clark Gable in *This Side of Heaven*, 1933.

The New York Times TUESDAY, JUNE 25, 1946.

WILLIAM S. HART, 75, FILM VETERAN, DIES

'Wild West' Idol During Era of Silent Screen Was Figure on Stage for Many Years

AN EASTERN-BORN COWBOY

Considered Good Horseman—Contributed Old Pictures to Museum, Estate to Public

William S. Hart in *The Gun Fighter*, 1917.

LOS ANGELES, June 24 (AP)—William S. Hart, Eastern-born "wild west" movie actor of a quarter of a century ago, died here late last night in a hospital. His age was 75.

At the bedside was his son, William S. Hart Jr., who last Thursday was appointed co-guardian, with George Frost, of the actor's person. Young Hart's mother, Winifred Westover, from whom the actor was divorced twenty years ago, had been almost constantly at Mr. Hart's side.

Major Idol of Silent Screen

William S. Hart was known to a generation of motion-picture fans as the long-faced, iron-jawed he-man of the West, but he was also remembered by patrons of the "legitimate" theatre in the parts he took in "Ben-Hur," "The Virginian" and many other plays, including several Shakespearean dramas.

As the strong and silent cowboy hero he became one of the major idols of the screen and he amassed a fortune during the golden years, earning $1,000 a day for grinning into an unloaded .45 and galloping across the wide plains near Hollywood.

He was the hero of thousands of eager boys the world over, and he was the ideal of thousands of women. It was said that at one time in his motion-picture career he received as many as 200 love letters a day.

Mr. Hart did not marry until he was nearly 50, but his matrimonial venture was not successful. He and his wife were separated five months after marriage and after long-drawn divorce proceedings the marriage was dissolved. His wife, who gave birth to a son, William S. Hart Jr., was Winifred Westover, a motion-picture actress of San Francisco.

Later in life Mr. Hart tried his hand at writing. He turned out a couple of books for boys and an autobiography, "My Life East and West," but the main successes in his career were in Hollywood as the two-gun terror of bad men and savior of maidens in distress.

He was born at Newburgh, N. Y., on Dec. 6, 1870, but his parents moved West when he was still an infant. His father was a builder of flour mills, and the family lived in Minnesota and Dakota until the lad was 15 years old. They moved to New York, where William began his career as a clerk in the postoffice at Park Row.

Made Stage Debut in 1889

Sorting mail, however, was irksome work, and he spent much time going to theatres and became infatuated with the stage. He applied for a part in a play for some time in vain, but finally made his debut at the People's Theatre, New York, on Jan. 21, 1889, in "Austerlitz," with Daniel Bandmann. Subsequently he played many parts with Lawrence Barrett.

After that he joined R. D. McLean and Marie Prescott and appeared at the Union Square Theatre in November, 1891, as Phesarius in "The Gladiator," and also in "Antony and Cleopatra," "The Merchant of Venice," "Othello" and other classical plays.

He then toured with Ada Rehan, playing Shakespeare in "When Bess Was Queen." For some time he was associated with Mme. Modjeska, taking such parts as Armand Duval in Dumas' "Camille," Julian Grey in "The New Magdalen," Benedick in "Much Ado About Nothing," Macbeth and Mark Antony in "Antony and Cleopatra."

Mr. Hart appeared at the Garrick Theatre in New York with Mme. Modjeska as Angelo in "Measure for Measure," Armand Duval, and the Duke of Malmsbury in "Mistress Betty." In 1897 he toured in "Under the Polar Star," and the next year, at the People's Theatre in New York, he played the dual parts in "The Man With the Iron Mask."

In 1899 he played Romeo to Julia Arthur's Juliet, and in November of that year he created the role of Messala in "Ben-Hur," a part he played for two years. In 1903, at the Broadway Theatre, he took the part of Patrick Henry in "Hearts Courageous."

He had been unwilling to leave the legitimate stage until 1914, when he turned his attention to the cinema. From early parts, for which he earned $75 a week, he quickly became a favorite of the screen, and he was presently as much discussed as Charlie Chaplin, Mary Pickford and other stars of the day. His first picture was "The Bargain," and this was followed by "The Disciple."

Mr. Hart was an excellent horseman. With his long, imperturbable but almost sinister face, he made a first-class Western hero of the plains. Always calm and showing the utmost sang-froid, he was exceptionally suited to the pantomime of the silent pictures.

Some of the films which he created were "The Toll Gate," "Square Deal Sanderson," "Wagon Tracks," "Sand," "White Oak," "Tumbleweeds" and "Singer Jim McKee." His pinto pony Paint became almost as famous as he himself.

Many of the pictures were made by Mr. Hart. He had his own studio in Hollywood and was generally surrounded by motion-picture cowboys and cowgirls.

Instead of tearing up his fan letters, Mr. Hart kept those which expressed admiration, love and offers of marriage. He was never averse to showing specimens of letters from women admirers. A characteristic one read as follows:

"Dear Mr. Hart:

"I love you!

"I simply must write this letter and tell you of what I know is a hopeless love. I cannot help it. You are so splendid, so wonderful in your last picture. Do you remember that scene where you were tied to the stake and the wretch who had stolen your sweetheart was lighting the fire? Ah, I nearly cried when I saw your agonized face. And I was with father and mother in the theatre, too. What would they have thought if I had not been able to restrain myself?

"I know you must get many letters from foolish, romantic girls like myself, but, believe me, Mr. Hart, the love I bear you is a spiritual love. There is nothing vulgar or mundane (is that the right word?) in it—my love, I mean.

"I do not hope for an answer, but won't you please put an article in one of the moving-picture magazines saying you are not married? Oh, I do hope you are not. I would be quite sick if I thought you were.

ALICE."

Mr. Hart admitted that he was sentimental. He said once:

"I am pretty sentimental. The chief reason for my success was my mother. She was—well, just mother. I went to her with all my troubles and came to her for advice all my life."

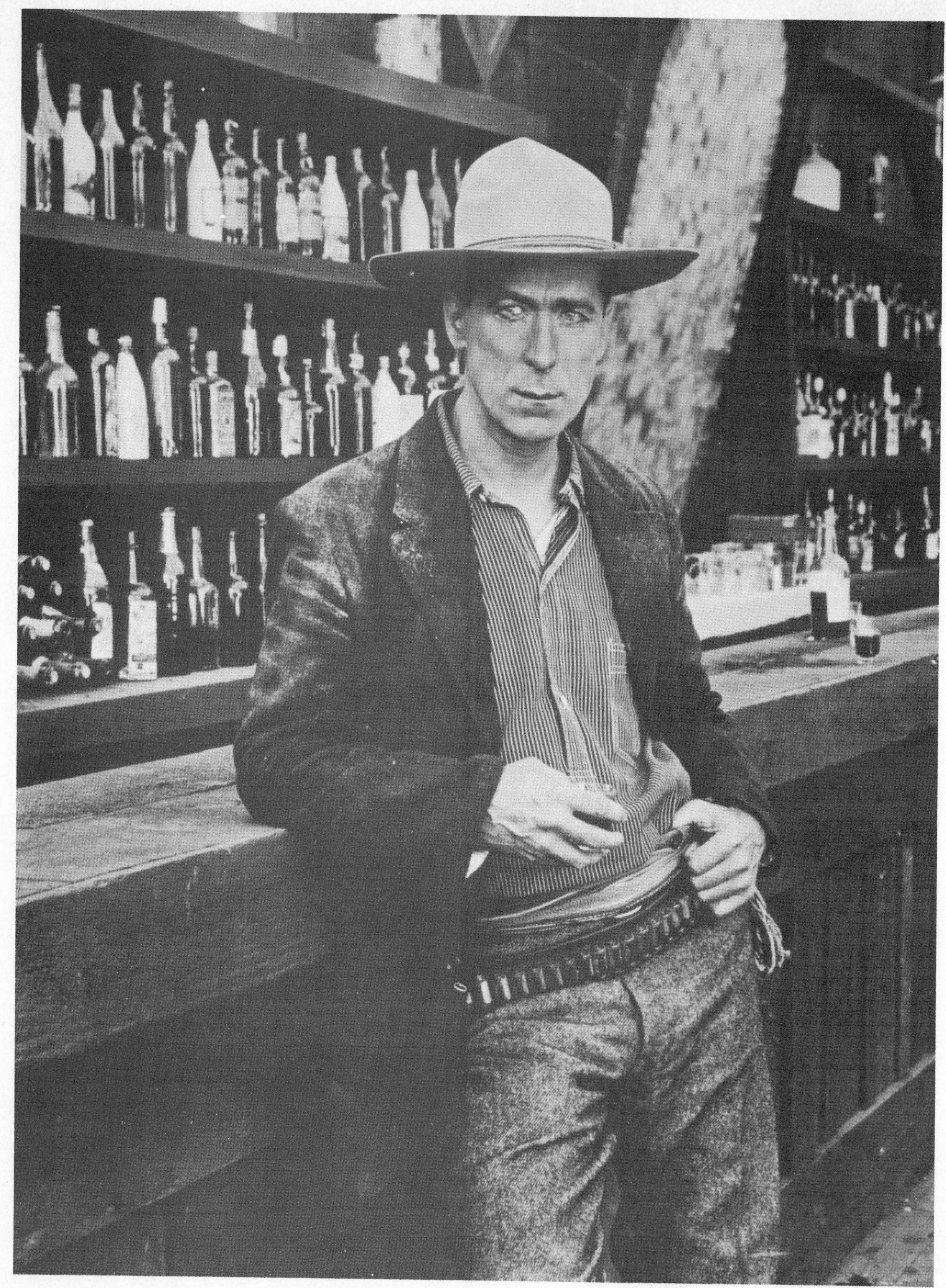

William S. Hart

The New York Times TUESDAY, NOVEMBER 27, 1973

Laurence Harvey, Screen Actor, Is Dead at 45

Attained Stardom With Role in 'Room at the Top'

Special to The New York Times

LONDON, Nov. 26—Laurence Harvey, the actor, died of cancer here at his home last night. He was 45 years old.

Mr. Harvey, had undergone surgery and cobalt ray treatment in Los Angeles last May.

The Screen's Perfect Cad

By PAUL GARDNER

With his clipped speech, cool smile and a cigarette dangling impudently from his lips, Laurence Harvey established himself as the screen's perfect pin-striped cad. He could project such utter boredom that willowy debutantes would shrivel in his presence. He could also exude such charm that the same young ladies would gladly lend him their hearts, which were usually returned utterly broken.

He had already appeared in about 30 European films when he found his niche as an actor —and stardom too— in "Room at the Top," the film which brought him to the attention of American audiences in 1958. His performance as a surly, self-serving chap who dumped his mistress (Simone Signoret) to marry the boss's daughter and ride off into the sunset in a Rolls-Royce limousine, won him an Academy Award nomination.

Enigmatic Flamboyance

In "Butterfield 8," he played a millionaire with a 10-room Fifth Avenue apartment and "caves all over town," whose beastly behavior toward his mistress, Elizabeth Taylor, drove her to suicide.

The image Mr. Harvey carefully fostered for himself off-screen was not far removed from some of the roles he played. "I'm a flamboyant character, an extrovert who doesn't want to reveal his feelings," he once said. "To bare your soul to the world, I find unutterably boring. I think part of our profession is to have a quixotic personality."

Mr. Harvey was a fastidious connoisseur of antiques, food and wine. His baronial manner, cheeky wit and upper-class British accent gave the impression that he was of aristocratic birth. But Mr. Harvey, whose real name was Larushka Mischa Skikne, was born in Joniskis, Lithuania, of Jewish parents.

Elizabeth Taylor and Laurence Harvey in *Butterfield 8.*

His father was a building contractor who moved the family to Johannesburg, South Africa, in 1934 when Mr. Harvey was about 6. "When I was 14 I ran away from home and joined the Royal South African Navy. I was always lying about my age—I still am," Mr. Harvey told an interviewer for Esquire several years ago.

During World War II, he served in the African and Italian campaigns. After discharge in 1945, he enrolled for three months at the Royal Academy of Dramatic Arts in London before joining a repertory company in Manchester, England. In the fifties he toured the United States with the Old Vic production of Henry V. In 1952, he did a season with the Royal Shakespeare Company in Stratford-on-Avon, where he met his future wife, the actress Margaret Leighton.

Their marriage, in 1957, lasted about four years. In 1968, he married Mrs. Joan Cohn, widow of Harry Cohn, a founder of Columbia Pictures. They were divorced in 1972. "What I've got is a mother fixation," Mr. Harvey once said, explaining his marriages to older women.

In the same year as his second divorce, however, he married a young fashion model, Paulene Stone, the mother of his three-year-old daughter, Domino.

An Arrogant Manner

Mr. Harvey's close friends included Rex Harrison and Elizabeth Taylor, who co-starred with him in his last film, "Nightwatch." But his sometimes arrogant manner did not endear him to other colleagues. After appearing with him in "Walk on the Wild Side," a steamy Southern drama, Jane Fonda remarked, "There are actors and actors—and then there are the Laurence Harveys. With them, it's like acting by yourself."

Such comments never fazed him. "Someone once asked me, 'Why is it so many people hate you?' and I said, 'Do they? How super!' I'm really quite pleased about it."

In the mid-sixties, while making a number of films that included "The Manchurian Candidate," in which he played a soldier hypnotized by Communists into committing a political murder, Mr. Harvey returned to the stage. He appeared at the Edinburgh Festival in a production of "A Winter's Tale" and in the London production of "Camelot."

Simone Signoret and Laurence Harvey in *Room at the Top.*

The New York Times THURSDAY, JULY 19, 1973

Jack Hawkins, the Actor, Is Dead at 62

Special to The New York Times

LONDON, July 18 — Jack Hawkins, one of the most distinctive and durable British film and stage actors, died here today in St. Stephen's Hospital. He was 62 years old.

A spokesman for the hospital, to which Mr. Hawkins was admitted more than a month ago, said the cause of death was "a secondary hemorrhage, which occurred after an operation to fit an appliance to improve his speaking voice."

Seven years ago, Mr. Hawkins, a versatile actor then at the height of his movie career, had his larynx removed in an operation for cancer of the throat. The operation deprived him of his natural voice, but with the help of a therapist, he developed a new "voice" and acted in half a dozen more films.

Thoroughly British

Over a period of four decades, beginning with his first appearance on the London stage at the age of 13, the slender, ruggedly handsome and—to American audiences, at least—thoroughly British Mr. Hawkins appeared in more than 60 plays and nearly as many films.

He had a wide variety of roles, but most often he was cast as the solid, responsible British military man or police inspector, a reassuring image of the Royal Air Force, the Army, the Navy or Scotland Yard at their best.

In "The Bridge on the River Kwai" he played the leader of the commando unit sent to blow up the bridge laboriously constructed by prisoners of the Japanese during World War II. In "The Cruel Sea," he starred as the doughty captain of a corvette in the heat of the Battle of the Atlantic. In "Lawrence of Arabia" he had the role of General Allenby.

Not all his film appearances required him to portray figures of Establishment respectability, however. In "The League of Gentlemen" he was the organizer of a gang of elegant but shady Army veterans who turned to robbery after being demobbed. And he played an occasional heel or cad in run-of-the-mill comedy-dramas.

It was early in 1966 that Mr. Hawkins's career appeared to be ended when he was found to have throat cancer. But a year after his larynx had been removed, Mr. Hawkins returned to films. He had learned to speak by using his diaphragm and stomach muscles, which served him sufficiently for delivering brief lines. When longer speaking parts were called for another actor's voice was dubbed for him.

Jack Hawkins as Quintus Arrius in *Ben Hur*.

The voice he had lost was a distinctive one—a film critic once described him as "the actor with a voice like a dinner gong." When he had relearned to speak by gulping in air and burping out the words, he took a characteristically philosophic view of the result.

"The most I can hope for is to vary the pitch of the sounds," he said. "The actual croaking quality, I'm afraid, is here to stay. It's a damned nuisance, but there you are."

Among his most recent films, in all of which his voice was dubbed, were "Nicholas and Alexandra," "Young Winston," "Waterloo" and "Jane Eyre."

Last April, in New York, surgeons attempted to restore Mr. Hawkins's speaking capability by implanting an artificial voice box in his throat. But the operation was not a success, and he was hospitalized in London for another operation.

Made Debut in 1923

Born in London on Sept. 14, 1910, Mr. Hawkins made his first appearance at the Holborn Empire Theater in December, 1923, in a walk-on part in "Where the Rainbow Ends."

The next year, when he was 14 years old, he was auditioned by George Bernard Shaw and played the role of the page in the playwright's "Saint Joan."

By the age of 18 he was performing regularly in shows in London's West End. At 19 he appeared with Laurence Olivier (now Lord Olivier) in "Beau Geste" and, on Broadway, in "Journey's End."

From then until the beginning of World War II he appeared regularly on the London and New York stages. In 1940 he joined the Royal Welsh Fusiliers and served in India. He became a colonel in charge of the British equivalent of the U.S.O., arranging entertainment for troops stationed in India.

Among his other post-World War II films were "Ben-Hur" and "Oh, What a Lovely War!"

Mr. Hawkins married twice. He was divorced from his first wife, the actress Jessica Tandy, whom he married in 1932. They had one daughter. He married Doreen Lawrence, a former actress, in 1947 and they had two sons and a daughter.

In 1958, in recognition of his achievement in the theatrical world, he was made a commander of the Order of the British Empire.

Geoffrey Horne, Jack Hawkins and William Holden in *The Bridge on the River Kwai.*

Jack Hawkins in *The Cruel Sea.*

The New York Times SUNDAY, NOVEMBER 25, 1973

Sessue Hayakawa Is Dead at 83; Silents Star Was in 'River Kwai'

Japanese Aristocrat Acted in More Than 120 Movies—Nominated for '57 Oscar

TOKYO, Nov. 24 (UPI) — Sessue Hayakawa, the motion-picture star who won an Academy Award nomination for his role as the Japanese prison-camp commandant in "The Bridge on the River Kwai," died last night at Kyoundo Hospital of a cerebral thrombosis complicated by pneumonia. He was 83 years old.

Silent Lover and Villain

By PAUL L. MONTGOMERY

In Hollywood's heyday, before talking pictures and the graduated income tax, Sessue Hayakawa was one of the silent screen's leading figures. He starred as lover and villain in more than 120 films, made $7,500 a week in 1920 and played host at his 32-room castle to such friends as Francis X. Bushman, Rudolph Valentino and Mary Pickford.

Though younger filmgoers knew him solely as a figure of menace in such films as "The Bridge on the River Kwai," for their parents Mr. Hayakawa's reputation had been established 42 years before, in 1914, when he starred in "Typhoon" with Bessie Barriscale. For some, the darkly handsome leading man was the first Japanese they had ever seen.

Mr. Hayakawa's career had many stages. After the days of Hollywood opulence, with the advent of sound, he became an impoverished unknown; for 12 years he lived quietly in France, subsisting by doing oil paintings on silk. After his comeback in "River Kwai," there were a few years of new stardom and then another falling off. The actor ended his days in a modest five-room bungalow in an unfashionable suburb of Tokyo, teaching acting and devoting his time to Zen Buddhism.

"Today in maturity nothing annoys me," the actor said in an interview 15 years ago. "I pity the man who tries to hurt me. Never am I angered. I feel only pity."

Of Aristocratic Lineage

He was named Kintaro Hayakawa at his birth, June 10, 1890, in the township of Naaura on the island of Honshu in Japan. His father, of a long aristocratic line, was the governor of Chiba prefecture, one of Japan's 47 administrative districts.

He was brought up in the strict warrior code of Bushido and planned a career in the Navy until a ruptured eardrum in a diving accident ended his hopes. His family sent him to the University of Chicago in 1909 to learn banking.

He was graduated in 1913 with a degree in political science. On his way home, he stopped in Los Angeles and became involved in the Japanese Theater in the Little Tokyo section of the city. He adopted the name Sessue for acting purposes and, in 1914, married the actress Tsura Aoki.

That year, a motion-picture producer saw him in his own adaptation of "Typhoon" and signed him for the film version. With his starring role with Fannie Ward in Cecil B. De Mille's 1916 film "The Cheat," his career was firmly established.

No Hero to His Family

Mr. Hayakawa's good looks and expressive gestures — a heritage of the Japanese theater—were perfectly suited to bringing silent epics to life. It was years, however, before he could tell his family what he was doing; for them acting represented a loss of status.

In 1918, with $1-million borrowed from the family of a Chicago classmate, Mr. Hayakawa founded the Haworth Pictures Corporation and by 1920 was netting $2-million a year. He was near the center of Hollywood's fast life, entertaining lavishly and buying a gold-plated Pierce-Arrow to outdo Fatty Arbuckle. He attributed part of his social success to the fact that he had bought and stored a carload of liquor before Prohibition.

In the nineteen-twenties, he met Presidents Warren G. Harding and Calvin Coolidge, performed for the King of England, toured in plays in France and in vaudeville in the United States.

In 1926, he said, he lost $965,000 in one night at the casino in Monte Carlo. The same night, a Japanese businessman ruined himself at the tables and committed suicide. For several years the rumor persisted that Mr. Hayakawa was the suicide, though he was always around to deny it.

In 1928, after a tour with Mr. Hayakawa, the vaudeville star Ruth Noble gave birth to a son, Yukio. The Hayakawas subsequently adopted the boy.

Sessue Hayakawa in *Bridge on the River Kwai.*

By the early thirties, with the arrival of the talking picture, which was unsuited to his talents, and a growth of anti-Japanese feeling, Mr. Hayakawa found his career on the wane. He appeared in the film "Yoshiwara" in Paris in 1937 and co-starred there with Erich von Stroheim in "Macao" in 1939. The war trapped him, and much of his income came from painting during the German occupation.

He returned to the United States in 1949 to appear with Humphrey Bogart in "Tokyo Joe," and subsequently had other roles in a variety of war movies. He regarded his role as Colonel Saito in "The Bridge on the River Kwai" in 1956 as the high point of his career.

There was a brief Hayakawa revival thereafter. He appeared in a Jerry Lewis movie and with Audrey Hepburn in "Green Mansions," and co-starred on the New York stage with Ben Piazza in the two-character play "Kataki."

Ordained a Zen Priest

By the end of the nineteen-fifties, however, Mr. Hayakawa was back in Tokyo with few prospects. He taught acting, played golf, lived modestly and enjoyed life with his children—Yukio, an engineer; Yoshiko, an actress, and Fujiko, a dancer.

Mr. Hayakawa had long been interested in Zen, and after the death of his wife in 1961 he became immersed in it. He was ordained a Zen priest, appearing before a court of six Zen masters to answer his test koan — a riddle in Zen that is at once unanswerable and all-encompassing.

In his 1960 book, "Zen Showed Me the Way," Mr. Hayakawa wrote:

"Destiny has brought me much. She has been kind. But it has been left to me to fashion the acumen of deeds in the pattern destiny has drawn, to solve the great koan of life for myself."

Sessue Hayakawa and Fanny Ward in *The Cheat.*

The New York Times SATURDAY, MARCH 15, 1975

Susan Hayward Dies at 55; Oscar-Winning Movie Star

LOS ANGELES, March 14 (AP)—Susan Hayward, the red-haired actress who won a 1958 Academy Award for her role in "I Want to Live," died today at her home in Beverly Hills, Calif. She was 55 years old.

Miss Hayward had been suffering from a brain tumor for two years. She died after having suffered a seizure, her physician said.

The Brooklyn-born actress appeared in more than 50 films and was one of the most sought-after stars in Hollywood in the nineteen-fifties.

Miss Hayward's motion-picture career began to taper off in the sixties. When she made "Valley of the Dolls" in 1967, it was her first Hollywood film in four years.

She starred in "The Revengers" in 1971 with William Holden, and most recently made two motion pictures for television that were pilots for projected series. They were "Heat of Anger" for CBS, in which she played a lawyer, and "Say Goodbye, Maggie Cole" for ABC, in which she was a doctor.

Survivors include two sons, a grandson and a granddaughter.

A Life Like the Movies

By LAWRENCE VAN GELDER

THE TIME: The late nineteen-thirties.

THE PLACE: A Manhattan modeling agency.

ENTER: Edythe Marrener, graduate of Public School 181 and Girls Commercial High School in Brooklyn, daughter of a transit company worker — young, poor, stagestruck, ambitious and beautiful.

RECEPTIONIST: A redhead! Come on in. We just got a call for a girl with red hair.

Her life was like so many of her movies.

In scores of films that made her one of the world's most popular stars, Susan Hayward, who began her career as Edythe Marrener, created an indelible impression of brassy charm, pert sexiness and a spirit that soared on success and met tragedy with throaty defiance.

Catalogue of Events

To sketch her life in swift scenes would be to create a catalogue of events that seem like clichés culled from a thousand movies: the lucky break that started her modeling career; the director who saw her picture in a magazine and offered her a screen test; a rejection for the role of Scarlett O'Hara in "Gone With the Wind"; hard times in Hollywood and a bicycle accident that cast her onto the lawn of an agent who changed her name to Susan Hayward; the starlet routine with cheesecake stills but no roles; the gutsy appeal to a convention of distributors that set her career rolling; stardom; Academy Award nominations; an Oscar; public triumph but personal tragedy—an unhappy marriage; a custody battle over twin sons; divorce; attempted suicide; a taste of scandal; a second, apparently happy marriage; her husband's death, and the final years, marred by illness.

"I never dreamed this could happen to a girl from Brooklyn," she once said.

It was an utterance made on a festive occasion. The time was January, 1959. The place was Sardi's Restaurant. Miss Hayward had just accepted the New York Film Critics Award for her performance in "I Want to Live." A few months later, at the RKO Pantages Theater in Los Angeles, she was awarded an Oscar for that same portrayal—Barbara Graham, the B-girl accused of murder, railroaded to a conviction and executed in a gas chamber.

Miss Hayward, in the opinion of Bosley Crowther, who reviewed the film for The New York Times, played the role superbly. "From a loose and wise-cracking B-girl," he wrote, "she moves onto levels of cold disdain and then plunges down to depths of terror and bleak surrender as she reaches the end. Except that the role does not present us a precisely pretty character, its performance merits for Miss Hayward the most respectful applause."

Five Award Nominations

Her Academy Award nomination for "I Want to Live" was Miss Hayward's fifth. She received the others in 1947 for her portrayal of an alcoholic in "Smash-Up"; in 1949 for the romantic drama "My Foolish Heart"; in 1952 for her depiction of the singer Jane Froman, in "With a Song in My Heart," and in 1955 for her appearance as Lillian Roth in "I'll Cry Tomorrow."

Once her Hollywood career began in earnest—she made her debut as Isobel Rivers in the 1939 remake of "Beau Geste," starring Gary Cooper — it seemed she was constantly at work.

There were films like "Reap the Wild Wind," "Adam Had Four Sons," "The Hairy Ape," "Jack London," "Canyon Passage," "The Fighting Seabees," "They Won't Believe Me," "Deadline at Dawn," "Tap Roots," "I Can Get It for You Wholesale," "Rawhide," "David and Bathsheba," "Lusty Men," "White Witch Doctor," "The President's Lady" "Demetrius and the Gladiators," "Tulsa," "Snows of Kilimanjaro," "Garden of Evil," "Where Love Has Gone" and a remake of "Back Street."

Fans the world over flocked to her films. She worked for David O. Selznick (who tested her for Scarlett O'Hara and dropped her option), for Warners, RKO, 20th Century-Fox and independent producers, like Walter Wanger. The American Beauticians Congress voted her "the most beautiful girl in the world." The Foreign Press Association of Hollywood voted her and John Wayne the "world favorite" screen stars of 1952.

During the attenuated proceedings that led to her divorce in 1954 from Jess Barker, an actor she married on July 23, 1944, Miss Hayward put her income at $17,000 a month. When the divorce was finally granted, she was awarded custody of their twin sons, Timothy and Gregory, and assets totalling $1,293,319. At one point, 20th Century-Fox figured its current investment in Miss Hayward at $12.5-million, nearly a quarter of the studio's production budget.

"Miss Hayward," declared an executive, "is our most valuable player."

Away from the studio, life for Miss Hayward was less rewarding. There was the divorce, the kind some people call "messy." And then, in the spring of 1955, there was the suicide attempt: sleeping pills; a hysterical telephone call to her mother, Ellen, in Brooklyn; a call by Mrs. Marrener to the police; two detectives kicking in the door of Miss Hayward's home in Sherman Oaks, Calif.; the finding of the unconscious star; the race to the hospital; the newspaper photos—closed eyes, tousled hair, the hospital blanket; a tongue depresser jutting from between lax lips.

Later that year, the taste of scandal: An actress named Jill Jarmyn charges Miss Hayward with attacking her when Miss Jarmyn walks in unannounced to find a pajama-clad Miss Hayward and Donald Barry, an actor, together in his bedroom. Miss Hayward accuses Miss Jarmyn of being insulting.

"Being Irish, this infuriated me," said the star.

Moved to Georgia

And then, in 1957, Miss Hayward married Floyd Eaton Chalkley, a lawyer with varied business interests. They made their home in Carrollton, Ga., near his work. They lived in a big house in a pine grove, overlooking a man-made lake. They danced at the Carrollton Country Club and gave small dinner parties. "He was the first man I had met that I felt I could lean on completely," said Miss Hayward. They seemed happy.

In 1965, Mr. Chalkley became ill in Rome, where Miss Hayward was making a film. He returned to the United States, entered a Fort Lauderdale, Fla., hospital, was treated and discharged. A week later, with his wife at his bedside, he died.

Miss Hayward returned to California.

Susan Hayward as Lillian Roth in *I'll Cry Tomorrow.*

The New York Times SATURDAY, JULY 24, 1971

Van Heflin, Actor, Dead at 60; Won Fame in Film and on Stage

Remembered for 'Shane' and 'Airport' Roles—Depicted Nizer in 'Libel' Here

HOLLYWOOD, July 23 (UPI) — Van Heflin, one of Hollywood's most versatile actors, died at Cedars of Lebanon Hospital today at the age of 60.

Mr. Heflin, a husky outdoorsman, avid fisherman and hunter, was found clinging to a ladder in the swimming pool at his apartment house after suffering a heart attack June 6. He swam 20 laps a day, rain or shine. He lapsed into unconsciousness and never regained use of his faculties.

The actor left instructions that no public or private funeral be held, and that his remains be cremated and scattered over the Pacific Ocean, where he loved to sail and fish.

His last major movie was "Airport," in which he played a crazed bomber on a plane. He also recently did a television movie called "The Last Child," which has not yet been seen.

Talent Surfaced Early

Van Heflin's enduring talent as an actor was recognized early on Broadway and in Hollywood, where he won an Oscar as best supporting actor in "Johnny Eager" (1942) and later attained distinction in "Shane" and many other successes.

In 1950 he declared his independence from Hollywood's binding commitments, branching out into Broadway and television. Although few of the movies attained great critical acclaim, Mr. Hefflin clearly preferred this pattern of professional life to the rigidities of Hollywood.

Emmet Evan Heflin Jr. was born on Dec. 13, 1910, the son of a dentist, in Walters, Okla. His college career at the University of Oklahoma was interrupted by numerous voyages, as a merchant seaman and by his first Broadway credit — in October, 1928—as Evan Heflin playing Junior Jones in Channing Pollock's "Mr. Moneypenny."

After receiving his degree from Oklahoma in 1931, Mr. Heflin gained experience in Philadelphia's Hedgerow Theater, at the Yale School of Drama and from a season of stock in Denver. He was an understudy in the Broadway musical "Sailor, Beware."

With his rugged but boyish countenance—and demonstrated stage talent—he appeared with Ina Claire in "End of Summer" and with Katharine Hepburn in "Philadelphia Story." Earlier she had picked him for a film, "A Woman Rebels," which was not a success. But "Philadelphia Story" was a hit, and Brooks Atkinson, The New York Times critic, wrote: "It would be hard to improve upon Van Heflin's honest and solid description of a tough-minded writer."

On a vacation from the long-running "Philadelphia Story," Mr. Heflin went to Hollywood for a Warner Brothers Western that played games with history entitled "Santa Fe Trail," in which Mr. Heflin had a chance to play a villain.

Mr. Heflin was quickly established in the film industry's thinking as a solid supporting character actor rather than a dreamboat. His Academy Award came for "Johnny Eager," a Metro-Goldwyn-Mayer gangster picture starring Robert Taylor and Lana Turner and directed by Mervyn LeRoy in which Mr. Heflin's drunker scholar gone to seed stole the show.

He was quickly promoted to lead roles and played the police-lab scientist in "Kid Glove Killer." A Times critic called it "another solid performance" adding, "although his wan smile and dry drawl have tended to 'type' him, he can create a character with intelligence."

In 1942, Mr. Heflin married Frances M. Neal, a film actress, and went off to war, serving as a combat cameraman with the Ninth Air Force in Europe.

Mr. Heflin returned in 1945 to the rapid-fire production of Westerns, war pictures and others in the prewar tradition. In 1950 he startled the Hollywood Establishment by asking M G-M to relieve him of a contract with two and a half years to run. The studio agreed to reduce his commitment to 12 weeks a year, so that he could be free to explore Broadway and television.

Paradoxically, it was during this retreat from Hollywood that Mr. Heflin had one of his greatest successes there — in the imaginative Western called "Shane" released in 1953, a Paramount picture directed by George Stevens in which Mr. Heflin played a homesteader and Alan Ladd was cast as a gunfighter.

In 1955 came a notable Broadway appearance as Eddie, a Brooklyn longshoreman doomed to self-destruction, in Arthur Miller's "A View From the Bridge." A film version of Rod Serling's play, "Patterns," about the television jungle, was well received in 1956.

Mr. Heflin's other motion pictures included: "They Came to Cordura," "Madame Bovary," "The Prowler," Tomahawk," "Weekend With Father," "My Son, John," "Wings of the Hawk," "Golden Mask" and "Tanganyika."

Also, "The Raid," "Woman's World," "Black Widow," "Battle Cry," "Count Three and Pray," "3:10 to Yuma," "Gunman's Walk," "Five Branded Women," "Under Ten Flags," "The Greatest Story Ever Told," "Once a Thief" and "The Wastrel."

Mr. Heflin's first marriage lasted six months. His second, to Miss Neal, ended in divorce in 1967. They had two daughters, Vana, now Mrs. Michael O'Brien, and Cathleen, now Mrs. Robert Westbrook, and a son, Tracy.

Alan Ladd, Jean Arthur and Van Heflin in *Shane.*

The New York Times MONDAY, OCTOBER 13, 1969

Sonja Henie, Skating Star, Dies

Olympic Winner Made Fortune in Movies

OSLO, Oct. 12 (AP)—Sonja Henie, ice-skating queen and film star, died tonight on an ambulance plane flying from Paris to Oslo. She was 57 years old.

Miss Henie had been suffering from leukemia for the last nine months. In Paris yesterday her condition worsened, and it was decided to fly her home.

Her husband, Neils Onstad, a Norwegian shipowner, said she "just slept away" halfway through the two-hour flight.

Champion and Star

Three times the Olympic figure-skating champion, Miss Henie won most of the major world skating titles from 1927 to 1936, when she turned professional.

A petite, glamorous woman with a taste for luxury and a shrewd business sense, she was immensely successful next with a series of her own ice revues, and prospered as a motion picture star.

After her marriage to Mr. Onstad, a childhood sweetheart, in 1956, she became interested in modern art. The Onstads gave Norway an art museum and 250 of their paintings in August 1968.

Two earlier marriages to Americans, Daniel Reid Topping and Winthrop Gardiner Jr., ended in devorces in 1946 and 1956. She had become an American citizen in 1941.
had a home in the Holmby Hills section of Los Angeles, an apartment in Lausanne, Switzerland, and an estate overlooking the Oslo fjord.

Skated as 6-year-old

Born in Oslo on April 8, 1912, Miss Henie received her first skates from her father, a Norwegian fur wholesaler, on the Christmas after her sixth birthday. She had already delighted in dancing, and—with her brother Leif giving her her first lessons—enjoyed skating even more.

While improving her skating, in the next few years, she also studied ballet with a former teacher of Anna Pavlova, and eventually she combined the two forms on ice.

She won the children's figure skating championship of Oslo when she was 8, and two years later, in 1923, she won the figure skating championship of Norway.

Practicing as much as seven hours a day, she studied with teachers in Germany, England, Switzerland and Austria. With her well-to-do father's backing, she studied ballet in London, and began applying choreography to her routines. Her mother traveled with her constantly, as she did throughout Miss Henie's career.

She won the first of 10 consecutive world skating titles at Oslo in 1927, captivating the crowd with her ballet style, a white silk and ermine costume and short skirt and a dimpled smile.

Over the next decade Miss Henie won Olympic titles at St. Moritz, Switzerland (1928), at Lake Placid (1932), and at Garmisch-Partenkirchen in Bavaria (1936).

She announced then that she was turning professional, and toured the United States in an ice show. She said her greatest hope was to become a movie star, and she soon did.

"I want to do with skates (in the movies) what Fred Astaire is doing with dancing," she said.

She signed with Darryl F. Zanuck and 20th Century-Fox, and her first skating film, "One in a Million," was released at the end of 1936.

It was a box-office smash, as were others she made in the following dozen years. The pictures were reported to have grossed $25-million.

She herself earned over $200,000 from her film work alone in 1937.

She also began staging and appearing in ice shows, in association with Arthur Wirtz, her business manager, and these, too, were very successful — with lavish costumes and spectacular routines.

These shows, the "Hollywood Ice Revues," were major attractions at Madison Square Garden for many years, up to 1952

Miss Henie was an exacting star. She once called Eddie Pec, the only person she permitted to sharpen her skates, in New York, to ask him to come to Chicago, where her show was to open.

He hopped on a train, reached Chicago the next day, rushed to her hotel, and sharpened the skates with a hand stone—a few minutes work.

"Anything else?" he asked.

"No, thank you," she said sweetly. "That's all."

And back he went to New York.

She broke with her manager in 1951, and began producing shows on her own, but gave them up after a block of seats at a Baltimore armory collapsed before a show in March, 1952, injuring more than 250 people.

Although later cleared of any responsibility for the accident, she did not stage any more arena-type shows. She appeared on several television shows in the next few years, including a one-hour special of her own.

Shows More Demanding

Commenting on the difference between skating in her shows and in competition, Miss Henie once said:

"When I was in championship competition I was on the ice for exactly four minutes. Now I arrive at the Garden at 6:45 and I never stop until 11:10. Besides, I can't quite imagine my doing the hula in the Olympics."

Sonja Henie in *Second Fiddle*, 1939, one of the musical films she starred in.

The New York Times SUNDAY, JUNE 3, 1956.

JEAN HERSHOLT, 69, IS DEAD ON COAST

Screen Actor for 50 Years Was Former President of Motion Picture Academy

KNOWN AS DR. CHRISTIAN

Civic Leader in Hollywood Created Role on Radio—Knighted by Denmark

HOLLYWOOD, Calif., June 2 (AP)—Jean Hersholt, the onetime Danish immigrant who was fifty years an actor, died of cancer today after a year-long siege of operations and illnesses. He was 69 years old.

Mr. Hersholt's philanthropies earned him the love of the film industry. He served for four years as president of the Academy of Motion Picture Arts and Sciences, from which he received two special "Oscars," in 1939 and 1941, for his activities on behalf of his fellow actors. He was past president of the Hollywood Bowl Association.

His success as the villain with Mary Pickford in "Tess of the Storm Country" made him one of the most sought-after heavies of the silent movies.

Hollywood paid tribute to Mr. Hersholt May 16 with a star-packed dinner. Although the long evening was a physical trial for him—he left a sickbed to attend and went into the hospital the next day—he told the big turnout:

"It is the most memorable evening of my whole life."

He had heard himself praised by Gov. Goodwin J. Knight, Miss Pickford, L. B. Mayer and in telegrams from President Eisenhower and Vice President Richard M. Nixon.

Consistently Successful

Mr. Hersholt once said he was an example of how long an actor could last in movies if he was careful not to become a star. Whether because of this philosophy or not, Mr. Hersholt's career as a screen actor was one of the longest as well as one of the most consistently successful in motion pictures.

He began playing screen parts in 1905, and continued until 1955, with a role in "Run for Cover." He portrayed more than 450 characters—in his earlier days he often took half a dozen parts in a single film—and his acting career ranged from the time movies were in their infancy to the era of the big screen.

Actually, Mr. Hersholt starred in a number of outstanding pictures, but he was famous chiefly as one of the cinema's foremost character actors. In his later years he branched out into radio and created the role of Dr. Christian in a drama series that continued for seventeen years.

Mr. Hersholt was born in Copenhagen, Denmark, on July 12, 1886. Although his parents were actors with the Danish Folk Theatre, he at first studied art and planned to be a painter. He was soon lured to the stage, however, and then into playing in the first motion picture made in Denmark.

After visits to the United States as a touring actor-manager in Danish shows, he took a Hollywood job with Thomas H. Ince in 1914 and from then on stayed with American movies.

Hired at $15 a Week

The story is told that he applied at the Ince office nattily dressed in spats, a cutaway and a derby and that the production manager wryly told him he would hire him for his costume at $15 a week.

Mr. Hersholt later worked for most of the major Hollywood studios and got into the top salary bracket for Hollywood actors. His first Hollywood picture was "Bullets and Brown Eyes," in which he played three roles.

In the heyday of silent pictures Mr. Hersholt was ranked as a character player with Erich von Stroheim and the late Lon Chaney.

Mr. Hersholt felt that "Greed" was the best silent picture in which he had appeared, and critics to this day rate it as one of the best made. The film was directed by Mr. von Stroheim, and Mr. Hersholt played a working-class character in a seamy drama based on the novel "McTeague" by Frank Norris.

Other silent pictures in which Mr. Hersholt played prominent roles included "Stella Dallas," "Grand Hotel," "The Beast of the City," "The Mask of Fu Manchu," "Abie's Irish Rose" and "Private Lives."

In the Nineteen Thirties, Mr. Hersholt gained fresh renown when he played the part of the physician in "The Country Doctor," a film about the Dionne quintuplets. The success started for him a succession of medical films, culminating in his creation of the "Dr. Christian" radio character.

A large man with broad, slightly bent shoulders, blue eyes and brown hair, Mr. Hersholt attributed much of his success to his friendly, good-humored outlook.

"I am not temperamental," he once said. "That is the chief reason I have survived so long."

Mr. Hersholt became an American citizen in 1918, but all his life maintained the closest links with his native Denmark. He was a student and admirer of Hans Christian Andersen and translated many of the Danish storyteller's tales into English.

The actor eventually accumulated the world's greatest collection of Andersen letters, manuscripts and first editions. He was also a collector of rare editions and manuscripts of other authors. He presented his most prized items some years ago to the Library of Congress, asserting that the donation was "in gratitude for what this country has meant to me and my family."

Mr. Hersholt married Danish-born Via Andersen in Canada shortly after he began his Hollywood movie career. Their son, Allan, was at one time a movie critic.

Mr. Hersholt devoted much of his time in the last fifteen years to philanthropic and civic activities. He was for eighteen years president of the Motion Picture Relief Fund and often participated in charities in this country for Danish causes.

King Christian X of Denmark knighted Mr. Hersholt in 1948. The Academy of Motion Picture Arts and Sciences presented a special award of merit to him in 1950 for his "many outstanding contributions to the motion-picture industry." Rollins College awarded to him the honorary degree of Doctor of Humanities in 1942, and Bowdoin College gave him the honorary degree of Master of Arts in 1943.

In March, 1955, at a luncheon in the Paramount Studios, Mr. Hersholt received a gold cup in honor of his fifty years as a motion-picture actor.

Jean Hersholt (left) with Gibson Gowland as McTeague and ZaSu Pitts as Trina, in *Greed*.

Shirley Temple and Jean Hersholt in *Heidi*.

"All the News That's Fit to Print"

The New York Times.

LATE CITY EDITION
U. S. Weather Bureau Report (Page 82) forecasts: Partly sunny, hot and humid today; fair, warm tonight and tomorrow.
Temp. range: 90—70; yesterday: 88—65.

VOL. CXIV..No. 39,217. NEW YORK, TUESDAY, JUNE 8, 1965. TEN CENTS

2 ASTRONAUTS DOWN SAFELY AFTER 4 DAYS; DOCTOR FINDS THEY ARE IN GOOD CONDITION; SPACECRAFT LANDS 56 MILES FROM CARRIER

ASSEMBLY ADOPTS SENATE'S REVISION OF CODE OF ETHICS

Bill, Sent to Governor, Bars Legislators From Practice Before Court of Claims

By SYDNEY H. SCHANBERG
Special to The New York Times

ALBANY, June 7 – A watered-down version of the strong code of legislative ethics that began its stormy journey through the Legislature five weeks ago won final passage tonight.

It was then sent to Governor Rockefeller, who is expected to sign it.

The Assembly also voted tonight to adjourn the 1965 session Thursday, June 17. The vote was 127 to 14. The Senate is expected to concur tomorrow.

Assembly Minority Leader George L. Ingalls wanted an amendment changing the adjournment date to next Wednesday. But the Democratic majority maintained that it wanted to avert the kind of frantic adjournment rush that marked previous years.

The severely amended legislative ethics measure, which was passed by the Senate 47 to 9 last Thursday, swept through the Assembly this evening by a similarly overwhelming margin, 120 to 19.

Debate Is Perfunctory

Assembly passage came after an almost perfunctory debate of only 23 minutes, which was in sharp contrast to the long and acerbic arguments that had erupted frequently over the issue in the last five weeks.

The conflict-of-interest bill had been amended in various ways in both houses, but there was only one major change—the Senate deleted half of what was considered the heart of the bill.

The section that the Senate struck from the measure would have barred legislators and legislative employes who are lawyers from appearing for a fee before most state agencies.

The half that was left intact – which is the bill sent to the Governor tonight—bars legislators and legislative employes from practicing for a fee before the State Court of Claims.

Bill Called Unnecessary

During tonight's brief debate, opponents of the ethics code again denounced it as unnecessary and a result of "an atmosphere created by some legislators and a small segment of the press."

The supporters of strong ethics legislation criticized the bill that was passed as too weak and nearly meaningless. Assemblyman Albert H. Blumenthal, Democrat of Manhattan, said bitterly after the vote: "This bill is a disgrace!"

The sponsor of the original, tougher version of the code, Assemblyman Daniel M. Kelly, also a Manhattan Democrat, said he was sorely disappointed that the bill had been weakened by the Senate.

"But," he said, "we are tak-

Continued on Page 27, Column 3

Drinking Age Bill Killed in Assembly

By R. W. APPLE Jr.
Special to The New York Times

ALBANY, June 7—The Assembly resoundingly defeated tonight a proposal to raise the state's minimum legal drinking age from 18 to 21 years.

After a show of hands indicated that no more than a quarter of the 150 members of the lower house supported the bill, it was withdrawn and sent back to committee.

The vote on the motion to recommit the bill was 106 to 35, with 20 Republicans and 15 Democrats voting "Nay."

The measure is considered dead for this session of the Legislature.

Governors of adjacent states had appealed for a revision of New York's law, which is the only one in the nation that permits the sale of liquor to per-

Continued on Page 26, Column 4

High Court Bars Curbs on Birth Control; Finds Connecticut Law Invades Privacy

7-to-2 Ruling Establishes Marriage Privileges —Stirs Debate

By FRED P. GRAHAM
Special to The New York Times

WASHINGTON, June 7—The Supreme Court struck down the Connecticut birth-control law today in a sweeping decision that established a new constitutional "right of privacy."

In a 7-to-2 ruling the Court invalidated the 1879 law, which

Excerpts from Court opinions will be found on Page 34.

forbids the use of contraceptives by anyone, including married couples.

The seven justices in the majority were divided on the proper constitutional provision to use in striking down the law, but they agreed that married couples had private rights that could not be abridged in such a manner.

The majority ruling was written by Justice William O. Douglas. It touched off a controversy as the two dissenters, Justice Potter Stewart and Justice Hugo L. Black, charged

Ju...

that ... Court's ... down ... ered ... the law ... cific ... tion.

The ... lieu of a ...

Continued on P...

Bill for Liberalizing New York Statute Goes to the State Senate

By PETER KIHSS

A bill to liberalize New York State's 1881 law against the dissemination of birth-control devices and information about them was reported out of ... State Senate Rules Co... yesterday ... chances ...

TV at Trials Limited As It Reverses Estes

Special to The New York Times

WASHINGTON, June 7—The Supreme Court threw out today the swindling conviction of Billie Sol Estes, Texas financier, because his trial in a Texas state court had been televised over his objection.

The Court laid down a rule that televising of "notorious"

Excerpts from opinions are printed on Page 30.

criminal trials is prohibited by the clause of the Constitution's 14th Amendment providing that no state "shall deprive any person of life, liberty or property without due process of law."

In a 5-to-4 decision, four justices said that "the time-honored principles of a fair trial" are violated when television is allowed in any criminal trial. A fifth member of the majority, Justice John ... Harlan, agreed that this was ... in the Estes trial because it w... one of "great notoriety." H... said, however, that he would reserve judgment on more routine cases.

Four dissenting justices objected to the blanket ban on television on constitutional grounds at this stage of the medium's development. They said there was insufficient proof that Estes' rights had been violated in this case.

The decision does not affect Estes' current term in the Federal Prison at Leavenworth, Kan., on a 15-year United

5-4 Ruling Says Co... in 'Notorious' ... Violates Constitut...

... lo... ti... co... room ... photo... ant's ... fair t... Texas ... televisio... Reading...

Continued...

MAYOR TO PROPOSE P. R. VOTING PLAN

Move Is Seen as Indication He Will Seek 4th Term

By CLAYTON KNOWLES

Mayor Wagner will propose reinstating proportional representation as the method of electing City Councilmen.

He said yesterday that he would have a detailed statement "within a day or two" on the proposal, which is highly controversial in organized politics but warmly supported by minority, labor and good-government groups.

"This is something that should be put before the people," the Mayor asserted.

His disclosure of his intention, elicited in an interview, was taken as the strongest indication yet that he plans to run for a fourth term for Mayor. He intends to announce his political plans in the next 24 hours.

Still another strong indication was the fact that two men sworn into office by the Mayor yesterday—Vincent L. Broderick as Police Commissioner and Robert H. Connery as Deputy City Administrator — left top posts in other fields to enter the administration.

Mr. Broderick was chief assistant United States Attorney in the Southern District of New York, while Mr. Connery was professor of public administration at Duke University. Neither would have been interested in a six-month job which, in effect, they might have been taking if they did not believe the Mayor would run.

"I've never had any doubt of

Continued on Page 20, Column 3

U.S. Will Promote Little Urban Parks, Udall Says Here

By SAMUEL KAPLAN

Secretary of the Interior Stewart L. Udall announced here yesterday that his department would concern itself with neighborhood parks as well as national parks.

During a hectic tour of the city by auto and helicopter, he said his office intended to look "deeply and seriously" into the recreation and open-space needs of urban areas such as New York City. Federal aid would be made available for such needs, the Secretary indicated.

He also announced that Philip Johnson, the New York architect, has been selected to design a national park on Ellis Island.

The Secretary stopped on his tour at a 30-by-100-foot Harlem playground, on 128th Street between Lenox and Fifth Avenues. He said the vest-pocket park probably served more people than some large national parks in the West.

Mr. Udall said at a news conference that the Interior Department would work with the Housing and Home Finance

Continued on Page 24, Column 2

NEWS INDEX

2 APPEA... IN EVIDEN...

High Court Says ... Is Not Retroa...

Special to The New York ...

WASHINGTON, Jun... Supreme Court held t... a 1961 decision based ... Fourth Amendment's p... tion against the admissi... of illegally obtained evidence in state trials will not be applied retroactively to void old convictions.

Ruling for the first time that a right guaranteed to defendants by the Bill of Rights will not be given retrospective effect, the Court indicated that in rendering decisions on criminal trial procedures it would take into consideration the effect on state administration of criminal justice.

The Court, in its 7-2 decision, ruled on the appeals of Victor Linkletter, who had been convicted of burglary by a Louisiana court in 1959, and George Angelet, who was convicted of possession of narcotics by a New York court in 1951. Both men maintained that their convictions were void because illegally obtained evidence was introduced at their trials.

Their claim was based on the Supreme Court's 1961 decision in the case of Mapp v. Ohio that evidence obtained in violation of the Fourth Amendment's prohibition against unreasonable searches and seizures is not admissible in state trials. The Court ruled in 1914

Continued on Page 32, Column 6

SENATE SUPPORTS JOHNSON REQUEST ON NEW ASIAN AID

$89 Million for Economic Help Is Approved, 42-26 —Morse Is Scornful

...FELIX BELAIR Jr.
...ial to The New York Times

...NGTON, June 7—The ...oved today Presi...'s request for $89 ...ional foreign aid ... for South Viet... ...d Thailand. The ...26.

... adding the ...pending $3.35 ...uthorization ...cted a pro... ...ayne Morse ...nal funds ... aid cate... ...45 to 22. ... Senate ...Relations ...rization ...2.18 bil... $1.17 ...tance ...ing ...il... ...n

...ticular, ...ettled at his double ... in the committee, he also impugned the motives of some members who voted against him.

There were a "considerable number" of Senators, he said, who "wish the Government

Continued on Page 4, Column 4

Red China Today: Leaders Are Aging

This is the second of a series of articles by Mark Gayn, author and editorial writer for The Toronto Daily Star, who has just completed a visit to Communist China.

©1965 by The Toronto Daily Star

CANTON, China — China is governed today by a regime of oldsters, bound together by memories of shared danger, suffering and triumph.

It is a remarkable group, unreceptive to yielding its power to younger leaders. Its unchallenged chief, Mao Tse-tung, is one of the great revolutionaries of all time, a maker of history, a legend in his own lifetime. His companions are able, tough, resourceful and confident.

In the last month I had the opportunity to see all of them but Chairman Mao at very close range. They appeared self-as-

Continued on Page 10, Column 1

Associated Press Radiophoto

...NE THE WORSE FOR WEAR: Maj. Edward H. White 2d, left, and Maj. James A. ...ivitt as they stepped from helicopter aboard carrier Wasp after four-day flight.

...LOR SUPPORTS ... OF BOMBINGS

...ashington, Set ...alt or Sharp ...nam Raids

...GGUTH
...rk Times

...nam, June ...xwell D. ... Wash... ...to op... ...n the ... air ...m. ...in... ... in ...h ... the ...aids on in... ...ts around Hanoi

One Vietnamese proposal has called for four days of solid hits on factories and mills, followed by a pause to permit an overture from the Communist leadership.

Premier Under Attack

Such intensified air strikes would also serve to bolster the position of Premier Phan Huy Quat. The Premier is under attack by Roman Catholics on the ground that he favors a neutralist solution to the war. Harsher bombing might help to silence his critics for a time.

Two hundred elderly Catholic men and women began a sit-in tonight at the office of the chief of state, Phan Khac Suu, at the Presidential Palace. They accepted food but said they would not leave until Premier Quat had been replaced.

By evening, however, the demonstrators appeared to be tiring.

Since the present series of air strikes began on Feb. 7, the Ambassador has resisted impatient critics who felt the pace was too slow.

Asked why the United States was not bombing Hanoi, the capital of North Vietnam, he said, "I am just a former military man. I don't enjoy killing civilians."

The Ambassador would be completely opposed to ending the strikes, however. From the beginning he has said that the strategy would require months to prove itself.

Lately he has begun to talk

Continued on Page 8, Column 3

Success of Gemini Gives New Impetus To Lunar Program

By WALTER SULLIVAN
Special to The New York Times

HOUSTON, June 7—The dramatic successes of the Gemini 4 space flight, which ended today, have suddenly made the far more ambitious projects that are imminent seem probable and believable.

It was typical that, as the spacecraft plunged across Florida in its descent to the sea, a booster was being hoisted into position at Cape Kennedy for the next Gemini shot in mid-August.

The tempo of manned flights promises to grow apace. They will overlap and before the end of the year are scheduled to include such feats as joining two rockets in space, one of them radio-controlled from the other.

Within months, flights will begin that are to culminate in the landing of two Americans on the moon. The performance of Gemini 4 today led officials of the National Aeronautics and Space Administration to reaffirm their prediction that the lunar landing would come before the end of 1969.

Within about four years it

Continued on Page 23, Column 1

Judy Holliday, 42, Is Dead of Cancer

Judy Holliday, whose portrayal of a junk dealer's doxy in "Born Yesterday" created a new kind of beautiful-but-dumb blonde, died of cancer yesterday. She was 42 years old.

In one line, she managed to forge the image of an intellectually vacuous young woman with a peasant shrewdness and a hard honesty:

"Do me a favor, will ya, Harry?" she told her boorish lover in the comedy. "Drop dead."

With an immaculate sense of timing, some venom and a good deal of passion, she made it the most memorable line of the play that became a hit of Broadway and Hollywood. Where such a role was usually characterized merely by gum-chewing, sinuosity and unalloyed brassiness, she made it

Continued on Page 37, Column 1

Judy Holliday, 42, Is Dead of Cancer

Judy Holliday, whose portrayal of a junk dealer's doxy in "Born Yesterday" created a new kind of beautiful-but-dumb blonde, died of cancer yesterday. She was 42 years old.

In one line, she managed to forge the image of an intellectually vacuous young woman with a peasant shrewdness and a hard honesty:

"Do me a favor, will ya, Harry?" she told her boorish lover in the comedy. "Drop dead."

With an immaculate sense of timing, some venom and a good deal of passion, she made it the most memorable line of the play that became a hit of Broadway and Hollywood. Where such a role was usually characterized merely by gum-chewing, sinuosity and unalloyed brassiness, she made it

Continued on Page 37, Column 1

NEW U.S. RECORDS

McDivitt and White Are Hungry, Thirsty and Bearded

Excerpts from Gemini radio conversations, Page 22.

By EVERT CLARK
Special to The New York Times

HOUSTON, June 7—Maj. James A. McDivitt and Maj. Edward H. White 2d landed safely in the Atlantic today after a four-day orbital flight. They had been aloft three times as long as the total logged by all previous American astronauts.

Their Gemini 4 spacecraft splashed down 56 miles from the aircraft carrier Wasp, about 10 miles from their original aiming point, at 1:14 P.M. Eastern daylight time.

Fifty-five minutes later they stepped from a helicopter onto the carrier's deck, still in their spacesuits. They were hungry, thirsty, bearded and happy.

Despite 97 hours and 58 minutes of space flight, they also were healthy, the doctors said. Major White did have a moment of seasickness as the capsule bobbed on the water before they were lifted from it.

One Hatch Left Intact

The two young Air Force pilots left the capsule through the hatch of the command pilot, Major McDivitt. They wanted to leave Major White's hatch as it was. It had proved difficult to close after his 20-minute excursion into space, and it must be examined to find out why.

A computer that was to have helped Major McDivitt fly the spacecraft to a precise landing failed in the last day in orbit, but it posed no danger to the pilots. They used old tricks perfected by earlier Mercury space pilots to bring themselves home.

Dr. Howard Minners, a space agency physician, said after two hours of medical testing that the pilots had "no problems."

He said they were "active, very talkative and cheerful."

Another space agency official said "they can sleep as long as they damned well please" after

Continued on Page 22, Column 1

Judy Holliday, Actress, Is Dead of Cancer at 42

Continued From Page 1, Col. 7

not only funny but also human and moving.

For the film of Garson Kanin's "Born Yesterday," the role she had created on Broadway, Miss Holliday won an Academy Award in 1950 as the best actress.

Six years later, her performance as the wish-fulfilling telephone operator in Broadway's "Bells Are Ringing" won her the Antoinette Perry Award as the outstanding female lead in a musical.

In all, Miss Holliday appeared in only five Broadway shows between 1945, when she made her debut in "Kiss Them for Me" and 1963, when she starred in the short-lived musical "Hot Spot." She made a number of movies but always felt that she was not a "Hollywood type." She was a native New Yorker and never took herself away from the metropolis for very long.

Had a High I.Q.

Acting was work to her, partly perhaps because it was not what she had set out to do (she wanted to be a writer and director) and partly because she was a perfectionist. Her stage stupidity was in contrast to an extremely alert and high intelligence, attested to early in life by a score of 172 in a public school intelligence quotient test.

Adolph Green and Betty Comden, two of the The Revuers, the group in which they and Miss Holliday rose from obscurity to fame as entertainers in Greenwich Village, recalled years later that when "Bells Are Ringing" was in its final weeks and set for closing, the actress would still call rehearsals to keep the cast from getting sloppy.

"I'm not an 'instant actor,'" Miss Holliday once said. "To really do anything I've got to try it five or six or a dozen times."

Miss Holliday was shy and never anxious to be known as a star anywhere but in her performances. She rarely indulged in lavish clothing and she fought a perennial war against a waistline that tended to expand and threaten her 5-foot 7-inch, 125-pound figure that went so well with her large expressive brown eyes and natural blond hair.

Her life was a succession of breaks predicated on talent and determination, but rarely in overconfidence. She encouraged her friends to see her and tell her how she did. When she went before her first audiences in 1938, at the Village Vanguard in 1938, she became so nervous that she became sick.

In 1945 she was chosen at auditions by Herman Shumlin

Judy Holliday starred in *Born Yesterday.*

for the role of a prostitute, in "Kiss Them for Me." She was frightened at the possibility that her low-pitched voice would not reach the back of the house. Mr. Green recalled that she came to him and Miss Comden and confessed, "I don't know if I can make it."

"She did," said Mr. Green. "The whisper became a roar." For her efforts she won the Clarence Derwent Award as the best supporting actress that year.

Her performance in this show caused Max Gordon to think of her when "Born Yesterday" ran into trouble a year later just before trying out in Philadelphia. Jean Arthur, who had been chosen to star in the show, fell sick.

Learned Part in 3 Days

"The minute she walked in I knew she was it," Mr. Gordon wrote in his memoirs. "I listened to her talk—even without giving her a script to read — and was certain that she would make an ideal replacement if she were needed."

She was needed, and only a few days later, when it became certain that Miss Arthur could not go on. Miss Holliday memorized the script in three days and the show opened in Philadelphia that weekend.

The late Paul Douglas and Gary Merrill played opposite her in the stage comedy, which ran for three years. Broderick Crawford and William Holden were in the film of "Born Yesterday."

Judith Tuvim, who was born on June 21, 1922, took Holliday as her stage name. It is a variation of the Hebrew translation of her family name, which means holiday.

Her father, Abraham Tuvim, was active in Jewish organizational affairs. Her mother, Helen, was a music teacher. Her parents were divorced when she was a child.

Young Judy grew up in a house in Sunnyside, Queens. She soon showed that she had been endowed bountifully with brains and drive. She read voraciously (adult books when her contemporaries were going through "The Bobbsey Twins"). Her mentor was an uncle, the late Joseph Gollomb, who was an author of novels and biography.

Although she was shy, she plunged into group activities at school. She wrote a Christmas play, "The Tucker Family's Christmas," which she also directed and starred in. She edited the school newspaper and one of her early literary efforts won an essay-contest prize: "How to Keep the Streets, Parks and Playgrounds of Our City Clean."

She was graduated from Julia Richman High School and then, because she could not enter the Yale Drama School, set about getting into show business from the bottom. The bottom was the switchboard, which she was hired to manage backstage at the Mercury Theater, then under the direction of Orson Welles.

It was one of the few assignments she failed. Calls became snarled and six months later she left, but with memories that later helped her play the dreamy operator in "Bells Are Ringing."

Her mother took her to a Catskill resort on vacation and she met Adolph Green, who was then performing in the Borscht Belt. The two became good friends.

That fall, in 1938, Miss Holliday took refuge from a sudden downpour in the Village Vanguard, a type of place that served soft drinks and hard poets who declaimed their works.

Max Gordon (not the Max Gordon who put her on stage) was the proprietor. He was impressed by her manner and intellect and they struck up a friendship.

"She was a Village kid, just like all the kids, even today," Mr. Gordon said yesterday. "She was very bright. I wanted some entertainment in the place and asked her if she could get a group together to go on Sunday nights for $5 apiece for each show."

Miss Holliday assembled Mr. Green, Miss Comden, Alvin Hammer and John Frank. They were all very nervous, Mr. Gordon said.

"None of us were what you might call actors," Mr. Green remembered.

From the very start, The Revuers, as they called themselves, scrounged for material. When they could not get enough, they began writing it themselves. They did take-offs and skits. They memorialized the man who invented the shoehorn and they made fun of Joan Crawford fans. Most of what they did went over well.

From there, all roads went up—for a while. They played the Rainbow Room and other top clubs. An agent hinted to them that Hollywood held out promise. With nothing more than this lead, the group entrained for the West Coast in 1943. There were no film jobs in Hollywood, but they played the Trocadero, where movie executives caught their acts, laughed and came up with little except offers to hire Miss Holliday.

"All the companies wanted her," Mr. Green said. "Nobody wanted us."

It was, according to all concerned, like a Grade B movie plot. Miss Holliday refused to enter films without her friends. They urged her to accept and, finally and reluctantly, she did, with an agreement that provided for The Revuers to have a part in the first film and for her to remain for six more.

In the first movie, The Revuers ended on the cutting room floor and Miss Holliday did not create any stir in her own role. Her other early experiments were also less than rewarding, although she drew a good review in "Winged Victory."

In 1944, she had one line as a wartime welder in "Something for the Boys." She later said that the filmmaker wanted someone who could speak quickly and that she had whipped through a 3-minute bit in 30 seconds.

In 1945 she returned, dispiritedly, to New York, where Mr. Green and Miss Comden had a hit in "On the Town." They encouraged her to apply for the part in "Kiss Them for Me."

After the role of Billie Dawn in "Born Yesterday," demands for her came from Broadway and Hollywood. She was in the films "The Solid Gold Cadillac," "Adam's Rib," "The Marrying Kind" and "Phfft."

On Broadway she also performed in "Dream Girl" and "Hot Spot." She persuaded Sydney Chaplin, now starring in "Funny Girl," to audition to play opposite her in "Bells Are Ringing." Mr. Chaplin, son of the famous movie comedian, had difficulty getting started in the theater. However, she worked with him and he got the part.

In 1948, she was married to David Oppenheim, a musician and head of the classical recording division of Columbia Records. The couple moved into the Dakota, at Central Park West and West 72d Street, where the actress continued to live after they were divorced in 1957.

The New York Times

TUESDAY, OCTOBER 10, 1972

Miriam Hopkins Is Dead at 69; Screen and Stage Star of 1930's

Miriam Hopkins, the vivacious blond star of "Becky Sharp" and some 35 other motion pictures, most of them in the 1930's, died early yesterday morning at the Alrae Hotel, 37 East 64th Street. She would have been 70 years old on Oct. 18.

Miss Hopkins, who had also starred in a number of Broadway productions, came to New York last July 12 to open a special retrospective showing of films at the Museum of Modern Art to mark the 60th anniversary of Paramount Studios. The retrospective was showing "The Story of Temple Drake," the film adaptation of William Faulkner's "Sanctuary," in which Miss Hopkins starred in 1933 with Jack LaRue.

Soon after arriving here, she fell ill and was admitted to the Harkness Pavilion of Columbia-Presbyterian Medical Center for treatment of a coronary condition. She was released from the hospital Sept. 9 and thereafter underwent medical treatment at her hotel suite. She died at 5 A.M. yesterday from what was tentatively diagnosed as a massive coronary attack.

Set Goal for Herself

"I want to know about things. I want to make something worth while of myself."

The words come out of a publicity release issued by Paramount Pictures in 1930, where, after a career in the theater, she was working on her first film and they accurately reflected the attitude Miriam Hopkins carried with her through life. Middle-aged movie fans remembered her as one of the brighter golden girls of the Hollywood dream factories with her striking blond hair, peaches-and-cream complexion and Georgia-tinted drawl. In reflection, her friends recalled her as an extremely warm, witty and intellectual woman who loved to recite poetry aloud to the circle of friends she invited to her elegant parties.

Traces of Southern Heritage

The late John O'Hara, who knew them well, once wrote that her parties were unlike most of those given by movie stars. "Most of her guests were chosen from the world of the intellect," he noted, and they were there "because Miriam knew them all, had read their work, had listened to their music, had bought their paintings. They were not there because a secretary had given her a list of highbrows."

The petite blond actress was born Ellen Miriam Hopkins on Oct. 18, 1902, in Bainbridge, Ga., and retained traces of her affection for the South—and her drawl — throughout a long career. After graduation from Syracuse University, Miss Hopkins came here to study dancing and was signed to go to South America with a ballet troupe. On the day the company was ue to sail she broke an ankle, however, and was forced to look for other work in the theater.

She decided to join the chorus of the first Music Box Revue in 1921 on Broadway. After that, parts came quickly. She made her greatest success in the theater in the 1930's in a succession of roles in "Jezebel" (1933) and "Wine of Choice" in Chicago in 1937. Then, against the advice of friends, she took over the role of Sabina in "The Skin of Our Teeth" from Talullah Bankhead after some years away from the stage. Her last appearance on Broadway was in "Look Homeward, Angel" in 1958. She was quoted at the time as saying that she would do everything differently if she were starting her career over.

Cited Her 'Bad Judgment'

"I've always had bad judgment about plays and movies," she said. "I turned down 'Broadway' and I turned down 'Twentieth Century,' and I also turned down the movie, 'It Happened One Night,' which won Claudette Colbert an Academy Award. I said it was just a silly comedy."

Despite such reservations, Miss Hopkins was one of Hollywood's top stars during its most glamorous era. Following her film debut in 1930 in "Fast and Loose," she appeared in a succession of pictures and was already a major star when she was offered the highly coveted role in "Becky Sharp" in 1935. Although she did not receive good notices, the film was a landmark as the first full-length feature produced in Technicolor.

Some of her other films included "Dr. Jekyl and Mr. Hyde" (1931), "Design for Living" (1933), "These Three" (1936), "Men Are Not Gods" (1937) and "The Heiress" (1939). She co-starred with Bette Davis in "The Old Maid" (1939) and in "Old Acquaintance" (1943). Her latest major films were "Fanny Hill: Memoirs of a Woman of Pleasure" (1965) and "The Chase" (1966).

Miss Hopkins was married four times—to Brandon Peters in 1926, to Austin Parker in 1928, to Anatole Litvak in 1937, and to Ray Brock in 1945. She was divorced from Mr. Brock in 1951.

For many years prior to 1966, Miss Hopkins lived in a townhouse she owned at 13 Sutton Place. Recently, however, she had lived in Los Angeles.

Miss Hopkins's sister, Mrs. Ruby Welch of Forest Hills, Queens, said funeral arrangements were being made by the actress's adopted son, Michael, who is a sergeant in the United States Air Force, stationed in California. In addition to her sister and her son, Miss Hopkins is survived by a grandson, Thomas.

Miriam Hopkins in *Splendor,* 1935.

Joel McCrea and Miriam Hopkins in *Woman Chases Man.*

The New York Times THURSDAY, OCTOBER 1, 1970

Edward Everett Horton Is Dead; Comic Character Actor Was 83

Star of Stage, Film and TV Played 'Befuddled' Role in a 60-Year Career

Special to The New York Times

ENCINO, Calif., Sept. 30—Edward Everett Horton, a character actor who was a master of comic befuddlement, died last night at his home in the San Fernando Valley. He was 83 years old.

The cause of death was not given, but Mr. Horton's family asked that in his memory donations be made to the American Cancer Society. Mr. Horton had been hospitalized at Glens Falls, N. Y., several weeks ago, and had only recently returned to his California home.

Instant Recognition

In an acting career that spanned more than 60 years, Edward Everett Horton, on the stage, the screen and on television, made an institution of the Nervous Nellie character. He was instantly recognizable as the jittery, worrying fussbudget who could utter a mild "Oh, dear" and make it sound like the end of the world.

Mr. Horton was one of those dependable, solid character actors who seldom found stardom but always had a job. He was a dedicated actor who lent authority and comic inventiveness to any role he took. "I have my own little kingdom," he once said of his work in the movies. "I do the scavenger parts no one else wants, and I get well paid for it."

He was constantly busy. When not appearing in movies—he made more than 150 of them—he toured the summer circuit, notably in the four-character farce "Springtime for Henry," in which he played a prissy double-taking Henry Dewlip who seemed always in a dither. He first appeared in the play in 1939, at the Bucks County Playhouse, and through various revivals played the title role more than 3,000 times.

Mr. Horton was born in Brooklyn on March 18, 1887, the son of Edward Everett Horton and the former Isabella Diack. After attending Boys High School he studied at the Polytechnic Institute of Brooklyn, Oberlin College in Ohio, and Columbia University, but

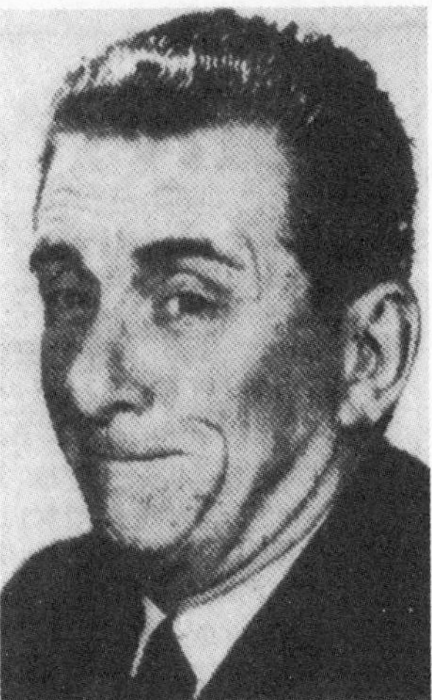

Edward Everett Horton

was graduated from none of them. He made his acting debut with Columbia's dramatic club, playing a corseted female despite the fact he was a manly 6 foot 2 inches tall.

Sang on Broadway

In 1907 he joined the Dempsey Light Opera Company, doing "The Bohemian Girl" and "The Mikado" on Staten Island. A baritone, he later sang in the chorus of a Broadway musical, and in 1908 he joined the Louis Mann troupe, in which he perfected his acting techniques over three years. Stock companies were thriving at the time, and Mr. Horton was regularly employed.

In the nineteen-twenties, while he acted in and managed the Majestic Theater in Los Angeles, with his brother and business manager, George, Mr. Horton appeared in dozens of silent movies, but did not hit his stride until the advent of sound. His first talkie was "The Front Page" and subsequently he was seen as Fred Astaire's sidekick in half a dozen Astaire-Ginger Rogers films, including "Top Hat." He also appeared as the Mad Hatter in "Alice in Wonderland" and as a crook in "Lost Horizon."

Seldom did a year pass, until the advent of television, when Mr. Horton did not appear in at least five or six films. And when the new medium did come along, he made the transformation to television with ease.

Well into his seventies, he was still being seen in movies (he appeared last year in "2000 Years Later") and on the stage. In 1963 he toured the straw-hat circuit with "Miss Pell Is Missing," in which he played the dramatic role of a mousy little man dominated by his sister. He appeared on Broadway in "A Funny Thing Happened on the Way to the Forum" and was seen as the Starkeeper in the 1965 revival of "Carousel" at the New York State Theater.

Pulled a Muscle

Mr. Horton's last televison appearance will be broadcast Oct. 14 on the series "The Governor and J. J.," in which he plays a crusty old physician. When he reported to work for the program several weeks ago, the octogenarian actor was limping slightly and he explained he had pulled a muscle playing tennis.

In recent years Mr. Horton had been doing off-screen voices for cartoon and television commercials, and he even presided as master of ceremonies at the Westminster Kennel Club's dog show in Madison Square Garden.

"It's not that I really need the money," he explained, "it's simply that I like money — lots of it. I must admit I'm sometimes over-frugal."

That was putting it mildly, according to some of his friends, one of whom recently described Mr. Horton as "prudent to a fault." Not long ago the actor was observed sitting alone in Sardi's Restaurant, carefully entering in a small lined ledger his daily expenses — carfare, taxi, "12 cents stamps," lunch expenses, and so on.

He and his brother George pieced together 22 acres of land in the San Fernando Valley, calling the estate Belleigh Acres. Mr. Horton lived there with his mother, who died several years ago at the age of 102. He did not marry.

Mr. Horton said that he was able "on the money I made from 'Springtime for Henry' alone" to buy his Adirondack summer home on Lake George, near Glens Falls, N. Y. He owned an antique collection said to be valued at half a million dollars.

Edward Everett Horton, Isabel Jewell, John Howard, Ronald Colman and Thomas Mitchell in *Lost Horizon.*

"All the News That's Fit to Print."

The New York Times.

LATE CITY EDITION
Continued warm with thundershowers in afternoon; moderate winds.
Temperatures Yesterday—Max., 83; Min., 63
Sunrise, 5:27 A. M.; Sunset, 8:21 P. M.

VOL. XCII..No. 31,176. Entered as Second-Class Matter, Postoffice, New York, N. Y. NEW YORK, THURSDAY, JUNE 3, 1943. THREE CENTS IN NEW YORK CITY

ROOSEVELT STUDIES COAL CRISIS AFTER THE WLB REFERS IT TO HIM; IT BARS TALKS TILL MEN RETURN

BRITISH SHIPS SHELL PANTELLERIA TWICE AS PLANES POUND IT

Island Garrison Reported on Alert for Invasion Seen as Imminent by Italians

FLEET SUFFERS NO LOSS

Weak Reply Made by Shore Guns—Fortresses and Lightnings Range Mediterranean

Wireless to THE NEW YORK TIMES.

ALLIED HEADQUARTERS IN NORTH AFRICA, June 2—The mightiest sea and air weapo the Mediterranean British fleet Force—combi batter Italy's of Pantelleria tons of bombs day.

It was the first by sea and air ag ernmost of the isl the Italian mainlan tresses blasted shippi air. Then late in the Britain's naval guns, sp thunderous salvos, sent s shell crashing into the A racks and shore batteries enemy retaliated lightly w shore guns, but the Royal had "no casualties."

This was the second naval bardment of Pantelleria in days. On Sunday night a Brit squadron shelled the island's on harbor heavily, with many shell falling in the harbor area. The enemy did not return the fire and there were no British casualties or damage.

[The garrisons of Pantelleria have been put on an emergency basis in expectation of an imminent Allied invasion that, Italian officials fear, may also strike at Sardinia and Sicily, according to French advices to Madrid quoted by The United Press. The Italian fleet is ready to put to sea at an hour's notice, the dispatches added.

[Another United Press dispatch from Madrid, quoting reports from France, said that Pantelleria was virtually isolated from Italy, with no ships able to enter the harbor and difficulty in maintaining air communications. Madrid said that Axis submarines were no longer putting in at Pantelleria].

American planes ranged the mid-Mediterranean area from Pantelleria to Northern Sardinia bombing and machine-gunning the shipping on which the enemy's supply system is based now that Allied fighters are hampering his transport planes' use of the airways. Eight Axis ships, one of which exploded, were damaged in these raids.

Fighter-Bombers Take Part

Ships and other targets in the Pantelleria harbor were hit by bombs from Fortresses and Lightning fighter-bombers. Formations of Lightnings then swept down to strafe targets in the area and observed the damage to the ships in the harbor from the Allied bombs. One formation hit boats in the harbor with a machine-gun fusillade.

Pantelleria has been raided thirteen times in the past sixteen days, a series of attacks that dwarfs in intensity the Axis air assault on Malta last Autumn.

Mitchells assaulted the harbor at Terranova, in Northern Sardinia, dropping high-explosive bombs among several ships. The formation was attacked by about ten enemy fighters, which used a coordinated attack in which they darted at the bombers simultaneously from the sides and below. No enemy planes were shot down in this or other operations during the day, but one Allied aircraft was lost.

The Marauders damaged a large merchant vessel in the harbor of Porto Ponte di Romano, in Southern Sardinia. Like Terranova, this is an important Axis supply center. Bombs also burst on the custom house and causeway road. Lightnings escorting the bombers strafed two gun positions and a sixty-foot naval vessel, which exploded.

At Porto Torres, other Lightnings carrying bombs hammered shipping, damaging two vessels. A pier and docks were also hit in this attack.

A railroad bridge at Balestrate, in Northwest Sicily, was bombed by still another formation of

Continued on Page Four

Ethiopians Ask Task Of Vanguard in Italy

By The United Press.

LONDON, June 2—Belata Ayela Gabre, Ethiopian Minister to Britain, urged today that a picked group of Ethiopian Commandos, fully equipped with long knives and a long-standing thirst for vengeance, should be allowed to spearhead an Allied invasion of Italy.

"The Fascist blood would turn to water," he said. "The Ethiopians remember the thousands of their comrades who died on the hot desert sands in 1936 and they will never be satisfied until they can rip an Italian gullet."

Ethiopia would like nothing better than to lead an Allied invasion, he said, for Commando-type fighting was familiar to th average Ethiop eye teeth

Italy, N Di

Kuban Ba

One German b International Inform a propaganda agency that the Germans ha seventy-eight more Rus in the Caucasus, but th remnants" of one Soviet Temryuk on the Axis left f

Casualties and an undisc amount of damage were ackn edged by the Russians at Kur which is a feeder point for R Army units long threatening Or to the north and the southern ap proaches of Bryansk to the north west.

Both sides have strong forces assembled in this critical triangular area above the German-held Ukraine stronghold of Kharkov, which the Germans lost, then recaptured in their counter-offensive last Winter. This same area formed the base from which the Germans began their big 1942 push, which rolled deep into the Caucasus and into Stalingrad before the Red Army drive nullified its gains.

Dispatches from Stockholm quoted Berlin military circles as saying that they believed any large-scale joint Russian and British-American offensive from east and west might not begin until

Continued on Page Eight

NAZIS HIT AIRLINER; LESLIE HOWARD PUT AMONG 17 MISSING

Transport Is Shot Down Over Bay of Biscay En Route From Lisbon to England

ACTOR ON OFFICIAL MISSIO

Film Director Washingto

NAZIS HIT AIRLINER; LESLIE HOWARD PUT AMONG 17 MISSING

Transport Is Shot Down Over Bay of Biscay En Route From Lisbon to England

ACTOR ON OFFICIAL MISSION

Film Director and Reuter's Washington Correspondent Also Are Feared Lost

By The Associated Press.

LONDON, June 2—A British Overseas Airways transport plane, with the actor Leslie Howard reported among its thirteen passengers, was officially declared overdue and presumed lost today after reporting in a final message at 11 A. M. yesterday that it was being attacked by an enemy aircraft while en route from Lisbon to England.

It was apparently the victim of German planes on unusually active reconnaissance along the seldom-molested air transport lane from neutral Portugal.

The names of the passengers and crew of four were withheld from the British Overseas Airways Corporation's announcement of the plane's presumed loss, but Lisbon reports said Mr. Howard was aboard.

In their daily communiqué, broadcast from Berlin and recorded by The Associated Press, the Germans said: "Three enemy bombers and one transport were downed by German reconnaissance planes over the Atlantic."

The Airways' announcement issued here tonight said:

"The British Overseas Airways Corporation regrets to announce that a civil aircraft on passage between Lisbon and the United Kingdom is overdue and must be presumed lost.

"The last message received from the aircraft stated that it was being attacked by an enemy aircraft.

"The aircraft carried thirteen passengers and a crew of four.

"Next of kin have been informed."

The plane left Lisbon yesterday morning and was due in England early last night.

It was the second British civil plane to be reported attacked on the Lisbon run. The first attack occurred last April, when a Netherland pilot evaded an ambush of six Heinkels and returned to Lisbon with none of his passengers injured and with one wing of his British airliner damaged.

Operate at Own Risk

While planes operate between Lisbon and England at their own risk, it was pointed out in reliable circles that it was generally understood they carry only civilian passengers. These sources said there was a slim chance that the plane could have been mistaken for a military transport.

Allied and Axis transport planes often idle side by side in the neutral Portuguese port.

Continued on Page Four

Britain's his wife, an London film Mr. Howard.

Later unoffi Lisbon identified as a Mrs. Hutch

Continued

Homes Miss Milk Quotas; OPA Plans Price Cut Here

Skip-a-Day Order Generally Obeyed in City Area—Mayor Seeks to Get Larger Supplies to Stores

al compliance with the or- e Office of Defense Trans- for skip-a-day milk de- reported yesterday for metropolitan area by Clark, ODT regional charge of motor trans- lk dealers carried out of no doorstep de- day.

Two million homes in the metropolitan area failed to receive their milk yesterday.

In the afternoon Mayor La Guardia conferred with Ralph T. Seward, impartial chairman of the Metropolitan Milk Distributors Commission. The Mayor said Mr. Seward informed him that milk deliveries to stores were carried out yesterday without difficulty, but the lack of deliveries to homes caused inconvenience to many.

"I am a little hopeful today," the Mayor said, as he left City Hall last night. "Store deliveries were okay. On home deliveries there was great inconvenience felt by a very large number of consumers."

The Mayor said he talked over the telephone with Chester Davis, Food Administrator, on the milk-delivery problem and that he would confer with Washington officials by telephone today.

Action by the War Labor Board

Continued on Page Twelve

Tax Bill 62-19, White House

CRIDER

ss ended its long labors over en the Senate adopted it by ouse. Favorable action by Congress. The Senate's 62

ROCAL TRADE NDED 2 YEARS

23, Adopts House hich Is Sent to e House

SUMMONS LEADERS

President Confers After Labor Board Attacks Strike Coercion

LEWIS DENOUNCES MOVE

He Declares Action Is Illegal —Miners Say Settlement Had Been in the Making

Text of War Labor Board's order on coal parley, Page 10.

By LOUIS STARK

Special to THE NEW YORK TIMES.

WASHINGTON, June 2—President Roosevelt acted swiftly today to put an end to the coal strike.

He called an emergency conference attended by Secretary Ickes, James F. Byrnes, Director of War Mobilization, and eight members of the War Labor Board. It was reported later that the Chief Executive had supported the board's order, issued earlier in the day, calling on the 530,000 bituminous and anthracite miners to return to work before continuance of collective bargaining conferences.

[Although mine whistles blew in patriotic appeals to coal diggers, little response to the government-sponsored back-to-work movement was noted, according to reports yesterday from Pittsburgh and other mining centers. Moreover, the stoppage spread to a few mines in Illinois, employing members of the Progressive Mine Workers of America, the A. F. of L. union, which has officially refused to join the U. M. W. strike.]

Appeal to Miners Is Hinted

Mr. Roosevelt was understood to be giving further consideration to the strike situation tonight, but no inkling was permitted to leak out as to his next course of action. He is expected to make a statement tomorrow.

It was considered possible that the President would request the miners to return to the pits. The terms under which the miners would work, according to these reports, would be the same as those offered by the WLB, with retroactive payments to April 1 if wage adjustments were made under collective bargaining.

How soon the miners would be expected to return was not indicated, but if such an appeal is made in a day or two it is unlikely that the strikers would be requested to report before Monday.

What steps might be taken if the miners refrained from obeying the request of the Chief Executive were not indicated.

The nation-wide coal strike was d over to the White House second day, when the WLB the dispute to the Presi- appropriate action after the Appalachian Joint and the United Mine America to cease all on the issues referred them by the board's order of May 25, "until the mine workers return to work" in compliance with the board's directive.

Telegram Interrupts Conferees

The White House meeting, which lasted an hour and three-quarters, ending soon before 7 this evening, was the culminating event of a hectic day of developments which began with resumption of the conferences.

In the midst of the session this morning the conferees were advised that Wayne L. Morse, compliance officer of the WLB, had sent a telegram to the parties by unanimous decision of the board, declaring that any agreement on the issues "while the workers are on strike and under the pressure of this strike coercion will not be considered or approved by the board."

The conference recessed at noon and resumed at 3 P. M. Upon adjournment at 5 the Southern operators' negotiating committee, of

Continued on Page Ten

Coast Guard Cutter Sinks U Captures 40 of Crew in Epic

Special to THE NEW YORK TIMES.

WASHINGTON, June 2—A "paper-skinned" Coast Guard cutter, commanded by a skipper from New York City, recently shepherding a large and important convoy across the North Atlantic, outmanoeuvred, out-shot and sank a German submarine, then plucked from the water forty Nazi seamen who were screaming "Halp!" and "Wasserbombs!" the Navy Department disclosed today.

The cutter was the 2,000-ton, 327 foot Spencer, one of the Hamilton class of ships that have distinguished themselves in previous anti-submarine actions. Her skipper is Commander Harold S. Berdine. The Navy indicated that it considered the action, which took place only a few weeks ago, the epic anti-submarine enco of the war.

The Spencer's fight was gra cally recorded for naval annals, on deck with three cameras rea just as the action broke was Chi Boatswain's Mate Jack January, former St. Louis newspaper pho tographer. January started "shooting" as soon as the guns went into action, and the result was a series of battle shots that the Navy considers among the best of their kind.

Before the battle was over an untold number of Nazis, whose heads dotted the water like dark corks bobbing in a tub, had perished, but forty thoroughly frightened survivors of the furious battle

Continued on Page Three

merican daylight bombing and asked for e help of the same kind. [5:5.]

Pope Pius exhorted the belligerents again to respect the laws of humanity in the conduct of aerial war. He implied that other countries might soon be drawn into the conflict. [5:1.]

U-boats did less damage and suffered more in May than at any previous time, First Lord of

nd reported sualties in the [6:3.]

British and American omats had sought to compose the differences separating General de Gaulle and General Giraud, it was announced in Algiers that the executive committee would meet again today. [1:4.] In Washington it was felt that French unity was still far off. [4:6.]

The United Nations Food Conference, which ends its meetings at Hot Springs, Va., today, was said to be a historic event demonstrating the possibility of Allied post-war agreement. [12:2.]

sed; es to Begin Sunday

Special to THE NEW YORK TIMES.

TON, June 2—Be- e beef slaughter during the st month was 10 per cent less than expectations, preferred cuts of beef, such as steaks and roasts, will call for surrender by the housewife of from 2 to 3 points a pound more after this Saturday, but many kinds of lamb, veal and variety meats will be rated at 1 point less, the Office of Price Administration announced today.

This new schedule of point values means that consumers who wish to eat as much meat as hitherto will have to take less beef and more veal, lamb and pork. Most pork cuts are unchanged as to point value, because pork, currently, is more plentiful than beef.

Commenting on the situation, a spokesman for the OPA said that "consumers who eat more pork, veal and variety meats during the next four weeks and probably throughout the Summer—will be able to get just about the same number of pounds of meat for their rationing points as they did during the last ration period."

New tables of point values for meats, fats, fish and cheese, which are valid from June 6 to July 3, include the newly rationed evaporated and condensed milk, with a point per pound point value. A new cheese group also has been added to cover creamed soft cheeses, which have been inserted in the rationed list. Four categories of canned fish—crabmeat, sea herrings, sea mussels and the half dozen other unimportant types

Continued on Page Twelve

IAZIS SHOOT DOWN BRITISH AIRLINER

Continued From Page One

Besides Mr. Howard, among ıose reported to have been aboard 'ere Kenneth Stonehouse, 35 years ld, Washington correspondent of ritain's Reuter news agency, and is wife, and Alfred T. Chaenhall, ondon film director and friend of Ir. Howard.

Later unofficial reports from isbon identified other passengers s a Mrs. Hutcheson and her two laughters, Bertha, 11 years old, nd Caroline, 2 years old; Mrs. Cecilia Paton, Cuban-born wife of n Englishman, and T. M. Sherington, said to be a director of the Shell Company and for eighteen 'ears a resident of Portugal.

An unverified report in Lisbon aid the craft was shot down over he Bay of Biscay. Other reports aid a rough sea would have lessened the passengers' chances of scaping in rubber boats.

Mr. Howard had been in Spain ecently canvassing the possibility of producing films there. He also ad been lecturing in Spain and Portugal on how films are made. He had been expected to return ome soon to supervise personally he final stages of a new film, "The Lamp Still Burns," which his rganization is producing.

Loss Confirmed in Lisbon

LISBON, Portugal, June 2 (U.P.)—A British Overseas Airways plane arrying Leslie Howard and twelve other passengers, including three small English children, was shot lown over the Bay of Biscay while n route to England, it was reported today at the office of the British press attaché here.

HOWARD WON FAME IN ROMANTIC ROLES

Peak of His Art Achieved in 'The Petrified Forest' and 'Of Human Bondage'

HIS MANAGER ALSO LOST

Another Victim, Stonehouse of Reuter Washington Bureau, Was a South African

As an actor, motion picture director and producer here and in England for more than a generation, Leslie Howard was equally successful on the stage and screen and equally popular on both sides of the Atlantic. Especially noted for his romantic roles, he divided his time between this country and England until 1939, when he returned to England to make a series of war pictures for the British Government.

Last April he stopped work on a new film to undertake an extensive lecture tour of Spain and Portugal under the auspices of the British Council. It was that mission that took him to Lisbon.

Mr. Howard was born Leslie Stainer, son of a stockbroker, in London, April 3, 1893. After graduating from Dulwich School, in London, he worked as a bank clerk until the outbreak of World War I, when he joined the British Army. After having been invalided out of the army in 1918 he determined to become an actor and changed his last name to Howard.

Started Career on Tour

He toured the British provinces in "Peg o' My Heart" and "Charley's Aunt," then made his London debut in a play called "The Freaks" in 1918. He came to the United States to take a role in "Just Suppose" at the Henry Miller Theatre in 1920.

There followed a succession of other appearances in Broadway hits and Mr. Howard's success was quickly assured. He remained in this country so long that the British referred to him as "that American actor," but to his American public he was always thoroughly and romantically British

Between his Broadway appearances he managed to make trips back to England to play in London productions. In 1930 he made his first motion picture, "Outward Bound." He was an immediate success as a motion picture actor and from then on he passed most of his time in Hollywood.

His last stage appearance in New York was in his own production of "Hamlet," at the Imperial Theatre in 1936. Mr. Howard's "Hamlet" was not a success, as he himself acknowledged after much public discussion of its merits.

One of Mr. Howard's favorite roles was that of Alan Squier in "The Petrified Forest"—a role that did much to enhance his stature as an actor both on the stage and screen. He also won renown for his portrayal of Philip Carey in W. Somerset Maugham's "Of Human Bondage."

Mr. Howard was married to the former Ruth Evelyn Martin while on leave as a soldier during World War I. They had two children, Ronald Howard, now in the Royal Navy, and a daughter, Leslie.

Kenneth Stonehouse, Reuter correspondent in Washington, was returning to London with his wife, the former Peggy Margetts of London, having left the United States in the middle of May.

Born in Cape Town, South Africa, in 1909, he attended school there and joined the South African Railways and Harbors Board, serving it in Cape Town and elsewhere. He then went to London as correspondent for a South African newspaper chain and later joined Reuter's London bureau.

Howard falls in love with Ingrid Bergman in *Intermezzo*, 1939, his last American film.

Leslie Howard with Vivien Leigh in *Gone with the Wind*.

The New York Times TUESDAY, JANUARY 3, 1950

EMIL JANNINGS, 63, VETERAN OF FILMS

German Actor Who Achieved Success Here in 'Way of All Flesh' Is Dead in Austria

STROBL, Austria, Jan. 2 (UP)—Emil Jannings, thick-set German who was a leading movie actor for many years, died tonight in his home at Lake Wolfgang at the age of 63.

The actor, who made Hollywood history in his younger days and later became a state actor for the Nazi Propaganda Ministry, had been suffering from cancer of the liver complicated by pneumonia. For the last few days he had realized his death was near and he called his friends to his bedside to tell them farewell while members of his family looked on.

Jannings became famous in Hollywood for such pictures as "The Patriot" and "The Way of All Flesh." He already had achieved fame in Germany with "Variety," a picture described as one of the best ever made.

The German actor, whose heavy mobile face could be subtle and eloquent, launched the film career of Marlene Dietrich in 1932 with the picture "The Blue Angel."

At his bedside when he died were his wife, his daughter, his brother and his physician.

A Favorite in Germany

Until the rise of Hitler, Emil Jannings enjoyed tremendous prestige in this country, though not quite as much as in Germany, where he was perhaps the favorite movie actor.

However, during the second World War, it became apparent that Jannings had become a favorite of the Nazi regime, particularly since he was one of a handful of people entrusted by Propaganda Minister Joseph Goebbels with running that phase of the movie industry most closely dominated by the Hitler regime.

After the war the actor, whose fine performance in "The Blue Angel" had attracted almost as much attention here as his artistic portrayals in "The Last Laugh," "Passion" and "Variety" had brought him in Germany, was seldom seen on the screen in this country.

Born in Brooklyn, son of a kitchen-ware manufacturer, Jannings had to go to Switzerland as an infant because of the illness of his mother. When he was 10 he was taken to Germany, where he was raised by his grandparents.

Went to Sea as Youth

A poor student and an inveterate mountain-climber who broke both arms and legs in the Swiss Alps, he spent his boyhood doing his best to evade the discipline of his teachers. His first ambition was to be an actor. But a close friend was in the Navy, and his presence, all decked out in blue and gold, caused Emil to run away and go to sea.

Albert Ballin, a founder of the Hamburg-American Lines, found him wandering the London docks, took pity on him and sent him back to his forgiving parents. They wanted him to go to college and become an engineer. For a short time he tried to obey the parental wishes, but again he ran away, this time as billposter and prop boy for a road show company. The police found him, but this time his father thought a good dose of theatrical hardship would cure him of his romantic notions.

For several years he traveled with one company or another in wagons. He visited all the provinces. Then he became a member of a stock company at Gardeleden Theatre, and later he appeared in stock at Bremen and Leipzig. He was an accomplished Shakespearean actor, and always held that Germans could act Shakespeare better than the English. For some time he was with the Darmstadt Royal Theatre in Berlin, where he played in Shakespeare, Ibsen, Strindberg and Goethe plays.

There this actor made the acquaintance of Robert Wiene, who a few years later was to make a name for himself throughout the world as the producer of "Caligari." To Jannings was given the part of Riessler opposite Erna Morenas.

He next played in a series of one-reelers in which a young member of the German theatre first tried his hand at directing. The young man was Ernst Lubitsch.

Other pictures of that era in which Jannings played included the famous "The Last Laugh," in which, as an old man who sees his world fall about him, he caused critics to rave about him. Besides this were "Deception," "The Loves of Pharaoh," "Peter the Great," "Faust" and "Variety," all made by Ufa in Germany. He won the Academy Award in 1928 for his performance in "The Way of All Flesh."

Then he came to this country, still before the film had become spoken, and for Paramount appeared in "The Way of All Flesh," "The Street of Sin," "The Last Command," "The Patriot" and "Sins of the Father." When talking pictures came into production he became one of that group of foreign film actors who, because of their accent, suddenly became homesick for their fatherlands. He returned to Germany. Later he did for Paramount "Betrayal" and "The Blue Angel." But most of his work after that was done in Germany.

He married Gussie Hill, a retired European variety hall artist.

Emil Jannings and Ruth Chatterton in *Sins of the Fathers.*

Emil Jannings with Evelyn Brent in *The Last Command.*

"All the News That's Fit to Print"

The New York Times.

LATE CITY EDITION
Gradual clearing today; fair and seasonable tonight, tomorrow.
Temperature Range Today-Max.,60; Min.,45
Temperatures Yesterday—Max.,55; Min.,49
Full U. S. Weather Bureau Report, Page 33

VOL. C No. 33,876. Entered as Second-Class Matter. Post Office, New York, N. Y. NEW YORK, TUESDAY, OCTOBER 24, 1950. Times Square, New York 18, N. Y. Telephone LAckawanna 4-1000 FIVE CENTS

U. N. DRIVE ADVANCES SLOWLY ON APPROACH TO MANCHURIA; U. S. CAPTIVES' TRAIL FOUND

LIBERATED AMERICANS CELEBRATE

Lieut. Alexander Makaroumis, left, and Capt. William D. Locke, second from right, are joined by friendly North Koreans on a street in Pyongyang. Associated Press Wirephoto

MANY REDS GIVE UP

Surrender Record Is Set —Allies Cross River, Drive on Mountains

PATROLS MOVING FORWARD

Advance Guards Reported 25 Miles From Kanggye at the Closest Point to Border

By LINDESAY PARROTT
Special to The New York Times.

TOKYO, Tuesday, Oct. 24—United Nations forces, moving ahead more slowly after their dash to within fifty miles of the Manchurian border, today slashed at the heels of the routed Communist People's Army from two directions.

[The United Press reported that the South Korean Sixth Division had picked up the trail of a large number of United States prisoners of war near the Manchurian border and was trying to find them, according to United States military advisers.]

On the west coast they thrust across the wide Chongchon River on the main highroad toward Sinuiju, on the Yalu River boundary between Korea and Manchuria. South Korean Republican forces struck northeastward toward mountain strongholds south of the Yalu, in the rocky central spines of the Korean peninsula around the communications center of Kanggye.

River Crossing by British

A river crossing was made north of Sinanju, near the mouth of the Chongchon, by the British Twenty-seventh Brigade of the Argyll and Sutherland Highlanders, Australians and men of London's Middlesex Regiment. Front-line reports said that Sinanju itself, an important settlement on the south bank, where the highway and coastal railroad cross the stream, was being cleared.

The British, from mop-up duties south of the captured Communist capital at Pyongyang, had moved north, joined hands with the United States 187th Airborne Regiment, which dropped from the skies at Sukchon last week, and become the leading element of the United Nations advance along the main highway.

[The United Press reported that a third crossing of the river had been made by the Republican First Division in the area of Yongbyon, town captured by its Twelfth Regiment.]

To the north, troops of the Republican Sixth Division crossed the river near occupied Anju and swept to the vicinity of Pakchon, on the farther bank, in an advance of about eight miles against scanty enemy resistance. They stood about sixty-five air miles from the border at Sinuiju.

In the center, the Republican

Continued on Page 3, Column 1

U.S. OPENS ROUND-UP OF 86 AS ALIEN REDS; BOARD IS APPOINTED

Party Workers Are Accused of Engaging in Propaganda —20 Arrested So Far

TRUMAN IMPLEMENTS ACT

Appoints Richardson Head of Subversive Control Panel— Communists Don't Register

By WILLIAM S. WHITE
Special to The New York Times.

WASHINGTON, Oct. 23—The Department of Justice began today a country-wide round-up of eighty-six persons accused of being alien Communists especially active in propaganda work for the party.

[Twenty arrests had been made up to late Monday night, according to The Associated Press.]

The department's drive was started under the Internal Security Act of 1950, which President Truman implemented today by naming the bipartisan Subversive Activities Control Board. He put a Republican, Seth W. Richardson, at its head.

The board is required by the so-called McCarran anti-subversive law, which Congress passed over the President's veto.

The department's drive on the eighty-six aliens was aimed at deporting them wherever the country of origin would accept them, and failing that to put them under the six-month detention provided in the security act.

If after six months deportation still is impossible, the aliens will be subject to indefinite surveillance by the Immigration Service.

Reds Refuse to Register

Today was the last day for Communist organizations to register voluntarily with the Department of Justice under the act, and they carried out their threat to refuse to do so.

[At national headquarters of the Communist party in New York, a spokesman said Monday that the party leadership was unconcerned about passage of the registration deadline.

["We stand on everything we've said previously," he said. "We don't fit the bill. We're not foreign controlled. We're not a conspiracy. We'll join with the growing number of people working to repeal it as a menace."]

Under the terms of the law, the department must now appeal to the Subversive Activities Control Board. The board must hold hearings and permit the accused associations the right of counsel and of cross-examination, before making a finding of record as to whether or not they are subversive. From any board conclusion, an appeal may be carried to the Federal Supreme Court.

Fines, Imprisonment Possible

The officers of the Communist party, Federal officials said, had a duty under the law to register the party today, but that as individuals they could free themselves from personal liability by coming forward with a registration for it within ten days.

A department spokesman told reporters that the case against known Communist organizations would necessarily have to be a comprehensive one, rather like making a major prosecution in court. It thus would involve a great deal of paper work that would take much time.

For failure to register, after a final determination that it is subversive and after exhaustion of all appeals, an organization may be fined $10,000 a day and its responsible officers—the four top ones in each case—may be imprisoned for five years.

On the subversive control board with Mr. Richardson, who is retiring as chairman of the Federal Loyalty Review Board, the highest appeals body in the program by which the Government tests the loyalty of its employes, President Truman appointed the following:

For two-year terms — Peter Campbell Brown of New York and Charles M. La Follette of Virginia.

For one-year terms—David J. Coddaire of Massachusetts and Dr. Kathryn McHale of Indiana.

Mr. Richardson's tenure as chairman will run for three years. Along with all his associates, he will receive $12,500 a year, and like them, he must give up all private employment.

Like Mr. Richardson, Mr. Coddaire, a Boston and Haverhill, Mass., attorney, is a Republican.

Mr. La Follette, though once a Republican member of Congress from Indiana, was formerly executive director of Americans for Democratic Action, an organiza-

Continued on Page 17, Column 2

DeSapio Says Impellitteri Offered Deal to Quit Race

Wanted Judgeships for Himself and 3 Aides, Tammany Chief Declares—Mayor Calls Charge a 'Contemptible Lie'

Contradictory versions of the negotiations that preceded the selection of the Democratic Mayoralty nominee were offered yesterday by Carmine G. DeSapio, leader of Tammany Hall, and by Acting Mayor Impellitteri.

The Tammany leader declared that Mr. Impellitteri had asked for a Supreme Court nomination for himself and three other judicial posts for his supporters as his price for ending the threat of running for Mayor as an independent. Mr. DeSapio denied the charge previously made by Mr. Impellitteri that a Supreme Court nomination actually had been offered him.

This version brought from Mr. Impellitteri the declaration that it was an "unmitigated, unabashed, contemptible lie." He said that Mr. DeSapio "unquestionably was compelled at political gunpoint to lend his name to such a self-debasing falsehood."

Mr. DeSapio told a story of a noon conference at Tammany Hall, a second, that started just before midnight a few days later and ended in the early hours of the morning, and a third at Mr. DeSapio's home one morning at 8:30 o'clock. He contended that at all of them Mr. Impellitteri pressed his claim to the Democratic Mayoralty nomination, but eventually offered to settle for less.

Mayor Impellitteri repeated his statement, made in a radio broadcast several weeks ago, that at the breakfast conference on Sept. 5, when Mr. DeSapio was about to start for the Rochester State Convention, Mr. DeSapio offered him the judgeship and admitted making the offer to a meeting of Tammany leaders in Rochester, three days later.

The DeSapio charge, designed to destroy what the Democrats c... the "myth" of Mr. ... independence, first ... radio broadcast ...

Con...

Statements by DeSapio ...

Corsi Challeng... To Enlist the A...

Edward Corsi, Republican cand... of his opponents, Acting Mayor Vincen... Ferdinand Pecora, last night why they ... of f... O'Dwye... paign.

"The ... who manag... istration of ... the Cohens, t... kelsteins and ... ning Pecora's ... biggest slush f... any local camp... said.

"And in Imp... Well, the Sampso... the Dan Finns ... Brickmans, all T... warts, deposed but ... back with Impy.

"Now my two T... ponents are experts, ... other phony game—do... tions, hemming and ha... double-talking, instead ... fair and frank with the p... the city."

Before ridiculing Mr. I... teri, who is the Experienc... candidate, and Mr. Pecora... Democratic-Liberal nominee, ... broadcast over Station WOR, ... Corsi denounced the Liberal pa... for its "violent political some... sault" in supporting Mr. Pecora and accused high police officials of profiting in the sale of taxica... licenses through the operation o... "a black market" in taxicab medallions.

"In this family battle, the poor fellow who is getting a terrible raw deal is none other than our Ambassador to Mexico," Mr. Corsi said in his broadcast. "He sits in his penthouse at the Hotel Carlyle waiting for a call from the Tammany speakers' bureau, but there is no call. Poor Bill—'the greatest Mayor New York ever had'—no one wants him, not even the 'greatest candidate for Mayor New York has ever had,' Ferdie Pecora.

"Bill O'Dwyer is in the doghouse. He is the great untouchable of this campaign. Why? Because my two Tammany opponents are trying to have the people of New York for-

Continued on Page 23, Column 6

HIGH COURT GRANTS REVIEW TO 11 REDS

It Limits Arguments to Legality of Smith Act, Under Which They Were Convicted

By LEWIS WOOD
Special to The New York Times.

WASHINGTON, Oct. 23—The fate of the eleven Communists, convicted in New York of conspiracy to overthrow the Government by force and violence, will be decided by the Supreme Court, under an order issued today granting a review of their appeal. Arguments in the case were set for Dec. 4.

Although agreeing to examine this central case, the high court postponed until Nov. 7, at least, a decision whether to review the contempt convictions of the Communists' six lawyers for contumacious conduct during the turbulent nine-month trial.

In consenting to hear the Communist conspiracy case, the Supreme Court acceded to a Government request. It commanded that the arguments must be limited to the question of Constitutionality of the Smith Act, which makes it a criminal offence to advocate or teach the overthrow of the Government by force or violence. The Communists were convicted of breaking this law.

Limitation of the arguments threw into the discard a number of complaints made by the Communists in a seventy-eight-page mimeographed brief. These included such allegations as hostility by Federal Judge Harold R. Medina, who presided at the trial, and

Continued on Page 16, Column 3

Gambling Raiders Seize $127,000 In Jersey as State Starts Inquiry

The New Jersey investigation of gambling in Bergen County opened auspiciously yesterday with the seizure of more than $127,000 in cash and large quantities of gambling paraphernalia in two raids conducted by Nelson F. Stamler, Deputy State Attorney General.

With a blanket search warrant signed by Superior Court Judge J. Wallace Leyden, Mr. Stamler led a police party to the home of J. W. Donaldson, alias Leo Link, 50 years old, at 479 Beatrice Street, Teaneck. Donaldson is at liberty in $25,000 bail on bookmaking charges. The $127,000 was found in his home, along with a note that led to the finding of additional funds, which were not immediately tallied, and the gambling devices, in a warehouse in Palisades Park.

Meanwhile, in Brooklyn, seven witnesses appeared before the grand jury investigating gambling.

In the Teaneck raid the officials had a map showing the location of a cellar safe, The Associated Press reported. They reached the Donaldson home just before noon. Donaldson, aroused from bed, came downstairs in his bathrobe and pajamas and watched Mr. Stamler search the ground floor rooms.

The Deputy Attorney General then led the way down into the expensively finished cellar.

"Where's the safe?" he inquired, but without waiting for Donaldson to reply, he took out the map and went into the liquor room. Pushing back a removable shelf filled with cans of food, he uncovered the object of his search.

Donaldson said he was too nervous to recall the combination, whereupon Mr. Stamler asked a police mechanic to drill it open. This caused the owner to remember the combination, and the safe was opened in the ordinary way.

Inside were neatly stacked bun-

Continued on Page 22, Column 3

GERMANS EXHAUST THEIR TRADE CREDIT IN PAYMENTS UNION

Organization Facing a Crisis as Result of Bonn Deficit After Only 3½ Months

DEBT EXCEEDS $320,000,000

Effect Is Seen on Cooperation in Europe—France Shows Surplus in Same Period

By SYDNEY GRUSON
Special to The New York Times.

THE HAGUE, The Netherlands, Oct. 23--West Germany has used up in three and a half months all the credits allotted to th... B... Administration for ... ation of th... Unio...

VISHINSKY CHARGES TRUMAN'S POLICIES ARE LIKE HITLER'S

Says San Francisco Address Laid Down Nazi Course of Guns Rather Than Butter

SPEAKS BEFORE U. N. BODY

Russian Indicates a Position Closer to West on Issue of Control of Atomic Bomb

Excerpts from the Vishinsky address are printed on Page 8.

By THOMAS J. HAMILTON
Special to The New York Times.

...E SUCCESS, Oct. 23—Sovi... ...ign Minister Andrei Y. ... charged today that Pres... ...man laid down the Nazi ...guns rather than butter" ...h at San Francisco on ... Vishinsky also re... earlier attacks on ...les" in the United

... hand, Mr. Vishin... a two-hour speech ...itical and Security ...he United Nations ...y that the Soviet ...anted peace and ...xistence of cap...istic countries, ...make further ... resolve the

...nsky came ...represen... ...ccepting ...ty plan ...ng un- ... the op- the ...der ...ech ...er- ...al

... of Uni... report... [1:8: ...]

The ... Ministe... prepare... in the ... atomic ... ment cam... speech cha... tions of Uni... ment and Pre... fore the United ... Assembly's Politic... He said the Presid... were like the Nazis ... "guns rather than b...

This is United ... commemorating th... versary of the ... founding. President ... deliver a major fo... address before the G... sembly at 11:30 A. M... Diplomats the world over hailed the day, some stressing that united action in Korea had spared the United Nations the fate met by the League of Nations. [11:1.] In this city's East Side a United Nations flag was raised at Madison House. [13:1.]

At a secret meeting of the Big Five of the Security Council the following names were proposed for Secretary General of the United Nations: Trygve Lie, Brigadier General Romulo of the Philippines, Dr. Luis Padilla Nervo of Mexico, Sir Benegal N. Rau and Sir Ramaswami Mudaliar, both of India. [12:2.]

The European Payments Union faced a crisis as the result of Western Germany's exhausting its full year's credit allotment in three and one-half months, it was disclosed. [1:4.]

...racy ... eleven Communist ..., but only on the consti-...onality of the Smith Act under which they were found guilty. [1:2.] The Court granted partial review of the Wisconsin utility anti-strike law. [17:5.]

Consumer prices rose half of 1 per cent in the month ending Sept. 15 [25:3.] All-out price and wage controls are not yet needed, Chairman Symington of the National Security Resources Board said; curbs on credits and use of materials should have a fair trial. [25:1.]

Defense Secretary Marshall ordered the armed services to free reservists from forced service as early as possible. [20:2.]

Index to other news appears on Page 30.

Truman Will Address U. N. On Its Anniversary Today

By GEORGE BARRETT
Special to The New York Times.

LAKE SUCCESS, Oct. 23—The United Nations has shaped final plans—with special security measures—for a packed house tomorrow when President Truman appears before the General Assembly at Flushing Meadow ...o deliver a major address.

The Presidential speech, com-...emorating the fifth birthday of ... world peace organization, will ...Mr. Truman's second important ...since his meeting with Gen. ... MacArthur on Wake Is-...ere is intense interest here ...Mr. Truman may have to ...he growing United Na-... world affairs, as ex-... the Korean crisis.

...2,500 seats are ex-...ed in the Great Hall ...uding the galleries ...d radio cubicles ... the high cham-...eat breakdown ...ol's use, which ... persons, del-... members of ...y; 347 for ...sentatives ...orld; 600 ...in floor ...ernates; ...nmental ... public

...eventy-... "gen-... no ...ers. ...ted ...ng ...e ...as ...as

...3

AL JOLSON DEAD AFTER KOREA TOUR

Noted Singer of Stage, Screen Has Heart Attack as He Plays Cards—Was 64

By The Associated Press.

SAN FRANCISCO, Oct. 23—Al Jolson, "The Jazz Singer," died at the St. Francis Hotel here tonight. He had recently returned from Korea after entertaining troops there.

Death came just after 10:30 P. M. (1:30 A. M. Tuesday, Eastern standard time) as Mr Jolson was playing cards in his room with friends. He was in San Francisco to be the guest star on the Bing Crosby radio program scheduled to be recorded Tuesday night.

[According to The United Press, Mr. Jolson, who was 64 years old, died of a heart attack.]

Mr. Jolson checked in at the St. Francis today. He was playing gin rummy with Martin Fried, his arranger and accompanist, and Harry Akst, song writer and long-time friend.

They said that he complained he

Continued on Page 26, Column 3

AL JOLSON DEAD AFTER KOREA TOUR

Noted Singer of Stage, Screen Has Heart Attack as He Plays Cards—Was 64

By The Associated Press.

SAN FRANCISCO, Oct. 23—Al Jolson, "The Jazz Singer," died at the St. Francis Hotel here tonight. He had recently returned from Korea after entertaining troops there.

Death came just after 10:30 P. M. (1:30 A. M. Tuesday, Eastern standard time) as Mr Jolson was playing cards in his room with friends. He was in San Francisco to be the guest star on the Bing Crosby radio program scheduled to be recorded Tuesday night.

[According to The United Press, Mr. Jolson, who was 64 years old, died of a heart attack.]

Mr. Jolson checked in at the St. Francis today. He was playing gin rummy with Martin Fried, his arranger and accompanist, and Harry Akst, song writer and long-time friend.

They said that he complained he

Continued on Page 26, Column 3

...an Gives Garment District Biggest Traffic Relief in 10 Years

Truck traffic in the congested garment district began operating yesterday under new voluntary rules that brought "the best improvement in ten years," according to Hugh C. Sheridan, chairman of the special committee that formulated the regulations.

A tour of the area by Mr. Sheridan and Lloyd B. Reid, traffic commissioner, disclosed only half a dozen violations by tractor-trailers and no tie-ups in the city's densest traffic area.

Customary snarls at cross-sections along Seventh and Eighth Avenues from Thirty-ninth to Thirty-fifth Streets were missing during the one-hour tour from 3 to 4 P. M.

Both Mr. Sheridan and Commissioner Reid said that trucks were moving in and out of the area with greater rapidity. There were almost no trucks circling back and forth through one-way streets to find parking space while other parked vehicles stood by in idleness. Pleased by the lack of tie-ups at the avenue crossings, Mr. Reid declared that the new plan was "off to a very good start."

If the "staggered-hour" regulations continue to work, no further rules may be necessary, he remarked after the tour. He emphasized that the plan did not mean to do away with curb parking by trucks. He characterized this as impossible because of the nature of the garment business where almost all merchandise "rolls twice" —once in and then out again.

Under the new plan tractor-trailers are to leave the area extending to the east side of Ninth Avenue by noon. The rules call for pick-ups and deliveries by specialized trucking units at varying hours of the day. The waste paper collecting vehicles are scheduled to start at 6 A. M., earliest among the fourteen categories set-up by the committee. These categories,

Continued on Page 22, Column 2

Red China Delegates Will Come to U. N.

By The United Press.

TOKYO, Tuesday, Oct. 24—Chinese Premier Chou En-lai has asked Trygve Lie, United Nations Secretary General, to make arrangements for a Peiping delegation to attend Security Council talks on Formosa, a Peiping radio broadcast said today.

General Chou, who is also Foreign Minister, asked Mr. Lie to facilitate the delegation's entry into the United States, the broadcast said. He suggested that entry arrangements be made at Prague, Czechoslovakia, to which the Peiping group will go.

This was a complete about-face for General Chou. Last Wednesday the Peiping radio said that the Premier had rejected the Security Council's invitation to take part in the discussion of Formosa Nov. 15.

WASHINGTON, Oct. 23 (UP)—A State Department spokesman said he thought it was probable that the delegation would be admitted to this country despite the new Internal Security Act, which bars Communists and other totalitarians.

Al Jolson Dies in San Francisco After Tour of Korea

Continued From Page 1

was not feeling well and lay down to rest. He felt no better after a short rest, they added, and asked for a doctor. They called Dr. Walter Beckh, the hotel physician.

Was Popular Everywhere

Al Jolson was one of the most attractive figures the theatre has given recently to the country. Essentially a minstrel, he was everywhere popular. Such was his ability and reputation that he could—and occasionally did—dismiss his show's supporting company and then carry on all by himself for hours. It was he who created the genre of the "Mammy" song of some years back. Although there was a legion of imitators, none reached him. Finally, he is credited with having, single-handed, saved the movies. Without "The Jazz Singer" to lead them, there would have been no talking pictures.

Mr. Jolson's real name was Asa Yoelson and he was born in Washington, D. C., on May 26, 1886. His father was a Jewish cantor who hoped that the son would follow his profession. The boy lacked enthusiasm, however, and ran away. Shipped home from New York, he stayed still for a short time and disappeared again. The Spanish-American War regiment to which he attached himself as mascot gave him an apple and sent him back to Washington. Trip No. 3 was with Al Reeves' burlesque troupe, but that ended like all the others—back home.

During this semi-roving boyhood young Al made his first stage appearance as a member of the mob in Zangwill's "Children of the Ghetto." He also sang for a time in a Washington cafe. He also joined his brother and a friend and went into vaudeville in the team of Jolson, Palmer and Jolson. The troupe arrived in San Francisco at about the same time as the earthquake—a fact that had no great significance to Mr. Jolson. A little later the singer put on burnt cork for the first time, becoming the black-face comedian of later fame. The cork, for the records, was first used in Brooklyn.

Minstrel at $75 a Week

In November, 1909, Mr. Jolson hired himself out to Dockstader's Minstrels at the weekly wage of $75. Two years later J. J. Shubert heard him sing with the minstrels and hired him for the Winter Garden shows. That theatre had just been built and the Shuberts were looking for talent. They found it in Erastus Sparkler of "La Belle Paree"; Claude of "Vera Violetta"; Gus of "The Whirl of Society"; Gus of "The Honeymoon Express"; Gus of "Dancing Around"; Gus Jackson of "Robinson Crusoe Jr.," and Sinbad of "Sinbad." At the Winter Garden he sang "Mammy" for the first time and so set the whole nation howling for the Southland. And it was at the same theatre, some years later, that "The Jazz Singer" turned the tide of amusement.

Along came 1921, and Mr. Jolson—by that time recognized as America's greatest single entertainer—had a theatre named for him. He played "Bombo" there—it was up on Fifty-ninth Street—for a season and then toured with the show for the next two. Nineteen Twenty-five found Gus back at the Winter Garden in the show called "Big Boy."

The movies had been after him in the old silent days, of course, but with the Winter Garden so much nearer than Hollywood, he was reluctant to attempt a new medium. He had tried it briefly once before under the direction of D. W. Griffith and the samples were so unfortunate that he confessed himself "unnerved" and broke his contract.

Appears in "The Jazz Singer"

But in 1927 the advent of sound films put a different face, or voice, on the matter. The first and electric result was "The Jazz Singer," in which, singing his way through a story that followed that of his own life, he was an instant success. Legend has it that the film grossed the record sum of $5,000,000. Certainly, its American success scarcely overshadowed its triumph in England, France and Germany.

A new epoch in the Jolson career was now launched and he pursued it melodiously and with high profits the next year in "The Singing Fool." It was in this show that he first sang "Sonny Boy," which was to resound through the land even more insistently than in earlier days had "April Showers" or "Avalon." With its sale of a million phonograph records, it even challenged "Mammy." That meant immortality, as Tin Pan Alley knows the word.

Other films—and all of them, of course, found him singing—followed at regular intervals until, in 1931, he turned once more toward the legitimate stage. Save for a concert tour and a few appearances in "Artists and Models" at the Winter Garden in 1926, he had not met an audience face to face since "Big Boy." It was "Wonder Bar," in March, 1931, which brought him back, this time to the Bayes Theatre. Though he discarded burnt cork for the first time in his career, he was once more the Winter Garden's hero, playing a one-man show, recalling to audiences the familiar Jolson tricks of old—the dynamic gestures, the emotional "delivery," the intimate conversational style.

Toured in "Wonder Bar"

When "Wonder Bar" closed here after a three months' run curtailed by illness, he toured across the country in it. He was not expected again to be lured by the grind of regular stage appearances, for which he developed an increasing reluctance. More films—"The New Yorker," "Hallelujah, I'm a Bum" and "Wonder Bar" were some of them—comprised his professional life, together with radio programs. Horse racing was his greatest outside enthusiasm, nor was this the hobby of an amateur. He had his own stable.

Wherever he was he could generally be found in the news. Nervous and alert, he was also pugnacious, and at least one of his fistic encounters reached headlines everywhere in the country. Considering that his wife's feelings had been injured by a scenario written by Walter Winchell, the columnist, he knocked him down in full sight of thousands in the Hollywood Bowl. There was talk of a damage suit for $500,000. Mr. Jolson, proud of his prowess, grinned and enjoyed the whole affair.

He was married four times, all the unions ending in divorce. His first two wives were Henrietta Keller and Alma Osborne Carlton, who was known on the stage as Ethel Delmar. The third, Ruby Keeler, he married in Port Chester, N. Y., in September, 1928, after a Broadway courtship.

His fourth wife was Erle Galbraith, a 22-year-old film extra from the South, whom he married on March 24, 1945, after an elopement to Quartzsite, Ariz. He had met her a year before when he was touring a Hot Springs (Ark.) hospital where she was an X-ray technician.

Former Wife Also in Show

The dancer had a part, however, in "Hold Onto Your Hats," the musical show in which Mr. Jolson returned to Broadway in September. 1940. She appeared in the show while it was on the road earlier in the year, but left in Chicago before the Broadway opening. On Oct. 29, 1941, Miss Keeler was married to John Lowe, a California broker. She and Mr. Jolson had adopted Al Jolson Jr. as an infant in 1935.

Mr. Jolson quit "Hold Onto Your Hats" after a successful Broadway run in February, 1941, because of ill health. He had suffered attacks of grippe and pneumonia. In August of that year he reopened 'Hold Onto Your Hats" in Atlantic City, and continued on the road until November, when the show closed after the death of his manager, Bobby Crawford.

Then came Pearl Harbor, and Mr. Jolson immediately volunteered for war service. He had toured every war front, singing the old songs, "Mammy" and "Sonny Boy," which he found to be favorities with the troops, from Alaska to the South-

Al Jolson in his starring role in *Mammy.*

west Pacific, and from England North Africa, India and Brazil. I appeared under the banner of t USO, but went out of his way al to give independent shows at a post that had an audience of tv or more, paying his own expense He was in Sicily soon after t first invasion barges, and left the to return home by clipper at t end of September. He was d scribed as looking fit but tir on his arrival here.

His tours were officially reco nized as having been morale buil ers of great value. Mr. Jolson wo a uniform resembling a private' although he had refused a commi sion and was not in the service.

Soon after returning from ente taining soldiers on three fronts October, 1943, he became ill wi a combination attack of pneum nia and malaria.

Mr. Jolson joined Columbia as producer in February, 1944. H first assignment, in March of th year, was as supervisor of the ne version of the late George Mank Watters' play "Burlesque," sta ring Rita Hayworth. He al played himself in the mov "Rhapsody in Blue," the story George Gershwin's life. He w supposed to have his voice dubbe in in the song of the leading role a screen unknown to play his part I wrence Hazard's screenplay his life, "The Jolson Story," pr duced by Sidney Skolsky.

"The Jolson Story" proved to one of the top money-makin movies in Hollywood history. T combination of young Larry Park playing the title role, and Jolson voice dubbed in singing the son which made him famous combin to make the picture an immedia box office success. It is estimat that the picture grossed more th $13,000,000 since its release in 194

Al Jolson in *The Singing Fool*.

"All the News That's Fit to Print"

The New York Times.

LATE CITY EDITION

Weather: Partly sunny, cold today clear tonight. Fair, cold tomorrow. Temp. range: today 33-25; Monday 38-30. Full U.S. report on Page 77.

VOL. CXVIII ... No. 40,554 — NEW YORK, TUESDAY, FEBRUARY 4, 1969 — 10 CENTS

Boris Karloff Dead; Horror-Movie Star

Camera Press-Pix

Boris Karloff

Special to The New York Times

LONDON, Feb. 3 — Boris Karloff, who chilled millions in film and stage horror roles, died yesterday in Midhurst, Sussex, of a respiratory disease. He was 81 years old and lived in Bramshott, East Hampshire.

In addition to his wife, the former Evelyn Helmore, he leaves a daughter, Sara Jane.

Role Changed His Life

By ALDEN WHITMAN

Without uttering a single intelligible word, a gentle British-born actor achieved virtually

Continued on Page 36, Column 1

PRESIDENT MOVES TO RESTRICT ROLE OF POVERTY BOARD

Meets With Urban Council on Taking Some of Major Functions From O.E.O.

ACTION DUE NEXT WEEK

Head Start May Be First to Go—Nixon Asks Aides to Review Legislation Plan

By ROBERT B. SEMPLE Jr.

Special to The New York Times

WASHINGTON, Feb. 3—The Nixon Administration moved forward today with its plans to strip the Office of Economic Opportunity of some of its major functions and transfer them to other agencies.

Informed sources disclosed that although no "final" decisions had been taken on the antipoverty agency's future there would be an "interim" announcement sometime next week stating that at least one of the agency's major programs — presumably Head Start — was to be transferred to another department of the Government.

Reflecting his concern for an early resolution of the status of the antipoverty program, President Nixon met for most of this morning with his Urban Affairs Council.

Few Details Released

The White House released almost no details about the session, which reportedly focused on the fate of the poverty agency and the future alignment of the Administration's own efforts in the antipoverty field.

"The antipoverty program is our Middle East," one council member commented afterward, suggesting that the subject was receiving the same priority in the domestic field that the President and his advisers had placed on the Arab-Israeli dispute in the foreign field.

In a related action on the domestic front, the White House disclosed that Mr. Nixon had issued 15 more directives to Cabinet officers, agency heads and special advisers asking them to review and comment upon proposals for legislative action made by the President during the campaign and by his special teams during the transition period.

Wide Range Under Study

The 15 directives, described briefly in a White House statement released by Ronald L. Ziegler, press secretary, brought to 29 the number of orders dispatched by Mr. Nixon to his principal Government officials.

They ask for review and comment on proposals ranging from elaborate changes in the welfare system to studies of the "rising costs" of Medicare to suggestions for agricultural reform.

Among the directives was one aimed at the Secretary of Health, Education and Welfare, Robert H. Finch, and the Department of Labor asking for "studies into the need for substantive changes in O.E.O. programs and approaches."

But on the basis of information available today it was clear that such studies were already well under way both in these agencies and in the Urban Affairs Council.

Not only did the council meet on the question of the antipoverty program this morning, but a special subcommittee of the council has already met twice to consider changes in the antipoverty effort.

The basis of all these deliberations—and the best available guide to the probable shape of the Administration's final disposition of the anti-

Continued on Page 22, Column 1

NEWS INDEX

OIL SLICK CENTER: Th... was taken from the pla...

A Request by ... Drilling Off S...

Secretary Inspects Slick

By United Press International

SANTA BARBARA, Calif., Feb. 3 — Secretary of the Interior Walter J. Hickel said today that all oil companies concerned had complied with his request that they voluntarily suspend drilling in the Santa Barbara Channel because of a huge oil slick menacing some of Southern California's finest beaches.

Mr. Hickel asked for the voluntary suspension of drilling until the pollution crisis had been studied. He made the request after a two-hour aerial survey today of the slick of reddish-brown crude oil that had spread across the blue waters of the Pacific along the coast.

In announcing that the six oil companies drilling in the area had agreed to his request, Mr. Hickel said:

"This procedure will afford a breathing spell until it can be determined whether corrective measures are necessary."

After surveying the slick from the air, Mr. Hickel said that "the pollution is much more severe than I had anticipated."

But Mr. Hickel, confronted with his first major problem since taking office with the Nixon Administration, did not order a halt to drilling in the channel. He has the power to

Continued on Page 78, Column 1

... Senator Muskie and ... supporters of stiffer antip... tion legislation were enc... aged today that the coincide... appearance of the huge ... slick off the California co... would focus attention on th... issue and improve prospects fo... Congressional action.

The toughest provisions of the legislation on which the Muskie subcommittee opened hearings today would set up

Continued on Page 78, Column 2

Allen Gets U.S. Schools Post; Hannah Is Chosen for Aid Job

Nixon Hails New Yorker

By RICHARD L. MADDEN

Special to The New York Times

WASHINGTON, Feb. 3 — President Nixon today picked Dr. James E. Allen Jr., New York State Education Commissioner for 13 years, as the nation's top education official.

Dr. Allen will take over two previously separate jobs—that of United States Commissioner of Education and that of Assistant Secretary for Education in the Department of Health, Education and Welfare. He will assume the posts "as soon as he can fulfill his obligations in New York State," or by May 1, the President said in a statement.

The 57-year-old Dr. Allen, who was introduced to newsmen in the Fish Room of the White House by Robert H. Finch, the Secretary of Health, Education and Welfare, promptly pledged to continue the sometimes controversial policies he pursued in New York.

He said he believed strongly in desegregation of schools and was "firmly committed" to community involvement in the schools, although he did not think that decentralization was the only answer to urban school problems.

"I favor busing students if it means getting students to a

Continued on Page 20, Column 1

Development Shift Seen

By FELIX BELAIR Jr.

Special to The New York Times

WASHINGTON, Feb. 3—President Nixon has offered Dr. John A. Hannah, president of Michigan State University, the post of administrator of the Agency for International Development.

The choice was interpreted by development experts as signaling a revision of the foreign aid program.

These experts foresee increased emphasis on technical assistance and less emphasis on capital outlays through government-to-government loans for large-scale projects such as factories, transportation systems and hydroelectric sources.

At Michigan State in East Lansing, Dr. Hannah said that he did not plan to retire from the university soon and that he would discuss the possibility of a shared-time arrangement when he meets with the university's trustees at 6 P.M. tomorrow.

He has been president of the university since 1941. In the past he received leaves of absence from the university when he accepted Federal assignments, and he commuted between East Lansing and Washington.

Dr. Hannah, 66 years old,

Continued on Page 20, Column 4

Continued on Page 58, Column 2

SHANKER IS GIVEN 15-DAY SENTENCE IN SCHOOL STRIKE

U.F.T. Is Fined $220,000—Degnan Gets 3 Days—All Sides in Dispute Scored

By ROBERT E. TOMASSON

The United Federation of Teachers was fined $220,000 yesterday and its president, Albert Shanker, was sentenced to 15 days in jail after being found guilty of criminal contempt of court in the defiance of court orders to end three ...wide school strikes last fall.

... imposing a fine far below ... maximum of $620,000, and ... jail sentence only half the ... sible length, State Supreme ... Justice Francis J. Blou... said he had found "ex... provocation" by repre... ...es of the Board of Edu... and others "in official ...

... night of a heart attack. He would have been 71 Wednesday.

Mr. McGill, who won the 1959 Pulitzer Prize for editorial writing, suffered the attack about 10 P.M. as he was leaving a private dinner party and early birthday celebration in his honor at the home of John B. Lawhorn. He was dead on arrival at Holy Family Hos-

Continued on Page 26, Column 1

U.S. Finds Nasser's Plan Positive and Encouraging

But Israeli Sources in Washington Call Egyptian Leader's Statements 'Cobweb of Half-Truths and Inconsistencies'

By JUAN de ONIS

Special to The New York Times

WASHINGTON, Feb. 3 — United States officials said today that they considered President Gamal Abdel Nasser's latest proposals for a Middle East settlement positive and encouraging, and hoped that Israel would react the same way.

Israeli diplomatic sources, however, dismissed the Egyptian leader's statements in an interview with Newsweek magazine as a "cobweb of half-truths and inconsistencies" that opened no new avenues to peace negotiations.

Mr. Nasser's proposals, contingent upon Israeli withdrawal from occupied Arab areas, included the offer of a declaration of nonbelligerence, the recognition of the right of each country to live in peace, the territorial integrity of all Middle Eastern countries and freedom of navigation on international waterways.

The contrasting reactions to the Egyptian proposals came as the United States officials drafted a reply that is expected to be favorable to the suggestion by President de Gaulle that four permanent members of the Security Council — the United States, the Soviet Union, Britain and France — meet through their United Nations representatives on new initiatives toward a Middle East settlement.

United States officials said that the reply would be delivered soon — presumably this week.

The American readiness to go along with the French initiative,

Continued on Page 13, Column 4

Latin Economy Advances In Alliance for Progress

Special to The New York Times

WASHINGTON, Feb. 3—Latin-American countries participating in the Alliance for Progress enjoyed a general upturn in economic growth last year, compared with the relative doldrums in the region's development since 1966.

According to the Inter-American Committee of the Alliance for Progress, the growth in the region's gross national product was 5.5 per cent last year, compared with an average of 4.3 per cent for the two previous years.

The gain was the result of increased exports, higher levels of domestic savings leading to larger public investments, and larger foreign transfers of public and private capital, the committee's survey said.

Population Up 6%

Exports, which reached ...11.4-billion in 1968, were 2.8 ...r cent higher than in 1966. ... the intervening year, Latin ...erica's population rose by ... than 6 per cent.

... a result of this rapid ...ation growth, the per ...rise in the gross na... ...duct reached only 2.5 ... last year. But this ... annual target of ... for Progress after ...tive years in which ...owth was only 1.4

MORE CONCESSIONS ARE HINTED BY KY

He Proposes Private Talks and Indicates New Moves if They Prove Fruitful

By PAUL HOFMANN

Special to The New York Times

PARIS, Feb. 3 — Vice President Nguyen Cao Ky said today that the South Vietnamese regime was willing to "hold private talks now" with representatives of the North Vietnamese Government.

Mr. Ky, the political coordinator of South Vietnam's delegation at the peace talks here, affirmed that Saigon had already made many concessions to the other side, and added:

"I am ready to make more concessions, in any field, if we are sure to reach some result."

Willingness Affirmed

The Vice President spoke to reporters in an improvised news conference in the lobby of his residence in suburban Neuilly this afternoon after an hour-long conference with Ambassador Henry Cabot Lodge, the head of the United States delegation. Mr. Ky also had a short talk with Senator John G. Tower. The Texas Republican, a member of the Senate Armed Services Committee, who stopped here on his way home from a visit to West Germany.

While stressing that he was in accord with President Nguyen Van Thieu and the Saigon Government, the Vice President, who is of North Vietnamese stock, sounded as if he personally wanted to get involved in confidential contacts with the Hanoi Government.

"I am willing to talk with any of their people who want

Continued on Page 9, Column 1

...cross Sound ... Court Ruling

... bridge ... Sound be... ...Rye and Oyster Bay ...as ruled unconstitutional yesterday.

Justice Samuel M. Gold of the State Supreme Court said a 1967 state law authorizing construction of the six-mile bridge-causeway by the Metropolitan Transportation Authority was illegal because the M.T.A. was not authorized to build bridges or highways under the 1965 act that created the agency.

Its jurisdiction covers trains, planes, buses and boats, but not bridges and highways, the court ruled. A spokesman for the M.T.A. said there would be an "automatic appeal" of the decision to the Court of Appeals. Sources on both sides of the issue predicted that the case eventually might reach the United States Supreme Court.

Proponents of the bridge project could seek new legislation in Albany that would specifically empower the M.T.A. to build bridges.

Civic leaders of Rye, a Westchester County community about 30 miles north of New York City, and Oyster Bay, 35

Continued on Page 31, Column 5

U.S. IS DEFERRING ACTION FOR TALKS ON MISSILE CURBS

Decides to Await 4-Power Mideast Parley and Senate Vote on Nuclear Treaty

TEST OF CLIMATE IS AIM

Nixon Wants Signs Moscow and American Public Are Ready for Agreement

By PETER GROSE

Special to The New York Times

WASHINGTON, Feb. 3—The Nixon Administration is deferring its decision about starting missile disarmament talks with the Soviet Union until the results are in on two forthcoming tests of the domestic and international political climate.

The President plans to ask this week for Senate approval of the treaty to ban the spread of nuclear weapons. The extent of opposition will be regarded by some Presidential advisers as a measure of domestic attitudes toward the Russians. Senate consideration of the treaty was postponed last year amid bitter feelings provoked by the Soviet-led invasion of Czechoslovakia.

Key advisers hope that a Soviet interest in reducing world tensions will become apparent during four-power meetings at the United Nations to discuss a Middle East settlement.

Reply to Be Sent Soon

The National Security Council decided Saturday to accept a French proposal for such meetings. State Department officials said the formal reply to President de Gaulle would probably be sent this week.

Though missile talks and the Middle East need not be directly related in their substance, the Administration is understood to believe that the mood created by the Mideast discussions could be significant in determining whether missile talks would be fruitful.

Since neither of these steps could be taken for some weeks yet — the Senate is not likely to take up the nuclear treaty until early in March — an early decision to open the missile talks is not considered likely.

Preliminary Talks Urged

Some advisers are urging, however, that at least preliminary technical talks with the Russians not be delayed into the summer, as Defense Secretary Melvin R. Laird hinted last month.

The Johnson Administration set up the talks last summer aimed at limiting and eventually reducing both superpowers'

Continued on Page 10, Column 1

Boris Karloff Dead; Horror-Movie Star

Camera Press-Pix
Boris Karloff

Special to The New York Times

LONDON, Feb. 3 — Boris Karloff, who chilled millions in film and stage horror roles, died yesterday in Midhurst, Sussex, of a respiratory disease. He was 81 years old and lived in Bramshott, East Hampshire.

In addition to his wife, the former Evelyn Helmore, he leaves a daughter, Sara Jane.

Role Changed His Life

By ALDEN WHITMAN

Without uttering a single intelligible word, a gentle British-born actor achieved virtually

Continued on Page 36, Column 1

Boris Karloff, Master Horror-Film Actor, Dies

Continued From Page 1, Col. 8

nstant motion-picture stardom, creating at the same time a genre from which he never escaped. The actor was Boris Karloff; the role was The Monster in "Frankenstein," a Universal film of 1931, and the genre was that of the horror movie.

"'Frankenstein' transformed not only my life but also the film industry," Mr. Karloff said later in his well-tailored voice. 'It grossed something like $12-million on a $250,000 investment and started a cycle of so-called boy-meets-ghoul horror films."

Mr. Karloff appeared in many of these, including several extensions of his original triumph—"Bride of Frankenstein," "Son of Frankenstein," 'House of Frankenstein" and 'Frankenstein 1970," the last issued in 1958. In other memorable films he was the Chinese detective, James Lee Wong, and the clever Dr. Fu Manchu.

On the strength of his sensitive film portrayals—that Mr. Karloff was an elegant actor was sometimes overlooked—he went on to a triumph on Broadway as Jonathan Brewster, the zesty international murderer, in Joseph Kesselring's "Arsenic and Old Lace" and as Mr. Darling and Captain Hook in James M. Barrie's "Peter Pan."

But it was as a movie horror man that Mr. Karloff attained lasting celebrity. He looted graves in "The Body Snatcher," wielded the ax as the leering executioner in "Tower of London," frightened people to death in "The Walking Dead," cheated death in "The Man They Could Not Hang," invoked the curse of the pharoahs in "The Mummy," was the sadistic prison warder in "Bedlam" and corrupted Jackie Cooper as a narcotics peddler in "Young Donovan's Kid."

Boris Karloff with Elsa Lanchester in *The Bride of Frankenstein.*

'Nothing to Write About'

Chance opened Mr. Karloff's path to stardom. He was 42 years old and unrenowned ("I quit writing home—for I had nothing to write about") when he got his break one lunchtime in the Universal studios' commissary.

Recalling the incident 30 years afterward, Mr. Karloff said in his low whispery voice: "Someone tapped me on the shoulder and said, 'Mr. Whale would like to see you at his table.' Jimmy Whale was the most important director on the lot. 'We're getting ready to shoot the Mary [Wollstonecraft] Shelley classic, 'Frankenstein,' and I'd like you to test—for the part of the Monster,' Whale said.

"It was a bit shattering, but I felt that any part was better than no part at all. The studio's head make-up man, Jack Pierce, spent evenings experimenting with me. Slowly, under his skillful touch, The Monster's double-domed forehead, sloping brow, flattened Neanderthal eyelids and surgical scars materialized. A week later I was ready for the test. I readily passed as a monster."

As The Monster, the soulless creation of Frankenstein from parts of cadavers, Mr. Karloff wore make-up that took four hours to apply and that was excruciating to work in. Even so, he was initially so subordinate to the stars of the film, Colin Clive and Mae Clarke, that he was not invited to the West Coast premiere, on Dec. 6, 1931.

Nor when the film opened at the Mayfair in New York was Mr. Karloff especially remarked upon. For example, Mordaunt Hall's comment in The Times was spare. "Boris Karloff undertakes the Frankenstein creation," he wrote, "and his make-up can be said to suit anybody's demands."

The movie's producers believed at the time that their melodrama might be overly horrifying for young eyes, but it turned out that teen-agers and even children found "Frankenstein" absorbing and Mr. Karloff fascinating. He became a folk hero to young and old in the tradition of Lon Chaney, the repellent Quasimodo in "The Hunchback of Notre Dame." And he was responsible in part for the rise of two other horror actors—Bela Lugosi and Peter Lorre, with both of whom Mr. Karloff played in 1941 in an indifferent picture called "You'll Find Out."

The Monster became Mr. Karloff's shadow. Not only did fans send him voodoo dolls, but he was also made the butt of a good deal of Hollywood gallows humor. For years Groucho Marx's standard greeting was, "How much do you charge to haunt a house?" On a more serious professional level, J. B. Priestly almost rejected him for the part of the kindly Professor Linden in the 1948 production of "The Linden Tree."

"Good God, not Karloff!" Mr. Priestley told Maurice Evans, the producer. "Put his name up on the marquee and people will think my play is about an ax murder."

Only Mr. Karloff's solemn assurance that he possessed inner tender sentiments persuaded the playwright to withdraw his objections.

'A Tragic Part'

Although The Monster typecast the actor (it also made him wealthy), he insisted that he liked the role. "Favorite role?" he said in reply to an interviewer. "Frankenstein's Monster, I guess. He had no speech and hardly any intelligence, yet you had to convey a tragic part."

Mr. Karloff became an actor for want of a vocation as

(continued)

a diplomat. Named William Henry Pratt at his birth in London Nov. 23, 1887, he was the youngest of eight sons of Edward Pratt, a member of the British Indian Civil Service, and Eliza Sara Millard Pratt. His parents died when he was a child and he was reared in serene circumstances by a stepsister and his elder brothers, who wanted him to enter the diplomatic service.

He began to veer from that objective when he was 9 and acted The Demon King in "Cinderella" in a school play. He attended King's College, London, but so unnotably that the family exported him to Canada in 1909. There he worked briefly as a farmhand and as a ditch-digger in Vancouver, British Columbia.

"Then one day in an old copy of 'Billboard,'" he recounted, "I came across the advertisement of a theatrical agent in nearby Seattle. His name was Kelly. I went to him and shamelessly told him I'd been in all the plays I'd ever seen. Two months later, while chopping trees, I received a brief note, 'Join Jean Russell Stock Company in Kamloops, B.C. — Kelly.' I left my ax sticking in a tree."

Invented Name

On the journey to Kamloops, the actor invented his stage name, taking the "Karloff" from a maternal relative and the "Boris" from thin air. He made his debut in Ferenc Molnar's "The Devil" and from 1910 to 1916 he learned the acting profession in a series of stock companies that played western Canada and the United States.

"In some towns we stayed a week; in others we settled down for a run," he said. "It was in Minot, N. D., that we stayed 53 weeks and I played 106 parts. I was a quick study and the quickest study got the longest parts."

In 1917 Mr. Karloff found himself in Los Angeles and without funds, a state to which he had become inured as a stock player. He got a job piling sacks of flour in a storeroom. "Then I wandered into the movies, via a $5-a-day extra role as a swarthy Mexican soldier in a Doug Fairbanks Sr. film, 'His Majesty, The American,'" Mr. Karloff recalled.

Between extra roles the actor drove a truck until his fortunes improved and he received some bit parts, mostly those of sweet and kindly characters. But what brought him to Mr. Whale's notice was his portrayal of Galloway, the convict-killer, in "The Criminal Code."

"Frankenstein" was Hollywood's first monster film of any significance, and it was produced with some trepidation lest it might not pass the Hays Office, the censorship agency of the time. Two endings were filmed, one faithful to the famous 19th-century gothic novel, in which Frankenstein died, and another, contrived, in which he lived. The second ending was ultimately used in order to elicit sympathy for the young scientist.

In both endings, however, The Monster was consumed in a crackling windmill fire that the villagers set. The awful mistake became quickly evident as Depression audiences flocked to see the film and demanded more of The Monster.

Hollywood's best brains proved equal to the contretemps. Drumbeaters for the sequel, "Bride of Frankenstein," explained that The Monster had not actually been burned to death, but had instead fallen through the flaming floor into the cool waters of the mill-pond below.

"The watery opening scene was filmed with me wearing a rubber suit under my costume to ward off the chill," Mr. Karloff recalled. "But air got into the suit. When I was launched into the pond, my legs flew up in the air and I floated there like some sort of an obscene water lily while I, and everyone else, hooted with laughter. They finally fished me out with a boat hook and deflated me."

Stage Debut in 1941

After 10 years of Hollywood fun and games, Mr. Karloff was pleased to be able to make his New York stage debut at the Fulton Theater on Jan. 10, 1941, in "Arsenic and Old Lace." The Russel Crouse-Howard Lindsay production ran for 1,444 performances.

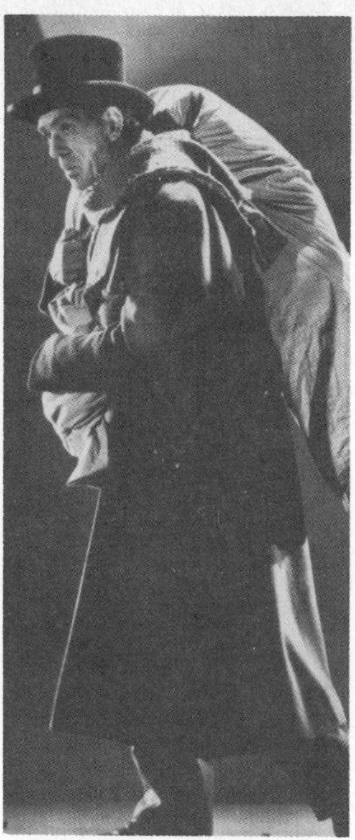

Boris Karloff starred in *The Bodysnatcher.*

Appearing with Josephine Hull and Jean Adair, as the two sweet and kindly Brewster sisters of Brooklyn who poisoned lonely old men, Mr. Karloff was their homicidal brother, whose victims' remains were scattered around the world. "As the evil one, Mr. Karloff moves quietly through the plot and poisons without resorting to trickeries," Brooks Atkinson of The Times wrote in his notice of the comedy.

Mr. Karloff became almost as much attached to his stage role as to his film one, for he played Jonathan Brewster on the road for years, venturing as far afield as Alaska. As late as 1961 he was in a television revival of the play with Dorothy Stickney.

After "Arsenic and Old Lace" Mr. Karloff was a hit with Jean Arthur in "Peter Pan." As Captain Hook, he was a favorite with children in the audience.

"After the show I'd corral as many [children] as my dressing room would hold and ask 'Would you like to try on my hook?' Even little blond angels would reply, 'Yes, sir,'" he said.

Mr. Karloff's professional life was enormously busy. He was in a dozen legitimate plays and 130 films. His last movie was "Targets," released here last year, when he was 80. In it he played a character similar to himself, a genteel, aged monarch of Hollywood shockers and a late-late show idol who wants to call it quits.

Quiet Private Life

In his inconspicuous private life, the actor was an affable, urbane 6-footer with a wry sense of humor. In late life his hair was gray, as were his bushy eyebrows and his colonial mustache. He bore himself with impeccable dignity and he enjoyed watching cricket, rugby football and field hockey, sports in which he had indulged as a younger man.

Mr. Karloff's first wife was Dorothy Stine, from whom he was divorced in 1946 after 17 years of marriage. His second wife was Evelyn Hope Helmore, whom he married in 1946.

In his later years the actor lived in and near London. His films were still billed as horror movies, although he objected to the adjective.

"I never liked the word horror," he explained. "It should have been terror. They needed a word [in 1931] to describe what we were filming, but they picked the wrong one.

"Horror means something revolting, but I don't think there's been anything revolting in the parts I've played.

"I believe in fear and excitement, in shock that emerges from the story, in terror — not horror."

Karloff with Peter Lorre and Vincent Price in *The Raven.*

"All the News That's Fit to Print"

The New York Times.

LATE CITY EDITION

Clearing today after early snow; fair, cold tonight and tomorrow. Temp. Range: 32—25; yesterday: 34—19

VOL. CXV. No. 39,456. NEW YORK, WEDNESDAY, FEBRUARY 2, 1966. TEN CENTS

SECURITY COUNCIL WEIGHS VIETNAM; DEFERS VOTE ON U.S. AGENDA ITEM; HANOI BARS ANY U.N. INTERVENTION

CATHOLIC CHURCH BIDS LEGISLATURE DELAY ON DIVORCE

Senator Who Led Drafting Panel Views Action as 'Declaration of War'

REFORM FEARED DEAD

Wilson Attack on Letter to All Members Brings Hot Reply From Leaders

By SYDNEY H. SCHANBERG

Special to The New York Times

ALBANY, Feb. 1—The Roman Catholic Church has sent a letter to all state legislators calling on them not to take any immediate "affirmative action" on the bill to reform the state's divorce law.

Senator Jerome L. Wilson, head of the joint legislative committee that drafted the bill, viewed the letter as "seemingly a declaration of war . . . opposition to meaningful divorce reform." It puts the bill "in deep trouble," the Manhattan Democrat declared.

The leaders of the Legislature took a less alarmist view and told Mr. Wilson there was no need for him to get excited. Nevertheless, almost everyone in the Capitol agreed that the move by the Catholics had not helped the bill.

Letter From State Group

The letter, dated yesterday, came from Charles J. Tobin Jr., secretary of the New York State Catholic Welfare Committee, the spokesman for the church in the state.

The Catholic Church does not recognize divorce and in the past has successfully opposed any liberalization of the state's 179-year-old divorce law, which provides only one ground for divorce—adultery.

The letter was actually a missive to the chairmen of the committees handling the bill in both houses—Senator John H. Hughes, head of the Senate Judiciary Committee, and Speaker Anthony J. Travia, who runs the Assembly Rules Committee. However, copies were sent to all the other lawmakers.

While the letter did not register outright opposition to the Wilson bill, it asked the Legislature to "postpone" any action until more "supporting data and explanations" were available.

"We are confident that there are many groups in our state who will be seriously disappointed in and critical of the

Continued on Page 38, Column 3

MOLLEN TESTIFIES IN STATE INQUIRY

Tells of Meeting With 2 Who Figured in Housing Case

By EDITH EVANS ASBURY

The State Investigation Commission heard testimony yesterday that a Brooklyn insurance salesman received $75,000 and insurance contracts after arranging a meeting between the applicant for a housing project and Milton Mollen at Mr. Mollen's home.

Mr. Mollen, chairman of the Housing and Redevelopment Board at the time of the meeting, denied that the meeting had figured in approval of the state-aided project.

Mr. Mollen said he had known the insurance salesman only as a rabbi and did not know he had any personal interest in the project.

The meeting at Mr. Mollen's home at 4618 Avenue H in Brooklyn took place on an evening in January or February of 1963, according to the testimony of Mr. Mollen and the other two participants. They were Reuben Glick, the builder, and Philip Gruberger, the insurance salesman.

It had been arranged, according to all three witnesses, to discuss a charitable event, "Music Under the Stars," to be held in Madison Square Garden in June, at which Mr. Mollen was scheduled to be a guest of honor.

During the discussion, "inadvertently it turned to the subject of housing," according to Mr. Gruberger.

The specific housing was Brightwater Towers, a proposed $16-million, 735-family develop-

Continued on Page 42, Column 2

PRESIDENT URGES WORLD AID DRIVE, BUT TRIMS FUNDS

Request for Foreign Help Is $3.4-Billion—Self-Help Is Key to Poverty Attack

Excerpts from aid message appear on Page 4.

By FELIX BELAIR Jr.

Special to The New York Times

WASHINGTON, Feb. 1—President Johnson told Congress today that the appalling conditions of the underdeveloped half of the world "challenge our security and threaten ..."

New Midwest Storm Moves Into the East

By BERNARD WEINRAUB

A new storm piled up snow and ice across the Midwest yesterday and moved into the East last night, dusting New York City with a wet layer of snow.

Snow flurries began at 11:20 P.M. and the Weather Bureau predicted "moderate amounts"—two to four inches—of snow by this morning. At 2:30 A.M. the snow measured less than an inch.

"It won't be anything like it was Sunday" said one forecaster, taking note of the storm that froze crops in the South, stranded motorists in the Midwest and buried parts of the Atlantic Coast under drifts of up to 30 feet.

Commissioner of Traffic Henry A. Barnes, who had lifted the

Continued on Page 20, Column 2

The New York Times (by Patrick A. Burns)

... ISSUE: Arthur J. Goldberg, U.S. ... far left is Nikolai T. Fedorenko, the ... is seated next to Mr. Goldberg.

JORDAN HOLDS KEY

Russians and French Opposing Move—Ballot Due Today

Excerpts from statements in Security Council, Page 14.

By DREW MIDDLETON

Special to The New York Times

UNITED NATIONS, N.Y., Feb. 1—Jordan held the key tonight to whether the Security Council could debate a draft United States resolution seeking peace in Vietnam.

Jordan's delegate, Waleed M. Sadi, obtained a postponement of the voting until 3 P.M. tomorrow while he seeks instructions from his Government in Amman.

The decision to delay the vote followed a series of sharp exchanges in the Council between Arthur J. Goldberg, the United States representative, and Nikolai T. Fedorenko of the Soviet Union, who bitterly denounced the United States. The Soviet Union and France opposed action on the resolution.

Seven other members of the newly enlarged 15-member Council support the United States proposal to place on the agenda a resolution calling on the Council to arrange a conference that would achieve a durable settlement of the war in Vietnam. The resolution also looks to the restoration of stability in neighboring Laos and Thailand.

Nine Votes Required

A ninth vote, Jordan's, is necessary for a majority in support of placing the item on the agenda. Since the question is procedural, the veto power of the permanent members cannot be exercised. If the issue is placed on the agenda, any action on it will then be subject to veto by the Soviet Union or France.

Supporting the United States are Britain, New Zealand, Argentina, the Netherlands, Nationalist China, Japan and Uruguay. Bulgaria, like the Soviet Union and France, is opposed to the agenda move, and Mali, Nigeria and Uganda are expected to abstain.

Mr. Goldberg, who spoke twice during the long, increasingly sharp debate, said he expected that the United States proposal would win the necessary votes.

The virulence of the Soviet and Bulgarian opposition, the cool rejection by France and the wavering of the African delegations foreshadowed hard passage for the resolution if it gets to the stage of debate in the Council.

The resolution, some diplo-

Continued on Page 15, Column 1

'54 PACT IS CITED BY NORTH VIETNAM

...ement Says That Only ...ties to Geneva Parley ...an Join Negotiations

FAILURE FOR U.S. SEEN BY GEN. GIAP

...oi's Defense Chief Says ...e of Force Is Irrelevant

Excerpts from Giap article will be found on Page 16.

By MAX FRANKEL

Special to The New York Times

WASHINGTON, Feb. 1—North Vietnam's Defense Minister, Gen. Vo Nguyen Giap, has issued an analysis of American war aims that predicts inevitable failure for the United States regardless of the size of its commitment.

Granting American military superiority, General Giap does not forecast a battlefield victory of the kind scored over the French at Dienbienphu in the Indochina War. He expects a long and hard war, but insists that the United States can never triumph because it cannot win over the people of South Vietnam, occupy enough of its territory or create a viable army and government there.

The long analysis by the general, who is also a Deputy Premier of North Vietnam, sug-

Continued on Page 16, Column 6

By TOM WICKER

Special to The New York Times

WASHINGTON, Feb. 1—Republican Congressional strategists believe divisions within the Democratic party and the prospect of an expanding land war in Vietnam may be giving them a winning political issue against President Johnson.

They believe the country may eventually turn against a President whose party does not fully support him and whose war policy may produce long casualty lists without military victory or a negotiated settlement.

To take political advantage of this, the Republican leaders are pulling back from direct criticism of the Johnson policy and are de-emphasizing their former

Continued on Page 11, Column 1

... in Vietnam snarled traffic in Times Square last night at the rush hour.

Thirty-two demonstrators, who made themselves limp, were carried to police vans. They were arrested on charges of disorderly conduct after sitting and lying on the slush-covered streets.

The protest was carried out by at least 1,000 persons who marched into Times Square from the United Nations Plaza. They ringed the Allied Chemical Building and the armed forces recruiting station at 43d Street

The demonstrators, shouting and chanting, arrived in Times Square at 6:20 P.M. and were herded behind police barricades where many had participated in a silent 24-hour vigil against President Johnson's decision to resume bombing North Vietnam.

Others marched in a long line in front of the bookstores

Continued on Page 18, Column 2

... would not include the representatives of either side in Vietnam, unless they, as nonmembers, were specifically invited to participate.

The North Vietnamese statement denounced the United States initiative in calling a Security Council meeting. It declared:

"As on previous occasions, this time the United States is seeking again to use the United Nations to cover up expansion of the war of aggression in Vietnam and to force on the Vietnamese people a settlement of the Vietnam question, according ...

Continued on Page 15, Column 5

NEWS INDEX

Buster Keaton, 70, Dies on Coast; Poker-Faced Comedian of Films

By The Associated Press

HOLLYWOOD, Feb. 1—Buster Keaton, the poker-faced comic whose studies in exquisite frustration amused two generations of movie audiences, died of lung cancer today at his home in suburban Woodland Hills. His age was 70.

Someone once remarked of Buster Keaton that he looked like the kind of man that dogs kick.

A mournful little fellow, sad-faced as a basset, usually wearing a saucer-brimmed porkpie hat, oversized suit and floppy bow tie, Joseph Francis Keaton stood with Charlie Chaplin and Harold Lloyd as one of the three great clowns of the silent screen.

In 30 or more films, mostly two-reelers filled with pratfalls and custard pie slapstick, Buster Keaton established an unforgettable character—the sad and silent loner who persevered stoically against a mechanized world.

Unlike Mr. Chaplin, he was never sentimental and he never resorted to maudlin pathos. He turned a granite face to the wildly comic and nightmarish cries that befell him—and he always prevailed over impending doom.

Buster Keaton

His strength was his ability to survive. He displayed that perseverance not only in his comic characterizations but also in his private activities.

For his life was marked by periods of triumph and frustration—wealth, a descent into

Continued on Page 32, Column 3

BUSTER KEATON, FILM CLOWN, DIES

Continued From Page 1, Col. 4

poverty and alcoholism, and then, in his twilight years, a return to riches, recognition and contentment.

His period of greatest productivity was in the early and mid-1920's. In those light-tax days, Buster's salary soared to $3,500 a week, and he built a $300,000 house in Beverly Hills.

A great pantomimist, the equal of Mr. Chaplin in comic inventiveness, he was held even superior to "the little tramp" in acrobatic grace. Mr. Keaton never used a double. His ability to take a violent fall without breaking a bone was the marvel of the day.

Most of Mr. Keaton's films were made without a script. "Two or three writers and I would start with an idea and then we'd work out a strong finish and let the middle take care of itself, as it always does," Mr. Keaton recalled in an interview two years ago. "Sometimes, we'd work out a gag in advance; other times, it would work itself out as we went along. In those days we didn't use miniatures or process shots. The way a thing looked on the screen was the way you'd done it."

When the movies began talking, Buster Keaton dropped out of sight. The public wanted voices, and Buster's pantomime technique failed to hold up.

Hard times and marital troubles piled up. After 11 years of marriage (and two sons), he and Natalie Talmadge, sister of the beautiful actresses Norma and Constance, were divorced in 1932. His second marriage, to Mae Scribbens, ended in divorce in 1935.

In 1934, filing for bankruptcy, Buster listed assets of $12,000 and liabilities of $303,832.

Mr. Keaton was down but never quite out. Just when life seemed as hostile as a paranoid's nightmare, things began to look up. His third marriage, to Eleanor Norris, a 21-year-old dancer, in 1940, brought stability. She survives him, as do his two sons.

Video Star in Britain

British television rescued him from obscurity in the early 1950's. It brought him fresh fame, a comfortable income and a new public. He appeared on most major television shows in London and was paid from $1,000 to $2,500 for each performance.

In 1956 Paramount paid him $50,000 for the rights to "The Keaton Story," a film tracing Mr. Keaton's rise from vaudeville to Hollywood stardom, with Donald O'Connor playing the title role.

Mr. Keaton used the money to buy a ranch-type house and an acre and a half of farmland in the San Fernando Valley. He kept busy, making several filmed television shows in Hollywood and appearing in several acting engagements.

But it was his old silent movies that brought in the gold. Mr. Keaton had had his own producing company in the 1920's and he retained ownership of his old films. He had the film quality restored and a sound track of music added. The pantomime remained intact and the old subtitles were kept.

The first reissue was of "The General"—a slapstick classic of a bumbling Civil War spy—in 1962. It played all over Europe. People laughed harder than they did in 1927, when the film first came out.

Mr. Keaton wrote the story and continuity of "The General," directed it, cut it and played the leading role. It was shot in 18 weeks at a cost of $330,000. It contained one of the great chases in movie history: Mr. Keaton's attempt to tame a runaway train during the Civil War.

Mr. Keaton's renaissance reached an artistic peak last October at the Venice Film Festival, when "Film," an arty 22-minute silent he made in New York in 1964, was accorded a five-minute standing ovation. Fighting back tears, Mr. Keaton told a correspondent: "This is the first time I've been invited to a film festival, but I hope it won't be the last."

Critics differed on "Film," Samuel Beckett's first screenplay, a story of an old, obsessed man who shuts himself up in a room to thwart fate.

But there was no dissension over the wonderfully comic image Mr. Keaton gave the world in his old two-reelers such as: "The Cameraman," "Steamboat Bill Jr.," "The Passionate Plumber," "Sherlock Jr." and in a full-length classic, "The Navigator."

"The Navigator" contained the unforgettable scene of Mr. Keaton trying to shuffle stuck-together cards. And then there was the memorable sequence when he launches a ship: he stood at attention on deck, resplendent in admiral's uniform, riding it down the ways, never blinking or wavering as it sank slowly out of sight.

Early in his career Buster Keating learned that a stoic countenance drew laughs.

He was born to the stage. His parents, Joseph and Myron Keaton, were appearing in a tent show with Harry Houdini, the magician, when the future comedian arrived on October 4, 1895, while the show was playing Piqua, Kan. It was Houdini who coined the nickname.

"What a buster!" Houdini is supposed to have exclaimed when the six-month-old baby fell downstairs.

That was only the first of countless pratfalls. In the family act, which became one of the roughest knockabout low-comedy turns in vaudeville, Buster was tossed around by Pop with murderous abandon while Mom, oblivious to the chaos, essayed a saxophone solo downstage.

It was around that time that Buster perfected his stoic mask while still a child performer. Hit on the face with a broom, he would wait five or six seconds without moving a facial muscle, and then say "Ouch." It always brought down the house.

The Keatons did their last variety turn at the Palace in 1917. They were signed by the Shuberts for "The Passing Show of 1917" but Buster was sidetracked by Roscoe (Fatty) Arbuckle, who talked young Keaton into taking a supporting role in a two-reeler called "The Butcher Boy." In this opus Buster was dumped in molasses, bitten by a dog and hit with an apple pie.

Soon Buster became an expert on the composition of slapstick pies. "First, you had to make it with a double crust on the bottom, so you could get a good hold on it without your fingers going through," he once recalled. "Then you made the filling of the pie out of flour and water uncooked, so it would be sticky and stringy, and you topped it off with, say, blueberries and whipped cream, or perhaps a nice meringue. I never threw a pie in any of my feature-length pictures. By then we thought pies were pretty silly."

Dignity in Deadpan

Buster Keaton's Impassive Demeanor Cloaked Elusive and Complex Charm

By BOSLEY CROWTHER

There are sure to be assorted recollections of Buster Keaton as the stone-faced little man in a long list of silent film comedies who tore through successive confrontations with torpid humans and irrascible machines with all the zip and conclusiveness of a buzz-saw.

An Appraisal

No doubt a great many people will fondly and confidently recall that the essential element of his humor was the passiveness of his deadpan in the face of horrendous upheavals and the most startling and shocking contretemps. Others will first remember the ludicrousness of his costumes, especially that frequent and familiar (but not inevitable) pie-plate hat. Some will remember that the secret of his peculiarly distant charm was his aggressive independence and his avoidance of loquacity. And a few will most fondly think back on his singular attitude toward girls: he accepted them as a convention, but usually found them nuisances and bores.

All of these characteristics and physical aspects were apparent in the man—the strange little individual—that Buster represented on the screen. He was deadpanned, impassive, independent, skeptical of women and bizarre. And, what's more, he had a built-in recoil to sentimentality and sham.

Buster was elusive and complex as a silent comedian. That's why he was never as popular as his contemporaries, Charlie Chaplin and Harold Lloyd. Where Charlie came through cleanly and clearly as the invariably tragi-comic Little Tramp, eternally hopeful of hoisting himself out of his stoic loneliness, and Harold was the unmistakably bumptious go-getting All-American boy, Buster was devious and different. He was something of a comic mystery, and to understand and appreciate him fully required a certain spiritual sensitivity.

But those who had it—and there were plenty of them, as there are still plenty of them today—were generally inclined to rate Buster as the greatest of the great comedians. At least, they recognized him as the most subtle and suggestive satirist—the keenest comic ridiculer of our social system and our mechanical age. This is an estimation with which I entirely agree.

What you had to respond to in Buster was his inherent dignity and pride, his genuinely wholesome ambition and his absolute belief in himself. In "The General," "The Navigator," "Sherlock Jr." and all the rest of his most characteristic pictures, he started out with confidence and trust, assured that he could do what he wanted through diligence, perseverence and common sense. He made no bones about it. He merely tried to forge ahead. He was solemn and sometimes gullible. But that was because of his simplicity.

The disposition of Buster that baffled many of his viewers was his way of displaying disillusion or disgust at the end of his films. He had had it by then; he was fed up with eccentricity and stupidity. He could walk away from the irrational, still closeting his pride and dignity.

The reason that Mr. Keaton never made it to any real extent in talking films was that the producers—and maybe he himself—did not realize his essential personality. They seemed to feel that the essence of his humor was in the gravity of his great stone face, as opposed to the phiz of Jimmy Durante or others with whom he was teamed. They did not see that the Keaton mystique was rooted in the confidence and pride with which he flung his funny-looking person against a perverse and crazy world, nothing loathe and nothing daunted—just bored with it at the end.

Buster Keaton with Marceline Day in *The Cameraman*, 1928.

The New York Times THURSDAY, JANUARY 30, 1964.

Alan Ladd, Actor, Dies at 50; Appeared in 150 Movie Roles

Became Famous for Part of Killer in 'This Gun for Hire' —Was Hero of 'Shane'

PALM SPRINGS, Calif., Jan. 29 (AP)—Alan Ladd, the film star, was found dead today in his home here, apparently of a heart attack. He was 50 years old.

In view of the circumstances of Mr. Ladd's death, Deputy Coroner Robert L. Drake said that an autopsy would be performed tomorrow.

Surviving are his widow, the former Sue Carol; a son by his first marriage, Alan Jr., a daughter, Alana, and another son, David, and a stepdaughter, Mrs. Carol Lee Veitch.

Wanted to Be Film Star

Alan Ladd was neither a brilliant Broadway actor lured to the motion pictures nor a soda jerk snatched from a Kansas drugstore. He was a child of Hollywood, ambitious to get into pictures.

As an actor he was famous for being a cold, calm killer or a cold, calm good guy, who was nearly a bad guy. The Ladd screen smile was never gay, always cynical and cool, and one studio press agent wrote that his eyes "go through you like two icicles."

He made the trenchcoat his symbol.

That the old fashioned motion picture gangster with his ugly face, gaudy cars and flashy clothes was replaced by a smoother, better looking and better dressed bad man was largely the work of Mr. Ladd.

He became an instant success in 1941 when he appeared as a psychopathic killer in a low budget sleeper, "This Gun for Hire," which also starred Veronica Lake, who was to be his screen romantic interest in many other pictures.

In all, Mr. Ladd appeared in about 150 movies.

Alan Walbridge Ladd was born on Sept. 3, 1913, in Hot Springs, Ark., but his family moved to North Hollywood when he was 7.

Track Star at School

He was graduated from North Hollywood High School, where he had been a swimming and track star, and immediately was discovered by talent scouts from Universal Studios.

Universal made him a member of a small group of youngsters the studio hoped, by proper training, to convert into movie stars. After two weeks, this experiment was disbanded and Mr. Ladd was dropped by the studio. Another young man named Tyrone Power was a member of the group and he also was dropped.

Studio Laborer

Mr. Ladd then went to work for The San Fernando Valley Sun-Record, but still desirous of being an actor, he took a job as a studio "grip"—laborer—which he held for two years.

But no director dangled a fat contract in front of the handsome laborer and no feminine star demanded that he become her leading man so Mr. Ladd retired from manual labor and enrolled at the Bard Dramatic School.

Mr. Ladd's big break came in 1939 when he met Sue Carol, a motion-picture actress turned agent. She heard him on a radio program and signed him as one of her first clients.

His first motion picture part was in 1939 as a seasick voyager in "Rulers of the Sea." But it was "This Gun for Hire" that made him famous.

Mr. Ladd and Miss Carol were married on March 15, 1942.

A number of critics sought the explanation for Mr. Ladd's quick popularity. Bosley Crowther of The Times said, "apparently it is his tight-lipped violence that his fans love."

A New Yorker critic wrote that Mr. Ladd seemed "to be an agreeable killer ... a different kind of mug, smooth and with even a parlor manner."

In "The Glass Key" in 1942 Mr. Ladd played a killer who redeemed himself at the end of the picture and for a reward won Miss Lake. In "Lucky Jordan" in 1943 he was a killer who, seeing his evil ways, joined the Army and became a good soldier.

Among his better pictures were "The Great Gatsby" and "Shane."

His portrayal of the gunfighter in "Shane" is generally regarded as one of the best performances ever given in a Western movie.

He served in the Air Force in World War II and came out of it as much in demand as ever. His last picture was completed last summer, "The Carpetbaggers," filmed at Paramount, where Mr. Ladd's career started.

Mr. Ladd was a slim 150-pounder who stood only 5 feet 7 inches tall and often had to stand on a box while playing love scenes on the screen.

Alan Ladd and Veronica Lake in *This Gun for Hire*.

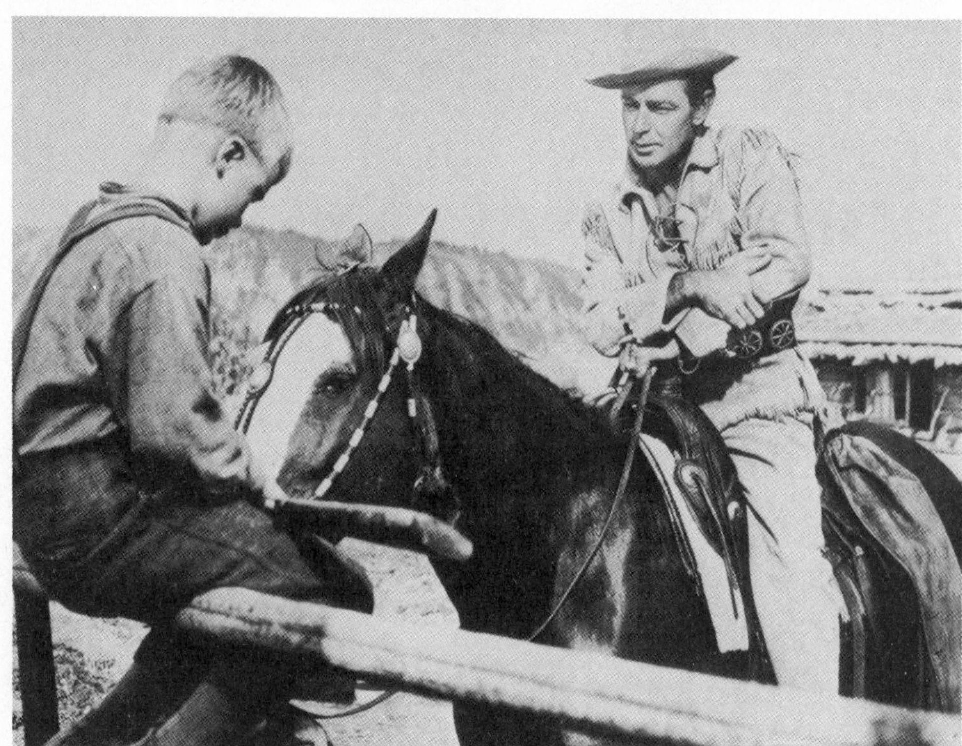

Alan Ladd in his classic performance in *Shane*, with Brandon De Wilde.

"All the News That's Fit to Print"

The New York Times

LATE CITY EDITION

Weather: Mostly sunny today; partly cloudy tonight. Cloudy Wed. Temp. range: today 55-32; Monday 47-33. Full U.S. report on Page 94.

VOL. CXVII..No. 40,127 — © 1967 The New York Times Company. — NEW YORK, TUESDAY, DECEMBER 5, 1967 — 10 CENTS

MAKARIOS ASKING GUARANTEE BY U.N. AGAINST INVASION

Cyprus Leader, Replying to Thant, Hints He Wants Role in Control of Force

TURKS UPHOLD REGIME

Greeks Send Ship to Island as First Step in Carrying Out Peace Agreements

By DREW MIDDLETON

Special to The New York Times

UNITED NATIONS, N.Y., Dec. 4—The President of Cyprus, Archbishop Makarios, said today that guarantees against military intervention in Cyprus should be insured through the United Nations Security Council.

This suggestion, which shadowed a deeper involvement for the world organization in the Mediterranean island's security, was made in a letter replying to the peace appeal Secretary General Thant issued Sunday.

The Secretary General sent appeals to Greece and Turkey, which had been at the brink of war over the situation on the island, as well as to Cyprus. The Greeks and the Turks have announced acceptance.

[Greece, taking the first steps to implement the agreements reached last week, sent a ship to start the withdrawal of her troops from Cyprus. Page 2. In Ankara, the National Assembly rejected a motion critical of the Turkish Government's handling of the situation. Page 3.]

'Broader Functions'

The proposal by Archbishop Makarios that the Security Council underwrite guarantees against military aggression was balanced by his qualified references to the role to be played by United Nations forces on the island. Mr. Thant had suggested enlarging the force's mandate to give it "broader functions."

The future role of these forces or the "enlargement of their mandate," the Archbishop said, will have to be considered by the Council "with due regard to the sovereignty" of Cyprus. His Government, he said, looks forward to the measures to be taken—"with the contribution" of these forces—to establish peace and security on the island.

Diplomats interpreted this as meaning that the President would consider a larger role for the United Nations force and, perhaps, its reinforcement, as long as he was able to exercise

Continued on Page 2, Column 4

3,600 an Hour File Past Spellman Bier

By EDWARD B. FISKE

Crowds that reached the rate of 3,600 persons an hour filed past the purple-draped funeral bier of Cardinal Spellman yesterday as his body lay in state in the nave of St. Patrick's Cathedral.

During the noontime rush the line of mourners backed up into the streets and at times nearly encircled the cathedral.

The line was interrupted periodically for special masses, including a low mass at 2 P.M. for thousands of children from the 443 schools of the New York Archdiocese.

The body of the Cardinal, who died Saturday of a

Continued on Page 50, Column 1

DISPARITY FOUND ...

... J... Hosp... who ... ment... discr... hospita...

Mr. Co... before th... Committee... and Medica... though a B... except one... policy—paid... his general h... period cove... was reimburse... only for a cer... percentage of t... Medicare and... burse hospitals f... for their patients,... mum of 11.5 per... search, repairs a... cence.

Mr. Colman res... the persistent ques... State Senator Se... Thaler, a Queens... who asked why Blu... rates were sometimes... cent less than Medicaid... Mr. Thaler, ranking... of the legislative com... noted that Long Island... Hospital was reimbursed... a day—the highest figure... state—for Medicaid pat... who are housed in war... Mr. Colman said he did n... have the Blue Cross figure.

"Our rates are computed

Continued on Page 52, Column ...

Associated Press Wirephoto

...n. Harold K. Johnson, Army; Gen. Earle G. ...as H. Moorer, Navy, and Gen. Wallace M. ...et was topic at session in Cabinet Room.

PRESIDENT DENIES OTHERS IN CABINET INTEND TO LEAVE

He Asserts That Rumors of Impending Changes Were Spread by 'Some Kids'

JAB AT KENNEDYS SEEN

Johnson Brushes Off Race by McCarthy and Invasion Proposal of Eisenhower

Transcript of President's news conference is on Page 20.

By MAX FRANKEL

Special to The New York Times

WASHINGTON, Dec. 4—President Johnson said today that he knew of no other impending changes in his Cabinet despite the rumors that had been spread by "some kids."

With this and other acerbic comments, he finally let show his annoyance at the reaction of the followers and relatives of the late President Kennedy to the scheduled departure of Secretary of Defense Robert S. McNamara. [Question 15, Page 20.]

Mr. Johnson also brushed aside the challenge to his renomination by Senator Eugene J. McCarthy, Democrat of Minnesota. He said that he thought everyone had a right to run for any office if he wished. [Question 9.]

Reaction to Eisenhower

And with a sharp "no comment," he held aloof from former President Dwight D. Eisenhower's suggestion that American troops temporarily invade the territory of North Vietnam. In a second thought, Mr. Johnson added that he would rather handle that through his commander in the field than on television—as General Eisenhower had. [Question 12.]

These and other subjects were placed before the President at an informal news conference. He dealt routinely with taxes and budget questions, avoided any lengthy repetition of his views on Vietnam and said that he thought his prior statement on Mr. McNamara's departure had contained his best explanation.

Vietnam Policy Explained

The President did, however, deal with Vietnam at length and with considerable force in a speech this evening to a foreign policy conference of business leaders at the State Department. He said that this country was helping Vietnam not only in order to repel aggression but also to give all Asia time and opportunity to develop without fear of Communist China.

And in recent years, the President said, this help from the United States has eliminated the "paralysis of will" all around the periphery of China.

A lot of people in the United States are looking for the "fire escape—the easy way out," he said, just as they did back in the time of Mussolini and Hitler. But there can be no peace in the world so long as half of

Continued on Page 20, Column 1

...Names Chapman ...ines' Commandant

...y JOHN W. FINNEY

...cial to The New York Times

...ec. 4—President Johnson brought an ...he Marine Corps by announcing today ... Gen. Leonard F. Chapman Jr. as ...ndant. ...w the ... will ... M. ...year

MARTIN ATTACKS RELIANCE ON GOLD

Federal Reserve Chief Says U.S. 'Must Not Bow Down to Idol' in Inflation Fight

By EILEEN SHANAHAN

Special to The New York Times

WASHINGTON, Dec. 4—William McChesney Martin Jr., the ...man of the Federal Re...ard, said tonight that ...d States "must not ... to the idol of gold" ...y discipline against ... national economic

...d the reliance on ... he called "this ...tal," as "the be-all ...f national mone-

...before the offi...e and national ...f the American ...n, Mr. Mar...eal of the ...quires gold ...nt of the

... that he ...complete ... in the ...m. ...d about ...eppered ...s un...al for ... of his

French Train Rides on Cushion of ...

United Press International Cablephoto

French "aerotrain" during its record-breaking performance at Gometz-la-Ville, France

By JOHN L. HESS

Special to The New York Times

PARIS, Dec. 4—France's wheel-less "aerotrain" roared along its concrete rail at 215 miles an hour today and its builders claimed a world record for track vehicles. Actually, the sleek aluminum car is reliably reported to have done 250 miles an hour in lonely sprints along its 4.2-mile track at Gometz-la-Ville, south of Paris. The test today, in the presence of three Cabinet Ministers and hundreds of newsmen, was to be ceremonial. But fog covered Gometz-la-Ville, and by the time it lifted, the Ministers and nearly all the newsmen were gone. Then the helmeted crew went for the record anyhow in "Le Zinc," as they call the car. With a jet engine backed up by two rocket tubes, they made it easily. Over the roar of the engines, the crew

Continued on Page 3, Column 2

...police... ...to add to the present force of 28,228, Norman Frank, the group's community relations counsel, said yesterday.

Mr. Frank said that residents of Harlem and Brooklyn and Queens Negro communities were also seeking more policemen. "The very underprivileged communities which Mayor Lindsay says were upset by this demand are echoing that call," he said. Another call for more

Continued on Page 41, Column 1

Bert Lahr, Comic Actor, Dies; Played Burlesque and Beckett

By ALDEN WHITMAN

Bert Lahr, the comic actor whose flexibility enabled him to star as the Cowardly Lion in "The Wizard of Oz" and as a hobo in "Waiting for Godot," died yesterday at the age of 72.

A trouper who never wanted to retire, Mr. Lahr was acting in "The Night They Raided Minsky's," a film about the golden age of burlesque—that he himself represented—when he was hospitalized Nov. 21 for a back ailment. At the Columbia-Presbyterian Medical Center, he later developed pneumonia. His death was attributed to a massive intestinal hemorrhage.

A low comedian with a high talent, Mr. Lahr was a memorably antic figure in show business. He starred in vaudeville and burlesque, reigned as the comedy king of Broadway in the late nineteen-twenties and thirties, made movies, appeared on radio and television, and, in a stage comeback, played tragi-comedy on Broadway with distinction.

He was a buffoon, a clown, one of the vanished breed who, like W. C. Fields, Sliding Billy Watson, Ed Wynn, Bobby Clark and Victor Moore, were schooled in the dingy halls of burlesque. As he once said of himself, "I have developed a technique that might be called a style."

His round face, bat ears, bulbous nose, baffled blue eyes and gravelly voiced ululations stirred generations of audiences to laughter. The musical revue, skit or play might be thin—and they frequently were—but Mr. Lahr surmounted such trivialities with an art and versatilities with an art and versatil-

Continued on Page 51, Column 2

Associated Press

Bert Lahr

...edian with a high talent, Mr. Lahr was a memorably antic figure in show business. He starred in vaudeville and burlesque, reigned as the comedy king of Broadway in the late nineteen-twenties and thirties, made movies, appeared on radio and television, and, in a stage comeback, played tragi-comedy on Broadway with distinction.

He was a buffoon, a clown, one of the vanished breed who, like W. C. Fields, Sliding Billy Watson, Ed Wynn, Bobby Clark and Victor Moore, were schooled in the dingy halls of

Bert Lahr — Associated Press

burlesque. As he once said of himself, "I have developed a technique that might be called a style."

His round face, bat ears, bulbous nose, baffled blue eyes and gravelly voiced ululations stirred generations of audiences to laughter. The musical revue, skit or play might be thin—and they frequently were—but Mr. Lahr surmounted such trivialities with an art and versatil-

Continued on Page 51, Column 2

...raft Deferments ...Graduate Study

...y NEIL SHEEHAN

Special to The New York Times

WASHINGTON, Dec. 4—An interagency advisory committee has recommended that the National Security Council permit broad draft deferments for graduate students in natural science, mathematics, engineering and health.

There are now about 144,000 first-year graduate students. If the recommendation is accepted, about half of them will continue to be deferred after blanket graduate school deferments expire next year.

The National Security Council is expected to decide the question later this month. The council is headed by President Johnson and includes Vice President Humphrey, Secretary of State Dean Rusk, Secretary of Defense Robert S. McNamara and C. Farris Bryant, director of the Office of Emergency Planning.

In his draft message to Congress last March, President Johnson announced his intention of ending all graduate school deferments except for medical and dental students, the bulk of those in the health field.

The revised draft law subse-

Continued on Page 26, Column 4

NEWS INDEX

Bert Lahr, Comic Actor, Is Dead at 72

Continued From Page 1, Col. 6

ity that were closer to the pantomimist's than to the trigger-witted comic's.

Bellowing and cavorting his zany way through his material, he strove to create mood and build a character. The lines were less significant to him.

In a reflective moment, Mr. Lahr once appraised himself in this way:

"A comedian, he's got to be able to make you laugh even when he don't say a word. And if he can't make you cry as well as laugh, he's no real comedian. And he shouldn't just say jokes.

"I'm always happy when I find a good writer with all the accoutrements. But my kind of comedian is more like an actor. I'm just playing situations and characters. I put myself into situations and it's the feeling I get across about these people and their troubles—that's what you get the tears with. Nobody can teach that; nobody can write it for you. It's got to come inside from the heart, and either God gave it to you or you ain't got it."

In Mr. Lahr's case, however formidable as were his natural endowments, he worked mightily to improve upon them from the time he entered show business at the age of 15. He taught himself by making faces in a mirror, by trying out weird sounds and guttural inflections, by experimenting with trick ways of walking and rolling his eyes and by splaying his fingers around. He never ceased honing his celebrated skills of timing and stage presence.

Child of Immigrants

Mr. Lahr's family background was inauspicious. He was born Aug. 13, 1895, at First Avenue and 81st Street, in the Yorkville section of Manhattan, the eldest child of Jacob and Augusta Lahrheim, immigrants from Germany. He was named Irving, and later altered his name for the stage.

His father was an upholsterer with a Prussian sense of discipline; his mother was high-strung and hypochondriacal. Bert attended P.S. 77 and Morris High School, but not much, for he was more often out of school than in, singing ballads in a quavery tenor in pick-up backyard quartets for nickels and dimes.

In 1910 he joined a child vaudeville act on the strength of his rendition of the sentimental "Garland of Old-Fashioned Roses." But it was a time when low-Dutch acts were the rage, and on stage young Lahr began to sprinkle his speech with "achs," "unds," "odders"

Bert Lahr as the Cowardly Lion in film "The Wizard of Oz"

and "shpeak op, bleases." For several years he toured the United States with small-time vaudeville troupes, often playing 14 shows a week for uncertain wages, but learning, too, from the older comedians.

'Boy Wonder' of Burlesque

He was snatched from obscurity in 1915 by Billy K. Wells, a skit writer for the Columbia Burlesque Circuit, who saw Mr. Lahr perform at the Olympic Theater in Brooklyn. He was hired for $35 a week, appearing with a troupe called the Roseland Girls, and by the third year he was "the boy wonder of burlesque," earning $100 a week and perfecting his Dutch character type.

After brief service as a seaman second class in World War I, Mr. Lahr expanded one of his burlesque skits into a 12-minute vaudeville act, "Lahr & Mercedes — What's the Idea?' and moved into big-time vaudeville at $350 a week. In the skit with Mercedes Delpino, a brunette dancer who became his wife, Mr. Lahr was a drunken Dutch comedy cop while his partner played a hootchy-kootchy dancer whom he was trying to arrest.

In this act and others, he developed the leer, grimace and wild cry of glahng-glahng that was to be his stock in trade. The grimace was abetted by some inexpert suturing of a gape in Mr. Lahr's forehead, the result of a streetcar accident on Avenue A as a child.

Mr. Lahr made his Broadway debut Nov. 28, 1927, in "Harry Delmar's Revels," but he made no splash. A review of the capering, in The New York Times the following day, remarked tartly that "there was also a vaudeville comic named Bert Lahr, who is entitled to about a C" for his performance.

In 1928, however, he became Broadway's darling overnight as Gink Schiner, a punch-drunk fighter, in "Hold Everything!" The Vinton Freedley and Alex Aarons musical, also starring Betty Compton, had the songs "You're the Cream in My Coffee" and "Don't Hold Everything," and it played 413 performances.

"New Comedy King Born" read one headline over a review, and all at once taxi drivers, speakeasy proprietors and columnists recognized Mr. Lahr on sight. In addition to his stage stint, he played the Palace, vaudeville's hall of fame, three times in six months at $4,500 a week.

Thereafter, Mr. Lahr was an established star in stage attractions, firmly endearing himself in "Flying High" in 1930. Of him in that musical Brooks Atkinson wrote in The Times:

"He is immensely funny. Nearly everything is against the sort of comedy Lahr cultivates; the elastic-face brand of slapstick is the most elementary. But Lahr goes at it uproariously, twisting his face into such fantastic shapes and bawling such outlandish sounds at the top of his voice, that you are soon blown down into a sort of helpless consent.

"In his burlesque clowning, he is a cross between a mugg and a sap. Here he is made over into a flying fool who breaks an endurance record by blind luck and 10 minutes. 'Some fun, hey kid?' he blurts out as he prances wildly about the stage."

Mr. Lahr saved his prancing and his humor for the stage. Off it, he was a dolorous man, given to melancholy, shyness, worry, superstition and hypochondria. For him, his years in the theater were a dogged, lifelong struggle against myopic critics, fickle audiences and the horror of obscurity.

"To begin with," Mr. Lahr once said, "I am a sad man. A plumber doesn't go out with his tools. Does a comedian have to be funny on the street?"

Despite his incessant fretting, his fear of heights and of flying and his off-stage air of sad bewilderment over the vagaries of his profession, Mr. Lahr was seldom at liberty. After playing Rusty Krause in "Flying High," he appeared in "Hot-Cha!" in 1932; in "Life Begins at 8:40" in 1934—a musical in which he sang "The Woodchopper's Song," a merciless travesty of concert baritones; in "The Show Is On" with Beatrice Lillie in 1936, and in "DuBarry Was a Lady" with Ethel Merman in 1939.

In that year he also appeared in his only enduring Hollywood role, that of the Cowardly Lion in "The Wizard of Oz." Although Mr. Lahr had parts in more than a score of motion pictures, starting in 1931, he never attained the peak of characterization that he managed as a lion. He departed Hollywood and his $85,000 home there without bitterness, remarking, "After all, how many lion parts can you get in pictures?"

The Broadway musical comedy of the 1940's, with its Rodgers and Hammerstein emphasis on operettas with a story line and romance, was not Mr. Lahr's bottle of beer. He played summer stock, toured in the road company of "Harvey" and was heard on radio.

He reappeared, this time in his first dramatic role, in a revival of "Burlesque" in 1946, which ran for more than a year. In 1951 he again found a musical comedy that fitted his talents, "Two on the Aisle," in which Dolores Grey was the co-star. Afterward he appeared on television frequently as a guest.

Then he was chosen for the role of Estragon in Samuel Beckett's metaphysical tragicomedy "Waiting for Godot." Although he professed not to understand the play, Mr. Lahr was a big hit.

The New York Times SUNDAY, JULY 8, 1973

Veronica Lake, 53, Movie Star With the Peekaboo Hair, Dead

Box-Office Favorite of 1940's Made 26 Pictures and Then Vanished From Limelight

By EDWARD HUDSON

Veronica Lake, one of the screen's leading box-office favorites of the early nineteen-forties, instantly recognizable for her long blond hair falling over her right eye, died yesterday in Burlington, Vt. She had been hospitalized there since June 26 for treatment of acute hepatitis. The movie star was 53 years old.

In her movie career, which ended in the early fifties, the diminutive and sultry-looking Miss Lake — she was 5 feet 2 inches and weighed 100 pounds —became one of Hollywood's most glamorous stars, playing in 26 motion pictures.

Then her acting career went into decline, and she wound up years later working as a barmaid in the Martha Washington Hotel, 29 East 29th Street. In recent years, she had been playing summer stock and stage roles in Britain.

Miss Lake preferred to describe herself as a "sex-zombie," rather than a "sex symbol."

"That really names me properly," she told an interviewer two years ago. "I was laughing at everybody in all of my portraits. I never took that stuff seriously. I will have one of the cleanest obits of any actress. I never did cheesecake like Ann Sheridan or Betty Grable. I just used my hair."

Hazard for Rosie the Riveter

Her seductive peekaboo hair style set a fashion. So much so that during World War II a Government agency asked her not to wear it long because many women were catching their tresses in factory machinery.

Miss Lake was the daughter of a ship's master. She was born in Brooklyn on November 14, 1919, named Constance Ockelman and spent her girlhood in Lake Placid, N. Y., and Miami. She studied at McGill University as a premedical student.

Encouraged by winning third prize in a Florida beauty contest and an ambitious mother who was later to sue her daughter for nonsupport, Miss Lake moved to Hollywood. She was cast in bit parts, finally landing a leading role in "I Wanted Wings" in 1941, playing a nightclub singer.

The movie was a hit, and she was quickly cast with Joel McCrea in "Sullivan's Travels." This was followed by another hit, "This Gun for Hire," co-starring Alan Ladd, who wasn't much taller than she was. This was only the first of the "tough guy" movies they made together.

Played Witch Roles

Other films in which Miss Lake starred were "The Glass Key," "I Married a Witch," "Star-Spangled Rhythm, "So Proudly We Hail," "The Hour Before Dawn," "Bring On the Girls," "Hold That Blonde," "Out of This World," "Miss Susie Slagle's," "Isn't It Romantic," "The Sainted Sisters," "Saigon" and "Slattery's Hurricane."

She married four times. In 1940 she was married to John Detlie, a studio art director. They had a daughter, Elaine. A year after her divorce from Mr. Detlie in 1943, Miss Lake married André de Toth, a movie director. They had two children, André and Diane. The couple were divorced in 1952. Three years later she was married to Joseph A. McCarthy, a music publisher and song writer, but this marriage, too, ended in divorce, about 1960. In later years, she said she rarely saw or heard from her children.

Her fourth husband was Robert Carelton-Munro, an Englishman, to whom she was married in Fort Lauderdale, Fla., in the spring of 1972. Friends said the couple had been in the process of divorce.

No Regrets

Miss Lake had made her home in Ipswich, England, for some years in the late nineteen-sixties and early seventies.

In her autobiography, "Veronica," published in 1971, the movie star admitted she drank a lot in her post-fame years. Showing some sensitivity about the subject, she told an interviewer: "To each his own. At least I'm not a mainliner, and it's more fun getting high without a needle. At least you can get over the booze."

She said she would not have lived her life any differently. "How would I learn to be a person otherwise?"

Veronica Lake in the early 1940's.

Veronica Lake with Robert Preston in *This Gun for Hire*.

The New York Times TUESDAY, AUGUST 3, 1976

Fritz Lang, Film Director Noted for 'M,' Dead at 85

By ALBIN KREBS

Friz Lang, the Viennese-born film director best known for "M," a terrifying study of a child killer, and for other tales of suspense, died yesterday in Los Angeles at the age of 85. He had been ill for some time, and had been inactive professionally for a decade.

The film world of Mr. Lang, whose innovative craftsmanship influenced hundreds of younger directors and put an indelible stamp on the art of cinema, was populaed largely by psychopaths, master criminals, prostitutes, cuckolds, child murderers, sadists and the insane.

"I am profoundly fascinated by cruelty, fear, horror and death," he once said. "My films show my preoccupation with violence, the pathology of violence."

Mr. Lang, who first won his fame as one of the giants in the golden age of German films, in the 1920's, made "M" in 1931, two years before he fled Nazi Germany. But in Hollywood he also directed many notable films. Among them were "Fury," a burning indictment of lynch law and mob rule; "You Only Live Once," "Man Hunt," "Hangmen Also Die!," "The Woman in the Window," "Scarlet Street" and Clifford Odets's "Clash by Night."

In the movie industry Mr Lang was much admired for his crisp, inventive pictorial style. He was a pioneer in the dramatic use of sound—the chirrup of crickets, the drone of a passing automobile, muffled footsteps in the night. Often he was called, approvingly, "a director's director."

'Hated Perfectionist'

On the set, however, many who worked for Mr. Lang found him to be an unbearable martinet, an egocentric despot. Mr. Lang waved such accusations aside with the comment, "I was something that is always hated in Hollywood—a perfectionist; nobody likes a perfectionist, you know."

He was a massive-featured man whose entire appearance bore witness to a curious mingling of strength and softness. His slightly sardonic blue eyes were given the lie by a childlike mouth. His hands, broad and heavy across the palms, had the long and restless fingers of a sensitive artist. He was very tall and carried himself like a soldier.

It was not until several years after he came to the United States that Mr. Lang exchanged his monocle for thick-lensed spectacles. He began wearing a monocle, which underscored his aura of aloofness, when he served in the Austrian Army in World War I.

Mr. Lang wa born on Dec. 5, 1890, in Vienna, the son of Anton Lang, an architect, and the former Paula Schlesinger. In acordance with his father's wishes, he enrolled in Vienna's Technical High School to study architecture. He was not happy, however, and ran away from home to study painting in Munich and Paris.

That soon became boring, and Mr. Lang set out on a tour, with very little cash in his pocket, through Germany, the Low Countries, Asia Minor, North Africa, China, Japan and the South Seas. During this time he supported himself by painting postcards, selling pictures and drawing cartoons for newspapers.

Wrote in Hospital

In 1914, when he was back in Paris, and soon after the opening of an exhibition of his canvases, war broke out. Mr. Lang returned to Vienna, where he was conscripted into the army. He was wounded four times and spent a year's convalescence in a hospital in Vienna. There the young lieutenant began writing short stories and screenplays.

Mr. Lang sold several scripts, mostly crime stories, to Berlin filmmakers before he was given his first directorial assignment, in 1919. The film, which he also wrote, was "Halbblut" ("The Weakling"), and it concerned a man destroyed by his love for a woman—a theme that kept cropping up in Lang movies.

In 1920 Mr. Lang married a popular writer of thrillers, Thea von Harbou, who collaborated with him on the screenplays of all the films he was to make in Germany.

Their first popular success was "Der Müde Tod" ("The Tired Death"), released in 1921 and shown in the United States under the title "Destiny." Douglas Fairbanks Sr. thought so highly of the film that he bought American rights to it for $5,000 and copied many of its spectacular special effects for his 1924 production of "The Thief of Baghdad."

Shown on Two Evenings

"Dr. Mabuse Der Spieler" ("Dr. Mabuse, the Gambler"), a Lang silent screen classics, was released in 1922. A two-part film shown on consecutive evenings, it featured Mr. Lang's master villain, an archcriminal animated by a lust for power, who leads a gang of killers and cutthroats. The director photographed the film in expressionist settings, using painted shadows on the walls.

Other Lang hits of the 20's were "Die Nibelungen," a two-part film based on the Siegfried and other Norse sagas; "Frau im Mond" ("Woman in the Moon") and "Spione" ("The Spy").

Some years ago Mr. Lang took credit for inventing the countdown, now used in spacecraft launching, during the production of "Woman in the Moon," the 1929 film for which Willy Ley, the space writer, and Dr. Hermann Oberth, the pioneer rocket scientist, served as technical advisers.

"It came from a dire necessity," he said. "When I shot the takeoff I said, 'If I count 1, 2, 3, 4, 10, 50, 100, an audience doesn't know when it will go off; but if I count down—10, 9, 8, 7, 6, 5, 4, 3, 2, 1, ZERO!—then they will know. Thus the countdown."

In 1924, during a brief visit to the United States, Mr. Lang was detained for several hours aboard ship in New York Harbor. Gazing upon the city's brightly lighted skyscrapers, he conceived the idea for "Metropolis," a controversial and highly successful film released in 1927.

In "Metropolis," he used expressionism of a broad sort, offering a lunatic but compelling version of the struggle between capital and labor in a futuristic "Big Brother" society in which the machines rule the people who created them. The film remains in all major film collections as an innovative classic, but Mr. Lang hated it.

In an interview in 1965 with Peter Bogdanovich, film maker and critic, Mr. Lang said:

"I didn't like the picture—thought it was silly and stupid—then, when I saw the astronauts—what else are they but part of a machine? . . . Should I say now that I like 'Metropolis' because something I have seen in my imagination comes true—when I detested it after it was finished?"

The working title of "M," Mr. Lang's great film (and his personal favorite), was "Murderers Among Us." Since he was already held in suspicion by the Nazis when it was produced as Germany's first talking picture, efforts were made to prevent him from filming it.

"The Nazis feared the "murderers' would be thinly veiled persons the audience would recognize as Nazis," Mr. Lang said years later. "When they found I was concerning myself with mere child murderers," he added sardonically, "they said, 'Oh, go right ahead, Herr Lang.' go right ahead, Herr Lang.' The pigs."

Two generations of film buffs have been fascinated by Mr. Lang's creative use of film and sound in "M," which he based on the true case of a psychopathic child killer in Düsseldorf. For example, in the film, a little girl's mother steps out of her apartment calling "Elsie, Elsie," while across the screen pass pictures of the empty stairwell up which the child has been carried to her death, Elsie's unused plate on the kitchen table, a remote patch of

(continued)

Fritz Lang

grass with her ball lying on it, a balloon caught in the telephone lines—the very balloon the killer had given her to win her confidence. The effect is sinister.

Equally terrifying is the whistling by the murderer (Peter Lorre) of a few bars from a Grieg melody. It threads through the film, ominously foreboding his appearances.

The film that followed "M" led to Mr. Lang's exile from Germany. A sequel to his 1922 movie about Mabuse, the master criminal, it was called "Das Testament Des Dr. Mabuse" ("The Last Will of Dr. Mabuse"). Into the mouths of the evil characters in the film, Mr. Lang put many Nazi slogans. After the picture was completed in 1932, he was summoned to the office of Joseph Goebbels, the Nazi Minister of Propaganda, who told the director the film had been banned by the Third Reich.

A Bid From Hitler

Goebbels was in a forgiving mood, however. "He told me that, many years before, he and the Führer had seen my picture 'Metropolis' in a small town," Mr. Lang said, "and that Hitler had said at that time that he wanted me to make pictures for the Nazis. Then Goebbels actually offered me the job of heading the Nazi film effort."

It was the last job Mr. Lang wanted, for he hated Nazism fiercely. In addition, he feared the Nazis might discover some Jewishness in his mother's background (he was a Roman Catholc) and thus concluded he was not sufficiently Aryan to work for Hitler.

As soon as the interview with Goebbels was over, Mr. Lang hurried home and jammed as many of his possessions as possible into his overcoat pockets. Then he took a train to the French border. (Thea von Harbou divorced him, joined the Nazi movement and later wrote several Nazi films.)

In Paris Mr. Lang directed "Liliom," (1934), Ferenc Molnar's tragicomic fantasy about a ne'er-do-well who dies and goes to heaven. Soon after it was released, David O. Selznick, then chief of production at Metro-Goldwyn-Mayer, signed him to a one-picture contract and he moved to Hollywood. For two years Mr. Lang did nothing at M-G-M except sit around and learn slangy English, which he used zestfully for the rest of his life.

Mr. Lang's first Hollywood picture, "Fury," was, for its time (1936), an uncompromisingly bold examination of mob violence. Although it was filmed on a low budget, it was an immense critical success. The film was laced with memorable scenes, including one in which pictures of gossiping women dissolve into pictures of a gaggle of honking geese.

During the filming of "Fury," as well as all his other American movies, there were quarrels aplenty involving Mr. Lang, his actors and the production staffs. He came from a European movie-making tradition that gave the director dictatorial control, even over the hours at which personnel had lunch or quit for the day. And so there were temperamental outbursts on the sets of Lang pictures.

Mr. Lang's Hollywood cycle of films more often than not dwelled on his favorite themes: society's maltreatment of the unfortunate, such as ex-convicts ("You Only Live Once," "You and Me"); the inexorability of fate ("Man Hunt," "Human Desire"); the good man ruined by the sluttish woman and her paramour ("The Woman in the Window" and "Scarlet Street").

Fascinated by the American West, Mr. Lang took several vacations in Arizona and Wyoming, sometimes living for weeks among the Indians. The Viennese directed three competently made, if not memorable, westerns, "The Return of Frank James," "Western Union" and "Rancho Notorious," starring Marlene Dietrich. (The director and star had stopped speaking by the time "Rancho Notorious" was finished.)

Mr. Lang's favorite of his American films was his second-to-last, "While the City Sleeps," released in 1956. That same year he directed "Beyond a Reasonable Doubt." He had so much trouble with the producers, he said years later, that he concluded, "I think I'll step out of this rat race; I decided not to make pictures here any more."

He returned to Germany in 1959 and made two penny-dreadful movies, one yet another variation on the Dr. Mabuse theme. Both were shown in truncated, badly dubbed English versions in this country, under the titles "Journey to the Lost City" and "The 1,000 Eyes of Dr. Mabuse."

In recent years Mr. Lang lived frugally in his Beverly Hills home. His fortunes had declined, and he was no longer in demand as a director. But, a friend said a few years ago, "He's just as opinionated, straight-backed, tyrannical and difficult as ever, and still sure he'll yet make the greatest movie ever some day."

A scene from Fritz Lang's *M*, 1931.

Fury, 1936, was Fritz Lang's first Hollywood film.

The New York Times SATURDAY, DECEMBER 23, 1944.

HARRY LANGDON, 60, SCREEN COMEDIAN

Film 'Dead-Pan,' Who Began With Mack Sennett, Dies—Once Paid $7,500 a Week

LOS ANGELES, Dec. 22 (AP)—Harry Langdon, veteran comedian of the stage and screen, died today of a cerebral hemorrhage. His age was 60. He had been ill for several weeks.

Mr. Langdon, former Mack Sennett comedian and recently a film writer, attained to a $1,000,000 film contract in 1925 from a beginning as an amateur vaudeville actor at the age of 12. He played in carnivals, circuses, tent shows, vaudeville and musical comedies and made his film debut in 1923 with Mr. Sennett.

He had fat jowls and wide eyes that gave him a bewildered look, and an odd little mannerism with his hands that spelled helplessness. They added up to a funny, human character for which the movies once paid Harry Langdon $7,500 a week.

Started in Two-Reelers

Mr. Langdon started in two-reelers and ended in them. Between, he had great success and failures and the tribulations that come with marriages and divorces and too much money. His best pictures were "Tramp, Tramp, Tramp," with Joan Crawford as his leading lady; "The Strong Man," both made in 1926, and "Long Pants," in 1927. He created a cinematic sensation in the latter by having his heroine play a blind girl.

"A man of many talents," as Col. Frank Capra, former film director, said today, Mr. Langdon could play any musical instrument by ear, was a ventriloquist and a cartoonist—so good, friends said, that William Randolph Hearst once offered him $3,000 a week to draw a daily strip. The comedian was too successful and too busy, he said, to draw cartoons.

Mr. Langdon never became bitter when his money was gone and he was earning "$22 a week—some weeks," as he testified in one alimony suit. Four wives divorced him. His fifth divorced him, too, but they were remarried, after a few months, in 1938. She and their daughter, Virginia, survive, together with his son Harry, Jr., the child of his third wife, Helen.

Known as "Dead-Pan"

Harry Langdon rose to the top as a laugh-getter of the short-reel silent film comedies because of his comically sad face, which, he once revealed in an interview, was not a mask at all, but quite natural. His whole appeal was a consummate ability to look inexpressibly forlorn when confronted with manifold misfortunes—usually of the domestic type. He was what was known as "dead-pan."

Born in Council Bluffs, Iowa, Mr. Langdon started life as a newsboy in the theatrical district of Omaha and first made a hit on the stage through an amateur night performance, when his worried look—due to the perfectly real difficulties of his trade—panicked the audience.

Thereafter he played small-time vaudeville for years without attracting unusual attention, and had almost decided to quit the stage and enter his father's business, which was painting scenery, when the feeble smile and owlish blink which had become his stock-in-trade caught on in a big way, and he skyrocketed to fame and fortune.

He soon became entangled in a series of domestic difficulties, however, and finally was forced admit that they upset him too much to act at all. He went into obscurity after the advent of the talkies.

In 1938 he made a comeback by entering the comedy writing field, and had a part in the production of several successful Laurel and Hardy shorts. In 1941 Monogram Pictures signed him to make a series of shorts.

Harry Langdon in *The Strong Man*, 1927.

Harry Langdon in a typical predicament.

MARIO LANZA DIES; SINGER, ACTOR, 38

Tenor Who Starred in 'The Great Caruso,' Other Films Was Recording Artist

ROME, Oct. 7 (UPI)—Mario Lanza, singer and film star, died today of a heart attack at the Gullia Clinic here. He had been in the hospital for a week and his heart ailment had been complicated by pneumonia and phlebitis. His age was 38.

Hefty Performer

Mr. Lanza—a weightlifter and an amateur boxer in his high school days, then a piano mover—began to study voice when he was 20 years old. At the age of 29, he had achieved fame as a tenor the world over mainly through his motion pictures and records.

His recording of "Be My Love" for RCA Victor sold about 1,500,000 copies. Another recording, "Loveliest Night of the Year," sold more than 1,000,000. His motion pictures grossed in the millions. "The Great Caruso" ran for ten weeks at Radio City Music Hall, a record at that time.

Despite this success, critics were divided on his voice. Some called it a "a great voice, full of power," while others said it lacked musical taste and discipline.

A handsome man with dark, curly hair, Mr. Lanza was a controversial figure in Hollywood. Time and again, he was involved in arguments with motion-picture producers because of his excessive weight.

On occasion, he tipped the scales at more than 250 pounds and was compelled to go on rigid diets to lose as much as sixty pounds in a short time in order to appear before the cameras.

Worked in Europe

Several times film production was delayed because he did not slim down in time. In 1957 he shed more than seventy-five pounds and embarked on a new career in Europe, interspersing movie work with concert tours.

Alfred Arnold Cocozza, the future Mario Lanza, was born in South Philadelphia, the son of Antonio and Maria Cocozza. His father was an avid collector of opera records and the boy listened to them by the hour.

It was his father who convinced the boy that he should study voice. His first voice coach was Irene Williams. Later, Mr. Lanza, who adopted his mother's maiden name of Lanza, studied with Grant Garnell and Enrico Rosati.

The late Serge Koussevitzky, conductor of the Boston Symphony Orchestra, became interested in Mr. Lanza, who went on a scholarship to the 1942 Tanglewood Music Festival at Lenox, Mass. Critics heard him sing and were impressed.

Also impressed was Columbia Concerts, Inc., which signed the singer for a nationwide tour. It was while on tour that Mr. Lanza was drafted into the Army Air Forces in 1942.

He first was assigned to the military police but later transferred to a special service unit. Before receiving his honorable discharge in September, 1945, he appeared in "On the Beam" and the Moss Hart production, "Winged Victory." The same year RCA Victor signed him to a recording contract, which he did no work on until 1948.

Meanwhile, a wealthy realtor, Sam Weiler, took an interest in Mr. Lanza's career, assuming the singer's debts and making him resume his studies. The young singer drew record crowds for solo appearances in 1946 at Grant Park in Chicago and the next year at the Hollywood Bowl. A total of 76,000 persons attended his two Grant Park performances.

Pictures Listed

His first picture was "That Midnight Kiss" in 1949. Other films made by him were "The Toast of New Orleans," 1950; "The Great Caruso," 1951; "Because You're Mine," 1952; "Student Prince," 1954, and "Serenade," 1958. Before the Caruso picture was released, more than 100,000 albums of the operatic numbers that Mr. Lanza sang in this film had been sold.

Metro-Goldwyn-Mayer instituted a $5,000,000 suit against Mr. Lanza for his failure to report for work on "The Student Prince." It was settled when Edmund Purdom, British actor, took the title role, and Mr. Lanza dubbed the voice for the operatic arias.

Mr. Lanza also was once sued by a Las Vegas night club, after he had failed to appear for a performance. In 1954 he made news of another sort when he starred in a television spectacular, and it was learned later that his songs were recorded. He had mouthed the lyrics, but later, to prove that he had not lost his voice, Mr. Lanza did another show, singing live.

His last film was "For the First Time," made in Europe. He was scheduled to return to this country to appear in a television series, and also to fulfill film contracts. The schedule was expected to keep him busy until 1961.

In addition to his parents, Mr. Lanza is survived by his widow, the former Betty Hicks, and four children.

Mario Lanza made his debut opposite Kathryn Grayson in *That Midnight Kiss.*

Jarmila Novotna with Mario Lanza in *The Great Caruso.*

The New York Times MONDAY, DECEMBER 17, 1962.

Charles Laughton Is Dead at 63; Character Actor for 3 Decades

By The Associated Press

HOLLYWOOD, Dec. 16 — Charles Laughton, whose outstanding performances over three decades made him the movies' top character actor, died yesterday of cancer. He was 63 years old.

The British-born performer, succumbed at his home. He had been in a coma for some time.

His wife, Elsa Lanchester, the actress, was at the bedside as was his brother Frank, a retired hotel man from England.

Mr. Laughton had entered the hospital here last July 30 after previous treatment at New York's Memorial Hospital for Cancer and Allied Diseases. He underwent surgery for a collapsed vertebra, and afterwards it was announced that he had cancer of the spine. He went home from the hospital Nov. 30.

His death came at a time of year in which he frequently had been in the public eye for his Christmas season readings of Dicken's "A Christmas Carol."

A Master Character Actor

NEW YORK.

Special to The New York Times.

From the start of his acting career, Mr. Laughton strenuously fought against being "typed." However, many of the characters, historical and fictitious, that he portrayed here have become typed in the public mind as Charles Laughton by virtue of his powerful style.

His personality left an indelible mark on a generation of moviegoers who identified him as the gluttonous, lusty, chicken-bone-waving Henry VIII or as the ponderous martinet, Captain Bligh. To perhaps a lesser degree, the perfect gentleman's gentleman of "Ruggles of Red Cap" will alway be Mr. Laughton.

Many will remember his readings from the Bible to bedridden veterans and to the general public during and after World War II and his reading in 1951 with Charles Boyer, Agnes Moorehead and Sir Cedric Hardwicke of George Bernard Shaw's "Don Juan in Hell."

Mr. Laughton's appearances on the stage, in films and television won for him critical and popular acclaim. However, his interpretation of King Lear at Stratford in 1959 resulted in divergence of opinion. W. A. Darlington, the London critic, said of his performance:

"There is not a scrap of majesty in him. If he resembles a king at all, it is the Old King Cole of the nursery rhyme."

Mr. Laughton was born in Scarborough, England, the son of middle-class Yorkshire hotel keepers.

He became an actor, but only after he had attended Stoneyhurst College, a Jesuit institution; had trained at Claridge's in London to learn hotel work, been gassed and wounded while serving as a private in World War I, and failed to adapt himself to family business.

He entered in 1925 with parental consent The Royal Academy of Dramatic Art in London. His first professional role was in "The Government Inspector" the next year. There followed a variety of roles in plays by Ibsen, Chekhov and others.

In 1929 Mr. Laughton married a young actress, Elsa Sulivan Lanchester. Two years later the couple opened "Payment Deferred," which became a hit in London and later in New York.

There followed another New York role, "The Fatal Alibi." Upon his return to London, Mr. Laughton made his first motion picture, "The Devil and The Deep." There followed his long association in both England and Hollywood in films, interspersed until 1936 with appearances on stage with the Old Vic-Sadler's Wells Company.

Among his early films were "The Old Dark Horse," Cecil B. De Mille's "The Sign of The Cross" (in which he played Nero) and, in 1933, "The Private Life of Henry VIII," for which he won an Academy Award. "Ruggles of Red Gap" "The Barretts of Wimpole Street" and "Les Meserables" were followed in 1935 by "Mutiny on the Bounty."

After the war he continued his film work, but more and more he became active in reading and work in other fields. After his adaptation in 1953 of Stephen Vincent Benet's "John Brown's Body" for reading, he directed in 1955 "The Caine Mutiny Court-Martial," appeared often on television and resumed acting on the London stage after an absence of more than two decades.

In 1950 Mr. Laughton and his wife became American citizens.

Charles Laughton in *The Barretts of Wimpole Street.*

Charles Laughton as Captain Bligh, facing the mutineers in *Mutiny on the Bounty.*

The New York Times WEDNESDAY, FEBRUARY 24, 1965

STAN LAUREL DIES; MOVIE COMEDIAN

Teamed With Oliver Hardy in 200 Slapstick Films—Played 'Simple' Foil

Special to The New York Times

SANTA MONICA, Calif., Feb. 23—Stan Laurel, the sad-faced, scalp-scratching fall guy of the movie comedy team of Laurel and Hardy, died of a heart attack today in his apartment. He was 74 years old.

His partner of more than 200 slapstick films, Oliver Hardy, died in 1957. Mr. Laurel had been retired since 1955 when he suffered a stroke. He had declined to appear in public after Mr. Hardy's death.

A Screen Favorite

Laurel and Hardy were often acclaimed as masters of the careful slapstick, geniuses of a woman-dominated society. Critics placed them close to, but not quite on a par with, Charlie Chaplin, Buster Keaton and others who gained fame as comic singles. Yet their doubles act was the highlight of many a Saturday afternoon at the movies, not to mention the rest of the week, during the late nineteen-twenties and through the thirties.

On the screen, Mr. Laurel, who was 5 feet, 9 inches tall, blue-eyed, and had sandy-brown hair, spoke in a querulous voice that made everyone tremble for his survival vis à vis the 250-pound, 6-foot 1-inch, aggressive Hardy. Yet it was Laurel who often came out the winner. While Hardy was being soundly thrashed by his screen wife, a weepy Laurel would be getting the sympathetic caresses of his movie helpmeet.

The pair had such a vogue that they often did not have time to hammer out stories.

"Nobody ever thinks of giving us a plot," Mr. Laurel once said. "All they do is tell us how funny we are and then push us in front of a camera. We go into the front office and beef and the producers slap down a long list of figures that say we were smash hits at the box office. So they want to know, why do we want to bother with writing our own stuff?"

The pair dressed somberly on screen, as though they were an ill-assorted butler duo. The bowler was their hallmark and they used it as their main prop. Their comedy was frantic on the whole but rarely in part. A fight would start with a slap, move to a slow return slap, followed by another slap and so on as a graceful prologue to a full-scale brawl and headlong flight.

Hardy was the idea man, the fellow with plans for a night out, for a get-rich-quick scheme. Laurel was the sidekick, honest and simple, who inevitably thwarted the deal and plunged the two into catastrophe.

Became a Team in '26

The drawling Lancashire-born Laurel and the high-pitched Georgia-born Hardy teamed up in 1926. They were always anxious for their two and three-reelers to be polished pieces of work.

"We had a rough idea of schedule," Mr. Laurel was quoted as saying in John McCabe's biography "Mr. Laurel and Mr. Hardy." "But our prime worry was whether or not the picture was going to be good.

"We would start out with an idea, go along working on it as we were shooting. If something went wrong with what we were doing, we'd just 'cut' and laugh about it. It was damned fine fun and damned hard work in those days when we were making ourselves a well-known team. Come to think of it, it was always fun."

A typical piece of buffoonery had them on a fire escape. Hardy wanted to get to the next fire escape but couldn't make it, as the villain was hot on their trail. Laurel lost his balance and fell, with toes hooked on to the first fire escape and fingers on the second, a perfect bridge for the chubby comic to walk across.

Jean Harlow appeared with Laurel and Hardy in one film. Laurel slammed a car door on the blonde's dress and as she walked away, she gradually lost most of her clothing. Miss Harlow went from Laurel and Hardy to "Hell's Angels," more dramatic but less fun.

"Humor is the truth; wit is an exaggeration of the truth," Mr. Laurel said in explaining their approach to comedy.

The big organization did not appeal to them. Mr. Laurel shared in the generally unfavorable criticism of their last film, "Atoll K," which they made in France in 1949.

Arthur Stanley Jefferson (Stan Laurel) was born in the little English town of Ulverson on June 16, 1890. He was born into show business. "My family were all theatrical," he once explained.

He followed the trouper's traditional route—circuses, musicals, vaudeville. He arrived in the United States at the age of 20, a member of the Karno "Night in the English Music Hall" troupe. Another British actor in the cast was Charlie Chaplin. At times, Mr. Laurel was his understudy and he said later, "I don't think there's any greater in the business or ever will be."

Mr. Laurel barnstormed for a bit before settling in Hollywood. He found it was tougher to get jobs as a comic than it was to write comedy. In 1917, he joined Hal Roach's studio and wrote, produced and directed.

The big break came in 1926 by accident, one that befell Mr. Hardy, whom Mr. Laurel was directing in a movie. Mr. Hardy, a trencherman and gourmet, burned his arm while cooking a leg of lamb at home.

"We tried to get someone else for the part but nobody was available," Mr. Laurel recalled. "Mr. Roach then asked me to play Hardy's part. Of course we had to rewrite it, but when the picture was finished, Roach liked it, and he asked me to write myself into the next one. By then Hardy was ready to go into the next picture and I appeared with him in it."

They made other films, but not as partners. Mr. Roach observed that they were supplementing each other in fine style and suggested that the movies be called Laurel and Hardy comedies.

The team had tremendous success. There were two million people enrolled in European fan clubs. They had their imitators, too, but none stood up for very long.

Their antics made for a hard day's work. What with the pummeling and the running, they should have been winded when the quitting whistle blew. According to Mr. Laurel, Mr. Hardy was more of a "playboy" who enjoyed going out or playing golf, while Mr. Laurel took care of the editing and the team's business affairs. He said that they did not see too much of each other off the job.

The team was among the few who made the jump from silents to sound.

"We had decided we weren't talking comedians and, of course, preferred to do pantomime, like in our silents," Mr. Laurel said. "So we said as little as possible—only what was necessary to motivate the things we were doing. If there was any plot to be told, we generally would have somebody else tell it. After a while we really liked sound, because it emphasized the gags, and, as time went on, we became a little more accustomed, and did more talking than we first intended."

The partners never had any argument that made headlines. Mr. Laurel once quipped, "We had different hobbies. He liked horses and golf. You know my hobby—and I married them all."

He married four women eight times and was sued by a fifth who wanted to be recognized as his wife. One of his former wives observed, "Stan's a good boy, really, but he has a marrying complex."

Stan Laurel and Oliver Hardy surrender themselves to laughter in *Leave 'Em Laughing.*

Laurel and Hardy in *Bonnie Scotland*.

"All the News That's Fit to Print"

The New York Times

LATE CITY EDITION

Weather: Chance of showers this evening; fair tonight, tomorrow. Temp. range: today 87-67; Sat. 82-64. Temp.-Hum. Index 75; Sat. 74. Complete U.S. report on Page 63.

SECTION ONE

VOL. CXVI. No. 39,978

NEW YORK, SUNDAY, JULY 9, 1967

60c beyond 50-mile zone from New York City, except Long Island. Higher in air delivery cities. 40 CENTS

VIVIEN LEIGH, 53, IS DEAD IN LONDON

Friedman-Abeles

Vivien Leigh

Special to The New York Times

LONDON, July 8 — Vivien Leigh, the stage and screen actress, was found dead in her London apartment this morning. Theater lights in the West End were blacked out for an hour tonight in tribute to her.

Miss Leigh, who was 53 years old, was confined to her apartment on Eaton Square, Belgravia, four weeks ago with a recurrence of tuberculosis, an illness from which she had suffered since 1945.

Her death was reported to the coroner, but it is considered unlikely that an inquest will be held, since indications are that she died a natural death.

Before her illness, Miss Leigh planned a return to the West End in Edward Albee's "A

Continued on Page 60, Column 6

MAYOR REQUESTS CONTINUOUS TALKS ON TEACHERS' PACT

He Urges Round-the-Clock Negotiations to Reach a Contract by Sept. 11

UNION SAYS IT'S WILLING

It Accuses School Board of Lagging—New Round of Bargaining Scheduled

By PAUL HOFMANN

Mayor Lindsay appealed to the United Federation of Teachers and the Board of Education yesterday to step up their contract talks and, if necessary, start round-the-clock sessions.

"The schoolchildren and their parents are the third party at the bargaining table and neither side can be allowed to forget that for one minute," the Mayor said.

He urged both parties in the current negotiations to meet as often and as long as was needed "so that the school year can begin with a contract already signed." The previous two-year contract, which covered salaries and working conditions of about 54,000 teachers in the city's school system, expired June 30.

The union says that a new agreement must be reached by Aug. 1 if the schools are to reopen on time in September.

Agrees With Mayor

The Mayor said in a statement yesterday that the issues in the present contract talks were numerous and complex "and will not be quickly resolved . . . even by men of good faith unless a maximum effort is made." He declared that the negotiations "must come to grips at once with the hard-core issues" and that the overriding concern for both sides must remain "the continuing quality education of the children of our school system."

Asked for comment, the teacher union's president, Albert Shanker, agreed with the Mayor that the issues to be settled in the contract talks were many and complex, and said: "We are therefore prepared to engage in round-the-clock negotiations." Mr. Shanker had accused the Board of Education 10 days ago of frittering away critical bargaining time.

Board of Education and un-

Continued on Page 30, Column 1

MRS. KING RETAINS WIMBLEDON TITLE

U.S. Tennis Star Also Wins Doubles, Mixed Doubles

Mrs. Billie Jean King of Long Beach, Calif., retained the women's singles championship and shared two other titles yesterday in the all-England lawn tennis championships at Wimbledon. Mrs. King defeated Mrs. Ann Jones of Britain, 6-3, 6-4, to become the first woman to win in successive years since Maria Bueno of Brazil in 1959 and 1960.

Mrs. King also teamed with Rosemary Casals of San Francisco to win the women's doubles and with Owen Davidson of Australia to capture the mixed doubles. She was the first woman to share three Wimbledon titles since 1951.

TRACK AND FIELD

Jim Ryun of Kansas ran the 1,500-meters in 3 minutes 33.1 seconds, breaking the world record by 2.5 seconds, in the United States-British Commonwealth meet in Los Angeles.

THOROUGHBRED RACING

Alden Branch Farm's Exceedingly upset heavily favored Damascus in the $54,100 William du Pont Handicap at Delaware Park. George M. Humphrey's Indian Sunlite won the $57,600 Sheepshead Bay Handicap at Aqueduct.

BASEBALL

The New York Mets beat the Atlanta Braves, 3-2. The Baltimore Orioles downed the Yankees, 12-5.

Details in Section 5.

Eastern Will Move Reservation Center From City to Jersey

The New York Times July 9, 1967

Old site (1) and new (2)

By MALCOLM W. BRO...

Eastern Airlin... move its region... tions center out of ... City because it ne... to expand.

The line has a... campus-like site of ... in Woodbridge To... N. J., to replace its ... reservation offices ... Hippodrome Building... West 44th Street. The ... employs about 700 pers...

Eastern thus joined a gro... ing list of companies pla... ning or considering moves from New York City to the suburbs.

Jerome Full, an Eastern public relations official, said that only the reservations center would move, and that the rest of the line's New York City facilities would remain

Continued on Page 32, Column 1

POLICE SHORTAGES DISTURB SUBURBS

Pay Scales, Residence Laws and Tests Turning Men to Jobs in Industry

By MARTIN GANSBERG

A number of New York's suburban communities are losing young patrolmen to private industry and are finding it difficult to get replacements.

Many municipal officials say that the problem is caused by low salaries, residence requirements, age restrictions and tough recruitment examinations for the policemen.

"We have difficulty attracting men and we have difficulty holding them," said Mayor Thomas G. Dunn of Elizabeth, N. J., explaining last week why his police force was short 31 men of its required 300. Eight more men are leaving soon, he said.

Shortages Widespread

A random survey of 64 suburban communities showed that 53 had a shortage of patrolmen. Some reported they were putting men on overtime to cover the shortage.

The Nassau and Suffolk County Executives said there was no problem on Long Island except in 13 communities at the eastern end of Suffolk. The other parts of the Island are covered by county or local forces.

The situation has become so serious in New Jersey that State Senator Richard R. Stout, Monmouth County Republican, said he would introduce a bill in the Legislature to raise municipal pay scales, with state help, on the basis of population.

"Police salaries must be drastically improved," he said, "if our communities are to attract

Continued on Page 22, Column 1

Baltimore's Schools Censured by N. E. A.

Special to The New York Times

MINNEAPOLIS, July 8 — Sanctions against the Baltimore public school system were invoked today by the executive committee of the National Education Association.

The committee's action, based on the charge that the system was so "deficient" that it denied minimum levels of educational opportunity to many of the city's children, was the first of its kind ever to single out a major city's school system.

In Baltimore, Mayor Theodore R. McKeldin termed the sanctions an attempt by the association "to get even" for the loss of a bargaining election last month by its local

Continued on Page 25, Column 3

REPUBLICANS FACE 4 KEY PRIMARIES FOR PRESIDENCY

Romney and Nixon Expected to Battle in the First—Reagan Likely in Others

By WARREN WEAVER Jr.

Special to The New York Times

WASHINGTON, July 8—Th... line-up is very ...

... which ... can co... another ... these ... candidate... hazardou... empted by ... didates.

In the la... fornia, wher... feller of New ... Barry Goldwa... primary of ... however, Gove... run as a favori... that ordinarily st... didates from com...

Other prospect... sons—men who are ... Presidential aspirants ... as such for the honor ... or to avoid a party ... primary—include Gov. ... Volpe of Massachusett... mond P. Shafer of Pennsy... and Claude R. Kirk J... Florida.

In general, primary compe... tion will probably be confin... to the Republican party. Pres... dent Johnson will either b...

Continued on Page 29, Column 1

VIVIEN LEIGH, 53, IS DEAD IN LONDON

Friedman-Abeles

Vivien Leigh

Special to The New York Times

LONDON, July 8 — Vivien Leigh, the stage and screen actress, was found dead in her London apartment this morning. Theater lights in the West End were blacked out for an hour tonight in tribute to her.

Miss Leigh, who was 53 years old, was confined to her apartment on Eaton Square, Belgravia, four weeks ago with a recurrence of tuberculosis, an illness from which she had suffered since 1945.

Her death was reported to the coroner, but it is considered unlikely that an inquest will be held, since indications are that she died a natural death.

Before her illness, Miss Leigh planned a return to the West End in Edward Albee's "A

Continued on Page 60, Column 6

Troops Enter and Villagers Leave After Hong Kong Border Incident

...rontier between Hong Kong and Red China, walking past policeman yesterday

United Press International Radiophotos

...try Brigade patrol a road near the troubled border town

... The United State... said that two mari... had made beach ... ter assault landings ... the demilitarized zo... and Tuesday to su...

Continued on Page 4, C...

South Kor...

Special to The New York Times

SEOUL, South Korea, J... 8—South Korea's Central I... telligence Agency said toda... that it had arrested about 7... members of a large-scale Communist espionage network organized by North Korean intelligence officials in East Berlin beginning in 1953.

In addition, 37 persons are said to be under investigation and facing possible arrest.

Kim Hyung Wook, director of the Central Intelligence Agency, said at a news conference that physicians, musicians and painters, several newspaper reporters and many students studying in West Germany and other European countries were in-

... Un... Sou... as D... ng, a Korea... at Frankfurt University, two artists in France and a Paris correspondent of a Seoul newspaper are said to be among them.

Said to be still at large are approximately 50 Korean students abroad, most in West Germany but three in the United States, who refuse to

... some of ... Seoul after "abduction."

According to his account, intelligence officials at the North Korean Embassy in East Berlin began organizing a pro-Pyongyang network nine years ago among South Koreans studying in West Germany and France. Seven leading members were said to have been taken to Pyong-

Continued on Page 3, Column 3

... Secessionists ...orted Captured ...igeria in East

...D FRIENDLY Jr.

...e New York Times

...geria, July 8—...en Nigerian Army ...ces of the seces-... Region entered ...day, with both ...y had inflicted ...the other and ...ting of con-...

60 FEARED KILLED BY CONGO TROOPS

5 Europeans Reported to Be Among the Slain After Recapture of Bukavu

By The Associated Press

KAMEMBE, Rwanda, July 8—Congolese Government troops who had been routed by rebels aided by white mercenaries on Wednesday returned to the border city of Bukavu yesterday and killed more than 60 persons, including five Europeans, in a wild rampage of revenge, diplomatic and Red Cross officials reported today.

They said disciplined Congolese paratroopers then brought calm to Bukavu after their arrival by air from Kinshasa, the Congolese capital.

The reports from Bukavu reached this neighboring nation as the Congolese radio announced that forces loyal to President Joseph D. Mobutu had ...efeated mercenaries and rebels ... Bukavu, in Kisangani, the ...mer Stanleyville, and in ...u.

...go-Rwanda Border Shut

... radio said the fighting ...tarted Wednesday had ...with Government forces ...ol. President Mobutu ...rebels had begun the ... as part of an at-...oup plotted in Spain ... Premier Moise ...ho is now in cus-...ria.

...d plane was hi-...flying over the ...and diverted to ...ngo seeks his ... execute him. He ... convicted of charges of treason and subversion.

Refugees reaching Kamembe, two miles across the border from Bukavu, said the Bukavu area was now in the hands of loyal forces. The border between the Congo and Rwanda remained closed to Europeans, however.

About 1,500 Europeans live in Bukavu. United States officials in Rwanda said they knew of

Continued on Page 8, Column 1

ISRAEL AND EGYPT CLASH ONCE MORE IN THE CANAL AREA

Tel Aviv Says Its Jets Cross Canal to Bomb U.A.R. Guns —Cairo Claims Victory

MIG REPORTED DOWNED

Planes Clash Over Sinai—Security Council Meets at Request of Both Sides

By TERENCE SMITH

Special to The New York Times

TEL AVIV, July 8—Israeli jet fighters crossed the Suez Canal today to knock out Egyptian artillery positions on the west bank, according to a communiqué issued here.

An army spokesman said the Egyptians opened fire at 9:25 A.M. on Israeli positions in the occupied territory on the east bank of the canal near Ras el Ish. After several hours of shelling by Egyptian artillery and tank guns, Israeli officers called in the aircraft, he said.

Israeli and Egyptian jet fighters clashed later over the Sinai Desert, according to an Israeli communiqué. The Israelis reported downing an Egyptian MIG-21 in the dogfight, which further shattered the fragile peace in the Suez Canal area.

[The Cairo radio reported that the Egyptian units had turned back an Israeli ground attack at Ras el Ish and repulsed air attacks on Port Fuad and Port Said, but the Egyptians acknowledged the loss of one plane. Page 14.]

[At the request of both the Israeli and United Arab Republic Governments, the United Nations Security Council met Saturday to consider the latest incidents. It adjourned until Sunday without taking action. Page 15]

4 MIG's Reported in Clash

The aerial dogfight was reported to have taken place over the northern Sinai, at a point about eight miles east of the Israeli-occupied town of Qantara, on the east bank of the canal.

According to the statement issued here, four Soviet-supplied MIG-21's crossed the canal and penetrated the air space over the Sinai at 5 P.M.

After the MIG's roared over Israeli Army positions at Qantara, heading east, two Israeli Mirage jet fighters encountered them and "engaged them in a fight," the statement said.

"The MIG's turned west," it asserted, "but one was hit and was seen falling south at Port Said on the western bank. Neither of the Mirages was hit."

The clashes across the Suez Canal were the first since Monday, when intermittent fighting stopped after three days of sporadic shelling.

According to the Israeli account, the Egyptians kept up a heavy barrage of artillery and tank fire for several hours today, killing two Israelis and

Continued on Page 14, Column 1

Today's Sections

*Included in all copies in the New York metropolitan area and adjacent territory.

Index to Subjects

Vivien Leigh, British Actress, 53, Dies

Continued From Page 1, Col. 3

Delicate Balance." The play, scheduled to open in August, was postponed until the fall. Miss Leigh continued rehearsals in her apartment with Sir Michael Redgrave, who was to co-star.

Miss Leigh's last appearance in the West End was about five years ago. She appeared on Broadway last year in Chekhov's "Ivanov," with Sir John Gielgud.

Despite her illness, Miss Leigh had held a number of dinner parties and had received many visitors recently, a porter at her home said. "She seemed very gay and happy," he added.

Sir Laurence Olivier, her former husband, spent about half an hour at the three-bedroom apartment this morning after learning of Miss Leigh's death. Sir Laurence was her second husband. They were married in 1940 and divorced 20 years later.

One daughter survives from Miss Leigh's first marriage in 1932, to Herbert Leigh Holman, a London barrister.

Clark Gable and Vivien Leigh in *Gone With the Wind.*

A Dedicated Actress

Behind fragile beauty and sophisticated charm, Miss Leigh harbored a feverish dedication to acting and a tough business sense that drove her to develop constantly an originally modest talent until she became one of the century's great stars.

She could have begun to relax long ago, instead of searching endlessly for taxing roles. Her fame was made worldwide early in her career by her performance as Scarlett O'Hara, in the film version of "Gone With the Wind," in which she starred with Clark Gable.

The review of that performance by the late Frank E. Nugent, then movie critic for The New York Times, was typical. of the praise she received.

"She is so perfectly designed for the part by art and nature," he wrote, "that any other actress in the role would be inconceivable. Technicolor finds her beautiful, but Sidney Howard, who wrote the script, and Victor Fleming, who directed it, have found in her something more: The very embodiment of the selfish, hoydenish, slant-eyed miss who tackled life with both claws and a creamy complexion, asked no odds of any one or anything—least of all her conscience—and faced at last a defeat which, by her very unconquerability, neither she nor we can recognize as final.

"Miss Leigh's Scarlett is the pivot of the picture, as she was of the novel."

For this role Miss Leigh won the first of two Oscars — the second was in the film version of Tennessee Williams's "A Streetcar Named Desire," in which she captured the complex sensitivity and desperate tragedy of Blanche du Bois.

Although Miss Leigh appeared in other films from time to time—"Waterloo Bridge," "That Hamilton Woman," "A Yank at Oxford," "Caesar and Cleopatra," "Anna Karenina," "The Deep Blue Sea," "The Roman Spring of Mrs. Stone," "Ship of Fools"—she always reserved much of her time for the stage.

Her Cleopatra to Sir Laurence's Caesar, in Shaw's "Caesar and Cleopatra," was memorable on Broadway, as well as in England. On alternating nights, they would do Shakespeare's "Antony and Cleopatra."

In the former she was coy, kittenish, the adolescent becoming the woman. In the latter she was the mature ruler, in which love was balanced against practical considerations.

Of Miss Leigh's girlish Cleopatra, Brooks Atkinson, then drama critic of The Times, wrote:

"Slight and animated, she brings a cameo beauty to the part. Her Cleopatra, ravishingly costumed, is quick-witted, adroit, disarming and uncommonly decorative."

Of her Shakespeare-created Cleopatra, he wrote:

"Miss Leigh's Cleopatra is superb. We all knew that she would be every inch a queen. But it is a pleasure to report that she also has captured the infinite variety of the ruler of the Nile. She is smoldering and sensual, wily and treacherous, but she is also intelligent, audacious and courageous."

Away from work Miss Leigh was, according to some who knew her socially, excellent company, sparkling with anecdotes that she told well, and a good listener. She was a woman of poise and education. Her heart-shaped face, green-gray eyes, and mobile lovely face were captivating, even after years of illness.

A young woman whose family she often visited recalled:

"She was sensitive to how children felt. She was very good at drawing you out. She also would answer your questions. She would take me up to her room to show me wigs she wore in public. "And I remember she was a whiz at crossword puzzles and Scrabble. There was something else I never forgot. She was always speaking with enormous admiration of how Olivier was always growing as an actor and how great he was."

Though Miss Leigh could, while smiling at curtain calls, curse under her breath at a dull audience, she could also vent her fury upon critics she considered too lavish in their praise.

Thus, looking back on reviews of one of her first successes — in an English flop, "The Mask of Virtue"—the British actress told Lewis Funke and John E. Booth, in an interview for their book, "Actors Talk of Acting":

"Some critics saw fit to be as foolish as to say that I was a great actress. I thought that was a foolish, wicked thing to say because it put such an onus and such a responsibility onto me, which I simply wasn't able to carry."

To moviegoers, Miss Leigh

(continued)

Vivien Leigh with Robert Taylor in *Waterloo Bridge.*

Vivien Leigh

was known mainly for melancholy, if not tragic roles, but to theatergoers — especially in Britain—she was famous for a comic style with a perfect sense of timing, keen intelligence and her customary intensive preparation.

This showed to excellent advantage in revivals of Shaw's "The Doctor's Dilemma," Thornton Wilder's "Skin of Our Teeth," and Sheridan's "The School for Scandal."

It was in frivolous roles that her career was started and as recently as 1963, she won a Tony here for playing the Russian grand duchess in the musical version of "Torvarich," from the French comedy by Jacques Deval, which Robert E. Sherwood adapted.

She considered comedy more difficult than tragedy. "It's much easier to make people cry than to make them laugh," she once remarked while she was in Jean Giraudoux's comedy "Duel of Angels."

Miss Leigh's success in winning the role of Scarlett O'Hara demonstrated her resourcefulness as well as her talent. At a time when a world search was on for someone to play Margaret Mitchell's heroine, with major film stars up for consideration, she had quietly begun angling for the part from London.

At that time Mr. Olivier was in Hollywood where "Wuthering Heights" was being filmed. Both were waiting for divorces so they could be married. She hurried to Hollywood.

Though Mr. Olivier's influence, she was allowed on the set where the burning of Atlanta was already being shot for "Gone With the Wind." She met the producer, David O. Selznick, and impressed him forcibly. He gave her a screen test and the part.

Miss Leigh's desire to be an actress began in childhood. She was born in Darjeeling, India, Nov. 5, 1913, to an Irish mother, Gertrude Robinson Hartley, and her English husband, Ernest Richard Hartley, a stockbroker. She was sent to a convent in London for early schoolingand there, in her first school plays became certain she wanted to spend her life acting. Her schooling was continued in France, Italy and Germany as well as in England, and she began studying acting as an adolescent.

This early training was begun in the Royal Academy of Dramatic Art, where she did not do too well, and augmented by private instruction in Paris

Her first marriage, to Herbert Leigh Holman, interrupted her career only briefly, while she had her only child, Suzanne. It was from this marriage that she acquired the name by which the world came to know her.

Miss Leigh's first stage role was in the London suburbs in 1935, a small part in "The Green Sash." Though the play never reached the West End, she attracted the attention of a producer, Sydney Carroll, who cast her as a cocotte in "The Mask of Virtue," that prepared the way for a long career.

But instead of going from one frivolous show to the next, she became involved in serious drama, with the encouragement of Mr. Olivier. She worked with the Old Vic in Shakespeare. She also toured with other groups in a wide variety of plays.

Her marriage to Mr. Olivier took place at Ronald Colman's ranch, near Santa Barbara, Calif. Thereafter, the couple tended to avoid publicity as much as possible.

Only once in Miss Leigh's career was she spurned by her audience. This happened in 1957, when, with Sir Laurence, she attended a debate in the House of Lords and rose to protest the destruction of a theater. Amid frigid looks from the peers, she was escorted out of the chamber by the Gentleman Usher of the Black Rod, or sergeant at arms.

To the very end, Miss Leigh kept a sense of perspective about drama. She once remarked, after having acquired her two Oscars, that though "Gone With the Wind" had greatly helped her career, her role was very shallow compared to Shakespeare's 'Cleopatra.'"

Vivien Leigh in Bernard Shaw's *Caesar and Cleopatra.*

Marlon Brando and Vivien Leigh in *A Streetcar Named Desire.*

"All the News That's Fit to Print"

The New York Times

LATE CITY EDITION

Weather: Partly sunny today; clear and cold tonight. Sunny tomorrow. Temp. range: today 37-23; Monday 36-31. Full U.S. report on Page 73.

VOL. CXX. No. 41,317 — NEW YORK, TUESDAY, MARCH 9, 1971 — 15 CENTS

Frazier Outpoints Ali and Keeps Title

Muhammad A...

U. S. BACKS THANT ON BID TO ISRAEL FOR WITHDRAWAL

Comment Is Said to Parallel Private Efforts for Full Pullout From Egypt

By HEDRICK SMITH
Special to The New York Times

WASHINGTON, March 8 — The United States today endorsed Secretary General Thant's appeal for a pledge by Israel to withdraw her forces from all Egyptian territory.

The public... the State...

Court Forbids Job Tests That Screen Out Negroes

Rules, 8 to 0, That '64 Rights Law Bars Examinations That Do Not Relate to Qualifications to Perform Work

Special to The New York Times

WASHINGTON, March 8 — The Supreme Court ruled 8 to 0 today that employers cannot use job tests that screen out Negroes without realistically measuring their qualifications to do the work.

In the Court's...

The exception declared that it would not be illegal to use "any professionally developed ability test," provided that it was not designed or used to discriminate against a certain group.

Today's case grew out of applications for promotion by 13 ...lack laborers at the Duke ...wer Company's Dan River ...er Station at Draper, N. C. ...efore the civil rights law ...passed, the company em... ...Negroes only as labor... ...en these Negroes asked ...e up to jobs as coal ...they were confronted ...ew requirements that ...high school equiva-

...on Page 21, Column 1

DRAFT EXEMPTION BARRED TO CRITICS OF A SINGLE WAR

High Court Rules Objection Cannot Be Based on the Vietnam Action Alone

DECISION ON AN 8-1 VOTE

Douglas Calls Guarantee of Religious Freedom Shield Against 'Unjust' Conflict

Excerpts from Court opinions are printed on Page 20.

By FRED P. GRAHAM
Special to The New York Times

WASHINGTON, March 8 — The Supreme Court ruled today that young men were not entitled to draft exemptions as conscientious objectors if they objected only to the Vietnam conflict as an "unjust war" and did not oppose all wars.

In an 8-to-1 decision, the Court held that Congress had acted constitutionally when it ruled out "selective" conscientious objection by authorizing exemptions only for those men who were "conscientiously opposed to participation in war in any form."

The majority opinion, written by Justice Thurgood Marshall, said that this did not unconstitutionally favor religious denominations that teach total pacifism or did not infringe the freedom of religion of those who believe that only "unjust" wars must be opposed.

Rule Called Neutral

Justice Marshall declared ...hat the rule against selective ...scientious objection was es... ...ially neutral in its treat... ...of various religious faiths ...that any "incidental bur... ...felt by particular ...s were justified by ...vernment's interest in ...g the manpower neces... ...military purposes."

...e dissenter, Justice ...). Douglas, said: "I ...ed that the welfare ...le human soul was ...test of the vitality ...Amendment." ...that whether an ...horrence of kill...

...States ...effort by ...Nations. He was

...tinued on Page 20, Column 1

By ...
Spec...

WASH... Capt. Er... commande... fantry co... through the... was orde... stand trial o... meditated mu... with a dangerou...

One of the... brought against... Army alleges tha... "an unknown... unidentified Vietna... sons, not less tha... means of shooting [t... machine guns, rifles... weapons."

The specifications of... allege that he shot at... dentified Vietnamese... "while interrogating susp... enemy personnel."

If he is found guilty, ... 34-year-old Army captain cou... be sentenced to death or life imprisonment. A death sentence could not be carried out without the approval of President Nixon.

The decision to court-martial Captain Medina was made by his commander, Lieut. Gen. Albert O. Connor, the commanding general of the Third Army, at Fort McPherson, Ga.

The announcement of the general's decision was made at Fort McPherson and at the Pentagon. The Army said that no date had been set for the court-martial.

In a statement issued at Fort McPherson, Captain Medina said:

"I am innocent of the charges. I am surprised and dismayed that the Army has taken this action. Now pending before the United States Court of Military

Continued on Page 6, Column 1

The... Court... swear... ernor... pointed... week by... hammad...

The Chie... diqui, was c... terday's call... Rahman, th... nationalist le... long strike in... fices and the cou... military administ... eastern province. T... ernor, Gen. Tikka K... last night.

Since today was... holiday here, Gover... fices and businesses...

Protests Interrupt City Wel...

By PAUL L. MONTGOMERY

The Apollo 14 astronauts, interrupted occasionally by demonstrations for better schools and welfare housing, received the honors of the city yesterday.

The chilled, smiling adventurers—Capt. Alan B. Shepard Jr., Capt. Edgar D. Mitchell and Lieut. Col. Stuart A. Roosa—rode in a motorcade past scattered crowds on Fifth Avenue and Broadway and were presented with the city's gold medal by Mayor Lindsay on the steps of City Hall.

"What I'm saying today is give us a break," Captain Shepard said at the presentation ceremony as demonstrators in the background chanted "Crumbs for the children and millions for the moon" and held up signs saying "Welfare ... —the new-style concentra... camps."

"When total budget is ...cussed, take a look at what... spent to improve our domesti... conditions and what's spent on space," Captain Shepard said. "You'll be surprised at the ratio."

The leader of last month's voyage to the moon gave no specific figures. The $229.2-

th... wh... bac... citie... told... chanc... and y... ...sources— ...at home, not by ending the space effort but by expanding its scope and purpose. Perhaps the worst enemy of our best hopes is the belief that we cannot succeed."

The astronauts, accompanied

Continued on Page 34, Column 2

NEWS INDEX

...sey Clark and Paul O'Dwyer Join Defense in Berrigan Case

By LINDA CHARLTON

A team of four lawyers—Ramsey Clark, Paul O'Dwyer, Leonard Boudin and Addison Bowman—has agreed to undertake the defense of the Rev. Philip F. Berrigan and his five co-defendants when they stand trial on charges of conspiring to kidnap a Presidential aide and blow up heating tunnels in Government buildings in Washington.

Reports of a tentative agreement among three of the lawyers were confirmed last night by Mr. Boudin, who spoke in a telephone interview from Cambridge, Mass., where he is living during a year of teaching advanced constitutional litigation at Harvard Law School.

There is "nothing tentative" about the agreement, he said. He said also that Mr. Bowman, a lawyer practicing in Baltimore and Washington, would represent the Rev. Joseph R. Wenderoth, one of the six defendants.

Mr. Boudin said that while he had been associated with Mr. O'Dwyer "in several cases before," he had not previously been associated with Mr. Clark "except in the sense that, of course, he was Attorney General during the time of the Spock case, so I suppose that's an association."

Mr. Boudin represented Dr.

Continued on Page 22, Column 1

Harold Lloyd, Screen Comedian, Dead

By The Associated Press

HOLLYWOOD, March 8—Harold Lloyd, whose portrayals of a bumbling, bespectacled youth in impossible situations made him one of the great comedians of silent films and later of the talkies, died today of cancer at the age of 77.

He leaves three children, Harold Lloyd Jr., Mrs. Peggy Patten and Mrs. Gloria Guasti. His wife, the former Mildred Davis, was his leading lady in the twenties. She died in 1969.

A funeral service is scheduled for Thursday morning at the Scottish Rite Temple in Los Angeles, followed by burial at Forest Lawn Memorial-Park, Glendale.

Horn-Rims His Trademark

By MURRAY ILLSON

A pair of inexpensive horn-rimmed eyeglass frames without lenses, the shy expression of a somewhat bewildered adolescent and a single-track ambition made Harold Clayton Lloyd the highest-paid screen actor in Hollywood's golden age of the nineteen twenties.

Mr. Lloyd's closest rivals during that dazzling decade were Charlie Chaplin, Douglas Fairbanks, Mary Pickford and Gloria Swanson. But before the horn-rimmed spectacles were to become his trademark, known wherever movies were shown two generations ago, Mr. Lloyd had been a lowly paid extra and a run-of-the-mill slapstick comedian.

After having experimented with various character roles, Mr. Lloyd, in 1917, donned the lenseless frames that were to make him the fumbling but lovable silent-screen youth who overcame peril and frustration just in time to win the girl in the last reel.

Americans of all ages and audiences the world over ate it up, so much so that by 1926 a news story from Hollywood reported that Mr. Lloyd's earnings had advanced to "about $40,000 a week, or $2-million a year." And this was at a time when income taxes were low. He made nearly 500 films, from one reel to full-length, which earned more than $35-mil-

Continued on Page 40, Column 1

Gene Kornman

Mr. Lloyd as he was known to millions of moviegoers.

Associated Press

Harold Lloyd in 1971 photo

...ecade ...glin, Douglas ...ary Pickford and Gloria Swanson. But before the horn-rimmed spectacles were to become his trademark, known wherever movies were shown two generations ago, Mr. Lloyd had been a lowly paid extra and a run-of-the-mill slapstick comedian.

After having experimented with various character roles, Mr. Lloyd, in 1917, donned the lenseless frames that were to make him the fumbling but lovable silent-screen youth who overcame peril

Harold Lloyd in 1971 photo

Mr. Lloyd as he was known to millions of moviegoers.

and frustration just in time to win the girl in the last reel.

Americans of all ages and audiences the world over ate it up, so much so that by 1926 a news story from Hollywood reported that Mr. Lloyd's earnings had advanced to "about $40,000 a week, or $2-million a year." And this was at a time when income taxes were low. He made nearly 500 films, from one reel to full-length, which earned more than $35-mil-

Continued on Page 40, Column 1

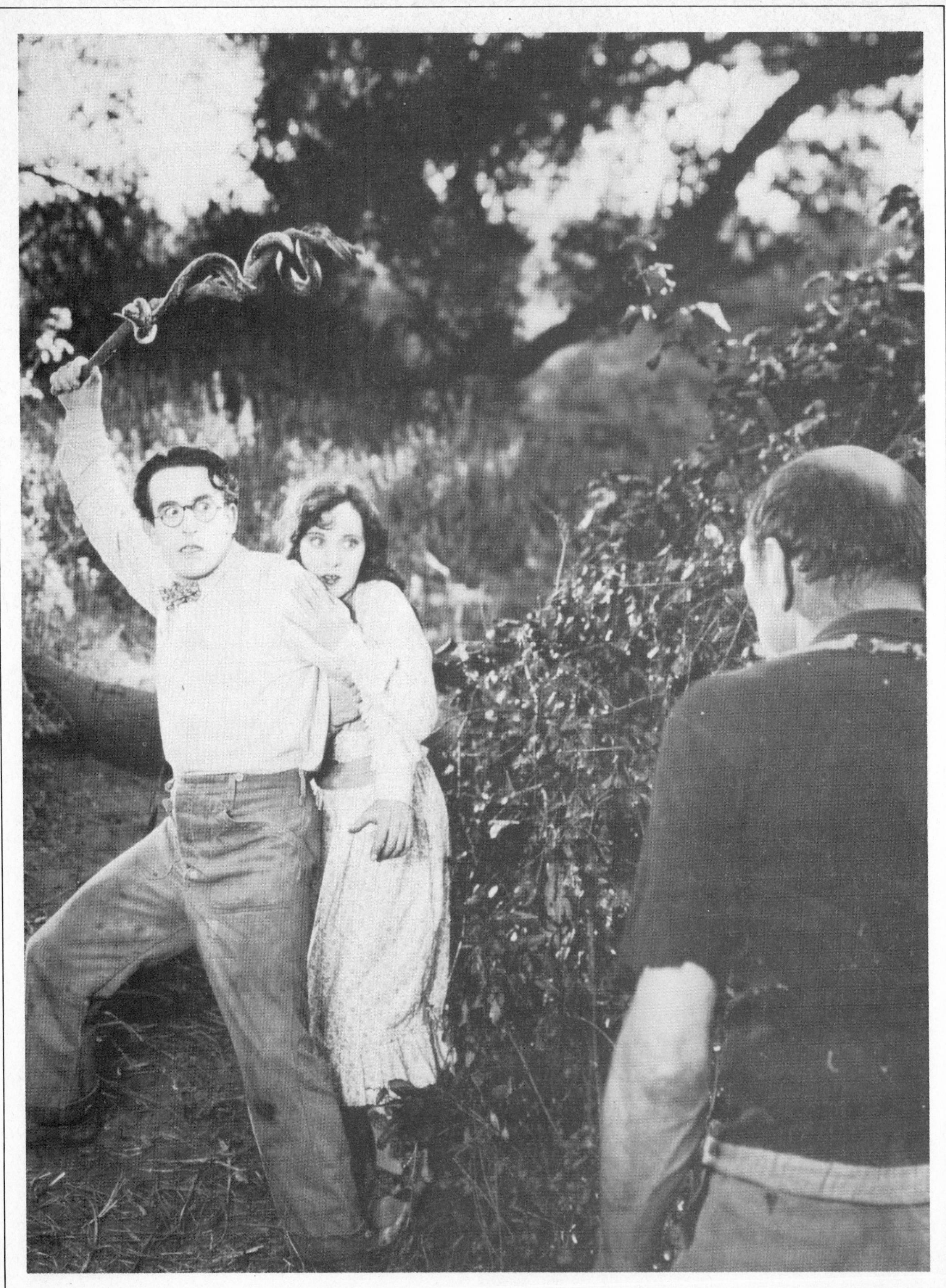

Harold Lloyd and Jobyna Ralston in *The Kid Brother*.

Harold Lloyd, Screen Comedian, Dies at 77

Continued From Page 1, Col. 6

lion in old-fashioned hard dollars.

In an autobiographical series that appeared in The Saturday Evening Post in 1928, Mr. Lloyd told how he found the horn-rims that he adopted as his own. The first pair he tried were too heavy, the second too large. The third pair, which proved to be just right, were finally found in a Los Angeles optical shop.

"I remember hunting through a tray containing probably 30 pair before coming on the right one," Mr. Lloyd recalled. "I wore them for a year and a half, guarding them with my life. When the frame broke from wear and tear I went on patching it with everything from paste to spirit gum, for three months, until progressive dissolution forced us to send them East to an optical-goods manufacturer for duplication.

"The manufacturers shipped us back 20 pairs tailored to the measure of the old faithfuls and returned our check. The advertising we had given tortoise-shell rims, they wrote, still left them in our debt. Since then all our rims have been tailor-made by this firm."

Lloyd with Jobyna Ralston in *Girl Shy*, 1924.

Insured for $25,000

The original lensless horn-rims were eventually to be insured by Mr. Lloyd with Lloyd's (no relation) of London for $25,000. The comedian wore them as a good-luck charm in the first scene of each of his pictures and then used substitutes.

Mr. Lloyd described his birth as "one of the least interesting things that ever happened to me." He was born on April 20, 1893, in a frame cottage in the Nebraska town of Burchard, which had a population of 300. He was the second of two children, five years younger than his brother Gaylord.

The Lloyd family lived in seven Nebraska and Colorado towns during Harold's first 15 years. His father had been an unsuccessful photographer, a shoe store clerk, a sewing machine salesman and finally the proprietor of a pool hall and lunch counter in San Diego, Calif., where young Harold finished high school.

Harold Lloyd once described himself as having been stage struck "as far back as memory serves, and to the exclusion of all else." He worked at odd jobs around local theaters, got occasional minor roles and then, in 1913, started in one-reelers in San Diego, playing bit parts for $3 a day.

100 Lonesome Lukes

The next year, in Hollywood, Mr. Lloyd was hired by Hal Roach, who also had been an extra but who had set up his own producing company with a recent inheritance of several thousand dollars. Mr. Lloyd played a character for Mr. Roach called "Willie Work" and later invented "Lonsome Luke."

As "Lonesome Luke," Mr. Lloyd wore clothes that were too small, a switch on the successful Charlie Chaplin, whose clothes were to large. About 100 "Lonesome Luke" one-reelers were produced, one, and at times two and three, a week. Of them, Mr. Lloyd had this to say:

"Whatever the plot, the picture always ended with 200 feet of chase. I was pursued by dogs, sheriffs, angry housewives, circus tigers, motor cars, baby carriages, wild bulls, trolleys, locomotives and, of course, legions of cops."

After having adopted his horn-rim glasses to suggest a new character that would be "quiet, normal, boyish, clean, sympathetic, not impossible to romance," Mr. Lloyd played the role in one one-reel picture a week for five years for Roach and Pathé.

Two years later, he started to make two-reelers that ran 20 minutes. In that year he was severely injured by a property bomb that exploded in his hand, and he was away from the cameras for about a year.

Married Leading Lady

In 1922, Mr. Lloyd decided to extend the length of his pictures to five reels or more. Then followed "Grandma's Boy," "Doctor Jack," "Safety Last," "Why Worry," "Girl Shy," "Hot Water," "The Freshman," "For Heaven's Sake," "The Kid Brother," and "Speedy." All were silent pictures, made up to 1928.

While "Why Worry" was being made in 1923, Mr. Lloyd married Miss Davis. His stunts in "Safety Last," also produced in 1923, made him known as the screen's most daring comedian. The plot required him to climb up the face of a 14-story building and to dangle from the hands of a giant clock at the top of the building.

These hair-raising scenes, which had audiences screaming and laughing at the same time, were done without the help of a double. The star was protected from a possible fall by an extended platform two floors below.

The comedian's first talking movie was "Welcome Danger," made in 1929. Thereafter, until 1945, with time out for a retirement of several years, he made for various studios "Feet First," "Movie Crazy," "The Milky Way," "The Cat's Paw," "Professor Beware" and "The Sin of Harold Diddlebock," which was a sequel to his famous 1925 film, "The Freshman."

"The Sin of Harold Diddlebock" eventually reached Broadway as "Mad Wednesday." It was described in The Times as "a curious mélange of comic spirit and apathy."

Owned Films Outright

Mr. Lloyd owned his later films outright and re-released several of them in subsequent years. In 1962 he issued a compilation of scenes from his old movies under the title "Harold Lloyd's World of Comedy."

When it was shown at the Cannes Film Festival in May that year, it was reported at the time that the audience "took a nostalgic look at the past and loved what it saw." Mr. Lloyd, who was present, was greeted by a standing ovation when the lights went up at the festival palace after a sell-out performance.

(continued)

Mr. Lloyd in "The Freshman"

Reviewing the film compilation for The New York Times when it was shown here, Bosley Crowther described Mr. Lloyd as "a wonderfully skillful and appealing comedian" and "a comedian of joyous elasticity and boundless invention."

Mr. Lloyd, he observed, was the "sometimes timorous but always tenacious 'average guy,' rushing into and out of all kinds of trouble and taking heroic punishment from all sides."

Of his roles in the movies, Mr. Lloyd had this to say of himself some years ago.

"I think my character represented the white-collar middle-class that felt frustrated but was always fighting to overcome its shortcomings. We had a big appeal for businessmen. They're always telling me they loved that boy because he was good for a laugh—you came away refreshed and you didn't have to do any heavy thinking.

"I think the new generation needs that kind of laughter. My God, the pictures they're making today are not for kids. They even put up signs in the box office—'For adults only.' And those French pictures! Many of them are fine, sure! But I can't take my grandchildren to see them."

Frequently Unrecognized

Mr. Lloyd recalled on occasion that in the old days of his movie fame he frequently would walk down a street unrecognized because he did not wear his world-renowned horn-rims off screen.

"I'd be with Doug Fairbanks and Mary Pickford, and heck, I'd get pushed out of the way," he noted. "The people wanted them, not me. Without the glasses, no one ever recognized me."

Another of Mr. Lloyd's close friends in Hollywood was W. C. Fields, who had developed an awesome repute for his consumption of martinis. Mr. Lloyd reminisced a few years ago:

"I used to play golf with Fields, and it wasn't easy, because he liked to drink. He didn't get that red nose for nothing. He bought it.

"I guess I bought mine a little, too, though I was never much of a drinker. Anyway, at the end of the first nine, we'd have to stop and drink. Fields insisted, and he poured stiff drinks. For me, the second nine was all uphill."

Lloyd's most famous sequence was in *Safety Last,* 1923.

Harold Lloyd with Mildred Davis in *Dr. Jack.*

The New York Times MONDAY, APRIL 1, 1957

GENE LOCKHART OF STAGE, SCREEN

Actor of Supporting Roles in Films Dies—Had First Broadway Part in 1916

SANTA MONICA, Calif., March 31 (AP)—Gene Lockhart, actor who became a familiar figure on motion picture screens in dozens of supporting roles, died today of a coronary thrombosis. He was 66 years old.

With him at his bedside in St. John's Hospital here were his wife, Kathleen, and daughter, June Lockhart, actress.

Mr. Lockhart, born at London, Ont., made his professional debut at the age of 6 when he appeared with the Kilties Band of Canada. At 15, he played in sketches with Beatrice Lillie.

In his later movie career, Mr. Lockhart appeared in more than 300 pitcures. Some of the best known included "The House on 92d Street," "Leave Her to Heaven," "The Shocking Miss Pilgrim," "Joan of Arc," "I'd Climb the Highest Mountain," "The Foxes of Harrow," "Miracle on 34th Street," "Vanishing American," "Carousel," and "The Man in the Gray Flannel Suit."

A frequent television performer, Mr. Lockhart played in the series "His Honor Homer Bill." His six-decade career also included turns at concert and operatic singing, writing a newspaper column and composing songs. He composed "The World Is Waiting for the Sunrise" with Deems Taylor.

On Broadway, Mr. Lockhart appeared in "Ah Wilderness!" and "Death of a Salesman." He had been working at Twentieth Century-Fox on a television show called "The Great American Hoax." The program was being made for the General Electric television series.

Mr. Lockhart's recent activities included a tour last fall in which he gave dramatic readings at colleges and universities.

In addition to his widow and daughter, he is survived by a sister, Mrs. Helen Havel of Baldwin, L. I., and two grandchildren.

Played in 'Riviera Girl'

Mr. Lockhart's first Broadway appearance was in "Riviera Girl" in 1916. In a later revue, "Bunk of 1926," he not only was a star, but also was co-author of most of the sketches and music. The production played off-Broadway at the Heckscher Theatre, and later at the Broadhurst.

In "Death of a Salesman," Mr. Lockhart replaced Lee J. Cobb as Willie Loman in 1949. Brooks Atkinson praised in The New York Times his portrayal of the role, and recalled the skill with which Mr. Lockhart had played the amiable reporter in the late Eugene O'Neill's "Ah Wilderness" seventeen years before.

At one point in his varied career, Mr. Lockhart had been an instructor in stage technique at the Juilliard School of Music here. He also had sung in "Die Fledermaus" for the San Francisco Opera Association. He had written theatrical sketches, radio shows, special stage material, song lyrics and articles for stage and radio magazines.

Mr. Lockhart was educated in Canadian schools and at Brompton Oratory School in London, England. He became a United States citizen in 1939.

Spencer Tracy with Gene Lockhart in *Edison the Man.*

Frank McHugh, Barry Fitzgerald, Bing Crosby and Gene Lockhart in *Going My Way.*

"All the News That's Fit to Print."

The New York Times.

LATE CITY EDITION
Warmer today; no rain or snow.
Temperatures Yesterday—Max., 35; Min., 15

Copyright, 1942, by The New York Times Company.

VOL. XCI..No. 30,674. Entered as Second-Class Matter, Postoffice, New York, N. Y. NEW YORK, SATURDAY, JANUARY 17, 1942. THREE CENTS NEW YORK CITY and Vicinity

NAVY SINKS FIVE JAPANESE SHIPS; BRITISH CHECK ENEMY IN MALAYA; NA[ZI]S PREPARE FOR SPRING DRIVE

NELSON RECEIVES OVER-ALL POWERS; KNUDSEN, ARMY JOB

Roosevelt Gives Production Chief Unprecedented Rule Over Nation's War Effort

OPM HEAD TO RUSH ARMS

Will Be a Lieutenant General Directing Output—Both on New War Production Board

By W. H. LAWRENCE
Special to THE NEW YORK TIMES.

WASHINGTON, Jan. 16—President Roosevelt delegated to Donald M. Nelson today full power to mobilize American industry, labor and government for an all-out war production effort, and shifted William S. Knudsen to the War Department, where, as Director of Production with the rank of lieutenant general, he will expedite arms output in the field.

Mr. Nelson was appointed chairman of a war production board of nine members, but the President gave to the chairman, and not to the board, the following powers:

"Exercise general direction over the war procurement and production program.

"Determine the policies, plans, procedures and methods of the several Federal departments, establishments, and agencies in respect to war procurement and production, including purchasing, contracting, specifications and construction; and including conversion, requisitioning, plant expansion, and the financing thereof; and issue such directives in respect thereto as he may deem necessary or appropriate.

Will Report to President

"Perform the functions and exercise the powers vested in the Supply Priorities and Allocations Board by Executive Order No. 8875 of Aug. 28, 1941.

"Supervise the Office of Production Management in the performance of its responsibilities and duties, and direct such changes in its organization as he may deem necessary.

"Report from time to time to the President on the progress of war procurement and production; and perform such other duties as the President may direct."

These powers give Mr. Nelson all the authority that he desires. The Executive order as issued by the President was said to be exactly as it was prepared by the new production chief and his counsel, Milton Katz.

It was said authoritatively that Mr. Nelson had more power than President Wilson gave to Bernard M. Baruch when he made him chairman of the War Industries Board in 1918, and that the delegation of power in today's Executive order was the greatest in the history of the nation.

The shift of Mr. Knudsen to the post of War Department production director was announced by the White House late in the afternoon after Mr. Knudsen, as OPM director general, had lunched with the President.

President Extols Knudsen

Mr. Roosevelt in a statement said:

"Bill Knudsen is one of the great production men of the world and his acceptance of this new post means that he can give his entire time to the direction and expediting of production, a field in which he has no equal.

"The country is already immeasurably indebted to Mr. Knudsen and in accepting this assignment at my request, he is undertaking one of the most important tasks of the war.

"He will, of course, continue as a member of the new War Production Board."

The White House said that Mr. Knudsen "will have entire charge of directing and expediting the gigantic production involved in the War Department munitions program, with special emphasis on the production of airplanes, tanks, guns and ammunition." It was said that Mr. Knudsen and his staff would frequently visit "the great arsenals and munitions factories with the object of helping them constantly to improve and speed up their lines of production."

Among defense officials, it was felt that Mr. Knudsen, who came to the advisory commission from the presidency of General Motors Corporation in June, 1940, with a great reputation as a production man, had been put in a job where his special talents and knowledge

Continued on Page Nine

ON MISSING PLANE

Carole Lombard

21 ON A LOST PLANE; MISS LOMBARD ONE

TWA Airliner Vanishes After Leaving Las Vegas—Blast Heard, Fire on Peak Seen

By The Associated Press.

LOS ANGELES, Jan. 16—A Transcontinental and Western air luxury liner carrying eighteen passengers and a crew of three was feared to have crashed and burned thirty miles southwest of Las Vegas, Nev., tonight.

On the Douglas Sky Club plane were Carole Lombard, actress wife of Clark Gable, the actor; her mother, Mrs. Elizabeth Peters; Otto Winkler, Metro-Goldwyn-Mayer publicity man, twelve Army pilots and three other passengers.

Mr. Gable chartered a plane to go to the scene.

The airliner, Flight 3, which left LaGuardia Field, New York, at 11 o'clock Thursday night for Los Angeles via Albuquerque, left Las Vegas at 7:07 P. M. Thirty minutes later workers at the Blue Diamond Mine reported that they saw a flare, then heard an explosion about thirty miles southwest of Las Vegas.

Pilot Art Cheney of Western Air Lines later reported that he saw a large fire while flying over Table Mountain.

First report of the apparent crash was telephoned to the police at Las Vegas. Two ambulances

Continued on Page Thirty

RIO PARLEY TREND IS TO VOTE BREAK WITH AXIS POWERS

Argentina Expected to Agree to Program Though Castillo Still Opposes Move

U.

the
that it
ican R
Americ
intendi
war de
introduce
ably will e
that the s
their purp
Though
offered on
will not b
next week th
understanding
resolution has a
sections and tha

Joint Pled

The preamble
porates the Washin
that none of those b
lations will reestab
rately and will cons
establishing relations w
first section declares the
the United States cons
act of aggression again
Americas. Section 2
break in all relations.
declares for no separate
lishment of relations.
Obviously this means th
Western Hemisphere inter
take measures constituting
tions against the Axis and its s
lites.

As this and other resolut
were offered in the final day f
that procedure there were increas
ing indications that Argentina wa
preparing to get in line. There wa
an impression that she would

Continued on Page Six

The International Situation

SATURDAY, JANUARY 17, 1942

United States warships of the Asiatic Fleet have sent five more Japanese vessels to the bottom in a powerful blow against an enemy offensive that relies heavily on sea transport. The latest Japanese vessels sunk, the Navy announced yesterday, were two cargo vessels and three troop transports, bringing the toll of sea losses inflicted on Japan by American forces to twenty-six. [1:8*.]

In sea action closer to home, the Navy confirmed that a second tanker had been sighted Thursday in a sinking condition off Long Island, about 100 miles east of New York. The tanker, flying the flag of an American ally, was apparently the victim of a submarine attack, and an undisclosed number of survivors were picked up. The Navy warned that the U-boat menace along the East coast was "increasingly serious." [1:4.]

The new American naval successes in the Far East lent indirect relief to General MacArthur in the Philippines, where specially trained enemy shock troops maintained attempts to filter through the Bataan defense lines with the support of constantly attacking planes. [1:6 and 7.]

To the south, the Japanese struck again by air at bases in the Netherlands Indies. For the second consecutive day they raided the naval and air base of Amboina, which was disclosed to have suffered some damage from the previous raid. They also bombed the oil port of Balik Papan on the lower east coast of Borneo and the Medan airport on the northeast coast of Sumatra. [2:8, with map.]

Japan's Malayan offensive slowed down under the impact of Australian reserves and other fresh Imperial troops, it was reported from Singapore. The defenders knocked out twenty enemy tanks and ten armored cars and inflicted heavy casualties. British planes smashed a new landing attempt on the west coast. [1:7, Map, p. 3.]

Inside Burma's border with Thailand, north of Malaya, British forces engaged invading Japanese troops, but a communiqué from Rangoon gave no details of the clash. [1:6.]

All along the Russian front, Soviet sources reported gains. In the Crimea, they said, Russian parachutists broke the German hold on the approaches to Simferopol at fourteen key points. In the Ukraine, the Russians were declared to be bombarding Kharkov and Taganrog heavily. On the Moscow front, indications pointed to progress of the pincers threatening Vyazma. [7:1.]

Germany is mustering new strength, both in man power and production, for a Spring offensive against Russia, an American correspondent reported on leaving the Reich. His dispatch depicted the German people as stolidly apathetic to good news and bad alike. [1: 5 and 6.]

In Libya, advance British columns pushed slowly toward El Agheila in the face of stiff resistance. [5: 1.]

In Washington, President Roosevelt delegated to Donald M. Nelson, head of the new War Production Board, the broadest powers ever given any man to mobilize American industry and fix Federal defense policy. The President shifted William S. Knudsen to the War Department as director of production. [1:1.]

At the Inter-American Conference of Foreign Ministers, three Latin-American nations submitted a strong resolution calling for a break of all hemispheric ties with the Axis. There were increasing signs that Argentina would support it. [1:3.]

*Figures in brackets refer to page and column respectively.

Co
se
n
the
sinc
Navy
was h
ing. H
word
Naval D
New York
Coimbra.
"An unkno
vivors has b
the only clue
ly worded Na
to the men who
bra.

Near Scene of

The location of t
was placed at "app
miles east of New Y
in the same general
definitely establishe
attack that sank the t
ness early Wednesday
The time was given as 7
morning—one day after
ness sinking.

Nothing was said as to the
ber of men that may have peri
with the tanker in American w
ters. Neither was it disclosed wh
the survivors may have landed.
was learned that the Southampto
hospital at 3 o'clock Thursday af
ernoon had been told to prepare
there for victims last night, but no survivors had arrived, the hospital superintendent reported.

After warning earlier in the day of the "increasingly serious" submarine menace in east coast waters, the Navy clarified the confused situation concerning the second sinking in the following announcement:

"A tanker named Coimbra, flying the flag of a foreign ally, was observed in a sinking condition on the morning of Jan. 15. Its position was approximately 100 miles east of New York. An unknown

Continued on Page Four

BOMBS FELL ON THE BRITISH STRONGHOLD OF SINGAPORE

Carole Lombard

21 ON A LOST PLANE; MISS LOMBARD ONE

TWA Airliner Vanishes After Leaving Las Vegas—Blast Heard, Fire on Peak Seen

By The Associated Press.

LOS ANGELES, Jan. 16—A Transcontinental and Western air luxury liner carrying eighteen passengers and a crew of three was feared to have crashed and burned thirty miles southwest of Las Vegas, Nev., tonight.

On the Douglas Sky Club plane were Carole Lombard, actress wife of Clark Gable, the actor; her mother, Mrs. Elizabeth Peters; Otto Winkler, Metro-Goldwyn-Mayer publicity man, twelve Army pilots and three other passengers.

Continued on Page Thirty

...ge in a street in the Malayan city

Associated Press Cablephoto, passed yesterday by British censor

...ear Indifferent ...for New Blows

...KELSSON
...YORK TIMES.

I have just left a Germany
Spring offensive announced
ver other military efforts
n the four-hour journey

...SE ATTEMPT ...URMA DRIVE

...h With Foe Near ...er but Details ...Revealed

...d Press.
...a, Jan. 16—
forces clashed
s late yester-
miles from
ong, narrow
down the
commu-
Royal
to de-
orth-
miles
the
air-
it

10 per
That 10 per
good half of the
...es of peacetime life—for instance, tobacco and liquor—while the 90 per cent of civilians has to divide as best it can what remains.

The Germans are being constantly encouraged by their press to consider the war as a piece of good business. While the campaign against Russia was going in the right direction for the Germans, the people at home were constantly fed with statistics very similar to the profit-and-loss sheets of a prosperous corporation. Every bushel of grain and every ton of iron ore in captured territory were

Continued on Page Seven

...l Arms in Drive ...Arthur From Peninsula

Special to THE NEW YORK TIMES.

WASHINGTON, Jan. 16 — General Douglas MacArthur, Commander in Chief of the United States Armed Forces in the Far East, again today reported that severe fighting was in progress in Bataan Province on the Philippine island of Luzon.

General MacArthur's report today was a terse but none the less emphatic account of the battle. It said that the Japanese were using specially trained units in an effort to pierce the defense lines. The attack constantly was being intensified.

[That the United States-Filipino forces still controlled large areas in the Philippines was indicated in an announcement in New York yesterday by the Western Union Telegraph Company. It said messages could be transmitted and received from the island of Mindanao, except the city of Davao, and from the islands of Cebu, Bohol, Leyte, Negros, Panay and Samar.]

"Ground fighting of varying intensity continues all along the front line," the War Department reported in the single communiqué on the Philippines issued today. "Enemy shock troops with special training are attempting aggressive infiltration. Attack planes and dive bombers are being used incessantly by the Japanese against

Continued on Page Three

AUSTRALIANS DEAL HEAVY BLOW TO FOE

R. A. F. Strikes Its Hardest So Far as Stand Is Made Above Singapore

By The Associated Press.

SINGAPORE, Jan. 16 — Eager Australians and other fresh Empire troops dealt heavy blows to the Japanese in Southern Malaya today and the R. A. F. struck its hardest in the six weeks of the conflict as the British Command organized the final defense of Singapore.

Battling the invaders along a shortened line, mixed Imperial forces were reported to have knocked out fourteen Japanese tanks and ten armored cars along the west coast above the plain of Malacca.

The Australians, who had moved into the lines with jovial shouts and ribald songs, smashed six more enemy tanks in Eastern Negri Sembilan State and cut down the invader in heavy numbers. This clash occurred in an area just above Johore State.

R. A. F. bombers pounced on Japanese forces attempting to land from barges in the mouth of the Linggi River, twenty miles north of Malacca, utterly smashing this attempt.

[Claims that Japanese forces had occupied the port of Malacca, about ninety miles north of Singapore; had taken all of Negri Sembilan State, and had penetrated deeply into Johore were made in a Tokyo broadcast

Continued on Page Three

HART STRIKES FO

U. S. Fleet Destroys Transports, 2 Cargo Boats in Far East

ENEMY OFFENSIVE CURBE

Allied Naval Units Fightir on Japan's Lines to Indies, Philippines and Malaya

By CHARLES HURD
Special to THE NEW YORK TIMES.

WASHINGTON, Jan. 16—Ame ican warships reported today t sinking of five more Japane ships—two cargo vessels and thr transports—as the United Stat Asiatic Fleet, under Admiral Thos as C. Hart, naval commander f the United Nations in the Sout western Pacific, carried aggressi warfare to the Japanese.

The sinkings, announced by t Navy Department twenty-fo hours after news of the sinking a 17,000-ton Japanese liner, rais to twenty-six the total of Japane ships known to have been su by naval forces since Dec. 7.

The Navy identified the ne sinkings only by stating that t Japanese ships included "two lar cargo ships, two large transpo and one medium-sized transport

Most of the Japanese ships su heretofore have been small, exce for a battleship destroyed by Army plane off the Philippines, cruiser sunk by the Marines w defended Wake Island for sever weeks, and the liner accounted f yesterday.

Blow to Japanese Campaigns

The ships now added to Japa mounting list of losses are i portant, particularly in view the fact that the Japanese are wa ing war a considerable distar from home, which obviously quires all the transport they c lay hands on to press their par lel campaigns on the Malay Pen sula, in the Philippines and t Netherlands Indies.

No sinkings of American sh have been reported from the P cific region for several days, c spite the fact that the War a Navy Departments have sent lar numbers of ships with more troc and matériel to Hawaii and r merous indications have been giv of the movement of importa convoys to the Western Pacific cooperate with the British a Netherlands in meeting the Ja anese attacks.

The naval aggression by t United States and Allied forces the Southwestern Pacific has a rect connection with the persiste defense by United States-Phil pine forces in their stronghold Bataan Peninsula, on the island Luzon.

If General Douglas MacArthu troops can hold out, without i mediate reinforcement or reli there is some confidence here though expressions of it are que fied—that they might be reliev by the stemming of Japanese a tacks elsewhere in regions whe American, British and Netherla forces can get at the foe.

The Philippines battlefield i almost 1,000 miles from the nea est strategic territory held by t United Nations and is surround by Japanese-occupied regions the Philippine Islands. Whate assistance is given now to Gene MacArthur apparently must co indirectly in the form of All naval and military successes el where that will contribute to e feat of the Japanese.

Hart Taking Fight to Enemy

WASHINGTON, Jan. 16 (U.P.) Today's report that the Uni States Asiatic Fleet had sent f more Japanese ships to the botte indicated that Admiral Hart's r atively small force is disdaini Japan's naval preponderance Far Eastern waters.

The total number of Japan warcraft actually sunk thus far American naval forces, includi the gallant marine defenders Wake Island, includes eight tra ports, five cargo ships, four

Continued on Page Four

21 ON A LOST PLANE; MISS LOMBARD ONE

Continued From Page One

Mr. Gable chartered a plane to go to the scene.

The airliner, Flight 3, which left LaGuardia Field, New York, at 11 o'clock Thursday night for Los Angeles via Albuquerque, left Las Vegas at 7:07 P. M. Thirty minutes later workers at the Blue Diamond Mine reported that they saw a flare, then heard an explosion about thirty miles southwest of Las Vegas.

Pilot Art Cheney of Western Air Lines later reported that he saw a large fire while flying over Table Mountain.

First report of the apparent crash was telephoned to the police at Las Vegas. Two ambulances bearing doctors and searchers in some twenty-five automobiles left Las Vegas immediately for the scene, which was about half way between Goodsprings and Blue Diamond, Nev., about forty miles west of Las Vegas and four miles south of the Las Vegas-Los Angeles highway.

The reported location is in rugged country near the edge of the desert, at an elevation of about 8,100 feet. The ground is covered with heavy snow.

Searchers set out immediately from Blue Diamond, and others were ready there to guide the Las Vegas parties to the scene.

Miss Lombard, her mother and Mr. Winkler were returning from Indianapolis where yesterday they participated in a defense bond campaign.

Survived Many Misfortunes

Carole Lombard gained her success in motion pictures in the face of numerous misfortunes which harried the early years of her career.

Her face, later known to millions, was badly cut and torn in an automobile accident, and doctors told her that she would never again be beautiful. She called in a well-known Hollywood plastic surgeon, and about a year later she returned to the screen with nothing to show for the accident but two almost invisible white lines on the side of her face.

At this period Miss Lombard was advised by a numerologist to change her name from Carol to Carole, on the theory that the added "e" would bring her immediate success. Soon afterward she signed a profitable contract.

Born Carol Jane Peters on Oct. 6, 1909, in Fort Wayne, Ind., she was the daughter of English and Scottish parents. One of her grandparents was a director of the company that laid the first transatlantic cable.

When she was a girl of 7 the Peters family moved to Los Angeles, where Carol Jane attended the Cahuenga Grammar School and a Los Angeles high school. Her first public appearance was as Queen of the May in a school pageant.

Her success in that role caused her mother to plan a stage career for Carol Jane. She sent her to the Marian Nolks Dramatic School in Los Angeles for further training.

Her step into motion pictures came after a dinner at which she met an executive of the Fox Film Corporation. She made her debut in a picture opposite Edmund Lowe. It was called "Marriage in Transit." During the next year, she worked in minor roles for the company and had just started to attract the attention of producers in other film companies when the automobile accident occurred. This threatened to end her career.

On returning to the Fox studios, Miss Lombard found that her contract had lapsed. She had to start from scratch again. Mack Sennett hired her for a series of slapstick comedies with Sally Eilers and Daphne Pollard. Her beauty attracted Paul Stein, a director for Pathe, who signed her to a contract for the leading role in "Show Folks," with Eddie Quillan and Lina Basquette.

Final Turn in Her Luck

But bad luck continued to trail the young actress. Her contract was permitted to lapse and she became a free-lance player, appearing in minor roles for Fox and Paramount, in such pictures as "Ned McCobb's Daughter," "Big News," "The Packeteer," "Safety in Numbers" and "Fast and Loose."

At last, however, her break came. In spite of obscure roles, she began to win a public following and approached the edge of cinema fame. This time her luck stayed with her. Paramount gave her a star's contract.

She appeared at this stage in her career in such films as "Up Pops the Devil," "No One Man," "No More Orchids," "Brief Moment," "I Take This Woman," "The Eagle and the Hawk," "No Man of Her Own" and "Ladies' Man."

In 1934 she played opposite George Raft in "Bolero," John Barrymore in "Twentieth Century," Bing Crosby in "We're Not Dressing," Gary Cooper in "Now and Forever," George Raft in "Rumba" and William Powell in "My Man Godfrey."

Her co-starring days ended in 1936. She established her reputation playing the lead in "The Gay Bride" and "Lady by Choice" in 1934, followed by feature-player parts in "Hands Across the Table," "Love Before Breakfast," "The Princess Comes Across," "Swing High, Swing Low" and "True Confession."

Star of Sophisticated Comedy

Her fame mounted to new heights when she starred in "Nothing Sacred," a sophisticated comedy by Ben Hecht. She followed that picture with a series of similar comedies, the high spots of which consisted in the heroine being batted around in a set of mad-irresponsible goings-on.

She had the lead in "Fools for Scandal," "Made for Each Other," "In Name Only," "Vigil in the Night," "They Knew What They Wanted" and "Mr. and Mrs. Smith."

Last week she completed her work in a picture titled "To Be or Not to Be." In the production, which has not yet been released, she was co-starred with Jack Benny. Alexander Korda produced the picture and it was directed by Ernst Lubitsch.

On Thursday Columbia signed Miss Lombard to appear opposite Melvyn Douglas in the picture "He Kissed the Bride," which was to go into production next month.

Since the outbreak of the war Miss Lombard had taken an active part in the sale of defense bonds. In her visit to Indianapolis, from which she was returning at the time of the accident, she sold more than $2,000,000 worth of bonds.

In 1931 Miss Lombard was married to William Powell, the film actor. She obtained a divorce two years later and in 1939 she and Clark Gable were married at Kingman, Ariz. The two top-notch stars were considered one of the happiest couples in movieland.

Carole Lombard and Fred MacMurray in *True Confession.*

Carole Lombard and Clark Gable in *No Man of Her Own,* 1932.

The New York Times TUESDAY, MARCH 24, 1964.

Peter Lorre Dies in Hollywood; Symbol of Film Horror Was 59

Actor Who Made Debut in 'M' Also Portrayed 'Mr. Moto' —Movie Favorite 30 Years

HOLLYWOOD, March 23 (UPI) — Peter Lorre, whose mild manner and sinister voice sent shivers up the spines of moviegoers for three decades, died of a stroke today. His age was 59.

Own Brand of Evil

When Peter Lorre squinted his baleful brown eyes and took a slow sinister puff on a cigarette, moviegoers throughout the world squirmed in their seats.

On the screen, the actor seemed to be the image of subsurface malevolence, and his pale, almost pasty moonface seemed to conceal a homicidal maniac with a temporary but firm grip on himself.

From the time of his debut in the German produced "M" in 1931, through scores of Hollywood and television films, Mr. Lorre, a short (5 foot 5 inches), pudgy man, was able to dominate the screen with his own particular brand of evil.

Occasionally, he varied his roles and played humorous parts, but he was never at his best in those parts, and he always returned to the role of the sinister and smart bad man.

As one critic put it, Mr. Lorre made a reputation "by being as mean and as murderous as the Hays office [then the industry's censorship panel] would permit." Others described him as "one of the cinema's most versatile murderers," the "gentle-fiend," and a "homicidal virtuoso."

After the terror years of Lon Chaney, Peter Lorre and Boris Karloff became Hollywood's stalwarts of horror movies.

Discovered by Fritz Lang

Mr. Lorre was born in Rosenburg, Hungary, on June 26, 1904. He went to school in Vienna for a while but ran away at 17 to join a touring German theatrical troupe. With the exception of a short period as a clerk in a bank, he remained an actor for the rest of his life.

After the usual tour in bit parts on the German stage, the producer Fritz Lang saw him as the perfect actor for the role of a pathological killer of little girls in "M."

Mr. Lorre's portrayal in the film is ranked among the greatest criminal characterizations on the screen, and the film made Mr. Lorre and Mr. Lang famous.

Although he was fluent in several European languages and had made a number of films on the Continent, Mr. Lorre spoke no English when he went to Britain for a role in a film.

However, when he encountered Alfred Hitchcock, Mr. Lorre let the director do all the talking, and by smiling and nodding, convinced him that his English was adequate.

Mr. Hitchcock gave the actor a role in "The Man Who Knew Too Much," after the one-way interview, and Mr. Lorre later commented that it was two weeks before Mr. Hitchcock learned that he spoke no English.

By the time the film was completed, Mr. Lorre's English was nearly perfect, and in 1934 he went to Hollywood.

In his first years in Hollywood, Mr. Lorre was cast in the type of roles that had already made him famous. He was an insane doctor in "Mad Love," and played the seriously disturbed student in Dostoevski's "Crime and Punishment."

One of his most distinctive features was the soft, nasal quality of his voice, tinged with a European accent, which he used with chilling effectiveness.

In many of the roles, Mr. Lorre seemed to be a man of two sides, a quiet gentle man and a raving maniac.

In one film, "Island of Doomed Men," which is not considered among his best, Mr. Lorre played a prison warden who equally enjoyed listening to Chopin and flogging prisoners.

In a series of movies, Mr. Lorre appeared as the larcenous sidekick of the late Sydney Greenstreet, a film bad man with a booming laugh that neatly complemented Mr. Lorre's nervous giggle.

Together with Humphrey Bogart, they appeared in "The Maltese Falcon," and "Casablanca," screen classics of the early nineteen-forties.

Mr. Lorre also portrayed the Japanese detective "Mr. Moto" in a series of movies, but soon returned to more sinister roles.

In Hollywood, Mr. Lorre was known as a quiet, almost shy man, with a deadpan sense of humor. He had been bothered with heart trouble in recent years, but managed to keep up a fairly busy working schedule.

Among his other films were "Arsenic and Old Lace," "Confidential Agent," "Mask of Dimitrios," Beat the Devil" and "20,000 Leagues Under the Sea."

During the nineteen-fifties and sixties he made frequent television appearances. He also sought more comic performances after the British Broadcasting Corporation in 1949 had warned parents to send children to bed before he appeared on a late variety show.

But Mr. Lorre had a thoroughly professional attitude toward his career.

"What do I care if I'm a villain?" he once asked. "I'll be anything they want me to be—ghoul, goon or clown—as long as it's necessary."

With only a few exceptions, Hollywood found it necessary—and Mr. Lorre found it profitable—for him to remain sinister.

Early in his career, Mr. Lorre worked with Bertolt Brecht and later was considered an expert on the works of the German playwright.

An avid reader of books in several languages, Mr. Lorre was also a fan of Los Angeles's professional baseball and football teams.

The actor married three times; Cecilia Lvovsky in 1934, Karen Verne in 1945 and Annemaire Stoldt in 1953. The first two marriages ended in divorce.

Peter Lorre and Humphrey Bogart in *The Maltese Falcon.*

Peter Lorre pleads for mercy in the final moments of *M.*

The New York Times FRIDAY, AUGUST 17, 1956.

BELA LUGOSI DIES; CREATED DRACULA

Portrayer of Vampire Role on Stage and Screen Was Star in Budapest

LOS ANGELES, Aug. 16 (AP)—Bela Lugosi, who won international stage and screen fame in the title role of Bram Stoker's mystery, "Dracula," died tonight. He was 71 years old.

A year ago the Hungarian-born actor appealed for help to Los Angeles County authorities, saying he was a narcotics addict and wanted a cure. He was admitted to Metropolitan State Hospital at Norwalk to begin a three-month rehabilitation course. When he was released Mr. Lugosi said he was convinced that he had been cured forever.

During World War I Mr. Lugosi was a lieutenant in the Hungarian Infantry. He served for more than two years on the Serbian frontier and later in Russia. In 1921, after the war and the political revolution in Hungary, he went to New York. He organized a Hungarian dramatic company in which he was producer, director and star.

Mr. Lugosi was born in Lugos, Hungary, on Oct. 29, 1884, a son of an upper-class family. He studied at the Academy of Theatrical Art in Budapest and began his career as an actor in 1900. In 1911 he was leading man at the Magyar Szinhaz, a Budapest theatre, and two years later became leading man at the Royal Hungarian National Theatre.

He started playing Shakespearean roles in Hungary and had three years of classical roles, including Ibsen and others. He fled the Communist reign of terror of the post-World War I period, and came to this country, via Berlin.

He produced several Hungarian plays here and made his first appearance on the English-speaking stage at the Greenwich Village Theatre as Fernando in "The Red Poppy."

This was during the early Nineteen Twenties. It was followed by his appearance as the Sheikh of Hammam in "Arabesque" at Daly's Theatre. Many important roles came thereafter, including those of Sergius Chernoff in "Open House," Father Petros in "Devil in the Cheese," and at the Fulton Theatre in this city in October, 1927, as Count Dracula in "Dracula," which ran throughout the season and was followed by a tour of two years.

Mr. Lugosi virtually created the role of Dracula, the mad count who lured victims to his macabre castle in the Hungarian mountains and there turned into a vampire and murdered them.

In September, 1933, Mr. Lugosi appeared as Siebenkase in "Murder at the Vanities," and, in 1944 he returned to the stage, after a long absence, in the role of Jonathan Brewster in a touring company of "Arsenic and Old Lace."

Mr. Lugosi first acted in motion pictures in 1915, and since that time had appeared in a great many films, mostly in the role of a monster. Among these were "The Wolf Man," "The Ghost of Frankenstein," "The Body Snatcher," "Zombies of Broadway," "The Human Monster," "One Body Too Many," "Frankenstein Meets the Wolf Man" and "The Mark of the Vampire."

In 1939 he portrayed one of the Communist commissars in the film "Ninotchka," which starred Greta Garbo.

Boris Karloff, Bela Lugosi and Basil Rathbone in *Son of Frankenstein,* 1939.

Bela Lugosi as *Dracula.*

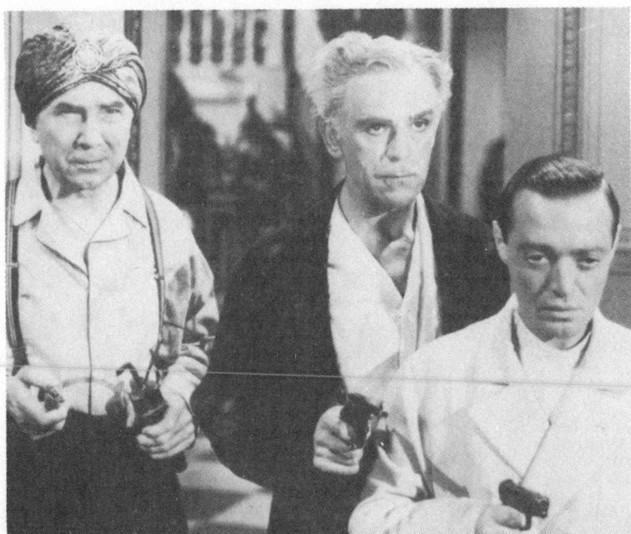

Bela Lugosi, Boris Karloff and Peter Lorre in *You'll Find Out,* 1940.

The New York Times TUESDAY, AUGUST 17, 1971

Paul Lukas, 1943 Oscar Winner, Dies

TANGIER, Morocco, Aug. 16 (Reuters) — Paul Lukas, who won an Academy Award as best actor in 1943 for his part in "Watch on the Rhine," died of heart failure in a hospital here last night. He was 76 years old.

Mr. Lukas, who starred in many movies in the 1930's and 1940's, came to Tangier in April.

Epitome of Suavity

In a career of more than half a century that included appearances in scores of films, on the stage, television and radio, Mr. Lukas won his greatest renown for his Broadway and Hollywood portrayals of Kurt Mueller in "Watch on the Rhine."

Although 25 years as an actor were behind him in 1941 when he undertook the role in the Lillian Hellman play of the anti-Nazi German who has come to America in 1940 to find peace and freedom, Mr. Luka's performance appeared to take many critics and the public by surprise.

The tall, cultivated, hazel-eyed actor, who epitomized Continental suavity, had appeared only once previously on the American stage, with Ruth Goldon in a revival of "A Doll's House." For the most part, he was known to the public from films in which he portrayed the villain or "the other man" in romantic triangles.

When "Watch on the "Rhine" opened at the Martin Beck Theater on April 1, 1941, Brooks Atkinson of The New York Times wrote: "As the enemy of fascism, Mr. Lukas's haggard, loving resourceful determination becomes heroic by virtue of his sincerity and his superior abilities as an actor." Later, the critic called the performance "a masterpiece, easily recognizable by every one who sees it."

The outpouring of praise from the critics was met by Mr. Lukas with amused calm, and he expressed the hope that it would not be the last time that he was discovered. He said of Miss Hellman's play, "The writing is so right you don't have to learn the part; it sticks to you. I amuse myself by changing a gesture occasionally."

With Bette Davis portraying his wife, Mr. Lukas re-created his stage role for Warner Brothers and was voted the best actor of 1943 by the New York film critics and by the Academy of Motion Picture Arts and Sciences, for which he was awarded the Oscar.

Bosley Crowther, The Times film critic said, "Mr. Lukas created a character—out of a richly written part, to be sure —which will live in the memory of this reviewer so long as it is possible to recall."

Mr. Lukas—the name was actually Lukacs, but Hollywood executives ordered it changed to spare audiences any difficulties in pronunciation—was born in Budapest, on May 26, 1895. The son of Janós Lukacs, an advertising executive, and the former Maria Zilahy, he said that he was born on a train as it pulled into the city.

In 1913, to avoid going into his father's business, he enlisted in the Austro-Hungarian Army. "I double-crossed the old man," he said once, "and the war double-crossed me."

After serving in the cavalry, he became an aviator, was wounded and was sent home. He had begun to perform in shows for soldiers and after leaving the service in 1915 he studied at the Hungarian Academy of Acting.

He made his formal stage debut in 1916 with a National Theater troupe and after two years moved to the Comedy Theater in Budapest, playing scores of characters in the works of Shakespeare, Chekhov, Shaw, Wilde and Moliere during the ensuing nine years.

Max Reinhardt, the noted director, took him as a guest artist to the theaters of Vienna and Berlin, where he made his film debut in "Samson and Delilah." Adolph Zukor, the American producer, was impressed by Mr. Lukas's performance in "Antonia" in Budapest, and brought him to the United States in 1927 to make his American debut with Pola Negri in "Loves of an Actress."

Mr. Lukas could barely speak English, and when talking pictures proved a success, Paramount offered to buy back his contract, but Mr. Lukas asked for a chance to take English lessons and within eight months achieved remarkable fluency.

Among his many films were "Address Unknown," "The Lady Vanishes," "Captured," "The Secret of the Blue Room," "Little Women," "Strange Cargo," 'Captain Fury," "The Three Musketeers," "Dodsworth," "Confessions of a Nazi Spy," "Uncertain Glory," "Deadline at Dawn," "Berlin Express," "Kim," "20,000 Leagues Under the Sea," "The Four Horsemen of the Apocalypse," "The Roots of Heaven" and "Fun in Acapulco."

His Broadway stage appearance included "Call Me Madam" and "Flight Into Egypt."

His first wife, the former Gizella Bense, known as Daisy, died in 1962. Mr. Lukas married Annette Driesens in 1963.

Paul Lukas, Bette Davis, and Beulah Bondi, in *Watch on the Rhine.* Lukas won an Academy Award for his role in the film.

Mary Clare with Paul Lukas in *The Lady Vanishes*, 1938.

The New York Times MONDAY, DECEMBER 22, 1975

William Lundigan, Actor, Dead; Made 125 Films Over 38 Years

William Lundigan, who appeared in more than 125 films during his 38-year career in Hollywood, died yesterday after a long illness in the City of Hope Medical Center in Duarte, a suburb of Los Angeles. He was 61 years old and lived in West Los Angeles.

Despite his active career in Hollywood, in which he appeared in an average of more than three films a year, including a handful of starring roles, critical acclaim largely eluded the lean, sandy-haired, blue-eyed actor.

A Critic's Description

A critic for The New York Times wrote 25 years ago, "He is more suggestive of a prep school football coach abruptly plunked down in the middle of the Rose Bowl, in the pink, but not quite seasoned to the shouting."

In the 1940's and 50's, Mr. Lundigan played the male counterpart to the-girl-next-door, a role that brought stardom to such actresses as Susan Haywood, Dorothy McGuire, Jane Greer and Jeanne Crain, all of whom he appeared with.

In 1951, after he appeared opposite Miss Haywood in "I'd Climb the Highest Mountain," the story of a Methodist circuit rider in the hills of Georgia, Mr. Lundigan described his first years in Hollywood.

After he signed a contract with Universal Pictures in 1937, "nothing much happened," he said in an interview.

"I was at Warners and Metro for two years each in pictures like 'Dodge City,' 'The Fighting Sixty-ninth' and 'The Old Maid.'

"I was always turning up as Olivia de Havilland's weak brother. Well, I got in a rut—that old bugaboo, type-casting—and made one quickie after another."

Mr. Lundigan was born in Syracuse, where he worked as a salesman in his father's shoe store. The elder Mr. Lundigan also owned the building that housed the local radio station, WFBL, and the actor-to-be often filled in as an announcer between stints as a pre-law student at Syracuse University.

After 13 years as an announcer, Mr. Lundigan was heard by a visiting film man, who was impressed by his crisp, resonant bass voice. He was sent to a movie studio in Astoria, Queens, for a screen test and soon he was in Hollywood.

"In, but not inside," he was to recall years later.

After making "Salute to the Marines," in 1942, he was drafted into the Marines and served two and one-half years, mainly with the First Division in the Pacific.

With Hedy Lamarr

After the war, the actor tried freelancing, with little success. The one exception was a supporting role in "Dishonored Lady," with Hedy Lamarr and his good friend, Dennis O'Keefe, with whom he often went duck hunting.

Two years later, Mr. Lundigan was cast in the Elia Kazan film "Pinky," starring Jeanne Crain.

Other films include "The Man Who Talked Too Much," "The Case of the Black Parrott," "Sunday Punch," "The Fabulous Dorseys" and "Mother Didn't Tell Me."

William Lundigan and Rhonda Fleming in *Inferno*.

Ethel Waters, Jeanne Crain and William Lundigan in *Pinky*.

The New York Times MONDAY, OCTOBER 27, 1952.

HATTIE M'DANIEL, BEULAH OF RADIO

Film Actress Who Won 'Oscar' for Role in 'Gone With the Wind' Succumbs at 57

HOLLYWOOD, Calif., Oct. 26 (AP)—Hattie McDaniel, portrayer of Beulah on radio and television and a Motion Picture Academy Award winner, died today after being ill with cancer for more than a year.

Miss McDaniel, who was 57 years old, succumbed at the Motion Picture Country House, in San Fernando Valley.

Miss McDaniel, who won her Academy Award in 1940 for playing the role of Scarlett O'Hara's mammy in "Gone With the Wind," was the first of her race to receive filmdom's coveted "Oscar." She had made her debut in films in 1931.

Miss McDaniel was born in Wichita, Kan., and was 15 when her family moved to Denver, where she won a gold medal at a contest sponsored by the Women's Christian Temperance Union for her eloquent recital of "Convict Joe." She performed without the benefit of a dramatic lesson and she never had one later, but from that contest-winning day Hattie was irremediably stage-struck.

She was 16 when her oldest brother, Otis, who wrote his own shows and songs, persuaded their mother to let Hattie go on the road with his company, which gave tent shows in small towns. Later Hattie sang with George Morrison's orchestra, and by 1924 she was a headline singer on the Pantages and Orpheum circuits.

In 1931, she went to California and was featured on a variety show on Los Angeles radio station KNX sponsored by a bakery that manufactured "Optimistic Donuts." The show ran for a year, aided by Hattie's singing.

"I used to get so enthusiastic singing," she recalled, "that I'd start to dance, too, and I'd dance right away from the microphone. Tom Breneman was the announcer and he'd have to lead me back to the mike. On our first show he gave me a nickname that he's never forgotten. I thought the cast would wear formal dress so I wore an evening gown. But everyone else wore street clothes, and when I arrived Tom said: 'Well, look at our High Hat Hattie.' He still calls me that."

Later Hattie appeared on the Eddie Cantor and "Amos 'n' Andy" shows on radio.

In addition to "Gone With the Wind," Miss McDaniel was seen in many other motion pictures, including "The Great Lie," with Bette Davis; "Maryland," "The Shopworn Angel," "In This Our Life," "George Washington Slept Here," "Since You Went Away," "The Little Colonel," with Shirley Temple; "Song of the South," "Judge Priest," "Saratoga" and "Nothing Sacred."

Hattie McDaniel received an Academy Award for her role in *Gone With the Wind.*

Paul Robeson, Hattie McDaniel, Irene Dunne, Charles Winninger in *Showboat,* 1936.

"All the News That's Fit to Print"

The New York Times.

LATE CITY EDITION
U. S. Weather Bureau Report (Page 85) forecasts:
Fair, then increasing cloudiness today. Snow tonight, tomorrow.
Temp. range: 25—10; yesterday: 37—12.

VOL. CXIV..No. 39,073.

NEW YORK, FRIDAY, JANUARY 15, 1965. TEN CENTS

U.S. PLANES WRECK KEY BRIDGE IN LAOS ON REDS' AID ROUTE

Raid Expected to Cut Deeply Into Flow of Supplies and Men From North Vietnam

SPAN HEAVILY DEFENDED

Washington Cloaks Incident in Tight Secrecy—Loss of 2 Craft Led to Disclosure

By JOHN W. FINNEY
Special to The New York Times

WASHINGTON, Jan. 14—A squadron of United States Air Force fighter-bombers yesterday knocked out a key bridge in Laos on the principal Communist supply route leading from North Vietnam.

The secret operation was described today as the largest, most successful air strike against Communist installations in Laos since the United States began attacking Communist supply lines several months ago.

The destruction of the bridge, it is believed, will result in drastically stemming the flow of men and supplies from North Vietnam into Laos and thence to South Vietnam.

However, Pentagon sources said that the primary purpose of the strikes has been to prevent the reinforcing and supplying of the Pathet Lao in Laos and only secondarily to harass a route also used by the Vietcong.

Defenses Aided by Radar

The large bridge knocked out yesterday was on Route 7, a road leading from the North Vietnamese coast into central Laos and the Plaine des Jarres, a stronghold of the pro-Communist Pathet Lao forces in Laos. The bridge is thought to be about 10 miles southeast of Ban Ban, where Route 7 crosses a tributary of the Son Ca River.

More than 20 fighter-bombers based in South Vietnam carried out the air strike. They attacked the most heavily defended Communist position in Laos. Machine guns protecting the bridge were aimed with the aid of radar.

Officials here had no comment on a report by Communist China that two groups of planes, totaling 24, had taken part in the bombing mission near Ban Ban. There were strong indications that the Chinese report was basically correct.

The Johnson Administration

Continued on Page 3, Column 5

The New York Times Jan. 15, 1965
SUPPLY LINE TARGET: A bridge was knocked out near Ban Ban (cross).

2 IRISH PREMIERS MEET FIRST TIME

Lemass Journey to Belfast Marks a Thaw, but Talks Exclude Political Issues

Special to The New York Times

BELFAST, Northern Ireland, Jan. 14 — The Prime Ministers of Northern Ireland and the Republic of Ireland met today for the first time since Ireland was partitioned, more than 40 years ago.

After the meeting, a Northern spokesman said, "Things will never be the same again."

He may have been overcome by the excitement of the occasion. But there was agreement throughout Belfast that Prime Minister Terence M. O'Neill and his guest from Dublin, Prime Minister Sean F. Lemass, had achieved a breakthrough that could soften the old bitterness of Irish politics.

They met in the Cabinet office at Stormont Castle, separated from the Parliament building by a quarter-mile of wooded estate. Mr. O'Neill extended the invitation to Mr. Lemass after a recent Washington meeting of the International Bank for Reconstruction and Development.

Communiqué Is Issued

After the talks there was a tea party, at which Mr. Lemass met other members of the Northern Irish Cabinet. Then both Prime Ministers issued the following communiqué:

"We have discussed matters in which there may prove to be a degree of common interest, and have agreed to explore further what specific measures may be possible or desirable by way of practical consultation and cooperation.

"Our talks — which did not touch on constitutional or political questions—have been conducted in a most amicable way, and we look forward to a further discussion in Dublin."

The subjects of the talks were believed to include trade and tourism, in which closer arrangements have been evolving for some time. The future of the Dublin-Belfast railroad, which is operating at a heavy loss, was also mentioned as a matter for urgent review.

Mr. Lemass's consent to come to the seat of government at Stormont is accepted in Belfast as a token of goodwill. Mr. O'Neill commented on television, "I regard it as a symbolic act."

Past statements of the Prime

Continued on Page 14, Column 2

SUKARNO FAVORS NEW BORNEO POLL ON MALAYSIA TIE

Pledges to Abide by a U.N. Survey Ruling or to Accept African-Asian Mediation

By SETH S. KING
Special to The New York Times

JAKARTA, Indonesia, Jan. 14—President Sukarno declared today that the only means of settling Indonesia's quarrel with Malaysia was to have another United Nations survey of political sentiment in Sarawak and Sabah, the Malaysian states on the island of Borneo.

He said he would "abide by" the findings of such a survey even though Indonesia had withdrawn from the United Nations.

If the United Nations does not choose to make this survey he will welcome appointment of an African-Asian conciliation commission to mediate the dispute, he said.

"Let us investigate the real feelings of the people of Sarawak and Sabah in a democratic manner," he said. "This is my answer when you ask if I have a peaceful solution."

He Talks to Newar

The Indonesi made gro his ma ter, come agree "Am he aske The In not discus rilla attack or Prince that these tro and a cease-fi before an Afr mission could fu

At Manila in Indonesia and t agreed to welcom a United Nations s that the people of S Sabah wanted to joi and Singapore in a ne nation. President Sukarn rejected the affirmativ ings of the United Natio

Suggestion at Tokyo

The African-Asian conc commission was sugges at a meeting of President S karno, Prince Rahman a Diosdado Macapagal, the Ph ilippine President, in Tokyo la June.

Mr. Sukarno told newsmen he had rejected a request this morning by D. N. Aidit, chairman of the Indonesian Communist party, for the arming of workers and peasants to defend the country against possible attacks by Malaysians and the British.

"I told him our own armed forces were strong enough to do this," the President said.

Indonesia's military leaders have always been opposed to

Continued on Page 3, Column 3

The New York Times (by Allyn Baum)
COMMENTING ON LEA FIGHT: Senator Robert F. Kennedy and alking with reporters yesterday after mocratic leadership stalemate Commodore Hotel.

Look onday

ed its ef- hopeful rly next

RT TY

sti nig ble over meeti cratic way out now are in In the be would succe the anti-Wa ing Mr. Bro majority leade

Continued on

63D STREET TUBE APPROVED BY CITY; HEARING HEATED

Transit Authority Is Backed Unanimously — O'Grady Rejects Further Study

By CHARLES G. BENNETT

The Board of Estimate approved yesterday the Transit Authority's proposal to build the controversial East Side subway tunnel at 63d Street instead of 64th Street as previously planned.

The board's vote was unanimous, but the nearly four-hour hearing that preceded the vote was acrimonious.

Tempers grew short in the white-painted Board of Estimate chamber as several rows of Queens civic workers, on hand to support the 63d Street route, became progressively more resentful as proponents of a 61st Street route emphasized their points.

Near the end of the hearing, Dr. David Bernstein, research director for the Citizens Union, warned the board it was "likely to be faced with legal action" because of its decision.

Assails 'Hasty' Decision

Anticipating board approval of the 63d Street route, he declared:

"The Transit Law requires adequate notice of a meeting of this kind and a full hearing. We have not had either. The law is designed to prevent a hasty, hysterical decision like this without adequate consideration."

The board was told by Joseph E. O'Grady, chairman of the Transit Authority, that the new tunnel would cost $28.1 million and that work would begin later this year.

Mr. O'Grady opposed suggestions by both William F. R. Ballard, chairman of the City Planning Commission, and the Citizens Budget Commission, a civic group, that the tunnel be studied further. The citizens get unit was one of the onents of an alternate route gh 61st Street.

u won't put a shovel in ound for several years if ing goes to a study," ady snapped.

90-Day Delay

had proposed that be delayed for 90 the Queens-Long Transportation Program to review of the ations south port back." ble connec- o existing tudy by gers and dem- Mr. ted uld permit tunnel and its about the same

Continued on Page 18, Column 4

MANHATTAN
WELFARE
ISLAND
QUEENSBORO BRIDGE
East River
QUEENS

The New York Times Jan. 15, 1965
SUBWAY TUNNEL: Solid line shows approved route. Cross marks island station.

ARENDS RETAINED; FORD REBUFFED

House G.O.P. Caucus Rejects Frelinghuysen as Whip Despite Leader's Plea

By JOHN D. MORRIS
Special to The New York Times

WASHINGTON, Jan. 14 — House Republicans disregarded the expressed wishes of their newly chosen leader today and re-elected Representative Leslie C. Arends of Illinois as minority whip.

It was a severe blow to the prestige and perhaps to the future effectiveness of Representative Gerald R. Ford Jr. of Michigan, who overthrew Representative Charles A. Halleck of Indiana as minority leader just 10 days ago.

Mr. Ford's announced choice for the job, which ranks second to his own in the party's House leadership structure, was Representative Peter H. B. Frelinghuysen of New Jersey.

Mr. Arends, a genial and popular survivor of the Old Guard, won on a secret ballot, 70 to 59, at a closed meeting of the Republican conference, or caucus, in the House chamber.

Byrnes Drops Post

In another development, Representative John W. Byrnes of Wisconsin resigned as the chairman of the House Republican Policy Committee in compliance with a new party rule.

This rule, adopted at today's caucus, prohibits the ranking Republican on any legislative committee from simultaneously holding a party leadership post in the House. Mr. Byrnes chose to continue as the senior Republican on the Ways and Means Committee.

Mr. Arends, who now has the same status on the Armed Services Committee, said he would step down to the second-ranking place among Republicans on that panel. Representative William H. Bates of Massachusetts will replace him.

Representative Arends attributed his victory over Mr. Frelinghuysen to a 21-year record of satisfactory service as whip under two leaders, Mr. Halleck and former Speaker Joseph W. Martin Jr. of Massachusetts.

Pledges Loyalty

"My loyalty to them was unquestionable," he said to Mr. Ford as the two stood, arm-in-arm, before television cameras. "It will be unquestionable to you. We will be doing the job to the best of our ability."

Mr. Ford said he did not regard the caucus vote as a "repudiation" of his leadership. Mr. Arends and Mr. Frelinghuysen agreed.

The minority leader conceded, however, that it was to some degree a "rebuff" in view of the fact that he had appealed to his colleagues in a speech at the caucus to follow his leadership and vote for Mr. Frelinghuysen.

Nevertheless, he said, "this

Continued on Page 16, Column 5

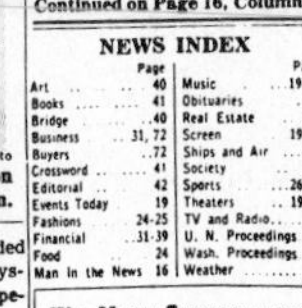

NEWS INDEX

The News Summary and Index appear today on Page 2.

PRESIDENT URGES FOREIGN AID FUND OF $3.38 BILLION

Request, Lowest in History of Program, Is Called the Necessary Minimum

PLEA MADE ON VIETNAM

Johnson Says He May Ask for More Money Later if New Situations Arise

Text of President's message is printed on Page 12.

By FELIX BELAIR Jr.
Special to The New York Times

WASHINGTON, Jan. 14 — President Johnson sought today Congressional approval for a $3.38 billion foreign aid authorization for the next fiscal year.

He said the program was designed to promote a world of stability, freedom and peace along with the security and well-being of the United States.

In a special message describing his program for the fiscal year 1966, beginning next July 1, the President reminded Congress that "this minimum request is the smallest in the history of foreign aid." He said it was "the lowest aid budget consistent with the national interest."

His request included $2.21 billion for economic loans and grants and $1.17 billion in military assistance to help independent developing nations remain free while acquiring the benefits of modern knowledge.

Reds' Aid Efforts Cited

The total cost would be $136 million less than the White House requested last year and the lowest since the first Marshall Plan installment of $7.4 billion in 1948.

Mr. Johnson said that the $500 million earmarked for military aid and supporting assistance to South Vietnam and Laos in the new fiscal year might not be enough.

Therefore he asked for an additional "open," or standby, authorization in these categories of aid, to be used only in Vietnam. Any such added amounts would be justified to the Congressional authorizing committees whenever an appropriation was requested, he said.

The President sought to counter criticism that the aid program was too widely scattered over a large number of coun-

Continued on Page 12, Column 7

PRESIDENT PLANS PAYMENTS ACTION

Special Message Expected on Worsening Deficit

By EDWIN L. DALE Jr.
Special to The New York Times

WASHINGTON, Jan. 14—In light of a sharp worsening of the deficit in the nation's international payments in the final quarter of last year, President Johnson will probably send a special message on the balance of payments to Congress in a few weeks.

The message would contain new measures for improving the balance of payments, though no final decisions on such measures have yet been made. The decision to send a special message is all but final, however.

A large, and probably temporary, bulge in the financing in the United States of new Canadian bond issues was the main factor in more than doubling the payments deficit in the fourth quarter over the average of the first three quarters, officials said today.

Preliminary figures for the fourth quarter indicate that the deficit, after a small seasonal adjustment, was more than $1 billion for the three months. This brought the deficit for the year as a whole above $2.5 billion, after earlier hopes it would be about $2 billion. The first three quarters averaged $500 million each.

The balance of payments measures the nation's transactions with foreign countries. It is the relationship between total payments to foreigners and total receipts from for-

Continued on Page 39, Column 6

1481 CRYPT YIELDS BODY OF PRINCESS

London Diggers Find Coffin of Historic Child Bride

By LAWRENCE FELLOWS
Special to The New York Times

LONDON, Friday, Jan. 15—Excavators on a building site in London have turned up a coffin with the remains of Anne Mowbray, the infant bride of the Duke of York, one of the two little princes murdered in the Tower of London in the 15th century.

The discovery was made Dec. 11 by workers breaking into a vaulted subterranean chamber of brick and chalk alongside St. Clare Street in Stepney, on the site of a medieval nunnery belonging to the order of St. Clare.

Since that time the lead sarcophagus and the remains in it have been under scrutiny by archaeologists, anatomists, osteologists and other experts, and they were identified by the London Museum today—the 487th anniversary of the marriage of Anne Mowbray to Richard, Duke of York.

She was then just over 5 years old; he was 4½.

At the wedding on Jan. 15, 1478, in St. Stephen's Chapel, where Parliament stands now, one of the honored guests was Richard's uncle, the Duke of Gloucester, who later became Richard III.

There, before a wall hung with carpets of azure covered with golden fleurs-de-lis, the Duke of Gloucester watched the celebration of mass at the high

Continued on Page 10, Column 1

Jeanette M'Donald, Star of 30's, Dead

Special to The New York Times

HOUSTON, Jan. 14—Jeanette MacDonald, the soprano who starred with Nelson Eddy in many popular Hollywood movies, died here today of a heart attack. Miss MacDonald, who was 57 years old, had been admitted to the hospital two days ago for heart surgery.

When Jeanette Anna MacDonald made her first stage appearance at the age of 3 in Philadelphia, she went on uninvited, recited "Old Mother Hubbard," and stole the show. Nineteen years later, in 1929, the red-haired beauty with sea-green eyes made her first movie, and from then on her

Continued on Page 43, Column 2

Jeanette M'Donald, Star of 30's, Dead

Special to The New York Times

HOUSTON, Jan. 14—Jeanette MacDonald, the soprano who starred with Nelson Eddy in many popular Hollywood movies, died here today of a heart attack. Miss MacDonald, who was 57 years old, had been admitted to the hospital two days ago for heart surgery.

When Jeanette Anna MacDonald made her first stage appearance at the age of 3 in Philadelphia, she went on uninvited, recited "Old Mother Hubbard," and stole the show. Nineteen years later, in 1929, the red-haired beauty with sea-green eyes made her first movie, and from then on her

Continued on Page 43, Column 2

Dr. Schweitzer Ha 90 in Jungle Town

He Hears Broadcast of Bach From His Alsatian Home

By United Press International

LAMBARENE, Gabon, Jan. 14—Modern technology carried music by Bach from Dr. Albert Schweitzer's birthplace of Kaysersberg, now in France, to this jungle village in Africa today as a special tribute to the physician and humanitarian on his 90th birthday.

Scores of guests came to take part in the celebration.

Dr. Schweitzer, an authority on Bach, was visibly moved as he listened to the Kaysersberg organ. The sound came through clearly on a special hook-up arranged by the French and Gabonese radio networks.

A motor-driven canoe brought Dr. Schweitzer here this morning from his jungle hospital a few miles across the muddy Ogooué River.

The ceremonies, sponsored by the Gabonese Republic, were attended by Americans, Europeans, Asians and Africans.

A strong sun bore down mercilessly on the equatorial rain forest. The deeply lined face of the doctor soon began to show signs of fatigue and he did not attend an official luncheon in his honor.

Instead, he returned to his hospital, where he ate with the medical staff. He canceled attendance at a dance recital in the evening to save his strength for the visits to be made to his hospital tomorrow by guests.

Among those who trekked to the village was Mayor Georges Ferrenbach of Kaysersberg. Kaysersberg, an Alsatian village, was in the German Empire when Dr. Schweitzer was born.

Lambaréné, the little hospital village Dr. Schweitzer founded in 1913, is "twinned" with Kaysersberg for the three-day period of celebration.

The Mayor of Lambaréné gave the reception and luncheon in

Continued on Page 2, Column 2

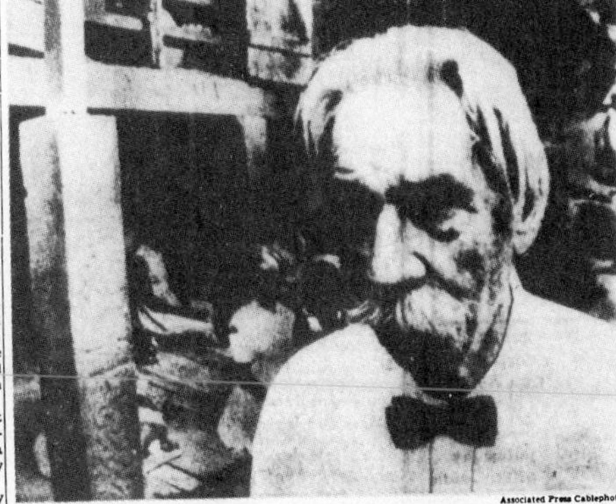

Associated Press Cablephoto
Dr. Albert Schweitzer as he appeared last month in a British Broadcasting Corporation television report on the doctor's work at his jungle hospital in Lambaréné, Gabon.

Jeannette MacDonald and Maurice Chevalier in *The Merry Widow*.

Jeanette MacDonald, 57, Dead; Starred in Hollywood Musicals

Continued From Page 1, Col. 2

soprano voice and wholesome charm enchanted thousands across the country.

Her first movie role was opposite Maurice Chevalier in the screen's first original operetta, "The Love Parade." Captivated audiences immediately latched on to rumors that she and Mr. Chevalier would soon be husband and wife. They denied the rumors but to no avail.

Later, in 1935 and 1936, when Miss MacDonald teamed with Nelson Eddy in two musical romances, "Naughty Marietta," and "Rose Marie," many fans again believed that a great love was in the making.

But in November of 1936, Miss MacDonald and Gene Raymond, the actor, announced that they would be married, stunning Hollywood fans and gossip-columnists.

They were married in June, 1937, in one of the fanciest weddings Hollywood had seen. Thousands of persons lined the streets for blocks behind more than 100 policemen to catch a glimpse of the stars.

In Hollywood, where romances often cooled quickly, theirs endured. Mr. Raymond was at his wife's side at her death.

A Long Love Song

It was in the summer of 1914 that young Jeanette got her first professional taste of show business, a taste that blossomed into a never ending love song. She accompanied her father on a business trip from their home in Philadelphia to New York and visited the Capitol Theater, where her sister Blossom was a member of the chorus.

Having taken some dancing and singing lessons and aspiring to a career in the theater, Jeanette did a few nervous steps and, she once recalled, "sang a popular melody" for the producer, who promptly offered her a job.

The MacDonald family then moved to New York. Young Jeanette was paid $20 a week in her chorus job.

She appeared in two Broadway shows shortly afterward, but then there was a dearth of parts and the theater she said "wasn't quite as bright, quite as gay."

She had an offer to be a professional model and accepted, only to find that she was modeling fur coats under hot lights in July.

"If it hadn't been for the coats, combined with the weather," she said, "I would never have had courage enough to take the next step in this Broadway career of mine."

Her first real break came when she was cast in one of the leading roles in a Greenwich Village Theater production of "Fantastic Fricasee."

The show was ill-fated, but Miss MacDonald gave it what life it had. She moved on to Broadway where her first show was "The Magic Ring." After that she appeared in "Tip Toes," "Bubbling Over," "Yes, Yes Yvette," "Sunny Days," "Boom Boom," and "Angela," all musical comedies.

The last show brought her to the attention of Ernst Lubitsch, the Hollywood director, who cast her opposite Mr. Chevalier. She impressed critics and audiences with her simple, easy, unaffected manner of delivering a song.

She played in two more Lubitsch-Chevalier films—"One Hour With You" in 1931 and "Love Me Tonight," a big hit in 1932. A third film, "The Merry Widow," an adaptation of the Franz Lehar operetta, opened in New York with great fanfare in October, 1934. Arc lamps threw a weird blue mist up and down Broadway and thousands crowded near the Astor Theater to see the array of movie stars. Miss MacDonald blew the crowd a kiss and told them her heart was full of gratitude.

Teamed With Eddy

After a European concert tour that attracted sell-out crowds, she returned to Hollywood and signed a Metro-Goldwyn-Mayer contract that resulted in her successful teaming with the baritone voice of Nelson Eddy.

"Naughty Marietta," with a score by Victor Herbert, was their first picture. It received an Academy Award in 1935 and the names of the two singers became household words. Miss MacDonald had not been enthusiastic about doing the film. She relented after Louis B. Mayer got down on his knees and began singing the Jewish lament "Eli, Eli" in an earnest manner.

As tears came to Miss MacDonald's eyes, Mr. Mayer got up humbly and said, "That's the way you should sing." She agreed to do the movie.

In 1936, the MacDonald-Eddy team made "Rose Marie," in which Mr. Eddy sang and yoohooed the now-famous "Indian Love Call" to Miss MacDonald.

They also teamed in "Maytime," "The Girl of the Golden West," "Sweethearts," "New Moon" and "Bittersweet." There were few romantics who did not lose their hearts to this handsome couple, singing enthusiastically as the falling apple blossoms showered them.

When their series was discontinued in the late 1930's, Miss MacDonald turned to a dramatic role and was acclaimed for her portrayal opposite Clark Gable in "San Francisco."

In 1942, she left the movies to make concert tours here and abroad, make recordings and appear on radio shows. She made her official grand opera debut in "Romeo and Juliet" in Montreal. This was followed by her American debut in "Faust" with the Chicago Civic Opera Company. She returned to films briefly in 1947 and after playing the role of a mother in one movie, said: "I'm through with the Valentine parts."

In recent years, she limited her appearances to occasional guest spots on television and some nightclub performances. Her films still appear on television.

Miss MacDonald was described by an associate in Hollywood as having suffered from a heart condition for the last five or six years. Just before Christmas she was stricken with abdominal adhesions, a Houston hospital official said.

Miss MacDonald and Mr. Raymond had no children.

Jeanette MacDonald and Nelson Eddy in *Sweethearts.*

Clark Gable and Jeannette MacDonald starred as Blackie Norton and Mary in *San Francisco,* a story about the 1906 earthquake.

The New York Times SUNDAY, NOVEMBER 8, 1959.

VICTOR M'LAGLEN, SCREEN STAR, DIES

Won 1935 Oscar as 'The Informer'—Capt. Flagg In 'What Price Glory?'

APPEARED IN 150 FILMS

Blustering Tough Guy for Lost Patrol,' 'Gunga Din' and Ford's 'Quiet Man'

HOLLYWOOD, Calif., Nov. 7 (AP)—Victor McLaglen, screen star and Academy Award winner, died today of a congested heart failure at his home in near-by Newport Beach. He was 72 years old.

His widow, Margaret; a son, Andrew, a television producer, and a daughter, Sheila, were at his bedside.

Directed by John Ford

Mr. McLaglen will probably be remembered longest for his finest achievement, the role of Gypo Nolan, the title part in "The Informer." The film, for which both he and John Ford, the director, won Oscars in 1935, is still revived frequently today.

Critics said that Mr. McLaglen submerged himself completely in the part of the brawling, drunken Irishman who sells out his comrades in the Irish underground and is agonized by conscience before he is slain.

He looked the part. He stood 6 foot 3, and his 220 pounds included little fat. He had the broken nose of a prize-fighter, and soulful eyes. He had the curly red hair and brogue of a native Gael.

But Mr. McLaglen was not an Irishman, not much anyway. His mother was of Irish descent, but his father was the Rev. Andrew McLaglen, an Anglican clergyman of Scottish and English ancestry, who later became Bishop of Clermont, South Africa. The son was born in Tunbridge Wells, a once-fashionable spa near London, on Dec. 11, 1886. He was never scholarly, like his father, but wildly adventurous and extroverted.

He ran away from home to enlist (by adding four fictitious years to his age) in the London Life Guards for service in the Boer War. It was three years before his parents found him and had him shipped home.

Prospected for Gold

Later the youth went to Canada to be a wheat farmer, but seized a chance, instead, to prospect for gold in the wild interior. Finding no gold, he earned a doubtful living as a professional boxer and wrestler.

In his biography, "Express to Hollywood," Mr. McLaglen estimated that he survived nearly 1,000 bouts.

He fought Jack Johnson, heavyweight champion of the world, in a six-round exhibition match in Vancouver, B. C., and earned $900. In another exhibition, Mr. McLaglen wrestled an entire football team, one man after another.

For several years he toured Canada with a traveling sideshow, offering any man in the crowd $15 to stay three minutes in the ring with him, or allowing his chest to be used as an anvil for men to break rocks on. Then he shipped about the South Seas, dived for pearls, got shipwrecked.

Mr. McLaglen was old enough to join the British Army for World War I. He served as a captain against the Turks and Germans in Mesopotamia, and also as provost marshal (military police chief) in Baghdad.

After the war, Mr. McLaglen got his start in show business, a rough-guy part in a British movie, "Call of the Road." It was a success, and he was signed for $150 a week. He progressed slowly in London until 1924, when he was called to Hollywood at double the salary. He became a citizen in 1933.

He had a minor part in Lon Chaney's horror film "The Unholy Three" in 1925. The next year came his first great success, in the role of Captain Flagg in the film "What Price Glory?" with Edmund Lowe as Sergeant Quirt and Dolores del Rio as the French girl the two Marines fought over.

The film did not approach the artistic excellence of the original stage play by Laurence Stallings and Maxwell Anderson, and the anti-war theme was subordinated to the sex. But it established Mr. McLaglen as a box-office favorite. For nine years, he and Mr. Lowe made a series of film comedies about Captain Flagg and Sergeant Quirt of the Marines. Mr. McLaglen was making $5,000 a week and—as he boasted—spending far more.

He acted in nearly 150 films before his death. None of his roles exceeded in popularity "What Price Glory?" or in artistic excellence "The Informer." He played memorable roles in John Ford's "The Quiet Man," a charming Irish comedy in 1952. He was a British platoon leader in "The Lost Patrol" and a British officer again in "Gunga Din."

When World War II ended, Mr. McLaglen, reduced to supporting roles, had squandered his fortune. He owed $250,000 in income taxes. But he paid it off with new earnings before he died.

Victor McLaglen won an Academy Award for *The Informer.*

Mr. McLaglen married three times. His first wife, Enid Lamont of London, died in 1942, leaving him two children, Andrew and Sheila. In 1943, he married his secretary, Suzanna Brueggemann. They were divorced in 1948. Mr. McLaglen then married Margaret Pumphrey of Berkeley, Calif.

Sam Jaffe, Victor McLaglen, Douglas Fairbanks, Jr., and Cary Grant in *Gunga Din.*

The New York Times THURSDAY, SEPTEMBER 27, 1973

Anna Magnani, the Actress, Dies at 65

Special to The New York Times

ROME, Sept. 26—Anna Magnani, who won an Oscar for her performance in "The Rose Tattoo," died tonight in a clinic. She was 65 years old.

The actress had been suffering from a tumor of the pancreas.

With her at her death were her son, Luca, and a long-time friend, the film director Roberto Rossellini.

Vesuvian Temperament

"The last of the great shameless emotionalists" was William Dieterle's description of Anna Magnani. Although the director's assessment contained some hyperbole, it was as the actress of Vesuvian temperament that Miss Magnani achieved her fame. There was, however, a genuine talent that matched her expressions of feelings; and the combination of the two won her critical praise for both her film and stage roles.

Her principal triumph in the United States was in the role of Serafina Delle Rose in the movie version of Tennessee Williams's "The Rose Tattoo" in 1955. The ardent and intense acting won her an Academy Award as well as the New York Film Critics' Award as best actress of the year.

"Miss Magnani sweeps most everything before her," wrote The New York Times film critic in describing her realism in playing a warm, full-bodied tragicomic character. "She overwhelms all objectivity with the rush of her subjective force," he said.

"The Rose Tattoo," which also starred Burt Lancaster, was Miss Magnani's first Hollywood film. But she had been known to American audiences for a decade for her starring roles in such Italian films as "Open City," "Angelina" and "Love," in which she was directed by Mr. Rossellini.

The woman that viewers saw was diminutive and slightly plump; she wore her raven hair long and mostly uncombed, and her face was set off by wondrous dark eyes. She had an ability to weep real tears, to laugh real laughter, to brawl fiercely; to be thunderous in anger, lusciously sensual in love. Searching for a word to encapsulate her, many critics fastened on "seething." It seemed to fit.

Miss Magnani's earthiness was a projection of her childhood. Born in Rome March 7, 1908, she was brought up in poverty by her maternal grandparents after her father disappeared and her mother departed for Egypt. As a slum child she absorbed the manners and language of the toughest children on the street.

After a stint in a convent school, Miss Magnani was able to enroll in the Academy of Dramatic Art in Rome. But she gained her real acting education by working in nightclubs, where she sang street songs in a torchy contralto. She tried vaudeville and then experimental plays. In one of these she came to the attention of Goffredo Alessandrini, a film director, who gave her parts in two unmemorable movies in the early nineteen-thirties and then married her.

She was away from both the theater and the camera for several years, then returned to the stage in undistinguished melodramatic roles.

Her first important film, "Teresa Venerdi" ("Friday Theresa") was directed by Vittorio de Sica in 1942. He has called her "Italy's finest actress and one of the most interesting actresses in the world."

Miss Magnani scored a public success with the American occupation of Rome in World War II, when she appeared in racy revues for servicemen.

About the same time Mr. Rossellini cast her in the leading feminine role in "Open City," in which incidents of the German occupation and the Italian underground were reenacted. The movie was an immediate hit in Italy, and it was then shown with English subtitles in the United States in 1946. Her performance won her the National Board of Review award as the best foreign actress of the year.

The following year Miss Magnani walked off with the Venice Film Festival award as the best international actress for both "Open City" and "Angelina," also directed by Mr. Rossellini. "Love," likewise a Rossellini picture, won Italy's Silver Ribbon for Miss Magnani in 1947.

Played Nun in 'Miracle'

This movie consisted of two unrelated segments—"The Human Voice" and "The Miracle." "The Miracle," in which Miss Magnani played the role of a nun, was shown in New York in December, 1950, and was almost immediately banned by the Commissioner of Licenses as "blasphemous" for its supposed irreverences.

The movie was among Miss Magnani's favorites. Among the others were "Open City" and "Rose Tattoo." This was the climax of her career, which afterward went into eclipse.

She returned to the stage in 1965 in "La Lupa" (The She-Wolf) under the direction of Franco Zeffirelli. Typically, she was the tempestuous, sensual heroine who seduces a young man, marries him off to her daughter, then taunts him until he slays her. It was a moderate success, as was her appearance as Medea in Jean Anouilh's "Medea," directed by Gian Carlo Menotti in 1966.

Four years ago Miss Magnani played opposite Anthony Quinn in "The Secret of Santa Vittoria." The critical reception was indifferent. Recently, she had been appearing in Italian television films.

Miss Magnani was separated from her husband for many years.

Anna Magnani and Burt Lancaster in *The Rose Tattoo.*

Anna Magnani

Anna Magnani in *The Secret of Santa Vittoria.*

The New York Times

FRIDAY, APRIL 11, 1975

Marjorie Main, Actress, Dies; Ma Kettle of Movies Was 85

By WILLIAM M. FREEMAN

Marjorie Main, a stage actress who topped her triumph as the mother in Broadway's "Dead End" in 1935 with more than 100 roles in Hollywood films, died yesterday in Los Angeles. She was 85 years old.

Miss Main, of the loping gait, the raucous voice and the breezy personality, was a comedian who could play tragic roles and a serious dramatic actress who was equally at home in light comedy.

Most of her motion-picture roles were in supporting characterizations, but she was invariably a standout, and had a devoted following. With Percy Kilbride, she made a number of films as Ma Kettle to Mr. Kilbride's Pa Kettle, and the films were among Universal-International's biggest money-makers.

Won Elocution Contests

Miss Main, the daughter of the Rev. Samuel J. Tomlinson and the former Mary McGaughey, was born in Acton, Ind., on Feb. 24, 1890.

She was educated in public schools in Elkhart, Ind., and at Franklin College and Hamilton College, Lexington, Ky.

This was followed by study of dramatic art in Chicago and New York, where her "odd voice," as it was called at the time, was remarked on, winning her some elocution contests.

She spent a year teaching dramatic art at Bourbon College, Paris, Ky., and then joined a Shakespearean repertory company playing a Chautauqua circuit.

It was on this tour that she met Dr. Stanley LeFevre Krebs, a Chautauqua lecturer, to whom she was married in 1921.

Played Stock in Fargo

She played stock in Fargo, N. D., where one of the productions was "The Family Ford," starring W. C. Fields, who brought the actress to New York's Palace Theater, then the No. 1 vaudeville house in the country.

On Broadway she appeared in "Cheating Cheaters," in 1916, in support of John Barrymore; "Yes or No," in 1917, in which she replaced Adrienne Morrison as the lead; "The Wicked Age," 1927; "Salvation," 1928, with Pauline Lord, and "Burlesque," with Barbara Stanwyck and Hal Skelly.

She left the stage for a time to be with her husband, whose lecture engagements were expanding, and returned to Broadway after his death as Mrs. Martin, mother of the killer, in "Dead End" in 1935.

A Hollywood Contract

Her next appearance, in Clare Boothe Luce's "The Women" in 1936, led to a Hollywood contract, where she repeated her "Dead End" role in the film, and succeeded Marie Dressler in films with Wallace Beery.

She played a lady blacksmith in "Wyoming" and a number of other roles in major films, among them a divorce-court judge in "We Were Dancing," 1942; a dance-hall operator with James Cagney in "Johnny Come Lately," in 1943; the wife of a Kansas beef operator in "Heaven Can Wait," with Don Ameche and Gene Tierney; also in 1943, and "Meet Me in St. Louis," with Judy Garland, in 1944.

Her appearance in 1947 as Ma Kettle in "The Egg and I," based on a true-life story, led to a succession of pictures in which she played with the late Percy Kilbride as her spouse, Pa Kettle.

While the critics thought little of the Kettle movies, which were made on a small budget, the public loved them. The first of the nine in the series, "Ma and Pa Kettle," following "The Egg and I," grossed something like $3.5-million, a record for the early nineteen-fifties.

Majorie Main and Percy Kilbride in *Ma and Pa Kettle at Waikiki.*

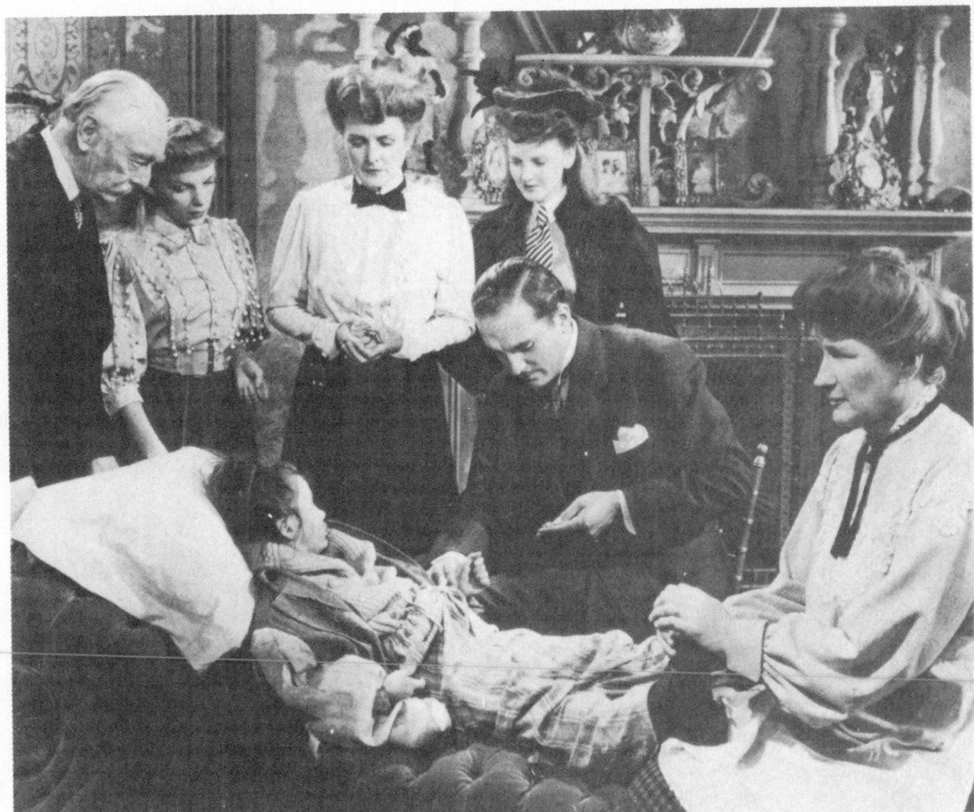

Left to right: Harry Davenport, Judy Garland, Mary Astor, Lucille Bremer, Donald Curtis, Margaret O'Brien (lying down) and Marjorie Main in *Meet Me in St. Louis.*

The New York Times FRIDAY, JUNE 30, 1967

Jayne Mansfield Dies in New Orleans Car Crash

Actress Parlayed Physical Attributes Into Film Career

Special to The New York Times

NEW ORLEANS, June 29—Jayne Mansfield, the actress, was killed instantly early this morning when the car in which she was riding hit the rear of a trailer truck on U.S. 90.

Killed with the 34-year-old performer were Samuel S. Brody, 40, of Los Angeles, her lawyer and companion, and Ronald B. Harrison, 20, of Mississippi City, Miss., a driver for the Gus Stevens Dinner Club in Biloxi, Miss., where Miss Mansfield was appearing.

Their auto plowed beneath the truck's trailer as it approached a mosquito-fogging machine. The driver apparently did not see the truck because of the thick white chemical used to spray mosquitces, the police said.

Three of Miss Mansfield's children, apparently sleeping on the rear seat were injured. They were Mickey Hargitay Jr., 8, who suffered cuts and a broken arm; Zoltan Hargitay, 6, who received cuts and bruises, and Marie Hargitay, who had head cuts and may require plastic surgery.

The children were taken to Charity Hospital by a passing motorist but were transferred to Ochsner Foundation Hospital at the request of Miss Mansfield's former husband, Mickey Hargitay, who telephoned from Los Angeles. Mr. Hargitay arrived this afternoon to be with his children, who were lated told of their mother's death.

Miss Mansfield had been playing the engagement in Biloxi, 80 miles from New Orleans, since June 23. She had left the club after an 11 P.M. performance Wednesday and was on her way to New Orleans for a television appearance at noon Thursday.

A Figure on Display

"To establish yourself as an actress," Jayne Mansfield once told an interviewer, "you have to become well known. A girl just starting out, I would tell her to concentrate on acting, but she doesn't have to go around wearing blankets."

Miss Mansfield didn't. Her statuesque figure, topped by flowing, platinum-blonde tresses and a provocative smile, was cheerfully and generously displayed in films, in newspaper and magazine photographs and on television.

This strategic avalanche of publicity made her one of the best-known glamour symbols of the last 10 years. Her unusual dimensions, 40-18-35, certainly helped.

"I've got to be a movie star." I've just got to make it," she told an interviewer soon after

Associated Press
Jayne Mansfield

arriving in Hollywood in 1954. "I've got to be a movie star." It took a while for her to succeed, but off-screen she played the role to the hilt.

She resided in a huge, pink mansion off Sunset Boulevard that became a tourist attraction, happily splashed for photographers in a heart-shaped pool and drove a pink car around the movie capital.

Her actual screen career consisted of about a dozen films, few of them memorable. She invariably played the role of a none-too-bright blonde who was victimized by unsavory characters.

Vera Jayne Palmer was born on April 19, 1933, in Bryn Mawr, Pa., the daughter of a lawyer. Her father died when she was 6 and she and her mother moved to Dallas. She later enrolled in Southern Methodist University, where she met and was married to a fellow student, Paul James Mansfield. She was 16 at the time and the following year, her daughter Jayne Marie was born. The Mansfields moved to Los Angeles and the young wife began making the studio rounds.

She had little success. As a candy vender in a movie theater, she got a small part in one television play that lead to a bit role in a film called "Female Jungle."

After hiring an agent and a publicity manager, she went on a promotional trip to Florida to help publicize a film titled "Underwater."

Photographs of the blonde Miss Mansfield in a red bathing suit all but put Jane Russell, the star of the movie, out of sight.

"I wanted to be a movie star ever since I was 3," Miss Mansfield said. "They told me I'd be another Shirley Temple, but I guess I outgrew it."

A deluge of revealing photographs soon flooded Hollywood and caught the eye of George Axelrod, playwright, who was casting "Will Success Spoil Rock Hunter?" for Broadway.

Miss Mansfield's playing of a voluptuous dumb movie star who captivates a milquetoast screenwriter, played by Orson Bean, was largely responsible for the comedy's run of 452 performances on Broadway. It opened in October, 1955, at the Broadhurst Theater.

During her nightly appearances, memorable for one scene in which she appeared only in a white towel, the baby-faced actress also managed to perfect an enticing, soft-voiced coo punctuated with squeals.

Her publicity campaign continued and she returned to Hollywood in triumph. Previously, she had been seen briefly in "Illegal, "Pete Kelley's Blues" contract at 20th Century-Fox, where she did the movie version of Rock Hunter," and "The Wayward Bus," "The Girl Can't Help It" and "Kiss Them for Me."

Her performance in the 1957 version of John Steinbeck's "The Wayward Bus," in which she played a wistful derelict, was generally conceded to have been her best acting.

In 1958, the actress divorced her first husband and was married to Mickey Hargitay, a former Mr. Universe. The wedding was attended primarily by a small army of press representatives. In 1963, Miss Mansfield obtained a Mexican divorce from Mr. Hargitay, by whom she had had three children.

Her third husband was Matt Cimber, a director, to whom she was wed in 1964. They were divorced last year. The actress was awarded custody of their child, Octabiano, now 2.

Two of Miss Mansfield's children were in the news recently. Last year Zoltan was mauled by a lion as the actress posed for pictures in a California animal compound. Two weeks ago, Jayne Marie went to the police and reported mistreatment at home. She was put in protective custody of juvenile authorities and released to relatives.

Jayne Mansfield

Jayne Mansfield and Tony Randall in *Will Success Spoil Rock Hunter?*

"All the News That's Fit to Print"

The New York Times

LATE CITY EDITION

Weather: Rain likely today, ending tonight. Fair and cool tomorrow. Temperature range: today 40-48; Monday 34-59. Details on Page 69.

VOL. CXXIV... No. 42,815 — NEW YORK, TUESDAY, APRIL 15, 1975 — 20 CENTS

Price higher in air delivery cities.

Fredric March Dies of Cancer; Stage and Screen Actor Was 77

By ALBIN KREBS

Fredric March, who appeared on the stage and in motion pictures over a span of 50 years, died of cancer yesterday at Mount Sinai Hospital in Los Angeles. Mr. March, who was 77 years old, had been hospitalized since April 5.

Mr. March was an actor of sometimes astonishing versatility who played juvenile leads in the Broadway era of David Belasco and crusty old characters in the movies of the nineteen-seventies. His career peaked in 1956 when he created the role of the brooding James Tyrone in "Long Day's Journey Into Night," but previously he had won two Academy Awards, in 1932 for "Dr. Jekyll and Mr. Hyde" and in 1946 for "The Best Years of Our Lives."

Mr. March, a tall, broad-shouldered man with a voice capable of booming with sonorous timbre, was rarely idle during most of his professional life. His most popular stage roles included appearances in

Sy Friedman, 1962

Fredric March

Continued on Page 38, Column 1

The New York Times/George Tames

Senate Foreign Relations Committee members getting ready for yesterday morning's meeting on evacuation of Americans and others from South Vietnam. From left: Howard H. Baker Jr., Republican, and John J. Sparkman and Mike Mansfield, Democrats.

SENATE UNIT BARS TROOPS AS GUARD FOR VIETNAMESE

Foreign Relations Committee Meets With President on the Evacuation Issue

By JOHN W. FINNEY

Special to The New York Times

WASHINGTON, April 14—The Senate Foreign Relations Committee balked today at the Ford Administration's request for broad Presidential authority to use American troops to protect the evacuation of the Americans and a number of Vietnamese citizens from South Vietnam.

After an executive session in the morning, the committee, at its request, met with President Ford in the afternoon at the White House and presented its objections to the use of Americans troops in the evacuation of anyone ... American citizens ...

Democratic ... House ...

REDS 3 MILES FROM PHNOM PENH; REFUGEES JAM MAIN ROAD TO CITY; SAIGON TROOPS HOLDING XUAN LOC

The New York Times/April 15, 1975

... Pochentong airport and, fighting also at Pochen... from Phnom Penh, less than three miles away. ... other rebels raised flag over factories.

AIRMAN DEFECTS

A Cambodian Bombs Own Headquarters, Killing at Least 7

By SYDNEY H. SCHANBERG

Special to The New York Times

PHNOM PENH, Cambodia, Tuesday, April 15—The Communist insurgents drove to within three miles of the western edge of the city yesterday. To the north, one report said, the insurgents raised their flags over factories less than five miles from the edge of the city, along Route 5.

Despite heavy bombing by the Government air force, the Communists pushed to less than a mile from the airport, which was closed to civilian traffic.

This correspondent, driving through the market of Pochentong town, two miles from the western edge of Phnom Penh, saw three soldiers in insurgent dress—black cotton shirt and trousers, a red-checked neck scarf, with ammunition bandoliers across their chests. They carried Chinese AK-47 rifles. They were just looking around, and the few civilians in the vicinity did not appear frightened.

Fighting Near Road

At 4 P.M. a battle was reported going on 500 yards from the Pochentong market. Cambodian reporters returning from the scene said the fighting was heavy.

This correspondent and others driving along the road to the airport, watched as single-engine bombers tried to stop the insurgent advance only a half mile or so north of the road.

The planes dived low, trying to drop their bombs exactly on target. The explosion and black clouds of smoke were a backdrop for a steady stream of refugees flowing out of side roads and jamming the main road into the city.

While the battle was raging, one pilot turned against the Government, veering his fighter-bomber toward the city and dropping two 250-pound bombs on command headquarters in the city center before flying off, presumably to land in insurgent territory.

Seven Persons Killed

The bombs fell on a military transport office inside the compound, killing at least seven persons and wounding many. Six ambulances were seen driving to and from the scene. No high-ranking commanders were reported hurt. The pilot was later identified as Lieut. Khiev Yos Savath.

It was difficult to get a coherent picture of the over-all situation. About the only thing that could be said definitely by late afternoon yesterday was that the insurgents had not entered the city in force.

The seriousness of the situation was suggested by jeeps carrying officers into and out of command headquarters, the radio antenna that the International Red Cross hurriedly set up on the roof of the Hotel Le Phnom to communicate with Geneva, and the crowd of Frenchmen and Cambodians who gathered at the French Embassy for sanctuary.

The insurgents' objective seemed to be to cut off the city from the airport, which is the last supply link with the outside world, and then to move on the city proper.

As darkness descended, the

Continued on Page 16, Column 1

... the Battle Nears

... unperturbed, her face a mask of calm.

Later a grimacing beggar entered the hotel lobby and began to assail all the foreigners in sight in a loud, whining voice. He rattled everyone's already frayed nerves so badly that they paid him handsomely just to go away. He probably got more in that five minutes than he normally does in a month.

At the front desk the receptionists were listening to the radio spew forth patriotic speeches and assurances that the armed forces would defend the capital against all assaults. As they listened

Continued on Page 16, Column 6

...ts Forces ... Loc Siege

... Nguyen Van Thieu ... a new Cabinet yesterday ... there was mount... that his Govern... tually paralyzed. ... the new Cabinet ... government of ... did not include ... e opposition ... ge 17.]

... the depot exploded,

Continued on Page 17, Column 6

U.D.C. 'FEAR' STOPS A BILLION IN WORK

Hospital and Health Projects Not Able to Get Financing From Wary Investors

By MAURICE CARROLL

Special to The New York Times

ALBANY, April 14 — Construction of more than $1-billion in nursing homes, hospital additions, facilities for the handicapped and other health projects has been held up, state officials said today, because investors have been frightened by the highly publicized fiscal problems of the Urban Development Corporation.

The local groups planning these projects had already spent $50-million in the expectation of state financing when they were told the money might not be there after all.

"They're out on a limb, and we're out on a limb with them," said Edward Strevy, assistant director of the financing program in the Health Department. "It's tragic."

'Not Even Justified'

These projects were to be financed by the same sort of "moral obligation" bonds that the U.D.C. had used—securities that lacked the "full faith and credit" of the state but that, state officials said, the state had a moral commitment to support.

But when the U.D.C., the vast housing construction agency born in 1968, when Nelson A. Rockefeller was Governor, teetered toward bankruptcy in the early days of the Carey administration and failed to pay back some of its bond-anticipation notes, the trouble spread to other agencies using the same financing device.

The State Housing Finance Agency, which borrowed money for less than 5 per cent two

Continued on Page 41, Column 3

Connally Denies Seeking Or Accepting Dairy Bribe

By JAMES M. NAUGHTON

Special to The New York Times

WASHINGTON, April 14—John B. Connally denied today from the witness stand that he had ever sought ... $10,000 ...

House ... To Save ...

WASHINGTON, April ... The House of Representatives passed today a bill that ... provide for the lending of ... eral funds to the unemployed to help them cover the mortgages on their homes if foreclosure were imminent.

The legislation, approved by a vote of 321 to 21, provides that unemployed workers who own homes would be eligible to receive loans of up to $250 a month for up to two years at an interest rate not to exceed 8 per cent.

The bill would authorize—but not appropriate — up to $500-million for the loans that, it was estimated, could help keep 300,000 families from losing their homes.

Israel Unveils the Kfir, a New S...

Associated Press

Israel's new Kfir, or Lion Cub, a supersonic, single-seat fighter plane, on display yesterday at Lydda

By TERENCE SMITH

Special to The New York Times

LYDDA, Israel, April 14—A new Israeli-designed and manufactured jet fighter, comparable to the French Mirage and Soviet MIG-21, was unveiled here today at a festive ceremony attended by Premier Yitzhak Rabin and most of the Israeli Government.

Dubbed the Kfir, or Lion Cub, the plane is the latest version of the supersonic Mirage family of aircraft to be manufactured in Israel. An earlier, less-sophisticated model was used successfully against the Arab air forces in the October, 1973, war. Today was the first time any of the planes had been shown in public.

The Kfir is similar in design to the delta-winged Mirage-5 but is driven by the powerful General Electric J79 engine used in the American Phantom F-4.

This combination, in the opinion of foreign air attachés here, puts the Kfir in a class with the latest versions of the MIG-21, the workhorse of the Egyptian and Syrian Air Forces.

But Egypt, Syria and Iraq are now also supplied with MIG-23's, supersonic variable-wing Soviet fighters. The MIG-23's are regarded by military experts as more maneuverable and slightly faster than the F-4, the mainstay of the Israeli Air Force.

Israel had been hoping to buy from the United States a squadron of F-15 Eagles, supersonic fighters that are faster than the MIG-23's. But negotiations

Continued on Page 3, Column 1

... an "adjustment ... excessive stocks" was a "precondition" for recovery in the economy, James L. Pate, Assistant Secretary of Commerce for Economic Affairs, said in a statement that the February figures were "an encouraging confirmation of a massive inventory adjustment during the early months of the year."

"Retail inventories were reduced appreciably in January, leaving durable goods—notably automobile stocks—as the principal inventory problems, Mr. Pated added. "The decline in automobile inventories in February suggests that the process of inventory liquidation is well under way."

Total business sales held up

Continued on Page 47, Column 2

A Rembrandt Stolen

A painting by Rembrandt, valued at $500,000, was stolen from the Boston Museum of Fine Arts by two men who fled in a car. Page 24.

Fredric March Dies of Cancer; Stage and Screen Actor Was 77

By ALBIN KREBS

Fredric March, who appeared on the stage and in motion pictures over a span of 50 years, died of cancer yesterday at Mount Sinai Hospital in Los Angeles. Mr. March, who was 77 years old, had been hospitalized since April 5.

Mr. March was an actor of sometimes astonishing versatility who played juvenile leads in the Broadway era of David Belasco and crusty old characters in the movies of the nineteen-seventies. His career peaked in 1956 when he created the role of the brooding James Tyrone in "Long Day's Journey Into Night," but previously he had won two Academy Awards, in 1932 for "Dr. Jekyll and Mr. Hyde" and in 1946 for "The Best Years of Our Lives."

Mr. March, a tall, broad-shouldered man with a voice capable of booming with sonorous timbre, was rarely idle during most of his professional life. His most popular stage roles included appearances in "The Skin of Our Teeth," "The Autumn Garden" and "A Bell

Sy Friedman, 1962

Fredric March

Continued on Page 38, Column 1

NEWS INDEX

Fredric March in the title role of *The Adventures of Mark Twain*.

Fredric March Dies of Cancer at 77

Continued From Page 1, Col. 7

"The Skin of Our Teeth," "The Autumn Garden" and "A Bell for Adano," and his film roles included "A Star Is Born," "The Adventures of Mark Twain" and "Anthony Adverse."

Mr. March's last professional appearance was in the four-hour movie version of O'Neill's "The Iceman Cometh," in 1973. It was his 69th film, and it won him praise for his portrayal of tough old Harry Hope.

Mr. March, who amassed a sum estimated at more than $2-million, was listed in 1937 as the fifth-highest-paid American, earning nearly half a million dollars a year. Although he could have retired 25 years ago, he detested idleness, and pushed himself to work at his craft.

When asked some years ago what he would do when he was no longer a star and could not get work, he replied: "I'd keep acting even if I had to get on the back of a truck. I'd act wherever there was a group of people."

Planned to Be a Banker

Born on Aug. 31, 1897, in Racine, Wis., and originally named Frederick McIntyre Bickel, Mr. March was the son of a small-time manufacturer, John F. Bickel, and the former Cora Brown Marcher. He worked as a bank teller during high school vacations and studied economics at the University of Wisconsin, and when he came to New York in 1919 after a year in the Army, it was not to be an actor but a banker.

This was in spite of the fact that he had always been interested in theatricals and had played leads on the university stage, had been a champion college debater and had had modest success as a part-time newspaper and magazine model. He had even quietly sent out résumés and photographs to agents and producers.

Fortunately for the theater, Mr. March had appendicitis shortly after his arrival here, and after an appendectomy, he applied for a recuperation leave of absence from his trainee's job at the National City Bank. His thoughts had turned increasingly to acting as a career. His professional debut, in 1920, came in Baltimore in Belasco's production of "Deburau," in which he was also seen on Broadway for the first time soon afterward.

By that time the young actor with the square-cut, all-American good looks had decided that Bickel was not a good name for a marquee. He dropped a couple of letters from his first name and adopted the first syllable of his mother's maiden name to come up with the stage name of Fredric March. Versatile, cooperative, eager, he was seldom without work.

In Denver in the summer of 1926, Mr. March joined a stock company whose leading lady was Florence Eldridge. While appearing together in Molnar's "The Swan," they fell in love, and were married in 1927 in Mexico. Their union, both personally and professionally, was to last for the rest of Mr. March's life.

In the late nineteen-twenties, the moguls of Hollywood were struck by a crisis with the advent of sound in movies—many of the dashingly handsome stars of the silent movie era possessed voices of startling squeakiness, nasalness or raspiness. Mr. March struck Hollywood as the answer to a prayer, for not only was he the possessor of a virile and handsome profile that could meet the most rigorous demands of the camera close-up, but also he had a rich, well-trained stage actor's voice.

Instant Film Success

His movie career began in 1929 with a featured role in "The Dummy." He was an instant success, and soon some of the top female stars were clamoring to have him in their pictures. In the nineteen-thirties Mr. March appeared opposite Clara Bow, Ruth Chatterton, Claudette Colbert, Miriam Hopkins and finally Greta Garbo in "Anna Karenina." Usually he was seen in romantic comedy or adventure roles, but in 1932 he switched to the serious dual role in "Dr. Jekyll and Mr. Hyde" and won his first Oscar.

At a peak in his movie popularity, Mr. March, much to the consternation of his film employers, returned to New York to appear opposite his wife in "Yr. Obedient Husband," a 1938 vehicle based on Samuel Pepys's diary.

The play failed so resoundingly that Mr. March, seldom without a sense of humor, felt constrained to make a public apology. He and Miss Eldridge bought advertising space in trade publications that showed a sketch depicting them as two trapeze artists missing each other's grip in midair. "Oops, sorry!" read the caption.

The Marches tried again in "The American Way" the following year, with better results, and from then on Mr. March was to deftly balance his work between movies and plays. "It has been my experience," he said years later, "that work on the screen clarifies stage portrayals and vice versa. You learn to make your face express more in making movies, and in working for the theater you have a sense of greater freedom."

In 1960, when the Marches appeared as William Jennings Bryan and his wife in the movie version of "Inherit the Wind," about the Scopes "monkey trial," Mr. March learned the whole script, theater-style, in advance, before rehearsals. And although he was still a man of imposing good looks, he quite willingly submitted to make-up that gave him a bald pate. He believed in immersing himself in a role.

Some of Mr. March's most memorable screen performances were in Noël Coward's "Design for Living," in which he played a flip sophisticate; as the poet Robert Browning in "The Barretts of Wimpole Street"; as the alcoholic and suicidal actor opposite Janet Gaynor in "A Star Is Born"; as the zany reporter in "Nothing Sacred"; as the widower in love with a much younger woman in "Middle of the Night" and, of course, as the war-weary veteran in "The Best Years of Our Lives."

(continued)

Janet Gaynor, Fredric March and Adolphe Menjou starred in the first version of *A Star is Born.*

Films in which he also appeared, with Miss Eldridge, were "Another Part of the Forest," "Christopher Columbus," and "An Act of Mercy." On stage the Marches appeared together in "The Skin of Our Teeth," Thornton Wilder's frolic, and O'Neill's "Long Day's Journey Into Night," which Mr. March considered the high point of his career.

A Serious Approach

A story concerning that major triumph illustrates how seriously Mr. March took acting, and the extent to which he would go to perfect his playing in an individual scene.

In the now famous card scene, Mr. March, in the role modeled after O'Neill's own actor father, was called upon to play solitaire while delivering highly charged, emotional lines intended to prepare the character Tyrone's two sons for some grave news.

A friend of Mr. March who was involved with the show recalled that during rehearsals the actor insisted on devoting an hour a day to that one scene, so that he could practice it alone. "He wanted to perfect his technique with the cards so he could concentrate on the timing of the lines," the friend recalled. "Even when we'd take a break he'd be working on the scene—that's the way we'd find him when we returned."

The actor's preparation for the role was well rewarded. There were universal critical accolades, with Brooks Atkinson of The New York Times writing: "As the aging actor who stands at the head of the family, Fredric March gives a masterly performance that will stand as a milestone in the acting of an O'Neill play. . .This is a character portrait of grandeur."

In his Hollywood heyday, Mr. March felt he was becoming type-cast as a "costume actor" and vowed that once his long-term contracts had run out, he would never sign another multiple-picture deal. That was in the nineteen-forties. He was also intensely, sometimes foolishly, selective about the Broadway roles he would consider.

For example, one script he was offered in the late nineteen-forties was about a traveling salesman who was a loser, and Mr. March rejected it because he found it, on a cursory reading, "too grim." The play was Arthur Miller's "Death of a Salesman," and the role of Willy Loman went to Lee J. Cobb, who became the season's toast of Broadway. The play won both a New York Drama Critics Circle award and a Pulitzer Prize in 1949.

Mr. March later explained that he was making a film in Rome when he received the play script and "I didn't have the time to read it properly. Boy, I sure blew that one." The producers of the movie version of the play gave Mr. March his second chance, and he won an Oscar nomination in 1951 for his film portrayal of Willy Loman.

As gifted and versatile an actor as he was—he could move with facility from light comedy to melodrama to tragedy, and was as believable as a hero as he was in a character role—Mr. March somehow never got around to playing the classics. He never undertook a Shakespearean role. "I don't know why I haven't, I really don't," he told an interviewer in 1973. "I should have done Romeo, and then Hamlet . . . I should have done Macbeth."

Hunt for Communists

In 1940 Mr. March was one of many Hollywood personalities who ran afoul of Representative Martin Dies, then chairman of the House Committee on Un-American Activities, who had started a widely publicized hunt for Communists in the film-making community.

Mr. Dies denounced Hollywood as a hotbed of radicalism, which struck Mr. March as "scattershot, unfair and ill-advised." He openly defended the film community and his having lent his name to pre-World War II liberal causes, and so incurred the wrath of Mr. Dies, who promised to take a searching look at Mr. March's own politics. The Congressman later apologized to Mr. March and placed him on a list of "politically clean" figures that included James Cagney, Humphrey Bogart and the writer Philip Dunne.

Harold Russell, Dana Andrews and Fredric March in *The Best Years of Our Lives.*

The Marches lived quietly, maintaining an apartment in New York and a 40-acre farm near New Milford, Conn. Mr. March loved the farm and liked to swing an ax to clear his land, but after illness beset him five years ago, he had to omit such activity. The couple sold the farm and moved into a Los Angeles condominium more than a year ago.

Mr. March underwent prostate surgery for the second time while filming "The Iceman Cometh" in 1973. By then, the debilities of age had forced him to walk with the aid of a cane.

The Marches adopted a son, Anthony, and a daughter, Penelope, now Mrs. Bert Fantcucci of Florence, Italy. Mr. March is also survived by his widow and four grandchildren. The funeral will be private.

Fredric March, Miriam Hopkins and Gary Cooper in *Design for Living.*

The New York Times SUNDAY, JANUARY 23, 1966

Herbert Marshall Is Dead at 75; Actor With a Sympathetic Air

His Characters Were Urbane, Impeccably Dressed and Benign Gentlemen

HOLLYWOOD, Jan. 22 (AP) —Herbert Marshall died of a heart attack today at his home in Beverly Hills. He was 75 years old.

The actor, whose career spanned half a century, had returned home eight days ago after two months as a patient in the Motion Picture Country House and Hospital.

A Gentlemanly Star

The plane was down in the middle of the Atlantic and heavy seas were washing over the limp bodies clinging to the wing. Here was the last chance for the villain to redeem himself by gallantry, and Herbert Marshall took it. He let go his hold on the wing and slipped away to a watery death.

That was in "Foreign Correspondent," a 1940 motion-picture thriller that gave Mr. Marshall the chance to display all the qualities that made him a star. In this film he happened to be a villain—a German agent who was plotting war while masquerading as the leader of a movement to save the peace of Europe—but he was such a sympathetic villain.

He was urbane, impeccably dressed, gentlemanly, almost ostentatiously upper class, intelligent, benign and fatherly to his daughter, Laraine Day, avuncular without being patronizing to the young hero, Joel McCrea, and, in the end, courageous enough to accept death as the price of the failure of his schemes.

A Secret Sadness

Those qualities, plus a secret sadness that seemed a permanent part of his makeup, were displayed in almost every role Herbert Marshall played in a film career that lasted 39 years. The stories were infinitely varied. He played drawing-room comedy, melodrama, science-fiction, detective thrillers, pirate romps, Westerns, musicals, romantic dramas, historical and costume pictures. He even found his way, somewhat to his embarrassment, into an Andy Hardy film with Mickey Rooney in 1944.

He played with and against the most glittering and glamorous female stars of the stage and the screen, among them Judith Anderson, Jennifer Jones, Bette Davis, Marlene Dietrich, Greta Garbo, Norma Shearer, Constance Bennett, Barbara Stanwyck, Margaret Sullavan, Jean Arthur, Merle Oberon, Simone Simon, Claudette Colbert, Mary Astor, Maureen O'Hara, Sylvia Sidney, Ann Harding, Katharine Hepburn, Helen Hayes, Joan Crawford, Rosalind Russell, Jeanne Eagels, Madeleine Carroll, Edna Best, who was his second wife, Deanna Durbin and even Shirley Temple.

The list is not exhaustive.

Played in Maugham Films

He seemed particularly well suited to screen plays based on Somerset Maugham stories and won critical acclaim for his performances in "The Painted Veil," "The Letter," and "The Moon and Sixpence." He played Maugham himself, the narrator who brings together all the skeins of the tangled plot, in "The Razor's Edge."

He was a versatile trouper and plied his profession in all the media open to him. He played in repertory companies, summer stock, on the London and New York stages, radio and television. He was particularly effective on radio, where his velvety voice and precise diction were employed on many programs. He played Ken Thurston in "The Man Called X," a popular radio adventure series.

Tried to Avoid Stage

Mr. Marshall once told an interviewer he found it amusingly ironic that he had had such a long acting career. "I am the only member of my family who did not want to go on the stage," he said. "My father and mother were both in the theater and I thought their choice of profession very mundane. You see, I wanted to do something glamorous when I grew up."

He thought of himself as a rolling stone, wandering back and forth across the United States and the Atlantic to work in Hollywood, New York and London. For many years, though his principal home was in Beverly Hills, he also maintained an apartment in London and was a member of the Garrick and Green Room clubs there. He had five wives to grace his homes.

His first wife was Mollie Maitland. He divorced her and married Miss Best, then his co-star on Broadway, in Jersey City in 1928. They had a daughter, Sarah Best Marshall, who became an actress.

He was divorced again in 1940 and married another actress, Lee Russell, and he was divorced a third time and married Patricia Mallory in 1947. Miss Mallory died in 1958. His last wife, the former Mrs. Dee Ann Kaufmann, survives.

He was born in England on May 23, 1890, and given the name Herbert Brough Falcon Marshall. His parents were Percy F. and Ethel Marshall, both theater professionals. He was educated privately and at St. Mary's College, Harlow.

Herbert Marshall and Bette Davis in *The Little Foxes*, 1941.

Tried Accountancy

When the time came for him to choose a career, he resisted the idea of the stage and decided to try business instead. He became an articled clerk to an accounting firm, Weamish and Blumberry, in the City, London's financial district.

More out of boredom than inclination, he joined a stage company in Brixton and in 1911 made his first appearance, as a man servant in "The Adventures of Lady Ursula." Two years later, he made his London debut as Tommy in "Brewster's Millions."

The First World War interrupted his career. He served in the British Expeditionary Forces from 1916 to 1918 in the 14th London Scots. Ronald Colman, another English actor who won fame in America, was a member of the same regiment.

Mr. Marshall was severely wounded and spent 13 months in an Army hospital. His leg was amputated, but he learned to walk so well on an artificial limb that few persons who saw him perform knew he was disabled.

The Important How-Not

He began to learn his craft in earnest in 1918, when he joined the Lyric Opera House Company in Hammersmith, London. "I studied the methods of the star and learned, not how to act, but how not to act, which was a beginning, anyway," Mr. Marshall said.

But in those years he played only American roles, because, he said, "our director thought I was the best American type he could find. It took Hollywood, and Samuel Goldwyn, to cast me in a role truly natural to me."

He made his first United States tour in 1921 and had his first important role in New York in 1925, in "These Charming People." Another memorable stage success here was "The High Road," in 1928, in which he played the Duke of Warrington.

In 1929 he began a long and profitable association with the producer, Gilbert Miller, appearing for him in plays in New York and in London. In many of those plays, he was co-starred with Edna Best. "Michael and Mary," "The Swan" and "There's Always Juliet" were among the plays they did together.

In Early Talking Films

He had been playing in silent films since 1926. His first talking picture was "The Letter," with Jeanne Eagels. Many years later, he played in a remake of that film, but in a different role, with Bette Davis.

In 1932 he appeared with Marlene Dietrich in "Blonde Venus," and followed that assignment with roles in "Trouble in Paradise," an Ernst Lubitsch production, and "Evenings for Sale."

He returned to London for a brief period and then came back to Hollywood to stay in 1933.

Among the films he made were "A Bill of Divorcement," "The Unseen," "The Dark Angel," "Duel in the Sun," "Rip Tide," "Girls Dormitory," "Till We Meet Again," "A Woman Rebels," and "Angel."

Mr. Marshall liked games "of every description," as he said in a capsule autobiographical sketch for the British "Who's Who," but poker was his favorite card game.

Though he was known as a formidable opponent across the green baize tables, he poohpoohed his abilities this way:

"The night I held these cards —deuce, four, five, six and king —I drew a trey from the deck. My hand trembled so that another player, holding three aces, refused to put up a guinea to see me."

The New York Times THURSDAY, OCTOBER 12, 1961.

Chico Marx, Stage and Film Comedian, Dies at 70

Oldest of 5 Brothers Took Role of 'Italian' Piano Player —Team Business Manager

HOLLYWOOD, Calif., Oct. 11 (AP)—Chico Marx, oldest member of the famed Marx Brothers who transformed low comedy on stage and in films into high art, died today of a heart ailment at his home. He was 70 years old.

Chico and his brothers—Groucho, Harpo, Zeppo and Gummo—created a brand of comedy all their own—wildly improbable, joyously irreverent, supremely illogical and almost painfully funny to lowbrows and intellectuals alike.

Their zany antics, with suggestive winks, leers, whistles and wisecracks, gave vaudeville and movie fans chuckles and belly laughs for nearly a half century.

They were considered masters of comedy, ranking with Laurel and Hardy, Charlie Chaplin, W. C. Fields and Will Rogers.

Deadpan Comic

Chico Marx was the brother with the pointed hat, the seedy velvet jacket, the sly smile, the deadpan face and the "Italian" accent. He was the pickpocket, the short-changer, the plot-thickener and the piano player.

Mark Brothers' admirers remember with delight one of Chico's best lines of dialogue. It came about after some tortured twists of plot to get an elephant into the scene.

"Hey, whatsa that?" Chico asked, rhetorically.

"That's irrelevant," the straight man said.

"Thatsa right," Chico said, triumphantly.

It was almost a certainty that in every Marx Brothers picture Chico would play the piano (as Harpo would play the harp). Chico played in two ways: in a kind of early Victor Borge manner, with little musical jokes and tricks, particularly with his right index finger aimed like a pistol; and in a dreamy, delicate way, with artistry. At such times his face would become rapt and moody.

His parody of an Italian offended no one because despite the farcial amorality of his activities, the character came through as an essentially kind and sweet person.

Chico's given name was Leonard. It was said that he received the name of Chico during a poker game many years ago. His brothers were dubbed, at the same time, Groucho, Harpo and Zeppo. A fifth brother, Gummo, was in show business briefly.

The Marx family lived in Yorkville section of New York, where Chico was born in 1891. In his book, "Harpo Speaks!" Harpo Marx, the girl-chaser who communicated with whistles and a bulb horn, wrote:

"All his life Chico has had an uncanny talent for turning up prospects. It was he who turned up the producer who first put us on Broadway, and made us nationally famous. It was Chico who turned up the producer — Irving Thalberg— who put us into grade-A movies."

The Broadway show was "I'll Say She Is," which opened at the Casino Theatre in 1924.

Chico and his brothers had spent fourteen years in vaudeville on the Orpheum circuit. Chico doubled as performer and business manager.

After "I'll Say She Is," the brothers went on to their second Broadway hit, "The Cocoanuts," with music by Irving Berlin and the book by George S. Kaufman and Morrie Ryskind.

In the early Nineteen Thirties—after the stock market crash—the brothers turned to the movies. Their film version of "The Cocoanuts" and their subsequent movies — "Animal Crackers," "Monkey Business," "A Night at the Opera," "A Day at the Races," "A Night in Casablanca," "The Big Store" and "Room Service"—were all successful comedy classics.

During World War II, when the brothers temporarily split up, Chico became the leader of a band. Besides the piano, Chico could play the coronet, the zither and the violin.

In recent years, Chico had been in poor health and rarely made professional appearances. In 1949 he and Harpo played a successful engagement at the Palladium in London. Chico also appeared on television shows. In 1956 he starred in the road company tour of "The Fifth Season."

Besides his brothers, he is survived by his widow, Mary, and a daughter by a previous marriage, Mrs. Maxine Culhane.

Lucille Ball and the Marx Brothers in *Room Service*.

The Marx Brothers in *A Night at the Opera*, 1935.

"All the News That's Fit to Print"

The New York Times.

LATE CITY EDITION
U. S. Weather Bureau Report (Page 86) forecasts: Cloudy and cool with periods of rain today, tonight and tomorrow.
Temp. Range: 59—49; yesterday: 67—50.

VOL. CXIV..No. 38,965. © 1964 by The New York Times Company. Times Square, New York, N. Y. 10036. NEW YORK, TUESDAY, SEPTEMBER 29, 1964. TEN CENTS

Harpo Marx, the Silent Comedian, Is Dead at 70

Blond-Wigged, Horn-Tooting Star Scored on Stage and in Films With Brothers

By The Associated Press

HOLLYWOOD, Sept. 28 — Harpo Marx, the blond-wigged, nonspeaking member of the Marx Brothers team, died tonight at 8:30 in Mount Sinai Hospital. He was 70 years old.

A hospital official said Mr. Marx died after surgery. [According to United Press International, a family spokesman said the comedian had entered the hospital earlier in the day for heart surgery.]

Mr. Marx, whose given name was Arthur, had been in semi-retirement for five years. In January, 1963, he announced that he was retiring completely.

The harp-playing comedian was the second of the theatrical brothers to die. Chico, the piano player, died in 1961.

The surviving brothers are Gummo, Zeppo and Groucho.

Mr. Marx leaves also his wife, the former actress Susan Fleming, to whom he was married for 28 years, and four adopted children.

A honking horn, facial expressions and gestures were

Continued on Page 52, Column 1

United Artists, 1946

Harpo in his battered plug hat, one of his trademarks.

CUSHING PRESSES FOR STRONG STAND ABSOLVING JEWS

Leads International Effort at Vatican for a Forthright Draft on Crucifixion

SEVEN OTHERS JOIN PLEA

Council Supports Formation of Deacons' Order to Aid Where Priests Are Few

Text of Cardinal Cushing's address is on Page 46.

By ROBERT C. DOTY
Special to The New York Times

ROME, Sept. 28 — Richard Cardinal Cushing, Archbishop of Boston, led today a broad international effort by Roman Catholic prelates to obtain a strong declaration by the Ecumenical Council that the Jews bear no special responsibility in the Crucifixion.

During today's session, the Council approved by a vote of 1,903 to 242 a pro... re-establishment... order of ...

... stron... church... bacy f...

In ... urged ... itself s... uity" ... gested ... "not many ... lifted" ag... mitted aga...

The chai... XII should ... forcefully aga... ocide of the J... Rolf Hochhuth... uty," has pro... debate on the r... time Pontiff.

Amended Dra...

The Boston ch... seven other Cardin... from the United St... one each from Austria, ... France, West Germa... Italy—urged the curre... sion of Ecumenical ... Vatican II to amend ... strengthen in liberal term... present draft declaration on ... attitude of the church towa... the Jews. Four other prelates of lesser rank also supported the move.

The opposition in the opening debate on the draft was limited to statements by a Cardinal from Antioch, Syria, speaking for four other Middle Eastern prelates, and by Ernesto Cardinal Ruffini of Palermo, Sicily, a member of the church's ultraconservative wing.

The heart of the issue is a statement on the role of the Jews in the Passion of Christ on the cross. A draft submitted to the Council last year made it clear that neither in Christ's time nor today did the Jews, as a people, have any special guilt in a sacrifice that was an atonement for the sins of all mankind.

Liberal Victory Forecast

For reasons that have never been officially explained, but probably for a combination of political and conservative theological considerations, this was changed to a more lukewarm exoneration of "the Jews of today."

Interpreting both the texts of the speeches today and the evident mood of the Council majority, qualified experts foresaw the final approval of a statement that would probably be more positive in its condemnation of anti-Semitism generally and of the Crucifixion-guilt theory than even the draft introduced last year but since diluted.

"In this declaration," Cardinal Cushing said, his strong, nasal voice and Boston-accented Latin evincing conviction, "in clear and evident words, we must deny that the Jews are guilty of the death of our Saviour except in-sofar as all men have sinned

Continued on Page 46, Column 3

School Buses Here Slowed for 2d Day; 5,000 Pupils Late

By LEONARD BUDER

Five thousand pupils in public and parochial schools missed classes or arrived late yesterday as school bus drivers again took part in what the Board of Education called a deliberate slowdown.

On some routes, including Queens Boulevard, the buses moved so slowly that they caused traffic jams, the board reported.

Many pupils were drenched by the morning rain as they waited at pickup points for school buses that came as much as 45 minutes late or did not come at all. Some children walked up to a mile and a half to school, some were taken to school by their parents, and many were kept home.

School officials and the bus company have said that the slowdown, which started Friday, results from a union jurisdictional fight.

The drivers involved are members of Local 1181 of the

Continued on Page 25, Col...

PRESIDENT WARY OF G.I.'S FIGHTING CHINA'S MILLIONS

Bars Taking Vietnam War to North 'at This Stage'—U.S. Aide Warns Reds

By United Press International

MANCHESTER, N. H., Sept. 28—President Johnson said tonight that he does not want to get American soldiers "into a war with 700 million Chinese."

In answer to suggestions by Senator Barry Goldwater and others that the United States carry the war in South Vietnam to the North, Mr. Johnson said:

"Before I start dropping bombs around the country, I would want to think about the consequences of getting American boys into a war with 700 million Chinese."

The President said the loss of 190 American lives in Vietnam was bad.

Crowds Greet Johnson in Providence and See Aides' Car Catch Fire

President Jo... the crowd

...VITES ...NS' AID

...r G.O.P. ...t Him ...our

NEW PANEL PLANS TO ACT SPEEDILY ON WARREN DATA

Hopes to Start Work Today—Will Study Proposals on the Secret Service

CONGRESS MOVE IS SEEN

Senators Weighing Measure to Make a Presidential Slaying a Federal Crime

Warren report appendix VII appears on Pages 28 and 29.

By ANTHONY LEWIS
Special to The New York Times

WASHINGTON, Sept. 28 — The special committee appointed by President Johnson to go over the Warren Commission's recommendations will probably hold its first meeting tomorrow.

Officials said today that the committee wanted to get to work as quickly as possible. It was unable to meet today because one of the four members, John A. McCone, director of the Central Intelligence Agency, was out of the country.

The other members are Douglas Dillon, Secretary of the Treasury; Nicholas deB. Katzenbach, Acting Attorney General, and McGeorge Bundy, special assistant to the President for national security af...

...hether there will be any ...l staff remains to be de... For the present, Mr. Dil... office is handling all ar...ents.

...re Agents Urged

...cret Service, which has ... responsibility for pro... President, is in the ...Department. It was ...rvice that received ...riticism yesterday ... the President's ... the Assassina...ent Kennedy, ... Justice Earl

... called for ... much more ... systems in ... Among ...anual files ... an elec...system. ...mittee, ... study ...rvice. ...roader ... an... ...and ...

...ongress in ... of this session. ...today he spoke of action ...ext January, after the new Congress convenes.

The Senate Judiciary Committee meets tomorrow, and there are indications that it might vote out the Senate's bill on making Presidential assassination a Federal crime. The Justice and Treasury Departments have endorsed it.

The Judiciary Committee may also take up a bill to provide Secret Service protection for Presidential and Vice-Presidential nominees. This is sponsored by Senator Mansfield and Senator Everett McKinley Dirksen

Continued on Page 29, Column 1

...ctory ...ets Rally Here

...ator who has ... the Democrats-for-Keating drive among intellectual Democrats, passed out a list of committee members who were behind the Keating drive. The list was dominated by writers, actors and well-known figures in the theatrical and labor worlds.

They included James Baldwin, the Negro writer; Herman E. Cooper, labor lawyer; Carey McWilliams, editor of The Nation magazine; Paul Newman, the actor; Joseph L. Mankiewicz, motion picture producer and writer; Joseph For..., president of Cafeteria Employes Union Local

Continued on Page 37, Column 3

By HOMER BIGART
Special to The New York Times

...ACA, N. Y., Sept. 28—...bert F. Kennedy canceled a rally scheduled for this morning in Union Square in New York. His aides said he did so because of the sorrowful memories evoked by the publication of the Warren Commission report on President Kennedy's assassination.

Instead of campaigning, he spent the morning with Mrs. John F. Kennedy, the widow of the President. "It's been a rough day for both of them," an aide said.

All morning assignments today were canceled, including a walking tour of 14th Street in Manhattan from Fifth Avenue to Union Square.

In the afternoon Mr. Kennedy flew to Ithaca for the start of a two-day tour of central and western New York. He spoke to a crowd of 200 at Ithaca Airport and to 1,000 persons at DeWitt Park in downtown Ithaca.

Mr. Kennedy seemed subdued and so did his audiences in this heavily Republican Finger Lakes region. Tompkins County, of which Ithaca is the seat, went for Richard M. Nixon in 1960. The vote was 17,061 for Mr. Nixon and 7,597 for Mr. Kennedy.

On the flight up from New York Mr. Kennedy sat by himself, staring out of the plane. Occasionally he smiled wanly during his speeches, which lacked fire.

However, Mr. Kennedy did reply spiritedly to Republican

Continued on Page 36, Column 3

Harpo ...

Blond-Wigged ... Star Scored ... in Films Wit...

By The Associate...

HOLLYWOOD, S... Harpo Marx, the blond... nonspeaking member ... Marx Brothers team, ... night at 8:30 in Moun... Hospital. He was 70 yea...

A hospital official sa... Marx died after surgery. ...cording to United Press In... national, a family spokesm... said the comedian had entere... the hospital earlier in the day for heart surgery.]

Mr. Marx, whose given name was Arthur, had been in semi-retirement for five years. In January, 1963, he announced that he was retiring completely.

The harp-playing comedian was the second of the theatrical brothers to die. Chico, the piano player, died in 1961.

The surviving brothers are Gummo, Zeppo and Groucho.

Mr. Marx leaves also his wife, the former actress Susan Fleming, to whom he was married for 28 years, and four adopted children.

A honking horn, facial expressions and gestures were

Continued on Page 52, Column 1

United Artists, 1946

Harpo in his battered plug hat, one of his trademarks.

NEWS INDEX

Harpo Marx, Silent Comedian, Dies

Continued From Page 1, Col. 2

Mr. Marx's only mode of communication as a performer on the stage and in films. He maintained professional silence until the end of his career.

His Silence Was Eloquent

A battered plug hat on his frizzled mop hair, a cretinous grimace on his innocent face, and his baggy pants and oversize raincoat filled with everything from ax handles to zebra skins, Harpo Marx kept audiences laughing for 50 years.

His trademark was his harp, which he played well, and his silence, which was funnier, sweeter and more eloquent than most comedians' noisiest chatter.

The cigar-chewing Groucho was the star of the team, but it was Harpo, tooting his horn while in pursuit of an attractive girl, who always seemed to draw the most laughs.

He was a great pantomimist who specialized in direct action. In a moment of peril he could be relied upon to produce from his huge coat pockets some device or tool with which to save the day—many times a scissors to straighten the hem of a woman's skirt or to cut phone lines.

The result was that the Marx Brothers became the most celebrated brother act in the history of motion pictures. Their wild chaotic world of improvisational humor was distinctly their own.

Among the films they made were "The Cocoanuts," "Animal Crackers," "Duck Soup" and "A Night at the Opera." Though they were produced in the nineteen-thirties, they are still popular and occasionally make the rounds of the art houses.

With his brothers Julius (Groucho), Leonard (Chico), Milton (Gummo) and Herbert (Zeppo), Harpo learned his profession through a childhood in vaudeville.

The team rose the hard way—starting as a musical act called the Six Musical Mascots (their mother was the sixth). Then followed the Three (later Four) Nightingales, until they reached a vaudevillian's peak—playing the Palace in 1918.

The brothers were the sons of an Alsatian tailor, Sam Marx, and the former Minnie Palmer, a German musician whose brother, Al Shean, was a member of the well-known comedy act of Gallagher and Shean.

Harpo was born in the Yorkville section of New York in a tenement on East 93d Street on Nov. 23, 1893. He attended Public School 86, but never got beyond the second grade.

After their success in the Palace, Gummo dropped out. But the team continued, traveling the vaudeville circuit for the next six years and adding to their popularity at every stop

In 1924, the brothers made their Broadway debut with "I'll Say She Is," a revue that brought them praise from Alexander Woollcott, who wrote:

"This man is a great clown. Harpo is the funniest man I have even seen on the stage."

The critic took a liking to Harpo, and introduced him to the crown of writers, actors, wits and wags that frequented the Algonquin Hotel. An ideal listener, Harpo became a favorite.

The team followed their stage success with "The Cocoanuts," a satire of the Florida land boom, and in 1928 with "Animal Crackers."

By that time, sound had arrived in motion pictures and the team made one of the first talking pictures from their show "The Cocoanuts." It was a smashing success. Others soon followed.

In 1936, after a long courtship, Harpo, married Susan Fleming, an actress who had the lead in a movie called "Million Dollar Legs."

Besides performing in films, Harpo made frequent concert tours. His act consisted of clowning combined with some excellent solos on the harp.

Zeppo dropped out of the team in the late nineteen-thirties to become an agent. Chico and Groucho remained with Harpo, and the three went on to new zany heights, starring in such films as "A Night at the Opera," "A Day at the Races," "At the Circus," "Go West," "Monkey Business," "Horsefeathers," "A Night in Casablanca," "Room Service" and "The Big Store."

In 1941, Harpo broke his silence on the stage by appearing in a summer production of "The Man Who Came to Dinner." He played the role of Banjo, speaking a line, but also honking his horns and chasing girls about the stage.

The Marx Brothers made their last movie, "Love Happy," in 1949. Groucho turned to radio as a quizmaster while Chico and Harpo took to the night club route.

Most of Harpo's time, however, was spent on his spacious ranch in California with his four children and assorted pets.

Groucho, Chico and Harpo Marx kept audiences laughing in *A Night at the Opera.*

The Silent Articulator

Harpo Marx Used Variety of Methods To Express Himself Without Dialogue

By BOSLEY CROWTHER

The "silent" Marx Brother was perhaps the least appreciative description of Harpo. For he provided the zany comedy team with an unusual and incomparable eloquence of pantomime.

With his huge, fuzzy, pink wig, large, bright eyes and broad, moon face, Harpo relied on rapid gestures, beaming expressions, beeping horns and high-pitched mouth whistles to say what few could articulate in words.

Groucho was the noise maker. He made with the gags, splattering the jokes and the grotesque comments all over in a verbal cascade. Chico, while less dynamic, was also adroit with words, tossing off humorous non sequiturs in tortured Italian dialect. Zeppo, the youngest brother, was a straight man while he was with the act. But Harpo said nothing—and, in doing so, he often said more than all the rest.

Bridged the Gap

The Marx Brothers' great success on the screen bridged the transition from silent to talking comedy. They arrived on the wing from vaudeville and the stage in the early 1930's to fill a peculiar vacuum that had been caused by the onrush of sound.

Where the great and popular silent comedians—Charlie Chaplin, Buster Keaton, Harold Lloyd—developed their humor with slight gags and pliant pantomime that revealed their separate characteristics, the first new comics who tried to be funny with sound were almost like stand-up comedians, laboring vainly to project humor with words. The sight gags were awkwardly downgraded. So was the artful pantomime. Dialogue was substituted and it was terrible.

Then came the zany Marx Brothers, who were neither silent-film comedians nor talking automatons of sound. They were an utterly crazy combination of nondescript characters, using verbal as well as physical slapstick and wisecracks mixed with pantomime. Each in his way represented a distinctly different comedy type, thrown together in a strange amalgam. Harpo was the soul of the act.

Close to Little Tramp

Obviously, he was the closest to the great comedians of silent films. In a way, he was esthetically related to Charlie Chaplin's Little Tramp. Harpo was full of mischief (as the Little Tramp certainly was), moving about with his boisterous playmates, chasing blondes and honking his auto horn, but he was also inevitably reflective of a tender poigancy. Being "mute," the heart of his nature and of his unspoken affection came out through his eyes.

While Groucho and Chico were concerned with the elaborate flip-flops of their plots, Harpo was having fun. He was always wise to their maneuvers, and would often offer an assist or a miraculously inspired suggestion to help the monkey business along. But invariably at some point in the scramble, Harpo and the pace would slow down and he would withdraw to the comfort of his harp. Then he would play sweet music. Love and bliss would shine in his eyes. And the pathos of being a cheerful misfit and a buffoon to maniacs would be revealed.

There was no common sense in the character. It was a whimsey, a hare-brained caricature. But it sweetly suggested life's derangements and something of its haunting mystery.

Unfortunately, his kind of expression is no longer seen in films.

The New York Times SUNDAY, MARCH 25, 1973

Ken Maynard of Westerns Dies

HOLLYWOOD, March 24 (UPI)—Ken Maynard, the white-hatted cowboy hero of some 300 Western movies, died yesterday at the age of 77.

Bashful and Wholesome

Sporting a broad-brimmed white hat and spangled boots, Ken Maynard played the bashful cowboy hero in scores of Hollywood Westerns in the nineteen-twenties and thirties. He never smoked or drank on screen, he strummed his guitar and sang soft ballads, he handled his horse, Tarzan, expertly, he tangled with bandits and Indians and, doing all these things, he flourished as one of the era's most popular movie stars.

Like Tom Mix, another leading Western screen idol, Mr. Maynard did all his own riding tricks on screen. They were tricks he had learned growing up in Texas and performing with circuses and Wild West shows, including those of the Ringling Brothers and Buffalo Bill Cody.

Square-jawed and dark-haired with a rangy build, Mr. Maynard achieved success with such movies as "The Red Raiders," "Songs of the Saddle," "Parade of the West," "Branded Men," "$50,000 Reward," "King of the Arena," "Fiddlin' Buckaroo" and "Strawberry Roan."

By his own estimate not long ago, there were roughly 300 films in all — mostly for First National Pictures and Universal Studios. At his peak, he was making up to $1,000 a week, helping to finance his own pictures, flying and sailing for recreation and living in a mansion in Los Angeles.

Later, the cowboy star went back to rodeo-circus shows that toured the country, giving demonstrations of the expert riding that had first landed him a job in motion pictures.

Ken Maynard was born July 21, 1895, in Mission, Tex., the son of William H. Maynard, a building contractor whose work kept him on the move. When the youngster was 8 years old, his family was living near the Matador Ranch in Texas, and there Ken learned his first riding tricks.

His real education in trick riding and roping came with his first attempts to join the circus. When he was 12, he ran away with a cheap wagon show and remained for three weeks before his father came and took him home.

Several more times, Ken ran away. Finally, h[illegible] father enrolled him in the Virginia Military Institute, where the boy who later would perform extraordinary feats of horsemanship look eventually graduated as an engineer. In 1914, he joined the Kit Carson show and then went to the Haggenback and Wallace Show, working there until enlisting in the Army in 1918.

After World War I, Mr. Maynard roped and rode as the star performer in Ringling shows and with Buffalo Bill. He recalled being with the Cody show when it was foreclosed in Denver.

In 1923, he drifted to Hollywood and was introduced to the movies by his friends Buck Jones and Tom Mix. His first role was as a horseman of another era, Paul Revere, in "Janice Meredith," a movie starring Marion Davies.

A review of one of his early movies in The New York Times praised him as a "good-looking" hero who "rides so well that he makes extraordinary feats of horsemanship look comparatively simple."

"I never drank nor smoked in a picture," Mr. Maynard said in retrospect. "I never made an issue of it either. In a saloon scene I just ignored it. I never objected. I did it because of all the kids who came to my pictures. I didn't think it was right for them to see drinking and smoking on the screen."

In his later years, Mr. Maynard toured with rodeos and also appeared at parades and was an occasional guest on television talk shows. He had a small role in "Bigfoot" in 1969, playing a retired movie star turned general-store owner.

For the last few years, Mr. Maynard lived alone in a trailer at a trailer court in the San Fernando Valley.

Sid Saylor and Ken Maynard in *Mystery Mountain*.

Ken Maynard and Hoot Gibson in *The Trail Blazers*.

The New York Times WEDNESDAY, OCTOBER 30, 1963.

Adolphe Menjou Is Dead at 73; Suave and Debonair Film Star

Mustached Actor Was Known for His Sartorial Elegance —Active in G.O.P. Politics

Special to The New York Times

BEVERLY HILLS, Calif., Oct. 29—Adolphe Menjou, suave, debonair actor in more than 200 motion pictures, died in his home today of chronic hepatitis. He had been ill nearly nine months. His age was 73.

The slick-haired, mustached actor was widely known for his sartorial elegance. Until a few years ago, Mr Menjou's name was consistently prominent on the annual list of the nation's best-dressed men.

In recent years, Mr. Menjou was more active in Republican party politics than in acting.

His wife, the former actress Veree Teasdale, whom he married in 1934, and their adopted son, Peter Menjou, were at his bedside when he died.

A funeral service will be held Friday at 11 A.M. at All Saints Protestant Episcopal Church in Beverly Hills. Private burial at Hollywood Memorial Park will follow.

Cast as Man of World

Adolphe Jean Menjou was credited with having been responsible for the use of the word "suave" as a noun. ("For this part we want somebody with plenty of suave — you know, the Menjou type.").

Perennially included among the world's "10 best-dressed men," he boasted that his wardrobe included about 2,000 articles. He once denied that he had 100 overcoats but added, "I'll admit to 15." Suits? The figure usually was around 100.

And, for about half a century, the Menjou mustache was a waxed, neatly trimmed symbol of male elegance.

In the nineteen-twenties, Mr. Menjou earned as much as $7,500 a week. Later, he was active in radio and television. Because of steady work and wise investments, he was reputed to have been one of Hollywood's wealthiest men.

At first Mr. Menjou was identified as the impeccable man of the world in sophisticated roles—lover, roué or villain. But later he played many types—an unscrupulous editor, a motion-picture producer, a flamboyant trial lawyer, a floor walker.

In his autobiography "It Took Nine Tailors" (1948), he said: "My career has been as full of luck as a crap-shooter's dreams."

Mr. Menjou was born in Pittsburgh on Feb. 18, 1890. His father, who had emigrated from France, was in the hotel and restaurant business.

After attending Culver Military Academy in Indiana, the younger Menjou went to Cornell University. His father wanted him to become an engineer, but he transferred to the College of Liberal Arts, and college theatricals took up much of his spare time.

Mr. Menjou left Cornell at the end of his third year and went to Cleveland to work in his father's restaurant. When the business failed, he came to New York, worked on a farm, on the Vincent Astor estate, in a haberdashery firm and at the Maison Menjou, a restaurant his father had opened.

In New York Mr. Menjou found his first screen job as an extra — a ringmaster in a picture called "The Man Behind the Door," which was made at the Vitagraph studio.

Soon he became a regular extra. "It was my mustache that landed jobs for me," he said. "In those silent-film days it was the mark of a villain. When I realized they had me pegged as a foreign nobleman type I began to live the part, too. I bought a pair of white spats, an ascot tie and a walking stick."

In World War I, Mr. Menjou enlisted in an ambulance unit, served in France and rose to the rank of captain. Shortly after his discharge, he went to Hollywood and appeared in small roles in Douglas Fairbanks's "The Three Musketeers," "The Sheik" with Rudolph Valentino and in Pola Negri's "Bella Donna."

A "milestone in my career," Mr. Menjou said, was his role as the wealthy Paris bon vivant in "A Woman of Paris," directed by Charles Chaplin in 1923. After that came such films as "The Grand Duchess and the Waiter," "The Marriage Circle" and "The Swan."

His appearances in these sophisticated comedies had much to do with establishing the actor's public image and trademark of sartorial splendor.

In 1930 Mr. Menjou was cast as the editor in "The Front Page." He said later this had been accidental. Another actor had been set for the part but died after 10 days of rehearsal.

"It was one of the luckiest things that ever happened to me," Mr. Menjou said.

For this fire-breathing starring performance, Mr. Menjou drew his one nomination for an Academy Award.

Several times he was told he was "all through" in Hollywood but each time he came back. His other films included "A Farewell to Arms," "Little Miss Marker," "The Mighty Barnum," "Sing, Baby, Sing," and "A Star Is Born."

In World War II, Mr. Menjou entertained troops overseas. He made broadcasts in French, Italian, Spanish, German and Russian for the Office of War Information.

A vigorous anti-Communist, Mr. Menjou testified before the House Committee on Un-American Activities in its investigation of Communist infiltration into the film industry in 1947. He named alleged Communists.

The actor's career continued to flourish after the war in prominent supporting roles. The best known were his portrayals of a political boss in "State of the Union" (1948); a Communist henchman in "Man on a Tightrope" (1953); a French Army officer in "Paths of Glory" (1957); and, unaccustomedly, an unkempt eccentric in Walt Disney's "Pollyanna" (1960), marking his last feature film role.

Ten years ago, Mr. Menjou served as host for a television series called "My Favorite Story."

Backed Nixon

In recent years, Mr. Menjou's public appearance had been limited mainly to political activities. He was a staunch member member of the John Birch Society. As an ardent Republican, he was a vigorous supporter of Vice President Richard M. Nixon in the latter's unsuccessful campaign for the Presidency.

The actor was the owner of estimable art and coin collections. Two of his paintings, by Utrillo and Dufy, drew top prices at an auction of modern art held in New York three years ago.

Mr. Menjou married three times. His first two marriages, to Katherine Tinsley and Kathryn Carver, ended in divorce.

William Holden, Don Beddoe, Adolphe Menjou and Barbara Stanwyck in *Golden Boy*, 1939.

***The Front Page* with Adolphe Menjou and Pat O'Brien.**

The New York Times SATURDAY, FEBRUARY 14, 1976

Sal Mineo Knifed to Death in Hollywood

HOLLYWOOD, Feb. 13 (UPI)—Sal Mineo, the actor who was twice nominated for Oscars, was stabbed to death last night as he returned home from rehearsing for a new play.

Sheriff's homicide detectives questioned apartment neighbors today. One unofficial source said they were checking on a "drug angle" in the case.

Mr. Mineo, who was 37 years old, was felled with a single knife thrust to the chest in the rear carport area of the West Hollywood apartment house where he lived just below the Sunset Strip.

The coroner's office reported that an autopsy showed the slim, dark-haired actor had "died of a massive hemorrhage due to stab wounds of the chest penetrating the heart." A "heavy type knife" was the death weapon, according to Don Drynan, assistant coroner, who said there were no other injuries aparent.

A white male with long hair and wearing dark clothes was seen fleeing the scene and detectives questioned residents in the hope of getting a full description.

Mr. Mineo's wallet was found intact on his body, but investigators said he could have been killed resisting a robbery attempt.

He cried out, "Help! help! Oh my God!" before he died and the assailant may have fled in fear of capture.

Mr. Mineo was returning from the Westwood Playhouse, where he was rehearsing for the play, "P. S. Your Cat is Dead," when he apparently was ambushed in the garage area.

Broadway Debut at 11

Sal Mineo made his Broadway debut at the age of 11 in "The Rose Tattoo" and went on to appear in more than 20 movies and dozens of television shows.

He became a teen-agers' idol in 1956 when he was seen as Plato, the switchblade-wielding, psychotic juvenile delinquent in the James Dean movie, "Rebel Without a Cause." Young people at the time seemed to identify with Plato, and the aura of smoldering, sensuous boyishness that the then 17-year-old actor brought to the role won Mr. Mineo an Academy Award nomination.

He was nominated for his second Academy Award for best supporting actor in 1961 for his performance as Dov Landau, the Nazi concentration camp survivor turned Zionist terrorist in Palestine in "Exodus."

In TV Series

Mr. Mineo recently appeared in TV episodes of the "Ellery Queen" and "Joe Forrester" series on NBC. His last stage appearance was in San Francisco last fall, in James Kirkwood's play, "P.S. Your Cat Is Dead."

Mr. Mineo, who played a comic bisexual burglar in that play, was to have begun a run in it at the Westwood Playhouse in Los Angeles beginning Feb. 19. He was killed upon returning home from a rehearsal.

Mr. Kirkwood said in New York yesterday: "Until I saw him last October in my play, I had dismissed Sal Mineo as an actor. But my admiration for him is inexpressible. He was a professional whose talent grew over the years, a dedicated actor, and there aren't many of those left."

Mr. Mineo's background as a boy in the Bronx helped prepare him for the roles that he was most identified with in the 1950's. Born Salvatore Mineo Jr. on Jan. 10, 1939, he was the son of a Sicilia born coffin maker who reared the family in a tough neighborhood on 217th Street in the Bronx.

Young Sal was in trouble as a gang member at age 8 and was dismissed from a parochial school for being a troublemaker. He later attended Christopher Columbus High School but never received a diploma.

When he was 9 years old, largely to keep him off the street, his mother Josephine signed him up for a dancing class. Two years later the Broadway producer Cheryl Crawford, looking for two Italian-American children for Tennessee Williams's "The Rose Tattoo," spotted him in dancing school and asked him to recite the line, "The goat is in the yard."

For a year, the boy led a goat across the stage of the Martin Beck Theater and recited his single line. Then he became the understudy for the young actor playing the Prince in "The King and I" and later succeeded him in the role.

Mr. Mineo's first film appearance was in "Seven Bridges to Cross," playing Tony Curtis as a boy, in 1955. Later movies included the title role in "The Gene Krupa Story," "The Young Don't Cry," "Dino" (again as a young delinquent), "Crime in the Streets," "Somebody Up There Likes Me" and "Giant." He was one of the major simians in 1971's "Escape From the Planet of the Apes."

In 1969, he directed "Fortune and Men's Eyes," which had a successful engagement in Los Angeles before it began a run here. The play, concerning prison life and including an onstage nude homosexual rape scene, led Clive Barnes to comment in this newspaper, "If this does sound like the kind of play you'd like, you need a psychiatrist a lot more than you need a theater ticket."

The play had a successful run, however, and Mr. Mineo later directed a screen version filmed in Canada.

At the height of his success in the 1950's, Mr. Mineo bought his family a $200,000 home in Mamaroneck, N.Y. from which his mother directed the answering of some 4,000 letters a week from Mineo fans. Mr. Mineo, described by a friend yesterday as "a bit of a loner," was a bachelor. He is survived by his mother, a sister, Sarina, and two brothers, Victor and Michael.

Sal Mineo and Susan Kohner in *Dino*.

Sal Mineo, James Dean and Natalie Wood in *Rebel Without a Cause*, 1955, one of the best of the alienated-youth films of the period.

Carmen Miranda Is Dead at 41; Movie Comedienne and Dancer

Prototype of Dynamic Latin, Noted for Her Garish Hats, Made Mark on Broadway

Special to The New York Times.

BEVERLY HILLS, Calif., Aug. 5—Carmen Miranda, the Latin dancer and comedienne celebrated for her fruit-basket hats, died unexpectedly early today at her home here. She was 41 years old.

She collapsed shortly after she had returned from performing with Jimmy Durante in the filming of one of his forthcoming television shows. The cause of her death was not immediately determined. A physician who had been treating her for a slight case of bronchitis since her recent return from Cuba said she had seemed in good health.

Miss Miranda, whose explosive, hippy dancing, thick-accented singing and garish costumes became a prototype of the dynamic Latin female, had been the wife of David Sebastian, a motion picture producer, since 1947. He was with her when she died.

Miss Miranda skyrocketed to fame fifteen years ago as "The South American Bombshell" through her performance in the Broadway show "The Streets of Paris." She had performed extensively in motion pictures, night clubs and television. Her first film was "Down Argentine Way," made in 1940.

Other pictures included "That Night in Rio," 1941; "Week-End in Havana," 1941; "Springtime in the Rockies," 1942; "The Gang's All Here," 1943; "Four Jills in a Jeep," 1944; "Greenwich Village" and "Something for the Boys," 1944; "Doll Face," 1946; "Copacabana," 1947; "A Date With Judy," 1948, and "Scared Stiff," 1953.

She was the only woman in America listed as having had an income of more than $200,000 in the fiscal year ended in 1945.

Although identified with Brazil, Miss Miranda actually was a native of Portugal. Her original name was Maria de Carno da Cunha. Her family moved to Brazil when she was a baby.

She attended a convent in the Brazilian capital and got a start in the direction of show business when she became a department store model at the age of 17.

Her flamboyant headgear compensated for her size: She was only five feet two inches tall and weighed only about 100 pounds.

She is survived also by her mother, Mrs. Maria Amelia Miranda de Cunha, who lived with her; two brothers, Mario and Oscar, and two sisters, Aurora and Cecilia.

Carmen Miranda

Carmen Miranda in *Down Argentine Way.*

Groucho Marx and Carmen Miranda in *Copacabana,* 1947.

The New York Times TUESDAY, DECEMBER 18, 1962.

Thomas Mitchell, Actor, Dead; Star of Stage and Screen, 70

Actor's Career in the Movies and in Theater Spanned a Half Century

BEVERLY HILLS, Calif., Dec. 17 (UPI) — Thomas Mitchell, Academy Award-winning character actor, died of cancer today at the age of 70—the second star to die in two days.

Charles Laughton died Saturday also of cancer. Ironically, both men had been patients of the same hospital during the fall in their unsuccessful battle against the disease.

Mr. Mitchell's wife, Susan, and daughter, Anne M. Lange, were at his bedside when he died at his home this afternoon. Mr. Mitchell, uncle of James Mitchell, former Secretary of Labor, was most fond of the stage but made his greatest success as an exuberant character actor in the movies. He had also appeared on television, last being featured on the Perry Como show.

Appeared in Many Films

• Mr. Mitchell appeared in a score of motion pictures, TV 'shows and Broadway plays. He is best remembered for his "Mayor of the Town" TV series, and his role as Scarlett O'Hara's father in "Gone with the Wind."

Mr. Michell was one of the few character performers, along with Walter Brennan, to reach top stardom. He won an Oscar in 1939 for his portrayal of the whiskey-soaked doctor in "Stagecoach."

He was born in Elizabeth, N. J., July 11, 1892, one of seven children of James and Mary Mitchell, both of whom were born in Ireland. His father was in the newspaper business, and his older brother, John, was a newspaper man. After graduating from Elizabeth High School, Mr. Mitchell also became a newspaper reporter, working for publications in Newark, Washington, Baltimore and Pittsburgh. He moved to show business by writing skits in his spare time.

He then turned to acting and by 1913 he had traveled throughout the United States with stock companies and had played in a Shakespeare festival in Madison Square Garden.

He spent the next two years touring the country with Charles Coburn's Shakespearean company performing at colleges.

His first Hollywood appearance was in the 1934 movie "Cloudy with Showers" in 1934. But it was not until 1936, when Mr. Mitchell played a character role in "Lost Horizons," that his career began to take shape. His best known pictures were "The Hurricans," "Mr. Smith Goes To Washington" and "The Hunchback of Notre Dame."

Mr. Mitchell was a noted collector of fine arts.

United Press International, 1959

Thomas Mitchell

Won Other Awards

BEVERLY HILLS, Calif., Dec. 17 (AP) — Mr. Mitchell also won an Emmy Awardd in 1952 as the best television actor. His performance in the Broadway production of "Hazel F'agg" won him the Antoinette Perry Award in 1953.

Vivien Leigh as Scarlett and Thomas Mitchell as Gerald O'Hara in *Gone With the Wind.*

Jack Carson, Paul Stanton, Thomas Mitchell and Jean Arthur in *Mr. Smith Goes to Washington,* 1939.

Tom Mix, 1921.

"All the News That's Fit to Print."

The New York Times.

LATE CITY EDITION
Fair and slightly warmer today. Tomorrow fair, with little change in temperature.
Temperatures Yesterday—Max., 75; Min., 54

Sections 1 AND 3

NEWS INDEX, PAGE 55, THIS SECTION

Copyright, 1940, by The New York Times Company.

VOL. XC...No. 30,213. Entered as Second-Class Matter, Postoffice, New York, N. Y. NEW YORK, SUNDAY, OCTOBER 13, 1940. Including Rotogravure Picture, Magazine and Book Review TEN CENTS | TWELVE CENTS Beyond 200 Miles, Except West of Pa.—South of Md.—North of Mass.

RUSSIANS MASS AT FRONTIER; NAZI TROOPS FILL BUCHAREST; R.A.F. BATTERS FRENCH COAST

RED ARMY MARCHES

Soviet Tanks Reported on Road as German Influx Grows

RUMANIAN WARSHIP SUNK

Protest to Moscow Is Planned —Nazi Forces in Bucharest Called Army 'Mission'

By C. L. SULZBERGER
Wireless to THE NEW YORK TIMES.

BUCHAREST, Rumania, Oct. 12—The Soviet General Staff was reported today to have begun massing troops on the Northern Bukovina frontier in the region of Hertza and Dorohoi. The main section of the town of Cernauti is reported to have been evacuated and motorized units, including hundreds of tanks, are said to be on the march. [Thirteen words deleted by Rumanian censor.]

At the same time the evacuation of German refugees from Bessarabia has been virtually halted on a Russian pretext and a Rumanian warship is reported to have been sunk by a Soviet destroyer.

Monitor No. 6, returning from Odessa, where she had taken some Rumanian experts, passed through Soviet waters en route to Constanta. For a week the passage of foreign vessels through Soviet waters has been forbidden and the ship was sunk. The crew was saved and a diplomatic protest is being prepared for transmission to Moscow. [Fifty-one words censored.]

The German military mission here is, to say the least, ubiquitous. One air division of the mission is arriving at Ploesti. Units of a Panzer [motorized] division have been seen. [Fifty-one words censored.]

Nazi Officers Crowd Hotel

It was scarcely necessary to issue a communiqué to let the inhabitants of Bucharest know there was a mission here. At one moment thirty-five of the mission's uniformed officers were standing in the lobby of the Athenee Palace Hotel tonight; one dining room was entirely occupied by them while an overflow of ten tables was seated in another dining room.

The Nazi flag is displayed over the hotel portal and two Rumanian soldiers are guarding the doorway. Inside stand dozens of Reichswehr officers and two private soldiers. [Forty-eight words censored.]

All day the mission's automobiles, bearing German license plates, have been driving around. This morning more than fifty Rumanian planes, including Heinkel and Blenheim bombers and P. Z. L. Polish chasers, roared overhead, honoring the mission. Tomorrow the mission is expected to bring its own planes.

Hundreds more of the mission's officers and men arrived at the Bucharest station today and one group was greeted by General Ion Antonescu, Rumania's military dictator, and Prince Luca Sturza, Minister of Foreign Affairs. At 5 o'clock a Junkers 52 transport plane delivered some more of the mission's officers, including Air Generals Speidel and von Schleich. Cavalry General Hansen arrived today. He also was present at Rotterdam with the German military mission last Spring. [114 words censored.]

British subjects are to begin leaving Rumania on Monday. On Thursday a special boat will take all those then left from Constanta. Only a few legation officials and the Minister are expected to remain. At 7 o'clock tonight conversations between the Foreign Office and the British began again. The Foreign Office is trying to induce the British not to break off diplomatic relations. [Thirty-two words censored.]

Axis Stroke Believed Near

BUCHAREST, Rumania, Oct. 12 (UP)—German airplanes, armored cars and infantry poured into Rumania tonight as diplomatic quarters predicted an imminent Axis stroke against Greece and possibly Yugoslavia.

[London sources reported Turkey had promised aid to Syria in the event of an Italian attack and was sounding out Moscow on the defense of Greece. The Soviet was expected at least to promise Turkey a free hand if she went to the assistance of Greece.]

Huge green-gray German army trucks rumbled into Bucharest with

Continued on Page Forty

The International Situation

The foreign policy of the United States, President Roosevelt said last night in a broadcast to the world, is total defense of this hemisphere and adjacent oceans, continued aid to Britain, insistence ... right of peaceful ... the Atlantic and ... appeasement of ... The people of all ... recognize the doct... appeasement for wha... said, "a major weapo... gressor nations." ... was construed as his ... the partition of the ... mally agreed on at ... Germany, Italy and ... Openly recognizing the ... tation that would be pla... his words, the President ... "I speak bluntly. I spe... love the American people... for freedom and liberty and ... cency and humanity." [Pag... Column 8.]

As German troops continu... to pour into Bucharest and othe... parts of Rumania, censored dis... patches from the capital said re... ports had come of large Russian troop movements along the mutual frontier and of the sinking by a Soviet destroyer of a Rumanian war vessel as it was passing through prohibited waters in the Black Sea. Diplomatic quarters believed the massing of Nazis troops in Rumania was only a preliminary to an Axis stroke against Greece or Yugoslavia, or both. A Rumanian communiqué said the Germans were there by invitation to "instruct" the Rumanians in methods of modern warfare. More were coming, the statement said. [Page 1, Column 1.]

The first official German confirmation of the military penetration of Rumania was a statement by D. N. B., the official news agency, which said the Nazi troops had been sent to protect the oil fields and to carry out the Axis guarantee of Rumanian borders given at Vienna and that they would return home after completing their task of instructing the Rumanian Army. How soon that would be was not stated. [Page 41, Column 1.]

Diplomatic circles in London said that Turkey, now potentially threatened by the Axis both from the north and the south, had promised aid to French Syria in case of an Italian attack and had sent its Ambassador to Moscow to inquire what the attitude of the Soviet would be if Greece should be attacked and Turkey should go to her defense. [Page 40, Column 1.]

Their way lighted by a harvest moon, British bombers returned to the attack on the Ger... vasion bases along ... coast last ...

... Japa... geste... part ... the ... sailed... steame... person... business ... firmed th... ton and M... uated seve... cans from ... prepared fo... the Far Ea... comment co... siderably les... United States ... viously, as di... Premier Konoy... umn 4.]

A study of Ita... tivities in the U... Professor Gaetano ... the American Coun... Affairs brought the... that 5 per cent of ... American population... United States was Fas... cent more who might ... that ideological direction ... first emergency. Ten per... Professor Salvemini found ... anti-Fascist. He urged c... supervision of the Italian ... bassador and consuls and dep... tation of proved propagan... agents. [Page 5, Column 1.]

TOKYO AMERICANS HEED U.S. WARNING TO FLEE FAR EAST

100 Wives and Children of Business Men Sail—Many Passages Are Bo...

Myron Selznick's Can't ... Continental Handicap at Ja... Knight was second, with F... Remsen Handicap for 2-yea... between Arnold Hanger's H... Stable's Mettlesome.

(Complete Details of These a... in Section 5.)

... down ... 30,000 ... Colum... looked ... was rou... to be ... nell swam... rally. Score...

Alabama	...		
Amherst	...		
Arkansas	...		
Auburn	...7		
Boston Coll.	..33		
Clemson	...39		
Colgate	...20	B...	
Columbia	...20	W...	
Connecticut	...6	W...	
Cornell	...45	Ar...	
Fordham	...20	Tu...	
Geo. Wash.	..20	W...	
Holy Cross	...18	W...	
Iowa	...30	Ind...	
Kansas	...20	...	
Lafayette	...26	Mu...	
Michigan	...26	Har...	
Mich. State	...20	Pur...	
Mississippi	...28	Duq...	
Missouri	...24	Kansas...	

ROOSEVELT PLEDGES TOTAL DEFENSE OF AMERICAS AND ADJACENT OCEANS; WILLKIE SCORES ATTACK ON FAMILY

NEW DEAL BERATED

Willkie Says Morgenthau Opposed 'a Break' for Munitions Makers

...ES DEFENSE 'DELAYS'

...t Talks Tolerance as ...y Raises Racial Issue, ...an Says at Albany

...of Mr. Willkie's ad... ...ny is on Page 28.

...A. HAGERTY ...EW YORK TIMES. ...12—Wendell L. ...unced as system... ...e attack upon ...used by the ...Democratic ...reported in ...EW YORK ...

...tic audi... ...n 15,000 ...aseball ...dential ...arance ...that ...d him ...d in ...

Democrats Accused of Distributing Official U. S. Books for Campaign

Willkie Backer Asks Gillette to Make Hatch Law Inquiry—Aiken Denies That Kits of Speakers Contain Pamphlet

Charging that there had been a clear violation of Section 2 of the Hatch act, Alan Valentine, executive director of the National Committee of Democrats for Willkie, yesterday asked Senator Guy M. Gillette of Iowa, chairman of the Senate Campaign Expenditures Investigating Committee, to inquire into the distribution by the Democratic National Committee of a booklet issued by the Federal Works Agency entitled "Millions for Defense."

The booklet, forty-eight pages long and profusely illustrated with photographs, came to the Democrats-for-Willkie committee as part of a "Speakers' Kit" distributed by the Speakers' Bureau of the Democratic National Committee. Others who called at the Speakers' Bureau on Friday for "Speakers' Kits" also received copies of the booklet.

Paul Aiken, director of the Speakers' Bureau, denied yesterday, when his attention had been called to Mr. Valentine's charge, that the booklet was being distributed by the Democratic National Committee. On a recent visit to Washington, he explained, he visited the Federal Works Agency and picked up a number of copies and brought them back to his office here.

Some of these, he added, were handed to visitors seeking kits, along with the kit itself. None, he said, was included in the kit.

"May I as executive director of the National Committee of Democrats-for-Willkie, the No Third Term branch of the Democratic party, call your attention to the fact that the Speakers' Bureau of the Democratic National Committee, the Third Term branch of the Democratic party, is issuing from its headquarters in the Biltmore Hotel in New York City, as part of a "Speakers' Kit," an elaborate booklet printed at government expense," Mr. Valentine said in his telegram to Senator Gillette.

"The booklet, entitled 'Millions for Defense,' consisting of forty-eight pages and cover, handsomely illustrated with twenty-two large photographs, is a product of the Federal Works Agency in Washington and bears the imprint of the United States Government Printing Office, 1940.

"Estimates by private printers put the cost of the eight by ten and a half inch booklet, with cover printed in two colors, at $51,000 for 1,000,000 copies. Evidently any one may obtain them and any temporary shortage at the Biltmore or other Democratic headquarters throughout the country is taken care of by the insertion of a card in each copy bearing this notation:

"'Additional copies of this publication may be had upon applica-

Continued on Page Twenty-five

TOM MIX, RIDER, DIES UNDER AUTO

...cus and Screen Equestrian, ...wboy Idol of Youth, Killed ...Arizona Car Upset

By The Associated Press. ...ENCE, Ariz., Oct. 12—... 60, cowboy-actor and ...Western thrillers of the ... killed eighteen miles ... today as he was ...er his overturned auto... ...highway detour. ...ose colorful career as ...mer, soldier, law en... ...and motion pic... ...him the idol of mil... ...over, was traveling ...n, Ariz., to Flor...

...agent for a ...o show soon in ...rrying $6,000 in ...avelers' checks ...jewels. ...oyes discovered ...alled State pa... ...ated the body. ... said that Mr. ...stantly after ...r. There will ... body was

...lvania ...Mix Run ...County, ...h he was ...e West, ...he was ...

...for twenty years of his career in

Continued on Page Forty-eight

DIVINITY STUDENTS FACE JAIL ON DRAFT

McDermott Threatens to 'Crack Down' on Them if They Fail to Register Wednesday

Colonel Arthur V. McDermott, Director of Selective Service for New York City, said yesterday he hoped the twenty 'conscientious objectors' at Union Theological Seminary, who have announced they will not register for the draft next Wednesday, would not "prove to be as foolish as their statement indicates them to be." If they do not register, the colonel added, "we will crack down on them without delay."

Informed of Colonel McDermott's remarks, William Lovell, president of the student body at the seminary and a leader in the movement to refuse to register, said he and his colleagues would study it and perhaps issue a rejoinder. There was no indication that the twenty youths would withdraw from their stand.

"The trouble with these young men," Colonel McDermott said, "is that their intellectual conceit is exceeded only by their immaturity of judgment. The law expressly exempts from service theological students who have completed their first year of study.

Ample Protection Afforded

"It provides ample protection for really sincere conscientious objectors.

"Yet, not satisfied with this, these so-called young intellectuals have smugly decided that their judgment and intelligence is so far superior to that of Congress and the American people that they propose to disdain the requirements of the law.

"The smug complacency of their statement that the American people * * * lack the imagination, the religious faith, and the precedents to make a proper decision in the face of threatened invasion, would be almost laughable if it were not for the grave consequence which will result from it.

...cannot say too earnestly that ... of these young men refuse ...ster they will be promptly ...orously prosecuted under ...l provision of the Selective ...ct. They will be subject ...nment up to five years ...ne up to $10,000, or both ...y firm intention to deal ...h obstructors speedily ...

...added that he had "a ...they will be good little ...

...ican Civil Liberties ...issued an appeal to Lieut. Col. Lewis B. Hershey, acting director of the Selective Service Act, for the appointment of a special central appeals board to hear the cases of conscientious o... ...tors.

John Haynes Holmes, chairman

Continued on Page Seven

REPLY TO THE AXIS

President at Dayton Is Blunt in His Talk on Dictator Nations

HEMISPHERE UNITY CITED

Appeasement Rejected, While No Line-Up in Europe or Asia Will Stop Our Aid to Britain

President Roosevelt's address will be found on Page 22.

By CHARLES HURD
Special to THE NEW YORK TIMES.

DAYTON, Ohio, Oct. 12—President Roosevelt stated the foreign policy of this country tonight to be the total defense of all the Americas and the adjacent oceans against any and all military or other attempts by dictator countries to encroach upon them or to influence them by indirect tactics.

Speaking by radio to the Western Hemisphere, but with obvious reference to Germany, Italy and Japan, he rejected any theory of appeasement, and grouped the American republics as a single unit within the neighborly defense program of this country.

"No combination of dictator countries of Europe or Asia," he said, "will stop the help we are giving to almost the last free people fighting to hold them at bay."

This country, he added, will defend now, as in 1798, the right of peaceful commerce in the Atlantic and Pacific Oceans.

The United States is keeping the nations of this hemisphere fully advised on defense preparations. Then the President said:

"We intend to encourage this frank interchange of information and plans because we shall be all for one and one for all."

On this Columbus Day, Mr. Roosevelt noted the widely varying racial origins of the Americans, among them Italian, German, Spanish and Portuguese, and pledged the might of the United States to perpetuate the friendly association of countries developed by their descendants.

Ocean Defenses First Factor

"We of the Americas," he said, "consider that this defense of these oceans of the Western Hemisphere against acts of aggression is the first factor in the defense and protection of our own territorial integrity. We reaffirm that policy, lest there be any doubt of our intention to maintain it."

Telling his diverse radio audiences that "the core of our defense is the faith we have in the institutions we defend," the President said:

"No combination of dictator countries of Europe and Asia will halt us in the path we see ahead for ourselves and for democracy.

"Our course is clear. Our decision is made. We will continue to pile up our defense and our armaments. We will continue to help those who resist aggression, and who now hold the aggressors far from our shores.

"Let no American in any part of the Americas question the possibility of danger from overseas. Why should we accept assurances that we are immune? History records that not long ago those same assurances were given to the people of Holland and Belgium.

"It can no longer be disputed that forces of evil which are bent on conquest of the world will destroy whomever and whenever they can destroy."

"I Speak Bluntly," He Remarks

The President recognized the interpretation that would be put upon his speech, when he said:

"I speak bluntly. I speak the love the American people have for freedom and liberty and decency and humanity."

Through the address ran the basic idea of maintaining the national integrities of the Western Hemisphere, and the national policy outlined indicated considerably more than passive resistance to threat.

"We are building a total defense on land and sea and in the air," the President said, "a total defense sufficient to repel total attacks from any part of the world. Forewarned by the deliberate attacks of the dictators upon free peoples, the United States, for the first time in its history, has undertaken the mustering of its men in peacetime.

"Unprecedented dangers have caused the United States to undertake the building of a Navy and an air force sufficient to defend all

Continued on Page Twenty-four

LONDON GETS LULL AFTER 200TH ALARM

Night Attack Slackens—All but Few Day Raiders Beaten Off in Heavy Fighting

By RAYMOND DANIELL
Special Cable to THE NEW YORK TIMES.

LONDON, Sunday, Oct. 13—For the 200th time London's air-raid sirens yesterday warned its people that German bombers were overhead.

Last night, as the sixth week of the intensive aerial assault on the central part of the town began with the customary buzzing of unseen engines, crumping of bombs and bark of guns, plans were announced for speeding the evacuation of mothers and children and for calling on troops and a pioneer corps to help clear the debris of buildings blasted from their foundations in the last month and a half. The night raiders seemed to be more numerous than usual in the early hours of darkness.

After midnight and before dawn [2:30 A. M., according to The United Press], sirens announced that the raiders had been driven off. The city's night cave dwellers sleeping in shelters paid the signal as little heed as Londoners pay to daytime alarms. They went on about their sleeping as in the daytime they go on about their business.

[Only eight or ten London districts reported hits and the German bombings were lighter than usual in the provinces, The Associated Press reported.]

Just before German planes yesterday resumed the intensive some-

Continued on Page Forty-four

NEW BERLIN RAID STAGED BY BRITISH

Channel Ports Are Attacked Above Mist—Germans Report Sea Fight Off England

By ROBERT P. POST
Special Cable to THE NEW YORK TIMES.

LONDON, Sunday, Oct. 13—In bright moonlight British bombers of the Royal Air Force attacked objectives along the French coast east of Boulogne during last night.

Observers on the Kentish coast said a dense mist hid the French shore so the bomb flashes could not be seen; but they watched a vast barrage from the Nazis' anti-aircraft guns bursting above the mist. They said explosions could be felt on the English side of the Channel.

[The R. A. F. during the night raided Berlin again after the German capital had had four quiet nights, according to dispatches from Berlin early today. Explosive and incendiary bombs were dropped, with some casualties.]

These nightly attacks—directed perhaps in part against some German long-range guns placed opposite Dover—have become regular.

During the afternoon, also, heavy explosions were heard from the direction of the French coast. The rumble was almost continuous and houses shook and doors rattled. The explosions may have been from air bombs or shelling or both.

Although the sun was brilliant the mist had hid the Channel coasts during the day, and it hung last night over the calm Strait of Dover.

Continued on Page Thirty-nine

TOM MIX, RIDER, DIES UNDER AUTO

Circus and Screen Equestrian, Cowboy Idol of Youth, Killed in Arizona Car Upset

By The Associated Press.

FLORENCE, Ariz., Oct. 12—Tom Mix, 60, cowboy-actor and hero of Western thrillers of the films, was killed eighteen miles south of here today as he was pinned under his overturned automobile on a highway detour.

Mr. Mix, whose colorful career as a circus performer, soldier, law enforcement officer and motion picture star made him the idol of millions the world over, was traveling alone from Tucson, Ariz., to Florence and Phoenix.

Serving as advance agent for a circus scheduled to show soon in Phoenix, he was carrying $6,000 in cash, $1,500 in travelers' checks and several valuable jewels.

Two highway employes discovered the upset car and called State patrolmen, who extricated the body. Coroner E. O. Devine said that Mr. Mix apparently died instantly after losing control of his car. There will be no inquest. The body was brought here.

Began Riding in Pennsylvania

Mr. Mix was born at Mix Run near Dubois, Clearfield County, Pennsylvania. Although he was generally associated with the West, he did not go West until he was 26 years old.

Until he was 18, when he enlisted in the Army to serve in the Spanish-American War, Tom worked at odd jobs in Dubois and as a water boy for lumberjacks in the Allegheny Mountain forests.

After serving two hitches in the Army, Tom went to Oklahoma where he joined the Miller Brothers "101" Ranch.

Continued on Page Forty-eight

Continued From Page One

Mrs. Emma Schwartz, 63, his oldest sister, recalled tonight at Dubois that he learned his horsemanship while helping their father, who managed a Dubois stable.

She told of how young Tom liked to play "Wild West," and of the time he stood a younger sister against a door and was preparing to throw hand-made knives about her when the family intervened.

Tom last visited Mrs. Schwartz in July. Mrs. Elizabeth Mix, his mother, died at Dubois in 1937.

Personality Brought to Screen

Tom Mix was an accomplished cowboy and a trick rider and roper and had been a soldier and a Western peace officer before he turned to the screen.

So when he anticipated the vogue for horse opera he brought to the motion pictures a compelling and realistic personality that kept its hold on the nation's youth to the end of his career.

For twenty years of his career in films he rode a horse named Tony. The magnificent animal developed a following of its own that won companion billing on theatre marquees with its master. Tony was retired in November, 1932, at the age of 23, to the Mix stables in Universal City.

The official biography of Mr. Mix had him born in Texas but that was evidently for publicity purposes. His Pennsylvania birthplace has been verified.

In 1898 he joined the Army and saw service in Cuba as one of Colonel Theodore Roosevelt's Rough Riders, and later he saw service with the American troops in the Philippines.

When the Boxer rebellion broke out in China Mr. Mix went there with the American forces. For distinguished service in the Orient he received a medal and a citation. He also did a turn as a soldier of fortune, going to South Africa and fighting with the British in the Boer War, taking part in the siege of Ladysmith.

Crack Shot Peace Officer

The Army did not sate his taste for adventure and, on returning to the United States, he became a law enforcement officer in Kansas, Oklahoma and Texas, where, even at that late day, the frontier spirit still survived and peace officers were obliged to be top-notch fighting men.

He served as Sheriff of Montgomery County in Kansas and of Washington County in Oklahoma, and also spent a term as deputy United States marshal and enforcement officer for the eastern district of Oklahoma.

After that he was a Texas Ranger for three years, an assignment that gave him ample opportunity to display his horsemanship and marksmanship. Four times he was critically wounded and to his death he carried in his body, as mementoes of this stage of his career, three slugs.

In 1906 he became livestock foreman at Miller Brothers' 101 Ranch, a Wild West show that toured the country with a bill featuring cowboys and Indians. Three years later he joined the Sells-Floto Circus for a season.

He won the national riding and roping contest for cowboys at Prescott, Ariz., in 1909, the year before

Tom Mix in the white hat and suit he made the uniform of the Hollywood cowboy of the Twenties.

he made his debut in the movies, and one at Canyon City, Col., in 1911.

Debut in Western Films

Around that time, after his turn in the circus, he was working as a hunting guide, and it was this that led to his first movie assignment.

The Selig Company had decided to make a few Westerns, which provided a chance to present a picture with sets yielded from the bounty of Nature, and had sent a company to Oklahoma to get some original atmosphere.

Mr. Mix was engaged to find locations and to supply cowboys, horses and the other paraphernalia of the Old West. The job aroused his interest in motion pictures and he offered to play a part in the horse operas. Soon he became the principal star of the Selig Company and eventually of the Fox Company.

He was credited with having foreseen the vogue of Western pictures and as a result made millions of dollars and became a hero to generations of small boys over the country as well as millions of juveniles and adults in various parts of the world where Westerns were taken to be typical of American civilization.

Being a hero to the country's boyhood he found something of a responsibility. He could never smoke a cigarette in a picture, nor could he enter a saloon except to deal justice to a "bad man."

His movie love affairs were always with the ranch foreman's daughter or the school teacher, and nothing ever happened that could not be explained by the small boy's mother at the table the night the minister had supper there.

Tom Mix was not a conservative person, especially as to clothes. When "all dressed up" he wore a platinum belt buckle with his initials in diamonds, as well as a diamond ring and pin. He wore a white evening suit at many of the movie parties in Hollywood and frequently was seen in a purple tuxedo.

He had his monogram in electric lights on both gates of his elaborate semi-Spanish house on a Beverly Hills knoll. Filled with cowboy trophies, the building became a museum of life on the range. Mr. Mix also maintained an old-time ranch.

Star of 370 Films in 24 Years

When the "talkies" came in Mr. Mix dropped out of pictures for two years and returned to the circus. Then, resuming screen roles, he made such features as "Destry Rides Again," "Destry of Death Valley," "My Pal, the King," and "Terror Trail.'

During the filming of a picture, "Oh, Promise Me," at a ranch near Lone Pine, Calif., in October, 1922, Mr. Mix's horse slipped, threw him and rolled on him. The actor suffered severe internal injuries.

The accident, one of a series, induced him to retire on Christmas Day, 1932, after he had finished work in his last picture, "The Rustler's Round-Up."

On his retirement he had appeared in motion pictures for twenty-four years and had starred in 370 feature productions. Afterward he toured with a show called "Tom Mix's Circus," and made vaudevi[lle] and rodeo tours of the world.

His first wife, Olive Stokes, [di]vorced him and he had brought [up] their daughter, Ruth. In 1917 [he] married Victoria Forde. They h[ad] one daughter, Thomasina. M[rs.] Victoria Mix obtained a divorce [in] 1930. In February, 1932, Mr. M[ix] married Mabel Hubbard Ward, [an] aerial performer in the Sells-Flo[to] Circus.

Gene Autry, movie player who [is] starring in the Rodeo at Madis[on] Square Garden, paid tribute la[st] night to Tom Mix as one who h[ad] "contributed a great deal to t[he] betterment of the American cowb[oy] and cowboy sports."

Tom Mix snatches Billie Dove from her wedding in *The Luck[y] Horsehoe*, 1925.

Tom Mix in a characteristic pose from *The Untamed*.

"All the News That's Fit to Print."

The New York Times.

THE WEATHER.
Fair, slightly warmer Thursday; Friday, fair, warmer; moderate winds, becoming south.
For full weather report see Page 22

VOL. CXI..No. 38,180. © 1962 by The New York Times Company. Times Square, New York 36, N. Y. NEW YORK, MONDAY, AUGUST 6, 1962. 10 cents beyond 50-mile zone from New York City except on Long Island. Higher in air delivery cities. FIVE CENTS

COMMON MARKET AND BRITISH VOICE HOPES IN IMPASSE

Both Sides Say Gains Were Made on Role for London Before Session Ended

OCTOBER MEETING SET

Failure to Settle Question of Commonwealth Exports Is Blow to Macmillan

By EDWIN L. DALE Jr.
Special to The New York Times.

BRUSSELS, Belgium, Aug. 5—Representatives of Britain and the European Economic Community expressed disappointment and some bitterness but no discouragement today over their failure to reach full agreement on the basis for British membership in the Community.

They stressed that substanti[al] progress had been made [on] major issues.

[...] fr[...] be [...] tari[...] tem [...] ain j[...] munity[...]

The p[...] modity [...] a "reaso[...] aimed a[...] duction a[...] ment to [...] treatment [...] monwealth [...] transition [...]

[The i[...] negotiation[...] Britain as a[...] Minister Mac[...] lieved he will [...] difficult to hol[...] servatives in li[...] an unqualified [...] the Commonw[...] Ministers when t[...] month.]

Key to the [...]

The key to the [...] conclude the matter [...] have been the last [...] troduction by Fra[...] highly complex finan[...] While hundreds of m[...] dollars are potentially [...] the issue has no [...] with the Commonwe[...] French made agreeme[...] point a condition for a[...] settlement.

The result of the wor[...] the last four days is that [...] British will have the "ma[...] part" of the terms of their e[...] try to present to the Common[...]wealth Prime Ministers when they meet in London Sept. 10, but not a full outline, as had been wished.

The British Government must deal with the political as well as the economic consequences [...]

Continued on Page 4, Column 5

Marilyn Monroe Dead, Pills Near

Star's Body Is Found in Bedroom of Her Home on Coast

Police Say She Left No Notes—Official Verdict Delayed

Special to The New York Times.

HOLLYWOOD, Calif., Aug. 5—Marilyn Monroe, one of the most famous stars in Hollywood's history, was found dead early today in the bedroom of her home in the Brentwood section of Los Angeles. She was 36 years old.

Beside the bed was an empty bottle that had contained sleeping pills. Fourteen other bottles of medicines and tablets were on the night stand.

The impact of Miss Monroe's death was international. Her fame was greater than her contributions as an actress.

As a woman she was considered a sex symbol. Her marriages to and divorces from Joe DiMaggio, the former Yankee baseball star, and Arthur Miller, the Pulitzer Prize playwright, were accepted by millions as the prerogatives of this contemporary Venus.

The events leading to her death were in tragic contrast to the comic talent and zest for life that had helped to make "Seven Year Itch" and "Some Like It Hot" smash hits all over the world.

Miss Monroe's physician had prescribed sleeping pills for her for three days. Ordinarily the bottle would have contained forty to fifty pills.

The actress had also been under the care of a psychoanalyst for a year, and had called him to her home last night. He had suggested she take a drive and relax. She remained home, however.

After an autopsy the Los Angeles coroner reported that Miss Monroe's "was not a natural death." He attributed it to a drug. He added that a toxicological study, to be completed within forty-eight hours, should yield more detailed information. He refused, until then, to list the death as a suicide.

Pending a more positive verdict by Dr. Theodore J. Curphey, the coroner, the Los Angeles police refused to call the death a suicide. They said they had no idea how many pills the actress might have taken, or whether any overdose might have been accidental. Miss Monroe left no notes, according to the police.

In addition to a physical autopsy, Los Angeles has a "psychological" autopsy. Two experts will look into the psychological history of Miss Monroe. However, the non-physical

Associated Press
Marilyn Monroe

Continued on Page 13, Column 6

PRESIDENT NAMES DEAN AT COLUMBIA TO POST ON A. E. C.

John G. Palfrey Is Second Lawyer Picked for Agency in Resolution of Dispute

Special to The New York Times.

HYANNIS PORT, Mass., Aug. 5 — President Kennedy announced today his intention to appoint John G. Palfrey, dean of Columbia College, New York, as a member of the Atomic Energy Commission.

He also announced his [...] tion [...]

Aug. 6, 1962

[...]sumed tests [...]lya (cross).

[...]ned [...]reau [...]hammed [...]cretary [...]n is [...]RS [...]A

RUSSIANS RESUME A-TESTING IN AIR; BLAST 2D BIGGEST

Explosion at High Altitude Over Arctic Island Is Put in 40-Megaton Range

U. S. DEPLORES ACTION

But Voices Hope Soviet Will Still Work for a Treaty—Stresses Pending Offer

By TAD SZULC
Special to The New York Times.

WASHINGTON, Aug. 5 — The Soviet Union resumed its nuclear tests in the atmosphere early today with a powerful high-altitude blast believed to have been in the forty-megaton range.

The blast, over Novaya Zemlya, in the Arctic, appeared to have been the second most potent nuclear explosion ever achieved. The record is held by the Soviet Union, which detonated last Oct. 30 a nuclear device with an explosive force estimated at the equivalent of fifty-eight megatons of TNT. A megaton is 1,000,000 tons.

The United States Government called the resumption a "somber episode," but expressed the hope that Moscow would nonetheless cooperate in working for an effective treaty prohibiting all tests of nuclear weapons.

This morning's test, at 5:08 A. M., Eastern daylight time, was first reported by Swedish and Japanese scientists. It was [l]ater confirmed, without details, [b]y the Atomic Energy Commis[si]on here. News of the test was [w]ithheld from the Soviet people.

[I]ssue Before Geneva Parley

[Th]e start of the Soviet test [...], forecast by Moscow two [...] ago, came on the eve of [...]xpected presentation be[fore t]he seventeen-nation dis[armame]nt conference in Geneva [...] and simplified United [...]posals for a test ban [...]

[...] broke a three-year [...]um on nuclear test[...] The United States [...] an extensive [...]nderground and [...]e.

[...]t made public [...]e State Depart[...] that, "despite [...] of atmospheric [...] we hope the [...]ill match our [...]te an effective [...]aty."

[...]oviet Union's [...]other series [...] — the sec[...]ess than a [...]egarded as [...]ssed that [...] even as

[Continued on Page ..., Co]lumn 5

[...]T [...]GO [...]es

[...] on June [...] 1960, there were only six major provinces in this huge country. With the sanction of Parliament, seven new provinces have been approved. A total of nineteen provinces is foreseen shortly.

Observers view the trend as essentially federalist and traditionalist and thus anti-nationalist and against the mainstream of pan-African political development. It marks, in effect, these observers believe, the failure of the late Patrice Lumumba and his nationalist movement to make any deep inroads into the traditional tribal alignment in the Congo.

There are, the observers note, about forty ethnic groups in the Congo, of which about twenty are major groups. The new provinces are generally being developed along major ethnic lines.

The new province of South Kasai, for example, is essentially a Baluba tribal area,

Continued on Page 8, Column 4

[...]s. No Soviet comment was immediately available. United States sources described the session as "inconclusive."

The hope among the neutralists in particular is that once the United States and the Soviet Union have completed their current tests they will consider their defense requirements satisfied and will be better prepared to compromise on a test

Continued on Page 3, Column 2

Charter Change U[...] Fiscal Power of Es[...]

The Citizens Budget Commission urged yesterday an early revision of the new City Charter to preserve the Board of Estimate's authority to control capital projects from the time a site is chosen through the appropriation of funds.

The present Charter gives the board this authority. In exercising it the board has followed a time-consuming procedure of holding public hearings on each aspect of a given capital project, from the planning stage on.

The Citizens Budget Commission recommended a single public hearing on each project, covering all its phases. It proposed that the Mayor should not initiate any project unless the Board of Estimate then approved it.

The civic organization pointed out that the new Charter, which becomes effective Jan. 1, provides for a public hearing by the Board of Estimate on all capita[l] [...] or initi[...] board no[...] them sinc[...] be held afte[...] proved.

The publi[...] group cont[...] fore be "fa[...]

It propos[...] be revised [...] giving the [...] authority to [...] final plans [...] major const[...] proposed bon[...] neces[sary] appropri[ations.]"

As it now stands, the new Charter provides for appropriation of funds for all projects in the city's capital budget when the budget is adopted by the Board of Estimate and the City Council. The Citizens Budget Commission contended this would leave actual initiation of any project listed in

Continued on Page 10, Column 6

[...]ciation [...]ed in building Negro caucu[se]s inside unions to exert internal pressure and has filed complaints with Federal and state anti-discrimination agencies against unions. The legal effort now in preparation is an extension of these efforts into a new field.

The first case, according to Mr. Hill, will begin as a petition to the National Labor Relations Board to decertify a union on

Continued on Page 22, Column 3

Associated Press Radiophoto

Prime Minister Sir Alexander Bustamante with Princess Margaret at National Stadium

By R. HART PHILLIPS
Special to The New York Times.

KINGSTON, Jamaica, Monday, Aug. 6—Jamaica became an independent nation with dominion status within the British Commonwealth today. Princess Margaret as representative of her sister, Queen Elizabeth II, witnessed the end of the 307 years of British colonial status. About 30,000 Jamaicans jammed the big new National Stadium and cheered the raising of the new flag. On the stroke of midnight, the huge spotlights were turned off and in silence and darkness, the British flag that had flown over the island was hauled down and the green, gold and black

Continued on Page 6, Column 2

NEWS INDEX

MARILYN MONROE DEAD, PILLS NEAR

Continued From Page 1, Col. 4

study will reach no conclusions as to whether she committed suicide. Nor will it have a bearing on the toxicological tests.

During the last few years Miss Monroe had suffered severe setbacks. Her last two films, "Let's Make Love," and "The Misfits," were box-office disappointments. After completion of "The Misfits," written by Mr. Miller, she was divorced from him.

On June 8 Miss Monroe was dismissed by Twentieth-Century-Fox for unjustifiable absenses during the filming of "Something's Got to Give," in which she was starred. Filming on the picture has not resumed.

Shortly before she was dismissed, Miss Monroe angrily protested to a reporter about attacks on stars. She said she had never wanted to do "Something's Got to Give."

"We're what's O.K. with the movie business," she asserted. "Management is what's wrong with the business. To blame the troubles of Hollywood on stars is stupid. These executives should not knock their assets around."

But a few weeks later, during which a $500,000 suit had been filed against her, Miss Monroe pleaded with Fox to let her return to work on the picture.

In low spirits she withdrew to her one-story stucco house in an upper middle-class section, which was far different from the lavish suites of the Beverly Hills Hotel that had been more typical of her. She died in the house at 12305 Fifth Helena Drive.

Housekeeper Last to See Her

The last person to see her alive was her housekeeper, Mrs. Eunice Murray, who had lived with her. Mrs. Murray told the police that Miss Monroe retired to her bedroom about 8 P. M. yesterday.

About 3:25 A.M. today, the housekeeper noticed a light under Miss Monroe's door. She called to the actress, but received no answer. She tried the bedroom door. It was locked.

Mrs. Murray went outside and peered into the bedroom through the closed French windows. Miss Monroe, she later told the police, looked "peculiar." An arm was stretched across the bed and a hand hung limp on a telephone, she said.

The housekeeper rushed back into the house and telephoned Miss Monroe's analyst, Dr. Ralph R. Greenson. When he arrived a short time later, he broke a pane of the French window and opened it.

He quickly examined the star. She was dead. He phoned Miss Monroe's personal physician, Dr. Hyman Engelberg. After his arrival, the police were called. This was at 4:20, almost an hour after the housekeeper had called Dr. Greenson.

Inspector Edward Walker of the Los Angeles police was asked if he regarded such a delay in calling the police as unusual. He said he did not think so.

"So far as the doctors were concerned, there was no evidence of crime, and the first doctor already knew she was dead," he said. "I have no critism to make of them."

Two radio patrolmen and a sergeant were the first policemen to arrive in the tree-lined neighborhood. Shortly afterward the case was taken over by Detective Sgt. R. E. Byron.

Room Simply Furnsihed

Sergeant Byron said Miss Monroe's bedroom was neat, but sparsely furnished. He estimated it at fifteen feet square.

"All she had in the room, so far as I can recall, was the bed, a little dressing table and the night table. And the telephone that she pulled on the bed."

After the police had completed their investigation, Miss Monroe's body was removed to the Westwood Village Mortuary. The house was sealed and placed under guard.

The body was later taken to the county morgue for the autopsy, which was performed by Dr. Tsunetomi Noguchi, a pathologist.

In the last two years Miss Monroe had become the subject of considerable controversy in Hollywood. Some persons gibed at her aspirations as a serious actress. They considered it ridiculous that she should have gone to New York to study under Lee Strasberg.

Miss Monroe's defenders, however, asserted that her talents had been underestimated by those who thought her appeal to movie audiences was solely sexual.

The disagreement about Miss Monroe took another form. One group contended she was typical of stars who had abused their privileges on sets.

An opposite group argued that Miss Monroe was an outstanding example of how Hollywood wanted to treat talent as just another commodity.

Her 23 Films Since 1950 Grossed $200,000,000

From the time Marilyn Monroe appeared in "The Asphalt Jungle," her first picture, in 1950 until her death yesterday, she had played in twenty-three films that grossed about $200,000,000.

They were:

1950—"The Asphalt Jungle," "All About Eve," "The Fireball" and "A Ticket to Tomahawk."

1951—"As Young As You Feel," "Let's Make It Legal" and "Love Nest."

1952—"Clash By Night," "We're Not Married," "Don't Bother to Knock," "Monkey Business" and "O. Henry's Full House."

1953—"Niagara," "Gentlemen Prefer Blondes" and "How To Marry a Millionaire."

1954—"River of No Return" and "There's No Business Like Show Business."

1955—"The Seven - Year Itch."

1956—"Bus Stop."

1957—"The Prince and the Show Girl."

1959—"Some Like It Hot."

1960—"Let's Make Love."

1961—"The Misfits."

Monroe and Tom Ewell in *The Seven Year Itch.*

Brilliant Stardom and Personal Tragedy Punctuated the Life of Marilyn Monroe

FIRST SCENE PUT HER IN LIMELIGHT

Actress Enjoyed Immense Popularity but Said She Was Seldom Happy

The life of Marilyn Monroe, the golden girl of the movies, ended as it began, in misery and tragedy.

Her death at the age of 36 closed an incredibly glamorous career and capped a series of somber events that began with her birth as an unwanted, illegitimate baby and went on and on, illuminated during the last dozen years by the lightning of fame.

Her public life was in dazzling contrast to her private life. The first man to see her on the screen, the man who made her screen test, felt the almost universal reaction as he ran the wordless scene. In it, she walked, sat down and lit a cigarette.

Recalled 'Lush Stars'

"I got a cold chill," he said. "This girl had something I hadn't seen since silent pictures. This is the first girl who looked like one of those lush stars of the silent era. Every frame of the test radiated sex."

Billy Wilder, the director, called it "flesh impact."

"Flesh impact is rare," he said. "Three I remember who had it were Clara Bow, Jean Harlow and Rita Hayworth. Such girls have flesh which photographs like flesh. You feel you can reach out and touch it."

Fans paid $200,000,000 to see her project this quality. No sex symbol of the era other than Brigitte Bardot could match her popularity. Toward the end, she also convinced critics and the public that she could act.

During the years of her greatest success, she saw two of her marriages end in divorce. She suffered at least two miscarriages and was never able to have a child. Her emotional insecurity deepened; her many illnesses came upon her more frequently.

Dismissed From Picture

In 1961, she was twice admitted to hospitals in New York for psychiatric observation and rest. She was dismissed in June by Twentieth Century-Fox after being absent all but five days during seven weeks of shooting "Something's Got to Give."

"It's something that Marilyn no longer can control," one of her studio chiefs confided. "Sure she's sick. She believes she's sick. She may even have a fever, but it's a sickness of the mind. Only a psychiatrist can help her now."

In her last interview, published in the Aug. 3 issue of Life magazine, she told Richard Meryman, an associate editor:

"I was never used to being happy, so that wasn't something I ever took for granted."

Considering her background, this was a statement of exquisite restraint.

She was born in Los Angeles on June 1, 1926. The name on the birth record is Norma Jean Mortenson, the surname of the man who fathered her, then abandoned her mother. She later took her mother's last name, Baker.

Family Tragedies

Both her maternal grandparents and her mother were committed to mental institutions. Her uncle killed himself. Her father died in a motorcycle accident three years after her birth.

Her childhood has been described as "Oliver Twist in girl's clothing."

During her mother's stays in asylums, she was farmed out to twelve sets of foster parents. Two families were religious fanatics; one gave her empty whisky bottles to play with instead of dolls.

At another stage, she lived in a drought area with a family of seven. She spent two years in a Los Angeles orphanage, wearing a uniform she detested.

By the time she was 9 years old, Norma Jean had begun to stammer—an affliction rare among females.

Her dream since childhood had been to be a movie star, and she succeeded beyond her wildest imaginings. The conviction of her mother's best friend was borne out; she had told the little girl, day after day:

"Don't worry. You're going to be a beautiful girl when you get big. You're going to be a movie star. Oh, I feel it in my bones."

Nunnally Johnson, the producer and writer, understood that Miss Monroe was something special. Marilyn, he said, was "a phenomenon of nature, like Niagara Falls and the Grand Canyon.

"You can't talk to it. It can't talk to you. All you can do is stand back and be awed by it," he said.

Marilyn Monroe as Cherie in Joshua Logan's *Bus Stop*, 1956.

This figure in the minds of millions was difficult to analyze statistically. Her dimensions—37-23-37—were voluptuous but not extraordinary.

She stood 5 feet 5½ inches tall. She had soft blonde hair, wide, dreamy, gray-blue eyes. She spoke in a high baby voice that was little more than a breathless whisper.

Heavy Fan Mail

Fans wrote her 5,000 letters a week, at least a dozen of them proposing marriage. The Communists denounced her as a capitalist trick to make the American people forget how miserable they were. In Turkey a young man took leave of his senses while watching "How to Marry a Millionaire" and slashed his wrists.

There were other symbols of success. She married two American male idols—one an athlete, one an intellectual.

Her second husband was Joe DiMaggio, the baseball player. Her third and last was the Pulitzer-prize winning playwright, Arthur Miller.

She was 16 when she married for the first time. The bridegroom was James Dougherty, 21, an aircraft worker.

Mr. Dougherty said after their divorce four years later, in 1946, that she had been a "wonderful" housekeeper.

Her two successive divorces came in 1954, when she split with Mr. DiMaggio after only

(continued)

nine months, and in 1960, after a four-year marriage to Mr. Miller.

She became famous with her first featured role of any prominence, in "The Asphalt Jungle," issued in 1950.

Her appearance was brief but unforgettable. From the instant she moved onto the screen with that extraordinary walk of hers, people asked themselves: "Who's that blonde?"

In 1952 it was revealed that Miss Monroe had been the subject of a widely distributed nude calendar photograph shot while she was a notably unsuccessful starlet.

Revealed Her Wit

It created a scandal, but it was her reaction to the scandal that was remembered. She told interviewers that she was not ashamed and had needed the money to pay her rent.

She also revealed her sense of humor. When asked by a woman journalist, "You mean you didn't have anything on?" she replied breathlessly:

"Oh yes, I had the radio on."

One of her most exasperating quirks was her tardiness. She was, during the years of her fame, anywhere from one to twenty-four hours late for appointments. Until lately, she managed to get away with it.

Her dilatory nature and sicknesses added nearly $1,000,000 to the budget of "Let's Make Love." The late Jerry Wald, head of her studio, simply commented:

"True, she's not punctual. She can't help it, but I'm not sad about it," he said. "I can get a dozen beautiful blondes who will show up promptly in make-up at 4 A. M. each morning, but they are not Marilyn Monroe."

The tardiness, the lack of responsibility and the fears began to show more and more through the glamorous patina as Miss Monroe's career waxed.

Speaking of her career and her fame in the Life interview, she said, wistfully:

"It might be kind of a relief to be finished. It's sort of like I don't know what kind of a yard dash you're running, but then you're at the finish line and you sort of sigh—you've made it! But you never have—you have to start all over again."

Monroe with Clark Gable in *The Misfits*.

Actress as a Symbol

Build-Up of Marilyn Monroe Tended To Obscure Her Artistic Capability

By BOSLEY CROWTHER

FOR all her acknowledged ability as a screen comedienne and, indeed, an apt dramatic actress in roles of a particular sort, Marilyn Monroe was not generally regarded as an artist submerged in her art.

She was popularly looked on and thought of as a lustrous, free body that floated above and only occasionally came in contact with the artistic element of the screen.

The persistence of this image of the exceptionally lovely movie star could be explained by the fact that, in the common view, she was more a symbol than an artist. Millions of ardent moviegoers, all over the world, and even people who had never seen her, were impressed with the established notion of a voluptuous and frivolous Marilyn Monroe.

Mention her name or, at one time, even the magical initials, M. M., and the image of the shapely, soft, blonde charmer would seductively swim into mind.

It was not the vision or thought of a skillful actress of the sort that the screen has often nourished, a glowing star such as Greta Garbo or Katharine Hepburn or Vivien Leigh. It was the image of feminine allurement, compounded of the silver-blonde tresses, the wide-eyed stare, the pouting lips, the baby-talk burble in a husky, sing-song voice and the remarkable body that were the physical attributes of Miss Monroe.

The irony of this popular image was that it tended to obscure in an excess of sheer sex symbolization the certain skills and competences of the star.

Although Miss Monroe was not a brilliant actress with extensive creative skills — nor, indeed, was she an altogether fluid and finished comedienne — she did bring to motion pictures a distinct personality and an ability to project a striking luster and rich feminine quality.

Potential Personality

This was not, by any means, entirely vulgar, as some observers of the Monroe image would have it seem, nor was it a mere emanation of sexual suggestiveness.

The Monroe personality, as established and developed over the years, was that of a generous young woman, healthy, good-humored, full of warmth and eager for honest self-improvement, despite intellectual limitations and crudities. It was a highly potential personality, apt for satire as well as farce and open, it seemed, for extension to drama and tragedy.

Indeed, it appeared from the appealing and poignant performance that Miss Monroe gave in "Bus Stop," directed by Joshua Logan, and from some of her tight and tender scenes in her last picture, "The Misfits," which her former husband, Arthur Miller, wrote and which has been said on good authority to have contained a subtle characterization of herself, that she was headed for stronger creations than her early comedies. It was thought by perceptive critics that she might shuck the Monroe symbol in time.

But the pathos of her situation was that she, too, soon became a glowing and glorious Galatea of the tyrannical movie medium. From her first minor memorable appearances in "The Asphalt Jungle" and "All About Eve," she was fashioned into the female image that was soon flashed as a symbol around the world.

Nurtured in Role

Striking at once as a "dumb blonde" of the sort that gentlemen prefer, she was nurtured, promoted, expanded and generally contained within this role.

She was given the big glamour build-up, the kind of romance-publicity that has always been a part of the calculated commerce and consequent culture of the screen.

She was made to become a part of the image, and as the image grew into a symbol, a standardization, there was no telling how much she had allowed herself and her own life to be merged and absorbed in it.

The dismal background and frequent tempests of her life were discovered and exposed as fodder for popular curiosity, not to explain her artistry or, at least, her early acknowledged and no doubt sincere pretensions to same.

Her marriages, divorces, exhibitions of temperament were widely publicized and were inevitably cooked into the image and then the symbol of Marilyn Monroe.

As with so many movie stars before her, in the days when glamorization was more intense and more consistent with the social environment than it might seem in this sophisticated age, Miss Monroe was a victim of and a gainer from the publicity aggrandizement of her job.

It remains for the philosophers, not the critics, to calculate what it did to her.

The New York Times

WEDNESDAY, MAY 1, 1974

Agnes Moorehead Dies at 67; Acclaimed in a Variety of Roles

Nominated for 5 Oscars — In 'Don Juan in Hell' on Stage and in 'Bewitched' on TV

By WILLIAM M. FREEMAN

Agnes Moorehead, the actress, died yesterday in the Methodist Hospital in Rochester, Minn., where she had been under the care of Mayo Clinic physicians. She was 67 years old.

The clinic declined to disclose the cause of her death; she had been hospitalized since April 9. Miss Moorehead's most recent appearance had been as Aunt Alicia in "Gigi," a Broadway musical based on the novel of that name.

Although Miss Moorehead was perhaps best known to modern audiences as Endora, the witch, in the television series, "Bewitched," she was a highly versatile actress who was equally at home on television or radio as on the stage and in the movies.

In discussing her career in a newspaper column that she wrote in 1965 as a substitute for vacationing Cynthia Lowry, an Associated Press writer, she commented:

"I have played so many authoritative and strong characters that some people are nervous at the prospect of meeting me for the first time. . . . There is a certain amount of aloofness on my part at times, because an actor can so easily be hurt by unfair criticism.

"I think an artist should be kept separated to maintain glamour and a kind of mystery. Otherwise it's like having three meals a day. Pretty dull. I don't believe in the girl-next-door image. What the actor has to sell to the public is fantasy, a magic kind of ingredient that should not be analyzed."

Versatile Star

Miss Moorehead was an established star in every medium. She had roles in such Broadway hits as "Scarlet Pages," "All the King's Men," "Courage," "Soldiers and Women" and "Candlelight," and appeared with Charles Laughton, Charles Boyer and Sir Cedric Hardwicke in "Don Juan in Hell," a 1951-52 dramatic reading of the third act excerpted from Bernard Shaw's "Man and Superman."

The reading, done in modern dress on a stage equipped with nothing more than chairs and a lectern, was repeated last year, with Miss Moorehead accompanied by Edward Mulhare, Ricardo Montalban and Paul Henreid.

The interpretation by the earlier acting group drew acclamation from critics, as the production toured England and the United States. The recent one did not do so well.

Although Miss Moorehead was often spoken of as a character actress, she could never really be typed. Her work ranged from comedy to tragedy, from portrayals of young girls to old ladies, to heroines and villainesses—roles she played with conviction and artistry.

The actress was born in Clinton, Mass., near Boston, in 1906, the daughter of John Henderson Moorehead, a Presbyterian minister, and the former Mary Mildred McCauley. Her ancestry was principally Irish.

Her first public appearance was at the age of 3, singing "The Lord Is My Shepherd" on a program sponsored by her father. Later, at 10, she appeared in summer stock and spent four years with the St. Louis Municipal Opera.

She attended school in Reedsburg, Wis., where her father had a pastorate, and Muskingum College in Ohio, which had been founded by an uncle.

Miss Moorehead earned an M.A. in English and public speaking at the University of Wisconsin and added a doctorate in literature at Bradley University. Later, she was the recipient of three honorary doctorates. In 1928-29 she studied here at the American Academy of Dramatic Arts, where she was an honor student.

At the same time she taught dramatics at the Dalton School and won parts in several Broadway plays, among them the Theater Guild's production of "Marco Millions."

When Broadway opportunities diminished during the Depression, Miss Moorehead turned to radio, appearing with just about every well-known star and on many major programs.

She was heard on "The March of Time," as Eleanor Roosevelt and as the girlfriend of "The Shadow," played by Orson Welles, and was featured with Fred Allen, Bert Lahr, Phil Baker, Bob Hope, Jack Benny and others. She played the nerve-tingling role of the bedridden woman about to be murdered in the radio suspense classic, "Sorry, Wrong Number."

With Mr. Welles and Joseph Cotten, she was a founder and a charter member of the famed Mercury Theater, and made her movie debut in Mr. Welles's film classic, "Citizen Kane."

Miss Moorehead made about 100 films and won five Academy Award nominations, the latest for her performance in "Hush, Hush, Sweet Charlotte" in the mid-sixties.

Her 1942 appearance in the Welles production of Booth Tarkington's "The Magnificent Ambersons" was judged the best female performance of the year by the New York Film Critics.

Miss Moorehead was married and divorced twice, and had an adopted son, Sean, now 25.

Tim Holt and Agnes Moorehead starred in Orson Welles' *The Magnificent Ambersons.*

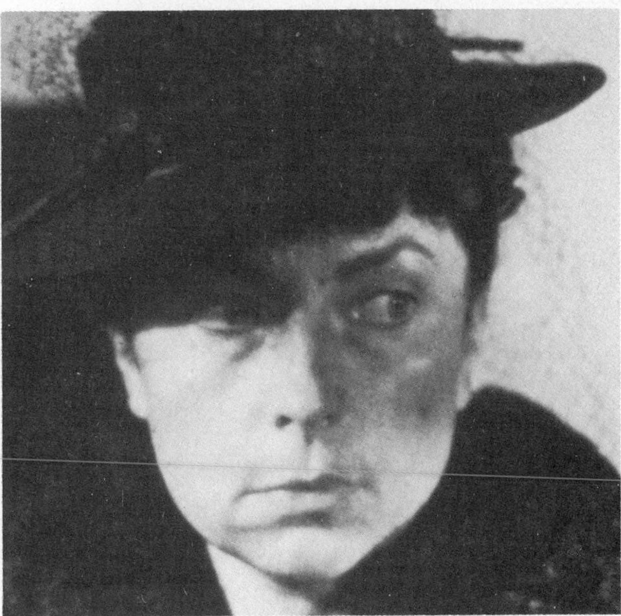

Agnes Moorehead in *Journey into Fear*, 1942.

The New York Times

SATURDAY, SEPTEMBER 12, 1970

Chester Morris Is Dead at 69; Created Role of Boston Blackie

In Hollywood, He Made Over 85 Films—Last Stage Part Was Capt. Queeg

Chester Morris, who created the role of Boston Blackie, was found dead of an overdose of barbiturates yesterday in his room at the Holiday Inn in New Hope, Pa. Mr. Morris, who was 69 years old, had been starring as Captain Queeg in "The Caine Mutiny Court-Martial" at the Bucks County Playhouse.

His last motion picture is the screen version of the Broadway play "The Great White Hope," in which he portrays Pop Morrison, the Boxing Commissioner. He returned from the filming location at Almeria, Spain, only a month ago. The film will begin previews on Monday.

Mr. Morris was almost literally, in the familiar show business phrase, "born in a trunk." His father was William Morris, a well-known actor at the turn of the century, and his mother was Etta Hawkins, a comedienne with the Charles Frohman Company. He appeared in a silent film when he was only 9 years old and made his stage debut in support of Lionel Barrymore in "The Copperhead" when he was only 15.

Born here on Feb. 16, 1901, and educated in public schools in Mount Vernon, N. Y., Mr. Morris, at the age of 17, was billed as "the youngest leading man in the country" when he toured in "Turn to the Right." This was followed by five years as a contract player with George M. Cohan's company.

In a Griffith Film

In 1928 he was signed by D. W. Griffith for his first screen starring role in "Alibi," and in the years that followed Mr. Morris made more than 85 films, including "The Big House," "Divorcee" and "Unchained." He was perhaps best known on the screen as the hero of 36 Boston Blackie detective stories.

Chester Morris

In many of his films, as well as his plays, Mr. Morris, who was square-jawed and wore his hair slicked back, played unsympathetic characters. He usually did so by choice, he said.

In an interview a few years ago, Mr. Morris, referring to his role in "The Caine Mutiny Court-Martial," said "Captain Queeg is a complete paranoic. He is a strange man, so offbeat. I like that kind of role. Anybody can play nice boys."

After 23 years in Hollywood, Mr. Morris toured in Sidney Kingsley's "Detective Story," in which he was seen as a neurotic policeman, and later starred on Broadway in "The Fifth Season," "Blue Denim," and "Advise and Consent." In 1967 he played the father in "The Subject Was Roses."

Even though Mr. Morris had grown frail in recent years and suffered from a stomach ailment, he remained active on the stage and in television.

Mr. Morris, whose home was at 176 East 77th Street, leaves his second wife, the former Lili Kenton, and their son, Kenton, of Chicago. Also surviving are two children of a previous marriage, Cynthia, who lives in Los Angeles, and Brooks, an Air Force officer.

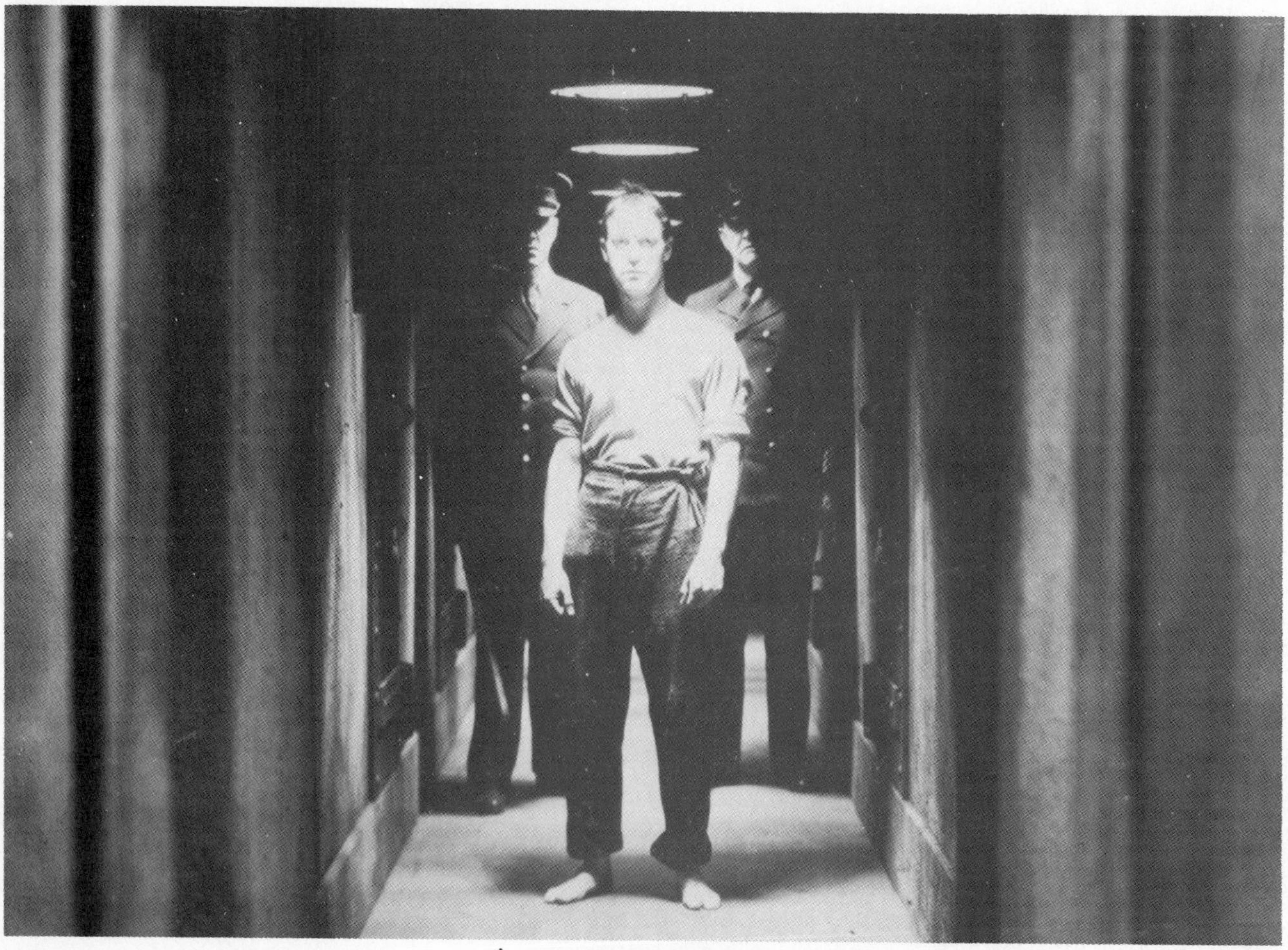

Chester Morris goes into solitary in *The Big House*, a 1930 box office smash.

"All the News That's Fit to Print"

The New York Times

THE WEATHER
Fair, slightly warmer Thursday; Friday, fair, warmer; moderate winds, becoming south.
For full weather report see Page 21

VOL. CXVI...No. 40,026

© 1967 The New York Times Company.

NEW YORK, SATURDAY, AUGUST 26, 1967

10 CENTS

INFLATION TREND FEARED AS PRICES RISE IN 2 SECTORS

Wholesale Industrial Index Climbs After a Record 5 Months of Stability

CONSUMER COSTS SPURT

Economic Events Expected to Strengthen Johnson's Case for Tax Increase

By EDWIN L. DALE Jr.
Special to The New York Times

WASHINGTON, Aug. 25—Consumer prices rose substantially in July, a normal experience for the month, the Labor Department reported today.

More worrisome to Government economists was a companion report that wholesale prices rose after a record-break months of stability. T cator is probably th closely watched as a si inflation.

Both increases will hel Administration's case for anti-inflation tax increase, n pending before Congress.

The consumer price increase for the month was four-tenths of 1 per cent. While this was the largest for a month this year, it was in line with the average experience for July during the last 20 years.

Seasonal Effects

For various seasonal reasons, the Consumer Price Index always goes up in July, according to Arnold Chase, Assistant Commissioner of Labor Statistics.

The index for July was 116.5, with average prices in the 1957-59 period taken as a base of 100. The June index was 116.0. Thus the index rose five-tenths of a point or four-tenths of 1 per cent in July.

The pace of price increases so far this year indicates a rise from the beginning to the end of the year of about 2.5 per cent or possibly slightly more, Mr. Chase said.

This is less than the 3.3 per cent of last year, but is well above the gentle rise in prices from 1958 through 1965.

Food Prices Climb

Higher food prices accounted for about half the July increase, today's report said. In the food area the chief cause of the rise was fresh fruits and vegetables, whose prices have been affected this year by short supplies because of bad weather in some parts of the country.

There were sizable July increases in apples, oranges, grapefruit, tomatoes, potatoes and lettuce.

Medical care costs rose sharply again, with hospital services up 20 per cent from a year ago. Other increases were recorded for used cars, cigarettes, some appliances,

Continued on Page 56, Column 1

BIGGER RISK FOUND IN LONG CIGARETTE

Surgeon General Charges Emphasis on Profits

By NAN ROBERTSON
Special to The New York Times

WASHINGTON, Aug. 25—The tobacco industry was accused today by Dr. William H. Stewart, Surgeon General of the Public Health Service, of carrying on an "unconscionable" campaign to promote longer cigarettes to get "longer profits."

Dr. Stewart said the industry's latest innovation, the 100-millimeter-long cigarette, increased the smoker's total dosage of tar and nicotine and thus the danger to his health.

In testimony before a Senate Commerce subcommittee, he also called for printing the amounts of tar and nicotine on cigarette packages and in advertisements.

In a corridor news conference following his testimony, Dr. Stewart said he favored establishing Federal standards to govern minimum permissible levels of tar and nicotine in cigarettes. Such a law could

Continued on Page 15, Column 2

AT... sh...

Ro... Ex...

ARLINGT... founder and l... by a sniper to...

GUN CURBS ... BY A RIFLE E...

Rep. Scheuer, Medal ... Tells City Hall Hea... Protection Is Urgen...

By DOUGLAS ROBINSON

A Bronx member of Congr... who has won four national cha... pionship medals from the Na... tional Rifle Association offere... support yesterday for city leg... islation to control the sale ... rifles and shotguns.

Democratic Representative James H. Scheuer told a City Council hearing that he owned two shotguns, three rifles and a .32-caliber revolver. He said he had a permit for the revolver, as required by state law.

"It's insanity to believe that my civil rights are being violated by having to have a pistol permit," he declared. He added that he would have no objection to a law requiring him to obtain a similar permit for his other weapons.

"No responsible citizen can in good conscience deny the urgent need to protect the public from arming the destructive, deranged, dangerous and irresponsible persons among us," he told the hearing.

Two-Day Hearing Ends

The National Rifle Association has consistently lobbied against any type of Federal, State or local control over the sale of rifles and shotguns.

Mr. Scheuer's testimony was given on the second and last day of hearings conducted by the Council's Subcommittee on Firearms Control and the State Joint Legislative Committee on Firearms Control at City Hall.

The Council is considering local laws that would require the registration and licensing of city residents who purchase or own any type of firearms. State law now demands that permits be obtained only for guns that can be concealed on the person.

Present laws also forbid a convicted felon to possess a rifle, define machine guns as

Continued on Page 14, Column 5

live... cha... in n... in V...

Th... was s... at abo... 1958 ... let ou... a shop... urban ... tomac ...

Accor... Nazi lea... laundry a...

Continued ...

Space W... Search ...

By WALTER ...
Special to The New ...

PRAGUE, Aug. ... tions of the "mys... nomenon" in the ... galaxy have shown ... emissions to display ... of the characteristics ... ficial interstellar communica-tions.

Scientists strongly suspect, however, that the emissions are being generated by a natural process that has not yet been adequately explained, rather than by intelligent beings.

The most recent observations in the nearby part of the galaxy, made simultaneously from California, Massachusetts and Britain, used almost the entire width of the earth as a baseline for measurement.

They have shown the spots in the sky producing the mys-

Continued on Page 10, Column 4

WORLD CHURCHES URGED TO ATTACK RACIAL PROBLEMS

Alarm Voiced on Civil Strife —Cardinal Konig Says U.S. Must Set an Example

By EDWARD B. FISKE
Special to The New York T...

CANDIA, Crete, A... Leaders of...

... Direction' ... of the meeting ... afternoon Mayor Richard S. Jackson told newsmen: "I think we're moving in the right direction to relieve the frustrations in the city, and we will continue to work here for the entire community."

Alfred Washington, principal spokesman for the Negroes in the recently formed Afro-American Unity Movement, said: "This is a step in the right direction, but it doesn't stop here. We'll have to see him again."

The Negroes had given an Aug. 31 deadline for City Hall to begin working on 30 de-

Continued on Page 22, Column 2

Paul Muni, Actor, Dies on Coast; Won Fame in Biographical Roles

Portrayed Darrow, Pasteur, Zola, Juarez and Gangster in Stage and Film Career

By United Press International

SANTA BARBARA, Calif., Aug. 25—Paul Muni, the celebrated screen and stage actor who won fame in many biographical roles, died at his home here today. He was 71 years old.

His wife was at his bedside. According to the family nurse, Mr. Muni had heart trouble.

In addition to his wife, Mr. Muni leaves two brothers, Joseph and Al, both of Los Angeles.

A funeral service will be held Tuesday afternoon in Hollywood Memorial Park with Rabbi Leonard Bierman officiating. Interment will follow in Beth Olam Cemetery.

As an actor of many talents, Paul Muni evoked acclaim from critics and enthusiasm from audiences.

He was a man of a simple face, intense, interested, probing; and he was a man of a thousand faces—Pasteur, Zola, Scarface, Juarez, the roles he portrayed. He was loved and he was hated by those who respected his talents, for he could make his audiences admire what he was doing but despise him while he was doing it.

For the stage or the screen, Mr. Muni's search for the reality to be reflected in the mirror was all-encompassing. When he

United Press International
Paul Muni

Continued on Page 27, Column 1

United Press International
Paul Muni

... his home ... He was 71 years

His wife was at his bedside. According to the family nurse, Mr. Muni had heart trouble.

In addition to his wife, Mr. Muni leaves two brothers, Joseph and Al, both of Los Angeles.

A funeral service will be held Tuesday afternoon in Hollywood Memorial Park with Rabbi Leonard Bierman officiating. Interment will follow in Beth Olam Cemetery.

As an actor of many talents, Paul Muni evoked acclaim from critics and enthusiasm from audiences.

He was a man of a simple face, intense, interested, probing; and he was a man of a thousand faces—Pasteur, Zola, Scarface, Juarez, the roles he portrayed. He was loved and he was hated by those who respected his talents, for he could make his audiences admire what he was doing but despise him while he was doing it.

For the stage or the screen, Mr. Muni's search for the reality to be reflected in the mirror was all-encompassing. When he

Continued on Page 27, Column 1

New Evacuations of Hanoi Ordered by North Vietnam

Declaration Says U.S. Intends to Bomb Center and Outskirts—All Civilians Except Vital Workers Included

By Agence France-Presse

HANOI, North Vietnam, Aug. 25—The Hanoi authorities announced measures today for the evacuation of all civilians ex... those vital to the city's ...tion and defense.

...plans were announced in ...oint declaration by the ...strative Committee. They ...arkedly more strict than ...dopted here in recent ...

...fall of night and the ... of air raids, wo... ...n and elderly men ...orners, with suit... ...akeshift pieces of ...heir feet. Buses, ...licabs transported ...hes of relatives ... countryside.

...on the Admin... ...tee said: "The ...sent intention ...nter as well ...Hanoi." The army and the people must remain "vigilant and ready to punish the American pirates as they deserve," it added.

The committee's declaration recalled that all old people, youngsters and school children between the ages of 6 and 10 had already been ordered to leave. Others now affected by the evacuation order include workers in light industry and craftsmen, who were told to leave the city with their families "according to the plan published by the Administration."

The earlier evacuation had restricted but not stopped normal city life. Bookstores had remained open and movie houses were full. A tailor could easily be found to make a shirt. The city's two antique

Continued on Page 6, Column 3

...ccused of a Plot ...Secrets to Soviet

...Press International

... 25—Two United States Army ...ted on charges of conspiring to ...nformation to the Russians, the ...y.

U.S. AGAIN BOMBS NEAR CHINA LINE

Rail Yard 18 Miles From ...order Raided — B-52's ...trike in Buffer Zone

...ial to The New York Times

...ON, South Vietnam, Aug. ...ghter bombers of the ...tes Air Force attacked ...yard 18 miles from ...f Communist China ...during continued ...orth Vietnam's rail ...esman said today. ...sed in Thailand, ...yards along the ...k with the Chi... ...hundershowers ...ar Hanoi and ... The spokes... ...kes had hit ...d 47 miles ...

...k twice ...g the ... and ...North ... were ...ering, ...onal ...ds ...ed ...of ...

...er military ...marily by small ... attack boats. The spokesman said a building in the base complex was heavily damaged.

Navy fighter-bombers also hit the Kepha airfield, 37 miles north-northwest of Haiphong, and Marine pilots, in an unusual raid deep in North Vietnam, struck the Hoalac MIG airfield, 15 miles west of Hanoi. The spokesman said the raids were at night, precluding damage assessments.

Marine planes also bombed the Longcon military area, 28 miles north of the North Viet-

Continued on Page 6, Column 1

NEWS INDEX

M'NAMARA DOUBTS BOMBING IN NORTH CAN END THE WAR

Differs With Military Chiefs on Escalation in Testimony Before Panel of Senate

OPPOSES NEW TARGETS

But Secretary Expects More Attacks to Be Authorized —Reaction Is Critical

Text of McNamara statement will be found on Page 4.

By HEDRICK SMITH
Special to The New York Times

WASHINGTON, Aug. 25 — Secretary of Defense Robert S. McNamara said today that, on the basis of "past reaction," there was no reason to believe that North Vietnam "can be bombed to the negotiating table."

The Defense Secretary argued vigorously against recommendations of Congressional critics and military commanders who have urged that the air war be widened with attacks against such new types of targets as North Vietnamese ports and air defense and control centers in populated areas, or a sweeping air offensive against North Vietnam's entire industrial infrastructure.

Would Not 'Shorten War'

Such attacks, he declared, would "not materially shorten the war" in Vietnam.

His testimony to the Senate Preparedness Investigations Subcommittee brought a broadside of sharp criticism from both Democrats and Republicans, indicating that they sided with military leaders against Mr. McNamara on the conduct of the air war.

After six hours of hearings in closed session, Mr. McNamara told newsmen that he expected "additional targets" in North Vietnam "to be authorized in the future."

But the general thrust of his opening statement to the committee, released to the press in a censored version, indicated that he disagreed with the Joint Chiefs of Staff over the kind of targets to be attacked. Several Senators said this was the gist of the secret testimony as well.

Extensive Defense of Policy

In the Administration's most extensive and detailed public defense to date of its bombing policy, Mr. McNamara specifically opposed for the present recommendations from military commanders that the port of Haiphong be mined and that other North Vietnamese ports be subjected to systematic bombing.

"It seems obvious," his prepared statement said, "that cut-

Continued on Page 5, Column 1

...HIEU ANNOUNCES ...RGE OF OFFICERS

... Eliminate Corrupt ... Inefficient Leaders

By The Associated Press

SAIGON, South Vietnam, Aug. 25—Lieut. Gen. Nguyen Van Thieu, the chief of state of South Vietnam and its leading presidential candidate announced plans today for a major purge of corrupt and inefficient military officers, including some generals.

One reliable report said that the purge was already under way and that five ranking generals had been marked for removal or transfer.

The reasons for the shake-up were not immediately made known. Premier Nguyen Cao Ky, who is running for vice president on General Thieu's ticket, said several weeks ago, however, that the armed forces would be overhauled and tightened up from top to bottom.

In a meeting with a small group of foreign newsmen today, General Thieu was asked if any generals had been fired for corruption. "Not yet," he replied. "We have a plan, not

Continued on Page 4, Column 6

PAUL MUNI, ACTOR, IS DEAD ON COAST

Continued From Page 1, Col. 6

was working in the movie "The Story of Louis Pasteur," he said:

"I read most everything that was in the library, everything I could lay my hands on that had to do with Pasteur, with Lister, with his contemporaries."

It was the same when he prepared for what many consider the acting plum of his career, his interpretation of Clarence Darrow, the great barrister, in the stage production of "Inherit the Wind."

He read what he could find about Darrow, talked to people who knew the lawyer and studied mannerisms he could detect from pictures.

The reason was clear to those who knew him best. To Paul Muni acting was not just a career, but an obsession. Despite enormous success on Broadway and in Hollywood, he threw himself into each role with a sense of dedication that prompted Arthur Miller, the playwright, to say that he was "pursued by a fear of failure."

Born into the theater, with acting parents, Mr. Muni learned his craft carefully and thoroughly. A Muni whisper could reach the last balcony of any theater; Muni makeup was a work of art. He followed no "method" as he perfected his control of voice and gestures into an acting style that was unique.

The Muni style had drawn into it the warmth of the Yiddish stage, in which he made his debut at the age of 12 playing an old man. The same tenacity of purpose gripped him in the theater and the movies as the years passed.

Critical raves and financial security did not lessen his self-searching. "I haven't had quite the pleasure, quite the boot from success that others get," he once told an acquaintance. "Many things I find difficult to explain to myself. I never wanted to be a star. I am still happier in the audience than on the stage."

Despite his dedication to precision, Mr. Muni was hard put to remember exactly how many roles he had played in the Yiddish theater, where he first attracted attention as Muni Weisenfreund.

The actor, born Sept. 22, 1895 in Lemberg when it was part of Austria, was brought to the United States by his parents in 1902 and made his stage debut in Chicago five years later.

As his fame spread among the tenements off Second Avenue in New York during the next decade, he was recruited by Maurice Schwartz for the Yiddish Art Theater here.

In this repertory, he attracted the attention of Max Siegal, coauthor of a play, "We Americans." Mr. Siegal persuaded Sam H. Harris, the producer, to give the actor his first English role. The play opened at the Eltinge Theater on Oct. 12, 1926.

Called to Hollywood

Good reviews led to a part the next year as a gangster in the Broadway production of "Four Walls." Hollywood summoned him after he appeared in this play, and film officials forced him to change his name.

Mr. Muni appeared in two little-remembered films. "The Valiant" and "Seven Faces," during those early days of the talkies. But in 1932, he made Hollywood history with "Scarface," which contrasted every acting talent he possessed.

His portrayal of an arrogant gangster called Tony Camonte in "Scarface" was considered a classic. With an ugly gash across his cheek, the actor snarled and pillaged as a brutal thug who displayed a streak of cowardice when taken by the law.

Mr. Muni also appeared in 1932 as the hunted James Allen in the memorable film "I Am a Fugitive From a Chain Gang." It was a grim and searing depiction of life in Southern prison camps, and it resulted in a nationwide reaction against inhuman prison conditions.

He broadened his range in the movies to include such diverse and distinguished films as "The Life of Emile Zola," "Juarez," "We Are Not Alone," "A Song to Remember" and "The Story of Louis Pasteur," for which he won an Oscar in 1936. After completing the role of Pasteur in 1935, he announced that he was quitting films to be idle for a while.

But that didn't last long. Two years later Mr. Muni appeared in the epical production of Pearl Buck's novel "The Good Earth," playing a simple Chinese peasant, a role that required nine makeups during the span of years covered by the film. After that he was billed by his studio, Warner Brothers, with Mr. in front of his name, a rare tribute.

Popularity on Wane

By the nineteen-forties, however, Mr. Muni's strength as a movie star was waning perceptibly, and as he failed to draw at the box office, producers found excuses to avoid using him. His own desire for perfection led him to reject offers to do Broadway plays he considered inadequate.

Herman Shumlin, producer-director of "Inherit the Wind,"

(continued)

Paul Muni in *Scarface: Shame of a Nation.*

Paul Muni in *The Story of Louis Pasteur.*

brought Mr. Muni out of the doldrums. He insisted that the actor read the play. Mr. Muni agreed overnight to do the drama, and Mr. Shumlin arranged for him to do his own typical research. The play opened on Broadway in 1955 and the actor was hailed by critics as "superb," "brilliant" and "inspired."

Mr. Muni's wife, the former Bella Finkel, told intimates at the time that this success was "vindication" for the actor after a decade of having been considered finished in the profession.

It was hard to believe that he had lost his talents. Broadway had welcomed his return in October 1930 after several movie successes, and he played a gangster in "This One Man." He also won applause soon after for "Rock Me, Julie," although the play closed after seven performances.

But in November, 1931, Mr. Muni was again hailed by critics and theatergoers when he appeared in Elmer Rice's "Counselor at Law," a heart-warming story of realistic humanity. The play had 258 performances, with Mr. Muni portraying a self-made Jewish lawyer filled with many human emotions.

In 1939, he scored another triumph on the stage in Maxwell Anderson's "Key Largo," winning the Drama League award for "the depth, the richness, the dignity and integrity" he gave to his role.

Shy in Public

Mr. Muni's consuming preoccupation with his art had reached perhaps its pinnacle back in 1921, on the day he married. As soon as the rabbi had finished the ceremony in downtown New York, the actor shook hands briskly with his bride and rushed off to do a matinee. He met her later that night, after the evening show, at a subway kiosk on 14th Street.

He took his bride home to her mother's and left her there. During the next 15 days he dutifully kept in touch with her by telephone. Their honeymoon began on the 16th day when they went on tour together in a show.

Away from the theater, Mr. Muni was exceedingly shy. When he was recognized while dining in restaurants, he would show apparent agony, his mouth twisted, his soft brown eyes pleading to be left alone.

His life was described as probably the least Bohemian of any actor. While living in a hotel suite during the run of a Broadway show, he would have breakfast with his wife in their room about 9 A.M. before doing some reading or going for a walk in secluded sections of Central Park. Sometimes they would go to a movie.

By 4:30 P.M., Mr. Muni would be ready for dinner. He would rest or read afterward, but was always at the theater before 7:30 P.M. to get ready for his performance. He would have a snack with his wife after the theater and then turn in.

Life at the Muni home in California was even more austere and retiring.

He and his wife had what amounted to a mania for privacy. They had few visitors at their estate, and Mr. Muni would busy himself in his den, which he called "Shangri-La."

Mr. Muni enjoyed spending his time among books, radios, tape recorders, cameras, television sets and recordings of broadcasts of music and speeches.

He had a fine collection of Toscanini concerts and his library of recorded speeches included ones by Hitler, Mussolini, Franklin D. Roosevelt, Winston Churchill and Robert Oppenheimer.

If Mr. Muni had a weakness, it was his desire to buy something any time he was in a stationery store. He would purchase erasers, pencils, paper clips, rubber bands, pads and notebooks for no apparent reason or need. "God forbid," his wife once said, "that I should throw anything out."

But for all his quietness, Mr. Muni was inflexible on matters of taste and principle. Thus, he was happy to end a movie contract that would have paid him $800,000 because he was not happy with the choice of films.

Mrs. Muni recalled her husband's reaction after he tore up the movie contract in the nineteen-thirties.

"That night," she said, "he did somersaults in the living room. Believe me. He jumped up and down, yelling, 'No one owns me. I'm a free man.'"

The actor, who was always precisely punctual for appointments, refused to tolerate tardiness in others. Explaining his unyielding attitude toward punctuality, he presented a variation of Shakespeare's lines that he who steals a purse steals trash.

"If a man steals money or property from you," Mr. Muni remarked, "that's one thing. But if he steals time, he steals a piece of your life."

Couldn't Explain Acting

He did not like to analyze his art. "I have been in the business for years," he told an interviewer, "but can't tell what acting is or how it is done. I know I have not tried to learn the 'art' of acting, whatever that may be." But he acknowledged that there was always something of himself in the roles he played.

Mr. Muni was starring in "Inherit the Wind" on Broadway when he was stricken with an eye ailment and taken to a hospital for surgery. Tests had shown that he had a tumor of the eye, and he was forced to quit the play. His performance won for him an Antoinette Perry Award in 1956 as the best dramatic star of the season.

The ailment ended his active career, although he did play a few roles in films afterward, including a moving performance as a doctor in Brooklyn in "The Last Angry Man."

But he had to resort to memories rather than performance. And his wife, who had always been the boss on his movie sets, settled down with him to a quiet life at home. No longer did he look to her at the end of each "take" for approbation or disapproval.

The Munis had no children. They spent their hours at home playing pinochle or painting. Mr. Muni also enjoyed the violin, which he had played for many years.

Luise Ranier and Paul Muni in *The Good Earth*, 1937.

Paul Muni in *I Am a Fugitive From a Chain Gang*, 1932.

The New York Times WEDNESDAY, FEBRUARY 25, 1970

Conrad Nagel, Actor, Dies at 72; Star of Stage and Silent Pictures

Made Transition to Talkies—Radio and TV Host Helped Found Academy Awards

Conrad Nagel, the actor, was found dead yesterday in his home at the Park Vendome, 340 West 57th Street. He was 72 years old.

A spokesman for the office of the Chief Medical Examiner said that Mr. Nagel's death was "due to natural causes," more specifically, a heart attack and emphysema. He added that no autopsy was planned.

The distinguished actor began his Broadway career in "Forever After" in 1918 and then went on to become one of the leading stars of the silent screen. He was also one of the few to make the transition to talking pictures.

In the next 14 years of making films he appeared in 150 features—the first, "Little Women," in 1919. Thirty-one of the films were made in a two-year period.

Among his more than 200 films were "Midsummer Madness" (1920), "What Every Woman Knows" (1921), "Tess of the D'Urbervilles" (1921), "The Jazz Singer" (1927) and "Stage Struck" (1958).

Returning to the theater in 1933, he appeared in "The First Apple," then toured in such shows as "The Petrified Forest" and "The Male Animal." Later, he appeared in such Broadway hits as the Pulitzer Prize-winning "The Skin of Our Teeth," "Tomorrow the World" and "State of the Union." He wooed Madeleine Carroll in "Goodby, My Fancy" and appeared with Gertrude Lawrence in a revival of "Susan and God" (1943).

New York Was Home

Between stage appearances, the blue-eyed, blond Mr. Nagel returned to Hollywood numerous times to make movies, but he regarded New York as his home.

Mr. Nagel recalled recently that when he went to Hollywood in 1919 "there wasn't even a restaurant there."

In a letter to the New York Times last year, he denounced as a "hoary myth" a much-quoted story about a silent film in which he lifts a girl and carries her to a bed. According to the story, the girl looked at him tenderly but actually said, "If you drop me, you bastard, I'll kill you.

Mr. Nagel recounted that the silent pictures were a source of great joy to many thousands of deaf people and that, being expert lip readers, they would have deluged Hollywood with letters of protest. However, he conceded that there was a basis in fact for the story. He said that during rehearsal another actor—Who was suffering from a hangover—had to lift an actress from the floor. She told him: "Use your breath, that's strong enough to do the job."

With Fred Niblo and Louis B. Mayer, Mr. Nagel founded the Academy of Motion Picture Arts and Sciences and he served on a committee that originated the Oscar awards. In New York he served as director and officer, governing performers in radio and television. Mr. Nagel himself received an Oscar in 1940 for his work on the Motion Picture Relief Fund.

Mr. Nagel had appeared frequently on radio and television. In 1937 his distinctive voice was heard as host of the Silver Theater radio broadcasts and of Radio Readers' Digest. In 1948 he became host of "Celebrity Time," a weekly show on the American Broadcasting Company television network.

Mr. Nagel was president of the Associated Actors and Artistes of America, and was a member of the national board of the American Federation of Television and Radio Artists, as well as of the union's local board. He also was a director of the Screen Actors Guild.

The future actor was born in Keokuk, Iowa, and graduated from Highland Park College in 1914. He made his professional debut that year with the Princess Stock Company in Des Moines.

He was a long-time member of The Lambs, the theatrical club at 128 West 44th Street and served for many years as chairman of its admissions committee.

He was married three times to Ruth Helms, Lynn Merrick and Michael Coulson Smith. All three marriages ended in divorce.

He leaves a daughter and son.

Aileen Pringle and Conrad Nagel in *Three Weeks*, 1924.

Greta Garbo and Conrad Nagel in *The Divine Woman*, 1928.

The New York Times SATURDAY, JANUARY 27, 1973

J. CARROL NAISH, ACTOR, 73, DEAD

Master of Dialects Starred in Radio's 'Life With Luigi'

LA JOLLA, Calif., Jan. 26 (AP) — J. Carrol Naish, the screen, television and stage actor who was a master of dialects, died Wednesday in Scripps Memorial Hospital. He was 73 years old.

His widow, Gladys, and a daughter survive.

Man of Many Parts

By DAVID A. ANDELMAN

In the 1940's it was not unusual for devotees of the double feature to watch a kindly Italian street-peddler bumble through the first half of the twin bill only to find the same man suddenly reappear a brief intermission later as a lecherous old despoiler of women and children.

For at that time, J. Carrol Naish was making 30 movies a year and played virtually every nationality in filmdom—Italians, Japanese, Hindus, Arabs, Chinese, Jews and Mexicans — every nationality in fact except his own: Irish.

During a stage, screen and broadcasting career that spanned 30 years, the entire era of the talkies, the black-haired, mustachioed Mr. Naish played supporting roles to every major actor from Humphrey Bogart to Sal Mineo. And to moviegoers of his era and late-show viewers of the 1970's, his face is almost equally familiar yet his name, to his death, remained a cipher to the viewing public.

"J. Carrol Naish is wrestling with a fame he doesn't fully appreciate," one Hollywood columnist wrote in 1949. "He has done Italian and Mexican parts so often his admirers have come to think of the dark-haired, stocky actor with his thin, Latin mustache as being of either nationality. This assumption has caused him no end of embarrassment."

Joseph Patrick Carrol Naish (pronounced "Nash"), was born in New York on Jan. 21, 1900. His Irish origins went back more than 750 years in County Limerick, his ancestors were listed in Burke's Peerage, and he was the great-great-grandson of the Lord Chancellor of Ireland.

He brawled his way through the Yorkville-Harlem area of the turn-of-the-century Irish with considerable success, being tossed out of one school after another. It was only because of his swarthy complexion, in fact, that he was never cast in a motion picture as an Irishman.

For his first 25 years, in fact, he never held a steady job for more than a few months at a time. During World War I he enlisted in the Navy, was promptly thrown in the brig, then sent to Europe. He deserted to join a buddy in the Army, flew missions over France with the Aviation Section of the Army Signal Corps and finally wound up with a discharge in Paris and $60 in his pocket.

For the next few years he roamed around Europe doing odd jobs, singing in occasional cafes and picking up a command of eight languages, six of which he spoke fluently.

A tramp steamer finally deposited him in Hollywood in 1926. After a succession of stunt and bit parts, he wound up as an understudy in a road company of a Broadway hit, "The Shanghai Gesture," where he met his wife, a beautiful Irish girl named Gladys Heaney. In 1929, when the play returned to Broadway, they married. Unlike many Hollywood marriages, theirs never broke up.

In 1932, Mr. Naish played in his first major film, a romanticized version of San Francisco's infamous Tong Wars called 'The Hatchet Man". Edward G. Robinson was the star. It was his first of many dialect films — he played an aging Chinese businessman who received a hatchet between the shoulder blades.

Other films followed quickly — "Her Jungle Love," of 1938, which starred Dorothy Lamour; a pirate role in "Captain Blood"; "Beau Geste," the great French Foreign Legion film of 1939, and "A Medal for Benny," for which he received an Academy Award nomination. Bosley Crowther of The New York Times described him as "warm and picturesque as the ignorant father of Benny."

During his film career he played in more than 250 movies but his name became a household word through radio. In 1948, the Columbia Broadcasting System inaugurated the comedy series "Life with Luigi." Luigi, played by Mr. Naish, was an Italian immigrant who settled in Chicago and took a look at the America around him.

J. Carrol Naish as one of the killers in *Violent Saturday.*

Boris Karloff as the mad scientist and J. Carrol Naish as the hunchback in *House of Frankenstein,* 1944.

"All the News That's Fit to Print."

The New York Times.

LATE CITY EDITION

THE WEATHER—Fairly cloudy today and tomorrow, not much change in temperature.

Copyright, 1931, by The New York Times Company.

VOL. LXXIX....No. 26,329. NEW YORK, MONDAY, FEBRUARY 24, 1930. TWO CENTS In Greater New York | THREE CENTS Within 200 Miles | FOUR CENTS Elsewhere Except 7th and 8th Postal Zones

BRIAND READY TO ACCEPT HOOVER SECURITY PLEDGE WITHOUT SENATE APPROVAL

NEW PRICE OF NAVY CUTS

Promise of Consultation by Us on War Threats Would Satisfy France.

OTHER PACT HANGS ON THIS

Mediterranean Accord Is Not Believed Likely Without Prior Assurance From America.

INTEREST AROUSED HERE

Irreconcilables Are Expected to Object to Move by President in Proclamation.

By CLARENCE K. STREIT.

Wireless to THE NEW YORK TIMES.

LONDON, Feb. 23.—The minimum political guarantees upon which ex-Premier Tardieu made dependent any reduction in the French naval program, and toward the obtaining of which Foreign Minister Briand on his return to the conference will direct his skill, can now be stated on high authority.

It can be further stated that the objections raised by the American Senators to the previously reported French political demands are not considered by informed circles here to apply necessarily to the real French aims.

It can be added that the bed rock situation, in which the conference faces the alternative of increased naval building all around or further organization of the machinery for the maintenance of peace, depends more for its solution on President Hoover individually than has been imagined.

Briand's Political Objectives.

M. Briand has two political objectives. One, and the only one directly involving the United States, boils down to the United States giving formal assurance that the precedent it set when it twice consulted the principal powers last year with regard to the Russo-Chinese threat of violation of the Kellogg pact would be followed whenever such a crisis arises in the future. Naturally the other big powers have to give the same assurance, but since the others here are already bound to consult each other by the League of Nations covenant the proposal really hinges on the attitude of the United States.

The French would prefer to have this assurance of immediate mutual consultation taken in the naval treaty, but it is stated authoritatively that if it came instead in the form of a solemn Presidential proclamation by President Hoover, not requiring Senate ratification, France would be sufficiently satisfied to reduce her naval program by some degree.

The other political objective is a Mediterranean agreement in which the French, contrary to many reports, do not consider American participation necessary but in which British participation is all important. A Mediterranean agreement would involve more than consultation for, since the Mediterranean powers belong to the League, they have to consult as it is. On the other hand it would involve less serious commitments than the Locarno treaties, the term "Mediterranean Locarno," it is stated, being very misleading as applied to the proposed arrangement.

League Pact to Be Guide.

The Mediterranean agreement would be modeled instead on the treaty of mutual assistance drafted by the League in 1923 along the lines proposed then largely by France. By this treaty, if any one of the contracting parties, after having reduced armaments, believes it is threatened by aggression it may lay the case before the League Council. If the council decides a menace exists, then all the contracting parties agree mutually to assist each other "in a form determined by the council," such as by executing any decision it took to apply economic sanctions or a blockade under Article XVI of the League covenant.

The prime object of the treaty as adapted to suit the Mediterranean situation would be to centre responsibility for the maintenance of peace in the Mediterranean upon the Mediterranean powers themselves, thus assuring each of them that the League would have a much quicker and more effective club at its disposal in an emergency in this region than it now has.

Such a Mediterranean treaty would entail a much greater French naval

Continued on Page Five.

Mayor Home Today to Attend Miss Curry's Bridal Tomorrow

Mayor Walker is due back in the city today from Florida where he has spent a vacation with a yachting party off Long Key.

The Mayor is understood to have cut short his vacation in order to be present at the wedding tomorrow of Miss Veronica Curry, daughter of Tammany Leader John F. Curry, who is to marry Edmund M. McCarthy, an attorney, of Springfield, Mass. The wedding will be in St. Patrick's Cathedral.

The party with whom the Mayor has spent his vacation in the South includes John McKeon and George S. Collins, his executive secretary.

LADY ASTOR APPEALS ON RADIO FOR PEACE

In Transatlantic Address She Predicts Naval Cuts by Britian and Us at Least.

ASKS WOMEN TO TAKE LEAD

She Warns That Another War Probably Would End Western Civilization.

The rôle which women should play in making world peace a reality was emphasized yesterday by Lady Astor in a radio broadcast from London in which she discussed the work of the five-power naval conference. Addressing herself specifically to the women of this country and of the British Empire, she urged them to "press on and force our countries to lead the way."

Charles F. Adams, Secretary of the Navy and a member of the American delegation to the conference, will speak on the radio next Sunday over the same international hook-up.

Lady Astor, announced as the first woman to deliver an international speech, spoke over the transatlantic telephone and the network of WABC and W2XE of the Columbia Broadcasting System. She began to speak at 12:34 P. M. and ended at 12:55 P. M. Her trained voice, with its Virginia drawl, came through distinctly. She was introduced by Frederic William Wile, Columbia observer at the parley. He referred to the fact that Lady Astor, born an American, was the first of her sex to enter the House of Commons, by introducing her as "Mother Parliament's first daughter."

Reminds of the Peace Pact.

The Kellogg peace pact must be kept to the fore at the conference, she said, adding that if some of the governments appeared to forget their signatures to the agreement, "it won't do any harm for the people to remind them that when they sign the pact, at least when we sign the pact, we mean business."

Lady Astor said that she was certain that every delegate at the conference and the countries they represented wanted peace, for "only a mad man or a mad country would want war." She spoke of the American delegates, saying that they had

Continued on Page Four.

SOVIET SENDS REPLY TO BORAH MESSAGE; 11 OF 14 RABBIS FREE

Senator Says He Believes the Three Others Are Safe From Execution.

JEWISH REDS DEMONSTRATE

Paraders Join Russian Outcry Against Religion, Calling the Rabbis Capital's Spies.

MOSCOW FEARS WAR AHEAD

Head of Army Cites New Weapons Here and Elsewhere as Signs of Capitalist Conspiracy.

Special to The New York Times.

WASHINGTON, Feb. 23.— ... three of the fourt... to have been ...

[partially obscured] ... "I hav... noon fro... sar of Fo... all of the ... rest have b... "Among ... stand is Rab... sonably cert... released are ... execution."

Senator Bora... terday appealin... ernment to rele... said he had so... many American... independently of ... ment because thi... no official relati... Russia. In sending ... Soviet Government ... merely asked for in... did not assert, as rep... rabbis were facing exe...

The Soviet Governme... friendly attitude tow... Borah because of his ... recognition in opposit... United States Governm... from the very day that th... retary of State Hughes de... phatically against recognitio...

Jewish Reds Reported Mar...

MOSCOW, Feb. 23 (Jewish ... graphic Agency)—Anti-religiou... ish street demonstrations, alle... have been organized by the J... population, were said today to ... progress in a number of towns ... in the Minsk, Mozir, Bobroisk ... Vitebsk regions.

The last synagogue in Krupke ha... been taken over by the authorities ... and a red flag waves over the synagogue in a township near Vitebsk. The Jews were said to be marching on the local Soviets asking for the conversion of the synagogues.

The newspaper Oktiabre, organ of the Jewish Communists in Minsk, declared that all rabbis in Russia play an important rôle in the present anti-Soviet crusade abroad. They are all spies for foreign counter-revolutionaries, the newspaper charges, and therefore "these holy damagers should be carefully watched."

The entire Soviet press, from Izvestia, the official government paper, to the smallest sheet, carried a furious official attack today on the Jewish Telegraphic Agency because of the

Continued on Page Six.

125 Patients Are Rescued in Hospital Fire At Providence, R. I.; 14 Babies Carried Out

Special to The New York Times.

PROVIDENCE, R. I., Feb. 23.—One hundred and twenty-five patients were rescued from a fire in St. Joseph's Hospital here early today which almost destroyed the five-story building.

Alarms summoned all the city's firemen and all police reserves to the scene, where acts of heroism marked the safe removal of all patients. There was no panic and no hysteria while nurses and firemen, drenched to the skin, carried surgical and maternity cases through flooded halls to ambulances, trucks and taxicabs.

The patients were transferred to other hospitals, to other Catholic institutions and to private homes.

The fire started from an undetermined cause in a linen chute which runs up through the four stories of the hospital. The flames mushroomed out into the children's ward on the fourth floor and burst through the roof. Everything below was drenched with water. Ceilings fell and plaster walls dropped apart. Instruments and almost all hospital equipment were destroyed or badly damaged.

A student nurse discovered the fire and gave the alarm to the Sisters of Mercy, who conduct the hospital, a Providence diocese institution. The nuns took charge and immediately started directing the removal of the patients.

By the time the firemen arrived many already had been carried from the point of immediate danger. Among those saved from the flames were fourteen babies, one less than an hour old. The mother of the newly born baby was carried out with it on a mattress by six firemen and then taken to another hospital.

As nurses approached to remove one young man he pointed to an aged patient in a corner and directed them to take him first.

Unofficial estimates of the loss ran from $100,000 to $300,000.

Doctors worked for hours after the fire aiding their patients in recovering from the shock and fright and from the effects of the drenchings which most of them suffered. It was feared that some of them might not ... effects.

BEACHE... [obscured] ...UND ARMED ...ER GUARDS

...He Killed Nine ...Knife on ...Here.

...TECTIVES

...Escape ...Poison

[remainder of these columns obscured by clipping]

Eight Dead, 100 Hurt, as Auto Derails Train Of Five Cars, Wrecks Freight, in Wisconsin

Special to The New York Times.

CHICAGO, Feb. 23.—Eight persons were known to have been killed and about 100 injured tonight when a southbound Chicago, North Shore & Milwaukee train struck an automobile and was derailed at a crossing in Kenosha, Wis.

The five-car electric passenger train was thrown into an eight-foot ditch at the west of the right-of-way, injuring practically every passenger and trainman on it.

Every available ambulance and automobile in Kenosha was rushed to the scene, carrying physicians. The injured were taken to inns and residences near by to await their turn to be carried to two Kenosha hospitals.

At midnight attendants at the Kenosha Hospital said twenty-five patients had been received there, most of them slightly injured. At St. Catherine's Hospital, thirty-five had been received.

The wreck occurred at 10:50 P. M. when the train, traveling to Chicago at a speed of about sixty miles an hour, crossed a State highway. The front car tossed the automobile, going east, directly into the path of a sixteen-car freight train, northbound, just as it passed the passenger train.

The automobile was apparently smashed to pieces, as no trace of it had been found in the wreckage. Roy Shaw of Kenosha, a motorist, who was only a short distance behind the car when it drove on to the tracks in the path of the speeding train, said that he thought there were four persons in the automobile. All are believed to have been killed instantly as the machine was crushed between the two trains.

As the front car of the passenger train hurtled from the tracks, derailed freight cars plunged into the rear coaches, sending them over the ditch. The two front cars on the passenger train were demolished. Most of the passengers who were killed or injured were riding in these cars, the rear coaches escaping the full force of the impact. All the passenger coaches remained upright.

Several of the freight cars burst into flames after the crash and rescuers worked by the light of the blazing cars.

The crash occurred at an hour when travel was heaviest on the interurban line, with crowds returning to Chicago from Milwaukee and other Wisconsin cities.

Motorman Hall of the passenger train, who was slightly injured, was the only member of the train crew who could be located after the crash. The others were believed to be among the injured taken to the hospitals.

Only three of the sixteen cars in the freight train remained on the track.

Continued on Page Eleven.

For more ... circling blind... dropping flar... his bearings, ... last, when his ... the ship down... cove without ... or the occupants ...

In the plane w... Kilgour Jr. of th... phone and Telegra... Frank Bartilino, ... waded ashore and ... the trip to New York ... aviators remained o... at Green Pond ...

J. Carlson of Clifton, ... airplane pilot, flying fr... Caldwell, had a some... experience. He was ca... Butler, N. J., and was forced to land blindly. He brought his ship down at Green Pond, scraping a tree in the descent. Neither he nor his passenger, Thomas Bottomley of Paterson, was injured. The plane was slightly damaged.

Highways Are Crowded.

Traffic on all roads leading from Long Island and New Jersey coast resorts was reminiscent of midsummer. By nightfall thousands of automobiles, headed for the city, were crawling along the slippery roads packed so close together that

... evidently ... He said al... probably will be ex... an alienist he regarded ... young man as normal.

Detroit Police Doubt Story.

Baker's confession was doubted by the Detroit police. According to them and his relatives, he was "a morbid egotist and a braggart and a liar." His mother, Mrs. Cyril Parks of Warren, Mich., told the Detroit authorities that he was kicked in the head by a horse when a youngster "and has acted funny ever since."

Several hours after Baker had been put in a cell on the charge of homi-

Continued on Page Sixteen.

MABEL NORMAND, FILM STAR, DEAD

The Comedienne Succumbs to Tuberculosis in California Sanitarium.

CONSCIOUS TO THE LAST

Began Career as Artists' Model, Intending to Study Art—Went Into Movies by Chance.

MONROVIA, Cal., Feb. 23 (AP).—Mabel Normand, whose private and film life offered strangely contrasting rôles of tragedy and comedy, died in a sanitarium here at 2:30 A. M. today. She had suffered from tuberculosis since the latter months of 1928. She was in her thirty-third year.

Blood transfusions recently resorted to in the hope that they would strengthen Miss Normand's weakened general condition failed, and after an almost imperceptible sinking spell late last night the comedienne died at the Pattenger Sanitarium. Only her secretary, Miss Julia Benson, and a nurse were at her bedside.

Continued on Page Twenty-one.

ROOSEVELT OBJECTS TO MASTICK'S PLAN FOR STATE PENSIONS

Governor Fears Provision for Local Control Would Result in Favoritism in Awards.

FINDS METHOD 'INADEQUATE'

And Points Out That Beneficiaries Would Not Be Required to Contribute to Fund.

MAY ACCEPT THE MEASURE

With This as Only a "First Step," the Whole Question Might Become Campaign Issue.

By W. A. WARN.

Special to The New York Times.

ALBANY, Feb. 23.—The satisfaction voiced in the Republican controlled Legislature with the old age pension plan recommended by a legislative commission, headed by Senator Seabury C. Mastick of Westchester, is not shared by Governor Roosevelt, who, in his first annual message to the lawmakers, took the initiative in the movement for old age relief.

In a statement made public today, Governor Roosevelt declares that since the report of the commission was made public, early last week, he has received many letters objecting to the Mastick commission plan on the ground that it fails to meet the real need of the situation and that the machinery provided to administer the old age pension system might lead to favoritism in dispensing the State's bounty and waste of the funds provided for relief purposes.

"Thousands of people will be disappointed in the recommendations of the commission; frankly, I share in this disappointment," the Governor says in his statement.

The Governor objects to the plan, not only on the ground that the commission has recommended merely an extension of local machinery already existing in the counties, and for the most part controlled by the Republicans, to administer the State's plan of old age relief, but on the further ground that prospective beneficiaries of the old age pension plan for dependent persons above the age of 70 would not be required to make any contribution to the pension fund ... under the circumstances ... come to them as a dole from ... State.

[Gr]ants Thrift Encouraged.

[The G]overnor expresses the opinion ... encourage thrift, an old age ... plan ought to provide for ... ributions on a graded scale, ... of the pension to be ... the size of the contribu... each instance, with a ... relief going to a non-... class of pensioners.

...'s stand on the old-... posal is certain to cre-... between him and the ... islature. Some time ... stick plan was com... Governor by the ... of the Legislature ... sent on grounds set ... nt statement, they ... fting his position ... ck a quarrel for ... e Republican ...

[remainder obscured by clipping]

24 Hours From Ice Pack; Seasick Till Gale Subsides

By RUSSELL OWEN.

Copyright, 1930, by The New York Times Company and the St. Louis Post-Dispatch. All rights for publication reserved throughout the world. Wireless to THE NEW YORK TIMES.

ABOARD THE BARK CITY OF NEW YORK, IN ROSS SEA, Monday, Feb. 24.—The City of New York, carrying Admiral Byrd and the members of his expedition, is making five to six knots through the Ross Sea toward the ice pack, which should be reached tomorrow.

The ship's position at noon today (we skipped a day when crossing the 180th meridian) is about Lat. 72.30 degrees S., Long. 178 degrees E. The sea is calm and there is a light favorable wind.

For three days the ship held one of the most seasick expeditions that ever put to sea. Only four or five were immune.

There was a lolloping head sea the first two days after leaving the Bar-

rier that made the City of New York quite lively, at least it seemed so to those who had not been on ship for a year.

But, fortunately, the gale which drove the ship so far to the west on its southern passage had blown itself out, and the passage so far has been surprisingly comfortable. It is quite warm today also, only 28 degrees above zero, Fahrenheit, and the remaining ice on the ship is melting.

Inasmuch as the ship's position at noon of the previous day was Lat. 74.50 degrees S., Long. 178 degrees E., she has moved northward about 120 miles further, making her about 384 miles northwest of Discovery Inlet.

HOOVER AGAIN CALLS PARTY CONFERENCE TO RUSH WORK ON THE BUDGET AND TARIFF

Drys Invite 156-Year-Old Turk To Come Here to Aid Cause

By The Associated Press.

CONSTANTINOPLE, Feb. 23.—"One hundred and fifty-six years old and never took a drink," is the boast of Zaro Agha, Turkey's longevity champion, who will abandon a job as doorkeeper at the City Hall here at the end of April to sail for New York at the invitation of the American Anti-Alcohol Society.

The society intends to exhibit the aged man throughout the United States, calling attention to the teetotaler's mental and physical vigor. Zaro, who has buried eleven wives, will leave his twelfth at home when he embarks for America.

MABEL NORMAND, FILM STAR, DEAD

The Comedienne Succumbs to Tuberculosis in California Sanitarium.

CONSCIOUS TO THE LAST

Began Career as Artists' Model, Intending to Study Art—Went Into Movies by Chance.

MONROVIA, Cal., Feb. 23 (AP).—Mabel Normand, whose private and film life offered strangely contrasting rôles of tragedy and comedy, died in a sanitarium here at 2:30 A. M. today. She had suffered from tuberculosis since the latter months of 1928. She was in her thirty-third year.

Blood transfusions recently resorted to in the hope that they would strengthen Miss Normand's weakened general condition failed, and after an almost imperceptible sinking spell late last night the comedienne died at the Pattenger Sanitarium. Only her secretary, Miss Julia Benson, and a nurse were at her bedside.

Despite her extremely weak condition, Miss Normand was conscious until the last few moments of her life. Scarcely more than an hour before her death she had taken some light nourishment.

Lew Cody, her husband, himself a motion picture star, was notified shortly after her death. Her mother, Mrs. Mary Normand, and her sister, Gladys, both of Staten Island, N. Y., also were informed. They telegraphed to Los Angeles that they would leave New York immediately for that city.

Except possibly to a few intimates, Miss Normand's death came as a surprise. Recently her physicians had issued bulletins declaring that her ravaged lungs were responding to treatment and that she was improving.

Entered Movies by Chance.

Mabel Normand came to New York from Atlanta, Ga., to become an art student and by chance drifted into the infant industry of motion pictures, in which she won her fame. She struggled through the customary days of the early comedies to become known as a talented comedienne, switched abruptly to a more serious type of picture and became equally successful in that field.

Her entry into motion pictures is the story of an ambitious and talented young art student forced to support herself by any means avail-

Continued on Page Twenty-one.

WILL MEET AT BREAKFAST

Mellon, Mills and Other Republican Leaders Are Called In.

FISCAL BILLS ARE A WORRY

President Seeks to Maintain Federal Employment, With Sound Revenue Basis.

TARIFF RESTS WITH SENATE

Statement by Executive Likely When Bill Is in Conference—Must Appease Regulars.

By RICHARD V. OULAHAN.

Special to The New York Times.

WASHINGTON, Feb. 23.—Further evidence of the concern of administration and Congressional party leaders over the delayed legislative situation, due to the Senate's protracted discussion of the tariff bill, was furnished this evening in an announcement from the White House that President Hoover would have another breakfast conference there tomorrow morning, when his guests will include the highest ranking officials of the treasury and leading Republican Senators and Representatives.

The President's guests will be Andrew W. Mellon, Secretary of the Treasury; Ogden L. Mills, Under Secretary of the Treasury; Senator James E. Watson, floor leader of the Senate; Senator Charles L. McNary, assistant floor leader; Senator Reed Smoot, chairman of the Finance Committee, who is in charge of the tariff bill; Senator Wesley L. Jones, chairman of the Committee on Appropriations; Representative Nicholas Longworth, Speaker of the House; Representative John Q. Tilson, the House floor leader; Representative Bertram L. Snell, chairman of the Committee on Rules; Representative William R. Wood, chairman of the Committee on Appropriations; Representative Willis C. Hawley, chairman of the Committee on Ways and Means, and Colonel J. Clawson Roop, Director of the Budget.

The make-up of the breakfast company indicates that the budget situation will be the chief topic for consideration, but it is evident that other matters of a more particular political slant will be discussed.

Appropriations Also in Issue.

The presence of the heads of the Senate and House committees which deal with the tariff and other revenue business suggests that the President will continue his effort to expedite the passage of the tariff bill, while it is equally apparent that he is concerned over the prospect that from 10,000 to 20,000 men employed on government works will have to be discharged if Congress does not appropriate more money by the first part of March for continuing public construction projects.

Last week, after the President had conferred at breakfast with some of the Congressional leaders, it became known that he had impressed on them that the government would be obligated to contribute to the unemployment situation unless additional appropriations were forthcoming for public works. It was his own estimate that from 10,000 to 20,000 men now employed by the United States would lose their jobs.

In addition to the money required for continuing work on the extensive public building program, the President has asked Congress for $12,000,000 for river and harbor improvements.

While it is accepted that the President and his breakfast guests will discuss the prospect of heavy appropriations in the light of their effect on the public finances, there appears to be confidence that the fiscal affairs of the government will be in sound shape at the end of the current fiscal year, June 30. Treasury officials expressed themselves as satisfied that the reduction of the corporation tax from 12 to 11 per cent, effective on last year's business and payable March 15, will have no serious effect on the government's internal revenue receipts. Whatever loss of revenue comes from this lowering of the corporation tax is likely to be overcome by heavy payments of income taxes during the earlier half of the fiscal year.

Big Revenue Due on Stock Sales.

While the revenue legislation of the recent extra session of Congress provided for reductions of income taxes applicable to last year's in-

MABEL NORMAND, FILM STAR, DEAD

Continued from Page 1, Column 7.

Despite her extremely weak condition, Miss Normand was conscious until the last few moments of her life. Scarcely more than an hour before her death she had taken some light nourishment.

Lew Cody, her husband, himself a motion picture star, was notified shortly after her death. Her mother, Mrs. Mary Normand, and her sister, Gladys, both of Staten Island, N. Y., also were informed. They telegraphed to Los Angeles that they would leave New York immediately for that city.

Except possibly to a few intimates, Miss Normand's death came as a surprise. Recently her physicians had issued bulletins declaring that her ravaged lungs were responding to treatment and that she was improving.

Entered Movies by Chance.

Mabel Normand came to New York from Atlanta, Ga., to become an art student and by chance drifted into the infant industry of motion pictures, in which she won her fame. She struggled through the custard pie throwing days of the early comedies to become known as a talented comedienne, switched abruptly to a more serious type of picture and became equally successful in that field.

Her entry into motion pictures is the story of an ambitious and talented young art student forced to support herself by any means available while the art studies waited. They continued to wait. While earning a living when she began her art studies she became a model, posing for James Montgomery Flagg, Charles Dana Gibson and Henry Hutt.

The death of P. F. Collier indirectly changed the course of her life. As she told of the incident later, she was released early by Mr. Gibson, for whom she was posing that day, when he was called down town because of Mr. Collier's death. She went to the Fashion Camera Studio, where many of the models used to obtain extra jobs posing for pictures as fashion models.

While there she met Alice Joyce, who tried to induce her to go to the Biograph Studios. Miss Normand was satisfied with things as they were and the new venture of motion pictures did not appeal to her, but on the next day, when Mr. Gibson was still unable to work, she reported at the studio and was put to work by D. W. Griffith. She worked through the Summer until the company went to California for the Winter and then shifted to Vitagraph, but returned to Biograph the next year.

It was not until she joined the Mack Sennett troupe turning out the famous Keystone comedies that she became generally known, however. Miss Normand contended that it was she who first noticed the work of Charles Chaplin and induced Mack Sennett to give him a contract. At that time she had become quite popular and was well on the way to stardom. Later she and Chaplin made many pictures together.

After several years in comedies she turned to more serious parts. This sudden shift, in which she left a field in which she had been successful to try a new and uncertain field, was regarded as foolish by many. But her success in the new field was just as great as it had been in comedies. As a Goldwyn star she increased her reputation.

A five-year stage contract with A. H. Woods was announced for Miss Normand in 1925.

Miss Normand's pictures became a storm centre in women's clubs throughout the country after the murder of William Desmond Taylor, a moving picture director, in February, 1922. Miss Normand was the last person who had seen him alive. He had escorted her to her car the night before his body was discovered.

After questioning at length by the police and District Attorney Miss Normand was cleared of all suspicion, the District Attorney announced. Meanwhile many cities had refused to permit her films to be shown.

She had another trying episode, although exonerated personally, when Courtland S. Dines, a wealthy Denver oil operator, was shot on New Year's Day, 1924, by Miss Normand's chauffeur. Miss Normand and Edna Purviance were at his apartment at the time.

Miss Normand was born on Nov. 10, 1897, at Quebec, the daughter of Mr. and Mrs. Claude C. Normand. She was married to Lew Cody early in the morning of Sept. 17, 1926, at Ventura, Cal., following a Hollywood party. Her father died three weeks ago yesterday at the family home, 125 St. Mark's Place, New Brighton, S. I., which Miss Normand had presented to her parents. Besides her mother, a sister, Gladys, and a brother, Claude, survive.

Mabel Normand in the title role of *Peck's Bad Girl*.

Ford Sterling, Fred Mace and Mabel Normand in *Mabel's Adventures*, a typical Mack Sennett Keystone comedy.

"All the News That's Fit to Print"

The New York Times

LATE CITY EDITION

Weather: Sunny, mild today; fair, cool tonight. Fair, mild tomorrow. Temp. range: today 60-39; Thurs. 55-36. Full U.S. report on Page 93.

VOL. CXVIII . No. 40,459 — © 1968 The New York Times Company. — NEW YORK, FRIDAY, NOVEMBER 1, 1968 — 10 CENTS

ATTACKS ON NORTH VIETNAM HALT TODAY; JOHNSON SAYS WIDER TALKS BEGIN NOV. 6

Ramon Novarro Slain on Coast; Starred in Silent Film 'Ben-Hur'

Special to The New York Times

LOS ANGELES, Oct. 31—Ramon Novarro, the Mexican-born star of scores of Hollywood movies made in the nineteen-twenties and thirties, was found bludgeoned to death in his $125,000 Hollywood Hills home early this morning. He was 69 years old.

The actor's nude body was discovered on the king-sized bed in the master bedroom at 8:30 A.M. by Edward Weber, 42, Mr. Novarro's private secretary and long-time friend.

According to detectives of the North Hollywood division of the Los Angeles police department, there was evidence that Mr. Novarro, a slightly built man, had put up a strong fight for his life. Furniture was overturned and vases and other small articles were broken in the den, living room and bedroom.

Several hours after the body was discovered, and while two dozen reporters and photographers were milling around outside the house, a young sightseer, Ted Grezlok, found a pile of bloody clothing in an ivy bed on the far side of the

Ramon Novarro

Continued on Page 43, Column 3

LINDSAY, SHANKER COOL TO HOLDING A SPECIAL SESSION

But Teachers' Union Leader Agrees to Public Hearing as Proposed by McCoy

By LEONARD BUDER

Mayor Lindsay and the president of the teachers' union both reacted coolly yesterday to a suggestion that Governor Rockefeller convene a special session of the State Legislature to deal with the city school crisis.

Informed of their reactions, Governor Rockefeller said:

"Wonderful. All they have to do is settle it. I certainly don't want to call a special session but I am deeply concerned about the children and the parents."

Mr. Rockefeller has been under increasing public pressure to summen a special session because of the school crisis, which has led to three citywide teachers' strikes this fall. City pupils have had only 12 days of regular schooling since the term began on Sept. 9.

Albert Shanker, the president of the teachers' union said last night he would be willing to take part in a public hearing as proposed by Rhody A. McCoy, the administrator of the Ocean Hill-Brownsville school district.

McCoy for Public Hearing

Mr. McCoy had suggested earlier in the day that a public hearing be held before "some responsible and high-ranking public official" that would go into union charges that its members have been harassed and threatened in the district.

At issue in the dispute is the reinstatement of a group of union teachers in the predominantly Negro and Puerto Rican Ocean Hill-Brownsville district in Brooklyn.

The district's governing board originally defied the city Board of Education and refused to reinstate the teachers, asserting that they were a detriment to the district. It has now agreed to permit the teachers to return, but the union has questioned the local board's sincerity.

Dr. James E. Allen Jr., the State Education Commissioner, said last night that he was con-

Continued on Page 32, Column 2

COST FOR WELFARE NOW TOP CITY BILL

Exceeds Outlay for Schools by Using 26% of Budget

By RICHARD PHALON

Welfare has supplanted education as the city's biggest expense item.

Controller Mario A. Procaccino's annual report, released yesterday, shows that welfare costs in the fiscal year ended last June 30 rose to 26.6 per cent of the city's $5.29-billion expense budget, while education declined to 21.4 per cent of the total.

A year earlier, when the total budget was $800-million less, education was the big expense item. It amounted to 22.7 per cent of all funds, compared with 20.7 per cent for welfare.

In all, the city last year spent $1.4-billion on such welfare programs as aid to dependent children and stipends to the aged and handicapped. This compared with $931.8-million the year before.

The outlay for education was $1.1-billion, an increase of $200-million over fiscal 1967.

The cost curves on welfare have continued to rise in this fiscal year. The Human Resources Administration, which administers the city's welfare and antipoverty programs, is budgeted at about $348-million over last year. That outlay rep-

Continued on Page 32, Column 2

Nixon Hopes Johnson Step Will Aid the Talks in Paris

By ROBERT B. SEMPLE Jr.

Richard M. Nixon expressed last night his hope that the halt in the bombing of North Vietnam would "bring some progress" in the Paris talks on the war.

But Mr. Nixon, who addressed a colorful and enthusiastic crowd of some 19,000 partisans gathered in lusty communion in Madison Square Garden, did not offer any further opinion on President Johnson's announcement of the bombing halt.

Pointing to Gov. Spiro T. Agnew of Maryland, his Vice-Presidential running mate, sitting on the stage behind him, the Republican Presidential nominee suggested ... would ...

stroy the chance of peace. We want peace," he said.

According to Nixon aides, the President telephoned Mr. Nixon at his New York apartment about 6 P.M., roughly four hours before the candidate spoke, to inform him of the substance of his address.

Mr. Nixon made his comments at what some observers called "the rally of all Nixon rallies." A man who has often been exposed to well-orchestrated gatherings, Mr. Nixon has not in this campaign seen a noisier and more demonstrative crowd.

One hour of the ... including the ...

STATE ... 4 HOS...

City to Run T... Centers and ... Projects Als...

A state corpora... by the 1968 Legis... build and outfit four... pitals, eight neig... health-care centers a... housing projects for ... staffs in this city at a c... $276.4-million dollars, ... Lindsay announced yeste...

The city will eventually... off the construction costs, ... ther in rents or by long-t... purchase of the buildings, ... the new plan can have the... ready for use within five year... as against 10 to 15 years ... the city were to build them... the Mayor said.

Mr. Lindsay said state and city health officials had resolved some legal and other problems and reached agreement that the new corporation, called the State Health and Mental Facilities Improvement Corporation, would finance the construction out of the $700-million bond issue authorized by the Legislature.

State and city officials will meet here Monday to work out remaining details, including de-

Continued on Page 32, Column 6

Ramon Novarro Slain ... Starred in Silent Film '...

Special to The New York Times

LOS ANGELES, Oct. 31—Ramon Novarro, the Mexican-born star of scores of Hollywood movies made in the nineteen-twenties and thirties, was found bludgeoned to death in his $125,000 Hollywood Hills home early this morning. He was 69 years old.

The actor's nude body was discovered on the king-sized bed in the master bedroom at 8:30 A.M. by Edward Weber, 42, Mr. Novarro's private secretary and long-time friend.

According to detectives of the North Hollywood division of the Los Angeles police department, there was evidence that Mr. Novarro, a slightly built man, had put up a strong fight for his life. Furniture was overturned and vases and other small articles were broken in the den, living room and bedroom.

Several hours after the body was discovered, and while two dozen reporters and photographers were milling around outside the house, a young sightseer, Ted Grezlok, found a pile of bloody clothing in an ivy bed on the far side of the

Ramon Novarro

Continued on Page 43, Column 3

CAUTION IS VOICED

U.S. Officials Expect the Sessions to Be Long and Difficult

By BERNARD GWERTZMAN

Special to The New York Times

WASHINGTON, Oct. 31—Administration officials cautioned tonight against expecting an early end of the war in Vietnam as a result of the agreement to stop the bombing of North Vi... nam announced by Pr... Johnson.

... for the atomic-... submarine and her crew of 99 officers and men.

The Scorpion was last heard from May 21. When she failed to arrive on schedule May 27 in Norfolk, Va., a vast air and sea search was begun.

In announcing the photographic sightings today, Adm. Thomas H. Moorer, Chief of Naval Operations, said that a seven-man Navy court of inquiry would be reconvened in Norfolk. He set no date.

Findings by an inquiry last June have not yet been released.

Admiral Moorer said that reports of the photographic sightings came last night from a United States Navy oceanographic research ship, the Mizar.

"Mizar reports that the submarine's location has been con-

Continued on Page 6, Column 1

... was seen on television yesterday

John Sotu for The New York Times

...of Tension Led ...ng Point in Talks

By PETER GROSE

Special to The New York Times

...—On Oct. 9, 1968, North Vietnam ... States some serious questions. ...merican replies dominated 22 days

... was festooned ... orange and black ... paper, and the stewardesses were wearing black sweaters and miniskirts in anticipation of a Halloween party.

"Happy Halloween," the Vice President exclaimed when he spotted the stewardesses. "We've had tricks—and look at the treats."

Chatting informally with the newsmen, he said that he planned to refer "in guarded phrases" to the Vietnam developments during the rest of his campaign.

He also insisted that he had received no word earlier this

Continued on Page 51, Column 7

NEWS INDEX

ROCKET ATTACKS ON SAIGON KILL 21

...st Victims at Early Mass — Hue Is Also Shelled, With 9 Feared Dead

By GENE ROBERTS

Special to The New York Times

..., South Vietnam, Fri... 1—A series of the ...t damaging rocket ... terms of human life ...gon last night and ... as President John... ...structing the mili... the bombing of ...

...mese police of... more than 20 ... fired, killing ...ese civilians ... than 70

...also fell on ...erial capi... ...ians and ... to Unit... ...okesmen. ... Mytho, ... Mekong ... heavily ...t that ...ualties

... official, ... knew that the ... halt was being ordered, seemed incredulous when he received his first word of the Saigon attack from a newsman.

"You can't be serious," he said. Seconds later, he recovered his composure and said, "I'm sure there won't be any comment on this—at least for a while."

Ton That Thien, the South Vietnamese Minister of Information, denied that these had been rocket attacks when he was awakened after midnight by newsmen calling for comment.

Then, after becoming convinced that the reports were true, he said, "Hanoi has ruined Vice President Humphrey's chances now."

Most of the casualties in Saigon occurred at 6:30 A.M. today when a rocket struck the Xom Moi Roman Catholic Church just before mass.

"Beaucoup deaths—women, children, men," said the Rev. Nguyen Van Tri in a mixture of French and English as he twisted a key ring over and over in his palm and paced back and forth near the debris.

The church and its yard

Continued on Page 13, Column 1

...resident Is Offered Million for Memoirs

Special to The New York Times

WASHINGTON, Oct. 31—President Johnson has received at least one, and possibly more, conditional offers of an advance in excess of $1-million for his memoirs.

One condition is understood to be that the first volume deal with the major events of his Administration, such as his decisions to begin the bombing of North Vietnam, to send American combat troops into the war, to announce that he would not seek another term and, now, to halt the bombing of North Vietnam.

Although the President has not firmly decided what he will do, he is said to have tentatively agreed to write such a volume in advance of a multi-volume series of memoirs. He also plans to write some magazine articles.

The President is understood to have indicated to prospec-

Continued on Page 22, Column 4

PEACE CALLED AIM

Saigon and N.L.F. Can Join in the Enlarged Paris Discussions

Text of the Johnson speech is printed on Page 10.

By NEIL SHEEHAN

Special to The New York Times

WASHINGTON, Oct. 31—President Johnson announced tonight that he was ordering a complete halt to all American air, naval and artillery bombardment of North Vietnam as of 8 A.M. Friday, Eastern standard time (9 P.M., Vietnam time).

"I have reached this decision on the basis of the developments in the Paris talks," the President said, "and I have reached it in the belief that this action can lead to progress toward a peaceful settlement of the Vietnamese war."

"What we now expect—what we have a right to expect," the President said in a television broadcast, "are prompt, productive, serious and intensive negotiations in an atmosphere that is conducive to progress."

Face Shows Fatigue

His face showed fatigue as he made the announcement culminating weeks of secret negotiations.

Mr. Johnson did not announce any reciprocal military commitments from North Vietnam, which he has often said he must have in order to halt the air and naval bombardment that began on Feb. 7, 1965.

[Word of the President's action reached Paris about 2 A.M. Friday, and North Vietnamese negotiators said they might have a statement later in the day. Page 11.]

Washington officials said the bombing of infiltration trails in Laos would continue and that there was no prohibition against reconnaissance flights over North Vietnam.

'Reason to Believe' Foe

Senior Administration sources said the United States had "reason to believe" North Vietnam would not escalate the war in South Vietnam as a result of the bombing cessation.

They said Hanoi "clearly understood" that Mr. Johnson would resume the bombing if it attacked South Vietnamese population centers or took military advantage of the demilitarized zone.

On its side, North Vietnam had apparently not obtained the unconditional bombing halt it has consistently demanded.

Mr. Johnson said that in exchange for the bombing halt Hanoi had agreed to accept participation of the South Vietnamese Government at the Paris talks and the United States had in turn accepted the

Continued on Page 11, Column 1

Channel 13 Ahead 20 Minutes on Talk

By MICHAEL T. KAUFMAN

Channel 13 broke an embargo and televised the President's speech 20 minutes before it was officially released last night.

The violation — which the educational station ascribed to honest error—resulted in angry and indignant protests by the White House and the commercial networks.

"No one told us that the film was embargoed," said Lee Hays, producer of Channel 13's nightly news show. He acknowledged that the unauthorized early showing of the film of Mr. Johnson's speech was put on the air at 7:40 P.M.

Neither he nor station officials were able to say whether the premature broadcast was picked up by any of the 16 other outlets of the Eastern Educational Network, which serves an area from Maine to Washington.

Within minutes after the em-

Continued on Page 10, Column 5

Ramon Novarro, Silent Era Star, Slain

Continued From Page 1, Col. 3

eight-foot steel fence protecting the Novarro property.

The police could not immediately determine whether the clothing—blue denim pants and jacket, T-shirt and undershorts—belonged to the movie actor or to his killer.

Gerald Lauritzen, a detective lieutenant of the North Hollywood division, reported that "we have at present no known suspects." He said there were no signs of forced entry and that a preliminary investigation seemed to rule out robbery as a motive.

Mr. Novarro, who never married, lived alone but was known to entertain often, including his four brothers and two sisters who live in the Los Angeles area. He also has two sisters living in Mexico and one in Spain.

Mr. Weber told reporters that he had last seen the victim at 6 P.M. yesterday and that "he seemed very well."

Lieutenant Lauritzen said that Mr. Novarro had apparently died of a severe beating about the head and upper part of his body, several hours before its discovery. No murder weapon was found.

Box-Office Svengali

Ramon Novarro was one of Hollywood's first great Latin lovers, a forerunner of generations of darkly handsome young men with flashing eyes who were considered sure-fire box-office Svengalis.

The Mexican-born star lured women to the movie houses of nearly a half century ago with such period spectaculars as "The Prisoner of Zenda," "Ben-Hur," "Scaramouche," "The Student Prince" and "The Midshipman."

He starred in dozens of films and, in the last 20 years, showed up as a character actor in several others, as well as on television shows such as "Bonanza."

He was idolized to the point that he drew the normal star's complement of police protection when he went out in public. Letters addressed merely to Mr. Ben Hur were easily expedited to him.

He co-starred with Greta Garbo ("Mata Hari," in 1932) and with Helen Hayes ("The Son-Daughter," in 1933) and was still in the radiant orbit of Hollywood beauty in 1960, when he drew good reviews for a smaller role in "Heller in Pink Tights," with Sophia Loren. His roster of leading ladies also included Norma Shearer, Myrna Loy and Alice Terry.

His fame crested in silent films and he never achieved the height of popularity in talking pictures. By 1934, Mr. Novarro, who had wanted to be an opera singer, had given up Hollywood and was devoting himself to giving concert appearances and to tending his real estate holdings.

In recent years, Mr. Novarro occasionally discussed the films of his heyday and more recent films and found that the new movies did not measure up.

"Now they kick a woman, pull her hair," he told an interviewer. "They are less of the gentleman. Our lovemaking was sexier, but it was subtle, a sentimental courtly variety. There is more vulgarity in love scenes now."

During his years of big earnings, he made $5,000 a week, much of which, untouched by income taxes in those days, he invested in real estate in the San Fernando Valley and in Mexico.

He never considered acting as the end-all of life and often confided that he wanted to direct films in order to get the feeling that what appeared was something that he himself had created. It was a feeling, he once said, that he could not achieve as an actor whose success depended upon director and cameraman.

He was always aware of the instability of popularity. He restricted himself to making two films a year in order not to wear out his welcome at the local Bijou.

"I am selling personality," he said in 1932. "When I have lost my vogue I have lost everything. Before it is too late I want to stop."

He stopped shortly after, having tried his hand at film directing and deciding to leave the movie world for good. In 1935, he produced, and appeared in, a play called "Royal Exchange." The audience and critics were scathing in the theater and in print. The venture cost him $10,000.

Mr. Novarro was born in Durango, Mexico, in 1899 into a well-to-do family. In 1913, his father, a dentist, brought his wife, five sons and four daughters to California to get away from a revolution that was sweeping the land. The first thing they found in the United States was poverty.

The star-to-be, then José Ramón Gil Samaniegos (he legally became Ramon Novarro after making it big in the movies) went to work in a grocery store and later became a theater usher, piano teacher and a bit actor in the young movie industry.

A dance impresario caught the youngster's singing act in a restaurant and hired him for her vaudeville show.

He went to New York for rehearsals, which did not pay a salary and the young actor went to work as a busboy in the Horn and Hardart Automat in Times Square to tide himself over.

When the vaudeville job was drawing to a close, the young actor got his big break, the title role in a movie called "Omar," about the Persian poet. He qualified because he was young, handsome and worked cheaply. The film was a success.

Rex Ingram, then a major Hollywood director, was beguiled by Mr. Novarro's performance and signed him to play the dashing Rupert of Hentzau in "The Prisoner of Zenda" in 1922. It was the start of a star-studded career that lasted for more than a decade.

Ramon Novarro as Ben-Hur in the 1927 silent version of the movie, with May McAvoy.

Ramon Novarro and Greta Garbo in *Mata Hari,* 1931.

The New York Times

SUNDAY, AUGUST 7, 1938.

WARNER OLAND, 57, SCREEN STAR, DIES

'Charlie Chan' of Films Victim of Pneumonia on Visit to Sweden, His Homeland

STOCKHOLM, Aug. 6 (AP).—Warner Oland, famous as an actor in Hollywood Oriental roles, died today at 3 P. M. (9 A. M., E. S. T.), at the age of 57. Death came at a Stockholm hospital where he had been ill of pneumonia.

The veteran character actor died in his homeland—he was Swedish by birth despite his Oriental features. He was stricken while on a holiday visit here.

In "The Perils of Pauline"

HOLLYWOOD, Aug. 6 (AP).—Twenty years ago movie fans sat breathless as Warner Oland tried with diabolic cunning, week after week, to kill Pearl White.

Both died in Europe, far from the scenes of the old silent movie serial thrillers in which they played—Oland near Stockholm today and Miss White in Paris two days before him.

They were the villain and heroine in the famous old serial "The Perils of Pauline."

A Native of Sweden

Warner Oland died in the land of his birth, although probably not one motion picture fan out of a hundred knew he was a native of Sweden. For so many years he had been identified with the Orient through his often sinister roles that Scandinavia, which produced Garbo, was rarely if ever credited with being the homeland of the man best known for his impersonation of Charlie Chan.

Nevertheless, Oland was a Swede. He was born in the tiny village of Umea, Vesterbotten, near the Gulf of Bothnia, on Oct. 3, 1880. He was named Johan Warner Oland, and accompanied his family to America when he was 13.

A recent studio biography credited the young Oland with a desire to be a judge. But on graduating from a Boston high school he apparently forgot it and enrolled in Curry's Dramatic School, where he sought to perfect his voice.

His first part, oddly enough, was that of Jesus. A group of Curry students were visiting backstage one day during a performance of "The Christian." The contact led to an offer to Oland to play the Saviour. He accepted, acted and sang the role successfully and subsequently made his road debut with it at $18 a week.

For fourteen years he was a trouper—in stock, in the "sticks," on Broadway. He specialized in Ibsen and Shakespeare, toured the forty-eight States and went abroad. He was still utterly unassociated with malevolent dope rings or fantastic Far Eastern detective stories, but soon, in the public mind, he was to emerge as a sort of Villain No. 1 in such tales.

Hollywood did that for him. His first screen engagement was with Theda Bara in "Jewels of the Madonna." Then came a serial called "Patria," filmed at Ithaca, N. Y., with a "Chinese general" called for. An unremembered Oriental performer was chosen, but was found too short. Oland, taller and bulkier, got the job.

That was the beginning of a career of assumed villainies which thrilled countless audiences and gave the native of a tiny Scandinavian town a chance to kill and die regularly, by knife, gun, poison or mysterious trapdoor. His films, which included some of Pearl White's, invariably pictured grotesque alleged Chinese statuary piled into unspeakable vice palaces; beaded curtains through which lethal darts flew; all manner of curved swords, venomous incense, drooping mustaches. And, of course, true to the movie code which still prevails to a certain extent, the villain had to get killed at the end. Oland got himself killed superbly in dozens of ways.

Thus it was the most dramatic paradox of his career that he should ultimately be remembered as a lovable, though improbable, detective than as a high priest of the make-believe forces outside the law. He had played Dr. Fu Manchu, a type of Oriental more in line with his previous experience, in a brief series of features prior to 1931. In March of that year he appeared as the lead in a routine film called "Charlie Chan Carries On."

Charlie Chan Carried On

He continued to play "heavies" in occasional non-Chan stories, but to a growing number of enthusiasts, he became closely identified with Earl Derr Biggers's philosophical super-sleuth. The hisses and grimaces of his long-nailed villains were swiftly forgotten as Chan's traditional "So sor-ry" and related politenesses, through Oland's reformed lips, became new box-office magic. Producers saw the handwriting; the villain Oland became increasingly a thing of the film museums. Charlie Chan carried on, even when Biggers, his creator, died on April 5, 1933.

Once in 1934 a Ronald Colman picture with Oland as an evil Oriental prince, and the gentle and righteous Chan in another adventure, reached Broadway simultaneously. But aside from such a brief session of incongruous competition with himself, Oland's Chan continued to make remarks like, "Perfect case, like perfect doughnut, has hole." while nobody even bothered to remember what he said as one of the wickeder Chinese. Charlie Chan not only routed the former stock conception of an Oland role, but virtually caused the actor to lose his own identity.

When late in his career he visited China, the ancient people whom he had imitated so successfully greeted him as Chan and apparently regarded him as a native—or at least so he reported on his return.

Last January he was suspended by Twentieth Century-Fox for having walked off the set. A few days later indications were that worry over a separate maintenance suit brought by his wife after thirty years of married life had led to a nervous breakdown. The "runaway" was found at his home in Hollywood—where he lived only while making a picture. He had a Connecticut farm and a Sout western island estate. Mrs. Olan who was about to go to his Stoc holm bedside when the news of h death came, was the former Edi Shearn, painter and actress.

Some of His Pictures

His pictures included "Don Q "The Jazz Singer," "Old S Francisco," "Chinatown Nights "Wheels of Chance," "The Myster ous Dr. Fu Manchu," "The Retur of Dr. Fu Manchu," "So This Marriage," "Riders of the Purp Sage," "Flower of the Night, "Don Juan" (pioneer Vitaphor film), "The Marriage Clause, "Tell It to the Marines," "Twinkl toes."

Also "Infatuation," "When a Ma Loves," "Stand and Deliver," " Million Bid," "Good Time Charley, "The Scarlet Lady," " Dream Love," "The Studio Murder My tery," "The Mighty," "Dangerou Paradise," "The Vagabond King, "The Black Camel," "Daughter the Dragon," "The Big Gamble, "Charlie Chan's Chance," "Shan hai Express," "A Passport to Hell."

Also "The Son-Daughter," "Cha lie Chan's Greatest Case," "Befor Dawn," "As Husbands Go," "Ma dalay," "Bulldog Drummond Strike Back," "Charlie Chan's Courage, "Charlie Chan in London," "Cha lie Chan in Paris," "The Werewo of London," "Charlie Chan i Egypt," "Shanghai," "Charlie Cha in Shanghai" (an entirely differer picture), "Charlie Chan's Secret, "Charlie Chan at the Circus, "Charlie Chan at the Opera, "Charlie Chan at the Racetrack, "Charlie Chan at the Olympics, "Charlie Chan on Broadway" an "Charlie Chan at Monte Carlo."

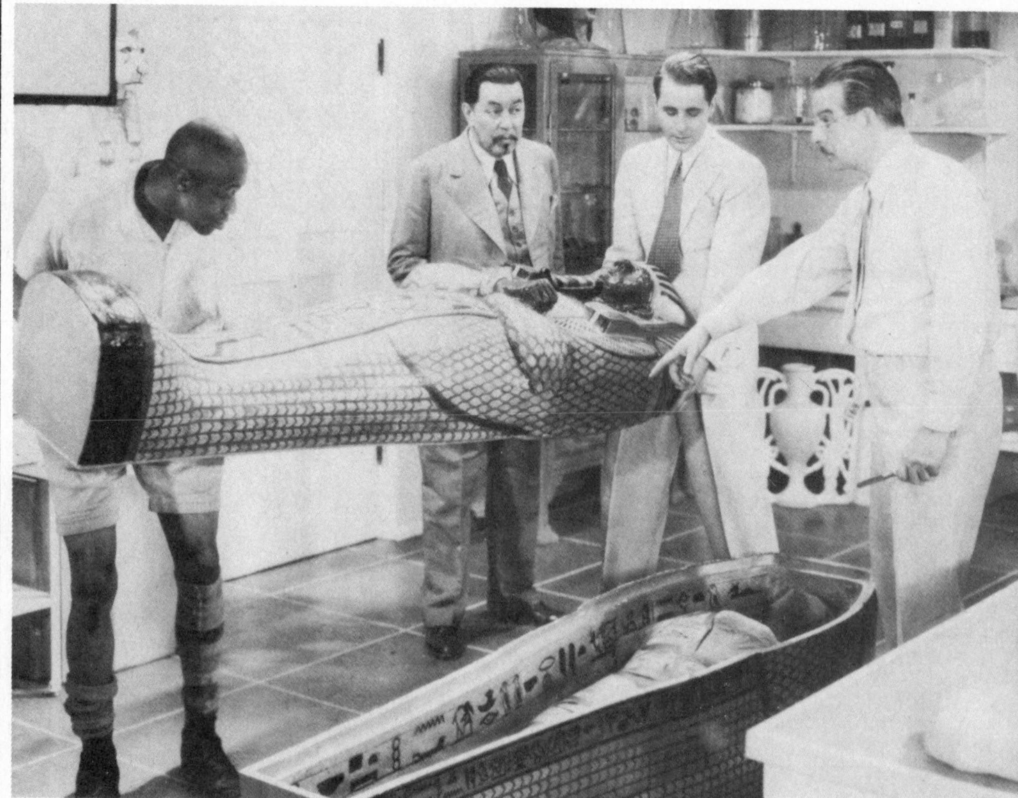

Charlie Chan in Egypt featured Stepin Fetchit, Warner Oland, Thomas Beck and Frank Conroy

The New York Times TUESDAY, APRIL 15, 1975

Larry Parks, Actor, Is Dead; Won Acclaim for 'Jolson Story'

Was the First Star to Admit Communist Membership in 1951 House Inquiry

Larry Parks, the actor who reached Hollywood stardom with his forceful performance in "The Jolson Story" in 1946 but whose acting career all but came to a halt in 1951 when he admitted past membership in the Communist party, died Sunday night of a heart attack in his home in Studio City, Calif. He was 60 years old.

With his acting career in decline after he became the first movie star to admit he had been a Communist, in an appearance before the House Committee on Un-American Activities, Mr. Parks found occasional stage and film work, but in recent years had made his living in real estate.

His wife, the actress Betty Garrett, whose career was also adversely affected by her husband's tearful admission that he had been a Communist from 1941 to 1945, although she was in no way connected with the party, is now seen regularly as Archie Bunker's neighbor Irene in television's "All in the Family" series.

Mr. Parks was born Dec. 3, 1914, in Olathe, Kan. Two childhood illnesses left him with a weakened heart and one leg slightly shorter than the other, but movie audiences were unaware of the latter defect because he wore special shoes.

The doctors who guided his recovery to good health inspired Mr. Parks to study medicine at the University of Illinois, but the acting bug bit him there and he wound up in New York, working as an usher at Carnegie Hall and a uniformed guide in Radio City while looking for work in the theater.

Mr. Parks became associated with the old Group Theater in the nineteen-thirties, playing small roles, and toured in summer stock. With the aid of the late John Garfield, he was signed on as a low-paid contract player at Columbia Pictures, where, beginning with "Mystery Ship" in 1941, he appeared in some 30 low-budget "B" pictures, with such forgettable titles as "The Boogie Man Will Get You," "Hello Mom," "Atlantic Convoy" and "Sergeant Mike."

How the hard-working Mr. Parks won the plum role in the Jolson biography reads like one of those stereotyped Hollywood star-is-born stories. It is said that Columbia interviewed and tested dozens of actors and Jolson-imitators for the Al Jolson role, and ended up finding the right man right there at Columbia.

In any event, the movie, in which Mr. Jolson did the actual singing of some two dozen songs "lip-synched" by Mr. Parks, was an enormous hit when it was released, and the new Columbia star was put immediately into "Down to Earth" opposite the studio's reigning queen of the lot, Rita Hayworth. And, following a protracted legal battle with Columbia over the money terms of his contract, Mr. Parks made the popular sequel "Jolson Sings Again" in 1948.

After his film carer went into eclipse following his "'confession," Mr. Parks appeared in a few pictures made abroad, including his last, John Huston's "Freud," in 1963, in which he had a feature role.

Besides Miss Garrett, whom he married in 1944, Mr. Parks is survived by two sons, Garrett Christopher and Andrew Lawrence.

Larry Parks with William Demarest in *The Jolson Story.*

Larry Parks as Al Jolson in *The Jolson Story,* 1946.

The New York Times

SATURDAY, JUNE 8, 1963.

ZaSu Pitts, Actress, Dies at 63; Talkies Turned Her to Comedy

Quavering Drawl Barred Her From Drama—Silent Role in 'Greed' Won Acclaim

Special to The New York Times

HOLLYWOOD, June 7—ZaSu Pitts, the motion-picture actress, died of cancer this morning at the Good Samaritan Hospital, where she was admitted yesterday. She was 63 years old.

The comedienne was the wife of John E. Woodall. She lived with her husband, a real-estate broker, in Pasadena.

A previous marriage, to Thomas S. Gallery, ended in divorce. The couple's daughter, Ann, was born in 1923. The same year, they adopted a boy, Don Mike, the son of the late actress Barbara La Marr.

Voice Evoked Laughter

ZaSu Pitts was a delicate, reedlike woman with plaintive eyes, a drooping mouth, fluttering hands and a whimpering drawl. From the beginning of talking motion pictures, the first syllable she uttered on the screen was a signal for audience laughter.

More than any of her other characteristics, the voice established her identity and turned her into one of the screen's most celebrated comediennes. It was also her voice that ruined her career as a serious actress—a career so promising that Eric Von Stroheim once called her "the screen's greatest tragedienne."

In 1925, when Miss Pitts was still a struggling ingénue in Hollywood, the temperamental German-born director cast her as the neurotic, avaricious Trina in his adaptation of Frank Norris's deterministic novel "McTeague." The film that emerged, "Greed," originally ran for eight grim hours but was cut by Metro-Goldwyn-Mayer to two.

Mr. Von Stroheim disowned the mutilated version, but film critics and historians long ago agreed that "Greed" was one of the finest films ever made, and that Miss Pitts's performance in it was an extraordinary achievement.

'Not Sexy Enough'

Later the actress liked to recall that the studio had complained about her casting, considering her "not sexy enough for the role."

It is true that neither "Greed" nor Miss Pitts attained box-office popularity during the silent era, but the director, undaunted, cast her as the pathetic lame princess in "The Wedding March." Again her performance earned critical acclaim.

When sound revolutionized the industry, Miss Pitts, like many other film players, thought her career was at an end. Her last silent role had been with Emil Jannings in a somber drama called "The Sins of the Father," but her high-pitched, cracking voice made similar talking roles unthinkable.

Her friend Ruth Chatterton recommended her for a comic supporting part in "The Dummy," and Miss Pitts found herself in a new career.

As a comedienne, she soon became more popular than ever. Audiences guffawed at her antics in slapstick farces with Thelma Todd. They liked her bits with Jeanette MacDonald in Ernst Lubitsch's "Monte Carlo" and with the Lunts in their only film appearance, "The Guardsman." In 1929 and 1930, her first two years as a "talking" actress, she made 21 films.

But when Miss Pitts attempted a return to serious drama, as Lew Ayres's bereaved mother in "All Quiet on the Western Front," she received a bitter disappointment. At a preview of the film, audiences could not reconcile her comic image with her role, and they laughed at her death scene.

The producers reshot her scenes with another actress, and Miss Pitts was typed as a fluttery comedienne for the rest of her life.

'Hundreds' of Roles

Miss Pitts appeared in more film roles than she could remember. In 1939, she estimated the number "in the hundreds."

Her first role, in 1917, was with Mary Pickford in "The Little American." Her last, as a telephone operator in "It's a Mad, Mad, Mad, Mad World," has not yet been released. Perhaps her best role as a comedienne was in "Ruggles of Red Gap," as the Western maid who married the perfect British butler, Charles Laughton.

Miss Pitts made her Broadway debut, after several unsuccessful tries out of town, in 1944 in "Ramshackle Inn." Critics thought the play deserved its adjective, but Miss Pitts received her usual good notices. In 1953, she starred in a short-lived revival of "The Bat." She also made many television appearances in the nineteen-fifties, most notably in "The Gale Storm Show."

ZaSu Pitts was born in Parsons, Kan., on Jan. 3 1900, and she moved with her family to Santa Cruz, Calif., as a child.

She attended the public schools of Santa Cruz, and a little later, armed with a gift of mimicry that had attracted attention among the family's friends, she went to Hollywood to look for a job.

Miss Pitts received her unusual first name, ZaSu, in an unusual way, and she was fond of telling the story. Her mother had two sisters, Susan and Eliza, of whom she was extremely fond. When the time came to christen the baby, Mrs. Pitts could not decide after which aunt to name the child, so she compromised by taking the first syllable of one name and the last syllable of the other.

ZaSu Pitts starred with Slim Summerville in *They Just Had To Get Married.*

ZaSu Pitts as Trina in *Greed.*

"All the News That's Fit to Print"

The New York Times.

THE WEATHER
U.S. Weather Bureau Reports (Page 8) forecast:
Los Angeles: Partly cloudy in morning, sunny in afternoon.
San Francisco: Fair.
Seattle: Fair in morning, cloudy in afternoon with a chance of rain.

VOL. CXII....No. 38,331. © 1963 by The New York Times Company. NEW YORK, FRIDAY, JANUARY 4, 1963. Air delivery in Alaska & Hawaii 25 cents. Air delivery in Canada & Mexico ... P TEN CENTS

FREEMAN MEETS WITH PRESIDENT ON FARM ISSUES

They Discuss Critical Need for Favorable Vote in '63 on Wheat Referendum

TALK OF FOREIGN SALES

Levels of Price Supports in Common Market Found Threat to Earnings

By TOM WICKER
Special to The New York Times.

PALM BEACH, Fla., Jan. 3 — President Kennedy and Secretary of Agriculture Orville L. Freeman conferred today on the crucial questions of maintaining United States farm sales in the Common Market, and new production controls for feed grains, butter and cotton.

Mr. Freeman submitted a year-end report to the President, setting forth what he called "very significant advances" in several areas.

Among them were the strengthening of farm income, a reduction by more than 700,000,000 bushels in the grain surplus and by more than $300,000 in the costs of handling the surplus, the maintenance of stable food prices to the consumer, and the beginning of a massive rural development program to counter rural poverty and convert productive farm land into grassland, forests and recreation area.

Critical Issues Discussed

But it was on three critical problems ahead for 1963 that Mr. Freeman and the President concentrated in their 90-minute conference at the holiday White House.

These were the wheat referendum scheduled in May or June; negotiations with the Common Market on maintaining United States sales in Western Europe, a major source of dollar earnings; and needed legislation for feed grains, dairy products and cotton.

The Secretary told reporters the referendum would be "critical and important." If two-thirds of the farmers voting fail to approve the Administration's program, already approved by Congress, wheat production would be unlimited, price supports would fall, and the price of wheat would tumble to $1 a bushel, Mr. Freeman said.

The result of such a glut of low-priced wheat, he added, would be disastrous to the farm economy and would have wide repercussions on the negotiations with the Common Market, on the international wheat agreement, and on United States relations with wheat

Continued on Page 3, Column 6

FARM PROBLEMS are di... and Agriculture Secreta...

Pentagon A... Of 14% for A...

By JACK ...
Special to The New York Times.

WASHINGTON, Jan. 3 — S... S. McNamara announced today ... for an average 14 per cent pa... for...

"F... elapsed... justmen... uniform... Namara... terim s... place in... compens... been a s... to the wage... wage e... economy."

About 1,600,... workers receive... per cent pay inc... two years after...

The proposed... would affect abo... members of the ac... and retired lists. If... an average of $1,70... year to Government... costs. The pay incr... been calculated in ca... mates of an expected... spending rise in the ne... year, beginning July 1.

Approval Is Expecte...

However, officials po... out that the impact of the rise, if approved by Congre...—as most officials expect—wo... be relatively small in the fir... fiscal period, since it would no... take effect immediately.

The proposal for the pay rise was based on a study at the Pentagon and recommendations by President Kennedy's advisory panel on Federal pay systems. The report of the panel, headed by Clarence B. Randall, retired chairman of the board of the Inland Steel Company, was issued at the White House today.

The Randall committee report stressed the importance of underscoring career incentives in military service but noted that "complete and sweeping reform in military compensation is neither feasible nor desirable at the present time."

Scales Not Disclosed

The Pentagon did not disclose the pay scales it would recommend after Congress convenes next week. A spokesman said only that most of the pay increases were designed to attract men and women who, having completed their military obligations as draftees or volunteers, were faced with decisions of whether to stay in military service.

Thus it appeared that the chief beneficiaries might be officers above the rank of a first lieutenant in the Army or Air Force or a lieutenant (junior grade) in the Navy. Such officers with three years service now receive $360 a month, plus $120 a month for living quarters with dependents or $95.10 a month without dependents, as well as a subsistence allowance of $47.88 per month.

The chief pay raise benefits were expected to go to officers in the rank of major with at least 12 years of service. They and their equivalents in the Navy, lieutenant commanders, now get $550 a month; $145.05 a month for living quarters, with dependents, and $120 a month, without dependents; and

Continued on Page 5, Column 2

CONGRESS STUDIES JET PLANE AWARD

Contract of Grumman and General Dynamics May Draw M'Clellan Inquiry

Special to The New York Times

WASHINGTON, Jan. 3 — The Pentagon award of an airplane development contract to the General Dynamics Corporation may be investigated by Congress. The Grumman Aircraft Engineering Corporation of Bethpage, L.I., is an associate contractor.

Senator John L. McClellan, chairman of the Senate Permanent Investigations Subcommittee, said today that members were gathering information, as a result of certain complaints, to determine whether a full-scale investigation was warranted.

At stake is a developmental contract in a multi-billion dollar program to build a new supersonic jet fighter plane. Officially designated the F-111, it has also been known as TFX (Tactical Fighter, Experimental).

The contract award, announced last Nov. 24, raised the prospects of heavier production schedules for both General Dynamics and Grumman.

Decision Still Pending

In addition, it was expected to bring jobs to Forth Worth, Texas, where General Dynamics Convair division has a major plant, to Bethpage, and to the communities of many subcontractors who have not yet been designated.

Senator McClellan, Democrat of Arkansas, stressed that he had not yet decided upon a full investigation. The precise nature of the complaint about the F-111 was not indicated officially. It was believed to involve charges that the contract was awarded over the objections of military officials at the Pentagon. The Boeing Aircraft Company of Seattle was a close competitor for the contract.

As usual with contracts of this kind, there have been many rumors in defense-contracting and political circles that the award was made to give economic assistance to the concerns and communities involved.

Under existing regulations, defense contracts may not be awarded on economic grounds, but must go to the bidders qualified by reason of price and quality.

According to a competent source at the Pentagon, the

Continued on Page 4, Column 4

KENNEDY'S BOARD CRITICIZES BOEING

Tells Company to Abandon Fight on Union Shop

By The Associated Press.

PALM BEACH, Fla., Jan. 3 — A Presidential board severely criticized the Boeing Company's attitude toward union security today and called on the aerospace firm to "abandon its stubborn insistence" on its views.

If it had arbitration powers (which it does not), the board said it would urge a union shop in which all employes would have to join the union. That is what the International Association of Machinists sought in the dispute on which the panel reported to President Kennedy today. Lacking such power, the board said, it could only appeal to Boeing to change.

Boeing's response to the union shop proposal has been a counter-demand to drop even the presently existing maintenance-of-membership clause, which requires members to stay in the union for the duration of the contract.

While union security was the chief issue, there was also a disagreement on money matters.

In that area the board went along with Boeing's general position, suggesting pay in-

Continued on Page 8, Column 6

NEWS INDEX

GOAL IN TAX CUT NOW IS 8 BILLION EFFECTIVE JULY 1

Kennedy Plan Would Offset Part of Sum by Reducing Gas-Oil Allowance

By United Press International.

WASHINGTON, Jan. 3 — President Kennedy will ask Congress this month to enact an $8,000,000,000 tax cut, with the first reduction in individual income taxes scheduled for July 1, Congressional tax experts predicted today.

They said the President would also propose tax reform... would yield the Trea... $3,500,000,0... by closi...

If... the-... all br... tion in... by a ... less wo... persons ... 000 it w... taxes a y...

At the... sons earni... would real... saving of $3...

United Press International Radiophoto

...O JADOTVILLE: United Nations soldiers scramble across demolished ...e Lufira River as they pressed the advance toward the key mining center ... secessionist Katanga Province. Yesterday the U.N. captured Jadotville.

...Y CAIRO ...Y U.S.

...ern at ...asis ...s

...ving ...narchy ...ohammad al-Badr. ...gnition was given as part ... broader plan to negotiate a disengagement of the outside powers, the United Arab Republic and Saudi Arabia, and thus to diminish the fighting between the royalist and republican forces.

U.A.R. to Remove Troops

Simultaneously with United States recognition, the Nasser Government declared it would withdraw its troops from Yemen provided Saudi Arabia ceased supplying arms and gold to the royalists.

But neither of the Arab states has made a move toward disengagement. On the contrary, reports reaching here indicate a build-up of United Arab Republic forces in Yemen.

At the same time, Crown Prince Faisal, premier of Saudi Arabia, apparently has been encouraged by limited battle successes of royalist tribesmen and has continued aiding them. He is said to hope that the royalists will eventually bleed the Nasser troops to the point where they will withdraw.

However, Prince Faisal was thought to be aware that the Yemen conflict was not popular in his officer corps and that a

Continued on Page 2, Column 3

U.N. Capture of Key City Contrary to Thant's Order

By THOMAS J. HAMILTON
Special to The New York Times.

UNITED NATIONS, N.Y., Jan. 3 — Reliable sources said today that the capture of Jadotville by United Nations troops was carried out either without the knowledge or against the orders of Secretary General U Thant.

A spokesman for Mr. Thant said today that it was a "source of regret" that during the Jadotville operation there was "a serious breakdown in effective communication and coordination" between the United Nations headquarters in New York and its office in Leopoldville.

The spokesman's written ...ement did not specify what ...akdown" had occurred. He ... however, that "steps are ... taken to determine the ... of this lapse and to en... ...at it will not recur."

...nche Due in Congo

...nited Nations field mis... ...d operations," the ... added, "are the re... ... and are under the ...he Secretary Gener... ... will be no excep... ... principle, in the ...ewhere."

...man, in a separate ..., said that Dr. ...che, Under Secre... ...al Political Af... ... of Mr. Thant's ...nts on the Con... ...during the night ... to the Congo. ...said that Mr. ...t with Rob... ... officer in ...ieut. Gen. ...mmander ... force in ...nber of ...y and ... the

...mn 5

...Agree to Changes After Federal Criticism

By JACK GOULD
Special to The New York Times.

NEW YORK.

The Federal Trade Commission has cracked down on the major popularity-rating systems, which can spell life or death for television and radio shows.

The commission charged that the A. C. Neilsen Company, Pulse and the American Research Bureau, the statistical bibles of the broadcast worlds, had misrepresented the accuracy of their ratings and used survey techniques that invited basic errors.

The three companies have concurred in consent orders halting a variety of practices that had attracted the commission's fire.

"The agreements are for settlement purposes only and do not constitute admissions by the respondents that they have violated the law," the commission noted.

The Neilsen concern, in commenting on the action, stressed the "amicable" nature of the consent agreements.

In a formal statement, Neilsen insisted that its research methods had not been chal-

Continued on Page 5, Column 5

FRANCE DELAYING POLARIS DECISION

De Gaulle Tells Kennedy Aim Is Still National Force—U.S. to Propose Aid

By HENRY GINIGER
Special to The New York Times.

PARIS, Jan. 3 — France will make no immediate decision to accept or reject the United States offer of Polaris missiles. While discussion proceeds, she will continue to build an independent atomic striking force.

President de Gaulle conveyed this reserved attitude to President Kennedy yesterday in a message delivered by Herve Alphand, the French Ambassador in Washington.

The fact that a reply had been sent to Mr. Kennedy's proposals of Dec. 21 was made public today. At the same time, its tenor was indicated by Alain Peyrefitte, Minister of Information, after a meeting of the Cabinet under General de Gaulle.

Bohlen Begins Talks

The French position was also outlined yesterday by Foreign Minister Maurice Couve de Murville to Charles E. Bohlen, the United States Ambassador, when the latter began the first of a probably long series of discussions with French officials on atomic and other questions affecting relations between Paris and Washington.

The discussions will continue tomorrow when Mr. Bohlen will be received by General de Gaulle. It was indicated that the President will have more to say publicly on the Polaris issue when he holds a news conference Jan. 14, his first since last May.

[In Bonn, it was announced that Chancellor Adenauer would visit Paris Jan. 21 and 22 to confer with President de Gaulle on putting closer French-German cooperation into practice. West German sources said the two men would also discuss President Kennedy's proposals for a NATO nuclear force.]

According to Mr. Peyrefitte, the Polaris offer has no "current interest," in the French view, because at present France lacks both the submarines to carry the missiles and the atomic warheads to arm them.

The United States has made a separate offer to provide atomic submarines.

As for bombs, President de Gaulle told the armed forces Tuesday that 1963 would see the appearance of France's striking force. Presumably France will have a few small atomic bombs by the end of the year, but the carrying force envisaged thus far is the Mirage IV supersonic plane, deliveries of which are expected to begin at the end of the year.

French hydrogen bombs are

Continued on Page 3, Column 2

U. N. FORCES MOVE INTO JADOTVILLE, KATANGA'S 2D CITY

Loss of Mining Center Seen as a Crippling Blow to Tshombe's Secession

HE FLEES WITH TROOPS

2 Belgian Women Killed as They Ignore a Command—Plant Is Sabotaged

By Reuters.

JADOTVILLE, the Congo, Jan. 3 — United Nations forces captured this key Kantangese mining center today with scarcely a shot. Observers said that the victory spelled the end of Katanga's claims to independence from the rest of the Congo.

The United Nations forces took the city after their Indian commander led a procession of jeeps by back streets into Jadotville, the second largest city in secessionist Katanga Province.

European and African civilians dispersed, and some stray Katangese gendarmes were disarmed and taken prisoner by troops under the command of Brig. Reginald S. Noronoa.

Two Belgian women were known to have been killed. They were shot by the Indian troops as their speeding car ignored signals to stop.

Power Plant Sabotaged

Katangese forces had retreated from the city before the United Nations troops arrived. They sabotaged the Jadotville power station as they left, but the city still had water.

The United Nations forces captured five Katanga mercenaries — four Belgians and a Hungarian—in their advance on Jadotville, Indian officers said today.

Capture of the town came after Brigadier Noronoa had led his troops into the city by way of a back entrance to the huge Belgian-owned Union Miniere mining installations here.

United Nations Infantry of the 4th Madras (Indian) Regiment set out shortly after dawn from their positions on the Jadotville side of Lifura bridge, which was sabotaged by Katanga forces.

Greetings Exchanged

The Indians advanced in jeeps, which were all they could get across the river by improvised raft. Brigadier Noronoa ordered his infantry to move on foot while he personally led three jeeps—two with machine-guns and one with a recoilless rifle—entering Jadotville.

The three jeeps made their lonely and exposed way over steep hills until they reached the plant of the Union Miniere du Haut-Katanga. Four Belgian employes of the company came out with their hands up.

Brigadier Noronoa jumped out of his jeep, shook hands with them, and wished them a happy new year.

The company's local manager, Joseph Derricks, and Brigadier Noronoa then led the jeeps into Jadotville.

The Brigadier and other United Nations officers went around shaking hands with residents

Continued on Page 3, Column 3

U.S. Embassy Beset By Sect in Moscow

By THEODORE SHABAD
Special to The New York Times.

MOSCOW, Jan. 3 — Thirty-two members of a Siberian religious sect forced their way into the United States Embassy here today, complained of "religious persecution" and asked to leave the Soviet Union.

Four hours later the Russians, many of them in tears, were driven from the embassy in a Soviet Government bus after United States aides had asked the Foreign Ministry to help remove the intruders from the compound.

A spokesman said the embassy had no authority to send Soviet citizens out of the country without Soviet permission. In answer to the reporters' questions, he added that it would require a legal expert to determine whether the group could have been granted asylum on embassy grounds.

The spokesman said the em-

Continued on Page 2, Column 6

Hollywood Stirred By Death of Powell

By MURRAY SCHUMACH
Special to The New York Times.

HOLLYWOOD, Jan. 3 — Hollywood's movie and television industries were stirred today by the death of Dick Powell, who had been so influential in both these aspects of show business.

Apart from having been a movie and television star, Mr. Powell became the head of Four Star, one of the most important producers of television shows in the world.

Mr. Powell died last night at his apartment of cancer at the age of 58. His death was made particularly poignant since it followed so closely on the death of Jack Carson earlier in the day, also of cancer.

The gloom was even more intense since it followed the recent deaths of Charles Laughton and Thomas Mitchell, and was within a year or so of the passing of Gary Cooper and

Continued on Page 4, Column 2

Hollywood Stirred By Death of Powell

By MURRAY SCHUMACH
Special to The New York Times.

HOLLYWOOD, Jan. 3 — Hollywood's movie and television industries were stirred today by the death of Dick Powell, who had been so influential in both these aspects of show business.

Apart from having been a movie and television star, Mr. Powell became the head of Four Star, one of the most important producers of television shows in the world.

Mr. Powell died last night at his apartment of cancer at the age of 58. His death was made particularly poignant since it followed so closely on the death of Jack Carson earlier in the day, also of cancer.

The gloom was even more intense since it followed the recent deaths of Charles Laughton and Thomas Mitchell, and was within a year or so of the passing of Gary Cooper and

Continued on Page 4, Column 2

Powell Death Stirs Hollywood; Service Is Set for Tomorrow

Continued from Page 1, Col. 4

Clark Gable. The death of Mr. Powell raised an important business question here. Would it mean the beginning of a new era in the operations of Four Star?

The shows made by Four Star, included Westerns, private eyes and dramatic anthologies. They helped set the pattern for United States television.

Mr. Powell had been the major force in creating and expanding the company he founded in 1952, with actors David Niven and Charles Boyer.

To guard against drastic alterations at Four Star, Mr. Powell took an important step last October after he knew he had cancer. He resigned as president of the company and became chairman of the board.

Television programs now being produced by Four Star include "The Dick Powell Show," "McKeever and the Colonel," "Ensign O'Toole," "The Rifleman," and "The Lloyd Bridges Show."

Earlier shows produced by Four Star have been "The Dick Powell Zane Grey Theater," "Wanted — Dead or Alive," "Robert Taylor's Detectives," "The June Allyson Show," "The Tom Ewell Show," and "Four Star Playhouse," the first of the programs by this company.

Mr. Powell's last appearance on television was as host on his show on New Year's Day. This was taped less than a month before his death.

When, because of doctor's orders, he had to stop acting, some of the most famous stars in Hollywood volunteered to act as host for Mr. Powell for the remainder of the 1962-1963 season. The substitutes waived their enormous acting fees.

Versatile Performer

Special to The New York Times.

NEW YORK.

Dick Powell was a phenomenon of show business. While other stars quickly faded in its successive revolutions, he stayed on top, passing nimbly from movie-house master of ceremonies to juvenile crooner to "tough guy" private eye to radio and then television star and director and producer.

"I started out with two assets," he once said, "a voice that didn't drive audiences into the streets and a determination to make money. I've always worked like a dog. If you don't keep working hard in this business, you're dead."

Mr. Powell failed to mention several other notable assets — charm, good looks, executive ability and the foresight and courage it took to switch careers in good times.

Richard Ewing Powell was born Nov. 14, 1904, in Mountain View, an Arkansas village nine miles from the nearest railroad station. Ten years later, his parents, Ewing and Sallie Thompson Powell, moved with their three sons to Little Rock, where Dick grew up.

As a boy in high school, he sang in choirs and with local orchestras, organized his own dance bands and worked at a variety of odd jobs. Singing whenever he could get a night engagement, he put in a year at Little Rock College and another as a collector of nickels from coin telephones.

He left that job to join a touring band, the Royal Peacocks, and married a Little Rock girl, Maude Maund. They were divorced two years later: his wife wanted her husband to stay home.

The Royal Peacocks expired in Indiana. Mr. Powell, by then able to play horns, piano and banjo as well as sing, joined the Charlie Davis orchestra in Indianapolis, took a fling at selling real estate in the Florida boom, and returned to the Davis orchestra.

Gradually, Mr. Powell developed skill and repute in a role in which he excelled to the end, as a master of ceremonies. From 1930 to 1933 he was M. C. "straight man," comedian and singer — the word "crooner" came into being about then — at Warner Brothers' Stanley Theater in Pittsburgh.

At the same time, he worked in some vaudeville tours, radio stints and recordings. At the end, Warners brought him to Hollywood and gave him a trial in the musical "Blessed Event." His wavy haired, dimple-cheek good looks made him an overnight star, and he appeared in such musical hits as "42nd Street," "The Gold Diggers" series, (1933, 1935, 1937), "Jubilee," "Naughty But Nice" and many others.

It was the heyday of network radio, and Mr. Powell found time also to conduct and star in a major weekly program. His one venture into serious acting in the Nineteen-Thirties was as Lysander in "A Midsummer Night's Dream." He was relunctant to take on the role, and the movie critics agreed that he had been miscast.

By the early Forties, Mr. Powell had witnessed the decline of film musicals and his obsolescence as a juvenile, and laid seige to producers for different roles. In 1945, he was reborn as the private eye in R.K.O.'s "Murder, My Sweet." The picture was a hit, and Mr. Powell was off on a new career.

Successive tough-guy roles in films, radio and budding television were not enough to satisfy Mr. Powell's drive. He produced and directed movies and, with David Niven and Charles Boyer, organized and headed what became one of the country's leading producers of TV shows, Four Star Television, Inc.

As a producer, Mr. Powell had a flair for unusual, and successful casting — Jack Carson as a beatnik cafe owner, Milton Berle as a blackjack dealer, Mickey Rooney as proprietor of an automobile laundry.

Of one of Mr. Powell's productions in 1961, Jack Gould, television critic for The New York Times, commented: "There's one thing that can always be said for Dick Powell: he's a pro."

In odd moments, he occupied himself with golf, sailing, flying, puttering with automobiles and politics. A Republican, he was active in the campaign of Richard M. Nixon for Governor of California, and shared in a venture aimed at introducing paid television to his hometown, Little Rock.

The turbulence of his activities ruffled Mr. Powell's home life. His second wife, Joan Blondell, divorced him in 1944 after eight years of marriage because, she said, his telephones were always ringing. His third wife June Allyson, obtained divorce papers early in 1962 on similar grounds, but the couple was reconcilled.

Miss Blondell had a son by a previous marriage, Norman whom Mr. Powell adopted, and they also had a daughter, Ellen. He and Miss Allyson had an adopted daughter, Pamela, and a son, Ricky.

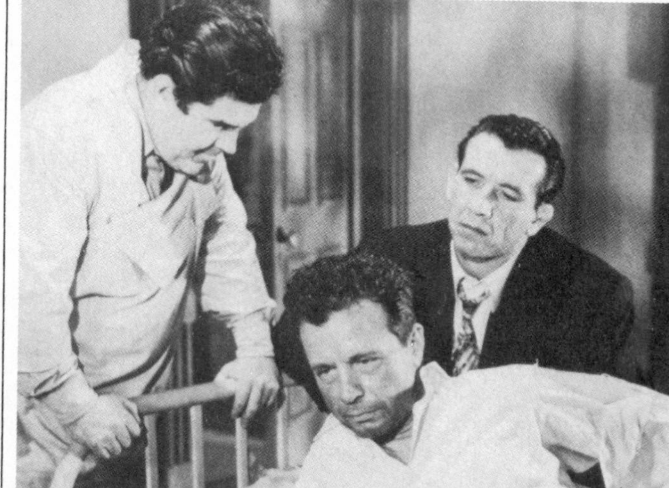

Dick Powell and Mike Mazurki in *Murder, My Sweet.*

Powell and Ruby Keeler in Busby Berkeley's *Gold Diggers of 1933.*

"All the News That's Fit to Print"

The New York Times.

LATE CITY EDITION

U. S. Weather Bureau Report (Page 95) forecasts: Partly cloudy, mild today. Partly cloudy, cooler tomorrow. Temp. range: 67-50. Yesterday: 60.6-54.8.

NEWS SUMMARY AND INDEX, PAGE 95

SECTION ONE

VOL. CVIII..No. 36,821. © 1958, by The New York Times Company. Times Square, New York 36, N. Y. NEW YORK, SUNDAY, NOVEMBER 16, 1958. TWENTY-FIVE CENTS

ECONOMISTS FIND NO SLOWING DOWN IN RECOVERY PACE

U.S. Aides Call Drop in Auto Output Temporary—Find Prospects Are Bright

SOME OTHERS DISAGREE

Slower Rise in Production, Consumer Spending and Re-employment Cited

By RICHARD E. MOONEY
Special to The New York Times.

WASHINGTON, Nov. 15—The nation's six-month-old recovery from its worst post-war recession has shown some apparent signs of slowing ... recent weeks. But ... here argue that the... not constitute a slow...

There has not been ... of a new dip. Moreo... talk of a slowdown bro... simple retort from one Go... ment economist:

"It's a lot of bunk."

The Federal Reserve Bank ... New York, in its November ... view of the business situati... said that the recovery was con... tinuing. But, it went on, "the pace of the expansion seems to have diminished somewhat since midsummer."

The review indicated doubts about what the major upward forces would be in the coming months.

It is generally assumed that any post-recession recovery will slow down some time after its initial burst.

Detroit Output a Factor

One argument raised against the belief in the slowdown is that the recent indicators cited were largely manufactured in Detroit. In the automotive city an early model change-over and sporadic strikes have produced a string of slow weeks. It is believed that the prospects for auto production this month and in the immediate future are bright enough to turn the indicators upward.

It is also argued that the initial burst of recovery was not quite so strong as advertised. Official, published estimates of the gross national product—the value of all goods and services—make it appear that three-quarters of the recession loss had been recouped by the end of September. However, unpublished estimates, which took price changes into account, put the recovery closer to one-third.

This adjustment did not alter the belief that the recovery has been widespread and strong.

The indicators that the slowdown theorists point to primarily are industrial production, employment and unemployment, and consumer spending. Gov-

Continued on Page 45, Column 1

Major Sports News

FOOTBALL

Princeton defeated Yale and Dartmouth beat Cornell yesterday to share the Ivy League lead. Scores of leading games:

Air Force	21	Wyoming	6
Alabama	17	Georgia Tech	8
Arkansas	13	S. M. U.	6
Army	26	Villanova	0
Auburn	21	Georgia	6
Boston Coll.	18	Boston U.	13
Brown	29	Harvard	22
Buffalo	34	Lehigh	26
California	12	Washington	7
Clemson	13	N. C. State	6
Dartmouth	32	Cornell	15
Duke	29	Wake Forest	0
Indiana	8	Michigan	6
Kentucky	20	Xavier	6
L. S. U.	7	Miss. State	6
Minnesota	39	Michigan St.	12
Navy	28	G. W'shington	8
Nebraska	14	Pittsburgh	6
Notre Dame	34	No. Carolina	24
Ohio St.	38	Iowa	28
Oklahoma	39	Missouri	0
Oregon St.	24	Stanford	16
Pennsylv'nia	42	Columbia	0
Penn St.	32	Holy Cross	0
Princeton	50	Yale	14
Purdue	23	Northwestern	6
Quantico	13	Rutgers	12
Syracuse	47	Colgate	0
T. C. U.	22	Texas	8
Tennessee	18	Mississippi	16
Texas A.&M.	28	Rice	21
Vanderbilt	12	Tulane	0
Wesleyan	22	Trinity	18
Williams	12	Amherst	7
Wisconsin	31	Illinois	12

HORSE RACING

Admiral Vee, $10.20, took the $38,000 Gallant Fox Handicap by a head at Jamaica.

Details in Section 5.

Leaders in Virginia

Gov. J. Lindsay Almond Jr.

Bisho... by 'S... Flow...

Text of state... is printed...

Special to The ...

WASHINGT... The Catholic ... United States ... what they said w... of "modern secular... the teaching of mora... the Roman Catholic Cl...

In a policy statemen... at their annual meeti... the Bishops reaffirme... they said was the ... "right to teach" the ... principles which flow from ... natural law and the posi... law of God."

The Bishops asserted that ... church not only had a right ... proclaim dogmatic truths bu... also to establish moral standards on such issues as birth control, divorce and education.

The statement said that there was "a genuine urgency" for dwelling on the teaching mission of the church at this time because "materialism and secularism" had made "heavy inroads on the official and popular thinking of men and nations."

The freedom of man "to accept the revelation of our Lord" is being "attacked and denied by modern secularism," the Bishops said. They said there was debate over the church's "freedom to assert her moral teaching in a world which has increasingly tended to acknowledge no objective standard."

Specifically, the Bishops noted that it had been questioned whether the church had a right to preach her own concept of

Continued on Page 70, Column 5

MOVES IN VIRGINIA HINT INTEGRATION OF SOME SCHOOLS

Almond Reported Preparing for Retreat From Massive Resistance to Mixing

By JOHN D. MORRIS
Special to The New York Times.

RICHMOND, Va., Nov. 15—The state administration has begun to prepare the ground for a probable retreat in the fight against racial integration o... public schools.

Officially Gov. J. Li... mond Jr. and his a... still ...

... ited ... been ... of inte... publishe... papers, ... nant Bry...

Almost ... Norfolk L... larly shifte... on the issu... papers hav... Norfolk Vi... posed mass... the start.

With the ... the state's ... are now adv... moderate appro...

It is unders... Richmond papers...

Continued on Page ...

Legislative Liaison Poses Key Rockefeller Problem

As Governor He Must Work With Heck and Mahoney, G. O. P. Chiefs Who Were His Rivals for Top Post

By WARREN WEAVER Jr.
Special to The New York Times.

ALBANY, Nov. 15—A task facing Governor-elect Nelson A. Rockefeller is the establishment of sound working relations with the veteran party leaders wh... will become his chief ai...

As loyal ... legisla...

...pects by accepting a position on the state ... was offered ...

NATO TO BE ASKED TO WARN RUSSIANS ON BERLIN THREAT

U. S. Also May Join Britain and France in Refusal to Leave the City

By JACK RAYMOND
Special to The New York Times.

WASHINGTON, Nov. 15—The United States plans to take the latest Soviet threats against the four-power status of Berlin to the North Atlantic Treaty Council.

The United States will seek ... have the Western alliance ... a firm declaration on Ber... ...hen the defense and for... ...inisters of the organiza... ...et in Paris next month. ...als here still believe ...ita S. Khrushchev, So... ...mier, has no intention ...ing up a military crisis ... They cited his an... ...ntention of offering ...soon on the future ...ded city.

... expected that not ...ited States, but also ... of the council, ...arn the Soviet ...rlin's status is ...rous than Leb... ...in its implica... ...eace.

...ions Cited

...ce in Ger... the general ...-West rela... ...ter World ... formation ...c Treaty ... here ... been ... and ... a ...af- ...y- ...iet

'Copter Crash Kills 7th Fleet Air Chief

Associated Press

Leonard B. Southerland

By The Associated Press.

NAHA, Okinawa, Nov. 15—Rear Admiral Leonard B. Southerland, commander of aircraft carriers of the Seventh Fleet, was killed in a helicopter crash today.

Comdr. John Coulthard and Lieut. (j.g.) John P. Loomis, pilot of the helicopter, also died in the crash.

The plane, reportedly flying into Okinawa from the aircraft carrier Lexington, came down at the edge of the

Continued on Page ., Column 3

TRAFFIC OF ALLIES AT BERLIN NORMAL

Army Convoys Are Flowing Smoothly Again Following Detention by Russians

By SYDNEY GRUSON
Special to The New York Times.

BERLIN, Nov. 15 — Allied military traffic flowed smooth...y along the rail and road ...ks between Berlin and West ...rmany today. Soviet control ...icers acted as if yesterday's ...ention of a United States ...y had never happened.

...ited States officials were ...d over how to interpret ...oviet authorities' behav... ...terday. The Russians ...e United States Army ...nd their drivers for ... one-half hours when ...can soldiers refused ...hem to inspect the ...cles.

...y trucks were ... and the Rus... ...tent to follow ...s. This meant ...ves to a look ...rders accom... ...r traffic of ...ins and ci... ...the special ... occupying ... no way ... Soviet ...rders ...kita ...re- ...of

U.S. AND RUSSIANS EACH SPURN PLANS ON NUCLEAR TESTS

Washington Says Moscow's Pact Halting Blasts Would Prove a 'Pig in a Poke'

SOVIET ACTS TOMORROW

Geneva Delegation to Reject West's Latest Move Aimed at Insuring Control of Ban

By E. W. KENWORTHY
Special to The New York Times.

WASHINGTON, Nov. 15—The United States rejected today the latest Soviet proposal for a permanent suspension of tests of nuclear weapons.

The State Department said in a statement that the rejection of a recently introduced Soviet draft treaty had been conveyed to the Soviet delegation to the current talks in Geneva on a test suspension.

[In Geneva, authoritative Soviet sources indicated that their delegation would reject on Monday the latest United States proposal for a cessation of tests under an inspection system. They said they suspected that the proposal would be used to delay negotiations while the West prepared a new series of test explosions.]

"The main intent of the Soviet treaty draft," the State Department declared, "is to conclude an agreement on permanent cessation of nuclear weapons without agreement being reached on a control system necessary to verify the paper pledge.

"In effect, the Soviet Union is asking the United States to buy 'a pig in a poke.'"

Control Issue Stressed

The State Department said, however, that this country stood ready to conclude an agreement provided that an adequate control system was specifically spelled out.

Persistent official hopes that the Soviet Union would finally agree to a control system as outlined last summer in Geneva by a meeting of experts of East and West were dimmed as the Moscow radio launched an all-out propaganda offensive for the five-point Soviet plan.

The plan as broadcast today was simply a restatement of the draft treaty introduced at the opening of the Geneva talks on Oct. 31 and made public last week by the Soviet delegation to the United Nations.

Semyon K. Tsarapkin, head of Moscow's delegation in the Geneva conference, has argued persistently for the plan in the sessions to date.

Under the Soviet plan, the three atomic powers, the United

Continued on Page 20, Column 3

MURRAY OPPOSES ATOMIC TEST BAN

Ex-A.E.C. Official Links U.S. Security to Small Arms

By JOHN W. FINNEY
Special to The New York Times.

WASHINGTON, Nov. 15—...as E. Murray, former ...ber of the Atomic Energy ...nission, urged today that ...United States continue ...testing to develop small ... weapons for limited ...

...ecurity vitally depends on continued progress in perfecting the technology of small weapons, and this progress cannot be assured without tests," Mr. Murray said.

In a speech before the annual homecoming dinner of the Alumni Association of Catholic University of America, Mr. Murray criticized the current Administration policy of seeking an atomic test suspension agreement with the Soviet Union.

Mr. Murray received the Cardinal Gibbons Medal, awarded annually for service to the

Continued on Page 19, Column 1

This section consists of 142 pages, divided into three parts. The news summary and index will be found on Page 95. Society news begins on Page 90 and obituary articles are on Pages 88 and 89.

Tyrone Power, 44, Dies in Spain; Stricken After Duel on Film Set

Associated Press Radiophoto

Tyrone Power, left, and George Sanders dueling yesterday

By The Associated Press.

MADRID, Nov. 15—Tyrone Power died here today of a heart attack after a dueling scene on a movie set of "Solomon and Sheba." His age was 44.

Mr. Power's death paralleled that of his father, Frederick Tyrone Power, who was stricken fatally on a Hollywood set in 1931. The acting tradition of the family began with his great-grandfather, Tyrone Power, who was a popular comedian on the Dublin stage in 1827. The baptismal name came from County Tyrone, Ireland.

A virtual stranger in recent years to Hollywood, where he made his fame and fortune, Mr. Power was starring in "Solomon and Sheba" with Gina Lollobrigida. He appeared on the set today for a dueling scene in the role of Solomon with George Sanders, playing the role of Solomon's older brother.

During the filming, Mr. Power complained of a pain in his left

Continued on Page 88, Column 2

Strike of TV and Radio Ac... Deferred to Tuesday in Pa...

By RICHARD F. SHEPARD

Negotiations to avert a nation-wide television and radio strike early this morning resulted in a seventy-two-hour extension of the strike deadline.

The four leading broadcasting networks and the American Federation of Television and Radio Artists "stopped the clock," keeping performers and announcers on the job despite the expiration of the old contract at midnight.

A new strike deadline was set for midnight Tuesday. A condition of the extension was that taped programs made between today and Tuesday could not be broadcast in the event of a strike.

Another negotiating session was set for 5 P. M. Tuesday.

"Quite a bit of agreement" was reported from the all-day session, which was held in the offices of the Columbia Broadcasting System at 485 Ma... Avenue. The talks were rece... at 2:45 A. M. today.

Progress toward a new co... tract was said to be "substan... tial." The talks centered o... counter-proposals made by the networks to the union's demands. Although there was still disagreement on many of the issues, no deadlock was reported.

Last week, authority was voted to the national board of directors of the 12,000-man federation to call a strike at any time after the midnight expiration time of the contract.

The dispute affects the radio and television networks of the American Broadcasting Company, the Columbia Broadcasting System and the National Broadcasting Company, as well

Continued on Page 87, Column 1

...ciated Press.

M... ...yrone Powe... today of a heart attack after a dueling scene on a movie set of "Solomon and Sheba." His age was 44.

Mr. Power's death paralleled that of his father, Frederick Tyrone Power, who was stricken fatally on a Hollywood set in 1931. The acting tradition of the family began with his great-grandfather, Tyrone Power, who was a popular comedian on the Dublin stage in 1827. The baptismal name came from County Tyrone, Ireland.

A virtual stranger in recent years to Hollywood, where he made his fame and fortune, Mr. Power was starring in "Solomon and Sheba" with Gina Lollobrigida. He appeared on the set today for a dueling scene in the role of Solomon with George Sanders, playing the role of Solomon's older brother.

During the filming, Mr. Power complained of a pain in his left

Continued on Page 88, Column 2

...WITKIN
...New York Times.

...v. 15—... has cleared up ...ystery that set the Caribbean island of Barbados abuzz last Oct. 17.

On that day the fishing boat Tip Top came upon an odd globular object bobbing in the water about two miles off shore.

It contained some miniature instruments and a plastic tape protected by a thick cover of foam rubber. It had two antennae jutting from the top and a lead weight at the bottom.

The crewmen broke open the sphere on the beach. But the owner of the boat had the foresight to stop this dismemberment and call the police. A security blackout was promptly imposed.

The Ballistics Missile Division of the United States Air Force told the story today. The object was a capsule ejected from the nose cone of an Atlas intercontinental missile launched on Aug. 2 from Cape Canaveral, Fla., seventy-six days before its recovery.

With all three engines functioning successfully for the first time in the Atlas program, the Atlas hurled its blunt, copper-tipped nose cone far past Antigua, to a point unofficially put at about 2,500 miles southeast of the launching site.

As the nose cone plunged earthward, it ejected a spherical capsule about a foot and a half in diameter.

A device inside was to record on tape information on how the

Continued on Page 19, Column 4

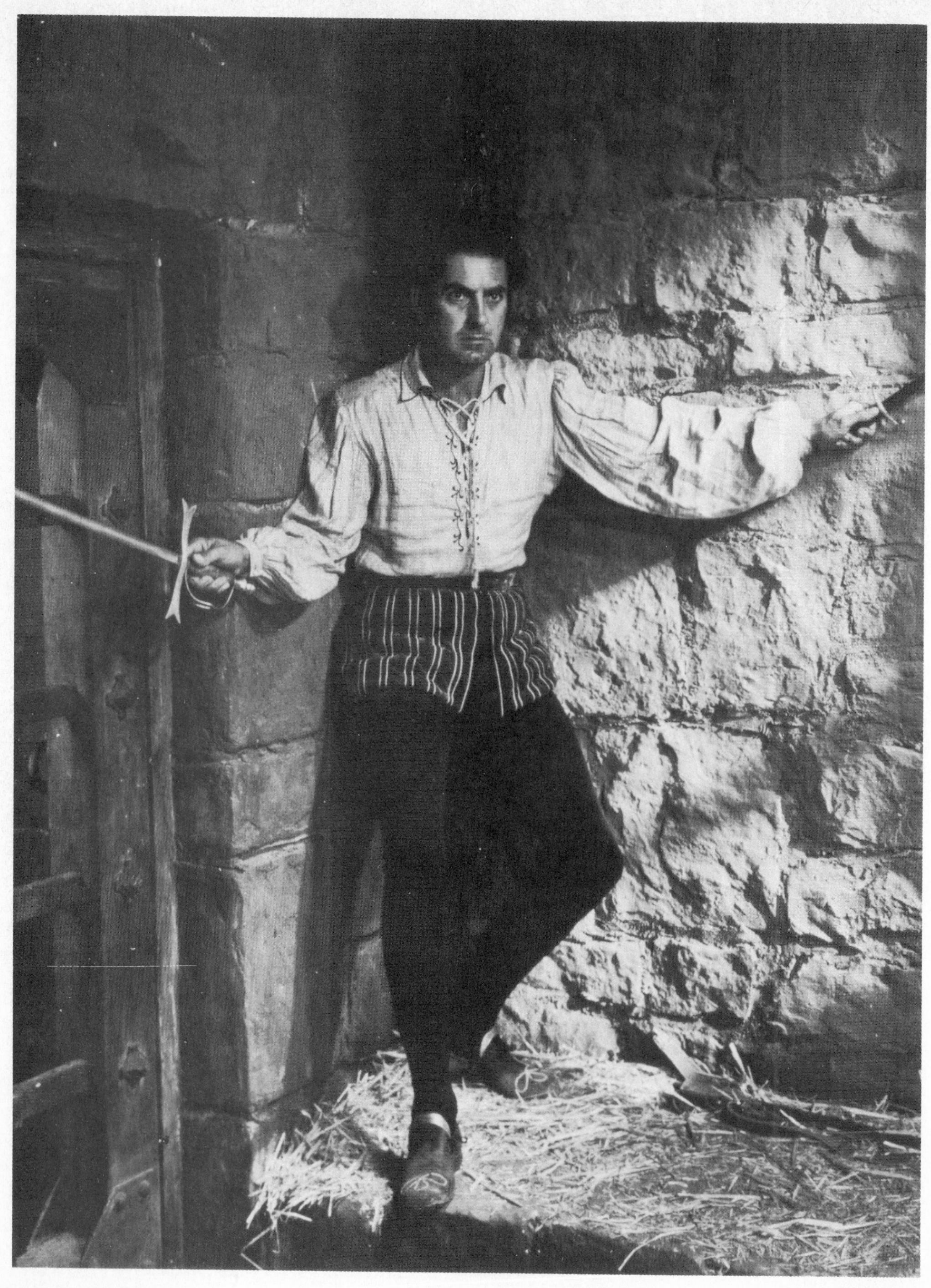

Tyrone Power in *The Captain from Castile.*

Tyrone Power, 44, Dies in Spain; Stricken After Duel on Film Set

Continued From Page 1, Col. 5

arm and abdomen. He was rushed to a hospital at 11:30 A. M., and died within an hour.

Mr. Power's third wife, the former Mrs. Deborah Minardos, was with him here. She is expecting a child in February. They were married early this year.

The body of the actor was transferred tonight by funeral coach from the hospital to the United States Torrejon Air Force Base. A funeral service will be held there tomorrow.

Mrs. Power intends to fly to Hollywood in a chartered plane with her husband's body. The date of departure has not yet been fixed.

In Palm Springs, Calif., Edward Small, producer of "Solomon and Sheba," said today it was too early to determine whether the film would have to be scrapped because of Mr. Power's death.

"It was about two-thirds completed," Mr. Small said. "We started shooting Sept. 15 and planned to finish Dec. 15."

He said films sometimes could be completed by a double if all close-ups had been made.

Won Reputation on Stage

Hollywood hardly noticed Tyrone Power when he started making the rounds of casting offices in 1931. Five years later, however, he was signed to a seven-year contract on the basis of his reputation as an actor on the Broadway stage.

Katharine Cornell gave Mr. Power his start here as general understudy to the three male leads in "Flowers of the Forest" in 1935. His salary was $30 a week. A year later he was seen as Benvolio in "Romeo and Juliet" and as Bertrand de Poulengy in "Saint Joan," with Miss Cornell as the star in both plays.

Then came the return to Hollywood to carry on the tradition set by Rudolph Valentino and Douglas Fairbanks Sr. Mr. Power won immediate success with one of his first pictures, "Lloyds of London," in 1936. In 1941 he played the bullfighter in "Blood and Sand," the role Valentino had in the original production twenty years earlier.

By this time, Mr. Power's success had added more than a few pounds to his lanky, 6-foot frame. But a year later he was back in fighting trim as a transport pilot with the Marine Corps. He spent four years on duty in the Pacific and at his death held the rank of major in the Marine Corps Reserve.

Mr. Power was born in Cincinnati on May 5, 1914. His grandfather, Harold Power, was a Shakespearean actor. At 7, he was a supporting player to his father in a play given at the San Gabriel Mission. While his father coached him in dramatics, his mother, whose stage name was Patia Power, helped him to perfect his voice and diction.

After the season with Miss Cornell, Mr. Power was signed to a contract with Twentieth Century-Fox. His association with the company spanned nineteen years, with time out for his war service.

Generally, Mr. Power was the dashing rescuer of the lady in distress. He was serious and rather stiff, but darkly handsome and always ready to swing across the courtyard, if necessary, to meet his pursuers in head-on battle.

Mr. Power broke away from Fox in 1955 to form an independent company, Copa Productions, with Ted Richmond, a Hollywood director, as his partner.

In the more than forty films in which Mr. Power starred, critics occasionally found fault with his characterizations and the unyielding solemnity with which he played each role. But his voice, with its vibrant deepness, was his greatest asset.

He used it to advantage when he returned to Broadway in 1953 to join Judith Anderson and Raymond Massey in a concert reading of "John Brown's Body." The production of Stephen Vincent Benét's poetic narrative at the Century Theatre was directed by Charles Laughton.

Although Mr. Power was a movie idol for the generation of bobby-soxers, and the top box-office star in Hollywood in 1940, he never felt far from the stage. In 1950 he spent six months in London playing the lead in "Mister Roberts."

In 1955 he played opposite Miss Cornell in Christopher Fry's verse drama "The Dark Is Light Enough" at the ANTA Theatre on Broadway. A year later he was in Shaw's "The Devil's Disciple" in Dublin. Early this year, he returned to Broadway again in Shaw's "Back to Methuselah."

However the bulk of Mr. Power's career was on film in such vehicles as "The Captain From Castile," "The Sun Also Rises," "King of the Khyber Rifles," "The Eddie Duchin Story," "Abandon Ship," and "Witness for the Prosecution." He also played Sgt. Marty Maher, West Point's venerable athletic trainer, in "The Long Gray Line."

Earlier pictures included "The Mark of Zorro," "Rose of Washington Square," "Suez," "Jesse James" and "Nightmare Alley." He also starred in "The Rains Came" and "The Black Swan," and had the lead roles in "The Razor's Edge," "An American Guerrilla in the Philippines," "The Mississippi Gambler" and "This Above All."

Mr. Power met his first wife, the French actress Annabella, when he joined her in the cast of "Suez." They were married in 1939 and divorced in 1948. A year later he married Linda Christian, another actress, in Rome, where his fans ran wild after the ceremony. Miss Christian is the mother of his two daughters, Romina Francesca, 7, and Taryn, 5. The marriage was dissolved in 1956.

Tyrone Power died of a heart attack while filming *Solomon and Sheba.*

Tyrone Power and Annabella in *Suez.*

The New York Times WEDNESDAY, MAY 31, 1967

Claude Rains, Film Star, Dead; Began Career on London Stage

'Caesar and Cleopatra' and 'The Invisible Man' Were Among Actor's Hits

SANDWICH, N. H., May 30 (UPI) — Claude Rains, the white-haired actor who rose from a $2-a-week page boy to become the first British stage and film star to earn $1-million for a single role, died of an intestinal hemorrhage today in nearby Lakes Region Hospital. He was 77 years old.

Mr. Rains received that sum for his portrayal of Julius Caesar in a 1944 film of Shaw's "Caesar and Cleopatra."

Survivors include two daughters.

World-Weary Aristocrat

Claude Rains failed the screen test for his first film in 1933. It was "the worst in the history of moviemaking," he said later.

But the director said "I don't care what he looks like, that's the voice I want," and Mr. Rains got the title role in H. G. Wells's "The Invisible Man" and his start in films.

He went on to more visible film roles—56 in the next three decades—and although his resonant, menacing voice remained a trademark, his face, too, became familiar to millions of Americans.

Mr. Rains was cast in his first films as a villain, but he soon showed he could handle varied roles. The dominant film-image of him, however, is probably as a suave world-weary aristocrat. "I can play the butcher, the baker, or the candlestick maker," he once said.

In his last film, in 1962, he played the British diplomat in "Lawrence of Arabia."

Mr. Rains was one of those film stars universally hailed as true professionals who somehow never won an Academy Award, although he was nominated four times—for his roles in "Mr. Smith Goes to Washington," "Casablanca," "Mr. Skeffington" and "Notorious." For what was perhaps his most distinguished portrait of cold-blooded villainy, his role in "Anthony Adverse," he was not even nominated.

Appeared Often on TV

At Warner Brothers in the late nineteen-thirties, Mr. Rains hit a prolific stride in featured characterizations that for color, flair and continuity could be matched by few players today.

And as his televised movies won him new following, he made frequent dramatic appearances in the newer medium and retained a firm foothold on his first love, the stage. In all three media, the 5-foot 7-inch actor projected a towering, dominant personality.

He was conscious of his shortness, however. (He played some scenes in "Notorious," with Ingrid Bergman, standing on a ramp. Mr. Rains once told a friend: "All the years in the theater I used to pray at night that I would wake up with about three inches added to my height."

Mr. Rains was born Nov. 10, 1890, in London, the son of a well-known stage player, Frederick Rains, and of Emily Rains. He made his first stage appearance at the age of 11 in "Sweet Nell of Old Drury."

He became a theater call boy, a prompter and a stage and company manager. He had little formal education.

In 1913 he made his first trip to this country, as an actor and company manager of a British repertory company. He served in a Scottish regiment during World War I and, upon returning to the London stage, won acclaim for roles in "The Government Inspector," "Julius Caesar" and "The Man of Destiny."

While teaching at the Royal Academy of Dramatic Art in 1926, Mr. Rains married one of his pupils, Isabel Jeans, whom American moviegoers know best as the briskly realistic aunt in the movie musical "Gigi."

The marriage ended in divorce (as did four of his five subsequent marriages). After the couple co-starred in the United States, in "The Constant Nymph." Mr. Rains remained here appearing in such Theater Guild plays as "Volpone," "Marco's Millions" and "The Apple Cart."

In "The Invisible Man," made at the Universal Studios, Mr. Rains was seen only briefly in the beginning and at the final moment, when the H. G. Wells scientist-hero materialized on his deathbed. Convinced that the picture would be a failure, Mr. Rains retreated East to his New Jersey farm and made a film in New York, "Crime Without Passion," which won critical praise, but failed at the box office.

In the meantime, "The Invisible Man" became a huge success "Anthony Adverse," in 1936, established the actor as a solid Hollywood fixture, complementing and bolstering a steady succession of features and teaming him with such stars as Bette Davis, Vivien Leigh, Ann Sheridan and Ingrid Bergman.

In 1946, when four films in which he was starring were showing on Broadway at the same time, Bosley Crowther of The New York Times quipped, "It never rains, but what it pours."

In 1951 Mr. Rains made a triumphant return to the Broadway stage in the dramatization of Arthur Koestler's novel, "Darkness at Noon."

His performance as the old Bolshevik who was imprisoned, forced to admit doctrinal errors and executed, won six of the year's most coveted stage awards, including the best-actor citation by the New York Drama Critics Circle.

In recent years Mr. Rains's television roles were numerous, ranging from a modern-dress version of "Antigone" to a lighthearted "Pied Piper of Hamelin." He also made dramatic recordings. Perhaps the most outstanding was the spoken commentary of Richard Strauss's "melodrama for piano" titled "Enoch Arden," with a piano counterpoint provided by Glenn Gould.

In 1964 Mr. Rains's contemplated return to the stage in "So Much of Earth, So Much of Heaven" was prevented by his own illness and by the death of his sixth wife, the former Rosemary Clark.

The couple resided in Sandwich, N. H., where Mrs. Rains had been helping her husband write his autobiography.

Mr. Rains's second wife was Marie Hemingway; his third, Beatrix Lindsay Thomas; his fourth, Frances Propper, by whom he had a daughter, Jennifer; and his fifth, Agi Jambor.

He became a United States citizen in 1938.

Although acting was his profession, farming was his avocation, and he owned a 350-acre farm in Bucks County for many years before moving to Sandwich a few years ago.

Stewart Granger, Basil Sydney, Vivien Leigh and Claude Rains in *Caesar and Cleopatra*.

Claude Rains and William Harrigan in *The Invisible Man*, 1933. Rains made his film debut in this movie in which his face was never shown.

"All the News That's Fit to Print"

The New York Times

LATE CITY EDITION

Weather: Warm, humid, chance of showers today, tonight. Fair, warm Sun. Temp. range: today 84-68. Fri. 80-68. Temp.-Hum. Index 75. Fri. 76. Full U.S. report on Page 52.

VOL. CXVI..No. 39,991 NEW YORK, SATURDAY, JULY 22, 1967 10 CENTS

DEFICIT IN BUDGET HITS $9.9-BILLION AS WAR COSTS RISE

Exceeds Johnson's Original Estimate for Fiscal Year 1967 by $8.1-Billion

BELOW REVISED FIGURE

$11-Billion Indicated in May —Final Total 2d Highest Since World War II

By EDWIN L. DALE Jr.
Special to The New York Times

WASHINGTON, July 21—The deficit in the Government's ordinary administrative budget in the fiscal year 1967, ended June 30, was $9.9-billion, the Treasury and Budget Bureau disclosed today.

This was the second largest deficit since World War II, exceeded only by the $12.4-billion deficit in the fiscal year 1959. But because the economy has grown tremendously in the last six years, this deficit was smaller in relation to the nation's total output than several earlier ones.

A $9.7-billion deficit was estimated last January, and an updated estimate of $11-billion was presented to Congress in May.

While these changes were relatively small, the deficit and the entire expenditure picture of the Government were drastically different from the original estimates for the fiscal year, presented in January, 1966.

Expenditures Higher

At that time the President estimated expenditures at $112.8-billion and receipts at $111-billion for a deficit of $1.8-billion.

Expenditures turned out to be $125.7-billion and receipts were $115.8-billion, for the deficit of $9.9-billion. By far the most important element in the higher expenditures was the cost of the war in Vietnam.

Defense expenditures were estimated 18 months ago at $58.3-billion, of which $10.4-billion was figured for Vietnam. These expenditures hit $68.4-billion, of which about $20-billion was accounted for by the war. There was no official separation of the war cost in today's report.

This miscalculation was essentially conceded by the time of last January's budget. This more recent estimate was $470-million below the eventual outlay, which was not considered a large difference in a total as big as $68-billion.

Decline in Spending

There were numerous other changes in the final results as compared with last January's estimates. The net change was a drop of $1-billion in expenditures.

Receipts were $1.2-billion below the January estimate, partly because personal income taxes were $700-million less than estimated.

Expenditures in the cash budget were put at $155.3-billion in the fiscal year 1967 and receipts at $153.5-billion, for a deficit of $1.8-billion.

This budget includes the operations of the Government's trust funds for such programs

Continued on Page 9, Column 5

Basil Rathbone, 75, Dies at Home Here

Basil Rathbone, the suave Shakespearean actor who won motion-picture fame in the early nineteen-forties as the detective Sherlock Holmes—and regretted the identification the rest of his life—died of a heart attack yesterday.

The tall, impeccably mannered actor, who was 75 years old, was found dead on the floor of his study at his home, 135 Central Park West, by his daughter, Cynthia. She said her father had suffered a heart seizure several years ago, but had appeared to be in good health.

Mr. Rathbone had been in the theater and the movies for more than 50 years, in roles that ranged from Shakespeare's Romeo to the snobbish Boston brahmin in "The Last Hurrah,"

Continued on Page 25, Column 4

Hatred and Pity Mix In Views of Whites On Newark Negroes

By RICHARD REEVES
Special to The New York Times

NEWARK, July 21—White citizens of this city's 405,000 residents speak with a confused mixture of hatred, fear and compassion about Negroes who rioted here for five days.

More than 150 interviews with white people—who form a minority of Newark's total population — showed that some residents and merchants are planning to leave, and that many homeowners are attempting to buy weapons. Most of the white people interviewed spoke of Negroes with open hatred.

But, at the same time, there were Newarkers who called Negroes "good people and good neighbors." And there were residents of the city and its prosperous suburbs who formed or joined organizations to help Negro victims of the riot.

Agnes Coleman, a real estate agent in the predominantly white North Ward,

Continued on Page 10, Column 3

ENGLEWOOD BES[ET] BY BRIEF VIOLENC[E]

3 Policemen Hurt Quelling Negro Youths—Troops Sent Into Minneapolis

Special to The New York Times

ENGLEWOOD, N. J., Saturday, July 22—A brief outbreak of violence began in the predominantly Negro section of this city late last night and spread to the main shopping area. Three policemen and a youth were injured and a dozen store windows were shattered.

But the disorders were quickly quelled by the police and public officials, who had been alerted to impending trouble by anonymous telephone calls earlier in the day.

[In Minneapolis, National Guardsmen moved into the racially troubled North Side as fire broke out for the third straight night. Page 11.]

By early this morning in Englewood, several hours after its first outburst, only a few Negroes were seen on the streets, and the main shopping area, along Palisade Avenue, was lined with policemen from Englewood and other Bergen communities and with Bergen County policemen armed with pump-action shotguns.

No Looting Reported

But the police reported early today that there had been no looting and no arrests.

City officials reported that no more than 150 Negroes, mostly teen-agers, were involved in the disturbance that began about 9 P.M., when rocks shattered a plate-glass window in a food market at William and Jay Streets, in the predominantly Negro Fourth Ward.

A burglar alarm, touched off by the breaking of the window in the market, brought policemen to the scene. They said they found a milling crowd of about 35 teen-agers. A scuffle ensued, the police said, that resulted in injuries to Patrolman Peter Timpone and Detective Kenneth J. Tinsley of the Englewood police, and to William Hillgardner of the Bergen County force.

The police said the three had been struck by objects thrown during the brief fight.

None of the three was seriously injured, although all were taken to Englewood Hospital for treatment. The hospital also reported that 20-year-old Roscoe Wilson Jr. of Englewood was knocked unconscious by a flying object and had been admitted for treatment.

A short time after the incident, some 15 youths gathered about eight blocks away and surged down Palisade Avenue,

Continued on Page 11, Column 3

M'KISSICK HOLDS END OF VIOLENCE IS UP TO WHITES

CORE Leader, at Meeting on Black Power, Warns of Further Rioting

By THOMAS A. JOHNSON
Special to The New York Times

NEWARK, July 21—Leaders of the National Conference on Black Power rejected today the concept that Negroes were solely responsible for preventing racial violence in Negro ghettos. They said the basic responsibility rested with white people.

"Bad conditions make for violence," said Floyd B. McKissick, chairman of the Congress of Racial Equality. "White people control the government, the money and the ghettos. They should be made to answer that question."

He made the statement to newsmen in behalf of a delegation of conference lead[ers] ... the Cathedral ...

... Negro newsmen are allowed to attend the workshop ses-

Continued on Page 11, Column 5

...oarding a raft in Great Bitter Lake, south of the Suez Canal, as they set out ...s in Israeli hands while the west bank is held by the United Arab Republic.

Associated Press Cablephoto

Albert Luthuli Kill[ed]; Zulu Won '60 Nobe[l]

Former Chief Led Nonviolent Resistance Against South Africa's Apartheid

Special to The New York Times

DURBAN, South Africa, July 21—Albert Luthuli, the former Zulu chief who won the Nobel Peace Prize in 1960, was struck by a train near his home today and died soon afterward in a hospital.

Mr. Luthuli, who was believed to be 69 years old, suffered from deafness and failing eyesight. He was walking over a narrow railroad bridge across the Umvoti River some 40 miles from here when he was struck.

Leader of the Oppressed

Albert John Luthuli, a Zulu only two generations removed from primitivism, was the acknowledged leader of millions of oppressed black men in South Africa. He was a moderate who advocated nonviolence and passive resistance.

Although he favored cooperation with whites to achieve equal citizenship for the blacks, he was spurned and reviled by the white-supremacist leaders of South Africa, whose policy of apartheid seeks to keep blacks and whites strictly segregated.

So fearful of Mr. Luthuli was the South African Government that since 1959 it had banished him to his 25-acre sugar farm near the Zulu village of Groutville. As an additional restriction, the Government forbade newspapers to quote his words. And it positively discouraged visits to him.

The ban on visits was grudgingly relaxed in June, 1966, when Senator and Mrs. Robert F. Kennedy were in South Africa. Shepherded by Government

Continued on Page 25, Column 1

Pictorial Parade
Albert Luthuli

...E LOSES ...RS COURT

...radition— ...-Premier ...Swiftly

... been detained in Al[ge]ria since June 30, when his plane was hijacked in midair and forced to land at an Algerian airfield.

Led Away by Guards

Mr. Tshombe was smiling when he turned to talk with Mr. Benabdallah. He was taken away by three security guards.

Bernardin Mungul Diaka, the Congolese Minister of State, who came here to present the extradition request, said at a news conference tonight that the extradition of Mr. Tshombe might take a month.

Mr. Diaka said that President Mobutu had told him in a long-distance telephone conversation that he might come to Algeria to express his gratitude to President Boumediene.

Before reading the decision, the presiding judge asked Mr. Tshombe if he had anything to say.

Mr. Tshombe, apparently sensing that the court's decision would be favorable to the extradition request, said, "The Algiers court wants to send me over."

Mr. Aoudia interrupted, and told Mr. Tshombe that he should not jump to conclusions

Continued on Page 6, Column 4

U.S. May Report to U.N. On Arms Sent to Mideast

By JOHN W. FINNEY
Special to The New York Times

WASHINGTON, July 21—The Administration is considering a plan under which the United States would report to the United Nations its arms shipments to the Middle East. The plan is aimed at imposing some psychological limitation on the Middle East arms race.

In discussing the plan today, State Department officials made clear that a resumption of United States arms shipments to Israel and to pro-Western Arab nations was imminent.

Shipments were suspended at the outbreak of the Arab-Israeli war last month, but officials said "very active considera[ti]on" was being given to a [re]sumption.

[T]he proposal for registration [of] arms shipments with the [Unit]ed Nations was first ad[vance]d by President Johnson [Ju]ne 19 as part of a five-[point pr]ogram for settling the [Isra]eli conflict.

[Call]ed 'a Beginning'

... possible military and political instabilities being created by Soviet arms shipments to such nations as the United Arab Republic, Syria, Iraq and Algeria. A Soviet airlift of weapons

Continued on Page 3, Column 1

Jersey Couple Wins 2 Times in Lottery

By RICHARD L. MADDEN
Special to The New York Times

ALBANY, July 21—An out-of-state couple—a Jersey City dental technician and his wife—became double winners in the New York state lottery today.

Although state officials figured the odds were almost 10 million to 1 against it, two consecutively numbered tickets, each bearing the names of Mary and Sol Levin, 124 Storms Avenue, Jersey City, were drawn about 10 minutes apart from a big blue and gold Y-shaped drum at the State Tax Department here.

The Levins' two tickets, plus each of the 1,545 others drawn yesterday and today, are assured of winning at least $150. Six of all the tickets sold will bring $100,000. But the

Continued on Page 23, Column 5

G.I. FORCE EVADES TRAP AND KILLS 90

Outnumbered Unit Puts Its Dead at 13—Ky Announces a 50,000-Man Build-Up

By TOM BUCKLEY
Special to The New York Times

SAIGON, South Vietnam, Saturday, July 22—A unit of the United States' 11th Armored Cavalry Regiment, outnumbered 3 to 1, reported having killed 90 Vietcong in a two-hour battle yesterday 30 miles northeast of Bienhoa.

The enemy force was said to have been a reinforced battalion of the 275th Regiment of the Ninth Vietcong Division, which has not been active in recent months.

[Premier Nguyen Cao Ky announced a 50,000-man increase in the South Vietnamese armed forces and an overhaul of the nation's defense structure, United Press International reported. Page 3.]

A United States spokesman said the Vietcong battalion in the battle yesterday had apparently been setting an ambush for the armored cavalry troop—the equivalent of a company, with 200 men—when the battle was joined near Route 20 in Longkhanh Province.

Support for Troop

The troop, equipped with tanks and armored personnel carriers, was reinforced by a second troop and was supported by helicopter gunships, artillery and tactical air strikes. When the enemy unit broke contact, it left behind a recoilless rifle and 25 individual weapons.

The Americans lost 13 killed and 59 wounded, the spokesman said. Damage to their equipment was described as light.

United States marines also ran into heavy fighting yesterday. Two companies of the Third Marine Regiment on a sweep in Quangtri and Thuathien Provinces, reported heavy engagements.

The first came when one company, after a barrage by mortars, recoilless rifles and rockets, was struck by a ground attack. Supported by naval gunfire and artillery, the attack was repulsed. Nine of the enemy and two marines were killed and 22 were wounded.

The second engagement came when a second company was apparently ambushed by an enemy force estimated at pla-

Continued on Page 3, Column 5

U.N., 63-26, TURNS CRISIS IN MIDEAST BACK TO COUNCIL

Soviet Fails in Effort to Get Assembly to Call for an Israeli Withdrawal

SESSION IS ADJOURNED

Arabs Reject a Compromise Worked Out by Russians in Talks With U.S.

By DREW MIDDLETON
Special to The New York Times

UNITED NATIONS, N. Y., July 21—The Soviet Union's campaign to win a General Assembly demand for the withdrawal of Israeli forces from the territory of three Arab states ended in failure tonight. The Assembly voted to send the Middle East issue back to the Security Council.

A resolution asking that the Council resume its consideration of the crisis "as a matter of urgency" was adopted by 63 votes to 26 with 27 abstentions.

The Assembly's emergency session was adjourned "temporarily" under the terms of the resolution, which authorized the Assembly President, Abdul Rahman Pazhwak of Afghanistan, "to reconvene the session as and when necessary."

Cries of 'Betrayal'

The session was closed "temporarily" at 10:35 P.M. by President Pazhwak with the air of the Assembly hall still heavy with Arab cries of "failure" and "betrayal."

The Soviet Government, which requested the emergency session, had hoped to obtain condemnation of Israel as an aggressor, withdrawal of Israeli forces and the payment of reparations for damages suffered by the Arab countries in the Middle Eastern war last month.

None of these objectives was attained, and the five-week session ended with relations between the Soviet Union and some of the Arab states noticeably strained, in the view of many diplomats.

Foreign Minister Andrei A. Gromyko, addressing the Assembly after the vote, put the blame for the Soviet setback on what he called the United States' "spirit of hostility" toward the Arab states and its support for Israel.

Goldberg Is Annoyed

Clearly irritated by this charge, Arthur J. Goldberg, the United States representative, retorted that Mr. Gromyko "more than anyone in this hall" knew that the United States had made every effort "to arrive at a meeting of the minds" on which the Assembly could concur.

This was an allusion to discussions held this week between Mr. Goldberg and Mr. Gromyko and Anatoly F. Dobrynin, the Soviet Ambassador to Washington, through which a compromise resolution on the Middle East was formulated by the Soviet delegates with the earnest cooperation of the chief American representative. The Soviet Union was attempting to salvage something

Continued on Page 2, Column 3

Eisenhower Scores 'War of Gradualism'

By DAVID R. JONES
Special to The New York Times

WASHINGTON, July 21—Former President Dwight D. Eisenhower believes that it is time for Congress to decide whether to declare war in Vietnam.

The general thinks that the United States cannot win a "war of gradualism" there, and that the nation's other goals should be relegated to second place. He also believes that a Federal tax increase would not be needed now if the nation had set its priorities earlier.

General Eisenhower's views were disclosed today in the weekly Newsletter published by the Republican Congressional Campaign Committee.

The Newsletter said his comments had been made in replies to questions from 34 first-term House Republicans at a meet-

Continued on Page 3, Column 1

Basil Rathbone, 75, Dies at Home Here

Basil Rathbone, the suave Shakespearean actor who won motion-picture fame in the early nineteen-forties as the detective Sherlock Holmes—and regretted the identification the rest of his life—died of a heart attack yesterday.

The tall, impeccably mannered actor, who was 75 years old, was found dead on the floor of his study at his home, 135 Central Park West, by his daughter, Cynthia. She said her father had suffered a heart seizure several years ago, but had appeared to be in good health.

Mr. Rathbone had been in the theater and the movies for more than 50 years, in roles that ranged from Shakespeare's Romeo to the snobbish Boston brahmin in "The Last Hurrah,"

Continued on Page 25, Column 4

Basil Rathbone Is Dead Here at 75

Continued From Page 1, Col. 1

the 1958 film about a political boss.

But for at least two generations of Americans, who saw his Sherlock Holmes pictures in theaters and later on television, Mr. Rathbone was instantly recognizable as the incarnation of the imaginary Holmes, magnifying glass, deerstalker hat, calabash pipe and all.

Although the role brought him fame and considerable fortune, Mr. Rathbone spoke derisively of it in almost every interview he gave after he stopped being Holmes.

"I played Holmes for seven years, and nobody thought I could do anything else," he once said. "When I would come onto a set or into a radio studio, it was never 'Hello, Rathbone.' It was always 'Hello, Holmes.' I simply threw away the pipe and hat and came back to Broadway. It was a simple question of survival—Holmes or Rathbone."

Actually, of the more than 100 films he made, only 16 were about the slightly smart-aleck eccentric of Baker Street who was forever fond of making the bumbling Dr. Watson appear the perfect ass. The role of Watson in the Holmes series was played by the late Nigel Bruce.

Skewered by Colman

Before the Holmes series began in 1939, with "The Hound of the Baskervilles," Mr. Rathbone had appeared in dozens of pictures, more often than not as the villainous man audiences love to hate. When Ronald Colman skewered him on a sword in "If I Were King," the moviegoers cheered.

Mr. Rathbone's first movie was a silent, "The Masked Bride," in 1925, but he achieved stardom with the advent of the talkies, in which his well-trained, crisply modulated voice stood him in good stead. His first "talkie" was "The Last of Mrs. Cheyney" in 1929.

Mr. Rathbone was born, the son of a mining engineer, on June 13, 1892, in Johannesburg, South Africa. The family lived in the Transvaal, and after young Basil narrowly escaped death at the hands of the Boers, his father decided to send him home to England to be educated.

When he was 18, Mr. Rathbone went to work for an insurance company, which he found "frightfully dull and uninvigorating," so much so that in 1911 he left it to join a theatrical company managed by his cousin Sir Frank Benson.

Mr. Rathbone's first stage appearance was at the Theater Royal in Ipswich, in "The Taming of the Shrew." He played Hortensio. He was good enough and—he said himself—close enough to his cousin to persuade Sir Frank to let him travel to the United States with the troupe in 1912.

The 6-foot 1-inch actor cut a dashing figure on Broadway, playing Fenton in "The Merry Wives of Windsor" and Paris in "Romeo and Juliet." He made his London stage debut as Finch in "The Sin of David," in 1914.

Although Mr. Rathbone won the Military Cross for his service in World War I as a captain with the Liverpool Scottish Regiment, the characteristically droll actor spoke of his feat later with disarming self-effacement.

"All I did, old man," he told one interviewer, "was disguise myself as a tree—that's correct, a tree—and cross no man's land to gather a bit of information from the German lines. I have not since been called upon to play a tree."

In 1922, Mr. Rathbone returned to this country to play Count Alexei in "The Czarina," and three years later he went to Hollywood, where he remained, except for occasional appearances on Broadway, until the mid-forties. By then, the Holmes series had run its course.

Mr. Rathbone's Hollywood career was spent mostly as a contract player at Metro-Goldwyn-Mayer and Universal Pictures. He seldom had starring roles in the more expensive films, but settled for meaty character parts that made an indelible impression on moviegoers. Among his films were "A Notorious Affair," "The Bishop Murder Case," "A Tale of Two Cities," "Anna Karenina," "David Copperfield," and "Son of Frankenstein," a "penny-dreadful," as he put it, in which Mr. Rathbone played the title role.

Revived Holmes on Radio

Mr. Rathbone liked to live well, and he did so, by staying busy most of the time. He supplemented his income with a Sherlock Holmes radio series in the late nineteen-forties and fifties, despite his distaste for the role.

In recent years, he appeared in the movies "Tales of Terror," based on three Edgar Allan Poe stories, released in 1962, and "Comedy of Terrors," a spoof of horror films in which he zestfully played a wealthy old miser given to reciting Shakespeare at the drop of a chopped-off head.

Mr. Rathbone was not above making "B" movies such as these, known in the trade as "exploitation pictures," but he was not very proud of them. They made money for him and gave him a chance to indulge in the kind of acting he really liked—recording the classics for Caedmon Records and touring campuses to read Shakespeare, Browning and other poets.

Mr. Rathbone loved acting and took roles, no matter how small, because he liked them. He summed up his philosophy last year during rehearsals of a "Hallmark Hall of Fame" television drama called "Soldier in Love," in which he had a brief role as the Duke of York.

"If you close your eyes during the first act you may very well miss me," he said. "But when it is no longer a matter of being a romantic star, an actor can play what he wants to play. And I wanted to play the Duke of York."

Besides his daughter, Cynthia, Mr. Rathbone is survived by his wife, the former Ouida Bergere, whom he married in 1926, and a son, Rodion, by his previous marriage, to Ethel Marian Forman, which was dissolved.

Basil Rathbone as Sherlock Holmes and Nigel Bruce as Dr. Watson in *The Hound of the Baskervilles*, 1939.

Rathbone, Vincent Price, Peter Lorre and Boris Karloff in *Comedy of Terrors, 1963.*

The New York Times FRIDAY, JUNE 11, 1971

Michael Rennie, Film and TV Actor, Dead at 62

Starred as Harry Lime in 'The Third Man' Series

Special to The New York Times

LONDON, June 10—Michael Rennie, the actor, who played Harry Lime in the television series "The Third Man," died today in Harrogate, Yorkshire. He was 62 years old.

Mr. Rennie, a United States citizen since 1960, was born in Yorkshire and was visiting his mother when he died.

Smooth and Debonair

Mr. Rennie was a smooth, debonair actor, who played a variety of roles in television and on the screen and stage.

He was probably best-known, however, for his suave and sophisticated portrayal of the romantic international spy, Harry Lime, in "The Third Man," one of the most popular television series ever made. The series was highly successful in Europe and Australia as well as here.

In 1961, Mr. Rennie co-starred as Dirk Winsten, a handsome film actor whose fortune was on the ebb, in the Jean Kerr comedy "Mary, Mary," and later took the same role in the movie of the play.

No allowance had been made for casting a Briton in the role. But this seemed to make no difference.

"It isn't that I have scarcely any accent," Mr. Rennie explained, "after spending years over here. The fact is that I arrived with little of what most people think of as a pronounced British accent. As I recall it, it seems to me that I never had much of it. At least not to the extreme that you sometimes hear.

"I was trained in British repertory companies and I learned to speak well. Then I made some British movies, felt I might have a future in films and realized that if I wanted to get ahead in that field I'd have to go to Hollywood eventually.

"And I knew that if I wanted to succeed there, I'd have to be able to play something besides British roles. So, even before I got my chance to go to Hollywood, I was consciously making an effort to erase what accent I felt I might have had at the time.

"Of course, I still get an occasional letter from my mother, who may see me in a film or in one of the television episodes, rather chiding me for talking so much like an American."

Mr. Rennie was born at Bradford, Yorkshire. He was English on his mother's side and Scottish on his father's.

A desire to leave his family wool business, which was started more than 150 years ago, led Mr. Rennie to the offices of Gaumont-British in London. His request to act in films was accepted, and the Cambridge-educated tyro performed a year before the cameras in a variety of roles at a minuscule salary.

Mr. Rennie then joined a Yorkshire stock company to expand his knowledge of acting. A little later he became the star of the York Repertory Company and performed contemporary works, including "Pygmalion," in which he played Professor Higgins many times.

His career was interrupted by World War II, in which he served as a flying officer in the Royal Air Force and as an instructor of American pilots in Georgia for several years.

After the war, he resumed film-making, appearing with Margaret Lockwood in "I'll Be Your Sweetheart," in which he sang. He also had a part in another of Miss Lockwood's British movies, "The Wicked Lady."

These pictures led to a 20th Century-Fox contract and Mr. Rennie's departure for Hollywood, where he made more than 50 films. Notable among his films were "Trio," "The Day the Earth Stood Still," "Desirée," "Third Man on the Mountain," "Seven Cities of Gold," "The Robe," "The Lost World" and "Les Misérables."

Others were "King of the Khyber Rifles," "Soldier of Fortune," "Rains of Ranchipur" and "Island in the Sun." Most recent were "Ride Beyond Vengeance," "The Devil's Brigade" and "The Power," the last in 1968.

Victor Mature as Demetrius and Michael Rennie as Peter in *The Robe*.

Michael Rennie and Patricia Neal in *The Day the Earth Stood Still.*

The New York Times

WEDNESDAY, FEBRUARY 5, 1969

Thelma Ritter, Versatile Actress With the Raspy Voice, Dies at 63

She Performed in Many Roles on the Stage, In Films and on TV

Thelma Ritter, a gravel-voiced housewife who became famous for her sharp, astrigent role as the disillusioned mother who argued with Santa Claus in the film "Miracle on 34th Street," died at 12:45 A.M. today from an apparent heart attack. She would have been 64 on Feb. 14.

The veteran character actress was admitted to Quens Hospital on Jan. 27 after being stricken at her home.

The one-time Broadway performer had kept her hand in the trade after retiring to a Long Island home with her husband and two children.

"Whenever 'Mr. District Attorney' needed a psycho, they put in a call for me," she said of her radio career that followed mariage.

When the film director George Seaton came here in 1946 to film "Miracle on 34th Street," he called Miss Ritter, a family friend for many years, and asked her to take the role.

"It isn't much of a part," he explained, "but it'll be fun and maybe you'll bring me luck."

After her success in that film, she played top roles in "All About Eve," and "A Letter to Three Wives."

In her television debut in 1955, she won an Emmy award as the Bronx housewife in Paddy Chayevsky's "The Catered Affair."

After finishing "Move Over, Darling" in late 1964, she made a try at retirement again. Hollywood beckoned once more, however, and she returned to the screen in 1965 in "Boing-Boing."

An Unassuming Housewife

Thelma Ritter was nobody's image of an actress. A short, gracious, unassuming and simply dressed woman offstage, she looked and behaved more like a suburban housewife—which she was.

When she wasn't appearing on Broadway, in films or on television, a housewife's role was one she happily played, rearing a son and a daughter and living with her husband, Joseph Moran, in a comfortable house in Forest Hills.

"We're only a block and a half from the subway," she liked to tell interviewers. "We came here in 1937 to see the tennis matches and decided that it was a nice place to live. We moved here and haven't been to the matches since."

Associated Press

Thelma Ritter

Even when she was making a film in Hollywood she preferred to do her own housekeeping in her hotel suite.

As an actress, she was reliable in whatever she did, regardless of the medium. She made her mark on the screen as a character played and Hollywood likened her to the late Marie Dressler.

She accepted the praise gracefully. But she would say, "It's always complimentary to be called another somebody—just so they don't make it stick. You know what happened to those youngsters who were billed as 'the second Garbo.' It's the kiss of death."

Miss Ritter usually turned up on the screen looking and acting like something the cat dragged in. Her forte was mostly comedy. She had a way with a line that was uproarious.

Three years ago she made one of her infrequent appearances on Broadway in a comedy caled "UTBU." The critic for The New York Times observed: "There are such phenomena as intrinsically funny people and Thelma Ritter is one. By any logic of expectation, she ought now to be less funny because there are few surprises left in her appearances. But all she need do is apply that umpire's voice and gravelly innocence to the most pallid of lines and it seems more humorous. With a good line she is irresistible . . . What helps keep her performance fresh is, of course, the fact that she is a very skilled technician."

But Miss Ritter also could play serious roles effectively as she did in "Birdman of Alcatraz," in which she appeared as Burt Lancaster's militant mother fighting for his release. Her portrayal won her an Oscar nomination in 1962. Prior to that she was nominated for Academy awards for appearances in "All About Eve" (1950), "The Mating Season" and "Pillow Talk" (1959). In 1957 she won an Antoinette Perry Award when she played Marthy in the musical "New Girl in Town," based on Eugene O'Neill's play "Anna Christie."

Born in Brooklyn on Feb. 14, 1905, Miss Ritter was the daughter of Charles and Lucy Ritter. Her father, she liked to relate, was a boy soprano and a soloist with the Garden City Cathedral. But, Miss Ritter said, being Dutch, he was frightened of a theatrical career. Instead, he eventually became the office manager of a shore company.

"He really was artistic," she said, "but fundamentally Dutch."

This, however, didn't interfere with Miss Ritter's own artistic inclinations. She was stagestruck in childhood and at 11 was playing Puck in "A Midsummer Night's Dream" with a semi-professional dramatic society. Subsequently she did readings around Brooklyn, at clubs and in churches.

With her eye on a theatrical career, she quit school to earn enough money to take courses at the American Academy of Dramatic Arts. But when she applied, she was advised to finish school and was graduated from Manual Training High School. Later she studied at the academy.

Her first professional experience was playing with stock companies around New York and in New England.

Romance Bloomed

A handsome young actor, Joseph Moran, joined a troupe with which Miss Ritter was appearing in 1926. He had just graduated from Johns Hopkins University. A romance developed and after what Miss Ritter called an "insidious" campaign, she agreed to marry him in 1927.

Miss Ritter made her first appearance on Broadway in 1926 in "The Shelf." Three years later she toured in "The Front Page." She played again on Broadway in "Sisters of the Chorus" (1931), and the same year in "Mr. Times Square." In 1932 she toured in "Counsellor-at-Law." But the Depression was hard on theatrical aspirations. Mr. Moran went into advertising, and Miss Ritter became a housewife.

After the children were born, Miss Ritter tried acting again. Her voice was heard on various radio shows. She was a fixture on such programs as "The Theater Guild of the Air," "Mr. District Attorney," "Big Town," "The Aldrich Family" and others.

The big break came in 1946. George Seaton, a director for Twentieth Century-Fox Films, came to New York in search of authentic characters for the movie "Miracle on 34th Street." He gave her a walk-on part as a harried housewife who berates Santa Claus for promising her son too much during the Christmas rush at Macy's. When Darryl Zanuck the producer, saw the film rushes he ordered her role built up. She was a hit. After that it was clear sailing to fame.

Thelma Ritter and Bette Davis in *All About Eve.*

"All the News That's Fit to Print"

The New York Times.

LATE CITY EDITION
Partly cloudy and cold today. Cloudy and warmer tomorrow.
Temperature Range Today—Max.,42; Min.,32
Temperature Yesterday—Max.,54; Min.,36
Full U. S. Weather Bureau Report, Page 39

VOL. XCIX..No. 33,544. Entered as Second-Class Matter, Postoffice, New York, N. Y. NEW YORK, SATURDAY, NOVEMBER 26, 1949. Times Square, New York 18, N. Y. Telephone Lackawanna 4-1000 THREE CENTS IN NEW YORK CITY | FIVE CENTS ELSEWHERE

TRUMAN DEMANDS LEAKS IN CONGRESS ON SECURITY HALT

Calls In McGrath, McMahon in Move to Safeguard Data Vital to National Defense

'SUPER-BOMB' TALK CITED

President Called Displeased by Senator Johnson of Colorado, Who Told of Atomic Work

By ANTHONY LEVIERO
Special to THE NEW YORK TIMES.

WASHINGTON, Nov. 25—President Truman moved today to plug u- national security leaks in Congress, apparently as a result of a statement by Senator Edwin C. Johnson. The Colorado Democrat said recently that considerable progress was being made on an atomic bomb 1,000 times deadlier than the one dropped on Nagasaki.

J. Howard McGrath, Attorney General, and Senator Brien McMahon, Democrat, of Connecticut, chairman of the Joint Congressional Committee on Atomic Energy, were summoned to the White House this afternoon. They said the President told them that he wished to continue to make secret data available to those entitled to it, but that he also wanted to make sure that the information remained protected in this period of tension with Russia.

Apparently no drastic steps or revision of the security laws are contemplated. Mr. McGrath and Senator McMahon were rather cryptic in discussing their Presidential interview with reporters.

Disclosures Irk Truman

Other sources cognizant of intelligence problems said that Mr. Truman's action was chiefly a reminder that he was watching the domestic intelligence situation and was displeased by a number of recent disclosures. They mentioned the Johnson statement, made to a television audience, as a major reason for today's meeting.

In confirming that no specific course of action was contemplated, Mr. McGrath did say, however, that security laws were as binding on members of Congress as on the public and officials of the Executive Branch of the Government.

In his television appearance, Mr. Johnson said that American atomic scientists had developed a bomb that was six times as effective as the Nagasaki bomb, with "considerable progress" made toward a "super-bomb" that would be 1,000 times more powerful.

"I didn't say anything on that broadcast that hasn't been said time after time by many officials," the Senator asserted tonight.

Mr. Johnson, who is a member of the atomic committee, said that disclosure that work was going on on a super-bomb was not secret, but that the construction of it was. He stressed that he had said nothing about that. He added that he had furnished a local newspaper twenty-five exhibits referring to

Continued on Page 7, Column 5

Capital Power Cut In Bomber Mishap

By The Associated Press.

WASHINGTON, Nov. 25—Six Air Force men escaped injury tonight when their B-17 plane wrecked a power line during a landing approach and put part of southeast and southwest Washington in darkness for two hours.

The pilots of the plane, from Omaha, Neb., blamed wind from the craft's propellors for breaking 4,000-volt power lines on a pole forty feet above the ground.

Power company crews found a pole broken about twenty feet from the ground. The pilots said the plane was undamaged and none of its occupants hurt in a normal landing at Bolling Field. They apologized for the public inconvenience they caused.

Homes in an extended residential section were plunged into darkness and customers in some stores were temporarily locked in until they could be checked out in orderly fashion with their purchases.

Lieut. Col. William Campbell, 32 years old, of Chicago, and Maj. Van R. Parker, 33, of Oakland, Ill., the pilots, said they did not believe the craft touched the power wires because "we didn't feel anything at the time we saw a flash of light." The lines were strung along a street over which the plane approached the field.

H. E. Howard, Coal Leader, Named Munitions Chairman

Truman Gives Long-Vacant Post to Chicagoan, Head of a Defense Board

By AUSTIN STEVENS
Special to THE NEW YORK TIMES.

WASHINGTON, Nov. 25—President Truman today named Hubert E. Howard, a Chicago coal company executive, to the long-unoccupied post of chairman of the Munitions Board of the Department of Defense. The appointment filled one of the most prominent of several vacancies that have occurred in the defense establishment.

The search for a chairman of the board, which under the amended National Security Act has broad authority in the planning of industrial mobilization for defense, has gone on since last June.

Several candidates have declined to serve in the $16,000-a-year position because of personal and business reasons. The Senate rejected the nomination of Carl A. Ilgenfritz, a vice president of the United States Steel Corporation, last September when Mr. Ilgenfritz would not renounce his $70,000 annual salary.

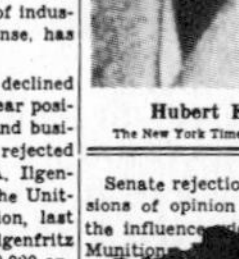

Hubert E. Howard
The New York Times (Washington Bureau)

Senate rejection followed expressions of opinion that ... the influence ... Munition...

Mayor ... R...

Mayor ... local law ... The measure ...

MINE OWNE[RS] ... TO RESUM[E] ...

Southern Bloc Infor[ms] ... It Will Meet Him A[...] —Coal 'Break' Hi[...]

Special to THE NEW YORK TIMES.

WASHINGTON, Nov. 25—... Southern Coal Producers Association unexpectedly made a dire[ct] offer to John L. Lewis tonight t[o] resume wage talks with the United Mine Workers.

This came at a time when Government officials were quietly redoubling their efforts to get the soft coal negotiations going again. There was no evidence that these efforts had met with any success. On the contrary, there was reliable information that many operators were resisting the overtures.

Joseph E. Moody, president of the Southern organization, made the offer in a telegram to Mr. Lewis. The offer did not contain any new terms. It stipulated that further negotiations would have to be based on principles previously outlined.

The significance of the message apparently lay in its timing. It indicated that the Southerners, or Mr. Moody, at least, suspected a break in the operators' solid front. If any negotiations are being conducted secretly, the Southern Coal Producers Association obviously is not part of them and is not even well-informed on them.

Mr. Moody's telegram would put his organization on record and would clear it, presumably, of any

Continued on Page 8, Column 2

... Walker. In t[he] ... Estimate fixed ... at $40,000, that ... at $35,000 and t[he] ... dent of the Board ... $25,000. Each o[f] ... Presidents received ... $20,000.

In 1933 a drastic e[...] resulted in sharp cut[s] ... of all city employes a[nd] ... including the eight me[mbers] ... Board of Estimate, wh[...] ... were fixed at the amoun[t] ...

Continued on Page 8, Co[lumn] ...

MAYOR INTERVENES TO BAR BUS STRIKE ON 3D AVE. SYSTEM

Meeting of Company and Union Heads Set This Afternoon as Halt Today Threatens

76 ROUTES ARE INVOLVED

Transit Aide Reports 40-Hour Week Might Be Warranted, Passes Up Wage Factor

Mayor O'Dwyer took action early this morning to prevent a threatened strike on buses of the Third Avenue Transit Corporation, which would affect 1,800,000 d[aily] users of its lines.

He invited both ... the Trans[port] ... CI[O] ...

ISRAEL TURNS DOWN MAKING JERUSALEM INTERNATIONAL CITY

Sharett Insists State Retain New Area, but Asks World Control of Arab Sector

OFFERS HOLY PLACES PACT

Egypt Also Scores U. N. Plan and Urges Compliance With Partition Resolution

Excerpts from ... Sharett and ...

VISHINSKY TAKES A WALK AT U. N.

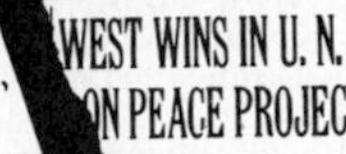

... in arm with Vladimir Clementis ... eeting that was discussing Chinese
Associated Press

[...] WEST WINS IN U. N. [...]ON PEACE PROJECT

...al Committee Votes 53-5 ... S.-British Text and ...jects Soviet Plan

... But ... [posi]tion is seated ... [A]ssembly and in the ... [Co]mmittee, full approval of the British-United States resolution and defeat of the Soviet motion will be in the nature of formalities.

As a parting shot at the end of the balloting today, Soviet For-

Continued on Page 4, Column 3

CHINA ASKS NATIONS TO INDICT MOSCOW, SHUN PEIPING TIES

Accuses Soviet of Threatening Peace in Asia—Vishinsky Rejects Any U. N. Finding

REFUSES DEBATE, LEAVES

Tsiang Holds Treaties Violated, Urges Action by Assembly Barring Aid to Red Regime

Excerpts from Dr. Tsiang's speech are printed on Page 3.

By A. M. ROSENTHAL
Special to THE NEW YORK TIMES.

LAKE SUCCESS, Nov. 25—China asked the United Nations today to find the Soviet Union guilty of jeopardizing the peace of Asia and to call on all fifty-nine members to refuse recognition and aid to the Chinese Communists.

The Soviet Union, for its part, announced point-blank in advance that it would not consider itself bound by any decision on China taken by the United Nations and would not even take part in the debate growing out of China's accusations against Moscow. The Chinese case was presented then by Dr. T. F. Tsiang in a bill of particulars charging Russia with widespread aggression and interference in China's affairs.

Foreign Minister Andrei Y. Vishinsky led the four other delegates of the Soviet bloc countries into a round of denunciations of the Chinese National Government and its delegation to the United Nations. He said the members of the delegation were the "fictitious representatives of a fictitious regime" and pointed to the Chinese Communists as the only legal Government of China.

Not a Walkout

Mr. Vishinsky and his supporters—the delegates of Czechoslovakia Poland, the Ukraine and Byelorussia—did not officially walk out of the Political and Security Committee of the General Assembly, where debate on China began this afternoon. But a few minutes after Dr. Tsiang had begun his case Mr. Vishinsky packed his brief case, left the table and motioned Deputy Foreign Minister Jacob A. Malik into the Soviet chair.

Dmitri Z. Manuilsky of the Ukraine, who spoke bitingly of "Kuomintang pettifoggery," revealed his own method of "not participating" in the debate. As soon as he had finished his denunciation of the Chinese National Government, he waved an aide into his seat, took an adviser's chair a couple of rows back, broke out a copy of Pravda and read it carefully and steadily while Dr. Tsiang spoke.

Yugoslavia's delegate, Dr. Ales Bebler, also questioned the authority of the Chinese delegation. He [s]aid the Chinese Communists had [the] right to represent China since [the]y had the confidence of the peo[ple]. Dr. Bebler suggested a vote on whether the Chinese delegation should sit for China but it was not acted upon and he did not follow up with an announcement of nonparticipation in the debate.

Non-Participation Tactic

It was the second time the Russians had announced a "no participation" attitude. The first came last year in Paris when Mr. Vishinsky sat silent in the Security Council during a debate on Berlin, but relented long enough to veto a motion.

Dr. Tsiang, who has been working on the presentation of his case ever since he put it on the Assembly's agenda two months ago, had before him a 17,000-word statement—plus some twenty-five pages of maps and annexes—when he began to speak. The gist of Dr. Tsiang's talk was that the Soviet Union was systematically violating the United Nations Charter and its 1945 friendship treaty with China by supplying arms and economic assistance to the Communists and by following a policy of aggressive imperialism against Chinese territory.

The Chinese delegate wound up with these four appeals to the committee and said he would present them later in the form of a resolution:

1. To pronounce judgment on the Soviet Union for blocking attempts by the Chinese Nationalists to re-establish their authority in Manchuria and for helping the Chinese Communists.
2. To recognize the cause of Chinese political independence and territorial integrity as a "cause

Continued on Page 3, Column 6

Bill (Bojangles) Robinson Dies; 'King of the Tap Dancers' Was 71

Bill (Bojangles) Robinson, the dancer, died at 7:28 P. M. yesterday in the Harkness Pavilion of the Columbia-Presbyterian Medical Center. The 71-year-old "King of Tap Dancers" had been admitted to the hospital on Nov. 14, suffering from a heart ailment.

Bojangles danced for pennies as a boy and for as much as $6,600 a week in the movies, but the money was secondary. He danced often at benefits for others, yet he himself frequently was broke. His earnings throughout the years have been put at more than $2,000,000, but at his death, a benefit performance for him was being arranged by his friends.

Not even his failing health kept him from dancing. About a year ago, he suffered a heart attack and had cataracts removed from his eyes, but he kept on performing despite the advice of his doctor. He continued dancing until three months ago, when he found he could not see the steps in his famous stair routine.

After he was admitted to the hospital, Robinson received more than 5,000 letters from his admirers, among them President Truman, members of the Cabinet, Congressmen and many state officials, as well as from his vaudeville, stage and screen fans.

With him at his death were his second wife, the former Elaine Dash, whom he married in 1944; her sister, Mrs. Dorothy Small, and his manager, Marty Forkins. A brother, Percy Robinson of North Carolina, also survives.

The body will lie in state tomorrow afternoon and Monday at the Abyssinian Baptist Church, 132 West 138th Street. A funeral service will be held there on Monday, and burial will be in Evergreen Cemetery, Brooklyn.

A group of newspaper columnists was making plans last night for a benefit performance to be held for Robinson's family at a Broadway nightclub on Dec. 12.

Continued on Page 10, Column 2

Bill (Bojangles) Robinson Dies; 'King of the Tap Dancers' Was

Bill (Bojangles) Robinson, the dancer, died at 7:28 P. M. yesterday in the Harkness Pavilion of the Columbia-Presbyterian Medical Center. The 71-year-old "King of Tap Dancers" had been admitted to the hospital on Nov. 14, suffering from a heart ailment.

Bojangles danced for pennies as a boy and for as much as $6,600 a week in the movies, but the money was secondary. He danced often at benefits for others, yet he himself frequently was broke. His earnings throughout the years have been put at more than $2,000,000, but at his death, a benefit performance for him was being arranged by his friends.

Not even his failing health kept him from dancing. About a year ago, he suffered a heart attack and had cataracts removed from his eyes, but he kept on performing despite the advice of his doctor. He continued dancing until three months ago, when he found he could not see the steps in his famous stair routine.

After he was admitted to the hospital, Robinson received more than 5,000 letters from his admirers, among them President Truman, members of the Cabinet, Congressmen and many state officials, as well as from his vaudeville, stage and screen fans.

With him at his death were his second wife, the former Elaine Dash, whom he married in 1944; her sister, Mrs. Dorothy Small, and his manager, Marty Forkins. A brother, Percy Robinson of North Carolina, also survives.

The body will lie in state tomorrow afternoon and Monday at the Abyssinian Baptist Church, 132 West 138th Street. A funeral service will be held there on Monday, and burial will be in Evergreen Cemetery, Brooklyn.

A group of newspaper columnists was making plans last night for a benefit performance to be held for Robinson's family at a Broadway nightclub on Dec. 12.

Continued on Page 10, Column 2

... [pe]ace" resolution ... for a Big Five ... Political and Security [Co]mmittee of the General Assembly approved a resolution, sponsored by the United States and Britain, urging all members to settle differences through international cooperation. [1:7.]

A compromise proposal by the United Nations Palestine Conciliation Commission for an international regime in Jerusalem was rejected by Israel's Foreign Minister Sharett, who declared that the New City of Jerusalem must remain in the hands of the Israelis. [1:5.]

Allied leaders in Germany were concerned over political developments in the Western German Republic. The Social Democratic party, whose leader, Dr. Kurt Schumacher, was expelled for twenty sessions of the Bundestag, said it would fight against Chancellor Adenauer's regime as authoritarian. [5:1.]

The French Assembly by 334 to 248 gave the Government a vote of confidence on Foreign

... [th]at ele... Arias to the ... has caused "profound [sho]ck" in this country, according to the State Department, which withheld diplomatic recognition from the new regime. [4:6.]

President Truman summoned Attorney General McGrath and Chairman McMahon of the Joint Congressional Committee on Atomic Energy to the White House for a conference on how to insure against leaks in Congress of security data. [1:1.]

The Chief Executive named Hubert E. Howard to the chairmanship of the Munitions Board of the Department of Defense, a position long vacant. [1:2-3.]

President John L. Lewis of the United Mine Workers was asked by Southern coal producers to resume wage talks. At the same time Government officials were trying, with some apparent success, to obtain resumption of negotiations in the soft coal industry. [1:2.]

Mayor O'Dwyer called a meeting for today of the Transport Workers Union, CIO, and the Third Avenue Transit Corporation to prevent a possible strike, which would affect 1,800,000 daily riders. [1:4.]

... [fo]llowed in ... but the agent re... he had the right to be ... Asked whether he possessed a warrant, he said he did not but

Continued on Page 6, Column 6

Rally at West Point to Beat Navy Stirs War Scare in Hudson Valley

Special to THE NEW YORK TIMES.

NEWBURGH, N. Y., Nov. 25—West Point cadets, using a B-25 bomber, an anti-aircraft searchlight and four or five remarkably loud-sounding cannons, staged a football rally at the Academy last night that alarmed this Hudson Valley community.

Citizens of Newburgh who retired early after Thanksgiving festivities were startled by a loud explosion at 11 P. M. There were about twenty such explosions in the next twenty minutes.

Those looking down the river to the Point, ten miles away, saw a large fire and an anti-aircraft searchlight pointing vividly in the darkness to a plane circling overhead. The explosions were louder than those that accompany usual Academy gunnery practice. Some reports said that Newburgh's windows were rattled and houses shook with each blast.

The immediate reaction of many in the city of 32,000 was that West Point was being bombed and that a sneak attack like Pearl Harbor was aimed at the Hudson Valley. The Newburgh telephone company recorded 1,200 calls in the first twenty minutes and 2,000 in half an hour. There may have been 3,000 during the night.

Word of the events was still reverberating today up and down the Hudson Valley like Catskill mountain thunder from Hendrick Hudson's legendary crew of ninepin bowlers which Rip Van Winkle came across deep in the hills. A formal note of protest was to be filed with Mrs. Katharine B. St. George, Republican Representative of the district in Congress and a cousin of the late President Franklin D. Roosevelt.

Early this morning high officers of the Academy left for Philadelphia and Saturday's annual Army and Navy game, which the rally preceded. Army's undefeated team will face Navy's team, de-

Continued on Page 30, Column 2

Bill (Bojangles) Robinson Dies; 'King of the Tap Dancers' Was 71

Continued from Page 1

Meanwhile, hospital expenses were paid by members of a Bill Robinson Fund, including Judge Jonah Goldstein, Msgr. James O'Reilly and Nobel Sissle.

For more than sixty years Bill (Bojangles) Robinson tap-danced, and, aided by an infectious smile, rolling eyes and a sparkling wit, won much acclaim.

Presidents of the United States and members of royal families lauded his talents. Some one gave him the name "Bojangles." No one seemed to know what the word meant or its source. "I like that name,' Bill often said.

"That man sho moves fast on his feet," his Harlem public would remark repeatedly. Other audiences could only murmur: "Oh!" and "Ah!" Then the applause would rock the theatre.

Robinson would alternate in the same evening between performances at a night club and in a musical comedy, crowding a benefit appearance between them. Once asked why his routines were so sharply different from each other, he said, with a grin:

"Folks, I goes home after dancin' and runs the tub half full of water as hot as I can stand. Then I pours in two quarts of gin. I soaks my feet in it for three hours and then wraps 'em up in cotton battin'. When I gets up in the morning, them feet—they's drunk. They don't know what they're doin'."

Never Took a Lesson

Bill never took a dancing lesson. "I just worked out my own steps when I would hear a new piece of music," he said.

Apart from his terpsichorean talents, Bojangles was known on Broadway as "a soft touch." Despite the high salaries he received for his dancing, and $6,600 a week for one year in 1937 for appearances in the motion-pictures, he never had much money because of his charitable enterprises. He averaged 400 benefits a year, often relinquishing professional dates, and sent many unsolicited checks to his home town, Richmond, Va., with the request that the money should be distributed to Negro and white charities alike.

Bill gave scholarships and money to schools and orphanages, and annually donated a prize to the graduating class of Public School 119 in Harlem. His wife, Fanny, was instrumental in saving some money and always on the alert for Bill "not to be a fall guy" for everyone. They were married in 1919, when she was working at a soda fountain in Chicago. She guided him financially until they were divorced in 1943. But she never could stop him from wandering into pool rooms, a deep-rooted hobby. He had another obsession, ice-cream. He would have ice-cream and hot biscuits for breakfast, ice-cream for lunch, and ice-cream and steak for dinner.

Born in Richmond, Va., on May 25, 1878, Bill was taken at an early date to live with his grandmother. His given name was Luther, which did not appeal to him at the age of 8, when he became an employe in a racing stable at Washington, so he changed it to Bill. At the end of a day's work in the stables, he would dance for pennies in saloons. He later hoofed around the country in vaudeville.

Perhaps because of his lack of formal schooling, Bill was particularly proud of having added a word to the language, though some etymologists asserted he had not coined the word, which was "copasetic," an equivalent of "okay." However, nobody could disprove his claim as word-coiner.

During a lull in his dancing career Bill was a waiter in a Richmond beanery when he spilled a plate of piping-hot oyster stew down the neck of Marty Forkins, the booking agent. Someone explained to Forkins that Robinson was a hoofer. Forkins consented to see him in action. This was in 1908. Later, when the team of Robinson and Butler, with Robinson the lesser light, appeared in Chicago, Forkins saw the act and immediately detected the great ability of Robinson. That was the beginning of a life-long friendship. Forkins became his manager. Robinson called him "The Boss."

As Robinson's fame grew his salary climbed to $2,000 a week, and he became the star in Negro musical comedies, notably in a number of the "Blackbirds" revues on Broadway. He scored an outstanding success in the swing version of Gilbert and Sullivan's "The Mikado."

He enjoyed equal success in the talking pictures, appearing in lead roles in "In Old Kentucky," "The Littlest Rebel," "One Mile From Heaven" and "The Little Colonel."

Bill had another outstanding accomplishment. He was famed for his ability to run backwards as fast as the ordinary man could run forward, and once held the world's record for this kind of running, doing seventy-five yards in 8 and 1-5 seconds.

Asked on one occasion how he managed to look so young, he said: "I suppose it's my dancing; I don't smoke and I don't drink, and dancing never makes me tired. I can keep right on doing it for hours and never get winded. I have no feeling for that slapstick dancing which a lot of people do. They have no respect for their feet: some of them come out and slap down their hoofs as if they were made of iron. No piano player would treat his hands that way, and I make music with my feet, so I just treat 'em with great respect. That's the reason they can do this." He then demonstrated a new step.

Bill "Bojangles" Robinson and Jennie Le Gon in *Hooray for Love.*

Edward G. Robinson, 79, Dies; His 'Little Caesar' Set a Style

By The Associated Press

HOLLYWOOD, Jan. 26 — Edward G. Robinson, whose tough, sinister appearance on movie screens concealed the soul of a gentle man, died today at the age of 79.

Mr. Robinson succumbed at Mount Sinai Hospital where he had undergone tests in recent weeks. The cause of death was not immediately determined.

Man of Great Kindness

By ALDEN WHITMAN

Edward G. Robinson was a skilled actor of the stage and screen whose vivid portrayal of motion - picture gangsters, among them Little Caeser, during the nineteen-thirties marked powerful mobsters who ruled the underworld during the Prohibition era.

So effective was the Robinson interpretation of the gangster that many of the underworld characters found themselves affecting the Robinson character—chomping down on cigar butts while snarling threats and orders out of the sides of their mouths.

But while Mr. Robinson was making his mark on others he, himself, remained strangely unaffected. In real life he was a man of great kindness and courtesy whose generosity scarcely knew bounds. Between 1939 and 1949 he made more than 850 contributions totaling above $250,000 to relief and entertainment agencies, to cultural, educational and religious groups.

His art collection comprised perhaps the outstanding group

Continued on Page 32, Column 3

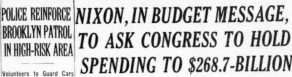

"All the News That's Fit to Print"

The New York Times

LATE CITY EDITION

Weather: Chance of rain today; cold tonight. Fair and cooler tomorrow. Temp. range: today 39-51; Friday 40-52. Full U.S. report on Page 56.

VOL. CXXII . . No. 42,007 — © 1973 The New York Times Company — NEW YORK, SATURDAY, JANUARY 27, 1973 — 15 CENTS

KISSINGER VOWS A CONGRESS ROLE IN AID FOR HANOI

Promises Consultation as He Briefs Members of Both Houses on Cease-Fire

CLOSED-DOOR SESSIONS

As He Speaks, Senate Gets a Bill to Curb Return of Troops to Indochina

Special to The New York Times

WASHINGTON, Jan. 26 — Henry A. Kissinger promised members of Congress today that the Nixon Administration would consult with them before making any firm commitments to North Vietnam on postwar aid programs.

On the eve of tomorrow's formal signing in Paris of the Vietnam cease-fire accord, Mr. Kissinger made an unusual trip to the Capitol to brief Senators and Representatives on the terms of the agreement that he and Le Duc Tho initialed in Paris Tuesday.

According to three who attended the two closed-door sessons—one for each House of Congress — Mr. Kissinger said that although the agreement called for the United States to contribute to "postwar reconstruction" in North Vietnam and other countries of Indochina, no commitments had yet been made.

Figure Put at $2.5-Billion

Last year, President Nixon said the United States was considering giving $7.5-billion in postwar assistance over five years, of which up to $2.5-billion would be earmarked for North Vietnam. But Mr. Kissinger at his news conference on Wednesday said that discussions about future aid would take place only after the implementation of the agreement "is well advanced."

At the same time as Mr. Kissinger was briefing Senators in a room off the Senate floor, two antiwar Senators, Frank Church, Democrat of Idaho, and Clifford P. Case, Republican of New Jersey, were introducing a bill on the floor aimed at prohibiting, without Congressional approval, the involvement of United States military forces in Vietnam, Laos or Cambodia after the last prisoners of war are released, which is to be 60 days after the cease-fire accord is signed.

Their bill was opposed on the floor by the assistant Republican leader, Robert P. Griffin of Michigan, who argued

Continued on Page 10, Column 3

TAY NINH REPORTS ATTACK BY ENEMY

Communists Forces Step Up Action as Truce Nears

Special to The New York Times

SAIGON, South Vietnam, Saturday, Jan. 27—Communist troops reportedly attacked Tay Ninh city west of Saigon this morning as they stepped up their assaults throughout South Vietnam in preparation for tomorrow's cease-fire.

The South Vietnamese command said that North Vietnamese and Vietcong troops made 160 attacks in the 24-hours ended at 6 A.M. today, the largest number since the height of the Communist offensive last spring.

Early reports from Tay Ninh said that fighting had broken out in the Cao Dai Temple and had spread to the rest of the city. Tay Ninh, about 55 miles west of here, is the center of the Cao Dai religious sect.

South Vietnam intelligence officials had predicted that the Communists might try to attack Tay Ninh in the last few days before a cease-fire in order to establish their capital for South Vietnam there. Other attacks were expected at Phan Thiet on the central coast and in the suburbs of Da Nang.

Allied forces also increased their activities as the cease-fire deadline neared. Three

Continued on Page 10, Column 5

Associated Press

Ralph E. Collins of Canada, standing, meeting in Ottawa with representatives of other countries that will make up the supervising commission in Vietnam. Clockwise from right: Djamin Gintings, Indonesia; Jozef Kustra, Poland, and Janos Bartha, Hungary.

CEASE-FIRE TEAMS AWAITED IN SAIGON

26 … mat… doub… comm… vise … Vietnam… establish… quarters… fied in… peace …

Accor… the head… ational a… hours af… which is to… Sunday, Saig…

The diplomat… thought it was… the commission… to install its … teams in posit… country within … start of the cease… lated in the proto…

"We don't even … people here yet," o… said. "There's going … of confusion."

Members of Old Com…

In his speech on We… announcing the cease-fire… dent Nguyen Van Thieu… the Communists believed… would take two weeks … month for the commission… be in full operation. And… warned that they might try … take advantage of this "confused period."

The Polish and Canadian diplomats in Saigon are members of the International Control Commission created at the 1954 Geneva Conference on Indochina. They assume that their delegations, which have shrunk over the years from several hundred to fewer than 20

Continued on Page 11, Column 2

For the Vietnam…

By MALCOLM W. BROWNE
Special to the New York Times

SAIGON, South Vietnam—For most of the people of South Vietnam the end of the war—if it *is* the end of *their* war—is coming far too late for rejoicing.

Few Vietnamese can even recall without a few moments' reflection when the war began. Most have spent the largest part of their lives at war.

For many Vietnamese the three decades of strife have worn away the old passions of nationalism, political hatred, revenge and even sorrow. There remains only a feeling of numb resignation to whatever the future may bring and a strong urge to escape into the traditional Vietnamese diversions of chess, gambling with cards and drinking baxide, a powerful rice liquor.

With probably around a million Vietnamese killed just in the time … began a… a family … least one … more have been … maimed.

Nor will the killing and maiming cease with the end of hostilities. Despite the passing of a generation, farmers are still killed on Okinawa and other battlegrounds of World War II by old mines and bombs. Vietnam has been seeded with far more of these lethal legacies than any other land.

… of the war … men, and in many ways South Vietnam now seems to be a nation dominated by hard-minded, lonely and sometimes bitter women, for whom idealism and even personal feeling appear to have been largely extinguished.

Two such women, both war widows, are Mrs. T., a 64-year-old former teacher originally from the Mekong Delta province of Kien Hoa, and her 35-year-old daughter-in-law, a slightly built woman named Lang.

Abroad, people receive news reports on the ending of war in Indochina, but neither Mrs. T. nor Lang took any interest in such things. When they are not busy preparing meals on a kerosene stove for the many children living with them, they

Continued on Page 11, Column 5

NEWS INDEX

POLICE REINFORCE BROOKLYN PATROL IN HIGH-RISK AREA

Volunteers to Guard Cars on Tours—Step Follows Wounding of Patrolmen

By ALFRED E. CLARK

Police Commissioner Patrick V. Murphy yesterday authorized 1,000 extra tours of duty for policemen in 11 precincts in the Brooklyn North Command during the next 30 days following the shooting of two policemen in Brownsville Thursday night.

Mr. Murphy said the two policemen, who are brothers and were reported to be in good condition in Brookdale Hospital, were attacked "without provocation and without warning." He noted that eight policemen had been shot within the last week.

The policemen on these special tours will be volunteers who will be mostly in … clothes and will ope… marked … man…

… in "unnecessary and wasted" Medicaid funds. The bill is backed by the Council leadership and the City Health Department.

It would require licensing of group practitioners and Medicaid discounters, or factors, who commonly receive 12 per cent of the bill in return for advancing cash to the practitioner who prefers not to wait several months for Medicaid reimbursement.

The bill would also set a limit on the number of Medicaid patients a doctor could see in one day and would require a Medicaid patient to attach his photograph to his Medicaid card.

Recently, Mr. Katz introduced a bill at the request of the Department of Health to halt "unethical" tie-ups between Medicaid practitioners and laboratories. Audits for the Health Department indicated that unnecessary tests had been ordered for patients to increase

The New York Times

Leon A. Katz

Medicaid payments. The department said the practitioners were receiving kickbacks from the laboratories.

As an example of the possible abuses in group Medicaid practice, Mr. Katz cited a recent visit he made to the Harlem offices of a medical group set up behind a pharmacy. Mr. Katz said he found an internist who had billed Medicaid for $106,000 in the first six months of last year—working part-time.

Mr. Katz said the internist

Continued on Page 59, Column 3

NIXON, IN BUDGET MESSAGE, TO ASK CONGRESS TO HOLD SPENDING TO $268.7-BILLION

Budget Chief Affirms Plan To Abolish Poverty Office

By JOHN HERBERS
Special to The New York Times

WASHINGTON, Jan. 26—The Nixon Administration confirmed today that it planned to abolish the Office of Economic Opportunity, the antipoverty agency established by the late President Johnson as one of the chief features of his Great Society.

Roy L. Ash, director of the Office of Management and Budget, acknowledged the development at a news conference, where he discussed President Nixon's proposals, announced today, to abolish … aller agencies — the … Emergency Prepared… Office of Science and … and the National … and Space Coun…

… these agencies is … esident's plan to … ber of employes … tive offices from … fewer than 2,000. … is expected to … rcussions than … f personnel. … to dismantle … gency is sure … in Congress, … on moves to … during the … been furi… the decision of the President to do without a science adviser in the White House aroused protests from a large segment of the scientific community, which felt that the role of science was being downgraded by the Administration.

Mr. Ash did not elaborate on plans to abolish the antipoverty agency. They will be detailed in the executive budget for the fiscal year 1974, which is to be released Monday. However, there have been reports in recent weeks that the agency is due to be dismantled under the many budget cuts that the Administration is proposing for the coming fiscal year, which begins next July. None of the reports has been denied.

The dismantling is to take three forms, according to informed sources. A number of the functions—health, aid to migrants, economic development, planning and research and others—are to be transferred to other departments and agencies. The Administration would make another effort in Congress to have legal services set up under a separate corporation.

But the largest component,

Continued on Page 26, Column 3

FIGHT IN PROSPECT

Democrats Worried by Plans to End Some Social Programs

By JAMES M. NAUGHTON
Special to The New York Times

WASHINGTON, Jan. 26 — President Nixon will ask Congress on Monday to approve a $268.7-billion budget for the fiscal year 1974.

The figure was disclosed today by Democratic Congressional leaders and was confirmed by Mr. Nixon.

But the Democratic leaders, while indicating their willingness to hold Federal spending to the level proposed by the White House, promised a battle to determine how the money should be allocated.

Reports circulated on Capitol Hill that Mr. Nixon's next budget would call for the elimination of the Job Corps and the Model Cities program, virtually dismantle the Office of Economic Opportunity and drastically cut the funding of health, housing, education and other social programs.

Leaders Are Briefed

"The question is whether they're legislating or we are when they abolish a whole program," Carl Albert, the Speaker of the House, declared after a briefing on the budget at the White House for Congressional leaders of both parties.

Mike Mansfield, the Senate majority leader, said that it was his feeling "we should try to work within that ceiling" outlined by Mr. Nixon at the meeting. But he pointedly added that Congress "should take the responsibility for so doing."

The White House announced that the President would make an 11-minute radio address on the new budget proposal at 6 P.M. Sunday from the Florida White House in Key Biscayne.

It was not known whether Mr. Nixon, on the eve of the formal submission of his budget to Congress, would specify any of his proposed allocations.

$25-Billion Deficit Seen

Mr. Mansfield said that, in a general discussion of the new budget this morning, the White House made clear that it would include a deficit of at least $12-billion. The Montana Democrat said that the Administration had also forecast a deficit of $25-billion for the current fiscal year, ending June 30.

In the current fiscal year, Mr. Nixon is authorized to spend some $260-billion but he is attempting in a variety of ways to hold the total to $250-billion. Against this, the plan to spend $268.7-billion in the next fiscal year would represent a modest increase.

Mr. Mansfield said that Congress would have to recognize that the 1974 proposal would include some $202-billion for "uncontrollable" items, which

Continued on Page 27, Column 3

…ld Nixon Aides …Watergate Fund

…TER RUGABER
… New York Times

… Reacting strongly to a remark by a defense attorney, the judge also said he would continue to examine witnesses …sonally whenever he felt …satisfied with the question… by either side.

…hen the prosecution finished … Mr. Sloan on Tuesday, … Sirica sent the jurors … courtroom and began … ine the witness on a … of financial points and … ssues.

… Sloan said he had "no … by the $199,000 in cash … turned over to G. Gor… a defendant in the … as then counsel to … arm of President … ical organization.

… ss said he had … e payments with … Stans, the former … Commerce, and … had in turn veri… ohn N. Mitchell, … rney General. … head of the … Re-election … d Mr. Stans … roup.

… t emerged … n by Earl … incipal assistant … es attorney, and the jury, thus, heard them for the

Continued on Page 19, Column 5

Edward G. Robinson, 79, Dies; His 'Little Caesar' Set a Style

By The Associated Press

HOLLYWOOD, Jan. 26 — Edward G. Robinson, whose tough, sinister appearance on movie screens concealed the soul of a gentle man, died today at the age of 79.

Mr. Robinson succumbed at Mount Sinai Hospital where he had undergone tests in recent weeks. The cause of death was not immediately determined.

Man of Great Kindness

By ALDEN WHITMAN

Edward G. Robinson was a skilled actor of the stage and screen whose vivid portrayal of motion - picture gangsters, among them Little Caeser, during the nineteen-thirties marked powerful mobsters who ruled the underworld during the Prohibition era.

So effective was the Robinson interpretation of the gangster that many of the underworld characters found themselves affecting the Robinson character—chomping down on cigar butts while snarling threats and orders out of the sides of their mouths.

But while Mr. Robinson was making his mark on others he, himself, remained strangely unaffected. In real life he was a man of great kindness and courtesy whose generosity scarcely knew bounds. Between 1939 and 1949 he made more than 850 contributions totaling above $250,000 to relief and entertainment agencies, to cultural, educational and religious groups.

His art collection comprised perhaps the outstanding group

Continued on Page 32, Column 3

Edward G. Robinson Is Dead at 79

Continued From Page 1, Col. 8

of privately owned paintings in the United States.

During the course of a marital settlement it was sold in 1957 for $3,250,000.

Mr. Robinson was born Dec. 12, 1893, as Emanuel Goldenberg in Bucharest, Rumania.

One of Mr. Robinson's brothers was hit on the head with a rock during a schoolboy pogrom and years later he died in America, probably from the effects of the blow.

To escape this persecution the family managed to scrape together the fare for steerage passage and came to the United States. "At Ellis Island I was born again," Mr. Robinson wrote later. "Life for me began when I was 10 years old."

Made Speeches to Friends

As a boy Mr. Robinson, as soon as he had mastered English, made speeches to his family and friends. His favorite was Theodore Roosevelt's second inaugural address, which he had committed to memory.

He hoped to become a criminal lawyer "to defend the human beings who were abused and exploited." With this purpose he entered Townsend Harris High School and after that City College. It was at City College that the youth decided to forego his law career to be an actor. He loved to perform before people.

But Mr. Robinson's study of the theatre told him that there had been many little men in the theatre. He won a scholarship at the American Academy of Dramatic Art with a sizzling and effective delivery of the Brutus and Cassius quarrel scene from "Julius Caesar."

He was 19 when he entered dramatic school and shortly thereafter changed his name to Robinson "a name I had heard while sitting in the balcony of the Criterion Theatre."

He played in stock in Cincinnati, in vaudeville as a Chinese man in a skit at Hammerstein's. He finally broke into the legitimate theater in 1915 in a play called "Under Fire." He got the part because he was multilingual, an attribute called for in the script. Role followed role and the youngster received many good notices.

He joined the Theatre Guild and played a great variety of roles in such productions as "The Adding Machine," "The Brothers Karamazov," "Right You Are, If You Think You Are" and "Juarez and Maximilian."

He was starred for the first time in "The Kibitzer"—a play of which he was the co-author.

In January, 1927, Mr. Robinson married Gladys Lloyd, an actress.

Mr. Robinson had experimented with several screen roles in silent pictures but he was not happy with the result. With the addition of sound to the shadows, however, Mr. Robinson's interest was renewed and he tried his first talking-picture "The Hole in the Wall."

There followed "The Widow from Chicago" and a short time later, in 1931, "Little Caesar." Of "Little Caesar" a critic for The New York Times wrote:

"'Little Caesar' becomes at Mr. Robinson's hands a figure out of a Greek tragedy, a cold, ignorant, merciless killer, driven on and on by an insatiable lust for power, the plaything of a force that is greater than himself."

The film contained a climatic line that itself became a classic, Little Caesar's parting words as he lay slumped under a billboard after he had been shot by the police:

"Mother of God, is this the end of Rico?"

It was sometimes said that Mr. Robinson was selected to play the role of Little Caesar because of a resemblance to Al Capone, the Chicago vice baron. Mr. Robinson doubted this theory, and there was no real-life resemblance. Hollywood makeup artists, however, always managed to make Mr. Robinson look as sinister as Capone was reputed to be.

A more reasonable theory was that Hollywood sought him out because of his success as Nick Scarsi, a character in a play called "The Racket." This play was so real, Mr. Robinson once remarked, that it could not be produced in Chicago.

In any event, his portrayal of Little Caesar came to be considered a classic, and there followed others in the curled-lip mold—"Smart Money," "Five Star Final," "Bullets or Ballots," "Kid Galahad" and "A Slight Case of Murder."

The actor thought "Five Star Final" one of his finest tough-guy pictures. In it he played Randall, the editor of a muckraking tabloid. This film, released in 1931, along with many of his other movies, has been revived from time to time on television.

Mr. Robinson's first real departure from his two-fisted type of role on the screen was "Dr. Ehrlich's Magic Bullet" in 1940, and even this film about syphillis was billed as "the war against the greatest public enemy of all."

From 1929 to 1966 Mr. Robinson appeared in more than 100 films. His name, until recent years, usually meant good box office. In all, his films grossed well over $50-million, and this figure is a modest estimate. His own earnings were high and he lived appropriately.

Mr. Robinson was the first Hollywood star to entertain in France after the invasion of Normandy. He sold war bonds and it was said he turned his regular weekly radio dramatic show "Big Town" into a soap box in favor of the American way.

The American Legion gave the program a citation and he was commended for his "outstanding contribution to Americanism through his stirring patriotic appeals . . ."

But because he had allowed his name to be linked with so many causes, inevitably there were those with a Communist tinge. Mr. Robinson was named in "Red Channels" in connection with 11 Communist front organizations.

But Mr. Robinson carried his case to the House Un-American Activities Committee and eventually won a clean bill of health.

After 28 years of marriage Mr. Robinson was sued for divorce in 1955 and his wife was granted an interlocutory divorce decree the next year.

After 28 years as a movie actor Mr. Robinson returned to the stage in "Middle of the Night" and scored a success. At the age of 63 he was a forceful and vital figure on the stage and the youthful cast said that they found it difficult to match his boundless energy.

In "Middle of the Night" he portrayed an aging widower who married a much younger woman. Early in 1958, while he was still appearing in the Paddy Chayefsky play, Mr. Robinson was married to Jane Bodenheimer, a 38-year-old dress designer known professionally as Jane Arden.

Appeared in 100 Films

After his stage success, the actor performed occasionally on television and played featured roles in several other movies. In all he appeared in 40 Broadway plays and more than 100 films. Among his most recent movies were "A Boy Ten Feet Tall," "Cheyenne Autumn," "The Cincinnati Kid" and "Sammy Going South." It was while making this picture in 1964 that he suffered a mild heart attack.

Mr. Robinson was an excellent actor and was to have received a special Oscar for his "outstanding contribution to motion pictures" at the Academy Awards ceremony March 27. It would have been his first Oscar.

Edward G. Robinson as Rico Bandello with the other members of the gang in *Little Caesar*.

"All the News That's Fit to Print."

The New York Times.

LATE CITY EDITION
WEATHER—Fair, continued warm today; tomorrow cloudy, showers.
Temperatures Yesterday—Max., 88; Min., 73

VOL. LXXXIV....No. 28,329. Entered as Second-Class Matter, Postoffice, New York, N. Y. NEW YORK, SATURDAY, AUGUST 17, 1935. P TWO CENTS In New York City. | THREE CENTS Within 200 Miles | FOUR CENTS Elsewhere Except in 7th and 8th Postal Zones.

WILL ROGERS, WILEY POST DIE IN AIRPLANE CRASH IN ALASKA; NATION SHOCKED BY TRAGEDY

WILL ROGERS, WILEY POST DIE IN AIRPLANE CRASH IN ALASKA; NATION SHOCKED BY TRAGEDY

ROOSEVELT CALLS CHIEFS TO ARRANGE CONGRESS WIND-UP

Conference Tomorrow Is Expected to Set Program for Adjournment Thursday.

FIVE MAJOR BILLS FAVORED

Wealth Tax, Banking, Coal, Alcohol Control and Gold Ban Measures Slated to Pass.

UTILITY DEADLOCK HOLDS

Holding Company Curb and Other Major Bills Likely to Wait Till Next Session.

By The Associated Press.

WASHINGTON, Aug. 16.—A semi-final conference of Democratic leaders to make arrangements for a prompt adjournment of Congress was called tonight by President Roosevelt for Sunday night.

The expectation of some of the party chiefs was that at that meeting the President would disclose which measures he was willing for Congress to drop and which he wanted enacted before adjournment.

Among those invited to the conference, beginning at 8:30, were: Vice President Garner, Speaker Byrns, Senator Robinson of Arkansas, the Democratic leader; Chairman O'Connor of the House Rules Committee, Chairman Harrison of the Senate Finance Committee and Chairman Doughton of the House Ways and Means Committee.

It was indicated by one of the conferees that any agreement reached Sunday night, however, would be subject to possible modification if particular pressure developed for the enactment of any measure.

Conjecture on Pro…

From what they … heard directly and indi… the President, some of … ees, talking privately, … meeting made more clear … bilities of an end to the pr… sion by the end of next we… latest.

Some were talking about … journment Tuesday, or T… Most agreed that it probabl… be the latter part of next we… fore everything could be wou… to their satisfaction or to tha… the President.

The expectation of some of … conferees was that the Preside… would renew his insistence up… enactment of:

1. The Guffey Coal Stabilization Bill, which proponents and some opponents say will pass the House Monday and be approved by the Senate early next week:
2. The Federal alcohol control plan.
3. The $250,000,000 Tax Bill.
4. The Omnibus Banking Bill, on which conferees reached an agreement late today.
5. The measure forbidding suits for gold payments on government contracts.

Six Bills May Be Shelved.

Their belief was that unless action was hastened the following would be left behind when this session ended, with their present status remaining the same until the next session:

1. The Utilities Bill;
2. The rivers and harbors legislation;
3. The measure expanding Federal control over food and drugs;
4. Railroad reorganization;
5. General oil regulation;
6. The Ship Subsidy Bill.

Leaders said the Utilities Bill probably would be left behind, not because the President did not want the legislation, but because the conference deadlock could not be broken.

A possibility was seen by some that the Rivers and Harbors Bill might be insisted upon because it would legalize the millions already spent by the Federal Government on a number of projects, such as the Parker Dam. And they added that they had but scant doubt that before Congress had adjourned it would ratify the oil compacts entered into in Dallas last February.

House Tax Conferees Named.

Special to THE NEW YORK TIMES.

WASHINGTON, Aug. 16.—A determined drive to adjourn Congress by Tuesday night, with Thursday as the latest alternate date, was started today following formal commitment of the Wealth-Tax Bill to conference and a conference agreement on the Eccles Banking Bill.

The promise of Tuesday adjournment was held out by Senator Robinson as the Senate voted to take a recess until Monday. Early in the day he had informed the Senate of his desire to quit at that time and in so doing issued a warning

Continued on Page Fourteen.

Davey Sets Ohio Vote for 1936, Defying Opponents of New Deal

Governor, Here, Denies Delaying Test on Advice of Roosevelt Forces, Gives Economy as Reason—He and President Are Accused of 'Conspiracy' by Republican Leader.

Governor Martin L. Davey of Ohio moved formally yesterday to defy Republican demands for a special State-wide election this year for Representative at Large to test New Deal sentiment in the State.

The Governor was visiting New York City during the day and telephoned his office in Columbus to frame an order in legal form setting the election for next year. All that remains to put the order into effect is the signature of the Governor, which he said he would affix when he reached Ohio tomorrow.

With the Republican national leaders, heartened by a victory in the Rhode Island Congressional elections, demanding that Ohio vote this November to fill the vacancy caused by the death of Representative Charles V. Truax, the Governor insisted that the election should be held next year to avoid imposition of from $500,000 to $600,000 special election costs on hard-pressed taxpayers of the State.

He ridiculed the charge made by his political adversaries that the election was being postponed until next year, apparently under advice from the Roosevelt forces at Washington, to prevent an early test of the New Deal in such a key State as Ohio.

"There is no moral justification of loading that extra cost for a special election on the units of the State," Governor Davey said at the Hotel Biltmore. "The good and ample reason for this order is that a recent referendum reducing the tax limit from 15 mills to 10 mills on the dollar has, with the aid of the depression, depleted the treasuries of the counties and the cities so badly that they could not well stand the expense of a special election.

"Now I want to point out that no district in Ohio will be without representation meanwhile, since this post is that of a Representative at Large. I have an excellent precedent for this action, since the same course was followed in my

Continued on Page Seven.

ROOSEVELT RESTS AT HYDE PARK HOME

Joins Family on Two-Day Visit to Celebrate 21st Birthday of Franklin Jr.

AVOIDS ISSUE ON HOOVER

President Intercedes for Man Caught at Baltimore Wh… Stealing Ride o…

… …ackle act… wh… he will retu… White House for a long se… of conferences with the individuals and groups representing the administration leadership on Capitol Hill.

A cheery confidence was radiated by Mr. Roosevelt today as he was subjected to a barrage of questions by reporters who clustered around his automobile in the bright morning sunlight.

Questioned on Utility Bill.

The questions dealt principally with the Utility Holding Company Bill, which has been deadlocked in conference between the House and Senate for some time, and the Tax Bill which was sent to conference yesterday after the Senate had approved a measure considerably different than the House bill.

Asked if he expected enactment of the Utility Bill this session, Mr. Roosevelt replied smilingly that he hoped so, with an inflection in his voice which some reporters interpreted as indicating that he intended to have this done.

Would he be willing, he then was asked, to accept the House bill, which differs from the Senate bill and administration recommendations in its omission of the celebrated "death sentence" section? At this question, Mr. Roosevelt smiled and closed the topic with the assertion that he could not comment on details.

A request for comment on the action of the Senate in passing the Tax Bill in changed form brought the rejoinder from the President that the Tax Bill had not been finally passed by Congress yet; that it was still an open question.

Renewed efforts by correspondents to get specific comment from the President on the recent statement by former President Hoover requesting Mr. Roosevelt to set forth definitely his plans regarding possible changes in the Constitution, elicited from the President only the reply that he had read Mr. Hoover's statement very hurriedly and therefore was in no position to comment.

Aside from the conferences Mr.

Continued on Page Fourteen.

CONFEREES AGREE ON BANK MEASURE

Glass and His Senators Win on Nearly All Points, Ending Long Battle on Bill.

ONE VICTORY FOR HOUSE

Effo…

… taken on the con… report in the House Monday. The conferees arranged to file formal reports to both branches tomorrow.

The end of the conference marks a long and bitter fight over the policies of Marriner S. Eccles, governor of the Federal Reserve Board, as expressed in the bill passed by the House, and the views of the Glass group as set forth in the Senate bill.

Opinion tonight was that Mr. Glass, veteran banking legislator, had once more come out the victor.

Reserve Board Is Increased.

He and the other Senate conferees succeeded in carrying out their views on the open market committee, particularly in the aspect that government securities must be purchased on the open market and not direct from the Treasury.

Likewise, Senate conferees prevailed in their insistence that the Federal Reserve Board must be increased from the present six to seven members, with the Secretary of the Treasury and the Controller of the Currency eliminated as members ex officio.

The suggested permission of the Senate bill for banks of deposit to underwrite securities was stricken out at the request of President Roosevelt, Senator Glass stated.

The provision of the Senate bill that bankers may serve on not more than two bank boards simultaneously was retained but made subject to the discretion of the Reserve Board, however.

A big feature of the bill is the arrangement for the open market committee, which would be composed of seven Reserve Board members and five representatives of the twelve regional Reserve Banks. This committee would have power to influence the flow of credit by purchase and sale of government bonds by the Reserve Banks.

Policy Is Mandatory.

The policy laid down by the committee would be mandatory upon the Reserve Banks.

Following the view of Mr. Eccles, the House gave complete voting control of open market operations entirely to the Reserve Board, with

Continued on Page Fourteen.

HOPSON ADMITS TRYING TO CONTROL PRESS WITH ADS

He Also Tells Senators He Urged Move to Kill Utility Bill in Conference.

ATTACK ON TIMES RENEWED

House Committee Told That His 1934 Income Was Between $300,000 and $500,000.

Special to THE NEW YORK TIMES.

WASHINGTON, Aug. 16.—Howard C. Hopson, who now admits that he was the guiding influence of the $900,000 lobby that the Associated Gas and Electric Company waged against the Wheeler-Rayburn bill, was forced to state before the Senate lobby inquiry committee today that the company had not hesitated to use the advertising columns of newspapers as a club to minimize unfavorable publicity.

He also said he had suggested to another high utility holding company official that a campaign be waged to kill the administration's utility program in conference of the two branches of Congress. As matters stand tonight every indication is that the Wheeler-Rayburn bill will die in conference, where for more than a month the conferees of the Senate and House have been deadlocked. All hope had not been given up by the measure's advocates, however.

Earlier in the day, be… House investigatin… Hopson …

… Com… was signed … Robertson, Mr. Hop… private secretary.

The telegram was in fact his own, said Mr. Hopson, explaining that it was his custom to have Mr. Robertson sign practically all of his messages to his New York office.

Messages to Hearst Admitted.

William Randolph Hearst was pictured before the committee as the writer of an editorial printed in the Hearst newspapers Sunday, June 2, which Senator Black asserted was strikingly along lines suggested by Mr. Hopson in a telegram to Mr. Hearst dated May 31.

Mr. Hopson admitted sending frequent messages to Mr. Hearst, who was dubbed by Senator Minton "the sage of San Simeon," but insisted that he had no reason to believe his messages inspired editorials or news articles in the Hearst papers.

Arthur Brisbane, Hearst writer, was pilloried, however, and documents placed in evidence showed

Continued on Page Twenty-six.

COAL BILL SPLITS HOUSE DEMOCRATS; PASSAGE HELD SURE

Widest Party Schism Since 'Death Sentence' Marks 'Must' Measure Debate.

VICTORY BY 30 CLAIMED

Administration Leaders Are Confident Despite Attacks as Unconstitutional.

Special to THE NEW YORK TIMES.

WASHINGTON, Aug. 16.—In the face of the most serious party schism which has yet confronted any of President Roosevelt's projects for industrial reform, the Guffey-Snyder Coal Bill was manoeuvred by House leaders tonight into a position for final action on Monday.

With general debate on the measure concluded, they planned to carry it through the amending stage tomorrow and adjourn before the vote on passage.

Not since the vote on the President's demand for the "death sentence" for utility holding companies has the rank and file of the Democratic majority been so thoroughly split as on the merits of the Guffey-Snyder measure, and leaders were working overtime to m… good their predi… would pa… Altho…

… whom … it, and …publican time. … been reported favor… the committee by a vote of 12 to 11.

The special rule for consideration of the bill was adopted 241 to 94, after a perfunctory debate. Representative McCormack, one of the two Democrats on the Ways and Means Committee who abstained from voting on reporting out the measure, said that he would vote for the rule but against the bill.

He told other members that there would be no inconsistency in such a position, and that he thought the bill should have a chance for consideration on the floor.

Representative Fuller of Arkansas called Speaker Byrns's attention to the distribution by pages in the hall of copies of the bill bearing typewritten slips which said:

"Bituminous Coal Bill as amended and reprinted. Controversial propaganda largely eliminated. Two-thirds of tonnage output operators favored bill and more than 95 per cent of labor."

Representative Snyder of Pennsylvania, co-author of the bill, said that he had pasted the slips on the measure and had instructed the

Continued on Page Seven.

Lawyer Charges Judge Downs Beat Him; Sues for $50,000 in Contempt Case Row

County Judge Thomas Downs of Queens was sued in the New York Supreme Court yesterday by Lorenzo C. Carlino, a lawyer, for $50,000 damages. The lawyer charged that Judge Downs, after finding him guilty of contempt of court in a trial, and fining him $250, had knocked him down and kicked him at the St. Albans Golf Club in Queens.

Mr. Carlino alleges that his appeal from the contempt order was based on the ground that it was a violation of the section of the Judiciary Act which requires that a contempt order cite the specific facts upon which it is based. The lawyer further asserts that he got an order from the Appellate Division restraining Judge Downs from making any change in the order pending the appeal.

Mr. Carlino served the order on Judge Downs at the golf club on May 7 last, he alleges, when the jurist was about to step into his car. He says that as soon as he showed a signature of Presiding Justice Lazansky on an injunction order, "the defendant, Thomas Downs, struck the plaintiff, knocked him down, then kicked him while on the ground and trampled upon the order which was served upon him. Defendant called plaintiff vile, filthy names and otherwise used vile and filthy language."

In addition to the suit against Judge Downs the lawyer asks $25,000 damages from Sheriff Peter J. McGarry of Queens for brutal treatment when he was arrested on the contempt order, which was later set aside by the Appellate Division.

Judge Downs denied last night he had assaulted Mr. Carlino.

"I was getting into my automobile parked in front of the clubhouse about 10 o'clock one night more than three months ago," the judge explained, "when a man I did not recognize in the darkness rushed out at me from some shrubbery. I was all alone and had received only a few days before an anonymous threat against my life. I hit the man at once. He fell down and a paper dropped to the ground. The man picked up the paper and ran away."

Sergeant Morgan's Report of the Death Of Rogers and Post as Seen by Natives

Special to THE NEW YORK TIMES.

SEATTLE, Wash., Aug. 16.—The radio message sent by relays from Point Barrow, Alaska, to Seattle, in which Staff Sergeant Stanley R. Morgan informed the world of the tragic death of Will Rogers and Wiley Post, read as follows:

"Ten P. M. native runner reported plane crashed fifteen miles south of Barrow.

"Immediately hired fast launch, proceeded to scene.

"Found plane complete wreck, partly submerged, two feet water.

"Recovered body Rogers, then necessary tear plane apart extract body of Post from water.

"Brought bodies Barrow. Turned over Dr. Greist.

"Also salvaged personal effects, which am holding. Advise relatives and instruct this station fully as to procedure.

"Natives camping small river fifteen miles south here claim Post, Rogers landed and asked way to Barrow.

"Taking off, engine misfired on right bank while only fifty feet off water.

"Plane, out of control, crashed nose on, tea… wing off and nosing over, forcing engine back … ne.

"Both apparently killed insta…

"Both bodies brui…

"Post's wri…

The…

…ain and France Hold That Frank Presentation of Demands Is Essential.

By FREDERICK T. BIRCHALL.

Wireless to THE NEW YORK TIMES.

PARIS, Aug. 16.—Throughout the day and until late this evening, with only an interval for luncheon, Premier Pierre Laval, Anthony Eden of Great Britain and Baron Pompeo Aloisi of Italy have been in conference at the Quai d'Orsay over the Italo-Ethiopian problem in an effort to avert a war, with its resultant repercussions in Europe.

The first day's deliberations closed tonight with one definite, positive step taken toward results. The British and French have made a joint formal request to the Italians to state fully and frankly their complaints against Ethiopia and their consequent claims upon her.

From a British source it is learned that the Ethiopian Government, which is not represented at this conference, has shown a disposition to concede several points that may go far toward satisfying the Italian claims when these are made.

Offers Security Guarantees.

The Addis Ababa government, for instance, has expressed willingness to provide the most complete guarantees of security from Ethiopian aggression for the present Italian colonies and such economic concessions as may be agreed upon, provided the guarantees expected fall short of military occupation.

Emperor Haile Selassie is willing to grant reasonable rights for developing mineral and commercial possibilities within the Ethiopian territory, specific concessions to Italy being made in both fields.

He is further willing to consider granting some rights to Europeans to settle in Ethiopian territory and develop it while maintaining their original nationality. This last point would go a long way toward compliance with the Italian wishes.

Finally, he is willing to renew and even extend by making further concessions the old understanding with Italy, giving her permission to undertake a certain amount of commercial road and railroad construction in this country. This again anticipates an obvious Italian demand.

No answer to the Franco-British query was forthcoming from Rome tonight. Indeed, an immediate response was not expected. Baron Aloisi agreed to submit the request to Rome and to report the result as soon as possible. He received assurance from the others that if Italy would comply with this re-

Continued on Page Three.

…nd to Post.

GARNER DEEPLY AFFECTED

Robinson Hails 'Best Loved Citizen'—Deaths 'Real Loss,' Speaker Byrns Says.

Special to THE NEW YORK TIMES.

WASHINGTON, Aug. 16.—The death of Will Rogers and Wiley Post shocked and saddened the capital, which knew Rogers as a frequent visitor and liked him as an amiable "josher" of politicians.

Legislative machinery stopped briefly in tribute. The Senate dropped other business to honor the humorist, a friend of Presidents, diplomats and political leaders. The House also listened to a speech of eulogy, while from all quarters came expressions of sorrow over his death.

As soon as the Senate convened, Senator Robinson, the Democratic leader, took the floor and said:

"Probably the most widely known private citizen in the United States and certainly the best beloved met his death some hours ago in a lonely, far-away place.

"We pause for a moment in the midst of our duties to pay brief tribute to his memory and to that of his gallant companion, Wiley Post.

"I do not think of Will Rogers as dead. I shall remember him always as a sensible, courageous, loyal friend, possessed of unusual and notable talents.

"He made fun for all mankind. In nothing that he ever said was there an intentional sting. He was kind, generous, patriotic.

"His companion was a courageous representative of a gallant group who, on wings of adventure, sought remote places and conquered long distances."

News Saddens McNary.

Senator McNary, the Republican leader, said:

"Mr. Rogers has brought happiness, joy and good feeling to the hearts of millions of Americans. In common with all his fellow-citizens, I regret his tragic end and that of his doughty and valiant companion."

Vice President Garner, a friend of long standing, who shared the humorist's dislike of ceremonial attire, could only say, when informed of his death:

"Awful bad! Awful bad!"

Mr. Rogers had boomed Mr. Garner for the Presidency three years ago, and the two had a gay time together Jan. 17 when the Vice President entertained for President Roosevelt.

Speaker Byrns, addressing the House, mentioned Mr. Rogers's in-

Continued on Page Four.

10-MINUTE HOP THEIR LAST

Engine Fails on a Take-Off for Final 15 Miles to Point Barrow.

LANDED TO GET BEARINGS

Startled Eskimos See Huge Bird Plunge to River Bank From 50 Feet Above Water.

ONE RUNS 3 HOURS TO TELL

Humorist Revealed as Financing a Trip Around the World With Famous Pilot.

(Copyright, 1935, by The Associated Press.)

POINT BARROW, Alaska, Aug. 16.—Will Rogers, beloved humorist, and Wiley Post, master aviator, were crushed to death last night when a shiny, new airplane motor altered and became an engine of tragedy near this outpost of civilization.

…oth were killed when their red …tic sky cruiser slipped and fell …feet head-on into a river bank. …50-horse-power motor, driven into the fuselage, snuffed out …es of the two men instantly. …ative runner raced to Point … with word of a plane … Sergeant Stanley R. Mor… the Army Signal Corps … to the scene to learn the full significance of the tragedy.

First he took the body of Rogers from the cabin. Then he was forced to tear the plane apart to recover that of the flier who twice had flown around the globe—once alone.

Bodies Are Taken to Barrow.

The bodies were brought here and given to the care of Dr. Henry W. Greist, a Presbyterian medical missionary.

It was a trifling ten-minute flight that ended the careers of two famous figures long accustomed to flying. Although Rogers—gentle master of the "wise crack"—never became a pilot, he was perhaps the world's foremost airplane passenger.

Resuming a happy-go-lucky aerial tour of Alaska, a prelude to a flight to Siberia and on to Moscow, the noted travelers left Fairbanks late yesterday for a 500-mile hop to Point Barrow, northernmost white settlement in America.

Fifty miles out they encountered fog. Post "sat down" on Harding Lake for a while, but resumed the journey soon.

Apparently uncertain of his bearings, he again brought his pontooned plane to the surface of a shallow river fifteen miles southwest of here to ask natives the way to Point Barrow.

Rogers chatted with the Eskimos. Post tinkered with the plane during the brief stop. Soon after 5 P. M. (11 P. M. Eastern daylight time) they took off for the last little hop.

Motor Misfires on Take-Off.

The natives told the story to Sergeant Morgan. They said the motor of Post's new specially built plane misfired soon after it rose. The pilot quickly banked to the right; then the ship plummeted nose first, out of control. It dived into the edge of the stream, where the water was only two feet deep.

When Sergeant Morgan arrived at the scene by launch, he said today, he found the monoplane a complete wreck, partly submerged. The right wing was broken off.

The soldier said Post's watch had stopped at 8:18 P. M., apparently the time of the accident. [The difference in time indicated by the aviator's watch and that reported by the natives probably is accounted for by the time zones through which he had flown.]

The runner arrived here at 10 P. M. with word of the tragedy. Recovering the flier's personal effects, Sergeant Morgan turned them over to Dr. Greist, awaiting instructions from Mrs. Rogers and Mrs. Post and from Morgan's superior, Colonel George E. Kumpe at Seattle.

The unrelenting Arctic, grave of other such noted fliers as Carl Ben Eielson and Frank Dorbandt, played a leading part in this new tragedy.

Rogers and Post had left Fairbanks in the face of poor flying conditions. The stop at Harding Lake enabled them to await the

Continued on Page Four.

ROGERS AND POST KILLED IN PLANE

(Copyright, 1935, by The Associated Press.)

POINT BARROW, Alaska, Aug. 16.—Will Rogers, beloved humorist, and Wiley Post, master aviator, were crushed to death last night when a shiny, new airplane motor faltered and became an engine of tragedy near this outpost of civilization.

Both were killed when their red Arctic sky cruiser slipped and fell fifty feet head-on into a river bank. The 550-horse-power motor, driven back into the fuselage, snuffed out the lives of the two men instantly.

A native runner raced to Point Barrow with word of a plane crash. Sergeant Stanley R. Morgan of the Army Signal Corps dashed to the scene to learn the full significance of the tragedy.

First he took the body of Rogers from the cabin. Then he was forced to tear the plane apart to recover that of the flier who twice had flown around the globe—once alone.

Bodies Are Taken to Barrow.

The bodies were brought here and given to the care of Dr. Henry W. Greist, a Presbyterian medical missionary.

It was a trifling ten-minute flight that ended the careers of two famous figures long accustomed to flying. Although Rogers —gentle master of the "wise crack" —never became a pilot, he was perhaps the world's foremost airplane passenger.

Resuming a happy-go-lucky aerial tour of Alaska, a prelude to a flight to Siberia and on to Moscow, the noted travelers left Fairbanks late yesterday for a 500-mile hop to Point Barrow, northernmost white settlement in America.

Fifty miles out they encountered fog. Post "sat down" on Harding Lake for a while, but resumed the journey soon.

Apparently uncertain of his bearings, he again brought his pontooned plane to the surface of a shallow river fifteen miles southwest of here to ask natives the way to Point Barrow.

Rogers chatted with the Eskimos. Post tinkered with the plane during the brief stop. Soon after 5 P. M. (11 P. M. Eastern daylight time) they took off for the last little hop.

Motor Misfires on Take-Off.

The natives told the story to Sergeant Morgan. They said the motor of Post's new specially built plane misfired soon after it rose. The pilot quickly banked to the right; then the ship plummeted nose first, out of control. It dived into the edge of the stream, where the water was only two feet deep.

When Sergeant Morgan arrived

Will Rogers

at the scene by launch, he said today, he found the monoplane a complete wreck, partly submerged. The right wing was broken off.

The soldier said Post's watch had stopped at 8:18 P. M., apparently the time of the accident. [The difference in time indicated by the aviator's watch and that reported by the natives probably is accounted for by the time zones through which he had flown.]

The runner arrived here at 10 P. M. with word of the tragedy. Recovering the flier's personal effects, Sergeant Morgan turned them over to Dr. Greist, awaiting instructions from Mrs. Rogers and Mrs. Post and from Morgan's superior, Colonel George E. Kumpe at Seattle.

The unrelenting Arctic, grave of other such noted fliers as Carl Ben Eielson and Frank Dorbandt, played a leading part in this new tragedy.

Rogers and Post had left Fairbanks in the face of poor flying conditions. The stop at Harding Lake enabled them to await the lifting of fog there. Then they encountered it again as they streaked further on toward the Pole.

They sighted the Eskimo camp southwest of here, an area described by Andrew Bahr, the reindeer driver, as one of the most desolate places in the world.

Obtaining directions, they set out on the little hop to Barrow. Here Rogers wanted to visit Charles Brower, known as "the King of the Arctic." Brower has lived in the Arctic fifty-one years. He is a trader and operates a whaling station near by.

The tragedy occurred during the height of the short Arctic Summer. Barrow is more than 300 miles inside the Arctic Circle, at the end of Alaska's northernmost point. Even yet its "harbor" is open only at intervals to shipping, and the Coast Guard cutter Northland is held in the icepack off Wainwright, seventy-five miles southwest of here, after her annual visit here.

Crosson Funeral Plane Pilot.

The bodies rested tonight in the Presbyterian Mission warehouse here, to be flown to Fairbanks by the flying friend of both men, Pilot Joe Crosson, who had advised them against taking off from Fairbanks because of bad weather.

Flying from Fairbanks, accompanied by Robert Gleason, local radio chief of Pan American Airways, Pilot Crosson arrived here this evening and planned to take off with the bodies on his return trip some time tonight.

Dr. Greist said the rescue party reported that "the plane débris was readily removed, as it was torn and broken to fragments by the plunge."

"The bodies," he said, "were dressed by Charles Brower, whom Rogers was flying to see; Sergeant Stanley R. Morgan of the United States Army Signal Corps, and myself."

As Dr. Greist understood the stories of the accident, Rogers and Post had landed on the river when the Arctic fog made them uncertain of their bearings on a 500-mile flight from Fairbanks to Point Barrow.

An Eskimo pointed out the way. A few seconds after the take-off the plane's engine spluttered. The ship dropped into the river, striking first on its right wing and then nosing into the bank head on.

"The Eskimo said he ran to the water's edge and called, but there was no answer," said Dr. Greist.

Will Rogers in *Lightnin'*, 1930.

"Alarmed, he turned and ran t Barrow and informed Sergean Morgan."

The Eskimo was three hours rur ning the fifteen miles to Barro over the rough tundra, with man small lakes to encircle and man streams to cross.

"The native runner," Dr. Greis went on, "in his excitement on firs arriving here, mumbled in his dia lect of a red plane 'blowing up close to his little camp.

"Sergeant Morgan immediatel set out in a whale boat for th scene, but darkness and ice mad progress slow.

"The bodies of the two men an their effects were placed in a ski boat and towed back here."

Post and Rogers had left Fair banks in the face of a report tha there was a dense fog along th route and the thermometer regis tered 45 degrees.

Friends quoted Post as saying, " think we might as well go, any way."

Rogers, they said, agreed, declar ing, "There's lots of lakes we ca land on."

ADVENTURE MARKED LIFE OF HUMORIST

Born in Indian Territory on Nov. 4, 1879, He Rose to Become 'Envoy of World.'

OFTEN ACCLAIMED ABROAD

Became a Familiar Figure to Broadway at Hammerstein's and the Follies.

Will Rogers had what it takes to tickle the national funny bone. His wry countenance, with its occasionally wistful expression, was comica to see, and his consciously culti vated drawl lent a rustic savor to his sophisticated quips. Most im portant of all, he had the knack o translating into trenchant phrase the inchoate thoughts of masses of "average" Americans.

He razzed Congress unmercifully twitted Presidents and Kings, kid ded the American public for falling for the blandishments of European borrowers, and he echoed the gen erally held impression that politi cians should do more and talk less He could be serious, too—putting into words the national pride that was stirred by the Paris flight of Colonel Charles A. Lindbergh and the public indignation that was felt over the murder of the aviator's in fant son. Characteristically, a few years ago he suggested the follow ing epitaph for his tombstone:

"I joked about every prominent man in my lifetime, but I never met one I didn't like."

America's foremost comedian, he had become, in recent years, one of

(continued)

its leading boosters of air travel. He wrote thousands of words in defense of the argument that it was safer to travel by plane than by train and demonstrated that he meant it by following his own advice.

As a passenger he flew back and forth across the continent, covered most of South America and got a birds-eye view of Europe and some of Asia. It has been estimated by aviation experts that he flew more than 500,000 miles in the past seven years.

He was in one crack-up before the one in which he lost his life, but that did not diminish his enthusiasm for the new means of transportation. The accident occurred at Las Vegas in June, 1928, when the rope-twirling raconteur was en route to the Republican National Convention. Rogers told the story of the crash in one of the brief dispatches he sent daily to THE NEW YORK TIMES.

"Wheel broke when she come down and turned over and lit on her head," he wrote. "Am the first candidate to land on his head, but being a candidate it didn't hurt the head."

William Penn Adair Rogers—to use all of it—has been called the lineal descendant of Artemus Ward. For years he watched the shifting American scene, noting its movements with flippancy and wisdom. While it is easy to call a spade a spade, he did so and yet made the spade like it—which is something else. His comments on life were widely followed and almost universally quoted. One of the most used American expressions was "Did you see what Will Rogers said?"

Before settling down as a philosophic jester, he had been almost everything else. He was a cowboy, a circus performer and an actor. Sometimes he denied this last, on the ground that he was "not smart enough to act." He starred in vaudeville and on the stage and in the movies after they became vocal. His attempts with the screen before it became audible were not overly successful. Finally, he was a lecturer and a writer, having to his credit an enormous output of pithy comment on the daily events.

He was once Mayor of Beverly Hills, Acting Mayor of New Orleans and Ambassador to the World —the last without portfolio. His name was mentioned for the Governorship of Oklahoma and for the Presidency of the United States a couple of times. Voting for Will Rogers became a habit with people; it was one of the best ways to file a protest without going Socialist.

Amassed Wealth in Work.

He had a tremendous financial success, and never mentioned it. When his friend, Fred Stone, was injured some years ago he dropped all his contracts—totaling some half-million dollars—in order to take his place until Stone recovered. He toured the country raising money for drought and flood relief and took part in hundreds of benefits. In his quiet way, he gave thousands of dollars of his private fortune to charity.

He was born at Oolagah, in Indian Territory, on Nov. 4, 1879, but he called Claremore, Okla., his 'home town." He had some Indian blood, and one of his more famous remarks came when, in a discussion of ancestry, he remarked that his ancestors had not come over in the Mayflower; they had "met the boat." He went to school at the Willow Hassell School at Neosho, Mo., and Kemper Military Academy at Booneville.

Difficult to interview at all times, he once replied to a question about education by saying: "I studied the

Kent Taylor, Will Rogers and Evelyn Venable in *David Harum*.

Fourth Reader for ten years." At all events, his mother saw in him a Methodist preacher, but she saw that quite alone. Will Rogers developed a passion for horses and he learned the use of the lariat. The chewing gum came later, when he was established. Talking about the days that followed the death of the Methodist dream, he once said:

"I was a kid in Oklahoma and had me a buddy and a little cattle ranch and I sold my cows for about $7,000 and took my buddy and went to New Orleans, figuring on catching a boat for the Argentine, because I had seen a map or read a dime novel or something. Well, there weren't any boats, so we took a boat for New York, figuring to catch one there.

"But New York didn't have any Argentine line either, so my buddy said I ought go to England; and we went to England and caught a boat there, and by the time we got to Rio I was just about broke and my buddy was homesick, so I paid his way back and got me a job on a ranch, thinkin' I could rope.

"Well, those gauchos down there taught me different, swishin' a lasso over my head from twenty feet behind and downin' a cow better than I can shoot a guy with a Winchester. So I worked awhile and then worked my way to South Africa on a cattle boat, and there I joined up with a little Wild West show, doing a roping act.

"From South Africa I went to Australia, where I worked with the Wirth shows, owned by Mae Wirth's daddy. Then I went to Japan and China, and then to San Francisco, and from there I bummed my way back home, and a feller told my dad he didn't think I had done so well because he heard I, came home wearing overalls for underdrawers.

"Well, that only goes to show the success magazines are full of bunk when they write about a fellow winning fame and fortune by working hard and sticking to one job. All of you know, as well as I do, it was some accident started you off on the right track, but you ain't going to tell the reporters that, the next time they interview you."

How He Won First Fame.

The "accident" seems to have been a cow. The tradition is that one day, while Mr. Rogers was playing in the Wild West show in New York, one of the animals got free. He captured it with the rope, got into the public eye and so was hired for a turn on the Hammerstein Roof. This was in 1905. He went from the roof to vaudeville, back to the roof and then to Ziegfeld, and was there almost ever after, at least as long as he remained on Broadway.

A legend has grown up on Broadway about the transition from pantomime to monologue in the early Rogers vaudeville act. One of his most difficult tricks was the double lassoing of a horse and rider. Two ropes and a good deal of concentration and hope were required, but the finer nuances of the job were lost on the drug store cowboys in the balcony.

He Finds His Voice.

Some one told Rogers that he ought to explain what he was getting at. He did and these are handed down as the first words ever spoken by the national commentator before an audience:

"Ladies and gentlemen, I want to call your sho nuff attention to this next little stunt I'm agoing to pull on you, as I am going to throw these two ropes at once, catching the horse with one and the rider with the other. I don't have any idea that I'll get it, but here goes."

The audience laughed and Rogers was angry. He had not meant to be funny. He was just being himself. For a long time afterward he could not be induced to say another word, but finally he did, and he said later it was "the luckiest thing" he ever did. For a while he confined himself to comments on the other acts in the show, but finally he began searching for other material.

He turned naturally to the newspapers, scanning the late editions of the evening papers and sometimes the early editions of the morning papers just before going on for his act, often managing to get off a pithy comment on some occurrence in the day's news before his audience knew of the event itself. This was the origin of one of his first widely quoted wisecracks:

"All I know is what I read in the papers."

In a little while Rogers was twirling his rope and amusing the patrons at Hammerstein's Roof with his comments on personalities and events. He appeared in Ziegfeld's "Follies" and the "Frolics" for more than six years and at the opening of one of them remarked:

"Yes, a first night at the Follies is quite a function. Every one brings his new wife to see the old one act."

Made Many Silent Films.

In 1919 Will Rogers abandoned the stage and went to Hollywood to make some silent pictures. Not unqualified successes, some of them were: "Two Wagons, Both Covered," "Doubling for Romeo," "Boys Will Be Boys," "Family Fits," "Jubilo," "Our Congressman," "Going to Congress," "Gee Whiz, Genevieve" and a series of shorts called "Strolling Through Europe With Will Rogers." In 1922 he returned to the "Follies" and remained on Broadway until the talkies came. Then he made "They Had to See Paris."

When Fred Stone was hurt, Mr. Rogers took his friend's place in "Three Cheers." Charles Dillingham, its producer, used to send the comedian his salary in the form of a signed check, permitting Mr. Rogers to fill in the amount. When the show went on the road he returned to Hollywood and appeared in "So This Is London," "Lightnin'," "A Connecticut Yankee," "Ambassador Bill," "Young as You Feel," "Business and Pleasure" and other pictures.

Other items, besides the usual collection of stories about him, were various. He was married in 1908 to Betty Blake of Oolagah and they had three children. Will Rogers got up a family polo team which did pretty well for a time. "Had to give it up," he said finally. "Mary [a daughter] went society on us." And then there was the undoubted fact that in Claremore is a hotel—"with more bathrooms than Buckingham Palace"—called The Will Rogers.

When he went to Hollywood his studio built him a place. There was a garden and adobe hut and cactus and an electric stove. He looked in, said it was "swell" and never went back until former President Coolidge and Mrs. Coolidge came later in the year to call. "Well," he explained after he had seen them there, "they had to sit somewhere, didn't they?" He played dangerous polo, "because you couldn't make my mug look any worse no matter how much I hurt it." He owned a hurdy-gurdy, the only instrument he could play.

In 1927 Mr. Rogers went to Mexico at the same time as Colonel Lindbergh and was the guest of Ambassador Dwight Morrow. When the drought struck the West in 1931 he started a campaign for money and barnstormed over the country raising it. It was he who in 1930 made the suggestion that a silver cup be awarded by the American people to the "world's most cheerful loser," Sir Thomas Lipton. This last was done. He went to Europe at least a half dozen times, receiving the welcome accorded mostly to crowned heads.

He contributed widely to magazines and newspapers and the "box" published daily in THE NEW YORK TIMES was syndicated to about 500 newspapers in the United States and Canada, as was a weekly article of comment. He wrote several books, among them, "Rogerisms," a collection of his wisecracks; "The Cowboy Philosopher on Prohibition, 1919," "The Cowboy Philosopher on the Peace Conference," and "What We Laugh At, 1920." In 1924 his "Illiterate Digest" was greeted as one of the funniest books of the year.

Once an interviewer asked him for his recipe for humor and Rogers replied:

"A gag to be any good has to be fashioned about some truth. The rest you get by your slant on it and perhaps by a wee bit of exaggeration, so's people won't miss the point."

A few years ago Mr. Rogers came one evening to THE TIMES office and was shown around by the publisher. They reached the composing room, where the comedian was recognized. A small crowd grouped around. Suddenly taking his hat in his hand and waving it, he yelled: "We want more pay and less work!"

It was that sort of scene he did best.

The New York Times THURSDAY, DECEMBER 24, 1970

Charles Ruggles, Actor, Dies

SANTA MONICA, Calif., Dec. 23 (UPI)—Charles Ruggles, the stage, screen and television performer whose wryly turned milquetoast image made him one of the most disarming comedians in show business, died in St. John's Hospital today at the age of 84. A member of the family said he had had cancer.

A funeral service will be held Saturday in the Church of the Recessional at Forest Lawn Memorial Park in Glendale. Jack Haley will deliver the eulogy.

Had a Quiet Flair

Of his more than 80 movie appearances, Mr. Ruggles's role in the 1932 Paramount film "If I Had a Million," an episodic, all-star package about changed lives, perhaps best indicated the quiet flair, gentle expertise and wistful air of lurking rebellion that the actor came to symbolize.

As a nervous employe in a high-class china emporium, he was continually being fined for breaking the fragile merchandise and his talkative wife belittled his longing to raise pet rabbits. Willed $1-million by a stranger, he enters the shop majestically, late for work and leading a white rabbit on a leash. He then marches through the store cracking the choicest crockery with a cane.

In his best-known movie roles, the kind-faced, wide-eyed Mr. Ruggles displayed an unmistakable personal trademark in a grimace that even suggested the twitching whiskers of a rabbit. Although he played drama in his initial stage career, and in several early talking pictures, the wry geniality prevailed.

This trademark colored his television series in 1954, "The World of Mr. Sweeney," his return to Broadway in 1958 after nearly 30 years in "The Pleasure of His Company" and his final movies for the Walt Disney organization.

"I'll always be grateful for my grounding in theater," he said during preparations for the television series. As he rehearsed for his stage comeback, a hit comedy that drew an ovation on opening night, he admitted that "the stage was my first and only love."

Slept Through Earthquake

Mr. Ruggles was born in Los Angeles, the oldest son of a wholesale drug salesman. He grew up in San Francisco, slept through the earthquake of 1906 and, to family disapproval, was playing in a stock company at the Alcazar Theater at 17.

He played in various stock and road companies, usually portraying old men and character roles, before joining the Oliver Morosco company and playing juveniles in Chicago and New York. After his Broadway debut in "Help Wanted," he appeared in "Rolling Stones," "Canary Cottage," "Battling Butler" and such musicals as "The Passing Show of 1919," "Queen High" and "Spring Is Here."

In Disney Features

His first screen role, in 1929, was that of a drunken reporter in "Gentlemen of the Press." But comedy won out in "The Lady Lies," "Charley's Aunt" and "Friends of Mr. Sweeney." He played henpecked-husband parts opposite Mary Boland in such vehicles as "Six of a Kind" and "Ruggles of Red Gap," the latter a comedy classic of the American frontier.

He also had featured roles in such sophisticated froth as "Trouble in Paradise," "Love Me Tonight," "The Smiling Lieutenant" and "One Hour With You."

Other Ruggles movies were "Honeymoon for Three," "Bringing Up Baby," "Our Hearts Were Young and Gay," "Anything Goes," "The Parson of Panamint" and "All in a Night's Work." Two of his last films were "The Ugly Dachshund" and "Follow Me, Boys!" both Disney features, in 1966.

Between his screen roles, Mr. Ruggles made appearances on radio and later on television. He won a Tony award for his portrayal of the father of Cornelia Otis Skinner in "The Pleasure of His Company." He also appeared on Broadway in 1964 in the short-lived "Roar Like a Dove."

Mr. Ruggles was a widower when, in 1942, he married Marion La Barba, former wife of Fidel La Barba, the boxer. The couple who resided in Brentwood, a suburb of Los Angeles, were childless.

Mr. Ruggles' brother, Wesley, also an actor, became a noted screen director of the late silent movies and the early talkies.

Mr. Ruggles in 1965

ZaSu Pitts, Charles Laughton and Charles Ruggles in *Ruggles of Red Gap.*

The New York Times MONDAY, NOVEMBER 29, 1976

Rosalind Russell Dies of Cancer; Star of Stage and Screen Was 63

By ALBIN KREBS

Rosalind Russell, long one of the brightest stars of the American stage and screen, whose witty sophistication as Auntie Mame was a natural extension of Roz, the woman, died yesterday of cancer at her home in Beverly Hills, Calif. The family gave her age as 63.

A spokesman for the family said Miss Russell's husband, the producer Frederick Brisson, and their son, Lance, were with her. He said the actress' long illness had been complicated by rheumatoid arthritis and that she had been in the hospital three months ago for surgery to replace her right hip joint.

Miss Russell was perhaps best known to the public for her long string of film roles as brassy, sassy, wisecracking career-woman sophisticates, such as the star reporter in "His Girl Friday."

But comparatively late in her career, she became a major Broadway star in "Wonderful Town," the musical version of one of her earlier movies, "My Sister Eileen," and followed that triumph as the free-spirited, free-living Mame in "Auntie Mame."

Miss Russell said she liked to believe—and many people who knew her concurred in the belief—that Mame, the exuberant, fast-talking eccentric, possessed a personality and outlook very much like Miss Russell's.

That viewpoint was exultantly expressed by Mame/Rosalind at the end of the play's first act, when she spread wide her arms and proclaimed: "Live, live, live! Life is a banquet, and most of you poor sons-of-bitches are starving to death!"

Like Mame, Miss Russell seemed to be a whirling, swirling, constantly animated bundle of energy, always on the verge of being ignited. She refused to retire, until she was forced to do so by the effects of crippling arthritis over the last decade.

Little Struggle in Career

Her Hollywood career, which began in the early 1930's, was a highly successful one, almost completely devoid of the usual tales of struggling-young-actress-finally-makes-good.

After several straight dramatic roles, Miss Russell emerged as one of the films' most expert comedians with her appearance, in 1939, in "The Women," in which she played the vacuous and vicious —but extremely funny gossip—Sylvia Fowler.

She came to look upon that success with mixed feelings in later years, however, for it led to her being typecast. "By 1951," she said, "I had grown weary of playing the eternal, successful career woman in films. I had played that role 23 times."

From all accounts, Miss Russell's tireless energy went back to her childhood in Waterbury, Conn., where she was born. Her father, James Edward Russell, a successful trial lawyer who had worked his way up through the Yale Law School, and her mother, the former Clara McKnight, named Rosalind, the fourth of their seven children, after a steamship on which they had traveled to Nova Scotia on a wedding anniversary.

Miss Russell was brought up in a pleasant, well-staffed 13-room Victorian house, and she attended a Roman Catholic academy before enrolling at Marymount College at Tarrytown, N. Y. Having been in her childhood an all-round tomboy athlete, with several broken limbs to prove it, she was more interested in riding and other sports than in her studies at Marymount, where, in her sophomore year, the acting bug bit her.

Carried Away in Role

Playing the role of St. Francis of Assisi in a school play, Miss Russell was called upon to beat herself with thongs. "I got so carried away with the self-flagellation that I drew blood on my legs," she recalled years later. "Anyone that hammy had to turn to acting."

Leaving Marymount to enroll in the American Academy of Dramatic Arts, Miss Russell glibly assured her straitlaced mother that she would receive voice training at the New York acting academy that would qualify her to teach. After graduating in 1929, she worked in stock productions for $150 a week, and a year later made her Broadway debut in "Garrick's Gaieties." Two more years of featured parts in the theater followed.

After being lured to Hollywood in 1933 by Universal Pictures, Miss Russell was let go without having appeared in a movie. Her debut in that medium came in 1934, with a featured role in M-G-M's "Evelyn Prentice."

Other roles, "none to get excited about," she said, followed, and then, in 1936, Miss Russell had her first hit in "Craig's Wife," as Harriet Craig, the cold, domineering perfectionist housewife. More dramatic roles followed, notably that of the frightened spinster in "Night Must Fall" and the gentle schoolteacher in "The Citadel."

George Cukor, noted as a "woman's director" in Hollywood, discerned a comedy streak in Miss Russell, and hired her for the 135-woman cast of "The Women." The highlight of her performance was the now classic hair-pulling, clothes-ripping, leg-biting fight scene with Paulette Goddard.

Request for an Introduction

Miss Russell was noticed in that film role particularly by Frederick Brisson, a Danish-born theatrical agent who saw "The Women" on a ship crossing the Atlantic in 1939. In Hollywood, he was the house guest of Cary Grant, who was then co-starring with Miss Russell in "His Girl Friday," a remake of Ben Hecht and Charles MacArthur's "The Front Page," and Mr. Brisson asked to be introduced to the actress.

Mr. Grant was best man at the couple's wedding in 1941.

Miss Russell's heyday years in Hollywood were in the late 1930's and 40's. Among her successes were "No Time for Comedy," "Take a Letter, Darling" and "My Sister Eileen."

But also, by her own admission, "there were plenty of duds along the way, as I played the same role over and over—the over-tailored, padded-shouldered, pompadoured, funny-hatted, sleek and tough career woman with the flip lines and the flinty heart that somehow melts in the clutches of the man I needed all the time —in the last reel, of course."

Among the flops were "The Velvet Touch," "Tell It to the Judge" and "Woman of Distinction." Also less than

(continued)

Norma Shearer, Joan Fontaine, Rosalind Russell, Paulette Goddard and Mary Boland in *The Women.*

Clark Gable and Rosalind Russell in *They Met in Bombay*, 1941.

successful were some of the roles Miss Russell assayed in an effort to shake her type-casting as a comedian, such as those in "The Guilt of Janet Ames" ("I rarely mention it except in an inaudible whisper," she said) and "The Casino Murder Case" ("I don't even mention it in a whisper").

Miss Russell's most spectacular dramatic failure, she admitted, was in the turgid film version of O'Neill's "Mourning Becomes Electra."

'Part of Life's Menu'

She was engagingly frank about all that. "I'll match my flops with anybody's," she said, "but I wouldn't have missed them. Flops are a part of life's menu, and I'm never a girl to miss out on any of the courses." With the waning of her movie career in the late 1940's—there was to be a resurgence later—Miss Russell stepped up her already heavy load of fund-raising activities for some two dozen charitable and religious organizations, many of them Roman Catholic-affiliated. (She was a dedicated Catholic, but never spoke publicly about her religious convictions. She was capable, however, of being mildly irreverent when speaking of her plushy Beverly Hills parish: "Our Lady of the Cadillacs, I call it.")

On the advice of an old friend, Joshua Logan, the director, a thoroughly bored Miss Russell, in 1950, joined the national touring company of the hit comedy "Bell, Book and Candle." She wanted to ascertain whether she could get back into the swing of stage acting after being in films exclusively for most of two decades.

"I learned I had become sluggish working with the camera," she said. "The stage demands that you use 42 new muscles, and you can't let down one minute. You have to relearn how to get laughs, to build 'em from the snickers to the belly to the boff."

Eighteen weeks on the road with the play limbered up Miss Russell sufficiently to allow her to accept the starring role in the 1953 Broadway hit "Wonderful Town," captivating The New York Times's drama critic, Brooks Atkinson, so completely that he felt compelled to demand that she be elected President.

Everyone, including Miss Russell, declared that she couldn't sing ("I gargle," she said), but that didn't seem to matter. "Instead of attacking a song," wrote the critic Walter Kerr, "she inhabits one, moving around in it with such confidence, grace and honest exuberance as to make it entirely her own."

Toast of Broadway

In 1956, Miss Russell again captivated Broadway in "Auntie Mame" and later repeated her performance for the hit movie version. Mame, the madcap, middle-aged terror of Beekman Place, had been created by Patrick Dennis, who made a fortune from his original novel, "Auntie Mame," and died three weeks ago of cancer at his Park Avenue home at the age of 55.

When Mame came into Miss Russell's life, the actress was still soignée and elegant, appearing, as always, taller than she actually was (5 feet 7 inches).

Being the toast of Broadway helped her movie career. She starred in Hollywood versions of the plays "Picnic," "Gypsy," "Five Finger Exercise" and "A Majority of One," as well as what she cheerfully called, in 1973, "a couple of unmemorable, unmentionable clinkers."

Miss Russell was particularly pleased to have been chosen by Joshua Logan for the role of the desperate schoolteacher in his movie version of William Inge's play "Picnic."

"Farewell, a career-woman role," she said. "Here was the opportunity to create a new image. Rosemary was a lonely old maid, who, with horrible shamelessness, wanted a man. I knew that to do the part, to show my face naked of makeup, to reveal a desperate woman with her guard completely down would take a certain amount of courage."

She received several film industry awards for her performance in "Picnic," but not an Academy Award, for which she had been nominated four times over the years.

With the onset of Miss Russell's arthritis, she grew more retiring and reclusive, which was far from her nature, friends said this year. She withdrew from active participation in the movie and play production company that she and her husband, Mr. Brisson, had organized in the late 1940's.

The actress's last professional appearance came in 1972, in a made-for-television movie called "The Crooked Hearts." She appeared puffy about the face and body, a condition said to be a reaction from cortisone and other drugs used to aid her in her fight against arthritis.

The New York Times — TUESDAY, MAY 23, 1972

Margaret Rutherford, 80, Fey Comedienne, Is Dead

Special to The New York Times

LONDON, May 22 — Dame Margaret Rutherford, the actress whose comedy roles delighted audiences for more than 40 years, died today at her home in Chalfont St. Peter, Buckinghamshire. She was 80 years old.

Dame Margaret, who had been ill for several weeks, spent six months in a hospital last year with a broken hip.

She is survived by her husband, the actor and producer Stringer Davis. They had four adopted children.

Stardom in Middle Age

By ALDEN WHITMAN

Creator of a notable gallery of film and stage eccentrics, Dame Margaret Rutherford was a comedienne with few peers who attained stardom in middle age as a result of granitic persistence in sharpening her acting talents.

Once established in her métier, she proceeded from triumph to triumph, winning an Oscar in 1964 for her role as a Shakespeare-quoting impecunious British aristocrat in "The V.I.P.s." Previously, she had been Madame Arcati, the wildly absurd spiritualist in Noël Coward's "Blithe Spirit," Miss Prism in "The Importance of Being Earnest," the evil Mrs. Danvers in "Rebecca," the formidable head schoolmistress in "The Happiest Days of Your Life," and the unquenchable, tweedy, bicycle-riding amateur detective, Miss Jane Marple, in four Agatha Christie films—"Murder She Said," "Murder at the Gallop," "Murder Ahoy" and "Murder Most Foul."

The whimsical, the fey, the dotty, the bombastic—these were the images she projected to the hilarious delight of millions; and to the point where, off stage or off camera, the actress was often confused with the private Dame Margaret.

"Everybody says one thing or the other—either I'm just what they expected or just the opposite," she remarked a couple of years ago. "Makes it difficult for me to tell whether it's a compliment or the other way! But I'm not displeased when people think I'm like my eccentric ladies—I love doing them."

Of ample build, Dame Margaret had bulbous eyes set in deep pouches, an impertinent nose and a fierce jaw that rested on an accordion of chins. "A splendidly padded windmill," one appreciative critic said of her, noting also that she was the master of the jolly, tart remark.

Actually, Dame Margaret was rather subdued in private life. She was a fresh-air buff, wore sensible shoes and an oversize cape, bicycled, indulged in nonexotic pleasures and twice a day—at precisely 11 A.M. and 3:30 P.M.—devoured a collation of hot milk and buttered biscuits.

Was she an eccentric? interviewers asked her. Her answer invariably was:

"I hope I'm an individual. I suppose an eccentric is a super-individual. Perhaps an eccentric is just off-center—ex-centric. But that contradicts a belief of mine that we've got to be centrifugal."

In all, Dame Margaret appeared in more than 100 plays and 30 films. She was in New York for the first time in 1947 as Lady Bracknell in Sir John Gielgud's revival of "The Importance of Being Earnest." "As the juggernaut Lady Bracknell, she sails through the play like a heavily armed frigate, firing deadly salvos of snobbery from both sides," wrote Brooks Atkinson in The Times. "She sweeps the seas without once lowering her standard."

Dame Margaret returned in 1960 in "Farewell, Farewell Eugene," a play that failed to last. She was described then as "white-haired, gracious, observant and charming." Here again in 1963 with Stringer Davis, her actor-husband, she received an interviewer in a housecoat and a boudoir cap. Her avocation, she said then, was reading poems aloud to groups. "I love the sound of poetry as long as the words are lyrical and musical," she declared, adding, "No avant-garde for me."

Born in London, on May 11, 1882, Margaret Taylor Rutherford was the only child of William and Florence Rutherford. After her mother's death three years later, the child lived with two aunts with a passion for the theater and for staging children's plays. Although she made her debut at the age of 8, it took a quarter-century before she got on the adult stage.

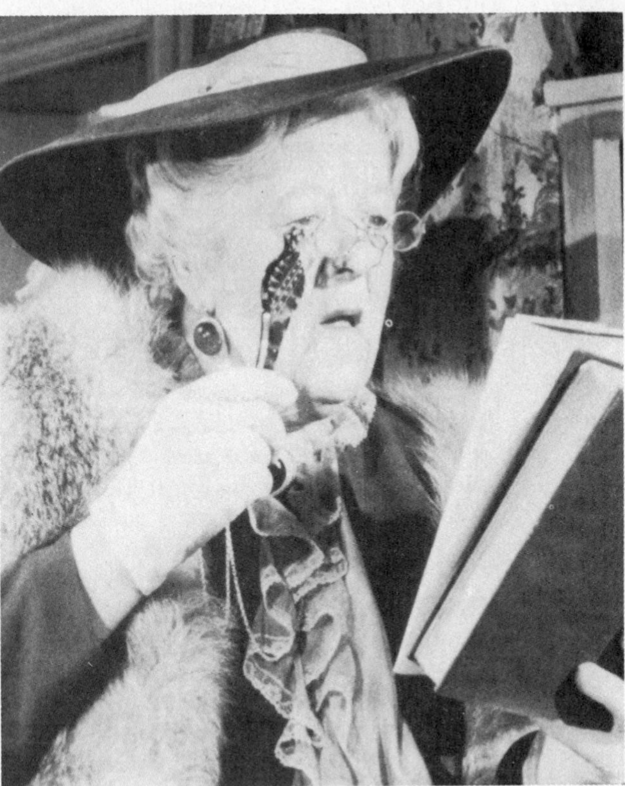

Margaret Rutherford in *I'm All Right Jack*, 1959.

Meantime, after some preliminary schooling, she spent six years studying the piano and became a licentiate of the Royal College of Music. For five years she pedaled from pupil to pupil in South London, a task she interspersed with the pleasure of reading poetry to British servicemen in World War I and acting with a Wimbledon amateur dramatic group. She also studied elocution with a Shakespearean actor and won a degree in the subject, which she taught for three years along with the piano.

When she was 33, Dame Margaret came into a small inheritance, gave up teaching and joined the Old Vic as a drama student. After nine months, her ambitions temporarily dashed, she went back to teaching the piano. Finally, in 1929, she caught on in repertory in the provinces, and went to London in 1933.

Initially, she was barely noticed by the West End critics, but in 1935 she appeared in Robert Morley's "Short Story," and her career was fairly launched when James Agate, a leading London critic, wrote that "as a ruthless village spinster [she] entrances and convulses the house every moment she is on the stage."

Three years later came stardom, and overnight, when she played a genteel old eccentric with a secret passion for wagering in the comedy "Spring Meeting." "Astonishing" was the word generally used for her performance, and for the first time she felt what it was like to be a lady of the theater, for beyond the praise there were photographs and interviews and requests for autographs.

Her triumph fed upon itself, for she got the part of Miss Prism in "The Importance of Being Earnest," which was followed by the role of Mrs. Danvers in Daphne du Maurier's "Rebecca." Dame Margaret topped that in 1941 as the bicycling clairvoyant in "Blithe Spirit," in the film version of which she also played in 1945. Two years afterward she was Lady Bracknell in "The Importance of Being Earnest," in which she toured the United States and Canada.

Dame Margaret's film career made her known throughout the world. Her roles included those of Professor Hatton-Jones in "Passport to Pimlico," Nurse Cary in "Miranda," the Duchess of Grand Fenwick in "The Mouse on the Moon," Jane Marple in the Christie thrillers, and the Duchess of Brighton, a crotchety old woman, in "The V.I.P.s," for which she won her Oscar as best supporting actress.

The New York Times

THURSDAY, JULY 12, 1973

Robert Ryan, Actor, Dies at 63

Made 90 Movies— Scored on Stage in O'Neill Drama

By ALDEN WHITMAN

Robert Ryan, the versatile and durable film and stage actor, died yesterday in New York Hospital. He was 63 years old and had lived at 135 Central Park West since the death of his wife last year. Previously, he had a home in the Dakota, at 1 West 72d Street.

He entered the hospital on July 3, and the cause of death was lung cancer, according to John Springer, his publicity agent and friend. Mr. Springer said that the actor had been treated for cancer several years ago and had believed that the disease had been arrested. Previously, he had been a heavy cigarette smoker, the agent reported.

Mr. Ryan had just completed two movies on the West Coast — "Executive Action" about the assassination of President Kennedy, for which Dalton Trumbo had written the script, and "The Iceman Cometh," based on Eugene O'Neill's play.

'Set-Up' Was Favorite

The husky rugged actor's renown was anchored in some 90 motion pictures in which he appeared over the last 30 years. He considered only four or five of them to be any good, he said in an interview a couple of years ago.

His favorite was "The Set-Up," which was released in 1949 and in which he played the role of Stoker Thompson, an aging but determined pugilist.

He also esteemed "Crossfire," a 1947 movie in which he portrayed a bigoted marine who kills a Jewish war veteran. The depiction was "frighteningly real," the critic for The New York Times wrote.,

Among other films Mr. Ryan thought well of were "Bad Day at Black Rock," in which he was a bullying rancher; "Lonelyhearts," in which he was a newspaperman, "The Professionals," in which he was a soldier of fortune, and "Wild Bunch," in which he was a bounty hunter.

3 Broadway Triumphs

Some filmgoers believed that the actor played only reprobates or sinners, a notion he disputed. "I've played a wider range of roles than most people have seen, apparently," he remarked recently. "That most people have the impression that all I've played is heavies and villains leads me to believe they never saw most of my pictures. Yet I've never stopped working, so I can't complain."

Although Mr. Ryan was on the stage only relatively infrequently, he scored at least three Broadway triumphs, the most recent being in 1971, when he was James Tyrone in a revival of O'Neill's "Long Day's Journey Into Night." "It is a great part, and Robert Ryan moves into it with care, love and understanding," said Clive Barnes of The New York Times.

In 1969 the actor captivated critics and audiences in the role of Walter Burns, the Machiavellian managing editor of "The Front Page," the classic newspaper play. The revival of the Ben Hecht-Charles MacArthur work was arranged by the Plumstead Playhouse, an organization that Mr. Ryan established with his friends, Henry Fonda and Martha Scott.

Wrote During Depression

In 1962, Mr. Ryan was President Stephen Decatur Henderson in Irving Berlin's musical, "Mr. President," which was written by Howard Lindsay and Russel Crouse. He had been proposed for the lead singing role by his friend Katharine Hepburn, with whom he co-starred in 1960 in the American Shakespeare Festival's revival of "Antony and Cleopatra."

Mr. Ryan came to acting from writing plays. The son of a prosperous builder, he was born in Chicago on Nov. 11, 1909. He attended Dartmouth College, from which he was graduated in 1932. He was a fraternity brother of Governor Rockefeller. For lack of jobs as a writer in the Depression, he toiled as a day laborer in Chicago, stoked coal on a freighter and herded horses in Montana. Ultimately he joined a Little Theater group in Chicago, but his playwriting did not succeed and he decided to try his hand at acting.

First Movie in '43

He went to Hollywood, where he studied at the Max Reinhardt Workshop and made his stage debut in 1940. He came cast to play in stock, a step that led to a part in 1941 in Clifford Odets's "Clash by Night." Favorable reviews caught the eyes of Hollywood scouts, and he was signed by RKO Radio Pictures.

His first movie was "Bombardier," released in 1943. In his film career the actor appeared in a distressing number of pot-boilers, and he never achieved epic stardom. Rather, he was a reliable and accomplished feature player, prized for his handsome features and "American" look.

Mr. Ryan was a politically engaged actor from the late nineteen-forties until his death. He was one of the founders of Sane, the Committee for a Sane Nuclear Policy, and he served on the board of the American Civil Liberties Union. He also took part in the work of the American Friends Service Committee.

When a number of film writers, known as the Hollywood 10, were being called by the House Un-American Activities Committee in the late forties, he enlisted himself in their support. In recent years he campaigned for liberal causes on the West Coast and here.

"When [Senator Joseph R.] McCarthy started, I expected to be a target simply because I was involved in things he was throwing rocks at," he said. "I never was a target. Now, looking back, I suspect my Irish name, my being a Catholic and an ex-marine sort of softened the blow."

Mr. Ryan was married to Jessica Calwalder, a fellow drama student, in 1939. She died last year. He leaves two sons and a daughter — Timothy, Cheyney and Lisa.

Robert Ryan and Sam Levene in *Crossfire*.

Woody Strode and Robert Ryan in *The Professionals*, 1966.

The New York Times WEDNESDAY, APRIL 26, 1972

George Sanders, Film Villain, a Suicide

BARCELONA, April 25 (UPI) —George Sanders, the suave sophisticate of the movies, died today in a nearby resort hotel of an overdose of sleeping pills. He left two notes, one saying he was committing suicide "because I am bored . . . and have lived enough."

The 65-year-old actor, who delighted playing the cynic and was typecast many times as a blasé lover and man of the world, was found dead in his room in the seaside hotel Rey Don Jaime at Castelldefels.

A police spokesman said five empty tubes of Nembutal were found in Mr. Sanders's room.

One note read: "Dear World: I am leaving because I am bored. I feel I have lived long enough. I am leaving you with your worries in this sweet cesspool—good luck." The other, written in Spanish, asked that Mr. Sanders's sister in London be notified of his death.

The Consummate Cad

By JOHN DARNTON

With the dissolute air of a cynic, the impeccable British diction of a fop and a sneer that marked him as a cad with a soul beyond redemption, George Sanders became one of Hollywood's busiest and best-paid cinema villains.

In a remarkable career that began as something of a lark, he appeared in at least 90 films since the 1930's. In all but a handful, he played "the heavy"—the man who stole another man's wife, escaped with the money, betrayed his best friend or achieved all three simultaneously.

His villains were so villainous —such an artful blend of charm and cruelty — that they are practically the prototype for the evildoer who masks his motives under a cool exterior.

The role had been his ever since his American motion picture debut as Madeleine Carroll's pernicious husband in "Lloyd's of London," in 1936.

In 1950, Mr. Sanders won an Academy Award as the best supporting actor for his portrayal of a vicious drama critic who escorted Marilyn Monroe in "All About Eve."

His last film was "The Kremlin Letter," in 1970, in which he played an ancient drag queen who becomes the darling of Moscow's homosexual-literary set.

In between, there were dozens of other memorable performances, in "Lancer Spy" (1937), "Rebecca" (1940), "The Picture of Dorian Gray" (1945), "Samson and Delilah" (1949), "Ivanhoe" (1952), "Village of the Damned" (1960), "A Shot in the Dark" (1964) and "The Quiller Memorandum" (1966).

In "The Moon and Sixpence" (1942), he was the Gauguin-like artist. In "The Lodger" (1944), he was the detective on the trail of Jack the Ripper. In two roles that departed from his customary fare, he played the loyal reporter-friend in Alfred Hitchcock's "Foreign Correspondent" (1940) and a hen-pecked hero in "Uncle Harry" (1945).

"Call Me Madam" (1953) was one of the few films in which Mr. Sanders, the possessor of a fine baritone, sang.

Off camera, Mr. Sanders maintained with minimum effort a reputation that dovetailed with his screen image: the indolent critic whose acerbic remarks—usually delivered from a supine position, it seemed—rivaled his characters for a sense of wit and mal de siècle.

"I am content with mediocrity," he once noted, in the midst of an explanation that he had entered the acting profession solely for its financial rewards.

"I hate interviews because I do not get paid for them. I hate to give autographs and never do. I am always rude to people. I am not a sweet person. I am a disagreeable person. I am a hateful person. I like to be hateful."

The 6-foot 3-inch actor, with deep-set eyes beneath a broad forehead, came to his profession almost as an afterthought.

He was born of British parents in St. Petersburg, Russia, on July 3, 1906. His father was a rope manufacturer and his mother a renowned horticulturist. During the Communist revolution the family fled to England.

The young man attended Brighton College, where he was known as being something of a rascal, a good swimmer and boxer and an inventive entrepreneur. He specialized in textiles at Manchester Technical School, and later was discharged from a mill for setting up a competing business.

Mr. Sanders next signed up for an abortive venture in the tobacco business to South America. While there, he lost one job when he appeared at his employer's betrothal soaked in alcohol and another when he fought a pistol duel with a jealous swain.

Returning to England, he followed the advice of an uncle and took up a singing career, despite the fact that he had never sang. He managed to attract the attention of a London producer at a party, who signed him for a three-man piano act in a short-lived musical called "Ballyhoo."

For the next three years Mr. Sanders was successful in cabaret work, chorus jobs and understudy roles. His success, he said later, was in the "volume" of his voice and his predilection for getting the principals drunk.

His first motion picture was "Strange Cargo." Then followed H. G. Wells's "The Man Who Could Work Miracles," in which he appeared briefly as a nude god riding a horse across the Milky Way. After several other British pictures, Mr. Sanders was cast as the villain in "Lloyd's of London," with another newcomer, Tyrone Power.

In addition to the succession of villain roles, Mr. Sanders starred in a series of detective films based on "The Saint." When he dropped the series in the early 1940's, the role fell to his brother, acting under the name of Tom Conway, who died several years ago.

Mr. Sanders married four times. His first wife was Elsie Poole, who divorced him in 1948. His second was Zsa Zsa Gabor, the actress, with whom he shared a $90,000 fourteen-bedroom mansion in Beverly Hills. "I lived there as a sort of paying guest," he said upon their divorce in 1954 after five years of marriage.

In 1959, Mr. Sanders wed Benita Hume, the widow of the actor Ronald Colman. After her death, Mr. Sanders married Magda Gabor, the sister of Zsa Zsa, but they subsequently separated. The sisters' mother, Jolie Gabor, said at the time: "I always liked George, but when a son-in-law comes back I really like it."

Judith Anderson, George Sanders, Joan Fontaine, Laurence Olivier and C. Aubrey Smith in *Rebecca*, 1940.

Hurd Hatfield and George Sanders in *The Picture of Dorian Gray*.

The New York Times WEDNESDAY, JANUARY 22, 1964.

Joseph Schildkraut, Actor, Dies; Played Father of Anne Frank

Praised for Stage and Film Portrayals—Won Oscar in '38 as Capt. Dreyfus

Joseph Schildkraut, the actor, died last night of a heart attack at his home, 171 East 62d Street. He was 68 years old.

Mr. Schildkraut, whose stage and screen career spanned 50 years, twice won Oscars for motion picture roles. He was to start rehearsals next month for his first musical, "Cafe Crown," due on Broadway in April.

He won his Academy Awards as the best supporting actor for his portrayal of Capt. Alfred Dreyfus in "The Life of Emile Zola" in 1938 and for his characterization of a weaver in "The Tell-Tale Heart" in 1942.

Mr. Schildkraut's most recent principal role was that of Anne Frank's father, which he played in the stage and screen productions of "The Diary of Anne Frank."

The play opened on Broadway on Oct. 5, 1955. The movie version was released in 1959. Mr. Schildkraut was acclaimed by theatrical and motion-picture critics for both performances.

Father Also an Actor

The son of an internationally famous actor, Rudolf Schildkraut, and the former Erna Weinstein, Mr. Schildkraut was born in Vienna on March 22, 1895.

His parents, who wanted him to be a concert violinist, had a villa in an artists' colony known as the Cottage Quarters. Other tenants there were Arthur Schnitzler, Ferenc Molnar, Gerhart Hauptmann and Richard Strauss.

Young Schildkraut attended the Imperial Academy of Music in Berlin where he studied piano and violin. But his love for the theater led him to Albert Basserman, a great character actor of the day, who coached him in the theater.

The elder Schildkraut came to the United States in 1910 to perform in New York. During his engagement Joseph studied at the American Academy of Dramatic Arts, where two of his classmates were William Powell and Paul Muni. He was graduated in 1913.

Returning to Berlin, he made his debut in "The Prodigal Son" under the direction of the great Max Reinhardt. On his next visit to the United States, Mr. Schildkraut was engaged to play the lead opposite Eva Le Gallienne in Molnar's "Liliom," which opened in April, 1921.

Mr. Schildkraut next appeared in the title role of "Peer Gynt" in 1923, for which he received great critical praise. This was followed by his portrayal of Benvenuto Cellini in "The Firebrands," which was acclaimed as "vivid."

D. W. Griffiths's production of "Orphans of the Storm" in 1922 was the actor's first film. In 1927 he went to Hollywood to play Judas in "The King of Kings" and remained until 1931. While on the Coast he managed the Hollywood Playhouse and starred in 25 movies, including "Show Boat," the second "talkie."

Among the plays in which Mr. Schildkraut appeared on Broadway were "Clash by Night," 1941; "Uncle Harry," 1942; "The Green Bay Tree," 1951, and "Love's Labor's Lost," for which he won the New York Shakespeare Society Award in 1953.

He also appeared as a host and star on his own dramatic television series in 1953.

Last year Mr. Schildkraut was a lecturer and guest director at the University of California, where he produced Ibsen's "Peer Gynt." Peer Gynt was one of his favorite roles, the other having been Richard II.

During his career Mr. Schildkraut appeared in more than 60 motion pictures, two dozen plays and at least 80 television shows.

He was nearly 6 feet tall and slender. In his early motion pictures and plays he was cast as a leading man by virtue of his brown hair and eyes and elegant appearance.

Mr. Schildkraut, whose permanent residence was in Beverly Hills, Calif., became an American citizen in 1926.

He an Elise Bartlett, an actress, were wed in 1923 and divorced in 1931. The next year the actor married Mary McKay, who died in 1961. Last year Mr. Schildkraut married Leonora Rogers, who was with him when he died.

H. B. Warner, Rudolph Schildkraut and Joseph Schildkraut in *The King of Kings*.

Joseph Schildkraut, Gusti Huber, Millie Perkins, Lou Jacobi, Shelley Winters, Richard Beymer, and Diane Baker in *The Diary of Anne Frank*.

"All the News That's Fit to Print"

The New York Times.

LATE CITY EDITION

U.S. Weather Bureau Report (Page 82) forecasts: Fair, hot and humid today, tonight; partly cloudy, warm tomorrow. Temp. Range: 90—70; yesterday: 91—68. Temp.-Hum. Index: about 79; yesterday: 80.

VOL. CXIV..No. 39,232. © 1965 by The New York Times Company. Times Square, New York, N.Y. 10036 NEW YORK, WEDNESDAY, JUNE 23, 1965. TEN CENTS

David O. Selznick, 63, Producer Of 'Gone With the Wind,' Dies

Special to The New York Times

HOLLYWOOD, June 22—David O. Selznick, one of the leading producers in the motion picture industry, died of a coronary occlusion this afternoon at Mount Sinai Hospital.

Mr. Selznick, who was 63 years old, was stricken in the office of his lawyer, Barry Brannen, in Beverly Hills, and was rushed to the hospital. His wife, Jennifer Jones, the actress, was with him at the time of the attack.

Mr. Selznick, who produced "Gone With the Wind," the movies' biggest money-maker, and his wife had returned to their Beverly Hills home last week after spending three months in New York City.

Mercurial, shrewd, self-confident and enormously gifted, David O. Selznick climbed to the pinnacle of power and success in Hollywood with films that are now classics and actors who are considered screen immortals.

His films included "Intermezzo," "Rebecca," "David Copperfield," "Little Women," "The Prisoner of Zenda," "Dinner at Eight," "A Star Is Born," "Duel in the Sun," and, the epic, "Gone With the Wind."

He was instrumental in spurring the careers of such actors as Clark Gable, Vivien Leigh, Ingrid Bergman, Joseph Cotten, Gregory Peck, Katharine Hepburn, Joan Fontaine, Fred Astaire, Leslie Howard, Myrna Loy and his wife, Miss Jones.

Mr. Selznick, a 6-foot 1-inch 200-pounder, moved quickly, spoke rapidly and worked tirelessly. He produced quality films with three trademarks: top stars, the finest writers and no expense spared.

Even in the twilight of his career, he remained wide-eyed and even brash, although a trace of pessimism and melan-

Associated Press

David O. Selznick

Continued on Page 38, Column 1

ASSEMBLY PASSES CITY FISCAL BILLS; SESSION NEAR END

Wagner Package, the Last Block to Adjournment, Is Voted With G.O.P. Aid

EXTRA BUDGET ADOPTED

It Includes an Added $1,000 Allowance for Legislators and Payment on L.I.R.R.

By WARREN WEAVER Jr.
Special to The New York Times

ALBANY, Wednesday, June 23—One of the longest, most disorganized, most controversial yet most productive sessions of the Legislature crept toward adjournment this morni[ng] ...

Through a haze o[f] ... smoke and dilatory ... chambers carpeted ... carded bills and ne[w] ... the Senate and Assem[bly] ... tinued after midnight t[o] ... the last of the more than ... bills before them.

The Senate recessed a[t] ... A.M. and the Assembly at ... Both were to meet agai[n] ... 10 o'clock this morning to w[ind] up the session, which be[gan] Jan. 6 and is the longest ... since 1911.

Before the recess, the lawmakers took two major steps: they bailed New York City out of its fiscal crisis and they added a record $72 million to the state's current spending program.

Borrowing Authorized

The city fiscal package was approved by the Assembly last night with the key measure—authorizing Mayor Wagner to borrow $255.8 million against future tax receipts—passing by a vote of 79 to 63, just three votes more than needed.

The two other bills authorize the Mayor to borrow $46 million to balance this year's budget and begin action on an amendment to the State Constitution to increase the city's real estate tax revenue by about $250 million a year.

All three measures had been passed by the Senate earlier. Assembly action on them was the last major obstacle to adjournment.

In one sense, the 1965 session ended as it began, with the Republicans giving the Democrats the majorities they could not muster themselves. The key New York City fiscal bill was passed only when five Republican Assemblymen dropped their opposition.

The supplemental budget that

Continued on Page 24, Column 1

NEW RACING PLAN LEADS TO THREATS

Legislator Tells of Calls—Quarter-Horse Bill Loses

By SYDNEY H. SCHANBERG
Special to The New York Times

ALBANY, June 22 — The sponsor of a quarter-horse racing bill brought a stunned hush to the Assembly chamber today when he disclosed that he and his family had been threatened by anonymous telephone calls and that the last call had been traced to the Assembly switchboard.

Assemblyman Clarence D. Lane, his voice quavering slightly, told his colleagues: "My family has been through hell this past week."

Many of the legislators were touched by the Greene County Republican's story and several rushed to his side to offer sympathy. The quarter-horse bill was later defeated by the Assembly for the second time.

The margin of defeat this time, however, was only two votes. The first time the bill came up, two weeks ago, it lost by eight votes. The second defeat killed the measure for this year. It would have authorized pari-mutuel betting on quarter-horse racing at up to eight tracks in the state.

The quarter horse is a cross between the American mustang and the thoroughbred and is named and noted for its ability to run a quarter mile at high speed. Mr. Lane had estimated that the state would receive more than $4 million from the additional tracks.

Assemblyman Lane told of the threatening phone calls at the close of his speech in defense of his bill. The state police,

Continued on Page 25, Column 1

GO... CO...

Says It ... Deterren[t] ... Public ...

By RONA[LD] ...
Special to The ...

ALBANY, Ju[ne] ... Rockefeller quo[ted] ... D. Roosevelt toda[y] ... vetoed a Democra[tic] ... that would have ... strictions against ... public employes.

"It is fundamental t[o] ... ment that public emplo[yes have] no right to strike," Mr. [Rocke]feller said. He then quo[ted a] statement that he said [was] made by President Roosevel[t in] 1937:

"A strike of public employe[s] manifests nothing less than a[n] attempt to prevent or obstruc[t] the operations of governmen[t] until their demands are satisfied. Such action, looking toward the paralysis of government by those who have sworn to support it, is unthinkable and intolerable."

Dismissal Mandatory

Restrictions against strikes by public workers are embodied in the Condon-Wadlin Act, which calls for the immediate dismissal of strikers.

The Democrats, in fulfilling a campaign pledge, tried to take the teeth out of the law by throwing out the automatic dismissal provision.

The Democrats also attempted to mandate for the first time collective bargaining between the state, New York City and all other communities and public workers, except the police.

In his light-blue veto message (yellow means approval) the Governor said that the Democrats "would have set up an involved and ineffective procedure which would (1) undermine the deterrent to strikes by public employes; (2) be unworkable and probably unconstitutional in certain of its aspects; and (3) impair vital functions of state and local government."

Prohibition Retained

Actually, the Democratic measure retained the prohibition against strikes. But it dropped the present law's automatic dismissal provisions in favor of milder sanctions in the Civil Service Law. However, a striking worker could still be dismissed at the discretion of the government.

This, said Mr. Rockefeller, would mean that the law "would contain no effective deterrent to a strike against the people." He said that "it is the certainty of a sanction, rather than its severity, that brings about compliance with a law

Continued on Page 23, Column 2

... sa[v] ... the ... stock ...

Lat[e] ... interv[iew] ... Schiff ... survive ... Asked if ... sold if the ... settled, she ...

"Yes, tha[t] ... forever if n[ot] ... it. I'm not ... hat to foot de[ath] ...

In the compo[sing room yes]terday, eight ... asked to process ... an International B[usiness Ma]chines Company comp[uter] ...

The men refused ... the tape that runs thr[ough] ...

Continued on Page 23, C[olumn] ...

Suffolk Aide S... Gangster Influen[ce] ...

Special to The New York Times

PATCHOGUE, L. I., June ... Charles T. Matthews, 39-ye[ar-]old Republican assistant distri[ct] attorney in Suffolk County bolted his party tonight to accept the Democratic designation for county prosecutor.

Mr. Matthews, accepting the Democrats' support at a convention here, charged that "sinister underworld influences have moved into Suffolk."

The Suffolk Democratic Committee made its surprise selection of a candidate two hours before 800 delegates opened a convention here. The delegates approved Mr. Matthews unanimously.

Mr. Matthews, a lawyer of Cold Spring Harbor and chief of the appeals bureau of the District Attorney's office, has been a Republican committeeman from Huntington for the last decade. He was refused the

Continued on Page 22, Column 4

CITY'S DIRTY AIR CALLED A FACTOR IN RISING DEATHS

Cars, Factories and Heating Listed as Contributors in Special Council Study

By ... [...]ER

... the ... een ... ce ...

Diplomat Indicates Soviet May Admit Vietnam Panel

In Conversation With Reporter, Russian Hints at Cooperation With Efforts for Peace by Commonwealth

By ANTHONY LEWIS
Special to The New York Times

LONDON, June 22—A Soviet diplomat here has indicated that his Government will let the Commonwealth peace mission on Vietnam visit Moscow.

A statement to that effect was made by the diplomat in a conversation yesterday with [a]n American correspondent. It [w]as one of several talks with [W]estern journalists arranged on ... notice by Soviet Embassy [perso]nnel.

... Russians had long talks, ...r request, with three ...correspondents. A re... Paris said a similar ...ad been made to a ...nt for Le Monde. ...rsations in London ...derably from one ...nly one did the ...ial make an af... ...ement that in the ...he Soviet Union ...dmit the Com... ...on.

But all of the talks had an inquiring character, with the Russians seeking to explore the origins of the Commonwealth peace mission and its possible results. In all, there was the impression of Soviet uneasiness about the expansion of the Vietnam war.

One of the Soviet diplomats even raised the possibility that American troops would seal off South Vietnam and then negotiate with the Vietcong.

With varying degrees of frankness, the Russians distinguished their attitude from the Chinese Communists'. They said they did not think the United States was a paper tiger that could readily be humiliated in Vietnam.

One of the Russians, in another recent talk that he sought with an American correspond-

Continued on Page 2, Column 2

...n Ends Suspension ...d Aid for U.A.R.

By [F]ELIX BELAIR Jr.
Special to The New York Times

... 22—President Johnson has de... ...nal interest to send the United ... in surplus farm products still

ALGERIAN REGIME GAINING SUPPORT

Ben Bella Aides Said to ... to It—Nasser and Back Parley Now

By [PET]ER BRAESTRUP
Special to The New York Times

... June 22 Amid ...orts on the pros... ...ing the Asian... conference here ...Col. Houari Bou... ...day-old regime ...how continuity ...gain recogni...

...dent Gamal ...e United ... Premier ...mmunist ... Algiers ...ed on ...

...n of ...ian ...n a ...for... ...en ...st ...

...alm ... through ...day's spo... ...ing demonstrations [sta]ged in favor of Mr. Ben Bella by 50 to 200 students and some women.

But shortly before 9 o'clock tonight, a new demonstration, apparently organized by Communists and other left-wingers, was begun in downtown Algiers.

About a thousand demonstrators, mostly teen-agers, moved across the square in front of the central post office yelling, "Down with Boumedienne!" A

Continued on Page 4, Column 1

... June 22 ... [pa]ssed legislation ... to require that cigarette packages carry a warning that smoking may be hazardous to health.

The measure, approved by voice vote, was similar to one passed by the Senate last week. Both bills call for a label reading: "Caution: Cigarette smoking May be Hazardous to Your Health."

The House measure would permanently ban the Federal Trade Commission from extending the warning to cigarette advertising, as it has proposed to do effective July 1.

The commission felt that advertising was the chief means of encouraging young persons to begin smoking and should be regulated.

The Senate measure would prohibit action against adver-

Continued on Page 62, Column 4

U.S. JETS ATTACK NORTH OF HANOI, NEAR RED CHINA

Planes Strike Ammunition Dump and Barracks Area Beyond the Capital

SHIFT IN TACTICS SEEN

A Readiness to Raid Major Military Facilities in New Zone Is Now Indicated

By JACK LANGGUTH
Special to The New York Times

SAIGON, South Vietnam, June 22 United States Air Force jets flew north of Hanoi today to bomb a North Vietnamese ammunition dump and a barracks area, the latter 80 miles from the Chinese Communist border.

The selection of the targets indicated that the United States was now prepared to raid the large and important military targets in the northern third of the country.

Since the bombing of North Vietnam began last Feb. 7 almost all the raids have been below the 20th Parallel, which is 70 miles south of Hanoi.

Eight F-105 Thunderchiefs struck the Bannuocchieu ammunition depot 70 miles west-northwest of Hanoi today.

Pilots reported only moderate damage from the 17 tons of 750-pound bombs and rockets they dropped.

Raiders Are Escorted

Another group of eight Thunderchiefs struck the Sonla army barracks, which are 110 miles west-northwest of Hanoi. The pilots said they had destroyed nine buildings and damaged 20 others at the site, with 17 more tons of the same type of bombs and rockets as those used at Bannuocchieu. Escorts of 25 Air Force planes supported the raiders on both missions.

[Sonla was first raided June 18 but was not designated as north of Hanoi at that time, The Associated Press reported. A communiqué had located Sonla as west-southwest of Hanoi. The Pentagon said this was a clerical error.]

The pilots who bombed Bannuocchieu said they had encountered some antiaircraft fire but did not see any enemy aircraft. All of the planes returned safely to their bases.

The United States mission here does not disclose the Southeast Asian land bases used in strikes against North Viet-

Continued on Page 2, Column 6

JAPAN AND KOREA RESUME FULL TIES

[T]reaty's Foes Clash With Police in 2 Capitals

By ROBERT TRUMBULL
Special to The New York Times

[TO]KYO, June 22 Japan and [South] Korea today signed a ... 20 related documents ... full diplomatic rela... ...a lapse of 55 years. ...was a result of 14 ...termittent negotia...

...pants in the his... ...y wore plain ...s, exchanged hand... ...in Occidental fashion instead of making Oriental bows and drank a toast in champagne brought in after the ceremony by white-coated waiters.

The police estimated that 10,000 left-wing unionists and students, under Communist leadership, marched through downtown Tokyo today in a protest against the agreement.

About 30 policemen and demonstrators were injured in scuffles, the police said.

[In Seoul 200 Opposition leaders and 8,000 students were involved in clashes with the police and 573 students were arrested. Page 3.]

The demonstrators in Tokyo, who were relatively orderly, asserted that the rapprochement with South Korea was likely to involve Japan in the Vietnam war through the participation of Korean troops in the conflict on South Vietnam's side.

The leftists were also dissatisfied with a clause in the agreement under which Japan recognizes the administration in Seoul as the "only legal government" in Korea. Tokyo has no official relations with the Com-

Continued on Page 3, Column 2

de... ...ted, Dav[id] ...bed to the ...er and success [in Holl]ywood with films that are now classics and actors who are considered screen immortals.

His films included "Intermezzo," "Rebecca," "David Copperfield," "Little Women," "The Prisoner of Zenda," "Dinner at Eight," "A Star Is Born," "Duel in the Sun," and, the epic, "Gone With the Wind."

He was instrumental in spurring the careers of such actors as Clark Gable, Vivien Leigh, Ingrid Bergman, Joseph Cotten, Gregory Peck, Katharine Hepburn, Joan Fontaine, Fred Astaire, Leslie Howard, Myrna Loy and his wife, Miss Jones.

Mr. Selznick, a 6-foot 1-inch 200-pounder, moved quickly, spoke rapidly and worked tirelessly. He produced quality films with three trademarks: top stars, the finest writers and no expense spared.

Even in the twilight of his career, he remained wide-eyed and even brash, although a trace of pessimism and melan-

Associated Press

David O. Selznick

Continued on Page 38, Column 1

NEWS INDEX

News Summary and Index, Page 43

DAVID SELZNICK, PRODUCER, DEAD

Continued From Page 1, Col. 5

choly became apparent in recent years.

"Nothing in Hollywood is permanent," Mr. Selznick said in 1959 on a Hollywood set, as Tara, the mansion built for "Gone With the Wind," was being dismembered and shipped to Atlanta, Ga. "Once photographed, life here is ended. It is almost symbolic of Hollywood. Tara has no rooms inside. It was just a facade. So much of Hollywood is a facade."

Mr. Selznick spoke in quick, staccato sentences. While working on a film, he virtually exhausted himself, laboring round-the-clock, seeking perfection to the minutest detail and stubbornly insisting on his own ideas.

David O. Selznick's most gargantuan achievement was *Gone with the Wind*, 1939.

Fighting Perfectionist

As a producer, Mr. Selznick was preoccupied with quality, and his perfectionism led him to many fights with directors.

"Gone With the Wind" started with George Cukor directing. He was replaced by Victor Fleming.

"A Farewell to Arms" saw a classic feud between Mr. Selznick and John Huston. "It was a case of one Alp and two Hannibals," said Mr. Huston after he had been replaced in Italy by Charles Vidor.

"I asked for a violinist," Mr. Selznick shot back, "and, instead, in John, got a soloist."

As one of Hollywood's most famous memo writers, Mr. Selznick dictated more than 1.5 million words of memos to two exhausted stenographers during the filming of "Gone With the Wind." At one point, he sent a message to Vivien Leigh that weighed half a pound and took the actress 10 days to reply to.

Mr. Selznick was born in Pittsburgh, on May 10, 1902, the son of Lewis J. Selznick, a Russian immigrant who had earned and lost a fortune in the movie business.

With unbounded confidence in the abilities of his two sons, Myron and David, the elder Selznick spared little expense in rearing them as prodigals. Myron, who later became a Hollywood agent, was given an allowance of $1,100 a week at the age of 21. The younger, David, was given $300 a week at 18.

David Selznick attended public and private schools and, for a brief period, Columbia University. He developed an interest in filmmaking in his early teens.

The Selznick family fortune was swept away in the stock market crash. L. J. (as he was called in Hollywood and New York) moved from a 22-room apartment on Park Avenue to three furnished rooms where Mrs. Selznick did the cooking. All the family possessions, including Mrs. Selzinck's jewels, were sold.

Job as a Reader

With zest and self-confidence, the younger Selznick got his first movie job by cajoling Harry Rapf of Metro-Goldwyn-Mayer into hiring him, nominally as a reader of scripts at $100 a week at a two-week trial.

Mr. Rapf had initially protested. "Readers don't get that kind of money," he said.

"I know they don't," Mr. Selznick retorted. "But I'll do more for you than read scripts. I'll help you fix them. I'll write titles. I'll do everything that has to be done to them."

Mr. Rapf hired him. Within several weeks, Mr. Selznick's pay was doubled and he was given a permanent job. A few months later, his salary was increased to $300 and he was appointed Mr. Rapf's assistant on the production of the Tim McCoy Western films.

Mr. Selznick next went to Paramount, offering himself on a similar trial arrangement. He received a $300 job and became an assistant to B. P. Schulberg, head of the studio, who had told him early:

"You're the most arrogant young man I've ever known."

In April, 1930, Mr. Selznick married Irene Mayer, Louis B. Mayer's younger daughter. Mr. Mayer, the head of M-G-M, was furious when the young Selznick courted his daughter. He even refused to speak to him at the wedding.

Shortly afterward, however, when the young man walked away from his job at Paramount, Mr. Mayer did have a few words to say to his new son-in-law.

"How dare you give up that contract," he yelled. "And you married to my daughter."

Mr. Selznick left Paramount to make films on his own, becoming vice president, in charge of all production at R.K.O.-Radio. It was there that he started producing such quality films as "A Bill of Divorcement," to which he brought Katharine Hepburn and George Cukor, the director, to Hollywood; "The Animal Kingdom," with Ann Harding, and the famous "King Kong."

After planning, "Little Women," Mr. Selznick resigned from R.K.O. to return to his father-in-law's studio, M-G-M, as vice president and head of his own production unit.

Mr. Selznick was greeted coolly by most of the executives there. Many felt that he was using his relationship with Mr. Mayer to get ahead.

"The son-in-law also rises," became one of the gags around Hollywood at the time.

In an incident related by Bosley Crowther, film critic for The New York Times, in "The Lion's Share," Mr. Selznick was treated so coldly by M-G-M executives that, at one point, he went home, threw himself on the bed and cried.

His wife comforted him. "Let them yammer," she said. "You can still take the best that the studio has to work with. Serve your term—and make some films!"

Mr. Selznick's early films at M.-G.-M. included "Dinner at Eight," "Dancing Lady" and "Viva Villa." Freddy Bartholomew was discovered by the producer and made famous in "David Copperfield."

In 1935, the producer left M-G-M to form an independent company. He was backed by Cornelius V. Whitney, John Hay Whitney; his brother Myron; Robert and Arthur Lehman, the bankers; John Hertz and Irving Thalberg and Norma Shearer (Mrs. Thalberg). Mr. Selznick did not invest any money but he owned a little more than half of the company.

In the early summer of 1936, Mr. Selznick was busy with "The Garden of Allah," with Marlene Dietrich, when a wire reached him from Kay Brown, the New York story editor, urging him to buy film rights to a new Civil War novel. It was "Gone With the Wind," by Margaret Mitchell, an unknown in the literary world.

At the time, the feeling in Hollywood was that the Civil War had been played out with "The Birth of a Nation." Mr. Selznick, however, was interested, although he had misgivings about the problems of producing a novel of such length (1,037 pages). Finally the novel was purchased for $50,000.

As winter came and the sales of the novel soared, the reading public, spurred by Mr. Selznick's publicity, became interested in the cast of the film. Tallulah Bankhead, Norma Shearer and Bette Davis were mentioned for the leading role of Scarlett O'Hara.

So strong was the public interest that when Miss Shearer declined to play Scarlett, The New York Times regretted her decision in an editorial.

Curfew on Memos

Vivien Leigh, a hazel-eyed, brown-haired British actress, was finally chosen in almost typically dramatic fashion. In order to clear the studio's lot

(continued)

for the building of Tara, the movie plantation, a maze of old sets had to be removed. It was suggested that instead of tearing down the sets, they should be burned and used to represent the dramatic highlight of the film, the burning of Atlanta. Mr. Selznick agreed.

While the cameras were shooting the scene, and as flames rose in the studio's night sky, the producer felt a tug on his sleeve. He turned and saw his brother, Myron, accompanied by a beautiful girl.

"I want you to meet Scarlett O'Hara," Myron said dramatically. Mr. Selznick stared at Miss Leigh and promptly signed her for the role.

The picture went before the cameras officially on Jan. 26, 1938. During the 22 weeks of shooting, Mr. Selznick's work habits became legend. He worked at times at three-day stretches without sleep, feeding himself Benzadrine and thyroid extract and playing poker and roulette to relax.

His memos became more prolific. At one point Clark Gable, the film's Rhett Butler, was routed out of bed at 3 A.M. by a messenger who presented him with a document—a memo on the portrayal of the role. Mr. Gable and the others finally revolted and established a 9 P.M. curfew on memos.

At the time, the film was the most expensive ($4,250,000) and one of the longest (3 hours and 45 minutes) ever produced. It has since grossed in excess of $50 million and has been reissued several times.

In seeking Mr. Gable for the film, Mr. Selznick agreed to a financial arrangement with M-G-M, the star's studio, in which M-G-M put up half the production costs in return for a share in the film's profits.

"I have never regretted it," Mr. Selznick once said. "I wouldn't have made the movie without Clark."

At the peak of his career, Mr. Selznick was voted for 10 successive years as the No. 1 producer of box-office successes by motion-picture exhibitors of the country.

Despite this, Mr. Selznick was notably unsuccessful, at times, in hiring top actors and producers. On receiving an overture from the producer, Nunnally Johnson wrote:

"I should certainly like to work for you, although my understanding of it is that an assignment from you consists of three months' work and six months of recuperation."

A Hollywood saying was, simply, "Selznick eats directors, writers and secretaries."

Since 1948, Mr. Selznick had been generally inactive in Hollywood, and in recent years had been involved in European film distribution, the sale of his films to television and several stage plays. None of the stage plays came to fruition.

In 1949 Mr. Selznick married Jennifer Jones, and he became involved in the production of most of her recent films.

Miss Jones, who had been married to the late actor Robert Walker, had starred in several of Mr. Selznick's films, including, "Duel in the Sun," and "Since You Went Away."

The producer and his wife lived in an elegantly rustic home on an estate atop a hill overlooking Beverly Hills. They also maintained an apartment at the Waldorf Towers in New York.

"Very few people have mastered the art of enjoying their wealth," Mr. Selznick remarked several months ago. "I have mastered that art and therefore I spend my time enjoying myself."

Gregory Peck and Jennifer Jones starred in Selznick's *Duel in the Sun*, 1947.

The Selznick Legacy

As a Creative Producer, He Endowed That Function With Taste and Fidelity

By BOSLEY CROWTHER

David O. Selznick's contribution to American films—outside of his singular achievement with "Gone With the Wind"—was his taking on and giving meaning and importance to the role of creative producer, which is peculiar to Hollywood. Where the production of motion pictures in other countries—and in this country, too, before the consolidation of the big studios—has been mainly under the control of the directors, who make the big decisions, in Hollywood it has been in the hands of the producers, the liaisons with financing. It is these men who pick the stories, oversee the preparation of the scripts, hire the casts, select the directors and designers, birddog the filming and master-mind the selling campaigns, which are a large factor in American motion pictures.

An Appraisal

It is this function, which, when fully accomplished, requires a maximum of intelligence and taste, not to mention an abundance of know-how and familiarity with all phases of the art and industry, that David Selznick, along with Samuel Goldwyn, Irving Thalberg and a handful of less qualified men, helped to establish and endow with standards, traditions and ideals.

Even though he was short on formal education (not because his father could not afford to give him as much as he wanted, but because he was too eager and impatient to get to work), the young Selznick was an avid reader and wide-eyed devotee of American and English literature. This taste and familiarity were reflected in the films he produced.

Filmed Literary Classics

As a young producer, right after the adoption of sound and the imposition of the requirement of a certain literate quality in films, he regularly picked his story properties from the library shelves—"Anna Karenina," "David Copperfield," "Tale of Two Cities," "Little Lord Fauntleroy." And his assiduously overseen productions were conspicuous for fidelity and taste.

It was his taste and much more than that—his fervor and his impassioned exercise of the creative urges of a writer and director—that dominated him during the three years of preparation and production of "Gone With the Wind." These were commanding factors in making for the richness of this film. Dave Selznick, along with the author, Margaret Mitchell, was the parent of this screen classic. He had more to do with the making of it than anyone who worked on it.

A tendency of critics and others has been to underrate and make fun of the Hollywood producer. Very few ever tried to make sport of Dave Selznick, except to tease or joke with him about his bursting enthusiasms and his rampant energies.

Devoted to Quality

On these topics, he was sometimes touchy. He had a lively sense of humor, except about himself. He didn't like to have writers trifle with his hard-earned and well-deserved reputation.

His ingrained and persistent devotion to quality in films was manifested by his establishment and maintenance of the annual giving of Golden Laurel awards to the outstanding productions of foreign countries. While he himself was not creatively disposed to the kind of moderate-cost, esoteric pictures that are generally made abroad, he admired and encouraged their production and he was as sensitive in his appreciation of the best as any writer, director or producer in Hollywood.

In recent years, the creative producer as such has been slowly deposed and his functions absorbed into the compound of the producer-director or the producer-actor who now have their own independent companies. Only a few of the old breed—the breed that David O. Selznick personified—remain or are active. But the new class of multihatted film men have abiding regard for the model and the standard that he set. It is not likely that his name and his achievements will soon be forgotten in notoriously short-memoried Hollywood.

"All the News That's Fit to Print"

The New York Times.

LATE CITY EDITION
U. S. Weather Bureau Report (Page 96) forecasts: Partly cloudy today; mostly cloudy, rain tonight. Clearing tomorrow. Temp. range: 50—38; yesterday: 52.1—46.

SECTION ONE

NEWS SUMMARY AND INDEX, PAGE 95

VOL. CX—No. 37,542. NEW YORK, SUNDAY, NOVEMBER 6, 1960. THIRTY CENTS

25c outside New York City, its suburban area and Long Island. 30c in 17 Western states, Canada; higher in air delivery cities.

U. N. CONGO GROUP TO TRY TO REVIVE PARLIAMENT RULE

Advisory Commission Said to Feel Legislative Void Increases Confusion

IT BACKS DAYAL REPORT

Kasavubu Plans to Fly Here to Protest to Assembly Against 'Interference'

By LINDESAY PARROTT
Special to The New York Times.

UNITED NATIONS, N. Y., Nov. 5—A United Nations conciliation committee on the Congo was instructed today to try to re-establish parliamentary government in the strife-torn African nation.

The directive to the committee of fifteen African and Asian members came from Sec[retary] General Dag Hammarsk[jold's] advisory commission on [the] Congo.

[Meanwhile, it was an[nounced] in Leopoldville that the Congo's President, Joseph Kasavubu, planned to leave Sunday for New York to protest against United Nations "interference" in the Congo.]

The Congo advisory commission consists of representatives of all eighteen nations that have contributed troops to the United Nations force in the Congo.

Commission Reviews Report

The mediation committee, named last week from among the commission's membership, consists only of the group's fifteen Asian and African nations.

The commission met here this morning to review a report by Mr. Hammarskjold's representative on the scene, Rajeshwar Dayal of India. He was present at the meeting.

No official announcement of the result of the session was made. Reliable diplomatic sources said, however, that the decision to seek a return to parliamentary government in the Congo was based largely on Mr. Dayal's report.

The Indian official returned here from the Congo yesterday and conferred at length with Mr. Hammarskjold at United Nations headquarters.

Parliament in Abeyance

According to reports that filtered from the closed meeting of the advisory commission, the consensus was that political rivalries, tribalism and confusion in the Congo had been increased by the inability of the Congo Parliament to act.

The Parliament now is in abeyance, with the country under the working control of the United Nations force and the Chief of Staff of the Congo Army, Col. Joseph D. Mobutu.

One source here emphasized that the commission's recommendation was not intended to favor one faction over another in the Congo, but rather to seek a generally agreed decision

Continued on Page 3, Column 4

WELCOME TO MOSCOW: Liu Shao-chi ... ceived in the capital by Premi[er] ...

GA[ITSKELL] ... PO[LARIS] ...

Wants ... 'Provoc[ative] ... Defends ...

By DREW ...
Special to The New York Times.

LONDON, ... Gaitskell dema[nded] ... cient British c[ontrol] ... States missile-f[iring] ... to prevent their ... vocative missions' ... Britain.

The newly re-ele[cted] ... the Labor party ... the nuclear subm[arines] ... United States Nav[y] ... use an anchorage at ... in Scotland, should not ... course and their acti[ons] ... any danger of war."

Mr. Gaitskell's con[cern] ... shared by others in both political parties and in the ... papers. It echoes the ... aroused by the flights o[f] ... United States U-2 spy plane ... the RB-47 reconnaissance p[lane] ... earlier this year.

Matter Is Put Bluntly

"To put the matter bluntly," an editorial in The Times of London said today, "the British people do not want the submarines to be going from Holy Loch to Holy Cape—the point near which the Russians claim to have shot down the RB-47."

Mr. Gaitskell, who believes in the Western nuclear deterrent, extolled the Polaris missile to be carried by the submarines as more effective, less dangerous to civilian populations, less likely to lead to war and more likely to preserve peace than any other nuclear weapon hitherto available.

But Britain, he said, must distinguish between control of submarines in peace and war.

Mr. Gaitskell's speech to a Labor party conference at Manchester was repeatedly interrupted by Labor party members who oppose him and support the resolution calling for unilateral nuclear disarmament for Britain approved at the

Continued on Page 12, Column 1

KENNEDY APPEARS TO LEAD IN STATE; RELIGION A FACTOR

Estimates of Margin Range Up to a Million—Catholic Issue May Be Decisive

By LEO EGAN

Senator John F. Kennedy appears to have a distinct edge over Vice President Nixon for New York's forty-five electoral votes, according to most of th[e] usual political criteria.

Estimates of th[e] ...

KENNEDY TOURS CITY AREA, CROWDS GREET HIM IN RAIN; NIXON SETS 4-HOUR TV TALK

The New York Times
[S]enator John F. Kennedy addresses crowd here. At left is Senator ... [In] center is Michael H. Prendergast, Democratic State Chairman.

Mack Sennett, 76, Film Pioneer Who Developed Slapstick, Dies

Keystone Kops, Custard Pies and Bathing Beauties Were Symbols of His Movies

Special to The New York Times.

WOODLAND HILLS, Calif., Nov. 5—Mack Sennett, the film pioneer whose name was synonymous with slapstick comedy, died today at the age of 76.

The director-producer of the Keystone Kops comedies died at the Motion Picture Country Home in this San Fernando Valley suburb.

Mr. Sennett underwent surgery yesterday. It was his second operation in a year for a kidney ailment.

During the movies' formative era, Mr. Sennett made about 1,000 films, many of them two-reelers and most of them comedies. From 1910 to 1929 he directed and developed such stars as Charlie Chaplin, W. C. Fields, Gloria Swanson, Harold Lloyd, Marie Dressler, Ben Turpin, Roscoe (Fatty) Arbuckle, Louise Fazenda, Chester Conklin, Polly Moran, Buster Keaton and Wallace Beery.

A friend, Reece Halsey, an agent, was with Mr. Sennett when he died. Mr. Halsey said Mr. Sennett was outlining a plot for a play before he entered surgery. For several months he had been working on ideas for a television series.

Associated Press
Mack Sennett

Made the World Laugh

Mr. Sennett was a key figure in the history of the motion picture.

His comedies made the world laugh. The Keystone Kop, the bathing beauty, the squash and ooze of a custard pie on an

Continued on Page 88, Column 1

...s in the West; ...r of Inflation

...RENCE
...rk Times.

...Vice President Nixon an[nounced] ...onal television appearance ...is final-day drive for the ...idency. The "telethon" ... originate from Detroit.

...e Vice President's televi[sion] appearance on 125 affili[ated] stations of the American ...casting Company will last ... P. M. to 6 P. M., East[ern] ...dard time, with listen[ers] ...s the nation telephon[ing] ...

[T]he Nixon statement [is prin]ted on Page 64.

...s to Mr. Nixon. No ...andidate has ever ...o long a time on ...radio.

... today in Cali[fornia] ...on warned resi[dents] ...ome state that ...d by his Demo[cratic] ... Senator John ...d bring "Ken[nedy] ...d a "Kennedy ...

...tonight, Mr. ...

...g right up ...

...ing, jam[med] ...00 in the ...

...cast na[tional] ...program ..., with ...resent ...

SENATOR IS HAILED

Renews Peace Pledge at Climactic Rally in the Coliseum

Text of the Kennedy address is printed on Page 67.

By HARRISON E. SALISBURY

Senator John F. Kennedy last night pledged himself—if elected—to be a fighting President, dedicated to laying the foundations of peace for future generations.

Mr. Kennedy made this vow before an overflow crowd of 9,000 at the New York Coliseum and a nation-wide television audience. His running mate, Senator Lyndon B. Johnson, flew up from Texas and introduced him at the rally.

"Let us remember on Tuesday," Senator Kennedy said, "when the last hurrah is over, that this is a solemn decision. We are not engaged in a name-calling contest. We are not voting for an image, or a team or a protégé. We are voting for a President of the United States."

His partisan audience shouted its appreciation after nearly every sentence of his speech, which was televised nationally by the Columbia Broadcasting System.

2 Factions on Platform

On the platform behind him were the leaders of both the regular Democratic organization here and the insurgents who have been trying to oust them—united publicly for the first time in the current campaign.

The rally marked the close of [Se]nator Kennedy's campaign in [the] city and the climax of his ... for New York's forty-five [elec]toral votes. It was preceded [by] a whirlwind electioneering ... of the metropolitan area ... by a motorcade through Times Square, past thousands cheering in a cold, driving rain.

Spirited crowds turned out to see Senator Kennedy—especially in Nassau County—despite the rain. The Democratic nominee rode in an open convertible, bare-headed, with only a light topcoat.

So heavy were the crowds that he fell nearly two hours behind schedule. He was forced to skip appearances at two Manhattan rallies.

Time and again Mr. Kennedy's cavalcade was engulfed by throngs of well-wishers who threw the timetable of an extraordinarily crowded schedule out of kilter.

The crowds that turned out to cheer him were comparable in enthusiasm with those the Democratic candidate had drawn in previous appearances in the New York area. The pelting rain, however, may have kept them from equaling the size of earlier throngs.

Mr. Kennedy appeared before

Continued on Page 67, Column 1

Sports News

FOOTBALL

Army beat Syracuse yesterday, but Navy was upset by Duke for its first defeat. Minnesota toppled Iowa in a battle of unbeaten teams. Scores of leading games:

Army	9	Syracuse	6
Boston	7	West Va.	7
Brown	7	Cornell	6
Bucknell	12	Colgate	8
Dartmouth	22	Columbia	6
Duke	19	Navy	10
Florida	22	Georgia	14
Ga. Tech.	14	Tennessee	7
Michigan	8	Illinois	7
Mich. St.	17	Purdue	13
Minnesota	27	Iowa	10
Missouri	16	Colorado	6
N'western	21	Wisconsin	0
Ohio St.	36	Indiana	7
Penn St.	28	Maryland	9
Pittsburgh	20	Notre Dame	13
Princeton	14	Harvard	12
Rutgers	36	Lafayette	8
Washington	34	So. Calif.	0
Wesleyan	22	Williams	12
Yale	34	Penn	9

HORSE RACING

Divine Comedy set a track record of 1:55 4/5 for one mile and three-sixteenths in the $56,600 Romer Handicap at Aqueduct. Divine Comedy won by eight lengths and paid $6.20 for $2. Good Move, paying $38.40, took the $61,470 Selima Stakes and lowered the track record to 1:44 3/5 for one mile and a sixteenth at Laurel, Md.

Details in Section 5.

Reds in Vietnam Kill U.S. Aide in Ambush

Special to The New York Times.

SAIGON, Vietnam, Nov. 5—An American official of the United States Operations Mission in South Vietnam was killed early this morning when his jeep was ambushed by Communist terrorists.

The ambush took place near the seacoast resort of Long Hai east of Saigon. The jeep driver was also killed.

[In Washington, the dead official was identified as Dolph B. Owens of Tuscaloosa, Ala.]

It was the second time in sixteen months that personnel of the United States aid program here have fallen victim to increasing Communist guerrilla activities. A spokesman for the

Continued on Page 15, Column 1

Mack Sennett, 76, Film Pioneer Who Developed Slapstick, Dies

Keystone Kops, Custard Pies and Bathing Beauties Were Symbols of His Movies

Special to The New York Times.

WOODLAND HILLS, Calif., Nov. 5—Mack S[ennett, the film] pioneer whose na[me was synon]ymous with slap[stick comedy,] died today at the [age of 76.]

The director-pro[ducer of the] Keystone Kops co[medies died] at the Motion Pictu[re Country] Home in this San [Fernando] Valley suburb.

Mr. Sennett under[went sur]gery yesterday. It wa[s his sec]ond operation in a ye[ar for a] kidney ailment.

During the movies' fo[rmative] era, Mr. Sennett made [about] 1,000 films, many of them two-reelers and most of them comedies. From 1910 to 1929 he directed and developed such stars as Charlie Chaplin, W. C. Fields, Gloria Swanson, Harold Lloyd, Marie Dressler, Ben Turpin, Roscoe (Fatty) Arbuckle, Louise Fazenda, Chester Conklin, Polly Moran, Buster Keaton and Wallace Beery.

A friend, Reece Halsey, an agent, was with Mr. Sennett when he died. Mr. Halsey said Mr. Sennett was outlining a plot for a play before he entered surgery. For several months he had been working on ideas for a television series.

Associated Press
Mack Sennett

Made the World Laugh

Mr. Sennett was a key figure in the history of the motion picture.

His comedies made the world laugh. The Keystone Kop, the bathing beauty, the squash and ooze of a custard pie on an

Continued on Page 88, Column 1

...yesterday by ... policemen and firemen urged them to vote Republican on Tuesday as a protest against the Democratic city administration.

Police Commissioner Stephen P. Kennedy immediately ordered an investigation to determine whether any policemen or any of the department's line organizations were responsible for the letters.

The communication was mailed Friday under the sponsorship of the "Committee for a Square Deal for Policemen and Firemen," with the address, Suite 1, 42 East Sixty-fourth Street. The suite mentioned is

Continued on Page 31, Column 1

... spoke ... confidence of Senator Kennedy's winning by up ... 100,000 votes and carrying Mr. Lord to victory with him.

They noted that Mr. Case had been openly opposed by Old Guard Republicans who found his brand of Republicanism "practically Democratic."

New Jersey Republicans, conceding nothing in the election, recall that the state last went for a Democratic Presidential nominee in 1944. They acknowledged that the state was politically volatile, but they said that Vice President Nixon, running on the peace and prosperity issue, would prevail on the basis of experience and maturity.

The Democrats banked on translating concern over loss of national prestige and influence in many areas into a victory.

Continued on Page 27, Column 1

SENNETT IS DEAD; FILM PRODUCER, 76

Continued From Page 1, Col. 4

actor's face were the trademarks of a Mack Sennett comedy.

Mr. Sennett first worked for D. W. Griffith and then, after working as an extra for a while, he struck out on his own. During those days he carried his meager equipment with him in a street car, a far cry from the large studios that later grew in Hollywood.

Working side by side, Mr. Griffith developed the melodramatic motion picture and Mr. Sennett the broad comedy and burlesque.

"The first picture I directed," Mr. Sennett said later, "was in Fort Lee, N. J., in 1910. A gentleman with the name of Ishnuff, a Russian and a prototype of the late Czar down to the imperial beard was the camera man. We had a skinny bankroll and were filming all our scenes outdoors.

"I sales-talked a Fort Lee housewife into letting us use her front lawn by promising her a Rembrandt like still picture of herself and her family. Ishnuff cranked the camera very slowly in order to save film, which cost 4 cents a foot.

"Neither Ishnuff nor I knew that when you cranked slowly the film would be speeded up on the screen. When we finally developed the film and showed it in a projection room there was a blur of jerky figures whizzing across the screen as if jet-propelled.

"I lost my bankroll of $2,500 and had to pawn a $3,500 diamond ring for $800 to start all over again."

Guarantee of Fun

However, once Mr. Sennett moved to Hollywood and learned the proper speed of rolling a movie camera, patrons came to recognize the legend "A Mack Sennett Comedy," as a guarantee of robust fun.

People would chase each other up and down, in and out; a gorilla might put in an appearance; the heroine would fall in the water and would emerge with her dress clinging fetchingly; custard pies would fly and all would end well.

Among the Keystone Kops were Charlie Chase, Billy Gilbert, Slim Summerville, Edgar Kennedy and Fatty Arbuckle.

Mr. Sennett said of his work, "We never make sport of religion, politics, race or mothers. A mother never gets hit with a custard pie. Mother-in-laws—yes. But mothers—never."

It all started in Danville, Que., where Mr. Sennett was born on Jan. 17, 1884. His name then was Michael Sinnott. When he was 17 the family moved to East Berlin, Conn. Here, the youth, a strapping fellow over 6 feet tall and weighing 210 pounds, got a job as an iron worker.

But the lure of the big city was stronger than iron. At the age of 20 Mr. Sennett arrived in New York. He changed his name and decided on a stage career.

The youth's first public appearance was as a bass singer in a church. He succeeded in landing some small Broadway parts, including a two-line role in "The Boys of Company B." John Barrymore was also in the cast.

Entered Movies in 1909

Mr. Sennett also played the hind legs of a horse, one of the principal reasons for his going to the Biograph Studios in 1909 in search of a job. Most stage people frowned on Edison's new invention, but Mr. Sennett said:

"Imagine staying in New York, sending a roll of film all over the world and getting back money for it."

Before he transferred operations to Hollywood, Mr. Sennett produced one successful picture called "Cohen in Coney Island" and got a name for his motion picture production outfit—the Keystone Company. He happened to see a sign saying Keystone in the vicinity of Pennsylvania Station in New York.

When the company arrived in Los Angeles they ran into a Shriners parade. In almost typical fashion they set up a camera, and Mr. Sennett instructed one of the troupe, Mabel Normand, the actress, to race across the street, buy a shawl and a doll.

Then he told her to run up and down the line of march as if she and her baby had been deserted by a wicked man. The camera recorded it all and also the Los Angeles police, who tried to chase they away from the paraders.

Mr. Sennett said later that those police were the original Keystone Kops.

Miss Normand was also responsible for the custard-pie routine. She was on the set while they were having difficulty filming a scene with Ben Turpin.

Tired of the repetition, Miss Normand picked up a custard pie belonging to some workmen and pushed it full in the face of Mr. Turpin. Mr. Sennett later wrote:

"No one expected this memorable heave, least of all Turpin. The grinding camera was full on him. When the custard smote him, Ben's face was as innocent of anticipation as a plate. His aplomb vanished in a splurch of goo that drooled and dripped down his shirt front; his magnificent eyes emerged batting in stunned outrage in all directions."

The scene was so successful that it was repeated countless times in Sennett comedies. It was always employed most successfully when the victim had no idea the pie was to be pushed in his face.

The Sennett studio closed in 1928, and his corporation went into bankruptcy in 1933. There were many promises of a comeback, but nothing really materialized.

In 1956 a report from Washington showed that Mr. Sennett's dependable income was $227 a year from a retirement fund. His yacht and his two mansions in Hollywood were only memories.

The movie industry did not entirely forget. In 1938 the Academy of Motion Picture Arts and Sciences bestowed on him a special award for "his lasting contribution to the comedy technique of the screen."

In an interview last year, Mr. Sennett said he was saddened by what he considered the decline of good comedy-making in Hollywood. He said pantomine had been sacrificed for "gag-lines" and that modern producers did not know how to make slapstick comedies.

"Maybe people are paying too much attention to grammar today," he declared. "I don't think there's too many belly laughs in grammar."

Mr. Sennett never married. "My work is my wife," he used to say.

But at his death he had become almost a stranger on the Hollywood scene. There was no place for him in the industry. People brushed past him on the crowded Hollywood streets without ever knowing who he was.

The Keystone cops in Mack Sennett's *In the Clutches of a Gang*. Fatty Arbuckle is at right.

Chester Conklin and vintage Sennett beauties, 1913.

The New York Times SUNDAY, JANUARY 22, 1967.

Ann Sheridan, Actress, 51, Dies; Career Spanned 33-Year Period

'Man Who Came to Dinner' and 'Kings Row' Among Her Many Films

HOLLYWOOD, Jan. 21 (AP) — **Ann Sheridan, the actress, who was once billed as "the oomph girl," died today after a long illness in her San Fernando Valley home. She would have been 52 years old Feb. 21. The cause of her death was not divulged.**

Miss Sheridan had recently returned to the limelight as star of the television series, "Pistols 'n' Petticoats" on the Columbia Broadcasting System.

Beauty Contest Winner

Ann Sheridan, with her reddish-gold hair and youthful face and figure, was one of the very few beauty-contest winners ever to be heard from again after arriving in Hollywood.

She was one of 33 young girls brought to Hollywood in 1933 by Paramount Pictures as part of a promotional campaign for a picture called "Search for Beauty," and she was the only one who developed a career out of this publicity stunt.

During a Hollywood career in movies and television that spanned more than 30 years she was often suspended by studios—or went on strike as she used to call it—either because she felt she was not getting enough money or did not like the roles chosen for her.

In 1941, she went on a six-month strike against Warner Brothers because she wanted more than the $600-a-week they were paying. But she lost and went back to work.

After World War II, she stayed out of pictures for 14 months because she was not allowed to choose her own roles. She took another sabbatical in 1956.

But eight years ago, her film career waning, Miss Sheridan turned to the stage and toured in "Kind Sir" with Scott McKay, whom she married last June.

At Home in Many Roles

In her acting roles — which began with a one-picture contract she signed after winning the beauty contest—Miss Sheridan was equally adept as a schoolmarm, dance hall queen, gangster's moll or comedienne. Before moving to Warner Brothers in 1939, she made five Westerns for Paramount, then quit to freelance.

As a relative newcomer to screen in 1935, Miss Sheridan played in "Car 99," the story of a manhunt, opposite Fred MacMurray.

Another early role cast her in 1939 as a rowdy frontier dance-hall hostess with Errol Flynn and Olivia De Havilland. in "Dodge City."

By the early 1940's Miss Sheridan had reached stardom. One of her best-known roles was that of the feline actress in "The Man Who Came to Dinner" who tries to steal a young man from an unsophisticated Bette Davis.

Also in that 1942 screen version of the George S. Kaufman-Moss Hart comedy were Monty Woolley, Jimmy Durante and Billie Burke.

In the same year she starred as the wife of Jack Benny in "George Washington Slept Here," which is revived each Washington's Birthday on television.

Miss Sheridan appeared opposite Zachary Scott in "the Unfaithful," and James Cagney in "Angels with Dirty Faces."

In the wartime comedy, "I was a Male War Bride," her leading man was Cary Grant.

Among her other films were "Kings Row"—one of several in which she starred with Ronald Reagan—"Shine on Harvest Moon" with Dennis Morgan and Jack Carson, and "The Opposite Sex."

In 1940, the Harvard Lampoon created a stir by characterizing her as the actress of the year who was "the most unlikely to succeed," to which she quipped back, "Harvard is the home of the unadulterated heel—and you may quote me."

She often admitted that she had no idea what "oomph" meant and described it as "what a fat man says when he leans over to tie his shoelace in a telephone booth."

Ann Sheridan was born Clara Lou Sheridan on Feb. 21, 1915 in Denton, Tex., a small town northwest of Dallas.

Miss Sheridan first married S. Edward Norris, a stage actor, in August 1936. They were divorced in October, 1937 having separated after just 375 days of marriage. Her second marriage, to George Brent, another actor, on Jan. 5, 1942, lasted only 263 days.

In the 1940's she was linked romantically to the publicity agent Steve Hannagan. They were often reported about to be married, but Hannagan died a bachelor in 1953. He left Miss Sheridan nearly $250,000.

Ann Sheridan, Ronald Reagan and Robert Cummings in *King's Row.*

Ann Sheridan, Frank McHugh, James Cagney and Anthony Quinn in Anatole Litvak's *City for Conquest,* 1940.

"All the News That's Fit to Print"

The New York Times.

LATE CITY EDITION
U. S. Weather Bureau Report (Page 24) forecasts: Mostly fair today, increasing cloudiness later. Rain tomorrow. Temp. range: 40—30; yesterday: 40.6—27.8.

VOL. CIX..No. 37,233. © 1960, by The New York Times Company. Times Square, New York 36, N. Y. NEW YORK, SATURDAY, JANUARY 2, 1960. 10 cents beyond 50-mile zone from New York City except on Long Island. Higher in air delivery cities. FIVE CENTS

BUS PACT REACHED TO ASSURE 2 YEARS OF TRANSIT PEACE

Seven Private Lines Agree to Contract With Smaller Increase Than Subways'

FARE RISE IS RULED OUT

Mayor and Transit Officials Say Rate Will Be Held—Bergen Routes Struck

By STANLEY LEVEY

The Transport Workers Union and seven private bus companies reached an agreement early yesterday, thus completing the structure for two years of transit labor peace.

The bus settlement came at 4 A. M., following by several hours an accord between the union and the Transit Authority. Both agreements kept the buses and subways running after a strike deadline of 5 A. M.

The earlier agreement ... announced at 12:42 A... had been known lo... that. A two-year pact p... wage rises and other be... 40 cents an hour, it will ... Transit Authority $35,0... Twenty-nine thousand w... are involved.

The later bus agreement c... for wage increases of 22 ce... an hour over a two-year perio... for 8,000 employes. Fringe benefits brought the value of the package to about 36 cents an hour.

Strike in Jersey

Meanwhile, in Bergen County, N. J., 350 drivers employed by three bus companies went on strike early yesterday after the expiration of their contract. The lines serve 10,000 commuters, and two of them operate between points in Bergen County and New York City.

Despite the size of the authority-union settlement here, responsible officials insisted that the 15-cent fare could be preserved. Mayor Wagner said without qualification that the fare would not go up for two years. Charles L. Patterson, chairman of the authority, and Joseph E. O'Grady, a member, agreed.

How this would be accomplished was not obvious. The new contract, which was even larger than the 32½-cent package won by the union two years ago under similar conditions of crisis, ate up the agency's surplus of $12,500,000 and the $13,000,000 pledged by the city to pay for the authority's police force.

This arithmetic would indicate that the authority must now look around for $10,000,000 more. Actually, the differences

Continued on Page 4, Column 5

SYRACUSE ELEVEN TOPS TEXAS, 23-14

Mississippi, Washington and Georgia Also Win in Bowls

Syracuse University, college football's national champion, defeated Texas, 23 to 14, yesterday in the Cotton Bowl game at Dallas.

Syracuse's triumph, its first in a bowl, was marked by two fights among players. Ernie Davis, a sophomore halfback, starred for Syracuse. He scored two touchdowns and four conversion points. Ger Schwedes and Davis combined in the first period on an 87-yard touchdown pass play, the longest ever in a major bowl.

The results of other leading bowl games:

SUGAR BOWL

Mississippi blanked Louisiana State, 21 to 0, at New Orleans, avenging its only defeat of the season. The three Mississippi touchdowns were made on passes.

ROSE BOWL

Washington routed favored Wisconsin, 44 to 8, before a crowd of 100,809 at Pasadena, Calif. It was the West Coast's first victory over a Big Ten team there since 1953.

ORANGE BOWL

Georgia topped Missouri, 14 to 0, at Miami. Francis Tarkenton passed for both touchdowns. Three Missouri drives were stopped by Georgia inside its 20-yard line.

Details on Pages 8 and 9.

Margaret Sullavan Dead; Overdose of Pills Is Hinted

New Haven Coroner Says Death of Actress May Have Been Accidental

Special to The New York Times.

NEW HAVEN, Jan. 1—Margaret Sullavan, the actress, was found unconscious in her room at the Taft Hotel today and was dead on arrival at Grace-New Haven Community Hospital. She was 48 years old.

James J. Corrigan, New Haven County Coroner, said the actress' death might have resulted from an accidental overdose of barbiturates. Some pills were found in her room, which was locked from the inside.

"I do not believe it was a suicide," Mr. Corrigan said.

Miss Sullavan was appearing here in a tryout of "Sweet Love Remember'd." She became ill after her performance last night and Dr. Rafi Tofig, a New Haven physician, was summoned at 2 A. M. He said he found her nervous and depressed. He visited her again later in the day.

Margaret Sullavan

The actress had been resting in her ro... P. M., Mr. Co...

...hav... ye... ried... bers... have... cording... authority...

The di... Jack R. G... December b... of sitting a... for things to...

Four of the... part of the city... ects are not b... sixty-eight other... part of the wee...

The centers ... games and other ... tivities under tra... They serve childre... and the elderly.

11 Centers Will Be...

The authority a... Mayor for $2,447,724 a... operate all seventy-two... seven days a week.

Mr. Reid said last night... eleven more centers would... available in projects to be c... pleted in 1960-61. He said $55... 000 a year more would ... needed to operate them.

"We recognize with you tha... there is no panacea for the juvenile delinquency problem," the authority members said in their letter to the Mayor, "but our being able to provide a full and enriched community-center program is a significant part of the answer."

The members of the authority besides Mr. Reid are Francis V. Madigan and Ira S. Robbins.

Mr. Goldberg was hired by the authority last April to fill the new post of director of social and community services.

The basic purpose of his job

Continued on Page 4, Column 5

A.M.A. Aide Scores Warnings on Food

By HAROLD M. SCHMECK Jr.

The Government's recent warnings about cranberries, hormone-treated chickens and candy colored with carbon black have caused the public "undue alarm," according to the editor of The Journal of the American Medical Association.

The criticism was voiced by Dr. John H. Talbott in an editorial titled "Cranberries, Charcoal and Chickens." It appears in the Jan. 2 issue of the weekly journal, which goes to about 180,000 members of the medical profession.

"When next fall rolls around, we hope that cranberries will be permitted for the festive dinners, that licorice and jelly beans will be for sale at the candy counter, and that Southern fried chicken will be a permissible menu item," the editorial said.

Present laws are sometimes

Continued on Page 4, Column 2

COSTS CURB U. S. IN EFFORT TO PUT MEN INTO SPACE

Schedule of Initial Flights and Related Programs Feel Budget Squeeze

By JOHN W. FINNEY
Special to The New York Times.

WASHINGTON, Jan. 1—The National Aeronautics and Space Administration has been forced to scale down or delay plans for manned space flight because of a tight budget and rising costs.

Plans to keep the first astronauts in orbit around the earth for up to twenty-fou... hours have been aband... least temporari... first...

France Introduces a New Franc Worth 20 Cents

The 5-franc note, which is good for 500 old francs, has portrait of Victor Hugo.

Cardinal Richelieu is depicted on the note for ten new francs, or 1,000 old.

On 50-f... is shown

Napoleon is on note for 100 new francs

...gh the new currency ... to effect today, no one ... ide and his nine dis... d fellow-citizens got ... d on any of it. The ... France will start ... banknotes in denomi... of 100, 50, 10 and 5 ... nday and franc and ... oins at a later date. ... laude, who lives in Hérimoncourt in eastern France, got into the act because a radio station suggested that a special occasion should mark his birth last May, which brought the population of continental France to exactly 45,000,000. The radio station arranged a New

Continued on Page 3, Column 6

...wed Terrorism Mars ...f State of Cameroon

By The Associated Press.

... Cameroon, Jan. 1—Renewed violence ... of Cameroon's first day of independence ... s were killed and eight injured on the ... The new ... rought to ... er killed ... e kill... eroon ... litical ... re... ur

CATHOLIC DEPUTY WARNS GOMULKA

Pole Tells Parliament Nation Can Solve Problems Only in Democratic Climate

By M. S. HANDLER
Special to The New York Times.

...ENNA, Jan. 1—A leading ... n Catholic Deputy in Po... Parliament has warned ... law Gomulka's Commu... vernment that it cannot ... country's economic ... without creating a ... climate.

...ty, Dr. Stanislaw ... ued the warning ... g a discussion of ... budget in Parlia... mma belongs to ... parliamentary ... Znak. ... nformal group ... puties not af... the three estab... The word znak

...ield Futile

... Dr. Stomma's ... racted little ... , was pub... Catholic ... ecchy of ... overn... govern... ent of ... urn to ... istra... olve ... es ... the ... economic tasks. ... believe, and I repeat

Continued on Page 3, Column 8

British Defend Hold On Arab Desert Fort

By DANA ADAMS SCHMIDT
Special to The New York Times.

WASHINGTON, Jan. 1—The Buraimi story starts with Bhalib Ibn Ali, the Imam of Oman, and his brother Talib.

If it weren't for the Imam, who claims independence, and the oil the British and the Saudi Arabians think his realm contains, there would probably be much less quarreling over Buraimi—or so it seemed on a recent visit by this correspondent.

Buraimi is the collective name of a group of nine lush oases whose misfortune it is to lie athwart the main route into Oman. Until the British moved in, the Saudis had used it for centuries as a jumping-off place for sallies into Oman and down to the pirate and slave-trading ports at the southern end of the Persian Gulf.

Ironically, Iraq Petroleum

Continued on Page 3, Column 6

KHRUSHCHEV SAYS SOVIET MAY START DISARMING ALONE

Indicates Moscow Will Not Wait if West Refuses to Reach Agreement

TROOP CUTS PROMISED

Premier Declares Country Would Depend More on Nuclear Weapons

By OSGOOD CARUTHERS
Special to The New York Times.

MOSCOW, Jan. 1—Premier Khrushchev declared in a toast to the New Year in the Kremlin early today that if the West did not agree to disarm, "maybe we will disarm unilaterally."

He said that at any rate the Soviet Union should further reduce its armed forces and rely more on rockets and nuclear weapons to defend its borders.

The Soviet leader's words were promptly seconded by Marshal Rodion Y. Malinovsky, the Soviet Defense Minister, who asserted:

"It would be a great honor for me to disarm and as Minister of Defense to make this my swan song."

These impromptu declarations were made before 1,500 Soviet officials and foreign diplomats in the dazzling St. George's hall of the Great Kremlin Palace shortly after the bells in the Spasky Tower of the Kremlin had chimed midnight and a forty-foot evergreen tree with hundreds of red and yellow lights had been lighted.

Nine Toasts Offered

Sitting at the head table with the rest of the ruling Presidium of the Soviet Communist party, Mr. Khrushchev rose nine times to offer toasts: to the outgoing year, which he said had been a good one for the Soviet people; to the friendship of the Communist countries; to peace; to the whole world; to the Ambassadors present; to the inevitability of world-wide communism; to the trade unions; to the Communist youth; to women, especially Soviet women, and to the Soviet armed forces.

The Soviet Union does not need such large armed forces, Premier Khrushchev said in a jovial holiday mood. Its armed forces are overburdened with heavy firing power, he asserted. It has already reduced its forces by 2,140,000, he added, and is willing to disband its army altogether and everyone would welcome such a move.

Then, turning to Marshal Malinovsky, the Premier declared, thrusting a forefinger in the air for emphasis:

"We must reduce our armed forces more."

The numbers of troops do not

Continued on Page 2, Column 2

SHAH ACTS TO END IRANIAN SERFDOM

Backs a Land Reform Bill to Revolutionize Farming

By RICHARD P. HUNT
Special to The New York Times.

TEHERAN, Iran, Jan. 1—Shah Mohammed Riza Pahlevi is preparing a frontal assault on Iran's feudal land tenure system, which holds more than 1,000,000 farm families in serfdom.

With his active support, a bill has been put before Parliament to reduce drastically the holdings of absentee landlords and to create a class of peasants and small farmers who will own the soil they till.

The bill carries the promise of a sweeping revolution in the way of life in 40,000 to 50,000 villages. Making the land reform work is likely to become a central concern of the Shah's Government in the coming years.

The stated purpose of the land reform bill is to increase farm production and spread social justice. The measure seems to foreshadow a broad shift of

Continued on Page 3, Column 2

Associated Press Wirephoto

Gen. David M. Shoup, center, the new commandant of the Marine Corps, takes his place with other members of the Joint Chiefs of Staff. They are, from left, Admiral Arleigh A. Burke, Navy; Gen. Nathan F. Twining, the chairman, Air Force; Gen. Thomas D. White, Air Force; and Gen. Lyman L. Lemnitzer, the Army Chief of Staff.

By The Associated Press.

WASHINGTON, Jan. 1—David M. Shoup, a fighting man, became commandant of the Marine Corps today. He also became a four-star general. The 55-year-old general distinguished himself in action against the Japanese at Tarawa, winning the Medal of Honor. Peacetime assignments have included a year as Inspector General of the corps and three years as fiscal director. When President Eisenhower appointed General Shoup commandant in August, to succeed Gen. Randolph McC. Pate, General Shoup was a major general. He was jumped over five three-star lieutenant generals into the four-star post at the head of the corps. The Marine Corps commandant sits with the Joint Chiefs of Staff when matters pertaining to the Corps are discussed. He was a colonel at Tarawa atoll in the Gilbert Islands in 1943 when

Continued on Page 2, Column 8

NEWS INDEX

Margaret Sullavan Dead; Overdose of Pills Is Hinted

New Haven Coroner Says Death of Actress May Have Been Accidental

Special to The New York Times.

NEW HAVEN, Jan. 1—Margaret Sullavan, the actress, was found unconscious in her room at the Taft Hotel today and was dead on arrival at Grace-New Haven Community Hospital. She was 48 years old.

James J. Corrigan, New Haven County Coroner, said the actress' death might have resulted from an accidental overdose of barbiturates. Some pills were found in her room, which was locked from the inside.

"I do not believe it was a suicide," Mr. Corrigan said.

Miss Sullavan was appearing here in a tryout of "Sweet Love Remember'd." She became ill after her performance last night and Dr. Rafi Tofig, a New Haven physician, was summoned at 2 A. M. He said he found her nervous and depressed. He visited her again later in the day.

Margaret Sullavan

The actress had been left resting in her room about 2 P. M., Mr. Corrigan said. She was found unconscious by her husband, Kenneth Arthur Wagg, and the play's co-producer,

Continued on Page 26, Column 1

MISS SULLAVAN, ACTRESS, IS DEAD

Continued From Page 1, Col. 3

Henry M. Margolis, on their return some three hours later.

When Miss Sullavan did not respond to their calls and they were unable to open the door they summoned the assistant hotel manager, Frank Donovan. He opened the door with a master key, but was unable to enter because the door was secured with a chain on the inside. The hotel engineer sawed through the chain.

Mr. Corrigan said the specific cause of Miss Sullavan's death would not be known until laboratory tests were completed in about four days. "No one at this moment can call it death from barbiturates," he said.

Miss Sullavan was starring with Kent Smith at the Shubert Theatre here in "Sweet Love Remember'd," by Ruth Goetz, which opened Monday. Critics were unenthusiastic, but they called her performance "eloquent." The play was scheduled for its New York première at the Billy Rose Theatre on Feb. 4.

Tonight's performance was canceled an hour and a half before curtain time. Later it was announced that the play would resume tomorrow with Priscilla Gillette, Miss Sullavan's stand-by, filling the role.

Left Comedy in 1956

"Sweet Love Remember'd" was to have marked Miss Sullavan's return to Broadway after an absence of nearly four years.

Early in 1956, she withdrew from the hit comedy "Janus," pleading ill health. That fall, she disappeared on the day of a scheduled "Studio One" television broadcast on the Columbia Broadcasting System.

Miss Sullavan was listed as star of a play, "The Pilot," based on the story of Sister Mary Aquinas, a Roman Catholic nun and teacher who learned to fly a plane. The nun herself and sixty-four actors in costume waited in vain for Miss Sullavan, and C. B. S. substituted a film.

The actress' husband, Mr. Wagg, said at first that she had been taken ill and was in a hospital. Later this was denied. Three days after the scheduled performance, Miss Sullavan issued a statement apologizing for the incident.

She said that after ten days of rehearsal, she had decided that she was unable to give the role "the kind of performance" it deserved, and had so informed the producer, Felix Jackson. There was, however, a "misunderstanding" about whether she would appear, she added.

Shortly thereafter, Miss Sullavan spent several weeks in a sanitarium specializing in treatment of neuroses. Then she returned to her role as housewife and mother in Greenwich, Conn.

Attracted by Role

Last fall Miss Sullavan was attracted by the part in "Sweet Love Remember'd" of a woman in her late thirties, deeply in love with her husband, who has died.

"I read the play on Wednesday," she said, "and on Thursday I knew I wanted to be in it, desperately. I haven't been as anxious to go to work in a play since I was young and just beginning."

Reviewers had been praising her acting since her Broadway debut in 1931 in "A Modern Virgin," a Lee Shubert production. She often related that she had won the role because she was suffering from laryngitis, and her husky voice reminded Mr. Shubert of Helen Morgan and Ethel Barrymore.

Miss Sullavan cultivated the voice Mr. Shubert and the critics liked and, she said, "after several months of mistreating my vocal cords, I found it stuck."

Miss Sullavan said she had been stage-struck since the age of 6, when she gave performances in the parlor of her home. That was in Norfolk, Va., where she was born May 16, 1911, the daughter of Cornelius H. Sullavan, a broker, and the former Garland Council.

Her parents resisted her dramatic ambitions while she attended three private schools and Sullins College in Bristol, Va., but finally yielded and permitted her to go to Boston, where she briefly studied dancing and then enrolled in the E. E. Clive Dramatic School.

Miss Sullavan earned her way by selling books in the Harvard Cooperative Store. In the summer of 1928 she joined the University Players Guild, a community theatre at Falmouth, Mass., on Cape Cod. Another member was Henry Fonda.

That winter Miss Sullavan returned to Norfolk to make her social debut, but she went back to Falmouth for another season and then made her debut as the lead in the Southern touring company of "Strictly Dishonorable," by Preston Sturges.

After the run she rejoined the University Players in Baltimore, where it had begun a season of stock. There she and Mr. Fonda were wed. The marriage terminated in divorce in less than a year.

Her first four plays on Broadway were all failures. But one reviewer commented, "Some day someone will find a real part for her—and then——!"

"Some day" was 1933, when Miss Sullavan took over the lead in "Dinner at Eight." During its run, she signed a contract with Universal Pictures, which starred her in "Only Yesterday."

She did not like Hollywood.

Margaret Sullavan co-starred with Robert Taylor in *Three Comrades.*

"Acting in the movies is just like ditch-digging," she said. And when she saw the rushes of her first film, she offered Universal $2,500 to release her from her contract. The picture, however, was a triumph for the star and the studio.

In 1935 Miss Sullavan was married to William Wyler, who was directing her in "The Good Fairy." They were divorced two years later.

Meanwhile, she appeared in the films "So Red the Rose," "Next Time We Love" and "The Moon's Our Home." But on the expiration of her contract in 1936 she returned to Broadway for a nonstarring role in "Stage Door." During its run she was married to her agent, Leland Hayward, later a producer.

Miss Sullavan left the play to have her first child, a daughter, Brooke, in 1937. Brooke Hayward made her debut as an actress last Tuesday evening in "Marching Song" at the Gate Theatre. Last night's performance was canceled.

Had Second Daughter

The Haywards had a second daughter, Bridget, in 1939, and a son, William Leland Hayward, in 1941. Their marriage ended in 1947. In 1950, Miss Sullavan was married to Mr. Wagg, a British industrialist. He has four children of a previous marriage.

Perhaps Miss Sullavan's greatest triumph was in "The Voice of the Turtle," in 1943. The John van Druten play was named best of the season in The Billboard's first annual Donaldson Awards, and the actress received an award for a best lead performance. The play also was honored by the New York drama critics in a poll conducted by Variety.

Miss Sullavan played the role of Sally Middleton, an aspiring actress who had an Army sergeant as a week-end guest in her New York apartment. Her Sally was composed of a young girl, an actress who was hoping for that leading part, and a girl from Missouri who liked to be busy around the house. Elliott Nugent was the sergeant.

The title was biblical, noting that when the turtle's voice was heard spring was upon the world—even in the small apartment in the East Sixties, near Third.

She left the comedy the next spring, and was not seen again on Broadway for eight years, although, as The New York Times reported in 1948, "any producer would give his right arm for the services of Margaret Sullavan." She did appear in "The Voice of the Turtle" in London in 1947, but the critics were cool to both play and star, and it quickly closed.

However, Miss Sullavan's acclaim grew in this country. She called television "hellish," but she starred in the first "Studio One" production in 1948 and in several other TV dramas thereafter.

Also Appeared in Films

She also performed in occasional motion pictures. Bosley Crowther of The Times said of her performance in "No Sad Songs for Me" (1950):

"Plainly Miss Sullavan is someone who can give to a needy role the fullness of personality that will bring it to life and form."

The New York Times MONDAY, NOVEMBER 26, 1973

Constance Talmadge, 73, Dead; A Film Star of the Silent Era

Special to The New York Times

LOS ANGELES, Nov. 25 — Constance Talmadge, a film star of the silent era, died Friday in California Hospital here, according to friends. She was 73 years old, the widow of Walter M. Giblin, a New York stockbroker, who died in 1964.

The funeral will be on Tuesday at 1 P.M. at the Pierce Brothers Mortuary in Hollywood.

Followed Her 2 Sisters

Miss Talmadge grew up in Brooklyn and followed her older sisters, Norma and Natalie, into early films shot at the Vitagraph studio on Avenue W in the Flatbush section.

She achieved success in the high-speed productions of the World War I era. With Norma, who was then married to Joseph M. Schenck, who managed both of them, she shared studios at 318 East 48th Street until 1921. That year, they moved their operations to what the newspapers called Los Angeles but soon was pinpointed in the world's imagination as Hollywood.

In an interview that year Miss Talmadge sought to dispel ideas of a glamorous life at the studios. Asked if a girl was subject to more temptation than elsewhere, she replied:

"Most of the studios are run today by big companies on a clockwork schedule. . . . Why, everything with us is just work, work, work. . . ."

And she recalled her beginning earnings as an extra in Brooklyn as $5 a day.

One of her great successes was "Her Sister From Paris," a 1925 production directed by Sidney Franklin in which a new British actor named Ronald Colman was her leading man. It suffered—not too acutely at the box office—from news reports of censorship trouble in Chicago over subtitles such as "I hope you have a good night's rest."

Miss Talmadge did not seek to extend her career into the era of sound.

Her first three marriages, to John T. Pialoglou, a New York tobacco importer, Capt. Alastair MacIntosh, a British officer, and Townsend Netcher, a Chicago merchant, ended in divorce. She was married to Mr. Giblin in 1939.

Constance Talmadge in *The Duchess of Buffalo.*

Constance Talmadge and Ronald Colman starred in *Her Sister from Paris,* 1925.

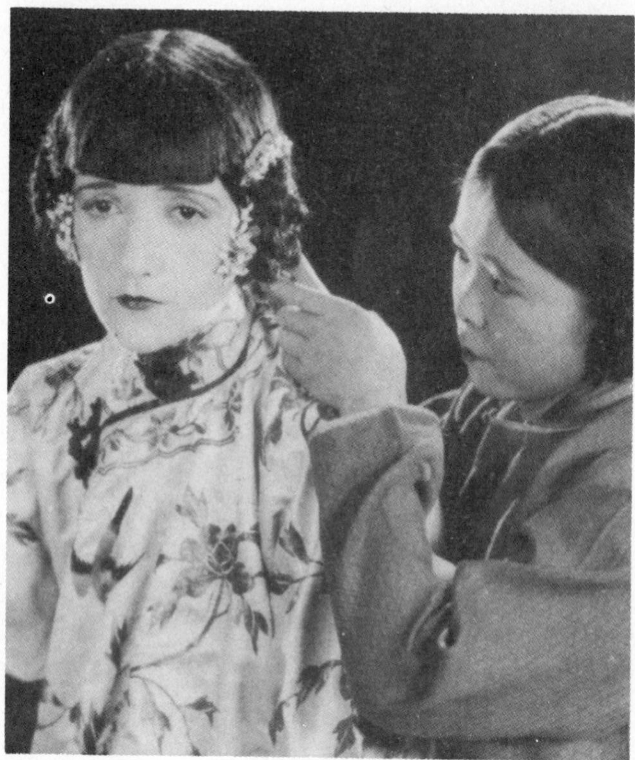

Constance Talmadge in *East is West,* 1922.

The New York Times WEDNESDAY, DECEMBER 25, 1957.

NORMA TALMADGE, FILM STAR, DEAD

Noted Actress of the Silent Screen, 1911-30—Made Her Movie Debut at 14

Special to The New York Times.

LAS VEGAS, Nev., Dec. 24—Norma Talmadge, one of the great stars of the silent screen, died in her sleep here this morning. Her age was 60.

Death came at her palatial home, 2047 West Charleston Boulevard, where she had lived in virtual seclusion. She had been confined to a wheel chair for the last several years with acute arthritis.

For some years she had divided her time between this city, Palm Springs, Calif., and Tucson, Ariz. But since 1946, when she was married to her third husband, Dr. Carvel James, she nad remained here a major portion of the time.

Appeared in Scores of Films

Not even Miss Talmadge herself knew, when she withdrew from cinema activity in 1930, how many motion pictures she had appeared in. She had risen from a $2.50 a day extra girl of 14 at the old Brooklyn Vitagraph studios in 1911 to the glamorous film stai who earned at least $5,000,000 in the last eight years of her career.

The film record books list sixty-seven, starting with her first ingénue lead in "The Dixie Mother" with Florence Turner in 1911. Her other great successes include "The Battle Cry of Peace," "Smilin' Through," "Camille," "Love or Hate," "The Woman of Vengeance," "Kiki," "Song of Love" and others, to her retirement after "DuBarry, Woman of Passion" in 1930.

In the beginning, her zest for her work was whetted by family need. Her father, Fred Talmadge, was an advertising salesman who had been finding it difficult to support his three growing daughters and their mother. At 13, while she was a student in Erasmus Hall High School in Brooklyn, Norma found that she could help a little by posing for colored slides that illustrated the songs plugged in the pits of the nickelodeons of 1910.

Then her mother registered her at the old Vitagraph studio on Avenue W in Flatbush. The first assignments were for occasional extra work, but as the volume of this increased the 14-year-old girl left high school, won her way into the Vitagraph stock company and within the year had played her first ingénue lead, in "The Dixie Mother." The salary in those days was $25 a week.

Norma Talmadge

Thenceforth, as her ability became established, she rose to $50 weekly, and at the end of her apprenticeship, in 1915, was earning $250 weekly, after the pronounced success of her first feature-length film, the nine-reel "Battle Cry of Peace."

Her First Picture

Norma's first picture was called "A Four-Footed Pest." Her second ingénue lead was with John Bunny and Charles Kent in "In Neighboring Kingdoms" and her first full-fledged lead was opposite Maurice Costello in "Mrs. 'enry 'awkins." Thereafter she was cast prominently at Vitagraph in "The Way of a Maid with a Man," "The Tale of Two Cities," "Counsel for the Defense," "The Fortunes of a Composer" and the Belinda series.

The first part written especially for her was in "Under the Daisies," with Leo Delaney, in 1913.

The success of "The Battle Cry of Peace" brought offers from Hollywood, the most attractive being that of the newly formed National Pictures Company. The next year (1916) found Norma in Hollywood under contract at $400 a week, with work guaranteed for Constance, who had been playing bits at Vitagraph.

Donald Keith and Norma Talmadge in *Secrets,* 1924.

A few months later Miss Talmadge regretted leaving behind the Brooklyn lot because National Pictures made one film with her, "Captivating Mary Carstairs," and subsided. She then made two films for Fine Arts.

After a time she and Constance joined the David Wark Griffiths unit at Triangle, Constance to drive a Babylonian chariot in "Intolerance" and Norma to make "Missing Links," with Bobby Harron and Elmer Clifton; "The Children in the House," "Going Straight" and "The Devil's Needle."

She was married to Joseph M. Schenck, producer, in Connecticut in October, 1917, and thereafter Mr. Schenck guided her considerably in pictures. "Panthea," "Poppy," "The Moth," "Ghosts of Yesterday," "By Right of Purchase," "De Luxe Annie," "The Safety Curtain" and "Her Only Way," her popular series with Eugene O'Brien, were released through Selznick between 1917 and 1920.

Shortly thereafter she set up her own unit, with Mr. Schenck as president and producer, and, releasing through Associated First National, entered upon her most successful years.

By 1930 Miss Talmadge, her family well provided for, her sisters established as screen players in their own right, decided to escape from the artificial world that had been created for her in pictures. She had begun as a comedienne, but in the late years perhaps "Kiki" in 1926 was the only gamin role in a welter of glamour and heavy drama—the "lady of the great indoors," they were calling her.

In April, 1934, she divorced Mr. Schenck in Mexico shortly after the death of her mother. She then came East and was married to George Jessel, vaudeville and radio comedian, late in the same month.

In June, 1939, Miss Talmadge announced that she and Mr. Jessel had separated. Two months later she obtained a divorce.

Miss Talmadge as "Rose of All the World" and Arthur Edmund Carewe in *Song of Love,* 1924.

The New York Times TUESDAY, SEPTEMBER 19, 1972

Akim Tamiroff, Actor, Is Dead; Had Screen Career of 35 Years

Expert in Character Roles Was Guerrilla Leader in 'For Whom Bell Tolls'

PALM SPRINGS, Calif., Sept. 18 (AP)—Akim Tamiroff, who played hundreds of roles in a movie career of more than 35 years, died yesterday at the age of 72, a family spokesman said today.

Twice Oscar Nominee

Mr. Tamiroff was nominated twice for an Academy award the first as the Chinese general in "The General Died at Dawn," the second as Pablo, the guerrilla leader, in "For Whom the Bell Tolls," starring Gary Cooper and Ingrid Bergman.

Born in Baku on the Caspian Sea, where his father was working in the oil fields, he grew up in Moscow and qualified as a youth for training in the rigorous school of the Moscow Art Theater. Admitted to the famous repertory company, he came to the United States when it toured here in 1923 and decided not to return.

The young emigré joined Balieff's Chauve Souris troupe, did Russian nightclub acts with his wife, Tamara Shayne, in Chicago, conducted a make-up academy in New York and appeared in "Wonderbar" with Al Jolson on Broadway. After a part in "Miracle at Verdun," also on Broadway, he and his wife went to Hollywood to try the world of films.

Bit parts won demands for his services in character roles in many of his successes of the 1930's. Some of the parts were in a swashbuckling vein, as in "The Soldier and the Lady," based on Jules Verne's novel "Michael Strogoff," in which Mr. Tamiroff played a Tatar rebel. Frank S. Nugent, reviewing its opening here in The New York Times, said he was "such a villainous villain that the audience — shame on it — was sophisticated enough to applaud him."

Often, Mr. Tamiroff was called on to play slapstick mad-Russian parts, as in "You Can't Take It With You." His strong Russian accent, which became a kind of trademark with the public, was sometimes an embarrassment to him. But he would tell interviewers later that when he offered to take lessons to get rid of it, he was told by studio executives that he would be dismissed if he did.

Mr. Tamiroff also found that the Moscow Art Theater discipline of studying and developing even a small part with great thoroughness stood him in good stead in Hollywood. The discontinuity of shooting a picture never found him uncertain as to the character he was portraying: his own consistency in a part was built in from the start.

His early successes in Hollywood included "Lives of a Bengal Lancer" and "Anthony Adverse." Later ones included "Outpost in Morocco," "Funeral in Berlin," and, perhaps inevitably, the screen version of "Anastasia." As a shady Russian banker in Paris, he was "in fascinating form," according to The Times critic Bosley Crowther.

In 1959, Mr. Tamiroff returned to Broadway and had a solid run playing the lead in "Rashomon."

Akim Tamiroff, Sheldon Leonard, Spencer Tracy, John Garfield and Hedy Lamarr in *Tortilla Flat.*

Orson Welles, Akim Tamiroff and Janet Leigh in *Touch of Evil,* 1958.

"All the News That's Fit to Print"

The New York Times

LATE CITY EDITION

Weather: Cloudy, chance of showers today. Fair tonight and tomorrow. Temp. range: today 72-62; Sunday 82-63. Temp.-Hum. Index yesterday 73. Complete U.S. report on Page 94.

VOL. CXVIII ... No. 40,679 | NEW YORK, MONDAY, JUNE 9, 1969 | 10 CENTS

NIXON TO REDUCE VIETNAM FORCE, PULLING OUT 25,000 G.I.'S BY AUG. 31; HE AND THIEU STRESS THEIR UNITY

A MIDWAY ACCORD

Leaders Agree First Cutbacks Will Begin Within 30 Days

Text of the joint communiqué is printed on Page 16.

By HEDRICK SMITH
Special to The New York Times

MIDWAY ISLAND, June 8—President Nixon met with President Nguyen Van Thieu of South Vietnam today and announced that 25,000 American soldiers would be withdrawn from Vietnam before the end of August.

After the first two hours of five hours of talks on this Pacific island, Mr. Nixon emerged to declare that the Presidents had agreed that troop withdrawals would begin within 30 days.

And with Mr. Thieu standing at his side, Mr. Nixon held out the hope of further reductions in the 540,000-man American force when this first phase was completed.

Replacements Available

He said that the equivalent of a combat division could leave Vietnam because of progress in the training and equipping of South Vietnam's Army.

Both President Nixon and President Thieu underscored the point that the American forces being withdrawn would be replaced in the field by South Vietnamese forces.

Mr. Nixon termed the withdrawal a "significant step forward" toward a lasting peace in Vietnam. At the end of the five-hour conference, Mr. Thieu said that the step was "good news for the American people that Vietnamese forces replace United States combat forces."

Both in announcing the troop withdrawal and in presenting a joint statement to the press at the end of their meeting, the two leaders sought to emphasize their solidarity.

Differences Not Mentioned

Their joint communiqué made no allusion to differences in approach to the Paris negotiations, and President Thieu remarked afterward that it was "not true" that he had come to Midway to thresh out differences with the new American Administration. But little was noted in the public statements of either man that might quiet Saigon's fears about the ultimate intentions of the United States leadership.

Although the announcement of the troop withdrawal was aimed at placating domestic critics of the war and putting pressure on North Vietnam and the Vietcong to negotiate more seriously in Paris by seeking to demonstrate South Vietnam's growing strength, Mr. Nixon mentioned neither American war critics nor the enemy.

As if pleading for more patience from the American pub-

Continued on Page 16, Column 3

VAGUE ON ISSUES

Statement Is Believed Unlikely to Dispel Saigon's Unease

By TERENCE SMITH
Special to The New York Times

...WAY ISLAND, June 8—...t Nguyen Van Thieu de...or Saigon today armed ...joint communiqué that ...to do little to relieve ...spread uneasiness that ...n South Vietnam over ...tes intentions con...war.

...word joint state...the two Presi...clusion of their ...ce appeared ...of much use ...oncern that ...olitical and ...South Viet...rican plan ...ment to ...livered ...leasc ...outh ...to ...re

Associated Press

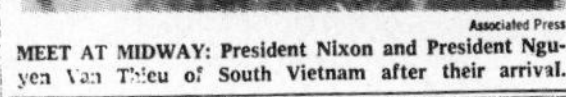

MEET AT MIDWAY: President Nixon and President Nguyen Van Thieu of South Vietnam after their arrival.

Aid to Vietnam Delayed To Force Inflation Control

By B. DRUMMOND AYRES Jr.
Special to The New York Times

SAIGON, South Vietnam, June 8—The United States ...en applying economic pressure on the South Viet... Government to convince it of the need to control

...ing to American offi... ...0-million in United ... was withheld from ...ring much of April ...hile intense discus... under way over ... price increases ... deficits.

... May, the South ...eed to take ...ation, and the ...d.

...months prices ...se stores and ...risen about ...have risen ...every 12 ...

...ecently, ...sugar... ...5 pi... ...that ...nth ...The ...18 ...he ...0

SOVIET GAIN SEEN IN MIRV PROGRAM

Pentagon Analysis of Tests Bolsters U.S. Advocates of Continued Testing

By WILLIAM BEECHER
Special to The New York Times

WASHINGTON, June 8 — A new analysis of Soviet missile tests in the Pacific is reinforcing arguments of those within the Administration who favor continuation of United States tests of multiple warheads.

The analysis, by intelligence experts in the Pentagon primarily, suggests that multiple warheads now being tested by the Russians may be capable of ...eing guided to three scattered ...rgets and powerful enough to ...troy hardened missile silos.

...il now, United States spe... had believed the Rus... ...ere testing a three... ...iple warhead all three ... of which landed in a ...t, predictable pattern ... another, attacking ... target.

...new intelligence in... ...iable sources say, ... Russians are fur... ...than previously ... development of

...ge 35, Column 1

PLAN WOULD HELP BIG STOCKHOLDERS TAKE HIGH OFFICE

Sales of Shares to Treasury Aimed at Removing Link to Conflict of Interest

SENATORS PREPARE BILL

McIntyre's Proposal Gives Appointee Chance to Serve Without Financial Loss

By WARREN WEAVER Jr.
Special to The New York Times

WASHINGTON, June 8—A novel plan that would permit millionaire stockholders to serve in high Federal office without risking conflict of interest or financial loss is being drafted in the Senate.

The plan is designed to meet the situation that arose when President Nixon named David Packard Deputy Secretary of Defense. He held $300-million worth of stock in an electronics concern that does about a third of its business with the Pentagon.

Mr. Packard, answering Senate criticism, set up a charitable trust for 3,550,150 shares of Hewlett-Packard Corporation stock with the Bank of America as trustee.

Under the new plan, an appointee would sell his stock to the Treasury, which, in turn, would gradually resell it in small pieces.

Bipartisan Backing

The legislative proposal, developed by Senator Thomas J. McIntyre, Democrat of New Hampshire, has bipartisan backing among leaders of the Senate Banking and Currency Committee. Senators William Proxmire, Democrat of Wisconsin, and Edward W. Brooke, Republican of Massachusetts, have endorsed the measure.

Senator McIntyre's idea has been submitted to President Nixon's top domestic advisers in the White House, and they were sufficiently interested in it to schedule a personal presentation to the President shortly.

If the plan wins the approval of Congress and the President, its first beneficiary may be Ray Watt, a California builder who was in line for appointment as the Federal Housing Administrator. He has been plagued by serious conflict-of-interest problems.

Mr. Watt and Mr. Packard both owned huge blocks of stock in corporations doing sub-

Continued on Page 37, Column 1

PREPARING FOR DEBATE: A s... phone before the start of the p...

New School Bo... Of 'Disaster' in ...

By LEONARD BUDE...

The new interim Board of Educati... statement, warned yesterday that the ... faced "major disaster" next fall becaus... ...ating funds.

The five-... which took offic... ago, said the indic... pense budget for th... starting July 1 wou... system to reduce c... ices by $96-million.

"We are shocked ... prospects facing our s... the next school year be... the most drastic bud... ever received by the city... system," the board said.

Plea for Aid Made

The budget reduction, which has already stirred an outcry from school, parent and community groups, would have the following impact, according to school officials:

¶The elimination of 4,427 needed teaching and supervisory positions.

¶An expected increase in class sizes in many schools by an average of two pupils for each class.

¶A one-third reduction in the free lunch program for poor children.

¶A cutback in pupil transportation services.

"Even at this late date," the board said, "we hope earnestly that the city, state and Federal Government can help restore the budget at least to the point that will enable our schools to

Continued on Page 67, Column 4

...tele... wit... a d...

In... him ... Mayor ... while not... had "star... be done." ... he said, p... "can be go... Mr. Linds... mayoral ca... Liberal party, ... addition of me... force, new subw... a balanced bu... years running an...

Continued on Pag...

POLICE IN U.S. SEEK TO EASE HOSTILITY

Survey Finds That a Rise in Efforts to Reduce Racial Tension Sometimes Fails

By JOHN HERBERS
Special to The New York Times

WASHINGTON, June 8—In cities across the nation, white policemen and black militant leaders have been holding "confrontation sessions" in which they probe each other's motivations and prejudices in an effort to lower the level of hostility between the two groups.

Many police departments have opened storefront centers in the slums, at which residents can voice complaints against the police or other public employes to policemen who have a reasonably sympathetic ear.

Virtually every department has stepped up efforts to hire more Negro policemen, and there have been a number of new community relations efforts, such as Operation Handshake, in which a new patrolman must spend several days in the community making friends before he begins enforcing the law.

An Explosive Issue

Despite these efforts, however, the hostility between the police and the Negro communities has worsened in some cities and in others remains the most explosive issue in race relations.

This information is based on a New York Times survey of 13 cities and on interviews with national leaders familiar with the situation. The cities surveyed were Boston, New York, Philadelphia, Chicago, Detroit, Pittsburgh, St. Louis, Houston, Miami, Kansas City, Mo.; Los Angeles, San Francisco and Oakland, Calif.

In the last year, the police departments have made efforts to institute new community relations programs, many of them following the recommen-

Continued on Page 37, Column 1

ROBERT TAYLOR, 57, IS DEAD OF CANCER

Associated Press

Robert Taylor

Special to The New York Times

SANTA MONICA, Calif., June 8—Robert Taylor, a Hollywood star for more than 30 years, died this morning of lung cancer at St. John's Hospital. He was 57 years old. With him was his wife, the German actress Ursula Thiess.

Hollywood's studio-sponsored star system created one of its most durable luminaries in Robert Taylor, who in 70 feature films, personalized the glamorous leading man adored by movie fans between the two World Wars.

Despite a shock of black, wavy hair, complete with an eye-catching widow's peak, a

Continued on Page 47, Column 2

NEWS INDEX

News Summary and Index, Page 49

United Press International

FLEE BATTLE IN TAYNINH: Refugees jamming road near the provincial capital 60 miles northwest of Saigon as allied troops sought to oust several hundred North Vietnamese who had taken a nearby hamlet. Article is on Page 17.

...rtmouth Are Troubled ...ing Echoes of Protest

By MICHAEL STERN
Special to The New York Times

...een ... sum- ...ng in here ... a sweet som- ...spell over the hearts and minds of Dartmouth men.

But this year, many of those hearts and minds are deeply troubled by still-fresh memories of chaotic springtime protests over R.O.T.C. on campus and the calling in of 90 state troopers last month to arrest students who had occupied Parkhurst Hall, the college administration building.

Vivid reminders of those events showed up here last week when 36 students—several with jailhouse haircuts—returned to the campus after having served 26 days of 30-day sentences for having defied ...—In a court order to leave the administration building. They got time off for good behavior.

Four others, whose trials had been delayed, left the campus this last week to begin their 30-day sentences and will not be released until July.

Still to come, beginning tomorrow, are hearings before the College Committee on Standing and Conduct, hearings that some condemn as a double jeopardy for the arrested students. The hearings are to determine what penalties will be imposed on those who overstepped Dartmouth's ground rules on free expression and dissent.

"Now is when the agony begins," said Prof. W. W. Ballard, chairman of the committee, as

Continued on Page 67, Column 2

ROBERT TAYLOR, 57, IS DEAD OF CANCER

Robert Taylor

Special to The New York Times

SANTA MONICA, Calif., June 8—Robert Taylor, a Hollywood star for more than 30 years, died this morning of lung cancer at St. John's Hospital. He was 57 years old. With him was his wife, the German actress Ursula Thiess.

Hollywood's studio-sponsored star system created one of its most durable luminaries in Robert Taylor, who in 70 feature films, personalized the glamorous leading man adored by movie fans between the two World Wars.

Despite a shock of black, wavy hair, complete with an eye-catching widow's peak, a

Continued on Page 47, Column 2

Robert Taylor and Dana Wynter in *D-Day the Sixth of June.*

Robert Taylor, 30 Years in Films, Dies

Continued From Page 1, Col. 1

trim, 6-foot frame and classically handsome features that verged on prettiness and often overshadowed his roles, he was a painstaking professional, if unspectacular, artisan quietly dedicated to his work.

Some 32 years after he made his film debut in 1934, he confided in a rare interview that he had "no complaints." "I can't think of anything I'd rather do, or rather have done," he said. "I'm just as nervous the first day of a picture as I was at the beginning, but perhaps I calm down a little faster. I'm still like a race horse when a picture starts. I can't wait to get going."

Richard Thorpe, who directed Mr. Taylor in six films at Metro - Goldwyn - Mayer, which first signed him and where he was under contract for more than a quarter of a century, said he was a no-nonsense, untemperamental actor who efficiently and quickly learned his lines. "Bob is really a nice guy," he said, "and it comes through on screen."

Shelley Winters, with whom Mr. Taylor appeared in the 1964 film "A House Is Not a Home," was equally complimentary. "Like Ronald Colman, he was the sweetest man to work with," she said. "By that I mean he was cooperative and understanding in contrast to most leading men today, who try either to elbow you out of camera range or are off in a corner somewhere practicing 'Method' acting."

'Luckiest Guy'

Mr. Taylor's personal evaluation of his ability to maintain his star status over the years was self - effacing. "Darned if I know," he told a reporter in 1957 while he was still at M-G-M. "I've been wondering about it myself for years. I guess the most important thing is to get a good picture once in a while. Acting is the easiest job in the world and I'm the luckiest guy."

The pictures, among them some good, big and spectacular ones such as "Camille," "Quo Vadis" and "Billy the Kid," began coming his way a few years after he signed with M-G-M as a handsome, largely untried 23-year-old actor from Nebraska.

He was named Spangler Arlington Brugh by his parents, Dr. Spangler Arlington Brugh and Ruth Adelia Stanhope Brugh. He was born on Aug. 5, 1911, in Filley, Neb., a village the family left for Beatrice, Neb., where the youth received his high school education and learned to play the cello. He also was a member of the track team and won the state oratorical championship.

Robert Taylor and Greta Garbo in *Camille.*

After his freshman year at Doane College in Crete, Neb., he followed his music teacher to Pomona College in Claremont, Calif., where he added to his academic and music studies roles in such Pomona collegiate plays as "Camille" and "The Importance of Being Earnest." An M-G-M talent scout saw his performance in the starring role of Captain Stanhope in the World War I drama "Journey's End" and signed him to a seven-year contract starting at $35 a week.

After graduation, young Brugh, whose name was changed by the studio, was farmed out to the Fox studio, where he made his movie debut in a small supporting role in "Handy Andy," a comedy starring Will Rogers. Within three years, starting with the lead in an M-G-M "crime-does-not-pay" short subject called "Buried Loot," Mr. Taylor appeared in 18 features, among them the 1937 "Camille," in which he played the love-smitten Armand to Greta Garbo's Camille.

'Surprisingly Good'

"Robert Taylor is surprisingly good as Armand," The New York Times critic said, "a bit on the juvenile side at times, perhaps, but certainly not guilty of the traditional sin of many Armands of the past—callowness."

Among the other films in which he appeared, and which helped boost his salary into the $5,000-a-week class, were "There's Always Tomorrow," "Society Doctor," "West Point of the Air" and the musical "Broadway Melody of 1936," in which he was the romantic lead, with Eleanor Powell and Jack Benny. However, it was his role opposite Irene Dunne in the tear-stained 1935 drama, "Magnificent Obsession," for which he had been lent to Universal Studios, that made him a top star.

He attended the President's Birthday Ball in Washington with Jean Harlow. Fans mobbed him in public places for several years thereafter and likened him to the late Rudolph Valentino as the movies' major matinee idol. His popularity was on a par with that of Clark Gable, Shirley Temple and the team of Fred Astaire and Ginger Rogers, the box-office favorites of the period.

But as a serious actor who yearned for artistry in his craft, Mr. Taylor managed eventually to escape the glamour boy classification by playing more muscular roles. These included the tough title character in the 1940 "Billy the Kid," the officer-gentleman opposite Vivien Leigh in "Waterloo Bridge," the hard-bitten prizefighter in "The Crowd Roars" and the noble killer in "Johnny Eager."

World War II put the actor's flying ability to use. An experienced amateur pilot, he was sworn in as a lieutenant in the Navy's air transport division but was deferred until he completed "Song of Russia" at M-G-M. He was then assigned to duty as a flight instructor. He also directed 17 Navy training films and did the narration for "The Fighting Lady," a documentary about an aircraft carrier. The commentary, one critic noted, was done in "a stern, self-effacing voice with no trace of the movie star."

The postwar years brought roles marked by steadfast professionalism. There were serious, workmanlike stints as a secretive mental patient in "The High Wall" (1947) and as a Secret Service man in "The Bribe" (1949). And there were variations in the Western genre. In "Ambush," he played a brusque frontiersman guiding the cavalry against the Apaches, and in "Devil's Doorway" he was a Shoshone Indian Medal of Honor winner who lost his fight against encroaching white settlers.

As one of the stars, along with Deborah Kerr, Leo Genn and Peter Ustinov, who spent much of 1950 working in Italy on the $7-million remake of "Quo Vadis," Mr. Taylor played a decided second fiddle to the superspectacle of Nero's Rome. Like the other principals in this moneymaker, the actor, cast as Marcus, the Roman centurion who falls in love with the captive early Christian portrayed by Miss Kerr, was "anything but inspired," according to The Times's critic.

Following the pattern set by other film stars, Mr. Taylor also was featured in his own television series, the 1961-62 "The Detectives." As the upstanding, no - nonsense sleuth, he reminded moviegoers that he also had played a hard-fisted, venal detective in the 1954 film "Rogue Cop." He also appeared on other TV shows, including "Death Valley Days."

Offscreen, Mr. Taylor led a singularly unglamorized, scandal-free life. He married Barbara Stanwyck in May, 1939, in San Diego. They had made two films together, the 1936 "His Brother's Wife" and the 1937 "This Is My Affair." They were divorced in February, 1951, but remained friends and co-starred again in 1965 in "The Night Walker," a lightweight suspense thriller.

In May, 1954, Mr. Taylor married Ursula Thiess in Jackson, Wyo. The actress, who had been divorced from George Thiess, a German director, had been featured in several American films before their marriage but later abandoned her screen career.

The New York Times THURSDAY, SEPTEMBER 19, 1968

Franchot Tone, Who Portrayed Sophisticates on Stage and Screen, Dies at 63

Franchot Tone, the actor whose many Hollywood roles as a dashing cafe society sophisticate were often only a pale echo of his wild and elegant private life, died at his home here yesterday. He was 63 years old.

Mr. Tone had been seriously ill for months, yet he remained actively interested in films and the theater despite his knowledge that he was suffering from cancer of the lung.

Only last Saturday, he sold his interest in Theater Four, where the hit play "The Boys in the Band" is running. He explained to his old friend Burgess Meredith that "the play is going to run so dammed long that I won't be able to use my theater for the kind of experimentation I want to do."

He had also purchased the film rights to "My Father, Renoir" by the French painter's son, Jean Renoir, the film director. Mr. Tone wanted his final movie role to be a portrayal of Renoir's vivid life.

In recent years, Mr. Tone spent far more time in New York, where he lived at 158 East 62d Street, than in Hollywood. His roots were in the East, his affection for Broadway and Off Broadway theater grew with age, and he wanted easy access to his house in Point Comfort, Quebec, where he spent the summer hunting and fishing.

Stanislas Pascal Franchot Tone, the son of a prosperous chemical engineer, was born on Feb. 27, 1905, in Niagara Falls, N.Y. His father, Frank Jerome Tone, who was of French-Polish ancestry, had been called to Niagara Falls by Dr. Edward G. Acheson, the founder of the Carborundum Company of America, and after a time as a technical supervisor he became president of the multi-million dollar corporation.

The Tone family moved often, and young Tone attended several private schools, including the Hill School in Pottsville, Pa., before enrolling at Cornell University. There he received outstanding grades and a Phi Beta Kappa key along with his degree, which he earned in Romance languages in three years.

After studying for a summer at the University of Rennes in France, he returned t the United States prepared to teach. Instead, he gave in to his passion for the theater and joined a stock company in Buffalo. Soon he was in New York as a member of the New Playwrights Company in Greenwich Village and not long thereafter he was chosen for a part in "The Age of Innocence" starring Katharine Cornell.

He was tall, wealthy, witty, intelligent and gracefully handsome—a perfect matinee idol of the time. He loved nightclubbing and he could usually be found, flanked by beautiful women, in the best watering places in town.

In 1932, after playing in several Theater Guild productions, including "Green Grow the Lilacs," Mr. Tone joined the revolutionary Group Theater and became a star, notably for his role in "Success Story."

As happened with so many theater actors, he was swept up in the vortex of Hollywood. He made his film debut in 1932, billed as "the millionaire star," in "Today We Live" with Joan Crawford and Gary Cooper.

He married Miss Crawford in 1935 and suffered the barbs of the gossip columnists, who liked to refer to him cuttingly as Mr. Joan Crawford. Their marriage was tempestuous, what with the fans who constantly mobbed them and Miss Crawford's career, which left them with only a few hours alone each day. They were divorced in 1939.

In the fall of 1941 he married Jean Wallasek, who was known as the actress Jean Wallace (and who is now Mrs. Cornel Wilde). During their seven years of marriage they had two sons. In a rather bitter custody fight after their divorce Mr. Tone was granted custody of the children.

His career—to the dismay of his friends—was tarnished in 1951 by a headlined escapade in which an ex-boxer and sometime actor named Tom Neal badly mauled him in a fist-fight over the affections of a blond actress named Barbara Payton. After some extensive plastic surgery, Mr. Tone married Miss Payton and, 53 days later, sued her for divorce in an action that filled gossip columns with spicy material for weeks.

His final fling at matrimony was a secret marriage to a budding actress, Dolores Dorn, that was disclosed in 1958—two years after the fact. A year later Miss Dorn got a Mexican divorce.

The film that Mr. Tone liked best of the three score or so he made was "The Lives of the Bengal Lancers."

Almost every year he would go to the Museum of Modern Art and ask to have it screened for him. He was also proud of his part in "Mutiny on the Bounty" and "The Three Comrades."

Mr. Tone's recent stage appearances here were in "Oh Men! Oh Women!," "Moon for the Misbegotten" and "Strange Interlude." On the screen, he was seen recently in "The Good Soup," "Mickey One" and in "In Harm's Way." He portrayed the President of the United States who dies in office in "Advise and Consent."

No More Ladies starred Robert Montgomery, Joan Crawford and Franchot Tone.

Robert Taylor, Margaret Sullavan, Franchot Tone and Robert Young in *Three Comrades*, 1938.

The New York Times SATURDAY, OCTOBER 19, 1968

Lee Tracy, Actor, Is Dead at 70; Played Fast-Talking Newsmen

Starred on Broadway Stage in 'The Front Page' in '28 —Was in 'Best Man'

SANTA MONICA, Calif., Oct. 18 (AP)—Lee Tracy, whose machine-gun delivery typified the breezy spirit of the talkies when sound came to the movies, died today. He was 70 years old.

The actor succumbed to cancer of the liver at St. John's Hospital here. He underwent surgery several months ago, but had been staying at his ranch home.

He leaves his wife of 30 years, the former Helen Thomas Wyze.

The Brash Newsman

On the stage, screen and television, William Lee Tracy was the typical example of the fast-talking, wisecracking, scoop-hungry newspaperman that he first created to popular acclaim in the Ben Hecht-Charles MacArthur hit "The Front Page" in 1928.

In an acting career that spanned nearly half a century, it seemed that he was fated again and again to portray the indefatigable newsman, and although countless other roles fell to him, it seemed that the city room was his natural habitat and the big story his prey.

He was cast as Eddie Haines, "invincible newshawk," in "Behind the Headlines"; Buckley Joyce Thomas, "ace of correspondents" in "Clear All Wires"; a "typical newspaper reporter" in "What's Your Number," and a performer of feats of "reportorial derring-do" in "I'll Tell the World," to list only a few of his films. Although the names and the places changed, the roles were all descended from Hildy Johnson of Chicago and "The Front Page."

Occasionally, too, the job altered slightly. In "Blessed Event," his Alvin Roberts was a gossip columnist and his Toby Prentis in "Advice to the Lovelorn," which was suggested by Nathaniel West's novel "Miss Lonelyhearts," counseled aching hearts.

Once he even moved up to the post of managing editor, playing Walter Burns in a scene from "The Front Page" for a group of newspapermen; and on the stage, in "Metropole," he portrayed the editor in chief of a slick magazine not unlike The New Yorker.

Even in television, he was a newspaperman, in the short-lived series "New York Confidential."

As life sometimes imitates art, he actually played the role of reporter at least once, during a Hollywood fire, and received at least one recorded byline, in The New York Daily Mirror in 1937.

The fire took place at the Voltaire apartment building in Hollywood, and Mr. Tracy was driving by when he noticed flames spurting from the windows. The fire routed out of bed such well-known people in the Voltaire and nearby buildings as Kathlyn Williams, Maureen O'Sullivan and Alan Hale.

Mr. Tracy telephoned a newspaper office and was instructed to get more information and call back.

The actor rushed up to a man clad in a bathrobe and demanded, "Who are you?"

"Alan Hale" was the answer.

"I never saw you look like this before," the actor-newspaperman turned acting newspaperman remarked.

In a moment, he recognized Miss O'Sullivan and then another pajama-clad man appeared. Mr. Tracy demanded his name and then learned it was John Farrow, whom he also knew.

"Why the heck don't you guys dress so you can be recognized!" Mr. Tracy yelled.

Under his byline in The Mirror, he wrote: "If the day ever comes that I step out of films, I should be aligible for a nice fat job on the staff of some metropolitan newspaper.

"I've covered police, City Hall the courts and every other run on a daily during my screen and stage career. I know all the ropes of the game, have staged a dozen original methods of scooping the boys on the opposition sheets and always 'bring home the bacon' in the last act."

"There's just one catch in my celluloid newspaper work," he acknowledged. "I never write a line. But then, a good 'leg man' is as valuable as the rewrite man, and so I guess I still rate a job on the city side."

Many years later, however, he told an interviewer, "I should have quit playing newspapermen after three or four parts in the movie. But the money kept coming in and I like it."

Despite his non-Method approach to his profession, Mr. Tracy was generally well received by the critics, for he brought energy and style even to less than weighty roles.

He created the role of an aging President, Arthur Hockstader, on Broadway in Gore Vidal's "The Best Man," in 1960, and when he re-created it for the screen was honored with an Academy Award nomination in 1964.

When he appeared in a revival of Robert E. Sherwood's "Idiot's Delight" at the City Center in 1951, Brooks Atkinson, then drama critic for The New York Times, observed that Mr. Trace had given "another of his irresistible performances" in the role of Harry Van, the song-and-dance man.

Mr. Tracy, who was the son of William Lindsey and Ray Griffith Tracy, was born in Atlanta on April 14, 1898. His father was a railroader, and the family lived a perpipatetic existence. The future actor grew up in Atlanta, Louisville, Kansas City and St. Louis, attended the Western Military Academy and Union College in Schenectady, New York, where he undertook to study electrical engineering.

But when World War I engaged the United States, he joined the Army and rose to the rank of second lieutenant. He also served in the army as an officer during World War II.

After World War I, he decided to become an actor, gained some experience in vaudeville and stock, then landed on Broadway in 1924 in "The Show Off" and achieved stardom in 1926 in "Broadway."

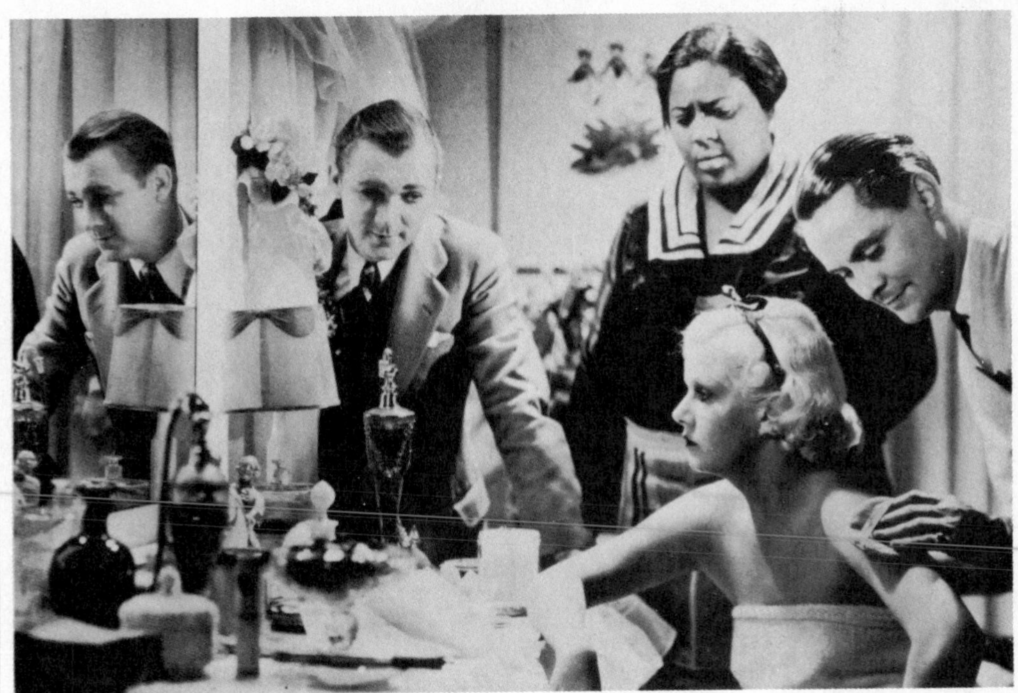

Lee Tracy (left), Louise Beavers, Jean Harlow and Franchot Tone in *Bombshell.*

Spencer Tracey and Mickey Rooney in *Boys Town.*

"All the News That's Fit to Print"

The New York Times

LATE CITY EDITION

Weather: Fair and continued quite warm through tomorrow. Temp. range: today 90-63; Sat. 91-66. Temp.-Hum. Index: today 78; Sat. 78. Full U.S. report on Page 95.

SECTION ONE

VOL. CXVI . No. 39,950 NEW YORK, SUNDAY, JUNE 11, 1967 35 CENTS

CEASE-FIRE IN SYRIA ACCEPTED; ISRAELIS HOLD BORDER HEIGHTS; SOVIET BREAKS TIES TO ISRAEL

Spencer Tracy Dies at Age of 67; A Hollywood Star for 37 Years

Special to The New York Times

HOLLYWOOD, June 10—Spencer Tracy, whose calm manner and rough-hewn face symbolized the justice-driven American man of action in scores of movies, died of a heart attack today in his Beverly Hills home. His age was 67.

Mr. Tracy recently completed "Guess Who's Coming to Dinner," his ninth film with Katharine Hepburn, a friend of many years.

He was stricken at 6 A.M. and died before a physician arrived with Carroll Tracy, his brother. The actor had suffered from a heart ailment for nearly 10 years.

Arriving shortly afterward were Mr. Tracy's estranged wife, Louise; their son, John, and daughter, Susan. They were followed by Miss Hepburn and George Cukor, the director, and the actor's business manager, Ross Evans.

Mr. Tracy was one of the last screen titans of a generation, a star whose name alone spelled money at the box office. And

United Press International

Spencer Tracy

Continued on Page 86, Column 1

LINDSAY VETOES BUDGET CHANGES; CHARGES POLITICS

Rejects Cuts and Additions Made by the Democrats on the Council and Board

WARNS OF NEW TAXES

O'Connor and Ross Accuse Him of 'Smokescreen' for His Campaign in '69

By THOMAS P. RONAN

With one exception, Mayor Lindsay vetoed yesterday all the reductions and additions made in his $5,183,508,877 expenditure budget for 1967-68 by the Democratic-controlled Board of Estimate and City Council.

The two bodies cut about $25.2-million from the Mayor's proposals, and added $19.3-million of their own projects, for a net reduction of $5,995,000. In both cases the Democrats have the required two-thirds votes to override the vetoes. They have until June 20 to do so.

The biggest cut, and t... to which the Mayor, a ...lican, objected most stren... was one of $23-million th... had set aside for expe... raises for city employes.

He called this action a "fisc... 'time bomb'."

The Democrats also eliminated $250,000 requested for Little City Halls, cut the Department of Buildings' proposed budget by $250,000 and reduced the amounts allotted to the Highways Department and Office of Labor Relations.

More for Education

Among the largest increases were $7-million for the Board of Education, mostly to expand kindergartens in depressed areas; $5-million for 50 additional day-care centers, where mothers on welfare could leave their children, and $4.4-million more to the City University to increase professors' pay and to provide for other services.

In the one exception to the vetoes, the Mayor accepted a $10-million cut in the $648.3-million budgeted for principal and interest payments on city loans. Controller Mario A. Procaccino has said other funds will be available to offset this reduction.

In his veto message the Mayor charged again that Board and Council had yielded "to political temptation." and that their actions could lead to new or increased taxes, or to deficit financing.

Frank D. O'Connor, the City Council President, and David Ross, its majority leader, countered with the accusation that the Mayor was "trying to set

Continued on Page 44, Column 1

To Our Readers

Beginning next Sunday, June 18, the newsstand price of the Sunday New York Times in the New York metropolitan area and all of Long Island will be 40 cents.

Beyond the 50-mile metropolitan area the price will be 60 cents.

Nitze Will Replace Vance at Pentagon

CIT... PLAN...

Many-Pro... List Enter... Offers ...

By THOMAS ...

Although it wa... Harlem's hot an... Street between ... Eighth Avenues ... people and was almos... as day.

Percy Malloy, sitti... glare of the 10 new ... spotlights installed as ... of the city's multimillion ... effort to avert violence ... slums this summer, gav... cards a loud shuffle on a ... in the gutter between ... parked cars.

Having just drubbed Jam... Gilliard in a game of tonk, ... simple form of gin rummy, he now threw out a challenge to the block's almost-undisputed tonk champion, Walter Birdsong.

"I'm the greatest," Mr. Malloy boasted. "I'm the Cassius Clay—the Muhammad Ali of the card table."

Mr. Birdsong took Mr. Gilliard's seat on a garbage can, picked up his cards and then laid them down in one spread after another on the clearly lighted table to win the game.

"These new street lights are

Continued on Page 78, Column 5

U.S. PLANES BOMB A PLANT IN HANOI; ONE JET DOWNED

3 Attacks on Capital Area—Missile and Motor Depots Struck at Same Time

By TOM BUCKLEY

Special To The New York Times

SAIGON, South Vietnam, June 10—Navy planes from the carrier Bon Homme Richard today bombed North Vietnam's most important electric power plant, which is only 1.1 miles from the center of Hanoi.

It was the third strike of the war against the plant on the banks of the Red River. The previous raids took place on May 19 and 21. In the first attack, moderate damage was reported. In the second, direct hits were said to have been scored on the generators and boiler house.

No reports on the extent of damage in the raid ... immediately ava...

Plane...

A 30-HOUR BATTLE

Syrian Zone 12 Miles Wide Cleared Near Sea of Galilee

By SYDNEY GRUSON

Special to The New York Times

TEL AVIV, June 10—Israeli sources said today that after less than 30 hours of fierce fighting, Israel's armed f... had won a major ... Syria ...

LEBANON Damascus El Quneitra SYRIA Haifa Sea of Galilee Mediterranean Sea ISRAEL Tel Aviv Amman Jerusalem GAZA STRIP Dead Sea JORDAN El Arish NEGEV Aqaba SAUDI ARABIA Strait of Tiran Red Sea

June 11, 1967

...t had wiped out past armistice ...ve to change. Area overrun ...rea (cross) was accepted.

U.N.'S TERMS MET

But an Air Raid Near Damascus Sets Off a Bitter Debate

U Thant's reports to the U.N. will be found on Page 33.

By DREW MIDDLETON

Special to The New York Times

UNITED NATIONS, N. Y., Sunday, June 11 — Syria and Israel have accepted United Nations arrangements for a cease-fire, but a heated Security Council debate over alleged truce violations continued into this morning.

At 2:40 A.M., when the Council finally adjourned, no action had been taken on the charges, or on three draft resolutions dealing with the cease-fire and the disposition of Arab refugees.

Secretary General Thant first announced the cease-fire at a morning session of the Council, informing the members that the peace had come to the last Middle Eastern battleground.

Syrian and Israeli representatives said they considered that the cease-fire was effective. But during the evening session, convened at the Soviet Union's request, Mr. Thant disclosed that United Nations observers reported bombing in the area of Damascus 17 minutes after the truce deadline.

Shelling Also Reported

Quoting a report from Lieut. Gen. Odd Bull, Chief of Staff of the United Nations Truce Supervision Organization, Mr. Thant also cited other reports of shelling from Syria into Israel and of Israeli occupation of El Quneitra, in Syrian territory.

General Bull informed the Secretary General that no Israeli troops were closer to Damascus than those at El Quneitra. But the Israeli-Syrian Mixed Armistice Commission reported that Israeli paratroops had been dropped at Tsil, about 20 miles east of Lake Tiberias (the Sea of Galilee), and at Rafid, 12 miles south-southeast of El Quneitra.

The Secretary General later read to the Security Council a cablegram from Foreign Minister Abba Eban of Israel. It said that truce orders had been issued in accordance with the Council's cease-fire resolution yesterday "at 1830 hours local time" (12:30 P.M., New York time, or 1630 Greenwich mean time), and that the cease-fire was "effectively enforced" and had continued uninterrupted.

A few minutes before this information reached the Council, Arthur J. Goldberg of the United States presented a new draft resolution demanding compliance with the Council's cease-fire order.

The United States resolution

Continued on Page 33, Column 1

...to Frontiers

...She also may try to keep ...me Jordanian territory ...st of the Jordan River. ...Old City of Jerusalem ...the West Bank of the ...n were captured from ...ian forces.

...has rejected pres... ...rom the Soviet Union ...the Israelis to return ...r previous borders. ...announced today ...was breaking diplo... ...tions with Israel. ...lle referred to the

...Page 32, Column 4

...REATENS ...'' MOVE

...Warns ...Other ...ly

...y and ...uld undertake ...ctions if Israeli forces failed to observe the United Nations cease-fire.

[Czechoslovakia and Bulgaria followed the Soviet Union in severing ties with Israel, and Hungary said she would do the same, according to news-agency dispatches. In Tel Aviv, Israeli officials declined comment on the diplomatic developments.]

Moscow's decision came after the Soviet Union had rallied a strong pro-Arab commitment from six East European Communist nations in a meeting here yesterday. Diplomatic analysts regarded the obtaining of the commitment as an effort to shore up a threatened erosion of Soviet influence in the Arab world.

Informed sources said the Communist bloc accepted a general responsibility to re-equip the United Arab Republic's battered army and air force for the gradual restoration of a military balance in the Middle East.

About 200 MIG jet fighters, for instance, were earmarked to replace the aircraft destroyed in the first hours of fighting last Monday, according to these informants.

The joint statement yesterday by leaders of the Soviet Union, Bulgaria, Czechoslo-

Continued on Page 99, Column 7

...seri... ...s week's

...nued on Page 31, Column 1

Sports News

BASEBALL

Gary Peters, a left-hander, hit a home run and pitched a four-hitter as the Chicago White Sox routed the Yankees, 9-0, yesterday at Yankee Stadium. It was Peters's sixth consecutive victory over the Yankees since Sept. 10, 1965. Don Buford also contributed a home run to the White Sox attack on three Yankee pitchers. Thad Tillotson took the loss, his first in the major leagues.

The Mets were rained out at Chicago after taking an early lead against the Cubs. Earlier, the Mets traded Jack Hamilton, a right-handed relief pitcher, to the California Angels for Nick Willhite, a left-handed starter.

The Cincinnati Reds, the National League leaders, got 14 hits as they coasted to a 9-4 victory over the Houston Astros.

THOROUGHBRED RACING

Mrs. Edwin K. Thomas's Furl Sail, ridden by Jacinto Vasquez, scored a wire-to-wire victory in the $97,800 Mother Goose Stakes at Aqueduct. In this second of the New York Racing Association's three-race series for 3-year-old fillies, Furl Sail scored by three lengths over Quillo Queen. Furl Sail returned $3.40, $2.60 and $2.40 for $2 across the board.

Mrs. Henry Obre's Lucky Turn and George M. Humphrey's Indian Sunlite won sections of the feature handicap at Monmouth. Potomac captured the Christiana Stakes at Delaware Park in 1:03 4/5, a track record for 5½ furlongs.

Details in Section 5.

...tai... ...nor...

...Cont...

...tribe... ...woun... ...son R... ...Traini... ...north ... ...rounds ... ...the casu... ...children ... An An... ...three mile...

Continued o...

Spencer Tracy Dies at A... A Hollywood Star for 3...

Special to The New York Times

HOLLYWOOD, June 10—Spencer Tracy, whose calm manner and rough-hewn face symbolized the justice-driven American man of action in scores of movies, died of a heart attack today in his Beverly Hills home. His age was 67.

Mr. Tracy recently completed "Guess Who's Coming to Dinner," his ninth film with Katharine Hepburn, a friend of many years.

He was stricken at 6 A.M. and died before a physician arrived with Carroll Tracy, his brother. The actor had suffered from a heart ailment for nearly 10 years.

Arriving shortly afterward were Mr. Tracy's estranged wife, Louise; their son, John, and daughter, Susan. They were followed by Miss Hepburn and George Cukor, the director, and the actor's business manager, Ross Evans.

Mr. Tracy was one of the last

United Press International

Spencer Tracy

screen titans of a generation, a star whose name alone spelled money at the box office. And

Continued on Page 86, Column 1

...banon and ...most of the oil ...ab countries, which feed ...pplies to Western Europe.

The canal and pipeline shutdowns disrupted the flow of oil equivalent to the capacity of 1,350 T-2 tankers that hold about 150,000 barrels of oil each. The Middle East supplies 10.3 million barrels of oil a day to non-Communist countries. This is one-third of the world's daily oil consumption.

J. Cordell Moore, Assistant Secretary of the Interior, who issued the emergency declaration, called a meeting of representatives of major oil companies here next Tuesday to begin work on plans that will assure a continued flow of oil where needed. The United States gets less than 5 per cent of its oil needs from the Middle East and would not be affected unless

Continued on Page 25, Column 1

...rdinal Ritter, 74, Dies; Liberal Archbishop of St. Louis

Special to The New York Times

ST. LOUIS, June 10 — Joseph Elmer Cardinal Ritter, a progressive leader in the Roman Catholic hierarchy in the United States and one of the principal figures of Vatican Council II, died here today. He was 74 years old.

Cardinal Ritter had suffered a mild heart attack on Monday and a more severe one Wednesday. He died at DePaul Hospital early this morning. "His heart just failed," said his physician, Dr. Christopher G. Vournas.

A religious vigil had been kept at the hospital since Wednesday. The Cardinal's sister, Sister Marie Catherine Ritter of the Sisters of Charity of Nazareth, arrived from Bardstown, Ky. A brother, Dr. Harry N. Ritter of Louisville, Ky., a retired eye specialist, was advised not to make the trip here because of his own heart condition.

A concelebrated funeral mass

Joseph Cardinal Ritter

for Cardinal Ritter will be offered at 11 A.M. Thursday at the St. Louis Cathedral. Burial will be at Calvary Cemetery

Continued on Page 86, Column 3

Today's Sections

Index to Subjects

Spencer Tracy Dies on Coast at 67

Continued From Page 1, Col. 3

although the former stage actor was partly eclipsed by younger and more prolific talents in his last years, his trademark of taciturn, unglamorized confidence remained a durable, salable commodity.

Mr. Tracy won two Oscars: as the Portuguese fisherman of "Captain Courageous" in 1937 and as Father Flanagan, the tough priest of "Boys' Town," the next year.

During 37 years of moviemaking he was repeatedly nominated for the award, for roles in such films as "The Old Man and the Sea," "San Francisco," "Father of the Bride," Bad Day at Black Rock," "Inherit the Wind" and "Judgment at Nuremberg." His last picture before the vehicle with Miss Hepburn was "It's a Mad, Mad, Mad World," completed in pleted in 1963.

Skill Made It Look Easy

At a press conference in Berlin in 1961, Spencer Tracy was asked what advice he would give a young actor just starting his career. Mr. Tracy thought a moment and then answered: "Learn your lines."

It was a typical response from the veteran film star, who disliked interviews and who always publicly denied there was any mystique about his profession. Yet Spencer Tracy was regarded as an actor's actor, a man whose great skill made his performances seem effortless.

He jealously guarded his private life and when interviewers asked what he thought were silly questions, he would answer in kind. To a reporter who questioned him about what he looked for in a script, he said simply, "Days off," and when another asked him what makes a woman attractive, he responded:

"Young man, I'll give you 30 seconds to think of another question." The reporter couldn't, and the interview was terminated.

Mr. Tracy, who appeared in more than 60 films in his long, very profitable career, was of the old school, having reached stardom while under contract for 20 years to Metro-Goldwyn-Mayer.

It was at M-G-M, which was known as the "studio of the stars," that he made his Oscar-winning films and "Libeled Lady," "Boom Town," "Test Pilot" and "Dr. Jekyll and Mr. Hyde." His co-stars included the most glamorous actresses in Hollywood—Myrna Loy, Jean Harlow, Joan Crawford, Hedy Lamarr and Lana Turner.

Signed in by Fox

In 1942, he was teamed with Miss Hepburn in the comedy "Woman of the Year," which began a close personal and professional association that was to last the rest of his life. Together they made "Keeper of the Flame," "State of the Union," "Without Love," "Sea of Grass," "Adam's Rib" and "Pat and Mike."

The actor, having begun as a contract player at Fox in 1930, reached the peak of his popularity in the 1940's and 1950's. But while Hollywood went through cycles of boom and bust, and the influence of the major studios declined, his career seemingly was unaffected. In 1960, on his 30th anniversary as a film actor, he commented on his freelance status:

"I miss the friends I made over the years in Metro. At the same time, I like the freedom I have. I pick my pictures now. But when I was at Metro, I did only a couple of pictures I didn't like."

Of the bad pictures, he said: "You make a bad picture and you know it's bad. You go up to see the head men and they say: 'What's the matter with you?' They show you the figures which prove your bad picture is making money hand over fist. A thing like that kind of baffles you. Makes you unhappy."

With the exception of his trip to Berlin in 1961 to attend the world premiere of "Nuremberg," Mr. Tracy had steadfastly refused to make personal appearances in recent years.

"You know what's wrong with this industry?" he once observed. "In the old days if you wanted to see Laurette Taylor, you went to the theater and paid $4. Now actors are refereeing football games and opening drug stores."

Mr. Tracy was able to maintain his popularity without opening a drug store. He seemed to fit naturally into the role of the strong man, no longer young, who could overcome adversity and fear by an inner toughness.

His role as the rugged one-armed hero in "Bad Day at Black Rock" in 1955 showed him fighting his way alone against overwhelming odds. The same was true of his portrayal in "The Old Man and The Sea." And all the wit and toughness he had gained through the years came through in Frank Skeffington, the old-time Boston politician he played in "The Last Hurrah."

Mr. Tracy was born on the right side of the tracks in Milwaukee on April 5, 1900, the son of a sales manager for a large trucking company. His early schooling was haphazard and marked by frequent truancy. When the United States entered the war, he followed his friend, Bill O'Brien, who later became Pat O'Brien of the movies, into the Navy.

After the war, which he sat out at the naval base in Norfolk, Va., he spent three semesters at Ripon (Wis.) College, before leaving to try his luck as an actor. He enrolled at the American Academy of Dramatic Arts in New York and shared a seedy West Side hotel room with Mr. O'Brien.

His first Broadway part was a bit as a robot in Karel Capek's "R.U.R." He later graduated to a featured role and toured with the show. There were plenty of low-paying acting jobs then if an actor was willing to travel.

Of those years, he later wrote: "In the old days, you had to go at it the long, hard way. Trains were as bumpy as a frog's back. Hotels were boot camps for bedbugs and roaches. And an actor's yearly salary would fluctuate like a broken spring."

It was while he was on the road that he met a young actress, Louise Treadwell. They were married a few weeks later, on July 28, 1923.

The actor, who stood 5 feet 10 inches tall and weighed about 170 pounds, looked like a tough but kind Irishman. The late J. P. McEvoy, the writer, once said that the lines in his face "would hold two days of rain." As his hair turned gradually from red to brown to snow white, Mr. Tracy maintained his position as a Hollywood individualist.

More and more in recent years he was moody, uncommunicative and often unpredictable even to his co-workers, with one exception, Miss Hepburn.

In personal crises, she invariably appeared near him. When the actor was intermittently hospitalized, Miss Hepburn would maintain a vigil at his bedside.

Film people in New York still recall how the actress coaxed Mr. Tracy back onto a plane bound for Germany, after he abruptly balked at filming "Nuremberg."

According to a United Artists official, "She said a few simple, tactful words, and that did it. Nobody else could handle him."

Spencer Tracy and Katharine Hepburn appeared together for the first time in *Woman of the Year*, 1942.

"All the News That's Fit to Print."

The New York Times.

THE WEATHER
Showers today; tomorrow fair, slight change in temperature.
Temperature Yesterday—Max. 73; Min. 63.
For weather report see Page 42.

VOL. LXXV....No. 25,049. NEW YORK, TUESDAY, AUGUST 24, 1926. TWO CENTS In Greater New York | THREE CENTS Within 200 Miles | FOUR CENTS Elsewhere in the U. S.

PEACE HOPE FADES AS MEXICAN BISHOPS REJECT COMPROMISE

Prelates Refuse to Negotiate Further Till Calles Suspends Religious Regulations.

WON'T RESUME SERVICES

Boycott Will Continue to Be Pressed, Says Bishop Diaz, as Catholics' Legal Right.

DOUBLE-DEALING CHARGED

President Is Accused of Altering the Episcopate's Statement and Shifting on Registry of Priests.

Special Cable to THE NEW YORK TIMES.

MEXICO CITY, Aug. 23.—Unless the Mexican Government suspends all regulations of the penal code affecting religion and the order for the registration of the priests, the Episcopate will not continue negotiations for an adjustment of the controversy between the Church and the State.

This position was taken by the prelates today when they rejected the formula for a compromise advanced in the conference of their delegates with President Calles late Saturday night.

The President, they said at the time, had assured them that the registration of the priests was entirely administrative in purpose, but later they discovered that he gave out a statement to a newspaper saying that returning priests would be "subject to the laws." The Bishops also charged that the statement which they issued after the conference, at the President's request, had been altered in its wording at the Chapultepec Palace.

As a result of the breakdown in negotiations, the Episcopate has dropped its tentatively considered project for resuming services in the churches.

Episcopate Decides to Fight On.

The Episcopate held a meeting tonight and unanimously decided to carry out the orders first issued when the Calles decrees were published, suspending all church services. It was decided that further conferences were useless as the prelates were convinced that the present Government was playing for time and was unwilling to suspend the penal regulations and the order requiring the registration of priests.

The bishops are confident that four weeks more of the boycott will bring the Government to terms, as Catholics in all parts of the republic report that the whole country is showing the effects.

Bishop Diaz Explains Situation.

Bishop Pascual Diaz of the State of Tabasco, who as Secretary of the Episcopate is the spokesman of the Church in Mexico, explained to THE NEW YORK TIMES correspondent today the reasons for the conference with President Calles and the significance of the result.

Moved by a desire to place themselves on record as having protested against the religious regulations in person to President Calles, he said, a committee of the episcopate, comprising Archbishop Leopoldo Ruiz y Flores of Michoacan and Bishop Diaz, readily accepted the invitations extended by Eduardo Mestro to meet the President.

Bishop Diaz added that the episcopate always had been ready and anxious to accept mediation in a form that would satisfy the Catholics and would permit the renewal of religious worship.

The members of the episcopate were consulted, and after a discussion it was agreed that Archbishop Ruiz and Bishop Diaz should explain to President Calles the exact position of the Church, and, if possible, arrive at a conclusion that would permit the faithful to use the churches and at the same time settle once for all the difficulties under which the Catholic Church had been working for many years. It was believed that through personal contact with President Calles the Catholic questions would be placed before the Chief Magistrate in such a form that an agreement would soon be reached.

Calles's Power to Act at Issue.

When ushered into the presence of the President in the Chapultepec Palace, Bishop Diaz found him in unusually good humor. The conference began immediately. During the conversation, which lasted for two and a half hours, no decision was reached, as both sides continued firm in their positions.

Archbishop Ruiz, presenting the Church side of the problem, told the President that if Señor Calles, in the exercise of his extraordinary powers which were granted by Congress and through which he issued the penal decrees and the order for all priests to register, would suspend the regulations, the prelates would immediately reopen the churches, resume services and use their personal influence with the faithful to end the present agitation.

President Calles in reply said that he personally could not use these same powers, as Congress would be in session within the next few days.

Bishop Diaz then pointed out that as Congress did not meet until Sept. 6 President Calles still enjoyed the usage of these privileges and that it was an easy matter for the President to suspend the regulations until Congress could find time to study the question and through the proper legal channels amend the articles to which the majority of Mexicans objected.

Dependence on Rome's Consent.

Bishop Diaz further informed the President that unless the regulations were suspended church service could not be resumed, at least until consent

Continued on Page Four.

Callizo, French Flier, Rises 41,811 Feet, World's Record

BUC, Versailles, France, Aug. 23 (AP).—M. Callizo is reported to have broken the world's altitude record today, reaching a height of 12,800 metres (41,811 feet). The record had stood at 12,066 metres (39,576 feet) a mark made by the same aviator. Callizo took off at the airdrome at 5 o'clock this afternoon and landed at Le Bourget two hours and twenty-five minutes later.

His instruments will be officially tested by the Air Ministry [...]row, but experts here are co[...] that the record will stand[...] mark he set is approximately [...] miles.

Lieutenant John A. Macr[eady] holds the American altitude rec[ord] 38,704 feet, made on Jan. 19. He [at]tempted to break Callizo's reco[rd] March 13, but reached only 37,5[..] feet.

PANGALOS CAUGHT; PRISONER IN ATHENS

Destroyer on Which He Was Fleeing Quit When Threatened With Destruction.

TWO AIDS ARE ALSO TAKEN

Attempt to Hide in Wireless Turret Has Brought Ridicule on Former Dictator.

Special Cable to THE NEW YORK TIMES.

ATHENS, Greece, Aug. 23.—The destroyer Leon, which had been sent by the new Condylis régime to prevent the escape of General Pangalos, deposed President, found the destroyer Pergamos, on which he was fleeing, near Cape Matapan last night. The Pergamos refused to heave to at first, but after warning shots had been fired she surrendered. The crew of the Pergamos intended to surprise the Leon by using hand grenades until they saw from the first fusillade that resistance was impossible.

General Pangalos was found hiding on board in spite of the commander's denials. The warships returned here about 6:30 o'clock this morning. Pangalos is now confined under close guard in the military hospital here.

General Condylis, leader of the revolution, addressed a popular demonstration yesterday which was called to celebrate the suppression of General Pangalos's "tyrannical rule." He was repeatedly interrupted by the crowd, which demanded immediate formation of a coalition Government and announcement of a general election. This General Condylis promised to do. He declared that those who had been responsible for the tyranny now suppressed must be held fully responsible for their action and that their punishment was a duty to the nation.

Demand Punishment as Example.

A similar demonstration held in Saloniki demanded that the army return to its work and that exemplary punishment be meted to those responsible for the Pangalos Government as an example for posterity and as the end of all dictatorships.

General Condylis today called a conference of party leaders to discuss formation of a new coalition Cabinet, but it probably will not be held until tomorrow, to give the parties time for discussion.

Admiral Conduriotis was expected to return this evening to take up his duties as President of the republic.

General Pangalos will be put on trial before the High Court of Justice with the other deposed Ministers. While a prisoner on board the Pergamos he was interviewed by Representative Eleftheros Typos, who once supported him. Pangalos expressed sorrow and surprise because his former friends and supporters had betrayed him and encompassed his downfall. He said he had had definite plans to bring about normal conditions and to announce holding elections. He said he had a clear conscience and had done his duty

Continued on Page Five.

HALL SUSPECTS STAY IN JAIL AS BAIL PLEA IS SHIFTED BY COURT

Justice Gummere Refuses t[o] Act, Holding Case [...] for J[...]

[...] C. Stevens, who are incarcerated in the Somerset County Jail because of the charge of murder on Sept. 14, 1922."

Asks Why They Come to Him.

"Why do you make the application to me?" asked the Court.

"Because Justice Parker, who sits in that circuit, is away and will not return until September, I understand, and also because Judge Cleary, the local Judge, has no jurisdiction to hear such an application."

Justice Gummere paused, and then said:

"I heard an application some two weeks ago to release Mrs. Hall on bail, probably connected with the same crime, according to the theory of the State. I had no knowledge of the application going to be made until it was made.

"Justice Parker, having observed in the newspapers—there has been some little notoriety given to this case in the newspapers now and then—wrote telling me that if at any time before his normal period of return any matter

Continued on Page Eight.

Berry Ousts Two Chief Aids, Tammany Men; General Shake-Up of His Office Forecast

A general shake-up of the higher officials of the city's Finance Department was forecast yesterday when it became known that Deputy Controller John J. Sullivan and Hans P. [...] chief of the Burea[u ...] justment, had [...]

[...] many or was due to the recent differences of opinion between the Controller and Mayor Walker over transit and bus policies.

Mr. Sullivan entered the employ of the Finance Department in 1924. He [wa]s chief of the Law and Adjustment [Bur]eau until last January, when he [was] promoted to Deputy Controller by [Contro]ller Berry on recommendation of [Tam]many. The Law and Adjustment [Burea]u is considered one of the most [import]ant in the department. [...]

$45,000,000 [...]NUM SUIT

[...]es Directors [...] Executors [...] Action.

[...]ENDANT

[...] Plaintiff [...] as a [...]

Continued on Page Nine.

Vault Built to Withstand Mobs and Bombs To Hold State's $200,000,000 in New Building

Special to The New York Times.

ALBANY, Aug. 23.—A most modern vault for holding $200,000,000 in cash and gilt-edged securities owned by the State will be built in the new twenty-six-story office building which the State is to erect just west of the Capitol. In case of fire it can be flooded with water. State Architect Sullivan W. Jones declared today it would be the safest vault that human ingenuity could devise. It will contain alarms connected with sirens outside the building and also with Albany Police Headquarters and the bankers' protective system.

Plans for the vault are being drawn by the State Architect's force. Its proposed location is being kept a secret and the specifications and details of the construction are confidential. It will measure approximately 50 by 50 feet.

On Wednesday Governor Smith and members of the State Building Commission will open bids for the wrecking of the buildings that now occupy the site where the new office building is to be built. By Jan. 1 next it is proposed to have the site cleared, test borings completed and the final program for construction ready for presentation to the Legislature.

Departments of the State Government that now have large sums on hand or hold large blocks of securities hire strong boxes at the local banks, but when the new building is ready and all the State departments are housed under one roof this will not be necessary.

While the State carries no insurance, the new vault will be so designed and built that it would take the lowest insurance rate. It will be fire and burglar proof and as near drill proof as it can be made, and will offer the greatest resistance to bombs and explosives or to mob attack.

The walls, floors and roof will be of flint concrete forty-eight inches in thickness, reinforced by an armor mat of high grade cold-drawn steel fabric. The doors will be of the circular type, two feet in thickness, with a time lock opened and closed with a concealed electric engine.

The day gate will be of hardened steel, equipped with a spring-bolt cylinder lock. A corridor will run all around it and mirrors will enable guards to see all sides. Three shifts of armed guards will be on duty every minute of the day and night. The expectation is that they will be former service men, former policemen and detectives.

Only accredited representatives of State departments will have access to the vault, and they will be triply identified by photographs, signatures and fingerprints. State troopers, it is expected, will provide additional guards.

Small vaults will be built into the structure for the use of departments such as the Controller's, Banking and Insurance.

VALENTINO PASSES WITH NO KIN AT SIDE; THRONGS IN STREET

Three Doctors and Two Nurses See "Film's Greatest Lover" Die After Long Coma.

MANAGER WEEPS IN HALL

Crowds Blocking Traffic, Held Back by Police Reserves, Rush to Funeral Church.

ASSOCIATES PAY TRIBUTES

Actor Dead at 31 Left Little of Huge Earnings—Arrangements for Funeral Yet Unmade.

Rudolph Valentino, motion picture actor, died at 12:10, yesterday afternoon, at the Polyclinic Hospital where he had undergone a double operation for acute appendicitis and gastric ulcers on Aug. 15. He was thirty-one. His youthfulness and rugged constitution aided him in making a valiant fight even after his five doctors had given up hope. Peritonitis and septic endocarditis, an affection of the heart tissues, were the immediate causes of death.

When the end came, the street in front of the Polyclinic Hospital was blocked by thousands of the actor's admirers and the curious, awaiting the latest bulletins from his bedside. The hospital switchboard was swamped by endless calls from persons anxious for the latest news.

Valentino lost consciousness several hours before he died. Shortly before the end came, a priest was called and administered the last rites of the Roman Catholic Church.

Continued on Page Three.

VALENTINO PASSES WITH NO KIN AT SIDE; THRONGS IN STREET

Three Doctors and Two Nurses See "Film's Greatest Lover" Die After Long Coma.

MANAGER WEEPS IN HALL

Crowds Blocking Traffic, Held Back by Police Reserves, Rush to Funeral Church.

ASSOCIATES PAY TRIBUTES

Actor Dead at 31 Left Little of Huge Earnings—Arrangements for Funeral Yet Unmade.

Rudolph Valentino, motion picture actor, died at 12:10, yesterday afternoon, at the Polyclinic Hospital where he had undergone a double operation for acute appendicitis and gastric ulcers on Aug. 15. He was thirty-one. His youthfulness and rugged constitution aided him in making a valiant fight even after his five doctors had given up hope. Peritonitis and septic endocarditis, an affection of the heart tissues, were the immediate causes of death.

When the end came, the street in front of the Polyclinic Hospital was blocked by thousands of the actor's admirers and the curious, awaiting the latest bulletins from his bedside. The hospital switchboard was swamped by endless calls from persons anxious for the latest news.

Valentino lost consciousness several hours before he died. Shortly before the end came, a priest was called and administered the last rites of the Roman Catholic Church.

Last Words Gave Cheer.

The actor closed his thoughts against death almost to the end. His last rational words were spoken to Joseph M. Schenck, Chairman of the Board of Directors of the United Artists Corporation, who was at his bedside at [...] A. M.

"Don't worry, Chief," said Valentino. "[I] will be all right."

[Dr.] Harold G. Meeker, who operated [on] Valentino, said that the actor [ga]ve up his thoughts of a vaca[tion ...] sure was he that he would [...] the complications which fol[lowed th]e operation.

"[He] passed peacefully," said Dr. [Meeker]. "He didn't know he was [...] At 3:30 this morning, he turned [...] and said cheerily: [...]

Friend Says Valentino Had Premonition of Dying Young

LOS ANGELES, Cal., Aug. 23 (AP).—Rudolph Valentino, who died today in New York, had a premonition of an early death and welcomed it in preference to living to a decrepit old age, it was revealed here today by John W. Considine, producer of his pictures.

Considine said: "Valentino several times remarked to me, 'I shall die young. I know it, and I shall not be sorry. I would hate to live to be an old man.'

"Valentino's prophecy has been fulfilled, but it has been a terrific blow to his friends. I found Rudolph a man of great courage and unquenchable spirit. He will be greatly missed."

COURT FINDING HALTS VOTE MACHINES HERE

Their Use in Fall Elections Is Doubtful, Knapp Contract Being Held Illegal.

ONLY HOPE LIES IN APPEAL

Justice Crain Finds Secretary of State Violated Charter in Acting as City's Agent.

Unless a decision by Supreme Court Justice Crain, handed down yesterday, is reversed by the higher courts before the November election, no voting machines paid for by the city's funds will be used here during the Fall balloting. This is the result of a ruling that the contract made by Secretary of State Florence E. S. Knapp, in behalf of the city, with the Automatic Registering Company of Jamestown, N. Y., is in violation of the city charter and constitutes a waste of city funds.

The contract called for the installation of about 3,000 machines, to cost $848.65 each, in the voting precincts of New York City over a period of three years.

Justice Crain grants an injunction in the suit of Adolph Hill, a taxpayer, who alleged waste of city funds amounting to about $200 on each machine because of the manner in which the contract was let. The Court upholds this contention and finds that under the requirements for the purchase of city property the machines could have been bought for less money.

City's Opposition Lethargic.

Although the question was taken before the court in the guise of a taxpayer's action and it was made evident that it was in behalf of the Shoup Voting Machine Company, an unsuccessful bidder on the voting machine contract, who asserted that the terms were so drawn that only the Automatic Company's machine fulfilled the requirements, the members of the Tammany City Administration involved were not active in opposing it.

Controller Berry, as disbursing officer of the city's funds, was made a main defendant with the Secretary of State, but the argument before Justice Crain was made by Deputy Attorney General Obermeier in behalf of the Secretary of State.

Temporary Victory for City.

The result of the suit is a temporary victory for the city officials in opposing action by the State Legislature to compel the installation of voting machines in New York City. The bill requiring the city to buy and use them was passed four years ago, and contained a provision that if the city officials did not act the Secretary of State had authority to do so.

During the Hylan régime Commissioner of Accounts Hirshfield declared that the cost of the Jamestown machines was excessive by $200, and the Administration refused to buy.

Justice Crain's decision is based upon his findings that, although the Legislature succeeded in one respect in circumventing the New York City charter in empowering the Secretary of State to buy supplies for the city, by making ineffective the charter provisions as to the purchase of "patenter articles," the lawmakers failed to overcome other requirements as to making contracts for city supplies. Justice Crain accordingly said:

"It is conceded that the provisions of the charter were ignored by the Secretary of State in the making of the contract. She did that which the applicable charter provisions did not permit her to do, and omitted to do that which the applicable charter provisions required her to do. Her action was illegal and it will incidentally involve an outlay of money in excess of that which the city would have been called upon to make had the charter provisions been followed.

"The Secretary of State's motives [in] doing what she did are not involved

Continued on Page Two.

[...]w York Tonight [...]eading Motor Ride

[...] Times.

[...]d a wonderful trip over on [...] We are seeking now a rest [...]le vacation. I am at peace [...] world and I hope everybody [...] as we are. We only want [...] to be happy and to be left [al]one."

Mr. Berlin said he had to get back to Broadway soon to begin work on a new musical piece. Mrs. Berlin is so weary from the long motor ride from Quebec that they shrink from going by motor to New York.

At Mr. Berlin's apartment at 29 West Forty-sixth Street it was said yesterday that no word had been received from him, and at the music publishing house the same information was given.

[...] leave by train [tomor]row night for New York, taking [a] sleeper at Watertown or Syracuse. They motored to Alexandria Bay from Quebec. Mrs. Berlin remained indoors today, but Mr. Berlin, with Mr. Winslow, played nine holes of golf on the Municipal Links, and went shopping in the village. Mr. Berlin, wearing white flannels and a silk shirt, turned in at the neck, said:

REPUBLICAN CHIEFS WILL CONFER TODAY ON GOVERNORSHIP

Wadsworth, Koenig and Morris to Discuss Candidates at Meeting in Saratoga.

KOENIG CONSULTS COOLIDGE

County Chairman Lays the New York Political Situation Before the President.

CROPSEY MEN RENEW HOPE

Leaders at Work Up-State to Win Convention Delegates Who Will Be "Harmonious."

Special to The New York Times.

PAUL SMITH'S, N. Y., Aug. 23.—Samuel S. Koenig, Chairman of the New York County Republican Committee, conferred with President Coolidge today on State politics, but their discussion did not result in determining who should be the party nominee for Governor this Fall.

Mr. Koenig left this afternoon for Saratoga, where he will meet tomorrow Senator Wadsworth and Chairman Morris of the Republican State Committee. The conference of these party leaders is expected to lead to more positive results on the Governorship.

The conferences held here with President Coolidge have been intended only to demonstrate that the President is vitally interested in New York State affairs, and to help soften, if possible, the opposition of the drys, among whom the President is strong.

Cropsey and Hilles Lead List.

After today's conference between the President and Mr. Koenig Supreme Court Justice Charles J. Cropsey and Charles D. Hilles appeared to be leading the list from which the nominee for Governor will be selected. It was indicated that Justice Cropsey seemed to satisfy more sections of the State than others who had been considered, and that he would be acceptable to the party leaders if he agreed to enter the race.

In his half-hour conference with the President, who is greatly interested in the New York situation because of the national politics involved, Mr. Koenig told him that the Republicans would gain four members of Congress in Greater New York and the party would control the next delegation from the State.

Mr. Koenig also assured Mr. Coolidge that prosperity was going to be a big asset favoring Senator Wadsworth's re-election, assuring him support from Democrats sufficient, in his opinion, to overcome the loss from up-State Republican drys.

Mr. Coolidge is not interfering in any way in New York politics, Mr. Koenig made it clear after the conference, but is interested in seeing that the Republicans increase their hold in Congress and retain the Wadsworth seat in the Senate. He will make no speeches in New York and do nothing to aid the party here, except what he may do before the November election in the way of a general statement on the trend of politics.

Mr. Koenig declined to commit himself on the Governorship, but admitted that Justice Cropsey seemed to be coming to the front. He said he felt that Cropsey, Attorney General Ottinger or Charles D. Hilles would make a strong standard-bearer in the State fight.

As to what the candidate would represent as between the wets and drys, Mr. Koenig declared he would not be a wet.

Suggests Campaign Issues.

"The issue of the Republican candidate for Governor will be the extravagance of the Smith Administration and the splendid record the Republican Legislature made last year," he said. "The wet issue will figure only incidentally, but still as a live and vital question. There will be other economic matters that are going to appeal to the voters, and, as the situation now stands, the Republicans enter the field with excellent chances.

"As for Senator Wadsworth, he will present the business prosperity brought about by the Republican Administration and stand on the accomplishments of the party. His chief appeal will not be modification of the Volstead amendment, but that and more far-reaching issues.

"I see no reason to feel that Mr. Wadsworth will be defeated. He is going to get a large vote in New York, much larger than the normal Republican vote. It will come from Democrats and ought to be large enough to overbalance his losses to the dry candidate for the Senate. There are thousands of dry Republicans, Democrats and independents who will vote for him to sustain the National Administration; then, too, the referendum will bring to his support wets who have been generally aligned against the Republican Party on State issues.

"The Republicans will not wage their campaign on the sole issue of prohibition. Senator Wadsworth will discuss national issues, and the candidate for Governor will stress the failures of the Smith Administration and the work done by the last Legislature.

Won't Be "Tool of the Drys."

"This is the first election in years that the Republican organization has not had to carry the load of being the tool of the drys. The agitation against Senator Wadsworth up-State is going to help him in New York City. The more the drys declare they are going to beat him, the greater his strength will become among the wets, with a consequent weakening of the Democratic candidate for the Senate."

It became known after Mr. Koenig's visit that there is a well organized movement under way to defeat Representative LaGuardia of New York,

VALENTINO PASSES WITH NO KIN AT SIDE

Continued from Page 1, Column 6.

The actor closed his thoughts against death, almost to the end. His last rational words were spoken to Joseph M. Schenck, Chairman of the Board of Directors of the United Artists Corporation, who was at his bedside at 6 A. M.

"Don't worry, Chief," said Valentino. "I will be all right."

Dr. Harold G. Meeker, who operated upon Valentino, said that the actor never gave up his thoughts of a vacation, so sure was he that he would conquer the complications which followed the operation.

"He passed peacefully," said Dr. Meeker. "He didn't know he was going. At 3:30 this morning, he turned to me and said cheerily:

" 'Doctor, do you know the greatest thing I am looking forward to?'

" 'What is it?' I asked.

"Valentino smiled and said: 'I am looking forward to going fishing with you next month. I hope you have plenty of fishing rods. Mine are in California."

Valentino left no fortune from his very large earnings. Mr. Schenck said the actor had spent practically all of his last year's income, which totaled close to $1,000,000. It is not yet known whether he left a will His life insurance, totaling $200,000, goes to the United Artists Corporation as beneficiary. Reports that Valentino's insurance amounted to $1,000,000 were erroneous.

No Relatives at His Side.

Despite the fact that Valentino had been cited as an illustration of the fact that "all the world loves a lover," he died alone save for his three doctors and two nurses. His brother and sister are in Europe. His first wife, Jean Acker, remained in New York in order to be in constant communication with the sick bed, but was not at the hospital when Valentino died. His second wife, the former Winifred Hudnut, known on the stage as Natoha Rambova, is in Europe.

Pola Negri, who recently had been reported engaged to Valentino, is in California. By long distance telephone she had made many inquiries concerning his condition. Her last call to the Polyclinic Hospital was at 4:25 A. M. yesterday. She tried to get the actor's manager, S. George Ulmann, and failing in that, tried to communicate with others near Valentino for the latest information concerning him.

Unnerved by his long and patient vigil, Mr. Ulmann was unable to remain in the sickroom before the end came. He had not slept for four nights and four days. He stood just outside the door so as to be near Valentino while the actor's life ebbed away. Mr. Ulmann broke down when he was informed that Valentino was dead. Doctors ordered him to bed. Before withdrawing, he expressed appreciation of the solicitude shown for Valentino. He said:

"Mr. Valentino was greatly cheered during his last days by the thousands of messages sent him by his friends and motion picture admirers, and while he was too weak to read all of them, it was a great comfort to him to know that so many friends were interested and sympathetic. I know he would want me to express the gratitude he felt. Personally I want to thank the physicians and nurses and the hospital attaches who worked so hard and conscientiously to save his life. Everything humanly possible was done for him."

Throughout the night a watch at the bedside of the patient was maintained by Dr. Meeker and Dr. William Bryant Rawls, house physician of the Polyclinic Hospital, and two nurses, Pearl Franks, who had been in attendance upon Valentino from the second day that he was in the hospital, and Jean Littlefield, who was called in on the case Sunday, after Valentino had taken a second turn for the worse.

At 3:30 A. M. the doctors gave the patient a hypodermic to induce sleep. Valentino slept until about 6 o'clock. Soon afterward Mr. Schenck and Mr. Ulmann entered the sick room. When Mr. Ulmann started to lower the window shade, Valentino objected, saying:

"Don't pull down the shade. I am feeling fine."

Valentino's condition remained virtually as it was on Sunday, but at 9 A. M. there was a slight rise in temperature to 104.5, according to Mr. Ulmann. At that time his pulse was 105 and his respiration 30.

The last rites of the Catholic Church were administered to the dying actor at 10 o'clock by Father Joseph M. Cangedo of the Church of the Sacred Heart of Jesus and Mary. Father Cangedo came to America from the little town in Italy where Valentino was born. He had known Valentino since the actor's boyhood. Father Cangedo had heard Valentino's confession and granted him absolution on Sunday, after the screen star's condition had taken a sharp turn for the worse.

Two Priests Summoned.

When the surgeons saw that Valentino was sinking rapidly they called, in addition to Father Cangedo, Father Edward F. Leonard of St. Malachi's Roman Catholic Church. After the last rites had been administered, Father Leonard and Father Cangedo left, thinking that the actor's death might be delayed. When Father Leonard was called a second time, he arrived just after Valentino had passed away.

According to Dr. Meeker, Valentino did not speak a word in English after 6:30 o'clock. At intervals he cried out in Italian which no one at his bedside understood. At 8 o'clock he went into a coma. Death, according to Dr. Meeker, was directly due to peritonitis and septic endocarditis. Peritonitis was caused by ulcers of the stomach and endocarditis followed the development of pleurisy in the left chest on Saturday.

Dr. Meeker said when Valentino suffered an attack of stomach trouble six weeks ago, he had not considered the

(continued)

Valentino as He Appeared in "The Son of the Sheik," His Latest Pictu[re] on Broadway, a Sequel to the Film in Which He Scored His Greatest Success.

Valentino in his death scene from *Blood and Sand.*

rouble as serious. The gastric ulcers which brought on the operation and esulted in death were probably manifesting themselves at the time of that ttack, the doctor said.

Mr. Schenck said he believed that Valentino's appeal to women motion-picture fans was to be explained by a personality which typified most women's ideal of romance.

Mr. Schenck said that Valentino had eft no fortune out of the large amounts of money he had made in motion pictures. He said that Valentino was a mere boy in money matters, and spent as fast as he earned. In explaining how Valentino's earnings in 925 totaled about $1,000,000, he said hey included $200,000 a picture and 50 per cent. of the profits on three pictures he made for United Artists, and $200,000 which he was paid by J. D. Williams for "Cobra."

Valentino's 1926 contract with United Artists Corporation provided for a payment of $200,000 a picture and 25 per cent. of the profits.

Mr. Schenck said that Valentino spent a large amount of money when he visited Europe last year. He toured he shops of art and antique collectors and bought a large collection for his home in Beverly Hills, Los Angeles.

Mr. Ulmann, Mr. Schenck, and Father Leonard departed from the hospital soon after Valentino died. The wo nurses left the death bed, and preparations were made to take the body to the Campbell Funeral Parlors, Broadway and Sixty-sixth Street.

Crowds Block Traffic.

News of Valentino's death spread hrough the hospital and to the streets with amazing rapidity. The crowds outside the hospital building continued o grow until it blocked traffic. The hospital authorities called up the West Forty-seventh Street Police Station, and requested the police to take charge of the situation. Not until the police arrived was traffic resumed through West Fiftieth Street between Eighth and Ninth Avenues. Many of the curious adopted all kinds of ruses to get into the hospital, but they were turned out as fast as they got through he entrance.

The body of Valentino was placed in a plain wicker basket, covered with cloth of gold, and taken to Campbell parlors. The crowds remained in front of the hospital, hoping in vain to see he removal of the body, which was aken from the building through a private entrance on West Fifty-first Street.

After the body was taken to the undertaking establishment, the crowds began to collect there in such numbers hat a guard had to be posted by the police. No plans for the funeral have been made. Friends of Valentino are awaiting instructions from his brother, Alberto Guglielmi.

Mr. Schenck cabled Mr. Guglielmi in Paris on Sunday that Valentino was dying, and received a cablegram that he actor's brother would sail for New York on the first ship. Mr. Schenck said last evening that he had heard nothing further from him. Valentino's sister, who was in Turin, also was advised by cable of the star's approaching end.

No word has been received from her.

The Valentino death certificate was filed with the Board of Health at 3:50 in the afternoon. It gave "ruptured gastric ulcer and general peritonitis" as the cause of death, and specified "septic pneumonia and septic endocarditis" as contributing causes. Valentino's name, "Rudolfo Guglielmi" was entered upon the death certificate, and his age was given as 31. A slight delay in filing he certificate was occasioned by difficulty in getting data as to his age.

One of the first persons who tried o view Valentino's body at the undertaking rooms gave his name as Camillo Santomero, 210 Stanton Street, and described himself as a traveling salesman and a cousin of the dead actor. He had failed in repeated attempts to get into the Polyclinic Hospital, and pleaded to get into the undertaker's by saying he had not seen Valentino for five years. He asserted that his mother was a sister. He was accompanied by Guido Valenti, who claimed to have been a boyhood friend of Valentino.

Body May Lie in State.

In response to constant inquiries, employes of the establishment announced that no definite information as to whether the body would be permitted to lie in state could be given. They said that the Gold Room was being held in readiness for such purpose if instructions were received. They were sure that no one would be permitted to view the body before 2 o'clock this afternoon, if at all. After that time they expressed the belief that close friends of the actor would be permitted to view the body.

Early in the evening a woman, who said she was Valeria Samel, a niece of Victor Neeler, antique dealer, 9 East Fifty-fifth Street, went to the undertaker's with a 14-inch nickel crucifix, inlaid with a mosaic of forget-me-nots. She said that her uncle was a long and close friend of Valentino and desired the crucifix to be placed on the chest of the dead actor. The crucifix was received, but the employes could not tell what disposition would be made of it.

The first floral offering, a modest spray of gladioli, tied with lavender ribbon, was received with a card signed "Rose Fellman." Women in the crowd at the funeral parlors greatly outnumbered the men and boys. Some of them pleaded several times to be permitted to see the body.

Crowds waiting before the doors of the Campbell establishment last night in an effort to view the body of Valentino were dispersed by five policemen detailed from the West Sixty-eighth Street Station, who ordered them to move on.

Rudolph Valentino in the famous tango scene from *The Four Horsemen of the Apocalypse*.

VALENTINO'S FAME A TRIUMPH OF YOUTH

Actor Wanted to Be a Gardener and Went to California to Get Work on a Farm.

BECAME "THE SHEIK" AT 26

Once Worked as Laborer in Central Park—Later Got Job Dancing at Maxim's and on Stage.

Rudolph Valentino was born on May 6, 1895, in Tastelameta, Italy, the son of Giovanni Guglielmi, a veterinary doctor. After taking an "agriculturalist's" diploma from the Royal School of Agriculture in Genoa, Italy, he came to this country in December of 1913 to seek work as a gardener.

He did not find what he wanted, he said later, although it is understood he worked a while on the Long Island estate of Cornelius Bliss Jr. His next position was as an apprentice landscape gardener in Central Park. He found something much more attractive to him in the dance halls and cafés of the city, and in them picked up the accomplishment of dancing. For some time he was practically penniless, accepting such odd jobs as shining brass on automobiles, sweeping and the like.

The head waiter at Maxim's first employed him as a dancer, and thus began his professional career. As dancing partner of Bonnie Glass, and later to Joan Sawyer, he attained some reputation. But at that time he still was bent on farming, and his fruitful journey to California, he told friends, was made with the idea of becoming a farmer there. He reached the Coast by joining a musical comedy troupe, which stranded him in San Francisco.

Valentino was advised by a friend he had known in the East, Norman Kerry, to try motion pictures, and on the bounty of Kerry he traveled to Los Angeles. He obtained only occasional jobs as an extra about the movie lots of Hollywood until June Mathis selected him for the rôle of Julio in "The Four Horsemen of the Apocalypse." In that he made his first triumph. That was in 1921. A feature of the picture was the Argentine tango as danced by Valentino, for the tango was then enjoying some of the popularity that has since been accorded the Charleston.

He gained his nickname from "The Sheik," a screen version of another best-seller. One of his earlier pictures was "Camille" in which he played opposite Nazimova. Official stardom came to him after "Beyond the Rocks," a Paramount picture from the story of Elinor Glyn in which he appeared with Gloria Swanson, "Blood and Sand" was his first starring vehicle—hitherto he had been a featured player only.

Valentino's last film was "The Son of the Sheik," which opened in New York on July 25 of this year.

Trouble Over Divorce.

The screen idol's marital difficulties brought him into the public eye almost as much as did his pictures. In 1919, when he was still a struggling and often hungry young film aspirant, he married Jean Acker, an actress who, although not a star, had met with some success. Miss Acker obtained an interlocutory decree of divorce from him in January of 1922.

Valentino waited only a few months before slipping across the Mexican border at Tia Juana to marry Miss Winifred Hudnut, stepdaughter of Richard Hudnut, millionaire manufacturer of perfumes. Miss Hudnut was also known as Natacha Rambova, Winifred de Wolf and Winifred Shaughnessy. It was while playing Armand in "Camille" that Valentino met Miss Hudnut. She was at that time working for Nazimova, and had designed the settings for the younger Dumas' melodrama.

Valentino came back to California with his bride, only to learn that he faced a charge of bigamy. The "divorce" won by his first wife, Miss Acker, would not be complete, according to law, until a year from the granting of the interlocutory decree.

The film star was freed of the bigamy charge in a preliminary hearing, and a Grand Jury that investigated it later dropped it with no action. The couple were remarried at Crown Point, Ind., on march 15 of the following year after the interlocutory decree had became absolute.

In January, 1926, Miss Hudnut obtained a final divorce decree from Valentino in Paris, and since then rumors have been current that Rudolph was going to wed Pola Negri.

Challenged Editorial Writer.

A month ago the "Shiek" became indignant over an editorial appearing in The Chicago Tribune entitled "Pink Powder Puffs." He resented the imputation that he was the cause of American men using face powder, and issued a challenge to the author of the editorial.

When the Chicago editorial writer would not reveal himself, Valentino said he considered the silence vindication.

After the war Valentino heard from a brother that he was rated a "slacker" in Taranto, Italy, because he had not fought for the United States. As a matter of fact, his services were refused on account of poor eyesight. He waited until he had cleared his name in Italy before taking out first citizenship papers in New York in November, 1925.

In 1922 and 1923 Valentino became involved in a dispute with his employers, Famous Players-Lasky Corporation. He broke with the company but patched things up soon afterward.

When Valentino became famous in "The Four Horsemen," many stories

(continued)

began to circulate about his early life. It was popularly supposed that he had supported himself after his arrival in America by working as a bus boy, a dish washer, and even a barber. All of which Valentino rose to deny.

He had, he said, been educated at Dante Alighieri College at Tarento, Italy, and at the military college della Sapienza in Perugia. He tried to enter the Government Naval Academy, but failed to pass the tests owing to a chest that was an inch short of the required measurement. After attending the agricultural school, he came to New York as a first-class passenger on the S. S. Cleveland of the Hamburg-American line.

He knew nothing of the language, and, failing to get work as a gardener, he became the dancing partner of Bonnie Glass and Joan Sawyer. He even appeared on the legitimate stage in minor rôles. His acting in "The Eyes of Youth," a C. K. Young production, attracted the attention of June Mathis, who had just finished her adaptation for the screen of "The Four Horsemen." She decided that Valentino was just the type to play Julio Desnoyers, and with his engagement for the rôle he leaped from obscurity to fame almost overnight.

Wrote Book of Poems.

Besides his better known successes, Valentino appeared on the screen in "Passion's Playground," "The Wonderful Chance," "Moran of the Lady Letty," "The Young Rajah," "Frivolous Wives," "A Rogue's Romance," "Monsieur Beaucaire" and "A Sainted Devil."

In 1924 Rudolph evinced activity in another sphere: he published a book of verse. "Day Dreams" was the title and it was brought out by MacFadden Publications. The poems were described as "jig-saw" verses on love, passion, kisses and kindred topics.

Some of Valentino's pictures were great money-makers. "The Four Horsemen of the Apocalypse" is said to have earned more than $2,000,000 and "The Sheik" more than $1,000,000. Valentino always insisted "The Sheik" was his idea of a poor performance.

Valentino in *The Sheik*, 1921.

MOVIE WORLD PAYS VALENTINO TRIBUTE

Will Hays Calls Actor's Death "on Verge of Greater Things" a Great Loss.

POLA NEGRI IS PROSTRATED

Producers and Actors in Eulogies of Star's Talents and His Qualities as a Man.

The death of Rudolph Valentino caused a deep shock to the motion picture and theatrical professions. Producers and artists of both the screen and stage paid high tribute to the art and character of Valentino in expressing their sense of loss.

Will H. Hays, President of the Motion Picture Producers and Distributors of America, telegraphed from Indianapolis to his New York office, 469 Fifth Avenue, the following statement:

"I deeply regret Mr. Valentino's death. He has had a distinguished career and was prepared to do yet greater things. His death is a great loss."

Joseph M. Schenck, Chairman, and Hiram Abrams, President of the United Artists Corporation, which had a contract with Valentino to release his pictures, issued the following statement:

"We are grieved and shocked at the great loss. Every one hoped for the best, especially since the boy had waged so brave a fight against the huge odds. The loss is a great one to us personally because he was our friend, and surely a real blow to the motion picture industry, in which he stood so high."

David Belasco: "I was saddened to learn of Mr. Valentino's death. I thought he was a great artist. The screen has lost one of its radiant personalities."

Adolph Zukor, President of Famous Players-Lasky Corporation, which formerly had Valentino under contract, said: "Rudolph Valentino was a great artist. In all my contracts with him I knew him as a gentleman of the best type. He was a credit to his profession."

Jack Dempsey, world's heavyweight champion, who met Valentino in the course of film productions, and whose wife, Estelle Taylor, was to have played opposite Valentino in his next photoplay, said: "The news was a real shock to me. I liked him tremendously. The screen has lost a dandy fellow and a talented actor."

Marcus Loew, President of Loew's, Inc., and Metro-Goldwyn-Mayer Pictures, who starred Valentino in "The Four Horsemen," said: "I cannot express my grief over the loss of Valentino. He was a friend."

Gloria Swanson, who co-starred with Valentino in "Beyond the Rocks," was visibly affected by the news of his death. "He was a real leader in his profession," she said, "and his loss will be keenly felt. May the thoughts and prayers of the millions who loved Rudy help him on his journey to the unknown. As a personal friend and admirer, my humble prayers follow him."

Gloria Swanson as the unhappy wife Valentino charms in *Beyond the Rocks.*

The New York Times MONDAY, MAY 13, 1957.

VON STROHEIM, 71, FILM ACTOR, DIES

Succumbs Near Paris After 6 Months' Illness—Made Last U. S. Movie 8 Years Ago

HOLLYWOOD, Calif., May 12 (AP)—Erich von Stroheim, the actor best known as a monocle-wearing, arrogant Prussian Army officer, died today in a hospital near Paris. He was 71 years old.

His sons, Erich Jr. and Josef, were notified of his death by telegram.

Mr. von Stroheim had been hospitalized for six months with a spinal ailment.

He had lived in France for the last eight years, since his last American movie, "Sunset Boulevard." In that film he portrayed a faithful retainer to a faded film star depicted by Gloria Swanson.

Recently he had appeared in French and Italian movies and was writing a novel and a biography.

Mr. Von Stroheim was known to audiences of World Wars I and II as a villainous German Army officer. In real life he had received the French Legion of Honor for his services to the film art. He attempted to enlist in the French Foreign Legion at the outbreak of World War II.

Starred in 'Grand Illusion'

Mr. von Stroheim was known to millions of early-day moviegoers as "the man you love to hate."

A star in such great productions as the French classic, "Grand Illusion," the Vienna-born actor-writer-director turned out "Greed," "Foolish Wives," "The Merry Widow" and "The Wedding March." He starred in three of these.

Mr. von Stroheim, who later became an American citizen, was the son of a colonel in the sixth regiment of dragoons in Austria.

Young Erich was an officer in the Austrian cavalry at 17 and served in the Army for seven years. He decided to end soldiering and seek his fortune in the United States in 1909.

Joins U. S. Cavalry

But in the United States he found himself again soldiering. He served two years with the United States cavalry and also in the Mexican Army against the bandit Pancho Villa. Finally he reached Los Angeles, and got a part as an extra—acting six different roles—in D. W. Griffith's "Birth of a Nation."

A painstaking artist concerned with meticulous detail, Mr. von Stroheim became Mr. Griffith's assistant director. By 1925 he was a leading director in his own right.

He would spend hours to get one small sequence correct. He gave his extras real liquor in drinking scenes and had the soldiers in "The Merry Widow" wearing un-seen underwear with a royal crest.

"Foolish Wives" was publicized as "The First Million Dollar Picture Ever Made," a slogan that won for Mr. von Stroheim a reputation for extravagance—a reputation that later ruined his directing career.

He was directing "Queen Kelly," starring Gloria Swanson, when he had to stop the film milday because sound had suddenly revolutionized the industry.

He continued acting, but he gradually disappeared from the Hollywood sets. By 1935 he was bankrupt.

Unable to get jobs even as an actor, Mr. von Stroheim quit Hollywood at the age of 51 to accept acting jobs in French films. Soon he became there one of the top box office stars.

Billy Wilder lured Mr. von Stroheim back to Hollywood twice, in 1943 to act in "Five Graves to Cairo" and in 1949 for "Sunset Boulevard."

Erich von Stroheim and Greta Garbo in *As You Desire Me.*

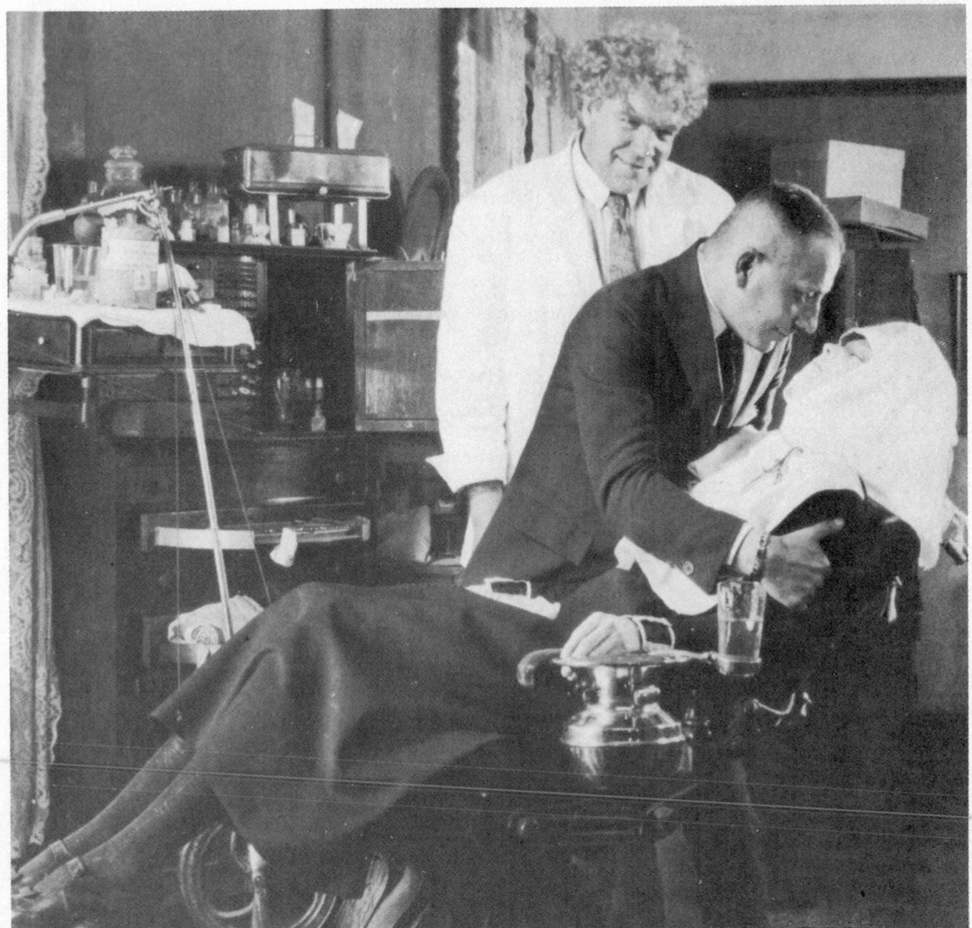

Von Stroheim demonstrates how he wants McTeague (Gibson Gowland) to embrace Trina (ZaSu Pitts) in *Greed.*

The New York Times SATURDAY, OCTOBER 15, 1966

Clifton Webb, 72, Dies on Coast; Movies' Dignified Mr. Belvedere

Broadway Comedy Star Won Fame on Screen in the Role of a Baby Sitter

BEVERLY HILLS, Calif., Oct. 14 (AP)—Clifton Webb, a child actor who became the star of smart Broadway shows and went on to win his greatest fame in the movies, died last night of a heart attack.

Mr. Webb had been retired and in ill health since 1961. He had reported his age as 69, but records indicate he was 72 and perhaps older.

In 1963 the actor underwent abdominal surgery, and last May he had an operation to remove an intestinal block. His secretary, Helen Mattews, his physician and his nurse were with him at his home here when he died at 9 P.M.

Oatmeal and Stardom

After having been a leading man on Broadway for decades and a familiar figure of menace for several years in a series of Hollywood films, Clifton Webb finally achieved his status as a star of mass appeal in 1948 when he dumped a bowl of oatmeal over the head of a small child.

The film was "Sitting Pretty," in which the debonair actor, then 55, played a baby sitter who was as formidable as he was unlikely. Of that performance, which started a new career for Mr. Webb, Bosley Crowther of The New York Times wrote:

"Yet there slyly protrudes through his arrogance a flickering spoof of pomposity and a tentative benevolence toward humanity, of which he generously agrees to be one. A student of the fine shades of kidding will find a lot to admire in Mr. Webb."

The actor repeated that success in a sequel, "Mr. Belvedere Goes to College," and in a series of similarly light-hearted comedies that resulted, in 1950, in his selection by the country's motion-picture exhibitors as one of the year's top 10 money-making stars.

Lived With His Mother

Mr. Webb, whose original name was Webb Parmalee Hollenbeck, immensely enjoyed the fame and money that came to him in his middle years. A bachelor, he settled in Beverly Hills with his mother, Mrs. Maybelle Webb, who was his constant companion until she died six years ago, at the age of 90. They were one of the most popular "couples" in the film colony's social set.

He subsequently appeared in a number of films, among them "For Heaven's Sake," "The Silver Whistle," "Cheaper by the Dozen," "Titanic," "The Man Who Never Was," "Boy on a Dolphin" and, as John Philip Sousa, in "Stars and Stripes Forever."

One of his last film appearances was in Leo McCarey's "Satan Never Sleeps" in 1961, when his health was beginning to fail. He played a Catholic priest in the violent melodrama. It was not a success.

Mr. Webb, whose theatrical career spanned more than half a century, was known for his impeccable diction and his elegant taste in clothes. He was credited with having introduced into the American man's wardrobe such items as the white messcoat dinner jacket, the double-breasted vest and the red carnation boutonniere.

Dancing at Age 3

He was born in Indianapolis. His mother, whom he once described as "not a bit like Whistler's," had had her own theatrical ambitions, which she transferred to her son at an early age. Mr. Webb seldom spoke of his father, and there have been reports that his mother left her husband when their son was 3 to enter show business.

It is known, however, that at that age, "young Webb," as his mother always called him, was taken to New York and sent to dancing school. When he was 7, he attracted the attention of Malcolm Douglas of the Children's Theater.

He made his formal theatrical debut as "Cholly" in "The Brownies" at Carnegie Hall in 1900. Next he played the title role in Oliver Twist, followed by "The Master of Carlton Hall." He also began studying singing and painting and gave his first one-man art show at the age of 14.

Opera Debut in 1911

But singing became a career, first in grand opera, then in operetta. At 17, after studying with Victor Maurel, Mr. Webb made his operatic debut at the Back Bay Opera House in Boston, in December, 1911, in "Mignon." Appearances with the Aborn Opera Company ranged from "Madama Butterfly" to "Hansel and Gretel." In 1913 he switched to operetta, appearing as Bisco in "The Purple Road" at the Liberty Theater here.

Mr. Webb's ability as a dancer attracted such attention in appearances at the Winter Garden and other leading Broadway theaters that Bonnie Glass invited him to team up with her. He accepted, earning $250 a week during his first dance engagement.

On the side Mr. Webb conducted private dancing classes. His mother served as secretary and manager of the Webb Dance Studio. When the team of Vernon and Irene Castle created the ballroom dance craze, Mr. Webb was a close second, with partners ranging from Jenny Dolly of the Dolly Sisters to Mae Murray.

Co-Star of Peggy Wood

The first musical comedy in which he starred was "Love O'Mike," in 1917, with Peggy Wood. This was followed by "Listen Lester" and "As You Were," with Irene Bordoni. He also played a dramatic role opposite Mary Boland in "Meet the Wife."

But Mr. Webb could not lay aside his dancing shoes. His nimble footwork successively graced "Sunny," starring Marilyn Miller; "She's My Baby," with Beatrice Lillie, and "Treasure Girl," with Gertrude Lawrence. He also appeared in "Three's a Crowd," "Flying Colors" and "As Thousands Cheer."

It was in 1942, while he was touring in Noël Coward's "Blithe Spirit," that he received a call from 20th Century-Fox to come to Hollywood to appear in "Laura." This was actually his second call to Hollywood. In 1936 Metro-Goldwyn-Mayer put him on a salary of $3,000 a week. He stayed in Hollywood for 18 months without ever making a picture.

His debut in "Laura," in which he played an acerbic, Alexander Woollcott type of character, set the pattern for subsequent roles in such films as "The Razor's Edge" and "Dark Corner." He was doomed to playing the slightly prissy, sharp-tongued villain until his talents as a comedian were fully utilized in the immensely popular "Sitting Pretty."

Clifton Webb as Mr. Belvedere in *Sitting Pretty*.

Harper Carter, Barbara Stanwyck, Audrey Dalton and Clifton Webb in *Titanic*.

The New York Times FRIDAY, AUGUST 5, 1938.

PEARL WHITE DEAD; EX-STAR OF MOVIES

Famous Actress in 'Perils of Pauline' and Other Silent Film Thrillers Was 49

EXECUTED DARING STUNTS

Saved Fortune and Retired to Paris in 1923—Spurned Offer for 'Comeback' Last Year

Pearl White

Crane Wilbur rescues Pearl White in *The Perils of Pauline.*

Wireless to THE NEW YORK TIMES.

PARIS, Aug. 4.—Pearl White of "Perils of Pauline" fame died today at the American Hospital after an illness which had kept her in bed for three weeks. Her age was 49. News of the illness of Miss White did not become publicly known until July 23 when the star of silent film thrillers had been in the hospital for several days.

She was then surrounded with secrecy by her friends and representatives. It was explained that she suffered from the after effects of a spine injury she received in her dangerous movie work more than twenty years ago. Hospital authorities said the funeral would be strictly private, with burial in Paris. This is said to be in line with her deathbed statement to her American lawyer, Bertram Winthrop, that she wanted to be buried quietly and with "no fuss made over my dead body." Knowing herself that she was dangerously ill and realizing the imminence of death she is reported to have been so anxious regarding the privacy of her funeral that she conferred even with her undertaker shortly before she died.

Pearl White came to France in 1923 after her retirement from the movies and she divided her time between her Paris home and her Rambouillet villa where she lived fastidiously, which was made possible by having wisely managed her large earnings. She kept a racing stable and won many important stakes on French tracks. She was the center of a fashionable group migrating between Cairo, Biarritz, the Riviera and other resorts. She once took over the Hotel Palais in Biarritz, which she transformed into a casino.

Father Says She Was 41

SPRINGFIELD, Mo., Aug. 4 (AP). —Pearl White's 84-year-old father said today she was 41 years old, not 49—explaining that she added a few years "to keep ahead of Mary Pickford."

She was born March 4, 1897, Edward G. White said, at Green Ridge, Mo., and the family moved here five years later. Mr. White said his daughter left home when she was 17 or 18 years old and joined a stock company.

Played in Serial Film Thrillers

Pearl White achieved fame and fortune as a serial star in the early days of the silent films. In the vernacular of those days she was known as the "lady daredevil of the fillums." She was one of the first women to attain stardom in the movies in America, and a pioneer of serial picture leading ladies. Her stunts were among the most daring ever performed before the camera.

She made her début in the thrilling serial screen portrayals in 1914. "The Perils of Pauline," produced that year by Pathé, established her at once as a film star extraordinary.

Miss White's hair-raising adventures did not always occur in films. In April, 1917, in war days, draped in an American flag, she made a perilous journey on a swaying steel girder to a height of twenty stories on a building being erected in Forty-second Street, near Broadway. From this height she dropped circulars to attract attention to the United States Recruiting Service.

When she descended she cried to the crowd, "I've done my bit. Now do yours."

Three years later she did a flying stunt in catching a steamship eight miles out of Hamilton, Bermuda, after finishing the last scene for the "Woman or Tiger," which was being filmed there. From a monoplane over the steamship she climbed down a rope ladder into a lifeboat, and was put aboard the ship. Later she inaugurated an airplaine service between Paris and Havre. She missed death perhaps by a few inches when an iron weight crashed from the flies of the Théâtre Casino de Paris as she stood on the stage bowing to the plaudits after swinging out over the audience in an airplane. Once she was lost for two days in the Pyrenees, an experience she recounted as the most exciting episode in her life.

Never Used a Double

Miss White was credited by her film managers as always acting in daring stunts herself, never employing a double.

At the height of her career she was famous throughout the world. She was among the first of the cinema actresses to receive a large salary, reputed to be $5,000 a week, and in less than ten years she is said to have earned close to $2,000,000.

In 1923 she announced that she had become tired of "being swung from cliffs and dropped from burning houses down into sewers," and was planning to enter a convent in France for a rest. Her eyesight had also been impaired by the film studio lights. For a brief period she was in a convent in the French Alps, but her desire for retirement did not long survive the attractions and plaudits of Paris. She drew crowds to the Montmartre Music Hall and led in the new Parisian fashion of wearing wigs. She became a notable figure at the race-track and gay nightlife places, and besides appearing in theatres in Europe she made a tour in Asia Minor and Egypt. Some years ago she was co-featured with George Carney in a revue in London.

On Miss White's final visit to the United States last year three Hollywood studios, still remembering that once her name on a theatre marquee meant a lot of money in a box office, offered to promote a return to the screen. She turned them down.

Recently she was questioned again as to a possible comeback in the movies. Her answer was: "Why should I? I have plenty of money. I'm happy now. Why should I go to Hollywood? Do I look crazy?"

Miss White made her stage debut as Little Eva in "Uncle Tom's Cabin" at the age of 6, was a bareback rider in the circus at 13 and left home with a traveling stock company when she was 17. Her first movie contact was in 1913.

She was twice married. She divorced her first husband, Victor Sutherland, an actor, and was married to the late Major Wallace McCutcheon, actor and author, whom she divorced in Providence, R. I., in 1921.

Wally McCutcheon was for a time one of Broadway's most colorful and popular figures. Early in the World War he enlisted as a private in a British regiment and was promoted for bravery until finally commissioned a major. Shortly after his divorce he disappeared for two years. His strange disappearance, and the death of John Stevenson, who had played with Miss White in pictures and was killed while performing a stunt in this city for her serial thriller, "Plunder," both contributed, it was said at that time, to her breakdown when she retired from the pictures.

Major McCutcheon, whose name she retained after her divorce, was finally located after two years in a private sanitarium, and resumed his career on the stage and screen. He died in 1928.

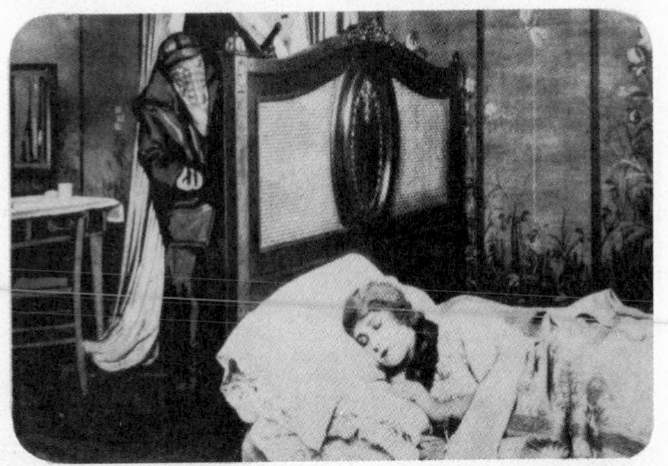

Pearl White in episode one of *The Exploits of Elaine,* 1915.

The New York Times

SATURDAY, FEBRUARY 4, 1961

Anna May Wong Is Dead at 54; Actress Won Movie Fame in '24

Appeared With Fairbanks in 'Thief of Bagdad'—Made Several Films Abroad

HOLLYWOOD, Feb. 3 (AP)—Anna May Wong, the actress who was among the first Chinese on the American movie screen, died of a heart attack tonight at her home in Santa Monica. She was 54 years old.

Miss Wong's film career spanned three decades, during which she was acclaimed as a versatile and talented performer.

Her last one, "Portrait in Black," with Lana Turner and Anthony Quinn, was recently released.

She also had appeared recently in television dramas.

Unforgettable Figure

Tall, slim and sloe-eyed, her blue-black hair worn in a bang that reached almost to her evenly arched eyebrows, Anna May Wong was one of the most unforgettable figures of Hollywood's great days—the Nineteen Twenties and Thirties.

Her Chinese name, Wong Liu Tsong, meant Frosted Yellow Willow. Her complexion, once described as "rose blushing through old ivory," shone on the screen like the texture of an old Ming vase.

The Chinese-American actress—she was born in Los Angeles, the daughter of a local laundry man—wore oriental costumes with a refinement of style that made her a stand-out in every picture in which she appeared.

Miss Wong began her career as a model for a firm of Los Angeles furriers. A picture of her, in a magnificent mink coat with her legs encased in brocaded silk ankle-length pantaloons, appeared in an advertisement printed in the rotogravure section of a Sunday newspaper.

A Brother's Comment

"My father was so impressed by my elegance that he cut the picture out and sent it to my half-brother in China," Miss Wong afterwards related. "My brother wrote back, 'Tsong is indeed very beautiful, but please send me the dollar watch printed on the other side.'"

Miss Wong, whose unusually keen sense of humor was well-known in Hollywood, added, "the moral of the story is—a fur coat doesn't tick."

The picture in the paper enabled James Wang, a cousin who played Chinese character roles in Western films, to persuade Marshall Neilan, the director, to give Miss Wong a part in a picture called "Linty."

Miss Wong rose to stardom in 1924 in "The Thief of Baghdad," which featured Douglas Fairbanks. From that time on she reigned as a movie symbol of "the mysterious East." Recognized as one of the most beautiful women on the screen, she quickly became a leading box office attraction.

Some Earlier Roles

"Forty Winks," "Old San Francisco," "Shanghai Express," and "Toll of the Sea" were among her earliest pictures. Esther Ralston, Dolores Costello, Warner Oland, and William Boyd were among her fellow-players in those days. In the late Nineteen Twenties she went abroad, making pictures in London and Berlin and touring many parts of Europe.

Miss Wong paid her first visit to China in 1936. Two years before that she had sent her parents, Mr. and Mrs. Wong Sam Sing, and their other children, on a trip to China at her expense.

While in Europe during the Nineteen Twenties Miss Wong learned to speak French and German well enough to use those languages in talking pictures. She also wrote and acted in a musical play called "Tschun-Tshi," which was produced in Vienna. But after two years she became so homesick for "L. A." that she could stay abroad no longer and in 1930 she returned.

"On the Spot," "The Flame of Love," "Daughter of the Dragon," "Chu Chin Chow," "Java Head," "Daughter of Shanghai," "King of Chinatown," "Limehouse Blues" and "When Were You Born" were among her picture vehicles of the Nineteen Thirties. She also found time at this period to write a series of articles for The New York Herald-Tribune, describing her experiences on her trip to China.

Miss Wong appeared in several films at the start of World War II, including "Bombs Over Burma" and "Ellery Queen's Penthouse Mystery." But from that period until two years ago when she emerged to try a comeback, she had been comparatively inactive.

Anna May Wong in *Limehouse Blues*, 1934.

Anna May Wong and Marlene Dietrich in *Shanghai Express*.

The New York Times TUESDAY, MAY 7, 1963.

Monty Woolley, Actor, 74, Dies; 'Man Who Came to Dinner' Star

Stage and Screen Player Noted for Sheridan Whiteside Role —Director Taught at Yale

SARATOGA SPRINGS, N.Y., May 6 (AP) — Monty Woolley, who was best known on stage and screen for his portrayal of the crotchety invalid in "The Man Who Came to Dinner," died this morning in an Albany hospital of kidney and heart ailments. The veteran actor and director had been a patient for a month. His age was 74.

A funeral service will be held at 11 A.M. Wednesday in the Bethesda Protestant Episcopal Church here. Burial will be in the local Greenridge Cemetery.

Memorable Role

It was as the arrogant, waspish, murderously comic and strangely lovable Sheridan Whiteside in "The Man Who Came to Dinner" that Monte Woolley achieved a probably enduring theatrical fame.

Making only his third Broadway appearance, he starred for two seasons in the George S. Kaufman-Moss Hart comedy about a world-famous lecturer, resembling the late Alexander Woollcott, immobilized by a leg fracture in a small town in Ohio.

Mr. Woolley went on to play the same role in the highly successful film version in 1941. He confined his activities to Hollywood for several years thereafter, and emerged as a first-rate performer in films as diverse as "Life Begins at 8:30," in which he played the leading role of a drunken old actor, "The Bishop's Wife," "Miss Tatlock's Millions" and "When Irish Eyes Are Smiling."

But is was as Whiteside that he remained in the national consciousness. In 1949, in fact, when he arrived at Cambridge, Mass., to appear in a revival of the play, he was greeted by members of the Harvard Dramatic Club, faculty members and even a few Radcliffe girls wearing false beards.

Most people found it difficult, if not impossible, to think of the performer without his splendid white Van Dyke and flaring mustaches. Mr. Woolley, who throughout his life had a deserved reputation as a wit, often spoke in defense of beards. In an article he wrote in 1942 for The Times he termed the beard "the historic trademark of genius."

"Take the beards off Santa Claus and Bluebeard and what have you?" he went on. "Nothing but a pair of middle-aged, overstuffed bores."

Monty Woolley

Edgar Montillion Woolley became a member of the fashionable world at birth, which took place in the old Bristol Hotel at Fifth Avenue and 42d Street. The hotel was owned by his father, who was also the proprietor of the fabled Grand Union Hotel in Saratoga Springs.

In the elaborate dining rooms and salons of the two establishments the boy met Lillian Russell, Sarah Bernhardt and just about every other theat l and social celebrity of the era. of the era.

Mr. Woolley attended the Mackenzie School in Dobbs Ferry, N. Y., and entered Yale in 1907. One of his classmates was Cole Porter, the composer, with whom he formed a lifelong friendship. This was depicted in the 1946 screen biography of Mr. Porter, "Night and Day," in which Mr. Woolley played himself.

Around the two undergraduates formed a group of admirers of the theater and high life in general that specialized in elaborate parties and frequent trips from New Haven to Manhattan.

Mr. Woolley became president of the Yale Dramatic Association and remained after graduation to get his master's degree. He then went to Harvard for further study under Prof. George Lyman Kittredge, the Shakespearean scholar, before returning to Yale as an instructor in English.

In 1916 he enlisted in the National Guard for service in the Mexican border campaign but got no farther than a remount station at Tobyhanna, Pa. Later he served in France as a lieutenant in intelligence on the General Staff.

After the war he went back to the Yale faculty as an assistant professor of drama. Under his influence student theatricals blossomed. But in 1927, when the Yale experimental theatre was established, Prof. George Pierce Baker of Harvard was brought in to head it, and Mr. Woolley resigned.

For a while he rusticated in his family's Victorian mansion in Saratoga Springs—the home he returned to late in life—and grew his beard, which originally had a pinkish tinge. Then he headed for Broadway. With Mr. Porter's help he soon established himself as a successful director. Among his credits were Mr. Porter's "Fifty Million Frenchmen," the second "Little Show" and "Jubilee."

Meanwhile Mr. Woolley was making a reputation as a wit, partygoer and man about town that kept many persons, perhaps including himself, from taking his theatrical career seriously.

In 1937 he went to Hollywood for the first time, and appeared in several films, including the notable "Nothing Sacred."

In recent years Mr. Woolley curtailed his activities. Among his final films were "As Young as You Feel," in 1951, which The Times's critic described as "a vastly superior entertainment."

His television appearances were infrequent and not notably successful. More than a decade ago he said, "For five minutes on a Fred Allen show I rehearsed for nine or 10 days. I was nervous and watched the clock constantly. I thought it was all terrible."

Monty Woolley in *Holy Matrimony*, 1943.

Ann Sheridan, Richard Travis, Bette Davis, and Monty Woolley in *The Man Who Came to Dinner*.

FILMOGRAPHY

The New York Times Film Review Index was the reference used for compiling these listings.

Abbott, Bud
One Night in the Tropics 1940
Buck Privates 1941
In the Navy 1941
Hold That Ghost 1941
Keep 'Em Flying 1941
Ride 'Em Cowboy 1942
Rio Rita 1942
Pardon my Sarong 1942
Who Done It 1942
It Ain't Hay 1943
Hit the Ice 1943
In Society 1944,Ag
Lost in a Harem 1944
Here Come the Co-Eds 1945
Naughty Nineties, The 1945
Abbott and Costello in Hollywood 1945
Little Giant 1946
Time of Their Lives, The 1946
Buck Privates Come Home 1947
Wistful Widow of Wagon Gap, The 1947
Noose Hangs High, The 1948
Abbott and Costello Meet Frankenstein 1948
Mexican Hayride 1949
Africa Screams 1949,My 5,34:2
Abbott and Costello Meet the Killer Boris Karloff 1949
Abbott and Costello in the Foreign Legion 1950
Abbott and Costello Meet the Invisible Man 1951
Comin' Round the Mountain 1951
Jack and the Beanstalk 1952
Dance With Me Henry 1956

Adorée, Renée
Eternal Struggle, The 1923
Women Who Give 1924
Bandolero, The 1924
Excuse Me 1925
Man and Maid 1925
Parisian Nights 1925
Exchange of Wives 1925
Big Parade, The 1925
Black Bird, The 1926
Boheme, La 1926
Tin Gods 1926
Flaming Forest, The 1926
Show, The 1927
Mr Wu 1927
Back to God's Country 1927
Certain Young Man, A 1928
Cossacks, The 1928
Michigan Kid, The 1928
Forbidden Hours 1928
Mating Call, The 1928
Spieler, The 1929
Pagan, The 1929
Redemption 1930
Call of the Flesh 1930

Anderson, Gilbert
Shootin' Mad 1918

Arbuckle, Roscoe (Fatty)
Moonshine 1918
Good Night, Nurse 1918
Fatty and Mabel Adrift 1918
Waiters' Ball, The 1918
Cook, The 1918
Love 1919
Desert Hero, A 1919
Back Stage 1919
Life of the Party, The 1920
When Comedy Was King 1960
Days of Thrills and Laughter 1961

Arlen, Richard
In the Name of Love 1925
Enchanted Hill, The 1925
Behind the Front 1926
Padlocked 1926
Rolled Stockings 1927
Blood Ship, The 1927
Wings 1927
She's a Shiek 1927
Feel my Pulse 1928
Ladies of the Mob 1928
Beggars of Life 1928
Manhattan Cocktail 1928
Man I Love, The 1929
Four Feathers, The 1929
Thunderbolt 1929
Dangerous Curves 1929
Virginian, The 1929
Burning Up 1930
Dangerous Paradise 1930
Light of Western Stars, The 1930
Border Legion, The 1930
Sea God, The 1930
Sante Fe Trail, The 1930
Only Saps Work 1930
Conquering Horde, The 1931
Gun Smoke 1931
Lawyer's Secret, The 1931
Secret Call, The 1931
Touchdown 1931
Wayward 1932
Sky Bride 1932
Guilty as Hell 1932
Tiger Shark 1932
All American, The 1932
Island of Lost Souls 1933
Song of the Eagle 1933
College Humor 1933
Three-Cornered Moon 1933
Hell and Highwater 1933
Alice in Wonderland 1933
Come on Marines 1934
She Made her Bed 1934
Helldorado 1935
Let 'Em Have It 1935
Calling of Dan Matthews, The 1936
Mine With the Iron Door, The 1936
Secret Valley 1937
Great Barrier, The 1937
Silent Barriers 1937
Artists and Models 1937
Murder in Greenwich Village 1937
No Time to Marry 1938
Call of the Yukon 1938
Straight, Place and Show 1938
Missing Daughters 1939
Mutiny on the Blackhawk 1939
Tropic Fury 1939
Legion of Lost Flyers 1939
Hot Steel 1940
Black Diamonds 1940
Devil's Pipeline, The 1940
Mutiny in the Arctic 1941
Power Dive 1941
Aerial Gunner 1943
Lady and the Monster, The 1944
Storm Over Lisbon 1944
Big Bonanza, The 1945
When my Baby Smiles at Me 1948
Kansas Raiders 1951
Hurricane Smith 1952
Sabre Jet 1953
Mountain, The 1956
Warlock 1959
Last Time I Saw Archie, The 1961
Best Man, The 1964
Law of the Lawless 1964
Black Spurs 1965
Fort Utah 1967

Arliss, George
Devil, The 1921
Disraeli 1921
Ruling Passion, The 1922
Man Who Played God, The 1922
Green Goddess, The 1923
$20 a Week 1924
Green Goddess, The 1930
Millionaire, The 1931
Alexander Hamilton 1931
Man Who Played God, The 1932
Successful Calamity, A 1932
King's Vacation, The 1933
Working Man, The 1933
Voltaire 1933
House of Rothschild, The 1934
Last Gentleman, The 1934
Cardinal Richelieu 1935
Transatlantic Tunnel 1935
Mister Hobo 1936
East Meets West 1936
Man of Affairs 1937
Dr Syn 1937

Arnold, Edward
Okay America 1932
Afraid to Talk 1932
Rasputin and the Empress 1932
Whistling in the Dark 1933
White Sister, The 1933
Barbarian, The 1933
Jennie Gerhardt 1933
Her Bodyguard 1933
Secret of the Blue Room, The 1933
I'm no Angel 1933
Roman Scandals 1933
Madame Spy 1934
Unknown Blonde 1934
Thirty Day Princess 1934
Sadie McKee 1934
Hide-Out 1934
Million Dollar Ransom 1934
President Vanishes, The 1934
Wednesday's Child 1934
Biography of a Bachelor Girl 1935
Cardinal Richelieu 1935
Glass Key, The 1935
Diamond Jim 1935
Remember Last Night? 1935
Crime and Punishment 1935
Sutter's Gold 1936
Meet Nero Wolfe 1936
Come and Get It 1936
John Meade's Woman 1937
Easy Living 1937
Toast of New York, The 1937

Blossoms On Broadway 1937
Crowd Roars, The 1938
You Can't Take It With You 1938
Idiot's Delight 1939
Let Freedom Ring 1939
Man About Town 1939
Mr Smith Goes to Washington 1939
Earl of Chicago, The 1940
Johnny Apollo 1940
Slightly Honorable 1940
Lillian Russell 1940
Meet John Doe 1941
Penalty, The 1941
Lady From Cheyenne, The 1941
All That Money Can Buy 1941
Nothing but the Truth 1941
Unholy Partners 1941
Design for Scandal 1942
Johnny Eager 1942
Eyes in the Night 1942
War Against Mrs Hadley, The 1942
Youngest Profession, The 1943
Standing Room Only 1944
Janie 1944
Kismet 1944
Mrs Parkington 1944
Main Street After Dark 1945
Hidden Eye, The 1945
Week-End at the Waldorf 1945
Ziegfeld Follies 1946
Janie Gets Married 1946
Three Wise Fools 1946
No Leave, No Love 1946
Mighty McGurk, The 1947
Dear Ruth 1947
My Brother Talks to Horses 1947
Hucksters, The 1947
Three Daring Daughters 1948
Big City 1948
Wallflower 1948
Command Decision 1949
John Loves Mary 1949
Take Me Out to the Ball Game 1949
Big Jack 1949
Dear Wife 1950
Yellow Cab Man, The 1950
Annie Get Your Gun 1950
Skipper Surprised his Wife, The 1950
Dear Brat 1951
Belles on Their Toes 1952
City That Never Sleeps 1953
Living It Up 1954
Ambassador's Daughter, The 1956

Auer, Mischa

Something Always Happens 1928
Marquis Preferred 1929
Benson Murder Case, The 1930
Inside the Lines 1930
Just Imagine 1930
Women Love Once 1931
Unholy Garden, The 1931
Yellow Ticket, The 1931
Delicious 1931
Midnight Patrol, The 1932
No Greater Love 1932
Scarlet Dawn 1932
Dangerously Yours 1933
Sucker Money 1933
Infernal Machine 1933
Corruption 1933
After Tonight 1933
Cradle Song 1933
Girl Without a Room 1933
Wharf Angel 1934
Stamboul Quest 1934
Bulldog Drummond Strikes Back 1934
Mystery Woman 1935
Lives of a Bengal Lancer, The 1935
Clive of India 1935
Murder in the Fleet 1935
House of a Thousand Candles, The 1936
One Rainy Afternoon 1936
Princess Comes Across, The 1936
My Man Godfrey 1936
Gay Desperado, The 1936
Winterset 1936
That Girl From Paris 1937
Three Smart Girls 1937
Top of the Town 1937
We Have our Moments 1937
Pick a Star 1937
Marry the Girl 1937
Vogues of 1938 1937
100 Men and a Girl 1937
Merry-Go-Round of 1938 1937
It's all Yours 1938
Rage of Paris 1938
You Can't Take It With You 1938
Service de Luxe 1938
Little Tough Guys in Society 1938
Sweethearts 1938
East Side of Heaven 1939
Unexpected Father 1939
Destry Rides Again 1939
Alias the Deacon 1940
Sandy Is a Lady 1940
Public Deb No 1 1940
Spring Parade 1940
Seven Sinners 1940
Trail of the Vigilantes 1940
Flame of New Orleans, The 1941
Hold That Ghost 1941
Moonlight in Hamaii 1941
Hellzapoppin 1941
Twin Beds 1942
Around the World 1943
Lady in the Dark 1944
Up in Mabel's Room 1944
Royal Scandal, A 1945
Brewster's Millions 1945
And Then There Were None 1945
Sentimental Journey 1946
She Wrote the Book 1946
Sofia 1948
Sky Is Red, The 1952
Monte Carlo Story, The 1958
Mam'zelle Pigalle 1958
Foxiest Girl in Paris 1958
Dog, a Mouse and a Sputnik, A; Pied, a Cheval et un Sputnik, A 1960
Mr Arkadin 1962
Christmas That Almost Wasn't 1966

Bainter, Fay

This Side of Heaven 1934
Quality Street 1937
Soldier and the Lady, The 1937
Make Way for Tomorrow 1937
Jezebel 1938
White Banners 1938
Mother Carey's Chickens 1938
Arkansas Traveler, The 1938
Shining Hour, The 1939
Yes, My Darling Daughter 1939
Daughters Courageous 1939
Our Neighbors-The Carters 1940
Young Tom Edison 1940
Our Town 1940
Bill of Divorcement, A 1940
Maryland 1940
Babes on Broadway 1942
Woman of the Year 1942
War Against Mrs Hadley, The 1942
Journey for Margaret 1942
Human Comedy, The 1943
Presenting Lily Mars 1943
Salute to the Marines 1943
Cry Havoc 1943
Heavenly Body, The 1944
Dark Waters 1944
3 Is a Family 1944
State Fair 1945
Virginian, The 1946
Kid From Brooklyn, The 1946
Secret Life of Walter Mitty, The 1947
Deep Valley 1947
Give my Regards to Broadway 1948
June Bride 1948
President's Lady, The 1953
Childrens Hour, The 1962

Bara, Theda

Carmen 1915
Serpent, The 1916
Gold and the Woman 1916
Eternal Sapho, The 1916
East Lynne 1916
Her Double Life 1916
Romeo and Juliet 1916
Cleopatra 1917
Salome 1918
Kathleen Mavourneen 1919

Bankhead, Tallulah

Tarnished Lady 1931
My Sin 1931
Cheat, The 1931
Thunder Below 1932
Devil and the Deep 1932
Faithless 1932
Stage Door Canteen 1943
Lifeboat 1944
Royal Scandal, A 1945
Main Street to Broadway 1953
Die! Die! My Darling 1965

Barker, Lex

Farmer's Daughter, The 1947
Crossfire 1947
Return of the Badmen 1948
Tarzan's Magic Fountain 1949
Tarzan and the Slave Girl 1950
Thunder Over the Plains 1953
Away all Boats 1956
Girl in the Kremlin, The 1957
Dolce Vita, La 1961
Code 7...Victim 5 1965
Place Called Glory, A 1966
Woman Times Seven 1967
Shatterhand 1968

Barrymore, Ethel

White Raven, The 1917
Call of her People, The 1917
Our Mrs McChesney 1918
Rasputin and the Empress 1932
None but the Lonely Heart 1944
Spiral Staircase, The 1946
Farmer's Daughter, The 1947
Moss Rose 1947
Paradine Case, The 1948
Night Song 1948
Moonrise 1949
Portrait of Jennie 1949
Great Sinner, The 1949
That Midnight Kiss 1949
Pinky 1949
Red Danube, The 1949
Secret of Convict Lake, The 1951
Kind Lady 1951
It's a big Country 1952
Deadline U S A 1952
Just for You 1952
Story of Three Loves, The 1953
Main Street to Broadway 1953
Young at Heart 1955

Barrymore, John

Lost Bridegroom, The 1916
Red Widow, The 1916
Raffles 1918
On the Quiet 1918
Here Comes the Bride 1919
Test of Honor, The 1919
Dr Jekyll and Mr Hyde 1920
Lotus Eater, The 1921
Sherlock Holmes 1922
Beau Brummell 1924
Sea Hunt, The 1926
Sea Beast, The 1926
Don Juan 1926
When a Man Loves 1927
Beloved Rogue, The 1927
Tempest 1928
Eternal Love 1929
Show of Shows 1929
General Crack 1929
Man From Blankley's, The 1930
Handsome Gigolo, Poor Gigolo 1930
Moby Dick 1930
Svengali 1931
Mad Genius, The 1931
Arsene Lupin 1932
Grand Hotel 1932
State's Attorney 1932
Bill of Divorcement, A 1932
Rasputin and the Empress 1932
Topaze 1933
Reunion in Vienna 1933
Dinner at Eight 1933
Night Flight 1933
Counsellor-At-Law 1933
Long Lost Father 1934
20th Century 1934
Romeo and Juliet 1936

Maytime 1937
Bulldog Drummond Comes Back 1937
Night Club Scandal 1937
True Confession 1937
Bulldog Drummond's Revenge 1937
Bulldog Drummond's Peril 1938
Romance in the Dark 1938
Marie Antoinette 1938
Spawn of the North 1938
Hold That Co-ed 1938
Great Man Votes, The 1939
Midnight 1939
Great Profile, The 1940
Invisible Woman, The 1941
World Premiere 1941
Playmates 1941

Barrymore, Lionel
Copperhead, The 1920
Master Mind, The 1920
Enemies of Women 1923
Unseeing Eyes 1923
Eternal City, The 1924
America 1924
I Am the Man 1925
Barrier, The 1926
Splendid Road, The 1926
Temptress, The 1926
Show, The 1927
Body and Soul 1927
Thirteenth Hour, The 1927
Drums of Love 1928
Sadie Thompson 1928
Decameron Nights 1928
Lion and the Mouse, The 1928
Alias Jimmy Valentine 1928
West of Zanzibar 1928
Mysterious Island, The 1929
Free Soul, A 1931
Guilty Hands 1931
Yellow Ticket, The 1931
Mata Hari 1932
Man I Killed, The 1932
Arsene Lupin 1932
Grand Hotel 1932
Washington Masquerade, The 1932
Rasputin and the Empress 1932
Sweepings 1933
Looking Forward 1933
Stranger's Return, The 1933
Dinner at Eight 1933
One Man's Journey 1933
Night Flight 1933
Christopher Bean 1933
Should Ladies Behave? 1933
This Side of Heaven 1934
Carolina 1934
Girl From Missouri, The 1934
Treasure Island 1934
David Copperfield 1935
Little Colonel, The 1935
Mark of the Vampire 1935
Public Hero No 1 1935
Return of Peter Grimm, The 1935
Ah, Wilderness! 1935
Voice of Bugle Ann, The 1936
Road to Glory, The 1936
Devil Doll, The 1936
Gorgeous Hussy, The 1936
Camille 1937
Family Affair, A 1937
Captains Courageous 1937
Saratoga 1937
Navy Blue and Gold 1937
Yank at Oxford, A 1938
Test Pilot 1938
You Can't Take It With You 1938
Young Doctor Kildare 1938
Let Freedom Ring 1939
Calling Dr Kildare 1939
On Borrowed Time 1939
Secret of Dr Kildare, The 1939
Dr Kildare's Strange Case 1940
Dr Kildare Goes Home 1940
Dr Kildare's Crisis 1940
Bad Man, The 1941
Penalty, The 1941
People vs Dr Kildare, The 1941
Dr Kildare's Wedding Day 1941
Lady Be Good 1941
Dr Kildare's Victory 1942
Calling Dr Gillespie 1942
Tennessee Johnson 1943
Guy Named Joe, A 1943
Three Men in White 1944
Since You Went Away 1944
Between Two Women 1945
Valley of Decision, The 1945
Three Wise Fools 1946
It's a Wonderful Life 1946
Secret Heart, The 1946
Duel in the Sun 1947
Dark Delusion 1947
Key Largo 1948
Down to the Sea in Ships 1949
Malaya 1950
Right Cross 1950
Lone Star 1952
Main Street to Broadway 1953

Barthelmess, Richard
Hope Chest, The 1919
Boots 1919
Girl Who Stayed Home, The 1919
Three Men and a Girl 1919
Peppy Polly 1919
Broken Blossoms 1919
I'll Get Him yet 1919
Scarlet Days 1919
Idol Dancer, The 1920
Love Flower, The 1920
Experience 1921
Tol'able David 1922
Seventh Day, The 1922
Sonny 1922
Bond Boy, The 1922
Bright Shawl, The 1923
Fighting Blade, The 1923
Twenty-One 1924
Enchanted Cottage, The 1924
Classmates 1924
New Toys 1925
Soul Fire 1925
Shore Leave 1925
Beautiful City, The 1925
Just Suppose 1926
Ranson's Folly 1926
Amateur Gentleman, The 1926
White Black Sheep, The 1926
Patent Leather Kid, The 1927
Drop Kick, The 1927
Noose, The 1928
Kentucky Courage 1928
Wheels of Chance 1928
Out of the Ruins 1928
Scarlet Seas 1928
Weary River 1929
Drag 1929
Young Nowheres 1929
Show of Shows 1929
Son of the Gods 1930
Dawn Patrol, The 1930
Lash, The 1931
Way Down East 1931
Finger Points, The 1931
Last Flight, The 1931
Alias the Doctor 1932
Cabin in the Cotton 1932
Central Airport 1933
Heroes for Sale 1933
Massacre 1934
Modern Hero, A 1934
Midnight Alibi 1934
Four Hours to Kill 1935
Only Angels Have Wings 1939
Spy of Napoleon 1939
Man Who Talked too Much, The 1940
Spoilers, The 1942
Mayor of Forty-Fourth Street, The 1942

Baxter, Warner
Those Who Dance 1924
Female, The 1924
Garden of Weeds, The 1924
Christine of the Hungry Heart 1924
Golden Bed, The 1925
Air Mail, The 1925
Welcome Home 1925
Awful Truth, The 1925
Son of his Father, A 1925
Best People 1925
Mannequinn 1926
Miss Brewster's Millions 1926
Runaway, The 1926,Ap 27
Aloma of the South Seas 1926
Great Gatsby, The 1926
Telephone Girl, The 1927
Singed 1927
Three Sinners 1928
Ramona 1928
Danger Street 1928
Craig's Wife 1928
West of Zanzibar 1928
In old Arizona 1929
Thru Different Eyes 1929
Behind That Curtain 1929
Romance of Rio Grande 1929
Happy Days 1930,F 14,20:1
Such Men Are Dangerous 1930
Arizona Kid, The 1930
Renegades 1930
Doctors' Wives 1931
Daddy Long Legs 1931
Squaw Man, The 1931
Cisco Kid, The 1931
Surrender 1931
Amateur Daddy 1932
Man About Town 1932
Six Hours to Live 1932
Dangerously Yours 1933
42d Street 1933
I Loved You Wednesday 1933
Paddy the Next Best Thing 1933
Penthouse 1933
As Husbands Go 1934
Stand up and Cheer 1934
Such Women Are Dangerous 1934
Grand Canary 1934
Broadway Bill 1934
Hell in the Heavens 1934
One More Spring 1935
Under the Pampas Moon 1935
King of Burlesque 1936
Prisoner of Shark Island, The 1936
Robin Hood of El Dorado, The 1936
Road to Glory, The 1936
To Mary-With Love 1936
White Hunter 1936
Slave Ship 1937
Vogues of 1938 1937
Wife, Doctor and Nurse 1937
Kidnapped 1938
I'll Give a Million 1938
Wife, Husband and Friend 1939
Return of the Cisco Kid, The 1939
Barricade 1939
Earthbound 1940
Adam Had Four Sons 1941
Crime Doctor 1943
Lady in the Dark 1944
Shadows in the Night 1944
Crime Doctor's Courage, The 1945
Prison Warden 1949

Beery, Noah
Red Lantern, The 1919
Woman Next Door, The 1919
Louisiana 1919
In Mizzoura 1919
Fighting Shepherdess, The 1920
Go and Get It 1920
Dinty 1920
Mark of Zorro, The 1920
Bob Hampton of Placer 1921
Bits of Life 1921
Wild Honey 1922
Crossroads of New York, The 1922
Ebb Tide 1922
Soul of the Beast, The 1923
Main Street 1923
Wandering Daughters 1923
Spoilers, The 1923
Stephen Steps Out 1923
Call of the Canyon, The 1923
Heritage of the Desert, The 1924
Fighting Coward, The 1924
Wanderer of the Wasteland, The 1924
Lily of the Dust 1924
Female, The 1924
Welcome Stranger 1924
North of 36 1924
East of Suez 1925
Contraband 1925
Light of the Western Stars, The 1925
Wild Horse Mesa 1925
Coming of Amos, The 1925
Vanishing American, The 1925
Lord Jim 1925
Enchanted Hill, The 1925
Crown of Lies 1926

Padlocked 1926
Beau Geste 1926
Paradise 1926
Rough Riders, The 1927
Evening Clothes 1927
Love Mart, The 1927
Dove, The 1928
Beau Sabreur 1928
Two Lovers 1928
Hell-Ship Bronson 1928
Noah's Ark 1929
Godless Girl, The 1929
Careers 1929
Four Feathers, The 1929
Isle of Lost Ships, The 1929
Isle of Escape 1930
Under a Texas Moon 1930
Murder Will Out 1930
Song of the Flame 1930
Golden Dawn 1930
Way of all Men, The 1930
Renegades 1930
Tol'able David 1930
Bright Lights 1931
Millionaire, The 1931
Soldiers Plaything, A 1931
Honeymoon Lane 1931
Riders of the Purple Sage 1931
Homicide Squad 1931
Stranger in Town 1932
Stoker, The 1932
Kid From Spain, The 1932
She Done Him Wrong 1933
Woman I Stole, The 1933
Madame Spy 1934
David Harum 1934
Cockeyed Cavaliers 1934
Caravan 1934
Kentucky Kernels 1935
Sweet Adeline 1935
King of the Damned 1936
Crimson Circle, The 1936
Strangers on a Honeymoon 1937
Bad Man of Brimstone, The 1938
Mutiny on the Blackhawk 1939
Torpedoed 1939
Tennessee Johnson 1943
Salute to the Marines 1943
Barbary Coast Gent 1944
This Man's Navy 1945

Beery, Wallace

Unpardonable Sin, The 1919
Love Burglar, The 1919
Life Line, The 1919
Victory 1919
Behind the Door 1920
Virgin of Stamboul, The 1920
Mollycoddle, The 1920
Rookie's Return, The 1920
Last of the Mohicans, The 1921
Tale of Two Worlds, A 1921
Golden Snare, The 1921
Wild Honey 1922
Robin Hood 1922
Ashes of Vengeance 1923
Drifting 1923
Spanish Dancer, The 1923
Eternal Struggle, The 1923
Richard the Lion-Hearted 1923
Sea Hawk, The 1924
Signal Tower, The 1924
Red Lily, The 1924
So Big 1925
Devil's Cargo, The 1925
Lost World, The 1925
Great Divide, The 1925
Coming Through 1925
Adventure 1925
Night Club, The 1925
Wanderer, The 1925
In the Name of Love 1925
Pony Express, The 1925
Behind the Front 1926
Volcano 1926
Four Horsemen of the Apocalypse, The 1926
We're in the Navy Now 1926
Old Ironsides 1926
Casey at the Bat 1927
Fireman, Save My Child 1927
We're in the Air Now 1927
Wife Savers 1928
Partners in Crime 1928
Big Killing, The 1928
Beggars of Life 1928
Chinatown Nights 1929
River of Romance, The 1929
Big House, The 1930
Billy the Kid 1930
Lady's Morals, A 1930
Min and Bill 1930
Way for a Sailor 1930
Stolen Jools 1931
Secret Six, The 1931
Champ, The 1931
Hell Divers 1931
Grand Hotel 1932
Flesh 1932
Tugboat Annie 1933
Dinner at Eight 1933
Bowery, The 1933
Viva Villa! 1934
Treasure Island 1934
Mighty Barnum, The 1934
West Point of the Air 1935
China Seas 1935
O'Shaughnessy's Boy 1935
Ah, Wilderness! 1935
Message to Garcia, A 1936
Old Hutch 1936
Good Old Soak 1937
Slave Ship 1937
Bad Man of Brimstone, The 1938
Port of Seven Seas 1938
Stablemates 1938
Sergeant Madden 1939
Thunder Afloat 1939
Man From Dakota, The 1940
Twenty-Mule Team 1940
Wyoming 1940
Bad Man, The 1941
Barnacle Bill 1941
Bugle Sounds, The 1942
Jackass Mail 1942
Salute to the Marines 1943
Rationing 1944
Barbary Coast Gent 1944
This Man's Navy 1945
Bad Bascomb 1946

Begley, Ed

Boomerang 1947
Sitting Pretty 1948
Street with no Name, The 1948
Deep Waters 1948
Sorry, Wrong Number 1948
Tulsa 1949
It Happens Every Spring 1949
Great Gatsby, The 1949
Backfire 1950
Dark City 1950
Wyoming Mail 1950
Stars in my Crown 1950
U S S Teakettle 1951
Lone Star 1952
On Dangerous Ground 1952
Boots Malone 1952
Deadline U S A 1952
Turning Point, The 1952
Patterns 1956
12 Angry Men 1957
Odds Against Tomorrow 1959
Green Helmet, The 1961
Sweet Bird of Youth 1962
Unsinkable Molly Brown, The 1964
Oscar, The 1966
Warning Shot 1967
Billion Dollar Brain 1967
Firecreek 1968
Wild in the Streets 1968
Hang 'Em High 1968

Bendix, William

Woman of the Year 1942
Wake Island 1942
Glass Key, The 1942
Who Done It 1942
Star Spangled Rhythm 1942
Crystal Ball, The 1943
Taxi, Mister 1943
China 1943
Hostages 1943
Guadalcanal Diary 1943
Lifeboat 1944
Hairy Ape, The 1944
Greenwich Village 1944
Abroad With two Yanks 1944
It's in the Bag 1945
Bell for Adano, A 1945
Don Juan Quilligan 1945
Sentimental Journey 1946
Dark Corner, The 1946
Blue Dahlia, The 1946
Two Years Before the Mast 1946
White Tie and Tails 1946
I'll Be Yours 1947
Blaze of Noon 1947
Calcutta 1947
Web, The 1947
Where There's Life 1947
Time of your Life, The 1948
Babe Ruth Story, The 1948
Race Street 1948
Connecticut Yankee in King Arthur's Court, A 1949
Life of Riley, The 1949
Streets of Laredo 1949
Big Steal, The 1949
Johnny Holiday 1950
Kill the Umpire 1950
Gambling House 1951
Detective Story 1951
Submarine Command 1952
Girl in Every Port, A 1952
Macao 1952
Blackbeard the Pirate 1952
Dangerous Mission 1954
Crashout 1955
Deep Six, The 1958
Portrait of a Sinner 1961
Boys' Night Out 1962
For Love or Money 1963
Law of the Lawless 1964
Johnny Nobody 1965

Bennett, Constance

Cytherea 1924
Into the Net 1924
Goose Hangs High, The 1925
Code of the West 1925
My Wife and I 1925
Goose Woman, The 1925
Sally, Irene and Mary 1925
This Thing Called Love 1929
Son of the Gods 1930
Common Clay 1930
Three Faces East 1930
Sin Takes a Holliday 1930
Easiest Way, The 1931
Born to Love 1931
Common Law, The 1931
Bought 1931
Lady With a Past 1932
What Price Hollywood 1932
Two Against the World 1932
Rockabye 1932
Our Betters 1933
Bed of Roses 1933
After Tonight 1933
Moulin Rouge 1934
Affairs of Cellini, The 1934
Outcast Lady 1934
After Office Hours 1935
Ladies in Love 1936
Topper 1937
Merrily We Live 1938
Service de Luxe 1938
Topper Takes a Trip 1938
Tail Spin 1939
Submarine Zone; (Escape To Glory) 1941
Law of the Tropics 1941
Two Faced Woman 1942
Wild Bill Hickok Rides 1942
Sin Town 1942
Paris Underground 1945
Centennial Summer 1946
Unsuspected, The 1947
Angel on the Amazon 1948
As Young as You Feel 1951
It Should Happen to You 1954
Madame X 1966

Benny, Jack

Chasing Rainbows 1930
Transatlantic Merry-Go-Round 1934
Broadway Melody of 1936 1935
It's in the Air 1935
Big Broadcast of 1937, The 1936

College Holiday 1936
Artists and Models 1937
Artists and Models Abroad 1938
Man About Town 1939
Buck Benny Rides Again 1940
Love Thy Neighbor 1940
Charley's Aunt 1941
To Be or not to Be 1942
George Washington Slept Here 1942
Meanest Man in the World, The 1943
Hollywood Canteen 1944
Horn Blows at Midnight, The 1945
It's in the Bag 1945
Guide for the Married Man, A 1967

Berkeley, Busby (Director)
She Had to Say Yes 1933
Dames 1934
Gold Diggers of 1935 1935
Bright Lights 1935
I Live for Love 1935
Stage Struck 1936
Go Getter, The 1937
Hollywood Hotel 1938
Men Are Such Fools 1938
Garden of the Moon 1938
Comet over Broadway 1938
They Made Me a Criminal 1939
Fast And Furious 1939
Forty Little Mothers 1940
Strike up the Band 1940
Babes on Broadway 1942
For Me and My Gal 1942
Gang's All Here, The 1943
Cinderella Jones 1946
Take Me Out to the Ball Game 1949

Bickford, Charles
South Sea Rose 1929
Dynamite 1929
Hell's Heroes 1929
Anna Christie 1930
Passion Flower 1930
River's End 1931
Squaw Man, The 1931
Pagan Lady 1931
East of Borneo 1931
Men in her Life 1931
Panama Flo 1932
Scandal for Sale 1932
Thunder Below 1932
Last Man, The 1932
Vanity Street 1932
No Other Woman 1933
Song of the Eagle 1933
This Day and Age 1933
White Woman 1933
Little Miss Marker 1934
Wicked Woman, A 1935
Under Pressure 1935
Notorious Gentleman, A 1935
Farmer Takes a Wife, The 1935
Rose of the Rancho 1936
Pride of the Marines 1936
Red Wagon 1936
Plainsman, The 1937
High, Wide and Handsome 1937
Night Club Scandal 1937
Daughter of Shanghai 1937
Thunder Trail 1938
Gangs of New York 1938
Valley of the Giants 1938
Storm, The 1938
Stand up and Fight 1939
Romance of the Redwoods 1939
Street of Missing Men 1939
Our Leading Citizen 1939
One Hour to Live 1939
Mutiny in the Big House 1939
Thou Shalt Not Kill 1940
Of Mice and Men 1940
South to Karanga 1940
Girl From God's Country 1940
Burma Convoy 1941
Tarzan's New York Adventure 1942
Mr Lucky 1943
Song of Bernadette, The 1944
Wing and a Prayer 1944
Captain Eddie 1945
Fallen Angel 1946
Farmer's Daughter, The 1947
Duel in the Sun 1947
Woman on the Beach, The 1947
Brute Force 1947
Babe Ruth Story, The 1948
Four Faces West 1948
Johnny Belinda 1948
Command Decision 1949
Roseanna McCoy 1949
Whirlpool 1950
Guilty of Treason 1950
Riding High 1950
Branded 1951
Jim Thorpe - All American 1951
Elopement 1951
Star is Born, A 1954
Prince of Players 1955
Not as a Stranger 1955
Court-Martial of Billy Mitchell, The 1955
Mister Cory 1957
Unforgiven, The 1960
Days of Wine and Roses 1963
Big Hand for the Little Lady, A 1966

Blue, Ben
Follow Your Heart 1936
College Holiday 1936
Top of the Town 1937
Turn off the Moon 1937
High, Wide and Handsome 1937
Artists and Models 1937
Thrill of a Lifetime 1937
Big Broadcast of 1938
College Swing 1938
Cocoanut Grove 1938
Paris Honeymoon 1939
Panama Hattie 1942
For Me and My Gal 1942
Thousands Cheer 1943
Broadway Rhythm 1944
Two Girls and a Sailor 1944
Two Sisters From Boston 1946
Easy to Wed 1946
My Wild Irish Rose 1947
One Sunday Afternoon 1948
It's a Mad, Mad, Mad, Mad World 1963
Russians are Coming the Russians are Coming, The 1966
Guide for the Married Man, A 1967
Busy Body, The 1967
Where Were You When the Lights Went Out? 1968

Bogart, Humphrey
Up the River 1930
Devil With Women, A 1930
Body and Soul 1931
Bad Sister 1931
Women of all Nations 1931
Holy Terror, A 1931
Big City Blues 1932
Three on a Match 1932
Midnight 1934
Petrified Forest, The 1936
Bullets or Ballots 1936
China Clipper 1936
Black Legion 1937
Great O'Malley, The 1937
Marked Woman 1937
Kid Galahad 1937
San Quentin 1937
Dead End 1937
Stand-In 1937
Swing Your Lady 1938
Crime School 1938
Men Are Such Fools 1938
Amazing Dr Clitterhouse, The 1938
Racket Busters 1938
Angels With Dirty Faces 1938
King of the Underworld 1939
Oklahoma Kid, The 1939
You Can't Get Away With Murder 1939
Dark Victory 1939
Roaring Twenties, The 1939
Return Of Doctor X, The 1939
Invisible Stripes 1940
It all Came True 1940
Brother Orchid 1940
They Drive by Night 1940
High Sierra 1941
Wagons Roll at Night, The 1941
Maltese Falcon, The 1941
All Through the Night 1942
Big Shot, The 1942
Across the Pacific 1942
Casablanca 1942
Action in the North Atlantic 1943
Thank Your Lucky Stars 1943
Sahara 1943
Passage to Marseille 1944
To Have and Have Not 1944
Conflict 1945
Big Sleep, The 1946
Dead Reckoning 1947
Two Mrs Carrolls, The 1947
Dark Passage 1947
Treasure of Sierra Madre 1948
Key Largo 1948
Knock on any Door 1949
Tokyo Joe 1949
Chain Lightning 1950
In a Lonely Place 1950
Enforcer, The 1951
Sirocco 1951
African Queen, The 1952
Deadline U S A 1952
Battle Circus 1953
Beat the Devil 1954
Caine Mutiny, The 1954
Sabrina 1954
Barefoot Contessa, The 1954
We're no Angels 1955
Left Hand of God, The 1955
Desperate Hours, The 1955
Harder They Fall, The 1956

Bow, Clara
Down to the Sea in Ships 1923
Black Oxen 1924
Maytime 1924
Poisoned Paradise 1924
This Woman 1924
Capital Punishment 1925
Eve's Lover 1925
Kiss Me Again 1925
Keeper of the Bees, The 1925
Best Bad Man, The 1925
Dancing Mothers 1926
Runaway, The 1926
Mantrap 1926
Plastic Age, The 1926
Kid Boots 1926
It 1927
Children of Divorce 1927
Rough House Rosie 1927
Wings 1927
Hula 1927
Get Your Man 1927
Red Hair 1928
Ladies of the Mob 1928
Fleet's In, The 1928
Three Week Ends 1928
Wild Party, The 1929
Dangerous Curves 1929
Saturday Night Kid, The 1929
Paramount on Parade 1930
True to the Navy 1930
Love Among the Millionaires 1930
Her Wedding Night 1930
No Limit 1931
Kick In 1931
Call Her Savage 1932
Hoopla 1933

Brennan, Walter
Law and Order 1932
Half a Sinner 1934
Wedding Night, The 1935
Lady Tubbs 1935
Man on the Flying Trapeze 1935
Barbary Coast 1935
Seven Keys to Baldpate 1935
Three Godfathers, The 1936
These Three 1936
Moon's our Home, The 1936
Fury 1936
Come and Get It 1936
Banjo on My Knee 1936
When Love Is Young 1937
Wild and Woolly 1937
Buccaneer, The 1938
Adventures of Tom Sawyer, The 1938
Texans, The 1938
Mother Carey's Chickens 1938
Cowboy and the Lady, The 1938
Kentucky 1938

Story of Vernon and Irene Castle, The 1939
They Shall Have Music 1939
Stanley and Livingstone 1939
Joe and Ethel Turp Call on the President 1940
Northwest Passage 1940
Maryland 1940
Westerner, The 1940
Meet John Doe 1941
Nice Girl 1941
Sergeant York 1941
This Woman Is Mine 1941
Swamp Water 1941
Rise and Shine 1941
Pride of the Yankees, The 1942
Stand by for Action 1943
Slightly Dangerous 1943
Hangmen Also Die 1943
North Star, The 1943
Home in Indiana 1944
To Have and Have Not 1944
Princess and the Pirate, The 1945
Dakota 1945
Stolen Life, A 1946
Nobody Lives Forever 1946
My Darling Clementine 1946
Scudda-Hoo! Scudda-Hay! 1948
Red River 1948
Blood on the Moon 1948
Green Promise, The 1949
Task Force 1949
Brimstone 1949
Ticket to Tomahawk, A 1950
Singing Guns 1950
Curtain Call at Cactus Creek 1950
Surrender 1950
Along the Great Divide 1951
Best of the Badmen 1951
Return of the Texan 1952
Lure of the Wilderness 1952
Four Guns to the Border 1954
Bad Day at Black Rock 1955
Far Country, The 1955
At Gunpoint 1956
Proud Ones, The 1956
Way to the Gold, The 1957
Tammy and the Bachelor 1957
God Is my Partner 1958
Rio Bravo 1959
Those Calloways 1965
Oscar, The 1966
Gnome-Mobile, The 1967
Who's Minding the Mint? 1967
One and Only Genuine Original Family Band, The 1968

Brice, Fanny
My Man 1928
Night Club 1929
Be Yourself 1930
Great Ziegfeld, The 1936
Everybody Sing 1938
Ziegfeld Follies 1946

Brown, John Mack
Fair Co-ed, The 1927
Divine Woman, The 1928
Soft Living 1928
Play Girl, The 1928
Our Dancing Daughters 1928
Lady of Chance, A 1929
Woman of Affairs, A 1929
Coquette 1929
Valiant, The 1929
Single Standard, The 1929
Jazz Heaven 1929
Undertow 1930
Montana Moon 1930
Billy the Kid 1930
Great Meadow, The 1931
Secret Six, The 1931
Last Flight, The 1931
70,000 Witnesses 1932
Saturday's Millions 1933
Female 1933
Son of a Sailor 1933
Belle of the Nineties 1934
Wells Fargo 1937
Chip of the Flying U 1940
West of Carson City 1940
Ride 'Em Cowboy 1942
Stampede 1949
Short Grass 1951

Burke, Billie
Gloria's Romance 1916
Peggy 1916
Let's Get a Divorce 1918
In Pursuit of Polly 1918
Make-Believe Wife, The 1918
Good Gracious, Annabelle 1919
Misleading Widow, The 1919
Bill of Divorcement, A 1932
Christopher Strong 1933
Dinner at Eight 1933
Only Yesterday 1933
Finishing School 1934
Where Sinners Meet 1934
We're Rich Again 1934
Forsaking all Others 1934
Society Doctor 1935
After Office Hours 1935
Becky Sharp 1935
Doubting Thomas 1935
Feather in her Hat, A 1935
She Couldn't Take It 1935
Splendor 1935
My American Wife 1936
Piccadilly Jim 1936
Craig's Wife 1936
Parnell 1937
Topper 1937
Bride Wore Red, The 1937
Navy Blue and Gold 1937
Everybody Sing 1938
Merrily We Live 1938
Young in Heart, The 1938
Topper Takes a Trip 1938
Zenobia 1939
Bridal Suite 1939
Wizard of Oz, The 1939
Eternally Yours 1939
Remember? 1939
And One Was Beautiful 1940
Irene 1940
Dulcy 1940
Hullabaloo 1940
Topper Returns 1941
One Night in Lisbon 1941
Man Who Came to Dinner, The 1942
What's Cookin' 1942
In This our Life 1942
They all Kissed the Bride 1942
Girl Trouble 1942
Hi Diddle Diddle 1943
Cheaters, The 1945
Breakfast in Hollywood 1946
Bachelor's Daughters, The 1946
Barkleys of Broadway, The 1949
And Baby Makes Three 1949
Father of the Bride 1950
Three Husbands 1951
Father's Little Dividend 1951
Small Town Girl 1953
Young Philadelphians, The 1959
Sergeant Rutledge 1960
Pepe 1960

Bushman, Francis X
Romeo and Juliet 1916
Masked Bride, The 1925
Ben Hur 1925
Marriage Clause, The 1926
Lady in Ermine, The 1927
Thirteenth Juror, The 1927
Grip of the Yukon, The 1928
Once a Gentleman 1930
Ben Hur 1931
Hollywood Boulevard 1936
David and Bathsheba 1951
Sabrina 1954
Story of Mankind, The 1957

Cantor, Eddie
Kid Boots 1926
Special Delivery 1927
Whoopee 1930
Palmy Days 1931
Kid From Spain, The 1932
Roman Scandals 1933
Kid Millions 1934
Strike Me Pink 1936
Ali Baba Goes to Town 1937
Forty Little Mothers 1940
Thank Your Lucky Stars 1943
Show Business 1944
Hollywood Canteen 1944
If You Knew Susie 1948

Carson, Jack
Music for Madame 1937
Stand-In 1937
Crashing Hollywood 1938
She's Got Everything 1938
Law of the Underworld 1938
Saint in New York, The 1938
Vivacious Lady 1938
Go Chase Yourself 1938
Having Wonderful Time 1938
Carefree 1938
Mr Doodle Kicks Off 1938
Legion of Lost Flyers 1939
Escape, The 1939
Destry Rides Again 1939
Honeymoon's Over, The 1939
I Take This Woman 1940
Young as You Feel 1940
Shooting High 1940
Enemy Agent 1940
Alias the Deacon 1940
Typhoon 1940
Girl in 313 1940
Queen of the Mob 1940
Lucky Partners 1940
Love Thy Neighbor 1940
Mr and Mrs Smith 1941
Strawberry Blonde 1941
Love Crazy 1941
Bride Came C O D, The 1941
Navy Blues 1941
Blues in the Night 1941
Male Animal, The 1942
Larceny, Inc 1942
Wings for the Eagle 1942
Gentleman Jim 1942
Hard Way, The 1943
Thank Your Lucky Stars 1943
Princess O'Rourke 1943
Shine on Harvest Moon 1944
Make Your own Bed 1944
Doughgirls, The 1944
Arsenic and old Lace 1944
Hollywood Canteen 1944
Roughly Speaking 1945
Mildred Pierce 1945
One More Tomorrow 1946
Two Guys From Milwaukee 1946
Time, The Place And The Girl, The 1946
Love and Learn 1947
April Showers 1948
Romance on the High Seas 1948
Two Guys From Texas 1948
John Loves Mary 1949
My Dream Is Yours 1949
It's a Great Feeling 1949
Bright Leaf 1950
Good Humor Man, The 1950
Groom Wore Spurs, The 1951
Mr Universe 1951
Dangerous When Wet 1953
Red Garters 1954
Star is Born, A 1954
Phffft 1954
Ain't Misbehavin' 1955
Bottom of the Bottle, The 1956
Tattered Dress, The 1957
Tarnished Angels, The 1958
Cat on a Hot Tin Roof 1958
Rally Round the Flag Boys! 1958
Bramble Bush, The 1960
King of the Roaring Twenties 1961

Chandler, Jeff
Johnny O'Clock 1947
Invisible Wall, The 1947
Roses Are Red 1947
Sword in the Desert 1949
Abandoned Woman 1949
Broken Arrow 1950
Two Flags West 1950
Deported 1950
Bird of Paradise 1951
Smuggler's Island 1951
Iron Man 1951
Flame of Araby 1951
Battle at Apache Pass, The 1952
Red Ball Express 1952
Because of You 1952
Great Sioux Uprising, The 1953
Yankee Pasha 1954
Sign of the Pagan 1955
Foxfire 1955
Female on the Beach 1955

Spoilers, The 1955
Toy Tiger 1956
Away all Boats 1956
Pillars of the Sky 1956
Tattered Dress, The 1957
Jeanne Eagels 1957
Man With a Shadow 1958
Lady Takes a Flyer, The 1958
Raw Wind in Eden 1958
Stranger in my Arms 1959
Thunder in the Sun 1959
Second to Hell 1959
Return to Peyton Place 1961
Mad Dog Coll 1961
Merrill's Marauders 1962

Chaney, Lon
Miracle Man, The 1919
Paid in Advance 1919
Victory 1919
Treasure Island 1920
Nomads of the North 1920
Penalty, The 1920
Bits of Life 1921
Oliver Twist 1922
Blind Bargain, A 1922
Quincy Adams Sawyer 1922
Hunchback of Notre Dame, The 1923
He Who Gets Slapped 1924
Monster, The 1925
Unholy Three, The 1925
Phantom of the Opera, The 1925
Tower of Lies, The 1925
Black Bird, The 1926
Outside the Law 1926
Road to Mandalay, The 1926
Tell It to the Marines 1926
Mr Wu 1927
Unknown, The 1927
Mockery 1927
London After Midnight 1927
Big City, The 1928
Laugh, Clown, Laugh 1928
While the City Sleeps 1928
West of Zanzibar 1928
Where East Is East 1929
Thunder 1929
Phantom of the Opera 1930
Unholy Three, The 1930

Chaney, Lon Jr
Accent on Youth 1935
Angel's Holiday 1937
Wild and Woolly 1937
Mr Moto's Gamble 1938
Passport Husband 1938
Jesse James 1939
Union Pacific 1939
Frontier Marshal 1939
Charlie Chan in City in Darkness 1939
Of Mice and Men 1940
One Million BC 1940
North West Mounted Police 1940
Man Made Monster 1941
Billy the Kid 1941
Badlands of Dakota 1941
Wolf Man, The 1941
North to the Klondike 1942
Ghost of Frankenstein, The 1942
Eyes of the Underworld 1942
Mummy's Tomb, The 1942
Frankenstein Meets the Wolf Man 1943
Son of Dracula 1943
Crazy House 1943
Calling Dr Death 1944
Weird Woman 1944
Cobra Woman 1944
Ghost Catchers 1944
Mummy's Ghost, The 1944
Dead Man's Eyes 1944
House of Frankenstein 1944
Here Come the Co-Eds 1945
Mummy's Curse, The 1945
Frozen Ghost, The 1945
Strange Confession 1945
Daltons Ride Again, The 1945
House of Dracula 1945
Pillow of Death 1946
My Favorite Brunette 1947
Albuquerque 1948
Abbott and Costello Meet Frankenstein 1948
16 Fathoms Deep 1948
There's a Girl in my Heart 1950

Captain China 1950
Once a Thief 1951
Inside Straight 1951
Only the Valiant 1951
Behave Yourself 1951
Flame of Araby 1951
Thief of Damascus 1952
High Noon 1952
Springfield Rifle 1952
Black Castle, The 1952
Lion Is in the Streets, A 1953
Jivaro 1954
Casanova's Big Night 1954
Passion 1954
Big House U S A 1955
Not as a Stranger 1955
I Died a Thousand Times 1955
Indian Fighter, The 1955
Pardners 1956
Rebellion in Cuba 1961
Haunted Palace, The 1964
Law of the Lawless 1964
Black Spurs 1965
Johnny Reno 1966
Welcome to Hard Times 1967

Chevalier, Maurice
Innocents of Paris 1929
Love Parade, The 1929
Paramount on Parade 1930
Big Pond, The 1930
Playboy of Paris 1930
Petit Cafe, Le 1931
Smiling Lieutenant, The 1931
One Hour with You 1932
Love Me Tonight 1932
Bedtime Story, A 1933
Way to Love, The 1933
Merry Widow, The 1934
Folies Bergere 1935
Homme des Folies Bergere, L' 1936
Beloved Vagabond, The 1937
With a Smile 1939
Man of the Hour, The 1940
Break the News 1941
Personal Column 1941
Man About Town 1947
Royal Affair, A; (Roi, Le) 1950
Ma Pomme 1951
My Seven Little Sins 1956
Love in the Afternoon 1957
Gigi 1958
Count Your Blessings 1959
Can-Can 1960
Breath of Scandal, A 1960
Pepe 1960
Fanny 1961
Jessica 1962
In Search of the Castaways 1962
I'd Rather Be Rich 1964
Monkeys Go Home 1967

Clift, Montgomery
Search, The 1948
Red River 1948
Heiress, The 1949
Big Lift, The 1950
Place in the Sun, A 1951
I Confess 1953
From Here to Eternity 1953
Indiscretion of an American Wife 1954
Raintree County 1957
Young Lions, The 1958
Lonelyhearts 1959
Suddenly, Last Summer 1959
Wild River 1960
Misfits, The 1961
Judgment at Nuremberg 1961
Freud 1962
Defector, The 1966

Cobb, Lee J
Golden Boy 1939
This Thing Called Love 1941
Men of Boys Town 1941
Paris Calling 1942
Moon Is Down, The 1943
Tonight We Raid Calais 1943
Song of Bernadette, The 1944
Winged Victory 1944
Anna and the King of Siam 1946
Boomerang 1947
Johnny O'Clock 1947
Captain from Castile 1947
Call Northside 777 1948
Miracle of the Bells, The 1948
Luck of the Irish, The 1948
Dark Past, The 1948
Thieves' Highway 1949
Man Who Cheated Himself, The 1951
Sirocco 1951
Fighter, The 1952
Tall Texan, The 1953
Yankee Pasha 1954
Gorilla at Large 1954
On the Waterfront 1954
Racers, The 1955
Left Hand of God, The 1955
Man in the Gray Flannel Suit, The 1956
12 Angry Men 1957
Garment Jungle, The 1957
Three Faces of Eve, The 1957
Brothers Karamazov, The 1958
Man of the West 1958
Party Girl 1958
Trap, The 1959
Green Mansions 1959
But Not for Me 1959
Exodus 1960
4 Horsemen of the Apocalypse, The 1962
How the West Was Won 1963
Come Blow Your Horn 1963
Our Man Flint 1966
In Like Flint 1967
Coogan's Bluff 1968
Lawman, The 1971
Man Who Loved Cat Dancing, The 1973
Exorcist, The 1973

Coburn, Charles
Boss Tweed 1933
Of Human Hearts 1938
Yellow Jack 1938
Vivacious Lady 1938
Lord Jeff 1938
Idiot's Delight 1939
Made for Each Other 1939
Story of Alexander Graham Bell, The 1939
Bachelor Mother 1939
In Name Only 1939
Stanley and Livingstone 1939
Road to Singapore 1940
Florian 1940
Edison the Man 1940
Three Faces West 1940
Lady Eve, The 1941
Devil and Miss Jones, The 1941
Our Wife 1941
Unexpected Uncle 1941
H M Pulham, Esq 1941
Kings Row 1942
In This our Life 1942
George Washington Slept Here 1942
More the Merrier, The 1943
Constant Nymph, The 1943
Heaven Can Wait 1943
My Kingdom for a Cook 1943
Princess O'Rourke 1943
Knickerbocker Holiday 1944
Wilson 1944
Impatient Years, The 1944
Together Again 1944
Royal Scandal, A 1945
Rhapsody in Blue 1945
Over 21 1945
Shady Lady 1945
Green Years, The 1946
Colonel Effingham's Raid 1946
Lured 1947
Paradine Case, The 1948
B F's Daughter 1948
Green Grass of Wyoming 1948
Impact 1949
Everybody Does It 1949
Doctor and the Girl, The 1949
Yes Sir, That's my Baby 1949
Peggy 1950
Louisa 1950
Mr Music 1950
Has Anybody Seen My Gal 1952
Monkey Business 1952
Trouble Along the Way 1953

Gentlemen Prefer Blondes 1953
Long Wait, The 1954
How to be Very, Very Popular 1955
Power and The Prize, the 1956
Around the World in 80 Days 1956
How to Murder a Rich Uncle 1957
Story of Mankind, The 1957
Remarkable Mr Pennypacker, The 1959
Stranger in my Arms 1959
John Paul Jones 1959
Pepe 1960

Colman, Ronald
White Sister, The 1923
$20 a Week 1924
Tarnish 1924
Romola 1924
Her Night of Romance 1925
Thief in Paradise, A 1925
His Supreme Moment 1925
Sporting Venus, The 1925
Dark Angel, The 1925
Stella Dallas 1925
Lady Windemere's Fan 1925
Kiki 1926
Beau Geste 1926
Winning of Barbara Worth, The 1926
Night of Love, The 1927
Magic Flame, The 1927
Two Lovers 1928
White Sister, The 1928
Rescue, The 1929
Bulldog Drummond 1929
Condemned 1929
Raffles 1930
Handsome Gigolo, Poor Gigolo 1930
Devil to Pay, The 1930
Unholy Garden, The 1931
Arrowsmith 1931
Cynara 1932
Masquerader, The 1933
Bulldog Drummond Strikes Back 1934
Clive of India 1935
Man Who Broke the Bank at Monte Carlo, The 1935
Tale of Two Cities, A 1935
Under Two Flags 1936
Lost Horizon 1937
Prisoner of Zenda, The 1937
If I Were King 1938
Light That Failed, The 1939
Lucky Partners 1940
My Life With Caroline 1941
Talk of the Town, The 1942
Random Harvest 1942
Kismet 1944
Late George Apley, The 1947
Double Life, A 1948
Champagne for Caesar 1950
Around the World in 80 Days 1956
Story of Mankind, The 1957

Cooper, Gary
Winning of Barbara Worth, The 1926
Children of Divorce 1927
Wings 1927
Beau Sabreur 1928
Legion of the Condemned, The 1928
Doomsday 1928
Lilac Time 1928
First Kiss, The 1928
Shopworn Angel, The 1929
Wolf Song 1929
Betrayal 1929
Virginian, The 1929
Seven Days' Leave 1930
Only the Brave 1930
Texan, The 1930
Man From Wyoming, A 1930
Spoilers, The 1930
Morocco 1930
Fighting Caravans 1931
City Streets 1931
I Take This Woman 1931
His Woman 1931
Devil and the Deep 1932
If I Had a Million 1932
Farewell to Arms, A 1932
Today We Live 1933
One Sunday Afternoon 1933
Design for Living 1933
Alice in Wonderland 1933
Operator 13 1934
Now and Forever 1934
Lives of a Bengal Lancer, The 1935
Wedding Night, The 1935
Peter Ibbetson 1935
Desire 1936
Mr Deeds Goes to Town 1936
General Died at Dawn, The 1936
Plainsman, The 1937
Souls at Sea 1937
Bluebeard's Eighth Wife 1938
Cowboy and the Lady, The 1938
Beau Geste 1939
Real Glory, The 1939
Westerner, The 1940
North West Mounted Police 1940
Meet John Doe 1941
Sergeant York 1941
Ball of Fire 1942
Pride of the Yankees, The 1942
For Whom the Bell Tolls 1943
Story of Dr Wassell, The 1944
Casanova Brown 1944
Along Came Jones 1945
Saratoga Trunk 1945
Cloak and Dagger 1946
Unconquered 1947
Good Sam 1948
Fountainhead, The 1949
Task Force 1949
Bright Leaf 1950
Dallas 1951
U S S Teakettle 1951
Starlift 1951
Distant Drums 1951
It's a big Country 1952
High Noon 1952
Springfield Rifle 1952
Return to Paradise 1953
Blowing Wild 1953
Garden of Evil 1954
Vera Cruz 1954
Court-Martial of Billy Mitchell, The 1955
Friendly Persuasion 1956
Love in the Afternoon 1957
Ten North Frederick 1958
Man of the West 1958
Hanging Tree, The 1959
They Came to Cordura 1959
Wreck of the Mary Deare, The 1959
Naked Edge 1961
Adventures of Marco Polo, The 1965

Costello, Lou
One Night in the Tropics 1940
Buck Privates 1941
In the Navy 1941
Hold That Ghost 1941
Keep 'Em Flying 1941
Ride 'Em Cowboy 1942
Rio Rita 1942
Pardon my Sarong 1942
Who Done It 1942
It Ain't Hay 1943
Hit the Ice 1943
In Society 1944
Lost in a Harem 1944
Here Come the Co-Eds 1945
Naughty Nineties, The 1945
Abbott and Costello in Hollywood 1945
Little Giant 1946
Time of Their Lives, The 1946
Buck Privates Come Home 1947
Wistful Widow of Wagon Gap, The 1947
Noose Hangs High, The 1948
Abbott and Costello Meet Frankenstein 1948
Mexican Hayride 1949
Africa Screams 1949
Abbott and Costello Meet the Killer Boris Karloff 1949
Abbott and Costello in the Foreign Legion 1950
Abbott and Costello Meet the Invisible Man 1951
Comin' Round the Mountain 1951
Jack and the Beanstalk 1952
Dance With Me Henry 1956

Crawford, Joan
Old Clothes 1925
Sally, Irene and Mary 1925
Tramp, Tramp, Tramp 1926
Paris 1926
Taxi Dancer, The 1927
Understanding Heart, The 1927
Unknown, The 1927
Twelve Miles Out 1927
Spring Fever 1927
West Point 1928
Rose-Marie 1928
Across to Singapore 1928
Four Walls 1928
Our Dancing Daughters 1928
Dream of Love 1928
Duke Steps Out, The 1929
Hollywood Revue, The 1929
Our Modern Maidens 1929
Untamed 1929
Montana Moon 1930
Our Blushing Brides 1930
Paid 1931
Dance, Fools, Dance 1931
Laughing Sinners 1931
This Modern Age 1931
Possessed 1931
Pente, La; Dance Fools Dance 1932
Grand Hotel 1932
Letty Lynton 1932
Rain 1932
Today We Live 1933
Grand Hotel 1933
Dancing Lady 1933
Sadie McKee 1934
Chained 1934
Forsaking all Others 1934
No More Ladies 1935
I Live my Life 1935
Gorgeous Hussy, The 1936
Love on the Run 1936
Last of Mrs Cheyney, The 1937
Bride Wore Red, The 1937
Mannequin 1938
Shining Hour, The 1939
Ice Follies of 1939 1939
Women, The 1939
Strange Cargo 1940
Susan and God 1940
Woman's Face, A 1941
When Ladies Meet 1941
They all Kissed the Bride 1942
Reunion in France 1943
Above Suspicion 1943
Hollywood Canteen 1944
Mildred Pierce 1945
Humoresque 1946
Possessed 1947
Daisy Kenyon 1947
Flamingo Road 1949
Damned Don't Cry, The 1950
Harriet Craig 1950
Goodbye, my Fancy 1951
ThIs Woman is Dangerous 1952
Sudden Fear 1952
Torch Song 1953
Johnny Guitar 1954
Female on the Beach 1955
Queen Bee 1955
Autumn Leaves 1956
Story of Esther Costello, The 1957
Best of Everything 1959
What Ever Happened to Baby Jane? 1962
Caretakers, The 1963
Strait Jacket 1964
I Saw What You Did 1965
Berserk! 1968

Dandridge, Dorothy
Lady From Louisiana 1941
Sun Valley Serenade 1941

Bahama Passage 1942
Drums of the Congo 1942
Hit Parade of 1943 1943
Bright Road 1953
Carmen Jones 1954
Island in the Sun 1957
Decks Ran Red, The 1958
Porgy and Bess 1959
Tamango 1959
Malaga 1962

Darnell, Linda
Hotel for Women 1939
Daytime Wife 1939
Star Dust 1940
Brigham Young - Frontiersman 1940
Mark of Zorro, The 1940
Chad Hanna 1940
Blood and Sand 1941 Poe, The 1942
Rise and Shine 1941
Loves of Edgar Allan
Buffalo Bill 1944
It Happened Tomorrow 1944
Sweet and Low Down 1944
Summer Storm 1944
Hangover Square 1945
Great John L, The 1945
Fallen Angel 1946
Anna and the King of Siam 1946
Centennial Summer 1946
My Darling Clementine 1946
Forever Amber 1947
Walls of Jericho, The 1948
Unfaithfully Yours 1948
Letter to Three Wives, A 1949
Slattery's Hurricane 1949
Everybody Does It 1949
No Way Out 1950
Two Flags West 1950
Thirteenth Letter, The 1951
Guy Who Came Back, The 1951
Night Without Sleep 1952
Blackbeard the Pirate 1952
Second Chance 1953
ThIs is my Love 1954
Dakota Incident 1956
Angels of Darkness 1956
Zero Hour 1957
Black Spurs 1965

Davies, Marion
Cecilia of the Pink Roses 1918
Restless Sex, The 1920
Buried Treasure 1921
Beauty's Worth 1922
When Knighthood Was in Flower 1922
Little Old New York 1923
Yolanda 1924
Janice Meredith 1924
Zander the Great 1925
Lights of Old Broadway 1925
Beverly of Graustark 1926
Red Mill, The 1927
Tillie the Toiler 1927
Fair Co-ed, The 1927
Quality Street 1927
Patsy, The 1928
Cardboard Lover, The 1928
Show People 1928
Hollywood Revue, The 1929
Marianne 1929
Not so Dumb 1930
Florodora Girl, The 1930
Bachelor Father, The 1931
It's a Wise Child 1931
Five and Ten 1931
Polly of the Circus 1932
Blondie of the Follies 1932
Peg o'my Heart 1933
Going Hollywood 1933
Operator 13 1934
Page Miss Glory 1935
Hearts Divided 1936
Cain and Mabel 1936
Ever Since Eve 1937
Show People 1967

Dean, James
East of Eden 1955
Rebel without a Cause 1955
Giant 1956

DeMille, Cecil B (Director)
Ten Commandments, The 1956

De Sica, Vittorio
Passa L'Amore 1933
Tempo Massimo 1936
Canzione del Sole, La 1936
Amo Te Sola 1936
Mazurka di Papa, La 1940
Due Madri, Le; Two Mothers, The 1940
Manon Lescaut 1941
Lost in the Dark 1949
Peddlin' in Society 1950
Escape into Dreams 1950
Heart and Soul 1950
My Widow and I 1950
Doctor, Beware 1951
Miracle in Milan 1951
Tomorrow is too Late 1952
Times Gone By (The Trial of Frine) 1953
Earrings of Madame De. The 1954
Hello Elephant 1954
Bread, Love and Dreams 1954
Gran Varieta 1955
Bed, The ; Divorce, The 1955
Frisky 1955
Too Bad She's Bad 1955
Gold of Naples (The Gambler) 1957
Miller's Beautiful Wife, The 1957
Scandal in Sorrento 1957
It Happened in the Park 1957
Farewell to Arms, A 1958
Monte Carlo Story, The 1958
Bigamist, The 1958
Tailor's Maid, The; (Patri e Figli) 1959
Holiday Island; (Vacanzie a Izchia) 1959
Anatomy of Love 1959
Always Victorious 1960
It Started in Naples 1960
Angel Wore Red, The 1960
Fast and Sexy 1960
General Della Rovere 1960
Millionairess, The 1961
Wonders of Aladdin, The 1961
Lafayette 1963
Amorous Adventures of Moll Flanders, The 1965
Biggest Bundle of Them All, The 1968
Shoes of the Fisherman, The 1968

De Sica, Vittorio (Director)
Shoe-Shine 1947
Bicycle Thief, The 1949
Doctor, Beware 1951
Indiscretion of an American Wife 1954
Umberto D 1955
Gold of Naples (The Gambler) 1957
Gold of Naples (Theresa) 1957
Gold of Naples (The Racketeer) 1957
Gold of Naples (Pizza on Credit) 1957
Roof, The 1959,My 13,43:4
Two Women; (Ciociara, La) 1961
Boccaccio '70 (The Raffle) 1962
Condemned of Altona, The 1963
Yesterday, Today, and Tomorrow (Part III-Mara Rome) 1964
Yesterday, Today and Tomorrow (Part 1-Adelina Naples) 1964
Yesterday, Today and Tomorrow (Part II-Anna Milan) 1964
Marriage Italian Style 1964
Young World, A 1966
After the Fox 1966
Woman Times Seven 1967

Devine, Andy
We Americans 1928
Red Lips 1928
Naughty Baby 1929
Hot Stuff 1929
Spirit of Notre Dame, The 1931
Three Wise Girls 1932
Law and Order 1932
Impatient Maiden, The 1932
Man Wanted 1932
Man From Yesterday, The 1932
Radio Patrol 1932
Tom Brown of Culver 1932
All American, The 1932
Cohens and Kellys in Trouble, The 1933
Song of the Eagle 1933
Big Cage, The 1933
Midnight Mary 1933
Doctor Bull 1933
Saturday's Millions 1933
Chance at Heaven 1933
Stingaree 1934
Upper World 1934
Let's Talk It Over 1934
Million Dollar Ransom 1934
Gift of Gab 1934
Wake up and Dream 1934
President Vanishes, The 1934
Hell in the Heavens 1934
Hold 'Em Yale 1935
Chinatown Squad 1935
Farmer Takes a Wife, The 1935
Way Down East 1935
Fighting Youth 1935
Coronado 1935
Small Town Girl 1936
Romeo and Juliet 1936
Big Game, The 1936
Flying Hostess 1936
Mysterious Crossing 1937
Star Is Born, A 1937
Road Back, The 1937
Double or Nothing 1937
You're a Sweetheart 1937
In Old Chicago 1938
Doctor Rhythm 1938
Yellow Jack 1938
Personal Secretary 1938
Men With Wings 1938
Storm, The 1938
Swing That Cheer 1938
Stagecoach 1939
Spirit of Culver 1939
Never Say Die 1939
Mutiny on the Blackhawk 1939
Tropic Fury 1939
Legion of Lost Flyers 1939
Little Old New York 1940
Geronimo 1940
Buck Benny Rides Again 1940
Torrid Zone 1940
Hot Steel 1940
When the Daltons Rode 1940
Black Diamonds 1940
Devil's Pipeline, The 1940
Trail of the Vigilantes 1940
Flame of New Orleans, The 1941
Mutiny in the Arctic 1941
Badlands of Dakota 1941
South of Tahiti 1941
Kid From Kansas, The 1941
North to the Klondike 1942
Between Us Girls 1942
Sin Town 1942
Frontier Badmen 1943
Corvette K-225 1943
Crazy House 1943
Ali Baba and the Forty Thieves 1944
Ghost Catchers 1944
Bowery to Broadway 1944
Frisco Sal 1945
Sudan 1945
That's the Spirit 1945
Frontier Gal 1945
Canyon Passage 1946
Michigan Kid 1947
Vigilantes Return, The 1947
Slave Girl 1947
Fabulous Texan, The 1947
Old Los Angeles 1948
Last Bandit, The 1949
Traveling Saleswoman 1950
Never a Dull Moment 1950
New Mexico 1951
Montana Belle 1952

Island in the Sky 1953
Pete Kelly's Blues 1955
Around the World in 80 Days 1956
Adventures of Huckleberry Fin, The 1960
Two Rode Together 1961
Man Who Shot Liberty Valance, The 1962
It's a Mad, Mad, Mad, Mad World 1963
Ballad of Josie, The 1968
Robin Hood 1973

Disney, Walt (Producer)
Snow White and the Seven Dwarfs 1938
Fantasia 1940
Reluctant Dragon, The 1941
Three Caballeros, The 1945
Fun and Fancy Free 1947
Melody Time 1948
Alice in Wonderland 1951
Men Against the Arctic 1956
White Wilderness 1958
Sleeping Beauty 1959
Kidnapped 1960
Absent-Minded Professor, The 1961
Parent Trap, The 1961
Greyfriars' Bobby 1961
Moon Pilot 1962
Big Red 1962
Almost Angels 1962
Legend of Lobo, The 1962
In Search of the Castaways 1962
Son of Flubber 1963
Savage Sam 1963
Tiger Walks, A 1964
Mary Poppins 1964
Moonspinners, The 1964
Winnie the Pooh and the Honey Tree 1966
Follow Me, Boys! 1966
Happiest Millionaire, The 1967

Donat, Robert
Private Life of Henry VIII, The 1933
For Love or Money 1934
Count of Monte Cristo, The 1934
Men of Tomorrow 1935
Thirty-Nine Steps, The 1935
Ghost Goes West, The 1935
Knight Without Armor 1937
Citadel, The 1938
Goodbye Mr Chips 1939
Young Mr Pitt, The 1943
Adventures of Tartu, The 1943
Vacation From Marriage 1946
Captain Boycott 1947
Winslow Boy, The 1950
Magic Box, The 1952
Lease of Life 1956
Inn of the Sixth Happiness, The 1958

Donlevy, Brian
Mother's Boy 1929
Barbary Coast 1935
Mary Burns, Fugitive 1935
Strike Me Pink 1936
13 Hours by Air 1936
Human Cargo 1936
Half Angel 1936
High Tension 1936
36 Hours to Live 1936
Crack-Up 1937
This Is my Affair 1937
Born Reckless 1937
In Old Chicago 1938
Battle of Broadway 1938
We're Going to Be Rich 1938
Sharpshooters 1938
Jesse James 1939
Union Pacific 1939
Beau Geste 1939
Behind Prison Gates 1939
Allegheny Uprising 1939
Destry Rides Again 1939
Great McGinty, The 1940
When the Daltons Rode 1940
Brigham Young - Frontiersman 1940
I Wanted Wings 1941
Billy the Kid 1941
Hold Back the Dawn 1941
South of Tahiti 1941
Birth of the Blues 1941
Remarkable Andrew, The 1942
Two Yanks in Trinidad 1942
Gentleman After Dark, A 1942
Great Man's Lady, The 1942
Wake Island 1942
Glass Key, The 1942
Nightmare 1942
Stand by for Action 1943
Hangmen Also Die 1943
Miracle of Morgan's Creek, The 1944
American Romance, An 1944
Duffy's Tavern 1945
Virginian, The 1946
Canyon Passage 1946
Our Hearts Were Growing Up 1946
Two Years Before the Mast 1946
Beginning or the End, The 1947
Song of Scheherazade 1947
Trouble With Women, The 1947
Kiss of Death 1947
Heaven Only Knows 1947
Killer McCoy 1948
Southern Yankee, A 1948
Command Decision 1949
Lucky Stiff, The 1949
Impact 1949
Shakedown 1950
Kansas Raiders 1951
Fighting Coast Guard 1951
Hoodlum Empire 1952
Big Combo, The 1955
Cry in the Night, A 1956
Cowboy 1958
Never so Few 1960
Pigeon That Took Rome, The 1962
How to Stuff a Wild Bikini 1967

Douglas, Paul
Letter to Three Wives, A 1949
It Happens Every Spring 1949
Everybody Does It 1949
Big Lift, The 1950
Love That Brute 1950
Panic in the Streets 1950
Fourteen Hours 1951
Guy Who Came Back, The 1951
Angels in the Outfield 1951
When in Rome 1952
Clash by Night 1952
We're not Married 1952
Never Wave at a Wac 1953
Forever Female 1954
Executive Suite 1954
High and Dry 1954
Green Fire 1954
Joe Macbeth 1956
Leather Saint, The 1956
Solid Gold Cadillac, The 1956
This Could Be the Night 1957
Beau James 1957
Mating Game, The 1959

Dressler, Marie
Agonies of Agnes, The 1918
Callahans and the Murphys, The 1927
Joy Girl, The 1927
Breakfast at Sunrise 1927
Bringing Up Father 1928
Patsy, The 1928
Divine Lady, The 1929
Hollywood Revue, The 1929
Vagabond Lover, The 1929
Chasing Rainbows 1930
Anna Christie 1930
Girl Said No, The 1930
One Romantic Night 1930
Caught Short 1930
Let Us Be Gay 1930
Min and Bill 1930
Reducing 1931
Politics 1931
Emma 1932
Prosperity 1932
Tugboat Annie 1933
Dinner at Eight 1933
Christopher Bean 1933

Dunn, James
Bad Girl 1931
Sob Sister 1931
Over the Hill 1931
Dance Team 1932
Society Girl 1932
Handle with Care 1932
Sailor's Luck 1933
Hello Sister! 1933
Girl in 419 1933
Hold Me Tight 1933
Arizona to Broadway 1933
Take a Chance 1933
Jimmy and Sally 1933
Hold That Girl 1934
Stand up and Cheer 1934
Change of Heart 1934
Baby, Take a Bow 1934
Have a Heart 1934
365 Nights in Hollywood 1934
Bright Eyes 1934
George White's 1935 Scandals 1935
Daring Young Man, The 1935
Bad Boy 1935
Pay-Off, The 1935
Don't Get Personal 1936
Two-Fisted Gentleman 1936
Come Closer, Folks 1936
Mysterious Crossing 1937
We Have our Moments 1937
Shadows Over Shanghai 1938
Government Girl 1944
Tree Grows in Brooklyn, A 1945
Caribbean Mystery, The 1945
That Brennan Girl 1946
Killer McCoy 1948
Bramble Bush, The 1960
Hemingway's Adventures of a Young Man 1962
Oscar, The 1966

Duryea, Dan
Little Foxes, The 1941
Ball of Fire 1942
Pride of the Yankees, The 1942
Sahara 1943
Man From Frisco 1944
Mrs Parkington 1944
None but the Lonely Heart 1944
Main Street After Dark 1945
Great Flamario, The 1945
Woman in the Window, The 1945
Ministry of Fear 1945
Valley of Decision, The 1945
Along Came Jones 1945
Lady on a Train 1945
Scarlet Street 1946
Black Angel 1946
White Tie and Tails 1946
Black Bart 1948
Another Part of the Forest 1948
River Lady 1948
Larceny 1948
Criss Cross 1949
Manhandled 1949
Too Late for Tears 1949
Johnny Stool Pigeon 1949
One Way Street 1950
Winchester 73 1950
Underworld Story, The 1950
Al Jennings of Oklahoma 1951
Thunder Bay 1953
Rails Into Laramie 1954
World for Ransom 1954
Silver Lode 1954
ThIs is my Love 1954
Foxfire 1955
Storm Fear 1955
Battle Hymn 1957
Night Passage 1957
Slaughter on Tenth Avenue 1957
Kathy O' 1958
Platinum High School 1960
6 Black Horses 1962
He Rides Tall 1964
Taggart 1964
Flight of the Phoenix, The 1966
Hills Run Red, The 1967

Eagels, Jeanne
Man, Woman and Sin 1927
Letter, The 1929
Jealousy 1929

Eddy, Nelson
Student Tour 1934
Naughty Marietta 1935

Rose Marie 1936
Maytime 1937
Rosalie 1937
Girl of the Golden West, The 1938
Sweethearts 1938
Let Freedom Ring 1939
Balalaika 1939
New Moon 1940
Bitter Sweet 1940
Chocolate Soldier, The 1941
I Married an Angel 1942
Phantom of the Opera, The 1943
Knickerbocker Holiday 1944
Northwest Outpost 1947

Evans, Edith
Queen of Spades, The 1949
Dolwyn 1949
Importance of Being Earnest, The 1952
Nun's Story, The 1959
Look Back in Anger 1959
Tom Jones 1963
Chalk Garden, The 1964
Young Cassidy 1965
Whisperers, The 1967
Fitzwilly 1967
Prudence and the Pill 1968
Doll's House, A 1973

Fairbanks, Douglas
Habit of Happiness, The 1916
Good Bad Man, The 1916
Reggie Mixes In 1916
Flirting With Fate 1916
Half Breed, The 1916
Manhattan Madness 1916
American Aristocracy 1916
Matrimaniac, The 1916
Americano, The 1916
In Again, Out Again 1917
Man From Painted Post, The 1917
Reaching for the Moon 1917
Mr Fix-It 1918
Say, Young Fellow 1918
Bound in Morocco 1918
He Comes Up Smiling 1918
Arizona 1918
Knickerbocker Buckaroo, The 1919
When Clouds Roll by 1919
Mollycoddle, The 1920
Mark of Zorro, The 1920
Three Musketeers, The 1921
Robin Hood 1922
Thief of Bagdad, The 1924
Don Q, Son of Zorro 1925
Black Pirate, The 1926
Gaucho, The 1927
Iron Mask, The 1929
Taming of the Shrew, The 1929
Reaching for the Moon 1930
Mr Robinson Crusoe 1932
Private Life of Don Juan, The 1934
Days of Thrills and Laughter 1961

Fields, W C
Janice Meredith 1924
That Royle Girl 1926
It's the old Army Game 1926
So's Your Old Man 1926
Potters, The 1927
Running Wild 1927
Two Flaming Youths 1928
Fools for Luck 1928
Her Majesty, Love 1931
Million Dollar Legs 1932
If I Had a Million 1932
International House 1933
Tillie and Gus 1933
Alice in Wonderland 1933
Six of a Kind 1934
You're Telling Me 1934
Old-Fashioned Way, The 1934
Mrs Wiggs of the Cabbage Patch 1934
It's a Gift 1935
David Copperfield 1935
Mississippi 1935
Man on the Flying Trapeze 1935
Poppy 1936
Big Broadcast of 1938
You Can't Cheat an Honest Man 1939
My Little Chickadee 1940
Bank Dick, The 1940
Never Give a Sucker an Even Break 1941
Follow the Boys 1944
Song of the Open Road 1944
Sensations of 1945 1944
W C Fields Comedy Festival 1966

Finch, Peter
Miniver Story, The 1950
Massacre Hill 1950
Rats of Tobruk, The 1951
Train of Events 1952
Story of Robin Hood, The 1952
Gilbert and Sullivan 1953
Elephant Walk 1954
Detective, The 1954
Heart of the Matter, The 1954
Warriors, The 1955
Make Me an Offer 1956
Simon and Laura 1956
Pursuit of the Graf Spee 1957
Town Like Alice, A 1958
Windom's Way 1958
Nun's Story, The 1959
Kidnapped 1960
Trials of Oscar Wilde, The 1960
Operation Amsterdam 1960
Sins of Rachel Cade, The 1961
No Love for Johnnie 1961
I Thank a Fool 1962
In the Cool of the Day 1963
Girl With Green Eyes 1964
Pumpkin Eater, The 1964
Judith 1966
Flight of the Phoenix, The 1966
10:30 PM Summer 1966
Far From the Madding Crowd 1967
Legend of Lylah Clare, The 1968
Red Tent, The 1971
Sunday Bloody Sunday 1971
Lost Horizon 1973
Nelson Affair, The 1973
England Made Me, 1973
Abdication, The 1974
Network, 1976

Fitzgerald, Barry
Juno and the Paycock 1930
Plough and the Stars, The 1937
Ebb Tide 1937
Bringing Up Baby 1938
Four Men and a Prayer 1938
Dawn Patrol 1938
Pacific Liner 1939
Saint Strikes Back, The 1939
Full Confession 1939
Long Voyage Home, The 1940
San Francisco Docks 1940
Sea Wolf, The 1941
How Green Was my Valley 1941
Tarzan's Secret Treasure 1941
Amazing Mrs Holliday, The 1943
Two Tickets to London 1943
Corvette K-225 1943
Going my Way 1944
I Love a Soldier 1944
None but the Lonely Heart 1944
Incendiary Blonde 1945
Duffy's Tavern 1945
And Then There Were None 1945
Stork Club, The 1945
Two Years Before the Mast 1946
California 1947
Easy Come, Easy Go 1947
Welcome Stranger 1947
Naked City, The 1948
Sainted Sisters, The 1948
Miss Tatlock's Millions 1948
Top o' the Morning 1949
Story of Seabiscuit, The 1949
Union Station 1950
Quiet Man, The 1952
Tonight's the Night 1954
Catered Affair, The 1956
Rooney 1958
Broth of a Boy 1959

Flynn, Errol
Case of the Curious Bride, The 1935
Don't Bet on Blondes 1935
Captain Blood 1935
Charge of the Light Brigade, The 1936
Green Light 1937
Prince and the Pauper, The 1937
Another Dawn 1937
Perfect Specimen, The 1937
Adventures of Robin Hood, The 1938
Four's a Crowd 1938
Sisters, The 1938
Dawn Patrol 1938
Dodge City 1939
Private Lives of Elizabeth and Essex, The 1939
Sea Hawk, The 1940
Santa Fe Trail 1940
Footsteps in the Dark 1941
Dive Bomber 1941
They Died With Their Boots On 1941
Desperate Journey 1942
Gentleman Jim 1942
Edge of Darkness 1943
Thank Your Lucky Stars 1943
Northern Pursuit 1943
Uncertain Glory 1944
Objective Burma 1945
San Antonio 1945
Never Say Goodbye 1946
Cry Wolf 1947
Escape me Never 1947
Silver River 1948
Adventures of Don Juan 1948
That Forsyte Woman 1949
Montana 1950
Rocky Mountain 1950
Kim 1950
Adventures of Captain Fabian 1951
Mara Maru 1952
Against all Flags 1952
Master of Ballantrae, The 1953
Warriors, The 1955
Istanbul 1957
Big Boodle, The 1957
Sun Also Rises, The 1957
Too Much, Too Soon 1958
Roots of Heaven, The 1958
Cuban Rebel Girls 1959

Francis, Kay
Gentlemen of the Press 1929
Cocoanuts, The 1929
Dangerous Curves 1929
Illusion 1929
Marriage Playground, The 1929
Behind the Makeup 1930
Street of Chance 1930
Notorious Affair, A 1930
For the Defense 1930
Raffles 1930
Let's Go Native 1930
Virtuous Sin 1930
Passion Flower 1930
Scandal Sheet 1931
Ladies' Man 1931
Vice Squad, The 1931
Transgression 1931
Guilty Hands 1931
Twenty-Four Hours 1931
Girls About Town 1931
Strangers in Love 1932,
Man Wanted 1932
Street of Women 1932
Jewel Robbery 1932
One Way Passage 1932
Trouble in Paradise 1932
Cynara 1932
Keyhold, The 1933
Storm at Daybreak 1933
Mary Stevens, M D 1933
I Loved a Woman 1933
House on 56th Street, The 1933
Mandalay 1934
Wonder Bar 1934
Dr Monica 1934
British Agent 1934
Living on Velvet 1935
Stranded 1935
Goose and the Gander, The 1935
I Found Stella Parish 1935
White Angel, The 1936
Give Me your Heart 1936
Stolen Holiday 1937
Another Dawn 1937
Confession 1937
First Lady 1937
Women Are Like That 1938
My Bill 1938
Secrets of an Actress 1938

Comet over Broadway 1938
King of the Underworld 1939
Women in the Wind 1939
In Name Only 1939
It's a Date 1940
When the Daltons Rode 1940
Little Men 1940
Play Girl 1941
Charley's Aunt 1941
Feminine Touch, The 1941
Always in my Heart 1942
Between Us Girls 1942
Four Jills in a Jeep 1944
Allotment Wives 1945

Gable, Clark

Easiest Way, The 1931
Painted Desert, The 1931
Dance, Fools, Dance 1931
Finger Points, The 1931
Secret Six, The 1931
Free Soul, A 1931
Laughing Sinners 1931
Night Nurse 1931
Sporting Blood 1931
Susan Lenox; Her Fall and Rise 1931
Possessed 1931
Hell Divers 1931
Pente, La; Dance Fools Dance 1932
Polly of the Circus 1932
Strange Interlude 1932
Red Dust 1932
No Man of her Own 1932
White Sister, The 1933
Hold Your Man 1933
Night Flight 1933
Dancing Lady 1933
It Happened One Night 1934
Manhattan Melodrama 1934
Men in White 1934
Chained 1934
Forsaking all Others 1934
After Office Hours 1935
China Seas 1935
Call of the Wild 1935
Mutiny on the Bounty 1935
Wife vs Secretary 1936
San Francisco 1936
Cain and Mabel 1936
Love on the Run 1936
Parnell 1937
Saratoga 1937
Test Pilot 1938
too Hot To Handle 1938
Idiot's Delight 1939
Gone With the Wind 1939
Strange Cargo 1940
Boom Town 1940
Comrade X 1940
They Met in Bombay 1941
Honky Tonk 1941
Somewhere I'll Find You 1942
Adventure 1946
Hucksters, The 1947
Homecoming 1948
Command Decision 1949
Any Number Can Play 1949
Key to the City 1950
To Please a Lady 1950
Across the Wide Missouri 1951
Lone Star 1952
Never Let Me Go 1953
Mogambo 1953
Betrayed 1954
Soldier of Fortune 1955
Tall Men, The 1955
King and Four Queens, The 1956
Band of Angels 1957
Teacher's Pet 1958
Run Silent, Run Deep 1958
But Not for Me 1959
It Started in Naples 1960
Misfits, The 1961

Garfield, John

Four Daughters 1938
They Made Me a Criminal 1939
Blackwell's Island 1939
Juarez 1939
Daughters Courageous 1939
Dust Be my Destiny 1939
Castle on the Hudson 1940
Saturday's Children 1940
Flowing Gold 1940
East of the River 1940
Sea Wolf, The 1941
Out of the Fog 1941
Dangerously They Live 1942
Tortilla Flat 1942
Air Force 1943
Fallen Sparrow, The 1943
Thank Your Lucky Stars 1943
Destination Tokyo 1944
Destination Tokyo 1944
Between Two Worlds 1944
Hollywood Canteen 1944
Pride of the Marines 1945
Postman Always Rings Twice, The 1946
Nobody Lives Forever 1946
Humoresque 1946
Body and Soul 1947
Gentleman's Agreement 1947
Force of Evil 1948
We Were Strangers 1949
Under my Skin 1950
Breaking Point, The 1950
He Ran all the Way 1951

Garland, Judy

Pigskin Parade 1936
Broadway Melody of 1938 1937
Thoroughbreds Don't Cry 1937
Everybody Sing 1938
Love Finds Andy Hardy 1938
Listen, Darling 1938
Wizard of Oz, The 1939
Babes in Arms 1939
Andy Hardy Meets Debutante 1940
Strike up the Band 1940
Little Nellie Kelly 1940
Ziegfeld Girl 1941
Life Begins for Andy Hardy 1941
Babes on Broadway 1942
For Me and My Gal 1942
Presenting Lily Mars 1943
Thousands Cheer 1943
Girl Crazy 1943
Meet Me in St Louis 1944
Clock, The 1945
Harvey Girls, The 1946
Ziegfeld Follies 1946
Till the Clouds Roll By 1946
Pirate, The 1948
Easter Parade 1948
Words and Music 1948
In the Good Old Summertime 1949
Summer Stock 1950
Star is Born, A 1954
Judgment at Nuremberg 1961
Gay Purr--ee 1962
Child Is Waiting, A 1963
I Could go on Singing 1963

George, Gladys

Red Hot Dollars 1919
Home Spun Folks 1920
Straight Is the Way 1934
Valiant Is the Word for Carrie 1936
They Gave Him a Gun 1937
Madame X 1937
Love Is a Headache 1938
Marie Antoinette 1938
I'm From Missouri 1939
Here I Am a Stranger 1939
Roaring Twenties, The 1939
Child Is Born, A 1940
House Across the Bay, The 1940
Way of all Flesh, The 1940
Lady From Cheyenne, The 1941
Hit the Road 1941
Maltese Falcon, The 1941
Crystal Ball, The 1943
Hard Way, The 1943
Christmas Holiday 1944
Minstrel Man 1944
Best Years of our Lives, The 1946
Flamingo Road 1949
Bright Leaf 1950
Undercover Girl 1950
Lullaby of Broadway 1951
He Ran all the Way 1951
Detective Story 1951

Gibson, Hoot

Flaming Frontier, The 1926
Long, Long Trail, The 1929
Powdersmoke Range 1936
Last Outlaw, The 1936
Horse Soldiers, The 1959

Gilbert, John

Shame 1921
Monte Cristo 1922
His Hour 1924
He Who Gets Slapped 1924
Snob, The 1924
Wife of the Centaur, The 1925
Merry Widow, The 1925
Big Parade, The 1925
Bardelys The Magnificent 1926
Flesh and the Devil 1927
Show, The 1927
Twelve Miles Out 1927
Love 1927
Man, Woman and Sin 1927
Cossacks, The 1928
Four Walls 1928
Masks of the Devil, The 1928
Woman of Affairs, A 1929
Desert Nights 1929
Hollywood Revue, The 1929
His Glorious Night 1929
Redemption 1930
Way for a Sailor 1930
Gentleman's Fate 1931
Phantom of Paris, The 1931
Downstairs 1932
Fast Workers 1933
Queen Christina 1933
Captain Hates the Sea, The 1934
Show People 1967

Gish, Dorothy

Jordan Is a Hard Road 1915
Little Meena's Romance 1916
Hearts of the World 1918
Hun Within, The 1918
Battling Jane 1918
Hope Chest, The 1919
Boots 1919
Peppy Polly 1919
Nugget Nell 1919
Nobody Home 1919
Turning the Tables 1919
Mary Ellen Comes to Town 1920
Remodeling her Husband 1920
Little Miss Rebellion 1920
Country Flapper, The 1922
Bright Shawl, The 1923
Romola 1924
Night Life of New York 1925
Beautiful City, The 1925
Clothes Make the Pirate 1925
Nell Gwyn 1926
London 1926
Madame Pompadour 1927
Wanted Men 1936
Our Hearts Were Young and Gay 1944
Centennial Summer 1946
Whistle at Eaton Falls, The 1951
Cardinal, The 1963

Goldwyn, Samuel (Producer)

Street Scene 1931
Greeks Had a Word for Them, The 1932
Kid From Spain, The 1932
Dodsworth 1936
Stella Dallas 1937
Goldwyn Follies, The 1938
They Shall Have Music 1939
Real Glory, The 1939
Raffles 1940
Westerner, The 1940
Little Foxes, The 1941
Ball of Fire 1942
Pride of the Yankees, The 1942
North Star, The 1943
Up in Arms 1944
Princess and the Pirate, The 1945
Wonder Man 1945
Kid From Brooklyn, The 1946
Best Years of our Lives, The 1946
Secret Life of Walter Mitty, The 1947
Bishop's Wife, The 1947
Song Is Born, A 1948
Enchantment 1948
Our Very Own 1950
Edge of Doom 1950

I Want You 1951
Hans Christian Andersen 1952
Guys and Dolls 1955
Porgy and Bess 1959
Adventures of Marco Polo, The 1965

Grable, Betty
Hold 'Em Jail! 1932
Child of Manhattan 1933
What Price Innocence? 1933
Student Tour 1934
Collegiate 1936
Follow the Fleet 1936
Don't Turn 'em Loose 1936
Pigskin Parade 1936
This Way Please 1937
Thrill of a Lifetime 1937
College Swing 1938
Give Me a Sailor 1938
Campus Confessions 1938
Man About Town 1939
Day the Bookies Wept, The 1939
Down Argentine Way 1940
Tin Pan Alley 1940
Moon Over Miami 1941
Yank in the R A F, A 1941
I Wake up Screaming 1942
Song of the Islands 1942
Footlight Serenade 1942
Springtime in the Rockies 1942
Coney Island 1943
Sweet Rosie O'Grady 1943
Four Jills in a Jeep 1944
Pin Up Girl 1944
Billy Rose's Diamond Horseshoe 1945
Dolly Sisters, The 1945
Shocking Miss Pilgrim, The 1947
Mother Wore Tights 1947
That Lady in Ermine 1948
When my Baby Smiles at Me 1948
Beautiful Blonde From Bashful Bend, The 1949
Wabash Avenue 1950
My Blue Heaven 1950
Call Me Mister 1951
Meet Me After the Show 1951
Farmer Takes a Wife, The 1953
How to Marry a Millionaire 1953
Three for the Show 1955
How to be Very, Very Popular 1955

Greenstreet, Sydney
Maltese Falcon, The 1941
They Died With Their Boots On 1941
Across the Pacific 1942
Casablanca 1942
Background to Danger 1943
Passage to Marseille 1944
Between Two Worlds 1944
Mask of Dimitrios, The 1944
Conspirators, The 1944
Hollywood Canteen 1944
Pillow to Post 1945
Conflict 1945
Christmas in Connecticut 1945
Three Strangers 1946
Devotion 1946
Verdict, The 1946
That Way With Women 1947
Hucksters, The 1947
Woman in White, The 1948
Velvet Touch, The 1948
Ruthless 1948
Flamingo Road 1949
Malaya 1950

Griffith, D W (Director)
Escape, The 1914
Birth of a Nation, The 1915
Sable Lorcha, The 1915
Greatest Thing in Life, The 1918
Idol Dancer, The 1920
Love Flower, The 1920
Orphans of the Storm 1922
One Exciting Night 1922
White Rose, The 1923
America 1924
Isn't Life Wonderful? 1924
That Royle Girl 1926
Sorrows of Satan, The 1926
Drums of Love 1928
Battle of The Sexes, The 1928
Lady of the Pavements 1929
Abraham Lincoln 1930
Struggle, The 1931

Hardwicke, Cedric Sir
Dreyfus Case, The 1931
Rome Express 1932
Ghoul, The 1934
Orders Is Orders 1934
Lady is Willing, The 1934
Power 1934
Bella Donna 1935
Miserables, Les 1935
Becky Sharp 1935
Nell Gwyn 1935
Peg of Old Drury 1936
Things to Come 1936
Tudor Rose 1936
Nine Days a Queen 1936
Green Light 1937
King Solomon's Mines 1937
On Borrowed Time 1939
Stanley and Livingstone 1939
Hunchback of Notre Dame, The 1940
Invisible Man Returns, The 1940
Tom Brown's School Days 1940
Howards of Virginia, The 1940
Victory 1940
Suspicion 1941
Laburnum Grove 1941
Valley of the Sun 1942
Ghost of Frankenstein, The 1942
Invisible Agent 1942
Forever and a Day 1943
Moon Is Down, The 1943
Cross of Lorraine, The 1943
Lodger, The 1944
Wilson 1944
Wing and a Prayer 1944
Keys of the Kingdom, The 1944
Sentimental Journey 1946
Imperfect Lady, The 1947
Ivy 1947
Lured 1947
Beware of Pity 1947
Nicholas Nickleby 1947
Tycoon 1947
Woman's Vengeance, A 1948
Song of my Heart 1948
I Remember Mama 1948
Rope 1948
Connecticut Yankee in King Arthur's Court, A 1948
Winslow Boy, The 1950
White Tower, The 1950
Mr Imperium 1951
Desert Fox, The 1951
Green Glove, The 1952
Salome 1953
War of the Worlds, The 1953
Botany Bay 1953
Commandos Strike at Dawn 1954
Diane 1956
Helen of Troy 1956
Richard III 1956
Gaby 1956
Vagabond King, The 1956
Power and The Prize, the 1956
Around the World in 80 Days 1956
Ten Commandments, The 1956
Story of Mankind, The 1957
Baby Face Nelson 1957
Five Weeks in a Balloon 1962
Pumpkin Eater, The 1964

Hardy, Oliver
Wizard of Oz, The 1925
Rogue Song, The 1930
Pardon Us 1931
Pack up Your Troubles 1932
Devil's Brother, The 1933
Sons of the Desert 1934
Hollywood Party 1934
Babes in Toyland 1934
Bohemian Girl, The 1936
Our Relations 1936
Way out West 1937
Pick a Star 1937
Swiss Miss 1938
Block-Heads 1938
Zenobia 1939
Flying Deuces, The 1939
Chump at Oxford, A 1940
Great Guns 1941
Air Raid Wardens 1943
Jitterbugs 1943
Nothing but Trouble 1945
Bullfighters, The 1945
Fighting Kentuckian, The 1949
Riding High 1950
Utopia 1954
When Comedy Was King 1960
Days of Thrills and Laughter 1961
30 Years of Fun 1963
Laurel and Hardy's Laughing 20's 1965
Further Perils of Laurel and Hardy, The 1968

Harlow, Jean
Hell's Angels 1930
Iron Man 1931
Public Enemy, The 1931
Secret Six, The 1931
Goldie 1931
Platinum Blonde 1931
Three Wise Girls 1932
Beast of the City, The 1932
Red Headed Woman 1932
Red Dust 1932
Hold Your Man 1933
Dinner at Eight 1933
Bombshell 1933
Girl From Missouri, The 1934
Reckless 1935
China Seas 1935
Riffraff 1936
Wife vs Secretary 1936
Suzy 1936
Libeled Lady 1936
Personal Property 1937
Saratoga 1937
Further Perils of Laurel and Hardy, The 1968
Queen, The 1968

Hart, William S
Disciple, The 1915
Apostle of Vengeance, The 1916
Captive God, The 1916
Patriot, The 1916
Return of Draw Egan, The 1916
Truthful Tolliver 1916
Blue Blazes Rawden 1918
Selfish Yates 1918
Shark Monroe 1918
Riddle Gawne 1918
Border Wireless, The 1918
Branding Broadway 1918
Poppy Girl's Husband, The 1919
Money Corporal, The 1919
Toll Gate, The 1920
Sand 1920
Cradle of Courage, The 1920
O'Malley of the Mounted 1921
White Oak 1921
Hollywood 1923
Wild Bill Hickok 1923
Singer Jim McKee 1924
Tumbleweeds 1925

Harvey, Laurence
Black Rose, The 1950
Man on the Run 1952
Wall of Death 1952
Cairo Road 1952
I Believe in You 1953
King Richard and the Crusaders 1954
Romeo and Juliet 1954
Innocents in Paris 1955
I Am a Camera 1955
Storm over the Nile 1956
Truth About Women, The 1958
Room at the Top 1959
3 Men in a Boat 1959
Expresso Bongo 1960
Alamo, The 1960
Butterfield 8 1960
Two Loves 1961
Summer and Smoke 1961
Walk on the Wild Side 1962
Jungle Fighters 1962
Wonderful World of the Brothers Grimm, 1962
Manchurian Candidate, The 1962
Girl Named Tamiku, A 1963
Running Man, The 1963
Ceremony, The 1964
Of Human Bondage 1964

Outrage, The 1964
Darling 1965
Life at the Top 1965
Spy With a Cold Nose, The 1966
Dandy in Aspic, A 1968
Escape to the Sun 1972
Night Watch, The 1973

Hawkins, Jack
Good Companions, The 1933
Autumn Crocus 1934
Phantom Fiend 1935
Peg of Old Drury 1936
Next of Kin 1943
Fallen Idol, The 1949
Black Rose, The 1950
State Secret 1950
No Highway in the Sky 1951
Bonnie Prince Charlie 1952
Small Back Room, The 1952
Outpost in Malaya 1952
Story of Mandy, The 1953
Cruel Sea, The 1953
Murder on Monday 1953
Fighting Pimpernel, The 1954
Angels One Five 1954
Malta Story 1954
Intruder, The 1955
Front Page Story 1955
Land of Fury 1955
Land of the Pharaohs 1955
Prisoner, The 1955
Touch and go 1956
Third Key, The 1957
Bridge on the River Kwai 1957
Two-Headed Spy, The 1959
Gideon of Scotland Yard 1959
Ben Hur 1959
League of Gentlemen, The 1961
Two Loves 1961
Five Finger Exercise 1962
Lawrence of Arabia 1962
Lafayette 1963
Rampage 1963
Third Secret, The 1964
Zulu 1964
Guns at Batasi 1964
Lord Jim 1965
Masquerade 1965
Judith 1966
Poppy is Also a Flower, The 1967
Shalako 1968

Hayakawa, Sessue
Alien Souls 1916
Dragon Painter, The 1919
Bonds of Honor 1919
First Born, The 1921
Where Lights Are Low 1921
Daughter of the Dragon 1931
Tokyo Joe 1949
Three Came Home 1950
House of Bamboo 1955
Bridge on the River Kwai 1957
Geisha Boy, The 1958
Green Mansions 1959
Hell to Eternity 1960
Swiss Family Robinson 1960

Hayward, Susan
Girls on Probation 1938
Beau Geste 1939
Our Leading Citizen 1939
$1,000 a Touchdown 1939
Adam Had Four Sons 1941
Sis Hopkins 1941
Among the Living 1941
Reap the Wild Wind 1942
Forest Rangers, The 1942
I Married a Witch 1942
Star Spangled Rhythm 1942
Hit Parade of 1943
Jack London 1944
Fighting Seabees, The 1944
Hairy Ape, The 1944
And Now Tomorrow 1944
Deadline at Dawn 1946
Canyon Passage 1946
Smash-Up, The Story of a Woman 1947
They Won't Believe Me 1947
Lost Moment, The 1947
Tap Roots 1948
Saxon Charm, The 1948
Tulsa 1949
House of Strangers 1949
My Foolish Heart 1950
Rawhide 1951
I Can Get It for You Wholesale 1951
I'd Climb the Highest Mountain 1951
David and Bathsheba 1951
With a Song in my Heart 1952
Snows of Kilimanjaro, The 1952
Lusty Men, The 1952
President's Lady, The 1953
White Witch Doctor 1953
Demetrius and the Gladiators 1954
Garden of Evil 1954
Untamed 1955
Soldier of Fortune 1955
I'll Cry Tomorrow 1956
Conqueror, The 1956
Top Secret Affair 1957
I Want to Live 1958
Thunder in the Sun 1959
Woman Obsessed 1959
Marriage-Go-Round 1961
Ada 1961
Back Street 1961
I Thank a Fool 1962
Stolen Hours 1963
Where Love Has Gone 1964
Honey Pot, The 1967
Valley of the Dolls 1967
Revengers, The 1972

Heflin, Van
Woman Rebels, A 1936
Outcasts of Poker Flat, The 1937
Flight From Glory 1937
Annapolis Salute 1937
Saturday's Heroes 1937
Santa Fe Trail 1940
Feminine Touch, The 1941
H M Pulham, Esq 1941
Johnny Eager 1942
Kid Glove Killer 1942
Grand Central Murder 1942
Seven Sweethearts 1942
Tennessee Johnson 1943
Presenting Lily Mars 1943
Strange Love of Martha Ivers, The 1946
Till the Clouds Roll By 1946
Possessed 1947
Green Dolphin Street 1947
B F's Daughter 1948
Tap Roots 1948
Three Musketeers, The 1948
Act of Violence 1949
Madame Bovary 1949
East Side, West Side 1949
Tomahawk 1951
Prowler, The 1951
My Son John 1952
Shane 1953
Wings of the Hawk 1953
Golden Mask, The 1954
Tanganyika 1954
Raid, The 1954
Woman's World 1954
Black Widow 1954
Battle Cry 1955
Patterns 1956
3:10 to Yuma 1957
Tempest 1959
They Came to Cordura 1959
Five Branded Women 1960
Under ten Flags 1960
Cry of Battle 1963
Wastrel, The 1963
Greatest Story Ever Told, The 1965
Once a Thief 1965
Stagecoach 1966

Henie, Sonja
One in a Million 1937
Thin Ice 1937
Happy Landing 1938
My Lucky Star 1938
Second Fiddle 1939
Everything Happens at Night 1939
Sun Valley Serenade 1941
Iceland 1942
Wintertime 1943
It's a Pleasure 1945

Hersholt, Jean
Tess of the Storm Country 1922
Red Lights 1923
Woman on the Jury, The 1924
Goldfish, The 1924
Sinners in Silk 1924
Greed 1924
So Big 1925
Her Night of Romance 1925
Fifth Avenue Models 1925
If Marriage Fails 1925
Dangerous Innocence 1925
Don Q, Son of Zorro 1925
Woman's Faith, A 1925
Stella Dallas 1925
Greater Glory, The 1926
Four Horsemen of the Apocalypse, The 1926
It Must Be Love 1926
Alias the Deacon 1927
Student Prince, The 1927
13 Washington Square 1928
Secret Hour, The 1928
Abie's Irish Rose 1928
Battle of The Sexes, The 1928
Give and Take 1928
Girl on the Barge, The 1929
Younger Generation, The 1929
Case of Sergeant Grischa, The 1930
Mamba 1930
Hell Harbor 1930
Cat Creeps, The 1930
Viennese Nights 1930
Soldiers Plaything, A 1931
Daybreak 1931
Transatlantic 1931
Susan Lenox; Her Fall and Rise 1931
Sin of Madelon Claudet, The 1931
Phantom of Paris, The 1931
Private Lives 1931
Emma 1932
Beast of the City, The 1932
Grand Hotel 1932
Night Court 1932
New Morals for Old 1932
Unashamed 1932
Skyscraper Souls 1932
Mask of Fu Manchu, The 1932
Flesh 1932
Crime of the Century, The 1933
Song of the Eagle 1933
Dinner at Eight 1933
Christopher Bean 1933
Cat and the Fiddle, The 1934
Men in White 1934
Fountain, The 1934
Painted Veil, The 1934
Mark of the Vampire 1935
Break of Hearts 1935
Murder in the Fleet 1935
Country Doctor, The 1936
Tough Guy 1936
Sins of Man 1936
His Brother's Wife 1936
Reunion 1936
One in a Million 1937
Seventh Heaven 1937
Heidi 1937
Happy Landing 1938
Mr Moto in Danger Island 1938
I'll Give a Million 1938
Alexander's Ragtime Band 1938
Five of a Kind 1938
Meet Doctor Christian 1939
Courageous Dr Christian, The 1940
Stage Door Canteen 1943
Dancing in the Dark 1949
Run for Cover 1955

Holliday, Judy
Winged Victory 1944
Adam's Rib 1949
Born Yesterday 1950
Marrying Kind, The 1952
It Should Happen to You 1954
Phffft 1954
Solid Gold Cadillac, The 1956
Full of Life 1957
Bells Are Ringing 1960

Hopkins, Miriam
Fast and Loose 1930
Smiling Lieutenant, The 1931
Twenty-Four Hours 1931

Dr Jekyll and Mr Hyde 1932
Two Kinds of Women 1932
Dancers in the Dark 1932
World and the Flesh, The 1932
Trouble in Paradise 1932
Story of Temple Drake, The 1933
Stranger's Return, The 1933
Design for Living 1933
All of Me 1934
She Loves Me Not 1934
Richest Girl in the World, The 1934
Becky Sharp 1935
Barbary Coast 1935
Splendor 1935
These Three 1936
Men Are not Gods 1937
Woman I Love, The 1937
Woman Chases Man 1937
Wise Girl 1938
Old Maid, The 1939
Lady With red Hair 1940
Gentleman After Dark, A 1942
Old Acquaintance 1943
Heiress, The 1949
Mating Season, The 1951
Outcasts of Poker Flat 1952
Carrie 1952
Childrens Hour, The 1962
Fanny Hill 1965
Chase, The 1966

Horton, Edward Everett
Too Much Business 1922
Ruggles of Red Gap 1923
To the Ladies 1923
Man Who Fights Alone, The 1924
Beggar on Horseback 1925
Marry Me 1925
Boheme, La 1926
Poker Faces 1926
Taxi, Taxi 1927
Terror, The 1928
Miss Information 1928
Sonny Boy 1929
Hottentot, The 1929
Aviator, The 1930
Wide Open 1930
Holiday 1930
Once a Gentleman 1930
Reaching for the Moon 1930
Kiss Me Again 1931
Lonely Wives 1931
Front Page, The 1931
Six Cylinder Love 1931
Smart Woman 1931
Age for Love, The 1931
But the Flesh Is Weak 1932
Roar of the Dragon 1932
Trouble in Paradise 1932
Bedtime Story, A 1933
Its a Boy 1933
Way to Love, The 1933
Design for Living 1933
Alice in Wonderland 1933
Easy to Love 1934
Sing and Like It 1934
Success at any Price 1934
Woman in Command, The 1934
Kiss and Make-Up 1934
Ladies Should Listen 1934
Merry Widow, The 1934
Gay Divorcee, The 1934
Night is Young, The 1935
Biography of a Bachelor Girl 1935
All the King's Horses 1935
Devil is a Woman, The 1935
In Caliente 1935
Top Hat 1935
Little Big Shot 1935
His Night Out 1935
Your Uncle Dudley 1935
Singing Kid, The 1936
Nobody's Fool 1936
Hearts Divided 1936
Lost Horizon 1937
King and the Chorus Girl, The 1937
Shall We Dance 1937
Oh, Doctor 1937
Great Garrick, The 1937
Perfect Specimen, The 1937
Angel 1937
Danger-Love at Work 1937
Hitting a new High 1937
Bluebeard's Eighth Wife 1938
College Swing 1938
Holiday 1938
Little Tough Guys in Society 1938
Paris Honeymoon 1939
That's Right, You're Wrong 1939
You're the One 1941
Ziegfeld Girl 1941
Sunny 1941
Here Comes Mr Jordan 1941
Week End for Three 1941
Body Disappears, The 1942
Magnificent Dope, The 1942
I Married an Angel 1942
Springtime in the Rockies 1942
Thank Your Lucky Stars 1943
Gang's All Here, The 1943
Her Primitive Man 1944
Arsenic and old Lace 1944
Summer Storm 1944
San Diego, I Love You 1944
Brazil 1944
Lady on a Train 1945
Cinderella Jones 1946
Earl Carroll Sketchbook 1946
Down to Earth 1947
Her Husband's Affairs 1947
Story of Mankind, The 1957
Pocketful of Miracles 1961
It's a Mad, Mad, Mad, Mad World 1963
Sex and the Single Girl 1964
Perils of Pauline, The 1967

Howard, Leslie
Outward Bound 1930
Free Soul, A 1931
Never the Twain Shall Meet 1931
Five and Ten 1931
Devotion 1931
Reserved for Ladies 1932
Smilin' Through 1932
Animal Kingdom, The 1932
Secrets 1933
Captured 1933
Berkeley Square 1933
Of Human Bondage 1934
Lady is Willing, The 1934
British Agent 1934
Scarlet Pimpernel, The 1935
Petrified Forest, The 1936
Romeo and Juliet 1936
It's Love I'm After 1937
Stand-In 1937
Pygmalion 1938
Intermezzo, A Love Story 1939
Gone With the Wind 1939
Mister V 1942
Invaders, The 1942
Spitfire 1943
Of Human Bondage 1965

Jannings, Emil
All for a Woman 1921
Vendetta 1921
Loves of Pharaoh 1922
Othello 1923
Peter the Great 1923
Passion 1923
Last Laugh, The 1925
Quo Vadis 1925
Three Way Works, The 1926
Variety 1926
Faust 1926
Way of all Flesh, The 1927
Tartuffe 1927
Husbands or Lovers 1927
Last Command, The 1928
Street of Sin, The 1928
Power 1928
Fortune's Fool 1928
Patriot, The 1928
Sins of the Fathers 1929
Betrayal 1929
Darling of the Gods; Liebling der Gotter 1930
Blue Angel, The 1930
Grosse Tenor, Der 1931
Stuerme der Leidenschaft; Storms of Passion 1932
Alte und der Junge Koenig, Der 1935
Traumulus 1936
Zerbrochene Krug, Der; Broken Jugi, The 1938
Robert Koch 1939

Jolson, Al
Vitaphone 1926
Jazz Singer, The 1927
Singing Fool, The 1928
Say It With Songs 1929
Mammy 1930
Big Boy 1930
Hallelujah, I'm a Bum 1933
Wonder Bar 1934
Go Into Your Dance 1935
Singing Kid, The 1936
Rose of Washington Square 1939
Swanee River 1939
Rhapsody in Blue 1945

Karloff, Boris
Parisian Nights 1925
Her Honor the Governor 1926
Soft Cushions 1927
Two Arabian Knights 1927
Love Mart, The 1927
Behind That Curtain 1929
Unholy Night, The 1929
Criminal Code, The 1931
Cracked Nuts 1931
Donovan's Kid 1931
Smart Money 1931
Public Defender, The 1931
Five Star Final 1931
I Like Your Nerve 1931
Mad Genius, The 1931
Yellow Ticket, The 1931
Guilty Generation, The 1931
Frankenstein 1931
Tonight or Never 1931
Business and Pleasure 1932
Alias the Doctor 1932
Miracle Man, The 1932
Behind the Mask 1932
Scarface, The Shame of the Nation 1932
Night World 1932
Old Dark House, The 1932
Mask of Fu Manchu, The 1932
Mummy, The 1933
Ghoul, The 1934
House of Rothschild, The 1934
Lost Patrol, The 1934
Black Cat, The 1934
Bride of Frankenstein, The 1935
Raven, The 1935
Invisible Ray, The 1936
Walking Dead, The 1936
Charlie Chan at the Opera 1936
Man Who Lived Again, The 1936
Night Key 1937
Juggernaut 1937
West of Shanghai 1937
Invisible Menace, The 1938
Mr Wong, Detective 1938
Son of Frankenstein 1939
Mister Wong in Chinatown 1939
Man They Could Not Hang, The 1939
Tower of London 1939
Fatal Hour, The 1940
British Intelligence 1940
Black Friday 1940
Man With Nine Lives, The 1940
Devil's Island 1940
Doomed to Die 1940
Before I Hang 1940
You'll Find Out 1940
Ape, The 1940
Devil Commands, The 1941
Boogie Man Will Get You, The 1942
Climax, The 1944
House of Frankenstein 1944
Body Snatcher, The 1945
Isle of the Dead 1945
Bedlam 1946
Secret Life of Walter Mitty, The 1947
Lured 1947
Dick Tracy and Gruesome 1947
Unconquered 1947
Tap Roots 1948
Abbott and Costello Meet the Killer Boris Karloff 1949
Strange Door, The 1951
Black Castle, The 1952
Haunted Strangler, The 1958
Days of Thrills and Laughter 1961
Raven, The 1963
Corridors of Blood 1963
Comedy of Terrors, The 1964
Venetian Affair, The 1967
Targets 1968

Keaton, Buster
One Week 1920
Saphead, The 1921
Scarecrow, The 1921
Neighbors 1921
Hard Luck 1921
High Sign, The 1922
Paleface, The 1922
Our Hospitality 1923
Sherlock Jr 1924
Navigator, The 1924
Seven Chances 1925
Go West 1925
Battling Butler 1926
General, The 1927
College 1927
Steamboat Bill, Jr 1928
Cameraman, The 1928
Spite Marriage 1929
Hollywood Revue, The 1929
Free and Easy 1930
Dough Boys 1930
Parlor, Bedroom and Bath 1932
Passionate Plumber, The 1932
Speak Easily 1932
What! No Beer? 1933
Hollywood Cavalcade 1939
Forever and a Day 1943
San Diego, I Love You 1944
That's the Spirit 1945
You're my Everything 1949
In the Good Old Summertime 1949
Sunset Boulevard 1950
Limelight 1952
Around the World in 80 Days 1956
When Comedy Was King 1960
Adventures of Huckleberry Fin, The 1960
It's a Mad, Mad, Mad, Mad World 1963
Sound of Laughter, The 1963
30 Years of Fun 1963
Seven Chances 1965
Sergeant Deadhead 1965
Funny Thing Happened on the Way to the Forum, A 1966
How to Stuff a Wild Bikini 1967

Ladd, Alan
Rulers of the Sea 1939
Beasts of Berlin 1939
Black Cat, The 1941
Reluctant Dragon, The 1941
Gangs Incorporated 1941
Joan of Paris 1942
This Gun for Hire 1942
Glass Key, The 1942
Star Spangled Rhythm 1942
Lucky Jordan 1943
China 1943
And Now Tomorrow 1944
Salty O'Rourke 1945
Duffy's Tavern 1945
Blue Dahlia, The 1946
O S S 1946
Two Years Before the Mast 1946
Calcutta 1947
Wild Harvest 1947
Saigon 1948
Beyond Glory 1948
Whispering Smith 1949
Great Gatsby, The 1949
Chicago Deadline 1949
Captain Carey U S A 1950
Branded 1951
Appointment With Danger 1951
Red Mountain 1952
Iron Mistress, The 1952
Thunder in the East 1953
Shane 1953
Desert Legion 1953
Botany Bay 1953
Paratrooper 1953
Saskatchewan 1954
Hell Below Zero 1954
Black Knight, The 1954
Drum Beat 1954
McConnell Story, The 1955
Hell on Frisco Bay 1956
Santiago 1956
Big Land, The 1957
Boy on a Dolphin 1957
Deep Six, The 1958
Proud Rebel, The 1958
Badlanders, The 1958
Man in the Net, The 1959
All the Young Men 1960
One Foot in Hell 1960
13 West Street 1962
Carpetbaggers, The 1964

Lahr, Bert
Flying High 1931
Merry-Go-Round of 1938 1937
Love and Hisses 1938
Josette 1938
Just Around the Corner 1938
Zaza 1939
Wizard of Oz, The 1939
Sing Your Worries Away 1942
Ship Ahoy 1942
Meet The People 1944
Always Leave Them Laughing 1949
Mr Universe 1951
Rose Marie 1954
Second Greatest Sex, The 1956
Sound of Laughter, The 1963
Night They Raided Minsky's, The 1968

Lake, Veronica
I Wanted Wings 1941
Hold Back the Dawn 1941
Sullivan's Travels 1942
This Gun for Hire 1942
Glass Key, The 1942
I Married a Witch 1942
Star Spangled Rhythm 1942
So Proudly We Hail 1943
Hour Before the Dawn, The 1944
Bring on the Girls 1945
Out of This World 1945
Duffy's Tavern 1945
Hold That Blonde 1945
Miss Susie Slagle's 1946
Blue Dahlia, The 1946
Ramrod 1947
Saigon 1948
Sainted Sisters, The 1948
Isn't It Romantic? 1948
Slattery's Hurricane 1949

Lang, Fritz (Director)
Between Worlds 1924
Siegfried 1925
Beyond the Wall 1927
Metropolis 1927
Dr Nabuse 1927
Spione; Spies 1928
Kriemhild's Revenge 1928
Spies 1929
By Rocket to the Moon 1931
M 1931
Liliom 1935
Fury 1936
You Only Live Once 1937
You and Me 1938
Return of Frank James, The 1940
Western Union 1941
Man Hunt 1941
Last Will of Dr Mabuse, The 1943
Hangmen Also Die 1943
Woman in the Window, The 1945
Ministry of Fear 1945
Scarlet Street 1946
Cloak and Dagger 1946
Secret Beyond the Door 1948
House by the River 1950
American Guerrilla in the Philippines 1950
Rancho Notorious 1952
Clash by Night 1952
Blue Gardenia, The 1953
Big Heat, The 1953
Human Desire 1954
Moonfleet 1955
While the City Sleeps 1956
Beyond a Reasonable Doubt 1956
Journey to the Lost City 1960
Testament of Doctor Mabuse, The 1973
Metropolis 1974

Langdon, Harry
Picking Peaches 1924
Tramp, Tramp, Tramp 1926
Strong Man, The 1926
Long Pants 1927
His First Flame 1927
Three's a Crowd 1927
Chaser, The 1928
See America Thirst 1930
Soldiers Plaything, A 1931
Hallelujah, I'm a Bum 1933
My Weakness 1933
There Goes my Heart 1938
Zenobia 1939
Days of Thrills and Laughter 1961
Sound of Laughter, The 1963
30 Years of Fun 1963

Lanza, Mario
That Midnight Kiss 1949
Toast of New Orleans, The 1950
Great Caruso, The 1951
Because You're Mine 1952
Serenade 1956
Seven Hills of Rome 1958
For the First Time 1959

Laughton, Charles
Piccadilly 1929
Day Dreams 1930
Devil and the Deep 1932
Old Dark House, The 1932
Payment Deferred 1932
Sign of the Cross, The 1932
If I Had a Million 1932
Island of Lost Souls 1933
Private Life of Henry VIII, The 1933
White Woman 1933
Barretts of Wimpole Street, The 1934
Ruggles of Red Gap 1935
Miserables, Les 1935
Mutiny on the Bounty 1935
Wanted Men 1936
Rembrandt 1936
Beachcomber, The 1938
Jamaica Inn 1939
Hunchback of Notre Dame, The 1940
Sidewalks of London 1940
They Knew What They Wanted 1940
It Started With Eve 1941
Tuttles of Tahiti, The 1942
Tales of Manhattan 1942
Stand by for Action 1943
Forever and a Day 1943
This Land Is Mine 1943
Man From Down Under, The 1943
Canterville Ghost, The 1944
Suspect, The 1945
Captain Kidd 1945
Because of Him 1946
Paradine Case, The 1948
Arch of Triumph 1948
Big Clock, The 1948
Bribe, The 1949
Man on the Eiffel Tower, The 1950
Blue Veil, The 1951
Strange Door, The 1951
O Henry's Full House 1952
Salome 1953
Young Bess 1953
Hobson's Choice 1954
Witness for the Prosecution 1958
Under ten Flags 1960
Spartacus 1960
Advise and Consent 1962

Laurel, Stan
Rogue Song, The 1930
Pardon Us 1931
Pack up Your Troubles 1932
Devil's Brother, The 1933
Sons of the Desert 1934
Hollywood Party 1934
Babes in Toyland 1934
Bohemian Girl, The 1936
Our Relations 1936
Way out West 1937
Pick a Star 1937
Swiss Miss 1938
Block-Heads 1938
Flying Deuces, The 1939
Chump at Oxford, A 1940
Great Guns 1941
Air Raid Wardens 1943

Jitterbugs 1943
Nothing but Trouble 1945
Bullfighters, The 1945
Utopia 1954
When Comedy Was King 1960
Days of Thrills and Laughter 1961
30 Years of Fun 1963
Laurel and Hardy's Laughing 20's 1965
Further Perils of Laurel and Hardy, The 1968

Laurel and Hardy
A-Haunting We Will Go 1942
Dancing Masters, The 1943
Big Noise, The 1944

Leigh, Vivien
Fire Over England 1937
Dark Journey 1937
Yank at Oxford, A 1938
Storm in a Teacup 1938
Gone With the Wind 1939
Sidewalks of London 1940
Waterloo Bridge 1940
21 Days Together 1940
That Hamilton Woman 1941
Caesar and Cleopatra 1944
Anna Karenina 1948
Streetcar Named Desire, A 1951
Deep Blue Sea, The 1955
Roman Spring of Mrs Stone, The 1961
Ship of Fools 1965

Lloyd, Harold
Be my Wife 1919
Now or Never 1921
Among Those Present 1921
I Do 1921
Grandma's Boy 1922
Doctor Jack 1922
Safety Last 1923
Why Worry? 1923
Sailor-Made Man, A 1923
Girl Shy 1924
Hot Water 1924
Freshman, The 1925
For Heaven's Sake 1926
Kid Brother, The 1927
Speedy 1928
Welcome Danger 1929
Feet First 1930
Movie Crazy 1932
Cat's Paw, The 1934
Milky Way, The 1936
Professor Beware 1938
Mad Wednesday 1951
Freshman, The 1953

Lockhart, Gene
Star of Midnight 1935
Crime and Punishment 1935
Garden Murder Case, The 1936
Brides are Like That 1936
Times Square Playboy 1936
Gorgeous Hussy, The 1936
Devil is a Sissy, The 1936
Wedding Present 1936
Come Closer, Folks 1936
Make Way for Tomorrow 1937
Something to Sing About 1937
Of Human Hearts 1938
Sinners in Paradise 1938
Men Are Such Fools 1938
Algiers 1938
Meet the Girls 1938
Listen, Darling 1938
Blondie 1938
Christmas Carol, A 1938
Sweethearts 1938
I'm From Missouri 1939
Story of Alexander Graham Bell, The 1939
Hotel Imperial 1939
Bridal Suite 1939
Tell no Tales 1939
Our Leading Citizen 1939
Blackmail 1939
His Girl Friday 1940
Geronimo 1940
Abe Lincoln in Illinois 1940
Edison the Man 1940
South of Pago-Pago 1940
We Who Are Young 1940
Dr Kildare Goes Home 1940
Dispatch From Reuters, A 1940
Meet John Doe 1941
Sea Wolf, The 1941
Billy the Kid 1941
All That Money Can Buy 1941
International Lady 1941
One Foot in Heaven 1941
Juke Girl 1942
Gay Sisters, The 1942
You Can't Escape Forever 1942
Hangmen Also Die 1943
Mission to Moscow 1943
Northern Pursuit 1943
Desert Song, The 1943
Action in Arabia 1944
Man From Frisco 1944
That's the Spirit 1945
House on Ninety-Second Street, The 1945
Leave Her to Heaven 1945
Scandal In Paris, A 1946
Shocking Miss Pilgrim, The 1947
Strange Woman, The 1947
Honeymoon 1947
Miracle on 34th Street 1947
Cynthia 1947
Foxes of Harrow, The 1947
Her Husband's Affairs 1947
I, Jane Doe 1948
Apartment for Peggy 1948
Joan of Arc 1948
That Wonderful Urge 1948
Down to the Sea in Ships 1949
Madame Bovary 1949
Inspector General, The 1949
Red Light 1950
Riding High 1950
Big Hangover, The 1950
I'd Climb the Highest Mountain 1951
Rhubarb 1951
Girl in Every Port, A 1952
Hoodlum Empire 1952
Secret Sharer, The 1953
Androcles and the Lion 1953
Lady Wants Mink, The 1953
Down Among the Sheltering Palms 1953
World for Ransom 1954
Carousel 1956
Man in the Gray Flannel Suit, The 1956

Lombard, Carole
Me, Gangster 1928
Power 1928
Show Folks 1928
Ned McCobb's Daughter 1929
Big News 1929
Racketeer, The 1930
Arizona Kid, The 1930
Safety in Numbers 1930
Fast and Loose 1930
Pays to Advertise It 1931
It Pays to Advertise 1931
Man of the World 1931
Ladies' Man 1931
Up Pops the Devil 1931
I Take This Woman 1931
No One Man 1932
Sinners in the Sun 1932
Virtue 1932,O 25,24 5
No Man of her Own 1932
No More Orchids 1933
From Hell to Heaven 1933
Supernatural 1933
Eagle and the Hawk, The 1933
Brief Moment 1933
White Woman 1933
Bolero 1934
We're not Dressing 1934
20th Century 1934
Now and Forever 1934
Lady by Choice 1934
Gay Bride, The 1934
Rumba 1935
Hands Across the Table 1935
Love Before Breakfast 1936
Princess Comes Across, The 1936
My Man Godfrey 1936
Swing High, Swing Low 1937
Nothing Sacred 1937
True Confession 1937
Fools for Scandal 1938
Made for Each Other 1939
In Name Only 1939
Vigil in the Night 1940
They Knew What They Wanted 1940
Mr and Mrs Smith 1941
To Be or not to Be 1942

Lorre, Peter
M 1933
Was Frauen Traeumen; What Women Dream 1933
Schuss im Morgengrauen 1934
Man Who Knew too Much, The 1935
Mad Love 1935
Crime and Punishment 1935
Secret Agent 1936
Crack-Up 1937
Nancy Steele is Missing 1937
Think Fast, Mr Moto 1937
Lancer Spy 1937
Thank You, Mr Moto 1938
Mr Moto in Danger Island 1938
Mr Moto's Gamble 1938
Mr Moto Takes a Chance 1938
I'll Give a Million 1938
Mysterious Mr Moto of Devil's Island 1938
Mr Moto's Last Warning 1939
Mr Moto Takes a Vacation 1939
Strange Cargo 1940
I Was an Adventuress 1940
Island Of Doomed Men 1940
Stranger on the Third Floor 1940
You'll Find Out 1940
Face Behind the Mask, The 1941
Mr District Attorney 1941
They Met in Bombay 1941
Maltese Falcon, The 1941
All Through the Night 1942
Invisible Agent 1942
Boogie Man Will Get You, The 1942
Casablanca 1942
Background to Danger 1943
Constant Nymph, The 1943
Cross of Lorraine, The 1943
Passage to Marseille 1944
Mask of Dimitrios, The 1944
Arsenic and old Lace 1944
Conspirators, The 1944
Hollywood Canteen 1944
Hotel Berlin 1945
Confidential Agent 1945
Three Strangers 1946
Black Angel 1946
Chase, The 1946
Verdict, The 1946
Beast With Five Fingers, The 1946
My Favorite Brunette 1947
Casbah 1948
Rope of Sand 1949
Quicksand 1950
Double Confession 1953
Beat the Devil 1954
20,000 Leagues Under the Sea 1954
Congo Crossing 1956
Around the World in 80 Days 1956
Buster Keaton Story, The 1957
Silk Stockings 1957
Story of Mankind, The 1957
Sad Sack, The 1957
Big Circus, The 1959
Scent of Mystery 1960
Voyage to the Bottom of the Sea 1961
Tales of Terror 1962
Five Weeks in a Balloon 1962
Raven, The 1963
Comedy of Terrors, The 1964
Muscle Beach Party 1964
Patsy, The 1964
Torn Curtain 1966

Lugosi, Bela
Silent Command, The 1923
Rejected Woman, The 1924
Such Men Are Dangerous 1930
Renegades 1930
Dracula 1931
Women of all Nations 1931
Black Camel, The 1931
Murders in the Rue Morgue 1932

White Zombie 1932
Chandu the Magician 1932
Island of Lost Souls 1933
Death Kiss, The 1933
International House 1933
Black Cat, The 1934
Best Man Wins 1935
Mysterious Mr Wong, The 1935
Return of Chandu 1935
Mark of the Vampire 1935
Raven, The 1935
Invisible Ray, The 1936
Son of Frankenstein 1939
Gorilla, The 1939
Ninotchka 1939
Saint's Double Trouble, The 1940
Black Friday 1940
Human Monster, The 1940
You'll Find Out 1940
Black Cat, The 1941
Invisible Ghost, The 1941
Spooks Run Wild 1941
Wolf Man, The 1941
Ghost of Frankenstein, The 1942
Night Monster 1942
Frankenstein Meets the Wolf Man 1943
Return of the Vampire, The 1944
One Body too Many 1944
Zombies on Broadway 1945
Body Snatcher, The 1945
Abbott and Costello Meet Frankenstein 1948

Lukas, Paul

Two Lovers 1928
Three Sinners 1928
Loves of an Actress 1928
Night Watch, The 1928
Woman From Moscow, The 1928
Manhattan Cocktail 1928
Shopworn Angel, The 1929
Wolf of Wall Street, The 1929
Half Way to Heaven 1929
Behind the Makeup 1930
Slightly Scarlet 1930
Young Eagles 1930
Benson Murder Case, The 1930
Devil's Holiday, The 1930
Grumpy 1930
Anybody's Woman 1930
Right to Love, The 1931
Unfaithful 1931
City Streets 1931
Vice Squad, The 1931
Women Love Once 1931
Beloved Bachelor, The 1931
Strictly Dishonorable 1931
No One Man 1932
Tomorrow and Tomorrow 1932
Thunder Below 1932
Passport to Hell, A 1932
Downstairs 1932
Rockabye 1932
Grand Slam 1933
Kiss Before the Mirror, The 1933
Sing Sinner Sing 1933
Captured 1933
Secret of the Blue Room, The 1933
Little Women 1933
By Candlelight 1934
Countess of Monte Cristo, The 1934
Glamour 1934
Affairs of a Gentleman 1934
I Give my Love 1934
Fountain, The 1934
Casino Murder Case, The 1935
Age of Indiscretion 1935
Three Musketeers, The 1935
I Found Stella Parish 1935
Dodsworth 1936
Ladies in Love 1936
Espionage 1937
Dinner at the Ritz 1937
Lady Vanishes, The 1938
Mutiny of the Elsinore, The 1939
Confessions of a Nazi Spy 1939
Captain Fury 1939
Strange Cargo 1940
Ghost Breakers, The 1940
Monster and the Girl, The 1941
Chinese Den 1941
They Dare not Love 1941
Lady in Distress 1942
Watch on the Rhine 1943
Hostages 1943
Uncertain Glory 1944
Address Unknown 1944
Experiment Perilous 1944
Deadline at Dawn 1946
Temptation 1946
Whispering City 1948
Berlin Express 1948
Kim 1950
20,000 Leagues Under the Sea 1954
Roots of Heaven, The 1958
Scent of Mystery 1960
Tender is the Night 1962
55 Days at Peking 1963
Fun in Acapulco 1964
Lord Jim 1965
Sol Madrid 1968

Lundigan, William

Armored Car 1937
Black Doll, The 1938
Wives Under Suspicion 1938
Missing Guest, The 1938
Three Smart Girls Grow Up 1939
Dodge City 1939
They Asked for It 1939
Forgotten Woman, The 1939
Old Maid, The 1939
Legion of Lost Flyers 1939
Fighting 69th, The 1940
Three Cheers for the Irish 1940
Man Who Talked too Much, The 1940
Sea Hawk, The 1940
East of the River 1940
Santa Fe Trail 1940
Case of the Black Parrot, The 1941
Highway West 1941
International Squadron 1941
Bugle Sounds, The 1942
Courtship of Andy Hardy, The 1942
Sunday Punch 1942
Andy Hardy's Double Life 1943
Salute to the Marines 1943
Dishonored Lady 1947
Fabulous Dorseys, The 1947
State Department-File 649 1949
Follow Me Quietly 1949
Pinky 1949
Mother Didn't Tell Me 1950
I'll Get by 1950
I'd Climb the Highest Mountain 1951
House on Telegraph Hill, The 1951
Elopement 1951
Down Among the Sheltering Palms 1953
Inferno 1953
Riders to the Stars 1954

McDaniel, Hattie

Judge Priest 1934
Little Colonel, The 1935
Alice Adams 1935
Gentle Julia 1936
Show Boat 1936
Hearts Divided 1936
High Tension 1936
Star for a Night 1936
Valiant Is the Word for Carrie 1936
Crime Nobody Saw, The 1937
Saratoga 1937
Nothing Sacred 1937
45 Fathers 1937
True Confession 1937
Battle of Broadway 1938
Shopworn Angel, The 1938
Mad Miss Manton, The 1938
Shining Hour, The 1939
Zenobia 1939
Gone With the Wind 1939
Maryland 1940
Great Lie, The 1941
Affectionaly Yours 1941
Male Animal, The 1942
In This our Life 1942
George Washington Slept Here 1942
Johnny Come Lately 1943
Thank Your Lucky Stars 1943
Since You Went Away 1944
Janie 1944
3 Is a Family 1944
Margie 1946
Never Say Goodbye 1946
Song of the South 1946
Flame, The 1948
Mickey 1948
Family Honeymoon 1949

MacDonald, Jeanette

Love Parade, The 1929
Vagabond King, The 1930
Monte Carlo 1930
Let's Go Native 1930
Lottery Bride, The 1930
Don't Bet on Women 1931
Annabelle's Affairs 1931
One Hour with You 1932
Love Me Tonight 1932
Cat and the Fiddle, The 1934
Merry Widow, The 1934
Naughty Marietta 1935
Rose Marie 1936
San Francisco 1936
Maytime 1937
Firefly, The 1937
Girl of the Golden West, The 1938
Sweethearts 1938
Broadway Serenade 1939
New Moon 1940
Bitter Sweet 1940
Smilin' Through 1941
I Married an Angel 1942
Cairo 1942
Follow the Boys 1944
Three Daring Daughters 1948
Sun comes up, The 1949

McLaglen, Victor

Beloved Brute, The 1924
Percy 1925
Unholy Three, The 1925
Winds of Chance 1925
Men of Steel 1926
Beau Geste 1926
What Price Glory 1926
Loves of Carmen 1927
Girl in Every Port, A 1928
Mother Machree 1928
Hangman's House 1928
River Pirate, The 1928
Captain Lash 1929
Strong Boy 1929
Black Watch, The 1929
Cock Eyed World, The 1929
Hot for Paris 1930
Happy Days 1930
Hot for Paris 1930
On the Level 1930
Devil With Women, A 1930
Dishonored 1931
Three Rogues 1931
Women of all Nations 1931
Annabelle's Affairs 1931
Wicked 1931
Gay Caballero, The 1932
Devil's Lottery 1932
Guilty as Hell 1932
Rackety Rax 1932
Hot Pepper 1933
Laughing at Life 1933
No More Women 1934
Lost Patrol, The 1934
Wharf Angel 1934
Murder at the Vanities 1934
Captain Hates the Sea, The 1934
Under Pressure 1935
Great Hotel Murder, The 1935
Informer, The 1935
Professional Soldier 1936
Klondike Annie 1936
Under Two Flags 1936
Magnificent Brute, The 1936
Nancy Steele is Missing 1937
Sea Devils 1937
This Is my Affair 1937
Wee Willie Winkie 1937
Battle of Broadway 1938
Devil's Party, The 1938
We're Going to Be Rich 1938
Pacific Liner 1939
Gunga Din 1939
Let Freedom Ring 1939
Ex-Champ 1939
Captain Fury 1939
Full Confession 1939
Rio 1939
Big Guy, The 1940
South of Pago-Pago 1940
Diamond Frontiers 1940
Broadway Limited 1941
Call out the Marines 1942
Powder Town 1942
China Girl 1943

Tampico 1944
Roger Touhy, Gangster 1944
Princess and the Pirate, The 1945
Rough, Tough and Ready 1945
Love, Honor and Goodbye 1945
Whistle Stop 1946
Michigan Kid 1947
Foxes of Harrow, The 1947
Fort Apache 1948
She Wore a Yellow Ribbon 1949
Rio Grande 1950
Quiet Man, The 1952
Fair Wind to Java 1953
Prince Valiant 1954
Many Rivers to Cross 1955
Trouble in the Glen 1955
Bengazi 1955
Lady Godiva 1955
Around the World in 80 Days 1956

Magnani, Anna
Tempo Massimo 1936
Cieca di Sorrento, La 1936
Open City; Citta Aperta 1946
Before Him all Rome Trembled 1947
Revenge 1947
Angelina 1948
Woman Trouble 1949
Bandit, The 1949
Peddler and the Lady, The 1949
Peddlin' in Society 1950
Ways of Love; Miracle, The 1950
Doctor, Beware 1951
Scarred 1951
Bellissima 1953
Volcano 1953
Golden Coach, The 1954
Anita Garibaldi 1954
Rose Tattoo, The 1955
Wild Is the Wind 1957
Awakening, The 1958
Of Life and Love 1958
Fugitive Kind, The 1960
Made in Italy 1967

Main, Marjorie
Music in the Air 1934
Stella Dallas 1937
Dead End 1937
Shadow, The 1937
Boy of the Streets 1938
Penitentiary 1938
King of the Newsboys 1938
Test Pilot 1938
Prison Farm 1938
Little Tough Guy 1938
Girls' School 1938
Lucky Night 1939
They Shall Have Music 1939
Angels Wash Their Faces 1939
Women, The 1939
Another Thin Man 1939
I Take This Woman 1940
Women Without Names 1940
Dark Command 1940
Susan and God 1940
Turnabout 1940
Wyoming 1940
Trial of Mary Dugan, The 1941
Woman's Face, A 1941
Barnacle Bill 1941
Shepherd of the Hills, The 1941
Honky Tonk 1941
Bugle Sounds, The 1942
We Were Dancing 1942
Jackass Mail 1942
Tish 1942
Tennessee Johnson 1943
Heaven Can Wait 1943
Johnny Come Lately 1943
Rationing 1944
Meet Me in St Louis 1944
Gentle Annie 1945
Murder, He Says 1945
Harvey Girls, The 1946
Bad Bascomb 1946
Undercurrent 1946
Show-Off, The 1947
Egg and I, The 1947
Wistful Widow of Wagon Gap, The 1947
Big Jack 1949
Ma and Pa Kettle 1949
Summer Stock 1950
Mrs O'Malley and Mr Malone 1951
Ma and Pa Kettle Back on the Farm 1951
Law and the Lady, The 1951
Mr Imperium 1951
It's a big Country 1952
Belle of New York, The 1952
Ma and Pa Kettle at the Fair 1952
Long, Long Trailer, The 1954
Rose Marie 1954
Friendly Persuasion 1956

Mansfield, Jayne
Illegal 1955
Hell on Frisco Bay 1956
Girl Can't Help It, The 1957
Wayward Bus, The 1957
Will Success Spoil Rock Hunter 1957
Kiss Them for Me 1957
Sheriff of Fractured Jaw, The 1959
George Raft Story, The 1962
It Happened in Athens 1962
It Takes a Thief 1963
Guide for the Married Man, A 1967

March, Fredric
Dummy, The 1929
Wild Party, The 1929
Studio Murder Mystery, The 1929
Jealousy 1929
Paris Bound 1929
Footlights and Fools 1929
Marriage Playground, The 1929
Sarah and Son 1930
Ladies Love Brutes 1930
True to the Navy 1930
Manslaughter 1930
Laughter 1930
Royal Family of Broadway, The 1930
Honor Among Lovers 1931
Night Angel, The 1931
My Sin 1931
Dr Jekyll and Mr Hyde 1932
Strangers in Love 1932
Merrily We Go to Hell 1932
Smilin' Through 1932
Sign of the Cross, The 1932
Tonight Is Ours 1933
Eagle and the Hawk, The 1933
Design for Living 1933
All of Me 1934
Death Takes a Holiday 1934
Good Dame 1934
Affairs of Cellini, The 1934
Barretts of Wimpole Street, The 1934
We Live Again 1934
Miserables, Les 1935
Anna Karenina 1935
Dark Angel, The 1935
Mary of Scotland 1936
Road to Glory, The 1936
Anthony Adverse 1936
Star Is Born, A 1937
Nothing Sacred 1937
Buccaneer, The 1938
There Goes my Heart 1938
Trade Winds 1939
Susan and God 1940
Victory 1940
So Ends our Night 1941
One Foot in Heaven 1941
Bedtime Story 1942
I Married a Witch 1942
Adventures of Mark Twain, The 1944
Tomorrow the World 1944
Best Years of our Lives, The 1946
Another Part of the Forest 1948
Live Today for Tomorrow 1948
Christopher Columbus 1949
Death of a Salesman 1951
It's a big Country 1952
Man on a Tightrope 1953
Executive Suite 1954
Bridges at Toko-Ri, The 1955
Desperate Hours, The 1955
Alexander the Great 1956
Man in the Gray Flannel Suit, The 1956
Middle of the Night 1959
Inherit the Wind 1960
Young Doctors, The 1961
Condemned of Altona, The 1963
Seven Days in May 1964
Hombre 1967
Iceman Cometh, The 1973

Marshall, Herbert
Letter, The 1929
Murder 1930
Secrets of a Secretary 1931
Calendar, The 1931
Michael and Mary 1932
Blonde Venus 1932
Trouble in Paradise 1932
Evenings for Sale 1932
Faithful Heart 1933
Solitaire Man, The 1933
I Was a Spy 1934
Four Frightened People 1934
Riptide 1934
Outcast Lady 1934
Painted Veil, The 1934
Good Fairy, The 1935
Flame Within, The 1935
Accent on Youth 1935
Dark Angel, The 1935
If You Could Only Cook 1935
Lady Consents, The 1936
Till We Meet Again 1936
Forgotten Faces 1936
Girls' Dormitory 1936
Woman Rebels, A 1936
Make Way for a Lady 1936
Angel 1937
Breakfast for Two 1937
Mad About Music 1938
Always Goodbye 1938
Woman Against Woman 1938
Zaza 1939
Bill of Divorcement, A 1940
Foreign Correspondent 1940
Letter, The 1940
Adventure in Washington 1941
Little Foxes, The 1941
When Ladies Meet 1941
Kathleen 1941
Moon and Sixpence, The 1942
Forever and a Day 1943
Flight for Freedom 1943
Andy Hardy's Blonde Trouble 1944
Enchanted Cottage, The 1945
Unseen, The 1945
Crack-Up 1946
Razor's Edge, The 1946
Duel in the Sun 1947
Ivy 1947
High Wall 1947
Underworld Story, The 1950
Anne of the Indies 1951
Captain Black Jack 1952
Angel Face 1953
Riders to the Stars 1954
Gog 1954
Black Shield of Falworth, The 1954
Virgin Queen, The 1955
Stage Struck 1958
Fly, The 1958
College Confidential 1960
Midnight Lace 1960
Fever in the Blood 1961
Five Weeks in a Balloon 1962
List of Adrian Messenger, The 1963
Caretakers, The 1963
Third Day, The 1965

Marx, Chico
Monkey Business 1931
Horse Feathers 1932
Duck Soup 1933
Night at the Opera, A 1935
Day at the Races, A 1937
Room Service 1938
At the Circus 1939
Go West 1941
Big Store, The 1941
Night in Casablanca, A 1946
Love Happy 1950
Story of Mankind, The 1957

Marx, Harpo
Too Many Kisses 1925
Monkey Business 1931
Horse Feathers 1932
Duck Soup 1933
Night at the Opera, A 1935
Day at the Races, A 1937
Room Service 1938
At the Circus 1939
Go West 1941
Big Store, The 1941
Stage Door Canteen 1943

Night in Casablanca, A 1946
Love Happy 1950
Story of Mankind, The 1957

Maynard, Ken
Janice Meredith 1924
Senor Daredevil 1926
Red Raiders, The 1927
Parade of the West 1930
Branded Men 1931

Menjou, Adolphe
Faith Healer, The 1921
Marriage Cheat, The 1921
Three Musketeers, The 1921
Fast Mail, The 1922
Bella Donna 1923
Rupert of Hentzau 1923
Woman of Paris, A 1923
Spanish Dancer, The 1923
Marriage Circle, The 1924
Shadows of Paris 1924
Broadway After Dark 1924
For Sale 1924
Broken Barriers 1924
Sinners in Silk 1924
Open all Night 1924
Forbidden Paradise 1924
Fast Set, The 1924
Swan, The 1925
Kiss in the Dark, A 1925
Are Parents People 1925
Lost-a Wife 1925
King on Main Street, The 1925
Grand Duchess and the Waiter, The 1926
Social Celebrity, A 1926
Sorrows of Satan, The 1926
Ace of Cads, The 1926
Blonde or Brunette 1927
Evening Clothes 1927
Service for Ladies 1927
Gentleman of Paris, A 1927
Serenade 1927
Night of Mystery, A 1928
His Tiger Lady 1928
Tiger Lady, The 1928
His Private Life 1928
Marquis Preferred 1929
Fashions in Love 1929
Forbidden Paradise 1929
Mon Gosse de Pere 1930
Enigmatique Monsieur Parkes, L' 1930
Morocco 1930
New Moon 1930
Easiest Way, The 1931
Front Page, The 1931
Men Call it Love 1931
Parisian, The 1931
Great Lover, The 1931
Friends and Lovers 1931
Forbidden 1932
Prestige 1932
Bachelor's Affairs 1932
Night Club Lady, The 1932
Blame the Woman 1932
Farewell to Arms, A 1932
Circus Queen Murder, The 1933
Morning Glory 1933
Worst Woman in Paris, The 1933
Convention City 1933
Easy to Love 1934
Trumpet Blows, The 1934
Journal of a Crime 1934
Little Miss Marker 1934
Great Flirtation, The 1934
Human Side, The 1934
Mighty Barnum, The 1934
Gold Diggers of 1935 1935
Broadway Gondolier 1935
Milky Way, The 1936
Sing, Baby, Sing 1936
Wives Never Know 1936
One in a Million 1937
Star Is Born, A 1937
Cafe Metropole 1937
100 Men and a Girl 1937
Stage Door 1937
Goldwyn Follies, The 1938
Letter of Introduction 1938,
Thanks For Everything 1938
King of the Turf 1939
Golden Boy 1939
That's Right, You're Wrong 1939
Housekeeper's Daughter, The 1939
Bill of Divorcement, A 1940
Turnabout 1940
Road Show 1941
Father takes a Wife 1941
Roxie Hart 1942
Syncopation 1942
You Were Never Lovelier 1942
Hi Diddle Diddle 1943
Sweet Rosie O'Grady 1943
Step Lively 1944
Man Alive 1945
Heartbeat 1946
Bachelor's Daughters, The 1946
I'll Be Yours 1947
Mr District Attorney 1947
Hucksters, The 1947
State of the Union 1948
My Dream Is Yours 1949
Dancing in the Dark 1949
To Please a Lady 1950
Tall Target, The 1951
Across the Wide Missouri 1951
Sniper, The 1952
Man on a Tightrope 1953
Timberjack 1955
Ambassador's Daughter, The 1956
Bundle of Joy 1956
Fuzzy Pink Nightgown, The 1957
Paths of Glory 1957
I Married a Woman 1958
Pollyanna 1960

Mineo, Sal
Six Bridges to Cross 1955
Private War of Major Benson, The 1955
Rebel without a Cause 1955
Crime in the Streets 1956
Somebody up There Likes Me 1956
Giant 1956
Dino 1957
Young Don't Cry, The 1957
Tonka 1959
Private's Affair, A 1959
Gene Krupa Story, The 1959
Exodus 1960
Escape from Zahrain 1962
Longest Day, The 1962
Cheyenne Autumn 1964
Greatest Story Ever Told, The 1965
Escape From the Planet of the Apes 1971

Miranda, Carmen
Down Argentine Way 1940
That Night in Rio 1941
Week-End in Havana 1941
Springtime in the Rockies 1942
Gang's All Here, The 1943
Four Jills in a Jeep 1944
Greenwich Village 1944
Something for the Boys 1944
Doll Face 1946
If I'm Lucky 1946
Copacabana 1947
Date with Judy, A 1948
Nancy Goes to Rio 1950
Scared Stiff 1953

Mitchell, Thomas
Craig's Wife 1936
Adventure in Manhattan 1936
Theodora Goes Wild 1936
When You're in Love 1937
Man of the People 1937
Lost Horizon 1937
I Promise to Pay 1937
Make Way for Tomorrow 1937
Hurricane, The 1937
Love, Honor and Behave 1938
Trade Winds 1939
Stagecoach 1939
Only Angels Have Wings 1939
Mr Smith Goes to Washington 1939
Gone With the Wind 1939
Hunchback of Notre Dame, The 1940
Swiss Family Robinson 1940
Three Cheers for the Irish 1940
Our Town 1940
Long Voyage Home, The 1940
Angels Over Broadway 1940
Flight From Destiny 1941
Out of the Fog 1941
Joan of Paris 1942
Song of the Islands 1942
Moontide 1942
This Above All 1942
Tales of Manhattan 1942
Black Swan, The 1942
Immortal Sergeant 1943
Bataan 1943
Flesh and Fantasy 1943
Sullivans, The 1944
Buffalo Bill 1944
Wilson 1944
Dark Waters 1944
Keys of the Kingdom, The 1944
Within These Walls 1945
Captain Eddie 1945
Adventure 1946
Three Wise Fools 1946
Dark Mirror, The 1946
It's a Wonderful Life 1946
High Barbaree 1947
Romance of Rosy Ridge, The 1947
Outlaw, The 1947
Silver River 1948
Alias Nick Beal 1949
Journey Into Light 1951
High Noon 1952
Secret of the Incas 1954
While the City Sleeps 1956
By Love Possessed 1961
Pocketful of Miracles 1961

Mix, Tom
Just Tony 1922
Deadwood Coach, The 1925
Dick Turpin 1925
Riders of the Purple Sage 1925
Rainbow Trail, The 1925
Lucky Horseshoe, The 1925
Everlasting Whisper, The 1925
Best Bad Man, The 1925
Yankee Senor, The 1926
My Own Pal 1926
Tony Runs Wild 1926
Last Trail, The 1927
Circus Ace, The 1927
Under a Texas Moon 1930
My Pal the King 1932
Terror Trail 1933

Monroe, Marilyn
Love Happy 1950
Asphalt Jungle, The 1950
All About Eve 1950
As Young as You Feel 1951
Let's Make It Legal 1951
Clash by Night 1952
We're not Married 1952
Don't Bother to Knock 1952
Monkey Business 1952
O Henry's Full House Cop and the Anthem, The 1952
Niagara 1953
Gentlemen Prefer Blondes 1953
How to Marry a Millionaire 1953
River of no Return 1954
There's no Business Like Show Business 1954
Seven Year Itch, The 1955
Bus Stop 1956
Prince and the Showgirl 1957
Some Like It Hot 1959
Let's Make Love 1960
Misfits, The 1961
Marilyn 1963

Moorehead, Agnes
Citizen Kane 1941
Magnificent Ambersons, The 1942
Big Street, The 1942
Journey Into Fear 1943
Youngest Profession, The 1943
Government Girl 1944
Jane Eyre 1944
Since You Went Away 1944
Dragon Seed 1944
Seventh Cross, The 1944
Mrs Parkington 1944
Tomorrow the World 1944
Keep Your Powder Dry 1945
Our Vines Have Tender Grapes 1945
Her Highness and the Bellboy 1945
Dark Passage 1947
Lost Moment, The 1947
Woman in White, The 1948

Summer Holiday 1948
Johnny Belinda 1948
Stratton Story, The 1949
Great Sinner, The 1949
Caged 1950
Without Honor 1950
Fourteen Hours 1951
Show Boat 1951
Adventures of Captain Fabian 1951
Captain Black Jack 1952
Story of Three Loves, Jealous Lover, The 1953
Scandal at Scourie 1953
Those Redheads From Seattle 1953
Main Street to Broadway 1953
Magnificent Obsession 1954
Untamed 1955,Mr 12,11:6
Left Hand of God, The 1955
All That Heaven Allows 1956
Meet Me in Las Vegas 1956
Conqueror, The 1956
Swan, The 1956
Revolt of Mamie Stover, The 1956
Pardners 1956
Opposite Sex, The 1956
True Story of Jesse James, The 1957
Jeanne Eagels 1957
Story of Mankind, The 1957
Raintree County 1957
Night of the Quarter Moon 1959
Tempest 1959
Bat, The 1959
Pollyanna 1960
Bachelor in Paradise 1961
Jessica 1962
How the West Was Won 1963
Who's Minding the Store? 1963
Hush...Hush, Sweet Charlotte 1965
Singing Nun, The 1966

Morris, Chester
Alibi 1929
Fast Life 1929
Woman Trap 1929
Show of Shows 1929
Second Choice 1930
She Couldn't Say No 1930
Case of Sergeant Grischa, The 1930
Playing Around 1930
Divorcee, The 1930
Big House, The 1930
Bat Whispers, The 1931
Corsair 1931
Cock of the Air 1932
Miracle Man, The 1932
Sinners in the Sun 1932
Red Headed Woman 1932
Blondie Johnson 1933
Infernal Machine 1933
Tomorrow at Seven 1933
King for a Night 1933
Let's Talk It Over 1934
Gay Bride, The 1934
Society Doctor 1935
Princess O'Hara 1935
Public Hero No 1 1935
Three Godfathers, The 1936
Moonlight Murder 1936
Frankie and Johnnie 1936
Counterfeit 1936
They Met in a Taxi 1936
Devil's Playground 1937
I Promise to Pay 1937
Flight From Glory 1937
Law of the Underworld 1938
Sky Giant 1938
Smashing the Rackets 1938
Pacific Liner 1939
Blind Alley 1939
Five came Back 1939
Thunder Afloat 1939
Wagons Westward 1940
Girl From God's Country 1940
Meet Boston Blackie 1941
Confessions of Boston Blackie 1941
No Hands on the Clock 1941
Canal Zone 1942
I Live on Danger 1942
Aerial Gunner 1943
Secret Command 1944
One Mysterious Night 1944
Rough, Tough and Ready 1945
Unchained 1955

Muni, Paul
Valiant, The 1929
Seven Faces 1929
Scarface, The Shame of the Nation 1932
I Am a Fugitive From a Chain Gang 1932
World Changes, The 1933
Hi, Nellie! 1934
Bordertown 1935
Black Fury 1935
Dr Socrates 1935
Story of Louis Pasteur, The 1936
Good Earth, The 1937
Woman I Love, The 1937
Life of Emile Zola, The 1937
Juarez 1939
We Are not Alone 1939
Hudson's Bay 1941
Stage Door Canteen 1943
Song to Remember, A 1945
Counter-Attack 1945
Angel on my Shoulder 1946
Stranger on the Prowl 1953
Commandos Strike at Dawn 1954
Last Angry Man, The 1959

Nagel, Conrad
Midsummer Madness 1920
Lost Romance, The 1921
Fool's Paradise 1921
Impossible Mrs Bellew, The 1922
Grumpy 1923
Bella Donna 1923
Lawful Larceny 1923
Name the Man 1924
Three Weeks 1924
Rejected Woman, The 1924
Tess of the D'Urbervilles 1924
Sinners in Silk 1924
Married Flirts 1924
Snob, The 1924
So This Is Marriage 1924
Excuse Me 1925
Cheaper to Marry 1925
Pretty Ladies 1925
Sun Up 1925
Lights of Old Broadway 1925
Only Thing, The 1925
Dance Madness 1926
Memory Lane 1926
Waning Sex, The 1926
Tin Hats 1926
Quality Street 1927
Girl From Chicago, The 1927
London After Midnight 1927
If I Were Single 1928
Tenderloin 1928
Glorious Betsy 1928
Michigan Kid, The 1928
Mysterious Lady, The 1928
State Street Sadie 1928
Caught in the Fog 1928
Redeeming Sin, The 1929
Idle Rich, The 1929
Kiss, The 1929,N 1
Sacred Flame, The 1929
Dynamite 1929
Second Wife 1930
Ship From Shanghai, The 1930
Redemption 1930
Divorcee, The 1930
One Romantic Night 1930
Numbered Men 1930
Lady Surrenders, A 1930
Du Barry, Woman of Passion 1930
Today 1930
Free Love 1930
East Lynne 1931
Right of Way, The 1931
Bad Sister 1931
Son of India 1931
Reckless Hour, The 1931
Pagan Lady 1931
Hell Divers 1931
Man Called Back, The 1932
Divorce in the Family 1932
Kongo 1932,N
Fast Life 1932
Ann Vickers 1933
Marines are Coming, The 1935
Wedding Present 1936
Navy Spy 1937
Gold Racket, The 1937
Mad Empress, The 1940
One Million BC 1940
I Want a Divorce 1940
Vicious Circle, The 1948
All That Heaven Allows 1956
Stranger in my Arms 1959
Man Who Understood, The 1959

Naish, J Carroll
Good Intentions 1930
Royal Bed, The 1931
Gun Smoke 1931
Homicide Squad 1931
Hatchet Man, The 1932
Beast of the City, The 1932
It's Tough to be Famous 1932
Mouthpiece, The 1932
Famous Ferguson Case, The 1932
Two Seconds 1932
Week-End Marriage 1932
Crooner 1932
Tiger Shark 1932
Kid From Spain, The 1932
Frisco Jenny 1933
No Other Woman 1933
Infernal Machine 1933
World Gone Mad, The 1933
Past of Mary Holmes, The 1933
Elmer the Great 1933
Arizona to Broadway 1933
Devil's in Love, The 1933
Captured 1933
Avenger, The 1933
Mad Game, The 1933
Murder in Trinidad 1934
Upper World 1934
Hell Cat, The 1934
Return of the Terror 1934
British Agent 1934
Hell in the Heavens 1934
Lives of a Bengal Lancer, The 1935
Black Fury 1935
Under the Pampas Moon 1935
Front Page Woman 1935
Special Agent 1935
Little Big Shot 1935
Captain Blood 1935
Exclusive Story 1936
Robin Hood of El Dorado, The 1936
Charlie Chan at the Circus 1936
Leathernecks Have Landed, The 1936
Moonlight Murder 1936
Special Investigator 1936
Absolute Quiet 1936
Anthony Adverse 1936
Ramona 1936
Charge of the Light Brigade, The 1936
We Who Are About to Die 1937
Crack-Up 1937
Border Cafe 1937
Think Fast, Mr Moto 1937
Bulldog Drummond Comes Back 1937
Hideaway 1937
Sea Racketeers 1937
Night Club Scandal 1937
Daughter of Shanghai 1937
Thunder Trail 1938
Tip-Off Girls 1938
Her Jungle Love 1938
Hunted Men 1938
Prison Farm 1938
Bulldog Drummond in Africa 1938
King of Alcatraz 1938
Illegal Traffic 1938
Persons in Hiding 1939
King of Chinatown 1939
Hotel Imperial 1939
Undercover Doctor 1939
Beau Geste 1939
Typhoon 1940
Queen of the Mob 1940
Golden Gloves 1940
Down Argentine Way 1940
Night at Earl Carroll's, A 1941
That Night in Rio 1941
Mr Dynamite 1941
Blood and Sand 1941
Birth of the Blues 1941
Corsican Brothers, The 1942
Gentleman at Heart, A 1942
Sunday Punch 1942
Dr Broadway 1942
Jackass Mail 1942
Pied Piper, The 1942
Tales of Manhattan 1942
Man in the Trunk, The 1942
Good Morning, Judge 1943

Behind the Rising Sun 1943
Sahara 1943
Gung Ho! 1944
Calling Dr Death 1944
Voice in the Wind 1944
Whistler, The 1944
Jungle Woman 1944
Dragon Seed 1944
Enter Arsene Lupin 1944
House of Frankenstein 1944
Medal for Benny, A 1945
Southerner, The 1945
Strange Confession 1945
Getting Gertie's Garter 1946
Bad Bascomb 1946
Beast With Five Fingers, The 1946
Humoresque 1946
Carnival in Costa Rica 1947
Fugitive, The 1947
Joan of Arc 1948
Kissing Bandit, The 1948
Canadian Pacific 1949
That Midnight Kiss 1949
Black Hand 1950
Annie Get Your Gun 1950
Please Believe Me 1950
Toast of New Orleans, The 1950
Rio Grande 1950
Mark of the Renegade 1951
Across the Wide Missouri 1951
Denver and Rio Grande, The 1952
Clash by Night 1952
Woman of the North Country 1952
Beneath the 12-Mile Reef 1953
Saskatchewan 1954
Sitting Bull 1954
New York Confidential 1955
Hit the Deck 1955
Violent Saturday 1955
Desert Sands 1955
This Could Be the Night 1957
Young Don't Cry, The 1957

Normand, Mabel

Venus Model, The 1918
Fatty and Mabel Adrift 1918
Back to the Woods 1918
Sis 1919
Sis Hopkins 1919
Upstairs 1919
Molly O 1921
Suzanna 1923
Extra Girl, The 1924
When Comedy Was King 1960
Days of Thrills and Laughter 1961

Novarro, Ramon

Prisoner of Zenda, The 1922
Trifling Women 1922
Where the Pavement Ends 1923
Scaramouche 1923
Thy Name Is Woman 1924
Arab, The 1924
Red Lily, The 1924
Midshipman, The 1925
Ben Hur 1925
Lovers 1927
Student Prince, The 1927
Road to Romance, The 1927
Across to Singapore 1928
Certain Young Man, A 1928
Forbidden Hours 1928
Flying Fleet, The 1929
Pagan, The 1929
Devil May Care 1929
In Gay Madrid 1930
Call of the Flesh 1930
Daybreak 1931
Son of India 1931
Ben Hur 1931
Mata Hari 1932
Huddle 1932
Son-Daughter, The 1933
Barbarian, The 1933
Cat and the Fiddle, The 1934
Night is Young, The 1935
We Were Strangers 1949
Big Steal, The 1949
Outriders, The 1950
Crisis 1950
Heller in Pink Tights 1960

Oland, Warner

Yellow Ticket, The 1918
Avalanche, The 1919
Witness for the Defense, The 1919
His Children's Children 1923
Fighting American, The 1924
So This Is Marriage 1924
Riders of the Purple Sage 1925
Don Q, Son of Zorro 1925
Flower of the Night 1925
Infatuation 1926
Don Juan 1926
Marriage Clause, The 1926
Tell It to the Marines 1926
Twinkletoes 1926
When a Man Loves 1927
Million Bid, A 1927
Old San Francisco 1927
Good Time Charley 1927
Stand and Deliver 1928
Wheels of Chance 1928
Scarlet Lady, The 1928
Dream of Love 1928
Chinatown Nights 1929
Studio Murder Mystery, The 1929
Insidious Dr Fu Manchu, The 1929
Mysterious Dr Fu Manchu, The 1929
Mighty, The 1929
Dangerous Paradise 1930
Vagabond King, The 1930
Vagabond King, The 1930
New Adventures of Dr Fu Manchu, The 1930
Dishonored 1931
Charlie Chan Carries On 1931
Black Camel, The 1931
Daughter of the Dragon 1931
Big Gamble, The 1931
Charlie Chan's Chance 1932
Shanghai Express 1932
Passport to Hell, A 1932
Son-Daughter, The 1933
Charlie Chan's Greatest Case 1933
Before Dawn 1933
As Husbands Go 1934
Mandalay 1934
Bulldog Drummond Strikes Back 1934
Charlie Chan's Courage 1934
Charlie Chan in London 1934
Painted Veil, The 1934
Werewolf of London, The 1935
Charlie Chan in Egypt 1935
Shanghai 1935
Charlie Chan in Shanghai 1935
Charlie Chan's Secret 1936
Charlie Chan at the Circus 1936
Charlie Chan at the Race Track 1936
Charlie Chan at the Opera 1936
Charlie Chan at the Olympics 1937
Charlie Chan on Broadway 1937
Charlie Chan at Monte Carlo 1937
Days of Thrills and Laughter 1961

Parks, Larry

Mystery Ship 1941
Harmon of Michigan 1941
Canal Zone 1942
Atlantic Convoy 1942
Flight Lieutenant 1942
Boogie Man Will Get You, The 1942
You Were Never Lovelier 1942
Reveille With Beverly 1943
Counter-Attack 1945
Renegades 1946
Jolson Story, The 1946
Down to Earth 1947,S
Swordsman, The 1947
Gallant Blade 1948
Jolson Sings Again 1949
Emergency Wedding 1950
Love Is Better Than Ever 1952
Freud 1962

Pitts, Zasu

Is Matrimony a Failure 1922
Poor Men's Wives 1923
West of the Water Tower 1923
Daughters of Today 1924
Triumph 1924
Goldfish, The 1924
Changing Husbands 1924
Wine of Youth 1924
Fast Set, The 1924
Greed 1924
Great Divide, The 1925
Pretty Ladies 1925
Woman's Faith, A 1925
Mannequinn 1926
What Happened to Jones 1926
Risky Business 1926
Her big Night 1926
Casey at the Bat 1927
Wife Savers 1928
Buck Privates 1928
13 Washington Square 1928
Wedding March, The 1928
Sins of the Fathers 1929
Dummy, The 1929
Squall, The 1929
Twin Beds 1929
Argyle Case, The 1929
Paris 1929
This Thing Called Love 1929
No, No, Nanette 1930
Locked Door, The 1930
Honey 1930
Devil's Holiday, The 1930
Little Accident 1930
Monte Carlo 1930
Squealer, The 1930
War Nurse 1930
Sin Takes a Holliday 1930
Lottery Bride, The 1930
Passion Flower 1930
Finn and Hattie 1931
River's End 1931
Bad Sister 1931
Beyond Victory 1931
Seed 1931
Woman of Experience, A 1931
Guardsman, The 1931
Big Gamble, The 1931
Penrod and Sam 1931
Secret Witness, The 1931
Man I Killed, The 1932
Shopworn 1932
Trial of Vivienne Ware, The 1932
Strangers of the Evening 1932
Westward Passage 1932
Is my Face red 1932
Make Me a Star 1932
Roar of the Dragon 1932
Back Street 1932
Blondie of the Follies 1932
Madison Square Garden 1932
Once in a Lifetime 1932
They Just Had to Get Married 1933
Out all Night 1933
Hello Sister! 1933
Professional Sweetheart 1933
Her First Mate 1933
Aggie Appleby, Maker of Men 1933
Meet the Baron 1933
Love, Honor and Oh, Baby! 1933
Mr Skitch 1933
Sing and Like It 1934
Private Scandal 1934
Dames 1934
Their big Moment 1934
Mrs Wiggs of the Cabbage Patch 1934
Gay Bride, The 1934
Ruggles of Red Gap 1935
13 Hours by Air 1936
Mad Holiday 1936
Plot Thickens, The 1936
Sing Me a Love Song 1936
Forty Naughty Girls 1937
52d Street 1937
Naughty but Nice 1939
Mickey, the Kid 1939
Nurse Edith Cavell 1939
Eternally Yours 1939
It all Came True 1940
No, No, Nanette 1940
Broadway Limited 1941
Week End for Three 1941
Mexican Spitfire at Sea 1942
Tish 1942
Let's Face It 1943
Breakfast in Hollywood 1946
Perfect Marriage, The 1947
Life With Father 1947
Francis 1950
Denver and Rio Grande, The 1952
Francis Joins the Wacs 1954
This Could Be the Night 1957
Teenage Millionaire 1962
Thrill of it All, The 1963

Powell, Dick

Street Scene 1931

Blessed Event 1932
Too Busy to Work 1932
King's Vacation, The 1933
42d Street 1933
Gold Diggers of 1933 1933
Footlight Parade 1933
College Coach 1933
Convention City 1933
Wonder Bar 1934
20 Million Sweethearts 1934
Dames 1934
Happiness Ahead 1934
Flirtation Walk 1934
Gold Diggers of 1935 1935
Wedding Night, The 1935
Broadway Gondolier 1935
Page Miss Glory 1935
Midsummer Night's Dream, A 1935
Shipmates Forever 1935
Thanks a Million 1935
If You Could Only Cook 1935
Colleen 1936
Hearts Divided 1936
Yours for the Asking 1936
Hollywood Boulevard 1936
Stage Struck 1936
Gold Diggers of 1937 1936
On the Avenue 1937
Another Dawn 1937
Singing Marine, The 1937
Varsity Show 1937
Hollywood Hotel 1938
Cowboy From Brooklyn 1938
Hard To Get 1938
Going Places 1939
Naughty but Nice 1939
I Want a Divorce 1940
Christmas in July 1940
Model Wife 1941
In the Navy 1941
Star Spangled Rhythm 1942
Happy Go Lucky 1943
True to Life 1943
Riding High 1943
It Happened Tomorrow 1944
Meet The People 1944
Murder, my Sweet 1945
Cornered 1945
Johnny O'Clock 1947
To the Ends of the Earth 1948
Pitfall 1948
Rogues' Regiment 1948
Mrs Mike 1950
Reformer and the Redhead, The 1950
Right Cross 1950
Cry Danger 1951
Tall Target, The 1951
Bad and the Beautiful, The 1953
Susan Slept Here 1954

Power, Tyrone
Black Panther's Cub, The 1921
Foot Falls 1921
Day of Faith, The 1923
Lone Wolf, The 1924
Janice Meredith 1924
Story Without a Name, The 1924
Where Was I 1925
Wanderer, The 1925
Regular Fellow, A 1925
Red Kimono, The 1926
Bride of the Storm 1926
Big Trail, The 1930
Tom Brown of Culver 1932
Girls' Dormitory 1936
Ladies in Love 1936
Lloyds of London 1936
Love Is News 1937
Cafe Metropole 1937
Thin Ice 1937
Second Honeymoon 1937
In Old Chicago 1938
Alexander's Ragtime Band 1938
Marie Antoinette 1938
Suez 1938
Jesse James 1939
Rose of Washington Square 1939
Second Fiddle 1939
Rains Came, The 1939
Daytime Wife 1939
Johnny Apollo 1940
Brigham Young - Frontiersman 1940
Mark of Zorro, The 1940
Blood and Sand 1941
Yank in the R A F, A 1941
Son of Fury 1942
This Above All 1942
Black Swan, The 1942
Crash Dive 1943
Razor's Edge, The 1946
Nightmare Alley 1947
Captain from Castile 1947
Luck of the Irish, The 1948
That Wonderful Urge 1948
Prince of Foxes 1949
Black Rose, The 1950
American Guerrilla in the Philippines 1950
Rawhide 1951
I'll Never Forget You 1951
Diplomatic Courier 1952
Pony Soldier 1952
Mississippi Gambler, The 1953
King of the Khyber Rifles 1953
Long Gray Line, The 1955
Untamed 1955
Eddy Duchin Story, The 1956
Abandon Ship 1957
Sun Also Rises, The 1957
Witness for the Prosecution 1958

Rains, Claude
Invisible Man, The 1933
Crime Without Passion 1934
Man Who Reclaimed his Head, The 1935
Mystery of Edwin Drood, The 1935
Clairvoyant, The 1935
Last Outpost, The 1935
Hearts Divided 1936
Anthony Adverse 1936
Stolen Holiday 1937
Prince and the Pauper, The 1937
They Won't Forget 1937
Gold Is Where You Find It 1938
Adventures of Robin Hood, The 1938
White Banners 1938
Four Daughters 1938
They Made Me a Criminal 1939
Juarez 1939
Daughters Courageous 1939
Mr Smith Goes to Washington 1939
Four Wives 1939
Saturday's Children 1940
Sea Hawk, The 1940
Lady With red Hair 1940
Four Mothers 1941
Here Comes Mr Jordan 1941
Wolf Man, The 1941
Kings Row 1942
Moontide 1942
Now, Voyager 1942
Casablanca 1942
Forever and a Day 1943
Phantom of the Opera, The 1943
Passage to Marseille 1944
Mr Skeffington 1944
Caesar and Cleopatra 1944
Strange Holiday 1945
This Love of Ours 1945
Notorious 1946
Caesar and Cleopatra 1946
Deception 1946
Angel on my Shoulder 1946
Unsuspected, The 1947
One Woman's Story 1949
Rope of Sand 1949
White Tower, The 1950
Where Danger Lives 1951
Sealed Cargo 1951
Paris Express, The 1953
Lisbon 1956
Earth Is Mine, The 1959
Lost World, The 1960
Lawrence of Arabia 1962
Twilight of Honor 1963
Greatest Story Ever Told, The 1965

Rathbone, Basil
Masked Bride, The 1925
Great Deception, The 1926
Last of Mrs Cheyney, The 1929
Bishop Murder Case, The 1930
Notorious Affair, A 1930
Lady of Scandal, The 1930
This Mad World 1930
Flirting Widow, The 1930
Lady Surrenders, A 1930
Sin Takes a Holliday 1930
Woman Commands, A 1932
After the Ball 1933
Loyalties 1934
David Copperfield 1935
Anna Karenina 1935
Last Days of Pompeii, The 1935
Feather in her Hat, A 1935
Tale of Two Cities, A 1935
Captain Blood 1935
Private Number 1936
Romeo and Juliet 1936
Garden of Allah, The 1936
Love From a Stranger 1937
Confession 1937
Make a Wish 1937
Tovarich 1937
Adventures of Robin Hood, The 1938
If I Were King 1938
Dawn Patrol 1938
Son of Frankenstein 1939
Hound of the Baskervilles, The 1939
Sun Never Sets, The 1939
Adventures of Sherlock Holmes, The 1939
Rio 1939
Tower of London 1939
Rhythm on the River 1940
Mark of Zorro, The 1940
Mad Doctor, The 1941
Black Cat, The 1941
International Lady 1941
Paris Calling 1942
Fingers at the Window 1942
Crossroads 1942
Sherlock Holmes and the Voice Of Terror 1942
Sherlock Holmes and the Secret Weapon 1943
Above Suspicion 1943
Sherlock Holmes Faces Death 1943
Spider Woman 1944
Scarlet Claw, The 1944
Bathing Beauty 1944
Pearl of Death 1944
Frenchman's Creek 1944
House of Fear, The 1945
Woman in Green, The 1945
Pursuit to Algiers 1945
Terror by Night 1946
Heartbeat 1946
Dressed to Kill 1946
Casanova's Big Night 1954
We're no Angels 1955
Court Jester, The 1956
Last Hurrah, The 1958
Tales of Terror 1962
Two Before Zero 1962
Comedy of Terrors, The 1964
Adventures of Marco Polo, The 1965

Rennie, Michael
Ships With Wings 1942
Tower of Terror 1942
Wicked Lady, The 1946
Golden Madonna, The 1949
Sanitorium 1950
Thirteenth Letter, The 1951
Day the Earth Stood Still, The 1951
I'll Never Forget You 1951
Phone Call From a Stranger 1952
Five Fingers 1952
Miserables, Les 1952
Sailor of the King 1953
Robe, The 1953
Dangerous Crossing 1953
King of the Khyber Rifles 1953
Princess of the Nile 1954
Demetrius and the Gladiators 1954
Desiree 1954
Mambo 1955
Soldier of Fortune 1955
Seven Cities of Gold 1955
Rains of Ranchipur, The 1955
Teenage Rebel 1956
Island in the Sun 1957
Omar Khayyam 1957
Third Man on the Mountain 1959
Lost World, The 1960
Mary, Mary 1963
Ride Beyond Vengance 1966
Hotel 1967
Power, The 1968
Devil's Brigade, The 1968
Young, The Evil and the Savage, The 1968

Ritter, Thelma
Miracle on 34th Street 1947
Letter to Three Wives, A 1949
City Across the River 1949
Father Was a Fullback 1949
Perfect Strangers 1950
All About Eve 1950
I'll Get by 1950
Mating Season, The 1951
As Young as You Feel 1951
Model and the Marriage Broker, The 1952
With a Song in my Heart 1952
Titanic 1953
Farmer Takes a Wife, The 1953
Pickup on South Street 1953
Rear Window 1954
Daddy Long Legs 1955
Lucy Gallant 1955,O 2
Proud and Profane, The 1956
Hole in the Head, A 1959
Pillow Talk 1959
Misfits, The 1961
Second Time Around, The 1961
Birdman of Alcatraz 1962
How the West Was Won 1963
For Love or Money 1963
New Kind of Love, A 1963
Move Over Darling 1963
Boeing Boeing 1965
Incident, The 1967

Robinson, Bill
Dixiana 1930
Little Colonel, The 1935
Hooray for Love 1935
Old Kentucky, In 1935
Littlest Rebel, The 1935
One Mile From Heaven 1937
Rebecca of Sunnybrook Farm 1938
Just Around the Corner 1938
Up the River 1938
Stormy Weather 1943

Robinson, Edward G
Bright Shawl, The 1923
Hole in the Wall, The 1929
Night Ride 1930
Lady to Love, A 1930
Outside the Law 1930
East Is West 1930
Widow From Chicago, The 1930
Little Casear 1931
Smart Money 1931
Five Star Final 1931
Hatchet Man, The 1932
Two Seconds 1932
Tiger Shark 1932
Silver Dollar 1932
Little Giant, The 1933
I Loved a Woman 1933
Dark Hazard 1934
Man With two Faces, The 1934
Whole Town's Talking, The 1935
Barbary Coast 1935
Bullets or Ballots 1936
Thunder in the City 1937
Kid Galahad 1937
Last Gangster, The 1937
Slight Case of Murder, A 1938
Amazing Dr Clitterhouse, The 1938
I Am the Law 1938
Confessions of a Nazi Spy 1939
Blackmail 1939
Dr Ehrlich's Magic Bullet 1940
Brother Orchid 1940
Dispatch From Reuters, A 1940
Sea Wolf, The 1941
Manpower 1941
Unholy Partners 1941
Larceny, Inc 1942
Tales of Manhattan 1942
Destroyer 1943
Flesh and Fantasy 1943
Tampico 1944
Mr Winkle Goes to War 1944
Double Indemnity 1944
Woman in the Window, The 1945
Our Vines Have Tender Grapes 1945
Scarlet Street 1946
Journey Together 1946
Stranger, The 1946
Red House, The 1947
All my Sons 1948
Key Largo 1948
Night Has a Thousand Eyes 1948
House of Strangers 1949
Operation X 1950
Actors and Sin; (Actor's Blood) 1952
Vice Squad 1953
Glass Web, The 1953
Black Tuesday 1955
Violent Men, The 1955
Tight Spot 1955
Bullet for Joey, A 1955
Illegal 1955
Hell on Frisco Bay 1956
Nightmare 1956
Ten Commandments, The 1956
Some Like It Hot 1959
Hole in the Head, A 1959
Seven Thieves 1960
Pepe 1960
My Geisha 1962
Two Weeks in Another Town 1962
Prize, The 1964
Good Neighbor Sam 1964
Robin and the 7 Hoods 1964
Outrage, The 1964
Cheyenne Autumn 1964
Boy Ten Feet Tall, A 1965
Cincinnati Kid, The 1965
Biggest Bundle of Them All, The 1968
Grand Slam 1968
Never a Dull Moment 1968
Soylent Green 1973

Rogers, Will
Laughing Bill Hyde 1918
Almost a Husband 1919
Jubilo 1919
Jes' Call Me Jim 1920
Cupid, the Cowpuncher 1920
Honest Hutch 1920
Guile of Women 1921
Boys Will Be Boys 1921
this edition; use 1921
Doubling for Romeo 1921
One Glorious Day 1922
Headless Horseman, The 1922
Fruits of Faith 1923
Texas Steer, A 1928
They Had to See Paris 1929
Happy Days 1930
So This Is London 1930
Lightnin' 1930
Connecticut Yankee, A 1931
Young as You Feel 1931
Ambassador Bill 1931
Business and Pleasure 1932
Down to Earth 1932
Too Busy to Work 1932
State Fair 1933
Doctor Bull 1933
Mr Skitch 1933
David Harum 1934
Handy Andy 1934
Judge Priest 1934
County Chairman, The 1935
Life Begins at 40 1935
Doubting Thomas 1935
Steamboat Around the Bend 1935
Old Kentucky, In 1935
Connecticut Yankee at the Court of King Arthur, A 1936

Ruggles, Charles
Peer Gynt 1915
Heart Raider, The 1923
Gentlemen of the Press 1929
Lady Lies, The 1929
Roadhouse Nights 1930
Roadhouse Nights 1930
Young Man of Manhattan 1930
Queen High 1930
Her Wedding Night 1930
Charley's Aunt 1930
Honor Among Lovers 1931
Smiling Lieutenant, The 1931
Girl Habit, The 1931
Beloved Bachelor, The 1931
Husband's Holiday 1931
This Reckless Age 1932
One Hour with You 1932
ThIs is the Night 1932
Love Me Tonight 1932
70,000 Witnesses 1932
Night of June 13th, The 1932
Trouble in Paradise 1932
Evenings for Sale 1932
If I Had a Million 1932
Madame Butterfly 1932
Murders in the Zoo 1933
Melody Cruise 1933
Mama Loves Papa 1933
Girl Without a Room 1933
Alice in Wonderland 1933
Six of a Kind 1934
Melody in Spring 1934
Friends of Mr Sweeney 1934
Pursuit of Happiness, The 1934
Ruggles of Red Gap 1935
People Will Talk 1935
No More Ladies 1935
Anything Goes 1936
Hearts Divided 1936
Early to Bed 1936
Wives Never Know 1936
Turn off the Moon 1937
Exclusive 1937
Bringing Up Baby 1938
Breaking the Ice 1938
Service de Luxe 1938
Invitation to Happiness 1939
Balalaika 1939
Farmer's Daughter, The 1940
Maryland 1940
No Time for Comedy 1940
Public Deb No 1 1940
Invisible Woman, The 1941
Honeymoon for Three 1941
Model Wife 1941
Parson of Panamint, The 1941
Go West, Young Lady 1941
Friendly Enemies 1942
Dixie Dugan 1943
Doughgirls, The 1944
Our Hearts Were Young and Gay 1944
3 Is a Family 1944
Bedside Manner 1945
Incendiary Blonde 1945
Stolen Life, A 1946
Gallant Journey 1946
Perfect Marriage, The 1947
It Happened on Fifth Avenue 1947
My Brother Talks to Horses 1947
Ramrod 1947
Give my Regards to Broadway 1948
Look for the Silver Lining 1949
All in a Nights Work 1961
Pleasure of his Company, The 1961
Parent Trap, The 1961
Son of Flubber 1963
Papa's Delicate Condition 1963
I'd Rather Be Rich 1964
Ugly Dachshund, The 1966
Follow Me, Boys! 1966

Russell, Rosalind
Evelyn Prentice 1934
President Vanishes, The 1934
Forsaking all Others 1934
Night is Young, The 1935
West Point of the Air 1935
Casino Murder Case, The 1935
Reckless 1935
China Seas 1935
Rendezvous 1935
It Had to Happen 1936
Under Two Flags 1936
Trouble for Two 1936
Craig's Wife 1936
Night Must Fall 1937
Live, Love and Learn 1937
Man-Proof 1938
Four's a Crowd 1938
Citadel, The 1938
Fast and Loose 1939
Women, The 1939
His Girl Friday 1940
No Time for Comedy 1940
Hired Wife 1940
This Thing Called Love 1941
They Met in Bombay 1941
Feminine Touch, The 1941
Design for Scandal 1942
Take a Letter Darling 1942
My Sister Eileen 1942
Flight for Freedom 1943
What a Woman 1943
Roughly Speaking 1945
She Wouldn't Say Yes 1946
Sister Kenny 1946
Guilt of Janet Ames, The 1947
Mourning Becomes Electra 1947

Velvet Touch, The 1948
Woman of Distinction, A 1950
Never Wave at a Wac 1953
Picnic 1956
Auntie Mame 1958
Majority of One, A 1962
Five Finger Exercise 1962
Gypsy 1962
Trouble With Angels, The 1966
Oh Dad, Poor Dad, Mamma's Hung You in the Closet and I'm Feeling so Sad 1967
Rosie 1968
Where Angels Go-Trouble Follows 1968
Mrs. Polifax – Spy 1971

Rutherford, Margaret
Yellow Canary, The 1944
Blithe Spirit 1945
Adventure for Two 1945
Meet Me at Dawn 1948
Miranda 1949
Her Man Gilbey 1949
Passport to Pimlico 1949
While the Sun Shines 1950
Happiest Days of Your Life, The 1950
Importance of Being Earnest, The 1952
Castle in the Air 1953
Curtain Up 1953
Miss Robin Hood 1953
Runaway Bus, The 1954
Innocents in Paris 1955
Trouble in Store 1956
Alligator Named Daisy, An 1957
Smallest Show on Earth, The 1957
I'm All Right Jack 1960
On the Double 1961
Murder She Said 1962
Mouse on the Moon, The 1963
Murder at the Gallop 1963
V I P's, The 1963
Murder Ahoy 1964
Murder Most Foul 1965
Countess from Hong Kong, A 1967
Falstaff; Chimes at Midnight 1967

Ryan, Robert
College Widow, The 1927
Strong Boy 1929
Golden Gloves 1940
Bombardier 1943,Jl
Sky's the Limit, The 1943
Behind the Rising Sun 1943
Iron Major, The 1943
Tender Comrade 1944
Marine Raiders 1944
Walls Came Tumbling Down, The 1946
Trail Street 1947
Woman on the Beach, The 1947
Crossfire 1947
Berlin Express 1948
Return of the Badmen 1948
Boy With Green Hair, The 1949
Act of Violence 1949
Caught 1949
Set-Up, The 1949
Woman on Pier 13, The 1950
Secret Fury, The 1950
Born to be Bad 1950
Best of the Badmen 1951
Flying Leathernecks 1951
Racket, The 1951
On Dangerous Ground 1952
Clash by Night 1952
Beware my Lovely 1952
Horizons West 1952
City Beneath the Sea 1953
Naked Spur, The 1953
Inferno 1953
Alaska Seas 1954
About Mrs Leslie 1954
Her Twelve Men 1954
Bad Day at Black Rock 1955
Escape to Burma 1955
House of Bamboo 1955
Tall Men, The 1955
Proud Ones, The 1956
Back From Eternity 1956
Men in War 1957
God's Little Acre 1958
Lonelyhearts 1959
Odds Against Tomorrow 1959
Ice Palace 1960
Canadians, The 1961
King of Kings 1961
Longest Day, The 1962
Billy Budd 1962
Crooked Road, The 1965
Battle of the Bulge 1965
Professionals, The 1966
Busy Body, The 1967
Dirty Dozen, The 1967
Hour of the Gun 1967
Minute to Pray, A Second to Die, A 1968
Custer of the West 1968
Anzio 1968
Lawman 1971
Love Machine, The 1971
. . . And Hope to Die 1972
Lolly-Madonna xxx 1973
Iceman Cometh, The 1973
Executive Action, 1973
Outfit, The 1974

Sanders, George
Lloyds of London 1936
Love Is News 1937
Slave Ship 1937
Lancer Spy 1937
International Settlement 1938
Four Men and a Prayer 1938
Mr Moto's Last Warning 1939
Saint Strikes Back, The 1939
Confessions of a Nazi Spy 1939
Saint in London, The 1939
Nurse Edith Cavell 1939
Allegheny Uprising 1939
Green Hell 1940
Saint's Double Trouble, The 1940
Outsider, The 1940
Rebecca 1940
House of the Seven Gables, The 1940
Saint Takes Over, The 1940
Foreign Correspondent 1940
Bitter Sweet 1940
Son of Monte Cristo, The 1940
Saint in Palm Springs, The 1941
Rage in Heaven 1941
Man Hunt 1941
Date With the Falcon, A 1941
Son of Fury 1942
Falcon takes Over, The 1942
Her Cardboard Lover 1942
Tales of Manhattan 1942
Falcon's Brother, The 1942
Moon and Sixpence, The 1942
Quiet Please, Murder 1942.
Black Swan, The 1942
They Came to Blow up America 1943
This Land Is Mine 1943
Appointment in Berlin 1943
Paris After Dark 1943
Lodger, The 1944
Action in Arabia 1944
Summer Storm 1944
Hangover Square 1945
Picture of Dorian Gray, The 1945
Uncle Harry 1945
Scandal In Paris, A 1946
Strange Woman, The 1947
Private Affairs of Bel Ami, The 1947
Ghost and Mrs Muir, The 1947
Lured 1947
Forever Amber 1947
Fan, The 1949
Samson and Delilah 1949
All About Eve 1950
I Can Get It for You Wholesale 1951
Light Touch, The 1952
Ivanhoe 1952
Captain Black Jack 1952
Assignment-Paris 1952
Call Me Madam 1953
Witness to Murder 1954
King Richard and the Crusaders 1954
Jupiter's Darling 1955
Moonfleet 1955
Scarlet Coat, The 1955
King's Thief, The 1955
Never Say Goodbye 1956
While the City Sleeps 1956
That Certain Felling 1956
Death of a Scoundrel 1956
Seventh Sin, The 1957
From the Earth to the Moon 1958
That Kind of Woman 1959
Solomon and Sheba 1959
Last Voyage, The 1960
Touch of Larceny, A 1960
Bluebeard's Ten Honeymoons 1960
Village of the Damned 1960
Trouble in the Sky 1961
Call Me Genius 1961
Five Golden Hours 1961
Operation Snatch 1962
In Search of the Castaways 1962
Dark Purpose 1964
Shot in the Dark, A 1964
Amorous Adventures of Moll Flanders, The 1965
Quiller Memorandum, The 1966
Trunk to Cairo 1966
Warning Shot 1967
Good Times 1967

Schildkraut, Joseph
Song of Love, The 1924
Road to Yesterday, The 1925
Young April 1926
King of Kings, The 1927
Heart Thief, The 1927
His Dog 1927
Forbidden Woman, The 1927
Blue Danube, The 1928
Tenth Avenue 1928
Show Boat 1929
Mississippi Gambler, The 1929
Night Ride 1930
Cock O' the Walk 1930
Carnival 1931
Viva Villa! 1934
Sisters Under the Skin 1934
Cleopatra 1934
Blue Danube 1934
Crusades, The 1935
Garden of Allah, The 1936
Slave Ship 1937
Souls at Sea 1937
Life of Emile Zola, The 1937
Lancer Spy 1937
Lady Behave 1938
Baroness and the Butler, The 1938
Marie Antoinette 1938
Suez 1938
Idiot's Delight 1939
Three Musketeers, The 1939
Mr Moto Takes a Vacation 1939
Man in the Iron Mask, The 1939
Lady of the Tropics 1939
Rains Came, The 1939
Pack up Your Troubles 1939
Shop Around the Corner, The 1940
Phantom Raiders 1940
Rangers of Fortune 1940
Meet the Wildcat 1940
Parson of Panamint, The 1941
Flame of Barbary Coast 1945
Cheaters, The 1945
Monsieur Beaucaire 1946
Plainsman and the Lady, The 1946
Northwest Outpost 1947
Old Los Angeles 1948
Diary of Anne Frank, The 1959
King of the Roaring Twenties 1961
Greatest Story Ever Told, The 1965

Selznick, David O (Producer)
David Copperfield 1935
Vanessa: Her Love Story 1935
Reckless 1935
Anna Karenina 1935
Tale of Two Cities, A 1935
Little Lord Fauntleroy 1936
Star Is Born, A 1937
Prisoner of Zenda, The 1937
Nothing Sacred 1937
Adventures of Tom Sawyer, The 1938
Young in Heart, The 1938
Made for Each Other 1939
Gone With the Wind 1939
Since You Went Away 1944
Spellbound 1945
Duel in the Sun 1947
Paradine Case, The 1948
Portrait of Jennie 1949
Farewell to Arms, A 1958

Sennett, Mack
- Hollywood Cavalcade 1939
- Days of Thrills and Laughter 1961

Sennett, Mack (Director)
- Good-Bye Kiss, The 1928
- Hypnotized 1933

Sennett, Mack (Original Author)
- Suzanna 1923
- Hypnotized 1933

Sennett, Mack (Producer)
- No Mother to Guide Him 1919
- Submarine Pirate, The 1919
- Uncle Tom Without the Cabin 1919
- Down on the Farm 1920
- Molly O 1921
- Crossroads of New York, The 1922

Sheridan, Ann
- Wedding Bills 1927
- Behold My Wife 1935
- Car 99 1935
- Fighting Youth 1935
- Sing Me a Love Song 1936
- Black Legion 1937
- Great O'Malley, The 1937
- San Quentin 1937
- Footloose Heiress 1937
- Alcatraz Island 1937
- She Loved a Fireman 1938
- Patient in Room 18, The 1938
- Mystery House 1938
- Cowboy From Brooklyn 1938
- Letter of Introduction 1938
- Broadway Musketeers 1938
- Angels With Dirty Faces 1938
- They Made Me a Criminal 1939
- Dodge City 1939
- Naughty but Nice 1939
- Indianapolis Speedway 1939
- Winter Carnival 1939
- Angels Wash Their Faces 1939
- Castle on the Hudson 1940
- It all Came True 1940
- Torrid Zone 1940
- They Drive by Night 1940
- City for Conquest 1940
- Honeymoon for Three 1941
- Navy Blues 1941
- Man Who Came to Dinner, The 1942
- Kings Row 1942
- Juke Girl 1942
- Wings for the Eagle 1942
- George Washington Slept Here 1942
- Edge of Darkness 1943
- Thank Your Lucky Stars 1943
- Shine on Harvest Moon 1944
- Doughgirls, The 1944
- One More Tomorrow 1946
- Nora Prentiss 1947
- Unfaithful, The 1947
- Silver River 1948
- Good Sam 1948
- I Was a Male War Bride 1949
- Stella 1950
- Woman on the Run 1950
- Steel Town 1952
- Just Across the Street 1952
- Take Me to Town 1953
- Appointment in Honduras 1953
- Opposite Sex, The 1956

Sullavan, Margaret
- Only Yesterday 1933
- Little Man, What Now? 1934
- Good Fairy, The 1935
- So Red the Rose 1935
- Next Time We Love 1936
- Moon's our Home, The 1936
- Three Comrades 1938
- Shopworn Angel, The 1938
- Shining Hour, The 1939
- Shop Around the Corner, The 1940
- Mortal Storm, The 1940
- Back Street 1941
- So Ends our Night 1941
- Appointment for Love 1941
- Cry Havoc 1943
- No Sad Songs for Me 1950

Talmadge, Constance
- Veiled Adventure, The 1919
- Fall of Babylon, The 1919
- Temperamental Wife, A 1919
- Virtuous Vamp, A 1919
- Two Weeks 1920
- In Search of a Sinner 1920
- Mamma's Affair 1921
- Wedding Bells 1921
- Woman's Place 1921
- Primitive Lover, The 1922
- Dulcy 1923
- Dangerous Maid, The 1923
- Goldfish, The 1924
- Her Night of Romance 1925
- Learning to Love 1925
- Duchess of Buffalo, The 1926
- Venus of Venice 1927
- Breakfast at Sunrise 1927
- Venus 1929

Talmadge, Norma
- Battle Cry for Peace, The 1915
- Panthea 1917
- De Luxe Annie 1918
- Her own Way 1918
- Forbidden City, The 1918
- Heart of the Wetona, The 1919
- New Moon, The 1919
- Way of a Woman, The 1919
- Isle of Conquest, The 1919
- Woman Gives, The 1920
- Yes or No 1920
- Branded Woman, The 1920
- Passion Flower, The 1921
- Sign on the Door, The 1921
- Love's Redemption 1922
- Foolish Wives 1922
- Smilin' Through 1922
- Eternal Flame, The 1922
- Voice From the Minaret, The 1923
- Within the Law 1923
- Ashes of Vengeance 1923
- Song of Love, The 1924
- Secrets 1924
- Only Woman, The 1924
- Lady, The 1925
- Graustark 1925
- Kiki 1926
- Camille 1927
- Dove, The 1928
- Woman Disputed, The 1928
- New York Nights 1930
- Du Barry, Woman of Passion 1930

Tamiroff, Akim
- Sadie McKee 1934
- Great Flirtation, The 1934
- Whom the Gods Destroy 1934
- Chained 1934
- Here is my Heart 1934
- Lives of a Bengal Lancer, The 1935
- Winning Ticket, The 1935
- Naughty Marietta 1935
- Black Fury 1935
- Go Into Your Dance 1935
- China Seas 1935
- Big Broadcast of 1936, The 1935
- Gay Deception, The 1935
- Story of Louis Pasteur, The 1936
- Woman Trap 1936
- Desire 1936
- Anthony Adverse 1936
- General Died at Dawn, The 1936
- Jungle Princess 1936
- Her Husband Lies 1937
- Soldier and the Lady, The 1937
- King of Gamblers 1937
- Great Gambini, The 1937
- High, Wide and Handsome 1937
- This Way Please 1937
- Buccaneer, The 1938
- Dangerous to Know 1938
- Spawn of the North 1938
- Ride a Crooked Mile 1938
- Paris Honeymoon 1939
- King of Chinatown 1939
- Union Pacific 1939
- Magnificent Fraud, The 1939
- Honeymoon in Bali 1939
- Disputed Passage 1939
- Way of all Flesh, The 1940
- Untamed 1940
- Great McGinty, The 1940
- North West Mounted Police 1940
- Texas Rangers Ride Again 1941
- New York Town 1941
- Corsican Brothers, The 1942
- Tortilla Flat 1942
- Five Graves to Cairo 1943
- For Whom the Bell Tolls 1943
- His Butler's Sister 1943
- Miracle of Morgan's Creek, The 1944
- Bridge of San Luis Rey, The 1944
- Dragon Seed 1944
- Can't Help Singing 1944
- Pardon my Past 1946
- Scandal In Paris, A 1946
- Fiesta 1947
- Gangster, The 1947
- My Girl Tisa 1948
- Relentless 1948
- Outpost in Morocco 1949
- Black Magic 1949
- Desert Legion 1953
- Anastasia 1956
- Battle Hell 1957
- Touch of Evil 1958
- Me and the Colonel 1958
- Ocean's Eleven 1960
- Romanoff and Juliet 1961
- Mr Arkadin 1962
- Reluctant Saint, The 1962
- Trial, The 1963
- Topkapi 1964
- Lord Jim 1965
- Bambole; Dolls, The (Monsignor Cupid); 1965
- Alphaville 1965
- Lt Robin Crusoe, USN 1966
- Hotel Paradiso 1966
- Liquidator, The 1966
- After the Fox 1966
- Vulture, The 1967
- Rose for Everyone, A 1967

Taylor, Robert
- Handy Andy 1934
- There's Always Tomorrow 1934
- Wicked Woman, A 1935
- Society Doctor 1935
- Times Square Lady 1935
- West Point of the Air 1935
- Murder in the Fleet 1935
- Broadway Melody of 1936 1935
- Magnificent Obsession 1935
- Small Town Girl 1936
- Private Number 1936
- His Brother's Wife 1936
- Gorgeous Hussy, The 1936
- Camille 1937
- Personal Property 1937
- This Is my Affair 1937
- Broadway Melody of 1938 1937
- Yank at Oxford, A 1938
- Three Comrades 1938
- Crowd Roars, The 1938
- Stand up and Fight 1939
- Lucky Night 1939
- Lady of the Tropics 1939
- Remember? 1939
- Waterloo Bridge 1940
- Escape 1940
- Flight Command 1941
- Billy the Kid 1941
- When Ladies Meet 1941
- Johnny Eager 1942
- Her Cardboard Lover 1942
- Stand by for Action 1943
- Bataan 1943
- Youngest Profession, The 1943
- Song of Russia 1944
- Undercurrent 1946
- High Wall 1947
- Bribe, The 1949
- Ambush 1950
- Conspirator 1950
- Devil's Doorway 1950
- Quo Vadis 1951
- Westward the Women 1952
- Ivanhoe 1952
- Above and Beyond 1953
- I Love Melvin 1953
- Ride Vaquero 1953
- All the Brothers Were Valiant 1953
- Knights of the Round Table 1954
- Valley of the Kings 1954
- Rogue Cop 1954
- Many Rivers to Cross 1955
- Quentin Durward 1955
- Last Hunt, The 1956
- D-Day, The Sixth of June 1956

Power and The Prize, the 1956
Tip on a Dead Jockey 1957
Saddle the Wind 1958
Law and Jake Wade, the 1958
Party Girl 1958
House of the Seven Hawks, The 1959
Killers of Kilimanjaro 1960
Miracle of the White Stallions 1963
House is not a Home, A 1964
Night Walker, The 1965
Johnny Tiger 1966
Where Angels Go-Trouble Follows 1968

Tone, Franchot
Wiser Sex, The 1932
Gabriel Over the White House 1933
Today We Live 1933
Midnight Mary 1933
Stranger's Return, The 1933
Stage Mother 1933
Bombshell 1933
Dancing Lady 1933
Moulin Rouge 1934
Sadie McKee 1934
World Moves On, The 1934
Girl From Missouri, The 1934
Straight Is the Way 1934
Gentlemen are Born 1934
Lives of a Bengal Lancer, The 1935
Reckless 1935
No More Ladies 1935
Mutiny on the Bounty 1935
Dangerous 1935
Exclusive Story 1936
Unguarded Hour, The 1936
King Steps Out, The 1936
Suzy 1936
Gorgeous Hussy, The 1936
Love on the Run 1936
Quality Street 1937
They Gave Him a Gun 1937
Between Two Women 1937
Bride Wore Red, The 1937
Man-Proof 1938
Love Is a Headache 1938
Three Comrades 1938
Three Loves Has Nancy 1938
Girl Downstairs, The 1939
Fast And Furious 1939
Trail of the Vigilantes 1940
Nice Girl 1941
She Knew All the Answers 1941
This Woman Is Mine 1941
Wife Takes a Flyer, The 1942
Star Spangled Rhythm 1942
Five Graves to Cairo 1943
Pilot No 5 1943
True to Life 1943
His Butler's Sister 1943
Phantom Lady 1944
Hour Before the Dawn, The 1944
Dark Waters 1944
That Night With You 1945
Because of Him 1946
Honeymoon 1947
Lost Honeymoon 1947
Her Husband's Affairs 1947
Every Girl Should be Married 1948
Jigsaw 1949
Man on the Eiffel Tower, The 1950
Without Honor 1950
Here Comes the Groom 1951
Uncle Vanya 1958
Advise and Consent 1962
Bonne Soupe, La 1964
In Harm's Way 1965
Mickey One 1965
High Commissioner, The 1968

Tracy, Lee
Big Time 1929
Born Reckless 1930
Liliom 1930
She Got What She Wanted 1930
Strange Love of Molly Louvain, The 1932
Love Is a Racket 1932
Doctor X 1932
Blessed Event 1932
Washington Merry-Go-Round 1932
Night Mayor, The 1932
Half-Naked Truth, The 1932
Clear all Wires 1933
Private Jones 1933
Nuisance, The 1933
Dinner at Eight 1933
Turn Back the Clock 1933
Bombshell 1933
Advice to the Lovelorn 1933
I'll Tell the World 1934
You Belong to Me 1934
Lemon Drop Kid, The 1934
Carnival 1935
Two Fisted 1935
Sutter's Gold 1936
Wanted: Jane Turner 1936
Criminal Lawyer 1937
Behind the Headlines 1937
Crashing Hollywood 1938
Fixer Dugan 1939
Spellbinder, The 1939
Millionaires in Prison 1940
Betrayal From the East 1945
High Tide 1947
Best Man, The 1964

Tracy, Spencer
Up the River 1930
Quick Millions 1931
Six Cylinder Love 1931
Goldie 1931
She Wanted a Millionaire 1932
Sky Devils 1932
Disorderly Conduct 1932
Young America 1932
Society Girl 1932
Painted Woman, The 1932
Me and my Gal 1932
20,000 Years in Sing Sing 1933
Face in the Sky 1933
Power and the Glory, The 1933
Shanghai Madness 1933
Mad Game, The 1933
Man's Castle 1933
Show-Off, The 1934
Bottoms Up 1934
Looking for Trouble 1934
Now I'll Tell 1934
Marie Galante 1934
Murder Man, The 1935
Dante's Inferno 1935
Riffraff 1936
Whipsaw 1936
Fury 1936
San Francisco 1936
Libeled Lady 1936
Captains Courageous 1937
They Gave Him a Gun 1937
Big City 1937
Mannequin 1938
Test Pilot 1938
Boys Town 1938
Stanley and Livingstone 1939
I Take This Woman 1940
Northwest Passage 1940
Edison the Man 1940
Boom Town 1940
Men of Boys Town 1941
Dr Jekyll and Mr Hyde 1941
Woman of the Year 1942
Tortilla Flat 1942
Keeper of the Flame 1943
Guy Named Joe, A 1943
Seventh Cross, The 1944
Thirty Seconds Over Tokyo 1944
Without Love 1945
Sea of Grass, The 1947
Cass Timberlane 1947
State of the Union 1948
Edward my Son 1949
Adam's Rib 1949
Malaya 1950
Father of the Bride 1950
Father's Little Dividend 1951
People Against O'Hara, The 1951
Pat and Mike 1952
Plymouth Adventure 1952
Actress, The 1953
Broken Lance 1954
Bad Day at Black Rock 1955
Mountain, The 1956
Desk Set 1957
Old Man and the Sea, The 1958
Last Hurrah, The 1958
Inherit the Wind 1960
Devil at 4 O'Clock, The 1961
Judgment at Nuremberg 1961
It's a Mad, Mad, Mad, Mad World 1963
Guess Who's Coming to Dinner 1967

Valentino, Rudolph
Four Horsemen of the Apocalypse 1921
Conquering Power, The 1921
Sheik, The 1921
Moran of the Lady Letty 1922
Beyond the Rocks 1922
Blood and Sand 1922
Young Rajah, The 1922
Monsieur Beaucaire 1924
Sainted Devil, A 1924
Eagle, The 1925
Cobra 1925
Son of the Sheik, The 1926
Four Horsemen of the Apocalypse, The 1926

von Stroheim, Erich
Heart of Humanity, The 1918
Blind Husbands 1919
Wedding March, The 1928
Great Gabbo, The 1929
Three Faces East 1930
Friends and Lovers 1931
Lost Squadron, The 1932
As You Desire Me 1932
Crimson Romance 1934
Crime of Dr Crespi, The 1936
Grand Illusion 1938
Alibi, L' 1939
Boys' School 1939
Ultimatum 1940
I Was an Adventuress 1940
Thunder Over Paris 1940
Personal Column 1941
So Ends our Night 1941
Five Graves to Cairo 1943
North Star, The 1943
It Happened in Gibraltar 1943
Lady and the Monster, The 1944
Storm Over Lisbon 1944
32 Rue de Montmartre 1944
Marthe Richard 1944
Great Flamario, The 1945
Devil and the Angel, The 1949
Sunset Boulevard 1950

von Stroheim, Erich (Director)
Blind Husbands 1919
Foolish Wives 1922
Greed 1924
Merry Widow, The 1925
Wedding March, The 1928
Wedding March 1965

Webb, Clifton
Polly With a Past 1921
New Toys 1925
Heart of a Siren, The 1925
Laura 1944
Dark Corner, The 1946
Razor's Edge, The 1946
Razor's Edge, The 1946
Sitting Pretty 1948
Mr Belvedere Goes to College 1949
Cheaper by the Dozen 1950
For Heaven's Sake 1950
Mr Belvedere Rings the Bell 1951
Elopement 1951
Dreamboat 1952
Stars and Stripes Forever 1952
Titanic 1953
Mister Scoutmaster 1953
Three Coins in the Fountain 1954
Woman's World 1954
Man Who Never Was, The 1956
Boy on a Dolphin 1957
Remarkable Mr Pennypacker, The 1959
Holiday for Lovers 1959
Satan Never Sleeps 1962

***White, Pearl**
Mayblossom 1912
Girl in the Next Room, The 1912
Where Charity Begins 1913
Exploits of Elaine, The 1914
Perils of Pauline, The 1914
New Exploits of Elaine, The 1915
Romance of Elaine, The 1915
Hazel Kirke 1916

* Pearl White's films were not reviewed by *The New York Times*.

Iron Claw, The 1916
Pearl of the Army 1916
Fatal Ring, The 1917
Black Secret, The 1919
Lightning Raider, The 1919
White Moll, The 1920
Know Your Men 1921
A Virgin Paradise 1921
Tiger's Cub 1921
Thief, The 1921
Mountain Women, The 1921
Beyond Price 1921
Without Fear 1922
Breadway Peacock, The 1922
Any Wife 1922
Plunder 1923
Parisian Nights 1924
Perils of Paris 1925

Wong, Anna May

Bits of Life 1921
Toll of the Sea, The 1922
Thief of Bagdad, The 1924
Alaskan, The 1924
Peter Pan 1924
Forty Winks 1925
Mr Wu 1927
Old San Francisco 1927
Devil Dancer, The 1927
Chinese Parrot, The 1928
Song 1928
Piccadilly 1929
Wasted Love 1929
Flame of Love, The 1930
Amour Maitre des Choses, L' 1931
Daughter of the Dragon 1931
Shanghai Express 1932
Study in Scarlet, A 1933
Chu Chin Chow 1934
Limehouse Blues 1934
Java Head 1935
Daughter of Shanghai 1937
Dangerous to Know 1938
When Were You Born? 1938
King of Chinatown 1939
Ellery Queen's Penthouse Mystery 1941
Bombs Over Burma 1942
Impact 1949
Portrait in Black 1960

Woolley, Monty

Live, Love and Learn 1937
Arsene Lupin Returns 1938
Everybody Sing 1938
Girl of the Golden West, The 1938
Three Comrades 1938
Lord Jeff 1938
Young Doctor Kildare 1938
Midnight 1939
Man About Town 1939
Dancing Co-Ed 1939
Man Who Came to Dinner, The 1942
Pied Piper, The 1942
Life Begins at Eight-Thirty 1942
Holy Matrimony 1943
Since You Went Away 1944
Irish Eyes Are Smiling 1944
Molly and Me 1945
Night and Day 1946
Bishop's Wife, The 1947
Miss Tatlock's Millions 1948
As Young as You Feel 1951
Kismet 1955